ANGALKUT / SHAMANS IN YUP'IK ORAL TRADITION

Angalkut
Shamans in Yup'ik Oral Tradition

Alice Rearden, Marie Meade, and Ann Fienup-Riordan

CALISTA EDUCATION AND CULTURE

University of Alaska Press

FAIRBANKS

© 2025 by Calista Education and Culture

Published by University of Alaska Press
An imprint of University Press of Colorado
1580 North Logan Street, Suite 660
PMB 39883
Denver, Colorado 80203-1942

The University Press of Colorado is a proud member of Association of University Presses.

The University Press of Colorado is a cooperative publishing enterprise supported, in part, by Adams State University, Colorado School of Mines, Colorado State University, Fort Lewis College, Metropolitan State University of Denver, University of Alaska Fairbanks, University of Colorado, University of Denver, University of Northern Colorado, University of Wyoming, Utah State University, and Western Colorado University.

∞ This paper meets the requirements of the ANSI/NISO Z39.48-1992 (Permanence of Paper).

ISBN: 978-1-64642-729-1 (hardcover)
ISBN: 978-1-64642-730-7 (paperback)
ISBN: 978-1-64642-731-4 (ebook)
https://doi.org/10.5876/9781646427314

The Yup'ik and English text in part 2 of the ePUB edition is arranged so that each Yup'ik paragraph is followed by its English translation, whereas the print and PDF editions present the English translations to the left of the original Yup'ik text.

Library of Congress Cataloging-in-Publication Data

Names: Fienup-Riordan, Ann author | Rearden, Alice author | Meade, Marie author
Title: Angalkut/shamans in Yup'ik oral tradition / Ann Fienup-Riordan, Alice Rearden, Marie Meade.
Description: Fairbanks : University of Alaska Press, [2025] | Series: Calista education and culture | Includes bibliographical references and index.
Identifiers: LCCN 2024058213 (print) | LCCN 2024058214 (ebook) | ISBN 9781646427291 hardcover | ISBN 9781646427307 paperback | ISBN 9781646427314 ebook
Subjects: LCSH: Yupik Eskimos—Alaska, Southwest—Social life and customs | Oral tradition—Alaska, Southwest | Yupik languages—Alaska, Southwest | Yupik Eskimos—Alaska, Southwest—Rites and ceremonies | Shamans—Alaska, Southwest
Classification: LCC E99.E7 F437 2025 (print) | LCC E99.E7 (ebook) | DDC 979.8/4004971—dc23/eng/20250328
LC record available at https://lccn.loc.gov/2024058213
LC ebook record available at https://lccn.loc.gov/2024058214

Cover image by Jeffrey Dykes, Peabody Essex Museum

This book will be made open access within three years of publication thanks to Path to Open, a program developed in partnership between JSTOR, the American Council of Learned Societies (ACLS), University of Michigan Press, and The University of North Carolina Press to bring about equitable access and impact for the entire scholarly community, including authors, researchers, libraries, and university presses around the world. Learn more at https://about.jstor.org/path-to-open/.

CALISTA
EDUCATION
& CULTURE

Contents

· ·

Tarenrat Nunanguat-Ilu
Illustrations

· ·

Quyavikelput
Acknowledgments

Over thirty years between 1985 and 2015, my Yup'ik partners and I have been privileged to listen to many shaman stories—first as part of interviews carried out in preparation for the Yup'ik mask exhibit, *Agayuliyararput / Our Way of Making Prayer*, and later as part of gatherings organized by the Calista Elders Council (CEC) to document traditional (primarily nineteenth- and early twentieth-century) Yup'ik knowledge. In 2014 CEC was reorganized and renamed Calista Education and Culture—the "new CEC"—and our conversations about traditional healing continued. All of these conversations highlight the critical role *angalkut* (shamans) played in so many aspects of Yup'ik life—healing the sick, interpreting dreams and unusual experiences, requesting future abundance through masked dances and other ceremonies, protecting the lives of young children, dealing with the dead.

The books CEC has produced over the years include some of these stories, especially accounts of the central role *angalkut* played in masked dancing. Yet no single book has been devoted exclusively to *angalkut*. Nor have we shared the variety of their roles and the richness of elders' recollections of these remarkable men and women.

It took the COVID-19 pandemic, and our inability to work with living elders, to motivate us to revisit these stories. Mark John especially encouraged us to take up this rich and important topic, noting that CEC's Elder Committee had always wanted young people to better understand the role *angalkut* played in Yup'ik lives. Once Mark had figuratively opened the door, and Alice Rearden and I had a chance to read old transcripts and revisit the occasions on which these stories had been shared, we were struck by their variety and eloquence. Moreover, these were much more than general accounts of anonymous *angalkut*. Elders had shared detailed descriptions of their experiences with particular *angalkut*—men and women like Puyulkuk, Asgulria, Ayalpik, Tairtaq, Leggleq, and Teggalquq—giving us a vivid history of their practices and personalities. Sadly, not only are these *angalkut* gone, but all of those who witnessed and participated in their activities have also passed away. The value of the stories they left behind cannot be overemphasized.

Many organizations provided funding and support for the original recordings on which this book is based, including the Alaska Humanities Forum, the Anchorage Museum, the National Science Foundation, the National Endowment for the Humanities, the National Park Service, and the US Fish and Wildlife Service. A grant from the Rasmuson Foundation was critical in allowing us to turn rough transcripts from previous gatherings into a readable bilingual text. And major funding from the National Science Foundation, Arctic Social Sciences, gave us the resources we needed to edit the recordings as well as host two additional gatherings to clarify and expand on our previous work. NSF program officers Anna Kerttula

https://doi.org/10.5876/9781646427314.c000a

FIGURE 0.1. The Kuskokwim shaman Ayalpik and his wife. L. Waugh, 1935, National Museum of the American Indian, Smithsonian Institution, L2694.

de Echave and Erica Hill were particularly helpful, and we are in their debt. Invaluable assistance was also provided by the staff of Calista Education and Culture, including Denise Brown-Chythlook, Nicole Baski, and Robyn Kugtsun.

Photographs and illustrations also come from a variety of sources, including the Leuman Waugh Collection from the Smithsonian's National Museum of the American Indian in Washington, DC; the Alaska State Museum in Juneau, Alaska; the Anchorage Museum in Anchorage, Alaska; the Ethnologisches Museum Berlin in Berlin, Germany; the Sheldon Jackson Museum in Sitka, Alaska; the Peabody Essex Museum in Salem, Massachusetts; and the University of Washington Library Special Collections in Seat-

tle, Washington. Tim Troll, Ray Troll, James Barker, Barry McWayne, and Mary Woods also provided photographs as well as helpful comments and information, and Patrick Jankanish and Ian Moore prepared the book's maps.

Finally, thanks to Leon Unruh and the staff of both the University of Alaska Press and the University Press of Colorado, especially Nate Bauer, Laura Walker, Laura Furney, and designer Kristina Kachele. We're also indebted to two anonymous reviewers whose thoughtful comments helped us fine-tune the organization of the original manuscript as well as add elements—especially the list of shamans named in the text—to help readers better understand this fascinating but complex topic.

ANGALKUT / SHAMANS IN YUP'IK ORAL TRADITION

Yupiit Yuuyaraatnek Nallunrilnguut
Yup'ik Tradition Bearers

· ·

This list reflects Yup'ik protocol. Names are ordered by community, running north to south along the Bering Sea coast and upriver to Bethel. Within each community, individuals are listed by age (eldest to youngest); their Yup'ik names are in italics. In the text the first occurrence of each speaker's name is followed by place of residence, for example, Paul John (November 2000:81) of Toksook Bay. The gathering date and transcript page number of the statement follows the elder's name in parentheses.

Name	Residence	Birthplace	Birth Year
Nick Andrew / *Apirtaq*	Marshall	Iquarmiut	1933
Wassilie Evan	Pilot Station		1907
Paul Waskey / *Pugleralria*	Pilot Station	Qagatmiut	1920
Andy Kinzy / *Qut'raacuk*	St. Mary's	Qissunaq River	1911
Mary Mike / *Arrsauyaq*	St. Mary's	Uksuqalleq	1912
Jasper Louis / *Kaligtuq*	St. Mary's	Anagciq	1916
Johnny Thompson / *Cakitelleq*	St. Mary's	Tuutalgaq	1923
Andy Paukan / *Angalgaq*	St. Mary's	Akuluraq	1939
Willie Beans	Mountain Village		1908
Charlie Steve / *Anuaterkaq*	Stebbins		1910
Cecelia Foxie	Kotlik	Penguq	1912
Henry Teeluk / *Tiiluq*	Kotlik		
Margaret Andrews / *Kuqaa*	Kotlik		1921
Alma Keyes / *Apaliq*	Kotlik	Pastuli River	1922
Willie Kamkoff / *Uankaaq*	Kotlik	Nunapiggluugaq	1923
Martina Aparezuk / *Atangan*	Kotlik	Caniliaq	1932
Catherine Moore / *Akiuk*	Emmonak	Bethel	1920
Alex Bird / *Apaliq*	Emmonak		1921
Benedict Tucker / *Cikulraaciq*	Emmonak	Cingigmiut	1917
Mike Andrews Sr. / *Angauvik*	Emmonak	Amigtuli	1928

continued on next page

https://doi.org/10.5876/9781646427314.c000b

Name	Residence	Birthplace	Birth Year
Peter Moore / *Yak'utaaq*	Emmonak	Imangaq	1932
Maryann Andrews / *Tauyaaq*	Emmonak	Qip'ngayak	1933
Thomas Chikigak / *Cikigaq*	Alakanuk	Alarneq	1913
Joe Phillip / *Panigkaq*	Alakanuk	Alarneq	1923
Fred Augustine / *Qapuggluk*	Alakanuk	Engeliileq	1825
Barbara Joe / *Arnaucuaq*	Alakanuk	Nunam Iqua	1928
Agnes Tony	Alakanuk		1930
Edward Phillip / *Qavarliar*	Alakanuk	Alarneq	1933
Placid Joseph / *Qavarliaq*	Alakanuk		1933
Lawrence Edmund / *Paugnaralria*	Alakanuk	Peguumavik	1934
Denis Shelden / *Kituralria*	Alakanuk	Alakanuk	1944
Eugene Pete / *Aliuq*	Nunam Iqua	Marayaaq	1923
Anna Pete / *Ac'aralek*	Nunam Iqua	Nunallerpak	1930
Joe Ayagarak / *Ayagarak*	Chevak	Qissunaq	1915
Francis Charlie / *Acqaq*	Scammon Bay	Anagciq	1941
Helen Smith	Hooper Bay		
Elsie Tommy / *Nanugaq*	Newtok	Kaviarmiut	1922
Michael John / *Qukailnguq*	Newtok	Cevtaq	1931
Joseph John / *Arnaucuaq*	Newtok		
Joseph Patrick / *Agiyangaq*	Newtok	Nerevkartuli	1937
Mary George / *Nanurniralria*	Newtok	Cevtaq	1942
Susie Angaiak / *Uliggaq*	Tununak	Tununak	1923
Edward Hooper / *Maklak*	Tununak	Tununak	1925
Helen Walter / *Nasgauq*	Tununak	Tununak	1945
Brentina Chanar / *Papangluar*	Toksook Bay	Cevv'arneq	1912
Theresa Moses / *Ilanaq*	Toksook Bay	Cevv'arneq	1926
Paul John / *Kangrilnguq*	Toksook Bay	Cevv'arneq	1928
Lizzie Chimiugak / *Neng'uryar*	Toksook Bay		1930
Martina John / *Anguyaluk*	Toksook Bay	Nightmute	1936
Ruth Jimmie / *Angalgaq*	Toksook Bay	Umkumiut	1951
Magdalene John / *Missan*	Toksook Bay	Toksook Bay	
Tim Agagtak / *Akagtaq*	Nightmute		1903
Albertina Dull / *Cingyukan*	Nightmute	Qungurmiut	1918
Dick Anthony / *Minegtuli*	Nightmute	Cevv'arneq	1922
Dennis Panruk / *Panruk*	Chefornak	Cevv'arneq	1910
David Martin / *Negaryaq*	Kipnuk	Cal'itmiut	1914
Frank Andrew / *Miisaq*	Kwigillingok	Kuigilnguq	1917
Peter John / *Mumess'aq*	Kwigillingok	Papegmiut	1919
Roland Phillip / *Anguteka'ar*	Kwigillingok		1927
Noah Andrew / *Aiggailnguq*	Kwigillingok	Kuigilnguq	1951
John Phillip / *Ayagina'ar*	Kongiganak	Anuurarmiut	1925
Wassilie Berlin / *Uqsungiar*	Kasigluk	Tuntutuliak	1916
Annie Blue / *Cungauyar*	Togiak	Qissayaarmiut	1916
George Billy / *Nacailnguq*	Napakiak	Nanvarnarrlagmiut	1922

continued on next page

Name	Residence	Birthplace	Birth Year
Annie Nelson / *Amarr'aq*	Napakiak	Tekermialleq	1931
Jacob Black / *Nasgauq*	Napakiak	Qaurrayagaq	1940
Ralph Nelson / *Tutmaralria*	Napakiak	Napakiak	1962
Fannie Jacob / *Mayuralria*	Napaskiak	Luumarvik	1932
Nastasia Larson / *Apeng'aq*	Napaskiak	Napaskiak	1940
Yako Andrew / *Qaluk'aq*	Napaskiak	Akerpiim Painga	1943
Martha Evan / *Akiugalria*	Napaskiak		1945
Alexie Nicholai / *Apeng'aq*	Oscarville	Oscarville	1928
Nicholai Steven / *Paugyuk*	Oscarville	Bethel	1949
Dick Andrew / *Apaqutaq*	Bethel	Kayalivik	1909
Kay Hendrickson	Bethel	Ciguralegmiut, Nunivak Is.	1910
Elena Charles / *Nengqerralria*	Bethel	Nunacuarmiut	1918
Peter Jacobs / *Paniguaq*	Bethel	Cuukvagtuli	1923
Agatha Nevak / *Uassuuk*	Bethel	Tununak	
Joan Hamilton / *Pirciralria*	Bethel	Chevak	
Joshua Phillip / *Maqista*	Tuluksak	Akiachak	1912
Mary Napoka	Tuluksak		1916
Bob Aloysius / *Sliksuuyar*	Upper Kalskag	Iinruq	1935
Golga Effemka / *Ungagpak*	Sleetmute		1934
Peter Black / *Nanirqun*	Wasilla	Hooper Bay	1940
William Tyson	Anchorage	Pastuli River	1916
Raphael Jimmy / *Angagaq*	Anchorage	Kuiggarpak	1924
David Chanar / *Cingurruk*	Anchorage	Umkumiut	1946
Marie Meade / *Arnaq*	Anchorage	Nunapitchuk	1947
Ann Riordan / *Ellaq'am Arnaan*	Anchorage	Virginia	1948
Mark John / *Miisaq*	Anchorage	Nightmute	1954
Alice Rearden / *Cucuaq*	Anchorage	Napakiak	1976

Angalkullret
Past Shamans

Name	Residence
Aasasilek	Kangirnaarmiut
Agagliiyaq	Naparyarraq / Napakiak
Angassaar	Qissunaq
Angutekayak	Negtemiut / Nightmute
Angutvassuk	Kapuutelleq
Apalciq	?Ekvicuaq
Apangtak	Naparyarraq / Napakiak
Apaqassugaq	Qaluyaat / Nelson Island
Aparr'aq / Apar'aq	Tununeq / Tununak
Aqsarpak	Ayikatarmiut
Arnaqulluk	Qaluyaat / Nelson Island
Arnarayar	Kuigilnguq / Kwigillingok
Arnaruaq	Tuyuryaq / Togiak
Asgulria	Qaurrayagarmiut
Ayagina'ar	Ekvicuaq
Ayalpik	Mamterilleq / Bethel
Ayuqsar	Kuigilnguq / Kwigillingok
Cingarturta	Kuigilnguq / Kwigillingok
Cupungulria	
Egacuayaaq	Qaluyaat / Nelson Island
Esiseq	Kangirnaarmiut
Ingallak	Nanvarnarrlak
Ingamulria	Alarneq / Alakanuk
Ississaayuk / Ississaayuq	Cevv'arneq
Kaligtuq	Marayaaq / Scammon Bay
Keggsuli	Mamteraq / Goodnews Bay

Name	Residence
Keggutellek	Apruka'ar
Kencialnguq	Paimiut
Kenirmigpak	Qissunaq
Keplialleq	Akulirarmiut
Kinguqall'er	Qaluyaat / Nelson Island
Kiuryaq	Pastuliq
Leggleq	Nunallerpak
Luk'alleq	Qaluyaat / Nelson Island
Mancuaq	Qamiqumiut
Muiqerrilleq	Qaluyaat / Nelson Island
Murak	Qipneq / Kipnuk
Nagiiquyaq	Yuukiararmiut, Qaluyaat / Nelson Island
Nayangaraqtaq	Qaluyaat / Nelson Island
Neq'ayaraq	Qinarmiut
Nutgun	Imangaq / Emmonak
Pamsuq	Qipneq / Kipnuk
Pangalgalria	Qinaq
Paqricilleq	Kapuutelleq
Puyulkuk	Kangirnaarmiut, Anuuraaq
Qakerluilaq	Alarneq / Alakanuk, originally from Kotzebue
Qakurtaq	Taciurtalek, Alarneq / Alakanuk
Qaluvialler	Qinaq
Qamuutaq	Nanvarnarrlak
Qateryak	Negtemiut / Nightmute
Qumaqniq	Kuigilnguq / Kwigillingok

continued on next page

https://doi.org/10.5876/9781646427314.c000c

NORTON SOUND

ALASKA

Fairbanks

ANCHORAGE

Juneau

MAP AREA

Penguq • St. Michael
Stebbins

∴ Petmigtalek

Caniliaq
Kotlik
∴ Pastuliq
∴ Bill Moore Slough
Emmonak Hamilton
Kuiguk ∴
Alakanuk
∴ Kangilek
Nunam Iqua • ∴ Akulurak ∴ Fish Village

Uksqalleq ∴ Anagciq
Mountain
Village Andreafsky
Amigtuli ∴ St Marys
Black River Pitka's Pilot Station
Point
Scammon Bay • Marshall
Cape Romanzof
Askinuk Mts. • Russian Mission
Qissunaq R.

Yukon River

Anvik

Holy Cross
Paimiut

Kuskokwim River
Johnson R. Kalskag Aniak Sleetmute

Hooper Bay• • Chevak

Qissunaq ∴

Atmautluak Tuluksak
Newtok Kasigluk Akiachak
Ningliq River Nunapitchuk BETHEL Akiak
Toksook Bay Nelson I. Baird Inlet Kwethluk
Tununak (Qaluyaat) Napakiak Oscarville Kisaralik R.
Cape Vancouver Cakcaaq Napaskiak
Up'nerkillermiut
Mekoryuk• Umkumiut Qalvinraaq R.
Nightmute Dall Tuntutuliak Iinrayaq R.
Lake
Nunivak Chefornak Eek
Island Etolin Strait
Cape Kipnuk Kongiganak
Avinof Kwigillingok
Quinhagak

Kilbuck Mountains

Kuskokwim Bay

MILES
0 30 60
0 50 100
KILOMETERS

• Modern village
∴ Historic site

Ahklun Mountains
Togiak R. DILLINGHAM
Goodnews Bay ∴ Nushagak
Togiak • Manokotak

Cape Iliyussiiq R.
Newenham Nushagak Bay
Cape Hagemeister I.
Peirce Cape
Constantine

BERING SEA BRISTOL BAY

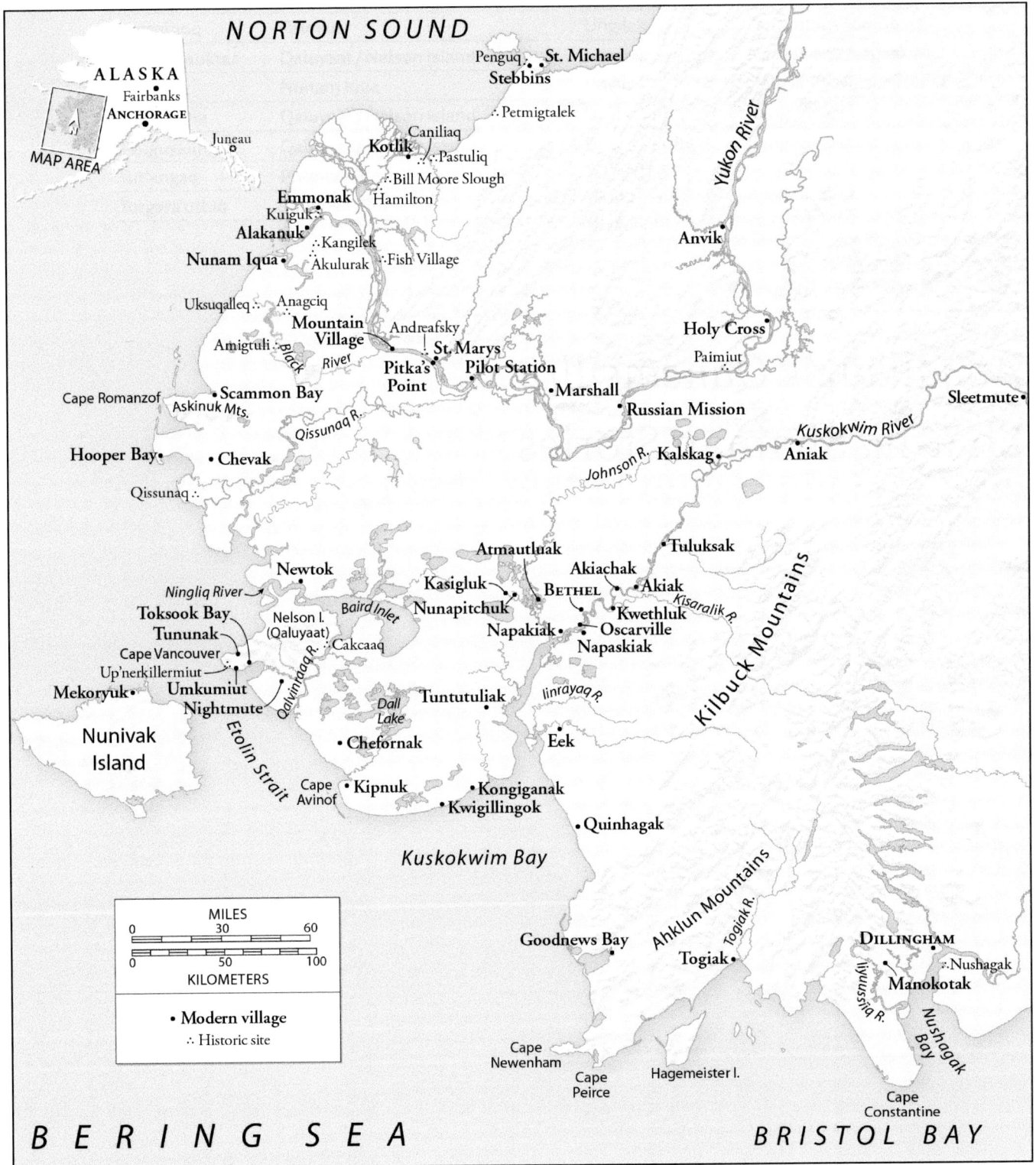

FIGURE 1.1. Southwest Alaska. Patrick Jankanish.

1

Kalikam Ayagnera
Introduction

In the early 1900s, *angalkut* (shamans) were ubiquitous in southwest Alaska. Born in 1903, Nelson Island elder Tim Agagtak (July 1985:37) recalled: "Their ancestors came from the ancient time. This business of shamanism has existed beginning from the first people." Indeed, shamanism has been practiced by men and women in southwest Alaska, as well as northern Eurasia and North America, for centuries. The derivation of the word *angalkuq* is unclear, although Thalbitzer (1930) suggested that it may be related to the Inuit word for mother's brother—*angak*. The term "shaman" comes from the Tungus word *saman* and has become a central theoretical concept in the study of religion (Eliade 1970; Laugrand and Oosten 2012:33). The literature on shamanism is vast, for both Alaska as well as other parts of the Arctic. Our intention is to contribute to that literature through a fine-grained presentation of unique first-person narratives rarely recorded or shared.[1]

While differing in important ways, Inuit and Yup'ik shamanic traditions—spread from the Bering Sea coast all across the Canadian Arctic and Greenland—share distinctive features. All across the Arctic, the shaman is viewed as someone who possesses the ability to locate animals, change the weather, and heal the sick, often with the assistance of helping spirits (Merkur 1991; Laugrand and Oosten 2012:xvii, 33).

Although contemporary healing practices still make use of shamanic techniques, including "poking" and the laying on of hands, the last generation of men and women recognized as shamans in southwest Alaska has passed away, as has the last generation of women and men with firsthand experiences of *angalkut*. Susie Angaiak (March 2007:1476) of Tununak mused: "When I think about what we experienced in the early days, it's like a dream. But we know what it's like since we experienced it." Elders also share what they heard from their own elders. Frank Andrew (October 2001:181) began one recording session with the disclaimer: "I speak of things that I heard from elders. . . . I cannot fabricate things, but I only reveal things that I have heard."

How and Why We Work Together: Topic-Specific Gatherings[2]

In 1997, Calista (the for-profit corporation for southwest Alaska) asked Mark John, born and raised on Nelson Island, to lead and reinvigorate the Calista Elders Council (CEC). CEC grew and thrived under John's leadership, taking on the job of documenting traditional knowledge in a part of Alaska rich in language and oral history. In 2014, CEC was reorganized and renamed Calista Education and Culture, and the "new CEC" remains the primary heritage organization in the Yukon-Kuskokwim delta region, a lowland delta the size of Kansas and the traditional homeland of Yup'ik people. At present

https://doi.org/10.5876/9781646427314.c001

11

the region's population of over 26,000 (the largest Native population in Alaska) lives scattered in 56 villages and the regional center in Bethel. Today this huge region is cross-cut by historical and administrative differences, including three dialect groups, three major Christian denominations, six school districts, two census areas, and three ANCSA (Alaska Native Claims Settlement Act) regional corporations.

The lack of commercially valuable resources (i.e., whales, fur bearers, mineral deposits) meant that the region attracted a resident non-Native population relatively late compared to other parts of Alaska. The first non-Natives to settle in significant numbers were Christian missionaries beginning in the 1880s (Fienup-Riordan 1990b, 1991, 2000; Oswalt 1963, 1973). Schools and churches were not established in many lower coastal communities until the 1930s. The elders we worked with were raised in small settlements where residents spoke the Yup'ik language and continued to harvest foods from the land and sea, as had their ancestors before them. Among the most significant changes in the twentieth century was the abandonment of these small settlements (ranging in size from 5 to 30 persons) and the gathering of people into 56 permanent villages between 200 and 1,200 persons. While these villages may seem small by urban standards, they represent unprecedented population concentration in the delta environment, with direct consequences for community viability.

As people gather closer together, animals and fish, although still abundant, are more distant. Now men often need to travel miles, either by gasoline-hungry snowmobile or skiff, to set their nets and traps. Many people still harvest from the fishing sites their parents used when they were young, but the cost is much higher. At a time when the market economy of southwest Alaska continues to founder, hunting and fishing activities become increasingly difficult to afford (Alaska Department of Labor 2010).

Both late contact and lack of commercial resources have meant that the Yup'ik region has retained many social patterns and knowledge of past practices—including direct experiences with shamans—that has been lost in other parts of Alaska. The Yup'ik language is second only to Navajo in numbers of speakers (14,000) of an Indigenous language in the United States (Krauss 1980). This continued cultural and linguistic vitality has contributed to the position of Yup'ik people as among the most traditional Native American groups.

Finally, lack of commercial resources has meant that the region is among the poorest in Alaska. Poverty and its attendant social problems, including suicide, alcoholism, and sexual abuse, continue to plague the region (Berman 2014). The process of social and economic change has accelerated since the 1970s, and efforts to understand these changes and how they are impacting the people of southwest Alaska are ongoing (Fienup-Riordan 1986, 1990a, 2000, 2010; Morrow 1990; Oswalt 1990).

A major breakthrough in understanding Yup'ik cultural history was the establishment of the Calista Elders Council (CEC) and the placement of heritage preservation efforts in local hands. A community-engaged approach has been the hallmark of CEC research since 2000. Elders and other community members are deeply concerned with maintaining their knowledge of past practices, which many feel is at the heart of their survival. CEC gatherings and resulting publications are viewed as important steps in ensuring that Yup'ik cultural perspectives are not only broadly shared but also preserved for future generations. CEC is a small organization. Mark John was CEC's original director and was largely responsible for realizing the vision of CEC as giving voice to Yup'ik knowledge holders. Alice Rearden and Marie Meade have been CEC's principal translators and language experts, along with men and women like David Chanar, Davina Carl, and Corey Joseph. I work as the team's anthropologist, helping to find funding for and provide assistance with CEC activities.

Mark, Alice, Marie, and I have worked together on a variety of CEC projects over decades. In the beginning all projects were initiated by CEC's board of elders, including nine Yup'ik-speaking men and women, representing villages throughout the region. Under the new CEC, this board has been replaced by a six-member elders committee, which continues to guide the work we do. Both the original CEC board as well as the new CEC elders committee actively support the documentation and sharing of their oral traditions, which they view as possessing continued value in today's world.

Almost from the beginning, CEC's primary information-gathering tool has been the topic-specific gathering. The CEC pioneered this format while working with elders between 2000 and 2005

FIGURE 1.2. Nelson Island place names. Ian Moore.

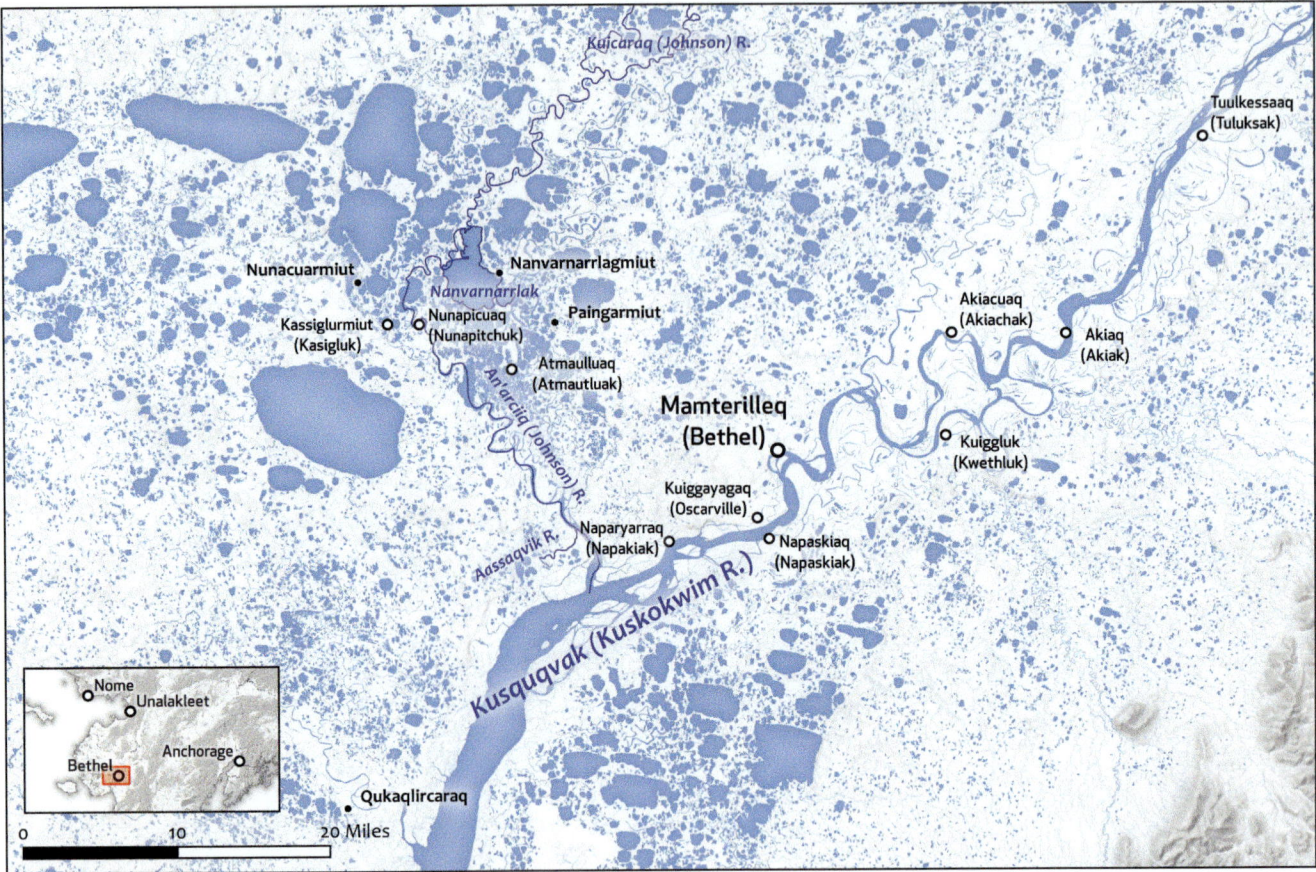

FIGURE 1.3. Kuskokwim River and Akulmiut place names. Ian Moore.

FIGURE 1.4. Canineq (lower Kuskokwim coastal area) place names. Ian Moore.

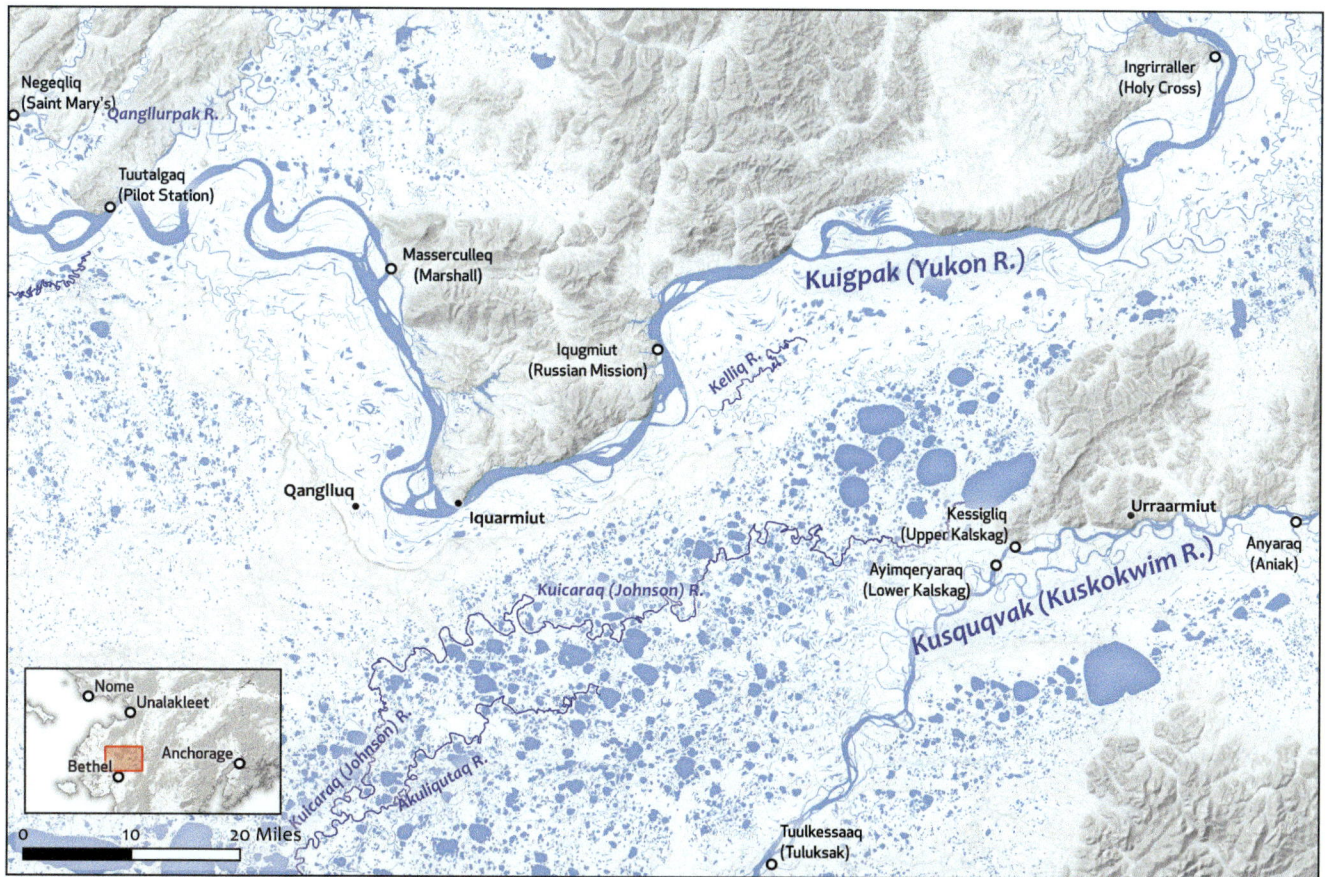

FIGURE 1.5. Middle Yukon and Middle Kuskokwim River place names. Ian Moore.

during a major Yup'ik traditional knowledge project funded by the National Science Foundation's (NSF) Arctic Social Science program. CEC staff found that meeting with small groups of elder experts, accompanied by younger community members, for two- and three-day gatherings devoted to a specific set of questions was an effective and rewarding way of addressing topics. We use the term *gatherings* to describe these open-ended exchanges between generations as opposed to the term *meetings*, which are more often viewed as goal-oriented, decision-making events. Gatherings are also unlike interviews, during which elders answer questions posed by those who often do not already hold the knowledge they seek. Gatherings (like academic symposia) encourage elders to speak among their peers at the highest level. CEC board member John Phillip (October 2006:284) of Kongiganak observed during one gathering: "Hearing the story you just told, I learned what I didn't know. It is like we are still learning."

CEC's gatherings always take place in the Yup'ik language, as the form in which information is shared is as important as the content. Alice and Marie then create detailed transcripts of each gathering, and we work together to turn these into bilingual publications and accompanying English texts (see p. 101 on "Transcription and Translation").

It is important to emphasize that these gatherings build on each other, and long and careful listening provides unique perspectives on Yup'ik knowledge. Over the past twenty years, CEC has hosted dozens of gatherings on numerous topics including: family values; traditional discipline; survival strategies; traditional technology; harvesting patterns; ocean hunting; snow and ice; and weather conditions. Our work together has resulted in more than 1,500 hours of recordings and 25,000 pages of transcripts. I'm reminded of the proverb: "If you want to go fast, go alone. If you want to go far, go together." These deep collaborations go beyond consultation and cooperation to the true co-conceptualization of knowledge.

In gatherings, elders teach not just facts; they teach listeners how to learn. They share not only what they know but how they know it and why they believe it is important to remember. CEC staff and Yup'ik community members value topic-specific gatherings not

FIGURE 1.6. Lower Yukon place names. Ian Moore.

merely as tools for documentation but also as contexts for cultural transmission, and youth often accompany the elders who attend. The gatherings themselves are meaningful events that enrich lives locally at the same time their documentation has the potential to increase cross-cultural understanding globally.

Some of our gatherings are held in villages, others in Bethel, and some at my home in Anchorage. During Anchorage gatherings, for example, elders arrive by air and stay as my guests—sleeping in the rooms vacated by our grown children. We all eat together in the morning, after which Mark, Alice, and Marie join us for the day. Sitting comfortably in our living room, and after an opening prayer giving thanks for our health and gratitude for being together, I turn on the tape recorder and we begin. Alice and Marie lead the discussions, with me chiming in with questions. Mark often brings seal meat or beluga to cook for lunch, and we all enjoy our shared meals. Time goes fast. By midafternoon, we stop for the day. After another shared meal, Mark may take the men home for a steam bath, while I take others shopping or to visit relatives at the Alaska Native Medical Center.[3]

CEC topic-specific gatherings and our work with elders are ultimately shaped by the concerns and choices of individual participants. When elders have been asked whether questions are appropriate in storytelling contexts, many said that stories should be "just told." Yet in our gatherings we have found elders ready and willing to answer our questions, especially when these questions show we have listened to what has gone before. It is difficult to adequately convey the compassion and loving spirit that fill their accounts. Mark John's father, Nelson Island leader Paul John, once told us that children should never be talked to harshly, as it blocks their minds and prevents them from learning: "If those who are giving them advice speak with compassion, it would be like giving them strong, healing medicine and would help bring them happiness." We remain deeply grateful for the gifts these elders have given us and their trust that we will treat these gifts responsibly and respectfully and share them in our turn.

The instrumental value of what we do is in the forefront of our work together. The image of the igloo-dwelling Eskimo still smiles out from many a gift shop window in Alaska. Though few elders directly confront this simple-minded and insidious stereotype, they sense that sharing their detailed narratives strikes its foundations, destabilizes it, and sends it crumbling down. Their contemporary narrative references to the past are active efforts to shape the future—a future in which they believe Yup'ik knowledge should be recognized and valued.

As noted, in gatherings Yup'ik elders are not just trying to *say*, but to *do* something. They know they possess a narrative tradition and knowledge system second to none, and they want others to give it the respect it deserves. In 2009, Paul John declared, "If white people see these books, they will think, 'These Yup'ik people evidently are knowledgeable and know how to take care of their own affairs through their traditional ways.'"

The Paradox of Talking on the Page

Yup'ik elders with whom we work are fluent in their Native language, and they were privileged to hear stories from their parents and grandparents as part of an oral tradition thousands of years old. In their article, "The Paradox of Talking on the Page," Tlingit scholars Nora and Richard Dauenhauer (1999) aptly compare this vibrant narrative tradition to the salmon running upriver and berries growing on the tundra—an abundance with the power to sustain us. But contemporary Yup'ik elders recognize that their younger generation is moving away from the rivers and tundra. It is for their sakes they support sharing knowledge in new ways.

Although the Yup'ik language remains strong in coastal and lower Kuskokwim communities, language loss has been severe in Yukon and middle Kuskokwim villages, where few young people are fluent speakers. Golga Effemka (January 2006:139) of Sleetmute sadly declared: "Upriver they don't comprehend in Yup'ik but only in English. It's because we elders don't teach them. When our parents raised us, they spoke to us in Yup'ik. They no longer speak [in Yup'ik] nowadays. And when speaking to them [in English], some get angry because they can't speak in Yup'ik." Although Yup'ik is second only to Navajo in numbers of speakers of an Indigenous language in the United States, its long-term survival is far from assured.

"Much of great importance is lost and added in translation," linguist A. L. Becker (2000:90) reminds us. The truth of his words captures both the strengths and weaknesses of the bilingual books that CEC has worked to produce over the past two decades.

Each translated text is at once less than the original telling—devoid of the shapes and sounds of the narrator's voice—and more. Through the double process of translation from Yup'ik to English and from oral to written form, something is inevitably lost. At the same time, readers gain access to a unique and compelling perspective on the world around them, as well as their place within it.

CEC staff and the elders we work with are enthusiastic about the books we do together. They are quick to point out, however, the importance of acknowledging the men and women who have contributed to our work, as well as of ensuring that their communities and youth benefit fully from their contributions. Although sharing knowledge is highly valued, responsibilities attend the process. Stories are not objects to be collected, classified, paginated, and sold for personal profit, and writing them down does not confer ownership. Elders also remind us that words are inherently powerful, having the capacity to create that which they describe. Words have never been used lightly within Yup'ik oral tradition, and CEC staff takes seriously the challenge of how best to translate and share these oral traditions in written form.

In documenting Yup'ik knowledge we work hard to ensure that the direct voice of individual elders always comes through. The anthropologist has a role to play, not as expert author but as translator, editor, and good listener. One technique we have developed as a way of sharing Yup'ik knowledge is to often do two books: one English for the general public and a bilingual companion volume in which quoted statements from individual elders are contextualized and shared at length. To date CEC has produced four sets of "paired" books—one English for general and scholarly audiences and the other bilingual for community use—setting new standards for academic publications resulting from collaborative projects.[4] Even in our English-language books, the decision to place Yup'ik voices front and center is the way we keep all of our books close to their sources.

Book-Making: How This Book Came Together

Having outlined how and why we work together generally, I want to share what this particular book includes and how it is organized. The book begins with a list of contributors as well as a list of specific shamans mentioned in the text. What follows is divided into two parts. As in our volumes on bow-and-arrow warfare and *ircenrraat* (other-than-human persons) (Fienup-Riordan and Rearden 2016; Rearden et al. 2021), Part 1: Sharing Shaman Stories provides an English introduction to the bilingual text, placing Yup'ik oral traditions in the context of shamanism in Alaska as well as in other parts of the Arctic. This English introduction is followed by first-person accounts in both Yup'ik and English, most recorded during elder gatherings that took place between 2000 and 2007. Part 2: Shaman Stories begins with elders' discussion of the importance of shamans and shamanism in general, good and bad shamans, and shamanism and Christianity. The narratives that follow are divided by regional group, including stories from Nelson Island, the Canineq (lower Kuskokwim coastal) area, and the Kuskokwim and Yukon Rivers. Over the years we have found that this format is the most accessible and meaningful to Yup'ik readers, who particularly value stories told by close friends and relatives from their own communities.

Narrators from different communities mix themes throughout their first-person accounts. While such "mixing" is not a problem for many Yup'ik readers, non-Native readers and some younger Yup'ik men and women unfamiliar with regional history may find this confusing. For this reason, the background and discussion of discrete topics in the English introduction is especially important. Following discussions of shamans as healers, separate chapters bring together information shared about shaman journeys, the shamans' role in masked dances requesting future abundance, powerful female shamans, shamans and *ircenrraat*, shamans and the dead, malicious shamans, shaman confrontations, becoming a shaman, and those who have shaman abilities today. These chapters promote interregional dialog, aiding readers in understanding shamanism more generally in southwest Alaska. The rich detail of individual accounts is the heart and soul of this book: As always, the English introduction is intended to help in their appreciation and enjoyment.

2

Angalkunek Elitelput
What We Learned about Shamans

In December 2003, a group of men and women gathered at the Yupiit Piciryarait Museum and Cultural Center in Bethel to examine and comment on the museum's collections. The group included Frank Andrew from Kwigillingok and his son Noah Andrew, Alex Bird from Emmonak, Margaret Andrews from Kotlik, as well as museum director Joan Hamilton from Chevak and CEC staff Mark John, Marie Meade, Alice Rearden, and Ann Riordan.

Toward the end of our gathering, Joan Hamilton brought out a small wood box containing a tiny carved figure. Its stomach was split open, and the figure was accompanied by a clear stone and a small piece of slate in the same box. Frank Andrew noted that the figure belonged to one with shaman powers, and Alex Bird agreed, briefly telling the story of the shaman Teggal-quq (lit., "Stone") from the mouth of the Yukon who encountered a female shaman and asked her to "do what men and women do" (have sex with him). When he was about to lay on her, he saw that the woman was slit open, and he understood that if he lay on top of her, she would kill him. Putting a log on top of his own stomach and pretending it was part of his body, he put it inside his adversary when they lay together, causing the woman to have stomach pains.

Agreeing that this was an object associated with shamans, Marie Meade then asked the group whether its picture, and the information shared by the elders during our meeting, should be made available to others—either through books or on the computer.

She noted that in the past such pieces would have been hidden and only seen by the person who owned them: "What do you think about the fact that this is going to be seen through that [video] and that what you are saying is recorded in [this tape recorder], and that it is accessible? It is being shown to those of us here. And what do you think of the possibility that it can be shown to those people out there in other far-away places when its information is written down along with its picture? What do you think: Is it good or bad?"

Margaret Andrews noted that it would be good to share, as young people today are curious about what shamans did. Alex Bird agreed, adding that people's dialects and ways differ, and that we should take time to fully understand these things before sharing them: "If you are thinking about [making it accessible to others], if you are not too anxious to put them on the computer, it would be better. That is what I think. You should try to understand them the best you can, meeting several times, and having different people, you will probably learn other things. Then you can put them into the computers." All agreed, and Marie reminded the group that we gather to record their words for future generations: "When you are gone, what you said will not disappear, [your words] will be put into books."

Marie continued, noting that objects like the one Joan was showing us still had power and should be treated with respect. Frank Andrew agreed, warn-

https://doi.org/10.5876/9781646427314.c002

ing of the dangers of mishandling things that were once the property of shamans. Frank concluded: "One with the ability and wisdom, one who is wise is an *angalkuq*, and he can use his abilities to accomplish things."

Angalkut Tungiitnun Umyuarteqellrat Cimirluni
Changing Views of Angalkut

Angalkut and their activities have not always been positively recalled. The discussion of *angalkut* at the Bethel museum differed markedly from accounts of shamans that I heard in the 1970s, as a young anthropologist doing fieldwork on Nelson Island and on later visits to Yup'ik communities. During those years few people spoke to me about *angalkut*. When they discussed them in private, the context was more often negative than positive. A notable exception was Paul John's storytelling at the Nelson Island High School in Toksook Bay in the winter of 1977, when he told a number of stories in Yup'ik about *angalkut* of the past. Students listened quietly. Only the students and a handful of Yup'ik teachers heard what he said, but soon that began to change.

During the 1980s, stories of shamans and their experiences were collected by Bethel High School students as part of a Foxfire-inspired oral history project. The Lower Kuskokwim School District (LKSD) published fifty of these stories in a bilingual book, *Yupik Lore / Yuut Qanemciit* (Tennant and Bitar 1981), which included three tales of *angalkut*: "Shamans and their powers" and "The shaman who was called Big Belly," both told by Alexie Andrew of Napaskiak, and "The good shaman Angamachuik," told by Mike Albert of Tununak. Neither narrator extolled or condemned the shamans' role but simply described them in the section entitled "Myths and Legends."

Three years after the publication of *Yupik Lore*, Elsie Mather of Bethel interviewed ten elders from eight Yup'ik communities to gather information on traditional ceremonialism for use in the classroom. Mather, a devout Moravian, subsequently published a detailed description of the traditional ceremonial cycle as *Cauyarnariuq [A Time for Drumming]* (1985), a book entirely in Yup'ik and intended for use in high school classes within the Lower Kuskokwim School District. Although Mather's book was never trans-

FIGURE 2.1. Yupiit Piciryarait Museum director Joan Hamilton holding a small wooden box containing a tiny figure said to have belonged to a shaman and asking the elders' advice as to how the object should be treated. The two small objects lying on the white glove are stones that the box contained. From left to right, Marie Meade, Margaret Andrews, Joan Hamilton, and Frank Andrew, December 2003. Ann Fienup-Riordan.

lated, cultural anthropologist Phyllis Morrow (1984) published an English summary for a non-Native audience. The curriculum committee (Yup'ik teachers and materials developers from the different LKSD schools) consulted with elders in their communities. The elders universally supported the project, and there was no sense that people might think poorly of them for contributing. On the contrary, it was hoped that a significant work available only in the Yup'ik language based on elders' knowledge of ceremonial traditions would be a strong draw for students and others literate in the standardized Yup'ik orthography.

As another example of Yup'ik attitudes toward shamanism, when the village of Alakanak experienced a suicide epidemic in 1986 that claimed the lives of seven young men and women in less than a year, some villagers blamed a powerful shaman, long dead, who was said to have appeared at the airstrip each time a death occurred. The suicides were widely publicized (Anchorage Daily News Staff 1986), but few outsiders heard this local explanation. In the 1990s, some deaths and mishaps as well as extraordinary occurrences were still being attributed to *angalkut*. Yet at the same time, many Yup'ik people, particularly in Catholic communities on Nelson Island and the lower Yukon River, also described *angalkut* positively as experts of extraordinary power. Moreover, their remembrances and explanations were often given publicly for the benefit of non-Native as well as Yup'ik listeners.

In the early 1990s, as elders shared their memories of masks and masked dancing in preparation for the Yup'ik mask exhibit *Agayuliyararput / Our Way*

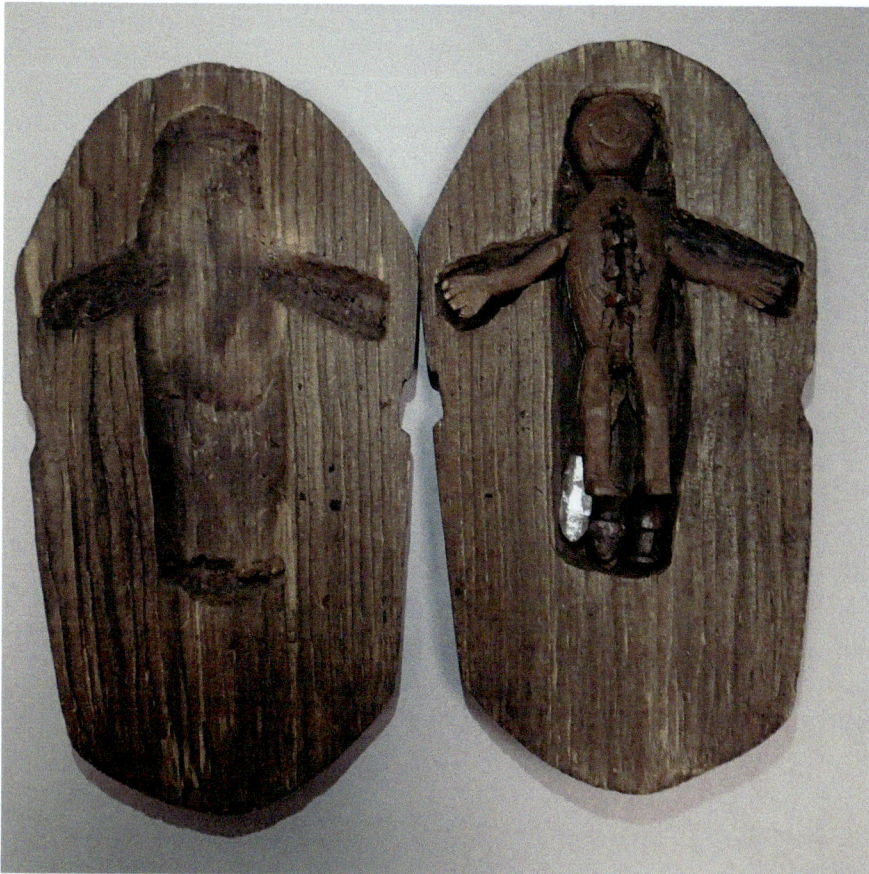

FIGURE 2.2. The shaman box contained this wooden figure with slit stomach lined with teeth and accompanied by a small crystal and piece of slate. Kilbuck School teacher John Snodgrass gifted the piece to the museum in 1970. Ann Fienup-Riordan.

of Making Prayer, a new appreciation of past *angalkut* emerged. Elders spoke of the *angalkuq* as a central figure in all masked dances, directing expert carvers to craft the masks and explaining their meanings to the people when the masks were presented. The *angalkuq* was also described as *tuunralek* (one with *tuunrat* or spirit helpers). According to Jasper Louis (February 1994:35) of St. Mary's: "There are masks for every animal we know that is potential prey, and some masks are even images of humans. The *angalkut* could have masks made of animals known to the people in the village if the animal had become the *tuunraq* [spirit helper] of that *angalkuq*. When the people heard the song with these two verses, an *angalkuq* could actually see the animals."

Angalkut Agayumaciq-llu
Shamanism and Christianity

Angalkut were both the primary spiritual leaders and healers in southwest Alaska until the arrival of non-Native missionaries. First came a handful of Rus-sian Orthodox priests in the early 1800s—too few to enforce strict adherence to their doctrines, yet plentiful enough to introduce new practices that would ultimately transform the Yup'ik way of life. Both Catholic and Moravian missionaries followed in the mid-1880s, in numbers that began to be felt (Fienup-Riordan 1988, 1990b, 1991; Oswalt 1963, 1990). These early missionaries had little positive to say about *angalkut*, and they actively worked to undercut the trust placed in them by community members. In an undated manuscript, Moravian missionary John Kilbuck described his archrival as an absolute power, more feared than loved: "They frame the superstition in vogue. . . . A shaman with a reputation for success gains quite an income by conjuring sick people. Like the Oracle of Delphi, the shaman's revelation bears two interpretations" (Fienup-Riordan 1988:38).

In his retrospective account of missionary work along the Kuskokwim River between 1885 and 1900, John Kilbuck wrote: "We openly attacked the shamans, and made a determined effort to discredit them before the people. Here is where we differed from the Greek [Orthodox] church. The [Orthodox] priest did not approve of shamaning, but he was so weak on this point that the people said that they could be good Greeks and still practice shamanism" (Fienup-Riordan 1988:72). As the Moravian mission's power in general increased along the Kuskokwim, the power and prestige of the shamans fell proportionately. When Kilbuck had first attempted to preach in the men's house, the shamans had ignored him and with their followers silently vacated the building. Allowing for occasional setbacks, by 1891 the tables were turning, and a Native helper reported that the shamans and their followers were the ones left alone when Kilbuck called the people to his home for services (Fienup-Riordan 1991:192). In fact, some of Kilbuck's most active and effective helpers were shamans who had recently converted (Fienup-Riordan 1991:146–64, 194).

Christian missionaries constituted a direct challenge to the power of the shamans, both as spiritual leaders and as healers. Their way had been paved by the social and ideological disruptions attending the epidemic diseases that ravaged Yup'ik people during the nineteenth century. The death toll resulting from the smallpox epidemic of 1838–1839 alone may have run as high as 60 percent of the Bristol Bay and Kuskokwim populations (Oswalt 1963:96–97). Had disease not preceded their arrival, the missionaries' message would probably have taken much longer to find fertile ground.

Though the shaman's role had been inextricably bound with healing, epidemic disasters alone would not necessarily have undone their claims to power. On the contrary, there is good evidence that increased disease produced a comparable increase in people's reliance on their traditional healers. Missionaries like Edith Kilbuck (1888) rightly feared the association of the arrival of disease with the arrival of the missionaries. The epidemics that followed the coming of the missionaries put a hard edge on the Natives' suspicions. Missionary power was ambiguous at best, as it could both help and harm. The attention the Kilbucks focused on the sick and dying reinforced these fears. Where their medicines worked a cure, however, the effect was profound and the Kilbuck's limited medical ministry reaped a rich harvest. In his 1889 report to his superiors in Bethlehem, Pennsylvania, John Kilbuck wrote: "The administering to the bodily ailments of our people has contributed not a little to the winning of the people. . . .

[W]e have been able to so help the sick, that the people nearly always come to us first, and do not go to their shamans."

Although disease provided a sober backdrop to the arrival of the Moravians, the missionaries' imperviousness to shamanic ritual action was also an effective tool in their behalf. In "The Hindrances," John Kilbuck noted that the shamans cut pieces from the missionaries' clothing and used them to make "bad medicine" with which to spoil the mission's power (Fienup-Riordan 1988:72–78). To the extent the missionaries ignored these threats and demonstrated their impotence, the efficacy of these shamanic acts of power was inverted and turned against the shamans themselves.

In his insightful discussion of shamans in southwest Alaska, Ahnie Marie Al'aq David Litecky (2011:79–86) points out that while missionaries offered many practical medicines for common illnesses, they could not provide cures for often deadly respiratory sicknesses, including influenza and pneumonia: "After the devastating double epidemic of measles and influenza in 1900, the Eskimos were disillusioned by the inability of their Moravian doctor [Herman Romig] to save them from the widespread death, and so, once again, turned to the shamans for answers and healing." While the shamans were also unable to cure these new epidemic diseases, they could offer both comfort and culturally comprehensible explanations in terms of traditional Yup'ik concepts of disease causation and cure (see chapter 3, "Shamans as Healers").

Although Christianity continued to gain ground, especially in villages near Bethel, shamanic healing remained an important part of Yup'ik life for many decades. As Litecky (2011:123–26) points out, shamans continued to outnumber missionaries and were often closer at hand to provide psychologicial counseling if not physical relief. Also, as diseases like tuberculosis became more common, people continued to consult shamans as missionaries had no medicines to cure them (Oswalt 1990:88). In 1918 a small hospital was established in Akiak, and access to Western medicine gradually increased. Yet the shamans' power as healers was slow to wane. According to Moravian missionaries stationed along the Kuskokwim, shamans still attended most illnesses in the mid-1920s (Gapp 1928:38). Stationed in Akiak beginning in 1936, Dr. Otto George expressed surprise that Yupiit still

FIGURE 2.3. Dancers in the Bethel *qasgiq* in the 1930s. The drummer on the far right is the well-known shaman Puyulkuk, who moved upriver to Bethel from the Canineq area, where both Frank Andrew and John Phillip had watched him performing when they were young. Ferdinand Drebert, National Museum of the American Indian, Smithsonian Institution L2710.

relied on shamans: "With the knowledge that there had been medical care for the area for the greater part of fifty years, I expected the natives to be pretty well acquainted with modern medicine, and that the native superstitions about medicine men had been replaced by modern ideas. I soon found I was badly mistaken" (George 1979:39).

Though slow to lose their influence, shamans gradually took a back seat as both Christianity and Western methods of healing spread and deepened in Yup'ik community life. Noting that he had listened to shamans practicing their powers three times in the *qasgiq*, Benedict Tucker (March 2011:902) of Emmonak recalled: "I saw shamans, but when there were few left. But these priests' influence was so strong, that eventually there were no longer any [shamans] around. At this time, [shamans] are no longer around, but they just attend church services."

Born in 1917, Frank Andrew (September 2005:178) also recalled the shamans of his youth:

The older folks back in those days weren't all converted yet when I was little. . . . They had not changed yet. There were some who were Russian Orthodox members and not yet Moravians.

Yes, they were still relying on shamans for guidance and support. However, though they relied on them, they were also members of the church.

When asked about the changes he had seen as he grew older, Frank continued:

People began to reject the medicine used by shamans, even though they still used them for healing.

More and more of them gradually turned to Christianity, and soon many became Moravians. When they became church members, the older ones were stronger in their faith in God then the younger folks. In the early days, the older Yup'ik people were easily persuaded into believing in the Word of God.

Whenever they could, missionaries forbid the masked dancing that was a central part of the winter ceremonial cycle and in which the shamans played a critical role. John Kilbuck (1892) continually exhorted his converts to "give up shamaning and the masquerade [masked dances]." The immediate response on the part of some ambivalent Yupiit was not to abandon their ceremonies but to take them underground, and other evasive tactics—such as holding annual dances without masks (figure 2.3).

Priests also considered *eyagyarat* (abstinence practices following birth, death, illness, and first menstruation) as superstitions related to the ways of the shamans. Martina John (March 2009:303) of Toksook Bay noted that when she first menstruated in the late 1940s, she didn't abstain, as priests had them stop those practices.

In the several instances where a shaman was converted, Edith Kilbuck (1894, 1895) testified to the extraordinary impact this had on their membership. In fact, John Phillip (January 2006:258) provided a brief but vivid description of the shaman Apangtak's conversion experience. Once when he was asked to speak in church, he replied that he had nothing to say and that people wouldn't believe him, knowing that he was a shaman. Then he dreamed that a voice told him to go outside, and when he did he saw a terrible person approaching from the river, whose face became first a dog, then a wolf. Before it reached him, the face became human again, then its tongue came out of its mouth and jumped over three villages, one after the other. The meaning was that gossip travels in the same way, and "this small tongue has no limit to how far it can reach." A voice told him that that was what he would speak of in church, and although he was Russian Orthodox, he heard and recognized a joyous Moravian hymn. Then he awoke, and from that time on abandoned his work as a shaman. John Phillip closed by saying that he had recalled this story when speaking of how shamans are actually good, made in God's image.

Christianity was well established throughout southwest Alaska by the mid-twentieth century. Fifty years later, however, community leaders were recognizing the slow but steady erosion of Yup'ik traditions generally, and came to blame some of this loss on the pressure missionaries put on people to forsake their old ways. At a Bethel elders' gathering in 2001, Paul John (April 2001:5–6) spoke about the importance of retaining these traditions, including the ways of the shamans:

> If those of us who are gathered here believe in God, when God made people, he made different races on this big earth and gave them all different traditions. . . . He actually gave us traditions to live by until the end of the world. . . .
>
> I do not want to think badly of Christianity, but I want to believe in it. . . . Christianity is a part of the reason why we are losing our traditions.

Paul John noted that Christianity had disrupted Yup'ik traditions given to them by God, replacing them with non-Yup'ik ways. This was a mistake made by Catholic priests and others who misunderstood Yup'ik spirituality, forcing converts to abandon their traditional ways, including their belief in *angalkut*. Paul John (October 2010:164) later added:

> Those two [priests] . . . said they also heard about those called *angalkut*; since they were asking questions [about our traditional ways], they also asked about those shamans.
>
> [The two priests] said those [shamans] had actually been given a gift by God so that those with an ability to heal people would help us. . . .
>
> From my perspective, I think what they did is true; priests, even though they were priests, made a mistake when they swept our way of life away, when they removed it like sweeping away things on top of the table.

Umyuaqellriit Umyuarrliqellriit-llu Angalkut
Good and Bad Angalkut

Paul John (April 2001:9) emphasized what many elders have shared over the years—that in the past there were good as well as bad shamans:

> And some of these Christians call *angalkut tuunrangayiit* [translated as Devils]. Not all [*angalkut*] had evil intentions because some of them were given powers by God. *Angalkut* used to help their people tremendously. . . .
>
> Indeed, when stories are told about those *angalkut* of the past, some of them did good works, healing their sicknesses, causing their ailments to heal. But some of them were evil toward their peers, trying to kill them.

David Martin (April 2001:10) from Kipnuk agreed with Paul John, using the word *tuunrangayiit* for shamans, and distinguishing those who were healers from those who harmed others and only made people worse: "I saw some *tuunrangayiit* from the later times in the *qasgiq*. Like he said, some did good works and healed some people's ailments. . . . But when I observed those who did deceitful works, it seemed that after they initially healed their ailment, . . . they would become sick again, worse than their previous sickness." Paul John objected to David Martin's use of the term *tuunrangayiit* for shamans: "We should not call them *tuunrangayiit*. But we should call those who helped others *piyunarqucilget* [those with abilities and authority]. It is because the name *tuunrangayak* is an unfavorable term."

Frank Andrew (December 2003:307) also stressed that shamans were not called *tuunrangayiit* in the past, but only *tuunralek* (one with a *tuunraq* [spirit helper]). Marie Meade noted that when missionaries arrived, they would talk about the Devil, translating it as *tuunrangayak*. Frank Andrew then spoke briefly about Asgulria from the Canineq (lower Kuskokwim coastal) area and Tairtaq from the upper Kuskokwim as good shamans: "At that time maybe God was helping someone who was like that because he did good works, even though he was known as a shaman. One who does good work doesn't come from anything else. That's how I think. One who wanted to help others was visible by the good he did back then."

Growing up near present-day Nunam Iqua, Raphael Jimmy (January 2013:358–61) extended Paul John's and Frank Andrew's view that good shamans were a gift from God. Raphael had no personal experience with shamans, but he recalled his mother saying that although there were many shamans in the past, there were two kinds—one good and one bad. When Jesus was born, he healed people, just like a shaman:

Jesus and the Devil, they are our shamans today. Jesus loves us greatly and tries to help us. But the other, the Devil, tends to constantly push us in the wrong direction. . . .

Those shamans gradually decreased in number. And it seems from up the Kuskokwim River and the Yukon River [they started becoming scarce] down toward the ocean, and today, we no longer have shamans, but only Jesus and the Devil.

During the Bethel gathering mentioned above, Frank Andrew (December 2003:302) also noted that some shamans were good while others were jealous:

They really believed in them, especially when they worked on what was ailing people in their lives. They would watch those who did that, too. . . . Some of the shamans got jealous and used their powers against those helpful shamans who received payment for helping people, and [other shamans] didn't receive any.

They say that is how it was. Those shamans who had abilities, ones who did a good job were held in high regard, and they would go and get them no matter where they were. It was because they actually had good healing powers.

Alex Bird agreed that there were two kinds of *angalkut*—one who worked like a doctor to help people, even doing surgery, while the second was jealous and would try to destroy the first one's power. Alex concluded: "Those two would be adversaries."

During a subsequent Bethel gathering, Alice Rearden (October 2006:166) commented that when she was growing up in Napakiak in the 1980s, she never heard of good *angalkut*. Roland Phillip of Kwigillingok responded that some *angalkut* were malicious, while others were good. George Billy, also from Napakiak, mentioned *umyuaqegcilria* (one with good wishes toward others, one who is thoughtful), adding that one with good wishes had a strong mind. John Phillip (October 2006:167) observed that the Moravian missionary Reverend Ferdinand Drebert had said that shamans shouldn't be criticized too much, as some helped people and had the ability to heal, just like Jesus.

One of the first Yup'ik Catholic deacons, Joe Phillip (December 2013:30–31) of Alakanuk, also understood *angalkut* as doctors—some able to heal people while others made people worse: "Those shamans who were good, I saw a number of them. . . . To be healed, they told a person to speak of how he was, like a confession of sins. If he didn't speak, he couldn't be healed, but if he spoke of how he was, the shaman could remove it." One should take care not to say or do anything to upset a shaman, as their negative thoughts could be dangerous: "They said a shaman would do that to us with his spirit powers. He would cause us to become ill or cause us to change. They used to be afraid of those [shamans]."

David Martin (January 2002:164) also spoke of two kinds of shamans—ones who could heal, and those who only pretended to remove sickness: "Our ancestors knew about the false shaman and called him *iqlungalria* [lit., 'a liar']. . . . Some of them really worked to get rid of the illness so that it never returned." Jasper Louis (February 1994:35) agreed: "Some *angalkut* were revered by the poor ancestors. They would know if he had a good mind and tried to the best of his ability to help others heal. Apparently, *angalkut* weren't the same. The ones who had slippery eyes, ones who didn't look at people straight, were not to be trusted."

Maa-i Umyuartequtiit Angalkugnun
Present Recollections of Past Shamans

Changes in contemporary Christianity have influenced elders' willingness to recall *angalkut* in a positive light, and their role is being discussed, reevaluated, and in some cases transformed. In lower Yukon and coastal villages north of and including Nelson Island, the Catholic Church encourages parishioners like Paul John and Joe Phillip to incorporate "traditional spirituality" into contemporary religious practice. This reappraisal is part of a general effort by Jesuit priests and their parishioners to come to terms with past suppression of traditional Yup'ik spirituality, including shamanism, that predated Vatican II. Beginning in the early 1970s, the Catholic church in southwest Alaska established its first Native deacon program to breathe new life into village churches by putting ownership and responsibility in the hands of local people. Fifty years later, two dozen Yup'ik deacons and their wives are leading the way toward an active reappraisal of beliefs and activities condemned by earlier missionaries as idolatry and "heathen superstition."

This new attitude is exemplified in the words of the late William Tyson (Fienup-Riordan 2000:142–43), originally from the lower Yukon River and one of the first Yup'ik deacons. His understanding of the changes he lived through is both clear-sighted and compassionate:

> The priests and nuns were saying that everything that we do was evil because it came from the Devil. We cannot follow them. . . .
>
> But then if you look at it, I cannot blame them. They work for Christ, and remembering the first commandment of God—"Thou shalt not have strange Gods before me"—well, they had to obey that. And everything else was not right. They had to tell us we had to obey that one. So are they wrong or what?
>
> So now what I've been thinking [is that] they should have studied our belief before they condemned it. Because those old medicine men, some of them were amazing in what they could do.

Today, selected pieces of the Yup'ik past are being revitalized and reevaluated. Once reviled by missionaries and rarely discussed in public, *angalkut* are reemerging as historical figures meriting respect and as men and women with special powers that they used for the good of the people.

Not only are people talking about things differently, they also are doing things differently. Today pre-Christian ritual acts and songs have been incorporated into the Catholic Mass. More remarkable is the extent to which devout Catholics are following the lead of priests, deacons, and community leaders like Paul John to bring parts of their past into the present, transforming and expanding on original meanings at the same time making the church uniquely their own. In this they demonstrate, as anthropologist Marshall Sahlins (1999:399) says so well, not the invention but the inventiveness of tradition.

This movement is not universally approved, and some are uncomfortable with such a repositioning. This reluctance is more common in Moravian communities to the south of Nelson Island. In Catholic communities, non-Native priests historically ministered to Native parishioners, many of whom stopped actively practicing the old "superstitions" but did not always inwardly deny them. In Moravian communities, however, beginning in the 1890s, missionaries handed the reins of church authority over to Native helpers, some of whom were themselves former shamans. Ironically, once converted, these Native helpers laid the foundation for a Yup'ik Christianity that, when rooted and grown, would be much less tolerant of traditional manifestations of Yup'ik spirituality than their Catholic contemporaries. Yet today many Moravian elders and community leaders speak more openly about past shamans, and the Moravian Seminary in Bethel has offered classes on shamanism so that Native clergy can better understand the role of these past "spiritual leaders."

Cultural pride in *angalkut* as men and woman of extraordinary power and abilities increasingly outweighs fear of them as "servants of the Devil." Secure in their Christian present, a generation removed from the emotional debate over shamanism that tore families and communities apart at the turn of the century, many Yup'ik people today can look at their pre-Christian past and see the positive aspects of what they lost. They extol the virtues of *angalkut* not to revive the practice of shamanism, but to revive pride in the Yup'ik past for future generations.

When Marie Meade and I began work on the Yup'ik mask exhibit in 1993 and visited the Yukon River village of St. Mary's to present our plans to village elders, I was prepared for complete rejection. I knew that the photographs of masks I brought to share depicted objects made by shamans and still closely associated with them. I feared contemporary elders would either be reluctant to speak of these past practices or unwilling to share their memories with a non-Native audience. Instead, the response was enthusiastic, with men and women sharing unprecedented remembrances (Fienup-Riordan 1996; Meade and Fienup-Riordan 1996).

In Catholic communities, this dramatic openness to re-own their past and their pride in presenting it to the outside world has been made possible in part by the post–Vatican II climate of apology and forgiveness, which itself developed in the context of increasingly liberal attitudes toward social and cultural diversity. The positive regard for *angalkut* also reflects a general revival of pride in all things Yup'ik, reinforced by increasing political and cultural ties with other Indigenous groups. Efforts toward cultural empowerment take a multitude of forms in the Yukon-Kuskokwim region today, including Yup'ik language immersion programs in the schools, multi-village dance festivals, and elders conferences. Cultural pride is also apparent in the words of village elders as they revisit their past. This is not an effort to turn back, but to ensure that Yup'ik history and oral traditions will be remembered.

This "speaking out" by elders came none too soon, as today none remain of the last generation to have personally witnessed dramatic shamanic performances and acts of healing. Their elderly status may have contributed to their desire to share their experiences. When Marie and I visited St. Mary's in 1993, Andy Kinzy closed his account of masked dancing by saying, "You have come just when I have stories to tell!" I never saw him again, as he died that spring.

Today many Yupiit proudly recall *angalkut* as the "scientists of our past," publicly proclaiming their strengths and virtues as healers and teachers. Their recollections open new vistas, countering descriptions of "heathen sorcerers" with public claims of *angalkut*, men and women alike, possessing extraordinary abilities, empowered by the Almighty.

3

Angalkut Yuungcaristengulallrat
Shamans as Healers

Angalkut yuungcaristekellruaput
Angalkut were our doctors

Today *angalkut* are remembered primarily as healers, men and women who could both interpret the cause of illness and help remove it from the patient's body. Paul John (June 1995) declared:

> The *angalkut* were not the leaders, but *angalkut* were their doctors. . . .
>
> In the stories told about them, the *angalkut* were important figures because they were their healers; they were not ridiculed or criticized, but a few complaints were made about them. They were able to perceive and reveal things that ordinary people could not comprehend.

Theresa Moses (April 2001:92) of Toksook Bay agreed: "The one who is healing those who are in pain, that *angalkuq* was like a doctor back then." Frank Andrew (December 2013:305) shared a similar view of shamans as healers: "[*Angalkut*] would help people. They really depended on them back before [Western] doctors became available. They really believed in them and always wanted them to be around. They didn't break any of their rules either. That's how it was."[1]

Like medical doctors today, *angalkut* were paid for their services. Tim Agagtak (July 1985:37) recalled that he was born in 1903 "just before they disappeared" when shamans still practiced their healing arts in every community and were considered the

equivalent of medical doctors. Tim described how parents would bring a sick child to a shaman with payment, noting that when a shrewd shaman wasn't satisfied with what was offered, his patient would die.

Naulluutem ayuqucia
What sickness is like

To understand the shaman's role as healer, one must first understand Yup'ik concepts of illness and wellness. These ideas reflected a view of the world as sentient and responsive to human action and intention. Illness was, first and foremost, a moral state—the body's physical response to the way a person chose to live life. People largely viewed disease as within their control. If they lived good lives, illness could not easily affect them. The rules for daily living promoted continued good health. Conversely, if people did not follow the rules, illness would "find them a comfortable place to lie on." People considered a sick person responsible for either knowingly or unknowingly disregarding the rules for living. Although illness did not always imply punishment, people believed that their offenses eventually came back to them.

People considered illness to be an animate force, and the way people chose to live determined whether or not sickness could enter their bodies. In the past, to succeed as a husband and hunter or wife and mother, men and women ideally performed all manner of

https://doi.org/10.5876/9781646427314.c003

tasks while keeping their minds focused on the animals they sought or the children they bore. Animals would not give themselves to a thoughtless or careless person. The lazy ran the double risk of ill health as well as loss of the animals' good will. According to Paul John (February 1977:2–4):

> They let illness have a saying. If an illness goes straight to the one who starts going about early . . . while the others are sleeping, one's illness is not comfortable staying with that person, because one doesn't stay put. . . .
>
> So then, the illness will think, "Alas, this one is not a comfortable place because this person does not stay put." . . .
>
> Then, when the illness looks around, over there is one who is lying in bed although it is time to be up and about.
>
> [Illness] will say, "That one over there seems like a good place."
>
> It will go to that person and find a comfortable place.
>
> Then while that person is lying in bed, he starts to feel sick. That person will wake up with a headache or having body aches or with some part of the body feeling sick.

Today people still speak of the importance of not giving in to illness. Annie Nelson (March 2017:204) of Napakiak clearly expressed this view: "When disease comes to a person and is welcomed, it will say, 'Let me stay since this person is happy that I'm here.' . . . When I remember such expressions, I've said to myself, 'I think I do fight sickness and disease when it comes.' . . . When disease comes to a person and is welcomed, that person will become immobile and not be able to do things."

People viewed all humans as susceptible to illness as a result of contact with unclean influences. Smithsonian naturalist Edward Nelson (1899:422) recorded the belief that epidemic disease came from the moon and that an eclipse of the moon foretold an epidemic, as during that time unclean influences descended to the earth. People sought to mitigate their effect by literally "shaking them off" through their activity. Moreover, if people did get sick, they could facilitate their cure by remaining as active as possible. If people lay down and gave themselves up to their illness, then it would continue to find them "a comfortable place," and they would not get well. According to Mary Mike (October 1992) of St. Mary's, "When you

get sick, always get up and do, and illness will get uncomfortable and go away from you. Don't give in to it, or it will think you welcome it. Laugh at it, and it will leave you."

The proscription against too much sleep, as well as the body's susceptibility to unclean influences following an eclipse, indicated a common cause of illness—the entry into the body of dangerous substances. Some people believed illness entered the unguarded body as a vapor. If a person lay too long abed, one made oneself susceptible to the entry into the body of *caarrluk* (that which one is going to have as an illness; lit., "dirt, debris, transgression, sin"). People employed a number of protective measures to frustrate or deflect the entry of disease into their bodies. Both men and women fought sleep, lest disease settle on them. The injunction to work ceaselessly at all manner of chores especially stressed the benefit of accomplishing the most repugnant. According to Dennis Panruk (December 1987:9) of Chefornak:

> Some worked hard like that, thinking about their future catch. Some did not wish to endure all forms of sickness.
>
> They swept the floors. They cleaned off the dogs' feces. Feces are a lot of mess. After they had swept and the refuse was taken out, they were told . . . not to be repelled by them but to carry them out in their laps.
>
> And after the refuse was dumped, even though our hands were filthy, they told us to lift up the hems of our parkas and wipe our hands on our stomachs.
>
> When I did that it was just cold against my skin. When one does that it is said that sickness is prevented.

Agnes Tony (March 1987) of Alakanuk noted that if people rubbed themselves with dirt from the entryway floor, the dirt would provide a path for sickness to leave their bodies: "Because everybody walks in and out like that, if you take that walking dirt, the sickness goes away, it walks out." Both the power of the minds of the people who had been helped as well as the power inherent in the dirt to "let the sickness walk out" provided a pathway for illness to leave the body. According to Joshua Phillip (June 1988:18) of Tuluksak: "At that time of sickness, the gratefulness of the people will make one live. And that person will be regarded by one's fellows as a person who cleans up the air. That is the nature of helping others, which is one of the *alerquutet* [admonitions]."

People could also expel sickness from their dwellings by exiting the house, circling it in the direction of the sun's course, and reentering.[2] Here exit and reentry created a passageway for illness to leave the body just as a pregnant woman's rapid exit from her home was said to make the child's exit from her womb easier. Rubbing the dirt floor of the house with a rock in a circular motion could prevent sickness. This action might also prevent the realization of something fearful that had been talked about.

Elders enjoined young men and women to diligently care for their homes and to employ the refuse they handled as a protective covering for their bodies. "Encasing" acts were likewise prescribed to keep contamination at bay (compare Morrow 1984). Young women wore belts following puberty, both to protect themselves and to prevent their unclean air from contaminating others. Similarly, young women were told to fold in the hems of their garments when passing a man and never to step over a child lest their bad air contaminate them. According to Theresa Moses (August 1987:3): "Females were warned never to step over a child. Watch the older women nowadays. They fold the hems of their dresses and pass the men. It is said in those days if females stepped over them, they began to have frequent bloody noses, and they began to have eye ailments. It is called *aurneraariluki* [from *aurneq*, 'mist or vapor, especially vapor rising from a warm object in the cold']. That is the way they lived."

Covering the body with refuse, clothing, paint, or ashes as well as encircling it with a belt or string had protective power in both everyday and transitional contexts, including birth, death, and first menstruation. Moreover, people's food and water must be carefully covered lest they be contaminated. For instance, Nelson Islanders routinely wiped their individual eating bowls clean with grass or moss after each meal and turned them upside down to prevent contamination from outside influences. Likewise, Nelson (1899:431) recorded that during an eclipse of the moon the people turned all of their utensils upside down to avoid contact with the unclean elements descending to earth during this period. Similarly, villagers emptied and refilled all water buckets following a human death, and close relatives of the deceased were required to hold water dippers under their parkas when taking a drink.

Covering the body and food and water containers protected against entry of disease. Keeping one's body covered also protected a person from the departure of one's life force or spiritual essence. Just as disease could be caused by contamination from without, it might also come from within. Nelson (1899:422) reported the belief that a person's *inua*, or shade, could be stolen, and accounts of soul loss survive in Yup'ik oral tradition.

People sometimes held encounters with apparitions responsible for illness. If a person heard a voice calling in the wilderness, one should not respond for it might be the spirit of a dead person calling the listener to join it. If a person encountered an apparition in the wilderness, one should ignore it as well, as to acknowledge its presence invited illness. Mary Napoka (May 1989:60–63) of Tuluksak shared a long account of a man who met an apparition and collapsed as he tried to flee. When found and returned to his village, he described his experience, then vomited a green substance, removing what was making him sick. In Mary's account, acknowledging the presence of the apparition allowed it to enter the man's body and to make him ill. Had he kept the encounter to himself, the experience might have killed him. Once the cause of his illness was discovered, however, he could expel it by vomiting until he completely recovered.

In the same way that encounters with apparitions must be confessed lest they cause illness, a person should always talk about bad thoughts, as to hold them inside would make the person sick. Helen Smith (1981) of Hooper Bay recalled: "Then my husband died. He didn't get sick. He shot himself. All those things went together, but I always try not to show it. Every time when it comes to my head I have to speak about it so I won't get sick."

As in so many aspects of Yup'ik cosmology, human action in the world focused on controlling the passage of spiritual essences from one realm to another. Disease prevention was essentially a boundary-making activity in which people concentrated attention on limiting the entry into the human body of outside contagions and, alternately, the departure of an inner spiritual essence. The rules for proper living were also the rules for healthy living insofar as they reinforced the separation between the sexes and an "active" attitude toward life that made it difficult for disease to settle on the body and find a passage inside.

Tuunrat
Spirit helpers

To heal a person, a shaman would call on his or her *tuunrat* (spirit helpers or familiar spirits). Paul Waskey (January 1996:1–2) of Pilot Station described his grandmother, Tut'angaq, who was a female shaman with two spirit helpers:

> My dear, old grandmother used to invite her *tuunrak* [two spirit helpers]. . . . *Tuunrat* talk like us, but they are a little hard to understand like they are talking from inside a tank [oil barrel]. One [of her spirit helpers] *meryiggluni* [spoke in the Chevak dialect], and the other *qaggluni* [spoke with a northern accent], like the Iñupiaq people. [The spirit] would talk from inside the seal-gut parka. Sometimes she would tell them not to be too close and to move farther away. . . .
>
> She understood the two because they were hers.

Willie Kamkoff (February 1994:3–4) of Kotlik described how a shaman's *tuunraq* (spirit helper) might enter the shaman's body, allowing him to remove the illness from his patient:

> They say back in those days, many *angalkut* had the wolf as their *tuunraq*. They also talked about a person named Nakacuk who operated on people. When Nakacuk removed the cause of the illness, his *tuunraq*, the wolf, entered him, and he would eat what he had removed as blood dripped down his mouth. . . .
>
> Iquvanrilnguq told that story in Marshall with a priest present. He said the shaman's patient was still alive. After the priest contemplated that for a while, he said he had begun to understand that the work of the *angalkuq* wasn't all bad. *Angalkut* were the only healers around, so some obviously did help people, yet they did not take care of their own relatives. Even today, medical doctors are reluctant to care for their own families. Our ancestors were like that, too.

Masks were sometimes made to represent a shaman's *tuunrat* and used both in healing ceremonies and masked dances. Jasper Louis (February 1994:39) declared: "*Angalkut* created masks in the images of their *tuunrat*. Some *angalkut* even had deceased humans as their *tuunrat*—deceased *angalkut*. The shaman used the *tuunraq* for healing purposes, and it was the only source used for healing."

Yuungcarat wall'u yungcarat
Ones treated by a shaman
while still in the womb

In the past, older women served as midwives during childbirth. Shamans also had a role to play in the health and well-being of a newborn. Even before the child's birth, a shaman was often called in to enable a couple to have a healthy child, known as a *yuungcaraq* (one who is doctored by a shaman while still in the womb and allowed to live), also pronounced *yungcaraq*. A shaman who played this role became the child's *urumavik* (one who helped in a child's conception, from *uruma-*, "to be warm [of a person]"). Frank Andrew (September 2005:247) explained: "When a couple conceived after previous failed pregnancies and they asked a shaman to intercede and help in the child's healthy development, and when the child known as a *yuungcaraq* was born, the shaman would be her or his *urumavik*."

The shaman's "doctoring" consisted of instructing the child's parents in carrying out or avoiding certain activities, as well as giving the child a *napan* or *napaneq* (amulet or name given by a shaman, lit., "support that keeps one up or alive," from *napa-*, "to stand upright"). Frank Andrew (December 2003:135) explained:

> And if he had a *napaneq*, he would join those things and stay alive, the various plants that are on the land. If he has one of those for a *napaneq*, he will stay alive with [the plant or animal] because he is one of them, be it of the water, of the air, or a land animal. They say that is how shamans are.
>
> [The child] would be taken from there. . . . He would grow up with that as a foundation.

Here the health and well-being of the *yuungcaraq* was analogically associated with the health and well-being of a particular plant or animal, which that person could not consume. Frank concluded: "This is what those with powers do. [The shaman] warned [Cauvakayak's] mother not to eat beluga whale. . . . His mother broke her admonition, and ate that to his detriment. She caused her child, the *yuungcaraq*, to end up a certain way. . . . He could not hunt, even though it was time for him to hunt."

Theresa Moses (August 1987:7) was a *yuungcaraq* and described her experience:

I was finally born. My older siblings kept dying before I was born. I had been taken special care of to be alive through the help of a shaman.

At that time that shaman *napanirlua* [gave me support to live] with wild celery.

When I was able to do things, I would gain weight when plants started to grow, and if the wild celery got hard I would become skinny again.

That is why even now wild celery tastes terrible to me. I don't like to eat them.

Theresa (April 2001:11) noted that she was also admonished not to cut her hair, and her parents were told not to eat certain foods if they wanted to have her for a child: "They took the admonishments of the *angalkut* very seriously because those *angalkut* who worked on people healed others honestly."

Maryann Andrews (April 2012:175–78) of Emmonak said that her husband's father, Quscuar, was an *angalkuq*, with a *kenriiq* (short-eared owl) as a *napan*. Once, when his children were lost in bad weather, he used his shaman powers and had a short-eared owl sit on them, like sitting on eggs, to keep them warm. Maryann also said that her mother had a walrus as a *naparta* (thing that held her up and allowed her to live) and that she snored loudly, like a walrus. When she was sick, however, she didn't snore. Her daughters asked her why this was so, and she told them that the walrus that kept her alive seemed to leave her when she wasn't feeling well.

During a Nelson Island women's gathering in Bethel, Elsie Tommy (March 2009:191–96) of Newtok explained her understanding of *yuungcarat*:

> They say when a shaman gives them protection from sickness, they use their powers to doctor them, then they give them *iinrut* [amulets], and that [child] gets big.
>
> The shaman also gave parents instructions to follow, such as not to pull her needle out of her sewing facing her child. If she does so, they say she will poke her child repeatedly with the needle, cutting his life.

Martina John agreed: "There were different requests made to the shamans. They would give instructions [to the parents of the children] who they had doctored to take care of a child a certain way. [The shaman] carries out their request, but the shaman would give instructions to the mother about how to take care of [the child]."

Frank Andrew (October 2001:182) noted that this was done when a woman was pregnant, and when her previous children kept dying: "The shaman decided on his own and named them after one of his *tuunrat*. [The child's] parents did not name them." Frank (December 2003:128) later elaborated:

> [The shaman] named [the children] of the ones who weren't able to have children after their powers [to allow them to live].
>
> However, . . . if the parents or grandparents of his *yungcaraq* do not ever give him goods, for some shamans, his mind would start to *?tunirugteng'arkauguq*. And he could cause his *yungcaraq* to become ill. That is why they were instructed . . . to always give that shaman something if he had done that to a child.
>
> And they talk about those and how they *cukalluku* [?hurry them up], he has him use his powers on him. That was the way of those who have *yungcarat*. They strengthen their powers and abilities like a satellite, going over to them. You know how they say they go over to satellites to strengthen the powers. They say those *yungcarat* are like that, too.

Frank Andrew (October 2001:182) explained how an *angalkuq* used his powers on a man from Tuntutuliak, while he was still in the womb, when his parents could not have children: "[The *angalkuq*] told them to name him Nauyartulria [lit., 'One who is growing'] when he was born." Nauyartulria turned out to be the shaman's term for spruce tree, which an eagle had landed on top of. Just as the spruce tree supported the eagle, the eagle became the child's support, and the parents were admonished to have the child sleep on an eagle's skin after birth. Frank also mentioned Bishop Jacob Nelson of Bethel, who was a *yuungcaraq*. Like Theresa Moses, Bishop Nelson used *ikiituk* (wild celery) as his *napan*, his foundation: "[The shaman] made him *ikiituk* [as a support]. And he told them to name him Ikiituguaq [lit., 'Something like *ikiituk*'] when he was born. It is obvious that his medicine was *ikiitut* [wild celery plants]."

Frank Andrew (December 2003:130) noted that children's foundations were all different:

> I know of a person they called Unguiq [lit., "One who comes back to life"] who was a *yungcaraq*. One with the moon up there for a *napaneq*. . . . They say that her condition was more serious when she was small. . . .
>
> You know how they say the moon dies when it goes dark [eclipses]. [The shaman] said not to pay any mind to her if she dies, that if [the moon] above goes back to normal, she would come to life following it.

They say that used to happen to her. . . . They said when the moon became dark . . . she would die for a short time, and she would come to life when it got bright. Her name was Unguiq.

Francis Charlie (January 2013:275–77) of Scammon Bay described a *yuungcaraq* named Tuuyuk who never caught animals. Once again, a couple's children continued to die: "Because they were tired of envying those around them with children, wanting to have a child, they evidently turned to a shaman. It seems he paid [the shaman] with his kayak, asking for a son." Raphael Jimmy added: "A shaman evidently put a baby inside that woman's stomach. Then he told them not to be critical of him, that he would not catch anything at all from the wilderness, nothing at all!"

Joe Phillip (December 2013:74–75) shared the story of Lawrence Edmund's parents, whose children tended to die. At Alakanuk, the shaman Qakerluilaq practiced his spirit powers and worked on the couple. Joe said that the shaman told them: "This is apparently what you are like. You get angry at one another. . . . And your child is between you two [when you get angry]." He said that having the child between them, they apparently made it die, and he admonished them not to be like that when they had another child. Lawrence was the first born after that, and he as well as his younger siblings lived.

As described in more detail below, the *urumavik*, the shaman who helped in a child's conception, was not only promoting the health of the *yuungcaraq* on the parents' behalf. In naming a *yuungcaraq*, the *angalkuq* was creating future shamans. Frank Andrew (December 2003:303) explained:

They say shamans would also use their powers to doctor a child while it was inside the womb, what they called *yuungcariluteng*, and [the children] would eventually become shamans.

Before a woman gave birth, while [the baby] was inside the stomach, [the shaman] would work on [the baby] using his powers and make the child a future shaman.

They would give [the child] a name that wasn't a namesake of a person. [The shaman] would give [the children] names of things, things that are amazing, or even great plant names. And killer whales were names, too. There was someone who was doctored by a shaman and given the name of Arrluyagaq [lit., "Little killer whale"].

A shaman would produce those [future shamans], those who would work to help people.

Tuunrilluki pilallrat naulluulriit
Healing the sick

A number of elders watched shamans healing the sick and described what they witnessed. Frank Andrew (October 2001:182) was among the most articulate. First he spoke about *angalkut* healing in homes, which he said he had watched because he was curious:

They would *tuunrilluki* [use their spirit powers to heal them]. He would let a woman sit on her bed, and he would crouch at her feet. And he would wrap himself with an *imarnitek* [seal-gut rain parka] and he would have her step on it; the *angalkuq* exercised his powers by going on his knees face down, with his knees flexed and legs folded toward the body when working inside the home. He would constantly move that [seal-gut parka] back and forth with his face covered behind the person who he was healing.

Frank (December 2003:135) later added detail: "They would crouch down at the edge of a sick person, what they called *yugtaarluteng*, and they would move these [seal-gut parkas] and not put them on." The shaman might also stand when using his powers. Frank (December 2003:135) continued: "However, when they [used their powers] standing up, they draped the [seal-gut parkas] . . . over their shoulders; they wore the seal-gut parkas making this constant motion when they used their powers."

Frank Andrew (October 2001:184–85) also described *angalkut* healing the sick in the *qasgiq*:

When they were [using their powers] in the *qasgiq*, when *nangrulluki* [they stand and work to heal a person in the *qasgiq*, from *nangerte-*, "to stand up"] they would have two drummers or three.

Then down on the floor planks, they would have the person they were healing sit on a mat in the back [of the *qasgiq*]. When they sang their *yuarulluut* [songs composed by shamans], when they were drumming, [the shaman] would dance. He would *takussagluni* [circle the person being healed] as they called it. The one down there would go in circles. When it was time, when he'd suddenly extend his arms, they'd suddenly stop [drumming]. He would talk about what the person who he was healing was like.

He would let the people in the *qasgiq* hear him. He used the *imarnitek* as a blanket. And they always circled in this direction [clockwise, *ella maliggluku*, lit., "following the direction of *ella* (universe, world)"]. . . .

And when they got all the way around, they would go toward the center. Then they would finally face the door of the *qasgiq*, the *kalvagyaraq* [tunnel entryway].

They call it *takussagluteng* [circling the patient]. I don't know how they do their work, but that is what they do. They would walk across, then they would back up, following their drumming. His steps would follow the drumming.

When he was ready, when he suddenly extended his arms, the drummers suddenly stopped. He would then squat and talk about what the person he was healing was like.

That's what they did in the *qasgiq*.

Frank noted that sometimes there were two or three *angalkut* helping one another. It was said to be very powerful, and the one who had been ill, or even dead, would walk away alive and well.

Many told stories of shamans exercising their healing powers. Elsie Tommy (March 2009:373) watched the Qissunaq shaman Angassaar heal a man's gunshot wound at Merr'armiut. After he accidently shot himself and a bullet lodged between his ribs, Angassaar used a hollow bird bone, moving it over the wound without touching it and sucking out blood. He periodically removed the bone and spit out the blood, until there was no more. Angassaar said that he could not remove the bullet but that he could clean the wound and the man would recover. Lizzie Chimiugak (June 2009:76) of Toksook Bay described how, following another hunting accident, the powerful shaman Apaq'aq healed a man who had shot himself by replacing his brain with moss, saving his life.

Several stories describe *angalkut* cutting open and operating on a patient using a wooden *yaaruin* (story knife)—a smooth blade commonly used by young girls to draw stories in the mud or snow while telling tales—then ingesting the sickness he found inside. Paul John (February 2014:70) spoke about an elderly woman in Tununak who a shaman had healed in that way:

> [Our late elder] said that after cutting open her stomach, when [the *angalkuq*] put a red-fox snout over his nose and mouth and ate her ailment, he made a loud crunching noise. And he said when he was done and put his mouth over that incision that he had made along the end, there was no longer an opening, but there was just a little bit of blood along part of it. . . . That elder really removed her ailment by cutting her open and eating her ailment, and his knife was a story knife.

Raphael Jimmy (January 2013:18–19) had heard of a shaman who used a story knife to cut open a woman during a difficult delivery, took the infant out, then healed her by closing his mouth over her wound: "They said that the shaman's [surgery] was just like the [surgery] that doctors carried out. . . . But they said when that shaman was about to use that story knife on her belly, he put it in his mouth. The people who watched said that the story knife was very sharp like a metal knife."

George Billy (October 2006:351–52) described how a female shaman used her story knife to heal people's injuries when a large *qasgiq* collapsed and many were injured: "It is said that their female shaman used her small wooden story knife to pierce the injuries of people who were hurt, and she healed them by allowing their wounds to bleed, removing the blood. It is said that the other shaman would also poke them with something, and he healed many people at that time." Finally, Frank Andrew (October 2001:199) told about the Kanirnaarmiut shaman Uyangqulriim Arnaan, who did surgery on those with broken limbs in the *qasgiq*, using a wooden knife, putting it inside her mouth, and cutting open the skin: "The knife was like steel to her."

Elena Charles (April 1997:433), originally from Nunacuarmiut, watched a shaman wearing a seal-gut parka and trying to heal her mother's father. Her grandfather had been sick for two years and couldn't swallow or eat. Working with his spirit helpers, the shaman sang a song.

> He was sitting on a short woven mat in the middle of the house floor. Also in the center of [the floor] was a man's wooden bowl. . . . In the middle of the bowl were three bearberries. . . .
>
> After he went around in circles, he stopped and said, "Hurry and let him swallow the middle one of those [bearberries]." My grandmother took it. . . . [My grandfather] couldn't swallow. I wonder how he swallowed it. After that, I don't remember anything.

Roland Phillip (October 2006:168–71) told how a shaman had Roland's father swallow a hailstone as a cure. When the family was living in Iiqaquq, his father was afflicted with dehydration for a long time. He tried different types of medicine, including beaver castor, cranberries, and the menstrual blood of girls who had their first menstrual period, without success. He then summoned the shaman Asgulria from a nearby fall camp. Without putting on a seal-gut garment, Asgulria told Roland's mother to get a *kavtak* (hailstone or piece of frozen snow) from outside and for Roland's father to put it inside his mouth, not biting it, but letting it melt and swallowing it along with his saliva: "After that, his condition improved. . . . His dryness stopped and he was healed from then on. That's something that I witnessed."

Our most detailed account of shamanic healing comes from Frank Andrew (February 2003:178–201), who heard the story from Aqumgaciq, who had witnessed it himself. Aqumgaciq had traveled with his father from Kwethluk to Iqugmiut (Russian Mission) on the Yukon River to attend a dance festival. When they arrived, they learned that the leader of Iqugmiut had a daughter who was ill, and that he had sent messengers to Tairtaq, the well-known shaman of Urraarmiut (just above Kalskag) to come to Iqugmiut to cure her. Aqumgaciq had heard of Tairtaq but had never seen him.

After the guests arrived, the leader's son came to tell the assembled group that his father had said to dance without him. His fellow villagers replied that they wouldn't dance properly without the sick girl's father attending, and that it was unfortunate that those who had gone to fetch the *angalkuq* Tairtaq from the Kuskokwim River area had not returned. That evening, however, the two messengers arrived, carrying Tairtaq, who was crippled. They brought him food in the *qasgiq*, but before he started to eat he asked if the spirit of the one he had come to work on was still with her. They answered that she was starting to lose her breath. Pushing his bowl aside, Tairtaq said that this was no time to eat, and he told them to bring her into the *qasgiq*, even if she was weak. They used a bearded-seal skin spread with grass mats to carry her in, then removed her clothing and covered her body.

Tairtaq covered himself with a seal-gut parka and began using his powers. He also told the girl's parents that he had allowed their daughter to die, but that it was okay, that he was catching up to her. He then said that the things that he had asked for as payment were too few for her path. As they left to bring in more goods, someone repeatedly called out, threatening that if he failed, they would bury Tairtaq along with her. They carried in more gifts as payment until Tairtaq said that they had brought in too many and to take some away. At first they wouldn't comply, but Tairtaq responded, "She will die before

becoming an old woman if some things are not taken away." They removed more until he said the payment was just right.

Tairtaq also admonished the girl's parents not to shed tears or show sadness. And he told the others to stay put and not to make noise, even if they were frightened. After giving these instructions, he finally started using his powers. Soon his legs stretched and he stood up, then walked in front of the *pall'itaak* (log frame entrance to the underground tunnel passageway into the *qasgiq*), faced forward, sang his song, then disappeared into the entryway. Before he left, he told them to uncover the dead girl.

After Tairtaq left, a boy would periodically check outside until he came in and reported that he saw a large dog running down in the air. The people stopped singing as a cold, white vapor spread into the *qasgiq*, and the head of a huge dog that was constantly sniffing came through the *pall'itaak*. Everyone tried to sit still, and Aqumgaciq recalled that he was so terrified that he could hear the thumping of his own heart.

The sniffing dog circled the *qasgiq*, first stopping near the girl's mother, then her father. Finally it sniffed all over the dead girl, then starting from her lower body, cut her in half and chewed her legs, with blood running down the corners of its mouth. The dog then chewed her upper body, continually stopping to listen. When it was done, it licked up all the blood, tilted up its head, sat back and howled, then disappeared through the door. Then vapor came out of the door, and the people resumed singing. Not long after, hands slapped onto the entryway, the people stopped singing, and they first pulled the girl into the *qasgiq*, then Tairtaq. She was no longer thin, and Tairtaq said that she would be healthy and could once again "be mischief" with her peers. The experience left Tairtaq crippled as before.

Frank Andrew followed with the story of how Tairtaq located and revived a boy who had drowned during summer. All fall, Tairtaq did not allow the place where the boy had drowned to freeze. Before he began to use his medicine, he advised the boy's parents and family members that if he revived their son, not to run to him and touch him before they brought him to the *qasgiq*. In this case, Tairtaq was assisted by two young helpers who went with him to the open water, as well as a "puller" in the *qasgiq* holding onto one end of a line in the water. When the drowned boy began to appear, the helpers held him by his wrists. They moved toward the *qasgiq*, both the puller and the helpers stopping when Tairtaq stopped his incantations. By the time they pulled the drowned boy into the *qasgiq*, he had come to life.

They said Tairtaq tried to revive the dead a second time, but the drowned person's mother ran to him and broke his efforts, and the drowned one moved back into the water. That one had broken Tairtaq's ability, and he said he could never revive anyone again.

Frank's story recalls a story told by Tim Agagtak (July 1985:28–34) of Nightmute. Like Frank, Tim had not personally seen the event but had heard the story. Tim described a couple whose children kept dying. When their child died once again, the parents asked a shaman to try to bring it back to life. Like Tairtaq, the shaman agreed and told them to bring the dead child to the *qasgiq* and lay it naked on the floor. He then told the parents to hide on each side of the *qasgiq*, covered with parkas. The shaman then dropped down into the tunnel entry hole and disappeared. Soon they saw the figure of a dog coming up, one with no fur but only hair on its paws and the tips of its ears and tail. As instructed, the drummers stopped, and the dog began to sniff all over the child. When it got to its feet, it started to eat them: "The huge dog ate the child's body, starting from the feet. . . . Though dead, it got bloody, and when the dog was done . . . it carefully licked up all the blood." After eating the child, the dog sniffed around, then plunged into the entry hole and disappeared.

Later the shaman came in, saying that the little child had almost finished off his medicine. Although he had tried again and again to revive the child, he had failed. The shaman noted that he had returned with barely any medicine left, and that he would never again practice his shaman powers: "He said he didn't want to go through what he experienced. If he had kept trying, he would have been defeated and would have died as well."

Joe Phillip (December 2013:75–78) also reported that some people were too difficult to heal, even by powerful shamans. Once the Yukon shaman Qakerluilaq was unable to heal his patient, although he blew on grasses to lengthen the patient's life:

> He told our father to bring some grass inside, ones used for insoles. . . . Then he dispersed them in front of him and would suddenly blow on them. . . .

They said they did it four times. . . . After gathering them, he told them to scatter them underneath that one in pain, along his mattress. . . . And he didn't practice his spirit powers on him. When he came over, he told him that he had added this much to his life. He said right after [the river] became free of ice, that person would die. He said he couldn't [lengthen his life further].

Many also shared first-hand experiences. John Phillip (October 2006:173–76) gave a vivid account of how the shaman Puyulkuk healed John's eye when John was a young boy living with his family at Anuuraaq. His right eye was swollen, and the center had turned white. John couldn't see, and his eye throbbed with pain, preventing him from sleeping for two nights. Then in the morning, Puyulkuk entered his home. John continued: "After laying me down on my back, . . . he placed his mouth over my eye. With his head down, he seemed to briefly touch [the eye] with the tip of his tongue. After touching it for just a second, when he removed it, the one up there started to chew just like he was crunching on candy. . . . After making crunching noises, he swallowed it. Then after a moment, he [put his mouth over my eye] again." Puyulkuk bent over John's eye five times—less each time—and after the fifth time, he got up and left. The throbbing pain stopped, and John was able to sleep. Later that day, when he went outside, his eye was dazzled by the sun: "The [eye] that previously had no vision had very good sight." After that, John's eye recovered and remained good throughout his life.

John Phillip (October 2006:177) also described witnessing Puyulkuk first injuring, then healing himself. As he entered the *qasgiq* after the men had taken a steam bath, he saw Puyulkuk take a knife out of his pocket:

> Since he would evidently constantly tease his *iluraq* [male cross-cousin], when he unfolded [the knife], after telling [his cousin] to look over at him, [Puyulkuk] cut his own index finger off, and it became covered with blood. Just as the blood started flowing out, he placed [his finger] inside his mouth. I was watching him, since I was in awe of someone doing that. This was after [he healed my eye]. . . . When he took it out, there was no cut here. . . . That's what that person did.

George Billy (October 2006:177–78) had also witnessed the shaman Qamuutaq healing cuts inside the *qasgiq*: "Then Qamuutaq took the adze from an area beyond him, and while he was chopping wood, he made an 'Eng!' noise. The [finger] that he had accidentally grazed with an adze was gone. We watched him when we were small. . . . Evidently, these shamans can place [cuts] inside their mouths and heal them."

Dick Anthony (January 1996:36–48), born in Cevv'arneq in 1922, was cured by a shaman when he was young. At the time, his family was living in a winter village on the Talarun River when his parents and older brother left him and his two sisters to attend a Messenger Feast at Kanerrlulegmiut, just north of Cevv'arneq. Dick was not concerned about their leaving until, when he was playing with his sled, he came to the place where his parents had prepared to leave. Suddenly he wanted to follow them, and he did so, passing a cross marking a tundra grave. As he continued, crying as he went, he heard his sister's husband following him. The man put Dick in his sled and brought him home. Although Dick said he was feeling fine, he had no appetite, even for tasty pancakes, which he normally craved. Dick mused: "Where was my insatiable appetite for pancakes? I absolutely did not want to eat them."

His parents returned from the feast, but Dick's appetite did not return, and his mother was frantic. His father then took him by dog team to Cakcaaq to visit his paternal uncle Qateryak, a known shaman. When food was served to the visitors in the *qasgiq*, Qateryak asked Dick to sit by him, which he did reluctantly, only eating a small bit of burbot liver. Qateryak expressed his gratitude to the boy for sharing his food; then after supper he had Dick sit on a grass mat, and he circled him, wearing a seal-gut parka and asking questions about what had happened to the boy, just as if he had been there watching him. Qateryak asked Dick if anything had disturbed his mind, and Dick said no. Qateryak told Dick that he was lying, and that the dead person buried at the mouth of the river had scared him.

When Qateryak finished inquiring about his experience following his parents' trail, he asked for a knife, then had Dick lie down in front of his father. Qateryak then came forward. Dick recalled:

I was really terrified because he needed a knife!
While I was lying down, he began to put his head down toward me!

Then when he got to a place where he was visible to me and he stopped, I could feel for sure that his lips came in contact with my throat. And I could feel the prickly whiskers around his mouth on my skin.

Then, when the shaman pulled, it seemed like something came off. The shaman then got up, took something from his mouth, showed it to Dick's father, and ate it, saying, "This is what has prevented him from eating!" After that, he was done. Although Dick did not immediately regain his appetite, he gradually started to eat again and recovered.

Dick Anthony (January 1996:49–51) also described how several shamans could work on a patient at the same time, with the stronger shaman giving the patient's sickness to the weaker one: "When there are three shamans or two of them doing an incantation at the same time on that sick person, when they start to dislike each other and counter one another, one who was watching them would say, 'For goodness sakes, Dudes! Pay attention to that person who you are doing the healing ceremony for!'" Although claiming to be working on the patient, the stronger shaman would continue trying to give the patient's sickness to the weaker shaman. And if three shamans were working on a patient, the two stronger ones would try to give the sickness to the weakest among them. Dick Anthony (January 1996:81–82) summarized his understanding of shamans when they exercised their healing powers:

They knew who their fellow *angalkut* were. Some were powerful; and some were not powerful. . . . Some always healed; some never saved. . . .
Even though they could cure them, they seemed not to do so. But if they were trying real hard and they were making medicine with another *angalkuq*, to whoever was weaker, [the more powerful *angalkuq*] kept having that weaker one take whatever ailed that patient.

Chuckling, he closed: "That is the way that I used to hear about them."

Descriptions of *angalkut* with varying degrees of power are common in discussions of healing as well as shamanic encounters generally. In some stories, the apparently weaker shaman turns out to be the most powerful. In other accounts, the shaman's power produced the opposite of the intended effect. Michael John (June 2008:255–60) of Newtok told the story of the elderly shaman who healed a young woman in hopes that she would become his wife. As her health improved, she would smile at him affectionately when he saw her, but after a while she began to run away from him. Angry, the shaman then attempted to kill her, but he couldn't catch her. Evidently, he had overdone it when he healed her, such that when he got close to her, his body heat pushed her away, against her will.

Iinrut
Amulets

Among the most important elements in a shaman's tool kit were the *iinrut* (commonly translated as amulets, charms, or medicines) he or she provided. Frank Andrew (September 2005:180) explained:

> Healers used different things, including carvings of miniature likenesses of people . . . made out of driftwood.
>
> They kept bundles of wild celery plants and some grass with the objects they used as medicine.
>
> They also used little rocks [as *iinrut*]. They would also tell people not to eat certain foods. People were also told not to drink from water that had a current. They were told to only drink water without a current, from lakes.

Elsie Tommy (March 2009:122–24) added detail on *iinrut* she had seen when she was young, growing up north of Nelson Island:

> They used to have handmade wooden *iinrut*.
>
> They say after shamans used their powers on them, they would give them *iinrut* that were models of various things, models of seals, models of people, models of birds, and they'd even give them models of kayaks as *iinrut*.
>
> They had males wear models of kayaks, models of seals, and girls had models of people for necklaces. There were three types of *iinrut* made for males—a seal model, a bird model, and then there was a small model of a person. And females only had one type of necklace—it was a small model of a woman. They say [that model] was a shaman.

Maryann Andrews (April 2012:178) said that her father was a *yuungcaraq* of the shaman Quscuar, who gave him a small rock as an *iinruq*, which his mother sewed into the cloth edge of his pillow.

Frank Andrew (December 2003:137) noted that *iinrut* varied and were always kept safely out of view: "I

saw many different kinds, when they administered *iinrut*. They watched over them carefully and paid close attention to them, and they did not place them out in the open, but only put *iinrut* in a safe place." Frank shared his experience observing a family care for their *iinruq*:

> Those families that I saw down in the winter village, that piece was probably clay, but I didn't know what it was since it was covered with woven grass mats, and I did not see it. . . . It was hanging high up at the edge of their bed, and it was covered.
>
> In December, during one evening, their father took it down, . . . and sitting, his children went to him, and they placed it in their center. He finally took the [sealgut] covering off of it. . . .
>
> I was not curious about it, and I didn't know what it was. It was their *iinruq*. When he was done with them, it was like he was unclothing his children and placing them all on the floor. They all did that, even both he and his wife. And he didn't say a word. He closed it after covering it, and making sure that it was completely covered, he hung it up in its place. They didn't say anything.

Listening to Frank's account, Alex Bird concluded: "It was probably their *iinruq*. . . . It was probably a way to give them strength. All *angalkut* had little *iinrut* back then, and they even kept stones in their pockets."

Some people kept their *iinrut* in their homes, while others brought them everywhere they went. According to Brentina Chanar (June 1989:31) of Toksook Bay:

> Any object [could be an *iinruq*]. They give them an *iinruq* that they will keep their whole lives . . . miniature weasels, miniature birds, small rocks, just anything. . . .
>
> They tell them that person has medicine from that thing.
>
> I also had an *iinruq* of a Arctic tern figure; but only its beak was visible, and the rest of it was bound up with a cloth. It was an Arctic tern but dead and dried up.
>
> We just let it stay. And then, when someone died from this village, my mother would rub that small Arctic tern all over my body. It is said that it was my medicine.
>
> All the children had *iinrut*. . . .
>
> That thing was kept hanging. Those *iinrut* were always hanging right above them where they slept.

As the influence of missionaries and priests increased, *iinrut* were burned, buried, or drowned. Mary George (March 2009:124) of Newtok said that her mother had a wooden model of a face as an *iinruq*, which she discarded when the priest told her to throw it away. Maryann Andrews (April 2012:176) recalled how the shaman Quscuar made a small wooden mask for a woman. Later he asked if she still had it, and told her to throw it in the river, which she did. Brentina Chanar (June 1989) recalled her mother's careful burial of her *iinruq* after the priest discouraged its continued use: "When we started believing in Catholicism, we dropped it. We stopped them by telling the *iinruq* to keep going back to its land/place. That is what my mother told my *iinruq*. She buried it in the ground. My *iinruq* is at Talarun."

Barbara Joe (April 2012:298) of Alakanuk gave a clear description of how the well-known shaman Leggleq visited her home, where he sensed that Barbara's mother's fetus might not live. So he practiced his shaman powers on the fetus, and the baby survived: "In our family that was the only person who [a shaman] practiced his powers on. . . . The child was born and seemed okay. . . . Leggleq evidently also gave him a small stone for his *iinruq*."

Yuum ayuqucia
What a human person is like

Iinruq is distinguished from *tarnaq*, defined as a person's soul or spirit, tiny visible likeness, or human figure resembling its owner. A *tarnaq* inhabited a person, not an object or charm. Frank Andrew (September 2005:180) explained: "When a [shaman] sleeps and loses conscious, through his *tarnaq*, he'll reach a level of awareness where he can experience things." *Tarnaq* (spirit, soul) is not an easy concept to understand, but Tim Agagtak (July 1985:39) provided a helpful clarification:

> [*Tarnat*] were little people of a certain height . . . who left [the person they had been inside] when he was about to die. [Shamans] would display [the little people] to others inside a seal-gut garment. The tiny things would be standing.
>
> Everyone has [a *tarnaq*]. . . . When [a shaman] retrieved the *tarnaq* from a normal person, even if he wasn't a shaman, they were able to see it.

To better understand the meaning of *tarnaq*, one needs to understand other aspects of the human person. Yup'ik cosmology possessed no simple, one-to-one body/soul dichotomy. On Nelson Island the word

yua (from *yuk*, "human being") applied to the "person" of an animal—its human aspect—that survived death and was destined for rebirth.[3] Coastal narrators also designated that aspect of the seals that rushed to their bladders at death to await rebirth as *unguvatii* (one's soul or life spirit, from *unguva*, "life"). Human beings were also believed to have *unguvatii*; however, this was only one of many aspects of a person's being, and each might have a different destination after death.

Each human person was thought to be accompanied through life by a *tarnaq* (also pronounced *tarneq*). *Tarnaq* probably corresponds to the *ta-ghun-u-g'ak* referred to by Nelson (1899:422) and described as an invisible shade in the shape of the human body. A person's *tarnaq* was both sentient and destined for future life, sometimes in the form of an animal and sometimes as a *tuunraq*, or shaman's spirit helper. Everyone had a *tarnaq*, but only shamans could detach them and take them from their owners. Linguist Steven Jacobson (2012:622) notes that *taru* or *taruq* translates as person or human being. *Taru* is used instead of *yuk* in some areas and may have been a shaman's word elsewhere.

According to some, the *tarnaq* corresponded to a person's visible ghost and was that part of the person that left the body at death: "When one sees a ghost, it is the *tarnaq* of a person—the one that does not die." Many people believed that a person's *tarnaq* might be stolen or leave one's body while the person slept, resulting in illness and ultimately death if it did not return. Waking someone up suddenly was strictly forbidden because if a person's *tarnaq* was elsewhere at the time, it would be prevented from returning. Illness was not only believed to be caused by the entrance of negative forces into the body, but also by the departure of a person's *tarnaq* or visible image. Accounts of "soul loss" occur in a number of stories. For example, Paul John (February 1977) described how his grandfather became ill following his encounter with a ghost, after which he vomited a black substance. Later, an *angalkuq* asked whose *tarnaq* kept wandering around, trying to find its human form. Displaying the *tarnaq* under his seal-gut garment, he had all the men in the *qasgiq* come down, one by one, to look in and see who it belonged to. When Paul's grandfather looked, the tiny figure moved, indicating it was his. Paul's grandfather then recalled and talked about his experience with the ghost. Paul said that his grandfather would have died had the shaman not found his *tarnaq* and returned it to his body (Shield and Fienup-Riordan 2003:523–51).

Mather (1985:105–108) and Morrow (1984:128) record that the terms *anerneq* (breath), *avneq* (felt presence, ghostly humming, shaman's helping spirit or "other half"), *yuuciq* (life, lifeline), and *puqlii* (its warmth, its heat) were also used to designate distinct aspects of the human person. Nelson Islanders also referred to a person's *umyuara* (one's mind) and *yuucian unguvii* (one's living spirit). Some people held that a person's "mind," "heat," and "breath" did not survive death. Others identified a person's *anerneq* or *yuucian unguvii* as capable of rebirth when a newborn received that person's name. But as with a person's *tarnaq*, all agreed that loss of either one's breath or heat brought death, just as their possession was essential to living.

Morrow (1984:128) helps to clarify the discrepancies between the different aspects of personhood, while admitting that the suppression of nineteenth-century Yup'ik concepts of the person by missionaries makes it unlikely that we can ever fully understand the significance of these distinctions. Also, as today, people in different parts of the region defined and used these concepts differently. What is clear is that there was no single correct term for a person's soul as distinct from the physical body. Rather, people believed that aspects of their being (one's mind, breath, heat, vision, voice, and visible image) possessed properties essential for life, both in the present and the future. Although the human person could not live without these aspects of being, they might exist separately from and independent of the human body.

As essential to life as one's thought, breath, heat, vision, voice, and visible image was the possession of an *ateq* (name). A nameless person was a contradiction in terms. When a child received a name, that aspect of the dead destined for rebirth entered the child's body. With the name, an essential aspect of the dead was transferred to the newborn. As the part recalls the whole, the dead were reborn through the gift of the name. The name of the deceased was not, however, usually bestowed on a single person. More than one child might be named after the same person (depending on the extent of the deceased's family and personal reputation), and most children received more than one name. An *atellgun* (from

ateq, "name," plus *-llgute-* "fellow") was one having the same name as another, usually those named after the same deceased person (Fienup-Riordan 1983:149–58).

Essential aspects of a person, like the *tarnaq*, separated from the human body at death and began to follow the path to the underworld. However it appears that the name, like the *yua* of the seal, was destined for rebirth. Nelson (1899:437) observed that hunters both propitiated and to some extent controlled the *yua* of sea mammals by keeping them with their bladders and later returning them to their watery world. In this way they produced more prey than if they let them go to the land of the dead or wander freely. The same belief extended to inanimate objects (furs, food, parkas, etc.) of which a small part could retain the essence of the entire article. Thus, a person could give away goods while retaining them in potentiality. By retaining the name of the deceased, a part of the dead was reborn at the same time a channel was opened between the worlds of the living and the dead.

Naulluun aug'arluku
Removing sickness from the body

The focus of Yup'ik concepts relating to sickness was on prevention rather than cure. "Keeping well" was an underlying motive behind the majority of *alerquutet* (admonitions) and *inerquutet* (prohibitions), with myriad rules prescribing how a person should live so as not to get sick. Homeopathic cures might be prescribed for relatively simple ailments such as headache, earache, cuts, and abrasions. But as anthropologist Margaret Lantis (1959:54) aptly points out, the strength of the Yup'ik system for disease control lay in keeping healthy rather than in getting well.

As described above, when precautions failed and a person became seriously ill, the *angalkuq* might be called in to take the sickness out of the patient's body. All the normal personal boundaries were inverted to accomplish this. During healing rituals the shaman's touch, sight, and breath were extended, as opposed to the rigorous control of these senses that normally circumscribed interpersonal relations. During these sessions grass mats might be used to cover the entrance and skylight. Devoid of the light required for normal vision, the *angalkuq* employed supernatural sight to determine the location and character of the patient's complaint. According to Joshua Phillip (June 1988), the shaman sometimes used a mask for this purpose.

> It was put on, using it as a mask. Then [the shaman] would pretend to be examining this person. . . . And [the shaman] would be able to see that person's ailment. Or if that person did something, or had been mischievous, or had intercourse with a woman, [the shaman] would be able to see it with that device. . . .
>
> When they became old, worn out, they made replacements of their likeness . . . that were identical, out of wood. . . .
>
> They said back then, no one tried any of the shaman's weapons, they were afraid of them because belief makes all things come true. If a person believes that a shaman has helped him, [that person] will be helped through his belief. That's how it is.

Frank Andrew (February 2003:274) had also seen the shaman Qaluvialler using a mask to save the life of his fellow shaman Yugauyulria: "After asking Yugauyulria to look toward him, he told him that if this [mask] hadn't saved him, he would not be seen there. He said [the mask] he was holding saved him. . . . That Yugauyulria was actually a shaman himself. . . . He would have died if [the mask] hadn't saved him."

Joshua Phillip (June 1988) described how the shaman Iluraksuar used his abilities to determine the cause of a woman's illness at Iquarmiut. Sitting in the qasgiq, Iluraksuar told his patient that the man sitting by the door was making her sick. The one by the door denied it, but Iluraksuar told him that he was lying and that he could see the man's weapon connected to the sick woman through the floor boards. Iluraksuar then took hold of the man's weapon and began tugging on it, causing the man to sway back and forth. When the man continued to deny that his weapon was tied to the woman, Iluraksuar asked for a knife and moved to cut the man's weapon. The person near the door began trembling and promised to untie his weapon from the woman. Joshua said that the man would have died if Iluraksuar had cut the link.

Caavtaatulit unatellget-llu
Those who feel around and find wounds and those who heal with their hands

Angalkut were called on both to find the cause of an illness and to remove it from the patient's body. In some cases, if the angalkuq determined the locus of disease was within the patient's body, he or she might remove the problem by either firmly holding or gently massaging the affected area. With hands providing a pathway, the healer then drew the illness out of the patient's body (see also Lantis 1966:114). A person—not necessarily a shaman—might acquire the power to heal in such a manner through an encounter with insects in a vole cache, which imparted the ability to heal. According to Brentina Chanar (June 1989:25):

> If one digs up melqurripsat [hairless caterpillars, lit., "ones without melquq (fur)"], one does this to the hem of their qaspeq [covers the insects with the lower part of the garment]. Yes [even though one is a male]. Do it like this on top of them. The person's hands will be extremely ticklish; and then when they stop squirming, one would take [the hands] off, and that storehouse of the vole would be completely empty . . . with nothing else inside! . . .
>
> [Those who found the insects] can feel [the ailment] with their hands. They put their hand on and feel the area that is in pain. And they say the hands get very stuck [to the skin]. They can't come off. . . . They move [their hands] around for a while. When [their hands] come off, they're done [healing the injury]. Then that person's injury goes away.

Elsie Tommy (June 1992:24–31) noted that there are two kinds of caterpillars, melqurripceret and uguguat (furry caterpillars), and that each imparts different abilities to the healer's hands. Also the healer will use a different plant helper depending on the kind of insects encountered. Those with "furry caterpillar hands" use Labrador tea as a plant helper, while a person who encounters melqurripceret uses salmonberry leaves as a plant helper: "They say since those kinds of insects stay on those kinds of plants they used to help them in their work" (see Fienup-Riordan, Rearden, and Meade 2017:334–41).[4] David Martin (April 2001:100–108) described his mother uncovering a vole's cache containing the bones of a human hand missing its index finger. His mother instructed David to place his hand over the bones, and then cover them with his cloth garment. He then felt a tingling sensation, and when he uncovered the cache, the bones had disappeared. From that time, his finger, which he referred to as *tuunrangayak* (little shaman) had the power to find the source of pain in a person's body. David's first patient was a woman with a painful breast. His mother instructed him to put his hand on top of her breast, which was warm to his touch. David's mother then got her *kapun* (poking instrument with a wooden handle and thin, metal tip), and when she pinched the skin and made an incision on the painful area, it oozed with water, then blood. In years to come, David said that he healed people by making incisions on them in the same way. David noted that his hands only allowed him to find the painful area, not to heal it.

Frank Andrew (October 2001:168–73) distinguished between *caavtaatulit* (healers who feel around with their hands and find wounds) and *unatellget* (ones with healing hands):

> Those *caavtaatulit* reveal the [wound or injury] after feeling around. . . .
>
> But those with broken bones, those *ayapetulit* [ones who lean down on their hands for support], those *unatellget* [ones with healing hands] work on those people. They fix their broken bones, welding them with their hands, healing them.

Frank noted that his grandfather was an *unatellek* who would put his hands on a patient, then pull them away. He would do it five times, then quit.

Alexie Nicholai (March 2017:288) of Oscarville also referred to healing with one's hands as *ayaperluku* (placing one's hands down for support): "You know how they dig the ground in search of mouse food. They say some people find those [insects]. . . . They say those [people] start to heal things that hurt the body by *ayaperluki* [leaning their hands down on them]."

Frank Andrew (October 2001:170) said that when they uncover *unatekat* (things that give one healing hands) in a vole cache, they are not to use them for one year. He also noted that frog bones found in cracks in the earth, not in a vole cache, are powerful as *unatekat*: "That one who uncovered frog bones. If a person has a broken bone, when [the healer] puts his hands on them while they are alive, they will not die. When he does that, his body makes crack-

ling noises . . . when his broken bones are repairing." Frank mentioned someone who was able to repair the bones of birds and animals in the wilderness, bones that were still connected, by throwing the animal in the air, and it would either fly away or run galloping, alive again.

Raphael Jimmy (January 2013) told the story of traveling when he was young with a companion who uncovered *pamyulget* (lit., "ones with tails") in a vole cache, tangled together and moving around. An elderly man advised his companion to cover them with his hands, but he was afraid and didn't comply. Raphael continued: "They say if a person had stabbing pains, . . . if that person was ill, that person, although he wasn't a shaman could run his/her hands over the place with the stabbing pain, that it would heal. . . . They say those *pamyulget* will suck out that person's illness, it will remove it. . . . That was evidently a good thing, but that person was afraid of it." Francis Charlie, who was listening, wished that Raphael had put his hands over the *pamyulget* so that he could have healed Francis's legs. "Indeed, if I don't make them worse," Raphael teased.

Yuvgermek atulallrat cupluki-llu pilallrat
Saliva and breath

The healers' hands were not the only part of the body that could be strengthened in such an encounter. If a person found and ate any type of food in a vole cache, such as berries or fish, the person would become a healer, able to use his or her saliva to heal the cuts, sores, and ailments of the human body. As the incorporation of the insects gave the healer's hands the power to draw out illness, the ingestion of food gave the healer's saliva comparable power. Supernatural touch drew disease out of the body in both cases. Brentina Chanar (June 1989:25–26) spoke from personal experience:

> If one finds two vole caches, when one opens the other, one will find it full of *tumaglit* [lowbush cranberries] only. And then that person must take one and eat it; swallow it. And then the person must leave all those other cranberries.
>
> Then they have what they call *paterturyaraq* [way or ability to suck out illness]. They would put saliva on them. They say it will give you the ability to use saliva [to heal]. . . .

They remove the saliva. They put it right on there also, or when they put it on the painful area, they suck it out.

They don't put saliva on it, they suck it out. Then they take out the pain on their flesh, and it comes out as saliva. [What comes out of the injury] is saliva, it is bloody water, it really looks like saliva. And they spit it out onto a cutting board. They also use a cutting board as a platform. I really watched when Apacualler sucked my leg. When it was hurt, I fell on my back.

I really watched. It was like his mouth really was stuck to [my leg]. I could feel it stuck on there. It was like he was [sucking up hot] tea when he would suck.

Then when he was done, they put a cutting board in front of him, and when he spit it out, it looked like saliva, it was watery and had blood in it.

Along with sucking or lifting illness out of the human body, the *angalkuq* also blew on the affected area to expel illness. *Angalkut* might combine these healing techniques, drawing the sickness out of a patient's body with their hands and then blowing on them to dispel the illness from their own bodies. Brentina (June 1989:27–28) continued:

A long time ago, the shaman made medicine for them. *Tuunrilluki* [using familiar spirits], they try to make them well. After *tuunrilluki*, they relate what is making them sick. Some of them did get well; they really got well.

They make them know what is making them sick which is called *elucira'arluki* [from *eluciq*, "shape, form, condition, what something is like"]. They point out what [the person] must do. It is said that they take it away.

That is called *elucira'arluki*. So while [the shaman] uses his spirit powers, he tells [the sick one] to blow. They really blow out when they blow. . . . When [the shaman] is behind that one he is making medicine for, he has a seal-gut garment as a covering.

I used to see them. They would blow out. But we could not understand what they said. Occasionally we understood what they said. And they say, "Whew." They seemed to say, "*Amitataar!*" And then soon, with a big "Whew," [the shaman] blows out!

When they did that, they *elucira'arluki*. . . . And after that shaman is finished, they feed [the shaman] with real good food.

Licking was also considered a healing act in many contexts, and saliva was often associated with long life. Alma Keyes (February 1993) of Kotlik described an extraordinary creature, the *uilurusak* (also *uiluruyak*, "meadow jumping mouse"), which was capable of licking people all over and giving them four lives:

They said if a person emanated light within their world, if it liked him it would come to him when he went down to the ocean in spring. They say that *uilurusak* has four ice holes. When a person came to them, one hole would be in the middle. When the mouse, *uilurusak*, came up on the ice it would get bigger and bigger.

As the person stood, the mouse would climb up on him and lick and slurp every aperture and blemish on his body. He would stand still, though he was petrified when the mouse came to him. Then it would enter him through his big toe and again in there. The person would remain though he was frightened. *Uilurusak* would turn into a mouse with a long snout. It would enter and lick every scuff and blister. It would come out, slowly, totally cleaning the person. Then it would turn into a person and ask him, "So, what do you wish for in your life? Would you like to become a great hunter? What do you want?" A person who was energetic would wish to become a great hunter and to become powerful through hunting. However, if a person had sense he should wish for a long life, realizing that he had already been cleansed by [the *uilurusak*]. (See also Nelson (1899:442) on Wi-lu-gho-yuk)

The act of licking can, like the healing touch, mend injuries and restore a person's senses. Similar to John Phillip's account, Wassilie Evan (March 1989) of Pilot Station described his experience when the shaman Irurpak licked his eyes, restoring his sight.

I was going blind. I could not open my eyes. My father had summoned Irurpak. When he arrived I thought he would chant for me. After he ate he told me to go to him so he could lick my eyes. As he proceeded to lick my eyes I noticed that his tongue felt like a file. After a while he told me, "Go outside and tell me what you have seen." When I first went out I did not see anything. It was still like a fog. I told him, "My sight did not improve."

Irurpak then licked Wassilie's eyes a second time, and when he went outside he could dimly see the Qissunaq shoreline across the river. Irurpak then licked Wassilie's eyes a third time, and when looking across the river, even the trees were clear. Wassilie concluded: "When I went back inside I told him, 'I can see the trees on the other side of the river just the way they are.' He told me that was enough. He stopped after the third time. He saved my sight and made my eyes open again."

Qalarutekluku
Speaking out and words of power

Along with powerful sight, touch, and air, loud noises—especially drumming and singing—were often employed to chase illness out of a patient's body. According to Brentina Chanar (June 1989:28):

> If they cannot [heal him] by that, they use their spirit powers to heal him in the qasgiq. They bring [the sick person] inside and seat him on the floor boards and sing for him like they do when dancing. [The angalkuq] repeatedly stomps his feet around [the sick person]. They say they are noticeable when they find out what is causing his ailment during the time they are bending over him; they start to jump up repeatedly, they jump around. It was when he found the source of his ailment, when they are going to remove [his illness].
>
> They jump around out of happiness, what they call takussagluteng [circling the one they are healing]. . . . Even though they were elderly men, they would be very spry, jumping around, . . . being really joyous over having found the source of his illness when he was about to remove [his ailment].

Angalkut were called on to heal mental as well as physical ailments, a task that many wise shamans excelled at. To do this the angalkuq encouraged the sick person to confess any transgressions that might have opened a path for illness to enter his body. The rules for right living created boundaries between human and nonhuman persons as well as between the living and the dead. When someone broke a rule, it opened the way for sickness to enter the body. The task of the angalkuq was to ferret out the breach. Once the shaman discovered the cause of the illness, the cure could begin. Joshua Phillip (June 1988:22–23) recalled:

> Then some of the angalkut asked them after they performed medicine on them, "Now, in your past life, you have not fooled around with another woman? Why is your sickness this way? Tell a little bit about yourself, even though it may be embarrassing. Reveal a little if you have been with another woman who is not your wife." . . .
>
> And some person will admit that he had been with this woman who was not his wife. And then that shaman would say, "Enough said! Because you have

volunteered to say it, you have saved yourself. Let me sing a song!"

By confessing their transgressions, patients reaffirmed the proper boundaries and were thereby freed from the negative consequences of their actions. A 1991 letter published in the Tundra Drums indicates that this belief outlived the activities of shamans. Susie Angaiak of Tununak wrote, "When a strong man has sex with a child, he will start becoming weak. . . . The elders would understand that the cause of his illness was what he did in secret. The only way he could heal was if he found someone he trusted and confessed to that person. When he confessed he would start to heal. . . . If this will help some young people, I will be glad."[5]

Public confession of misdeeds provided a framework for the social reintegration of the patient into the human community while it cleared away any obstacles that might block recovery. Only the patient was held to blame for the illness, and only personal confession could provide a cure. Meanwhile, other participants continuously expressed their sympathy toward the patient and urged that the consequences of the transgression be mild. Here the power of their minds was believed to positively affect the patient's condition. At the same time the patient must think only good thoughts and confess bad ones. Negative thoughts were as dangerous as negative deeds.

Transgressions were not the only things that might be confessed to provide a cure. People also believed that personal encounters with apparitions could cause illness if not communicated. One Nelson Island woman recalled an unusual experience she had while berry picking as a young girl. After she went home she started to bleed and became very ill. During a curing session in the qasgiq, the angalkuq determined that her illness had been caused by a ghost that she had encountered on the tundra at the time she had picked berries. Once he had established the nature of her encounter, she could recover. The angalkuq told her that if he had not discovered the cause of her illness, she would have died.

Joe Phillip (December 2013:71) also noted how people were encouraged to speak about things on their minds before they got serious: The shaman worked on those who kept things inside:

> And when they became worse in the past, saying that their condition had become serious, they would

let shamans use their spirit powers to work on them sometimes. . . .

That shaman would say, "If you don't speak of that, I cannot fix it." But when he spoke of it, he could remove that like one confessing his sins. That person would stop thinking about it . . . and would improve.

Eugene Pete (December 2011:35–42) from Nunam Iqua shared a long description of how, when the woman who raised him was dying, she told him not to cry for her, even if he was extremely sorrowful. Following her wishes, he didn't cry when she died, but in the days that followed he felt heavy and unable to eat. His neighbors thought he was suffering because he had been with a woman. But the shaman Leggleq visited him at home and told him to come to the *qasgiq* that evening so that he could find the cause of Eugene's condition. Eugene did so, and Leggleq put on a seal-gut garment and shook it, while others drummed and sang. Eugene recalled: "When he stopped shaking it, he said to me that my great sorrow had caused my condition, since I tried to hold it in and not cry. . . . That Leggleq really knew things, and that person would save people. I never heard that that person did anything malicious at all."

After Leggleq identified the cause of Eugene's condition—keeping his sorrow inside and not talking about it—Leggleq took Eugene across Qip'ngayak (Black River) and had him sit facing the sunrise, with Leggleq seated behind him, telling a *quliraq* (legend) and blowing on him four times. Eugene (December 2012:37–38) recalled: "He didn't sing but just talked. When he reached a certain point, he blew some air at me. I could feel the air that he was blowing back there. He told me that he would blow air at me four times, that the fourth would be the last time." Leggleq instructed Eugene to learn the *quliraq*, but he did not, although he told Leggleq that he had learned it. When Eugene returned home and went to bed that night, in his sleep he started to feel wind on his ears, then saw his bed hovering in the air, landing with a jolt. The next morning he told Leggleq about his amazing experience, and Leggleq expressed his satisfaction: "I'm go grateful. Yesterday, over there in the wilderness, I sang that *quliraq* to you. That evidently brought you to a good place." Indeed he wasn't lying, and Eugene no longer felt heavy but felt good and recovered.

Angalkut not only used words of power to cure but also to summon their *tuunrat* and to communicate with their *avneret* (helping spirits). The men and women we spoke with, and cite in this book, were not shamans themselves, but many vividly recalled shamanic performances and *qaniqutet* (ritual incantations invoking helping spirits and protecting one from illness). Lizzie Chimiugak (June 2009:84–98) told a long *quliraq* in which a family escaped danger aided by their shaman father's incantations (Fienup-Riordan 2018:468–85).

Lizzie Chimiugak (June 2009:208–16) also told about two women who married and moved north to the mouth of the Yukon. An old woman advised them to save their leftovers and bury food when they traveled, as someday they might need provisions when their husbands no longer wanted them. Sure enough, the time came when they had to return home, so they traveled south, using those provisions. Lizzie assumed the old woman was, in fact, a shaman who could see the future. Lizzie then mentioned something that she said she hadn't previously known—that people were told not to stay quiet without speaking or they would stop speaking altogether. As they traveled, one of the women stopped speaking, and she always turned her head, concealing her face and crunching her food when they ate. Her companion began to fear her, and when she looked at her face while she slept it was the face of a wolf. She crept away, unnoticed, then fled. Behind her, her companion who had transformed into a wolf began to howl, disappointed in losing its prey. Lizzie concluded that long ago shamans were responsible for having people change forms. Speech clearly had power, and silence could be dangerous.

Qelayaraq
Divination through lifting one's body parts

Over the years, elders have mentioned *qelayaraq* (divination through lifting one's body parts) but rarely described it in detail. One notable exception was a long, animated discussion between Eugene Pete, Mike Andrews Sr., and Lawrence Edmund (December 2011:245–51), all from the lower Yukon. Eugene had just finished telling a story about the shaman Terussaq, who was able to enlarge a *qasgiq* using his powers. Mike Andrews Sr. noted that Terussaq also practiced *qelayaraq*, a ritual in which a patient's ailment was determined by tying a string or piece of skin rope

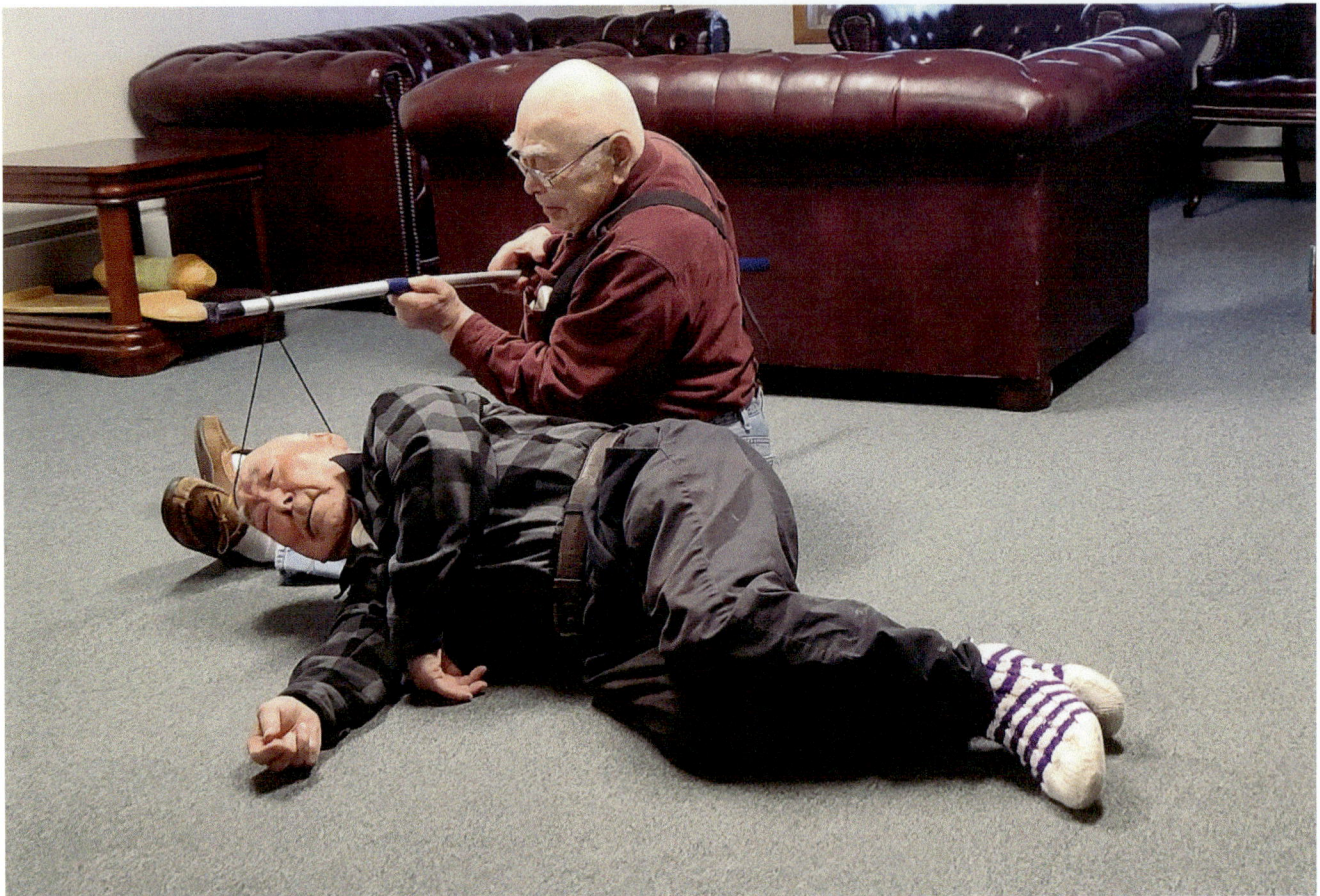

FIGURE 3.1. Nick Andrew and Francis Charlie demonstrating *qelayaraq*, a divination technique in which a patient's ailment is determined by tying a string around another person's head or foot and testing it by pulling on it to see if it could or could not be easily lifted. Here Francis is playing the part of the "head," which Nick is trying to lift, 2023. Ann Fienup-Riordan.

around another person's head or foot and testing it by pulling on it to see if it could or couldn't be easily lifted.

Eugene noted that sometimes the one performing *qelayaraq* could lift it and sometimes not. Mike Andrews Sr. explained: "They say if you lift it, even a person's head, it will mean yes [a positive sign]. But they say if you can't lift it, [it means no, a negative sign]." Mike noted that *qelayaraq* was used to heal the sick and that if the body part could not be lifted, the person could not be healed. Lawrence Edmund declared: "They call its name, their *qela* [spirit], talking to it, trying to heal a person with an ailment."

Mike Andrews Sr. said that the patient was not the one whose body parts were lifted and that his wife had been the "head" for one who was practicing *qelayaraq*:

Qakurtaq's second wife from up north carried out the practice of *qelayaraq*, and my wife's [head] was the head [she tried to lift]. . . .

Nothing was wrong with my wife, and she wasn't feeling differently, and nothing was wrong with her after that.

Eugene had tried to carry out *qelayaraq*, thinking that they might have lied, and a person pretended that he couldn't lift it. Although he tried, he couldn't get a divination. Lawrence had also tried it unsuccessfully. Mike Andrews Sr. described his experience when he pretended to *qelayaraq*:

At Nunaqerraq, it was spring and the days were longer. Aqevtan and I, since we were close friends, went down to the *qasgiq*.

When we entered [we said], "Let's try *qelayaraq* just to try." We said that, just the two of us.

We were across from one another, down on the floor on top of the floor boards, and I carried out the practice of *qelayaraq* on my leg. While I was [pulling], I [pulled this] and it couldn't [be lifted]. [*laughs*] I found out that the lace of my boot was caught and couldn't [pull up].

We suddenly stood up and quickly ran outside, making loud clanking noises!

The men didn't go inside again.

Edward Nelson (1899:433) recorded another instance of *qelayaraq*. He noted that when a person from south of the Yukon Delta became ill, *angalkut* would determine the character of the malady by tying a cord attached to the end of a stick to the patient's head or limb and lifting it. The part was very heavy if seriously affected, but it became lighter and easier to raise as the disease passed away. Here the invisible disease-causing agents that entered the body and made people ill were said to have weight. Margaret Andrews (December 2003:308) also described illness as having weight:

> I used to hear about *qelatulit* [those who used divination] on a person who had an illness. Even women did divination.
> They let the one who had an illness lie down on a pillow, and they tied him here around the head. They put a tether on that and put a piece of wood where it was tied. [The *qelatuli*] then sat on the floor and began to pull on it.
> They say that he would pull it toward him. They say when his sickness is not quite right, his head would be heavy. When that happens, [the *qelatuli*] stops and instructs [the patient] not to eat certain foods. . . .
> I call them "junior *tuunraq*."

Margaret Andrews asked Frank Andrew about *qelayaraq*, but he hadn't heard about it. As "head lifting" is a form of divination well known in the Canadian Arctic (Laugrand and Oosten 2012:307), it is possible that *qelayaraq* was present only on the Lower Yukon and not in the Lower Kuskokwim coastal area. As the elders who experienced this are gone now, we will probably never know.[6]

Angalkunek tarenrat
Images of shamans

In the early 1900s, John E. Thwaites took a series of intriguing photographs at Nushagak in Bristol Bay, including the now well-known image he titled "Eskimo Medicine Man, Alaska, Exorcising Evil Spirits for a Sick Boy" (figure 3.2). At the time, Thwaites was serving as mail clerk aboard the SS *Dora* during its mail runs between Valdez and Bristol Bay. Thwaites biographer J. Pennelope Goforth (2003) notes that while Thwaites made his living as mail clerk, his lasting contribution consists of what he called his hobby of "Kodaking in Alaska," creating a unique collection of hundreds of photographs of southwest Alaska from 1905 to 1912.

All of Thwaites's images of "medicine men" were posed with several different men wearing masks that likely had been brought to Nushagak to sell after they had been used in ceremonial dances the previous winter. In fact all of the masks, as well as the huge hands, ended up in the possession of collectors in the Lower Forty-eight states and abroad (see Fienup-Riordan 1996; Mooney and McIntyre 2019). The hands were purchased, along with several masks, by George Gustav Heye to add to his already substantial collection of Yup'ik material at the Museum of the American Indian in New York and transferred to the National Museum of the American Indian (NMAI) in Washington, DC, in 2004.

Although the image was posed and did not depict a real healing ceremony, the hands are a powerful evocation of the shaman's healing touch. In 1996, the hands were included in the Yup'ik mask exhibit, *Agayuliyararput / Our Way of Making Prayer*. After the exhibit, Tim Troll and others worked with NMAI to bring them back to Dillingham on long-term loan from the museum and to place them on display at the Samuel Fox Museum, where the Yup'ik descendants of those who created and modeled the hands could see them. While they were on display, John Dyasuk of Dillingham identified the man wearing the mask as his relative—the shaman Iyiayuk, whose English name was Andrew, and whose father, Dyueziak, came from Nelson Island. Iyiayuk was born around 1863 and died around 1959, and he was the father of Andrew Andrews. The museum's label also notes that Andrew used to deliver mail between Dillingham and Togiak, and that is likely how he became acquainted with Thwaites. Andrew was said to be "a strong person, both physically and [in his] personality" (Samuel Fox Museum 2021).

In his discussion of Thwaites photographs, Sean Mooney (2019:131) suggests that the shaman posing with the masks was also their creator. This is unlikely. Masks were typically created by expert carvers under the direction of a shaman, whose vision they represented. Alternately, if the man wearing the masks was their creator, then it is unlikely

FIGURE 3.2. "Working to Beat the Devil": Eskimo Medicine Man, Alaska, Exorcising Evil Spirits for a Sick Boy. According to John Dyasuk of Dillingham, the man wearing the mask was the shaman Iyiayuk, whose English name was Andrew and whose father, Dyueziak, came from Nelson Island. Iyiayuk was born around 1863 and died around 1959, and he was the father of Andrew Andrews. This is one of at least five photographs taken by John E. Thwaites of the same man posing with different masks. Thwaites probably posed the photographs during one of his several visits to Nushagak between 1906 and 1908. Alaska State Library, J. E. Thwaites Collection PCA-18-497.

FIGURE 3.3. Thwaites's photograph of the shaman Iyiayuk, without the mask he displayed in "Working to Beat the Devil." Alaska State Library, J. E. Thaites Collection PCA-18-496.

that he was a shaman. It is most likely that the man wearing the mask and hands in Thwaites's photograph was the same man—the shaman Iyiayuk—who commissioned their creation, as few would have been bold enough to display these once powerful objects, even in the secular, posed environment of the Nushagak trading post where the photos were made. Although we may never know the answer to the question of who it was who made the masks and hands, the photograph, as well as the hands themselves,

FIGURE 3.4. Thwaites's photograph of three men and a boy, entitled "Nushagak, Alaska." The man on the far right wearing the squirrel-skin parka and with his face blackened is the shaman Iyiayuk photographed wearing the mask and huge hands in "Working to Beat the Devil." The boy in the two photographs, identified by Thwaites as a Togiak Native, is also the same. According to John Dyasuk, the boy may be Robert Ayojiak, with Willie Byayuk and Pavila Byayuk standing beside him (Sam Fox Museum 2021). Alaska State Library, J. E. Thaites Collection PCA-18-122.

remain vivid reminders of the powerful role shamans played in the past, both to help and to harm.

Iqua
Conclusion

The treatment of the body in times of illness was as much a spiritual as a physical endeavor. People experienced a direct connection between physical problems and spiritual solutions. Conversely, physical ills directly reflected moral inadequacies. People brought on disease by transgressing the rules for right living, and only through correcting or confessing their offenses could they hope to remove illness from their bodies. Animal products used as medicines were primarily an attempt to restore and maintain the boundaries between the person and the world at large that the original transgression had broken.

In the case of serious illness, the patient employed the *angalkuq* to cure both mind and body. Significantly, all curing techniques involved the reversal of the interpersonal boundaries of everyday life. A person's senses were carefully restricted under normal circumstances—eyes averted out of respect, a woman's bad air avoided, and direct address carefully controlled so as not to injure another's mind. To draw an illness out of a patient's body, the *angalkuq* employed supernatural vision, powerful touch, "strong air," and confession, or "speaking out." Whereas people consumed animals to make their bodies healthy and strong, the shaman or his spirit helper (often in the form of a wolf or dog) might suck illness out of a person's body and devour it, making crunching noises, to restore good health. By obviating the normal boundaries between persons and between the human and nonhuman worlds, the *angalkuq* opened a pathway either for illness to leave the patient's body or for a lost spiritual essence to return.

4

Angalkurkat
Ones Who Would Become Shamans

Shamans passed on their abilities both before and after they died. Many spoke of the children of shamans inheriting their parents' abilities. Lizzie Chimiugak (June 2009:252) recalled: "They say that since my mother had a father who was a shaman, she almost became a shaman. They say when Egacuayak married her, her ability went away, making it so that she wouldn't become a shaman." Nightmute elder Albertina Dull (June 2009:252) agreed: "You know how today, the children of shamans will have some sort of ability."

Not all shamans wanted their children to inherit their powers. Frank Andrew (December 2003:125–26) spoke of the shaman Ayagina'ar, whose father, Apalciq, was a shaman. Because Ayagina'ar was his only son, Apalciq didn't teach him what he knew. However, another shaman who had died long before pursued Ayagina'ar outside at night, took hold of him, and turned him into a shaman:

> When he finally captured him, he showed him the abilities that he would acquire. He showed and explained to him what powers could be used for curing what illnesses. He explained what they were one by one.
>
> [Ayagina'ar] said that person [even though he had died] . . . turned him into a shaman. He said that he didn't know anything because he wasn't taught [by his father]. But he said when he followed that person's instructions, he became a shaman.

Frank Andrew went on to explain that when shamans were about to die, they started looking for their *mer'umavigkat* (lit., "ones who would give them a constant source of drinking water," from *meq*, "water"), ones who would receive them openly and without problems. The term likely derives from the fact that the dead generally were believed to suffer from hunger and thirst, which their descendants could alleviate through gifts of food and water. Frank continued:

> When [the shaman died], he would be visible through that person, he would have awareness there at his *mer'umavigkaq* [one who would give him drinking water], at his *mer'umavik*.
>
> And he didn't know who that person was because he had not seen him before. He came to learn later on that the [shaman who passed on his powers to him] was his great-grandparent.

Frank Andrew (December 2003:126) followed with the story of how Ayagina'ar's great-grandparent appeared to him inside a house in Eek and passed on his shaman powers. Ayagina'ar was sitting on a bed, to the right of the door, when he became aware that the dead shaman was sitting on the floor boards facing the door. Then Ayagina'ar began to hear something that sounded like a housefly, and the house began to shake as the sound got louder. The floor boards started to rise, and when the floor boards were about to reach his level, they suddenly parted and went down. The dead shaman faced away from him

https://doi.org/10.5876/9781646427314.c004

and told Ayagina'ar to grab hold of him. Ayagina'ar saw what looked like two bound spruce roots on his upper body and two on his hips, and the dead shaman instructed him to grab the bottom ones. Using a firm grip, Ayagina'ar easily moved in circles, but the dead shaman admonished him to stop messing with him, so he could show him something: "After doing that, you know how it becomes bright when the sun suddenly pours through the gaps in the wall when there are holes. Those [sun beams] suddenly shone in front of him." The dead shaman explained what they were and how they could be used to cure certain ailments. Ayagina'ar said that he allowed beams of light to shine on him three times, replacing them with others each time he was done. Frank concluded: "So [Ayagina'ar] would use his powers like he had been instructed. He couldn't [use his powers] as he pleased. He said that's what shamans are like. They can do things through the abilities they learned. Those who don't have powers can't do things."

Frank Andrew (December 2003:134) noted that mer'umavigkat could be women as well as men. Paul Waskey (January 1996) described his grandmother Tut'angaq's experience. When she was a girl, before she became an angalkuq, she loved playing alone at night, and once when she was outside playing she saw a person's figure. She began to run from house to house, but she would run into a face at every doorway and couldn't enter. As her body began to weaken she finally reached the qasgiq, and she remembered what to do. She began to push the shade's head down with the weight of her hand. But as she stepped over it, before it had totally disappeared into the ground, she was knocked down by a blow to her head. Her skull felt like it was cracked open: "As this was happening to her outside, an angalkuq inside knew exactly what had happened to her and helped her to regain consciousness. She became an angalkuq after that experience."

Albertina Dull (June 2009:122) said that long ago, some of those who would become shamans found out when they were still fetuses in the womb:

> Apar'aq said that he was aware when he was a fetus. He was thinking of going out, and when he would head down to his door, when he would see one of those, he would turn back. . . . His mother's labor would probably start and stop again.
>
> They say when he finally went out, when he was finally born, he went out and he had already grown teeth.

Lizzie Chimiugak added that the baby's namesakes probably caused that to happen.

Albertina Dull (April 2013:65–67) recalled that angalkurkat (lit., "ones who would become angalkut") sometimes saw things, such as faces on driftwood: "They are probably alairumanrilnguut [ones who keep themselves concealed]. They refer to those who don't practice their shaman powers [in public] as alairumanrilnguut. Although they know things, they keep themselves concealed."

At the beginning of his long account of the Urraarmiut shaman, Tairtaq, Frank Andrew (February 2003:178) described how Tairtaq encountered a yugaq, a nonhuman being of the wilderness who did things that shamans do. Tairtaq and the yugaq used their powers to fight one another all day, Tairtaq eventually running out of his powers. Tairtaq's companion then began fighting the yugaq, depleting its powers. Just before sunset, that yugaq started to hesitate, saying that it had run out and could not recall anything anymore. The young man told him not to worry, that they would not do anything to him. Relieved, the yugaq asked which of them wanted to be an angalkuq. Tairtaq's companion told the yugaq to give his powers to Tairtaq, who became a shaman after that encounter.

Some contemporary elders talk about how they declined offers shamans made to bequeath them their abilities. A shaman wanted to leave Nick Andrew (January 2006:249) of Marshall his abilities: "He pleaded with me all summer: that if I wanted to become a shaman, that he would leave me [his powers]. And he would tell me that if I wanted to be a good hunter, he could give me that ability." Nick declined but now regrets his decision, as he would now be able to heal broken bones: "That ability has been passed down to those people who can heal with their hands. They say if these angalkut don't misuse their ability, it will not lead them toward harm."

Jacob Black (March 2017:286–87) described how two shamans in his hometown of Napakiak, Apangtak (his great grandfather) and Agagliiyaq, both wanted to give him their abilities if he would accept them. Apangtak said that he didn't have much of an ability, but that in the past, someone had asked him to receive his powers, just as he was asking Jacob to receive them from him: "They explained to me that they have to teach them. They also warn them about the wrong way of practicing it. And when they've learned, they give over the entire [ability] to the one who wants to accept [it]." Jacob declined their offers. He said that before that he had heard about those two being shamans, but that they didn't cause anyone harm, using their abilities "in a good way": "They would become doctors. . . . They had no limitations, and although one's ailment was inside the body, they would remove it. They used to be extremely amazing."

Fred Augustine (March 2011:1084) of Alakanuk held a less positive view of shamans, noting that few were good: "Our late grandfather [who was a shaman] said that being a shaman isn't something to desire. . . . His fellow [shamans] tended to pursue him without him knowing. . . . He said that when he sensed them, he wouldn't let them kill him." Fred noted that when he was a boy he didn't want to be a shaman's helper back at Kapuutelleq, even though he didn't think shamans harmed people: "Sometimes today, I hear that I'm a shaman. But I'm not a shaman. But I don't mind [people thinking that] since it's not true."

Raphael Jimmy's (January 2013:358) mother always told him not to accept anything a shaman told him, as what a shaman did had a bad consequence: "She would also tell us, 'Although you don't catch things in the wilderness, even if a shaman wants to give you a *pissurcuun* [power source, lit., "something to hunt with"], don't receive it at all. It also has a bad consequence.'" Francis Charlie (January 2013:358) added that the late Kaligtuq wanted to pass down his *pissurcuun* to him: "I replied that being a careless person, although I'm pitiful, that I cannot accept it. He wasn't insistent, but agreed with me." Raphael then told about a person who had accepted a *pissurcuun* from a shaman, then approached and caught a fox that didn't sense him at all. By doing that, however, he was responsible for causing himself pain later in life.

Lizzie Chimiugak (June 2009:253) recalled that although they are shamans, they were told not to finish their future abilities: "Probably because it would shorten his life." Albertina Dull noted that although shamans had amazing abilities, when their time came they could not save themselves and died.

Arnat angalkut
Women shamans

Women like Paul Waskey's grandmother were, indeed, considered to hold great power. Charlie Steve (January 1996:46–50) of Stebbins described his grandmother, the powerful shaman Ungilak, who used a mask to look into the future and predict it. Every year she commissioned a wolf mask with a movable jaw containing sharp ivory teeth. As she danced with the mask, she would pull up her sleeves and begin biting her arms, continuing to dance even though she was bleeding. When Charlie visited his grandmother the next day, she would pull up her sleeves and show him her arm, which was totally healed. Charlie recalled: "She would tell me that our village was going to be okay. She would say there wouldn't be any deaths in our village in the days to come." The next year, his grandmother would have someone make a new wolf mask, and when she used it during a performance, she would bite herself again and bleed. When he visited her the next day, he would find her sitting with her arms inside her parka: "I'd ask to see her wounds again. Then she would tell me that her bites from last night hadn't healed. . . . It was believed that the wounds were unable to heal because of the *cangerlak* [epidemic] which was about to come to some people in the village." Charlie recalled with a chuckle that when she died and her relatives took her body out through the window on the side of the house, the window broke on one side, and her body fell: "Her younger sibling ran to her body . . . and said, 'What did you do with your shaman powers and fall?' He scolded his older sister, even though she was dead."

Paul John (May 2003:40–58) told the story of the female *angalkuq* from Kwethluk who had her fellow villagers make a bearded-seal mask, which she wore in honor of the coastal people who had traveled to Kwethluk for a dance festival: "She said she was grateful for the coastal people's gifts and was presenting the mask so their good fortune would continue when they went out hunting." She then disappeared into the underground entryway, from which came the sound of a *qalriq* (male bearded seal in rut). The coastal people were amazed that she was able to produce the exact sound of a bearded seal in rut, although she had never been to the ocean: "After the presentation, the men said she sounded so much like a bearded seal that they felt their foreheads open up and pull back from the experience." Paul John emphasized the exceptional character of the woman's performance. It was unusual for a woman to perform with a mask and particularly impressive that she embodied a bearded seal. A powerful female *angalkuq* possessing hunting knowledge contrasts dramatically with the male *angalkuq*, who was often a mediocre hunter.

Michael John (June 2008:40–41) told the story of a female shaman who, when she was about to die, asked to be buried holding a model of an *ussugcin* (a long, wooden land prying tool sharpened at one end), as she didn't want her grandchild to endure hardship when he portaged: "When she died she was holding a model of one of those, and the other a model of a *kaugtuutaq* [striking tool or club]. Then after she died, this [channel] evidently cut through the land and formed a new stream." Michael added that the edge of the new channel appeared as though it had been cut with a prying tool.

Joseph Patrick (June 2008:127) also had a grandmother who was a shaman remembered as having *tuunrat* (spirit helpers) who were white people: "I watched her maybe three times. When she'd put on her seal-gut rain garment and [use her powers], she would speak as those two white people, his wife and her husband. Then when she did that for the last time, when she was done, she said that those two white people had moved down to the Lower Forty-eight states, and she never [used her powers or spoke English after that]."

Some female shamans were malicious. Albertina Dull (April 2013:40) spoke of the female shaman Luk'aq, whose children continually died because she used them as shields: "They called that *qetulkelluki irniateng* [their children were too soft for them]." Elsie Tommy (March 2009:384) briefly spoke of a woman who had her grandchild give her a tattoo along her forehead, near her hairline, every time she heard that someone she had pursued had died. In the end, when Ap'alluk's father killed her, he pulled back her hair and saw many tattoos concealed underneath.

Elsie Tommy (January 2012:13) remembered seeing her grandmother who used her shaman powers to visit the sky in winter, returning and entering the *qasgiq* with a bucket filled with ripe salmonberries: "She said that she had picked some salmonberries from *ellam allngignaa* [the sky's open tundra]. And when she entered the *qasgiq*, she distributed them.

They smelled like salmonberries, they had turned red in their midst. That's the last time, she never went again."

Frank Andrew (February 2003:118) also recalled Arnarayar, the second wife of Cingarturta, who was not previously known to be an *angalkuq* when the couple lived in Kwigillingok. When her husband was unsuccessful at curing his brother-in-law, his wife confronted him, "You are just too much. . . . Even though you use your powers to try to heal him, he remains the same! You should treat him in earnest!" Cingarturta didn't reply, and Arnarayar then told him to give her his cloth *qaspeq*: "Using your heat, let me [doctor him]!" She then began to sing and cured her brother-in-law.

Martina John (March 2009:378) gave one explanation for why female shamans were so powerful: "They also said that these female shamans are more difficult to overpower than men because they have their menstrual blood to protect them. Women were more difficult to overpower, since they are cloaked by their menstrual blood." Discussing the powerful female shaman Uyangqulriim Arnaan, Frank Andrew (October 2001:199) also noted that female *angalkut* are too strong to kill: "They say it is because women *qagrumaluteng* [have exploded, referring to their menstrual periods]." Frank (December 2003:132) later elaborated: "They said that a female shaman is not easy [to kill]. . . . They say a female *angalkuq* cannot explode because she has already exploded. Women are not like us men, and they have regular menstrual periods. They said it is because they have exploded in that way, that an *angalkuq* cannot easily kill [women *angalkut*]."

According to Frank Andrew (October 2001:200), Uyangqulriim Arnaan was not only able to heal and perform surgery, she and her "little husband"—a man who she had operated on when he had tuberculosis—also saved the people of Kangirnaarmiut from a flood. As the water rose, the couple sat back-to-back in a kayak. Then she instructed the people to get two sealskin floats and two large rocks, connecting each rock to a float with a long sealskin line. Then she told the people to throw one inside the river and the other behind their village. The float that was filled with air sunk, while the rock floated:

> After letting them do that, she said that she had made a float for the village. And when the water reached a certain level, it stopped going up. But around the village, the water rose.

And those hills disappeared when the water got high. The area around the village was like this [bowl], and the village was down below. The water level around their village stayed at that level, but the water rose around them.

As she sat in the kayak, her face became that of a walrus, and her tusks were on the side of the kayak. Then after a while she turned back into her normal self. To this day, logs can be seen on the tops of hills near the old village site, showing how high the water rose during the flood.

Uyangqulriim Arnaan continued as a healer, even after she was too old to leave her home. She would have someone take a *taprualuk* (sealskin line) and bring it to her patient in the *qasgiq*, and she would suck out the illness from her home, taking out the bleeding with that *taprualuk* that was not hollow.

5

Cauyatuli
One Who Drums

. . . .

Tumaralriim apqara'arcuutii
Tumaralria's drum

During public events and gatherings over the past two decades, elders have repeatedly stressed the importance of the drum as a metaphor for the continued vitality of the Yup'ik way of life. During planning meetings for the Yup'ik exhibition, *Yuungnaqpiallerput / The Way We Genuinely Live*, Paul John (August 2003:24) declared: "I have said many times that God gave us our traditions to keep until the end of the world. That's how it is. Our ancestors were in that drum. When Christian religions came around, all of our ancestors came out of that drum. But nowadays, it is like you Yup'ik people are working toward putting us back inside that drum. We shouldn't think that our traditional ways are nothing. They are very valuable things." At the same gathering, Frank Andrew noted:

> The drum is indeed most important. Our ancestors used it in December [during dance festivals]. It was like they were giving thanks for the things that they harvested starting from January, and they were joyous, and the host village would invite other villages. All villages used the drum down on the coast and took part in dancing. That's why the drum is truly the most important item. Our ancestors kept the drum's sound alive, trying to follow its customary ways.

Frank concluded: "The reverberation of the drum kept everyone together."

Elders distinguish between *cauyat* (dance drums) and *apqara'arcuutet* (shamans' drums, lit., "devices for asking," from *apqara-*, "to ask about something"). Paul John (August 2003:27–29) spoke at length about how *angalkut* used these drums to heal people in the past and exercise their powers. Elders have examined and commented on a number of shaman drums in museum collections over the years, including a Nelson Island drum with a toothy cavity running down the length of its handle which Paul John identified as having belonged to the powerful Nelson Island shaman, Tumaralria (figures 5.1a and 5.1b).

Looking at the drum, Paul told the story of a man who, long after Tumaralria had died, constructed kayak parts below the old village of Tununak. The following winter he went to collect them, spending the night inside the deserted *qasgiq*. While he was trying to sleep, he felt the *qasgiq* jolt, and the floor suddenly detached so that he could see outside. As he watched, a person approached and told him that he had come to get him, as he didn't want him to be cold when he slept that night. The man recalled that if a person replied to a ghost, he would lose his ability to speak. When this thought came to his mind, the one who had come to get him replied, "You will not lose your ability to talk, even though you speak to me. I'm not a ghost."

The man followed his host inland, where he saw a village in a place where there usually was no village.

https://doi.org/10.5876/9781646427314.c005

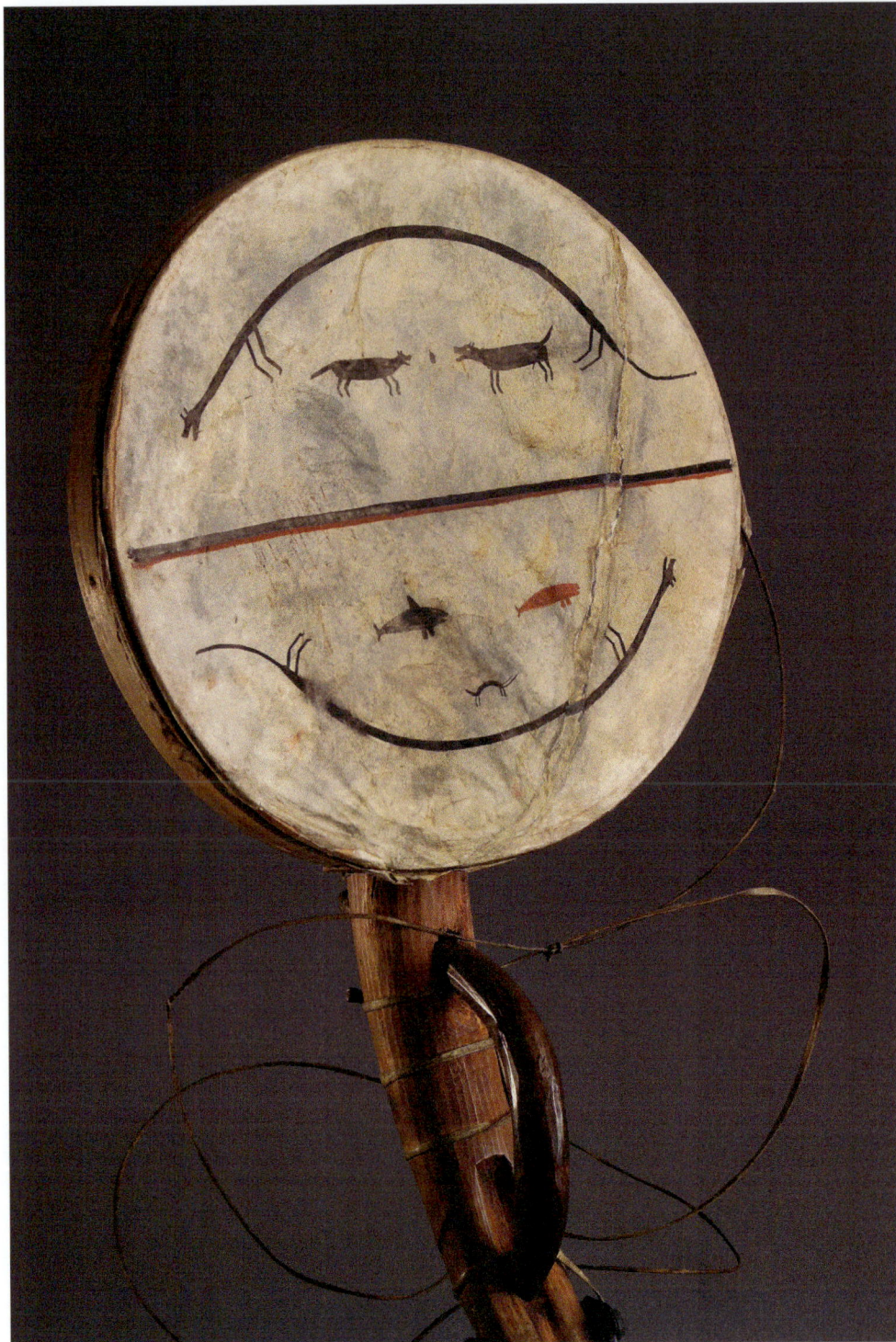

FIGURE 5.1A. Tumaralria's drum. While examining this drum collected on Nelson Island in the early 1900s, Frank Andrew noted: "The drum is indeed most important.... Our ancestors kept the drum's sound alive, trying to follow its customary ways." L. A. Lee, 1905, Peabody Essex Museum E13084. Photo by Jeffrey Dykes.

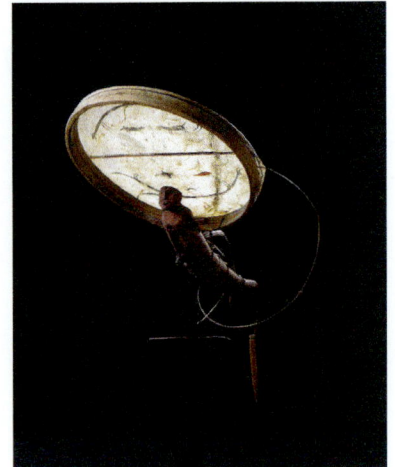

FIGURE 5.1B. The underside of Tumaralria's drum, showing the open cavity cut into the drum handle. L. A. Lee, 1905, Peabody Essex Museum E13084. Photo by Jeffrey Dykes.

They entered a warm *qasgiq* where he was offered food. First he was given a bowl of whitefish, which he accepted; then he was offered a bowl containing a child with its stomach split open, and teeth around the edges of the opening, which he did not accept. After the two ate together, his host told him it was time to return home. As they headed toward the *qasgiq* where they had first met, his host said, "Now, have you heard of the shaman of the people of Nelson Island, Tumaralria? I am him. Since I didn't want you to sleep in a cold place, I went to get you." Paul concluded: "When he told the story at home, those people said that since he wasn't a malicious *angalkuq*, he still had compassion for people." Whether or not the drum that elicited the story had actually belonged to Tumaralria, its Nelson Island origin and obvious association with once powerful *angalkut* gave it great value to those planning the Yup'ik exhibition. When *Yuungnaqpiallerput* opened at the Anchorage Museum in February 2008, Tumaralria's drum was the first thing visitors encountered (Fienup-Riordan 2007a).[1]

The striking design of Tumaralria's drum is not unique. Yup'ik shaman drums in other museum collections have similar handles. In 1989 Wassilie Evan and Willie Beans of Mountain Village visited the Sheldon Jackson Museum in Sitka, Alaska, and identified another extraordinary drum collected in the 1890s as belonging to the lower Yukon shaman, Irurpak (Long Legs). Like Tumaralria's drum, its handle was shaped like a human figure with a slash lined with fox teeth running the length of its body. Elders subsequently requested the drum for inclusion in the Yup'ik mask exhibition, *Agayuliyararput / Our Way of Making Prayer* (Fienup-Riordan 1996:180). The Sheldon Jackson Museum was unable to grant their request due to the drum's age and fragility. Yup'ik community members, however, were not deterred, and they commissioned John McIntyre of Bethel to make a replica of the drum. Like Tumaralria's drum, the replica drum was given a place of honor in the *Agayuliyararput* exhibition, and Andy Paukan of St. Mary's presented it to the people during opening ceremonies in Toksook Bay in January 1996 (figures 5.2 and 5.3).

The Norwegian collector Johan Adrian Jacobsen also collected a number of shamanic pieces displaying toothy cavities. He described one fish-shaped drum handle from Nushagak (IVA5428) with two perforated hands and an open belly studded with reindeer teeth as belonging to a shaman. Working in collections at the Ethnologisches Museum Berlin, Catherine Moore (September 1997) from Emmonak demonstrated how to hold the handle with the drum frame (fastened on the top of the fish's head) close to and covering her face (figure 5.4), and Wassilie Berlin of Kasigluk described its use:

> This handle does not look like those on regular drums. It's quite long. This looks like the size handle that would be held by *angalkut* when they went into meditative songs scrutinizing events. *Angalkut* used drums which were called *apqara'arcuutet* [lit., "devices for asking"].
>
> This was the handle of an *apqara'arcuun* [shaman drum]. The front is shaped like a mouth with teeth. Such drums were small, and I've seen them, too. They

FIGURE 5.2. Drum like that belonging to the shaman Irurpak, collected by Sheldon Jackson from Andreafski in the 1890s. Both Johan Adrian Jacobsen (IVA5428) and Edward Nelson (1899:442) collected wooden figures, each with a broad toothy mouth running down the chest. Nelson (1899:406) wrote that these toothy cavities showed that "the being represented was supposed to be provided with mouths all along these portions of its figure." Sheldon Jackson Museum IIS171.

FIGURE 5.3. John McIntyre of Bethel holding the festival drum he carved for the opening of the Yup'ik mask exhibit. The drum replicates one collected by Sheldon Jackson from Andreafski in the 1890s and said to have belonged to the shaman Irurpak. James H. Barker.

held them in front of their faces and struck their drumsticks toward them.

Wassilie Berlin then described how *angalkut* had special songs they sang *apqara'arluteng* (asking for things) when they communicated with their *avneq* ("other half," helping spirit). As the *avneq* spoke in song, only the *angalkuq* could understand what was said. Wassilie then held up the drum, and Catherine described a personal experience:

> The person I saw beating the drum toward herself had a drum with a short handle, and each day she sat and drummed and sang, covering her face with the drum. Her drum was small, but it was a genuine drum. Her mother told us not to go near her, but her mother would sit next to her as she drummed. The woman's skin had some kind of festering cuts. When I came in from playing, she would still be sitting at the same spot and singing. And the rest of the people in the house didn't complain about her singing and allowed her to do that. When she and her mother stayed with us for a short time, she did that. Perhaps she was an *angalkuq* because she drummed and sang every day.

Frank Andrew (December 2003:336–39) had also observed shamans using drums, and he described his understanding of what he had witnessed: "Those drums are a way for the *angalkut* to search and examine. . . . They say shamans inspect things by drumming and find a way to travel with a drum. They say these drums are a way for shamans to look around [and discern things]. Then when they stand without [using the drums], they can travel with their bodies, after examining their path with drums." Once, when the shaman Puyulkuk used a drum, Frank and his companion Qugan'aq crawled under the floor boards and watched Puyulkuk drumming in the back of the *qasgiq*.

> *Angalkut* who are drumming apparently don't keep their eyes open. He was singing away, he was dancing with his body. But when his song ended, when he started to sing faster, he started to [do something] without keeping his eyes open. While he was drumming . . . he would move his jaws from side to side, but he would not open his eyes, even when his song suddenly ended. I wonder what he was doing? His *tuunrat* [spirit helpers] probably made him do that.
> They apparently don't stay still. They say they search when they are drumming.
> When they started, they would take the drumstick and do this, not hitting [the drum].

> Probably when they were ready, they started to sing the song, continually [hitting the drum]. When they wanted to, they would drum faster and begin [the song]. When they got going, they then [hit the drum] like this, they struck [the drum] like regular drummers. But when the song was over, they'd [drum] faster.

Frank Andrew (December 2003:338) then explained that when *angalkut* communicate with their *avneq* (other half) it is referred to as *apqara'arluteng* or *apqara'ar* ("to ask about something"):

> They refer to it as *apqara'arluteng* when they are speaking to one another.
> That person, Akerpak, his *avneq* was very understandable when it spoke. They say his *avneq* took him.
> They apparently speak, but in a different way. But they are understandable. The shaman's *avneq* would speak through him in Yup'ik, but not clearly.

After a shaman dies, he can become the *avneq* of another shaman, referred to as the dead shaman's *mer'umavigkaq* (lit., "one who would give him a constant source of drinking water"). Frank Andrew (December 2003:339) explained:

> The ones who will become *avneret*, the shamans, when they are going to die, they start looking for what they call their *mer'umavigkat* [ones to whom shamans give their powers after death].
> And when they [go to] one who they consider to be bright, they take that one, and that one becomes his *mer'umavik*. [The shaman who died] would become his *avneq*.
> They always give them water. While they are using their powers, they ask for some water. Then he would stop using his powers, and he let them fill the dipper, and would have another person splash water on him. They say they are giving him water when he is thirsty. That is why shamans searched for what they called their *mer'umavigkat*.

Roland Phillip (October 2006:189–90) described witnessing a shaman perform, using his powers, at the request of a white doctor from Akiak, who had traveled to the old village of Akulirarmiut. Keplialleq was just a regular person, but he had an *urumavik* (shaman who helped in his conception), so he obtained an *avneq* and became a shaman as well. Roland explained that *avneret* were invisible guardians, and when other shamans tried to attack him, one's *avneq* would alert the person it resided in.

FIGURE 5.4. Catherine Moore holding a small shaman drum (IVA6990) and singing a song during her visit to the Ethnologisches Museum Berlin, September 1997. Ann Fienup-Riordan.

Roland said that when Keplialleq came to the qasgiq, he told the singers to sing. While they sang, he went along the back wall, removed and folded his seal-gut garment, and tossed it down on the floor, toward the entrance. When he threw it, a mink made "cer" noises, and when the parka stopped moving, it got quiet. The non-Native doctor admitted that he was unable to do anything like that.

Catherine Moore (September 1997) described how once she and a friend were alone in a house when a boy who was being trained by an angalkuq entered and asked if they wanted to hear his avneq as it came up from underground. He proceeded to cover his head with a seal-gut garment and to mumble something to summon it while rustling the garment. When the girls heard someone's low, muffled voice coming up from the ground, they ran from the house in terror: "His avneq was coming up to meet him as he was singing and mumbling words." Later the boy's grandfather stopped his training when he began mumbling and snickering to himself and acting strangely.

Fred Augustine (March 2011:1078–81) witnessed what was likely a shaman communicating with his avneq. As a young man, Fred accompanied his father to attend a dance festival at Kapuutelleq. After the guests left, a group of shamans stayed behind to practice with their spirit powers, and Fred went to the qasgiq to observe. One of the younger shamans, Angutvassuk, asked Fred to be his helper. Although reluctant, Fred's grandfather told him to help, and Fred obeyed. Angutvassuk lay face down, and Fred and another helper lay face down beside him, pressing down on him as hard as they could: "Then he started. They were drumming. That shaman spoke. It would reply to him. It was like it would reply to him from his mouth. They were talking back and forth. He was doing something, he continually made rumbling noises, he made noise like a fly, he was making loud rumbling noises." When the voices got quieter and left, the shaman's body went limp: "[The voices] were no longer there. And his body fell. But he had told us to press down on him hard, when we could hear his noise. Finally, after a long time, he started making noise from somewhere, from far away. When he started making noise, we did as he asked. His body was flat." Then the young shaman's body gradually went upright, his voice returned, and he went back to normal and was done. Fred wondered what the others watching would say, but they never said a thing.

Frank Andrew (December 2003:123) also described experiencing the powerful drumming of his cousin Mancuaq, his father's sister's son, who was an angalkuq. Frank was visiting their winter camp at Qamiqumiut. When he arrived, Frank didn't know that his cousin had gotten good at drumming. When it was time to lie down to sleep, he said he would sleep next to his cousin, in front of the door. Noticing a drum hanging nearby, he asked whose it was, and his cousin said it was his drum and that he would drum for him. Frank's cousin told him to sit below him, with his legs over the end of the bed and his back to Mancuaq. Frank continued: "After some time, I started to feel cold and to shiver, and my arms started to shake, and they were lifting. It seemed that my breathing was going inward sometimes. It started to get more powerful. Eventually, my voice started to come out unexpectedly, and I would make the sudden noise, 'Ee-ee.'" At that point Frank began to hear something and realized that the other people in the house were laughing: "When it got too powerful, I twisted the bottom part of my body and fell onto the floor. When I landed, it suddenly ended. . . . I told him that I was done, that I wouldn't do it again." Frank concluded: "They are powerful. People should not think that the abilities of angalkut are nothing."

Frank Andrew (February 2003:40) also described watching the female angalkuq Cupungulria conjuring, using a drum, describing her as both an igyararatuli (one who drums and sings to conjure her spirit powers, from igyaraq, "throat") and a cauyatuli (one who drums). Frank noted that her drum was small, the size of a sugar-cube box, and that when she drummed, the drumstick sometimes hit her face.

Paru was apparently her uicungaq [male teasing cousin]. Paru criticized her drum because the drumstick would hit her face. She replied that when her tari [another word for tuunraq, spirit helper] comes near her, her drum grows into a very large drum. . . .

Her spirit powers come to her, inhabit her. They call those who do that igyararalriit.

As a final testament to the essential role drums played in shamanic enactments of power, Frank Andrew (September 2006:271) told the story of the powerful angalkuq Arnaruaq (lit., "Pretend woman") who stole the drums of lesser shamans but was finally destroyed by one with a more powerful drum. Arnaruaq lived on the Togiak River and was known

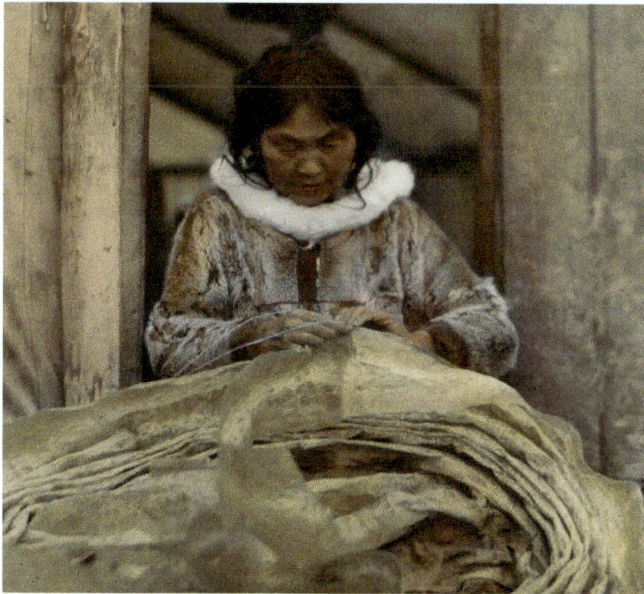

FIGURE 5.5. The shaman Cupungulria, sewing a seal-gut parka. Frank Andrew identified her as an *igyararatuli* (one who drums and sings to conjure her spirit powers). L. Waugh, 1935, National Museum of the American Indian, Smithsonian Institution L2738.

to instigate conflict between shamans. Arnaruaq had two husbands who were *nukalpiat* (great hunters). At night he turned into a woman, but during the day he was a man.

In Apruka'ar lived another shaman named Keggutellek (lit., "One with teeth") who would go on journeys with his drum there in his village. Then one day his drum disappeared. Time went by, and Keggutellek traveled down the coast to Togiak, where he encountered Arnaruaq. Arnaruaq invited Keggutellek to visit his home, and on entering Keggutellek saw a sleeping platform and four posts used as supports for the house frame. Many drum heads were tied along each post, and three drums hung above the sleeping platform, one of which was his. Arnaruaq said that after taking the drums from *angalkut* and realizing that their owners were not truly powerful, he took the drumskins off and hung them. He said that the drums hanging over his bed were real and that the drum hanging the farthest back—Keggutellek's drum—was the most powerful: "He told him that when he used it, he traveled out and couldn't get to all the places it could go. He said it was a drum [with real power]."

Arnaruaq then invited Keggutellek to visit him at night, but Keggutellek didn't respond. That night, however, Keggutellek left the *qasgiq* and summoned

his spirit helpers to find a way inside Arnaruaq's house. Eventually, he transformed himself into a down feather and dropped through the smoke hole, transformed into a human again, and saw Arnaruaq sleeping in the form of a woman. Arnaruaq woke, but Keggutellek escaped through the smokehole along with his drum. The next day Keggutellek left toward home. Arnaruaq pursued him as Keggutellek fled to his parents' home on the upper Yukon River. There Keggutellek's father gave him a bow, which he used to finally kill Arnaruaq when he looked in on them through their smokehole.

Qanerpak
The monstrous mouth

The toothy cavities appearing on both Tumaralria's and Irurpak's drums, as well as on other shamanic objects such as the tiny wooden figure with the open belly elders examined at the Yupiit Piciryarait Museum in 2003, have strong associations in Yup'ik iconography and oral tradition. Nonhuman persons, they say, possessed extraordinary sight, hearing, and smell, so that humans had to control their own vision, noise, and odor when dealing with them. The Yupiit also marshaled the forms and functions of the human mouth in their concepts of the spirit world.

Among the most distinctive and intriguing mask features are the wide, toothy mouths and teeth running along great cavities in the body or down the arm or leg. Nelson (1899:406) noted that the toothy grooves on one lower Kuskokwim mask indicated that the being represented had mouths all along those portions of its body. This may be a reference to the creature's predatory, carnivorous nature. Lantis (1990:173–76) contended that these toothy mouths symbolized the animals' revenge on human hunters. Jasper Louis (February 1994:32) said simply, "If the being they were creating had many teeth, they would make the mask look like it, too."

Lantis (1990:170–76) related the masks' toothy mouths to the story of a baby with a mouth stretching from ear to ear that consumed its mother and others as punishment for breaking admonishments (see also Andrew and Rearden 2007:64–83). The story of the big-mouthed baby is not the only tale featuring a creature with a toothy cavity or monstrous mouth. Cecelia Foxie (May 1993) of Stebbins gave a detailed account

FIGURE 5.6. One of two large wooden figures (IVA4464, IVA4196) from the lower Yukon with toothy cavities running along their backs. The collector, Johan Adrian Jacobsen, designated them both as Slaowikmiu-Tonnerak (Ellam Yua *tuunraq*, "Spirit of the Person of the Universe"). This figure was said to have been hung in the entryway of a house as protection for a child. Ethnologisches Museum Berlin IVA4196, Barry McWayne.

of a boy who disobeyed his grandmother and went to explore a nearby knoll, which he discovered was a house. Inside lived a hunter lying on his belly. Similar to Tumaralria's experience, a woman then served the boy a bowl. When she turned around, the boy saw a baby in the dish with its stomach slashed open, revealing canine teeth (see also Nelson 1899:496).

Frank Andrew (February 2003:106) told a comparable story about Kukukualek from Kipnuk, who was haunted by a ghost when he spent the night alone in the *qasgiq* at Iqukvaq. After he went to bed, he heard the voice of a woman in the porch, and wrapping his belt around his hand as a weapon, he climbed into the rafters. There he heard her say, "They have said a stranger has arrived! He must be hungry!" When she entered, she carried a plate containing a baby with its belly split. When her head appeared, Kukukualek whipped his belt in her face, lost consciousness, and awoke to find her gone.

The acts of eating and biting were fraught with associations for a people whose day-to-day lives depended on killing and eating animals, and they were often featured in scary stories of supernatural retaliation. As we have seen, licking was considered a healing act in many contexts, and saliva was often associated with long life. The toothy mouth of a dog or wolf was also associated with healing in some contexts. Recall Frank Andrew's (January 2004:146) description of the healing ceremony the shaman Tairtaq performed in the *qasgiq* during which a huge dog entered the *qasgiq*, crouched down at the sick girl's feet, and ate first the lower half, then the upper half, of her body. People could hear her bones being crunched between its powerful teeth and saw blood gushing through its jaws. The dog then licked the area clean and disappeared through the entryway. Soon after, fingers appeared in the entryway, and two men pulled up both Tairtaq and his patient—alive and restored to health.

At the Ethnologisches Museum Berlin in 1997, elders also examined two large wooden figures (IVA4464, IVA4196) from the lower Yukon with toothy cavities running along their backs (figure 5.6). The collector, Johan Adrian Jacobsen, designated them both as "Slaowikmiu-Tonnerak" (probably Ellam Yua *tuunraq*, "spirit of the Person of the Universe"). Jacobsen interpreted them as both "thunder devil" and "lightning spirit," and said they were hung in the entryways of houses as protective figures for children: "Among rich people the children are entrusted into the care of a shaman, meaning that he is responsible for keeping the children healthy. This is the reason for making such figures; then he forces the spirits under his power to go into the figure, which will then protect the children during his absence." Jacobsen said that the toothy cavity on the back of each figure was intended to "lock in the spirit of the lightning," among others, and marked it as a protective spirit. One (IVA4464) was also named "Inrok-Palok-Aderok-Nomnajorte" or *iinruq paluqtaruaq enem nayurtii* (spirit in beaver form guarding the house). These were valued items and not something people were willing to part with. Jacobsen candidly wrote: "I obtained this figure [IVA4196] in a house whose inhabitants had gone on a reindeer hunt; the protective god was left behind. This gave me the opportunity to obtain the seemingly unattainable figure, something I had tried for months" (Fienup-Riordan 2005b:222).

The dramatic toothy mouths inscribed on the handles of Tumaralria's and Irurpak's drums as well as other shamanic objects likely recall the supernatural senses of the shaman's *tuunraq* and the large-mouthed child of oral tradition—senses one dismissed at one's peril. The monstrous mouth was prominent both in the shamans' actions—biting and eating diseases—and in the objects they created. When Tumaralria's guest was presented with a bowl containing a child with slit stomach, the cavity lined with teeth, he refused it. Yet Tumaralria treated his guest with compassion. The powerful shaman, Irurpak, was also a healer. Drums like Tumaralria's played an essential role in shamanic enactments of power in southwest Alaska in the past. Today these shaman drums are neither rejected nor hidden but are given a prominent place in public statements and displays about the Yup'ik way of life.

6

Angalkut Tuunriluteng Ayagatullret
Shaman Journeys and Performances

....

Kit'ellriit
Shamans who travel underwater

Angalkut used drums to communicate with their *avneret*. They also used drums to travel to the sea or to the sky to obtain things for the people. According to Frank Andrew (September 2005:248):

> *Tuunritulit* [ones who conjured spirits] had drums. There's a ritual [shamans] do by standing up to conjure spirits, then there was the drum. They say the way of conjuring spirits by standing up was a way for a shaman to travel . . . physically in the flesh.
>
> He wouldn't be drumming, but it was a way of conjuring spirits [and travel].
>
> They say it was his way of going out and traveling. . . . In his mind he would travel. Even though his body stayed behind, he'd travel far away.
>
> But they say a shaman used the drum to look around. He would check his path ahead if he was asked to do so by the community.
>
> And if they asked him to *pinguarluku* [request an abundance of something using his spirit powers, lit., "pretend to do something"], he'd use his drum first and check out the path he would take, and find out what he would do if he encountered something.

Frank Andrew (September 2005:250–61) followed with the story of Aqsarpak, who lived in Ayikatarmiut many years ago. Once his two grandsons asked him to travel to the ocean where they would hunt during the coming season. First he used his drum to check the trail he would take, passing by Ayikatarmiut, located on a tributary of the Tagyaraq River. After he drummed for a long time, he told his grandsons that he wanted to wait, as a younger person was getting ready to go down to the ocean, but his grandsons kept pleading, and he reluctantly got ready.

In some cases, when a shaman was going to travel to the ocean, they wrapped him, naked with his arms by his sides, in a bearded-seal skin, referred to as *qilaraulluku*, tying him securely with walrus-skin line, then attaching the skin line of a spear as a tether when he took off. Some *angalkut* asked that a seal-gut parka be put next to them. After the shaman was wrapped, he would suddenly roll onto his belly, dart forward hopping on his arms and legs, and the dried seal-skin covering would suddenly get soft and appear to be the skin of a live seal, disappearing head-first down the entry hole, with the skin line following behind. A man stood at the back of the *qasgiq*, holding a wooden handle attached to the line, and pulled on the line to keep it taut. Then the line would suddenly get loose. Frank Andrew (December 2003:344) later added that when they pulled them back into the *qasgiq* and removed the binding, the shaman would be wearing the seal-gut parka and would be drenched: "They used to say that they would actually drown when they were pretending to do it."

Other shamans, including Aqsarpak, traveled out through ice holes rather than through entrance

https://doi.org/10.5876/9781646427314.c006

holes, wrapped in skin. Aqsarpak prepared by dressing in waterproof garments worn for ocean hunting. Then his helpers made a square hole in a lake, and five men accompanied him to the hole which he straddled, planting one foot on each side. No one else would be there. Even when he put his feet in the water, he wouldn't fall in. Then the men would all put their hands on the crown of his head, one on top of the other. As the weight got heavier, he slowly went down.

Frank Andrew (September 2005:254) clarified what Aqsarpak acquired when he traveled to the ocean: "He got the *tarnaq* [soul, tiny visible likeness] of the thing he had acquired, and he quickly pushed it behind the lace loop of his waterproof boots. But in his hand he held a mock-up piece of the real thing." Although battered by his adversary, Nagiiquyaq, Aqsarpak returned to his village, bringing the *tarnaq* of what his grandsons wished to acquire. (Aqsarpak's continued conflict with Nagiiquyaq is described below in chapter 9: "Malicious Shamans and Shaman Confrontations.")

Frank Andrew (September 2005:255) noted that when shamans went on journeys, they usually appointed a person who had the ability to see them as they traveled. The seer would sit in the *qasgiq* with a cover over him, looking into a bowl of water and watching the shaman out on the ocean: "Though the person wasn't a shaman, he had the power to see. . . . He would use the *tuunrat* [spirit guides] of the shaman, and . . . from inside the *qasgiq* he'd be able to see [the shaman] out in the ocean. . . . He'd tell the others what he was doing."

Kit'ellriit (shamans who traveled underwater, lit., "those who fall into water or drown") were aided by drummers and singers while they journeyed. Frank Andrew (December 2003:342) explained: "They say they sang all night when he was on his journey, resting periodically when they were tired and then going on. They would finally stop when he arrived." Those in the *qasgiq* sang *yuarulluut*, songs composed by shamans but that others performed when a shaman was taking a journey or using his power: "They call those [shaman songs] *yuarulluut*. They say [other people] sang for them when [angalkut] used their powers while standing. When [angalkut] used drums, they sang their own *yuarulluut*. But when they [used their powers] standing, those who weren't *angalkut* sang for them, because they knew their songs."

Many noted that *kit'ellriit* could not be without *imarnitet* (seal-gut rain parkas)—also essential gear for hunters traveling on the ocean. They would tighten the hood around the face to keep water out. Frank Andrew (December 2003:343) noted: "These were tools for *angalkut*; drums and seal-gut garments were their tools." During performances in the *qasgiq*, a shaman would drape the seal-gut garment over his shoulders, but he always put it on when he traveled.

Frank Andrew (December 2003:340–43) described how the shaman Pangalgalria, from the village of Qinaq, used five helpers when he went underwater. He had his helpers make a hole in the ice downriver from their village, at the river's mouth, and then clear the surface of the ice and cover it with woven grass kayak mats. After weighing down the mats' corners, they left. Then, when the five helpers took him down from the *qasgiq* and removed the weights from the grass mats, no ice was on the water's surface. Frank continued:

> They say they spread their legs out when they do that. They plant their feet on the edges of that hole in the ice, and he'd insert his walking stick on the sides. Then using their powers, when he did something, he would plant their feet next to his feet. They would push him farther toward the hole, and also the other person on the other side, narrowing his legs.
>
> After a number of times, he would suddenly get into the water. . . . He didn't go down in the water right away.
>
> And when he got to that point, he let them put their hands on him here [on top of his head], with their hands on top of each other. And he told them not to help him [put weight down on him]. But with just the weight [of their hands], just relaxed, with their [hands] on top of one another. And when they did that, they would finally start to go down. And the bottom of his seal-gut garment would reach the water.
>
> They would go down like that. And like he told them to, when [their hands] reached the water, they didn't remove them right away, but kept them there for a while. After he had done that, they'd return, when he had sunk.

People would sing all night while he was on his journey, resting when they got tired, then starting again, and finally stopping when he returned.

Some stories described the techniques shamans used during their performances. Elsie Tommy (March 2009:197–204) gave a lively account passed down from her husband's father, Tutgara'urluq, of the time a shaman asked him to be his helper when he used his powers in the *qasgiq* to check for seals in the ocean. The shaman instructed Tutgara'urluq to put on ringed-sealskin boots and mittens. Then, putting on his seal-gut rain gear, the shaman told Tutgara'urluq to go into the underground entryway and to sit facing the front of the *qasgiq*, which he did. When the men closed the door behind him, Tutgara'urluq went inside the draft hole (located just below the door). There he took hairs from his sealskin boots and placed them in the mouth of a small model seal that the shaman had given him. Tutgara'urluq then squeezed back out of the draft hole, into the entryway, and, just as the shaman stopped his song, slowly went inside. There he showed the model seal to the one who had asked him to go to the ocean, and the shaman replied, "Just as could be expected, there will be many seals this spring." Indeed, there were many seals that spring. Elsie explained: "They say that when seals are going to be scarce, the ones who he sent out don't obtain anything. And if seals are going to be [plentiful], he obtains something. [Tutgara'urluq] said that was a time when he was clever. He said that spring, seals were abundant." Laughing, Elsie concluded, "He said it turned out to be true. He said that the unseen one helped them." Elsie (December 2012:45–48) later added that although the shaman asked Tutgara'urluq to help him in future, Tutgar'aurluq declined: "That one thought he was a shaman, he really believed that he traveled to the ocean and used to try to get him to be his helper."

When asked if shamans really traveled through holes in the ice, Albertina Dull (April 2013:81–82) responded that she did not know: "When they practiced their shaman powers long ago, they would say they traveled to the ocean, and they would say they also tried to change the weather." Then she mentioned a large wooden grave marker at Umkumiut with a model walrus on top. The grave belonged to the shaman Kinguqall'er: "They say Kinguqall'er instructed them, that although he had died, they should call his name. My! That walrus model facing the ocean was probably something [powerful]."

Ellakun ayalallret
Traveling to the sky

Angalkut traveled up to the sky as well as down to the ocean. Thomas Chikigak (August 1987:76–79) of Alakanuk spoke of a shaman from his village who traveled to the sky to procure land animals for the people.

> He flew away using snowshoes. . . . From somewhere that he considered to be far away, he went to get that thing that people would use, and he returned.
>
> While he was traveling home up in the sky, he saw a tundra hare along the edge of a hole [den], along the edge of a star's hole . . . and the place where people were walking was visible underneath it.

Wanting to have that tundra hare for the people of his village, he approached it and swept it into the hole with his snowshoes, letting it fall to earth.

> When he returned home, after displaying that one that he had gone to get inside the *qasgiq*, he evidently told them—this was before I started going to the *qasgiq*—he said that while he was traveling up in the sky, as he was returning home, when he saw a tundra hare that could easily fall, suddenly desiring to have it for the people in his hometown . . . he swept it with his snowshoes. . . . He said that if he wasn't lying, during spring . . . those tundra hares would increase in number.

Indeed, that spring tundra hares were plentiful. Thomas said that his older brother was a boy then, and although the lever of a bird gun was almost too far for him to reach, he would travel and catch many tundra hares.

Mary Mike (October 1994:21–25) told the story of two shamans who met each other on the moon—Teggalquq from Paimiut at the mouth of the Yukon and another shaman from just below Marshall. Mary didn't recall why they traveled to the moon—a feat that was a recurrent theme in Inuit as well as Yup'ik oral tradition (Laugrand and Oosten 2012:148). She described how those flying to the moon were tied inside a bearded-seal skin, then placed in the firepit and covered with floor boards. Men sang *yuarulluut* and drummed in the *qasgiq*, trying to get the person to go: "[Shamans] left using their shaman powers. They weren't regular people but left with something; they probably also went in the form of their *tuunrat*." Mary continued, describing how the two shamans met on the moon, but got angry at one another and fought, Teggalquq finding his adversary weak: "[Teggalquq] evidently told him to his face that he wouldn't have let him return home alive, but that he wanted him to tell the story about him, that he was going to have him return home near death." In fact, Teggalquq returned unharmed, but his enemy returned with his body broken:

> It is said that when he returned home he told the people that he ran into a shaman up on the moon. He said he wasn't a person but evidently a rock, that he had broken his bones. . . .
> It was evidently Teggalquq [lit., "Rock"], Teggalquq was his name.

Eugene Pete (December 2011:98–99) also knew the story of Teggalquq, who would fly to the moon with his two dogs: "He would leave, having them tie him up inside a bearded-seal skin." When encountering the shaman from the north, Teggalquq put on his *amiq* (skin or cloak): "Although he hit him, it wouldn't go inside his body. . . . They say when he reached home, his northern counterpart told that he came upon a person, that he evidently wasn't human, that he was a rock." Fred Augustine (March 2011:1032) also spoke of Teggalquq, the indomitable shaman who could travel to Bethel with five dogs and arrive that night, running at the same pace as his dogs.

Lawrence Edmund (December 2011:99–100) talked about the shaman Qakurtaq, who was said to fly, riding his drum. Two men would tie him up and leave him on the far side of the Alakanuk River, along with his drum. Qakurtaq would fly across the river, getting faster each time. Once a woman looked through a small tear in her tent:

> They say she looked outside, and he was circling with his drum underneath him *cella maliggluku* [going clockwise, lit., "following the universe"] in the air.
> She said that after a while, back when they had seal-gut windows, he landed on that window and went inside the *qasgiq*.

Once, when they tied a rock to him as a drag, Qakurtaq became desperate and admonished them never to do that again, that the rock had almost caused him to fall. Lawrence (December 2011:101) added that they would also hide drums from him to no avail: "Once when they threw his drum in the water and had it float away, he made a snare and lowered it through a crack in the floor boards of the *qasgiq* and snared that drum by its handle and retrieved it."

Alexie Nicholai (March 2017:289) mentioned shamans who traveled to the moon to make animals more readily available. Yako Andrew of Napaskiak followed with a story of two shamans who said that they were going to the moon. The first one left the *qasgiq* to travel to the moon. When the second one followed him out of the *qasgiq*, he looked for a place to hide in the entryway, where he found the first shaman already hiding. Yako concluded with a laugh: "Then the one who had gone out second said to him, 'Are you here, too?' They pretended to travel to the moon, lying. That's an old story I used to hear."

Allat irr'inarqellriit tuunrilriit
Other extraordinary performances

Shamans were known to travel to the ocean and to the sky to obtain things people requested. Shamans also used their skills to perform a variety of feats. John Phillip (February 2014:187) watched a shaman who tried to change the weather. He turned the wind direction by moving a paddle inside the *qasgiq*, while having someone check outside:

> [The one who checked] would say that [the wind direction] reached this place where the paddle was pointing. Then when it reached the west, he told him to stop when the people told him to stop. The wind started blowing from that direction. They said the weather would improve after that. . . .
> He shifted [the wind] in a circle inside the *qasgiq* using a paddle, by continually moving it. And the wind followed and shifted.

Shamans sometimes traveled and performed with no purpose other than to entertain people. Frank Andrew (December 2003:344–48) described his experiences in the 1930s in the village of Kwigillingok when he watched the *angalkuq* Ayuqsar fly, seated on a rock. As when shamans traveled to the ocean, Frank and the others removed the shaman's clothing; then they tied him up and put him on top of a rock on the edge of the floor boards in the back of the *qasgiq*, with his body bent, his arms down by his ankles and wrists tied. They then took a large drum out into the porch, placing it sideways in the narrow space. Letting the drumstick fall through the cracks in the floor boards, they turned off the lights: "And just as [Ayuqsar] instructed them, the ones in the back [of the qasgiq] would make a noise [of slapping their tongues against the front part of their lips inside their mouths]. And the ones who were below, up front would constantly go, 'Shhhh, shhh.' " This was followed by a sudden loud noise, and then something made a drumming sound, which started coming in with the drumstick beating fast. The second time, the drumming sound came from above and suddenly went around the qasgiq. Finally the men sang loudly, and when their song ended, a loud noise came from below. When they turned on the light, they saw the shaman sitting on top of the rock, biting the drumstick with his teeth, with the edge of the drum leaning against his knees: "He would strike using his jaws, but here he was tied down. . . . And when the five times [of circling the qasgiq] were complete, we would turn the lights on and see his bindings down there still tied, but in a pile."

Frank Andrew (December 2003:347) then described his iluraq (male cross-cousin) Milton who took a fire poker and tried to reach out to Ayuqsar during his performance. Ayuqsar responded, "You will not touch me, even though you try to swipe at me. Do you think that I [fly] inside this qasgiq? I go in circles up there nunat anllugneratni [along the aura/mist of the village], where you cannot reach." When asked how he performed this feat, Ayuqsar pointed at the rock and said, "This takes me." He said that it also took him upside down, as it was really stuck to his buttocks.

Frank had witnessed this more than once: "Lerniq and Tengquq from Chefornak used to do that in my presence, and Ayuqsar as well." He added that they were told to tie them tightly, as loose bindings were painful, while they didn't feel anything with tight ones. Like the heavy rock allowing the angalkuq to fly, the tight bindings had the opposite effect—a common characteristic of shaman experiences. Frank added that this was only done during winter, for amusement: "I didn't hear that it was done for any purpose, but that it was done for fun."

Shamanic demonstrations of power varied, and stories of their performances were long remembered and recalled with considerable interest. Frank Andrew (February 2003:166–71) spoke of the Kwigillingok shaman Qumaqniq who let people burn him outside. Frank had not personally witnessed this, as it happened before he was born. Qumaqniq first drummed in the qasgiq looking for wood. When he finished drumming, he revealed the location of a log buried in the snow, with a snowy owl perched on top. The men cut the log and brought it back to the village. Qumaqniq then called on his spirit powers in the qasgiq. Just as the sun was setting, they brought him out of the qasgiq, dressed in a seal-gut parka with belt, fishskin mittens, wading boots, and holding two canes. They then piled the wood, with kindling at each corner: "When he got there, just before they were lit, on the north side of the corner, he would kneel down and bow his head, and circle farther following the direction of the universe, whenever he bowed on their corners." Qumaqniq then climbed on top of the wood pile, facing east. The men lit the wood, and the fire grew, engulfing the large pile: "So the flame completely engulfed that person. And the smoke started to go right straight upward. . . . The wind could not blow it away." Finally, the smoke split in two, and the two smoke columns were blown away.

Frank Andrew (December 2003:171) said that while in the fire, Qumaqniq became red hot like steel. When the stack of wood crumbled and fell, he also fell. Then people were told to go inside the qasgiq, and not to go in and out. Frank noted that Qumaqniq's clothing was insulated with highly combustible wood shavings and that he had a ruff made of material that was also easily singed. The ceremony continued throughout the night, with men beating their drums inside the qasgiq. When the sun rose, Qumaqniq arrived and was pulled up through the underground entryway wearing clothing that was neither burned nor singed. Qumaqniq was also said to have sat on five igneous rocks that had been heated until they were red hot, and once again he came away unscathed.

Frank Andrew and Kwigillingok elder Peter John (February 2003:175) discussed the powerful shaman Ingallak from Nanvarnarrlak, who was known to walk on water in the summer, using snowshoes and bundled up for winter weather. When he reached the land, his whiskers would be frosty. Peter John also recalled Ingallak making medicine in the qasgiq to obtain a snowy owl so that his fellow villagers could use its feathers to decorate masks for dancing. Ingallak succeeded, and when a messenger checked the hill near Nanvarnarrlak, the owl capsized as he watched, and they took it to the qasgiq.

Francis Charlie (January 2011:1032) spoke of piyugcetalget (ones who take a step and their path folds, shortening the distance to their destination, from *piyua-*, "to walk"). Although a village is far away, they can arrive there right away: "They say if he takes a step, [the ground] folds and he is able to land far away. . . . His path folds. He shortens his destination. They call those *piyugcetalget*." Raphael Jimmy added, "They say although a place is very far, some take two steps or three and arrive. Those *piyugcetalget* are like that."

Frank Andrew (December 2003:348) also described swimming through the ground, known as *kis'uka'arluni*, which he had witnessed in the *qasgiq*.

> When they swam through the ground, they were amazing to watch. . . . [One person in the *qasgiq*] would hold onto the sealskin rope. And down underground would be a person. When he would swim around, the skin line would move, cutting through the floor boards, and the wooden plank [that it had gone through] would fuse together after it passed. [The sealskin line] would turn in different directions, cutting across [planks]. . . .
>
> And there would be a person inside the ground swimming, what they called *kis'uka'arluni*. Another person would hold onto the sealskin rope. And suddenly, it would go toward the front of the *qasgiq*. When it got to the tunnel entrance, he would make noise and tell them to pull him out. They also tie them up when they do that.

Frank Andrew (December 2003:349) had also seen the shaman Puyulkuk place a drum on the edge of the skylight, hanging by its handle. He would then have others tie him and turn off the lights: "The drumstick would whistle, and after whistling, we couldn't sense him going up there; and immediately from the window above, there would be a loud drumming noise. After that, he would fly around and go down. When he landed on the floor boards, he would stop [making noise]." When they turned on the light, Puyulkuk would once again be tied down with the drum handle lying on one side.

John Phillip (October 2006:179), who had seen the shaman Puyulkuk exercise his powers a number of times, described watching Puyulkuk in the *qasgiq* when he took a knife and severed a piece of sealskin line that his *iluraq* had cut from a whole seal skin. His cousin was upset when he saw what he had done, but Puyulkuk only smiled, went to the rope, and after joining the two ends together, placed it inside his mouth and down toward his belly button: "When

he removed it, we saw that it was connected. He attempted to pull it apart and put it down. . . . I'm just speaking of Puyulkuk who exercised his powers in my presence."

Frank Andrew (December 2003:348–50) described other amazing feats that he had seen Puyulkuk perform:

> He would have us watch him as he was down in the center surrounded by us. And even though we were staring at something, as we were looking at it, it would disappear.
>
> And we would tear up a seal-gut parka, and he would gather all the pieces together and . . . cover them with his old *qaspeq*. After a while, he would open it up and take them out and they had already repaired; it would have no tears on it.

One time Puyulkuk had them burn twine in the stove. When the fire went out, he stuck his hand in and took it out, and the twine was in its original state. Puyulkuk also had them stare at a large, oblong rock in front of them: "As we were looking at it, it felt as though we just blinked, and when we looked at it, the rock was gone. After doing that, he did the same thing to us, and made [the rock] reappear."

After his performance, Frank said that Puyulkuk asked what they thought about what he had just done: "He asked if we thought that he merely moved it somewhere else. He said that they actually stay in their places, but that our eyes become blinded suddenly. That thing disappears, our eyes become unable to see it. He said that's what happens to them . . . even though it was still sitting in its original place." Puyulkuk noted that while some shamans are deceptive, he explains things without holding secrets: "[Puyulkuk] said that some shamans pretend to go on journeys, and they pretend to go underwater, by paying their helpers. And they paid them with animals, [saying] that they would give them those things. They would pretend to go on journeys and not really go. . . . They weren't truthful, they'd lie about going on journeys."

Finally, John Phillip (February 2014:189) told about Puyulkuk's reaction when he saw an airplane for the first time, along the mouth of the Kuskokwim River:

> Puyulkuk's *nuliacungaq* [man's female cross-cousin] apparently called to him while he was inside the tent, "My *uicungaq* [woman's male cross-cousin], come out, look at that one up there flying in the sky." After

saying that [she said], "Here you [shamans] say that you fly but you aren't seen. Come and look at this one flying." . . .

Being astonished, Puyulkuk apparently suddenly sat down and cried.

Puyulkuk was not the only shaman to perform amazing feats. Benedict Tucker (March 2011:778–82) described the Yukon shaman Angutvassuk performing at Cevv'artelleq, where Benedict and his mother were visiting his mother's sister. Benedict said that he was in awe, as he had never seen anything like it. First Angutvassuk took off his shirt, then swallowed a needle and took it out on his left side next to his heart, near his lungs. He displayed it, but there was no blood and he wasn't hurt. When someone asked him to do something else, he picked up a wood shaving from the floor and swallowed that as well: "After flexing it with his hands, he put it inside his mouth. . . . His mouth started to make clanking noises. I never forgot those two things. . . . It was evidently something that a person who was about to become a shaman just did for entertainment."

Eugene Pete (December 2011:49–51) also told the story of how the shaman Teggalquq performed an amazing feat, tethering a heavy kayak filled with ice to his eyes and somehow lifting it, having his eyes pull the kayak, when greeting guests arriving for a feast. Sometime later, Teggalguq evidently asked Kencialnguq to doctor his one daughter while she was in the womb so that she could live. Kencialnguq agreed, asking that Teggalguq teach him how to pull a kayak filled with ice with his eyes. Teggalguq acquiesced, but made Kencialnguq promise to follow all the steps exactly, leaving nothing out. Kencialnguq attempted to pull the kayak, but afterward couldn't remove one side of the tether and was in great pain. Teggalquq scolded him, saying he must have left something out. Chuckling, Eugene concluded: "Teggalquq who it belonged to removed it. But the one using it couldn't remove it."

Lawrence Edmund (December 2011:101–104) followed Eugene's account with the story of Qakurtaq, who removed his clothes and exercised his powers, shooting an unloaded gun in the qasgiq four times. When the men checked the next morning, bullets were found in the log walls. Lawrence exclaimed:

"That one was really fit to be a soldier." Lawrence noted that Qakurtaq gradually became more powerful after he married and his father-in-law gave him half his shaman powers. He would kill himself when he exercised his powers, planning to go to where the deceased were: "They say that's what he did, choking himself with a strip of sealskin hide. They say he would be extremely puffy and sick looking and his eyes were almost coming out. They say he would really die and his body would get stiff." Qakurtaq would stay like that in the qasgiq all night. In the morning, the sound of a fly could be heard, and when the sound reached Qakurtaq he would come back to life. Once Qakurtaq accidently shot himself while fox hunting. Since he couldn't recover, he had someone shoot him with an unloaded gun. First he exercised his shaman powers, then put on a seal-gut garment that they painted with a spot they would shoot at. Later, when he opened his rain garment, that charcoal smudge was a hole. Lawrence concluded: "They say they drummed all night. They say after a while, first as a fox, that one that sounded like a fly came up first. They say he circled the qasgiq as a fox first. And when he went all the way around, he became human again. And they say he never was bothered by that [gunshot wound] he was suffering from. That Qakurtaq evidently was amazing."

Finally, Albertina Dull (June 2009:73–74) described shamans who were cooked in a large pot, egavagluteng:

It wasn't boiling heavily. . . . They would heat those [iingarnat, pumice stones], probably along the qasgiq fire pit. [The stones] would be ablaze. That shaman would be sitting inside a large bowl filled with water. They say they would drop [pumice stones] in one by one, and when they put the last one in, . . . they would make noise. Then it would come to a heavy boil along with those pumice stones.

They say they would poke that shaman along his collarbone and check to see if he was done cooking.

Then when it didn't touch the bottom, they'd say that he wasn't cooked.

Wondering about the purpose of such performances, Ruth Jimmie commented that they were probably trying to astound people, and Lizzie Chimiugak said they were displaying their abilities as shamans.

7

Angalkut Pingualallrat
Shamans Requesting Future Abundance

··

Agayulallrat
Dancing with masks to request things

The *angalkuq* was a central figure in all masked dances, directing expert carvers to craft particular masks and explaining their meanings when the masks were presented to the people. The late Kay Hendrickson (January 1994:2–3), a well-known carver reared on Nunivak Island, remembered:

> These masks belonged to the *angalkut*. In preparation for the Messenger Feast, messengers were sent out to invite people from another village, and while they were gone the *angalkut* would have the carvers make masks which would be used in performance.
>
> The *angalkuq* composed a song and dance for each mask. The lyrics for the verses would be different.
>
> I observed people dancing with masks. Two dancers appointed by the *angalkuq* put on the masks and performed for the guests. Following the instructions of the *angalkuq*, they knelt on the floor. One said that he was at the crest of the daylight, as depicted by the mask. The other said that he was at the ocean floor. That was what they said, and after that they danced (figures 7.1 and 7.2).

Most masks, elders said, were made under the direction of *angalkut* to request an abundance of fish and animals in the coming season. Shamans did not wear these masks but instructed talented performers in how to use them. Mary Mike (October

1994:12–14) described the shaman Leggleq instructing others to make masks. She recalled seeing two people using wolf masks. At first they sat on top of the *qasgiq* howling like dogs. Then eventually they reached the porch, entered the *qasgiq*, and fought until bloody.

Frank Andrew (February 2003:272) reiterated that *angalkut* were the only ones who revealed the meaning of the masks.

> Those they called *angalkut* used to explain the masks after using them. No one made [masks] for leisure. Ordinary people did not use masks, but only *angalkut* revealed the masks, and they would let them wear them while dancing, and then they finally explained their purpose. . . . That is why there is an admonishment not to use a mask to dance when one isn't an *angalkuq*. The *angalkut* reveal them because they belong to them, and they let [others] wear them, and I used to see them as well.
>
> That is why those who were composing songs for dancing would compose songs ending with *ii-yirrii* . . . that were not ones that were for *angalkut*. And those *angalkut* would [compose] their own songs and would explain the meanings when possible and would appear with the masks, they would reveal them and let them wear them.

Frank Andrew (February 2003:272) noted that although the Moravians had stopped dancing in Kwigillingok in the early 1920s, he had witnessed masked dancing three times—once in Napaskiak,

https://doi.org/10.5876/9781646427314.c007

FIGURE 7.1. Men performing with masks representing animals of the land (the fox) and sea (seal and gull) at Qissunaq, 1946. Alaska State Library, Historical Collections. Alfred Milotte, neg. no. 1098.

FIGURE 7.2. Pair of masked dancers performing in the Qissunaq *qasgiq*, photographed by Alfred Milotte during the filming of Alaskan Eskimo, 1946. Alaska State Library, Historical Collections. Alfred Milotte, neg. no. 1103.

once in Bethel, and once in Qinaq. At Napaskiak, he listened to the shaman Unrapik describe the meaning of the masks:

It was a red fox mask along with a white fox mask. Two men danced wearing those masks. [Unrapik] said that they were his *aciliurcuutek* [lit., "two items used by a shaman to check below," in this case underwater or in the lower world]. Maybe they were for requesting an abundance of fish.

[The shaman] Ayalpik from Bethel also explained [the purpose of another mask]. He also said that the two [masks] were for requesting an abundance

of fish. . . . I don't know what the two were made to depict. The masks looked like humans.

Frank Andrew (February 2003:24–27) described how the shaman Qaluvialler constructed a mask to make an abundance of wood available in spring: "Yes, he constructed a mask. When the wind was blowing from the south, the wind smelled of wood pitch as the [many] logs [Qaluvialler had requested] were about to float ashore." Frank (September 2005:195) also recalled the song Qaluvialler composed, honoring the spirit of the wood: "He composed the song when he lived in Kwigillingok briefly . . . right before [driftwood was abundant in our area]. It was back in those days when a lot of driftwood used to drift ashore in our area. That one particular time [after he composed the song] lots of driftwood came to our area. He, great Qaluvialler, had decided to compose that particular song when driftwood was going to be abundant" (figure 7.3).

Eugene Pete (December 2011:1077) also spoke of watching Paqricilleq, who was blind, use a mask to

FIGURE 7.3A AND 7.3B. The shaman Qaluvialler from the lower Kuskokwim coastal area, photographed by Leuman Waugh in the 1930s. National Museum of the American Indian, Smithsonian Institution L2712.

request an abundance of wood: "His lyrics stated that he wanted to smell the odor of spruce pitch. Indeed, when those logs came out, they smelled of spruce pitch. Iicill'er [Excellent]! That one used to authentically [practice his shaman powers]." Paqricilleq also used masks to request an abundance of fish in the Qip'ngayak River. Eugene used to see Paqricilleq as an elderly man wearing a birdskin parka.

John Phillip (October 2006:197) noted that when people learned that a shaman had the ability to perform a ritual to request something, they would ask that shaman to do so. John followed with the story of how, when the village of Anuuraaq was planning to host a Messenger Feast and invited the people of Kipnuk to attend, Pamsuq of Kipnuk saw that his iluraq, Murak of Anuuraaq, was not listed as a gift-giver. Murak was not prosperous, but he was known to be a shaman. Pamsuq insisted that Murak be included, even though he had nothing to give. John Phillip noted that they usually requested things from one person in the family. So Pamsuq requested that seal pups be abundant in the name of Murak's eldest son, and he asked for calm, windless weather from Murak's younger son: "When he requested something from his iluraq, Pamsuq had evidently said that [Murak] had no gifts to give, but that he wanted to request something that wasn't seen or visible since

he had heard that he was a shaman. . . . [Pamsuq] requested those which had not yet arrived."

Before the Messenger Feast, Murak constructed a ellanguaq (model ella, "universe"), a round hanging device made from rings of slatted wood and decorated with long-tailed duck tail feathers, with a wooden model of a bearded seal pup in the center, that was hung in the qasgiq and moved up and down during the Messenger Feast. When the people of Anuuraaq went to Kipnuk to receive gifts in their turn, Pamsuq composed a song for Murak, and Murak took along another small ellanguaq and model seal that he had constructed. When the people of Kipnuk sang, asking Murak to bring forward the gifts they had requested, he first presented the model seal followed by the model ellanguaq, representing good weather. John continued: "When the song was over, his iluraq kingulluggluku [sang a song of ridicule to him] as they call it. . . . When he ridiculed that poor person in that way, Murak suddenly entered. When he came into view down there, he pretended to paddle down on the floor, facing those people, and he suddenly ran out. That's the ritual they asked him to perform to request and conjure something, a ritual that was done in my presence." That spring, sure enough, seal pups came in abundance and remained through the fall. And the wind stopped blowing

FIGURE 7.4. Dancing in the Kipnuk *qasgiq* in 1933. Note the line decorated with feathers hanging above the drums and known as a *ellanguaq* (model world or universe). When John Phillip (born in 1925) was young, he witnessed the presentation of a *ellanguaq* by the shaman Murak in the Kipnuk *qasgiq*, and this photograph may have been taken during that event. Augustus Martin, Martin Family Collection, Anchorage Museum, B2007.5.1.A23.

during the entire time they hunted that spring (figure 7.4).

Frank Andrew (February 2003:518) noted that *angalkut* used all kinds of models. He described how the shaman Neq'ayaraq had two wooden models of common loons hung beside each other along the sides of the skylight during the Qinaq dance festival:

> I used to see ones from Qinarmiut that were *pinguarcuutek* [two items shamans used to request an abundance of resources], that were *aciliurcuutek* [two used for checking what was below] that belonged to shamans, two wooden common-loon models.
>
> And in the summer, when salmon were going to be abundant on the Kuskokwim, some people would see those two as kayakers using wooden visors. They'd be down [on the water], especially across . . . from Tuntutuliak on the other side of the Kuskokwim River. . . .
>
> They say the two of them would appear to people there. Two kayaks would be down from the bank. But then they would start sinking. . . . Then after disap-

pearing for a while, a pair of common loons would appear farther away from shore. Then they'd fly away.

> They said they didn't do that all the time. They'd do that when the Kuskokwim was going to have an abundance of salmon. . . .
>
> They say those two common loon models were what he bequeathed to the people of Qinaq. He instructed them to use them when they'd have a Kassiyuq [Dance Festival].

Frank Andrew (February 2003:527) said that he had seen the hanging loon models twice during the Messenger Feast when he was young, before he married. He didn't know what they were, but someone explained them to him:

> The common loon models had just skin hangers. . . . He said they would store them away. They didn't mess with them and hung the two up.
>
> When they were hung, they would remain in place synchronized. And when they wanted, they would go in a circle and face each other . . . and remain still. And

when they didn't do that, they would be in opposite directions. They would [rotate] again when they wanted. He said they were amazing to see. Like that, they wouldn't hang still. Whenever they wanted to, they would rotate slowly, and stay in place with their backs to each other.

Frank concluded: "When they wanted fish to be abundant, they would let shamans *aciliurluki* [check what was below], and he wasn't the only one [to do that]. They were making what they would catch more available. . . . They call it *aciliurluteng*." Peter John added: "They wanted the entire Kuskokwim River to have an abundance of fish."

Neq'ayaraq was not alone in constructing objects intended to promote future abundance. Eugene Pete (December 2011:54–55) spoke at length about the Yukon shaman Leggleq, who constantly constructed *agayut* (masks to request things) in Eugene's presence. Leggleq also made a ball as an *aviukarqun* (offering) used to ask for certain things in the future:

There was a ball up there with a twine harness that extended to the edge of the *qasgiq*, and there was someone who watched over the end of the twine.

Then there were two people situated across from one another curled up. They were both polar bears sleeping.

Then that ball up there fell down. When it landed on the floor boards, it landed with a loud thud down there! Those two suddenly got up. They circled *ella maliggluku* [clockwise, lit., "following the universe"], walking and snarling. Those masks looked like real polar bears.

Eugene said that Mike Andrews's father was so moved he cried out: " '*Pikayakatartut!* [They are going to do something great!]' Then he let his voice out, and he cried without any restraint, letting out his feelings of being moved by what he saw." Eugene explained how the thud the ball made on the floor boards imitated the abundance of food that the offering would elicit: "You know how when they get a small bowl, they just take a pinch and give an offering. That thing that is hanging is one of those when it lands down there. They say it is a large amount. And the small contents of this, when a person sprinkles it, they say it lands as a large amount down there."

Angalkut performed other actions to promote successful hunting. Roland Phillip (October 2006:183–89) described his experience watching the shaman Cingarturta exercise his powers. Because he

was curious, Roland accompanied his father to the *qasgiq* at Iiqaquq when they heard that Cingarturta was going to perform. Some large drums were set out, and seal-oil lamps were in the corners of the *qasgiq* such that everything inside was very visible. Roland watched as Cingarturta went down to the floor, removed his clothing, and put on a seal-gut rain garment. Singers began to perform *yuarulluut* that Cingarturta had composed, while the shaman walked back and forth, using his hands to continuously rattle and shake his seal-gut parka from the inside. After a while he quickly moved across the room, and when he got to the tunnel entryway, he suddenly extended his arms, and his hands became visible:

After doing that three times, he went on his knees in the middle of the *qasgiq*, with one leg down on his knee and the other up, and he told the singers to stop singing. . . . When he removed the seal-gut garment that he was wearing, he took it by the bottom section along the opening. It appeared as though his right arm was inside the seal-gut garment, as though he was keeping his arm extended. . . . I watched in amazement.

After positioning himself in that way, he told people who wanted to see it to come and see it. . . . He also said, "But try not to breathe inside this seal-gut rain garment."

The men closest to the exit approached, putting their heads down and covering their mouths with the neck areas of their hooded garments. Roland, who was also wearing a hooded garment, covered his mouth and went down, accompanying his father:

I went down there. When it came into view as he was holding [the seal-gut garment] open, I saw that he held his hands together [in a cup]. . . .

There was water inside his palm, and there was a seal down there . . . moving around and swimming in a circle. And it would even move its hand flippers . . . inside that person's palm. And after putting its head down in the water, when it lifted its head up, its whiskers would drip water. . . .

Apparently, since its head was reddish in color, those who saw it said that it was an adult.

Everyone had a turn, and when there was no one else left to see it, Cingarturta said that he was going to place that seal in the upper part of the Ilkivik River, a river that flowed out into the ocean where men camped and hunted in spring. After saying that, he

FIGURE 7.5. One of several *nepcetaq* masks collected by Johan Adrian Jacobsen during his travels on the lower Yukon River in 1882–83. Jacobsen described it as an "imitation caribou mask" used to ensure an abundance of caribou in the coming season. The plague may represent the heavens, with caribou models looking through sky holes to the earth they will soon repopulate. Ethnologisches Museum Berlin IVA4410, Barry McWayne.

had them sing, then suddenly extended his arms again inside the *qasgiq*. Roland surmised: "He probably placed it at the upper part of the Ilkivik River [when he did that]."

Nepcetat
Ones that stick to the face

Kegginaqut (dance masks) were made and worn by men under the direction of shamans, and they were routinely destroyed after use, either burned in the fire bath or set out to rot on the tundra. Elders also described one striking exception—the *nepcetaq*, literally, "something that sticks to the face." Unlike dance masks, *nepcetat* were masks made and worn only by *angalkut*. All *nepcetat* were the property of *angalkut*, but not all *angalkut* had power enough to possess them.

FIGURE 7.6. Man carving a *nepcetaq* mask in a drawing made by lower Yukon artist Milo Minock. Anchorage Museum 1972.102.005.

Some say that the backboard typical of *nepcetat* represented the universe—water, air, or land, depending on the mask and the story it told. Again, according to the mask's particular story, the holes might represent skyholes or ice holes through which animals moved in their journey toward the human hunter. The carvings of birds, seals, whales, and caribou on the mask's surface were used to call forth or show gratitude to the animals represented. Many *nepcetat* in museums

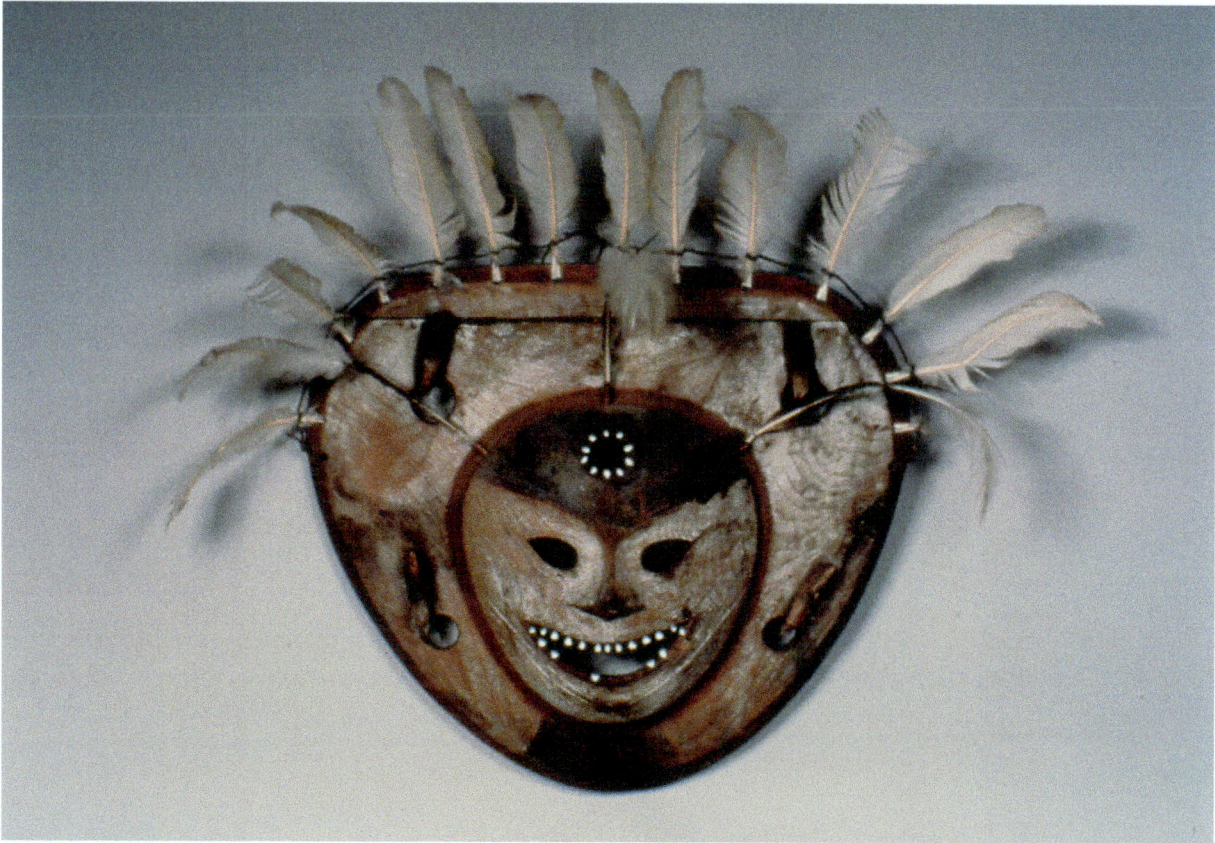

FIGURE 7.7. *Nepcetaq* mask collected by Sheldon Jackson at Andreafski. This mask was exhibited at Toksook Bay, Bethel, and Anchorage as part of the *Agayuliyararput* Yup'ik mask exhibit. Sheldon Jackson Museum IIB8.

FIGURE 7.8. Wassilie Evan (holding the Andreafski *nepcetaq* mask), Tim Troll, Andy Paukan, and Willie Beans during their visit to the Sheldon Jackson Museum in 1989. This museum visit set the stage for the 1989 Mountain Village Dance Festival, which in turn inspired the Yup'ik mask exhibit, *Agayuliyararput*. Tim Troll.

FIGURE 7.9. The Andreafski *nepcetaq* mask, as depicted in the poster Ray Troll made for the 1989 Mountain Village Dance Festival. Ray Troll.

today came from lower Yukon River villages such as Andreafski, but collectors acquired them from all over southwest Alaska. Unlike other masks, *nepcetat* were kept and used year after year. Johan Adrian Jacobsen collected a miniature *nepcetaq* said to represent a gull. He labeled it "a true imitation of the so-called shaman masks" of the lower Yukon and said that it was for children, as it had no holes for facial attachment (figures 7.5 and 7.6).

Jasper Louis (February 1994:5–8) gave a detailed description of the presentation of a *nepcetaq* that he had observed:

> *Nepcetat* were amazing. The mask was placed on the floor in front of the *angalkuq*. When he bowed, the mask rose up to his face. If the performance was a success, someone would suggest that a parka be placed over the mask. If the owner of the parka was destined not to live very long, it would not rise. And if they put down the parka of a person who was to live long, it would rise. Then they put down a second parka. Being parkas, they probably were heavy. When the shaman bowed again, his mask would begin to rise. They could not add any more after the third parka.
>
> Once the mask adhered to the face, the shaman used his hands to remove it like this [pushing down and away from the face]. And if that didn't remove the mask, they used both hands on the outside of the parka and pulled it away from the face. I observed those performances, but the people who owned those masks have been gone a long time.

In 1989 Yukon delta elders Wassilie Evan and Willie Beans, accompanied by Andy Paukan and Tim Troll, traveled to the Sheldon Jackson Museum in Sitka, Alaska, to choose objects from the museum's col-

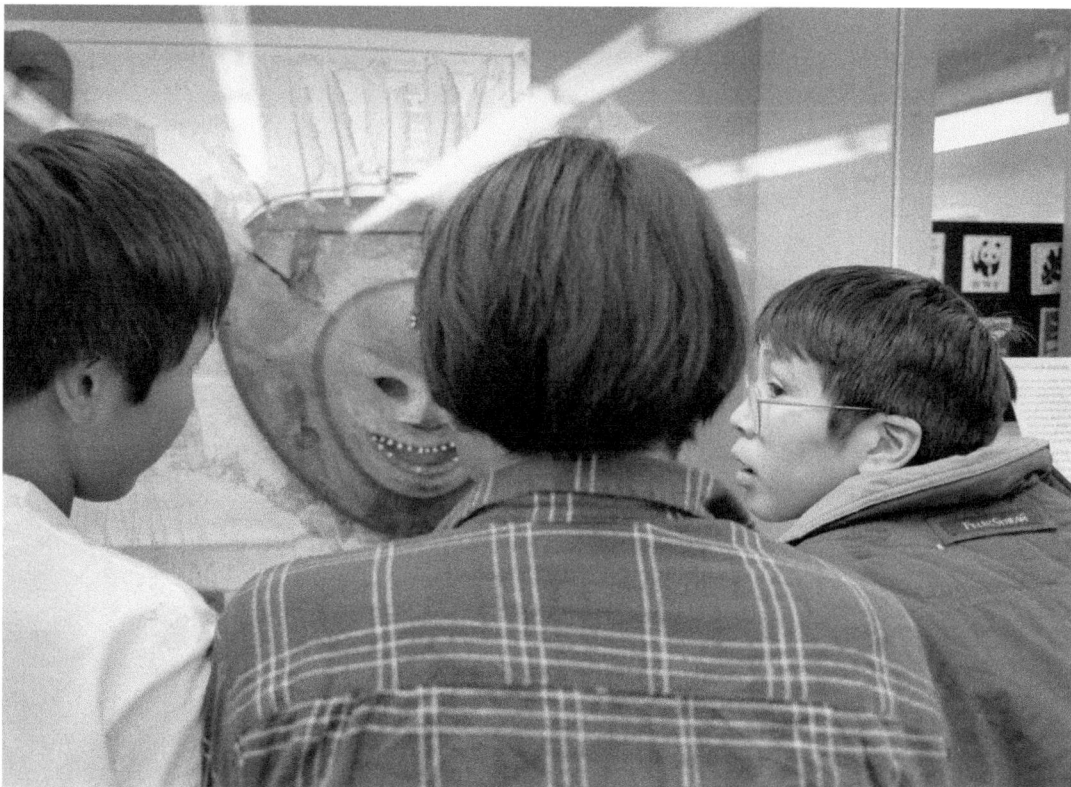

FIGURE 7.10. Young visitors looking at the *nepcetaq* mask displayed at the opening of the exhibition *Agayuliyararput* in Toksook Bay in January 1996. James H. Barker.

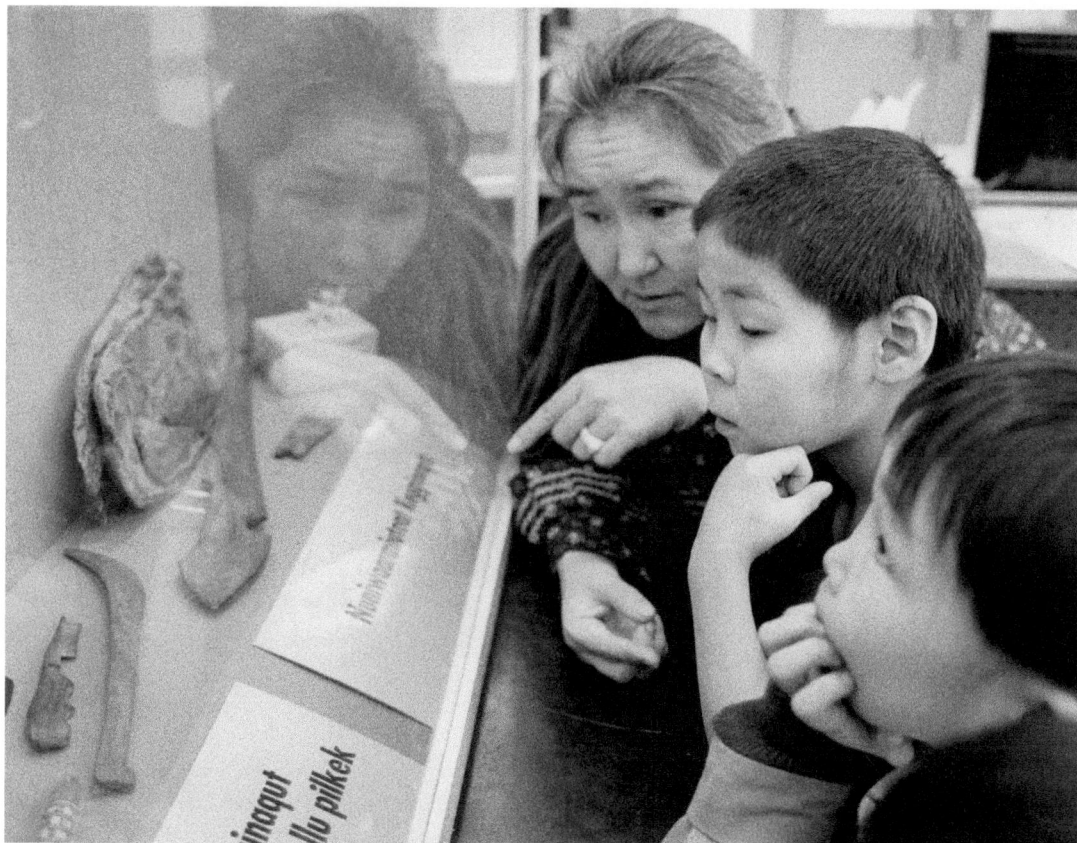

FIGURE 7.11. Youngsters listening while Marie Meade tells them about the objects displayed at the *Agayuliyararput* exhibit in Toksook Bay, January 1996. James H. Barker.

lection to bring home to Mountain Village to share during a four-day dance festival. Among the pieces they chose was a formidable *nepcetaq* collected from Andreafski in the 1890s. Its striking image appeared on posters and T-shirts all over the delta, advertising the Mountain Village Festival. At the opening of the mask exhibit, *Agayuliyararput / Our Way of Making Prayer*, in Toksook Bay in January 1996, this *nepcetaq* was again brought out and displayed, evoking intense interest among younger visitors and elders alike. Standing in front of the glass display case in which the Andreafski *nepcetaq* hung, Willie Kamkoff (January 1996) gave this account of *nepcetat* he had seen when he was young (figures 7.7–7.11).

> When I was a boy in Pastuliq, I used to see a mask like this in a shed. It was bigger than this piece. The area above its eyes was covered with carved pieces of all the land animals caught and used by people. And down below its eyes were sea mammal pieces. The one I saw didn't have eyes, though. Its face resembled the face of this piece.
>
> When the shaman Uqsuqaq got ready to use his *nepcetaq*, he first placed a seal-gut garment on it, then a woman's squirrel parka, then two caribou fawn skins. As Uqsuqaq began to bend forward over the mask, the mask flew up to his face. He danced with the mask on his face. They say the *nepcetaq* mask was used to look into the future.

Lawrence Edmund (December 2011:287–90) said that the shaman Teggalquq kept a *nepcetaq* mask inside his *angyaq* (boat) and another inside his kayak,

stored on top of a fish rack at the old village of Paimiut, and that during a great flood in the early 1900s that washed away many homes, the ice didn't touch them at all: "It was as if the ice showed respect to those two." Lawrence also noted that he had found a *nepcetaq* mask in a smokehouse in the old village of Kuimlill'er. He left it there, thinking that he would take it home later on another trip: "They say they put things out for people when that happens; I think they displayed those for me. I didn't take them and didn't touch them, thinking to take them when I arrived the next time. When I arrived . . . two years later, they were completely rotten."

Men were not the only ones who performed with *nepcetat*. Paul Waskey (January 1996:1–11) described his late grandmother's experience, also recorded during the Toksook Festival.

> She had a huge *nepcetaq* fully adorned. It was a big mask covered with different animals and fish. She used the *nepcetaq* when people gathered for a dance festival. When she got ready to use it, she would put on a seal-gut parka which she had soaked in urine [to soften it] and then dried. Her parka was so dry it made a loud crackling sound. When she performed with the *nepcetaq*, she placed four different parkas on it and had her hands tied back.
>
> Tut'angaq was an *angalkuq*, a female shaman. Women *angalkut* were very powerful. They were respected and feared by men. Men were wary of them. And I myself believed in shamans because I had watched them since I became aware. But since the arrival of the missionaries I stopped believing in them.

8

Angalkut Tuqullret-llu
Shamans and the Dead

Angalkut alangrut-llu
Shamans and ghosts

The living and the dead existed in close proximity in the past, and people often spoke to and gave gifts to their deceased relatives and friends. Albertina Dull (April 2013:67) recalled a woman who she observed giving tallow to a dead man: "The first one I saw was the late Nupigaq's mother. . . . [She] had a small piece of tallow. She instructed [the dead], and she constantly spoke to that dead person. And she told him that when he arrives to his older sister and she made *akutaq* [mixture of fat, fish, and berries], this would be the *tunuq* [caribou back fat] that she would use."

Aviukaryaraq (the process of giving an offering of food and water to the dead, to animals, or to the land), hoping for safe travel or future abundance, was common practice throughout southwest Alaska, and in many areas remains so to this day. *Aviukaryaraq* not only provided for the deceased, but ensured continued access to food for the living and might continue for years after a burial. According to Joshua Phillip (1988):

> Whenever they came across a burial, they would take a bit of their food, in little portions saying, "While I am traveling I would like to travel safely and I would also like to catch a lot. . . . Please place before me things to catch." They would talk to that person in that manner . . . They would place those things on graves

for their deceased relatives. . . . They say *aviukarluni* [they give them an offering] when they do that ritual, giving a food offering to that [dead] person.

Some people made requests from long-dead *angalkut*. Lawrence Edmund (March 2011:978–83) spoke at length about his experience placing an offering of food and water, as well as tobacco and candy, in the firepit of the *qasgiq* of the old village of Paimiut, the home of the deceased shaman Teggalquq. This was at a time when mink were scarce, and Lawrence asked Teggalquq to provide them: "I was thinking, 'Teggalquq probably used to call on his spirit helpers here.' This is what I told him first, that we are his descendants, . . . that we want him to provide us with mink that we will hunt all fall, but that we are daunted, that we cannot do anything about them." Lawrence spoke to Teggalquq, reminding him that when he was alive he used to obtain things for the people: "After giving him the offerings, . . . I told him again, 'Okay, be grateful because a person won't come to you from afar and give you water and food that you lack. Provide us the mink that we are going to hunt this fall.'"

Sure enough, after giving an offering to Teggalquq, mink trails appeared where they had not previously been found. Lawrence continued: "I finally realized [the offering I gave] had come to materialize. . . . In a period of four days, there were suddenly many mink around, . . . and all the people with me also caught many mink." Lawrence noted that this experience

https://doi.org/10.5876/9781646427314.c008

81

proved the efficacy of making an offering of food and water to the deceased.

The dead might appear and visit the living either as *alangrut* (ghosts, things that appear unexpectedly) or *aliurtut* (apparitions). Tim Agagtak (July 1985:35–36) shared instructions for what a person should do when encountering a ghost in a doorway. The ghost would stand elevated, looking like an actual human, with vapor flowing in from the entrance. *Amiingirluku* (from *amiik*, "door, entranceway") is the term used to describe this experience when a ghost blocks a person's path between the entryway or exitway of the tunnel leading into a *qasgiq* or home. Tim continued:

When they pushed down on them with their hand [to make them disappear], they'd first try to touch it on its skin here. [Ghosts] would feel very cold like ice.

They'd [push down on them] here with the weight of the arm. They say the ghost would begin to go down inside the ground when that was done. When they'd almost push down, it would come up a little.

When [the ghost] would disappear, the ground where it had stood would turn and twirl . . . until [the ghost] disappeared. [People who had seen ghosts] talked about it. It wasn't a good experience.

Like Tim Agagtak, Dick Andrew (August 1992:6) of Bethel said that a person should push down with the weight of one's arm until the ghost was flat against the ground, then step on it with one's feet. If the ghost was a woman, her face would be veiled, and one should put one's hand under the hem of her garment and touch her torso (figures 8.1a and 8.1b).

Shamans often acted as intermediaries, alternately promoting and eliminating hauntings. Albertina Dull (November 2007:164) noted that when dealing with a ghost *angalkut* were specially equipped: "You know how they say that when they were using their powers on ghosts, they used dog-fur gloves, wearing seal-gut rain garments." Dogs generally were considered more aware of ghosts and often alerted their owners to a ghost's presence by crouching down or whining. Alexie Nicholai (March 2017:239) mentioned that dogs barking could indicate a ghost: "Some people said that when they were about to encounter ghosts and dogs were making noise, they would go outside along the edge of the home and use an ax to make a cut across [the doorway]. And they would place a fish trap outside along their doorways. . . . They put them there because the [ghost] couldn't go past them."

Tim Agagtak (July 1985:36) noted that shamans were concerned about ghosts "belching" on them:

Long ago, when a ghost was about to enter a home or the *qasgiq*, vapor would first begin flowing in through the entrance . . . like it does when cold air suddenly hits warm air.

When a ghost was about to enter, vapor would "belch" [start flowing] in from the entrance and from the cracks between the wooden planks covering the firepit. [The vapor] would also enter from underneath.

And in a few minutes, you'd hear a big bang coming from the entrance area. It would sound like a rock crashing. The [ghost] entering would make that loud bang.

The ones who saw them in those days, when people were able to see ghosts of the dead, they said they were cold just like ice.

Many observed that *angalkut* were responsible for the appearance of the deceased in the form of ghosts, which people feared. Lizzie Chimiugak (June 2009:259) noted: "The poor things used to say that their mothers became ghosts. My, how scary. . . . This was back when shamans had the deceased walk around." Frank Andrew (September 2005:46) declared: "*Angalkut* did have the power to allow people to see *alangrut*. I, myself knew that shamans could do that, and I saw them doing it. Our deceased relatives, when living humans see them in their physical form they call them *carayiit* [fearsome things]. But since [ghosts] don't possess life, they can't walk or run . . . since it wasn't filled with its *tarnaq* [spirit]. But a shaman [with his power] helped it to move and go from here to there very easily."

Lizzie Chimiugak (June 2009:193–94) described how a shaman caused the person she was named after to haunt people as a ghost for a long time after she died. She told how the ghost followed a man back from Kanerrlulek when he went to retrieve things stored there, and as he traveled he began to hear her voice clearly from behind him. When he reached the village, the ghost entered the *qasgiq*, where his grandfather grasped her and brought her down: "He said that he was going to lower her [possibly from *iivkar-*, 'to lower from a height,' probably putting his hands on the ghost to lower it to make it disappear]. . . . A shaman was responsible for having them do things, taking their bodies. . . . She was whining and pleading down there."

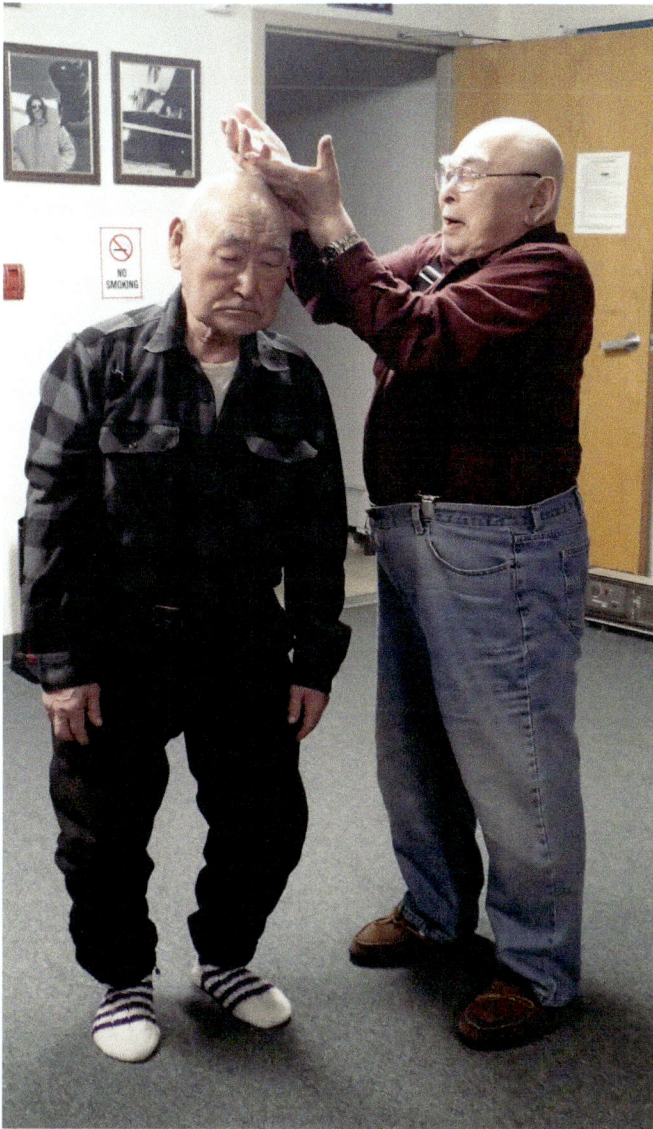

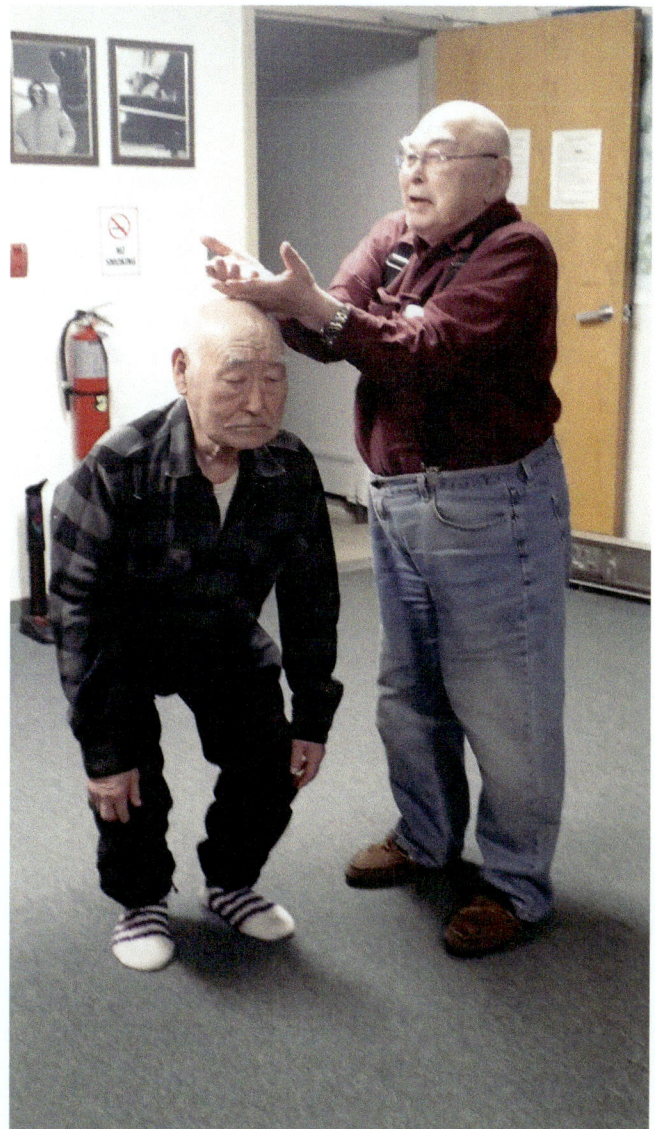

FIGURES 8.1A AND 8.1B. During a 2023 CEC gathering, Nick Andrew demonstrated how a person can use the weight of his hands to lower a ghost. Playing the role of ghost, Francis Charlie gradually lowered himself down to the ground. Note that Nick held his hands palms upward to accomplish his task. Ann Fienup-Riordan.

There are many accounts of shamans capturing or getting rid of ghosts that troubled their fellow villagers. Tim Agagtak (July 1985:35–36) recalled the Cevv'arneq shaman, Ussugan Atii, who was able to capture ghosts: "The ghosts he took would look like people. His arms would be visible clutching [the ghost]."

Speaking to students during a CEC Culture Camp, Paul John (June 2009:13–19) told the story of a man whose wife died in childbirth and was buried along with her baby. Because her husband didn't want to lose her, he purposely used a tool, breaking the admonishment not to do so for five days after a death. That evening his wife's ghost appeared through the under-

ground tunnel entrance, carrying her child, asking for her husband. Shamans seated in the qasgiq who were asked to help were fearful and retreated, but a Qissunaq shaman who people didn't consider competent came forward. The dead wife called for her husband, saying that by using his adze he had broken her trail. Putting on dog-fur gloves, the one considered unworthy stood in front of her in the tunnel entranceway, then grasped her, and together they gradually went down and disappeared. When he returned, he was covered in fine sand. He then told the people to make their qasgiq upright again. They say that if that shaman hadn't dealt with her, she would have turned the qasgiq inside out, causing the people to go underground.

John Phillip (January 2006:256) spoke about the shaman Apangtak, who was asked to deal with a ghost that had started appearing in Qukaqlircaraq, even during the day. Apangtak told John that his *apqaraun* (one that served him, means by which he did his work, from *apqara-*, "to ask about something") stayed beside him and told him what to do: "When [the ghost] got to that point [in his presence], after asking [the *apqaraun*] what to do, [Apangtak] told [the ghost] to confess who was responsible for his hauntings. [The ghost] named all the shamans inside the *qasgiq*, saying that he was being coerced by this person and by that person. The dead person asked [Apangtak] to let him go, [telling him] that he would never [haunt people] again."

There are also many stories of dead *angalkut* appearing as ghosts. Albertina Dull (June 2009:135–36) told about the shaman Tunguyailnguq, who people had killed when he came to Tununak to purchase caribou back fat. The two non-Natives who manhandled him died soon after, as the shaman had cursed the murderers after his death. Then his young wife, who had returned to her home in Kipnuk, encountered her husband's ghost when she and another young woman were searching for "mouse food" in the fall along the shores of Qass'urpak.

> As they were picking, when they heard a noise underneath an area that was eroding, something down there that was dark stood up.
>
> His parka was a muskrat parka, and his skin boots were made of unattractive wolf fur, and they say his walking stick had lines on it as designs. He stood and started shaking things from his body. Then after a while, he climbed up and started approaching.

The girls ran off, but he would appear in front of them wherever they turned. Looking back, they saw him as an ugly wolf. Then smoke started to rise from their village: "Evidently, there wasn't any smoke actually rising. But . . . [the shaman] Angutekayak had evidently been born. When a baby was born, a lot of smoke seemed to start rising, although there wasn't actually smoke rising there at all. The child who was born saved them."

Like many of his generation, Frank Andrew (December 2003:131) connected the decline in ghosts and ghostly encounters with the decline of shamans:

> We know that there were many shamans back then, and there were many *aliurtut* [supernatural

presences, apparitions]. They obviously used them in their work. When a person died, shamans used them as a weapon. [A shaman] would allow a person to be seen, even though he had died.
>
> As we see today, now that these *angalkut* are no longer seen, those ghosts are also no longer seen, there are no longer any.
>
> Those *angalkut* allow ghosts to appear. . . .
>
> And they said when they took [ghosts] in the *qasgiq* and asked them, they would say that this person [made them appear], they would name shamans who were responsible. However, they would cry when they were going to reveal the person. After crying, they would name that shaman who controlled them. Those experiences revealed that they were weapons for those shamans who had powers.

Frank Andrew (February 2003:106) told the story of Kukukualek from Kipnuk who was haunted by a ghost when he spent the night alone in the *qasgiq* at Iqukvaq. At the story's end, Frank concluded:

> When *angalkut* became scarce, [hauntings] became rare. That's why I think that those apparitions were caused by shamans. When there were no longer *angalkut*, . . . those ghosts didn't happen any more.
>
> They say that some *angalkut* deal with the dead. When they started to haunt people, they take them and no longer make them appear as ghosts. . . . Some [*angalkut*] do not deal with the dead because they do not have the expertise to deal with them.
>
> It is evident that *angalkut* make those [apparitions] appear].

Angalkut ataam utertetulit
Shamans coming back to life

Along with the close association between shamans and ghosts, shamans themselves were said to have the ability to come back to life. Joe Ayagarak (December 1987:41) of Chevak spoke of a shaman who would do flips and become young again: "They say after doing five somersaults, he'd stand as a young person, he would be very young."

Nick Andrew (January 2006:239–44) told of a known shaman living between the Kuicaraq and Akuliqutaq Rivers at a place called Kuvuartelleq. The man used to tell Nick stories when Nick and his wife stayed there and brought him fish. Nick recalled:

> He told a story and said that an *angalkuq* who was keeping watch over him had killed him. But he said

that in the spring when he paddled and spent a night out, when he gained awareness at that time, a small person was setting a *naneryaq* [deadfall trap]. . . .

Then suddenly a spear came toward him through the air. Although he tried to move, he couldn't move out of the way. They say that one died for . . . one week. His wife said that he never arrived for one week.

When he became aware of his surroundings, he searched for a way to return, and when he came upon a wild celery plant, he reappeared through there. The man then told Nick that if he died in his presence, to bind and hide his body, that he would return to life. The man added that Nick would know when he died, which Nick did.

A year later, the dead man's words came to mind, and Nick thought that he had probably come back to life underground. Then in winter, not far from the place where Nick and the man and their families had lived, it got stormy, and a hunter took shelter under a large hill along the Kuicaraq River:

As he was sitting there, during the evening, the sound of people talking appeared up there. He said that the one who I told the story about, the one who was supposed to come back to life, would refer to him as his grandchild. But he had never seen that person up at Nanvarnarrlak. He heard someone say, "Grandchild, do not feel desperate. Nothing will happen to you. I'm watching over you." He would look around, but there was no one there.

The dead *angalkuq* then gave the man directions to his camp, which the man followed, subsequently staying at the camp until the weather improved and he could return home. Months later, when the one who had been lost arrived at Nanvarnarrlak, he saw a man sitting outside: "When he was about to reach him, [the man] said to him, 'Hello grandchild. Have you forgotten my voice? When you were in a desperate situation during winter, I helped you.' He then recognized him through his voice."

Tim Agagtak (July 1985:20–27) told the story of the Qalulleq shaman who people repeatedly killed. Although they severed his legs and took apart his body, he kept coming back to life. Finally, they removed his eyes and hid them under a clay lamp, and the shaman was gone for some time. Then someone visiting Qalulleq when others were at fish camp encountered the shaman's ghost, still looking for his eyes. The ghost stood elevated above the ground,

wearing snowshoes and carrying two walking sticks, with a single eye in the middle of his forehead. When the ghost asked about his eyes, the man didn't respond, recalling that one who responded to a ghost would lose his voice. The ghost read his thoughts, however, and told him that nothing would happen to him if he answered. When the man said he didn't know where the eyes were, the dead shaman said that although he wanted to retaliate, he was holding back because he didn't want to hurt his family members. He added that he wouldn't return because children might be afraid of his one eye.

Sometime later, Tim said that people heard that some of the shaman's songs were being sung in the Nushagak area, and they were told that the people there had learned the songs from the child of a couple that couldn't previously conceive. Apparently the shaman had placed himself inside the wife and became their child.

Lizzie Chimiugak (June 2009:126–27) told another version of this story. She identified the shaman who couldn't die as Apaqassugaq, who became aware inside different things, including a tree, before he went inside a person and was born: "He said he came to be born dwelling inside everything." Lizzie described him as a person traveling through the air, looking for his eyes. Albertina Dull concluded: "We don't know [why he couldn't die] because, as you know, when people of other villages tell stories, they tell different versions." Lizzie agreed: "Since they are old [stories], they tell them in different ways."

Frank Andrew (February 2003:581–83) also told the story of Apaqassugaq who his fellow villagers repeatedly tried to kill, butchering his body, until finally they pried out his eyes and placed them inside a lamp turned upside down. When a man traveling in the wilderness encountered him, Apaqassugaq told him that he would not return home lest he startle children with his empty eye sockets. Apaqassugaq also said that there was already someone who would inherit his powers:

After a while, among those Kangirnaarmiut [down the coast from Platinum], one of them had a baby boy. When he got a little older, at a certain age, he began drumming . . . singing Apaqassugaq's *yuarulluut* [shaman songs].

That was his *mer'umavik*, the one who would inherit his powers. That is as much as I heard, because shamans are very powerful.

Angalkut ircenrraat-llu
Shamans and ircenrraat

Many stories attest to the connection between *angalkut* and *ircenrraat*. According to Frank Andrew (September 2005:282), *yuungcarat* (those doctored by shamans while still in the womb) especially belong to the *ircenrraat* and can seek help from them, as they are related. Dick Andrew (August 1992:37) identified *ircenrraat* as former shamans. Others said that when shamans die, they go to live among *ircenrraat*, who kick their feet and make rumbling noises to welcome them, as described for Kalukarmiut on Nelson Island. Susie Angaiak (March 2007:1246) explained: "They say those *ircenrraat* who live there, they kick their feet to make rumbling noises because they are grateful that one of their own who is living elsewhere is about to come."

Frank Andrew (October 2003:219–22) told the story of the shaman Cingarturta, who saw two *ircenrraak* passing during the night while he was camping on the Ilkivik River downriver from Qaurrarmiut. Everything brightened as they approached, then got dark again. In another story that Frank Andrew (September 2005:270–71) told, the shaman Aqsarpak had *ircenrraat* defend him against the dead shaman Ungaayacungaq, who was about to come after him during the night. Taking the form of wolves, his *ircenrraat* helpers demolished Ungaayacungaq's grave.

Paul Waskey (January 1996:1–4) described how his grandmother, the shaman Tut'angaq, did rituals in the *qasgiq*, inviting both her *tuunrat* (spirit helpers) as well as *ircenrraat*:

The *ircenrraat* came to us through the ground. When they came she would be very happy. She would let everyone know that since they were present, things would go well in the future.

She would say after she used shaman powers that they would let the *tukaratulit* [lit., "those who kick," another term for *ircenrraat*] come. When they came, they would be thankful. She said nothing [bad] would happen out there today.

Paul remembered sleeping beside her at her winter camp at Putukulek not far from Cuqartalek, and his grandmother telling him not to be scared, that she was going to look for a path for his future: "She would do that when she was going to ask for *tukaralriit* [the ones who kick]. I would believe her and stay still. I would wait for those who would 'kick.' . . . It would be such a sudden loud noise [coming from close-by, outside, underground]."

Shamans are also said to visit the world of *ircenrraat* to punish the inhabitants for their mischievous activity, as when the Kanaryararmiut shaman Luglaaq traveled to Qaurrarmiut to bring his children home. If angered, shamans had the power to turn the world of *ircenrraat* around. Conversely, dead shamans who had gone to live among *ircenrraat* sometimes greeted human visitors or, as in Elsie Tommy's (February 2010:69–74) story of the Tununak shaman Ayukuq, bring humans into the *ircenrraat* world to care for them. Frank Andrew (December 2003:132) declared that even *angalkut* who had been killed could go to live among the *ircenrraat*.

9

Angalkut Umyuarrliqelriit Calluutelallrat-llu
Malicious Shamans and Shaman Confrontations

Umyuarrliqelriit angalkut
Evil angalkut

Even those who advocated recognition of *angalkut* as powerful healers spoke of those who abused their powers. Frank Andrew (September 2005:280) described malicious shamans who were jealous of those who helped people: "They say that when a shaman did good work and healed people from sickness, the other shamans would become jealous and go against him and begin trying to cause trouble."

Jealousy, Frank noted, derived from the payments people gave shamans to do their work: "They'd award them for the work, giving them material things. Other shamans would become jealous of what they received. They'd lie about them and try to influence others who weren't shamans." Spreading gossip, malicious shamans prodded people to kill their rivals.

Many recalled with feeling the dangers of denying a shaman's request, lest a malicious shaman take revenge. Elsie Tommy (March 2009:380) told the story of a shaman who killed a child whose parents had failed to give him what he wanted: "They said that shamans would ask for items from people, and when they didn't comply with their requests, [the shamans] would place something underneath their child [or] their grandchild, revealing the item that they had asked for, what they call *atlirnirluki* [placing something underneath them, with the intention of making them sick]."

Elsie then told the story of the powerful shaman who asked for a small spotted-seal skin from Maacungaq, who denied his request. Then in the fall their grandchild became ill, and they asked Uqviir to cure him. Although Uqviir tried, he said that it was too difficult. However, he knew who had done it and told them that the child had a spotted-seal skin underneath him. The woman asked the shaman to remove the seal skin, as only the one who placed the tether could remove it, but he refused.

> Because of their refusal to [give him a spotted-seal skin], he placed a spotted-seal skin under that child and tethered it.
>
> [The child] died. And they say when he was about to die, . . . the small thing told his parents that when others asked for something from them, to give it to them without refusing.

Listening, Alice Rearden asked if people retaliated against malicious shamans, and Martina John replied that, although they knew who they were, people couldn't retaliate out of fear.

Shamans were said to kill not only the children but also the wives of those who refused to give them what they wanted. Lizzie Chimiugak (June 2009:148–49) told how a white man wanted her father to be a storekeeper, but his mother persuaded him not to do it,

https://doi.org/10.5876/9781646427314.c009

saying that a shaman might kill his wife out of jealousy: "They probably attempted to [kill] their family members . . . when they declined to give them something they wanted." Albertina Dull (June 2009:174–75) followed with the story of a shaman who claimed two otters to be his, although they were out in the wilderness and didn't belong to anyone. The family denied his request, and subsequently the shaman didn't allow two sisters to be doctored, and they died. Albertina maintained that the shaman who claimed the otters had caused their deaths. She concluded: "These shamans, after asking for something from someone, they were so irritating, sometimes they put a curse on a person. My, they were scary."

Many mentioned that shamans were responsible for the deaths of their own relatives. Lizzie Chimiugak (June 2009:225–27) told the story of the shaman Qateryak, who was believed to have caused the death of his nephew, Unangik. Albertina added: "They won't feel bad. If he wants to [kill him], he won't hesitate just because he is his relative." Lizzie (June 2009:234) also mentioned Mancuam Atti, who caused the death of his own daughter when she refused to give him a wolf skin that he wanted for a parka ruff. Ruth Jimmie exclaimed that shamans were such jealous people, and Albertina Dull agreed that they had no empathy at all. Martina John (March 2009:382) added: "They constantly killed their own children, trying to lengthen their own lives." Barbara Joe (April 2012:301) also spoke of shamans who, wanting to have a long life and considering themselves most important, took the souls of their own children, taking the lives they would have lived.

Just as it was dangerous to refuse a shaman's request for material possessions, it was also dangerous to refuse a shaman's request to marry one's daughter. Albertina Dull (April 2013:29) described how reluctant parents were forced to comply: "You know how long ago these shamans, when their partners died, they would get a partner for themselves, even if that person was young. It is said the parents would heed [the shaman's request] so that they would live. Even if [the shamans] were elderly, they would have them marry them. My goodness, how awful!" Lizzie Chimiugak (June 2009:147) told the story of a haughty person who refused to marry the son of a shaman, who cursed her as a result. Albertina added: "They say when they wanted to marry them, because they were concerned for their lives, they used to comply with their requests." Lizzie agreed: "Although they were reluctant to marry them, they were afraid of shamans." Lizzie (June 2009:255) spoke of a woman whose father refused the request of a shaman:

> They say that although men wanted to marry Paningayaq, her father never complied. Then they say Nayangaraqtaq, a powerful shaman, wanted to marry her.
>
> Her father didn't want her to marry him. They say when she was about to die, she mentioned Nayangaraqtaq, the shaman who had wanted to marry her. That one evidently killed her.

Many stories describe shamans cursing those who did not comply with their requests. George Billy (October 2006:171) spoke about *aniqlaayaraq* (putting a curse on someone): "They wish that person to come upon misfortune in the future, or they wish death upon that person. They threaten them. That's what malicious shamans are apparently like." Frank Andrew (September 2005:281) described one way this was accomplished using *nuyarniurcuutet* (devices to put a curse on someone and make him sick, from *nuyarnir-*, "to feel the body warmth of an unseen person"):

> The *nuyarniurcuutet* that shamans used were devices that they used to curse others. Without us knowing it, a shaman might put a curse on someone and make him sick; and what they put in that person would remain while he was living. They see the bad thoughts that a shaman has for someone [through their minds] as *nuyarneret*. [Normal] people couldn't see them, but only the shamans could see that it had been planted in a person, by his *nuyarneraralria* [the one who cursed someone].

Michael John (June 2008:54–63) told a long story about how the people of Engel'ullugarmiut, on Nelson Island, traveled to Qissunaq when they were experiencing food shortage, where they were humiliated and sent home. As they traveled, their shaman Tengesqauktar protected and guided them. Upset by their treatment at Qissunaq, he cursed the rivers of the people of Qissunaq:

> They say he had them draw their summer fishing sites, a number of rivers, onto the snow. Then he stepped on those rivers and went across them, and when he was done [stepping on] all of them, he was done [using his powers].
>
> When he was done, he told those people that he was offended by what happened, and that the following

summer fish wouldn't enter the rivers where they fished.

Indeed, the following year those rivers lacked fish and the people of Qissunaq experienced starvation in their turn.

Even shamans who were not malicious could be dangerous. Barbara Joe (April 2012:302) spoke of how sometimes a shaman, when filled with gratitude when someone gave him food but lacking something to repay the gift-giver, might coax them to take his powers: "He says out of gratitude, although he wants to repay that person who helped him with something small, that he has nothing to give. They say that is one who is trying to coax someone." People are told not to agree with that shaman, but to ignore him: "They say a shaman who coaxes someone is dangerous."

Edward Hooper (March 2007:1475) of Tununak noted that shamans were respected in the past because they could kill. He said that when shamans murdered someone, another shaman might search but couldn't track the person using his spirit powers: "Some [shamans] would constantly kill people without a trace." Michael John (June 2008:35) said that shamans who killed others might be killed themselves: "They evidently killed [shamans] back in those days after constantly admonishing them [not to kill people], when they had killed too many people. They say that when they were about to die, the ones they had murdered would name the shaman responsible for their condition."

Benedict Tucker (March 2011:911–13) told about how he came to understand the power of shamans. During the years when reindeer were plentiful along the lower Yukon, the Catholic priest, Father O'Connor, accused Tuucillngaq, a known shaman, of stealing and killing a reindeer: "After a short silence, that shaman replied to him—there were no wolves around here back then—'If my two wolves come to materialize, although you want to have reindeer, you won't have any reindeer.'" That spring, wolves arrived and decimated the herd, wolves that would only appear when people weren't watching, and eventually reindeer became scarce. Benedict concluded: "[The priest] hurt his feelings, and he probably hadn't [killed a reindeer]. They used to tell us not to mistreat those shamans."

Barbara Joe (April 2012:239) noted that the more shamans exercised their powers, the stronger they became and, potentially, the more dangerous: "It is

said *angalkut* want to try [exercising shaman powers] once in their minds. Then they say that person's mind gradually becomes powerful, they want to exercise shaman powers. . . . It is said if they want to try once and they try, they will gradually do it more and more."

Finally, some mentioned that even good shamans, when in a desperate situation, aren't good leaders. As an example, Joe Phillip (December 2013:138–42) described how three men were lost on the ocean ice all spring, including the shaman Qakerluilaq; the trio eventually landed near Nome and returned home by way of St. Michael. Qakerluilaq was originally their leader, but he didn't choose good paths to travel on: "They say he never recalled the possibility of using his spirit power when he became desperate. They say that's apparently what shamans do." Later, when the shaman's companion Qasqanayuk told the story, he said that when shamans are desperate, they aren't good leaders, because they panic: "They say they aren't to be depended on for support. . . . He said it was like he was trying to survive alone, wanting to be the only one to survive."

Eugene Pete and Lawrence Edmund (December 2011:89–92) described another shaman who panicked when a Christmas flood and gale-force winds pushed sea ice up through the marshland south of the Yukon, folding the land and carrying people and their homes away in the deluge. Eugene explained:

> Teggalquq, that shaman who was indomitable, they say he panicked. They say one of them brought him to his senses when he asked him why he was doing nothing. He told him to do something [with his shaman powers], not to just do nothing.
>
> They say he pierced the middle of his home down there with a knife, making a place for [the water] to leak out. They say the ice didn't enter it at all. They say he suddenly came to his senses; at first he panicked.

Angalkut qavanguqellrit
Shamans appearing in dreams

Many described encountering shamans and their "weapons" (often in the form of dogs) in their sleep. Frank Andrew (September 2005:282) noted that normal people are perceptive and can understand when things are not normal. A person will know immediately, through his dreams, if a shaman is not "thinking right" toward him, even if that shaman is being secretive. Frank explained that this is because shamans sleep on two levels, while normal people sleep only on one level:

Malrugnek-gguq qavaryarangqertuq angalkuq [A shaman can sleep on two levels]. He can sleep and get down very deep and stop breathing. And he can also sleep on the level that we normal people sleep. . . .

[When he sleeps,] he can stop breathing as if he is dead. But a normal person only sleeps in one way. That's why normal people can easily understand if a shaman has ill feelings toward them. A normal person will perceive [that it is a shaman] right away in his sleep.

Indeed, many elders describe encountering shamans in their sleep. Tim Agagtak (July 1985:21) explained: "[A shaman] might tell someone what he needed; if that person didn't comply, that person would soon get sick. [The shaman] would come to that person in dreams. The shaman was the one who was [making him sick]. That person would know through his dreams." Albertina Dull (April 2013:41) agreed: "[The shaman] would go into our dreams, and we would feel fearful. If [a shaman] tried to harm us, we would know."

Paul John (May 2003:42–58) provided a detailed account of how his grandfather sought support for his young grandson from Paul's mother's uncle, who was a shaman. Later, Paul woke up whimpering and told his grandmother that he had been frightened by the shaman's dogs in his dream. When his grandmother angrily confronted the shaman, he explained that he had been testing Paul, so that when another *angalkuq* tried to harass him later in life, Paul would know it. Indeed, years later the Nelson Island shaman Angutekayak confronted Paul with dogs in his dreams. In his dream, Paul picked up a rock and threw it at the female dog, hitting her on the side of her head. The next morning, Angutekayak's wife, who had gone to bed fine, woke with a pain in her head.

When discussing shamans with Mike Andrews, Eugene Pete (December 2011:440–41) said that the one who raised him told him that he would know if a shaman did something to him: "They say those [regular people], when a shaman [confronts or attacks them in their dreams], they will know for sure [that it was a shaman]. I also knew when a shaman was doing something to me." Eugene added that he used a club

as his weapon to fight back, and that he had fought dogs twice in his dreams, killing them when they approached him:

The second time, I had a dream about Thomas. A dog approached, and Thomas also walked outside. That dog approached me, snarling. The weapon I used suddenly appeared. I took it, and its weight was just right. When it arrived and I hit it, [the dog] fell face first, and that person [Thomas] entered. And I heard that Thomas wasn't feeling well. I think that person indeed used to mess [with people].

Maryann Andrews (April 2012:336–38, 347) told a story of how a shaman in the form of a dog had bothered her friend in her sleep. The woman got revenge by spreading her hands and putting saliva on them, then smearing saliva on the tips of her feet.

She said that when she took a step, that dog started making noise right away. She said when that one started to make noise, it was Leggleq. . . . She said he hunted her in his dream, but she countered him, and when she [took another step], he made even more noise.

As she continued approaching him, she saw fire burning behind him. She said that [shaman] was extremely desperate, and she was thinking to let him fall there. But she stopped and thought, "If you bother me again, I will let you fall."

She learned his identity on her own in her sleep. She said she used to see him as a dog.

Maryann noted that a person's saliva is powerful: "Since she had no knife, but she only had her saliva, she evidently used that as a weapon and confronted that [shaman] with it."

Many describe how shamans used dogs as their weapons, trying to kill people or make them ill. According to Theresa Moses (April 2001:94): "We used to hear they used dogs as their weapons, hunting them in their sleep. You hear that some people say that they were extremely afraid because they were being chased by dogs in their sleep. In that way, those *angalkut* disguised themselves as dogs and pursued people, making them ill."

In normal life, dogs doing unusual things might portend death. Barbara Joe (April 2012:373–74) noted that dogs that cry are sometimes referred to as *elpengcarilriit* (those that give signs that something is about to occur). Although Barbara hadn't heard of people killing dogs that cried, Peter Black (originally from

Hooper Bay) said that someone who was not a relative would kill it: "I think they had them do that through shamans, to have [the death] affect the dog and not the person." Albertina Dull (June 2009:139–40) told the story of two women who danced together and subsequently died. Before their death, a man had seen a female dog dancing, *takullugluni* (displaying unusual behavior portending someone's death).

Though closely associated with shamans and dreams, dogs also had positive associations. Albertina Dull (June 2009:136–37) told the story of a woman who was healed by her dog. As she stayed seated nursing her baby, the ghost of her dead mother entered her home. When the ghost left, the woman suddenly felt lethargic and turned to her dog, telling it that if she died it would also perish, as no one would feed it. The woman lay down, and when she looked again, she saw that someone was using shaman powers to heal her: "Just when she got up from where she lay, that dog that had been nursing its pups jumped from behind her onto the floor. They say her dog was using its powers [to heal her]." Albertina concluded: "My, some dogs were so wise in the past; when giving them commands, they would understand."

Although not always easy to interpret, many people viewed dreams as having real effects on their waking lives. Many understood what happened in their dreams as predictive of future events, at times providing advice or warnings. Among the Canadian Inuit, some said that in the past it was considered very important for children to tell their parents about their dreams (Laugrand and Oosten 2012:221). Though these are not topics that we have explored in depth, elders made clear that in the past shamans sometimes entered their dreams and communicated what was to come.

Angalkut calluutelallrat
Shaman battles

Many stories recall rivalries and battles between powerful shamans. Joe Ayagarak (December 1987:15–17) remembered three elderly men who faced each other in the *qaygi* (men's house) in Qissunaq and told stories, sometimes bursting out laughing as they really imagined what they were talking about. Among their recollections were stories about shamans:

When they caught up with the ones who they were pursuing, then they would capture them, flattening their *tuunriyarat* [ways of practicing their spirit powers]. They finished them.

And when there was no way for him to escape, they didn't let [that shaman] know, they didn't allow his body to be aware [that they had flattened his spirit helpers].

When a shaman realized that others had flattened his powers, he would inflate his spirit helpers and retaliate. But if the original attacker was paying attention, he would sense it and the two would confront each other. Joe Ayagarak (December 1987:17) explained:

They say when they do that, all those who are able to see using spirit helpers move toward the edge. They want to watch those two who are going to challenge one another.

They say those are just like movies, like watching TV. . . . They say only powerful shamans do that.

Joe said that when one shaman caught up to another, he would strip away his powers, take away his spirit helpers, and claim them as his own: "They would make it so that the one stripped of his powers would die before him. They will let him go with a time [to die]."

While Joe Ayagarak spoke of shamans generally, Frank Andrew vividly recalled particular conflicts and their outcomes. One such conflict was between the shaman Uyangqulria from Kangirnaarmiut and a Qinarmiut shaman who had requested and received Uyangqulria's boat as a gift during a winter dance festival. The next summer, however, Uyangqulria changed his mind and traveled across the Kuskokwim River to the Qinarmiut fish camp on the shores of Kuiguyuk. When he reached his old boat, he realized that he would die if he took it. Frank Andrew (October 2001:210) explained: "The one who came to own it used his powers to make it untouchable."

Uyangqulria learned that a grandmother and grandson staying at the fish camp wanted to travel to Kangirnaarmiut, and when Uyangqulria went to them and explained his problem, the old woman said that her grandson could touch the boat. After she put saliva on his hands, he went to the boat and turned it over. While the trio was getting ready to leave, the new owner arrived, raised his arms, and said, "I am sending Uyangqulria a pet." Uyangqulria saw a small rabbit in his hands that could not be taken, as it was the shaman's weapon, which the man then threw toward the north.

Uyangqulria and his companions started to cross the Kuskokwim, with the boy oaring and Uyangqulria steering. When they got to the middle of the river, the area to the north got dark with wind and rain. The grandmother again put saliva on her hands and ran them down her body and that of her grandson as protection. As the wind blew stronger, Uyangqulria saw that through the old woman's *pissuun* (power source) they were protected by a huge stickleback, which prevented waves from touching their boat. Then Uyangqulria took the form of a walrus, holding the boat with its tusks and pushing it across the river. They then saw a beluga whale, the weapon of the *angalkuq* they were fleeing, and they knew if it touched them they would die. Through his power, Uyangqulria created a huge person in a huge kayak, who harpooned the beluga and took it into the front of his kayak.

Uyangqqulria's boat finally arrived at the opposite shore where waves were exploding, but a person stood there shoveling the waves and creating a calm area for them to land in. Safe ashore, they covered the boat and slept inside. When they woke they found themselves on top of a hill above Kangirnaarmiut, with both the Kuskokwim River and the ocean far away. They walked home, leaving the boat there, where its wooden frame can be seen today.

Frank Andrew (October 2001:350) noted how jealous and vindictive shamans were in the past—definitely not approved social behavior: "These *tuunrangayiit* [shamans] are apparently always battling with one another when they are upset about something; if someone upset them, it is like a cut to them. . . . They would only try to get back at them with their powers." Frank followed with the story of Keggsuli from Goodnews Bay who ridiculed Aasasilek from Kangirnaarmiut, laughing at his attempts to cure his son-in-law, Puyulkuk, and displaying no compassion. When Aasasilek heard that he had been ridiculed in the *qasgiq*, he tried once again but was unable to cure Puyulkuk. Then he changed parkas with his son-in-law, who then faced Keggsuli and stripped him of his powers: "Even though Keggsuli tried to use his powers on him, [Puyulkuk] would take them and own them. That shaman from Goodnews Bay no longer was an *angalkuq* because his powers were all gone because this person finished them and had them for himself."

Frank Andrew (February 2003:34–37) also described the *angalkuq* Esiseq, who was regarded as an *alairumanrilnguq* (one who kept himself concealed, using his power secretly). Esiseq didn't like to hunt or go after animals. He lived along the Iluqaaqniq River in the fall harvesting blackfish, then moved to Kangirnaarmiut in winter: "He was totally unafraid of other *angalkut*, even though they were malicious. When he got a little agitated by them, he'd cast stronger force on them, pressing them down flat. The *angalkut* were wary of him and left him alone, even though he never used his power in public." Frank described Esiseq encountering a beluga, then a bearded seal, and finally a herd of caribou along the Ilkivik River. In each case, though his wife got excited, he disappointed her and let the animals pass:

> He never got excited when he saw animals, and he didn't try to catch them. Those who knew him have said that he never pursued animals that presented themselves to him like that because he knew they were placed there by the other *angalkut* [to try to kill him]. . . .
>
> He knew that if he struck the animals with a weapon, he would only hurt himself.

Frank Andrew (September 2005:200) also told about Murak and Pamsuq, who were *yuiratellriik* (two who provoked each other through song): "Those who try to take the spirit away from each other, *yuiratellriit* as they called it, composed songs to try and aggravate each other. In his song the person would mention little things that the other person had done to irritate him." When Murak composed a song to try to provoke his cousin Pamsuq, at first Pamsuq was afraid and ignored him since Murak was a shaman. Others told Murak to leave Pamsuq alone, warning that Pamsuq was clever and that when he answered back he would strike with greater power. Murak continued to ridicule his cousin, and indeed, when Pamsuq finally retaliated, he did it with great determination, singing a song he had composed, belittling Murak in turn. Pamsuq continued to humiliate Murak through songs, even after Murak died.

Angalkuq were also known to put spells on one another. Frank Andrew (September 2005:243) told how, before alcohol was introduced, the shaman Qateryak filled a ladle with plain water, and after drinking a little, he let Pamsuq drink the rest, making him intoxicated: "It was Qateryak who cast a spell on Pamsuq and allowed him to stay drunk [from plain water] . . . for a long time."

Frank Andrew (September 2005:250–61) provided unique details of the rivalry between shamans in his story of the Ayikatarmiut shaman, Aqsarpak (described in chapter 6: "Shaman Journeys and Performances"), who reluctantly traveled to the ocean at the request of his grandsons. There he encountered the shaman Nagiiquyaq from Yuukiararmiut, near Tununak, who severely beat him and left him for dead. On his way home, Nagiiquyaq saw a raven and gull fighting on the beach, but he didn't understand their significance. Then, rounding Cape Vancouver on Nelson Island, he saw a red fox and white fox playing a stick game, qip'artaalriik, the significance of which he also failed to grasp. When he got home, Nagiiquyaq boasted that he had killed a shaman and taken away what he had acquired. He also followed abstinence practices for when one shaman killed another, covering his head and wearing a belt.

Then Nagiiquyaq started to feel sick. He noticed two human eyes looking through the grass mat covering the entrance to the underground tunnel. He continued feeling ill, and when probing he saw that the shaman who he thought he had killed was about to kill him. He then understood that the raven and gull were actually fighting over his tarnaq, and that the eyes he'd seen were those of Aqsarpak. Meanwhile at Ayikata'ar, Aqsarpak would ask for a dog-skin hood and pair of gloves, and putting them on he would jump down into the entrance hole, causing dried soil to fly up from below. After being gone for a while, he would reappear from the back corner of the qasgiq, covered with dirt. When he did that he apparently would go and check on Nagiiquyaq at Yuukiararmiut.

One day when the men at Yuukiararmiut were having a fire bath, Nagiiquyaq went out and saw his two cousins playing a stick game behind the qasgiq, and they insisted he join them. When he jumped over the stick and landed on the other side, the impact sounded like a bladder popping and his nose suddenly started bleeding. When he looked at his cousins, he saw that they were actually the red fox and white fox he had seen previously, and he realized that he had been defeated and would soon die.

Not only did Aqsarpak kill the shaman of the people of Yuukiararmiut; he also belittled Nagiiquyaq and boasted of his feat when invited to Yuuki-

ararmiut for a Messenger Feast. In this way, Aqsarpak injured the minds of the people of Yuukiararmiut, who summoned their shamans to retaliate. Although Aqsarpak fell ill, his qatngun (close friend or partner) came to his defense, and Aqsarpak recovered. Vivid stories like these are long remembered, stories in which appearances are often deceiving and even shamans must carefully measure their strength against adversaries of equal or greater power.

Stories also speak of shamans forced to flee from their adversaries. Fred Augustine (March 2011:1082–83) talked about Qakerluilaq, an Iñupiaq shaman who had fled from the Kotzebue area: "They say Qakerluilaq constantly fled and moved from place to place. His fellow [shamans] tended to pursue him. But he would escape before they [killed him]. And he was alive for a while here [in Alakanuk] . . . but died in this village some time ago." Qakerluilaq was said to have been responsible for the death of another shaman, Angutvassuk, who died of stomach pains at Narullegarvik, but was himself killed by the shaman Qakurtaq.

Frank Andrew (September 2005:226) noted that sometimes when people thought badly of a particular shaman, he was forced to flee: "More than once, there were those who left their home areas and moved over to this [lower Kuskokwim coastal] area because of fear of being killed." John Phillip (October 2010:400–13) told the story of a shaman who moved to Qinaq as a son-in-law. Then, when sickness began to afflict the people of Qinaq, they suspected him of causing it, and mistreated him, forcing him to eat feces inside the qasgiq and cutting the skin along the soles of his feet. The shaman fled along the Avcaumciq River. As he traveled, one side of his footprints became wolf tracks, making the people of Qinaq reluctant to follow. Then he saw a house in the distance and approached it. Because he was moving so slowly (due to his injured feet) the grandmother living there thought he was other-than-human and advised her grandchild to first circle their house with a whetstone, then with a beaver castor, then with a stalk of wild celery, leaving each item on top of the other outside their home. When the shaman arrived, the house kept transforming into a rock, a beaver den, and a wild celery plant, preventing him from entering. He finally found a path to enter when the house transformed into a beaver den, and using his powers he dove inside. The grandmother felt guilty for blocking his way, saying that she had feared he wasn't human.

Before they went to bed, the shaman had the grandmother and grandchild place a blackfish trap in the entryway. In the morning, it was full of debris. John explained: "They say he didn't want sickness to afflict the people he was staying with, but he said that it had come from those people who were sick." The grandmother cared for him while his feet healed, making him two pairs of skin boots to use when he traveled. He told her that when he left, she should set the blackfish trap in the river down below their place: "They say that after setting the blackfish trap, they looked inside and saw that the blackfish had evidently already appeared. The blackfish trap was full of blackfish. They say those two pulled out blackfish from there that that person provided for them through his gratitude."

Just as shamans repaid those who helped them, they punished those who tried to harm them. Joe Ayagarak (December 1987:37–39) told the story of the Qissunaq shaman Kenirmigpak, who was pursued by Qip'ngayagmiut shamans. Kenirmigpak found himself trapped in the tunnel entryway of their *qasgiq*. When they began drumming inside, he headed toward the exit, but found his way blocked by people outdoors practicing their shaman powers: "When he closed his eyes and tried to think of what to do, he saw that they had already flattened his spirit helpers."

Then, when a woman inside the *qasgiq* struck her drum, two lengths of hair stretched out and encircled him, pulling him inside. He finally found a way to escape through a small hole in the skylight when a urine container spilled and the other shamans lost consciousness. Returning to Qissunaq, Kenirmigpak used his shaman powers to shorten the lives of his adversaries: "He *tekiterkirturluki* [?made a future for] all of them, he lined them up and put them in their places."

Frank Andrew (September 2005:282) also described how shamans could use their powers against someone, even after they had died and gone to live among *ircenrraat*. Once they had died, however, they could no longer run. Frank added that shamans who retaliate after they have been killed always win, even though they had been defeated while alive. Frank (December 2003:131) explained:

Even those who had been shamans in the past [and had died], their fellow shamans who were living used them as weapons. And a shaman, if two shamans were fighting, if [the other] was weaker, he would kill the one who he found weak.

They say if [the dead shaman] finally attacks him after he had died, he would find the one who [killed him] to be weaker than him. It would be hard for shamans to counter him after he died as a shaman. He could then easily kill the person who killed him.

10

Iqua
Conclusion

··

Angalkut ayuquciit
A shaman's powerful senses

Many stories emphasize the extraordinary senses shamans possessed, including powerful touch that could heal or harm, depending on their intent, and the ability to see into the future and travel between the human and nonhuman worlds. Paul John (June 1995) described the late Billy Lincoln's ability to hear songs in the sounds of the natural world.

> Your great-grandfather Apacuk mentioned that he was able to do that since he was a descendant of a line of *angalkut*. He was an offspring of people who had extraordinary perceptions. He said he could hear people singing when the wind blew against the house, making a whistling sound. Also he could hear people singing when the wind moved the grass. He said he learned some of the songs he had heard from the sounds of nature. The ability to hear such things was one of the capabilities of *angalkut*.

As described above, Yup'ik cosmology can be characterized by the opposition between restricted human senses and powerful supernatural ones. Masked dances directed by the *angalkuq* contrasted restricted human sight to powerful supernatural vision, the gloved human hand to supernatural touch, potentially dangerous human scent to cleansing smoke, restricted human speech to powerful songs, and the closed lips of attentive listeners to the spirits' wide, toothy mouths found on both masks and drum handles (Fienup-Riordan 1996:161–96). Dance performances combined movement, sound, light, song, smoke, and food to attract, to influence, and often to embody the spirit worlds. Often *angalkut* gained their special powers through restricting their own senses—binding their limbs, covering their bodies, lying motionless, and fasting for long periods. Like Paul Waskey's grandmother, who was able to interpret the different languages spoken by her *tuunrat*, *angalkut* restricted normal senses to gain the ability to see and hear things unavailable through ordinary human perception.

In their activities, shamans displayed special abilities that allowed them to perceive the world in ways normal people could not. Paul John (February 1994) pointedly described *angalkut* as the "scientists of our ancestors" with the ability to predict the future:

> White people mention biologists nowadays, the ones who keep records on fish. Some *angalkut* worked on the path of the fish the people were going to use. Wanting to ensure a plentiful supply when summer arrived, shamans would use their *tuunrat* to assist in removing all obstacles from the path of the returning fish. Some *angalkut* would go down into the ocean during winter to request plenty of seals or other sea mammals, so that springtime would bring an abundance when men were out hunting. With their extrasensory perception they could tell what the future held for others.

https://doi.org/10.5876/9781646427314.c010

FIGURE 10.1. Joe Chief Jr. of Bethel performing with a mask that tells the story of the shaman Ississaayuk, who foretold the coming of the first white people in a ship, represented on the mask by the carving atop the shaman's head. James H. Barker.

Angalkut played an important role in community life, functioning as intermediaries between the human and nonhuman worlds. The shaman was recognized as a person with special abilities that allowed him or her to journey for particular purposes with newly acquired agility and speed. Some were believed to die and subsequently be reborn, or they might be killed and come back to life.

Michael John (June 2008:260–67) shared the story of the powerful shaman Ississaayuk, who, as a young man, repeatedly came back to life after his enemies killed him. After moving to the coast, some of his fellows asked him to use his powers to summon *augtuaraat* (red phalaropes). He told them to make a model bird, then burn it completely along the ocean shore, which they did, and in the spring red phalaropes arrived. The second time he used his ability to sum-

mon spectacled eiders, and when he accompanied his companions to the small lakes along the marshland, they were full of spectacled eiders.

Later, as a grown man in the days before white people came to the area, people asked Ississaayuk to summon white people. He warned against it, saying that if he summoned white people, diseases would become widespread. But the people continued to plead with him and, once again, he told them to make a wooden model of a boat, and then burn it completely. When spring came, a large ship arrived with a caribou walking inside, and masks hanging on the sides, blinking periodically, said by John Phillip (October 2006:188) to be the boat's lighted portholes. John Phillip added that shamans always made wooden models of what they requested: "Before a ritual like that they always made something that represented what they were asking for. I watched [the shaman] Murak do that when someone asked for a bearded seal. I also heard that Ississaayuk had a wooden ship made with eyes on the side, and on that wooden ship there was a carving of a person standing at the bow of the boat with his finger pointing to the north" (figure 10.1).[1]

In times of food shortage shamans acted as food locators through the exercise of their clairvoyant powers and supernatural sight. John Phillip (January 2011:128) told about people from the Kuskokwim whose shaman, during a famine, led them to the Urrsukvaaq River near the coastal village of Chefornak to survive: "They say their shaman was looking at a bright light that was shining down on that place. . . . When they reached that river, that shaman told them to make an opening [along the ice]. It was evidently showing where the needlefish were." The people made a hole in the ice to harvest the needlefish, and those who ate survived. Placid Joseph (December 2013:248–50) from Alakanuk also mentioned his grandfather, a powerful shaman who brought his family north from the mouth of the Kuskokwim during a period of food shortage: "Since he was a shaman and knew, he traveled with his shaman power, probably at night. They say he saw fish vapor here at Iqalliarvik [on the Yukon River]. . . . He apparently told them to leave [the Kuskokwim] and travel to the place he saw."

Shamans might also be asked to divine the cause of bad weather or disease. Albertina Dull (April 2013:72) spoke of the Nelson Island shaman Yus'uk, who saw death appearing as darkness, coming from the headwaters of the Kuskokwim and Yukon Rivers: "He knew that he was going to die. The Yukon River, the Kuskokwim River got dark. He said the darkness was approaching. He said many people don't come out of that dark. . . . That dark was death, and he said that he himself won't come out of it. What he said turned out to be true."

Shamans were trained to have visions in which they might see the future in the surface of a pot of water, in a bowl of oil, or in the reflection from an animal's eye. People referred to this act of seeing as *tangrruarluni* or "something like seeing," and their visions were often fulfilled. Dreams told of the future and might foretell an individual's impending death. The shaman could tell by the "picture" or aura of a sick person whether that person would recover, remain ill for a long time, or die (Kawagley 1989:10). Mike Andrews (December 2011:438–40) told of how a shaman used his powers to track the trail of a person who stole gifts given to a guest from upriver during a dance festival at Alakanuk. He identified the thief as someone from Mountain Village, who was known to steal things: "The shaman evidently told the one who lost his things that [the thief] wouldn't live through the entire winter." In fact, the thief died before winter ended.

Angalkukuyuut
Those with abilities today

Many noted that some people possess extraordinary abilities to this day. In answering the question of how people became shamans, Paul John (January 2006:246) declared: "There are some people who have the capability to become shamans during our time now. But because they have no encouragement, since they know that people don't support them, they are in hiding, it's hard to distinguish who they are." Paul followed with the story of how once, while on his fishing boat anchored in Bristol Bay, his young helper had come into the cabin, worried about his family back in Toksook Bay. The next day, Paul got a radio message that the young man's child was seriously ill and that he was needed at home. This was decades before cell phones, and there was no way the young man could have known about his family's situation. Paul noted that from that experience he recognized that the young man had abilities, likely inherited from his ancestors.

Paul John's son, Mark John (October 2006:192–94), also spoke about encountering those with abilities. In the 1980s, while traveling through Anchorage on his way to Bristol Bay for fishing, one of his crew members slammed his fingers in a hotel-room door: "That person evidently said, 'How infuriating! I needed to use this hand, too!'" And when he displayed his fingers, they were healed. Mark noted that the man's mother's grandfather was also known to have abilities, although he always denied it, and his grandchild—Paul John's fishing helper—also had abilities. Mark concluded: "That's why when people say that there are people who could possibly [become shamans], I believe it since I hear of people who have those types of experiences nowadays."

Raphael Jimmy (January 2013) agreed that some people today still have shaman abilities, inherited from their ancestors, although not openly displayed. As noted, Albertina Dull (June 2009:252) used the term *alairumanrilnguut* (ones who keep themselves concealed) to designate those who had shaman powers but didn't use them in front of people. Roland Phillip (October 2006:195) agreed, adding that it is because they don't want to be noticed: "There are obviously people [with abilities], but those people aren't trying to be noticeable nowadays. That person briefly mentioned that [shamans can attack] people in their dreams. And those who enter people's dreams, sometimes even regular people injure those [shamans]." Roland concluded: "They say those of us who are just regular people [without powers] will know when shamans are meddling with us."

Stories of shamans and their activities provide us with insights into Yup'ik history. Eugene Pete witnessed shamans many times and spoke with obvious enjoyment about his encounters. Summing up a lifetime of experiences, Eugene (March 2011:1232) declared with a laugh: "I've seen them many times. Some are real, some aren't real. They just pretend to be shamans." The act of telling also reveals something about the present. These tales are shared with enjoyment and pleasure. Listening to Frank Andrew speak about his experiences, Alex Bird (December 2003:132) exclaimed, "You are fun to listen to. When someone is there to explain them well, they are easy to understand."

Part 2

Angalkunek Qanemcit

Shaman Stories

Yugtun Igautellrit Kass'atun-llu Mumigtellrit
Yup'ik Transcription and Translation

The Central Alaskan Yup'ik language is spoken on the Bering Sea coast from Norton Sound to the Alaska Peninsula, as well as along the lower Yukon, Kuskokwim, and Nushagak Rivers. It is one of four Yupik languages, all of which are closely related to the Inuit/Iñupiaq languages of the arctic coast of Alaska, northern Canada, and Greenland, although they are not mutually intelligible. Together, Inuit/Iñupiaq and Yupik constitute the Eskimo branch of the Eskimo-Aleut family of languages. No apostrophe is used when speaking of Yupik languages generally, but an apostrophe is used for Central Alaskan Yup'ik and its dialects.

There are five dialects of Central Yup'ik: Norton Sound, Hooper Bay / Chevak (Cup'ik), Nunivak Island (Cup'ig), Egegik, and General Central Yup'ik. All are mutually intelligible with some phonological and vocabulary differences (Jacobson 2012:35–46; Woodbury 1984:49–63).

The Central Yup'ik language remained unwritten until the end of the nineteenth century, when Russian Orthodox, Moravian, and Jesuit Catholic missionaries, working independently of one another but in consultation with Native converts, developed a variety of orthographies. The orthography that is used consistently throughout this book is the standard one developed between 1967 and 1972 at the University of Alaska Fairbanks and detailed in works published by the Alaska Native Language Center and others (Reed, Miyaoka, Jacobson, Afcan, and Krauss 1977; Miyaoka and Mather 1979; Jacobson 1995).

The standard orthography for Central Yup'ik represents the language with letters and letter combinations, each corresponding to a distinct sound as follows:

Consonants

	labials	apicals	front velars	back velars
stops	p	t, c	k	q
voiced fricatives	v	l, s/y	g (ug)	r (ur)
voiceless fricatives	vv	ll, ss	gg (w)	rr
voiced nasals	m	n	ng	
voiceless nasals	m	n	ng	

Symbols in parentheses represent the sounds made with the lips rounded.

Vowels

	front		back
high	i		u
mid		e	
low		a	

The apostrophe indicates consonant gemination, or doubling (and serves several other less important functions). There are also conventions for undoubling the letters for voiceless fricatives under certain circumstances (Jacobson 1995:6–7). This stan-

https://doi.org/10.5876/9781646427314.c011

dard orthography accurately represents the Yup'ik language in that a given word can be written in only one way and a given spelling can be pronounced in only one way. Note that certain predictable features of pronunciation, specifically automatic gemination and rhythmic length, are not explicitly shown in the spelling. Readers should also note that a question mark preceding a Yup'ik word or definition indicates that the meaning is unknown to the translator or that the recording was unclear.

Mumigtellrit
Translation

Most of the translations in this book were done by either Alice Rearden or Marie Meade with a handful of colorful contributions by David Chanar. As translators, Alice and Marie offer distinctive strategies for bridging differences between Yup'ik and English without erasing them. For both, the goal has been a natural-sounding, free translation, as opposed to either literal translation (at one extreme) or paraphrasing (at the other). Paraphrasing may communicate some of the sense of the original, but such interpretive translations modify the original to the point where the speaker's voice is alternately erased or transformed. Literal, word-for-word translation also falls short. At best, it is awkward, and at worst, it makes no sense. The narrator's choice of words is respected in this book, although translators may modify word order and sentence structure slightly to communicate original meaning. They do this in different ways. Marie Meade, for example, is freer with English word choice, paragraphing, and paraphrasing in contrast to Alice Rearden, who retains a more literal word choice and style.

Because their primary goal is communication, no translation in this book mechanically follows the structure of the original language. For example, Yup'ik word order is "English turned on its head," in which suffixes indicating tense, person, case, and other units of meaning are appended to verb and noun bases. Thus, the English phrase "my little boat" corresponds to the single Yup'ik word *angyacuarqa*, which consists of *angya-* "boat," plus *-cuar-* "little," plus *-qa* "my," so that the order of the parts within the Yup'ik word is "boat, little, my." In Yup'ik discourse, the object also typically precedes the verb. A literal

translation of *qaltarpaliunga* might read "bucket / big one / to make / I." A more natural translation would employ typical English word order, that is, verb followed by object, and would read "I / make / a big bucket." Thus, translation involves a continuous process of reordering.

Other characteristics of Yup'ik oratory have been carefully retained. For example, redundancies and repetitions are important rhetorical devices in Yup'ik narrative. Narrators frequently restate important points, often phrased somewhat differently, at the beginning and end of an account, both to enhance memory and to add emphasis and depth. Use of repetition gives Yup'ik texts a denser texture than typical English phrasings, which careful attention in the translation can retain. Structured repetitions are characteristic of Yup'ik narrative art and vital to its structural integrity. To smooth them over or omit them would impoverish the translations.

Several grammatical features of the Yup'ik language pose potential problems for translators. First, relatively free word order characterizes the Yup'ik language. For example, the meaning of the English sentence "The man lost the dog" can only be conveyed by placing the words "man," "lost," and "dog" in this order. A Yup'ik speaker, however, can arrange the three words *angutem* ("man"), *tamallrua* ("s/he lost it"), and *qimugta* ("dog") in any of six possible word orders with no significant change in meaning. Nevertheless, word order is not totally irrelevant to interpreting Yup'ik sentences. Word order may be the only key to appropriate interpretation when the ending alone is insufficient. For example, the sentence *Arnam atra nallua* (lit., "woman//his/her name//s/he not knowing it") can mean either "The woman does not know his name" or "He does not know the woman's name." The same three words in a different word order, however, are less ambiguous. *Arnam nallua atra* is commonly taken to mean "The woman does not know his name." In contrast with other languages that have a free word order, the relative position of postbases inside a Yup'ik word is very rigid. Consequently, syntactic problems may occur in words that occur only in sentences in translation.

Translation is further complicated by the fact that the Yup'ik language does not specify gender in third-person endings. The listener is left to deduce gender from the context of the account. When a speaker describes women's tasks, we have translated the pronominal ending as "she," as that is the way an English speaker can best understand the speaker's intent. Conversely, pronominal endings are translated as "he" when the speaker is describing a man's activities. In general discussions, we have used either "it" or "he," depending on the context. Readers should also know that Yup'ik orators sometimes mix singular and plural endings in a single oral "sentence," and we have retained these grammatical variations to reflect the complexity of the Yup'ik original.

Yup'ik verb tenses also differ from English tenses. Although some postbases place an action clearly in the future and others place action definitely in the past, a verb without one of these time-specific postbases may refer to an action that is happening in either the past or the present (Jacobson 1984:22). Accounts of events or customs that are no longer practiced in southwest Alaska have been translated in the past tense. Readers should also note that tense may vary within a paragraph, especially in discussions of *qanruyutet* (oral instructions) marked by the enclitic "-gguq," which can be translated "they said," "they say," or "it is said," depending on the context. Traditional *qanruyutet* that speakers indicate still apply are translated using the present tense.

Our narrators also frequently used nonspecific pronouns and phrases that are difficult for English readers to follow. For example, a speaker may say "that one who told the story," rather than naming a specific person. Narrators also often use phrases such as "he went down" or "he arrived" without specific places mentioned. Readers should note that the Yup'ik language has an elaborate set of demonstratives that situate listeners and that indicate relative placement of action and movement of people—often very specifically—without ever mentioning places directly. These include terms such as *pikavet* (toward the area up above), *piavet* (up the slope), *kanavet* (down the slope, toward the area down below), and *uavet* (toward the mouth of a river, toward the door), to name but a few (Jacobson 2012:963–67). Demonstratives also distinguish between things upslope, downslope, etc. that require more than a single glance to be seen, things that can be seen fully in a single glance, and things that are obscured from view. Where necessary we have tried to clarify these phrases using brackets to indicate the narrator's intent. We have used parentheses to designate passages where narrators themselves offer explanations

important for the reader but not necessarily part of the account.

Many narrators attach the postbase "miut" (people of) to the name of a river or slough to designate the people living there, as in Kusquqvagmiut (the people of the Kusquqvaq [Kuskokwim River]). The names of many villages also derive from the name of the river or lake where they are located, for example, the old village of Kaviarmiut on the Kaviaq River. However, narrators may also use the name Kaviaq for the village itself, and in fact often do so. Other village names may be rendered with or without the "miut" ending. The maps that accompany this text show the most commonly used place name. The text, however, reflects what narrators actually said, designating the place with or without the "miut" ending.

Yup'ik oral rendering values close attention to detail and consistent retellings, and whatever their stylistic preferences, Marie and Alice continue to work in that tradition. As Yup'ik scholar Elsie Mather (1995:32) notes, "The most respected conveyers of Yup'ik knowledge are those who express things that listeners already know in artful or different ways, offering new expressions of the same."

Igautellrit
Transcription

As if translation from one language to another were not challenging enough, this book involves the movement from oral to written language. Our starting point is the verbal artistry of individual elders, but critical to understanding their words is the transfer of their voices onto the page. Through the 1970s, little attention was given to reflecting the dynamics and dramatic techniques of the performance, including the speakers' shifts in tone and rhythm. The oral origins of texts were all but hidden from view. Texts were routinely transcribed in paragraph form, as if the paragraph were the "natural" form of all speech.

Beginning in the 1980s, when so many basic tenets of anthropology were being scrutinized, the ubiquitous paragraph came under attack, especially in the work of Dell Hymes (1981) and fellow linguist Dennis Tedlock (1983). Together Tedlock and Hymes inspired a generation of linguists and anthropologists who have since adopted and adapted their insights in a variety of sociolinguistic transcription styles, igniting a veritable "renaissance" in the translation of Native American literature (Swann 1994:xxviii). Although neither Alice or Marie have chosen to employ the "short line" verse format favored by many translators, they use the prose format with a new sensitivity. In their work, paragraphs are no longer arbitrary groupings disconnected from the speaker's original oral performance but are distinguished by prominent line-initial particles like *tua-i-llu* ("so then"), by cohesion between contiguous lines, and by pauses between units. This is by no means a mechanical process, however, and different translators make different choices about what markers require a new paragraph.

As we think about both the limitations and power of translation to communicate meaning across cultural and linguistic boundaries, it is useful to recall that translation is not the endpoint of understanding, but the beginning (Becker 2000:18). Similarly the reader is invited to engage these translations and use them as starting points for understanding and respecting the profound differences between literary traditions that, in turn, make it possible for us to better understand ourselves.

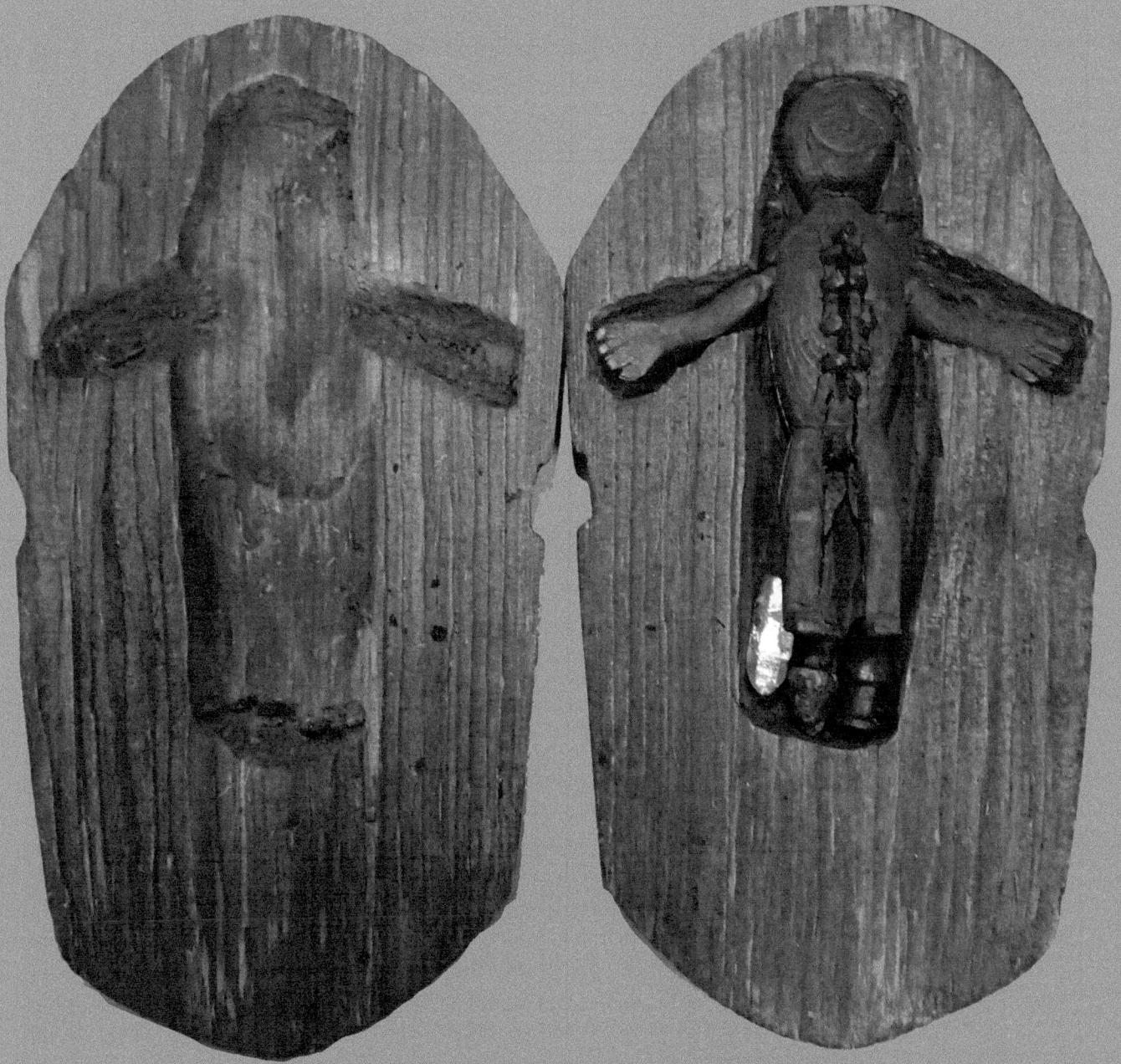

Contents of the shaman box Joan Hamilton shared with elders Frank Andrew,
Margaret Andrews, and Alex Bird at the Yupiit Piciryarait Museum in Bethel,
December 2003. Ann Fienup-Riordan.

Shamanism and Christianity

It would be good if they know it[1]

Frank Andrew, Margaret Andrews, Alex Bird, Joan Hamilton, Noah Andrew, Mark John, Marie Meade, and Alice Rearden, Bethel, December 2003

JOAN HAMILTON: It is only written on this box that these were used by shamans.

MARIE MEADE: Oh goodness, there is a small person inside there. A little human figurine.

MARGARET ANDREWS: I think it belongs to *tuunralget* [those with spirit helpers, those with shaman powers]. I think it's one of those. It shouldn't be touched.

ALEX BIRD: She has brought it because it can be handled, she has brought it probably because it could be touched. Everything can be handled.

FRANK ANDREW: Those belong to *tuunralget*.

ALEX BIRD: Some women had shamanic powers back then, and the same with men. I've heard of one woman with shaman powers. I forgot the name of that woman with shaman powers. I will talk about what I heard because the stomach of this [figurine] is open.

That shaman, they called that shaman Teggalquq [Stone]. They say this was up north. Back when there were shamans, that woman was bothering him because that woman was apparently a shaman. Because he was a shaman, that man asked her to do what men do, to have sex.

And because that man, Teggalquq, was a shaman, he was a shaman named Teggalquq. That woman was a shaman as well. When he was about to [lay on her], he saw that the woman was cut open from here to here [on her body], probably like this [figurine]. She was cut open. If he laid on top of her, that woman would [kill] him.

Because shamans are clever, because they are shamans, when he got an idea, he laid down with a log cloaking his body, and put that log inside that female shaman's [stomach].

https://doi.org/10.5876/9781646427314.c012

Angalkut Agayumaciq-llu

. . . .

Assirciqellria-wa nallunrilkuneng

Miisaq, Quuqan, Apaliq, Pirciralria, Aiggailnguq, Miisaq, Arnaq, Cucuaq-llu,
Mamterilleq, December 2003

PIRCIRALRIA: Uumi yaassiigmi igaumaluni taugaam angalkut-gguq ukut aturlallruit.
ARNAQ: Ila-i yuyaarmek imangqertuq. Yuguayaarmek.
QUUQAN: Tuunralget pikngataat. Tamakuciungatuq. Agtuyunaituq.

APALIQ: Agtuyunaqngan taiskii, taiskii-wa agturayunarqellian. Ca agtuyunaitenrituq ca tamarmi.

MIISAQ: Tuunralget pikait tamakut.
APALIQ: Tamaani ilait waten, arnat ilait tuunralgulartut tamaani ilait, angutet ayuqluteng.
  Arnamek tuunralegmek niitelartua ataucimek. Kitumeg' im' pilaryaaqaat arnaq tauna
  tuunralek. Tua-i waniw' niitellemkun qanrutkeciqaqa una wani ikingqallinian man'a,
  ikingqallinian man'a aqsii.
    Angalkuq tauna, Teggalqumek tua-i pilaraat tauna angalkuq. Qiini-gguq. Tamaani
  angalkungqellermeggni, tua-i tarikluku taum arnam uum, angalkuungami-llu una arnaq,
  angalkuulliniami taun' arnaq. Tua-i angalkuungami tua-i waten piciryaramek angutem
  aturyaraanek tauna angutem unayaqliniluku, arniuryaramek tamatumek unayaqliniluku.
    Tua-i-ll' angun taun' angalkuungami, Teggalquq, Teggalqumek atengqerrluni angalkuuluni.
  Taun' call' arnaq angalkuuluni. Tua-i waniwa, tauna arnaq tanglliniluku, waken-gguq ayagluni
  ullingqaluni ikingqalliniluni waten uutun tuar waten piciqellria. Ikingqaluni. Tuavet tua-i
  qainganun palureskan tua-i piarkauluku taum arnam.
    Tua-i imkut angalkut umyuartuameng, angalkuulaameng, umyuarteqngami, tua-i
  muragmek amirluni, muragmek waten amirluni palurtelliniluni tua-i qainganun, tua-i
  muragmek tamatumek iqmilirluku, imanirluku tauna angalkuk, taun' arnaq.

https://doi.org/10.5876/9781646427314.c012

Then he let go of [the log]. After a while, that woman started to have stomach pains, she was hurting inside because her fellow male shaman had put a log inside her. He pretended that that log was part of his body.

Shamans were clever back then. When they speak about shamans who were rivals, they always tried to be clever, trying to [attack] their fellows in some way.

I just recalled that story they used to tell. Because this [figurine] has an open [stomach], that is what I thought it was. That's the length of my story. He will probably tell another story about this object.

It's a shaman's object, this here is an object used by shamans.

MARIE MEADE: What do you think about objects like this, about our ancestors' objects and tools that are similar to this? This object is shamanic, it is obvious that this is a shamanic object. [What do you think about] how they will be talked about, how they will be shown to people revealing what they are, and displaying them like this, and writing down what was said about them?

These days, using computers, what we call computers, in any of the small villages and large cities and the whole world, if a person wants to know about something he can find it in the computers just by typing it in, and if it has information, it will appear. And the picture will appear, and a description of what it is will appear, and the stories that go with it will appear, and any person can read it from any place, whether they are in a small village, anyone with a computer. Everyone has access to it. And now, what do you elders think about the fact that the pictures and writings can be available to any person? What is your opinion on that?

Long ago, before the ways of the people [Yupiit] changed, these [figurines and shamanic tools] were probably hidden and would not be shown to people. Probably only the person who owned it could show it to those they wanted to. That person would be the only one to have it and would not let other people see it. And this figurine was probably treated that way as well.

She is asking what you think about that. What do you think about it these days, and at this time,

Tua-i-llu peggluku. Tua-i uitaqerluni tauna arnaq iluminek nangteqengluni, ilua qamna akngirtengluni tamatum muragmek imilliniani taum angalkullgutiin angutem. Elliin taun' temeknguarluku, temeknguarluku tamana murak.

Umyuartullruut imkut angalkut tamaani. Qanrutkaqamegteki qayuwa tuaten imkut inglukellriit, angalkut umyuartungnaqu'urluteng pitullruameng, ilateng qayuwa pingnaqluku.

Tua-i tauna neq'aqa'arqa una qanemciklallrat. Una wani ikingqallinian tamakuciuyukluku-llu tua-i. Tua-i tuaten taktalriamek qanemcikaqa wii. Uum taugaam qayuwa qanrutkeciqellikii una.

Angalkurtauguq, angalkurtaulkiaguq una.

ARNAQ: Qaillun umyuarteqceci waten makut ayuqellriit, augkut-wa tua-i ciuliamta aklullrit waten ayuqellriit? Angalkurtauluni una, nallunaituq waniw' angalkurtaullra. Waten qanrutkumallerkaat, nasvagluki yugnun aperturluki caullrat, waten-llu tangertelluku, igauliuku-llu qalarutekluku pillra?

Maa-i mat'um nalliini augkutgun computer-aatgun, apqeput augkut computer-aat, nunacuaraat, nunarpiit, maani-llu nunamta iluani nunaruat tamarmeng, ella-llu iluarrluku waten computer-aatgun yuum ca imna nallunrir[yukni] nalaqsugngaa negtaaqerluki ukut wani qaillun nallunrilkuni, tua-ll' alairrluni. Tua-ll' tarenraa-llu pugluni, caullra-llu alairluni, qanrutkumallra qanemcia pugqerrluni alairrluni tua-i kia piyugngaluku nanleng'ermi, nunacuarni uitang'ermi tuaten computer-aalgem. Yuut tamarmeng, yugnun tamarmeng ikingqaluni. Tua-llu-qaa elpeci ciulirnerni maa-i cangalkececiu waten makucit-llu tuaten tarenraitgun igaumallratgun-llu alaicugngallrat piciatun yugnun? Qaillun umyuartequceciu tamana?

Ak'a tamaani ciungani man'a yuut piciryaraat cimirpailgan makut maa-i iirumatullrullilriit yugnun tangercecimangaunateng. Taum taugaam kiimi pikestiin wall' kitumun aipaagni piyukminun-llu nasvagyugngaciqlikii. Kiimi taum tua-i avaliqarkauluku yugnun allanun tangercecuunaku. Aipaagni-llu waten una waten ayuqellria tayima tuaten ayuqucingqellrullilria, una waniwa.

Qaillun-gguq maa-i umyuarteqceci. Tua-i-wa qaillun umyuartequceciu maa-i-rpak, waniwa-llu

how [the object] is going to be seen in that [video] and what you are saying is recorded in [this tape recorder], and that it is accessible to everyone?

It is being shown to those of us here at this time. What do you think of the possibility that the information written about it and pictures will be shown to people out there in other places far away down there? Is it good or bad?

MARGARET ANDREWS: To me it is good. It will be good. They're probably curious about things when they hear about them, and even the young people [are curious] about what shamans did. It is okay with me.

ALEX BIRD: When you have gatherings, you gather in a group like this with other people. Then other people gather to speak about instructions as well. Some don't have the same language or dialect when they talk about them. Other people speak about these things in a different way. They are not exactly the same when people of other villages speak about shamans' ways. But they [speak about them] the way they heard them; I only talk about things the way that I heard them. They only speak about how they heard them.

If you are thinking about [making it accessible to others], if you are not too anxious and in a hurry to put them on the computer it would be better. That is what I think.

You should try to understand them the best you can first; when you meet a number of times with different people from different places, you will probably learn other things. Then you can put them into the computers so that others down states can view [them]. It would be okay to talk about them as we are doing now. In my perspective, it would be okay to talk about it [and record it] on TV, and have this person talk about it. What do you think about having our people here [have access to it]?

MARGARET ANDREWS: It would be good if they know it. . . .

MARIE MEADE: What he said seems to be good. If it is to be written down, we should not speak about it right away, but after we speak about it with our fellow Yup'ik people around us, and making it clearer, and it will be better if it is spoken of truthfully.

The things we are working on are always recorded in [this tape recorder], and then we write them down. And anyone who wants to can take it

ing'ukun alairturalria, uuggun-llu qanerturalci ek'urluni, ikingqaluni-ll' tauna?

Wangkutnun tua-i waniwa nasvaumalria. Qakemkunun yugnun allanun-llu nunanun yaaqvani akmani igaurrluku tarenraa-llu tapeqluku igaucimaluku qaillun umyuartequceciu tuaten piyugngarillerkaa? Assirtuq-qaa wall'u-qaa assiinani?

QUUQAN: Assirciqellria-wa wangni. Assirciquq. Cat paqnaklarngatait niigartaqameng yun'erraat-llu tamakut tuunralget calallrit. Wangni assirtuq.

APALIQ: Waten-wa quyurtaqavci quyurrlalriaci allanek yul'irluci. Ataam-llu ukut allat yuut ataam tailuteng quyurrluteng makunek ataam qaneryaranek. Ilait qanellguteksuitut qanemcikellrat. Iliin allaurqurluku waten qanemciku'urlarait makut cat. Ayuqeqapigcuitut nunanek allanek pilriani nalqigtellrit makut angalkuryarat. Taugaam niitellermegteggun; wii niitellemkun taugaam qanrutkelaranka. Niitellermegteggun qanruteklarait waten.

Tayim' elpeci umyuarteqkuvci tuaten ayuqluki, taugaam waten computer-aanun ekekuvciki pataganrilkuvciki assinrunayukluki. Wii umyuartequa wii tuaten.

Taringenqegcaararraarluki; qavcirqunek quyurtaanqiggluci allanek yul'irluci ataam eliciiqsugnarqerci naken piciatun. Tuaten nutaan tamakunun computer-aanun ekluku akmavet tangercecuumari[vkarluku]. Maani watua ping'ermi cangaituq. Umyuarteqlemni maani cangaicugnarquq, waten qanemcikluku TV-mun, uum-llu qanrutekluku pikani. Cangalkeciqsiu wangkuta yumtenun maani?

QUUQAN: Assirciqellria-wa nallunrilkuneng. . . .

ARNAQ: Taugaam-wa aug'um taum qanellra assirngacaaqellria. Waten egmianun waten-llu una, una waniwa ayuqellria igauluku pimaarkaukan, qalarutkelerpek'naku, taugaam waten yuullgutekluta wangkuta piurarraarluku nutaan assiriluku piciulriakun qanrutkekuni nutaan assinruciqlilria.

Maa-i iciw' wangkuta una caliarput caliuralalput uumun ek'uratuuq, igauqurluki makunun, igauqurluki-ll' tua-i wangkuta.

and read it. We've been gathering together like this so that they could be published in books. When you are gone, what you said will not disappear. [Your words] will be put into books, they will be made into books and a person can take them, open them, and read them.

The question that that person over there asked, because objects like this belonged to only one person who did not show them to others, but owned them and used them privately, [saying] that maybe we should be careful with these things because they were treated that way in the past. We should respect them, we should treat them with reverence.

FRANK ANDREW: We are cautioned about these items; this is their admonishment. Even though a person thinks nothing of [an object], he must not break it either.

There are many stories told about people, and about how a person's body [deteriorated] from damaging these items. Having no regard for them, a person physically fights those shamans, too, those with shaman powers.

Or because a *tuunraq* has power, [a shaman] can take away the loved ones of a person who is like that. Or he can make a person barren or crippled because a *tuunraq* [spirit helper] has power, because nothing is impossible for him.

MARIE MEADE: And so objects like these, is their strength or power still effective? And is this object here like that also?

FRANK ANDREW: A shaman told me about how he abandoned his *tuunrat*. He said one should not suddenly reject his powers. He said he will not be well if he does that. But he should gradually stop using this particular [ability], then this [ability]. He will only be well if he does that. That person died recently down river in Napakiak. And his son now lives in Kwigillingok, the one they call Mumuss'aq in Yup'ik.

He said one with the ability and knowledge is a shaman. He is able to work on things using his ability. But if he doesn't have the ability, he cannot work on it. If he knows those Yugtaat [Yup'ik skills] well, because shamans are always feuding, if his fellow shaman doesn't have that certain skill or ability, he can easily kill him. But if he was skilled

Tua-i-llu tua-i kia imum piyulriim teguluku naaqsugngaluku. Kalikaurtellerkaitnek iciw' kalikaurrluki pillerkaitnek maa-i waten quyurtaarturluta piuralartukut. Ukaniku elpeci elpeci-llu catairucimariluci, makut catairusngaitut qanerturalci. Kalikamun wani ek'arkaurciiqut, kalikaurrluteng, waten yuum-llu teguluki ikirrluki naaqsugngariciqluki.

Ing'um apyutkellra, makut maa-i waten ayuqellriit ak'a-w' tamaani atuullratni pikestaita ellaita kiimeng nasvaurpeknaki yugnun, ellaita kiimeng pikluki aturluki pitullrulliniata tamaani, tuaten ayuqellrat pitekluku, ayuqetullrat, mulngakluki makucit waten pillerkaat piciqsugnarqukut, pinaqsugnarqukut. Qigcikluki, imutun-wa qigcikellriatun piluki.

MIISAQ: Makut-wa inerquusngalriit; tua-i inerquusngaut waten. Caunrilkengermiu yuum navgurluku-ll' piarkaqenritaa.

Amlleq qanemciulartuq, qaillun-llu temii elliraqluni tuaten nangelrakilria makunek. Caunrilkellni maliggluku tua-i yagiraluki tuaten tamakut angalkut, angalkulget.

Wall'u tua-i piningqerrami tuunraq, tamaaggun ugayalriatun ayuqaqluku tuaten ayuqellria kenkekngainek. Wall'u yung'esciigalivkaumaaqluni, wall'u temii elluarrluni kangarciigalivkaumaaqluni, piningqerrami tuunraq, ca artunrilamiu tamalkuan.

ARNAQ: Maa-i-q' makut waten ayuqellriit tamana tuknillrat wall'u piniat cali ayuqlun' tuaten? Waten-llu una waniwa tuaten ayuqluni?

MIISAQ: Tua-ll' tuunraam aug'um qalarutaanga qanemcillua pegcillminek tuunraminek. Waten-gguq piyunaitelliniuq, alqunaq tua-i pegqualuku. Tuaten-gguq pikuni elluatuqngaitelliniuq. Taugaam-gguq una pinriraqluku, una pinriraqluku. Tuaten-gguq taugaam pikuni nutaan assirciqliniuq. Tua-i ukaqvani piunrillruuq tauna Naparyarrarni uani. Qetunraa-llu yaa-i Kuigilngurmi uitaluni, Yugtun Mumuss'amek pilaqiit.

Pissuutellek-gguq elisngalria, elisngalria tua-i angalkuulartuq. Elisngakni pissuun aturluku ca piyugngaluku. Pissuutailkuni-llu pisciiganaku tauna. Tamakut Yugtaat-gguq kangiit elisngakuniki, taumek-gguq tua-i tamakut nakukucameng tuunraat tuunraam uum tuunraullgutni tamakumek piilkan tua-i

in a way that the other shaman wasn't aware of, he can survive. They say a *tuunraq* is like that.

[God] gave us traditions to live by until the end of the world[2]

Paul John, Bethel, April 2001

PAUL JOHN: I would like to speak a little before we begin. If those of us who are gathered here believe in God, when God created people, he made different races on this earth and gave them all different traditions. There are many people in our world and beneath us. He actually gave us traditions to live by until the end of the world. We are supposed to live by the traditions that God gave the different races until the end of the world. If we believe in God and we have different racial backgrounds and we have a deep respect for our ancestors' traditions, we would not lose them and live by them until the world ends.

But like my *iluraq* [cross-cousin] here just said, at this time, it's like all of us are confused. Even though the traditions that God gave us are honorable and we were to continue following them and not lose them, because we became confused and lost sense, we no longer valued them and started to abandon them. And now we're at the point where we have started to value them again and brought them back from the brink of extinction.

I am not against Christianity at all, but I want to believe in it. Through the understanding that our two priests gave me, Christianity is part of the reason why we are losing our traditions.

The *kass'at* [non-Natives] first created their own form of Christianity using their own way of life. Then those who first created Christianity, when they came from across our land and came among us, they gave us Yupiit Christian traditions that were not our own, traditions that they, the *kass'at* created themselves.

What those two priests said was that we [Yupiit] were supposed to live by our traditional ways that

piqainitekluku piunriryugngaluku. Elisngakuni-gguq taugken elisngalriarukuni nallukiikun yuucini anausngayugngaluku. Tuaten ayuqniluku tuunraq.

Ellam piunrillran engeliinun piciryararkicaaqluta

Kangrilnguq, Mamterilleq, April 2001

KANGRILNGUQ: Ayagnirpailemta qancuaqeryugtua. Agayun ukvekekumteggu, wangkuta waniw' quyungqalriani ukvekekumteggu Agayutvut, Agayun yul'illermini yul'illruuq ayuqenrilngurnek yugnek piciryararkirluki-llu ayuqevkenaki ellarpallraam iluani. Maani ellamteni camani-ll' acimteni tayim' yug'ugaat. Ellam piunrillran engeliinun piciryararkicaaqluta. Ella taugaam piunriqan tauna imna Agayutem taitellra piciryaraq cakuciuluta yugni iquklicuumaarkauyaaqluk', nangyuumaarkauyaaqluku. Tuaten tua-i Agayun ukvekekumteggu cakuciuluta yuucimteggun ciuliamta piciryaraat pirpakluku tamarcetevkenaku ellam iquklitellranun egelrutarkaqsaaqelliniluku.

Taugaam ilu'urma uum ava-i qanqallratun tua-i watua aakulagtengelriatun yugni tamamta ayuqlua watua. Augna qigcignaqsaaqengraan Agayutmek piciryararkiutellerput tamarpek'naku aturturararkaqsaaqellerput aakulagtengelriatun, ellangpengelriatun ayuqellemteggun pikegtakenrirluku, tua-i pegtangitangluku. Kiituan' maa-i tamaqataryaaqellranek ataam nutaan maa-i utelmun pirpaksuumingyaaqluku ayagningyaaqluta.

Wiinga man'a Agayumayaraq ingluksugnaitelaraa umyuama tua-i ukveksugyaaqluku taugaam. Agayulirtegemta malruk taringarcetellriatun ayuqellrakun, man'a maani agayumaciq wangkuta piciryaramta tamautiin-llu ilakelriatun maa-i ayuqaa.

Ellait kass'at Agayumaciliqerraallruut ellaita pimeggnek yuuyarateng aturluku. Tua-i-llu tamakut agayumaciliqerraallret nunamta akmatiinek taingameng tekicamegtekut Yup'igni wangkuta piciryaraqenrilkemtenek Agayumacimek cikirluta ellaita kass'at piliameggnek Agayumaciliameggnek cikirluta.

Tamaa-i tamaggun-llu nutem piciryararput imutun ilumun taukuk agayulirtegemta qanellrak

their ailment, from what I observed, they would become sick again, worse than their previous sickness. That was the work of a shaman who did dishonest works.

But a person who did honest healing work would heal their sickness. They would heal them to where someone didn't have to work on them again.

But those who were doing deceitful works would heal a person, and they would initially get better. But later on, when they started to get sick again, it would be even worse than their previous sickness. One who did dishonest work was like that.

And like he just said, back when they didn't have doctors, these shamans were like their Gods because they believed in them. It is because some of them did good works. They were really like their Gods.

And some would go and get a shaman who healed others and lived in a different village; concerned about their child or partner who was very ill, they would go and get them, even if they lived in another village.

Those Eskimo ancestors of ours were like relatives when I first became aware of my surroundings. And because they didn't have many homes, and they did not have many buildings, a group of relatives lived in one house from what I saw.

And some of the houses did not have stoves before stoves became available. This was before this Western way of life was widespread. That is what I used to see because I've been around for a long time. I just added to what that previous speaker said.

THERESA MOSES: They said that I was born a *yungcaraq* [one who was doctored by a shaman while still in the womb], I was doctored by a shaman. My parents had restrictions.

They called the [things that kept them alive] *napanret*. They'd tell me that my *napaneq* was a wild celery. Because I really did, I got fat when they started to grow, and I got skinny when the plants hardened. That's what used to happen to me.

And I could not eat those wild celeries; now I am starting to eat them in small amounts. When I ate some, even in the smallest quantities, my breathing would get bad, and I did not like the smell of it. Apparently that is how I lived.

camek naulluutiinek wii murilkumallemki ataam ayanqigciaqluni arcaqanruluni taumi naulluutellra. Piciunrilngurkun calilria tuaten tuunrangayag'-am calitullrulliniuq.

Taugken piciulriakun calilriim cali apqucimek naulluutmek aug'aricillrem tua-i tayima tamartelluku tua-i tamana. Tua-i-w' pinqiggviirulluku yugmun taumun aug'arituluku.

Tuaten taugaam tamakut tamaa-i piciunrilngurkun-am calilriit tua-i piqarraami tauna aug'arilteng assirluni, assiriluni. Taugaam kinguqvaarni-am cali ayanqigcami arcaqanrurrluni ciuqlirmi tainqiggluni. Piciunrilngurkun calilria tuaten ayuqucingqellrulliniuq.

Tua-i-ll' ava-i qanellratun Agayutmek tamaani yungcaristetaitellrani, tuunrangayiit taugaam makut Agayutkelriatun tua-i piluki ukvekngamegteki tua-i. Ilait tuaten piciulriakun caliata. Agayutkelriatun tua-i.

Camiuni tuani tuunrangayak aug'arituli nunani allani uitalria aqvaluku-llu ilaita; yum'inek waten wall'u aiparminek naulluussiyaalriamek piaqami aqvaluku tauna camiungungraan pitullruluku.

Augkut ciuliat Eskimo-t ilakutellriatun ayuqellruut wii murilkessagutqerraallemni. Ner'ugarnek-llu waten anglanillrunrilameng, elaavkaarugarnek anglanillrunrilameng ilakutaqelriit enem'i ataucimi quyungqaluteng pitullruluteng, wii tanglallrenka.

Kaminiartaunateng-llu enet ilait, kaminiat paivngarivailgata. Kass'artaryaraq man'a paivngarivailgan. Wii tua-i tamana tanglallruaqa, ak'allaraurcan kinguneqa. Aug'um qanemcia ilaqerluku piaqa wii.

ILANAQ: Wiinga-llu cali yungcaraulua-gguq yuurtellruunga, angalkum tua-i yungcaraqlua. Caneg' inerquutarlutek angayuqaagka taumek.

Tua-i napanritnek pilarait cait tamakut. Wiinga taum ikiitumek-gguq taumek napanirlua qanrut'lallruanga. Pipiatullruama tua-i nauyugararqata-gguq uquringtuunga enriqata-llu-gguq kemgiayaurtenglua. Tuacetun tua-i pitullrulua.

Neresciiganaki-ll' wii tamakut ikiitut; waniw' tua-i neraksuaryaurtanka. Carraungraan nerqallrukumku tua-i anertevkaqlua ikiitugpagniq neqnialkelluki. Tuaten-am tua-i yuullrulliniunga wiinga.

And one time, when I fell down and burst my appendix, someone named Maklagaq healed me. He took it away, he healed the burst part. I fell down and burst my appendix and Maklagaq healed me. But they used to tell me that I was born a *yungcaraq*.

DAVID MARTIN: Shamans who did honest work used to heal [sickness].

THERESA MOSES: They used to call *tuunrangayiit angalkut*. They never called them *tuunrangayiit*, but only *angalkut*. They were *angalkut*.

PAUL JOHN: We should not call them *tuunrangayiit*. But we should call them *piyunarqucilget* [those with abilities]. It is because the name *tuunrangayak* is a judgmental term. We can call shamans *piyunarqucilget*.

THERESA MOSES: And I was admonished, my hair was not cut. My hair was not to be cut. And my parents would not eat certain foods. Trying to get me to live, the shaman would give admonishments for that particular [remedy].

And shamans would tell their parents not to eat certain foods, even though they found them delicious and had eaten them before. Because they followed his admonishments, they no longer ate that certain food. Even though they desired to eat it and found it delicious, they no longer ate what they were told not to eat.

And they took the admonishment of shamans very seriously because those shamans who worked on people healed others for real. But some intended to kill people, and people suffered due to them.

We used to hear they used dogs as their weapons. We heard that dogs were their main weapons, using them to hunt people in their sleep.

You hear that some people say that they were extremely afraid because they were being attacked by dogs in their sleep. Those shamans disguised themselves as dogs and pursued people. Many times, when they'd injure them, they would get a sickness. Shamans used those ways.

Those things we caught in life were good. The comparison that I make for our lives in the past, I say that the *qasgiq* was our church, and the elder men our priests. Only males stayed in the *qasgiq*.

Tuamtellu tua-i canemkun Maklagaam-gguq uum pallallemni-gguq kemka ciamqerrluni caniqamkun 'ggun tua-i tuunrillua. Tauna tua-i aug'allrua, ciamqercimalria mamtellrua. Caniqami wani paallaglua tua-i ca im' navegyaaqluku, tua-i tuunrillua ikayullruanga taum wani Maklagaam. Taugaam tua-i qanrut'lallruanga yungcaraulua-gguq wiinga yuurtellruunga.

NEGARYAQ: Tamaa-i tamana piciulriakun calilriit aug'aritulriit tuunrangayiit tamakut.

ILANAQ: Tuunrangayiit angalkunek pitullruit. Tuunrangayagnek piyuunaki, taugaam angalkunek. Angalkuuluteng.

KANGRILNGUQ: Tuunrangayagnek-wa tua-i pinarqenricaaqekput tamakut. Piyunarqucilegnek taugaam. Tuunrangayak una imuungami inglukilriaruami ateq. Tamakut tamaa-i angalkut piyunarqucilegnek taugaam wangkuta aperyugngayaaqekvut ikayuritullret.

ILANAQ: Tamaa-i-llu inerquutarlua wii, nuyanka kepsuunateng. Nuyanka kepngaitelliniluteng. Taukuk-ll' angayuqaagka caneg' nerngaitellinilutek. Taum tua-i yuuvkangnaqlua wiinga angalkuum taum inerquutainek inerquuciciqelliniut.

Tamakut-ll' angalkut una neresqevkenaku angayuqaagkenun neqnikengraagnegu, nertullrungraan'gu. Tua-i inerquutaag' atuagnegu tamana nerellra kepluni. Cucungermek tua-i neqnikellrung'ermegen'gu tua-i kepluni neryuirulluku taun' inerquutaat.

Cali-am tua-i inerquutait tamakut angalkut pirpakluki, aug'arituata pipiggluteng pitullruata tamakut calilriit angalkut. Ilait taugken tua-i yuut pitaqnaluki tuqutnaluki, caknerutektulliniluki.

Caskirluteng niitellrat qimugtenek. Qimugtet caskurpalluktullruit niitellrita angalkut tamakut qavaitni pissurluki.

Nauwa tua-i qavangurtulriani qimugtemek alingkacagalria pissaallrani. Tamaa-i qimugtenek amilirluteng angalkut tamakut yugnek pitullrulliniut. Pulengtaq tuaten akngirrluki-ll' piaqatki apqucingaqluteng. Tamakut tamaa-i angalkut tamaaggun, tamakutgun.

Angulput augkut assillruut. Wiinga-ll' tua-i ayuqekutetuaqa augna yuulput qasgiq-wa agayuvigput, angulluat-wa agayulirtait. Anguterrlainarnek tauna qasgiq yugluni.

The boys honored the admonishments of their priests. And we heard that they did not behave badly inside the *qasgiq*. It was filled with all young men. And their priests, their elder men admonished young men not to have sexual relations with women.

And those shamans would use their powers inside the *qasgiq* in the real way. They'd *neqnguarluteng* [request for food to be abundant using their shaman powers], having them ask for a partcular [food to be available]. They'd *taqukanguarluteng* [ask for many seals using their shaman powers]. When they did that, things would be abundant.

They would let them do healing work inside the *qasgiq*. They wouldn't let them [work] in just any place, but only inside the *qasgiq*.

But these days, if they want to laugh inside the churches that replaced [the *qasgiq*], they laugh, and they also clap their hands.

Hearing about the *qasgiq*, they did not play around, did not clap their hands inside the *qasgiq*. And there was nothing lavish inside there whatsoever. It's because we were not wealthy in the past. Because grasses were especially our source of wealth, we really valued them. Because I have not forgotten my past and I did not become aware of my surroundings being wealthy. . . .

Because I did not become aware of my surroundings being wealthy, I am starting to talk about my past. And when those shamans would *neqnguarluteng* [request an abundance of food using their shaman powers] and when they would heal a person, if they were going to heal a person, they would let that person go to the *qasgiq* and would not use just any mat but a kayak grass mat when they tried to heal his ailment. That is what that is.

And sometimes they would heal them in their houses. When they did real healing on them, they would work on them only inside the *qasgiq*. I just spoke of some of what I know.

PAUL JOHN: I briefly said earlier that if we believed in God, we would have held onto the traditions he gave us. What she just said was that God gave her parents the message that they should abstain from eating foods they ate if they wanted to have her for a child. Because they wanted their child to live, they sent that message to God through the shaman with abilities.

The parents followed the rules and stopped eating some foods they normally ate. Because they

Agayulirtemeng tamakut tan'gaurluut inerquutait qigcikluki. Iluani-llu akusrarcuunateng niitellrita qasgim iluani. Tan'gurrarrlainarnek yugluni. Arniuresqevkenaki tan'gurraat tamakut agayulirtaita angulluat inerqurluki.

Tamaa-i-ll' tamatum iluani tamakut angalkut tuunriaqluteng pipiggluteng. Neqnguarluteng cameg' uumek kaigavkarluki. Taqukanguarluteng. Cat tua-i nuuqitarkauvkenateng tuaten pikuneng.

Tamatum qasgim iluani calivkarluki. Nani-ll' allami pivkayuunaki qasgim taugaam iluani.

Maa-i taugken cimia man'a agayuviit makut iluani-ll' ngel'allagayukuneng ngel'allagaluteng patguuruciluteng tuaten unatmegteggun.

Tamakut niitellrit qasgiq akusrarcuunateng patguuruciyuunateng iluani tamatum qasgim. Tukuuvkenani-llu cataunani ilua. Tua-i augkut tukuullrunrilamta avani wangkuta. Can'get makut arcaqerluki tukuutekellruamteki pipiggluki can'get makut arcaqakluki. Wiinga taun' kinguneqa nalluyagutenrilamku tukuulua ellangellrunrilama. . . .

Tukuulua wii ellangellrunrilama kinguneqa qanemciksaurtaqa nutaan maa-i. Angalkut-llu tamaa-i neqnguaquneng yugmek-llu kitugcikuneng, kitugciqataquneng tauna qasgicelluku camek curiryugnaunaku ikaraliitnek curirluku aulukaqluku tamaa-i apqucianek aug'aritengnaqaqluku. Tamana tamaa-i.

Wani-ll' allami enaitni taugaam caaqameng tamaa-i tuunritevka[tullruit]. Pipiggluteng piaqamegteki tamaa-i qasgim iluani taugaam caliaqetulliniluki. Tua-i ava-i nallunrilkengama ilii qanrutkaqa.

KANGRILNGUQ: Ava-i qanqallrulrianga Agayun ukvekekumteggu tuag' piciryararkiutii man'a qeleksallemtenek. Ava-i-am Agayutem *message*-aallinikek angayuqaak ellii una yuksukan'gu nertukiignek iliinek nerenriisqellukek. Tua-i-am tamaa-i yuksuamegen'gu Agayutmun *message*-aartuq tauna angalkumek aprumalria piyunarqucilek tumekluku.

Tua-i maligtaqucamek angayuqaak nertukmek ilait neryuirulluki. Yuksuamegen'gu ukverlutek

wanted that child, the parents believed that God gave them ways to live by and their daughter was born.

He won't become a shaman if he isn't given that ability by God[4]

Paul John, Nick Andrew, Magdalene John, and Alice Rearden, Bethel, January 2006

PAUL JOHN: Now, what question were you about to ask earlier?

ALICE REARDEN: This person has a question.

MAGDALENE JOHN: How did they become shamans in the past?

PAUL JOHN: Although a person desires to become a shaman, he won't become a shaman if he isn't given that ability by God. Only one who God has given that ability will become one of those; only a person who God has given the ability.

There are some people who have the capability to become shamans during our time now, but because there is no one to encourage them, since they know that people aren't in support of them, and they are in hiding, it's hard to tell who they are.

There is also one person whom I suspect in my village [of Toksook Bay], one of the young men. Although it seems that he clearly has the capability to become one of those, because no one supports him, it's hard to know if he's one.

I came to realize [his ability] when I brought him to Bristol Bay with me when I went commercial fishing. I think he had one child or two; during that time he had one child.

When I got up in the morning, I made coffee. Since he was lying back there in the sleeping quarters, when the coffee was done, after it had boiled, I looked inside toward the back and said to him, "The coffee here is ready."

When he came out, when he sat on the small chair, sitting across from one another after filling our cups, when I sat down, he said to me, "I didn't sleep all night." I knew that his ancestors had [shaman] abilities. I said to him, "Why?"

"My child kept me from sleeping, as I was worried about him/her." That's all he told me. Then we drank our coffee, and when we were done, after sitting for a short while, an airplane overhead said

tua-i taukuk Agayutem yuucirkiutiinek angayuqaak, nall'arulluni tua-i unguvainanrani paniag' man'a tekilluni.

Angalkuurrngaituq piyunarqucirkicimanrilnguq Agayutmek

Kangrilnguq, Apirtaq, Magdalene, Cucuaq-llu, Mamterilleq, January 2006

KANGRILNGUQ: Tua-ll' camek apteqatarngacaaqellrucetek?

CUCUAQ: Una apyutengqertuq.

MISSAN: Qaillun-gguq angalkuurtelallruat?

KANGRILNGUQ: Yuk angalkuuyung'ermi angalkuurrngaituq piyunarqucirkicimanrilnguq Agayutmek. Taugaam Agayutem piyunarqucirkicimak'ngaa tamakuugarkauguq, kiimi; Agayutem tua-i piyunarqucirkicimastii, piyunarqucirkaanek piumakii.

Maa-i cali tamakut angalkuuyugngalriit pitangqerrsaaquq makuni ernemteni, taugaam cingumastailameng, nallunrilameng cingumanrilaceteng, iirumauraameng nallunaruartut.

Wiinga-ll' kanan' nunamni ataucimek kamakekngangqelartua, tan'gurraat iliitnek. Tua-i tamakuciuyugngaqapiaryaaqeng'ermi cingumastailami taugaam tua-i nallunalriatun ayuquq.

Taringellruaqa wii malikluku, Iilgayarmun wii ayaulluku neqsuryartullemni. Irniangellrungatuq ataucimek wall' malrugnek; atauciullruuq irniara tamatum nalliini.

Unuakumi makcama kuuvviilua. Tua-i-llu qavarvigmek kia-i inarngiin, kuuvviaq tua-i qaqican, taqngan, qallaterraartelluku, qinerlua kiavet piaqa, "Kuuvviaq-wa una pinarilria."

Tua-i anelraami estuulucuallermun aqumngan akiqliqa'arrlunuk caskapuk imirraarluki, aqumelrianga, pianga, "Unugpak qavanritua." Nallunrilamki-llu ciuliari tamakukuyuungata taum. Piaqa, "Ciin?"

"Irniama qavarcetenritaanga, peng'garrluku." Tua-i tuaten taktalriamek qanrullua. Tua-i-llu yuurqerlunuk taqlunuk uitauraqerlunuk, tengssuun pakem qanertuq, angyama atra

[on the radio] calling my boat's name, asking where it was located, that the wife of my fishing helper had asked him to return home because of an emergency, that his child wasn't well. He knew that his child who was at his village was ill [although he hadn't heard the news]. [*laughs*] I suspect that he has the ability to become one of those [shamans].

NICK ANDREW: That one, the one who I told the story about, the one who had the ability to come back to life; he had been pleading with me all summer at that time, that if I wanted to become a shaman, that he would leave me [his powers].

And he would tell me that if I wanted to be a good hunter, that he could give me the ability to become a good hunter. And he would tell me the following. I had one son [at the time]. "I will not leave my child anything; he has no sense. He will use [the powers] in the wrong way." He would plead with me, and I never agreed with him. He wanted to leave me [his shaman powers].

He did various things, and he would heal broken bones. And if a person's bone broke, he would repair it immediately if it hadn't been touched, if another person hadn't touched it.

And now I think, a while after he had asked me, that I should have agreed to take his power of healing broken bones. Like this person said, indeed a person who hasn't been given that ability will not become one of those.

Our Creator up in Heaven, and some of you have probably read in the Bible, when one of Jesus's disciples cut someone's ear off with a knife, he took it and touched [his ear], and when he let go, there was no cut and there was no blood surrounding it. That ability has been passed down to those people who have the ability to heal with their hands. They say these shamans, if they don't misuse their shaman ability, it will not lead them toward harm. That's it.

PAUL JOHN: My grandchild also asked just now how shamans attain their ability. God who has given us life, who is responsible for our existence, when he has given us life from the time we're inside our mothers' stomachs, he lays out before us the things we will experience until death, only to end when we die. That's why those who have the ability to become shamans, since part of their spirit comes from Him, only ones who he gave the ability to help people like these doctors could be [shamans]. They are called *angalkut*.

aperluku, nantellranek tayima, iqugteka-gguq nulirran *emergency*-rluku utercesqaa, irniara-gguq assiituq. Tua-i irniani kingunermini uitallra naulluullra nalluvkenaku. [*ngel'artuq*] Tua-i tamakuciuyugngalriaruluku tua-i kamakela'arqa.

APIRTAQ: Augna, taun' imna-w' ava-i qanemcikelqa, unguiryugnganilleq; kiagpak qaruqurallruanga tuani, angalkuurcukuma unicivikeciqnilua.

Pinauraanga-llu, picuyukuma-llu picullerkamnek cikirciqnilua. Pinauraanga-llu waten. Qetunrangqellruunga ataucimek. "Augna wiinga yuk'a camek unicivikngaitaqa; usviituq. Iqlutun aturciqaa." Tua-i qarutnauraanga tua-i, angyuunaku wii. Uniciviksuglua.

Catullruuq, enernek-llu tumarcituluni. Tua-i yuum-llu enra ayimeskan kitugciiqaa wanirpaagaq, agturamanrilkan, allam yuum agturallrunrilkaku.

Maa-i-am umyuarteqlartua, kingukuurcan taun' angellrunrilamku, tumarcissuutiinek. Ava-i uum wani nauwa qanelria, tamakuullerkamek cikiumanrilkuni tamakuurrngaitepigtuq.

Piliaqestemta pakmum, tayima-llu ilavci naaqelaryaaqngataa Bible-aani, Jesus-aam pistemi iliita ciutairillrani, nuussimek teguluku ellillrukii unatminek cavvluku, peggluku-llu kilinertaunani, augtaunani-ll' avatii. Tauna kinguvarluni tamakunun unatmegteggun tumarcitulinun kinguvallruuq, kinguvaumauq. Makut-gguq angalkut, angalkuucirteng iqlutun aturpek'naku pikuneng picurlautekarkaqenritaat. Tua-i.

KANGRILNGUQ: Una cali ava-i tutgarqa aptellria qaillun angalkut piuyugngallratnek. Uum Agayutem anerniumastemta yuurcimastemta, tua-i aanamta iluanek ayagluku anernirqamikut, yaavet tuqullemtenun ciunerkamtenun atu'urkaput ellitui, tuqukumta tua-i taugaam iquklitarkauvkarluki. Taumek tamakut tamaa-i angalkuuyugngalriit, elliin cali anernemi iliinek anernengqerrata, makutun maa-i *doctor*-aatun yug' ikayurarkauvkarluku ak'a picirkiumakngai taugaam tamakuuyugngaluteng. Angalkunek aprumaluteng.

That one they called Apangtak was a shaman[5]

John Phillip, Bethel, January 2006

JOHN PHILLIP: Let me add to what he said about that. Indeed, back then, you know the person they called Apangtak in Napakiak? Apangtak was Mumess'aq's father. That one, the one they call Apangtak. He was a shaman. He was a shaman, and I knew that he was.

And with his shaman abilities, he pulled out a dead person, when they asked him to in Qukaqlircaraq downriver back when there were people living there. He made one appear in the *qasgiq* and had them see the apparition, back when there were many shamans. I also saw those with that ability, or those who practiced.

That's something that he worked on. I asked him about it myself, since I heard that he had [taken] a dead person. He did it twice.

Since I asked that person questions directly, I asked him about what I heard when we took a steam bath one day. I said to him, "Apang, I hear that you took a dead ghost." I told him to tell the story if it was true. He laughed a little and replied to me, "My, what lies [you're asking about]!" He replied to me, "What lies." I said to him, "Since I heard about you, I want to hear about that now."

Then he told about what it's like to be a shaman. He said that shamans are like us. They are people like us. He said they aren't actually shamans, but the ones they call *apqarait* [ones that serve shamans], the ones by which they do their work; those stay next to them here, and are the means by which they do their work.

He said the means by which they do their work [makes them shamans]. (He explained what a shaman was like, since you my grandchild want to hear about it.) They watch the actions of that person. He said the means by which a shaman carries out his work, the one who he serves, is here.

He said that he used that ability with care when he was asked to [take] a ghost that had been reappearing at Qukaqlircaraq and one that was starting to be seen during the day.

You know how in the past they said they would encounter ghosts sometimes. And those ghosts

Apangtagmek pilaqiit angalkuullruuq

Ayagina'ar, Mamterilleq, January 2006

AYAGINA'AR: Qanrutkellra augkunek cali ilaqerluku piqerlaku wii. Ilumun wani avani, imna nallunritarci Naparyarrarmiuni Apangtagmek pilallrat-qaa? Apangtak ug'um aug'um Mumess'am aatii. Tauna, Apangtagmek pilaqiit. Tauna tua-i angalkuullruuq. Angalkuullruuq, nalluvkenaku-llu wiinga.

Tamaaggun-llu angalkuuyaramikun tuqumalriamek nugcillruluni, pisqengatni uani Qukaqlircarami tamaani yungqellratni. Pugciluni qasgikun tauna tangertelluku, alangruq imna tamaani angalkut amllellratni avani. Wiinga-ll' angullruamki tamakucilget, tamakucilriit.

Tauna tua-i caliaqellrulliniluku elliin. Aptellruaqa wii tungaunaku tauna taumek tuqumalriamek niitelaamku. Malrurqugnek pillruuq.

Aptelaamku wiinga wani tungaunaku ellii tauna, niitelqa caqerlua maqillemegni aptellruaqa. Piaqa, "Apang', niitelaramken tuqumalriamek alangrumek tegutellruniluten." Qanemcikesqelluku piciukan. Engelaq'erluni kiugaanga, "Aling iqlungruyagnek-lli!" Kiugaanga, "Iqlungruyagnek." Piaqa wii, "Tua-i-wa niitellruamken, tauna niicugluku waniw' pikeka."

Tua-i-gguq, nutaan nalqigtaa tamana angalkuuyaraq. Tamakut-gguq angalkut wangkucicetun ayuqut. Waten yuugut. Angalkuunricaaqut-gguq, tamakut-gguq taugaam imkut apqaraitnek pilarait, kevgiuqengait taukut; wantetuut caniatni tamakut, taukut, calissuutnguluteng.

Tua-i-gguq taum wani pissuutiita. (Nalqigtellrua waniwa angalkum ayuqucia, niicuavet tutgarqa.) Ayuqucia yuum taum murilkelaraa. Tua-i-w' taum yuum-gguq pinini tauna, tamakuulriim angalkuulriim tauna pissuutii tauna angalkuussuutii, kevgiuqengaa, wantuq.

Tuani-gguq nutaan elliin atullrua tamana, murilkelluku, taumek yugmek ellimerrumallermini alangrumek waten alaiqetaalriamek alaingelriamek Qukaqlircarami tangrruuluni-ll' waten erenrani pilriamek.

Iciw' avani iliini-llu unugmi alangrutullrunilaqait. Tamakut alangrut

At that point, he said to him, "Now get me something to retrieve with, two small gaffs made of wood." Using those two, watching his [apqaraun], he took them. That one would just tell him what to do. [Apangtak] said that he was just staying [and doing nothing]. That [apqaraun] was the speaker [who told him what to do]. That's the story he told about himself.

When he took hold of that dead person, he gradually lifted him. When he was about to get that one, he told them, "Because you will not believe it, I will let you see [the dead person]." He lifted it up in the center of all of them. That thing started to look frightening. And he said that the people of the qasgiq, although they were shamans, started to become frightened, and he was also afraid.

When he placed him, when he got to the center, since he was so afraid, [Apangtak] took off running away from it, as he was afraid of it. As he was running, he came upon it, and it was in the same place.

He said that he did that three times. He would run away from it, succumbing to his fear. After the third time [that he ran], that [apqaraun] said to him, "Why do you flee?" [Apangtak] said it was because he was afraid. The [apqaraun] told him not to be afraid, that he himself wasn't working on [the ghost], that [the ghost] wasn't going to do anything to him, to stay where he was.

It so happened that when [Apangtak] would take off, he would go along the periphery of the qasgiq, and he would circle it. And when he got to that place, he would see that one down there. That's how he told the story.

When [the ghost] got to that point, after he asked [the apqaraun] what to do, he told him to confess who was encouraging him to haunt people. [The ghost] named all the shamans inside the qasgiq, naming all of them, saying that he was being coerced by this person and coerced by that person. The ghost asked [Apangtak] to let him go at that time, [telling him] that he would never do it again.

He told him that he wouldn't let him go until he confessed. And he told him that if he didn't confess who it was, "If you don't confess, look at what is in your future." He said that [the ghost] became agonized about where he was going.

When he was done naming all of [the shamans], that dead person cried. He cried when he was about to confess who it was. When he cried, he said that it seemed that he bent down into a bucket filled with water and cried. This is what [Apangtak] said: *?qal-tauryiggluni* [?bending over a bucket to cry].

Nutaan tua-i pillinia, "Kitak' tegussuutekagemnek negcicuaraagnek malrugnek muraggagnek pilegnek." Tua-i-gguq taukugnek aturluni, elliin tangvaurluk' tauna pissuutni tegulukek. Qanrutaqluku taugaam. Ellii-gguq tua-i waten uitaluni. Qanertenguluni taugaam tauna. Tuaten tua-i qanemcikuq ellminek.

Tauna-gguq tua-i tuqumalria teguamiu mayuqaniraqluku. Qanrutlinii piqataamiu tauna, "Asgurayugciquci-ll'-am tangertelluku piciqaqa." Tua-i tuaten mayurtelliniluku qukakaaraagnun. Alingnariluni tauna. Ukut-llu-gguq qasgim yui angalkuungermeng alingengluteng, ellii-ll' tapqulluku alingluni.

Tuaten-gguq tua-i ellillrani, qukakaarallrani, alingvakaami ayakpalria aqvaqurluni qimagluni alingami ellminek. Maa-i-w' ayainanermini piinanermini tekiartaa imumi wani uitaluni.

Pingayurqunek-gguq tuatnallruuq. Qimalaryaaqluku, alingellni niilluku tauna. Tua-i pingayirian taum pillinia, "Ciin ayalarcit?" Alingami-gguq. Pillinia, alingevkenaku elliinun caliaqenritniluku qaill' pingaitniluk', uitauraasqelluku tuani eniini.

Cunawa-gguq-am tamaani ayagartaqami ellii maaggun qasgim mengliikun ekiarakun ayalallinilria, uivluni. Tauna-ll' imna tekicamiu, tauna kanani tangerqerluku. Tuaten tua-i qanemcikaa elliin.

Nutaan tua-i tuaten pitarian, apqerraarluku, pillinia, nalqigcesqelluku kitumun cingluku waten alangruucianek. Taukut-gguq angalkut iquitnek ayagluki aperturturqai, qaqitkacagarluki qasgimi tuani anglkut qaqilluki, taumun cingniaqluni, taumun cingniaqluni. Pegcesqessaaquq-gguq tuani pinqiggngaitniluni tauna tuqumalria.

Qanrutaa, nalqigpailgan peggngaitniluku. Nalqigtenrilkan-llu tua-i qanrutlinia-am taum, "Nalqigtenrilkuvet atam ciunerkan tangerqerru." Nangyaqitellruuq-gguq tauna ciunerkaminek.

Nutaan tua-i qaqicamiki taukut qialliniluni taun' tuqumalria. Nalqigteqataami qialliniluni. Tuarpiaq-gguq qiallermini imumun qaltamun mermek imalegmun pull'uni qialria. Waten-wa qanellrulria: qaltauryiggluni.

When he got up, he confessed that the shaman Ungelralria had coerced him. When he confessed, [Apangtak] said to him, "I am going to let you go to a place where you won't appear in your past life again." That one said to him, "I'm going to let you go to a place where you won't appear and terrorize people again."

He said that while [Apangtak] was watching [the dead person], that [apqaraun] who had worked on him threw him like this, using those [walking sticks], "Esss." He told me, "You know when the water first freezes during the fall, when throwing something at a lake, what is thrown makes noise as it's moving, when the ice is thin, it makes noise as it goes." He said that was how it sounded when he listened. [The ghost] cried and stopped making noise. He said that from that time on, that ghost never appeared again.

When he finished the story, he talked about a time one day on a Saturday when he was living downriver in Napakiak. As he was lying down in the evening, Cimiralria came inside, Joe Chimegalria's father. Cimiralria came inside. [Apangtak] said that he respected that person as he wasn't his piarkaq [teasing cousin]. When he went inside, he said to him, "Now, Apang', tomorrow..." Since he was going to lead the church service on Sunday, [he said] "I want you to help me, and I want you to say what you want to say, what you have in mind."

When he told him that, since all the people of that village knew that he was a shaman, he couldn't think of anything to say. When he would think about what to say, he would get held back [by the fact that he was a shaman]. He couldn't think of anything to say. He couldn't think of anything good to say, as they all wouldn't believe him, as they knew that he was a shaman.

He stayed, and when he tried to think of something good to say, he would end up with that thought. As he was sitting there, the surrounding area that he was looking at . . . I used to see his small home, the home that belonged to his son-in-law, his daughter's home. The inside of that little home wasn't good, and it wasn't attractive to look at.

As he was staying, and he said that he didn't seem to be sleeping, as he stayed like this, from the bottom up, that small house started to look better, and it started to look nicer inside, and the whole place started to look joyous. As he watched, when that whole house became that way as he watched,

Tua-i nutaan makcami nalqigtelliniluni taumun angalkugmun Ungelralriamun cingniluni. Nutaan-gguq nalqigcimarian qanrutlinia, "Kinguliurviilngurmun ayagcetqataramken." Taum tua-i pillinia, "Kinguliurviilngurmun ayagcetqataramken."

Tua-i-gguq ellii tangvaurallrani taum tua-i pistiin egeskii waten, taukugnek aturluni, "Esss." Pianga waten, "Iciw' uksuarmi qenuqerraarqami nanvaq milqaq'alriani qalriayaarluni angqin ayalalria, mamkitaqan ciku imna, qalriayaarluni ayalalria." Tuaten-gguq tua-i niicugnillrani. Tayima tua-i qialuni, nepngurrluni, nepailliniluni. Tua-i-gguq tuaken alangrunqigtevkenani tauna, alangruq tauna.

Nutaan iquklicamiu qanerluni, caqerluni waten Maqinermi uani Naparyarragni uitaluni. Atakumi waten inangqaurallrani imna wani Cimiralria itliniuq, Joe Cimiralriim atii. Cimiralria imna itliniuq. Takaqaa-gguq taun' piarkaqenritaa. Itrami pillinia, "Kitak' Apang' unuaqu wani..." Ciuliqagtelliniami Agayunermi, "Ikayuqsugluten piyullerpenek qanqaasqelluten elpet umyuaqekevnek."

Aling tua-i-gguq tang tuani qanrutellrani, una tua-i angalkuucini nallunrilatgu nunat taukut tamarmeng, qaillun qanerkaminek qanerkangesciigatellrulria. Tua-i-gguq umyuangcaryaaqaqami taumun naggnaurtuq angalkunun. Qanerkangesciiganani umyuamini. Pikangesciiganani assilriamek, ukveqngailatni tamarmeng ukut nallunrilatni angalkuucini, tamakuucini.

Tua-i uitaurluni umyuarteqsaaqaqami assiliramek qaneryugluni, tamatumun tut'aqluni. Uitaurainanrani-gguq man'a wani tangellra waten ... enecuallra-w' tanglallruaqa, nengaugan enellra, panian enekluku. Enecualler taum ilua assillrunrituq ilumun, assirpek'nani tangnirqevkenani-llu.

Uitaurallrani qavanrilngacaaquq-gguq uitaurallrani waten, ena man'a aciminek ayagluni assiriyartullinilria waten, waten tangniriinarluni, qaqilluni-ll' tua-i cakneq nunaniqluni tangellra. Tangvallra tua-i, qaqiteqertelluku, qaqican man' enem ilua tuaten tangvallrani, atam quliinek

from up above him, someone spoke, "Apang'," referring to him by name, "Apang', go outside and look at the person who is coming from the river down there."

Long ago there were homes that were situated across from one another in the village of Napakiak, and their church was located behind them. When that one asked him to go outdoors, he went outside that place. When he asked him to look toward the shore, he looked over. There was someone approaching from the direction of the river down there, a terrible person wearing dark clothing, dragging his long hair, the end of his hair being very long.

It was a person approaching down there. He was wearing dark clothing. While he was approaching, his face was that of a human. After a while, as he was watching his face, it transformed into the face of a dog, and it became the face of a wolf. As he watched it approaching, its face transformed into a dog, and it ate all of its surroundings. It put everything that it came across inside its mouth, even logs.

Also, before it reached him, when it stopped [eating everything], its face began to look better, and it became human. As he was watching it, just as it turned human, its tongue suddenly shot out. When it suddenly came out, he saw two villages beyond, and a third village beyond as he watched. When its tongue came out, it jumped over the two villages and landed on the third one.

When its tongue landed . . . when my wife was alive, he told us, this is what he told us. "Now, you two will gossip about people. You will gossip about people." He said when a person says a bad thing, that person . . . (you know how we sometimes say bad things). He said that no matter how far it is, this small tongue has no limit to how far it can reach. His tongue came out, jumped over two villages and landed on the third.

He said that's how it is when a person gossips. When they speak of bad things, when they speak badly about people, that this small tongue will reach a place even though it's far. That person told me those things. And he'd tell my poor wife, that if she tends to gossip about people, that her tongue would be like that. They also say that a tongue is like fire. You know how they liken it to a flame.

He then told him, "Apang', these are things that you will speak of tomorrow when it is your time to

pakmaken qanllinilria, "Apang'" aterpaggluku, "Apang', atam anluten unaken kuigem tungiinek yuk tagelria tangerrsartuqerru."

Naparyarrarmiut ugkut avani ciuqvaarni akiqliqluteng yuullruut enait, agayuviat-wa piani keluatni. Anesqengani taum wani qanrucani anlliniluni tuaken. Ketmun takuyaasqengani takuyalliniuq kuigem unaken tungiinek tagelria, yulkuk man'a tungulrianek aturarluni, nuyarpallrai qamurluni, nuyai tayima iquit takluteng.

Tua-i yuuluni uka-i tailuni. Tungulrianek aturarluni. Atam tainginanermini kegginaa im' yinrauyaaqluni tua-i. Piinanermini atam kegginaa im' tangvainanrani qimugcinraurtellinill', kegluninraurrluni-ll' tangvainanrani taillrani. Tangvainanrani taillrani tuaten elliami, kegginaa qimugcinraurcami, tekitellni makut iqmigluki tamalkuita nerluki. Tekitellni tamalkuita iqmigluki, muraungraata.

Tua-i-am cali tekipailegmi, tamakut pinriamiki kegginaa assiriyartulliniluni, yinraurrluni-ll' tua-i waten. Yinraurteqerluni-am elliin tua-i tangvallrani, yinraurteqerluni-am, ulua una anqertellinilria. Maaten-gguq anqercan piuq nunat ingkut malruin, ingkut-wa pingasuingit yaatiini elliin tuani tangvaurallrani tamaaggun. Ulua anqercami ayallinilria nunat ingkut malruin qeckarluk' pingasuingitnun-llu tull'uni.

Tuc'an ulua . . . aipaqa canritellrani piakuk, waten piakuk. "Kitaki, yuliularciqelriatek, yuliularciqelriaten." Yuk-gguq waniw' qanerrlugaqami assiitellriamek, yuk tauna . . . (tua-i qantulriakut iliini assitellriamek). Waten-gguq tua-i yaaqsingraan alunguksuar una yaaqsigliituq. Alungutii-gguq anelria, tua-i ayalria tuavet nunat malruin qeckarluk' pingasuingitnun-llu tull'uni.

Tuaten-gguq wani yuk qanerrlugaqami pituuq. Assinrilngurmek qalartaqami, yuliuraqami, yaaqsingraan alunguksuaraam uum tekitaarluku. Tamaa-i tua-i tamakunek qanengssitellruanga elliin. Tua-i aipaurluqa-ll' piaqluku tuaten ilumun yuliuryukan tuaten alungutii ayuqeciqniluku. Una-gguq alunguksuar kenertun cali ayuquq. Iciw' ayuqekutelaqiit kenertun.

Nutaan qanrutlinia, "Apang', makut maa-i unuaqu qanrutkarkaten pillerkan tekiskan

speak at church." Without speaking, he answered him in his mind. [Apang'] said that person spoke from above him and was not seen. He said to him, "I will forget those things." When he was thinking that, although he hadn't said anything, he said [he heard] from above, "You will not forget them, you will not forget them. You will speak of them."

After having said that, from up above him, they suddenly sang a song. That is a song from the Moravian church, and he had us [my wife and I] sing it briefly. It has the following words, "Our life will not be for long. It won't be long until Jesus comes. Those who died will be born again to Christ. They will praise the Savior by singing."

He had us sing that song until the end. It is one of our hymns at the Moravian church. They sang that song until it ended from up above him. He said they sounded very joyous. Apangtak is Russian Orthodox. He is Russian Orthodox. But he recognized it.

Since he was about to speak at the Moravian church, he heard that Moravian song. When it ended, he told him, "When you stand tomorrow, these are what you will speak of; you will speak of them from the beginning." When he initially thought, "I will forget them." He answered him in that way, "You will not forget them." When that ended, after speaking, he suddenly twitched. He said he didn't feel like he was sleeping. He said that home was in its usual state, the house that came to look nice inside. When he saw the home, it started to get bright first when he saw it.

That's what he said. Then he explained, that he abandoned his work [as a shaman] at that time. He said that after he spoke of that in church, he stopped practicing it. He abandoned [his ability] to where he would never use it again.

Then he said, he said that he was also told the following. He said that these shamans are okay; these shamans are okay. But you know how the Devil . . . you know how he [sent the ghost away using his powers]. He said that the Devil, however, is bad because he tends to meddle with people. That's how he explained it. He said that these shamans who can help their people are okay, [ones] who can heal people with their hands, through other means.

agayuvigmi." Umyuamikun qanerpek'nani kiullinia. Quliinek-gguq qanlartuq tauna tangrruvkenani. Pillinia, "Nalluyaguciiqekenka augkut." Tuaten-am umyuarteqngan qanenrilengraan quliinek qanrutlinia, "Nalluyagusngaitaten, nalluyagusngaitaten Qanrutkeciqaten."

Tua-i nutaan tuaten pirraarluni, quliinek pakmaken cali atuallalliniluteng yuarutmek. Tamana wani Moravian-aat yuarutkaat, wangkugnun-llu atuqertelluku. Aug'umek waten *word*-angqertuq tamana. "Ak'anurrlingaituq man'a unguvavut. Ak'anurrlingaituq Jesus-aam tekitellerkaa. Kristussaamun tuqulriit unguirarkaugut. Aturluteng Anirturta nanrarciqaat."

Tamana iquklilluku aturcetellrua wangkutnun. Yuarutemteni uitauq Moravian-aani. Iquklilluku tua-i yuarun tamana aturturcetliniluku, aturturalliniluku quliinek. Niitniqpiarluteng-gguq. Ellii tauna Kass'alugpiaruuq Apangtak. Kass'alugpiaruuq. Elitaqluku taugaam.

Tuani tua-i Moravian-aartarni qanqataami tamatumek yuarutmek Moravian-aartarmek pilliniluni. Iquklican-am qanrutlinia-am aug'utun, "Unuaqu nangreskuvet makut maa-i qanrutkarkaten; avaken ayagluki qanrutkeciqaten." Tuaten-am piyaaqellria, "Nalluyaguciiqanka." Aug'utun-am kiullinia, "Nalluyagusngaitaten." Tua-i tamana nutaan iqukliarcan, qanrraarluni, qunglullakalliniluni. Qavarngatenricaaquq-gguq. Man'a tua-i ayuqucia waten ayuqucimitun tua-i man' ayuqsaaqellinill', enecualler' taman' tangnirilleq. Ciumek tamana enem ilua tangniriluni tangellrani tuani.

Tuaten tua-i augna pitaluni qanerluni. Tua-ll' nutaan nalqigtaa, qanertuq, tuaken-gguq tamana tamakuliuryarani nutaan pegtellrua. Tuani agayuvigmi pirraarluni qalarqaarluni tamatumek pegtellrua. Kitak nutaan, ava-i nutaan peggluku tua-i atunqiggngairulluku.

Tua-ll' qanertuq, tua-i-gguq-am nalqigucimallruuq cali. Angalkut-gguq makut canritut; canricaaqut angalkut. Taugaam-gguq una Tuunrangayak . . . iciw' iivkallrukii. Taugaam-gguq un' Tuungrangayak assiituq yuliuryuami. Tuaten nalqigtellinia, nalqigtaa. Makut-gguq angalkut ikayuucugngalriit yum'eggnek, makunun ilameggnun canritut, unatmegteggun, naugg'un.

This person spoke of it earlier. I recalled that, I remembered what Jesus said, and let me use it as an example. You know how he went up to a blind person and just touched his eyes and cured him of blindness. I immediately recalled that, when he spoke of that. [Apangtak] said that those shamans are actually okay, ones who are able to help people around them, with their hands and through other means.

And from what I remember, I'm going to add to it. I suddenly recalled that when he spoke. It is no wonder that God said the following. I suddenly recalled the following. It is no wonder God said, it is said that God created a person in his image, made him capable, made him capable of working with his hands also, made it possible for him to work. This person said it exactly as it is, making him able to do things.

Indeed, we are made the way God made us. When God created a person, He created him, I suddenly remembered it, made him in his image. He said that he had created a person in his image, made him with a shape, made him able to do things, and able to create a person like himself. I came to understand that. My grandchild, because you asked, I'm telling you what I know about shamans.

I also saw shamans, and those using their spirit powers. I saw those. And I used to see ones who were trying to change the weather. I'm telling about those briefly, adding to what your grandfather said about shamans, mentioning the stories that shaman told me. I'm telling about that, what a shaman himself told me directly. Do you understand it?

How God is truly amazing[6]

Paul John, Bethel, January 2006

PAUL JOHN: But there is no one who can prevail over God. And He can easily overcome the Devil. I don't have any shaman powers. But while I was awake during the day like this, one who they said was a shaman targeted me. That shaman targeted me three times. I didn't sleep.

Tua-i ava-i qanrutkellrukii uum. Nutaan atam imna wii umyuaqeqaqeka, Jesus-aam qanellra taun' wangni umyuaqeqallruaqa taun' tuavet ellinguaqerluku. Cikmiumalria iciw' ullagluku iik agtuqainarlukek kiingan assirivkallrukii. Tauna egmian' umyuaqertellruaqa tuaten pillra, qanellrani tamana. Tamakut-gguq tua-i qanrutkai waten elliin, canricaaqniluki tamakut angalkut waten ilameggnek ikayuriyugngalriit, unatmegteggun, nauggun, tuaten.

Tua-i-ll' nutaan cali wii umyuaqerrluku, ilaqerluku piaqa waniwa. Umyuaqertaqa-am wii tauna qanran. Anirtima waten Agayun qanellruuq. Wiinga umyuaqertelqaqa una wani. Anirtima waten Agayun qanellruuq, Agayutem-gguq yuk taqellrua ellmitun ayuqluku, piyugngavkarluku, caliyugngavkarluku unataikun-llu, cayugngavkarluku. Ava-i uum qanrutkaa, cayugngavkarluku.

Tua-i ilumun tuaten taqumaukut Agayutem taqellrakun. Yuk taqngamiu Agayutem taqellrullinia, umyuaqertellruaqa man'a, qaqilluku ellmitun. Waten qanellruuq, ellmitun taqniluku yuk, elucingqerrluku, cayugngavkarluku, ellmitun-gguq yul'iyugngaluku. Tua-i nutaan tamana tuaten ayuqluku taringellruaqa wii nutaan. Aug'utun ava-i pitaluku angalkumek apengssiivet nallunrita'arqemnek tutgarqa qanrutamken aug'umek.

Angalkunek-llu wii tangaalallruunga, tuunrilrianek-llu. Tamakunek tangaalallruunga. Ellaliulrianek-llu tangrraqlua tamakunek. Tua-i augkut ava-i qanemcikqeranka ap'an ikayuqerluku augkunek wiinga aug'um anglkum pillrinek wangnun qanemciinek. Taumek qanemcitamken, qanemcistellemnek tungaunii angalkumek. Taringan?

Iillanarqellra Agayutem

Kangrilnguq, Mamterilleq, January 2006

KANGRILNGUQ: Taugaam Agayun anagngastaituq. Tuunrangayak-llu qacikaa. Wiinga, wii waniwa camek tuunraryaramek carraungraan avaliitua. Taugaam qavarpek'nii ernemteni tua-i waten caumakesciuryaaqellruunga angalkuunitukiitnek. Pingayurqunek cauyaaqlua taum angalkum. Tua-i qavarpek'nii.

MARIE MEADE: People began to doubt their validity.

FRANK ANDREW: Yes. More and more of them gradually turned [to Christianity]. Soon many of them became Moravians. [When they became church members], the older ones were stronger in their faith in God then the younger folks. In the early days, the older Yup'ik people were easily persuaded into believing [in the Word of God].

ARNAQ: Piukenrirluki.

MIISAQ: Ii-i. Caungiinarluteng mat'umun. Kiituan' tua-i Moravian-aanun ukunun pingut. Pingut tua-i ayagyuani uqgellruluteng tungiinun. Ukvertanruluteng ciulirneret tamakut.

Those who are shamans, God helps them in their work, because their work is for the good of all[9]

Frank Andrew and Marie Meade, Anchorage, September 2005

FRANK ANDREW: These shamans, even though they are shamans, God helps them in their work, because their work is for the good of all. I know [God] helps those who do good work for people.

In those days we all were told to listen to God's work very closely and not interfere in their work. That is the nature of their work.

Angalkuungraata Agayutem tua-i assilriamek calillrat pitekluku ikayuumalarai

Miisaq Arnaq-llu, Anchorage, September 2005

MIISAQ: Makut tua-i angalkut, angalkuungraata Agayutem tua-i assilriamek calillrat pitekluku ikayuumalarai. Ikayuumalarai nallunaituq yugnun assilriamek caliriit.

Tua-i imkut ellimertulallrukiikut tamalkumta tamakut caliarat man'a, Agayutem caliara, niicugnilaasqelluku murilkelluku, caliarat ellaita agturavkenaku. Tuaten tamaa-i-nguuq tamana.

Those shamans who had abilities, ones who did a good job were preferred[10]

Frank Andrew, Alex Bird, Joan Hamilton and Marie Meade, Bethel, December 2003

JOAN HAMILTON: Before the pastors and priests came what was *tuunrangayak* [shaman]?

FRANK ANDREW: They say they believed in [a shaman's] ability to heal ailments. And [other shamans] with those abilities would watch them. They say some of their fellow shamans would get jealous over the payments they were given in the form of goods. Some of them, because they did good and helped people using their shaman powers, they would slander and taunt him. They were jealous of him because they would pay him in goods. It's because they weren't given payment themselves. They say that's what they were like.

Those shamans who had abilities, ones who did a good job were preferred, and they would go and get them no matter where they were because they had good healing powers.

Tamakut tamaa-i pissuutellget-gguq tuunrangayiit assirluteng pitullret nakmikluki

Miisaq, Apaliq, Pirciralria, Arnaq-llu, Mamterilleq, December 2003

PIRCIRALRIA: Quliraartet agayulirtet-llu tekipailgata una tuunrangayak caullrua?

MIISAQ: Ukvekellruat-gguq tua-i makunek arenqiallugutnek calilallra. Tangvagluku-llu tua-i tuatnatulit. Ilaita-gguq taugaam tuunrangayaullgutaita ciknakluki aklunek cikirluki waten pilallrat nunulirluki pitekluku-am. Ilaita tamana tuunrangayagyaraat, assirluteng yugmeg' ikayuriluteng pilallrat tuunrangayamegteggun, ikiurrluku picetaarluku piaqluku. Tauna aklunek waten nunulirluku pilallrat pitekluku ciknakluku. Ellait tua-i piyunrilaceteng. Tuaten-gguq ayuqellruut.

Tamakut tamaa-i pissuutellget-gguq tuunrangayiit, assirluteng pitullret tua-i nakmikluki, nani-ll' uitangraata aqvaluki pitullruit assirluteng ikayuriluteng pilallrat pitekluku.

But that's what they would say about them. They said their fellow shamans would be jealous of them and taunt them to do wrong. They were jealous of them. That's why they would end up fighting using their shaman abilities.

ALEX BIRD: Yes, from what I heard, there were two kinds of shamans. One works by helping sick people like a doctor, and some healers even did surgery. They were like doctors.

[A shaman] would heal his sickness, and those *qumigualriit* [those whose fetuses died inside the womb], back then they'd say [women] *qumiguarluteng*, they weren't able to deliver their fetuses; [shamans] would take those out. That is how I heard it up north when they spoke of it.

But they say the other [shaman] was a jealous one; he tended to do things to people, giving them sicknesses. They were jealous of the ones who helped people, just like this person said.

They said they would pay the ones who were like doctors with a small amount of food, and even some tea and some tobacco, or whatever they wanted, with things they would be grateful for. When they had them come, they would [pay] those shamans. It was so that they would help that person, and when their child was ill or their other family members [were ill].

But his fellow shaman would get jealous of him and try to ruin his ability as a shaman in some way. Those two would be adversaries. That [other shaman] tended to counter him, and he would make people sick. He would make that person change in some way.

That's why it was a serious admonishment not to ever offend that person who had power; it was a serious warning back then. That shaman would retaliate against him. If it wasn't that person himself, he would give his family, or his children, or a relative some kind of sickness. Those shamans were malicious because they were jealous. That's how I've heard it.

Tuaten taugaam qanrutkelallruit. Ciknaklukigguq tuunrangayaullgutaita taugaam picetaarluki assinrilngurmek pitullruit. Ciknakluki tua-i. Taumek tuunrangayamegteggun anguyakulluteng pillrullinilriit.

APALIQ: Ii-i, wii niitlallemni malruuguk tuunralgek, tuunrangayak. Aipa yugnek ikayuqngetuuq waten nangteqellrianek-llu *doctor*-aatun waten, pilagturituluteng-llu ilait yungcartet. Yungcartetun ayuqluteng.

Nangyutiinek, imkut-llu qumigualriit, tamaani qumiguarnilaqait ancesciiganaki; tamakunek ancituluteng tua-i. Wii qiini niitaqamteng.

Una-gguq taugken aipaa ciknatarluni waten; waten cayugluki makut yuut, camek nangyutmek cikiryugluki. Tamakut ikayuqngetulit, uum qanellratun watua, ciknakluki tamakut.

Tamakut-gguq *doctor*-aartun ayuqellriit nunulira'arluki canek neqkarrarnek-llu amllenrilengraan, caayurrarnek-llu, cuyarrarnek-llu, canek piyullritnek, quyatekciqngalkaitnek. Taivkaraqamegteki pilarait tuaten tamakut. Ikayuqallerkaa tauna, irniarteng-llu nangteqaqan qang'a-llu cateng, ilateng piaqata avani pitekluku.

Taum taugken aipaan tuunrangayallgutiin ciknakluku tauna tamatum pillra cali, qayuwa tamana tuunraryaraa navgungnaqluku, navengnaqluku qayuw' tua tuaten. Ingluklutek taukuk. Taum tua ingluliumayugluku, waten yugnek canek nangyutaitnek-llu nangyuciryugluki yuut makut. Qayuwa ayuqlircetaqluku.

Tuatelluku inerquutnguuq taman' tuunraq caqaasqevkenaku kina cameg' un' pirralek; inerquutnguqapigtellruuq tamaani. Tua akiyugaa taum tuunralgem. Qayuwa tauna pinrilkuniu, ilii qang'a-ll' irniari, qang'a natii qang'a-llu camek apqucimek pivkararkauluku. Tamakut ikiurlurluteng ciknatarngameng. Wii tuaten niillarqa.

They never called them *tuunrangayiit* back then, only *angalkut*[11]

Frank Andrew, Alex Bird, Marie Meade, and Alice Rearden, Bethel, December 2003

MARIE MEADE: *Tuunrangayak, tuunralek, angalkuq.* If a person had [that ability] can he/she be called all those names? When they say he is a shaman?

FRANK ANDREW: They were *angalkut,* they had *tuunrat* [spirit helpers].

MARIE MEADE: *Tuunralek* [one with a *tuunraq* (spirit helper)], *tuunrangayak* [evil spirit, Devil], did they also call them *tuunrangayak?*

FRANK ANDREW: They didn't call them *tuunrangayiit* in the past, only *angalkut.*

ALEX BIRD: They also called them *tuunralget* [those with spirit helpers].

FRANK ANDREW: They called them *tuunralget.*

MARIE MEADE: What about the term *tuunrangayak?*

FRANK ANDREW: After Christian doctrine depicted them [as evil], they started calling [a shaman] *tuunrangayak.*

MARIE MEADE: Was *tuunrangayak* a term created after the adoption of Christianity?

FRANK ANDREW: Yes.

MARIE MEADE: Before that, did they not use the term *tuunrangayak?*

FRANK ANDREW: I never heard it before that. They didn't call [a shaman] that. They only called them *tuunralget* and *angalkut.*

ALEX BIRD: There was no term *tuunrangayak* back when they didn't have an Agayun [Christian God].

MARIE MEADE: Back when they never used the term Agayun [God].

ALEX BIRD: There was no Agayun [God] back then.

MARIE MEADE: No, back when they only used the term Ellam Yua [Person of the Universe], they never spoke of *tuunrangayiit.*

ALEX BIRD: They never said [those terms]. They only spoke of Esslam Yua [Norton Sound dialect]. I think they knew there was an Agayun [God] back then, and that was Esslam Yua.

MARIE MEADE: But when the priests who brought Christianity had arrived and they brought the Bible, the English term Devil, the one they call the Devil in English, they translated that [into the Yup'ik language] and started calling [the Devil] *tuunrangayak.*

Tuunrangayagnek apaayuitellruit tamaani, angalkunek taugaam

Miisaq, Apaliq, Arnaq, Cucuaq-llu, Mamterilleq, December 2003

ARNAQ: Tuunrangayak, tuunralek, angalkuq. Taukut-qaa, tauna yuk tuaten pitukan tamakunek tamalkuita apaayugngaat? Angalkuuniluku?

MIISAQ: Angalkuuluteng tua-i, tuunrarluteng.

ARNAQ: Tuunralek, tuunrangayak, tuunrangayagmek-llu-q' apaatullruluki?

MIISAQ: Tuunrangayagnek apaayuitellruit avani, angalkunek taugaam.

APALIQ: Tuunralegnek-llu.

MIISAQ: Tuunralegnek.

ARNAQ: Una-mi tuunrangayak?

MIISAQ: Tua-i nutaan mat'ukun agayu[macikun] nalqigtellrakun tauna tuaten aterpagtelangaat tuunrangayagmek.

ARNAQ: Mat'um-qaa nutaram piciryaram Agayumacim pugtellrua tauna tuunrangayak?

MIISAQ: Yaa.

ARNAQ: Ciungani-qaa tuunrangayak apaayuitellruat?

MIISAQ: Ciungani niicuitellruaqa. Apaayuitellruat. Tuunralegnek taugaam piaqluki angalkunek-llu.

APALIQ: Tuunrangayagtaunani Agayutaitellermeggni tamani.

ARNAQ: Agayun apaaluku qanyuitellermegni.

APALIQ: Agayutaitellruuq tamaani.

ARNAQ: No, Ellam Yuanek taugaam qanaatuluteng pitullermegni Tuunrangayagnek qanyuitellruut.

APALIQ: Qanyuunateng. Taugaam Esslam Yuanek taugaam tua-i. Nallunrilngurtun Agayucetangqellra tamaani pillruyugnarqut, tamana Esslam Yua.

ARNAQ: Taugaam Agayumacimek iluvautellriit agayulirtet tekicimariata ukunek qaneryaranek Bible-aanek tekiulluteng, Kass'atun pimallra una, Devil, Kass'atun pilallrat una Devil-aq qanrutkelallrat, taukut mumiggluku tuunrangayamek apaangluku.

ALEX BIRD: Because the ones who explained those terms are [people] of God, after [saying] they were from hell, [they] called the ones who are of hell *tuunrangayiit*.

ALICE REARDEN: What did they call shamans who did evil works, shamans who did evil works? Did they just call them *angalkut*? Did they have a name? Good shamans and those who didn't do good work, were they called something?

MARIE MEADE: The term *umyuarrliqellria* [one who has malicious or evil intent], one who is malicious, is *umyuarrliqellria* only used for *angalkut*? If a person does bad, is that [one] *umyuarrliqluni* [one with malicious or evil intent]?

FRANK ANDREW: Yes. *Umyuarrliqsaraq* [to have malicious or evil intent] is from Satan. That's why it is an admonishment. And [evil works] by Satan can work [in someone] when one hasn't talked about them. But one is friendly toward others, even though they think of them in [a malicious] way.

And now, they spoke of an old person named Asgulria, and also Tairtaq, a shaman from the Kuskokwim. [They spoke of] those two shamans who had good intentions. They say those two had no evil intentions toward people at all. And when people gave them goods for payment, they'd have them decrease the amount of goods saying there were too many goods given for their *?yugyarat*.

Tairtaq and Asgulria weren't the type to try to swindle someone. They say that Asgulria was from Canineq [the lower Kuskokwim coast]. And Tairtaq was from the upper Kuskokwim River.

They say those two had very good intentions, never thinking about harming anyone.

A person exposes how he is by what he does, by his actions. An elder, one who has a mind that isn't like ours can understand how he is. They told stories about those two; they were actually shamans.

But back in those days, I think God helped a person who was like that. It's because he did good works, even though he was referred to as a shaman. One who helps people in a good way doesn't come from anywhere else. That is how it was. That is what I think.

They say Tairtaq, even if they had drowned in water for a year, he would bring them back to life. And when they [drowned] in the fall, he wouldn't let the Kuskokwim River freeze where [they had drowned] back when he was a shaman. He kept it

APALIQ: Elliin Agayutem pikngamiki imkut nalqigcetellri taukut kenerpagmek nunaliraqluki, kenerpiim pikestai tuunrangagmek aciqai taukut.

CUCUAQ: Camek-mi angalkuut assinrilngurmek calialget aptullruitki, assiilngurnek caliaget angalkuut? Angalkunek-qaa kiingan piaqluki? Atengqellruut-qaa? Assilriit angalkuut, assilriamek-llu calinrilnguut atengqellruut?

ARNAQ: Una wani umyuarrliqellria, umyuarrliqluni, umyuarrliqellria angalkunun-qaa atauq? Assirpek'nani pikuni umyuarrliqluni?

MIISAQ: Yaa. Tuunrangayiim tamana pikaa umyuarrliqsaraq. Taumek inerquutaulria tua-i. Waten anteksaunaku-llu tua caliyugngaluni Tuunrangayiim pia. Tua-i taugaam yugnikluki-ll' makut tua-i tuaten umyuartequteng'ermiki.

Tua-i-ll' augna Asgulriamek atengqelleq ak'allaq qanrutkumalartuq, Tairtaq-wa cali tauna tuunrangayak Kusquqvagmi. Umyuaqellriignek taukugnek angalkugnek. Yugmek iqlutun umyuarrliquciyuitqapiarlutek-gguq. Aklunek-llu-gguq cikirturlukek akiliraqacetek ilangarcetaqluki, yugyaraatnun mat'umun anagarusnganiluki.

Teglessaalriaruvkenatek-gguq Tairtankuk Asgulria-llu. Asgulria-gguq Caninermiungullruuq. Tairtaq-llu pagkumiunguluni Kusquqviim kangrani.

Taukuk-gguq umyuaqegqapiaralriik, qaillun yugmeng umyuartequcinrilngurmek iqlutun pillerkaanek.

Yuk tua-i caliamikun manimatulliniami, caurallmikun. Ciulirnerem tua-i taringyugngaluku, wangkucicetun umyuangqenrilnguum. Taukuk tua qanemcikumalartuk; tuunrangayauyaaquk.

Taugken tamatum nallini tayima tuaten ayuqelria Agayutem ikayumalaryugnarqaa. Assilriamek calillra pitekluku angalkugmek aterpagingangraan. Ikayurilria assirluni naken kingunengqenrituq. Tua-i. Tuaten umyuarteq'lartua wii.

Tauna-gguq tua-i Tairtaq allrakurrluteng-llu kit'ellrungraata mermun unguirtelluki utercecitullruuq. Kusquqvak-llu uksuarmi piaqata cikuvkayuunaku taum nallii angalkuullermini tamaani. Piurluku-gguq elliin, taugaam

that way, but he wouldn't say anything. But when the people asked him [to save that person], he would then bring him back to life, he would give him breath.

They say Asgulria would do the same thing, too. He would also replace their lungs by operating in the *qasgiq* by cutting them open.

And Puyulkuk who I spoke of earlier, he used to heal big wounds on people. And he healed one who had a big cut in my presence. But he didn't heal [the wounds] all the way. They say [the wounds] throb when healed all the way. He would heal wounds.

He healed one who got a big cut down at Kwigillingok. He left a little bit [of the cut unhealed]. He said that's how he would treat them. [The wound] wouldn't throb in pain for those who were healed that way. But if he healed [the entire wound] it could throb in pain. But he would have them rest until the inside healed, even though he had healed them. He would tell them to abstain from work and to rest so it could heal.

qanyuunani. Ukut taugaam pisqelluku piaqatgu nutaan nangrutaqluku, utercetaqluku, ataam tua-i anernengevkarluku.

Tauna-llu-gguq Asgulria tuatnatullruuq cali. *Lung*-inqigtaqluki-llu, pugtautait cimiraqluki qasgimi pilagturluki.

Augna-ll' ava-i Puyulkugmek watua pilqa, kilirpalrianek mamcitullruuq. Takumni-ll' mamcillruluni kilirpalriamek. Taugaam qaqilluki mamcuitellinii. Ngell'ugtutuut-gguq qaqilluki piyaaqaqata. Mamcitulliniluni tua-i.

Uani Kuigilngurmi mamcillruuq kilirpalriamek. Carraquineq taugaam tua-i pinritqerluku. Tuatnalarai-gguq. Ngell'ugtuyuunateng tua-i tuatnalriit. Tamalkuan-gguq taugken pikani ngell'ugturyugngaluni. Tua-i taugaam uitavkatullinii qamna mamnatkaanun, mamteng'ermiki. Inerqurluki caliksaunaki uitasqelluki, mamciisqelluki.

Stories from Nelson Island

They killed that shaman again and again, but he'd return[1]

Tim Agagtak and Ruth Jimmie, Nightmute, July 1985

TIM AGAGTAK: The shamans of the past; once in a while some people became shamans in those days. I was born just before they disappeared. During their transformation and becoming visible to others as shamans, they continously used the drum, when they were about to become shamans.

RUTH JIMMIE: Did people like them?

TIM AGAGTAK: People liked them because they helped heal people just like they do at hospitals today. They were doctors.

They worked just like medical doctors. A person would be near death, but when just one shaman doctored him, or two doctored him, he would heal and get well again.

Today, [this type of healing] is prohibited. Today, we view this kind of healing as useless. We think of it as useless and evil.

When a person was sick, or if the child of a couple was sick, the parents of the child would bring him to a shaman with something as payment. [Shamans] didn't do work without payment. The amount of effort they put into their work was according to the payment they got.

They were shrewd. When [a shaman] wasn't satisfied, he would not save his patient, too. Sometimes, if he was satisfied, though the patient's condition was serious, he'd rescue the patient and save him from dying from a serious condition.

For instance, [a shaman] might tell someone what he needed; if that person didn't comply, that person would soon get sick. [The shaman] would come to that person in dreams. The shaman was the one who was [making him sick]. That person would know [it was the shaman] through his dreams.

All shamans did work like that. Some were evil. And some did good work. Some used their power to cast evil on others.

Down in Qalullermiut. . . . I knew his name, but I can't remember it now. The shaman who was killed over and over. After being killed, he'd return from the dead. It was down there below

https://doi.org/10.5876/9781646427314.c013

Qaluyaarmiut Qanemciit

. . . .

Tua-i-gguq tuqutelaryaaqaat tauna angalkuq, utertaqluni

Akagtaq Angalgaq-llu, Negtemiut, July 1985

AKAGTAQ: Tamakut angalkullret; yuut ilait caqalriit angalkuurtelalliniut tamakut.
Angumcakarluki ellma. Waten-gguq alairyugararqameng cauyarturangluteng,
angalkuurteqatarqameng.
ANGALGAQ: Assikaqluki?
AKAGTAQ: Assikluki anirtuituata *hospital*-aatun. *Doctor*-auluteng.

Doctor-aatun ayuqluteng. Yuk tua-i tuquqatarraartelluku tuunriskani angalkum
ataucirraam, iliini-llu malruulutek tuunriskagni, tauna yuk assiriluni.
Mat'um nalliini atuyunailnguuguq. Cakaunrilnguq mat'um nalliini. Caungairutellria,
assiilnguq.
Tua-i waten yuk una nangteqkan, wall'u irniarak ukuk assiilkan, tua-i taukuk
angayuqaagken camek atu'urkamek natkaanek ellimerrucirluku, nunulirluku tauna angalkuq.
Akiinateng piyuunateng. Ellimerruteteng taugaam aturluki.
Ikiuluteng. Iliita-gguq qatngunritaqami, anirturpek'naku-llu. Iliin-llu-gguq tua-i qatnguquni
anirtuyunailengraan assirivkarluku.

Tuamtellu tua-i, iliirarraarluteng yuut iliitnun; niitenrilkaceteng, tauna imna niitenritleq
ikiurrluni apqucingluni. Qavamikun qavanguqaqluku. Taum tua-i angalkum pivkarluku.
Qavamikun taugaam nalluvkenaku.

Tuaten tua-i ayuqluteng angalkut tamarmeng. Ilait ikiuluteng. Ilii-gguq taugken assirluni
tua-i. Ilii-gguq taugken umyuarrluuluni.
Uani-am Qalullermiuni. . . . atra nallunritellruyaaqaqa. Tauna tuqutaulguli angalkuq.
Tuquqaartelluni tua-i utertaqluni. Ug'um ua-i Qalullrem aciani. Tua-i-gguq tuqutelaryaaqaat

https://doi.org/10.5876/9781646427314.co13

Qalulleq. They killed that shaman again and again. As time went by, he woke up quicker and quicker from death.

I used to hear people talking about [that particular shaman].

One day they killed him. After they killed him, they gouged out his eyes. Numerous times they'd attack him and break him apart when they killed him, even severing his legs. After that, he'd return with no scars and no pain.

One time they killed him; in those days people used clay lamps for light. Once they killed him, they gouged out his eyes and put them in a clay lamp and placed that lamp upside down on a piece of wood. Back then, shamans were able to perceive everything. But this time the shaman didn't return and was gone for some time.

What was his name?

He was gone and never returned. Finally . . . this was at the time when people moved down the coast during harvesting time. The village of Qaluller-miut would be totally empty during that time.

One day one of the people went to Qalullermiut to get food that they had left behind. People had storage racks with thick split wood as a base. The split wooden panels were fixed on poles. The [elevated] storage cache was called a *mayurrvik*.

The person who was getting food, when he heard someone talking he stopped and listened and heard someone saying that he'd been looking for his eyes and had not seen them. [The shaman said,] "I wonder where they put them that I can't find my eyes?"

This was in summer. Right after summer came. The person looked, and there in front of the *mayurrvik* . . . I can't remember his name at this time. That shaman has a name. He was a bad shaman. Since they didn't like him, they would repeatedly kill him because he was malicious. But he'd return after he was killed.

The person looked and saw [the shaman] standing in front of the *mayurrvik*. He stood elevated above ground with snowshoes and holding a walking stick. He said, "Where have they put my eyes that I can't see them? Would you happen to know where they are?" [The shaman] asked the person.

Back in those days people were cautioned not to respond when the dead appeared and tried to communicate with them. They say when one responds verbally to their inquiry, one would be unable to speak anymore.

tauna angalkuq. Cukariinarluni-gguq taugaam unguillra.

Una tua-i qanemcik'lallruat.

Tua-i pivakarluku-am tuqutelliniluku. Tuqucamegteggu-llu iik ikugglukek. Navgurluku-llu-gguq piyaaqaqluku, tua-i navguk'acagarluku, iruk-llu keplukek. Utertaqluni calliqengsaarpek'nani.

Caqerluku tuani tuqucamegteggu; kenurrangqetullruut qikunek. Iik ikugglukek tamakucimun eklukek muriim qainganun palurutlinilukek. Cat nallungaunaki pituyaaqluteng tamaani tua-i angalkut. Tua-i tayima qayuwa utercuunani pilliaqellria tauna tua-i.

Atengqellria imat'anem kitumek tauna?

Tua-i tayima tua-i utercuunani. Kiituani . . . upagatullratni un'gavet ak'a tamaani. Yuirulluteng-llu tua-i ugkut Qalullermiut.

Caqerluni tua-i tauna yuut iliit aqvailria neqnek unitameggnek tuavet Qalullermun. Mayurrviggaat imkut, pikegkut tusngallrit muragat ellegluteng. Muragat imkut tusngalleqluki, kanagarluteng. Tauna mayurrvigmek piaqluku.

Tauna yuut iliit neqnek aqvailria qanelriamek niicami piqalliniuq, iigni imkut tayima yualaryaaqnilukek, tangerrsunritnilukek. "Natmun tayima pilriim iigka imkut nataqsunripakarcia?"

Kiagmi. Kianrakun. Piqalliniuq taum mayurrviim ciuqerrani . . . atra-am waniw' kis'arciaqa. Atengqertuq tauna angalkuq. Umyuarrliqellria ikiulria yuk. Kenkenrilamegteggu tua-i tuqucaaqaqluku assiilan. Taugaam tuquqaartelluni utertaqluni.

Piqalliniuq mayurrviim ciuqerrani nangerngalria. Ayarurluni ellarrlainarmi tanglurturluni. Qanellrani tua-i, "Natmun waniwa imkuk iigka pikegteng tangerrsunripakarcia? Nallunritqanritagken-qaa elpet?" Apcaaqluku.

Tamaani waten tangrraqameng tamakunek yull'ernek inerquutaqellrulliniat kiusqevkenaku. Tua-i-gguq kiukuniu yuk tauna qanernanrirluni, qanerciigaliluni.

He suddenly thought, "I've heard warnings not to respond to the dead when they come to you." Then at the end of that thought, the [shaman] out there said, "You will not lose your voice. Tell me where they are." Here he had not said what he was thinking. He then told him that he didn't know where they were.

[The shaman said,] "I'm holding back though I want to retaliate by putting poison on the food these people are eating." It was because the ghost had family and children there [in that village].

In those days, women became partners to some bad shamans out of fear. [Women] knew that they wouldn't let them live if they refused to marry them. They say [shamans] were evil. And here they couldn't even catch when they hunted. Animals, fish and food stayed away from them.

[The shaman] said that since he had gotten desparate, he was going to his *mer'umavigkaq* [one to whom he would pass on his powers].

When [the shaman] turned his head, the man saw one eye here [between his eyebrows]. [The eye] seemed to be rolling. [As he looked at the eye momentarily] it looked like it was rolling fast. [The shaman] said that though he wanted to return to the village, he wasn't going to because of his eye, that children might be afraid of him.

RUTH JIMMIE: These two eyes were gone?

TIM AGAGTAK: There were hollow spots where his eyes used to be. He just had one eye here. He said that because children might be afraid of him, he wasn't going to return [to the village]. He said he was about to leave and go toward Puqlanaaq to his *mer'umavigkaq*.

[The shaman] then lifted his walking stick on one side and poked it in the ground and lifted the other and poked it in the ground on the other side. He was wearing snowshoes.

Then he pulled his leg forward and stepped right in the air. And just as he pulled his other leg, the big wooden plank started springing back and forth, bending easily like the wooden rib of a fish trap. It was very pliable. [The wooden piece] was very thick and couldn't be bent by anyone.

[The shaman] started walking away elevated above ground, using his walking sticks and wearing snowshoes. When he poked his walking sticks on the side, they'd make a crackling sound. You know, when wood is poked into snow it makes a loud crackling sound. It sounded just like that. He started going away, making a loud crackling sound. He left.

Umyuarteqa'artelliniuq, "Makut-ggem waten tangrruugaqata tuqullret kiusqevkenaki inerquituut." Umyuarteqellra-llu-gguq iqukliyuciatun keggna qanlliniuq, "Qanernanrirciqenrituten. Aperturkek." Wall'u-gguq kiingan umyuartequq. Nutaan kiuluku nallunilukek.

"Tua-i-wa arenqialnguq waniwa tua-i ukut wani nunat neqiitgun akinauryungramki uitalrianga." Irniangqelliniami, ilangqelliniami tauna tamalkuuluni aiparluni-llu.

Tamakut-llu arnat ikiungraata tamakut aipaqsagutetulliniamegteki alikluki. Unguvavkarciqenrilani taum qessaksaaqekuniu. Ikiuyaaqut-gguq tua-i tamakut. Ima-llu-gguq-qaa pitetuluteng. Pitesciiganateng, cat paivngatevkenaki.

Waniwa tua-i mer'umavigkaminun ayakatarniluni arenqialami.

Takuyaqallrani-gguq tungminun, wani-gguq iinga atauciq. Tuarpiaq-gguq tang akalria tangvallra. Tua-i akagnganani. Waniwa-gguq utercung'ermi mikelngurnun taugaam tatamurratek'larnayukluni waniw' uterteqatanrituq una pitekluku iini, alikelarnayukluni.

ANGALGAQ: Ukuk-qaa cataunatek?

AKAGTAQ: Iillrek ukuk ilutulutek imaunatek. Uuggun taugaam iiluni ataucirrarmek. Tua-i waniw' mikelngurnun tatamurratek'larnayukluni uterteqatanritniluni. Waniwa tua-i ayakatarniluni amavet Puqlanaam tungiinun mer'umavigkaminun.

Tua-i maavet ayarumi aipaa kapulluku, inglua-llu cali kapulluku. Tangluturluni.

Irumi-llu aipaa cayugluku, ellamun maavet tull'uni. Inglua-llu cayukii, tamana imna muragpall'er petengllialliniluni, tuarpiaq-gguq cigyak. Tua-i qetutkacagarluni. Ellek'acagalria-gguq-wa yuum-llu perrngaunaku.

Ayangartelliniuq ellarrlainarkun ayarurluni tangluturluni. Tua-i-gguq ukuk ayaruk kaputaqatek qiaryiggnaurtuk. Iciwa imkut muragat qanikcarmun kaputaqameng qiarecpalalriit. Tuaten-gguq tua-i. Qiarespagtaarluni ellarrlainarkun ayangartelliniuq. Tua-i tayima.

So, not too far from that time, one of people who had gone to Nushagak said that over there . . . back then when people went to the place with a few white people.

I can't remember his name now. The name is easy to remember, but I can't remember it now. He has a name, too.

[In Nushagak] there was a drummer singing the song, and the middle parts of the songs he sang were the same ones that the shaman they killed used to sing. They were the songs [that shaman] sang. And no one [from the shaman's village] had traveled to that place.

So the person asked people there where they learned the songs. [They said,] "These are the songs of the child conceived by a couple who finally were able to conceive after a long time." [The songs were] from their only child.

[The shaman] seemingly had planted himself in the [woman] who couldn't have children, and he became the couple's child. In time their son became a shaman. He was from Qalulleq downriver.

RUTH JIMMIE: How did he go in [the woman] and disappear?

TIM AGAGTAK: He went inside the wife. They say that woman who couldn't conceive finally got pregnant with that child. When the baby was born, he was [that shaman].

The songs he sang were songs [the shaman] used to sing [when he was in his original body] when he drummed. Some songs were different, but when he started singing, the child sang the shaman's old songs.

Some people looked almost alike, just like they do today. There were shamans in every community.

I knew his name, but can't remember it now. Few things sink in my memory like now. I know his name will pop up in my head later on.

Long ago there were shamans among our people.

A couple who couldn't have children[2]

Tim Agagtak and Ruth Jimmie, Nightmute, July 1985

TIM AGAGTAK: I've heard another shaman story. There was a shaman . . . people tell stories about them because of their experiences. People tell

Amani, tua-i qakuan' yaaqsigpagpek'naku tamana, Iilgayarqaqelriit tamaavet iliit qanlliniuq, amani-gguq tang . . . ayagatullratni kass'aksuaraat tungiitnun.

Atra-tang-atak' kis'arciaqa. Nallunaitkacagaryaaquq taugaam nalluyaguartaqa. Atengqertuq atam cali tauna.

[Ilgayami] atulgat tauna cauyalria imum taum tuqutellrata, yuarutait pikuratullratni, ak'a tamaani atuaquratullratni, tamakunek tamaa-i akunlirturluki. Kia taum yuarutellri. Kina-llu im' ayaksaunani tamaavet.

Tua-ll' tua-i apteqerluki taum naken makut yuarutet elitellratnek. "Ingkuk-wa yungyuilnguuk yuagnek maa-i yuarutai." Irniaragnek ataucirraam.

Taukugnun yungyuilnguugnun pulalliniluni tua-i aanaklukek taukuk. Qetunraqngagni angalkuurrluni alairyuarluni pillinilria. Uaken ua-i kingunerluni Qalullermek.

ANGALGAQ: Qaillun-tam pulaluni?

AKAGTAQ: Tua-i-wa arniinun taumun. Tauna-gguq yungyuilnguq qingayuilnguq qingallruuq taumek tua-i. Anlliniuq taunguluni tua-i.

Makut-gguq maa-i yuarutai, taum tua-i atutukai cauyarqami, atulaq'ngai tua-i makut. Ilait-gguq allauyaaqut taugaam-gguq taum amani atularai.

Yuut ak'a tamaani ayuqerrlullruameng, waten tua-i maanicetun. Angalkurluteng tua-i yuut tamarmeng.

Atra-am nallunricaaqaqa taum. Waten kis'arcila'arqa carraq. Atam tua-i waniw' neq'aqerniarqa atra taum.

Waten tua-i ak'a tamaani cat tua-i piyaaqelriit angalkut.

Yungyuilnguuk

Akagtaq Angalgaq-llu, Negtemiut, July 1985

AKAGTAQ: Cali-am qanemcimek niitellruunga man'a maa-i angalkuq iqukluku. Angalkuq atam tauna . . . tua-i-wa atulallruata qanrutkelaqait,

stories about things they've seen and experienced and don't make up lies. They've also said that the land once had sinkholes where there were people.

Since [these stories] are old, and since it's been a while since I stopped hearing about them, I'm starting to forget some things. I have told [some stories], but not in their complete form.

I used to hear them telling this amazing story.

There was a couple who couldn't have children. Every time the wife delivered, the child would die. The babies would die not long after they were born.

The shamans carried out all kinds of work. And people believed in their work.

When their child died once again, when the infant died, the parents asked a shaman to try to bring it back to life.

[When he asked the shaman], since the father [of the child] was a successful hunter, he wanted to try [and work on the dead child] since he paid him many items. He offered the shaman everything a person would need since the successful hunter was a great provider. But he couldn't have children.

[In the *qasgiq* the shaman] had them put [the body of the child] down there. They laid him down on his back on the plank flooring over the firepit. [The child] was dead; he wasn't breathing and was dead.

I used to see shamans going in circles [around their patients] when they did their doctoring. They always had drummers and singers on the side singing ritual songs.

After [the shaman] did an incantation several times he said, "Now, would the child's parents . . ."

In the *qasgiq*, there were lamps. The lamps were put on stands they called *nanilrat*. Up on top, they'd have a little panel where the clay lamp would sit. I used to see [lamps] like that, too. There was one on each side of the room.

RUTH JIMMIE: Were they toward the entrance?

TIM AGAGTAK: No, they were across from each other midway on the sides of the room away from the entrance. The door was out there. They had lamps on the sides situated across from each other.

And sometimes if the *qasgiq* was large, there was a third lampstand toward the back. Seal oil was used for fueling the fire. I used to see [lamps like that] before gasoline was introduced. They used those for a while when I was little.

qanemcik'laqait. Iqluqutekevkenaki atulallermeggnek yuut qanemciuralalriit. Angayaangqellruyaaqniaqluku tuaten man'a nunavut Yup'ignek.

Ak'allaurtengvakaata, niitnanriuciat akaurpakaan ilait unimqaqunganka. Taugaam tua-i ilait qaqimaqapigtevkenaki qanrutkeqalaranka.

Tauna-am cali caperrnarqelria qanemcik'lallruat.

Taukuk-gguq yungyuilnguuk. Tua-i irniyaaqngami tauna tua-i irniara tuquaqluni. Ak'anivkenateng-gguq tamakut tuqunaurtut mik'nateng.

Qaillukuanrulliniameng tamakut angalkut. Tua-i yuut-llu ukvekngamegteggu.

Tauna-am tua-i yugtek tuquan, mikcuar tauna tuquan, ayumian-am utercetaaresqelliniat angayuqaagken.

Tua-i nukalpiaruami tauna atii piciatun ellimerrucirluku, tua-i naspaaqeryugluku, arenqialata tamakut aklut nunuliutai ellimerrutai. Tua-i piciatun yuum atu'urkai, nuuqitenritliniami tauna nukalpiaq. Taugaam yung'esciiganani.

Kanavet tua-i ellivkalliniluku waten. Kanavet taklarrluku nacitet qaingatnun. Tua-i tuqumaluni; tua-i anernerunani tuqumaluni.

Tua-i uivvaarluteng tanglallruunga angalkunek tuunrilrianek. Cauyarturluki taugaam yuarullugnek aturluteng.

Tua-i tamaa-i tuunriuraqerluni pilliniuq, "Kitak' tua-i ukuk wani angayuqaak . . ."

Kenurrangqetuameng tamakut qasgit. Nanilrarluteng, napautarrarluteng nanilranek piaqluki. Pikaggun kangmegteggun elliqeryararluteng qikurraat. Wiinga-ll' tanglallruluki tamakut. Akiqliqelriignek.

ANGALGAQ: Amiigata-qaa tungiini?

AKAGTAQ: Qang'a, maani taqumi amiigem tungkenrilkiini. Amik-wa uani. Maani taqumi akiqliqelrianek kenurrangqetuluteng.

Iliini-llu angkan qasgiq kiaggun cali pingayirlukek. Uqupianek uqirluki taqukinrarnek. Tanglallrulua-llu wii tamakunek kaassartaitellrani. Anguqacuaqerluki ellma.

Then [the shaman] told the couple to go behind the lamps, the husband on one side and the wife on the opposite side, behind the lamp. He asked them to be covered with people's parkas. He told them to cover them with only parkas, not other clothing items.

RUTH JIMMIE: The child?

TIM AGAGTAK: The parents. The parents of the small dead child were both covered with just people's parkas. So as instructed, they were covered with parkas.

So, there [they were all covered]. And the child was undressed and without clothes, laid on its back on the floor back there toward the wall.

I used to hear people telling this story. I didn't make this up, but only heard about it. People used to tell stories like this. They are stories from our people and not coming from white people.

When everything was situated, [the shaman] went down the entrance hole and disappeared.

The tunnel entryways, the doorways into the qasgiq, had wooden pieces along the sides to lean on going down, and they were quite high. An adult would bend forward and go in and out [through the passage].

It was a dugout tunnel entryway, made just like an underground seal poke storage place. They made them long like an underground burial. [A person would go and] come out through a hole into the porch. [The entrance and exitway] were the same. And when he entered, he would come up [and appear] through a hole [into the main room inside]. It was a deep dugout [tunnel entryway].

[The shaman dropped down into the entry hole] and was gone. [The drummers] kept singing. He had instructed them to stop singing when they saw or heard something unusual. He told them to sit and be completely silent.

Then after a moment they saw the top of a head popping up [through the entrance hole]. They saw that the figure coming up was a dog. It came up, and its body looked just like [the skin on our body]. It only had hair on its paws, at the tip of its ears, and also at the tip of its tail. It was a big old dog with no fur.

As it came up and stood up, they saw that it was a huge old dog. It only had fur at the tips of its paws and the top of its ears.

Once [the dog] was up inside, it started sniffing around and raising its head. Then after it stretched

Tua-i-llu ellisqelliniak angayuqaak kenurram keluanun, uinga ikavet, cali-ll' aipaa nulirra wavet cali akianun, kenurram keluanun. Yuut atkuitnek piciatun patuqtuurullukek. Yuut taugaam atkurrlainaitnek, atkuunrilngurmek pivkenakek.

ANGALGAQ: Mikelnguq-qaa?

AKAGTAQ: Taukuk angayuqaak. Taum tuqumayagalriim kanani angayuqaak tamarkenka patulukek tua-i, yuut atkuitnek taugaam. Tua-i atkugglainarnek patuqtuurullukek ellillinilukek.

Tua-i-ll' tayima. Tauna-llu mikelnguyagaq ugayarluku ugayak'acagarluku, kiaqvaarni kiavet elliluku taklarrluku.

Qanemcik'lallrat. Wii piliaqenritanka niitelallrenka taugaam. Qanemcik'lallrit yuut. Kass'artaunrilnguut Yupiat qanemciit.

Tayima tua-i tuaten qaqicata amiigmun kalevluni.

Waten amiiget makut, qasgim amiigi, avaperrukarluteng muraganek cakmavet tayima, qerturrarluteng. Yuk tua-i pusngaurluni egilraarkauluni.

Nayugluku amik, uquucillertun ayuqliriluki. Qungicillerkiuratun taklririluki. Cakmani-llu elaturrakun pugluni. Ayuqlukek. Cali-ll' itquni tuaggun pugluni. Ilutuluni.

Tayima tua-i. Tua-i tamaa-i aturluteng. Pillruluki camek alangrukata tamakut atunermek taqesqelluki. Tua-i nepengssagaunaki uitasqelluki.

Piinanratni tua-i piqerluni kakangcalkitliniluni cakemna. Maaten uavet tangvakalliniat qimugta. Mayulliniuq, qainga-w' tua-i waten. Ipimi nuugitgun taugaam melqurluni, ciutmi-ll' kangregken'gun, pamyumi-ll' nuvuakun. Melqungssagaunani qimulvangruyagpall'er.

Mayulliniuq, nangertelliniuq qimulvangruyagpall'er kan'a. Tua-i tuaten ciutek taugaam kangrak melqurlutek ipimi-ll' nuugitgun.

Tua-i mayuami ua-i naruralliniluni, ciugngaluni tuaten. Piuraqerluni kiatmun waten

its body toward the back a couple of times and sniffed, it started to head inside toward the body of the dead child.

When it reached the body it began to sniff [the body] back there. The dog smelled the child's whole body, and when it got to his small feet, it started to eat them.

The huge dog ate the child's body starting from the feet. The dog ate the whole body of the dead child. Though dead, as the dog consumed the body, it got bloody here and there, so again, when it was done eating [the child's] body, it started carefully licking all the blood.

RUTH JIMMIE: Were people watching?

TIM AGAGTAK: The drummers quickly stopped drumming as instructed [by the shaman]. It was completely quiet inside the *qasgiq*.

Then when it was done, it turned and slowly walked toward the front following the same path it had taken.

And when it got to where the lamps were located, it stopped and turned and looked at the lamp where the child's mother was covered and made movements forward. Although it started heading up, it didn't proceeed forward, but turned toward [the lamp] on the other side and moved forward again. It stopped again and didn't go to it and continued going toward the entrance hole.

And just as it plunged [into the hole], it screamed while its tail whacked the side of the hole. It did that because it was huge. It disappeared.

Sometime after, the shaman came up through the hole the same as he was before. Once he was inside he went toward the back.

As soon as he sat down he said he was done. He told everyone that he was done because he couldn't do anything else. He said the little one, the little child almost finished off his medicines. He told them that he did not want to go through the same experience again. He said he would not accept another offer again when asked. He said that he was very worried and had barely returned with a little bit of medicine left in him as they were almost finished. He vowed that he would never again [use his shaman medicine on anyone].

He said that he had tried his best to revive [the child] so that he could live until he would use a walking stick [as an elder]. He had tried to bring the child to elderhood, but [the child] was unable to pass through a certain point. He said every time the child went beyond that point, [the child] would immediately regress back to its starting point.

nengqetaarraarluni, narurarraarluni, ayumian itranga'artelliniuq taum tua-i tuqumayagalriim tungiinun.

Ayumian tekicamiu naru'urturalliniluku kia-i. Naru'urturaqerluku iquklican qainga, it'gayagai ukut tekicamiki nerngartellinii.

It'gainek ayagarrluku taum imum qimulvallraam nerrlinia. Tauna imna tuqumalria nerrlinia nangkacagarluku. Tuqumang'ermi-llu aunrallian tayima, tuamtellu taqngami, tamana auggluarii pairturalliniluku tua-i.

ANGALGAQ: Yuut-qaa tangssugluku?

AKAGTAQ: Yuut tua-i taq'errluteng cauyanriqerrluteng alerquuciatun. Nepengssagaunani tua-i qasgim ilua.

Tua-i-ll' taqngami ayumian tuamtell' anelralliniluni tumellmikun.

Tua-i-ll' taukuk kenurrak nallaiqerlukek ayumian arulairluni, taum tua-i arniin tungiinun patusngalriim tagyuguangartelliniluni. Tua-i-gguq tagevkenani tua-i tagemciraluni pirraarluni, tuamtell' akianun wavet tagyuguaralliniluni. Tua-i-gguq tagevkenaki tuamtell' tua-i anelrarluni tayima tua-i.

Kanaqauciatun aarpalria, pamyua-ll' pikavet piqrulluni. Angengami-gguq. Tua-i tayima.

Piqerluni imna ugna puggliniuq, imna angalkuq ayuqucirramitun. Pugngami-llu itrarluni.

Aqumngami qanlliniuq tua-i taqniluni waniwa. Tua-i cavigkairucami waniwa taqniluni. Tua-i-gguq tang aug'ucuaraam imumek, aug'uyagaam mikelngucuayagaam nangyarpiaqii tuunrainek. Tua-i-gguq waniwa cangiminrituq. Kia-gguq pingraani pinqiggngaitkacagartuq. Tua-i-gguq tang arenqialnguq, tua-i cassuutai nangyarpialriit. Tua-i pinqiggngaunani tua-i.

Taugaam-gguq tang tua-i ayarungellra tekilluku yuuvkangnaqa'arcaaqekii. Tauna-gguq tang tua-i pellugyunrilkii, ayarungllerkaa tekicunrilkii. Tua-i-gguq kiturluku piyaaqngani, maaten pinaura imutun ayuqliriqertellinilria. Tua-i pellugciiganani, tua-i-gguq tuatequaluku tua-i.

But their arms would just go right through, even wood.

And sometimes, when a ghost would come up through the entrance hole and go in, it would head toward the back and continue and go out and disappear through the back wall, even though there was no door there. That's another thing they say about them. After entering through the entranceway, it would exit through the back wall. It would then disappear.

They say the old village of Nunangyarmiut down there had many fearsome things. They say there were a lot of fearsome things in Nunangyarmiullret across there. In those days [ghosts and out-of-the-ordinary occurrences] were more common. Today we don't have those anymore.

And when [a ghost] was stuffed in the entryway, there would be no way for [a person] to walk through. When one of the people tried pushing it down, [the ghost] would come up more. There was no way [to move it].

But when they pushed down on them with their hand [to make them disappear], they'd first try to touch it on its skin here. [Ghosts] would feel very cold like ice.

They'd [push down on them] here with the weight of the arm. They say the ghost would begin to go down inside the ground when that was done. When they'd almost push down, it would come up a little.

When [the ghost] would disappear, the ground where it had stood would turn and twirl. The grasses and whatever was on the ground would twirl until [the ghost] disappeared. [People who had seen ghosts] talked about it. It wasn't a good experience.

Dogs were aware of [ghosts]. The dogs used their nostrils to sense them. When I heard people talking about ghosts back when they used to see them, I wasn't sure if I should believe their stories or not, but they do tell of real things they have experienced. They didn't lie. They talked about things they've gone through.

Tua-llu-gguq-am cam ilii, mayuquneng, tamakuciq, itrarciquq, kiugna-llu egkukacaaq amigtailengraan ciunemikun anluni. Waten-am cali qanrutkelarait. Uaggun itraaluni amigkun, kiaggun-llu egkukacaarkun anluni. Tua-i tayima tamarluni.

Kankut-gguq kana-i, kegkut Nunangyarmiullret carayagtulillret. Ika-i-gguq carayagtulillret Nunangyarmiullret. Cat-wa tamaani paivngiimeng. Maa-i tua-i catairutut mat'um nalliini.

Tuamtellu-gguq tuaten tua-i amiigmun keviuskata tua-i caviinani pekviinani. Negcaaqekaceteng yuut ilaita, pugkanirluni tauna. Cayunaunani tua-i.

Taugken-gguq tua-i negeskaceteng, makut kemgit agtungnaqa'arqaarluki. Tua-i-gguq imutun cikutun ayuqluteng.

Uuggun tua-i maaggun tallim uqamarriinek. Nutaan-gguq tua-i atrarciquq nevumun iterluni, tuatnakatni. Negcarpiarqatni yuraqaniryarpiaraqluni.

Tua-i-ll' tamaqan, kingunrat uivluni. Can'get piciatun nuna uivluni tamarnatkaanun. Tua-i cali qanemcikaqluku tamana. Assiinateng.

Qimugtet nalluvkenaki tamakut. Qengamegteggun taugaam tamaa-i. Tangaatullratni tamakunek qanemcikaqaceteng, tua-i-w' qanemcikengraitki ukvekeksaicaaqekenka tua-i taugaam pillruaqata qanemcik'laamegteki. Iqluquluteng piksaitut. Tua-i pillernek qanemcilartut.

People said Luk'alleq was a powerful shaman[4]

Tim Agagtak and Ruth Jimmie, Nightmute, July 1985

TIM AGAGTAK: They would try and save a person who was dying, they'd try to prevent him from dying. He'd use another person's life to cover himself, to cloak himself. The [other person] would die [instead].

This happened more than once. Even others besides Luk'alleq performed that which they called *capkuciryaraq* [using another person's life to cloak oneself].

Luk'alleq was my grandfather, and I was comfortable being with him and could talk to him with ease. One time I asked him questions about being a shaman. He said that he personally was not responsible, but that it was his *pissuutet* [helpers] who performed the work he did as a shaman.

He also said that if another shaman tried to kill him [his helpers] would protect him. And he said that since he wasn't the perpetrator, he'd have more power to fight.

This was what he would say to me. He said that if he had been the perpetrator, the opponent could have easily killed him, even though he wasn't as strong. He said there was strength in being genial and not instigating conflict. That was his reply to me.

How did they take flight? I never saw a flying shaman. But I heard them talking about those who flew. And they would say they'd travel around the globe. I never saw one [fly]. But they'd say they circle the globe.

Just like Tengesqauktar.

Tengesqauktar also . . . they would fly. I did not see one fly, but I heard them talk about those who flew. When they'd drum [as they flew], drumming sounds would come from the air. That's how they knew they were flying. [The drumming sounds] did not come from the ground, but they came from above, too.

Then one time . . . he was always truthful. People would say Luk'alleq was a shaman. They said he was a powerful shaman. Once I asked him, "In your work as a shaman did you ever see God?" He replied that he had never seen God in his work. He said he had gone around the world, but he had not seen any [God].

Angalkuunilallruat tauna Luk'alleq. Angarvaunilallruat

Akagtaq Angalgaq-llu, Negtemiut, July 1985

AKAGTAQ: Tuquqatalria yuuvkangnaqluku, tuqunricetaarluku. Yuum allam unguviinek capkucirluni, amilirluni. Taumun tut'arkauluni.

Pulengtaq. Luk'allrunrilngermi, capkuciryaraq.

Tauna-wa Luk'alleq takaqenritkacagallrukeka angullruamku, ap'akngamku. Apqangaqekeka tua-i angalkuullranek. Kiurluraanga-am, ellii-gguq piyuicaaquq, taugaam-gguq tamakut pissuutai, tamakut-gguq taugaam pilartut pissuutai, angalkuussuutai, calissuutai tamakut.

Cali-llu-gguq yuum tuqutessaakani, angalkum allam, tua-i pivkaryugnaunani. Elliin-gguq pinrilamiu, ciumek-gguq pinrilami pinirluni.

Waten-am kiulallruanga. Ellii-gguq taugaam ciumek pillrukuni, taum tua-i pik'ngaa pikeggnerunrilngermi tuquciiqaa. Tua-i-gguq waniw' piniruarcet'laraa ciumek piyuitellran. Tuaten tua-i kiulallruanga.

Ellakun cali tenguralartat qaillun? Tengelriamek tangellrunritua. Tengniaqluki taugken. Ella-ll' uivniaqluku. Tangeqsaitua. Amta-ll' qanraqluteng ella-gguq uivelaraat.

Tengesqauktartun.

Tengesqauktaraam-llu taum . . . tenguraluteng-gguq tamaa-i. Tengaulriamek tangeqsaitua, taugaam niitaqlua tengtuniluki. Tua-i-wa cauyarluteng piaqata, ellamek-llu maaken cauyalalliniameng. Tamaa-i tengaurutiit. Maaken nunamek pivkenateng, pagken tuaten.

Tua-ll'-am pivakarluku . . . tua-i tang iqlungaitellinilria. Angalkuunilallruat tauna Luk'alleq. Angarvaunilallruat. Aptaqa, "Waniwa-qaa ayagalallerpeni maani Agayutmek tangerqaqsaituten?" Kiugaanga, waniwa-gguq tang tua-i tangengssaaqsailnguq Agayutmek. Ella-llu-gguq uiveng'ermiu camek tangyuunani.

[He probably said that] because he was probably a real shaman. Then he extended his arm. However, he said that he had seen rosary beads hanging somewhere above in the middle of the sky. He said those were the only things he had seen.

Luk'alleq hadn't seen God whatsoever.

He always told me the truth. He said that people and even shamans will never see God. He said he had only seen rosary beads hanging somewhere up in the middle of the sky. He never lied. I was not reserved toward him [and was able to be with him and easily ask him such questions].

RUTH JIMMIE: At that time he knew what rosary beads were and what they were for?

TIM AGAGTAK: He knew what they were. Before he died he learned about rosary beads. He learned about rosary beads and what they were used for before he died.

Tiny visible images or souls[5]

Tim Agagtak and Ruth Jimmie, Nightmute, July 1985

TIM AGAGTAK: And also Tengesqauktar and his family, their ancestors came from the ancient time. Shamanism has existed beginning from the first people.

RUTH JIMMIE: So were Tengesqauktar and the others the first ones?

TIM AGAGTAK: They were the first ones. Shamans are people. They are people, but they could use power to do magic just like white people. That's what they are.

And they would take *tarnat* [souls] when those [*tarnat*] were no longer with [a person]. They were little people of a certain height. They were [little people] who left [the person they had been inside] when he was about to die. They'd display [the little people] to others inside a seal-gut garment. The tiny things would be standing.

RUTH JIMMIE: Whose life essence? Was it the entity or life essence inside the shaman?

TIM AGAGTAK: Everyone. They say [people] have *tarnat*. This is what they would say about them. When [a shaman] retrieved the *tarnaq* from a normal person, even if he isn't a shaman, they were able to see it. The shamans were the only ones who took them, and a normal person couldn't take it.

Tang ilumun angalkuulliami. Tua-ll'-am tallini nengtaa. Nani-gguq taugaam pakmani, ellam qukaani piicagnek agalrianek tanglartuq. Tua-i-gguq taugaam taukut tanglaq'ngai.

Tangerciqenritaa Luk'allrem Agayun, tangerrngaitkacagaraa.

Tua-i iqluksaitellruanga. Tangerciqenritaa-gguq kia yuum angalkuunrilngermi Agayun tauna. Taukunek-gguq taugaam piicagnek ellam qukaani nani pakmani agalrianek tanglartuq. Iqluyuitell'ertuq. Takaqenrilamku.

ANGALGAQ: Tamaa-i-qaa piiciit qaillun ayuquciit elliin nalluvkenaki?

AKAGTAQ: Tua-i-wa nallunritellrukai. Imumi tuquvailegmi nallunrillrukai piiciit makut. Piiciuryaraq nallunrillrua tuquvailegmi.

Tarnat

Akagtaq Angalgaq-llu, Negtemiut, July 1985

AKAGTAQ: Tamakut-wa cali Tengesqauktaraankut avani tayima ciuliarluteng yaaqvanun. Ak'a man'a tuunrangayak piurtellruami yuut maliggluki.

ANGALGAQ: Waniwa-qaa tamakut Tengesqauktaraankut ciuliaqluki?

AKAGTAQ: Ciuliaqluki. Yuuyaaqut makut angalkut. Tua-i yuuluteng, taugaam imkuuluteng, maa-i iciw' kass'at-llu makut *magic*-aatulinek ilangqelalriit. Tamakuugut, tamakuyaaqut.

Yuut-llu tarnanek-am pitulaqait tegutaqluteng, tamakut nayunrirqatki. Qaill' angtalrianek yucuayaarnek. Yugteng tauna tuquqata'arqan nayunriqaitnek. Maniluki imarnitek iluagni. Nangerngayagaqtarluteng miketkacagarluteng.

ANGALGAQ: Kia yua? Angalkut-qaa yuit?

AKAGTAQ: Yuum tamarmi. Tarnangqertut-gguq. Waten qanemcik'lallruit. Tarnaq-gguq tauna, yuum tarnaa, angalkuunrilngermi, teguaqatni tua-i alaitelartuq. Angalkut taugaam tegutuluki, yuum-llu teguyuunaku.

RUTH JIMMIE: Were they able to take the *tarnaq* from a person who was dying?

TIM AGAGTAK: Yes. [They were able to retrieve it] when it was no longer with the person it was in. They say every person has a tiny one of those. Even if he wasn't a shaman, [in every person] there was a *tarnaq*. It looks like that person, it looked exactly like him, even though it was very tiny. When they show their size, they say it's about this big.

RUTH JIMMIE: Did the tiny figure look like the person it was in?

TIM AGAGTAK: Yes, like the person it was in. It looked exactly like him, and it wore exactly the same tiny clothing. That's called a *tarnaq*. They used to talk about them in that way.

I still remember some stories I used to hear. When old men lived in the *qasgiq*, they told stories all the time. There seemed to be a lot of old men, and even though they were old men, they would take a long time to die. And they didn't urinate outside. They'd have small urine buckets. I'd always take their buckets and empty them outside. I'd splash them outside anywhere.

ANGALGAQ: Yuk-qaa tuquqata'arqan tamana tarnaat teguaqluku?

AKAGTAQ: Ii-i. Nayunrilliniaqatgu tauna yugteng. Yuut-gguq makut tamarmeng taucuayaartangqertut. Angalkuunrilngermi, tarnamek-gguq. Tautun ayuqluni yugtun, ayuqkacagayagarluni miketkacagang'ermi. Tua-i angtassiirqamegteki waten-gguq tua-i.

ANGALGAQ: Yullmitun-qaa tautun ayuqkacagarluni?

AKAGTAQ: Ii-i, yum'itun. Tautun ayuqkackacagarluni cangallruvkenani aturainek-llu aturayagarluni. Wagg'u-q' tarnaq. Qanemcik'lallruit-am waten.

Atam tua-i qanengssaaraat avauqsaitanka ilait augkut. Qasgingqetullratni augkut nepaicuitut angullugaat. Amllerngat'lallruut imkut angulluat, tuqusciigasngatnaurtut-llu angulluangermeng. Ellamun-llu yuqercuunateng. Qurruksuarluteng. Tua-i wii ciqicilguaqellrianga qurrutaitnek. Ellamun qagaavet piciatun ciqrutaqluki.

The time when I was the object of their curing ceremony[6]

Dick Anthony and Marie Meade, Toksook Bay, January 1996

DICK ANTHONY: That way of life that I caught, I didn't think we were poor, but when we were short of food, that's when we sensed that we were poor.

MARIE MEADE: Now about those shamans. So you were the object of their curing ceremony at that particular time . . .

DICK ANTHONY: Yes, those shamans, since this person who thinks I'm a shaman is asking me to record [the story], since she's asking me now, [*chuckles*] the time when I was the object of their curing ceremony, let me talk about that first.

Sickness was not with me at that particular time.

But my father and his younger brother, too, we had our own winter settlement up there at Talarun River, a tributary of the Qalvinraaq River. It was at Manignalek [lit., "Place with burbot"]. We were from Manignalegmiut. When people were going

---

Tuunricesciulqa

Minegtuli Arnaq-llu, Nunakauyaq, January 1996

MINEGTULI: Augna ava-i angulqa arrsauciiteurlullruukut taugaam tua-i waten neqmek nuuqilluta piaqamta nutaan arrsauyucirput elpekumanarqetullruuq.

ARNAQ: Tua-ll'-am imkut angalkut. Tuunritesciullrullinilriaten tuani . . .

MINEGTULI: Ii-i, angalkut cali augkut, angalkuuyuklua-w' uum tua-i imiricesqenganga, apcanga, waniw', [*ngelaq'erluni*] tuunricesciulqa una wii qanemcikqerraaqernauqa.

Tua-i apqucim wii tusngallrunricaaqaanga taum nalliini.

Taugaam ukuk aatagka uyurani-llu, allakarramta uksillengqerramta kiani wagg'u-q' Talarutmi, Qalvinraam avayaani. Manignalegmi tua-i. Manignalegmiunguluta tua-i. Manignanek taluyirtuumaarkaugaqameng carvani qavani

---

QALUYAARMIUT QANEMCIIT : 149

to set wooden traps to catch burbot, they'd stay up in the mountain streams. So we'd live there all by ourselves and [with my father's younger brother].

There came a time when this village of Kanerr-lulegmiut, just on this side of Cevv'arneq, since they were going to be the village where people were going to go to be guests [for the Messenger Feast], when they invited them, they went there; they went down, or they left.

At the time, my siblings were my three sisters, then there were me and my late older brother. So many of our siblings died when they were little. So there were that many of us who were alive at the time.

So when they left, when my parents were going to leave, they took along our youngest sibling.

When they were going to leave, they took our youngest sibling and my deceased older brother. And three of us stayed behind. I was with my two older sisters when I stayed behind.

Even when they were going to leave me behind, I had no desire to go with them. I was totally uncon-cerned, and when they were getting ready to go, I didn't mind.

So [my parents] left.

After they left, since I was the only boy there, I'd use my father's kayak sled and starting from just outside of our house, I would slide down. After sliding down, I would drag them up and slide down again.

Then after a while, I brought my sled farther up the hill from where I had been sliding.

When I slid, I reached a spot where my parents had prepared to go. That's where my sled stopped. So I stood there when I saw their tracks where they made preparations to leave.

Finally, at that instant, my urge to go with them hit me.

Right away, leaving that kayak sled where it was, I followed their trail and left.

The dog-team route would go up on the land to the lake, it would go down into the lake. Then they would continue on to [the lake's] end, and then going briefly over the land, they would descend into a river from there.

Just before I descended onto that lake, an urge to cry came to me; there was no one from where I had just come from.

uitatullrulriit. Tuantaqelriakut tua-i kiirraramta ellii-llu.

Tua-i caqerluteng ukut Kanerrlulegmiunek pitukengait, Cevv'arnermiut ukaqlirrait, tuani tua-i curukiuqataameng, aqviicetek ayagtuk; atrartuk, tua-i-w' ayagluteng.

Ilangqellrianga-wa arnat pingayun, wangkuk-wa ciuqliirutka-llu. Ilarugapuk mikelnguuluteng egmirluteng pitullrulriit. Taukuuluta tua-i anerteqelriaruluta.

Tua-i-llu ayiimek, taukuk angayuqaagka ayakataamek, taumek tua-i uyuqvaaramtenek malilirlutek.

Ayakataamek uyuqlikacaamtenek tua-i irnialirtuk, ciuqliirutemnek-llu. Wangkuta-ll' tua-i pingayuni unkarluta. Alqagemnek ilalua unkallrulrianga.

Uniteqatangraatnga-llu tua-i nacigmek tua-i qemangqaarunii. Tua-i cangalliurpek'nii, uptengraata-ll' cangalliurpek'nii.

Tayim' ayaglutek.

Tua-i kingunragni kiima tua-i tan'gurraungama aatama qamigautegkenek keggaken elatemtenek tua-i ellu'urtaaqelrianga. Tua-i-ll' ellu'urqaarlua qamurlukek tagullukek ataam elluraqlua, ellu'urtaqlua.

Tua-i pivakarlua qulvaqanirluku una ellulalqa, mayuullukek tamakuk ellu'urtaarcuutegka.

Ellu'urtellrianga imkut angayuqaagma uptellrat tekilluku. Tua-i ikamragka makuk arulairlutek. Nangerngaqertua ukut tumliallrit ayakatarluteng waniw' tangrramki.

Nutaan atam nacigyuum tekiskiinga.

Tua-i ayumian qamigautek tamakuk unillukek tumellritgun ayaglua.

Piavet nanvamun nunakun taglalriit ikamraryarat, nanvamun piavet kanarluteng. Ayakuneng-llu iquani yaani cali nunaliuqerluteng kuigmun aug'umun kanaquneng-llu kanarluteng.

Nanvaq tamana kanarniararluku iluteqem tekillua; yugtangssagailami-ll' tua-i kinguneqa.

When I descended into the lake, since I wanted to cry, I let out my voice. So crying, I went on following their trail to the end of it.

So when I got to its end while still crying, when I descended into that river, whenever we'd go up the river, down by its mouth, I would see an old cross. A grave, it was a grave. But there was a cross there.

When I descended, I lacked courage because of that [grave].

And as one goes along there, there is a trail also going toward the place where one gets firewood. Instead of following my parent's trail, using that firewood trail, when I crossed a high area, I approached their tracks toward the Qalvinraaq River.

The two cracks on the ice had been covered by light falling snow. As soon as I descended, my foot fell through that crack. I was still crying then. When my foot fell in, my urge to cry increased!

When I descended to their trail, I continued on following them.

When I got farther downriver, my crying noise seemed to be mixed with some other noise. But my curiosity not having been roused, I continued on still crying.

And then again, my crying seemed to have some other noise mixed with it.

And then I stopped crying and continued on, thinking I would hear that noise, but not hearing any other noise, since the urge to cry came again, I started crying.

While I was continuing on, a little bit louder, my crying was mixed with another noise. I ignored it, and I never even looked back.

As I was going along, even louder than before, I heard something. When I heard that and when I stopped, I looked back, and I saw a person coming behind me.

Ignoring the person, I continued on following their tracks.

So while I was going along, that person caught up to me.

When that person caught up to me, it was my brother-in-law, our older sister's husband.

He said to me, oh my, if the weather became inclement, I would be disoriented and not know where to go, that we should go home. He said if I got disoriented, I would get lost.

So I believed him and putting me in the sled—he had run after me using a hauling sled with handles

Nanvamun tua-i kanaama tua-i iluteqngama erinaka annluku. Qiaqcaarturlua iquvarluku tumaitgun.

Tua-i qianginanemni iquklicamku, tamaavet kuigmun kanaama, asgurqamta cakmani paingani ak'allar, augna kristaq tanglarqa. Qunguq tua-i, qunguuluni. Kristaq taugaam, kristartarluni.

Kanaama tua-i taumek tua-i umyuaqa caceskicugtuq.

Ukut-wa tua-i pilriani qugtaryarat cali tumyarat. Tuaggun tua-i tumayaratgun angayuqaagma tumelkek aturpek'nakek qugtaryaratgun tuaggun piama qertuuralria man' tev'arcamku, nutaan tumait ullagluki, Qalvinraam tungiinun.

Qulinrek imkuk mat'um qanuggluaraam patullrullinilukek. Tua-i atraqerlua murulua, murulua qulinermun. Qiaqcaarturlua tua-i. Muruama nutaan tua-i iluteqvallaangarrlua tua-i!

Tumait tua-i kanaamki tua-i tumaitgun ayaglua.

Uaqsigiuraqerlua qialqa tuartang wangni camek avungqeqalria. Paqnayullagpek'nii-ll'-am tua-i qiaqcaarturlua ayaglua.

Tuamtell' tua-i qialqa avungqeqernganani.

Tua-i qiavkenii, taqlua qianermek, ayaagaryaaqelrianga imna niitnayukluku, tua-i tayim' niipailemku, tuamtell' tua-i iluteqngama qialua.

Ayaagaqertua-am imum qasturikaninqelluku qialqa avungqeqaqili. Ilangcivkenaku, kingyayuilama-ll'.

Tua-i ayagturaqerlua ak'anivkenii imum qastunerpiinek cameg' imumek niillua. Niicama, arulairngama kingyartua, yuk man' kingunemni.

Tua-i ilangcivkenaku ayaglua tumaitgun.

Tua-i piinanemni angulua.

Anguanga maaten, nengauka, alqamta uinga.

Pianga, aren, ellaqerruskanga natuyaciiqnilua utercuglunuk. Atam-gguq pellaakuma tamarniartua.

Tua-i ukverlua ucikarrlua—qamigaukaraagnek augkugnek qulel'egnek apqiitnek

so that he could lean on them with his belly. So he put me in the sled, and I went home.

This was at the time when we craved for pancakes and we just couldn't get enough of them when our mothers used to give some to us in the morning. It was a time when we really craved to have more.

When we got up that next morning, when our late older sister gave me a pancake, where was my insatiable appetite for pancakes? I absolutely did not want to eat it.

I was feeling fine; I did not feel any illness whatsoever.

Because I didn't want to eat it, I didn't eat it.

So that was how I was for days to come as long as my parents were gone. I never ate. Even when they ate and though they prepared food for me, because I wasn't hungry, I never ate. And I was never hungry. But still, I was in good health; I would walk and go outside.

By and by, [my parents] came home.

You see after those people came back from the dance festival, they had lots of gifts: Flour, salted fish, sugar. So they would arrive with food that we craved. I wasn't a bit hungry for them, even when our mother offered some to me.

So my older sisters there told her it had been a long time since I stopped eating. But still, I was just fine . . .

My mother was frantic.

So in the mornings, because I wasn't hungry and because I didn't want to eat pancakes, I never ate pancakes. And I was never hungry either.

My late paternal uncle was living at Cakcaaq, one who was a shaman. They called him Qateryak, our late paternal uncle.

So pretty soon, because our mother insisted, having been frantic all this time, my father took me to Cakcaaq by dog team.

We arrived.

Even when he ate when we got there, I didn't even eat. This was back in those days when guests always stopped at the qasgiq.

So that night, pretty soon they brought in food to eat.

My late uncle there, when they brought him food, it was a cooked burbot head. When he took it across there, he got hold of a piece of wood and mashed it.

When he was going to have one man beside him share his food, he told me to come and eat with

palungqakarirluni malirqallinikiinga. Ucikurlua tua-i uterrlua.

Mukaat imumek aglumanaqkacagallret cangimirnarqetullrata uum nalliini cikirrautii unuakumi aanamta. Cangemlerqutek'lallemta nalliini.

Unuaquan tupiimta, assaliamek cikiryaaqekiinga alqairutma, aa naugg'unkiq imna nau imna mukaaryunqelqa? Tua-i neryuumiitkacagarluku tua-i.

Tua-i camek niiskengaicaaqua; apqucimek-llu niiskengauni.

Tua-i neryuumiilamku nerevkenaku.

Cunaw' tua-i ayuqucirkaqa uumirpak cataitellragnek angayuqaagma taktaciatun. Neryuunii. Nerengraata-ll' neqlirtungraagnga-ll' tua-i neryuumiitelaama, neryuunii. Kaiyuunii-llu. Amta-ll' tua-i cavkenii; kangarlua anqetaaraqlua ellamun.

Tua-i piinanemteni tekillutek.

Nauwa imkut curukaliyarraarluteng tekitaqameng minarugait: Mukaat, culunat, caarralat. Tua-i pituryuumikanirluteng tekitetullrulriit. Cayugnaunii, aglumayugnaunii maniicaaqekiinga aanamta.

Tua-i qanrulluku ukug' alqaagma akaurrniluku nernanriuciqa. Amta-ll' tua-i waten tua-i cavkenii . . .

Tua-i-am aanavut kapialuni.

Tua-i unuakutengraaki tua-i neryuumiitelaama mukaaryuumiitelaama-ll' mukaartuyuunii. Kaiyuunii-llu.

Una wani ataatairutka Cakcaamenani, angalkuulria. Qateryagmek piaqluku, ataatairutvut.

Tua-i pivakarlua, qepirpakartelluku aanavut un' kapiayagpakartelluku, aatama ayaullua Cakcaamun qimugtetgun.

Tua-i tekillunuk.

Tua-i tekiutangraan-llu cayugnaunii, neryugnaunii. Qasgimun ciunirturatullratni.

Tua-i atakumi piameng pivakarluteng payuggluteng.

Ellii tauna ataatairutka payugtaat manignaam qamiqurranek egaamek. Ika-i tua-i teguamiu, ika-i muragmek piluni, ciamlerrluku.

Tua-i caniqliminek neruteqataami taisqaanga cikiliryartuusqellutek. Niicugnaunaku kainrilama.

them. I absolutely did not obey him, because I wasn't hungry.

When my father told me to eat just a little bit, I went across to them. I sat down on top of the headrest in front of him, and when I saw his food, thinking of dog food, that is when I did not want to eat at all!

So my late uncle was really insisting that I eat. So turning to his plate, I saw a small piece of liver that he had not mashed, and it was barely sticking out. So I took it, pinched it with my thumb and index finger, putting it in my mouth, I stood up and went across and sat down below my father.

So my late uncle across from us said, "Oh my, I am grateful that one who has continually refused to eat has eaten!"

So he was really glad that I had eaten. "I am so grateful that one who has continually refused to eat has eaten!" So he went on about me refusing to eat; he was thankful that I had eaten.

Oh, I forgot to mention, my father had told him at that time about me having stopped eating, just before they were going to bring them food.

So [my uncle] said to [my father], he wanted to work on me after supper.

So after we had dinner, they brought in a grass mat for a kayak along with seal-gut rain gear. And then they spread the grass mat for the kayak out in the middle of the floor and just placed the rain gear there.

So then my father told me to go down and sit on top of [the grass mat] facing the door. So when I sat down facing the door, my late paternal uncle came down.

Then I could hear him taking and handling the rain gear behind me.

Before he went down, he told my father, "I have tried to cure your children before using my powers, but I have not been able to save them." He told him that he would surely save this one who has become precious to lose. "I will surely save this child who is now precious to lose." So he said that he had used his powers on his children before, but he had not been successful in saving them.

So he came down . . .
[While they are doing incantations], they usually walk around the person, and the people are drumming and singing. And before they finish

Tua-i aatama pianga, iqemkaryartuusqellua tua-i pianga, arvirlua. Akitem qainganun ketiinun aqumqerlua qantaa tangrraqa wangni qimugtem alungkait umyuaqeqerluku, nutaan tua-i neryugnaipallaarlua!

Tua-i-am qepirrluni tauna ataatairutka amci neresqellua. Tua-i takuyaumaurluku qantaa piunga tenguggaq una ciamlertellran qantaan imaani waten tua-i alaiteksuarluni. Tua-i teguqerluku, pupeskarluku, qanemnun pakmavet ellirraarluku, nangerrlua ikavet aatama ketiinun aqumlua.

Tua-i-am ikna ataatairutka piuq, "Aling quyanaqvaa-ll' nerenrilkurpakall' nerluni!"

Tua-i-am ika-i nerrlermini tua-i quyamaluni nerrlemnek. "Quyanaqvaa-ll' naa, nerenrilkurpakarluni nerluni!" Nerenrilkurtellemnek piluni; quyalun' nerrlemnek.

Tuani imat'am aatama qanruskii tua-i tamatumek neryuirutlemnek, waniw' tua-i payuggniarartelluki.

Tua-ll' piuq, qanrutaa atakutam taugaam kinguani piyuglua.

Tua-i atakutarraarluta ikaraliitet itrutait imarnitegnek taperlutek. Tuavet-llu kanavet natrem qukaanun ikaraliitet caggluki imarnitek-llu elliqerlukek.

Tua-i aatama atraasqenganga kankut qaingatnun aqumyartuusqellua uatmun caugarrlua. Uatmun tua-i caugarrlua aqumelrianga, ellii tua-i ataatairutka atrarluni.

Pama-i tua-i imarnitek pilkialukek, tegulalkialukek pama-i.

Atrarpailegmi aataka qanrutaa, "Waniw' irniarpenek tua-i waten tuunriskenglaryaaqelrianga tua-i, taugaam anirtuiksaitamken." Uumek waniwa qununarilriamek anirtuinrilngaiteqerniluku. "Anirtuinrilngaiteqaramken tua-i uumek qununarilriamek." Tua-i irniarinek tuunrisnguakenglaryaaqellruniluni anirtuqallrunritniluki.

Tua-i atrarluni . . .

Uivluku pilaameng pekluteng, cauyarluteng-llu ukut aturluteng. Tua-i-ll' yuarun iquklipailgatgu, "Aarrarrarraaqan," cauyalriit tua-i taqluteng.

singing the song, if he says "Aarrarrarraa," the drummers stop.

They face the one they are using their powers on to cure and say whatever they want to say to them.

When he'd continue [his incantation], they would start drumming and singing again.

When he'd say, "Aarrarrarraa" by raising his arms, they would stop drumming.

One of the times he squatted in front of me, he told me that now he was going to ask me questions; he told me not to lie to him. If he asked me if I had done something, he told me to say that I had done them, and if I had not done what he asked, he told me to say I had not done them.

Oh my, when he asked me, starting from the time I left, and here he had not watched me, it was like he had actually watched me!

[He told me] when I descended into the lake, it was that I had started wading in water, I was wading in water.

And when I descended into that river, he said I lost courage because of the dead person at the mouth of the river. [He asked,] "Were you scared?" Even though I lacked courage because [of the grave], I said to him that I had not been scared.

He said I was lying! He said it made me lose confidence.

And he said that I had gone on veering from my parents' trail on another trail. [He said that] just like one who had been watching [me]!

And so when I was just about to descend into Qalvinraaq, while I was crying, when I descended into Qalvinraaq, [when my foot fell in], I was really walking on more water.

When he asked me if my foot fell into water, I told him that my foot had not fallen into water.

He said I was lying!

He said that my foot fell down into the water! "Even though you say that your foot didn't fall into water, your foot fell into the water of Qalvinraaq!" [chuckles]

And then he talked about how I had traveled!

And as I continued on, he told me of that person who had pursued me.

MARIE MEADE: Yes.

DICK ANTHONY: He called it something when he had spoken. He told of when he caught up to me; then he talked about how I was taken home.

Tuunriskengarteng caugarrluku qanaaluteng tua-i qanaayullmeggnek.

Allamek ayagaqan, cauyarluteng piaqluteng aturpagaqluteng.

Aarrarrarraaqan yag'arrluni cauyanermek tua-i taqluteng.

Ciuqamnun-am uyungqerpakarluni pianga, waniwa-gguq apqaqataraanga; iqlusqevkenani. Pirrlainaqumki tamakut apyutni, pillruniluki piurasqellua pillrunrilkumki-ll' piksaitniluki tamakut apyutni pisqellua.

Aren tua-i aptaanga, tuaken tua-i ayakarraallemnek, tangvallrunrilkiinga-wa, tua-i tangvakapiarallrulua tuar'!

Tua-i-llu nanvamun tuavet kanaama, tua-i-ll' meliungellinilua-gguur maa-i, meliurturlua ayaglua.

Tauna-llu kuik kanaamku cakmumek nalamalriamek kuigem painganelngurmek caceskicullrullinilua, caceskicullrullinilua-gguq. "Alingellruuten-qaa?" Tua-i caceskeggiyuutekellrungramku piaqa alingellrunritnilua.

Iqluunga-gguq! Caceskiyuutekellruaqa-gguq.

Tua-llu-gguq maa-i angayuqaagma tumelkek avvlukek ayallinilua allat tumellritgun. Tua-i tangvakapiarallertun!

Tua-i-llu call' Qalvinraamun kanaqatarlua tua-i qiaqcaarlua tua-i pillemni, tua-i-llu-gguq maa-i Qalvinraamun kanaama mermun muruama, meliurpallaangartellinilua maa-i.

Mermun murullemnek apcanga, piaqa mermun muruksaitnilua.

Iqluunga-guuq!

Mernun-gguq murullruunga! "Mermun muruksaitniluten piningerpet, Qalvinraam mer'anun murullruuten!" [ngelaq'erluni]

Tuamtell' tua-i ayalqa!

Tuamtallu tua-i ayakartellua, tuamtell' tauna kingunrirturteka, tuamtell' qanrutekluku.

ARNAQ: Em-em.

MINEGTULI: Eriniallra-am cameg' acirluku piyaaqaa.

Tua-i anguvkarlua cali; tuamtall' ut'rutellua.

[He talked] as if he had actually watched me.

Then when he got to the end [of his questioning], and having circled me and performed his rites, he told me that he needed a knife. One of the men had a knife in his pocket.

Those men always had small knives with them.

MARIE MEADE: Yes.

DICK ANTHONY: So they gave him that small knife.

He told me to go up in front of my father, to lie on my back with my head on the log headrest. I lay on my back.

MARIE MEADE: Yes.

DICK ANTHONY: So just to the side of the light toward the door, I lay on my back resting my head on the log headrest. I was really terrified because he needed a knife!

While I was lying down, he began to put his head down toward me!

Then his lips, when he got to a place where he was visible to me and he stopped, then I could feel for sure that his lips came in contact with my throat. And I could feel his prickly whiskers that were around his mouth on my skin.

And here I was still looking at his mouth right there!

MARIE MEADE: [His mouth] was in midair?

DICK ANTHONY: It was in midair, it still hadn't touched me!

MARIE MEADE: Yes!

DICK ANTHONY: He was dancing at that time!

[Feeling like] it was being stretched upward, toward his lips, from his second lip where it was in contact with my throat, suddenly it came off, it came off!

When he got up, after he had taken his hand from his mouth, he showed it to my father, but I never saw what it was. [He told my father,] "This is what has prevented him from eating!"

MARIE MEADE: Yes.

DICK ANTHONY: I wonder what it was?

After he showed it like that, he took it, chewed it, and swallowed it! I don't know what it was. I never saw it.

After he had gone around in a circle so many times, he told me that he was finished with me.

The day after, they used to tell them not to use tools for five days after doing an incantation. They'd also caution the people in their family [not to use tools].

Tua-i tangvalqapiaramitun tua-i.

Tua-i tuaten iqukliciami, uiverraarlua-am tua-i tuunriluni pianga caviggaillitarluni. Caviggamek iliit qemangqaariluni.

Tua-i caviggarraicuitellruameng imkut angutet.

ARNAQ: Em-em.

MINEGTULI: Taumek tua-i cikirluku caviggarrarmek.

Tagesqaanga atama ketiinun, nevercesqaanga akin akitekqerluku. Neverrlua.

ARNAQ: Em-em.

MINEGTULI: Tua-i wavet kenurram ualirneranun neverrlua tua-i akin akitekqerluku. Alingkacagarlua tua-i caviggaillitallruan!

Tua-i-ll' tua-i qetengqainanemni, tua-i-ll' puc'imaartuq!

Cugg'ek-llu tua-i, natmun maavet tangvallemnun tua-i elliqerluni arulaiqertelluku, ayumian nallunaunatek tua-i wavet igyaramnun, cugg'ek tull'utek. Cali-ll' ungai nallunaiterpak tua-i kapuqcaarluteng tua-i qanran ceniini.

Amta-ll' qanra tua-i wavet tangvagluku!

ARNAQ: Qerrataluni?

MINEGTULI: Qerrataluni, nurvagluku!

ARNAQ: Ii-i!

MINEGTULI: Yurarlun' tua-i tamaani!

Nengetmun, qulmun cugg'egken tungiignun, igyarama una aipaa petgumallra piuraqerluni imumek alqunaqerluni aug'artellria, aug'arrluni!

Tua-i makcami unatni piluki, qanminun tua-i unatni manirraarluki, aatamnun un' mania, wiinga taugaam tangellrunritaqa. "Tang waniw' un' nerenrilkurutii!"

ARNAQ: Em-em.

MINEGTULI: Caullrua-kiq tayima?

Tuaten tua-i manirraarluku teguluku, tamualuku igluku! Caullrua-ll' tayim'. Tangellrunrilkeka.

Tua-i qavcirqunek uivaartaarturaqerluni, pianga tua-i taqnilua.

Unuaquan tua-i, tuunritellrata-am kinguani tamaa-i caskuyaasqevkenaki pitullrukait erenret ukut talliman aturluki. Kingunrit-llu inerqutullruit.

Even when we went home, when we went home the next day, I also didn't suddenly become hungry. I was still the same. And where was my insatiable appetite for pancake, I absolutely did not want to eat them!

On one of those occasions when I was prodded to eat, I took a small mouthful, just a very small mouthful. So that was the instant that I would start eating more. Then I came to eat, even though I did not finish all my food. Soon I began to eat.

So I know of that incident when I was the object of a shamanistic ceremony.

MARIE MEADE: Yes.

Tua-i-ll'-am utertengramegnuk, unuaquan utertengramegnuk, neryullagpek'nii-ll' tua-i. Ayuquciqa tua-i ayuquciqluku. Nauwa-ll' imna mukaaryunqekacaaralqa, tua-i aglumayuitkacagarluki!

Atam tua-i neresqevvakartellua iqemkalrianga, iqemkapigarrlua tua-i. Cunaw' tua-i nerqaqungellerkaqa ngelekluku. Kiituan' tua-i neqka nangenrilengramku neryaurtaqa. Kiituan' tua-i nerlangua.

Tuaten tua-i taumek tuunritesciullemnek nallunritaqa tauna.

ARNAQ: Ii-i.

And sometimes three [shamans] all [used their powers] on that person[7]

Dick Anthony and Marie Meade, Toksook Bay, January 1996

DICK ANTHONY: So this is how healers used their spirit powers on a person. If a male or female was no longer able to walk, they did what they called *akigarluku* [carrying something evenly between several people]. They'd carry him/her on a grass mat when they didn't have cloth. And when they began to have real cloth, well, even when they came to have cloth, they highly depended on grass mats. They sat a person on top of it, or lay him down, and they took that person to the *qasgiq*.

MARIE MEADE: A female?

DICK ANTHONY: Yes, or a male. Or even a young person. Even it was a young person, or a young boy, anyone who was unable to walk, seeing his state, that is how they brought one with an ailment to the *qasgiq*.

They only performed shamanistic ceremonies for people in the *qasgiq*. Every once in a while, when they didn't want them to do it in the *qasgiq*, inside a home, they said [a shaman] would get into a prone position behind [their patient] and perform a rite for him.

MARIE MEADE: Did they always face the door?

DICK ANTHONY: No, they did not face [the door] when they did it in the house.

So they did shamanistic ceremonies for people. Well anyway, I've witnessed several shamanistic ceremonies performed on people. They didn't always have shamanistic rituals. But I have seen a number of shamans doing rituals on people.

Iliini-ll' tua-i pingayuulluku

Minegtuli Arnaq-llu, Nunakauyaq, January 1996

MINEGTULI: Cunaw' tua-i tamaa-i waten tuunriskengtulriit, tuunriskengtullrulriit. Una tua-i angun wall'u arnaq tua-i kangarciigallikan apqiitnek akigarluku-gguq. Kevgucirluku tupiganek ellumarrallritlermeggni. Lumarralngameng-llu, tua-i-w' lumarralengqeng'ermeng tupigat tua-i tegullitaqluki pitullrukait. Qaingatnun tua-i aqumlluku kevegluku, taklarrluku-ll' wall', agulluku qasgimun.

ARNAQ: Arnauluni?

MINEGTULI: Ii-i, wall' angun. Wall' ayagyuarung'ermi. Ayagyuarungraan tauna tan'gurraqsigluni-ll' pingraan, tua-i-ll' kangarnanrilria nangteqellra niilluku, nangtequtellek tuaten tua-i qasgitetullruat.

Qasgirrlainarmi taugaam tuunritetullruit. Iliini-ll' tua-i qasgimi pivkaryuumiilkunegteki, nem'i, tunuatnun tua-i lavqerluku tuunritnitullrukait.

ARNAQ: Amiik-qaa caurrlainarluku?

MINEGTULI: No, cauvkenaku nem'i piaqameng. Tuunriskengtullrulriit-am. Takumni-w' tua-i qavcinek tuunriskengtullrulriit. Tuunrirrlainarluki piyuitellrulriit. Taugaam tua-i tuunriskengelrianek qavcinek tua-i tanglallruunga.

Sometimes two [shamans] would [do a healing ritual on a person]. And sometimes when there are three [shamans], they all [did a healing ritual on that person].

They said even if they were able to cure people, since material goods were scarce at the time, even if [a shaman] could cure a person, they decided not to [cure them] because of the material goods he required [to do a healing ceremony].

They tell stories about a person from the Akula area. Over to Cevv'arneq—and I didn't see this myself—he used to cure those he used his powers to heal.

And this resident of Arayakcaaq was a man's wife who had been sick all summer.

Soon she wasn't able to walk.

When they would do what they call *kacell'uteng* at their winter camp, when they'd gather at their winter settlement, those people would say they *kacell'uteng*.

Yes. It is said that they *kacell'uteng*. They gathered together.

They probably let their shaman do an incantation to cure her, I'm not sure. When it froze over, when the ice was safe, her husband told someone to get [that shaman].

Ice skating, he went to get him.

So when he arrived at that village, [that shaman] was not there.

Those people never went to houses first, even when they were guests, but always to the *qasgiq*. They only went directly to that *qasgiq* all the time.

Well, when they asked him [why he had come], he told them that he had been told by that person to get that [shaman].

A boat that had been completed the previous year—now what do they call those? He said that he is going to give [the shaman] a skin boat that he had built the year before as payment for his request.

After he had waited for him in vain, since nightfall would come before he arrived, he went home skating.

So that evening, they took [the sick person] to the *qasgiq* by using a stretcher, what they call *akigarluku*, by lifting her. They "poured" that boat to their shaman as payment instead of the other [shaman he had gone to get].

Iliini malruulluku. Iliini-ll' tua-i pingayuukuneng pingayuulluku.

Tamaa-i-am anirturyuumallining'ermegtekigguq cunaw', waten nunuliukaramegteggun, ca nurnarqellruan, ca-w' tua-i nurnaqluni pillruan, 'gguun nunuliukarani tamakut nunuliukaramikun aklungllagallni pitekluku tua-i, piyuumang'ermiu pinrilkurrngatetullrulliniit assirivkaryuumang'ermegteki.

Tauna-am qanemcik'laqiit Akulmiu. Yaavet Cevv'arnermun—wiinga-ll' tangvallrunrilkeka—tua-i-w' anirtuskengtuluni tuunriskengaminek.

Una-ll' Arayakcaarmiunguluni nangteqelria angutem nulirra kiagpak.

Tua-i kiituan' kangarnanrirtuq.

Tua-i uksillmeggnun apqiitnek kacetniaqameng, uksillmeggnun quyurtaqameng kacetniaqut augkut.

Ii-i. Kacell'uteng-gguq tua-i. Quyurrluteng.

Tuunritevkalaryaaqellikiit-wa taumun angalkumeggnun, qaill' piat. Waten tua-i cikuan, aarnairucan, arnaircan-wa tua-i, ellimeqlilliniluni taun' uinga tauna aqvasqelluku.

Tua-i kankiirturluni aqvalliniluku.

Tua-i tekicaaqelliniuq ayaumalliniluni.

Nen'un ciuniyuitellruameng augkut allanrung'ermeng, qasgirrlainarmun taugaam. Qasgirrlainaq taugaam taun' ciuneqluku.

Aren, tua-i aren apcatni, qanrutliniluki taumun tua-i ellimerrniluni augna aqvasqelluku.

Angyamek allragni taqlermek—Cakaqekait imat'anem? Ellimerrutekniluku tamana angyaq allragni taqellni qecik.

Tua-i utaqayaaqvigminek, unugarkaurcan tekipailgan, tuamtell' tua-i utertellinilun' kankiirturluni.

Tua-i atakuan qasgilluku tua-i apqiitnek akigarluku, kevegluku. Taumun tua-i angalkumeggnun taman' angyaq naivvluku, im'umun [pivkenaku].

MARIE MEADE: I know where you're comin' from . . .

DICK ANTHONY: So after supper, that [shaman] did an incantation on her.

When they'd seat them, when a shaman would fold the seal-gut rain gear and wrap his head with it up behind him, they say he *tuunrangcarrluni* [waited for his shaman powers or spirit helpers to come to him]. He would stay crouched down, even when they were singing, beating on a drum and singing, [the shaman] would stay there, and that is what they called *tuunrangcarrluni*.

When the third song was just finishing, that person out there—because they used to have doors on the floor where a person comes up when he enters—that [other shaman] he had gone to get appeared!

MARIE MEADE: Yes!

DICK ANTHONY: And night had fallen.

When he had come up, he said that as soon as he heard, he had come without eating his arrival meal and came there. He told them to get him a seal-gut rain garment.

When they got into a frenzy about the person who they are using their powers to heal, when they rapidly circled the subject, they would hit the drum and start singing.

So while [the shaman] is circling and he says "aarrarrarraa," like I said, they would stop singing and drumming. So [that shaman] down there would be talking about what was happening [to the subject].

It happened that on his third time circling, before the shaman from that village even got up from behind his subject, [the other shaman] asked [the shaman from the village], calling him by name, "You down there, when are you ever going to start using your powers?"

He did what they call *aniqlaaluku* [he cursed him], he threatened him. When they threaten them, they called it *aniqlaaluki* [they cursed them].

"You there, when are you going to use your powers? Now, while you are drinking water, look around and see how the water is and take a drink! And while you are still able to look around, look around and see how the world is!"

Then that wily [shaman] who had been crouching, taking his hat off and getting up, he said to that [other shaman], he called him by name as he was looking at him, "Passiilria! Are you threatening me now? You are dead!"

ARNAQ: Ya . . .

MINEGTULI: Tua-i atakutam kinguani tuunritliniluku taum.

Tamaa-i-am aqumtaqamegteki, imarnitet imkarluku qamiqumeggnun patukeqerluki tunuatni apqiitnek tuunrangcartaquq angalkuq. Tua-i lavngaurluni atuangraata tua-i, cauyarluteng atuangraata, tua-i tuantaurluni wagg'u-q' tuunrangcarrluni.

Tua-i yuarutet pingayuurteqertelluki, iquklitqertelluku, tua-i-ll' ugna—pugyaranek amiingqetullruameng—tua-i-ll' puggliniuq imna augna aqvayaaqellra!

ARNAQ: Ii-i!

MINEGTULI: Tan'geriluni-ll' qakemna.

Nugngami pilliniuq, tua-i waniw' niigarucirramitun tekiutarpek'nani-ll' tua-i waniw' tainiluni. Imarnitegnek aqvacesqelluni.

Tamaa-i im' ilungengaqameng-am taugaam, una tuunriskengarteng ilungutngaqamegteggu, tua-i cukamek uivqerrluku ayagareskata, kaugluteng-llu aturpagluteng.

Tua-i-llu uivvaarinanermini aarrarrarraaqan, tua-i aug'utun qanllemtun arulairrluteng tua-i atunermek tua-i taqluteng cauyanermek-llu. Kan'a tua-i qanerturluni waten qaillun pillranek.

Atam tuaten uivqerrartellermi pingayuagni, tauna tua-i nunalga makpailgan taum tuunriskengami tunuani, qanaarraarluni [?nunaleni] tauna pillinia arivvluku, "Kacuur, usuuq, qaku tuunriqataqsit?"

Apqiitnek aniqlaallinia, akeqnerrlualuku. Akeqnerrluagaqamegteki tamaa-i aniqlaanilaqait.

"Qaku usuuq tuunriqataqsit? Atak mer'umaurallerpeni, mer'em callra kiarrluku, mer'a! Cali-llu kiarcugngaurallerpeni, ellam callra cali caluku kiaresgu ella!"

Nutaan atam taunall'er lavngauralria nacani aug'arluku makluni, pillinia, aterpagtellinia wavet takuyarluku, "Passiilria! Waniwa-qaa aniqlaagarpenga? Tuquuten!"

He was what they call a *kitengkayuli* [one who kicks]. He does what they call *kitengkarluni* [he kicks]. They say when he was determined, he would kick. And his drumming had two beats. That was the length of his ritual.

When [the shaman] started, he said, "Two of them!"

When [the other shaman] started, shortly after they sang the song, they hit two beats and then he stopped and said "aarrarrarraa." Then they stopped [singing]! After he talked, once again . . . And that [shaman] who kept going around in circles down there, he suddenly crouched down on the floor boards of the *qasgiq*!

He prevented his counterpart who had been going around in circles from summoning his helping spirits!

They would beat [the drum] two times, then he would say "aarrarrarraa." That is the way he would stop.

MARIE MEADE: [The shaman] from the Akula area?
DICK ANTHONY: No, [the shaman] from the coastal region. When the inland [shaman] suddenly crouched down, he never stood up.

So sometimes after going around in a circle, he'd quickly head up to where the people were sitting.

MARIE MEADE: The one crouched down?
DICK ANTHONY: Exactly.

So while he was doing that, he said that he had no more medicine rites to perform, that he was done with [the person]. He told that person that he was using his helping spirits to cure to go home.

That one they had brought [on a stretcher], her husband brought her home by holding her arm.

So he was finished.

[That shaman] who had performed the real incantation for her, while they were lying down facing each other that night, his fellow villager asked him how far he had gone when he stopped doing the incantation.

So that wily shaman answered him that since he didn't want [the other shaman to die] in that village, he had given him one day [to live].

So they went to sleep. The next day, that [other shaman] went back to his village.

So time passed all through that fall.

When one of the men from Cevv'arneq arrived, and while he was at the *qasgiq* and had eaten dinner, he said that that person they had come to get

Apqiitnek taun' kitengkayuliuguq-gguq. Kitengkarluni-gguq wagg'u-q'. Umyuani tua-i cumikaqtarqan-gguq tua-i kitengkarquq. Cauyarluni cal' kaugtunregnek malrugnek. Tua-i tuunrillran amllertacia.

Ayagarcami qanlliniuq, "Malrugnek!"

Ayagarcan tua-i yuarun atuckaqerluku malrurqugnek kaugluku aarrarrarraarluni. Tua-i taqluteng tua-i! Qanerturauqaarluku tuamtell' tua-i . . . Kan'a-ll' imna uivqerrartetuli lavqerrluni qasgim nacitainun!

Tuunrangesciigatevkarluku tua-i aipani uivqerrartaqelria taun'!

Tua-i kaugaqluku malrurqugnek aarrarrarraarluni. Tua-i taquciqluku.

ARNAQ: Taun' Akulmiurtaa?
MINEGTULI: No, cenarmiuqlia. Nunamiuqlia lavqercami tua-i nangercuinani.

Tua-i uivqerpakartelluku iliini pavavet yugnun tagqercaaqellininaurtuq, yuut tam' aqumgallratnun pavavet.
ARNAQ: Lavingalria tauna?
MINEGTULI: Ii-i.

Tua-i, tua-i tuatnavakarluni qanlliniuq tuunritkartairutniluku tua-i, taqniluku. Agesqelluku kan' tuunriskengani.

Imna kevegluku taitellrat uingan tass'urluku agulluku.

Tua-i taqluni.

Tua-i tauna tuunritpiartellra, nunalgutiin tua-i waten cauqerluku atakurpak inaquuyaarallermegni kelutmun pilutek, aptellinia, aptevguarallinia qaillun pitaluku taqellranek.

Tua-i taum angalkullraam pillrallinia, pillinia maani pivkaryuumiilamiu ernermek ataucimek cikirniluku.

Tua-i qavarluteng. Ercan tua-i tayim' utertelliniluni tauna.

Tua-i tayim' uksuarpak.

Tua-i Cevv'arnermiut iliit tekican-am tua-i tekilluni qasgimi tua-i uitainanermini nerellmi kinguakun qanlliniuq uksuaq imna aqvallrat,

in the fall, in the evening, they had slept in the *qasgiq*, when they woke up they found that he had died.

He gave [the other shaman] just one day.

MARIE MEADE: Yes.

DICK ANTHONY: When there were three shamans or two of them doing an incantation at the same time on that sick person, when two shamans start to dislike each other and fight, one of the people who was watching them would say, "For goodness sakes, Dudes! Pay attention to that person who you are doing the healing ceremony for!"

When they keep telling them that, [the shaman] who was stronger would say, "We are making medicine for him now!" But from what they could see, they go on like they are disputing with each other.

It so happens the stronger [shaman] was giving the sickness of the person down there [who they were healing] to that other shaman who was weaker than him.

MARIE MEADE: Those two [shamans] were from the same village?

DICK ANTHONY: Right on!

MARIE MEADE: I knew it . . .

DICK ANTHONY: Even when they are from the same village or they have a guest from another village performing with them.

So they would save that person who had been heading toward his death.

There are three [shamans] sometimes when they work on a subject. And if there are three of them working on them, those two [shamans] would give the sickness of that subject down there to that weaker shaman.

MARIE MEADE: This cassette tape has become full already!

unuan qavarluteng tua-i qasgimi, maaten tua-i tupalliniut tuqullrullinilria.

Tua-i ernermek ataucimek ciki[rluku].

ARNAQ: Ii-i.

MINEGTULI: Tamaa-i-am pingayuulluku-llu, wall' malruulluku piaqamegteggu nangteqelria tauna, kenkenriqrullutek ukug' angalkuk ellmegnun, waten tua-i inglukuurullutek pingaqagnek, taun' tua-i tangvagtaita ukut ilaita pilalliniluki, "Aling! Tuunriskengartek atak tauna cumikluku tuunritgu!"

Tua-i pivakartellutek qanlarnilaqait, qanlernilaqiit tauna pininra, "Waniw' tuunritarpuk!" Amta-llu-gguq tua-i tangvanermi ellmegnun taugaam tua-i kenkenrilullutek pilutek.

Cunawa taum pininran tua-i nangtequtii taumun tua-i, kat'um nangtequtii tunlallinikii, cirlakekngaminun taumun angalkumun.

ARNAQ: Nunalguteklutek-qaa taukuk?

MINEGTULI: Ii-i.

ARNAQ: Em-em . . .

MINEGTULI: Tuaten nunalgutkeng'ermeng wall' allanermek ilangqeng'ermeng.

Tua-i anirturluku tauna tuqullerkami tungiinun ayagyaaqelleq.

Ilait-llu call' pingayuulluku piaqluku. Pingayuuskunegteggu-am cali tua-i tuaten ilaseng cirlakekunegnegu ukuk ilasek, tua-i call' tuavet tua-i tuaten tun'urluku tauna ikiutii taman' kat'um pitullrulliniluku.

ARNAQ: Ak'a-am un' muiqertelliniuq!

When they are training future *angalkut*, they also used to bind them[19]

Dick Anthony and Marie Meade, Toksook Bay, January 1996

DICK ANTHONY: These shamans, this is what they would say about shamans: Some shamans have malicious intent. And a person who is about to die blames him, well, they are tormented by [the shaman].

Angalkurkat tamakut qaillukuangaqaceteng, qillerqelluki tuaten piaqluki

---

Minegtuli Arnaq-llu, Nunakauyaq, January 1996

MINEGTULI: Waten-wa makut tuunrangayiit, waten angalkunek qantullrulriit: Angalkuulriim ilii, umyuarrliqtuluni. Cali uum tuquqatalriim avalillukluku, tua-i-w' kapiatekaqluku piaqluku.

They say that [the shaman] had put him in a situation where he would die. [The one dying] knew his attacker, even though he is not a shaman but just an ordinary person. He would be tormented by [the shaman]. That's what they would experience because of [the shaman]. That's what I used to hear.

When they were training the future shamans, they'd also tie them up. Some [shamans in training] used to prohibit people from tying them down to the floor boards over the fire pit of the *qasgiq*. They say it can make you malicious, it can cause you to be malicious.

MARIE MEADE: The ones who had been tied up?

DICK ANTHONY: They gave that reasoning. Being tied to the floor boards over the fire pit [in the *qasgiq*] makes one malicious. Some [shamans] told others that they could do anything to them, but never to tie them to the floor boards of the *qasgiq*. They said it can make one malicious. That is the way they were.

I have only heard stories about but not seen some shamans who dabbled in shamanistic activity.

Though they cured people or made things appear, when their time came to die, they died. [*chuckles*]

Cunawa-gguq tua-i taum tuqullerkaanun elliluku. Pistellni tauna tua-i nalluyuunaku angalkuunrilngermi waten yuunginaungermi. Kapiatekaqluku. Pitullrullinikiit tuaten. Tuaten tua-i ayuqluku niicugnilallruaqa.

Tamaa-i alairyugarararkamek, angalkurkat tamakut qaillukuangaqaceteng, qillerqelluki tuaten piaqluki. Tamaa-i ilait inerquutetullrullinilriit qasgim nacitiinun nacitmun qillerqucesqevkenateng. Umyarrluunarqut-gguq, umyuarrliqnarqut.

ARNAQ: Qillerqutellret?

MINEGTULI: Kangilirluku-w' tua tuaten pilallrukiit. Umyuarrliqnaqniluki nacitet qillerqut. Ilait-gguq tua-i inerquutetullruut qaillukuangraiceteng, qasgim nacitiinun qillerqucesqevkenateng. Umyuarrliqnarqut-gguq. Tuaten tua-i ayuqellriit.

Avani qanemcimek, tangvallrunrilkenka, qanemciuluki taugaam niitetullrukenka augkut qaillukuatulit angalkut ilait.

Anirtuilguluteng qaill' ca una alairtaqluku pitullrung'ermeng, tua-i taugaam tuqullerkarteng tekitaqan, tuqulallrulriit. [*ngelaq'erluni*]

I used to see shamans performing rituals using their powers in the *qasgiq*[9]

Dick Andrew and Marie Meade, Bethel, August 1992

DICK ANDREW: I used to see shamans performing rituals using their powers in the *qasgiq*. When I watched them, they would be singing the kind of songs we called *yuarulluut* [songs composed by shamans and performed by others when shamans use their power]. During this time, we dance some of their songs.

MARIE MEADE: Who were they working on using their powers when you watched them?

DICK ANDREW: When Tutgara'urluq was performing an incantation. Aparr'aq, too, the one who your grandmother helped to become a shaman, the person she helped to become one of those kind. I watched them work. Those shamans.

My father [and his siblings'] real *iluraq* [male cross-cousin], their cousin, he wrapped himself up in a bearded-seal skin. He had the others sew him up inside it using a harpoon line as a thread.

Angalkunek tuunrilrianek tangvatullruunga qasgimi

Apaqutaq Arnaq-llu, Mamterilleq, August 1992

APAQUTAQ: Angalkunek tuunrilrianek tangvatullruunga qasgimi. Tangvagaqamteng tua-i atuanaurtut tua-i yuarutnek augkunek yuarullugnek pitukaitnek. Maa-i-w' yuraqetukvut ilait yuarutaita.

ARNAQ: Kina tuani tuunrillrani tuunritellratgu tangvallrusiu?

APAQUTAQ: Tutgara'urluq tuunrillrani. Aparr'aq-llu, taum maurlurpet angalkuurtevkallra, pistellra, tamakuurtevkallra, tamakuurcetevkallra. Taukunek tangvatullruunga. Angalkut tamakut.

Atamta iluraat-gguq nakmiin tauna, *cousin-aarat*, maklagmun waten imgulluni. Usaamek yualirluk' waten mingqutevkarluni.

He would travel. When he'd travel, and when he'd travel to the ocean, they would use a harpoon line as a rope to hold him. He would leave his [seal-skin] covering at the doorway and they wouldn't know where he went.

He'd travel, *ayagluni* as they called it. That shaman Aparr'aq. He would leave his skin covering behind, the bearded-seal skin.

He would come back when he was ready. They would sing songs when he was gone, they would sing what they call *yuarulluut* [shaman songs].

Ayagaqluni. Ayagaqami, imarrluni-llu-gguq ayagaqami, usaamek uskurirluku. Ayagaqluni tua-i waten caqutuumarmi. Tua-i-ll' caquni unilluku amigmi tayima nanluciinani.

Tua-i-gguq ayagluni. Taun' angalkuq Aparr'aq. Amini taun' unilluku, makliim amia tayima.

Tua-i tekillun' tekicungaqami tekitaqluni. Kingunrani aturpaagaraqluteng yuarutnek, yuarullugnek-gguq aturpaagarluteng.

They say those apparitions would block the doorways from people[10]

Dick Andrew and Marie Meade, Bethel, August 1992

MARIE MEADE: Back when the apparitions were common, too.

DICK ANDREW: Yes. They say there were many apparitions in those days. They say those shamans would also use the bodies of those who died and would be seen as apparitions. They would use the body of a person though he had died. [chuckle]

MARIE MEADE: Do you know any *qulirat* [legends] about apparitions?

DICK ANDREW: They aren't *qulirat*, but they are *qanemcit* [stories, historical tales]. I had just told a geniune *quliraq* just a few minutes ago. However these [shaman and ghost stories] are *qanemcit*.

MARIE MEADE: The apparitions? Have you ever seen an apparition?

DICK ANDREW: Yes.

MARIE MEADE: Has anyone ever told you about his/her experience with an apparition?

DICK ANDREW: They say those apparitions would block the doorways from people, too. When they'd block doorways, if [the apparition] was a male, people were instructed to stick their hands in here [neck area] to try to touch it on the skin.

MARIE MEADE: On his neck?

DICK ANDREW: Yes. You would try to touch it. They say your hands would get very cold, they would be very cold. Their hands would sting after they briefly stuck them in there trying to touch its skin.

MARIE MEADE: Their shoulder?

DICK ANDREW: Yes. Then you would slowly push down here [placing the hand above the head] with the weight of your arm. If you come down too fast it would come back up. [One would only push down] with the weight of his arm.

Alangrut-gguq tamakut waten amiigituit-llu tamaani

Apaqutaq Arnaq-llu, Mamterilleq, August 1992

ARNAQ: Alangrut-llu-w' tamaani nurnaitellratni.

APAQUTAQ: Ii-i. Alangrut-llu-gguq nurnaitellruut tua-i tamaani. Makut-gguq, tamakut angalkut amilirluteng, tuunrat tamakut amilirluteng tuqullernek-ll' alangruutullruut. Amiqluku tauna tuqumangraan. [ngel'artuq]

ARNAQ: Alangrunek-qaa qulirarnek nallunrituten?

APAQUTAQ: Qulirauvkenateng-w', qanemciuluteng taugaam tua-i. Ava-i augkunek qulirapianek quliriunga ava-i. Makut taugaam qanemciugut.

ARNAQ: Alangrut? Alangruqaqsaituten-q' elpet?

APAQUTAQ: Ii-i.

ARNAQ: Kia-qaa qalamciteksaitaaten alangrullminek?

APAQUTAQ: Alangrut-gguq tamakut waten amiigituit-llu tamaani. Amiigirqaceteng-gguq, angutngulliniaqan uugg'un kauluku kemga agtungnaqluku.

ARNAQ: Uyaqurrakun?

APAQUTAQ: Mm-m. Agtungnaqluku. Tua-i-gguq unatairnarqut cakneq, kumlalluk' cakneq. Pupingquagaqluki-llu-gguq maavet kausngaqallrit kemgat agtuqangnaqluki.

ARNAQ: Tusgat?

APAQUTAQ: Mm-m. Tua-i-llu-gguq uugg'un waten negqurluki tallimi tua-i uqamii anagteksaunaku. Negpallakarqaku-gguq ataam utqaniraqluni. Taugaam uqamiinek tallimi.

Then when [his hand] is flat against the ground he'd step on it with his feet, and the apparition would disappear. Then he'd go back inside. That was what apparitions would do when they block the doorway on a person, *amiigirluku*.

MARIE MEADE: What about if [the ghost] was a woman?

DICK ANDREW: And if it's a woman, one would put his hand in down under the hem of her garment. He'd put his hand in and try to touch the top of her leg. They say that was what they did.

They say some of them would have a veil through here, and their faces would be covered with something. When they'd try to see them, they would slowly turn away, they'd turn and hide their faces. They say those have veils over their faces. Apparently, a long time ago, [when people died] they used to cover their faces.

MARIE MEADE: When they died?

DICK ANDREW: Yes. I don't know who [would be covered].

Tua-i-llu-gguq tuaten tua-i nunamun patguskan nutaan kan' it'gaminek piqerluku tua-i tayim' alangruq tamarlun'. Iterluni-ll' tua-i. Tuaten-gguq alangrut pitullruut amiigiqai, amiigirluku.

ARNAQ: Arnaukan-mi?

APAQUTAQ: Arnaukan-llu-gguq maaggun akuakun cali kauluku. Akuakun tua-i kauluku man'a iruan kangia agtuqangnaqluku cali. Tuaten-gguq cal' pitullruut.

Ilait-gguq patukutangqelartut maaggun, kegginait-llu patuluteng canek. Ilait-gguq waten igvaqangnaqaqaceteng-llu uivumalartut, tua-i uivumaarluteng qimagalluk' kegginateng. Tamakut-gguq patukutalget kegginait. Ak'a tamaa-i yuut patuluki-ll' kegginait pitullrulliniamegteki.

ARNAQ: Tuquaqata?

APAQUTAQ: Ii-i. Calriit tayim'.

It was probably Tumaralria's drum[11]

Paul John, Bethel, August 2003

PAUL JOHN: It was probably Tumaralria's drum. I've never heard any explanation about Tumaralria's drum, but they'd tell stories about him.

He was the strongest among all the shamans on the coast. There was no other [shaman] who was more powerful. [He] could do anything. And he could travel through the ground when he wanted to.

Long after he died, and that person—I shouldn't tell the story because I will take up your time—when that person was born, he used to hear of Tumaralria, a powerful shaman on Nelson Island.

He had become an adult then, and when he was able to construct a kayak, he was roughly cutting the shapes of his kayak parts during the summer but not finishing them, what they call *qanilqer-luki*, right below the first village of the people of Tununak, the rib parts, lower bow parts, stern bottom parts, those parts. He left the kayak parts that he constructed at their winter village when they moved [to spring camp].

Winter came, after the shorfast ice froze into a large mass . . . That person apparently had one dog. He went to get his kayak parts.

Tumaralriim-wa aipaagni cauyalqellikii

Kangrilnguq, Mamterilleq, August 2003

KANGRILNGUQ: Tumaralriim-wa aipaagni cauyalqellikii. Taugaam Tumaraliriim tauna cauyaanek qaneryararluk' niiteqaqsaitaqa, taugaam qanemciuluku qanrutkelallruat.

Kayutatailqurrakacagalleq unani angalkuni tamaitni. Tuknitataitqapiaralleq. Tua-i ca tamalkuan piyugngaluku. Nunam-llu akuliikun eglercugngaluni piyugaqami.

Tua-i-llu tuqullra akaurrluni tayima, tauna-llu yuk tauna—qanemcinrillii uamciiqamci—tauna yuk yuurcami niitelallliniluni tua-i taumek Tumaralriamek Qaluyaani angalkumek kayulriamek.

Tua-i taqnerurrluni tamaa-i, qayiyugngariami-ll' ellminek qayarkani-am tua-i kiaguluku, Tununermiut nunaqerraallrat uatiitni uani apqiitnek qanilqaarturluki taqenrilngermiki ayagarkat, cat amuvigkat, kagaalurkat tamakut. Uksiyarameggnun tua-i upiimeng unilluki taukut qayarkiurani.

Uksurluni, tuarpangan . . . Qiumugkarangqellliniluni ataucimek tauna. Aqvalliniluki taukut qayarkiurarkani.

They say that the only provisions he had were raw frozen blackfish from the inner funnel of the fish trap where it narrows and the hole leads inside the fish trap.

When he arrived at the old village of Tununak, down the coast from [the current village], he went inside the *qasgiq* and brought his dog inside, and they ate his provisions, and he even gave his dog something to eat. And they didn't finish their provisions from the bottom part of the inner fish trap funnel.

When he was done, he went to bed, and because he had eaten frozen fish, he was cold. And right below him, his dog was curled up right next to him.

As he was trying to sleep, when the *qasgiq* jolted, he suddenly woke. They say there was a full moon. The floor of the *qasgiq* suddenly detached all the way around and lifted, and he could go outside through there himself.

Back then when they used to encounter ghosts, since he heard about haunting occurances in stories, the part where the *qasgiq* detached, thinking that it might land back in place, he took their leftover and threw it underneath [the crack]. It just rolled outside, and nothing happened to the *qasgiq*, but it was still detached.

When he thought he heard crunching snow, when he thought he heard someone walking, he listened closely and heard snow crunching from the area near where Tununak would come to be established. He looked and saw a person coming from there.

When he arrived right outside, he entered through the area where there was usually a door up front, and when he stood in front of him, he told him, "Because I didn't want you to be cold when you slept here all night, I have come to get you so that you can sleep up there at a place where you won't feel cold."

He suddenly thought, "I thought they said that when they reply to these ghosts, they lose their ability to talk." And his dog didn't sense anything. His dog hadn't moved from his curled position. Even though they said that dogs are aware and can sense ghosts, his dog hadn't sensed anything and stayed curled where it was.

When he thought that, the one who went to get him replied, "You will not lose your ability to talk, even though you speak to me. I'm not a ghost. Just get up and come with me."

Taquara-wa-gguq waten ilulirallret kan'a igyaricartullrat, can'giirnek tua-i kumlanernek taukut taquarluni.

Tua-i tekicami Tununermiut nunallritnun uaqliitnun qasgimun-am tua-i iterluni, qimugkaarani-ll' taun' itrulluku nerrlinilutek taquaminek tua-i, qimugteni-ll' tauna neqkiurluku cikirluku. Tauna-llu-gguq nangevkenaku tua-i taquartek, ilulirat kan'a pillrat.

Aren maaten-gguq tua-i taqngami inartuq, kumlanertullruami-llu tua-i pacelluku. Tauna-llu-gguq call' qimugkarii waniw' ketiini ungelrumaluni tua-i wani.

Qavangnaqsaaqnginanrani qasgi man'a qatngican uigartelliniuq. Iralvagtuq-gguq, unugcuullugpagtuq. Qasgim man'a acia kevkartellinilria kassugarrluni tua-i-gguq anyuumaluni-ll' ellii tamaaggun.

Tua-i alangrutullratni tamaa-i alangrut qalangssauluk' niitelaamiki, ataam tamana qasgiq kevkartellra ataam, tut'ellerkaa umyuaqluku, tauna tua-i ilakuartek aciakun tamaaggun egcaaqellinikii. Ava-i-llu-gguq akagluni anengraan, qasgi taman' cakanirpek'nani kevkaringaluni.

Camek-gguq qerqiuggngalngurmek pektellriarngalngurmek niicami niicugnilun' pilliniuq, ikegkut ika-i Tununermiut nunaurrvigkaqlinikiita tungiinek, qerqiugtellinilria. Pilun' pilliniuq yug' man'a agiirtellria.

Tua-i kegga-i ellircami elatiinun pirraarluni, amingqerrsaraakun uaggun iterluni amiigakun ciuqerranun nang'ercami pillinia, "Nenglliuresqumanrilamken maani qavaquvet unugpak, nenglliunritarallerkarpeni qavaasqelluten pamani aqvaamken."

Umyuarteqa'artelliniuq, "Aren makut-ggem alangrut kiumraaqatki qanernanrirniaqait." Qimugtii-llu-gguq tauna tua-i cameg' nalluluni. Man'a tua-i ungelrumaarallra pekteksaunani qumugkarii tauna. Alangrut-gguq qimugtenun nalluyuitnilaryaaqekait, qimugtii taun' cameg' nalluluni tua-i ungulrumaurluni.

Tuaten-am umyuarteqngan taum aqvastiin kiullia, "Aren qanaateng'erpenga qanernanrirngaituten. Alangruunritua. Maligesnga taugaam makluten."

He got up and they went up together. When they went inland, he saw a village up ahead of them in a place where there was usually no village. And their *qasgiq* was visible, it was obviously a *qasgiq*. He brought him to the *qasgiq* and brought him in. They entered and it was very hot in there and wasn't cold whatsoever. When he laid down, he fell asleep.

After a while, the one next to him woke him up and told him, "It's time for you to get up. The one who is to offer us food is about to come in."

Just as he woke, the one who was giving them food handed it to the one who went to get him, and the bowl was filled with frozen whitefish. He said to him, "Don't feel squeamish about the next one that they will offer you, but accept it without any qualms."

When the next one arrived, she was holding a bowl. He looked inside it and saw that it was filled with a child with its stomach split open, and it looked as though the area where the stomach was split had teeth around it. Even though he had told him to accept it without being squeamish, he stayed and didn't extend his arms.

When he didn't extend his arms to take it, the one next to him told him, "So, you don't want to accept it. It's okay if you don't want to accept it." He told that one to take it back.

When she took it out, he faced him talking about the contents of his bowl, "Let's eat this together." He ate the whitefish with him.

When he was finished, he told him, "Now, you should return. I'll follow you when you go down." He put on his skin boots, and when he went out he went with him, and as they were going down toward the *qasgiq* where he slept at first, that one told him, "I wonder what you think I am. What do you think I am?" That person said he didn't know.

When he said he didn't know, he told him, "Now, have you heard of the shaman of the people of Nelson Island, Tumaralria? I am him. Since I didn't want you to sleep in a cold place, and since I wanted you to sleep warm, I went to get you. Now, when you return home, there are people still alive in your village who heard of me, tell them, 'Tumaralria had me sleep in a place where I wouldn't be cold.'"

When he got home, he told that story, since he had also heard of Tumaralria, the shaman of the people of Nelson Island.

When he told the story, those people said that since he wasn't a malicious shaman when he was

Tua-i makluni malikluku tagglinilutek. Kelutmurcamek-wa tua-i pilliniuq nunat pingkut ciunragni, nunatangqessuilnguq-wa-gguq. Qasgiat-llu-gguq yaa-i nallunaunani, qasgiq tua-i elitaqnaqluni. Tuavet tua-i qasgimun ciuniulluk'. Itliniuk, aa-gguq kiirpagluni naugg'un qerrutnaqsugnaunani. Aaa, inartellriim tayim' qavaqalliniluni.

Piinanrani uum tupagtellinia caniqlian, "Kiik amci maknariaten. Payugcetevuk itrarkaurtuq."

Tua-i makluni piqanrakun, tua-i-llu-wa payugtellria itrami, taumun tua-i aqvastellranun tunllinia qaurtunek imarluni urungnaarmek qantaq. Pillinia, "Kinguqlirkaan elpenun payugutkaa, qungvakevkenaku ciuniuqiu."

Kinguqlia pugngami pilliniuq tua-i tuaten qantamek tegumiarluni. Uyangtellinia mikelnguyagarmek imarluni aqsiik ullingqalutek, tuarpiaq-gguq keggutet ullingqallran avatiini. Aling tua-i qungvakevkenaku ciuniuresqessaaqellrungraaku, tua-i uitalliniluni yagtevkenani.

Yagtenrilan uum caniqlian pillinia, "Tua-i ciuniuryuumiitellinian. Ciuniunrilngerpegu canrituq." Ut'rutesqelluku taumun tua-i.

Tayim' anucaku, qantami tauna imaa pillinia caugarrluku, "Nerullunuk nernaurpuk." Tua-i nerlutek nerulluku qaurtumek.

Tua-i taqngan pillinia, "Kitek' nutaan kingutmuarturniartuten. Atraquvet maligqurciqamken." Tua-i piluguugni aqaarlukek, anngan-am maliggluku tuavet tua-i qasgimun inarvviksaaqellranun atrainanermegni, taum pillinia, "Aling cauyuklua-kiq tayima umyuan pia, cauyuklua pisia?" Naamikikaallinia taum.

Naamikiikaarani pillinia, "Tua-llu-qaa niicuitaquten tayima Qaluyaat ukut angalkullratnek Tumaralriamek? Wanguuq waniwa. Qerrutesqumanrilamken urumaluten qavallerkarpenek aqvallruamken. Kitak' kinguniskuvet niitetustellrenka kingunerpeni call' unguvaut, qanemcikina, 'Tumaralriim qerrutenritlerkamni qavaryarturcetellruanga.'"

Tua-i kingunicami taumek qanemcilliniluni, niitetuamiu-llu angalkullrat tauna Qaluyaarmiut Tumaralria.

Tua-i qanemcian taukut qanaalliniluteng, umyuarrluunritellruami-gguq tamaa-i

their shaman, he still had compassion for people. Those people were praising him for the fact that he took pity on him.

That was probably Tumaralria's drum if it's from Nelson Island.

There was a woman who had let someone make a bearded-seal mask[12]

Benedict Tucker and Paul John, Bethel, May 2003

BENEDICT TUCKER: And one time, the village of Emmonak made masks in recent times, but it was apparently the last time.

Those who made masks would make the masks using their powers, making the mask look like their vision.

[The mask] was a way for them to request things.

They explained what those [masks] were when the people arrived. They explained that that mask was a means for [that shaman to request things].

They would make sounds that were appropriate to the depiction of that mask.

That was what I saw.

PAUL JOHN: Oh, my! When they made masks at Kwethluk, the people from the muddy lowland coast, at the time, since the people of the muddy lowlands would move to the mouth of the Kuskokwim River to go salmon fishing, the people of Kwethluk asked them to come, and the people of Kwethluk probably partnered with the villages that were close to them.

There was a woman who had let someone make a bearded-seal mask; but that woman was a shaman.

After the guests arrived, that woman, since she was a shaman and had someone make a bearded-seal mask, after the guests had eaten, she showed that mask to the people of the coast. It looked like a bearded-seal model.

She said that because she was always so grateful when the coastal people gave her coastal food, so she had made this in support of the people from the coast and not for the people of her village. She said she made it thinking of the people from the coast.

They call it *qalrirluteng* [bearded seals in rut making their mating calls] when bearded seals make their calls after diving in the water.

angalkuqellratni, tua-i-gguq-am cali naklegyuumalliniuq yugnek makunek. Naklekellra tauna piluku ucuqluku tua-i tamakut yuut.

Aipaagni-ll' taun' cauyalqellikii Tumaralriim Qaluyaanek pillrukan.

Taumek arnamek maklaguamek kegginaqivkallrullinilriamek

Cikulraaciq Kangrilnguq-llu, Mamterilleq, May 2003

CIKULRAACIQ: Ataucirqumek-llu taukut Imangarmiut kegginaqillruut tua-i ukaqvaggun, nangermek cunaw' tua-i.

Kegginaqilriit tamakut kegginaquteng tua-i tamakut casuutmeggni tayim' ellaita, tangvallermegteggun ayuqeliluku kegginaqinaurtut.

Pissuutekluku, kaigassutekluku.

Tua-i tamakut aperturluki tuani yuut tekicata. Nalqiggluku, tauna tua-i kegginaquq taumun pissuutekniluku.

Tuacetun tua-i kegginaqum taum ayuqiinek qalriacianek.

Tua-i tauna, tangellruama.

KANGRILNGUQ: Aling! Tua-i kegginaqillratni kiani Kuigglugmi, unkumiut mararmiut, tuani-am mararmiut unkut Kusquqviim un'gavet painganun neqliayaqulaata, kiaken call' Kuigglugmek tungcillinikait, Kuigglugmiut-llu tayim' ikayungqellilriit mallgeskemeggnek.

Taumek arnamek maklaguamek kegginaqivkallrullinilriamek; angalkuuluni taugaam arnaq tauna.

Tua-i-gguq allaneteng tekicata tauna imna arnaq, angalkuulliniami, maklaguamek kegginaqivkalleq, allanret tua-i nererraartelluki tauna kegginaqivkallni maniuraa Cenarmiunun. Maklaguatun-gguq tua-i ayuqluni maklak.

Pilliniuq ellii waniwa quyalaami cakneq unkumiut unkumiutarnek cikiqerqatni, ellii waniwa una cingumatekluku unkumiunun, nunalgutminun umyuaqutkenritniluku. Unkumiunun taugaam umyuaqutekniluku.

Makliit qalrirniaqekait neplirqata mermun angllurraarluteng.

BENEDICT TUCKER: Yes.

PAUL JOHN: She said that she was going to make a mating call for that mask.

   As soon as she disappeared down through the underground tunnel entranceway, just as she went out of view, there came a sound exactly like that made by a bearded seal, like a *qalriq* [male bearded seal making its mating call]!

BENEDICT TUCKER: That elderly woman?

PAUL JOHN: Yes! Since those people from the coast were so amazed that she had produced the exact sound [of a male bearded seal in rut], some of them said it was like their heads split open and they felt tingling because they were so amazed! [*laughter*]

   Those people who I saw [before they died] told that story. It was because she made the exact sound of a bearded seal in rut making its mating call, even though she had never been to the ocean.

BENEDICT TUCKER: Those people did not do it themselves.

"I brought you here so that you could call our grandchild over there a name!"[13]

Paul John, Benedict Tucker, Martina John,
and Marie Meade, Bethel, May 2003

PAUL JOHN: My mother's uncle, because he was a shaman, I always called him "Tuunraruaqestekaa" [One who will be my *tuunraruaq* (pretend spirit helper)].

BENEDICT TUCKER: Okay.

PAUL JOHN: That was the only way I addressed him "Tuunraruaqestekaa."

   At the time, while I was sleeping next to my grandmother, his dogs . . . Oh no, I got ahead of myself. This may not be appropriate to tell at this time?

MARIE MEADE: It's cool!

PAUL JOHN: Back when I was a baby, he was my paternal grandfather's *iluraq* [male cross-cousin]. But that shaman was also my mother's maternal uncle.

   When he arrived while [my grandfather] was in the *qasgiq*, [my grandfather] asked him to go with him, "Let's go to my house so you may eat your arrival meal."

   When he was finished eating his arrival meal—my mother was nursing me then because I

CIKULRAACIQ: Ii-i.

KANGRILNGUQ: Waniwa-ll' elliin qalriuciliqatarniluku tauna.

   Qasgimi-gguq kalvagyaraanun cakma kalevngami ipteqerluni nepngumaartuq-gguq maklak'apiartun neperluni, qalritun!

CIKULRAACIQ: Arnangyaaq-qaa?

KANGRILNGUQ: Ii-i! Tuarpiaq-gguq tang unkumiut taumek imumek ucuryugtacirmeggni nepii ayuqelissiyaagpakaaku, ilaita-gguq man'a kevkarrnganan' tuarpiaq qakmallegtelalria-ll' qamiqurrat ugaan tua-i ucuryugyaaqem! [*ngel'artut*]

   Taumeg'-am tua-i qanemcingqetuqallruut augkut anguqallrenka. Tua-i ayuqelissiyaagpakarluku-gguq makliim qalriryaraa imarpigteqaqsaileng'ermi taum arnam neplircecaku.

CIKULRAACIQ: Tamakut-wa tua-i ellmeggnek-llu pilanrilnguut.

"Maavet taiculuugtamken tutgarpuk ikna tuqlungssaaraqaasqelluku!"

Kangrilnguq, Cikulraaciq, Anguyaluk,
Arnaq-llu, Mamterilleq, May 2003

KANGRILNGUQ: Aug'um-am aanama angiin angalkuungami tuqlurturatullruaqa "Tuunraruaqestekaa."

CIKULRAACIQ: Em-em.

KANGRILNGUQ: Kiingan tua-i tuqluutekluku, "Tuunraruaqestekaa."

   Tamaa-i maurlurma caniani qavallemni, qimugtainek . . . Qang'a tua-i patakartua. Qanemciknarqenricaaqelliaqa?

ARNAQ: Assirtuq!

KANGRILNGUQ: Tamaa-i-gguq mikelnguulua, taum apa'urlurma ilu'urqelliniluku, aatama atiin. Aanama taugken cal' angakluku tauna angalkuq.

   Tauna-gguq imna tekican qasgimelnginanermini, apa'urlurma taum unayaqaa, "Amani aglunuk enemni tekiutaryartuqaa."

   Tekiutanermek taqngan—ika-i-gguq aanama anqiitayagaulua aamarrlua—pillina taum

was just a newborn—my grandfather said to him, "Okay now, it was because of our grandson across there that I invited you here so that you would call him a name! I brought you here so that you could call our grandchild over there a name!"

Because he had little regard for himself, my mother's uncle said, "I do not want to 'call him a name' in here where no one will hear! But I will call him a name at the *qasgiq* where shamans can hear me! Let him be taken to the *qasgiq*!"

And so he went out and went to the *qasgiq*.

Shortly after he had gone into the *qasgiq*, my grandfather came up [through the tunnel entryway] with my mother right behind him. My mother had me bundled up inside her parka.

When they came in, my grandfather asked [my mother] to give me to him, then he brought me to his *iluraq*, my mother's maternal uncle. When he brought me over, he said, "Okay now, call our grandson a name. I have brought him so that you can call him a name!"

So when he took me and cuddled me, he said to me up close . . . That person, since he was not the type to put himself down, he never put himself down, looking at my face, he called me a name, "Tuunraruaqestekaa [One who will be my pretend *tuunraq*]!"

He told exactly about himself!

BENEDICT TUCKER: Yes.
PAUL JOHN: "One who will be my pretend *tuunraq*!"
And then starting from the side wall, he went all the way around the *qasgiq*! "Regardless of anything that all these shamans might do!"

When he said that he was through with me, as my grandfather went to fetch me and bring me back to my mother, he whispered to him, "My word! You have given him such a big name that makes him so concerning!"

And then he answered him in a loud voice, "It isn't concerning at all!" [*laughter*]

After that time, while I was sleeping beside my grandmother, I was totally frightened by his dogs [in my dream]!

BENEDICT TUCKER: Yes.
PAUL JOHN: When my whimpering woke me up, my grandmother asked me, "What's happening to you?"

I said to her, "Because my Tuunraruaqestekaq . . . I used to call him my Tuunraruaqestekaq just like he called me."

apa'urlurma, "Kitaki ikna ikani tutgarpuk unayaqluugtamken asvaingssaaraqaasqelluku, aren tuqlungssaaraqaasqelluku. Maavet taiculuugtamken tutgarpuk ikna tuqlungssaaraqaasqelluku!"

Taum-am aanama angiin, ellminek-llu pinritekluni, pilriarunritekluni, pillina, "Maani niitestauni tuqluryumiitaqa! Qasgimi taugaam angalkut niicetekluki tuqlurciqaqa! Qasgitevkaqiu!"

Tua-i-llu-gguq anluni qasgimun agluni.

Uitauraqertelluku-gguq apa'urluqa pug'uq aanamnek kinguqlirluni. Aanama-gguq tua-i qumiklua.

Tua-i-llu-gguq itramek ua-i apa'urlurma tungcirlua tegulua, taumun tua-i ilu'urminun, aanama angiinun, taitaanga. Tekiucamia-gguq tua-i, "Kitak' tua-i tutgarpuk tuqlungssaarqerru. Tuqlungssaaraqaasqelluku taitaqa!"

Taum-gguq tua-i teguamia kenirmiglua, wavet pillinianga . . . Tua-i-am ellminek tauna ellminek kinguvartelriarunritniitekluni qanellmikun, pillni man'a ellminek kinguvanqanrilami, kegginaqa tua-i tangvagluku tuqlullinianga, "Tuunraruaqestekaa!"

Tuaten-gguq ellmineg'-am tua-i ayuqeliqapiggluni qanemcilliuq!

CIKULRAACIQ: Ii-i.
KANGRILNGUQ: "Tuunraruaqestekaa!" Tua-llu-gguq tua-i caniqamek ayagarrluku qasgi uivaa! "Makut maani angalkut piksugtengraata!"

Tua-i-gguq taqnianga apa'urlurma ulliimiu, aanamnun tegulua tunyarturlua, pillinia-gguq apa'urluma agyumciararaa, "Aling! tegg'anernarivakarluku-llu-tam tuqlurpagciu!"

Elliin-gguq qastuluni call' kiugaa, "Tegg'arnernaituq!" [*ngel'artut*]

Tamaa-i kinguani qimugtainek maurlurma caniani qavallemni alingqapialqa cakneq!

CIKULRAACIQ: Ii-i.
KANGRILNGUQ: Cungiallagallma-ll' tupagcanga maurlurluma pianga, "Qaill' pisit?"

Piaqa, "Tuunraruaqestekama-wa . . . Uterceta'arluku wiinga-ll Tuunraruaqestekamnek tuqlutullruamku."

"Because I am frightened by my Tuunraruaqes-tekaq's dogs!"

Oh my, my grandmother exclaimed, "What does he think he's doing? Let him be now, he will come sometime!" He wasn't living in the village where we stayed.

BENEDICT TUCKER: I see.

PAUL JOHN: When he came later on that winter and he was taking off his outer garments calling me his pretend spirit helper. When he sat down, my grandmother went to him. As she stood not very far from him, like one who despised him, she said to him not in a quiet voice, "What did you do to him, you scoundrel?!" [laughter]

She shouted to him, "You disturbed his sleep by frightening him with your dogs!"

Oh, my! The awful one she confronted, after he had been looking down while she was talking to him, he looked up at her smiling, "It is done! When a shaman tries to harass him, he shall know it!" [laughter]

"In case he didn't know when a shaman was harassing him, I tested him!" [laughter]

And there was a time when my uncle and I came here [to Bethel] with a boat that used sails. And that shaman who was from our village was also here [in Bethel].

Our boat was docked at [Brown] Slough where the bridge is located now. And that shaman's boat was docked beside our boat, too.

While I was doing something around there, that shaman appeared. Then he began to come toward me.

BENEDICT TUCKER: He was living here [in Bethel]?

PAUL JOHN: No, he was from our village; he was visiting this place like us. They used to call him Angutekayak [Frank Amadeus].

Oh, my! As soon as he started coming toward me, the part of my body that was toward him started to feel ticklish! I understood right away: My, this person coming toward me doesn't have good intentions toward me!

That shaman's older sister used to have a house there just on this side of the bridge where the small mound is. His older sister had a sod house.

My, I ran away from him as he approached. When I looked back, I'd see that he had increased his speed, and I also increased my speed! I kept the distance between us constant.

"Tuunraruaqestekama-wa qimugtiinek alingelrianga!"

Aren, maurluqa tua-i qanpagtuq, "Caqtarta? Uitasgu tekiciiquq!" Nunalgutkenrilamteggu.

CIKULRAACIQ: Ii-i.

KANGRILNGUQ: Tua-i-am tekicami-am uksuumainanrani matarrluni tua-i-am uputaarlua Tuunraruaqestekaminek. Aqumngan maurlurluma ullagaa. Ciuqerranun tua-i yaaqsissaagpek'naku nangercami kenkenrilngurtun tua-i imutun erinani qaskitevkenaku, "Caqtallrusiu?!" [ngel'artut]

Wavet pia, "Qavarrluvtuavkarluku qimugtevnek alingcetaaqtarluku!"

Aren! Ciunellrii imna putrunga'arrluni uitarraarluni qanrutellrani, quuyurmi ciugtuq, "Tua-i! Angalkuum pingraani nallungaitellinia!" [ngel'artut]

"Angalkum pikaku nallunayukluku pitassiallruaqa!" [ngel'artut]

Tua-i-ll' tua-i maavirtukut angaka-llu tengalratulikun angyakun. Augna-llu nunalgutvut angalkuq cali maanelmiluni.

Kanani kana-i Slough-m imum' uum, bridge-arkam cunawa nuniini angyarpuk culungqauq. Tua-i-ll' angyaa call' taum angalkum nuniini angyamta uitauq.

Tamaani piinanemni tauna im' anglkuq igvartuq. Tua-ll' man'a tungemnun taiguq.

CIKULRAACIQ: Makurmiunguluni?

KANGRILNGUQ: No, nunalgutvut; cali maavingqaluni. Angutekayagmek aug' pilallruat.

Aren! Tungemnun taingarcan tunglirnera man'a qungvagyuaranga'artuq! Taringartaqa: Aren mat'um maa-i umyuaqegciluni wangnun pinritliniuq man'a!

Kanani taum angalkum alqaa kat'um kana-i bridge-am ualirnera kan' qerkunani qerturiqertelartuq. Nengqellruuq alqaa tua-i nepiarrarmek.

Aren, tua-i qimagaqa tungemnun taingan. Kingyaq'ernauqa ellii-llu cukarikanilria, wiinga-ll' cukarikaniqlua tua-i! Cakanirceteksaunaku.

When he said something in disgust, I looked back at him—we had passed his sister's house by then—when I looked back when he said in disgust, "Humph! The darn little thing is trying to go too fast!" He turned around toward his sister's house and then went back toward it.

Oh my! As I was going back toward the boat, panic struck quickly. I began to feel really terrible! I had diarrhea and I was throwing up black stuff!

After I had vomited and had diarrhea, I immediately began to feel fine.

When the time came to go back home, we went home. So things went on as usual. And my parents, even when I arrived, I didn't tell them [about that incident].

One day, my poor mom asked me, "What happened to you at Bethel?"

So I told her about that incident.

Then she said to me, "Your dear uncle told me that if he had not helped you, he would have brought you home dead." If he had not helped me . . .

But still, my uncle never said anything. People never mentioned that he had powers. Or did he help me by his prayer.

That time passed. After a while, reindeer were wiped out. [In the past] land down there had lots of reindeer once and also around here. So when there were no more reindeer, that wily person repeatedly said to me, "While you are still living, they will reappear again!"

I often think that it is these that are starting to appear around here . . .

BENEDICT TUCKER: Caribou?

PAUL JOHN: Yes. Because he repeatedly told me that, I asked him one time, "Since you are always mentioning them, show me where they are." He didn't show me. He put his head down and said, "Up that way some place!" [laughter]

MARIE MEADE: That person who tried to harm you, what was his older sister's name?

PAUL JOHN: Her English last name was Link, that very old woman. They called her Elia's mother. Nick Charles and his siblings' father's younger sister.

That shaman was the youngest sibling of Nick Charles's father. And their oldest sister, Kayanguculi, lived at Stebbins.

Kayanguculi, Ac'urunaq's mother.

Tua-i-ll' eng'alugcan kingyaartaqa—alqaan enii kitullruluku—kingyaartaqa eng'alugcan, "Eng! Cukangnaqeqtarluni!" Alqermi-ll' eniinun caqirrluni tayim' itrarluni.

Arenqiapaa angyamun uterteqerlua yuucirkairucartuqilii patak'apigmek tua-i. Ayuquciqa assiirrluni! Anarallaglua, miryaralua tuaten tungulriamek!

Tua-i miryariima anariima-llu utermun assiriinarlua.

Tua-i uterrnariakuk uterrlunuk. Tayim' tua-i. Angayuqaagka-ll' tekiteng'erma qanrutevkenakek.

Cat iliitni aanaurluma aptaanga, "Mamterillermi qaill' piyaaqellrusit?"

Tua-i taumek qanrulluku.

Tua-ll' pianga, "Angagurlurpet qanrucanga ikayunrilkuniten tuqumaluten tekiucallruniluten." Ikayunrilkanga-gguq . . .

Amta-ll' taun' angaka tua-i qaillun-llu qanyuunani. Yuut apyuunaku cakuyuggauniluku. Wall'u-r' agayullermikun ikayullruanga.

Tua-i tayima. Piqerluni tuntut nangkilit. Unkut tua-i tuntulilallrulria man'a-llu. Nangqercata-am taulleraam tua-i pinauraanga pulengtaq, "Unguvainanerpeni call' tuntut utermun alairciqut!"

Makuuyuk'laranka maa-i maani alaingelriit . . .

CIKULRAACIQ: *Caribou-t?*

KANGRILNGUQ: Ii-i. Pulengtaaqtarluni tua-i pilaanga caqerluku-am aptaqa, "Aperpakalaqten tuntut, apertuuteqernga nantellritnek." Tua-i tang apertuutenrilkiinga. Pusngauraqertuq, "Avani-w' tua-i!" [ngel'artut]

ARNAQ: Taum tua-i pisteksaaqellerpet alqaa kituuga?

KANGRILNGUQ: Imna kass'atun atra Link-amek *last name*-angqetullruuq arnaskacagalleq imna. Iiliam Arnaanek piaqluku. Imkut-wa Nick Charles-ankut atallrata nayagaa.

Tauna tua-i angalkuq kinguqlikacaalqaat Nick Charles-ankut ataita. Alqaqlikacagiit-llu, Kayanguculi, Taprarmiuni uitallruluni.

Kayanguculi, Ac'urunam Aanii.

MARTINA JOHN: That Ac'urunaq was an old woman. You know that she used to be the oldest woman of the dance group. You probably saw her. When they'd go to dance festivals, they'd always bring her along.

PAUL JOHN: She was their older sister Kayanguculi. And that Kakiaculi, who had a last name of Link, was her younger sister.

MARIE MEADE: Now it's starting to come together . . .

PAUL JOHN: And that one who attacked me was their youngest brother Angutekayak, a shaman.

MARIE MEADE: I see. Where did those people reside?

PAUL JOHN: They were from the coastal region. And then their oldest sister went up north, Kayanguculi . . .

And these two, Nick Charles and his siblings' father and their father's younger sister, whose last name was Link, moved here [to Bethel]. But their youngest brother there didn't move from that coastal region.

MARIE MEADE: He stayed there?

PAUL JOHN: Yes. Angutekayak. He stayed at Nightmute. At Nightmute, he was one of our fellow residents.

ANGUYALUK: Tauna Ac'urunaq arnassagauluni. Iciw' yuralriit arnassaganqurraqetullrukiit. Tangtullrulliken-wa. Yuraliyarqameng malikuratullrukiit.

KANGRILNGUQ: Tauna alqaqluku, Kayanguculi. Tauna-wa Kakiaculi, Link-amek *last name*-alek nayagaqluku.

ARNAQ: O-oh . . .

KANGRILNGUQ: Tauna-wa pisteksaaqelqa uyuqlikacagiit Angutekayak, angalkuq.

ARNAQ: O-oh! Camiungullruluteng taukut?

KANGRILNGUQ: Unkumiungullruut. Tauna-ll' tua-i alqaat negetmurrluni Kayanguculi . . .

Ukuk-llu malruk, Nick Charles-ankut atiit maavarluni, tauna-llu nayagaa Link-amek *last name*-alek. Tuana taugken uyuqlikacagiit unaken tua-i nugtartevkenani.

ARNAQ: Uitaurluni?

KANGRILNGUQ: Ii-i. Angutekayak. Negtemiuni uitauratuluni. Negtemi ilakluku wangkuta.

Why did shamans want to antagonize me?[14]

Paul John, Benedict Tucker, Martina John, Marie Meade, and Ann Riordan, Bethel, May 2003

PAUL JOHN: He also tested me with his dogs. He attacked me again in my dream.

His dogs; I recognized his dogs. And I recognized the mother of his dogs when they attacked.

When I looked around me, I saw that rocks were under me. I picked up rocks in both hands and looked about me.

So right in front of me, they were barking at me. My arms were poised to throw. Their mother was the closest.

I threw a rock at her, but I hit the side of her head with a glancing blow! When their mother took off howling in pain, her young ones followed suit.

After I woke up from having that dream, planning to go get firewood, as I was putting on my winter boots, one of his daughters came in.

My mother [was alive then]. When [his daughter] came in, she turned to my mother and said that her poor dear mother who went to bed feeling fine

---

Angalkut wii ciin caumaksugyaaqellruatnga?

Kangrilnguq, Cikulraaciq, Anguyaluk, Arnaq, Ellaq'am Arnaan-llu, Mamterilleq, May 2003

KANGRILNGUQ: Cali tua-i qimugtemikun-am pimiyaaqlua. Elliin taum pulengllua qavangumni.

Qimugtain; elitqaluki tua-i qimugtai. Aaniit-llu qimugtain elitaqluku curukpallratni.

Avateka kiaqertaqa acika tua-i man' teggalqutangqellinilun'. Inglugtun tua-i teggalqunek tegullua kiarrlua.

Tua-i wani ciuqamni qilugluteng. Wiinga-w' urniumalrianga. Aaniit tua-i arcaqerluni iluqsinruluni.

Tua-i wavet milpagyaaqekeka maaggun ?cetangcugluku! Aanaseng aaraluni ayagarcan irniarin maliggluku.

Qavangurtulqa-ll' tauna makcama, qugtarnalua waniwa upnginanemni, iqertallraagka asnginanemni, paniin iliit itertuq.

Aanaurluqa tua-i tamaa-i. Iterluni aanaka caungamiu piuq, aanaurlua-gguq-wam kiugna nat'liqengssaarpek'nani inarqaarluni

didn't get up that morning. She had acute pain on the side of her head!

When she went out, I said to my wife here, "If I had properly hit my dear *nuliacungaq* [female cross-cousin of a male] last night, I would have killed her!" [*laughter*]

MARIE MEADE: Oh, that [shaman] was a female?

PAUL JOHN: The wife of that shaman. She had gone to bed feeling fine but she didn't get up; one side of her head was in great pain. The night before, I had thrown a rock at their mother [on the side of her face].

MARIE MEADE: I see! Yes! It was her! It hit her?

PAUL JOHN: Yes. Why did shamans try to antagonize me so much?

In daytime, another one also did that in the steam bath while we were waiting for it to get hot. I caught something out of the corner of my eyes—he was also a shaman—as I caught a glimpse of something in his direction, I looked and he had his hands like this and was looking at my face like this!

I grabbed his arms on the wrist, and the door was near. Because they had mentioned that they would *?aakayagarluki* some people. I put his hand on the door, and I said to him, "If you want to go out, there is the door!"

When I let him go, he moved away. So I didn't pay any attention to him for a while. Again when I looked at him out of the corner of my eyes, he was doing the same thing! He was making this motion near my face.

I took [his wrist] again and like I had said before, "If you want to go out, there's the door!" I would put his hand on the door.

BENEDICT TUCKER: Yes.

PAUL JOHN: Then when I paid attention to him, he put his head down. After having his head down, I looked at him with the corner of my eye, and he lifted his arm again.

After he did that as he crouched down, I thought, "God would not allow Himself to be overpowered by the Devil." While he crouched, I made the sign of the cross twice over the hump of his neck.

Oh my! When I did that the third time . . . I compared [his reaction] to one receiving an electric shock, like receiving a shock.

Oh my! While he was still crouching, he shrieked! He really shrieked out loud! When he stopped, he said, "What did you do to me, [you fool]? What did you do to me?" Then he finally

maktenrilnguq. Qamiqumi-gguq ingluanek nangteqkacagarluni!

Tua-ll'-am tua anngan tuan' una piaqa, "Nuliacunga'urluqa piluaqallrukumku unuk tuqucalliniaqa!" [*ngel'artut*]

ARNAQ: Oh, arnauluni-q' tauna?

KANGRILNGUQ: Nulirra taum angalkuum. Inarqaarluni-gguq natlugtevkenani maktevkenani; qamiqumi ingluanek nangteqkacagarluni. Ukuk-wa tua-i tuani qimugtain aaniit milqallrukeka maaggun.

ARNAQ: Aa-a! Ii-i! Tua-i tauna! Taumun tull'uni?

KANGRILNGUQ: Ii-i. Angalkut wii ciin caumaksugyaaqellruatnga?

Erenrani call' allam aug'um qasgimi waten tua-i teggalquryaraq qasgiq puqlangnercirluku uitaqainanemteni. Qigcilkircama—tauna call' angalkuullruuq—qigcilkircama tunglirneranek takuyarqa waten tang tua-i unatni piluki kegginaqa wavet tua-i!

Unatai teguqerluki tayarnerikun amik canimelan. Caluku-ll' aakayagarluki-ll'-am ilait pinilaitki. Amik pategcetaqa qanrulluku, "Anyukuvet tua-i tang amik!"

Pegcamni latqertuq. Tua-i murilkevkenaku. Ataam-am qigcilkirtua-am piaqa, ataam-am tua-i! Kegginaqa waten.

Ataam-am teguqerluku tua-i-am tuavet qanllemtun, "Anyukuvet tua-i tang amik!" Pategcetaqluku amiik.

CIKULRAACIQ: Ii-i.

KANGRILNGUQ: Nutaan murilkartaqa palurcan. Wavet palungqauraqerluni qigelvaglua pikavet-am tua-i tallini piyartuqaraa.

Tuaten-am tua-i pirraarluni lavqaan umyuarteqa'artua, "Agayun-wa tuunrangayagmun cirlakevkarngailnguq." Palungqallrani-ll' tua-i malrurqugnek waten krisciqilaku pequrran tua-i pamavet qulii.

Aren! Pingayiriluku waten pilrianga . . . Ayuqekutellrukeka tang *electric*-amun caakalriamun, *shock*-alria.

Aren! Palungqainanermini aarcillagluni! Caknerpak aarcillapik aarcillagluni! Arulaircan qanertuq, "Calkugcia-w'? Caqtarcia-w'?" Amik-llu nutaan cauluku anluni. Maqivailemta.

faced the door and went out. This was before we took a steam bath.

BENEDICT TUCKER: Yes.

PAUL JOHN: I thought: After he goes out for a while, he'll probably come back in and take a steam bath. [giggles]

Because he didn't come in, we started taking a steam bath. When we got tired, we went out. And he went out after putting on his clothes and went home. He ended up not taking a steam bath.

And then there came a time when he was about to die; when I heard about it, I went to see him. Oh, my! It was that, as they say, he passed on in a very good way!

When I came in, he was laying down on his back. There were his daughter, his son-in-law, and my former *iluraq* Asuuluk. Then they said that they had alerted the priest and that he was going to come.

When the priest came in, he took a pinch of a small host and asked his daughter to get water. After he put the host in his mouth, when he gave him water, he swallowed. After he swallowed it, the priest opened his small book and prayed as he was reading. As he read, that shaman's breathing got weaker and weaker.

When he finished reading, the priest made the sign of the cross. Then he died.

From what I saw, it seemed to me that the prayer of the priest guided his soul. And when he made the sign of the cross, he died.

When they were getting ready to wash him, I went home. When [my wife here] woke up, I said to her, "I think I took away the *tuunrat* [spirit powers] of your grandfather. He had a good death!" [laughter]

He was [Martina John's] grandfather. He was her mother's maternal uncle.

MARIE MEADE: I see.

PAUL JOHN: My! I am telling you about things that are off the subject.

MARIE MEADE: No, they are cool.

MARTINA JOHN: But still, even though he had died, [my husband] managed to retaliate while he was taking him across [to Tununak] by going fast with him and letting him bump around!

PAUL JOHN: I thought what I did was crazy after it happened!

Once he was sealed in his coffin, his children said they wanted to bury him in his original village of Tununak near his former wife's grave. But they didn't know who would be willing to take him.

CIKULRAACIQ: Ii-i.

KANGRILNGUQ: Umyurtequa: Ava-i-w' tua anqerraarluni maqiyarciqlilria iterluni. [ngel'artuq]

Iteryunrilan maqingluta. Tua-i maqilngungamta anluta. Augna-ll' aturarturluni anlun' uterrluni. Maqinricenarluni.

Atam tua-i tuqu'urluqatalria; niicamku ullagluku. Aling! Tua-i tang apqiitnek ayakegtaaqapiaralria!

Itertua tua-i waniw' taklalria. Pania, nengauga, ilurairutka-wa Asuuluk. Tua-i-ll' qanertut agayulirta-gguq tayim' elpengcallruat, taiciquq.

Agayulirtem itrami akurtuquinrayagarmek pupsukaulluni, pania-ll' mermek pisqelluku. Qanranun tua-i akurtuq ellirraarluku merr'armek pikiini igluk' tua-i. Igumariaku kalikacuarani cilla'arrluki, agayulirta imna agayuuq naaqiurluni. Naaqiurallrani anernera kayuirusngiinartuq angalkuum taum.

Tua-i-llu naaqillni iquklican, kriscirluni agayulirta. Anernerirluni-llu.

Tuartang im' tangvallemni agayullran anernera agayulirtem ayauskii. Krisciani-llu tua-i anernerirluni.

Tua-i eruqatangarcatgu uterrlua. Una tupiin piaqa, "Apa'urlurluun tang tua-i tuunriillruyugnarqekeka. Tua-i tang tuqukegtaaralria!" [ngel'artut]

Apa'urluqellrua uum. Aaniin, aaniin angakluku.

ARNAQ: Em-em.

KANGRILNGUQ: Aren! Qanerkaunrilngurnek makunek qanemcitamci.

ARNAQ: No, assirtut.

ANGUYALUK: Tua-llu-wam tuqumarinrakun akinauqii arviutellerminiu cukalialluku qatngiapagcelluku!

KANGRILNGUQ: Tua-i tang usviilkessaaqelrianga kinguknerakun!

Caqumarian, caqukagkenun ekumarian qanertut nunapiaranun Tununermun nulirran-llu nuniinun qungisngavianun irniarin tua-i tuavet qungicugluku. Ayautestekaillitaraat.

When they didn't know who would take him, I said, "If you can't find anyone to take him, I could." His children were suddenly elated and grateful!

So they took [his coffin] outside. I took my sled outside their house. After they'd loaded it onto the sled, I waited for those who would come with us, but they would not come out.

MARIE MEADE: Oh, oh!

PAUL JOHN: They were taking so long getting ready to go.

ANN RIORDAN: . . . unthinkable; simply and absolutely unthinkable . . .

PAUL JOHN: I went in and asked them, "Where will I put that one out there, into the house or somewhere else?"

They told me to take him directly to the church. I said to them, "I should be on my way."

When they said yes, I left. And there was absolutely no one else who was on the trail with me.

When I got to just this side of Tununak, I saw that the trail was rough because the wind had been blowing and making it bumpy.

Then I thought to myself, "Now that person [in my sled] did harass me once. I think I will speed up with him and let him bounce around!" [laughter]

So I squeezed the throttle of my ski-doo all the way! Man alive! So I really took off—I'd become airborne, too! When I looked back at it, inside my sled [his coffin was bouncing]! [laughter]

Oh, my! How absolutely insane! Even after that, he never haunted me, he never got into my dreams! [laughter]

Tua-i-ll' tua-i ayucestekaillitaatgu piunga, "Wiinga-wa pistekailkan piyugngakeka." Iriari quyaqertut!

Anulluku. Ikamragka agullukek elatiinun. Ikamragemnun ekumariatgu qamkut maligkanka anenercingramteng anyugpek'nateng.

ARNAQ: Oh, oh!

KANGRILNGUQ: Upteturniinateng.

ELLAQ'AM ARNAAN: . . . em . . .

KANGRILNGUQ: Iterlua aptanka, "Keggna natmun piciqa, nem'un-qaa wall'u-qaa natmun?"

Piatnga agayuvigmun-gguq ciuniuskilaku. Pianka, "Wii atak tua-i ayagturlii."

Angratnga tua-i ayagtua. Kitumek-llu piullgutaunii.

Maaten tang tua-i Tununermiut ukatiit man' tekitaqa imuulun' tua-i anuqlillruami manianani qatngianarqellria.

Umyuartequa, "Ing'um-wa tua-i qaillukuallruyaaqekiinga wani. Cukanraulluku-w' tua-i petgavkaqumku!" [ngel'artut]

Ski-doo-qa qet'aqa ngellitkacagarluku! Aren! Tua-i ayagtua—tengqernaurtua-llu! Kingyarqa ikamrag' iluani! [ngel'artut]

Aling! Usvipaa-tam! Kinguani-ll' tayim' alangrukevkenaku, tua-i-w' qavamnun ekevkenani! [ngel'artut]

I used to hear shamans who were using their powers, singing inside the qasgiq, but we weren't inside[15]

Albertina Dull, Martina John, and Alice Rearden, Bethel, November 2007

ALICE REARDEN: Did you not see shamans doing things inside the qasgiq?

ALBERTINA DULL: I saw shamans inside the qasgiq, but I stopped. [laughter]

I used to hear shamans who were using their powers, singing inside the qasgiq, but we weren't inside.

MARTINA JOHN: You weren't curious to watch them?

Aturpagalrianek qasgini tuunrilrianek niitetullruyaaqua taugaam itrumavkenata

Cingyukan, Anguyaluk, Cucuaq-llu, Mamterilleq, November 2007

CUCUAQ: Angalkunek-qaa calrianek anguksaituten qasgim iluani?

CINGYUKAN: Qasgimi angalkunek cayaaqlua, taqlua. [ngel'artut]

Aturpagalrianek qasgini tuunrilrianek niitetullruyaaqua, taugaam itrumavkenata.

ANGUYALUK: Paqnakevkenaki?

ALBERTINA DULL: We'd dig the ground on top of the *qasgiq* and listen, watching.

MARTINA JOHN: The [shamans] who were using their powers to heal people?

ALBERTINA DULL: Yes, those who were using their powers to heal people.

They'd put on seal-gut rain garments. Like [a shaman] who was using his powers on ghosts, but they probably weren't wearing dog fur [gloves]. They used to say when they were using their powers on ghosts, they used dog fur gloves, wearing seal-gut rain garments.

CINGYUKAN: Nevuq tua-i elagluku niicugniluki qasgim qaingani, tangvagluki.

ANGUYALUK: Tamaa-i-q' tuunriskengelriit?

CINGYUKAN: Ee-m, tuunriskengelriit tamaani.

Imarnitnek all'uteng. Imucetun alangrumek pilria-llu nauwa, taugaam qimugtenek piinateng pillilriit. Iciw' alangrunek piaqameng qimugtenek-llu aliumatnek pinilaqait, imarniterluteng.

They say a shaman had [that bowhead whale] go up that river[16]

Michael John, Joseph John, and Alice Rearden, Newtok, June 2008

MICHAEL JOHN: Yes, and around here, close to here, is a bend on the river, they used to call it Qangllurpak [lit., "Deep hole in the river"], and it also used to be deep.

Then in the past, I heard a story that was told, when I heard the story being told, they said that an *arveq* [large whale or bowhead whale] went up that [river], a large whale. Then at that location, when it went around the bend, it got stuck. It couldn't bend [and turn around] and got stuck.

During the summer, when the people of Kayalivik found out it was there, they evidently tried to kill it. They say they'd stuff wood inside its breathing hole here and would strike them to insert them; when it would breathe, it would shoot them upward.

After a while, it died. When it eventually died, our ancestors used to announce that these large animals were caught by their elders. They announced that the eldest person in their village of Kayalivik, Apqalulleq, had caught it.

Then afterward, that time that they caught that large whale was used as a design on the window of their *qasgiq*.

They say a shaman had [that large whale] go up that river. And he had it go there. And when it got stuck there and couldn't move, they killed it. They say since that shaman had that [bowhead whale enter that river] they say seals and other animals cannot enter that [river].

Tauna-gguq tua-i angalkum tamaaggun asgurcetellrua

Qukailnguq, Arnaucuaq, Cucuaq-llu, Niugtaq, June 2008

QUKAILNGUQ: Ii-i, maani tua-i maani maaqvaarni ukatmun waten qip'artelleq qipneq, Qangllurpagmek pitullruat cali etuaqluni.

Tua-i-ll' avani qanemciuluku niitaqa, qanemcikevkarluku niitellemni niilluku, arveq tamaaggun asgullinilria, arveq. Tua-i-ll' tamaani tamaa-i qipcaaqelriim *stuck*-arluni. Tua-i qiptesciiganani *stuck*-arluni.

Nallunriamegteggu kiagmi taukut Kayalivigmiut tua-i tuqutengnaqliniluku. Uuggun-gguq aneryaarcuutiikun muragnek kevirluku tua-i kaugtuarluki tua-i piyaaqaqluk'; aneryaarqami-gguq nut'gutaqluki qulmun.

Tua-i pivakarluni tuquurainarluni. Tua-i tuquurainaan augkut ciulimata cat makut pitarkat angtuat ciulirnemeggnun tua-i pitaqevkarluku aprumaaqluku. Tauna tua-i Kayalivgmi Apqalullermun taumun ciuqlikacagameggnun pitaqevkarluku acillrulliniat.

Tua-i-ll' kinguakun qasgimun egaleranun tua-i tauna qaraliquralliniluku arvermek pitaqellerteng.

Tauna tua-i, tauna-gguq tua-i angalkum tamaaggun asgurcetellrua. Tuavet-llu pivkarluku. Tuavet tua-i *stuck*-aami, ayagciigalan, tuqulluku. Angalkum-gguq tamana taumek pivkallruani taqukat-gguq allat iterciigataat.

JOSEPH JOHN: I think it's this place here. Yes, where it becomes Naruyaq [River]. The place downriver from it has many bends. I'm not sure which one [of these bends] it is.

ALICE REARDEN: A large whale?

JOSEPH JOHN: Yes, a large whale. Like this person's story, they say it happened long ago.

You know how we fish there with gillnets; at that place there.

It's called Qanglluq. The place where the bowhead whale went around, and couldn't turn around and got stuck. They say long ago, that shaman had it go up Narukacuk there. And then it stopped here, unable to turn.

Like [Michael John] said, they tried to kill it, and they killed it.

At this time, the location of its head is a patch of grass in this area. It's a small mound, and there's grass on it, behind that [bend] there, on this side, on the north side of it.

ARNAUCUAQ: Uunguyugnarquq. Yaa, Naruyaurtellrani-w' tamaani. Man'a uatii qiptaartuq. Naliquciitaqa taukut, ukut.

CUCUAQ: Arveq?

ARNAUCUAQ: Ii-i, arveq. Uum tua-i qanemcikellratun, ak'a-gguq tamaani.

Tuani iciw' kuvyalalriakut; tuani tua-i.

Qangllumek. Arevrem tua-i tuani qiptagtellra, caqircesciiganani caltullra. Ak'a-gguq tamaani angalkum tua-i taun' asgurcetellrua Narukacuk tamana. Tua-i-llu-gguq wani arulairluni caqircesciiganani.

Qaill' ava-i tua-i qanemcikellratun tuqutengnaqluku tuqulluku.

Qamiqurra tayima uum nuniini maani evgurneruaraulartuq. Pengurrauluni tua-i evget naumaluku taum tua-i keluani, uum ukalirnermi, neglirnerani.

They evidently killed [shamans] back in those days, when they had killed too many people[17]

Michael John, Newtok, June 2008

MICHAEL JOHN: This is evidently Cingigartuli. And the old village of Nunangnerrarmiut is here. I think this is its name here.

When I first went muskrat hunting when my father brought me with him, I saw an old kayak that had belonged to a shaman at this location.

A shaman who people had killed, they evidently placed his kayak there, at this location. Along the shores of a lake. The lake faces inland, and I'm not sure how the water compares to that place. When I went to check on that [kayak] afterward, I saw that shaman's old kayak had eroded away, right after we moved to this village [of Newtok].

They evidently killed [shamans] back in those days after constantly admonishing them [not to kill people], when they had killed too many people.

They say the people [they had murdered], when their spirits were about to leave their bodies when they were about to die, they would name the shaman who had been responsible for their demise.

Maani maa-i tuqucitullrulliniut, yugnek tuqurqivakarqata

Qukailnguq, Niugtaq, June 2008

QUKAILNGUQ: Cingigartuliulliniuq. Cali waniwa Nunangnerrarmiullret maantut. Una ateqsugnarqaa.

Tamaa-i kanaqlagcuqarraallemni aatallma maliklua, angalkuum qayallranek wani tangellruunga.

Angalkuq tauna tua-i yuut tuqutellrat, qayallra tuavet tua-i ellillrulliniat, wavet. Nanvam ceniini. Qaill' tayim' nanvaq kelutmun caumaluni, meq-llu tua-i tamatum cangalqau. Kinguakun paqcaaqekeka tayim' taun' ussutellrulliniluku makumiungurrnemteggun qayaq tamana, qayallra angalkum.

Tamaani angalkut inerquryaaqvimeggnek, maani maa-i tuqucitullrulliniut, yugnek tuqurqivakarqata.

Tamakut-gguq tamaa-i pik'ngaita anernemeng uniteqatarqateng tuquqata'arqameng tauna tua-i pistellerteng angalkuq apertutullruat.

That elderly woman who was a shaman didn't want her grandchild to endure hardship when he portaged here[29]

*Michael John, Joseph John, and
Alice Rearden, Newtok, June 2008*

JOSEPH JOHN: They say long ago, this was the end of this [river]; there was no river here.

MICHAEL JOHN: I only heard stories about it. We started seeing this just as it became a traveling route, after it had become a river.

An elderly woman who was a shaman, when she was about to die, she didn't want her grandchild to endure hardship when he portaged to here, she had evidently said that when she died, [she wanted to be buried with] a model of a land-prying tool. The people in the past used to have land-prying tools that were pieces of straight-grained wood that were long, and they'd [sharpen] their ends like this, and our late fathers used them to pry the ground during summer.

When she died she was holding a model of one of those, and the other a pretend club.

Then after she died, this [river] evidently cut through the land and formed a new stream. When they looked at it, they saw that the edge of that channel appeared as though it had been [cut] with a land-prying tool. And they said that became a river. I only heard that as a story.

ALICE REARDEN: So it was once land, and this was a river?

MICHAEL JOHN: And this area was a long stretch of tundra. We also used to go tent camping there.

JOSEPH JOHN: When they tell stories about this place, they mention that Ukicivik was where this ended. They call this slough here Ukicivik.

The story of Engel'ullugarmiut[19]

Michael John and Alice Rearden, Newtok, June 2008

MICHAEL JOHN: Have you not heard the story about Engel'ullugarmiut that occurred long ago?

ALICE REARDEN: Yes, I haven't heard about it.

MICHAEL JOHN: This place evidently had many residents during that time, it had many residents. The people of Qissunaq invited them during winter when they were going to have a dance festival.

Tua-i arnassagaam angalkuum tuquqataami tauna tutgarani tua-i-w' cakviurluku maavet tevesqumavkenaku pilliniami

*Qukailnguq, Arnaucuaq, Cucuaq-llu, Niugtaq,
June 2008*

ARNAUCUAQ: Man'a-gguq ak'a mat'um iqukellrua; man'a kuigtaunani una.

QUKAILNGUQ: Qanemciuluku-w' taugaam. Tamaa-i man'a tumyaraurrnerrakun kuigurrluku tanglallruarput.

Taum tua-i arnassagaam angalkuum tuquqataami tauna tutgarani tua-i-w' cakviurluku maavet tevesqumavkenaku pilliniami, qanllinilria tuqukuni ussugcitnguamek [tegumiisqelluni]. Augkut muragnek ussugcitengqetullruut unrapigaat takluteng, iquit-llu waten piurluk' tua-i nunaliurcuutekluki kiagmi aatallemta.

Tamakucinguamek tegumiirluni aipaa-llu kaugtuutaruamek, tua-i tuquluni.

Tua-i-ll' tuqullran kinguani tamana maaggun man'a cevvliniluni. Piat-gguq avatii-gguq tua-i tamana kuinrem tua-i ussugcitlermek piluni. Kuigurrluni-llu-gguq tua-i tamana. Tamana qanemciuluku taugaam niitelallruaqa, niitellruaqa.

CUCUAQ: Nunaullruyaaqluni, kuiguluni-ll' man'a?

QUKAILNGUQ: Man'a-llu takluni nunapiuluni. Tamaani-ll' cali pelatekiyarluta pilallruukut.

ARNAUCUAQ: Man'a maa-i qanemcikaqamegteggu, una waniwa iqukellruniluku pilaraat Ukicivik. Ukicivigmek una pituat wani kuigaar, tauna.

Engel'ullugarmiut

Qukailnguq Cucuaq-llu, Niugtaq, June 2008

QUKAILNGUQ: Ukut qanemciit Engel'ullugarmiut avani ciuqvani, niiteqaqsaitatek?

CUCUAQ: Yaa, niiteksaitanka.

QUKAILNGUQ: Tamaa-i ukut yugyatullrulliniut tamatum nalliini yugyagluteng, yugyagaqluteng piaqluteng. Ukut Qissunamiut uksumi kelellinikait, yuraqatarluteng tamaa-i.

They say [the people of Engel'ullugarmiut] started to have a food shortage. Starting in February, when they started to lack food to eat when this area used to be cold, they evidently used to have a shortage of food.

Although they caught quite a bit of fish, since they and their dogs constantly consumed them, since they used their dogs for carrying out subsistence activities, they experienced shortages of food in the past.

Back when this land used to be cold, and even these lakes would freeze. Although [the lakes and rivers] had an abundance of fish, the fish [inside lakes and rivers] would go out to places where it doesn't freeze, to their wintering sites.

During that time, the fish along the coastal regions, fish from the ocean were much more abundant than fish from the land.

When the people of that village were about to have a dance festival and they went to get them, the people of Engel'ullugarmiut got ready and using dogs traveled to Qissunamiut.

When they arrived, when they were about to dance, their hosts told them to undress and dance, that if they didn't undress and dance, they wouldn't let them eat.

Although they were shy, they undressed and danced.

They also had a shaman named Tengesqauktaq among them.

I'm not sure how many days they had the dance festival at that time, or did they dance for three days.

When they were done, when they finished during the day, it was raining out. During a certain time of day, the elders [of Qissunamiut] told them that the weather had improved and started to tell them to leave.

When one of the elderly men went out, after going outdoors and coming back inside, he evidently said that Avamingnaq had become visible, that it was time to leave. And what was that place called Avamingnaq? He lied.

Then the elders of those people who had gone to attend the dance festival, since the people there started to treat them badly, they didn't want to spend a night there and wanted to leave.

They prepared, and before dark, they probably left during the day, during the afternoon; they left traveling one after the other.

Then after traveling for a short while, the village they had left disappeared from view.

Tua-i-llu neqmek-gguq tua-i nuqlitengluteng. Una avani tua-i February-q ayagluku tuaken tamaa-i nuqlitngaqameng man'a nengllitullrani, nengllitullrani tamaa-i neqmek nuqlitenglallrulliniut.

Tamaani neq'liqrang'ermeng qimugteteng-llu ilakluki neruralaameng, cassuutekngamegteki qimugteteng, tua-i neqmeggnek nurucetulallrulliniut.

Nuna man'a nengllitullrani, nanvat-llu makut tua-i cikuluteng. Neq'lillrung'ermeng neqait tamakut antullrulliniut tua-i cikuyuilkiinun uksivigkameggnun pitulallrulliniut.

Tamaa-i tamatum nalliini man'a cenam, cenam neqai paivngalngurpatulallrulliniut, imarpiim neqai nunam neqaini tamaa-i.

Tua-i taukut yuraqataameng aqvaiceteng Engel'ullugarmiut upluteng tua-i tamaa-i qimugteggun-llu tua-i Qissunamiunun ayallinilriit.

Tekicata tua-i ciunrita pilliniit yuraqataameng matarrluki yuraasqelluki, matarrluteng yuranrilkata nerevkarngaitniluki.

Tua-i talluryung'ermeng tua-i matarrluteng tua-i yuralliniluteng.

Cali Tengesqauktarmek angalkungqerrluteng.

Tua-i qavcini tuan' yurallruat, wall' ernerni pingayuni yurallruut.

Taqngata tua-i, taq'ut-gguq erenrani ellallirluni. Qaillun erneq pitariqerluku tamakut, taukut tua-i tegganrita assiriniluku ayaasqelluki pinglliniluki.

Angulluaraat iliit anngami qanlliniuq anrraarluni itrami qanlliniuq, Avamingnaq-gguq alairtuq ayagnariuq-gguq. Call' tayim' Avamingnaullrua? Iqluluni.

Tua-i tauna tamakut, taukut tua-i yuraliyallret tegenrita, ukut wani kenkenriiceteng tamaani qavaryuumiinateng pillinii, ayagyugluteng.

Tua-i upluteng tua-i tan'gerivailgan maani, erenrani-w' tua-i pillrullilriit, *afternoon*-ami; tua-i ayalliniluteng tua-i kinguqliqu'urluteng.

Taukut-llu tua-i ayacuaqerluteng kingunrit tamarluteng.

And during that time, it used to get [extremely] cold. It used to be [extremely] cold.

Then that shaman told his traveling companions that he wanted to stop for a while and shelter them from the wind using his *tunturyugpak* [big Ursa Major].

They gathered in one spot, and after the shaman covered the sled where they were all gathered, he used his powers using his ability.

While they were there, the weather outside became calm.

When they were done, they got ready and went out, and the area where they were situated was calm quite a ways out, and there was no blowing snow on the ground, and it was calm. They left, and the snow blowing along the ground was blowing intensely in the area surrounding them [at a distance].

ALICE REARDEN: But the area around them was calm?

MICHAEL JOHN: Yes, the area around their sleds. They traveled on. When it started to get dark, they stopped and built shelters.

They ate. When they were done eating, their shaman told them, their shaman said . . . I forgot to mention that immediately after those people left, the people of Chevak told their men to follow their tracks.

ALICE REARDEN: What did they ask them to do?

MICHAEL JOHN: They told them to follow their tracks, to kill them when they caught up to them.

When they left, their tracks had been covered. After following them for a while, they lost their trail.

When they lost them, they tried to return. They say some people got lost and missed their destination, probably many of them, and some of them actually arrived at that village.

When those people stopped, after eating and when they were done, their shaman told the others that he was upset by the people who had done that to them, since the people of Engel'ullugarmiut had never mistreated those people when they arrived.

He used his helping spirits to do an incantation. They say he had them draw their summer fishing sites [of the people of Qissunaq], a number of rivers, onto the snow.

When he was done, he stepped on those rivers and went across them, and when he was done [stepping on] all of them, he was done [using his powers].

Tuamtellu tua-i taum nalliini nengllitullrulria. Nengllitullruuq.

Tua-i-ll' taukut tua-i angalkum taum ilani pillinii arulaiqerluteng tunturyugpaminek uqruciryugluki.

Tua-i katurrluteng camek, taukuk tua-i patuluku ikamrak uitaviik angalkuum pirraarlukek tua-i tuunrilliniluni tayim' tamatumek calissuutminek.

Piinanratni-gguq tauna tua-i elliit qakemna kayukellilliniuq.

Tua-i taqngameng upluteng pilliniut anlliniut, tauna-gguq tang uitallrat avaqvaarnun maavet quunirluni natquigtevkenani kayukunani. Ayallinilriit avatiit-gguq natqugpalria.

CUCUAQ: Man'a-qaa taugaam avatiit assirturluni?

QUKAILNGUQ: Ii-i, ellaita ikamrat avatiit. Tua-i ayagluteng tua-i. Tua-i-ll' tan'geringarcan, tan'geriaranga'arcan tua-i arulairluteng tua-i enel'iluteng.

Tua-i nerluteng. Nernermek taqngameng, angalkuata taum pillinii, angalkuat qanlliniuq . . . imat'am taukut tua-i egmian' call' taukut ayagngata tayima Cev'armiut tamakut anguteteng pilliniit, tum'arcesqelluki.

CUCUAQ: Qaill' pisqelluki?

QUKAILNGUQ: Tumellritgun ayaasqelluki, angukatki tuqurqesqelluki.

Tua-i ayagyaaqelriameng tamakut-llu tua-i tumellrit patuluki. Maligtaquqeryaaqluki, tamarilliniluki tamakut.

Tamariamegteki uterqaqsaaqelliniluteng. Ilait-gguq tamaa-i unani uniurutaqluteng, amlleq pingatuq, ilait-llu tamakut nunanun taukunun tekilluteng.

Tua-i, tua-i arulairameng taukut, nererraarluteng taqngameng, angalkuata pillinii ingkunek pistemeggnek nekayugniluni, ellaita tua-i taukut tekitaqata qaillun eq'ukualuki-ll' piksailamegteki, Engel'ullugarmiut.

Tuunrilliniluni tua-i. Tamakut-gguq tamaa-i neqsurviit kiagmi qanikcamun igaucelluki tayim' kuiget qavcin.

Tua-i taqngami kuiget tamakut tut'aqluki arvilliniluki, tua-i-ll' qaqicata tua-i taqluni.

ALICE REARDEN: So when he was using his powers, he pretended to [step on the rivers]?

MICHAEL JOHN: Yes, on top of that snow on the ground, and after [stepping on] those [etchings of the rivers], he finished.

When he was done, he told those people that he was offended by what happened, and that the following summer fish wouldn't enter the rivers where they fished.

ALICE REARDEN: The people of Qissunaq?

MICHAEL JOHN: Yes, [the rivers] along this side of Qissunamiut.

The fish actually arrived, including chum salmon or other types of fish that are eaten, but some of those rivers, all of those rivers there didn't have [an abundance of] fish. They didn't obtain fish although they did obtain a small amount of some other foods.

They say the people of Engel'ullugarmiut had one great hunter who was good at catching seals.

When winter came, although they worked hard, they didn't obtain large amounts of fish.

Also starting in the month of February, when that month came, back when they used to experience starvation, they started to experience a shortage of food during that time.

I did catch the time when Alaska used to be very cold in the past, and it was indeed cold. Although there was an abundance of fish [when the weather was cold], even the lakes inland no longer had fish in them. The fish in them would go out to their wintering sites and even out to rivers.

The people of Chevak, when they started to lack food to eat, traveled to Engel'ullugarmiut to survive the famine.

When they arrived, they didn't let them eat large amounts of food.

They say the great hunter of the people of Engel'ullugarmiut constantly went seal hunting. After a while, he evidently caught a bearded seal. When he caught a bearded seal, and he arrived, he had his wife cook that meat.

When she started cooking . . . and what I observed in my old village up there, when they cooked food, they didn't cook them using stoves. And they didn't cook blackfish using stoves. But they cooked them in the porch, using willows as firewood to cook them. [laughs]

They also cooked inside their homes by opening their windows. They also used some sort of har-

CUCUAQ: Tuunrillermini-qaa, pinguarluni?

QUKAILNGUQ: Ii-i tamaavet qanikcaam qainganun natermun tua-i tamakut tayim' waten piaqluki piami tua-i taqluni.

Taqngami tamakut qanrutlinii nekayugniluni waniwa kiaku, neqsurviit tamakut neqmun iterngaitniluki.

CUCUAQ: Taukut-qaa Qissunamiut?

QUKAILNGUQ: Ii-i, Qissunamiut ukatiitni.

Tua-i tamaa-i neqet tekicaaqelriit iqalluut, cat neqngutulit piciatun, tua-i-gguq tamakut kuiget ilait, kuiget tamakut neqaunateng tamarmeng. Tua-i unangevkenateng neqkamek tua-i, canek tayim' calqurrarnek unangyaqellriit.

Taukut-gguq tua-i Engel'ullugarmiut nukalpiangqertut taqukaculimek ataucimek.

Uksuan tua-i caliyaaqelriameng neqmek amllermek unangevkenateng.

Tamaani cali tamaa-i February-q-gguq ayagluni, naugaqan, tamaa-i neqmek kaitullermegni, neqmek nuqlitngetullruut.

Alaska-q' man'a ilumun tamaani nengllitullra-ll' angullruaqa. Tua-i neq'litullrung'ermi pavani nanvat-llu neqairut'lallrulliniut. Neqait tamakut tua-i uitavigkanun uksurpak kuignun-llu anluteng.

Tua-i Cev'armiut taukut qaill' tamatum tayim' piani, tua-i neqmek nuqlitngengameng Engel'ullugarmiunun ukunun anangniyalliniluteng.

Tua-i tekicata tua-i cali tua-i anglanivkarpek'naki neqmek.

Tauna-gguq tua-i Engel'ullugarmiut nukalpiarat qamigarqelria. Qaill' tayim' pitariqerluku maklagtelliniluni. Maklagcami tua-i tekicami aipani tauna kenircetliniluku kemegnek tamakunen.

Tamakut-gguq tamaa-i keningarcan . . . avani-llu augkut nunallemteni pamani, neqnek keni'irqameng, caggun kaminiakun-llu keniyuitait. Makut-llu blackfish-at-llu keniyuunaki kaminiakun. Elaturrakun taugaam tua-i uqvigarnek tua-i murirluki keniraqluki. [ngel'artuq]

Tamaaggun egalerkun-llu, egaleteng ikirrluki tamaani kenitullrulliniut enem'egteggun. Cat-llu

ness and hung the pots on them, and then they'd lift them [over the fire].

When they were done cooking, the husband told his wife that the food of the people of Engel'ullugarmiut . . . they used to have wooden bowls that were pretty large, and [their sides] weren't very high. And some had very high bowls that were wooden that they made large. They would fill them with various things, and even seal meat.

They filled [the bowl of food] that would be eaten by their guests with meat, and they added a lot of seal oil to it.

In the past, I used to see when they added a lot of seal oil, although the [food] down on the bottom [of the bowl] was hot, those ones [with a lot of seal oil] don't let off steam. Steam didn't rise from them. They ate inside the *qasgiq*.

They say the people of Chevak ate too much and consumed too much seal oil and would die during that winter.

They would gather the people who died together out in the cold in a particular spot; they would place [their bodies] at a certain location.

But the people from their village ate with just the right amount [of seal oil in their food].

And those people consumed too much and died, they would die.

And they say when the shore ice was gone down in the ocean, those they call *terr'et* [sea anemones] that are along the shore on rocks, those used to be abundant. They would grow between the rocks, and they'd come out. Then when you touched them, when they suddenly retreated, they'd go in between rocks.

We would eat those raw and cooked when they first became available in the past.

They also ate those [sea anemones] and ate them raw, and started to obtain food to eat. They ate too much slime and they died when summer came.

They gathered [those dead bodies]. Since they didn't have coffins and they didn't bury them underground, they'd just place them [on the ground].

When people started moving [to spring camps] and I started observing things, up the coast from Engel'ullugarmiut, on top of a steep place, there were homes. Since those homes belonged to people, they would move to [those homes]. And when we'd move there sometimes, we would erect tents to live in; they would construct homes.

canek uskurirluki, egatiinun tuavet aga'arrluki, pirraarluni mayurrluki piuraqluki.

Tua-i uungaki taum angutiin alerquallinia aipani Engel'ullugarmiut neqkait . . . muragnek imkunek qantallruarpall'ernek pingqetullruut, qaill' cugtuvkenateng-llu tua-i piaqluteng. Ilait-llu cugtukayalrianek muraganek call' tamakucirpagnek, piliallermeggnek. Canek tua-i taqukanek-llu imiraqluki tamakut.

Tauna allanernun neqkaat kemegnek imirluki tua-i, uquarutii-gguq amllerrluku uqirluku.

Tamaani atam tangtullruunga uqipaagarluki piaqaceteng camkut uuqnarqeng'ermeng tamakut tamaa-i puyirciigatut. Puyirciiganateng. Tua-i nerluteng qasgimi.

Tua-i tamakut tamaa-i Cev'armiut nervallagaluteng-gguq uquqilluteng-gguq tua-i uksuuluku tuqulalliniluteng.

Tamakut tamaa-i tuqullret tua-i natmun kumlanermun katurrluki elliaqluki; elliaqluki-w' tua-i tuaten.

Taukut-gguq taugken tua-i nunalgutait pitalqeggluki nerluteng.

Cali tamaan' tamakut tua-i nervallagluteng tuquluteng, tuquaqluteng.

Tuamtellu-gguq tua-i tuariucan unegna, cali unkut cenami teggalqut akuliitni augkunek ternek pitukait tua-i paivngatullruut. Teggalqut akulaitni naugaqluteng anluteng. Tua-i-ll' agtuq'aquneng itqerreskuneng tua-i teggalqum akuliinun piluteng.

Qassarluki egaluki-llu tua-i alaiqerraarqata tamakunek nerlallruukut.

Tamakunek cali tamaa-i tua-i nerluteng, qassarluteng, nerumanga'arrluteng. Tamaa-i yuvgilluteng nervallagaluteng tua-i kiagurrluku-ll' tuquluteng.

Tamakut tamaa-i tua-i katurrluki. Tua-i caqukailameng elaguteksailamegteki-llu tuaten piaqluki.

Upagyaurcata-ll' tamaa-i murilkessaurrlua, Engel'ullugarmiut wani kiatiitni, qertulriim qaingani enet'angqellruuq. Tua-i yuut ilaita pikngamegteki upagvikaqluki tamaavet. Tamaani-ll' wangkuta iliini upagaqamta pelatekanek enel'iluta piaqluta; enel'iluteng tua-i piaqluteng.

Along the end of that home along the shore here, the log that I used to see, I'm not sure how it compares in size to this here, and it was a certain width. Toward it, behind it, there were skulls without any flesh on them situated next to one another there.

And in that story, when the sun started to get warm, the dead bodies that were gathered in one spot started to rot, and their hair started to come out. They say when the people down the coast would walk along the shore there when it was windy, hair even started to blow along the ground there. That's how I heard the story.

And right up the coast from that place, that area is like this.

ALICE REARDEN: Are you talking about Kelliruat?

MICHAEL JOHN: They used to call that place Ceturrsulleq. Yes, on top of here, on top of this steep place here. And that lake, I'm not sure how its size compares to this small lake here; it was pretty large.

That [lake] used to be there when I saw that place. There were a certain amount of bones inside it. They had evidently thrown the bones of those people who had died and rotted inside there.

ALICE REARDEN: Inside that lake?

MICHAEL JOHN: Yes, in the lake. On top of Ceturrsulleq. They called this tundra here where [the bones] are located Ceturrsulleq; that there.

ALICE REARDEN: Up the coast from Iqallugtuli?

MICHAEL JOHN: Up to this area here, it reaches the mountains up there.

At that place, down the coast, but [the lake] above it seemed to be empty. But that one there, the [lake] was filled with bones.

I think [those bones] are responsible for the destruction [of the land around] Engel'ullugarmiut. It is no longer habitable [today]. That's the story that I used to hear.

She had *tuunrat* who were white people, and she would speak in English[20]

*Michael John, Joseph Patrick, and
Alice Rearden, Newtok, June 2008*

MICHAEL JOHN: In the *qasgiq*, you probably heard of those two large boats that were selling furs during the spring.

Also this person's deceased grandmother was a shaman. Sometimes when she'd use her powers,

---

Taum tua-i, wani waniwa enem taum wani cenami iquani, murak tamana tanglalqa, mat'umkiq cangalqau qaill' ellegtaluni. Maani tua-i waten tua-i piqatallran maavet keluani qamiqukuyiit kemgunateng caniqliqu'urluteng tua-i uitaluteng.

Tua-i-ll' tamaa-i qanemcimi tamaani tamaa-i akerta puqlangan tamakut tamaa-i katungqalriit yuut aruluteng, arungluteng, nuyait-llu meqluteng. Tua-i-gguq ceni'irrluku anuqlirqan unegkut ceni'irrluku man' anuqlirqan nuyanek-llu natquigcaurtengluni. Tuaten tua-i qanemciuluku niitelallruaqa.

Cali-llu wani kiakaraatni tamana waten ayuquq.

CUCUAQ: Kelliruat-qaa?

QUKAILNGUQ: Tamana tua-i Ceturrsullermek acirluku piaqluku. Yaa, maani mat'um qaingani, uum qertulriim qaingani. Nanvaq-llu tamana qaill' mat'um-llu tayim' nanvarraraam cangalqau angtacia; angrrarluni.

Taukuk, qiall' tauna tuantellruuq tanglallemni. Qaill' tua-i pitalrianek enernek imarluni. Cunaw' tamakut tamaa-i tuquallret arullret enellrit tuavet tua-i egqaqellrullinikait.

CUCUAQ: Tuavet-qaa nanvamun?

QUKAILNGUQ: Ii-i, nanvamun. Qainganun Ceturrsullrem. Tauna tua-i Ceturrsullermek man'a nunapik uitaviat atengqelallruuq; tauna.

CUCUAQ: Iqallugtulim-qaa kiatiini?

QUKAILNGUQ: Waniw' una, una waniw' engelkarrluku natiikun pavavet ingrinun pimauq.

Tuani tua-i, uani tayim', keluqlia taugaam pingna imailngat'lallruuq. Tauna taugaam tua-i man'a tua-i muirumaluni enernek.

Tauna tua-i, ugkut tua-i taumek tamakut tamaa-i Engel'ullugarmiut tamakut navgurcessngatait. Tuani uitavigkaunrirluteng. Tauna tua-i qanemciuluku tuaten niitelallruaqa.

Tua-i tuunrangqerrluni kass'anek, qitevvluni qanraqluni

Qukailnguq, Agiyangaq, Cucuaq-llu, Niugtaq, June 2008

QUKAILNGUQ: Cali-llu angyarpiik tuani tua-i qasgimi niitelallrungatagken malruk tunenialriik melqulegnek up'nerkami.

Cali uum maurluirutii angalkuullruuq. Iliini tuunriaqami tua-i tuunrangqerrluni kass'anek.

she had *tuunrat* [spirit helpers] who were white people. She would speak in English. [*laughs*]

ALICE REARDEN: Really? Did you watch her when she used her powers?

JOSEPH PATRICK: I watched her maybe three times.

Yes, when she'd put on her seal-gut rain garment and would [use her powers], two white people would speak, a wife and her husband.

Then when she did that for the last time, when she was done, after doing that, she said that those two white people moved down to the Lower Forty-eight states. She never [used her powers or spoke English after that].

Maybe if holy water was splashed on [a shaman] while she was using her powers, they probably would have suddenly stopped. [*laughter*]

ALICE REARDEN: Did she have a drum?

JOSEPH PATRICK: No, she didn't drum, but she would wear a seal-gut rain garment. The seal-gut rain garment would make rattling noises.

Evidently he had overdone it when he healed her[21]

Michael John and Alice Rearden, Newtok, June 2008

MICHAEL JOHN: I used to hear a story that took place in the village of Kuiggluk [Kwethluk] up there, about those brothers. Those brothers had a younger sister, a girl. Since that girl would take care of the animals they caught, her older brothers watched over her.

Then one day, her health started to decline. They say there was a shaman among them. She eventually stopped getting up.

And her older brothers, since she helped them tremendously, including preparing the animals they caught into food, he didn't want to lose her, when she was about to die.

He told his younger siblings that he wanted to bring their younger sister to a shaman to heal her. If he healed her, they told him that he could marry her; she would be his payment.

And that shaman had become an older man. Their older brother informed him. That shaman was delighted, since he had no wife.

He evidently used his powers to heal her, using his full power and ability. [*laughs*]

Qitevvluni qanraqluni. [*ngel'artuq*]

CUCUAQ: Qaa? Tangvalallruan-qaa tuunriaqan?

AGIYANGAQ: *Maybe three times* tangvallruaqa.

Yaa, imarnitegnek all'uni piaqan, kass'ak augkuk qantullruuk, nulirra angutii-llu.

Tua-i-ll' tuani nangnermek tuani pillermini taqngami tuaten pirraarluni kass'ak taukuk akmavet upagnilukek Lower Forty-eight-aamun. Kinguakun tayima pinqigtevkenani.

Tamaani *holy water*-aamek ciqrekuni tauna tua-i tuunriinanermini kepsalliuq. [*ngel'artut*]

CUCUAQ: Cauyangqellruuq-qaa?

AGIYANGAQ: Nuu, cauyarpeg'nani, imarnitegnek taugaam. Waten kavcagglutek taukuk imarnitek.

Cunawa-gguq tang tua-i tamaa-i tuknirivallagluku ikayullrullinikii tauna

Qukailnguq Cucuaq-llu, Niugtaq, June 2008

QUKAILNGUQ: Kuigglugmiuni cali kiugkunek qanemcimek niitelallruunga, anngaqelrianek. Taukut anngaqelriit nayagarluteng nasaurlurmek. Taun' tua-i nasaurluq tauna, tua-i aklut makut, tamakut unangkengateng, pitarkateng cat caliaqelaaki, anngain taun' tua-i murikelluku.

Tua-i-ll' piuraqerluni assiirutliniluni. Angalkumek-gguq ilangqertut. Tua-i kiituan'-gguq maknanrirtuq.

Taum-llu tua-i anngaan tua-i, ikayurpiiteng tamaaggun cat pitalteng-llu neqkaurrluki call' ikayuutek'laitki tua-i qivrukluku tua-i tuquarkaurtenga'arcan.

Taukut uyurani pillinii, taukut angalkumun, angalkumun tauna nayagarteng kitugcetengnaqluku muucugluku. Tua-i assirivkaqaku elliinun nulirqesqelluku; elliinek akikluku.

Tauna-ll' tua-i angutngurtelliniluni-ll' angalkuq. Tua-i qanrutliniluku taum anngaata tua-i. Taun' tua-i quyaqerluni angalkuq nulirritliniami-llu.

Tua-i tuunritlinikii tua-i, tuknitacini aturluku. [*ngel'artuq*]

Then after a while . . . I forgot to mention that her older brother told him that if he healed her, he would become her husband, and she would become his wife.

Then after he used his powers to heal her, when she started to gain strength and energy, she started to gain strength. And that shaman loved her and planned to have her as his wife. He planned to take her as a wife when she started to move about and when she got better.

They say when that girl saw him, when she saw him somewhere, she would beam and smile affectionately at him.

Since she was to be that shaman's wife, he wanted to start having a relationship with her. He would go and see her, even in the evening at their home, but she would be gone. After going to see her, he would leave.

And when he saw her working outdoors, or doing something, or when he was about to come upon her as he walked, that girl would know that he was coming and would look over at him and smile at him affectionately.

Then after a while, that girl started to run away from him, she started to run away from him. That's what she would do to him.

After trying to heal her, he then attempted to try to kill her again, but he couldn't.

ALICE REARDEN: The shaman?

MICHAEL JOHN: Yes, the shaman. Evidently he had overdone it when he healed her.

He was planning to kill her. She started to run away from him. Evidently, he, the shaman, had overdone it when he healed her.

When he got close to her, long before he reached her, that shaman would push her away with his body heat. Although that girl didn't want to run away from him, she would run away from him. [laughs]

Then one day, when winter came, he evidently saw her getting water from the river down below their village. They say that the area down below the village was a deep spot in the river. There was no ice on it.

When she sensed that he was there . . . those water holes evidently had snow shelters over them, that were small shelters. Those were shelters that were built.

Tua-i piuraqerluni . . . anngaan-am imat'am tuani pikii tua-i assirivkaqaku elliinek, elliinek uingeciqniluku, elliin-llu nuliqsagulluku.

Tua-i taun' tuunritellran kinguani cegg'anga'arcami tua-i cegg'anga'arrluni. Taum-llu tua-i angalkuum tua-i kenekluku tua-i aipaqnaluku. Tua-i aipaqerkaurrluku tua-i pekngarcan assiriqercan-llu tua-i piluku.

Tua-i-gguq taum nasaurluum tangrraqamiu-llu, nani tangrraqamiu tua-i cakneq quuskegcitnauraa.

Tua-i-ll' taum-am tua-i angalkuum nulirkautekngamiu tua-i aipaqsaguteqatarluku ayagnirluku piyaaqellinikii. Paqcaaqellininauraa atakumi-llu piyaaqeciqellininauraa enem'eggni tayim' cataunani. Tua-i piyaaqerraarluku unitaqluku.

Tuamtellu tamaa-i ellami tangerquniu calivkarluku, cavkarluku-llu wall' pairacarturluku ullagciqlinia taum-gguq-am nasaurluum nalluvkenaku naken taikan takuyaquniu tua-i quuskegcilluku tua-i piluku.

Qaillun-llu-gguq tua-i pitariqerluku taum tua-i nasaurluum qimangliuranga'arrluku, qimangarrluku. Tuaten tua-i pilalliniaqluku.

Tua-i-am ikayungnaqraarluku cali maaten tuqungnaqsaaqellinia cali, tua-i tauna tua-i pisciiganaku.

CUCUAQ: Angalkuum-qaa?

QUKAILNGUQ: Yaa, angalkuum. Cunawa-gguq tua-i anagarulluku pill-iniluku, yungcallin-iluku.

Tua-i tuqutarkaurrluku piyaaqluni. Qimangliuranga'artelliniaqluku. Cunawa-gguq taum elliin anagarulluku taum angalkuum tuunritlinikii.

Tua-i-gguq canimelliaqamiu taun' cayugnaitarluku angalkuum puqlaminek cinglluku. Nasaurluum tua-i qimagyuumiileng'ermiu qimalalliniaqluku, tauna tua-i. [ngel'artuq]

Tua-i-ll'-am tua-i caqerluni kuik-llu-gguq tauna, uksuurrluku, uksuurrluku tua-i mertarluku tangllniluku unavet ketmeggnun kuigmun. Tauna-gguq nunat ketiit qanglluuguq. Tua-i cikuunani.

Tua-i elpeka'arcamiu . . . tauna-gguq elakat makut, tamakut caqungqelallrulliniut camek tua-i qanikcamek eneng'uluteng avani. Eneluki tua-i, taqumaluki.

He increased his speed and approached her.

He hurried, planning to seize her when he caught up to her inside there. That's what he did to her.

Once again, before he reached her, she held her water bucket and turned her head toward him and saw him.

When he was about to reach her, when she put down [her bucket], that shaman rushed toward her since that river had no ice, since she would flee toward [the river].

That girl, when he rushed toward her, when he ran toward her, when she noticed him, she quickly ran down toward that [open] water.

She ran, and that shaman ran faster since she would surely stop there. He ran after her.

When that girl came upon that river, upon the water, she didn't stop, but ran on top of the water, and the area across from where she was heading was a sandy bluff. And that shaman ran along the trail she had taken on top of the water. [laughs]

Since she appeared as though she wouldn't get up on top of that [bluff] across there when she reached it, he was thinking to catch her then.

When that girl reached that frozen sand bank, she didn't stop running, but she went inside it. When he quickly reached the place where she had entered, since he had no trail to take and couldn't go farther, he stopped. [laughs]

They say that girl disappeared. And he didn't know which way she escaped from him. He didn't see her.

Then after a while, [she was gone] all winter. Summer came after the winter, and during a certain time of year, a boat came down from upriver.

They saw that it was a man, and that woman had a large stomach, she was pregnant and soon would have a baby. They saw that it was that [girl] who had disappeard along that [bluff].

And although that shaman wanted to use his powers on her, he found it difficult to do so.

And that girl had cared for him at that time, and when he approached her and was about to reach her, she would flee from him, not following her own will. That shaman would evidently push her away with his body heat.

Cukangnaqa'arrluni tua-i ullalliniluku.

Tua-i-w' cukangnaqluni tua-i teguarkauluku tua-i taum iluani angukuniu. Tuaten pimaluku.

Tua-i-am tekipailgani mertarcuutni tegumiaqluku tua-i takuyaumaluku tanglliniluku.

Tua-i-ll' waniw' tekiteqataamiu waniwa, elliqerluk' tua-i tuavet pirraarluni, taum angalkum ullagartelliniluku un'a cikuilan kuik, tamatum tungiinun qimagciqngan.

Tua-i nasaurluum taum, taigarcan, aqvaqussuarluni taigarcan, elliin tua-i murilkarcamiu, aqvaqurluni atraqertelliniuq tamatum mer'em tungiinun.

Aqvaqurluni tua-i, elliin-llu tua-i taum angalkum pikanirluni tua-i tamaavet arulairciqngan. Malirqerluku ullagluku.

Imum taum nasaurluum kuik tamana meq tekicamiu cakanirpegnani mer'em qaingakun aqvaqulliniluni, agna-llu-gguq ciunra qaugyaq ekvigauluni. Taum-llu call' tua-i angalkum tumellrakun call' tua-i aqvaqurluni mer'em qaingakun. [ngel'artuq]

Agaavet cali tamaavet mayurngailan tangvallerminiu tekiskan nutaan tegunaluku.

Nasaurluq tamana-ll' ekvigaq kumlaneq qaugyaq tekicaaqekni, aqvaqullni cakanirpegnak' tayim' itliniluku. Ellii-ll' tua-i tekiarcaaqekii tua-i kingunra, qaill' tumkailami ayagciigali'ircami arulairluni. [ngel'artuq]

Tauna-llu-gguq tua-i tayim' nasaurluq tua-i tayima tua-i. Naugg'un-llu anallra nalluluku. Tangeqsaunaku.

Tua-i-ll' piuraqerluni, uksurpak. Uksuurraarluni kiagluni, qiall' tayim' pitariqerluku, angyaq tamana qamaken angyaq man'a anelralliniluni.

Maaten-gguq tua-i tauna piat, tauna tua-i angutngullinilria, tauna-ll' arnaq tua-i aqsarpauluni qingarluni tua-i irniarkaurrluni. Maaten-gguq imna pilliniat, tauna tua-i tuaggun tua-i tamalleq.

Tauna cali tua-i elliin angalkum qiallukuaryung'ermiu tua-i capeqluku.

Nasaurluum cali tua-i kenkelaryaaqekii tuani ullagaqani, tekitniararqan qimalliniaqluku tua-i umyuani aturpek'naku. Tamaa-i-gguq puqlamikun cinglalliniaqluku angalkum taum.

That [woman] gave birth. Along with their small son, when they had a child, they stayed there.

After a while, [the baby] started to move about.

That shaman was planning to kill her child, angry at his mother. Although he was angry, he couldn't do anything to that girl, and he couldn't attempt to kill her using his mind.

That small boy began to walk. [The shaman] began to watch for an opportune time to kill [the child].

Then while he was walking along, was it outside their home, he saw that boy was playing. He approached him.

And when [the child] noticed him, when he turned his head toward him, that child was smiling admiringly at him.

He approached him, and before he reached him, since he still wasn't able to walk too well, when he approached him, he started fleeing from him on foot.

Then as he was going, he fell face down. And when he fell face down, when he did something, he disappeared. And that shaman couldn't even see him, and here he had approached him to kill him.

Then someone mentioned what that shaman had said, "So that [child] also does this!" [laughs] I used to hear that story.

Since her older brother used [the girl] as payment [for healing her], although [the shaman tried to be with her], she couldn't do as he wanted. Evidently, he had overdone it when he had healed her. [laughs] I heard [that story].

Ississaayuk was evidently a powerful shaman[22]

Michael John and Alice Rearden, Newtok, June 2008

MICHAEL JOHN: I also heard the entire story of Ississaayuk from Kuiggluk [Kwethluk] from the one who told the story. His grandmother [gave him the ability].

They say when those two who were *ken'gutkelriik* [relational name used by cross-cousins] from Kuiggluk went to go and get firewood for the fire bath, they asked [Ississaayuk] to accompany them.

They loaded their sleds and left. And after loading it [with wood] when they were done, when they were about to return home, since the Kuskokwim

---

Tua-i taun' irniluni tua-i. Tauna-ll' tua-i qetunrayagii, irniangamek tamaani uitalutek.

Qaill' tayim' pitariqerluku pekngelliniluni.

Tua-i-am taum angalkuum nutaan taun' irniara tuqutarkauluku, tua-i taumek aaniinek nekayugluni. Taugken-gguq tua-i elliin taun' nekayung'ermi tauna nasaurluq qaillukuarciiganaku, umyuamikun-llu tuqungnaqesciiganaku.

Tua-i pekngarrluni tauna tan'gurra'ar. Tua-i nutaan tua-i asqikallerkaa kellutengllinia tuqutnaluku.

Tua-i-ll' cenirrluni piinanermini piqalliniuq eniita-qaa elatiitni tua-i tauna tan'gurra'ar akusrartellria. Ullalliniluku.

Taum-gguq elpeka'arcamiu takuyarcamiu quuskegcilluku, quuskegcilluku tua-i mikelnguum.

Tua-i ullagluku, tekipailgani tauna tua-i pektellni piyumanariksailaku, taingarcan pekluni qimatmun ayangartelliniuq.

Tua-i-ll' piuraqerluni paallagluni. Paallalriim, qiall' piqalriim tamaqerluni. Tua-i taum elliin-llu taum angalkuum tua-i tangvagciiganaku, tuqucarturluku ullagyaaqluku.

Angalkuq tauna tua-i taum qanruciiralliniluku qanellranek, "Augna-llu-wam cunaw' waten pitulria!" [ngel'artuq] Tua-i taumek tua-i niilluku qanemciuluku niitellruaqa.

Tua-i taum anngaata tua-i elliin akikellruaku, pingraani qaillun tua-i maligtaqusciiganaku. Cunawa-gguq tang tua-i tamaa-i tuknirivallagluku ikayullrullinikii tauna. [ngel'artuq] Taumek tua-i.

Ississaayuk taun' angalkuullra tuknillrulliniuq

Qukailnguq Cucuaq-llu, Niugtaq, June 2008

QUKAILNGUQ: Issiyssaayuk cali augna Kuigglugmiu tamalkuuluku cali tua-i qanemcikestiinek niitelallruaqa, niitellruaqa. Maurluanun.

Tauna tua-i Ississaayuk, taukuk ken'gutkelriik-gguq Kuigglugmiuk maqikassurlutek pillermeggni unayaqluku.

Tua-i waniw' tua-i ikamratek ucilirraarluki ayaglutek. Ucilirraarluk' taqngameng uterteqataamek, tauna tua-i tan'gurraq taun'

River ice was thin, after chopping it to make a hole with an ice pick, one of the men drowned that boy in the Kuskokwim River. They killed that [boy].

Then after [killing him], they returned home.

When they approached the village and were about to arrive, some children were having fun playing kal'utaq [a hockey-like game]. They were playing kal'utaq, having fun on top of the smooth ice.

When they arrived, they observed them and saw that they were playing with the one who they had drowned in the Kuskokwim River earlier. [laughs]

The other [man] said to him, "What are you doing [here]?" The one he asked said to him that since he didn't want to waste his time waiting for them, he had just left them and returned home. [laughs]

Then not long after, they asked him to accompany them again. He accompanied them, they brought him on their trip. They went moose hunting, they brought him moose hunting.

When they were about to return home, they killed him again. And after throwing him in the Kuskokwim River, they returned home.

Once again, as they approached the village and were about to arrive, his companion told his partner, "You know he will [be there]."

When they approached their hometown, those boys were ice skating. Once again, when they arrived, they saw that they were ice skating along with that boy. [laughs]

When they asked him again, he replied to the ones who had [killed him] that since he didn't want to waste his time waiting for them, he returned home.

They say that his grandmother, knowing that he was a shaman, was the one who had him [come alive again].

From that time on, since they would eventually kill him for good, his grandmother, toward the spring, using a kayak sled, they went down the Kuskokwim River.

They'd spend nights [as they traveled]. They traveled on down the river, and they traveled along the lower Kuskokwim coastal area, and after spending nights, they would continue on their journey.

They say when they reached the village of Cevv'arneq, she finally stopped there with him.

Kusquqvak qecigkilan tugerluku pirraarluku taum aipaan Kusquqvagmun kic'etlinluku. Taun' tuqulluku.

Tua-i-ll' pirraarluku uterrlutek.

Tekicarturakek-gguq taukut nunat mikelnguut augkut tua-i nunaniryugluteng canek kal'utalriit. Kal'utarluteng tua-i nunaniryugluteng, cikulraam taum tua-i qaingani.

Tua-i-am tekicamek pilliniuk, murilkelliniuk, watua una Kusquqvagmun kic'etlertek ilakluk' akusrartellriit. [ngel'artuq]

Aipaan pillinia, "Waq', qaill' pisit?" Ciunran kiullinia qariteksuumiilamikek-gguq ilangcivkenakek utertellruuq. [ngel'artuq]

Tuamtell' tua-i akaurpailgan tua-i, tuaten-am tua-i unayaqliniluku. Tua-i maliklukek, ayaulluku. Tuntuvagcurlutek, tuntuvagcuulluku.

Tua-i-am uterteqataamek tuaten cali tua-i, tuqutelliniluku. Kusquqvagmun-llu egqaarluku uterrlutek.

Tua-i-am tekicartuamek tekicarturlutek, taum tua-i aipaan aipani pillinia, "Tua-i-am imna piciquq."

Maaten-gguq tekicarturtuk tuavet, tuavet kingunellermeggnun kankiilriit tamakut tan'gurraat. Maaten-gguq-am tua-i tekituk tauna, tamana, tauna tan'gurraq ilakluku kankiilriit tua-i. [ngel'artuq]

Tua-i-am tuaten apcagni, kiulliniak taukuk pistegni, pillragnek qariteksuumiilamikek uterrniluni.

Tauna-gguq tua-i maurluan-llu angalkuucia nalluvkenaku tuaten pillrullinia.

Tua-i tuaken qaqiciqataikek-gguq, tua-i-w' tuquteqataan'gu, maurluan up'nerkanga'arcan, up'nerkatmun ayangarcan, qamigautegnek tua-i tamaa-i ikamrirlutek Kusquqvagkun cetullinilutek.

Tua-i qavartaraqlutek. Cetuurlutek tua-i ayaglutek kuigkun tamaavet, avaggun-llu Caninerkun call' tamaa-i tua-i qavartarraarlutek piaqlutek.

Cevv'arnermun-gguq tua-i tekicamek nutaan arulairulluku. Tuani-llu tua-i maurluan

periodically.

They headed up and anchored right down below them.

Their shaman admonished them, when they went to it, although there were many appealing items inside the ship, not to purchase them. But he told them that they should only [purchase goods] from the next [ship], when it arrived again, because they would run out of things to purchase goods with.

They approached [the ship]. When they reached the boat, they saw that [the ship] looked like the model that he had constructed. But although those people spoke, or maybe even in Yup'ik, they couldn't understand what they were saying. That's what they did.

Then when the tide was going out, it removed its anchor and left. The next day, when the tide came up again, it arrived, it arrived again. He told them that they should then [purchase things].

I forgot to mention that those people who had purchased goods, although he had admonished them against it, since they had appealing items. And [Ississaayuk] himself, when his own daughter wanted some beautiful necklaces, since she cried, he bought her one.

They went to sleep. The next day, when his daughter woke and searched for her necklace, they searched for it, but didn't see it. But there was something hanging. When they looked closer, they saw various things strung through coarse grass, including dog feces, and other debris evidently made into a necklace. [laughs]

And the people who purchased nice-looking items, their items turned out to be nothing, and even included debris from the ocean.

When it came a second time the next day, those [items] turned out to be genuine. They were very nice items and they purchased them, and they used their leftover [trade items] to purchase them.

When they woke after sleeping, they saw that they were as they had appeared before.

Ississaayuk was evidently a powerful shaman.

They say that his grandmother fled the village with him since the two who had been trying to kill him would kill him. That's what she did.

Tua-i itrarluteng ketiitnun kicarluteng.

Taum tua-i aug'um-wa tua-i angalkuata inerqullinii paqcatgu angyarpiim iluani cakegtaaraat amllengraata kipucesqevkenaki. Kinguqlianek taugaam tekitenqigeskan akikairutlerkait pitekluki, tamakunun navrucesqevkenaki.

Tua-i ullagaluku tua-i. Tua-i-llu tamaavet tekicaaqut, tauna tua-i uksuq calillracetun ayuqluni. Taugaam-gguq tamakut qaillun wall'u-q' Yugtun qanngermeng taringesciiganaki ellaita. Tuaten tua-i piluteng.

Tua-i-ll' encan kicairluni tayim' ayalliniluni. Tua-i unuaquan ulenqigcan tekilluni, tua-i-am tekilluni. Pillinii, nutaan.

Tuani imat'am kipurqelriit tamakunek tamaa-i inerqullrungraateng akluit assirngata. Ellii-llu, tauna panini uyamikegtaarnek cucuan tua-i qiangan kipuyutliniluku.

Tua-i qavarluteng. Unuaquan tua-i tauna pania uyamiminek tupiimi kiartelliniuq, kiarrluni piyaaqelriim, tangyuunaki. Ukut-wa cat makut agalriit. Maaten-gguq piit, kelugkarmek nevuterluteng cat qimugkauyaraat anait, caarrlugnek tuaten avuluteng tuaten uyamiulliniluteng. [ngel'artuq]

Tamakut-llu-gguq tua-i kipurqellret canek aklukegtaarnek cali akluut tua-i cauvkenateng, imarpiim tuaten caarrlukluki tamakut tamaa-i.

Nutaan tua-i kinguqlilirian unuaquan piameng tamakut tamaa-i piciuluteng. Cakegtaaraat tua-i kipuqluteng, kipurqelluki, tamakut-llu tua-i ilakualteng tamakunun tua-i kipulluk'.

Qavarraarluteng tupangermeng piyaaqelliniut ayuqucirramegcetun ayuqluteng.

Tua-i tauna Ississaayuk taun' angalkuullra tuknillrulliniuq.

Tua-i-gguq taum maurluan qimautellrua taukugnun tuqungnaqestiignun tuqutarkaurcan'gu. Tuaten tua-i pillruuq.

They say after shamans used their powers on them, they would give them *iinrut*[23]

Elsie Tommy, Martina John, Mary George, and Alice Rearden, Bethel, March 2009

ALICE REARDEN: Back when you became aware of life, did they have *iinrut* [amulets, medicine] that shamans made?

MARTINA JOHN: She's asking you about those *iinrut* that people kept that were handmade.

ELSIE TOMMY: They used to have wooden *iinrut*; some were models of seals, some were figurines of birds, some were figurines of small people. They were wooden handmade ones. They say they were made for them by the shamans.

That's what they used to do; they had those types of *iinrut*.

They say after shamans used their powers on them [to heal them], they would give them *iinrut* that were models of various things, seal figurines, small figurines of people, bird figurines; those kinds, and they'd even give them models of kayaks as *iinrut*.

They had males wear models of kayaks, seal figurines, and girls had figurines depicting people for necklaces. There were three types of *iinrut* made for males—a seal figurine, a bird figurine, and then there was a small person figurine. And females only had one type of necklace; it was a small female figurine. They say [that figurine] was a shaman.

MARY GEORGE: My mother showed me her *iinruq*. It was a wooden model of a face; it was this size. It was an oblong face figurine, and it had a thing here that was a certain length, and it had eyes. She said that was her *iinruq*.

And then at Cevtaq, when the priest first arrived there, the priest asked them what types of items they had associated with shamans. Then when he asked her to throw that away, she threw it away.

I saw that wooden figurine that was this size, but its face was oblong, it was thin. She evidently discarded that, when the priest [first arrived].

MARTINA JOHN: Was it when they discarded things, or rather when the priests started arriving?

MARY GEORGE: I don't know about the time when they first started arriving, but I saw that [priest],

Angalkut-gguq tuunriqaarluki iinruliraqluki

Nanugaq, Anguyaluk, Nanurniralria, Cucuaq-llu, Mamterilleq, March 2009

CUCUAQ: Tamaani-qaa ellangellerpeni canek iinrungqetullruut angalkut piliaritnek?

ANGUYALUK: Aptaaten pilianek qelkaanek yug' iinrungqerraqluni.

NANUGAQ: Iinrungqelallruut muraganek; ilait taqukaruaruaqluteng, ilait tengmiaruaruaqluteng, ilait yuguacualleraugaqluteng. Muragaarnek pilianek. Angalkut-gguq iinruliutait.

Tuaten pitullruut; tamakunek iinrurluteng.

Angalkut-gguq tuunriqaarluki iinruliraqluki tuaten, canguaruluki, taqukaruaruluki, yuguacuallerauluki, tengmiaruaruluki; tamakut tamaa-i, qayaruanek tuaten iinrukitaqluki.

Angutet qayaruanek taqukaruanek, arnat-llu yuguanek uyuamingqercetaqluki. Angutet taugaam ukut iinruit pingayuuluteng—taqukaruaq, tengmiaruaq, una-wa yuguacualler. Arnat-llu atauciuluni uyuamiat; arnalquaruaruluni. Tua-i-gguq angalkuq.

NANURNIRALRIA: Aanama iinruminek maniitellruanga. Muragaar' kegginaruar'; waten tua-i angtaluni. Taksuryiluni kegginaruar' uuggun qaill' tayim' pitalriamek piluni, iik-llu uitalutek. Tauna-gguq tua-i iinrua.

Tua-i-llu tuani Cevtarmi agayulirta tekiteqarraallrani agayulirtem apqaulliniluki canek angalkurtarnek pingqellritnek. Tua-i-ll' tauna egcesqengaku egtelliniluku.

Tangellruaqa tauna tua-i muragaar waten tua-i angtaluni, kegginaa taugaam tak'urluni, aminani. Tua-i-ll' taun' egtelliniluku, agayulirta [tekiteqarraallrani].

ANGUYALUK: Imumi-qaa egqaqillratni, callratni tamaa-i agayulirtet tekitengellratni?

NANURNIRALRIA: Wiinga-w' tua-i tauna tekiteqarraallrat nallukeka, taugaam wiinga

and I'm not sure who it was. They say that [priest] told them to discard those things associated with shamans. You had me recall that.

MARTINA JOHN: When that Father Fox and others first arrived. Those who arrived [in villages] from time to time were probably old [priests].

Priests considered [abstinence practices] to be related to the ways of the shamans[24]

Martina John, Bethel, March 2009

MARTINA JOHN: Evidently when I reached the time that I would have my first menstrual period, I had my first menstruation, but I didn't abstain from anything. They didn't tell me to follow abstinence practices. I think in those days, in our village especially, they had abandoned the abstinence practices.

When those priests arrived, they had them stop practicing their abstinence practices because they considered those practices to belong to the Devil, because they considered them practices related to the ways of the shamans.

They took away their practices, took away their abstinence practices, and no longer allowed them to follow abstinence practices. If we abstained, it was because we believed in the Devil and followed those abstinence practices, the ways of the shaman, his practices. They evidently had us stop practicing those things because they thought we would be practicing the shamans' ways.

Also, I became aware of life like this person, never seeing anyone dancing. But I'd only hear these elderly men singing *yuarulluut* [shamans' songs, ritual songs] holding a child; they'd start singing. I thought that they were songs to lull [children] to sleep, since I had never seen people dancing before. I used to think that they were songs to lull [children] to sleep.

---

tangerqerraallrukeka tauna, kituullrua-llu. Taum-gguq tua-i tamakut angalkurtaat cat egqaqesqelluki. Tauna neq'aqercetan.

ANGUYALUK: Imkut-wa tua-i Father Fox-at tamakut tekiteqaqu[lallret]. Ak'allaullilriit tamakut tekiteqaqulallret.

Agayulirtet angalkuuyaramun mat'umun pikekluki

Anguyaluk, Mamterilleq, March 2009

ANGUYALUK: Tua-i-ll' wiinga aunrallerkaqa tekitelliniamku cali tua-i aunraryaaqelrianga cameg' eyallrunritua. Eyasqellua pillrunritaatnga. Avani augkut, nunamteni-w' tua-i arcaqerluteng eyautet tamakut pegingallruyugnarqekait.

Tamakut tamaa-i agayulirtet tekicameng tamakut eyacunguaryarait pegtelluki, wagg'u-q' Tuunrangayagmun pikekluki, angalkuuyaramun mat'umun pikekluki.

Tua-i cairluki, eyautairulluki, eyagcecuirulluki. Tamaa-i eyakumta Tuunrangayak ukvekluku eyautet tamakut aturciqngamteki, tuunrangayiim piciryarai, aklui. Tamakut angalkut piciryarait aturciqngamteki tua-i tamakut pegcetellrullinikait.

Cali tua-i uutun ellanglua yuralriamek tangerqayuunii. Makunek taugaam angullugarnek yuarullugarnek atulrianek mikelngurmek tegumiarluteng; tua-i atuangnaurtut. Tua-i umyuarteqnaurtua qavangcarissuutnguyukluki, yuralrianek-llu tangerqayuilama. Qavangcarissuutnguyukluki umyuarteqaqlua.

One who has been doctored by a shaman while still in the womb and allowed to live[25]

Elsie Tommy, Martina John, Mary George, Ruth Jimmie, and Alice Rearden, Bethel, March 2009

ALICE REARDEN: Did they try different things in the past when their children constantly died, and consult with shamans?

ELSIE TOMMY: They didn't have me [consult with those shamans].

MARTINA JOHN: They didn't seem to blame shamans for those who constantly died. But when they started to try different things, wanting their children to live, although they didn't have any other children at all, they'd give [the baby] to another person, thinking that their child may live after that.

Like the baby would die, they'd give [the baby] to another person. Then since they anticipated [that it would live as a result] and since they believed in those practices in the past, starting from then, their children would start living. They'd start to try different things so that their children might live.

Some poor people in the past constantly had children, and they'd die, their children constantly died. And something I mentioned earlier, they didn't give [a child] a name.

Atrilnguq [lit., "One without a name"] who was born after the children who constantly died, when they named him Atrilnguq, he lived. Starting from then, his younger siblings started to live.

Then Naanguar [lit., "Play thing"], his older siblings constantly died also, and when he became Naanguaq, when they gave him the name Naanguaq, these two lived.

MARY GEORGE: Qilangaq also said that about Anerteqnguaq [lit., "One who pretends to live"]; they say after she gave him the name Anerteqnguaq, her [other children] started to live.

MARTINA JOHN: Yes.

RUTH JIMMIE: These different names, Elakautarkaq [lit., "One who will be buried"], Egcarpialler [lit., "One who was almost discarded"], those invented names, those invented names that they gave them.

MARTINA JOHN: Yes. Since they almost gave away our maternal aunt, the youngest, they called her Egcarpialleq [lit., "One who was almost discarded"].

Yuungcaraq

Nanugaq, Anguyaluk, Nanurniralria, Angalgaq, Cucuaq-llu, Mamterilleq, March 2009

CUCUAQ: Qaillukualallruut-qaa tamaani iciw' tuquigiurarqameng irniameggnek, iciw' angalkunek-llu?

NANUGAQ: Tamakunek piyuitellruatnga wiinga.

ANGUYALUK: Angalkunek-wa avalitaitellrullilriit tamakut tuquuralriit. Taugaam tua-i qaillukuangaqameng qaillun anerteqiiqeryugyaaqluteng, irniaritqapigteng'ermeng-llu yugmun allamun cikiutekluku, tua-i nutaan anerteqiinayukluni kinguakun.

Tua-i tuqucirkaatun allamun yugkiutekluku. Tua-i-ll' tamaani neryuniukluku pilaameng ukvekluki-ll' pilaameng, tauna tua-i ayagneqluku-ll' anertequ'uranga'artaqluteng. Qaillukuarluteng qaillun tua-i irniateng anerteqngellerkaatnek qaillukuangaqluteng.

Ilait avani irniuraurlutullruut tua-i egmirturluteng, tuquigurluteng, tuquurluteng. Tua-i-ll' camek makut maa-i ava-i qanrutkelqa augna, atermek acirpek'naku.

Atrilnguq ava-i augna tuquuralriit kinguatni Atrilngurmek aciatni anerteqluni. Ayagneqluku-llu kinguqlii anerteqengluteng.

Tuamtell' una Naanguar augna ciuqlii cali tuquurallruluteng, Naanguarurcami-ll' tua-i Naanguamek aciatni ukuk malruk tua-i anerteqlutek.

NANURNIRALRIA: Qilangaq-llu cali qanellruuq augna Anerteqnguaq; Anerteqnguarmek-gguq cali tua-i acirluku piani cali unguviingluni.

ANGUYALUK: Ee-m.

ANGALGAQ: Atret-wa tua-i makut Elakautarkaq, Egcarpialler, iciw' tamakut at'nguat, aciruarutellrit.

ANGUYALUK: Ii-i. Augna-w' anaanavuk uyuqlikacaar cikiutekqatallruyaaqelliniatgu-am tua-i Egcarpiallermek pilallrukiit.

RUTH JIMMIE: Was that her nickname?

MARTINA JOHN: It isn't her actual name. Her name is Cakiculi. They were about to give her away to someone. Then they called her Egcarpialleq.

In the past, how the parents of those giving away chldren didn't get attached and want to keep the babies afterward. After breast-feeding them, then when they were able to eat real foods, they'd give [the baby] away.

ALICE REARDEN: Or also when they mistook others for their parents.

MARTINA JOHN: And some would mistake others, their caretakers, their grandmothers and other relatives of their parents and prefer them.

I, too, was like a caretaker for these kids [Ruth and siblings] as I constantly went to visit them since I didn't have a real younger sibling. I'd even go to them immediately when I woke early in the morning. These kids would make it difficult for me to go out sometimes when they wanted me to stay and not leave.

When one is an only child, children are extremely noticeable. And when people from other villages had arrived with their children, when they were seen at the church, one really felt like taking and holding [children], but I was reserved toward them. It's not good not having a child [to take care of].

These ones [Ruth's family], including Alqa-cungaq ["Dear older sister"] and this person's [Ruth's] mother, were the only two who lived close to our place and constantly gave birth to children, but some died.

And this person's [Ruth's] sibling's constantly died when they were little babies. And Alqa-cungaq's children constantly died. After enjoying taking care of them, I would miss them [when they died].

Then when her children started living, when they'd turn a year old and they got younger sib-lings, this [child] would die. This was when they were going to start living. Since I always took care of them, I know about it.

Then that started to happen to her; when they'd get younger siblings, they'd die. Then after Paul Sunny down there was born, these three [younger siblings] lived.

ALICE REARDEN: Earlier I asked about that—I forgot what they call them—are they called *yuungcarat* [ones given life by shamans]? Those shamans—you know how they say that *yuungcarat* have *napartet* [things that keep them alive].

ANGALGAQ: Aterrlugaqluku-qaa?

ANGUYALUK: Atqenricaaqluku. Cakiculiuluni. Kitumun yugkiutekqataryaaqellrulliniluku. Tua-i-ll'-am Egcarpiallermek piaqluku.

Tamaani aling ak'a yugkiuskengelriit qunuyagucuipagtatki. Aamarqurarraarluki tua-i-llu neqnek-llu piyugngarikata nutaan tua-i cikiutekluku.

CUCUAQ: Wall'u-q' alartaqata-llu.

ANGUYALUK: Alartaqluteng-llu ilait, auluku'urtemeggnun, maurlurmeggnun cameggnun tua-i.

Ukut wani, wiinga-llu aulukelriatun ayuqellrukenka tua-i ullagturluki nakmiin uyurailama. Unuakuayaarmi-ll' tupakuma egmian' ullagluki. Ukut tua-i anllerkairutngaqlua iliikun qunukengaqatnga.

Man'a tua-i mikelnguum, tua-i kiimi yuulleq, cakneq atam mikelnguut mistuut. Allanret-llu waten tekitellruaqameng irniarluteng agayuvigmi tangrruugaqameng teguyukacaarnaqsaaqluteng, taugaam takarnaqluteng. Mikelngurmek kepqelleq assiituq.

Ukut tua-i, Alqacungaurluq-llu imna uum-llu aanii kiimek tua-i avatemni canimenatek irniuraurlulriik, ilait tuquyugluteng.

Uum-llu cali ilai tuquurluteng mikelngucuarauluteng. Alqacungaam-llu cali augkut irniari tuquurluteng. Aling piyugcalirraarlua tamaqerriaqlua.

Tua-i-ll'-am anerteqiingarcami, ak'a allrakungaqameng kinguqlingkuneng-llu tua-i una tuquluni. Tamaa-i anerteqngeqatallinillermeggni. Tua-i piuratullruamki nallunrilkenka.

Tuatmell' tua-i, tuaten-am pinga'arrluni; kinguqlingaqameng tuquaqluteng. Tua-i-ll' ava-i Paul Sunny-q' kan'a engelekluku ukut wani pingayun tua-i anerteqluteng.

CUCUAQ: Watua aug'umek apcaaqellruunga—canek im' acilaqait—yuungcaranek? Iciw' angalkut—napartengqenilaqait-llu canek yuungcarat.

MARTINA JOHN: You know how that person [Elsie] talked about it yesterday, how they had *iinrut* [amulets]. You know how she talked about it yesterday.

ELSIE TOMMY: They say when a shaman gives them protection from sickness, they use their powers to doctor them. Then they give them *iinrut*, and then that [child] would get big.

And there is the following instruction. [The child's] mother is given the instruction that while she is sewing, not to pull her needle out of her sewing facing the child when she is sewing. If her child faces her, she was told to put away what she is sewing and tend to her child. That's the instruction that the shaman gave the child's mother.

And if she didn't recall [the shaman's] instructions to her, if she faces the point of her needle toward her child, while the child is sitting there, if she pulls the needle out toward her child, they say that she will poke her child repeatedly with the needle, cutting his life.

MARTINA JOHN: My goodness!

ELSIE TOMMY: That was the instruction she was given. [The shaman] would doctor him and protect him from illness as he was growing, and to prevent any type of sickness from affecting him.

And when he was done [doctoring him], he would give him an *iinruq* that was a wooden figurine of a person or a model of a kayak or a model of a bow, or they'd give them *iinrut* resembling animals on the land.

Then after making an *iinruq* like that for him, he would tell the child's mother that if her child who he had doctored and protected from sickness approached her while she was sewing, he admonished her never to pull her needle out and point it toward the child. When her child faced her, he told her to put away her sewing and tend to her child.

They say if the child faces her while she is sewing, when she pulls out her needle, they say that she will repeatedly poke [the child's] face with a needle and it will cut his life.

MARTINA JOHN: There were different requests made to the shamans. They would give instructions [to the parents of the children] who they had doctored to take care of a child a certain way. [The shaman] carries out their request, but the shaman would give instructions to the mother about how to take care of [the child].

ELSIE TOMMY: Also, while she was cutting fish or food with her semilunar knife, when her child

ANGUYALUK: Akwaugaq iciw' taum qanrutkellrukii, iinrurluteng. Taum iciw' akwaugaq qanrutkellrukii.

NANUGAQ: Piyaircaraqamegteki-gguq angalkuum apqucimun piyaircaraqamegteki tuunrilluki. Tua-i-ll' iinrulirluki, tua-i-ll' tauna tua-i angturriluni.

Waten-llu alerquutarluni. Aanii alerquumaluni, irniara mingqenginanrani irniaran tungiinun mingqun caulluku waten amuqaasqevkenaku. Irniaran caukaku mingqekngaa tauna calligarrluku irniara pisqelluku. Taum angalkum tuaten aanii qanirturluku.

Tua-i-llu-gguq tamana qanirtuutaa neq'aqanrilkuniu, waten mingqutminek irniarmi tungiinun mingqutni cingilganek tungiinun waten irniara uitaluni, tungiinun mingqun amukaku irniara-gguq tua-i mingqutmek kapurciqaa, tua-i anernera kepluku.

ANGUYALUK: Ala-i!

NANUGAQ: Alerquutaqaqluku. Tuunrilluku piyaircarluku nangteqsuunaku anglisqelluku, camun apqucimun-llu agtuumayuunaku.

Tua-i-ll' taqkuniu nutaan camek tua-i muragamek yuguacuarmek wall'u-q' qayaruamek wall'u urluvruamek, canek tua-i makut nunam qaingani ungungssit ayuqaitnek iinrulirluki.

Tua-i-ll' tuaten iinrulirraarluku aanii tauna qanirturluku, mingeqnginanrani irniaran ullakaku tauna tuunrilluku cayairtullra, mingqutmek agu tunglirneranun mingqeqaasqevkenaku inerqurluku. Caugaqaku irniaran mingqekngaa calligarrluku pilaasqelluku.

Tua-i-gguq tuaten tua-i mingeqnginanermini caukani mingqutmek, minguqutem amullran kegginaa-gguq tua-i imkunek mingqutnek kapurciqaa tua-i, anernera-gguq tua-i kepluku.

ANGUYALUK: Ayuqevkenateng tamakut angalkumek kaigatet, ayuqevkenateng. Ellaita tua-i pikngait alerquraqluki qaillun tauna mikelnguq aulukesqelluku. Tua-i elliin kaigatii tauna tunluku, taugaam tua-i taum wani angalkum auluklerkaa aanii alerquraqluku, waten aulukesqelluku.

NANUGAQ: Cali-llu waten neq'liurluku waten pilagtuaqan taum irniaran ullakaku tauna

approached her, she was also told to drop what she was cutting and tend to [the child]. They say if she doesn't drop it, she will also cut his body with the semilunar knife.

The instructions that were given to the people who came before us were daunting to follow.

I know some [instructions] very well, and I do recall some of the instructions they gave, but these days, I'm forgetting some. They never used to come to mind, I also never recalled them when my children started living, I never recalled those instructions when my first children constantly died.

And those shamans would be on my mind, wondering if they could do something to keep them alive, and they have since died. I wanted to have one of my children live.

They say they had [Tutgara'urluq] go to the ocean at Kayalivigmiut[26]

Elsie Tommy, Martina John, Ruth Jimmie, and Alice Rearden, Bethel, March 2009

ELSIE TOMMY: The following is also something I happened to catch when shamans were around and something that I witnessed with my eyes. And also about how Tutgara'urluq went to the ocean although he wasn't a shaman. [*laughs*]

Since that's something that happened long ago, how [shamans] used their powers and had people go and check seals in their ocean toward the end of winter; since I recalled that story, it probably will be okay if I tell that story.

Shamans used their powers in the *qasgiq* to check to see if there were seals, having boys help them carry out the task.

Then the person he chose to carry out the task, the shaman would tell him, "You have some sort of ability. You will be good as the person to carry out the task."

He said that some shamans lie. This is what Tutgara'urluq said. He said that some shamans, those who people say are shamans, lie. He thought perhaps God helps them; although he isn't a shaman, they refer to him as a shaman. [*laughs*]

[Tutgara'urluq] said they had him go to the ocean at Kayalivigmiut.

MARTINA JOHN: Was Tutgara'urluq a shaman?

---

pilagtuaqengaa peg'arrluku cali pisqelluku. Peg'artenrilkaku-gguq tua-i call' tuaten kegginalegmek ceteqtarciqaa-gguq qainga tamana.

Alerquutait qanirtuutait augkut ciuqliit, ciuqliit caperrnarqellriarulallruut.

Tua-i-w' ilait nallunritkacagaryaaqekenka, qanerturluteng-llu waten qanruciluteng alerquatelput ilait tua-i neq'aktuyaaqekenka, taugaam ilait cali unimrayagluki cali pingluki maa-i. Umyuaqsuitetullruyaaqanka, tua-i umyuaqsuunaki tua-i irnanka ukut unguvangellratni-llu, umyuaqsuirulluki tamakut irnianka imkut ciuqliit tuquurallratni.

Tamakut-llu angalkut umyuamni uitaaqluteng qaillun unguvakaatnek cikiutekat tuqumariluteng-llu tayima. Qaillun unguvaiqeryugyaaqlua umyuarteqlua.

Ellii-gguq tua-i [Tutgara'urluq] imarpigcetelqaat Kayalivigmiuni

Nanugaq, Anguyaluk, Angalgaq, Cucuaq-llu, Mamterilleq, March 2009

NANUGAQ: Wiinga cali una angalkunek angulqa iigemkun-llu tangvalqa. Una-llu Tutgara'urluum angalkuunrilngermi imarpigtellra. [*ngel'artuq*]

Tauna cali tua-i akaartaungan, tuunriluteng waten iqukvaraqan imarpigteng taqukanek paqcet'lallrat; tauna cali tua-i umyuamnek neq'akngamku tua-i, tamana-llu-w' cali qanrutkekuni tayim' cangaitellilria.

Angalkut waten qasgimi tuunriluteng, taqukangqetassiarluku waten kevgirluteng tan'gurrarnek.

Tua-i-ll' kevgaa tauna taum angalkum piciqaa, "Tua-i-gguq carrangqelliniuten. Kevgaukuvet-gguq assirciquten."

Angalkut-gguq ilait iqlulartut. Tutgara'urluum qanellra. Angalkut-gguq ilait angalkuunikait iqlulartut-gguq. Agayutem-gguq ikayularngatai; angalkuunrilengraan angalkumek tuqlurluku. [*ngel'artuq*]

Ellii-gguq tua-i imarpigcetelqaat Kayalivigmiuni.

ANGUYALUK: Ellii-qaa tauna Tutgara'urluq angalkuuguq?

ELSIE TOMMY: He wasn't a shaman.

RUTH JIMMIE: Even though he wasn't a shaman, he probably told him that he had some ability as a shaman.

ELSIE TOMMY: That shaman said that he was a shaman, that he had some ability, and he told him that he should go down to the ocean.

MARTINA JOHN: [He told him] to use his powers?

ELSIE TOMMY: That shaman used his powers. He used him to carry out the task, telling him to go down to the ocean, wearing skin boots.

MARTINA JOHN: He told him to go for real?

ELSIE TOMMY: Yes, he actually told him to go down for real. They say they used to go down for real.

When they gave him a pair of ringed-seal skin boots, he said that his maternal aunt/stepmother had him put on the skin boots since he was to be the one to carry out the task on behalf [of the shaman].

And he said that he put on a skin binding for a belt. Then when he was done, his maternal aunt/stepmother told him, "Now go over to the *qasgiq*." And he said she gave him some ringed-seal skin mittens. Those ringed-seal [mittens] had a harness that they hung from.

Then when he went inside, they were getting ready. [The shaman] told him okay now, "Okay now, you won't have a difficult time when walking on the trail when you travel down to the ocean. When you go and check the seals, you won't have a hard time walking on the trail."

When he got the seal-gut rain garment that he used when he did incantations [he said,] "Well then, go down into the tunnel entryway." Then he went down into the tunnel entryway.

MARTINA JOHN: After he got ready?

ELSIE TOMMY: After getting ready, the door, its door was open, and there was nothing down there. When he told him to go down into the tunnel entryway, he went down. And when he told him to sit like this, he sat facing the front [of the *qasgiq*].

And he told him that when he let out his voice, to run outside.

MARTINA JOHN: So the one who was telling him what to do, told him to [run out] when he let his voice out?

ELSIE TOMMY: Yes. When he let out his voice, he stood and ran out. And he looked outside. And he said that they closed the door back there. And when they closed it, he went inside through the draft hole. [*laughs*]

ALICE REARDEN: Which way did he go inside?

NANUGAQ: Angalkuunrituq.

ANGALGAQ: Angalkuunrilengraan-wa angalkurrluuniluku.

NANUGAQ: Angalkurrlugaam taum angalkuuniluku carrangqerrniluku pissuukarangqerrniluku imarpigcesqelluku qanrutliniluku.

ANGUYALUK: Tuunriluku-qaa?

NANUGAQ: Tuunriluni tauna angalkuq. Kevgaqluku imarpigmun ayaasqelluku waten, pilu'ugluku.

ANGUYALUK: Pipiarluku-qaa ayasqelluku?

NANUGAQ: Pipiaryaaqluku, ee-m. Pipiarluteng-gguq ayatullruut.

Tua-i nayiignek piluguugnek cikiatni tua-i-ll' taum anaaniin-gguq piluguugnek acelluku kevgauqatallinian.

Naquggluni-llu-gguq tapengyagmek. Tua-i-ll' taqngami tua-i anaaniin taum pillinia, "Kitek' tua-i qasgimun agi." Nayirraagnek-llu-gguq kaumacirluku. Agangqerrlutek-gguq taukuk nayirraak.

Tua-i iterngan tua-i piut-gguq tua-i uptelliniluteng. Kitakiillinikii, "Kitaki, tumlliquangaituten imarpigmun atraqaquvet. Taqukat paqeskuvki tumlliquangaituten."

Tua-i tuunrissuutni imarnitek piakek, "Kitaki, kalevvluten." Tua-i-ll' amigmun tua-i kalevvluni.

ANGUYALUK: Upqaarluni?

NANUGAQ: Upqaarluni tua-i, amik, amiinga ikingqaluni, kanaggun pitaunani. Tua-i kalevcesqengani kalevvluni. Aqumesqengani-ll' waten tua-i aqumluni, uatmun cauluni.

Tua-i-ll' erinani aneskaku aqvaqurluku anesqelluku.

ANGUYALUK: Elliin-qaa taum ellimerrluku, ellimeqngaan erinani aneskuniu?

NANUGAQ: Ii-i. Tua-i erinani ancaku nang'errluni aqvaqurluni anqertelliniluni. Keggavet-llu uyanglluni. Amik-llu-gguq kiugna patuluku kia-i. Patuatgu-llu-gguq cup'urillrakun iterluni. [*ngel'artuq*]

CUCUAQ: Naugg'un iterluni?

MARTINA JOHN: Through the draft hole [of the firepit]. They used to have holes down below the door. They called those holes *cup'urillret* [draft holes]. The flames were visible through there back there, and the doorway, a hole, was up there. And underneath it, we used to watch the flame back there when it was lit. She said that he went inside through there. [*laughs*]

ELSIE TOMMY: When he went in through there, he said there was some ash down there. Since he was able to [enter through there], he said up there were [cracks].

MARTINA JOHN: Holes, cracks.

ELSIE TOMMY: Then he tried to take off a piece [of fur], and he placed it inside the model seal's mouth. He put on his mittens and took it, and he did this to its mouth.

MARTINA JOHN: The small seal model?

ELSIE TOMMY: Yes. He quietly went out trying not to make noise. He said that when he entered, since it was a little difficult for him to enter, since he almost got stuck, he suddenly struggled thinking that he might not enter. He turned, and when he took his head out . . . [*laughs*]

He finally got out. Then he stood along the side of the doorway of the porch and scanned the ocean, "I wonder how I went [to the ocean]? [*laughs*] I wonder how I could have gone?" Then when there were no longer any voices, he slowly went inside.

MARTINA JOHN: He didn't do anything?

ELSIE TOMMY: Yes, without doing anything, he slowly went inside. Then when he got to its doorway, he opened it and went up. When he went up and stood, he showed [the seal figurine] to the person who had asked him to go.

Then that one who was positioned like this, after shaking off his seal-gut rain garment, stood and took it, "Just as could be expected, there will be many seals this spring." [*laughs*] He said it was just as could be expected, and he was extremely happy.

My, [Tutgara'urluq], the one who had said that he would be walking along the sky, how . . . [*laughs*] The one who said that he would head down toward the ocean and not walk on the ground was wondering how he would travel there.

MARTINA JOHN: Did he tell him to run and immediately go down?

ELSIE TOMMY: Yes, he told him to run down and leave immediately. When he went down through the porch, he went up through the steps, and when he appeared, he stayed there.

ANGUYALUK: Cup'urillrakun. Ukinengqetullruut atam imkut kanaggun amiigem aciakun. Cup'urilleqniluki tamakut ukinret. Tuaggun tua-i kenret alaitaqluteng kia-i, amiik-wa pikani ukineq. Aciani tua-i kiaken, wangkuta-am tangssunglallrulriakut kenermek kiugumek kumaaqan. Tuaggun-gguq tua-i iterluni. [*ngel'artuq*]

NANUGAQ: Tuaggun tua-i iterngami kan'a-gguq kana-i aralleq. Tua-i-gguq una piyunarqellinia, pagkut-gguq-wa.

ANGUYALUK: Ukinret, qulinret.

NANUGAQ: Tua-i-gguq augautessaagluni tuavet taqukaruacuaraam qanranun ekluk' pilliniluku. Tua-i kaamautegni all'ukek teguqerluku tua-i, qanra-ll' tauna waten piqerluku-gguq.

ANGUYALUK: Taqukaruacuar?

NANUGAQ: Ii-i. Anqatassuarluni niumrugcaaqevkenani. Itlermini-gguq tuani tua-i-gguq iterciigaterrlugngami nagcarpiarami, tua-i-gguq itenritnayukluni nangteqa'arcaaqellruuq. Tua-i caqirrluni tua-i qamiquni ancamiu . . . [*ngel'artuq*]

Tua-i anlliniluni tua-i nutaan. Tua-i-ll' amiinga, taqurrani elaturram amiingan taqurrani nangerrluni tuani, imarpigmun kiartelliniluni, "Qaillun-kiq ayallrusia? [*ngel'artuq*] Qaillun-kiq ayallruyarcia?" Tua-i-llu erinataircan iterturalliniluni tua-i.

ANGUYALUK: Camek piurpek'nani?

NANUGAQ: Ii-i, tua-i camek pivkenani iterturalliniluni tua-i. Tua-i-ll' amiinga tekicamiu ikirrluku nugluni. Nugngami-ll' nang'ercami taumun ayaasqurteminun waten piqerluni maniitelliniluku.

Tua-i-ll' taum taukuk imarnitegni waten pimaurluni evcuggaarlukek nangerrluni tegulliniluku, "Qayumi taqukat up'nerkaqu amlleqatartut." [*ngel'artuq*] Qayumiirluni-gguq tua-i quyak'acagarluni tua-i.

Aren tua-i ellii, qaillun-llu-gguq qilagkun pekciiqnillra, qaillun . . . [*ngel'artuq*] Imarpiim-gguq tungiikun nunamun tutmarpek'naku atrarciqlilria, qaillun-gguq ellii tuavet ayagciqa.

ANGUYALUK: Tua-i-qaa imumek aqvaqusqessaaqluku egmian' ayagluku?

NANUGAQ: Ii-i, aqvaqusqelluku tua-i egmianun ayagluku. Elaturraakun anelraqaami akerteggun mayurluni, nutaan igvarcami-gguq tua-i uitaluni.

MARTINA JOHN: And did he return and then stay?

ELSIE TOMMY: After standing there for a while, he said when [the shaman] sang his incantation song, he could hear him clearly. He said when he got quiet, he slowly went in, trying not to [make noise].

ALICE REARDEN: Through the draft hole?

ELSIE TOMMY: He had gone out through the draft hole, after having gone out.

MARTINA JOHN: When he went out through the draft hole, he waited for the song to end.

ALICE REARDEN: Who was that person?

ELSIE TOMMY: The one who went was the deceased father of my husband, Tutgara'urluq. [laughs]

MARTINA JOHN: So when he showed him that, he said qayumi [just as could be expected]?

ELSIE TOMMY: Yes, he said qayumi, "Just as could be expected, this spring there will be many seals." [laughter]

Then that shaman put that [seal figurine] away carefully.

MARTINA JOHN: So that [seal figurine] had belonged to him?

ELSIE TOMMY: Yes, the small seal figurine belonged to that shaman.

MARTINA JOHN: So when he was about to let him go, he gave that to him?

ELSIE TOMMY: He gave it to him.

They say when seals are going to be scarce, the ones who he sent out don't obtain anything. And if seals were going to be [plentiful], he obtained something. [Tutgara'urluq] said that was a time when he was clever. He said that spring, there was an abundance of seals.

MARTINA JOHN: It turned out to be true?

ELSIE TOMMY: He said it turned out to be true. He said that the unseen one helped them. [laughs]

ALICE REARDEN: Where, at Kayalivik?

ELSIE TOMMY: At Kayalivigmiut.

ALICE REARDEN: Did you live for a time at Kayalivik?

ELSIE TOMMY: I used to stay there from time to time back when they used to dance; back when they used to dance, back when they had Messenger Feasts, we used to stay at Kayalivik.

ANGUYALUK: Tua-i-llu-q' ataam uterrluni uitaluni?

NANUGAQ: Tuani tua-i nangerngaurarraarluni yuarutmek-gguq tuunrissuutminek atullermini alaiteqallruuq. Tua-i-gguq nepairucan itqataarluni tua-i piyaaqevkenani.

CUCUAQ: Cup'urillerkun-qaa?

NANUGAQ: Cup'urillerkun anellruluni, anrraarluni.

ANGUYALUK: Cup'urillerkun anngami tua-i tuani yuarun iquklitnercirluku.

CUCUAQ: Kituullrua tauna?

NANUGAQ: Ayalleq wani aiparma atallra, Tutgara'urluq. [ngel'artuq]

ANGUYALUK: Tua-i-qaa tauna maniaku qayumiirluni?

NANUGAQ: Ii-i qayumiirluni tua-i. "Qayumi up'nerkaqu taqukat amlleqatartut." [ngel'artut]

Tua-i-llu-gguq-am tauna qemanqegcaarluku taum angalkum.

ANGUYALUK: Elliin-qaa pikellruluku tauna?

NANUGAQ: Ii-i taqukaruacuayagaq elliin taum angalkum pikluku.

ANGUYALUK: Tua-i-llu-qaa ayagcesqataamiu tauna tunluku elliinun?

NANUGAQ: Tunluku.

Tua-i-gguq taqukat nurnarqeqatarqata ayagcecillri unangyuitelartut. Taqukat-llu-gguq piarkaukata unangluni. Tua-i-gguq tauna piarkartuyartellra. Up'nerkaan-gguq taqukat amelkacagallruut.

ANGUYALUK: Piciuluni?

NANUGAQ: Piciuluni-gguq tua-i. Ikayurtengqellruuq-gguq tangvaumanrilngurmek. [ngel'artuq]

CUCUAQ: Nani, Kayalivigmi?

NANUGAQ: Kayalivigmiuni.

CUCUAQ: Tuani-qaa Kayalivigmi uitaqallruuten?

NANUGAQ: Uitaqalallruunga yuratullratni; yuratullratni kevgitullratni uitatullruukut Kayalivigmi.

When he cleaned [a wound] at Merr'armiut, I watched him[27]

Elsie Tommy, Mary George, and Alice Rearden, Bethel, April 2009

ELSIE TOMMY: I also watched a shaman down at Merr'armiut. Kangrilnguum Atii accidentally shot himself and lodged a bullet between his ribs. That Angassaar from Qissunaq had him lie on his back on top of a woven grass mat, and back when paper first came around, he had someone place a small white piece of paper on top of his body.

And using a *nuqaruaq* [upper wing bone] of a bird, one that is hollow in the middle, the ones they used to sniff snuff through their noses, and not touching his mouth, and also not touching his skin down there, while he was [lying] like this.

Not touching this, he went across it like this, and he made no noise at all. Then when he reached [the wound], he was not touching it at all [he sucked it].

Then he would remove the device that he used to suck with, and he would [place it] on top of the paper, and it would be blood.

When the [blood] that he spit out became less and less, and there was other substance in it, when there was no longer [any blood in it], he said that it was a little difficult for him to [extract] the bullet down there. He said that a shaman who was more powerful than he could remove it, but he said that his condition won't worsen although it isn't extracted.

When he cleaned [a wound] at Merr'armiut like that, I watched him.

ALICE REARDEN: Who was cleaning [a wound]?

ELSIE TOMMY: Angassaar from Qissunaq.

MARY GEORGE: Was Angassaar a shaman?

ELSIE TOMMY: Because he probably was, that's what he did; he was probably a shaman.

Carririllrani Merr'armiuni tangvallruaqa

Nanugaq, Nanurniralria, Cucuaq-llu, Mamterilleq, April 2009

NANUGAQ: Cali Merr'armiuni kanani angalkumek tangvallruunga. Tayima Kangrilnguum Atii, anqerrivikluni tulimag' akuliignun puuliaramek. Imum Angassaaraam Qissunamium taklarrluku tupigat qaingatnun taklarrluku, kalikat alaillrata tamaa-i, qainganun kalikaarmek qatellriamek elliivkarluku.

Tengmiam-llu nuqaruaranek cuplungqelriamek qengamegteggun iqmigssuutektullritnek tamakucimek, qanen'i-ll' agtuumavkenaku, kan'a-ll' ekia cali agtuumavkenaku, waten pimallrani.

Una agtuumavkenaku waten tua-i arviagurluku camek-llu tua-i nepmek-llu cangssagaunani. Tua-i-ll' nallaiquniu agtuumangssaarpeg'naku, piaqan, tauna tua-i agtuumangssaarpek'naku.

Tua-i-llu tauna melugcuutni aug'aqerluku kalikam qainganun [pikani] auguluni.

Tua-i-ll' tamana qecirturatni ikeglian, iciw' carrarmek-llu tua-i avuqetaangluni tua-ll' piirucan qanerluni elliin-gguq waniwa puuliq kan'a artucuararaa. Piuguranran-gguq angalkuunerraan piuguranran-gguq aug'aryugngayaaqaa, taugaam-gguq ikiurrngaituq aug'anrilngermi.

Tuaten carririllrani Merr'armiuni tangellruaqa, tangvallruaqa.

CUCUAQ: Kina tauna carririluni?

NANUGAQ: Angassaar Qissunamiu.

NANURNIRALRIA: Tauna-qaa Angassaar angalkuuluni?

NANUGAQ: Pilliami-w' tua-i tuaten pillrulria; angalkuullilria-wa.

They say that female shamans are more difficult to overpower than men[28]

*Elsie Tommy, Martina John, and
Alice Rearden, Bethel, April 2009*

MARTINA JOHN: They also used to tell stories about Ayaprun's late mother. My *acacungaq* [little paternal aunt] told about her this past winter. She said that her body was covered with peeling skin.

She said her entire body was covered with peeling skin. She would constantly drum and sing. Her mother continually tended to her body.

I used to see her when her skin appeared strange, it was different.

Those were her old sores. She said that she used to be in pain, that person used to be in great pain. I also used to see that person, and I used to see her small mother, but this was after [her skin] had healed. You know how the skin along places where sores healed looks different; that's how [her skin] looked.

She was James Sipary's late mother. His mother, since there were shamans around before our time, they say she also used to constantly drum and sing.

ELSIE TOMMY: She probably constantly used her powers to heal her.

MARTINA JOHN: Herself, that person [with sores] would constantly drum and sing herself.

ALICE REARDEN: I also heard that some women and elderly women who were shamans had drums, had small drums.

MARTINA JOHN: Those shamans would do that for sure.

They also said that these female shamans are more difficult to overpower than men because they have their blood to protect them, the blood they menstruated. Women were more difficult to overpower, since they are protected by their menstrual blood.

Some shamans were good, but some were malicious. They wanted people to die. But the other ones were people who helped others, we'd hear that they'd help people.

Arnat-gguq makut angalkut pingnaqellrit caperrnanruut angutni

*Nanugaq, Anguyaluk, Cucuaq-llu, Mamterilleq,
April 2009*

ANGUYALUK: Iciw' tua-i augna-llu Ayaprutem aanallra qanemcik'lallruat. Acacungama-ll'-am uksuq qanemcikqallrua. Tua-i-gguq qainga qelterluni tua-i, qelterluni.

Tua-i cakneq qainga-gguq tamarmi tua-i qeltenguaqluni. Cauyaqcaarturluni atuqcaarturluni. Aaniin tua-i piuraraqluku tamana qainga.

Iciw' tamaa-i tanglallrukeka kemga allayuuluni, iciw' allayuuluni.

Tamaa-i callarnellri. Nangteq'lallruuq-gguq tua-i nangteq'lallruuq tauna. Wiinga-ll' tanglallrukeka tauna aanacuarallra-llu cali tanglallruluku, taugaam mamumarinrakun. Iciw' imkut callarnret mamellret kemget qiallun ayuqelalriit; tuacetun ayuqluni.

Aug'um ava-i James Sipary-m aanallra. Aanii ciumteni tayima angalkut pilallruameng, ellii-ll' tua-i tauna cauyaqcaarturluni-gguq aturtuarnaurtuq.

NANUGAQ: Tuunriteqcaalallrullikii-wa.

ANGUYALUK: Ellminek, ellii tauna tua-i ellminek cauyarluni atuqcaartura'qluni.

CUCUAQ: Niitellruunga-llu-ggem ilait-gguq arnat arnassagaat-llu angalkuuluteng cauyangqetullruut cauyacuarluteng.

ANGUYALUK: Tua-i-w' piciqelriit tamakut angalkut.

Waten-llu qanernaurtut, arnat-gguq makut angalkut pingnaqellrit caperrnanruut angutni, tua-i-gguq-wa aumeggnek tunglingqerrameng, iciw' aunralallermeggnek. Arnat caperrnaqluteng tua-i tekisciigatnaqluteng, capengqerrameng-gguq tamatumek aunralallermeggnek.

Ilait angalkut assirluteng, ilait taugken ikiuluteng. Iciw' tua-i tuqusqumaituluteng. Makut taugken aipait ikayurilriaruluteng, ikayurilriaruluteng niitellrit.

*Elsie Tommy, Martina John, Mary George, and
Alice Rearden, Bethel, April 2009*

ELSIE TOMMY: They used to say that shamans would ask for items from people. And when they didn't comply with their requests, they would place something underneath their child, and if they had a grandchild, their grandchild, revealing the item that they had asked for, what they call *atlirnirluki* [placing something underneath them].

The father of Cuyanguyak and her siblings pursued and killed the first child of Angurvak, the deceased eldest sibling of Taguyangaq and his siblings. We know this.

At that time, he evidently asked Maacungaq for a small spotted-seal skin that had been dehaired to patch his kayak.

Then Maacungaq told him that since they only had enough kayak skins to cover a kayak, they couldn't give away any of their skins. Then he left her.

And they say toward fall time, her grandchild, the small son of Angurvak, started to become ill. Then when he became ill, Ap'aller asked Uqviir to come and examine his grandchild.

He used his powers to try to heal him inside the *qasgiq*. After going in circles around his head for a while, he would go around him starting over there, and he never went past his head. He would kill him if he went past his head. He went in circles around him like this using his powers.

MARTINA JOHN: Going back and forth?

ELSIE TOMMY: Yes. He evidently brushed off his sealgut rain garment that he was constantly shaking. And when he brushed them off by shaking them, he turned to Maacungaq and Ap'alluk, saying that [the boy] was a little too difficult for him to heal, but that he knows the person who did that to him.

He told them that he has a spotted-seal skin for an *atlirneq* [thing placed underneath him by a shaman]. Although he wanted to take it out, that he was held by some implement that he could not cut, that a shaman who was more powerful than he could cut them. He said that they were just a little too difficult for him.

---

*Nanugaq, Anguyaluk, Nanurniralria,
Cucuaq-llu, Mamterilleq, April 2009*

NANUGAQ: Angalkullret kaigatullrunilartatki cakameggnek ukunek. Tua-i-llu-gguq niitenrilkatki irniara, tutgarii, tutgarangqerkan tutgarii wagg'u-q' atlirnirluku, aperturluku kaigaviksaaqelteng, atlirnirluki-gguq tua-i.

Angurviim imna irniaqeqarraallra ukut Tagiyangankut ciuqliirutkeqarraallrat una, ingkut Cuyanguyiinkut atiita pitaqelqaa. Nallunritarput.

Tuani Maacungaq imna kaigaviksaaqelliniluku qayami callmagkaaraanek meqtarrarmek taquka'armek kaigaviksaaqelliniluku issurimek.

Tua-i-llu Maacungaam waten kiulliniluku, qayamek naacirturiameng ukut qeciggauteteng ilangarcesciigatniluki. Tua-i-llu-gguq unilluku.

Uksuaryartullrani-llu-gguq tua-i tauna tutgara'urlua Angurviim qetunrayagii nangteqenglliniluni tua-i. Nangteqngellrani-llu-gguq tua-i Ap'alluum Uqviir tungcirluku yurviqaasqelluku una tutgarani.

Tua-i qasgimi waten tuunritliniluku. Tua-i uivvaalnguamiu waten qamiqurra, yaaken ayagluni waten uivvaarluku, qamiqurra pelluyuunaku. Tua-i-gguq qamiqurra pellukuniu tapciiqngamiu. Uivvaarluku tua-i waten tuunriluni.

ANGUYALUK: Utqetaarluni?

NANUGAQ: Ii-i. Imarnitek taukuk waten arulaquraqngagni evcullinilukek. Evcugngamikek-llu tua-i taukuk tua-i Maacungaankuk Ap'alluk-llu caullinilukek, tua-i waniw' elliin caperqecuarniluku, taugaam pistii nallunritniluku, taringumaniluku waniw'.

Issurimek-gguq atlirniumauq. Elliin-gguq qaillun ancung'ermiu, ukugnun caskugnun kepesciigalkengaminun, tua-i-gguq angalkuunran-gguq taugaam taukuk kepsugngaak. Tua-i artucuarturnilukek.

He tried to go and get the [weapons]. Uqviir told [the shaman] that he is the one who is trying to kill that child down there. He said he can remove the spotted-seal skin that he placed underneath him, and asked why he was meddling with him.

He told him that the piece of seal skin used to patch a kayak is nothing, that he wasn't able to use a kayak any longer, that he was an elderly man.

He told him that saving that child down there won't be difficult for him, to remove the two weapons down there that he was using [to try to kill him]. He said he would try [to get it]. That thing continually headed up reacting vocally [to cold water].

Uqviir also told him that he was afraid of the kind of shaman powers and ways of pursuing people that he had observed in him. He said that he didn't have the type of shaman powers that he was afraid of, that his shaman powers were too cruel.

He didn't remove [the seal skin underneath the boy that caused his health to deteriorate]. Although he tried relentlessly, he didn't remove it.

Then Maacungaq told Uqviir, "If we gave him a spotted-seal skin, would he be able to remove it?" He said that he won't, that the weapon that is on her grandchild won't come off, but only the person who owns it could remove it.

MARTINA JOHN: So the one who put that on him could remove it?

ELSIE TOMMY: Yes. He said that spotted-seal skin is tethered to that child.

MARTINA JOHN: Was it because they had refused to give [to that shaman]?

ELSIE TOMMY: Yes, because of their refusal to [give him a spotted-seal skin], he placed a spotted-seal skin under that child and tethered him to it.

ALICE REARDEN: Then what happened to that child?

ELSIE TOMMY: He died. And they say when he was about to die, when he started speaking, the small thing told his parents that when others asked for things from them, to give it to them without refusing. They say this is what he told both of his parents. He didn't tell his grandparents, but his parents.

Dear Cuyanguyak and her siblings lived up at Kayalivigmiut all winter one time when Uqviir had someone go and get them. Angutengyaar went to get them. When he arrived, he used his powers on him, but he wasn't successful [in healing him].

Tua-i aqvayaaqlukek. Tua-i qanrutliniluku Uqviiraam mikelnguq kan'a elliinun pissuqengaqniluku. Issuriq atlirniutellra aug'aryugnganiluku elliinun, ciin qaillukuallranek.

Qayam callmagkaa caunritniluku qayarturnairutniluku angukara'urluurrniluku.

Kan'a kanani tan'gurraq elliinun arturngaitniluku, kankuk caskuk augaasqellukek. Tua-i-gguq pilaryaaqaa. Tauna-gguq tua-i imu'urtualuni tagyugtuq.

Tua-i-am cali Uqviiraam pilliniluku elliinun angalkuanek, elliin angalkuanek cumikellrani angalkuanun pissurcuutiinek nangyaryularniluku. Ellii tamakunek nangyaqekngainek ellii angalkungqenritniluni, elliin angalkua ikiussiyaagniluku cakneq.

Tua-i aug'arivkenaku. Cangraani pingraani aug'arivkenaku.

Tua-i-llu Maacungaam taun' Uqviir qanrucaaqelliniluku, "Issurimek-qaa tunkumegnegu aug'aryugngaciqaa?" Pingaitaa-gguq, caskuan-gguq kana-i kan'a tauna tutgariin caskuan aug'arngaunani tua-i, pikestiin-gguq taugaam aug'aryugngaluku.

ANGUYALUK: Pistellran-qaa aug'aryugngaluku?

NANUGAQ: Ii-i. Tauna-gguq tua-i issuriq tauvet mikelngurmun petuumauq.

ANGUYALUK: Taum-qaa qunutellni pitekluku taum?

NANUGAQ: Ii-i, qunutellni tua-i pitekluku mikelnguq taun' issurimek atlilirluku petugluku.

CUCUAQ: Tua-llu-q' qaill' tauna mikelnguq pia?

NANUGAQ: Tuquluni. Tuquqataami-llu-gguq qaneryaurcami angayuqaagni taukuk qanrutyagarlukek yuum pingraakek camek wani qunuvkenakek cikiqengaqlukek pisqellukek. Waten-gguq tua-i angayuqaagni qanrutellruak tamarkegenka. Maruluugni pivkenak' angayuqaagni taugaam.

Tua-i Kayalivigmiuni piani tua-i uksurpak uitaqallruut ingkut Cuyanguyagurluunkut Uqviiraam aqvavkarluki. Angutengyaaraam-llu aqvaluki. Tua-i tekican tua-i tuunriteurluryaaqlukek, unakevkenaku.

They say Uqviir did everything he could [to remove what was underneath him]. When they would start, and they'd quickly bite one another, he would suddenly head up crying out in pain reacting from a sudden chill.

When he would suddenly head up, Uqviir would tell him that his way of crying out from a sudden chill wasn't his own, that he cries out using his own weapon. He said he could remove it, but since he was trying to kill that child, that's probably what he did.

And Uqviir also knew what he had done.

MARTINA JOHN: So the one who had asked for [the seal skin] was a shaman?

ELSIE TOMMY: Yes, they say he was a very powerful shaman.

ALICE REARDEN: Those shamans who were too malicious and killed people, what did they do to them?

ELSIE TOMMY: They probably did as I just explained. But they say when they were about to die, they'd have visions of those who were trying to kill them, when they were about to die, and they would name who they were.

ALICE REARDEN: Rather, a shaman who was continually killing people in a village; did those people not retaliate against him?

ELSIE TOMMY: I don't know. Although they retaliated against him.

ALICE REARDEN: Or did they leave them alone?

MARTINA JOHN: They probably couldn't retaliate against them, out of fear, although they knew that they were responsible.

MARY GEORGE: That's probably what they did to them.

MARTINA JOHN: They also mentioned that shamans killed their own children. They killed their own children, trying to lengthen their own lives.

Uqviiraam-gguq cali caqeryaaqaa, piqeryaaqaa tua-i. Tua-i-gguq ayagniraqamek keglengareskunek imurtualuni-gguq tagqertaqluni.

Tagqertaqan-gguq Uqviiraam piaqluku, elliin imu'urtuavia pikenritniluku, elliin caskuanek imurtualarniluku. Aug'aryugngayaaqniluku taugaam, tua-i-wa tauna mikelnguq tuqungnaqngamiu pillrullilria tuaten.

Taum cali Uqviiraam nalluvkenaku tuaten tua-i pillra-gguq.

ANGUYALUK: Angalkuullruluni-qaa tauna kaigayaaqelria?

NANUGAQ: Yaa, angarvauluni-gguq angalkuullruuq.

CUCUAQ: Taukut anagarucessiyaagluteng tuquciaqluteng angalkut pitulit qaillun pilallruitki?

NANUGAQ: Tua-i-w' tuaten, aug'utun ava-i qanrutkellemtun pilallrullilriit. Taugaam tuquqata'arqameng tamakut pissurteteng qinuciakelalqait-gguq tuquqata'arqameng, aterpaggluki.

CUCUAQ: Aren, nunani una angalkuq iciw' tuquciuralria yugnek; tamakut-qaa yuut qaillun piksaitaat?

NANUGAQ: Naamikika. Tua-i-w' ping'ermegteggu.

CUCUAQ: Wall'u-q' uitat'lallruit?

ANGUYALUK: Alikluki-w', alikluki-w' nallunrilngermegteki qaill' pisciigat'lallrullikait.

NANURNIRALRIA: Pilallrullikait-wa tuaten.

ANGUYALUK: Makut-am tua-i angalkut tungengqerrninaurait, aling nakmiin-llu irniateng tuquurtelluki. Tua-i nakmiin irniateng tuquurtelluki ellmeng yuucirteng taktucangnaqluki.

That shaman, when people mentioned that the one she pursued had died, she would have her grandchild give her a tattoo[30]

Elsie Tommy, Martina John, Mary George, and Alice Rearden, Bethel, April 2009

ELSIE TOMMY: They say down there, the late Ap'alluk's grandfather killed a female shaman. [A person] would be delirious, naming [the female shaman], [saying] that she had killed him. Then that shaman, when people mentioned that the one she tried to kill had died, she would have her grandchild give her a tattoo here [along her forehead near her hairline].

She would have [her grandchild] give her a tattoo. She was counting [the people she had killed].

MARTINA JOHN: [The grandchild] would poke her, she got a tattoo.

They made a marking on her. Since they probably couldn't write them down, they made a mark that wouldn't disappear.

ELSIE TOMMY: Then they say when [the female shaman] was about to be killed, she once again killed a girl. She evidently said that she had enough [markings] for a parka now, that she was about to have enough [markings] for a parka, that she finally was going to have enough [markings].

MARTINA JOHN: By constantly killing people?

ELSIE TOMMY: Yes, by constantly killing people.

They say the late Ap'alluk's deceased father [killed her].

He hit her on the head with a woodworking implement. Her grandchild had given her a tattoo once again, since he probably knew that she was [a shaman]. When she suddenly went on her back, he pulled her hair back, and her tattoos that were lined [all along her forehead near her hairline] were beautiful; her tattoos were beautiful.

MARTINA JOHN: So were they covered by her hair all the time?

ELSIE TOMMY: Yes, they were concealed by her hair.

That's what the late Ap'alluk said happened to her when he'd tell stories. The late Ap'alluk, the ones named after him down there aren't like him at all.

Angalkuq tauna, tua-i pissuqengani tuqunikatgu tutgarminun eyarcelluni

Nanugaq, Anguyaluk, Nanurniralria, Cucuaq-llu, Mamterilleq, April 2009

NANUGAQ: Kanani-gguq kana-i Ap'alullrem tayima apa'urlullra angalkumek taumek tuqucillruuq arnamek. Tua-i qinuciakaqluku aterpaggluku taumun tuquvkarniluni pitaqniluni. Tua-i-llu-gguq tauna angalkuq, tauna tua-i pissuqengani tuqunikatgu tutgarminun maaggun eyarcelluni.

Eyarcelluni. Naaqluki.

ANGUYALUK: Iciw' kapluku, eyarluni.

Nallunailkucirluk'. Igarluk' pisciigatliameng tua-i tamarngailngurmek nallunailkucirluteng.

NANUGAQ: Tua-i-llu-gguq tuani tua-i tuqutaugarkaurtellermini, tua-i-am tua-i tuquciluni taumek nasaurlurmek. Tua-i qanlliniluni atkugkanek naaciqatarniluni, atkugkanek-gguq naaciqatartuq, naagurainariqatartuq.

ANGUYALUK: Tuquciurallermikun?

NANUGAQ: Ii-i, tuquciurallermikun.

Ap'alullrem-gguq tayima atallran.

Qamiqurrakun muragiurrsuutekun kaugturluku. Tua-i-gguq-am tua-i eyaryaaqelliniluku tauna, tutgariin eyaryaaqelliniluku tua-i nallunritliamiu, angalkuullrullian-wa. Taklaqercan tua-i nuyai ukut qakugartai qakitmun-gguq eyari tangnirpak-gguq; tangnirpak-gguq eyari.

ANGUYALUK: Tamaa-i-qaa nuyainek capumauraraqluteng?

NANUGAQ: Ii-i, nuyaminek capumauraraqluki.

Tuaten tua-i pinillrua-am Ap'alullrem tayim' qanemcingaqami-llu. Ap'alulleq taun' nakmiin kankut atqestain kankut aturyugnailkiit.

They say they would poke that shaman along his collarbone here and check to see if he was done cooking[31]

Albertina Dull, Lizzie Chimiugak, and
Ruth Jimmie, Umkumiut, June 2009

ALBERTINA DULL: These were the ways of the shamans. When they did this in the *qasgiq* . . . for what reason did they *egavak* [cook in a large pot]?

LIZZIE CHIMIUGAK: My, they were probably burning themselves; they never burned.

ALBERTINA DULL: *Egavagluteng* [They cooked in a large pot].

RUTH JIMMIE: Oh, so they got inside something that was boiling and stayed there?

ALBERTINA DULL: It wasn't boiling heavily. Those *iingarnat* [pumice stones], those rocks called *iingarnat*, you all know what *iingarnat* are. They'd heat those, probably along the fire pit of the *qasgiq* down there. [The stones] would be ablaze.

That shaman would be sitting inside a large bowl filled with water.

They say they would drop [pumice stones] in one by one, and when they put the last one in—probably because they weren't large—when they dropped inside, they would make noise. Then it would come to a heavy boil along with those *iingarnat*, it would come to a heavy boil.

LIZZIE CHIMIUGAK: My goodness!

ALBERTINA DULL: Then when they thought [the shaman] was cooked—I wonder what they do? They say they would poke that shaman along his collarbone here and check to see if he was done cooking.

Then when [he] didn't touch the bottom, they'd say that he wasn't cooked.

LIZZIE CHIMIUGAK: My goodness!

ALBERTINA DULL: They would do that again, and again. Then after doing that for a while, they would poke him here again. When he moved like this, when he touched the bottom of the bowl, they'd say that he was done cooking, *uuluku* as they say.

For what reason did they do that?

RUTH JIMMIE: They were probably trying to astound people.

ALBERTINA DULL: Yes, that's what they did.

LIZZIE CHIMIUGAK: And they probably were also displaying their ability as shamans when they did that.

Qutuita-gguq ukuakun kapluku taun' angalkuq uutassiarciqaat

Cingyukan, Neng'uryar, Angalgaq-llu, Umkumiut,
June 2009

CINGYUKAN: Tang maa-i angalkut cayarallrit. Tuatmellu waten piaqameng qasgimi . . . cassuulluteng egavalallruat?

NENG'URYAR: Ala-i eleggluteng-wa pilallrullilriit; elegyuunateng.

CINGYUKAN: Egavagluteng.

ANGALGAQ: Oh, ekluteng-qaa camun qallarvalriamun tua-i uitaluteng?

CINGYUKAN: Qallarvagpek'nani. Iingarnat, iingarnat imkut teggalqut; iciw' iingarnat nallunrilkeci. Tamakut puqlirluki, kat'um-wa qasgim kenillrani pilallilria. Kenrurtaqluteng.

Tauna-wa angalkuq qantarpallraam iluani mermi uitauralria.

Ekurciqaat-gguq nangneq-llu-gguq —angenrit'lalliata-w' pikait—maligarrluku qalrialuteng tuaten ek'arciiqut. Tua-i-ll' qallarvagluni, tamakut iingarnat ilakluki qallarvagluni.

NENG'URYAR: Ala-i!

CINGYUKAN: Tua-i-ll' uuyuklius[katgu] ala i qaill' pilartat? Qutuita-gguq ukuakun kapluku taun' angalkuq uutassiarciqaat.

Tua-i-llu terr'anun camavet agtuutenrilkan uuksaitniluku.

NENG'URYAR: Ala-i!

CINGYUKAN: Allamek tua-i tuaten piaqluku, tuaten tua-i piaqluku. Tua-i-ll' pivakarluku nutaan tua-i ugg'un cali-am kapluku. Waten elliuqan, qantam tua-i terr'anun cama-i tugruskaku wagg'u-q' uuluku.

Ala-i cangnaqluteng tuatelallruat?

ANGALGAQ: Iillanartaarluteng-wa pilallrullilriit.

CINGYUKAN: Yaa, tuaten.

NENG'URYAR: Maniluki-w' tua-i cateng angalkuutassirteng maniaqamegteggu pilallilriit.

One who easily flies[32]

Albertina Dull, Lizzie Chimiugak, and
Ruth Jimmie, Umkumiut, June 2009

ALBERTINA DULL: Those people including the late
father of Anaanangulluaq, you know how when
they told stories of Tengesqauktar, Tengesqauktar
who lived long ago, when they told stories about
him, I think they said it was up at Qanrangaq up
there, Tengesqauktaq's parents were ill.

  Then they say when they were going to die in
great numbers, Tengesqauktar had a drum for
an *iinruq*. They say the one who would come to be
called Tengesqauktar used it as a mattress.

LIZZIE CHIMIUGAK: The one who would become a
powerful shaman?
ALBERTINA DULL: Yes.
LIZZIE CHIMIUGAK: That was our great-grandfather.
The grandfather of my father.
ALBERTINA DULL: Then their mother died. And their
children died. Their father told him what to do
when he was about to die. He told him to always
use that drum for a mattress, to always use it as a
mattress when he slept.

  And there were sinews up there, and what type
of animal sinews were they, the ones hanging.
[And he told him,] "And from up there, when you
want to chew on some skin, take some from up
there and chew some. Here's a tool you can use." It
was an adze, his adze.

  My, did he not feel anguished?
LIZZIE CHIMIUGAK: Gee indeed, he could have cried
out of distress.
ALBERTINA DULL: They say as he stayed there, the
window up there started to drip water.

LIZZIE CHIMIUGAK: It started melting.
ALBERTINA DULL: It started melting. They say
following the instructions his father gave him . . .
my, they were probably high. He would take some
and place it on his pillow. When he would chop
with his adze, he said it looked like their faces were
clean. My, how awful.
LIZZIE CHIMIUGAK: Dead people.
ALBERTINA DULL: The dead people would move back
and forth. My, then while they were there, he went
to the partially underground storage cache, and
since it was dark, after continually feeling around
with his hand, since there was no food, since the

Tengesqauktar

Cingyukan, Neng'uryar, Angalgaq-llu, Umkumiut,
June 2009

CINGYUKAN: Augkut-am Anaanangulluam-llu
augna aatallra, imumi iciw' Tengesqauktar
augna akaartar imna Tengesqauktar
qanemcikaqamegteggu, kiani-gguq tuar-am
Qanrangami kiani naulluuquluteng taukuk
Tengesqauktaraankuk angayuqaak.

  Tua-i-gguq waten waniwa
tuquaqatallinillermeggni, tauna
Tengesqauktar-gguq cauyamek iinrungqellria.
Tua-i curuqura'arqekii-gguq taum tua-i
Tengesqauktaugarkam.
NENG'URYAR: Angarvagkaq?

CINGYUKAN: Ee-m.
NENG'URYAR: Amaurpuk-wa tauna. Aatama
apa'urluat.
CINGYUKAN: Tua-i-ll' aaniit tuquluni. Irniarit-llu-w'
tua-i tuquluteng. Aatiita tua-i tuquqatalliniami
alerqualuku. Tua-i una cauyaq tua-i-w'
curuqerrlainasqelluku, inarteqatarqan
curuqurluku qavalaasqelluku.

  Cali pagaa-i pagkut yualut, cat yualukatki
agalriit. "Pagaa-i-llu aaqassaaryugaqavet
pagaaken tegulluten aaqassaaraqluten. Waniwa
tang caskukan." Kepun, keputni.

  Aling iluteqsuituq-qaa?
NENG'URYAR: Ala-i ikika, nanikualuni qiaksaitell'.

CINGYUKAN: Kiituani-gguq tang tamaani
uitainanrani egaleq-llu pikna
kuciqniaryaurtenguq.
NENG'URYAR: Urungluggluni.
CINGYUKAN: Urungluggluni. Tamaa-i-gguq aatami
pisqutii aturluku tua-i . . . aling quyilalliut-ll'-am.
Tegulluni akitmun piluku. Keputequaqan tuar-
gguq avani qamiqurrit tua-i erulkeggluteng. Aling
ilalketar.

NENG'URYAR: Tuqumalriit.
CINGYUKAN: Tuqumalriit arulaluteng. Aling aren
tua-i-llu-gguq tuaten tua-i uitainanratni ca
elagyamun-llu agluni, tua-i tayim' tan'gercecan
caavtaaryaaqvigminek neqtailan, amiik tua-i
nallunailan, tua-i-am taumek keputmek piurluku
amik callarrluku.

door was noticeable, he used that adze to chop open the door.

When he went outside, they say Quuneq and their family's home was down from them. And he went to it, and he tore some part of it and looked inside, and he said it was the amount of a twined grass storage bag.

He brought that, after placing the drum inside first, he then went inside. The poor thing stayed there. He had a lot of food to eat inside that grass bag.

Then while he was there, he heard a person outside. When they found that he was there, they were surprised, and Quunrem Arnaan said that he had caused the fish to become graves, and she was mad at him and told him to get out.

When the poor thing went out . . .

LIZZIE CHIMIUGAK: Back when they followed taboos.

ALBERTINA DULL: One of them threw a spear at him. Because he wasn't deliberately trying to catch him, he didn't catch him. They say they didn't pay attention to the food at all, and he said that they had become graves and left them.

LIZZIE CHIMIUGAK: Back when they believed in taboos?

ALBERTINA DULL: Then they say Quuneq [lit., "Calm weather"], Tengesqauktaq probably had malicious thoughts toward him. Oh my, they said that Quuneq never caught anything, he couldn't catch animals at all. He was calm weather, he was calm. That's what [Tengesqauktaq] did to him.

Then while Aaqacugaq and family were there, they say that Aaqacugaq's parents who had gone to check their fish trap, they didn't return for a while. When her grandchild would run outside and search his surroundings from a high spot, he would say that a sled was coming their way, and that it had moved closer and had appeared.

Since his grandmother suspected that it wasn't a person, since it wasn't a person, when she told him to stop going outside, he stopped.

They say they had grass storage bags that had been brought inside the home. Those people, since it used to be cold, they used to have a supply that they brought inside their homes because they weren't Westernized at all [implying that they weren't easily offended by things].

My, they said that after a while, some people who had died came inside. It was Tengesqauktar and his sibling's father, and their mother was pregnant, and there was a girl. The one who had been

Anngami, Quunrenkut-gguq un'gani. Ullagluku tua-i-am natii allegluku qinertellinia, tuar-gguq naparcilluut amllertaciit.

Tua-i-am tauna ayulluku cauyar-am tua-i ciumek iterceqaarluku ellii iterluni. Tua-i tuanteurlurluni. Neqauterugai-wa tua-i tamakut naparcilluut.

Tua-i-ll' waten uitainanrani tua-i-ll' yulkitalliniluni ella qakemna. Aren tua-i elpekngamegteggu arenqianateng, tauna Quunrem Arnaan neqet qunguurrniluku-gguq kenkevkenaku anesqelluku.

Aneurluami-am tua-i . . .

NENG'URYAR: Piciruitullratni.

CINGYUKAN: Iliita-gguq tang narulkaryaaqekii tugermek. Pitaqessaanritliamiu-llu-gguq pitaqevkenaku. Aling aren neqet-gguq tang im' ilangcingssaarpek'naki qunguurrniluki uniskilitki.

NENG'URYAR: Piciruitullermeggni?

CINGYUKAN: Tua-i-llu-gguq tang tauna, Quuneq-gguq una, taum tua-i Tengesqauktaraam umyuarrlugcillrullikii. Aren, Quuneq-gguq tua-i tauna cacuitkacagarluni tua-i, picuitkackacagarluni. Quunruluni tua-i quunirluni. Tuaten-am tua-i pillrukii.

Tua-i-ll' taukut Aaqacugaankut uitainanratni, taukuk-gguq-am tua-i Aaqacugaam angayuqaak takuilriamek iteryugpek'natek tekicugpek'natek. Anqerrluni tua-i tauna tutgarrlugii anluni nacetararrarqami man'a ikamraq agiirrniaqekii ukaqvaqanirluku pugniaqluku.

Tua-i-am maurluan yuunrillekluku yuunrilan anqetaanermek taqesqengani taqluni.

Itertangqellriit-gguq naparcillugnek. Yuut imkut, caungameng nengllilaameng-llu itertangqetullrulriit kass'amircugnaiturluameng.

Ala-i, piqerluteng-gguq tang taukut tuqullret tang itqilit-gguq. Tauna tua-i Tengesqauktaraankut aatiik, aaniit-gguq-wa qumiyaalria, qumigluni, una-gguq-wa

going outside [to check on those arriving] was laying on his back. Although [the ghost] spoke, their grandmother never replied. You know how long ago, they used to tell them not to.

LIZZIE CHIMIUGAK: Not to speak to a ghost.

ALBERTINA DULL: Yes, not to reply to a ghost although it spoke, that they would lose their ability to speak if they did.

Their father, after repeatedly saying they were hungry, he then took a bowl and dished himself some food from that *naparcilluk* [grass storage bag]. They ate.

The girl there had very messy hair. Then while they were eating, he evidently said that although he wanted to take his family home . . . I forgot where they said they had moved. My goodness, where do their souls go?

LIZZIE CHIMIUGAK: Oh my.

ALBERTINA DULL: He said that they had moved to some village so that they would stay in contentment. He said that although he wanted to take his companions home, the girl prevented him from doing so because the gulls had removed her eye. My, here I thought she was inside the home.

LIZZIE CHIMIUGAK: Probably because he was afraid they would laugh and poke fun at her.

ALBERTINA DULL: Yes. And he would stroke that boy, "Although this darn one isn't sleeping, he is pretending to sleep."

When they were about to leave, they got ready, his grandmother told him, "Don't refuse to eat our leftover and eat it. Nothing will happen to you." My, that would probably be suspicious [to eat].

My goodness, that poor Tengesqauktar, they say while Tengesqauktar was there, a couple who couldn't have children probably went to get him to have him as a child. They say that poor thing was easily startled. That's why they called him Tengesqauktar [lit., "One who easily flies"].

LIZZIE CHIMIUGAK: That one is the grandfather of our father and Nuyarnerilnguq also. Tengesqauktar is our ancestor.

ALBERTINA DULL: Yes.

LIZZIE CHIMIUGAK: Maybe we're Tengesqauktar. [*laughing*]

ALBERTINA DULL: They say that he was easily startled.

cali nasaurluq. Tauna-w' tua-i anqetaalleq taklauralria. Qanengraan-gguq tua-i taumllu maurluata kiuqayuunaki. Iciw' ak'a inerqutullrukait.

NENG'URYAR: Carayak qanrutesqekvenaku.

CINGYUKAN: Ee-m, carayak kiusqevkenaku qanengraan, qanyuiruciiqniluki.

Qaneryaaqvigminek tauna atiit kaigniluteng qanenqigciryaaqvigminek, tua-i-ll' qantamek tegulluni neqliurluni tuaken naparcillugnek. Nerlutek.

Una-gguq-wa tang nasaurluq tua-i nuyavlugtek'acagarluni. Tua-ll' nernginanermeggni qanlliniluni, tua-i-gguq ukut ilani ut'rucungermiki taugaam . . . camiunun imat'am upagnilriit. Aling anernerit natmun ayalartat?

NENG'URYAR: Ala-i.

CINGYUKAN: Camiunun-gguq wavet upagtut elluanillerkameggnun. Ukut-gguq ilani ut'rucungermiki taumun taugaam nasaurlurrarmun naggluni naruyat-gguq-am iingiraraqallrulliniatgu. Aling enem'etellruuqggem tanem.

NENG'URYAR: Temciqutaqnayukluku-w' piurlullilria.

CINGYUKAN: Ii-i. Tauna-ll' tan'gurraq ellainauraa, "Una-ller qavanrilngermi qavangualleralria."

Tua-i anqataameng upluteng qanrucaaqelliniluku maurluan, "Una ilakuarput nerenrilkurtevkenaku nerkiciu. Cangaituci." Ala-i umyuarcurnarqeciqellilria.

Aling aren tua-i nauwa taunaurluq Tengesqauktar tuani uitainanrani irniangyuilnguuk-gguq taukuk tua-i irniaqsagulluku aqvallikiik-gguq. Tua-i-gguq tatamqeryuk'ackacagarluni taunaurluq. Taumek Tengesqauktarmek aciqiit.

NENG'URYAR: Aatamegnuk Nuyarnerilnguumllu apa'urluqaa tauna. Ciuliaqerpuk taun' Tengesqauktar.

CINGYUKAN: Ee-m.

NENG'URYAR: Wangkuk-kiq Tengesqauktaraulliukuk. [*ngel'artuk*]

CINGYUKAN: Tatamqeryuk'acagarluni-gguq.

Those who would become shamans, some find out when they are still fetuses[33]

Albertina Dull and Lizzie Chimiugak, Umkumiut, June 2009

ALBERTINA DULL: Long ago, those who would become shamans, some know when they are fetuses in the womb, I think they say they know. You know how they said Arnaqulluk knew when he was a fetus.

LIZZIE CHIMIUGAK: My Ilungkurpak?

ALBERTINA DULL: The father of Lincoln and his siblings, the father of Aliurtuq and his siblings was aware when he was a fetus in the womb.

LIZZIE CHIMIUGAK: Our father's brother.

Those who were tied[34]

Albertina Dull, Lizzie Chimiugak, and Ruth Jimmie, Umkumiut, June 2009

ALBERTINA DULL: What are *nemertayagaat* [those small ones who are bound]?

LIZZIE CHIMIUGAK: Those *qillerqayagaat* [small ones who are tied/bound].

Apar'aq used to tell stories about children who were ghosts who were *qillerqayagaat*. I didn't pay attention during that time; my deceased younger sibling and I used to play for a long time on the mattress. And here Apar'aq would tell stories and talk about *qillerqat* [those who were tied] and *qillertayagaat*. They were evidently children who had died.

I would have stories about those if I had paid attention during that time. I was terrible during that time, I had no sense.

ALBERTINA DULL: He said, when Qulvarkam Arnaan [Qulvarkaq's mother] told me about him, she said that he was aware when he was a fetus. He was thinking of going out, and when he would head down to his door, when he would see one of those, he would turn back.

LIZZIE CHIMIUGAK: A *qillerqayagaq*?

ALBERTINA DULL: Yes.

LIZZIE CHIMIUGAK: They evidently called children who were like that *qillerqayagaat*.

ALBERTINA DULL: Yes. He would turn back. [His mother's] labor would probably start and stop again. . . .

They say when he finally went out, when he was finally born, he went out and he had already grown teeth. Arnaqulluk had grown teeth.

Makut angalkurkat-llu nauwa qingaugaqata-ll' ilait nallunrilalriit

Cingyukan Neng'uryar-llu, Umkumiut, June 2009

CINGYUKAN: Ak'a makut angalkurkat-llu nauwa qingaugaqata-ll' ilait nallunrilalriit, nallunritningatelaqait. Iciw' augna-ll' ava-i Arnaqulluk qumiullra nallunritnillrukiit.

NENG'URYAR: Ilungkurpaka-qaa?

CINGYUKAN: Augna imna ukut aatiit Lincoln-ankut, Aliurtunkut aatiit qumiullra nalluvkenaku.

NENG'URYAR: Ataatapuk-wa.

Qillerqat

Cingyukan, Neng'uryar, Angalgaq-llu, Umkumiut, June 2009

CINGYUKAN: Nemertayagaat caugat?

NENG'URYAR: Qillerqayagarnek.

Qillerqayagarnek mikelngurnek alangrunek Apar'aq qanemcilallruyaaquq. Cumikellrunritua tamatum nalliini; kinguqliirutka-ll' akusrarcimalallruukuk acimi. Apar'aq-wa qanemciuralria qillerqanek, qillertayagarnek qanraqluni. Cunaw' mikelnguut tuqullret.

Tamaa-i tamakunek qanemcikangqerrsartua cumiketullrukuma tamaani. Ikiullrulrianga tamatum [nalliini], usviitellruunga usviitellemni.

CINGYUKAN: Tamaa-i-gguq, Qulvarkam Arnaan qanemcitlerminia taumek elliinek, qumiullni nalluvkenaku. Anen'aluni umyuarteqluni, anelraryaaqaqami amiiminun tua-i tamakucimek tangrraqami utertaqluni.

NENG'URYAR: Qillerqayagarmek-qaa?

CINGYUKAN: Ii-i.

NENG'URYAR: Tua-i tamaa-i mikelnguut tuaten qillerqayagarnek aptullrulliniit.

CINGYUKAN: Ee-m. Utertaqluni. Aipaagni tuani nepngerraarluni ataam arulairluni. . . .

Anyaqlirluni-gguq tua-i anyaqlirturainarluni an'uq keggutengllinilria. Tauna Arnaqulluk keggutengellrullinilria.

My, she probably had a hard time giving birth; he evidently grew large [while in the womb]. My, I thought they only grow teeth when they are a number of months old.

LIZZIE CHIMIUGAK: My goodness!

RUTH JIMMIE: I thought sometimes, some give birth to babies who already have teeth.

LIZZIE CHIMIUGAK: I forgot who they said was born when they had started to grow teeth. [The baby's] namesakes probably caused that to happen.

Although he was dead, he put a curse on them[35]

Albertina Dull, Lizzie Chimiugak, and Ruth Jimmie, Umkumiut, June 2009

ALBERTINA DULL: Did Aamecaaq not tell you the story about her late grandfather?

LIZZIE CHIMIUGAK: She never told us the story.

ALBERTINA DULL: Aamecaaq is named after her grandfather Tunguyailnguq, the one who they say the people of Tununak had someone murder.

They told someone to kill him.

My goodness! Those *kass'aruak* [two who were part non-Native] arrived, as those *kass'anguat* used to travel by sled.

LIZZIE CHIMIUGAK: Long ago; it was a long time ago.

ALBERTINA DULL: Yes, a long time ago.

Well, he stayed in Tununak for a brief time, but he had a young wife. His young wife was Kavkam Arnaukaq, or was it Qengmiulriim Arnaukaq, a girl.

While they were staying at Tununak, they say those *kass'aruak* arrived. They had a gun.

LIZZIE CHIMIUGAK: Maybe they were policemen.

ALBERTINA DULL: My, then they say the people of Tununak over there told someone to kill him.

LIZZIE CHIMIUGAK: My, how poor! Maybe those two were marshals.

ALBERTINA DULL: Then the people bought goods. It seems they were [purchasing] caribou back fat, the caribou back fat that they had obtained. My, did we have caribou? Was it caribou back fat [that they purchased]?

LIZZIE CHIMIUGAK: I don't know. You are telling the story; I don't know that.

ALBERTINA DULL: Poor, when the poor thing was purchasing some goods, the other one manhandled him because he had become frail and weak, and he shot him with a pistol.

Aling irnisciigatellruvagtuq; anglirillrulliuq. Aling qavciurtaqameng-ggem keggutenglartut taugaam.

NENG'URYAR: Ala-i!

ANGALGAQ: Caaqameng-ggem ilait piipingtuut *already have teeth.*

NENG'URYAR: Kina-ll' imat'am ak'a keggutengaarluku anen'illrukiit. Atrin-wa pillrullikiit.

Tuqumang'ermi cali kingullugglukek

Cingyukan, Neng'uryar, Angalgaq-llu, Umkumiut, June 2009

CINGYUKAN: Aug'umek-qaa Aamecaam aparrlugallminek qanemcicuitellruaci?

NENG'URYAR: Qanemcicuitellruakut.

CINGYUKAN: Tua-i-w' atqekii aparrlugani tauna Amecaam, Tunguyailnguq, Tununermiut tuqucetellrat-gguq.

Tua-i-w' ellimertuulluku tuqutevkarluku.

Ala-i! Nauwa kass'aruak taukuk iciw' tekillutek, ikamraraluteng imkut kass'anguat.

NENG'URYAR: Ak'a-w' tamaani; akaurtuq.

CINGYUKAN: Ee-m akaar tamaani.

Tua-i Tununermetqalria, nuliayaarluni taugaam. Kavkam Arnaukamek-qaa nuliayaarluni, wall'u-qaa Qengmiulriim Arnaukamek, nasaurlurmek.

Tununermetellragni taukuk tua-i kass'aruak-gguq tekillutek. Nutengqerrlutek.

NENG'URYAR: *Police*-aulliuk.

CINGYUKAN: Ala-i tua-i-llu-gguq Tununermiut ikegkut ellimertuutelliniluku tuqutesqelluku.

NENG'URYAR: Aling nakleng! *Marshal*-aulliuk-llu taukuk.

CINGYUKAN: Tua-i-llu-gguq kipussaaquluteng tua-i yuut. Tuar-am tunukunallrulriit, tunurtagkenek. Ala-i tuntungqellruukut-qaa? Tuntum-qaa tunugkenek piut?

NENG'URYAR: Nallukeka-w'. Elpet qanemci[uten]; nallukeka tang.

CINGYUKAN: Nakleng, kipussaagurlullrani tua-i aipaagnek calekcagaluku tuaten cirlaurcan, nutyaarkun nutkallinikii.

LIZZIE CHIMIUGAK: Poor thing!

ALBERTINA DULL: Then one of them yelled, "Let the one who told me [to kill him], as he is dead now, come and get him."

That one died. Evidently, like him, like himself, he wouldn't heed him because he was a shaman like himself. Because he was a shaman, the other, like himself, vomited blood, and something happened to the other person.

RUTH JIMMIE: The ones who killed him?

ALBERTINA DULL: The two who killed him [died] not long after.

RUTH JIMMIE: So although he was dead, he put a curse on them?

ALBERTINA DULL: Yes, he repaid them. Then his young wife returned home to Qipneq [Kipnuk].

Then during the fall, the dead person's young wife along with another girl her age, one who was younger and not as strong and fast as she was, they went to pry the ground in search of mouse food from underground caches during the fall along the shores of Qass'urpak.

They say the shore of Qass'urpak has a very steep bank. They were prying the ground in search of mouse food during the fall. As they were picking mouse food, when they heard a noise, underneath an area that was eroding something down there that was small and dark stood up.

LIZZIE CHIMIUGAK: My goodness!

ALBERTINA DULL: His parka was a muskrat parka, and his skin boots were made of unattractive wolf fur, and his walking stick—they say his walking stick had lines on it as designs.

He stood and started shaking things from his body. Then after a while, he climbed up down there, and he started approaching. [laughs]

He started approaching them.

LIZZIE CHIMIUGAK: My goodness!

ALBERTINA DULL: And since that was her dead husband, his former young wife was probably very afraid.

They say her companion, also, it was fortunate that that girl was a fast runner. My, they ran. They say the one who wasn't as fast would grab her. That one would try to let go of her grasp, and [her hand] would come off.

She tried to leave her behind.

RUTH JIMMIE: Probably because she was so creeped out.

ALBERTINA DULL: Yes, they say when they would turn this way, he would intercept them.

NENG'URYAR: Nakleurluq!

CINGYUKAN: Tua-i-llu-gguq qayagaurluni, naliak tayima, "Waniwa ellimertuutestellran waniw' tuqumariuq, aqvaliu."

Tauna tua-i tuquluni. Cunawa-gguq tua-i elliitun, ellmitun, ellmitun aipaa ak'a niicugnaunaku angalkuungami. Aipaa-gguq ellmitun augmek mirecpagluni, aipaa-llu cali qaill' piluni.

ANGALGAQ: Taukuk-qaa tuqucetellrek?

CINGYUKAN: Tuqucetellrek ak'aniyugnaunatek.

ANGALGAQ: Tuqumang'ermi-qaa cali kingullugglukek?

CINGYUKAN: Ii-i, akinaurlukek tua-i. Tua-i-llu-gguq tauna nuliayagii uterrluni Qipnermun.

Tua-i-llu waten uksuarmi taukuk tua-i nuliayaallra cali nasaurluullgutminek aiparluni, taugaam ayaniillminek aiparluni, pakissaaglutek, uskuarmi Qass'urpiim ceniini.

Tamana-gguq Qass'urpak ekvigenqekacaartuq cenii. Tamaa-i uksuarmi pakiurlutek avurlutek. Avuinanermegni caqalriamek niicamek piqalliniuk uss'aryuum aciani kanan' tunguyaalria nangertellria.

NENG'URYAR: Ala-i!

CINGYUKAN: Tevyuliit-wa atkui, keglunvialullraak-gguq-wa tang iqertiik, ayarua-gguq—ayarua-gguq keptarluni qaralirugaat.

Nangerrluni evcumyigtellria. Tua-ll' piqerluni kana-i mayurluni tua-i-ll' man'a agiirtenga'artellini-ll'. [ngel'artuq]

Agiirtenga'artelliniluni tungiignun.

NENG'URYAR: Ala-i!

CINGYUKAN: Aren tauna-llu uilqengamiu alingellilria cakneq nuliayaallra.

Tua-i-gguq tang malia-ll' tauna, anirta-gguq uqilallruuq-llu tauna nasaurluq, nasaurluulermini. Aren aqevlutek. Taum tua-i ayaniillran tauna teguqeraqluku. Taum-gguq tang pegleqrutsaagluku, aug'artaqluni.

Unitessaagluku.

ANGALGAQ: Qungvagyussiyaagngami-w' pillilria.

CINGYUKAN: Ee-m, ukatmun-gguq piaqagni narulmuarlukek piaqluni.

LIZZIE CHIMIUGAK: My goodness!

ALBERTINA DULL: While [they were running], smoke started to appear from their village down there. Since they were afraid, *?paivcivikurluku.* Then [the ghost] sat down. They returned home, the poor things keeping an eye out for him.

   Then after a while he stood, and he was an ugly wolf.

RUTH JIMMIE: My goodness!

ALBERTINA DULL: My goodness! Evidently, there wasn't any smoke actually rising from their village. But Iquyuilnguum Atii, [the shaman] Angutekayak had evidently been born. When a baby was born, a lot of smoke started rising, although there wasn't actually smoke rising there at all. The child who was born saved them.

They say her dog was using its powers [to heal her][36]

Albertina Dull, Lizzie Chimiugak, and
Ruth Jimmie, Umkumiut, June 2009

ALBERTINA DULL: Also a ghost that Yuguayiim Arnaan [Yuguayak's mother] used to tell about. She said there was a woman with a small baby. Then her husband died, and her mother also died.

   Her mother and her husband died. I'm not sure how they died. That woman had a small baby. She had a female dog who was nursing its pups. My, was she not afraid at that time?

   Then while she was sitting like this in the evening, a person evidently came inside. She saw that it was her deceased mother. And the dog down there didn't bark at all.

   After a while, [the ghost of her deceased mother] went out. When she went out, she suddenly started to feel lethargic. When they encountered ghosts in the past, you know how they felt lethargic and started to vomit. My, she suddenly started to feel lethargic.

   Then she looked over at the dog. They say it wasn't making any noise, what they call *niugilngarluku* [it wasn't making noise].

RUTH JIMMIE: It wasn't making any noise?

ALBERTINA DULL: It wasn't making any noise. It didn't bark at all.

   She looked over at her dog and said, "My, you over there, I'm probably going to die now. When I die, your pups will die, and you will probably die

NENG'URYAR: Ala-i!

CINGYUKAN: Tua-i pivakarlutek, tua-i-ll' kankut nunakek tua-ll' kankut puyungelliniluteng. Tua-i alingamek tua-i, paivcivikurluku. Pivakarluku tua-ll' aqumqertelliniluni imna. Tua-i uterrlutek kell'urutekuraurlurluku.

   Tua-i-ll' piqerluni nangertelliniuq keglunvialull'er.

ANGALGAQ: Ala-i!

CINGYUKAN: Ala-i! Cunawa-gguq tang takut nunakek puyingssaaranricaaqellinilriit. Imna taugaam iciw' Iquyuilnguum Atii imna Angutekayak yuurtellrullinill'. Piipiq tamaa-i yuurcan puyurpallinilriit, puyinrilengraata. Taum tua-i mikelnguum yuurtellriim anirturlukek.

Wagg'u-q' qimugtiin qaniqluku

Cingyukan, Neng'uryar, Angalgaq-llu, Umkumiut,
June 2009

CINGYUKAN: Cali aug' alangruq-am Yuguayiim Arnaan qanemcik'lallra. Tauna-gguq arnaq irniacuarangqellria. Tua-i-llu-gguq aipaa tauna tuquluni, aanii-ll' call' tuquluni.

   Aanii uinga-ll' tuqulutek. Callermeggni ukuk tuquak. Tauna arnaq irniacuarluni. Qimugtengqellria-gguq arnacalumek mugciluni. Aling alingeksaituq-qaa tuani?

   Tua-i-ll' waten uitainanrani atakumi yug' itliniluni. Maaten-gguq tang pia aanallra. Qimugta-llu-gguq tua-i kan'a tua-i caitqapik qilungssaarpek'nani-gguq.

   Tua-i calnguami tayim' anlliniluni. Anngan, aren tua-i ellii cayuumiitem tekilluku tua-i. Tua-i-w' alangruaqameng iciw' imumi cayuumiinateng miryaqungelalriit. Aren tua-i cayuumiitem tekilluku.

   Tua-i-ll' ikaviallinia qimugta. Wagg'u-q' tua-i niugilngarluku.

ANGALGAQ: Niugilngarluku?

CINGYUKAN: Niugilngarluku. Qilungssaarpek'nani.

   Qimugteni ikavialliniluku, "Aling aren iksuuq, waniwa tua-i wiinga tuquqatallilrianga. Tua-i tuqukuma irniaten tuquaciqelriit, elpet-llu

also; you will all go hungry." She lay down because she felt so sluggish, she lay down.

My, for some reason, she gained conciousness, and there was someone up there who was using his shaman powers [to heal her], *qaniqelria*, you know, he was practicing his shaman powers.

Just when she got up from where she lay, that dog that had been nursing its pups jumped from behind her onto the floor. They say her dog was using its powers [to save her].

LIZZIE CHIMIUGAK: My, [her dog] saved her life.

RUTH JIMMIE: So [the dog] was using its powers to [save her]?

ALBERTINA DULL: It was using its powers on her.

LIZZIE CHIMIUGAK: It was wise.

ALBERTINA DULL: My, some dogs were so smart in the past; when giving them commands, they would understand.

Those two stories she told, I was so frightened.

When he was about to obtain a sibling, he died[37]

Albertina Dull and Lizzie Chimiugak, Umkumiut, June 2009

ALBERTINA DULL: They say that Ayagina'ar was doctored to live by a shaman. They say it was declared that if he was about to get a younger sibling, he would die. My, how awful.

LIZZIE CHIMIUGAK: My, poor thing. I wonder why?

ALBERTINA DULL: Then they say when [his mother] became pregnant with Ayagina'ar, her [older child's] health deteriorated and he died.

LIZZIE CHIMIUGAK: Poor thing!

ALBERTINA DULL: They say because he had a *napaneq* [support that keeps one well or alive] that was an only child.

LIZZIE CHIMIUGAK: An only child?

ALBERTINA DULL: Probably one who was selfish. How awful, what were those shamans like? Since that was his situation, when he was about to obtain a sibling, he died. Why did they do that to him [take his body someplace else]?

---

piciqellilriaten; paluciqelriaci." Inarrluni tua-i cayuumiitellmi pitaciani, inarrluni.

Aren, tua-i qaillun pilriim ellangyartuqalliniuq, qaniqelria, qaniqelria pakemna, iciw' tua-i tuunrilria, tuunrilria.

Inangqallerminek uilluni piqanrakun keluanek qimugta taun' mugcilleq qeckalliniluni natermun. Wagg'u-q' qimugtiin qaniqluku.

NENG'URYAR: Ala-i, anirturluku.

ANGALGAQ: Qaniqluku-q' angalkilluku?

CINGYUKAN: Angalkilluku.

NENG'URYAR: Usvituluni.

CINGYUKAN: Atam usvitular ak'a qimugtet ilaitni; qanrutaqameng nalluvkenaku piaqluteng.

Taukugnek-am tua-i qanemcitqallranga, tua-i cakneq qungvagyuk'acagallrulrianga.

Aipangqataami tua-i tuquluni

Cingyukan Neng'uryar-llu, Umkumiut, June 2009

CINGYUKAN: Tauna-am tua-i iciw' tuunrangayagtaullinilria, tuunrangayakngaullrullinilria Ayagina'ar. Tua-i-gguq qanrumaluni tua-i-gguq uyurangqataquni tuquciquq. Aling ik'atak.

NENG'URYAR: Ala-i nakleurluq. Ciin-kiq?

CINGYUKAN: Tua-i-llu-gguq qingarluni aug'umek ava-i Ayagina'armek, tauna tua-i irniara assiirulluni tuquluni.

NENG'URYAR: Nakleng!

CINGYUKAN: Taumek-gguq napanengqerrami tua-i-w' kiimelngurmek.

NENG'URYAR: Kiimaulriamek?

CINGYUKAN: Tua-i-w' kiimurrsugmek pillilria. Ik'atak angalkut qaill' piat? Tuaten tua-i ayuqelliniami aipangqataami tua-i tuquluni. Ciin tuaten pillruatgu?

When they were afraid of shamans[38]

Albertina Dull and Lizzie Chimiugak, Umkumiut, June 2009

LIZZIE CHIMIUGAK: And again, Paningayaq used to tell me that Al'aruk, the deceased mother of Aaqaq, someone asked to marry her, but she didn't comply. They say Al'aq completely refused [to marry him].

ALBERTINA DULL: Are you talking about that awful person?

LIZZIE CHIMIUGAK: Yes, they say *angliriqerrluni* [she became haughty] as they say. She wouldn't [marry him]. Then they say the father of the one who had wanted to have her as a wife, since he was probably some sort of [shaman], he evidently said, "Let her be, she will grow as big as her haughtiness."

ALBERTINA DULL: My goodness!

LIZZIE CHIMIUGAK: And indeed, she grew large. You know how the doctors said that her bones grew large. "Let her be, she will grow as large as her haughtiness." My goodness!

ALBERTINA DULL: Shamans, long ago, for this reason . . .

LIZZIE CHIMIUGAK: Their curses became true.

ALBERTINA DULL: They say when they wanted to marry them, because they were concerned for their lives, they used to comply with their requests.

LIZZIE CHIMIUGAK: Although they didn't want to [marry them]; they were afraid of [shamans].

ALBERTINA DULL: Yes, that's how it was.

LIZZIE CHIMIUGAK: They only complied because they wanted to live.

ALBERTINA DULL: Yes, that's how they are.

LIZZIE CHIMIUGAK: I had forgotten that Aamecaaq had told me that Mancuam Atii [Mancuaq's father] told Gabriel that he wanted him for a son-in-law. He wanted him to marry Cakayak down there. They say that Gabriel couldn't decline thinking of his life. They say that he made him [his son-in-law], and here I think he was his relative.

ALBERTINA DULL: That's what I've heard throughout my life.

LIZZIE CHIMIUGAK: Carrup'ak evidently practiced the old tradition.

ALBERTINA DULL: Yes, for the sake of living.

LIZZIE CHIMIUGAK: When they were afraid of shamans.

Alikellermeggni angalkut

Cingyukan Neng'uryar-llu, Umkumiut, June 2009

NENG'URYAR: Tuamtell' Paningayam qanemcit'lallrukiinga Al'aruk augna Aaqam aanallra, kia-gguq taun' nulirrniaryaaqekii niitevkenaku. Al'am-llu qessakekackacagarluku.

CINGYUKAN: Aug'uruum-qaa imum?

NENG'URYAR: Ii-i, angliriqerrluni-gguq apqiitnek. Pingaunaku tua-i. Tua-i-llu-gguq taum nuliqsugteksaaqellran atiin caulliniami qanlliniluni, "Uitasgu angucirmitun angliriciquq."

CINGYUKAN: Ala-i!

NENG'URYAR: Ilumun-llu angliriluni. Nauwa yungcartet enerpaurrniluku pillrukiit. "Angucirmitun angliriciquq uitaciu." Ala-i!

CINGYUKAN: Tua-i waten angalkut akaar tamana, man'a maa-i pitekluku . . .

NENG'URYAR: Akqutiit piciugaqluni.

CINGYUKAN: Tua-i-w' nulirrniarqatki anernerriit-gguq pitekluku niitetullruit.

NENG'URYAR: Qessakeng'ermegteki; uluryaktullrulliniit.

CINGYUKAN: Ee-m, yaa, tuaten tua-i.

NENG'URYAR: Anernerraa taugaam pitekluku niiyutekluku.

CINGYUKAN: Yaa, tuaten ayuqut.

NENG'URYAR: Aamecaam-llu imat'am qanemcitellrukiinga Gabriel-aq-gguq nengauksugluku qanruskii Mancuam Atiin. Kat'umek Cakayagmek nuliangesqelluku. Tua-i-gguq elliin pinricesciiganaku anernera-gguq umyuaqluku, tauna Gabriel-aq. Tua-i-gguq piurcelluku, tungayakngacaaqekii-llu.

CINGYUKAN: Tua-i waten avanirpak tua-i niitaqelrianga tua-i.

NENG'URYAR: Akaarcetun Carrup'ak pillrullinilria.

CINGYUKAN: Ee-m, anernerrait pitekluki tua-i.

NENG'URYAR: Alikellermeggni angalkut.

[Shamans] killed the wives of storekeepers out of jealousy[39]

*Albertina Dull, Lizzie Chimiugak, and
Ruth Jimmie, Umkumiut, June 2009*

LIZZIE CHIMIUGAK: And my father, was it Eriq; was there a white man named Eriq? I forgot who he said it was. They say that white man desired him for a storekeeper for a long time. He said that he tried to persuade him to be his storekeeper for a long time. But he said his late mother used to tell him not to ever become a storekeeper although he asked him to become a storekeeper. She told him that the wives of many storekeepers don't live.

ALBERTINA DULL: Because they were jealous of them.

LIZZIE CHIMIUGAK: Yes, when [shamans] were jealous. Then he said that he was never a storekeeper [for that reason].

RUTH JIMMIE: So they'd kill their wives?

LIZZIE CHIMIUGAK: And also they say Aamecaaq, when her husband was a storekeeper, when he was a storekeeper for a short while, the late grandfather of Cimiugaq, Yulqiim Atra, *kuimartengyaaqellruuq* [something came to swim inside her body]. Her health deteriorated. A shaman did that to her, but another shaman evidently saved her life.

She said [the shaman] would say that she *?melqulkitarluni* like a muskrat.

RUTH JIMMIE: What do you mean, they killed the wives of storekeepers out of jealousy?

LIZZIE CHIMIUGAK: Shamans [killed them].

ALBERTINA DULL: They were jealous of them.

LIZZIE CHIMIUGAK: They probably attempted to [kill] their family members. They probably did that to them when they declined to give them something they wanted. They say that *kuimartengellruyaaquq* [something started swimming in her body].

ALBERTINA DULL: My goodness!

LIZZIE CHIMIUGAK: The one who [caused her to become ill] would say she *?melqulkitarluni*. Another shaman evidently did that to her, but they say another shaman saved her life. My goodness!

Kupcaat nulirrit tuqutaqluki ciknakluki

*Cingyukan, Neng'uryar, Angalgaq-llu, Umkumiut,
June 2009*

NENG'URYAR: Aataka-ll' wiinga Erim-qaa uum; kass'amek-qaa Erirtangqellruuq? Kitumun imat'anem. Taum-gguq kipucesteksuumirturallruyaaqaa kass'am. Kupcaaqsugluku-gguq qarucimayaaqekii. Taugaam-gguq aanallran pilallrua kupcaarurcesqengraaku kupcaaruqaasqevkenaku. Kupcaat amllerem nulirra unguvayuitniluku.

CINGYUKAN: Tua-i-w' ciknakluk'.

NENG'URYAR: Ii-i, ciknaaqameng. Tua-i-llu-gguq kupcaaruqallruvkenani.

ANGALGAQ: Nulirrit-qaa tuqutaqluki?

NENG'URYAR: Aamecaaq-llu-gguq cali aipallni kupcaarullrani, kupcaaruurallrani, Cimiugam im' apa'urluirutii Yulqiim Atra, kuimartengyaaqellruuq. Assiirulluni. Angalkum call' piyaaqluku, allam angalkum anirtulliniluku.

Melqulkitarninauraa-gguq taum tevyulitun.

ANGALGAQ: Qaillun, kupcaat-qaa nulirrit tuqutaqluki ciknakluki?

NENG'URYAR: Angalkut.

CINGYUKAN: Ciknakluk'.

NENG'URYAR: Cait-wa tua-i pissaalallrullikait. Qunuteqa'arqaceteng-llu-w' pilallilriit. Kuimartengellruyaaquq-gguq.

CINGYUKAN: Ala-i!

NENG'URYAR: Taum-gguq tua-i pistiin melqulkitarniaqluku. Angalkum allam pivkaryaaqelliniluku, taugaam-gguq cali angalkum allam anirtullrua. Ala-i!

Some shamans evidently had two wives[40]

Albertina Dull and Ruth Jimmie, Umkumiut, June 2009

ALBERTINA DULL: My goodness! That's why I say, "If someone talks about our past and says that they were wealthy, they will be lying. We never saw any wealthy people."

But some people who made great efforts at subsisting, some people evidently had two wives. My, I wonder why.

RUTH JIMMIE: Probably because if someone was a very skilled *nukalpiaq*, his wife wouldn't be able to keep up with the work if she was the only one. [*laughs*]

ALBERTINA DULL: My, but Muiqerrilleq [had two wives], probably since he was a shaman, the deceased father of Nina and her siblings, probably since he was a shaman. [He was married to] Inuuk and another. The mother of those ones, Louise and her siblings, was Inuuk. And the mother of Qalqarayak and her sibling was Niuk, Niuk. My goodness, and here some people tend to be jealous.

The shaman was responsible [for their death], he killed them[41]

Albertina Dull and Ruth Jimmie, Umkumiut, June 2009

ALBERTINA DULL: My goodness, long ago, since my mother was given to another family to raise long ago, my mother was evidently given away to Sophie over there, to Sophie's late grandmother at first.

Poor, she talked about the one who took care of her, the one who also took care of the deceased father of Allirkar and his siblings, those sisters. I seem to have told the story before, that because of those otters that that shaman had claimed to be his; although they were out in the wilderness, he lied and said that they belonged to him, probably since he was trying to find a motive for his wicked acts. Those two sisters, including the one who took care of my mother, and the others, he didn't allow the sisters to get doctored, and they were sick.

They say that their deceased parents were only trying to save the late mother of Allirkar and his siblings, they had a shaman use his powers on her to save her.

Ilait angalkut aipangqetullrullinilriit tang malrugnek

Cingyukan Angalgaq-llu, Umkumiut, June 2009

CINGYUKAN: Arenqiapaa-ll' tua-i! Taumeg'-am pilalrianga wiinga, "Kina imna kingunemtenek qanemcikuni tukuuniluni-ll' qanellrukuni iqluciquq. Tukurlimek tangeqsaitukut tua-i."

Man'a taugaam ilii pingnatupialriim ilii, iciw' tua-i aipangqerraqluteng tua-i ilait aipangqetullrullinilriit tang malrugnek. Ala-i, ciin-kiq.

ANGALGAQ: Tua-i-wa tauna nulirra nukalpiapiarukan atauciuluni angusngangailan pillilria. [*ngel'artuq*]

CINGYUKAN: Aling imna taugken tua-i Muiqerrilleq angalkuungami-w' pillilria imna Nina-nkut, Nina-nkut aatallrat, angalkuungami-w' pillilria. Ukugnek tua-i Inuunkugnek. Ikegkut ika-i aaniit Inuulria, Louise-ankut. Ukuk-llu Qalqarayiinkuk aaniik Niuguluni, Niuk. Aling aren, qungyarayulalriit-llu ilait.

Angalkuum pivkarlukek, pitaqlukek

Cingyukan Angalgaq-llu, Umkumiut, June 2009

CINGYUKAN: Aling aren tua-i, akaar waten, waten yugkiutngurlullrulliniami-ll' aanaka, tamaani aug'um Sophie-m ik'um, Sophie-m ik'um maurlullrinun yugkiutnguyaaqellrulliniuq.

Akleng, tua-i-gguq imna, una aulukestii ik'um-llu ukut Allirkaraankut aatallrata aulukestellra, alqaqelriik taukuk. Iciw' qanemcikellrungacaaqekeka, taukut cenkayagaat pitekluki taum angalkuum piklakuallri; yuilqurmiutaungraata pikninguarluki avalitkaaraminek kepeqngami ikiutekaraminek kepeqngami pillilria. Taukuk tua-i alqaqleriik, tauna aanama-ll' aulukestii, augkut-llu tua-i, alqaqelriik yungcavkarpek'naki, naulluulutek tua-i.

Tua-i-gguq ukut Allirkaraankut aanallratnun angayuqallregket, tauna taugaam anangnaqucaaqluku, iciw' tua-i tuunriqu'urcelluku.

But they say the one who raised my mother, it was as though they weren't paying any attention to her. It seems that my mother said that her adoptive father was the older brother of Nusail's late father.

Poor, my mother said that she got to a point where she didn't have skin boots to put on. My, she said some days, when her adoptive father probably felt sorry for her, he would tell her, "Now, put on my skin boots and go out and go and tell stories with a story knife." She said that she would just slip them on to go outside and tell stories with a story knife.

She said that she was lethargic, she wasn't vigorous. Poor thing, she said she would tell stories with a story knife. Then she said she eventually died one day, my, those two died.

RUTH JIMMIE: The shaman was responsible [for their deaths], he killed them?

ALBERTINA DULL: That shaman who had claimed [the otters] caused [their death]. They should have gone to him and struck him long before!

RUTH JIMMIE: So those two had stolen some otters?

ALBERTINA DULL: Some otters from the wilderness. They didn't belong to anyone but they were just out and available. My, why did he do that? That one told him that they belonged to him.

And also these shamans, after asking for something from someone, they were so irritating, sometimes they would put a curse on a person. My, they were scary.

That shaman probably caused her to begin walking around [as a ghost][42]

Albertina Dull, Lizzie Chimiugak, and
Ruth Jimmie, Umkumiut, June 2009

LIZZIE CHIMIUGAK: The dear person I was named after who they said haunted people as a ghost for a long time, Kumlilriim Atii [Kumlilria's father] evidently captured her.

ALBERTINA DULL: They said that they "pulled her" when they moved from the place where she had died before the specified time [after her death]. That caused her to haunt people as a ghost.

LIZZIE CHIMIUGAK: Because of shamans.

ALBERTINA DULL: Yes. They evidently went down to Kanerrlulegmiut probably before the specified days were over [following a death].

Tauna-gguq taugken tauna aanama aulukestellra tua-i imutun cumikenrilngurtun ayuqluku. Tuar-am ukut Nusailankut aatallrata anngaanek tauna aanaka aatanguangqellrunilria.

Akleng, tua-i-gguq pilugugmek-llu acuirulluni aanaka. Aling, tua-i-gguq cam iliini taum tua-i aatanguaran naklegyagutelliaqamiu piciqaa, "Kitek' pilugullraagemnek all'uten yaaruiyartua." Muruqerlukek-gguq anluni yaarui[luni].

Caullruuq-gguq atam tua-i uralaunani, uralaunani, tua-i-w' pirenqeggianani. Yaaruirlurnaurtuq-gguq tua-i. Tua-i-llu-gguq tang piqerluni tuquluni tauna, ala-i tuqulutek taukuk.

ANGALGAQ: Angalkuum pivkarlukek, pitaqlukek?

CINGYUKAN: Angalkum taum pivkarlukek piklakuallrem. Ak'a ullagluku kav'agnami!

ANGALGAQ: Taukuk-qaa tegutellrulutek canek cenkanek?

CINGYUKAN: Taukut cenkayagarmek yuilqumek. Pikumavkenateng ellmikun uitalrianek. Ala-i ciin taun' waten pia? Pikniluki-gguq elliin taum tua-i piluku.

Cali makut iciw' tuunrangayiit makut yugmek kaigarraarluteng nekanaqluteng iciw' umyuarrlugcirrluk' iliini. Aling, tua-i alingnaqluteng.

Tua-i-w' angalkum taum kangangevkallikii

Cingyukan, Neng'uryar, Angalgaq-llu, Umkumiut,
June 2009

NENG'URYAR: Tauna alangruuguraurlurnillrat atqa, tua-i Kumlilriim Atiin-am pitaqeurlullrullinia.

CINGYUKAN: Qimuutniluku-wam pillrukiit. Tamatum tamaa-i alangruungevkallrukii.

NENG'URYAR: Angalkungssiit-wa.

CINGYUKAN: Ee-m. Kanerrlulegmun-am atralliniluteng erenret tayim' naavailgata aipaagni pillilria.

You know how they used to wait until after a number of days had passed [after someone died]. . . . I think it was five days.

LIZZIE CHIMIUGAK: That shaman probably caused her to begin walking around [as a ghost].

ALBERTINA DULL: Yes, my goodness. . . .

LIZZIE CHIMIUGAK: Shamans. Cimiugaq and his family had a window that was Western-made at Cakcaaq. They said one night, when Arnaq told what happened, she said that the one I'm named after was looking through the window when they didn't close their window right away [when it got dark]. They say her ruff was about to cover the window; they suddenly closed it [with a curtain].

Then again, Yulqim Atii went to go and get various things from Kanerrlulek. The poor things would go and retrieve their things after leaving them. They say he went to get some things from there.

Then they say he got some old skin boots, a pair of skin boots, back when skin boots were their only footwear when they didn't have shoes. They say a piece of her clothing was somewhere near his skin boot or with his other things. They used to throw away all their clothing. Her piece of clothing was evidently there.

They say while he was traveling, he didn't see her there, but his dogs started traveling at a fast speed. [The dogs] started hunkering down, they were afraid. They say when he started traveling at a fast speed, when his dogs started running faster, he started to hear her voice from right behind him. When she'd speak, her voice . . . Is *kavyaitkacagaq* a good voice, or what?

ALBERTINA DULL: *Kavyaakiinani* means that her voice was clear.

LIZZIE CHIMIUGAK: Yes, they say her voice was clear. They said that her voice was very clear. He said that from behind him, when he started traveling at a fast speed, she started to make noise from behind him. She would make noise.

When he arrived, he arrived that evening, Cimiugaq was at the *qasgiq* when he was small. He said he happened to be there sitting next to his deceased grandfather when she came inside, when she came inside down there. She went inside [the *qasgiq*] that evening.

ALBERTINA DULL: My goodness!

LIZZIE CHIMIUGAK: And he'd hear her voice. Then [Cimiugaq] said his grandfather grasped [him] with his parka. Although he put him under his parka, he could hear what they were doing.

Iciw' naacirturatullrulriit. . . . Erenret talliman pilliut.

NENG'URYAR: Tua-i-w' angalkum taum kangangevkallikii.

CINGYUKAN: Ee-m, ala-i! . . .

NENG'URYAR: Angalkut. Waten-gguq egalengqellrulriit Cakcaami Cimiugaankut kass'allarmek. Atakut-gguq iliitni Arnam qanemciklermini atqa-gguq qinengqalria egaleteng patunaciallratni. Negilian-gguq mat'um patuqatalliniluki egalret; patulerluku.

Tuamtell' Kanerrlulegmek yaaken Yulqim Atii aqvaillinilria piciatun. Callrateng uniteurlurluki ayaggaarluteng aqvaingilallrulliniut. Aqvailria-gguq canek.

Tua-i-llu-gguq pilugull'ernek piluni, pilugugnek, pilugugugaat kiingita cap'akiitellermeggni. Aturaquinrayagii-gguq aturalquinrai-gguq cakuiner piluguum natiini wall'u-q' caini uitalliniluni. Aturait tamaa-i tamalkuita egtetullruit. Aturaquinrayagii-gguq uitalliniluni.

Ayainanrani-gguq qimugtai tamaani tangenrricaaqekii cukariluteng. Imumek tua-i elivkacagangluteng, alingluteng. Cukarillemini-gguq, tamaa-i-gguq qimugtai cukarillratni waken qamaneminek erinii niicaurrluku. Erinalkiagaqami-gguq erinii . . . Kavyaitkacagaq-qaa assilriaruuq, qiallun?

CINGYUKAN: Kavyaakiinani tua-i-w' erinakeggluni.

NENG'URYAR: Yaa, erinakegciluni. Erinalkitallri-gguq kavyaitkacagallruuq-gguq erinaa. Kingunranek-gguq cukanrarluni ayangellran kingunranek-gguq wavet qamanranek nepuaqaqungluni. Nepuaqengnaurtuq.

Tekican tua-i, tekilluni atakuan, Cimiugaq uitaluni mik'nani qasgimi. Apa'urluirutmi-gguq canian' tamaa-i itellrani nall'aringallrullinia, cakma cama-i itellrani. Atakuani iterluni qasgimun.

CINGYUKAN: Ala-i!

NENG'URYAR: Erinii-llu-gguq niitaqluku. Apa'urluan-llu-gguq tua-i atkumikun qumigluku. Qumingraani tua-i-gguq niitaqluki.

Ussugan Atii [Ussugan's father] was evidently there. Ussugan Atii went to [the ghost], and he probably went down to [the ghost] through the doorway.

ALBERTINA DULL: He probably took hold of her. Are you talking about Neng'uryar? My goodness.

LIZZIE CHIMIUGAK: Poor, he said that before they became muffled down there, she was speaking to him, saying that she was his niece.

He told her that she was actually his niece and that he should be treating her right, but that since she was asking for it, he was confronting her.

Poor, [Cimiugaq] said that she would talk, and then their voices became muffled. Eventually their voices were no longer heard. He said that he was going to lower her, *iivkarluku* [from *iivkar-*, "to lower from a height," probably putting their hands on ghosts to lower them to make them disappear]. What do they do?

ALBERTINA DULL: They say they lower them, *iivkarluki*. You know how they say when they want to lower them, [ghosts] cry.

LIZZIE CHIMIUGAK: My, how poor. A shaman is responsible for having them do things, controlling their bodies; they seemed to have [ghosts] do things. Then they said she stopped haunting people after that.

Since Cimiugaq was afraid, his grandfather, although they didn't see her, but just heard her voice, he said that she was whining and pleading down there. My goodness! I wonder which way he took her through the ground.

RUTH JIMMIE: Maybe he brought her to hell.

ALBERTINA DULL: My, I don't know where they lower them to.

LIZZIE CHIMIUGAK: Probably not to hell, since they came from shamans, but they probably lower them somewhere. Those poor people didn't know about hell, but to places created by shamans, and they were also afraid of shamans when they did things.

Shamans were responsible for having them [change form] like that long ago[43]

Albertina Dull, Lizzie Chimiugak, and Ruth Jimmie, Umkumiut, June 2009

LIZZIE CHIMIUGAK: My *acageurluq* [dear paternal aunt], the late grandmother of Maacuar,

---

Tuani tua-i Ussugan Atii uitalliniluni. Ussugan Atiin ullalliniluku, kalevviklikii-w' amigkun.

CINGYUKAN: Qumillikii-w'. Neng'uryar-qaa tauna? Ala-i tua-i.

NENG'URYAR: Nakleng cama-i-gguq umingurpailegmek qanerturauskii usruksaaqniluku waniwa elliin.

Usruksaaqniluku waniwa elliin arenqiakarkaqniluku, taugaam waniwa picetaaran piniluku.

Nakleng, erinalkiagaqluni-gguq, erinakek aling tayima-gguq tang umingurcartuqilik. Kiituan-gguq eriniik tamartuq. Iivkaqatarniluku. Calartat-llu tamakut?

CINGYUKAN: Iivkarnilaqait. Iciw' ilait iivkaryugaqatki iciw' qialaryaaqnilaqait.

NENG'URYAR: Aling, nakleng. Tuunrangayiim-wa calivkalaqai kemgit teguluki; calivkalarngatellrullinikait. Tua-i-llu-gguq alangruunermek taqluni.

Tamaa-i Cimiugaq alingan, apa'urluan, tangenrricaaqekseng, erinii taugaam, cungicaaqluni-gguq cama-i. Ala-i! Natetmurutau-kiq tayim' nevum akuliikun.

ANGALGAQ: Kenerpagmun-wa ayautellikii.

CINGYUKAN: Ala-i natmun iivkalartatki.

NENG'URYAR: Kenerpagmek-wa pivkenateng, angalkut pikngatki natmun iivkarnilallikait. Tamaa-i-ll' kenerpak nallu'urlullrukiit, wavet taugaam angalkut piliaritnun, cali-llu angalkut alikluki caaqata pitu'urlullrulriit.

Angalkut waten qaillukuarcecetullrulliniit ak'a

Cingyukan, Neng'uryar, Angalgaq-llu, Umkumiut, June 2009

NENG'URYAR: Acageurluma agkunek qanemciqurallruyaaqaanga uunguciirutanka,

Iquyuilnguq told me stories about those places across there, but I've forgotten them. She told me stories about those places across there, and she even told me about where Irniliingaq had lived. I have forgotten them.

Once, two women evidently married and moved with their husbands up north to the Yukon River area. I think some females married young, like you mentioned in your story.

Those girls who married and moved with their husbands to the Yukon River area, somewhere up north, they say an old woman instructed them, did she tell them to go inside her home? It was summer.

ALBERTINA DULL: An old woman from the Yukon River area?

LIZZIE CHIMIUGAK: Yes. She told those girls; they had husbands, their husbands probably went to get them. They say that old woman instructed them that when they started to travel when it was time to gather greens and berries from the land, to take many provisions with them, more food than they needed.

Then when they traveled, their leftover foods, or rather not their leftover food, to dig a hole and place some food inside it in places that they would recognize along the land that leads toward our area, toward this place [Nelson Island].

They say as she had instructed them, when they'd travel, they would bury [food] nearby, and they'd also bury some underground a great distance away like she had told them to. How [that elderly woman] knew what was to come.

ALBERTINA DULL: My, that's for sure.

LIZZIE CHIMIUGAK: They say she told them, "When they don't want you to stay here any longer, when you leave, you may go hungry." It was probably back when they used to tell people that they didn't want them to stay any longer. If they were in that situation, she told them that they both would know [about those buried foods], and that they would eat them.

Just as she said would happen, when they were in that situation, they returned home, walking, my goodness, from up north.

ALBERTINA DULL: Poor!

LIZZIE CHIMIUGAK: Or was it along the Yukon River area.

ALBERTINA DULL: My. Why did they obtain husbands from far away?

LIZZIE CHIMIUGAK: I think [they obtained husbands]

imum Maacuaraam Iquyuilnguum maurluirutiin. Agkunek qanemciqurallruyaaqaanga Irniliingaam-llu enellranek qanemciqurallruyaaqlua. Nalluyagulluki.

Taukuk-ll'-am ak'a qagaavet Kuigpagmun arnak ukurritlinilriik. Nasaurluut ak'a ayagyuarluteng tua-i ilait uingetullruyugnarqut qanemcillerpetun.

Taukuk nasaurluuk arnak ukurritellriik Kuigpagmun, nani-ll' tayim' qagaani, taum-gguq arnam arnassagaam alerquakek, enem'inun-qaa itresqellukek? Tamaa-i kiagluni.

CINGYUKAN: Kuigpagmium-qaa arnassagaam?

NENG'URYAR: Ii-i. Qanruskek taukuk arnak; tua-i uilutek uikakenka aqvallrullikegket. Taum-gguq tang arnassagaam qanruqu'urkek ayaganga'areskagnek waniw' makiranarikan amllernek taquilaasqellukek, taquarkakek cipluki.

Tua-i-llu-gguq ayakagnek cali ilakuakek neqet tamakut, tua-i-w' ilakuakegnek pivkenani neqmek elliilaasqellukek nevumun elakaulluku elkenka nallunritarkauluk' nunamta tungiinun, mat'um tungiinun.

Tua-i-gguq qanellratun tuaten ayagaqamek wavet elauciaqelriik tuamtell' yaaqvanun alerquuciatun elaulluki, elaugarcilutek. Nallunripaa-lli.

CINGYUKAN: Ala-i, ikika.

NENG'URYAR: Waten-gguq pilukek, "Qelkenriqacetek ayakuvtek kaigyuartutek." Tuaten tua-i ilait qelkinritullratni pillilriik. Tuaten pikagnek tamakut tamalkegnun nallunritarkaqniluki, nerlarciqniluki.

Apellratun-llu tua-i tuaten piamek, uterturlullinilutek kangarturlutek, ala-i qagken.

CINGYUKAN: Nakleng!

NENG'URYAR: Wall'u-q' Kuigpiim.

CINGYUKAN: Ala-i. Ciin yaaqvanek uingak?

NENG'URYAR: Kuigpiim ukatiinek piyugnarquk.

from this [south] side of the Yukon River area [closest to Nelson Island].

And the person who told the story said that long ago . . . I had never heard of this, I never heard this from my mother. And although other people told stories around here, I don't know about that.

[The person telling the story] said that long ago, they used to tell them not to stay quiet without talking, that if they stay [without speaking] that they will stop speaking all together. I don't know of this. But that's what that person said.

But that person [who told the story] knew about that. The person who told the story said that long ago, they instructed people not to stay silent without talking, that our tongues will stop speaking all together. I never heard that from my mother, or from Noni or Cangarraq.

ALBERTINA DULL: I don't know about that either.

LIZZIE CHIMIUGAK: This was a story told by the deceased younger sister of Panigaraam Atii [Panigaraq's father].

ALBERTINA DULL: You mean Panruk?

LIZZIE CHIMIUGAK: Yes. His daughter told me the story.

They say when they returned home, like the old woman had instructed them, they gathered those [buried foods] and ate them.

ALBERTINA DULL: My, what good memories they had.

LIZZIE CHIMIUGAK: My, they'd eat those dried fish. Yes, that [old woman] had told them to mark where they were. And she was right that they would tell them to leave, and she knew it. That's probably what they did.

ALBERTINA DULL: The animals probably ate them.

LIZZIE CHIMIUGAK: Probably so.

ALBERTINA DULL: My, how poor!

LIZZIE CHIMIUGAK: [That old woman probably instructed them to do that] because the people up north probably used to do that. They probably didn't want them for wives any longer.

RUTH JIMMIE: They probably didn't treat them very well since they weren't from their area.

LIZZIE CHIMIUGAK: The poor things probably weren't knowledgeable, not familiar with the northern region.

It is said while they were traveling, her companion stopped speaking. They'd sleep overnight in places along their journey.

They say her companion stopped speaking, and she was the only one who spoke. Her companion stopped speaking altogether, and eventually she started concealing her face from her.

Waten-llu qanemcikestii waten pillrulria ak'a-gguq . . . man'a niicuitaqa, aanamnek niitellrunirtaqa. Piciatun-llu qanemcing'ermeng maani cameg' tamana nalluaqa.

Waten piluku, piluni, ak'a-gguq qanresqevkenaki, qaneqsaunaki uitauraasqevkenaki pitullruit uitauralaqata qanernanrirciqniluki. Man'a nalluaqa. Tuaten taugken taum.

Taugken taum tauna nalluvkenaku tuaten pillrat. Waten qanemcistii pillruuq ak'a-gguq tamaani qaneqsaunata uitauraasqelallrunritaakut, uluput-gguq qanernanrirciqukut-gguq. Wiinga niitellrunritaqa aanamnek Noni-mek-llu call' Cangarrarmek-llu.

CINGYUKAN: Wiinga-ll' nalluaqa call' tamana.

NENG'URYAR: Panigaraam Atiin nayagairutiin qanemcia.

CINGYUKAN: Panruum-qaa?

NENG'URYAR: Ee-m. Panian qanemciqurallruanga qanemciatnek.

Utercamek-gguq tamakut tamaa-i taum arnassagaam qanellratun avurturluki neqkurluki.

CINGYUKAN: Ala-i unimssaipaa, capripaa.

NENG'URYAR: Ala-i neqerrluaraat ner'aqluki. Yaa, nallunairturluki-gguq taum pisqelallrui. Qelkenrillerkaak-llu man'a *right*-arluni, nalluvkenaku. Tuaten-wa pitullru[llilriik].

CINGYUKAN: Aipaagni-w' unguvalriaraat nernaurait.

NENG'URYAR: Tua-i.

CINGYUKAN: Aling nakleng!

NENG'URYAR: Tuaten-wa pitullrulliata-ll' qagkut. Nuliqsuumiitelliamegtekek-wa.

ANGALGAQ: Tua-i-w' nunalgutkenrilamegteki picaqsuitellrullikait piinanermeggni.

NENG'URYAR: Nallumciqeurlullrullilriit qagna nalluluku.

Ayainanragni-gguq aipaa qanernanringluni. Qavartaraqlutek.

Aipaa-gguq qanernanrirluni, ellii-gguq kiimi qanerturangluni. Aipaa qanengssaarayuirulluni, kiituan-gguq kegginani tangssiyaagcetnanriraa.

My, they say when she ate, she would turn with her back toward her and eat; that's how she began to eat when they ate a little. They say when she ate, she would chomp her food like an animal. That's how she began to eat their small amounts of food, crunching them. They say she never saw her face.

Then, since it was summer when they traveled, since it wasn't winter, the poor things returned home. . . .

One day, a mountain was visible, a mountain became visible along the place where they were heading. Once again, they slept overnight since it was summer.

ALBERTINA DULL: Poor.

LIZZIE CHIMIUGAK: She began to fear her companion. When she went to sleep, when she started falling asleep, she looked at her face and saw that it had transformed into a land animal's face.

ALBERTINA DULL: My goodness!

LIZZIE CHIMIUGAK: They say when she started sleeping with vigilance she cautiously crawled and started leaving toward the mountains. They say she crawled through the grass. Poor, when she was a great distance away, she finally stood and ran.

She ran nonstop. Then when she reached the mountains, she climbed up, and she reached the top and she would look back to check on her. They say just as she went down, that one started making noise, "I could have [killed] her already, but left her alone." She would make howling noises. My goodness!

ALBERTINA DULL: What did she say?

LIZZIE CHIMIUGAK: She had evidently transformed into a wolf. They say that she would make howling noises.

ALBERTINA DULL: My goodness!

LIZZIE CHIMIUGAK: She was extremely afraid. When she arrived, they saw that her face, her head had transformed into a wolf's head. My goodness! I wonder what they did to her.

Then [the person who told the story] said that they tell us not to stay quiet without speaking, that we would stop speaking altogether. That's the first time I heard that.

ALBERTINA DULL: [laughs] Probably because she thought that she would become a wolf.

LIZZIE CHIMIUGAK: She said our tongues would stop speaking.

ALBERTINA DULL: I thought there was another story about someone who was about to transform into a wolf, another person who was on a journey, and

Ala-i ner'aqami-llu-gguq tunulluku nernaurtuq; neryaurrluni tamaa-i nerqerqamek. Tua-i-gguq tang ner'aqami ungungssitun qangquraqluni. Tuaten neryaurrluni nerrluaraitnek qangqurluki. Kegginaa-gguq tangyuunaku.

Tua-i-ll', kiagan tamaa-i pillertek, uksuunrilan uterteurlullinilriik. . . .

Tua-i-ll' im' caqerlutek ingrir' ava-i alaunani, ciunrak ingriq alairluni. Qavartarlutek-am tua-i kiaguan.

CINGYUKAN: Nakleng.

NENG'URYAR: Alingengluni aiparminek taumek. Qavaan-gguq qavaryunga'arcan kegginaa piqaraa ungungssilinramek kegginangellrullini-ll'.

CINGYUKAN: Ala-i!

NENG'URYAR: Qavalria-gguq, qavaryungan-gguq cumikluku aurrurluni ayakataarluni ingrit tungiitnun. Can'get-gguq akuliitgun aurrurluni. Nakleng yaaqsigiami nutaan nangerrluni aqvaqurluni.

Aqvaqurturluni ayagluni. Tua-i-llu-gguq ingrinun tekicami mayurluni, qaklilluni paivcivitaqluku. Atraqanrakun-gguq augna nepualuni. "Ak'a pinami, uitaskeka." Marumcalleggnaurtuq-gguq. Ala-i!

CINGYUKAN: Qaillun qanerluni?

NENG'URYAR: Keglunrurcaaqelliniluni. Marumcalleggnaurtuq-gguq.

CINGYUKAN: Ala-i!

NENG'URYAR: Alingkacagarluni. Tua-i tekican paqnakluku piat kegginaa qamiqurra keglunrem qamiquqsagutelliniluku. Ala-i! Qaill' pillruatgu-kiq tayima.

Tua-i-llu-gguq piluni, piluni qaneqsaunata-gguq uitauraasqessuitaitkut qanernanrirciqukut-gguq. Nutaan niitaqa man'a.

CINGYUKAN: [ngel'artuq] Keglunrurrnayukluku-w' pillikii.

NENG'URYAR: Uluput-gguq qanernanrirciquq.

CINGYUKAN: Tauna-ggem tanem cali ca imna keglunrurteqatalria waten call' ayagturalleq cali, nalluani cali ayagluni. Tauna-w' pillilria.

she also escaped without the person knowing. It's probably that one.

LIZZIE CHIMIUGAK: It was probably her.

ALBERTINA DULL: When she howled, she only *?canimnaaraluni*, like she was disappointed over having lost her.

LIZZIE CHIMIUGAK: Yes, they say that she was disappointed in losing [her chance to kill her].

ALBERTINA DULL: I think it's that story.

RUTH JIMMIE: She was probably thinking of eating her.

LIZZIE CHIMIUGAK: Poor thing, she was probably thinking of eating her.

ALBERTINA DULL: She was disappointed that she had left her side. My, the shamans were probably responsible for their state.

LIZZIE CHIMIUGAK: Yes, shamans were responsible for having them [change form] like that long ago.

ALBERTINA DULL: Yes.

LIZZIE CHIMIUGAK: They were responsible for causing them to be in that state. A person transformed into something that they would never have become, back when they had faith in shamans. . . .

ALBERTINA DULL: But at this time, they don't transform into things.

LIZZIE CHIMIUGAK: Long ago, their elders . . . that old woman was probably a shaman. She had been telling them that when they didn't want them there any longer, when they left, she was worried that they wouldn't have any provisions. When summer came, when they [told them to leave], the poor things returned home walking.

They say they would gather greens and pick berries, and she would tell them to bring a large amount of provisions with them when they were gathering greens or picking berries. She told them to bury food and mark those places. Animals could have eaten them.

During summer, they returned home. Like that elderly woman had told them, they picked the foods when they'd come upon them and eat. But they say the other stopped speaking after she had the ability to speak, she stopped speaking completely. Her companion was the only one who spoke.

NENG'URYAR: Taungullilria-wa.

CINGYUKAN: Tua-i-gguq maruarayaaqelriim canimnaaraluni taugaam, qivrunganani.

NENG'URYAR: Yaa, tauna tua-i qivruknganaku-gguq.

CINGYUKAN: Taunguyugnarquq tua-i.

ANGALGAQ: Tua-i-w' tayima nernaluku piyaaqellilria.

NENG'URYAR: Nernaluku-wa piurluryaaqellill'.

CINGYUKAN: Caniminek ayallra qivrukluku. Ala-i tuunrangayiim-wa ak'a pivkalallrullikait waten.

NENG'URYAR: Yaa, angalkut waten qaillukuarcecetullrulliniit ak'a.

CINGYUKAN: Ee-m.

NENG'URYAR: Pillerkirluki tua-i. Piciryaraqsugnailkeminek yuk pingluni, angalkut tamaa-i agayutkellratni. . . .

CINGYUKAN: Mat'um-llu-w' taugken maa-i nalliini cat imkut caurcuunateng tua-i.

NENG'URYAR: Ak'a temirtait makut . . . arnassagaq-llu taun' angalkuulliuq. Aren tua-i-w' ak'a qanruqurallrukek qelkenriqatkek ayakagnek taquaritnayuklukek. Kiagan tamaa-i elliuciak, tuaten tua-i tayim' piicetek uterteurlurlutek kangarturlutek.

Makiraciquk-gguq amllernek taquilaasqellukek-gguq makirakagnek. Tua-i tamaa-i neqet nallunritarkaagnun elliuraasqelluki nallunailkucirturluki. Ungungssirraam-llu nereksailkai.

Tamaa-i kiagan uterrlutek. Aranassagaam taum alerqullratun tamakut tamaa-i avurluki tekitaqamegneki-ll' ner'aqlutek. Taugaam-gguq tua-i aipaa qanturraarluni qanernanrillruuq, qanyuirutkacagarluni. Ellii-gguq kiimi qanerturluni aipaa tauna.

The shaman said to him, "Gee whiz, your face looks like you're far from dying"[44]

Albertina Dull, Lizzie Chimiugak, and Ruth Jimmie, Umkumiut, June 2009

LIZZIE CHIMIUGAK: It barked for a while, and made its barking audible from the *qasgiq*. Then while we were there, his poor father, since the poor thing was spry, he appeared through the doorway of the *qasgiq*, smiling. He quickly came toward us, and we took Joseph out [of the sled]. The poor thing ran toward his father and hugged him right away.

ALBERTINA DULL: Poor thing!

LIZZIE CHIMIUGAK: He said, extremely happy, that when he recognized the dogs barking, he ran out.

   Then we ate, my late younger sibling and I ate. While we were having tea, while he was eating, Kumlilriim Atii [Kumlilria's father] came inside. The previous summer, he used to bring him along to places, wanting him to accompany him. He probably used to mess with him in his sleep.

   He went right up to Unangim Atii's [Unangiq's father's] face.

ALBERTINA DULL: Qateryak did that?

LIZZIE CHIMIUGAK: Yes. [He said,] "Gee whiz, your face looks like you're far from dying." My goodness, why did he say that?

ALBERTINA DULL: My goodness!

LIZZIE CHIMIUGAK: He would die not long after that. That's what Kumlilriim Atii [Kumlilria's father] said to him. He went up to his face, and he was sitting and eating like this. The shaman said to him, "Gee whiz, your face looks like you're far from dying."

ALBERTINA DULL: My goodness.

LIZZIE CHIMIUGAK: My, why did he do that? Then after we ate, since it was a while before it would get dark, Kicarraq loaded [our sled] with a grass container filled with dried herring that had been packed down, since his wife Tuquyuilnguq had prepared some provisions for him before he died.

   He loaded a container filled with dried herring [in our sled], he had us load up with that, and we returned home, we returned the same day, giving his dogs to him.

   His female dog was happy to see him. It was probably barking because it recognized him. Then

Waten piluku angalkum, "Aull' kegginan taun' tuquyugnaipagta"

Cingyukan, Neng'uryar, Angalgaq-llu, Umkumiut, June 2009

NENG'URYAR: Qiluk'aquuraqerluni erinani tua-i alaicelluku qasgimek. Tua-ll' tang piinanemteni ata'urlua qecengkeggurlullruami, qasgikun amiigakun yura'artuq quuyurmi. Taigarrluni Joseph-aq yuuluku. Ata'urluni curukii qes'arrluku-ll'.

CINGYUKAN: Nakleurluq!

NENG'URYAR: Qanerluni tua-i quyak'acagarluni, uum-gguq waniw' qiluk'aqullra elitaqa'arcamiu anqertuq.

   Tua-i-ll' nerluta, nerlunuk tua-i kinguqliirutka-ll'. Yuurqainanmegni nernginanrani-w' tua-i Kumlilriim Atii iterluni. Kiak call' maliksugluku ayautelallrukii. Qaillukualallruyugnarqekii-ll' tamaani qavaakun.

   Unangiim Atiin kegginaa ullagluku waten pia malkussaggluku.

CINGYUKAN: Qateryiim-qaa?

NENG'URYAR: Ii-i. "Aull' kegginan taun' tuquyugnaipagta." Ala-i ciin tuaten qanellrua?

CINGYUKAN: Ala-i!

NENG'URYAR: Waniw' cunaw' uumikuarqu tuquqatarluni. Tuaten tang pillrukii Kumlilriim Atiin. Kegginaa ullagluku, waten-wa uitalria nerluni. Waten piluku angalkum, "Aull' kegginan taun' tuquyugnaipagta."

CINGYUKAN: Ala-i!

NENG'URYAR: Ala-i, ciin-wa? Tua-i-ll' nererraarlunuk tua-i unugyugnailan tut'armek ucilirlunuk Kicarraam, aiparmi tua-i taquarkiullrulliniaku, Tuquyuilnguum, tuquvailgan.

   Iqalluarpautnek ucilirlunuk, ucilircellunuk, uterrlunuk, ut'rarrlunuk, qimugtai tua-i tunluki.

   Arnacaluan-llu taum wani aryuqluku. Elitaqiluni-w' tamaa-i qiluk'aqullilira. Uumikuan-

not long after, [Unangim Atii] died. Qateryak had said recently that he was far from dying. He evidently did that because he would die.

He didn't arrive from the wilderness during a nice day. I think he had a seizure. He had evidently been kicking his feet.

He had some provisions, and his camp stove had a lot of fuel in it, and his kettle was there, but he had caught a mink.

ALBERTINA DULL: Who uses mink as a means [to attempt to kill people]?

LIZZIE CHIMIUGAK: They seem to also use them as a means [to attempt to kill people].

ALBERTINA DULL: I think they are used as a means [to kill], weapons that shamans use. . . .

LIZZIE CHIMIUGAK: That summer, we went down the river, leaving [Unangim Atii]. I felt sorry for my mother, who didn't want to leave his grave. When we went to Tunuiruksuar, Uyanglin and Uliggaq died, Joseph's late older sister. Kicarraq was there also; they had come.

When Kumlilriim Atii arrived with a large boat, and Joseph and someone else had come accompanying Kumlilria and his family, coming to see us. As they were arriving, Kumlilriim Atii was facing the opposite direction. He had his back to the village.

RUTH JIMMIE: They probably knew.

LIZZIE CHIMIUGAK: My, probably so.

RUTH JIMMIE: That person probably [killed him].

LIZZIE CHIMIUGAK: I think he might have. He had said at the time that he was far from dying. He was evidently going to die soon after [when he said], "Gee whiz, your face appears as though it is far from dying."

My goodness! A shaman, and here he was actually our maternal uncle.

RUTH JIMMIE: Maybe he said the opposite of what he thought.

LIZZIE CHIMIUGAK: My, that's probably so!

ALBERTINA DULL: They won't feel bad. If he wants to [kill him], he won't hesitate on account of him being his relative.

llu ak'anivkenani tuquluni. Qateryiim tuquyugnaitnillruluk' uumi tua-i waniwa. Tuquqataan cunaw' pillinikii.

Yuilqumi tekitevkenan' ellakegpagmi. Qistellruyugnarquq. Tua-i-gguq tukarturallrulliniluni.

Tua-i-ll' taquaritevkenani kenircutii-ll' cali uqulirluni caaniiga-wa, taugaam imarmiutatellrulliniluni.

CINGYUKAN: Imarmiutaat makut kia caskuk'lartatki?

NENG'URYAR: Caskuk'laryugnarqait-llu.

CINGYUKAN: Caskuuyugnarqut, tuunrangayiim caskukluki. . . .

NENG'URYAR: Kiagan-llu cetuluta unilluku. Tua-i aanamnek naklegyuglua, unicuumiicaaqluku qungua, unicuumiicaaqluku. Tunuiruksuarmun-llu piamta Uyangliinkut Uliggaq-llu tuqulutek, Joseph-am alqairutii. Tamaa-i Kicarraq-llu uitaluni; taillruluteng.

Kumlilriim Atii tang tekicartulria angecpagkun Kumlilriinkut maliggluki Joseph-ankurluuk taillinilutek ullagluta. Kumlilriim Atii tang tekicarturtut iqlu caumaurluku. Nunat tunusngaurluki.

ANGALGAQ: Nalluvkenateng-wa tayim'.

NENG'URYAR: Ala-i pillilriit-wa.

ANGALGAQ: Elliin-wam tua-i taum pillrullikii.

NENG'URYAR: Pillruyugnarqaa.

Tuquyugnaitnillrukll-ll' tuani. Waniwa cunaw' tuquqatarluni, "Aull' kegginan taun' tuquyugnaipagta."

Ala-i! Angalkuq, angaksaaqluku-ll' wangkuta.

ANGALGAQ: Umyuarteqellmi-kiq mumigneranek qanellrulliuq.

NENG'URYAR: Ala-i kiika!

CINGYUKAN: Arenqiayugngaunateng. Piyukuniu tungelquqningaunaku.

Mancuam Atii evidently [killed] his daughter[45]

Albertina Dull, Lizzie Chimiugak, and
Ruth Jimmie, Umkumiut, June 2009

LIZZIE CHIMIUGAK: [whispering] You know how
Mancuam Atii [Mancuaq's father] evidently
[killed] his daughter.
ALBERTINA DULL: Yes, that's what he did also.
LIZZIE CHIMIUGAK: My, Mancuaq.
ALBERTINA DULL: He was responsible for her death.
LIZZIE CHIMIUGAK: Mancuaq. I didn't mention her
father's name on purpose, thinking that his
children might hear it. He was responsible for her
death.

They say that he had asked for some material
for a ruff, when he asked for a really nice wolf skin
from them. Then she told him that it was going to
be made into a ruff for Maksii.

Then, I think they said that she started growing
wolf hair along here. You see!

RUTH JIMMIE: Shamans were such jealous people.
ALBERTINA DULL: My, his daughter, my goodness, his
daughter, how awful!
LIZZIE CHIMIUGAK: My, how poor!
ALBERTINA DULL: My how poor, my they have no
empathy at all.

They say her first husband was Egacuayaaq, a shaman[46]

Albertina Dull, Lizzie Chimiugak, and
Ruth Jimmie, Umkumiut, June 2009

LIZZIE CHIMIUGAK: And my mother, the story that
my mother told, the time when she got her first
husband is a little aggravating. They say her first
husband was Egacuayaaq, a shaman.

The father of Aingassaaq and her sibling's
mother.
RUTH JIMMIE: Really?
LIZZIE CHIMIUGAK: Poor Aingassaaq and her siblings.
Nasgauq is Egacuyaaq's daughter.

She said the people there had her put on really
nice clothing, they had her put on nice clothing,
and she put on skin boots, she had every type of
clothing, and her beautiful parka.

Mancuam Atiin panini pillrullinikii

Cingyukan, Neng'uryar, Angalgaq-llu, Umkumiut,
June 2009

NENG'URYAR: [agyimciarluni] Iciw' Mancuam Atiin-
llu panini pillrullinikii.

CINGYUKAN: Ee-m tuaten call' tua-i.
NENG'URYAR: Ala-i Mancuam.
CINGYUKAN: Tuquvkarluku.
NENG'URYAR: Mancuaq. Apenrilkurtaqa atii
pitsaqevkenaku niitnayukluku irniarinun.
Tuquvkarluku.

Negilirkamek-gguq tamaa-i kaigayaaqelria,
keglunqegtaarmek piatek. Tua-i-llu-gguq piluku
Maksiimun negilirkaqniluku.

Tua-i-gguq natiini-ll' maani melqurrinek-llu-
qaa keglunrem makuni tuartang pinillrukii.
Tangrriu!
ANGALGAQ: Anglill' ciknataulallruvaa angalkugni.
CINGYUKAN: Ala-i panini, ala-i panini, aling ik'atak!

NENG'URYAR: Aling nakleng!
CINGYUKAN: Aling nakleng, ala-i naklegipaa-ll'
cakneq.

Egacuayagmek-gguq uingeqarraallruuq angalkugmek

Cingyukan, Neng'uryar, Angalgaq-llu, Umkumiut,
June 2009

NENG'URYAR: Aanaka-llu imna aanama qanemcia,
nekanarqerrlullruuq uingeqarraallrani.
Egacuayagmek-gguq uingeqarraallruuq
angalkugmek.

Imum wani Aingassankut aaniita aatiitnek.

ANGALGAQ: Qaa?
NENG'URYAR: Aingassankurluut. Taum panikaa
imna Nasgauq Egacuayaam.

Ayumian-gguq tang ukut at'eskilitgu
aturaqegtaarnek, aturaqegtaarnek-gguq ac'elluku
pilu'ugluni, qaqimaluni tua-i, atkukegtaara-gguq.

Then when she was done, they told her, I forgot what they had her refer to him as, that she had just acquired him for a husband. She suddenly felt regret. They told her to go and give him food.

My, how awful! I would have thrown the bowl! [laughter]

ALBERTINA DULL: After throwing it, I would have run off somewhere.

RUTH JIMMIE: Is it because her husband-to-be was ugly?

ALBERTINA DULL: Their parents would have them acquire spouses like that without them knowing about it.

RUTH JIMMIE: Why don't you like that man?

LIZZIE CHIMIUGAK: I feel sorry for my mother, who felt embarrassed. If you obtained a husband, if there was a qasgiq, we would put a bowl in your hands, and have you go and give that.

RUTH JIMMIE: I would throw that bowl. [laughter]

LIZZIE CHIMIUGAK: They told her that he was her husband now. That one.

She said they put a bowl filled with food in her hands. While she was standing, she was hesitant, they told her to go and give Egacuayaaq some food in the qasgiq.

The poor thing's name was Asgulria; they told her to go and give Asgulria some food. She said she stayed for a while, then her deceased mother, the one who raised her turned her body this way, turned her around toward the doorway.

Then she said she turned toward the back of the house. She couldn't go out. She said when her deceased maternal aunt turned her around without any sympathy, she couldn't refuse and went out. Poor, she went over and gave him food. My how awful!

They say when her family had her stop giving him food, she would give him food without their knowledge, going out from the porch.

RUTH JIMMIE: You mean her husband?

ALBERTINA DULL: Egacuayaaq.

LIZZIE CHIMIUGAK: She would go and give food to Asgulria. When Kicarraq found out, poor Kicarraq, she mentioned that she had given food to Asgulria. She said they admonished her not to give him food.

RUTH JIMMIE: I wonder why?

LIZZIE CHIMIUGAK: The people who had wanted him [to be her husband] didn't want him any longer since he was only good at hunting fur animals, and wasn't too keen on obtaining food.

Tua-i-llu-gguq taq'ercan piat, caneg'-im' tuqlurcelluk', taumek uingniluku. Qessanayullagluni-gguq. Payugcesqelluku.

Aling ik'atak! Qantaq-wa wii egcaqeka! [ngel'artut]

CINGYUKAN: Egqaarluku natmun ayagarcalrianga.

ANGALGAQ: Ikiungan-qaa taun' uikaa?

CINGYUKAN: Angayuqrita-w' tua-i waten aipangevkaraqluki nalluitni.

ANGALGAQ: Qaill' pian tauna angun assiilkessiu?

NENG'URYAR: Aanamnek talluryulriamek naklegyuglua. Elpet tua-i uingekuvet qasgitangqerkan qantamek tegumiirciqamteggen taumek payugcesqelluku.

ANGALGAQ: Qantaq-wa egcaqeka. [ngel'artut]

NENG'URYAR: Taumek uingniluku. Tamana.

Qantamek-gguq tegumiirluku neqnek imarluni. Nangerngaqaan-gguq, ancurturluni, payugcesqelluku tauna Egacuayaaq qasgimi.

Asgulriarurlu-ll'; Asgulria payugcesqelluku. Uitayaaqelria-gguq anaanairutiin anglicartiin ukatmun tuviggluku uivvluk' amiigem tungiinun.

Tua-i-llu-gguq kiatmun cauyaaqluni. Anesciiganani. Anaanairutiin-gguq aaqata'arpek'naku cauquangani taq'iviinani anluni. Nekleng agluni payuggluku. Aling ik'atak!

Tamaa-i-llu-gguq ilami payuggnanriatgu payuggnanricecatgu elliin-gguq nalluatni payugtaqluku, elaturramek anluni.

ANGALGAQ: Tauna-qaa uini?

CINGYUKAN: Egacuayaaq.

NENG'URYAR: Payugtelaryaaqluku taun' Asgulria. Kicarraam-gguq-am elpeka'arcamiu Kicarraurluum payugtellruniluku Asgulria qanerluni. Inerquqiit-gguq payugteksaunaku pisqelluku.

ANGALGAQ: Ciin-kiq?

NENG'URYAR: Tua-i-w' qessakengluku yuin taugaam-gguq melqulegcuarallni pikliniaku, neqmun cumigtessiyaagpek'nani.

When they obtained husbands, when their husbands were like that, and they didn't like them, they used to tell them to leave, since food was their only means of sustenance back when there were no store-bought foods.

Back in those days, they had difficult lives because they had no freezers. Her family didn't want him any longer and broke her marriage off with him, and here he was a shaman.

RUTH JIMMIE: How brave they were.

LIZZIE CHIMIUGAK: My, they say he said that Paniyaaq, they used to call my mother Paniyaar, "I am placing an old woman along the aura she's emitting." So that she would become an elderly woman early . . . maybe we're also experiencing that.

ALBERTINA DULL: These shamans never declined to react.

LIZZIE CHIMIUGAK: Then Unangiim Arnaan [Unangik's mother] evidently told Egacuayaaq, "Why have you placed an old woman along her aura to make life more difficult for her?"

He gave her something to think about, "If I don't do that, she probably would go underground or go into the air."

RUTH JIMMIE: Are you talking about his wife?

LIZZIE CHIMIUGAK: My mother. The poor thing wanted her for a wife. He did that to her with his shaman abilities. Unangim Arnaan evidently told him that, and he told her that if he didn't do that, she would go underground, or she would go into the air.

She thought that she experienced that on this side of Naruyamiut, as there is a large marshy area along this side of it, and there is an area where the marshland turns into tundra. There are many places to catch things, and there are many sloughs, and sometimes there are oxbow lakes.

And there are many oxbow lakes. She said as she walked along one day, she began to walk for a long time, and she didn't suspect anything. She said she walked for a long time.

She said that toward the area where the marshland turns into tundra, behind it, she said that there was a white fox that never moved, that was constantly wailing. It was constantly barking, it was very active; it was a white fox.

And she said it didn't seem to move from its spot. She said that she started continually hearing the wailing of a white fox.

Then after a while, she continued to walk without thinking anything. Then an Arctic tern

Waten wani uingaqata angutait waten ayuqaqata cangakaqamegteki ayagcecetullruluk', ak'a neqa'ar taugaam man'a kass'allartaitellrani neqkeurlullruamegteggu.

Tamaa-i tamatum nalliini ilalqerluteng kumliviinateng-llu. Ilain qessakluku uikenrircelluk', angalkuulria-gguq-wa.

ANGALGAQ: Alingipagtat.

NENG'URYAR: Ala-i, tua-i-gguq qanaalliniluni ellii tua-i Paniyaaq, Paniyaarmek aanaka piuratullrukiit, "Arnassagarmek anllugneranun elliilrianga." Arnassagaryararallekaanek . . . atulliarput-llu wangkuta.

CINGYUKAN: Waten taugaam uitqapigtevkenateng-llu angalkungssiit makut pinaurtut.

NENG'URYAR: Tua-i-ll' Unangiim Arnaan Egacuayaaq tauna qanrutliniluku, "Ciin-tam ilalqerluku-llu anllugneranun arnassagarmek elliillinisit?"

Uum-gguq neqaarturitenga'artaa, "Pinrilkumku nunanun aciirucartuq ellangqurrulluni-ll' aipaagni."

ANGALGAQ: Tauna-qaa nulirra?

NENG'URYAR: Aanaka. Nuliqsugeurluryaaqluku. Angalkumikun tamaa-i. Unangiim Arnaan qanrutliniluku, tuaten-gguq pinrilkuni nunanun aciiruciiquq wall' ellangqurrulluku.

Tua-i tamaa-i tamana tamaa-i aturyukellrua avani Naruyamiut-qaa ukatiitni, ukatiit marar' amllellria ingigucetarluni-ll'. Canguvigkar amllerrluni kuigaaraat-llu amllerrluteng, iliini-llu imkut taktuat im' kuiguat.

Kuigualirluni-llu. Ayalriim-gguq tang caqerluni ayangelria camek-llu-gguq piyuunani. Ayaumalria-gguq.

Pamna-gguq-wa ingigutem tungiinek pingna, keluanek-gguq cakaniyuilnganani uliir uarquralria. Qilugturalria tua-i, qepirqurluni; uliiq-gguq.

Cakaniyuilnganani-llu-gguq. Tua-i-gguq tauna niiskengaqsagulluku uarqurallra uliirem.

Tua-i-llu-gguq piinanermini camek pivkenan' ayangluni. Teqiyaaraam pugugarrluku, swooped down at her and hit her hard here. She said it was like she suddenly became aware. And she said that it cut her forehead. That *yungaq* [jaeger, possibly another name for the Arctic tern] brought her to her senses, probably since that *yungaq* was something to her.

She suddenly became aware, and there were oxbow lakes along the area that she had traveled through, different things, rivers, and oxbow lakes, ones whose ends were impossible to reach. She wondered how she had passed those.

She almost went into the sky. But that white fox and the Arctic tern, she said that white fox was trying to bring her to her senses for a long time. But she said when the Arctic tern finally hit her forcefully here with its beak and cut her, it seems that she suddenly became aware of what was happening.

RUTH JIMMIE: If she hadn't done that, if she hadn't come to her senses, what would have become of her?

LIZZIE CHIMIUGAK: She probably would have gone into the air.

ALBERTINA DULL: She would have disappeared.

LIZZIE CHIMIUGAK: She would have started walking in the air, and she would have started staying in the sky. Those two.

ALBERTINA DULL: These were their customs in the past, *ellangqurrulluni* [going into the sky], *aciirulluni* [going underground to the place below].

tugpagluku ukua. Tuar-gguq ellangartellria. Kakangcaa-llu-gguq kilirluku. Ala-i elpengcalliniluk' yungam taum, cakliani-w' yungaq-llu tauna.

Ellangartuq-gguq kuiguat makut kingunrani, piciatun kuiget kuiguat iquiyunailnguut. Qaillun-kiq-gguq tamakut-llu pellullruaki.

Ellangqurrucarpiarluni. Taum taugaam uliirem teqiyaaraam-llu, uliirem-gguq ellangcaumayaaqelliniluku. Teqiyaaraam-gguq taugaam uuggun tugpallrani cugg'egmikun kilirluni ellangarrnganani.

ANGALGAQ: Tayima tuaten pillrukan, ellangellrunrilkuni qaill' piyarta?

NENG'URYAR: Ellangqurrucallilria-wa.

CINGYUKAN: Tamarluni.

NENG'URYAR: Ellakun pekengluni, ella nunaksagulluku. Taukuk tua-i.

CINGYUKAN: Ala-i piciryarangssaarallrit-wa maa-i makut, ellangqurrulluni aciirulluni.

Shamans seem to make *qukviulriit* and *keggiarnat* appear[47]

Albertina Dull, Lizzie Chimiugak, and Ruth Jimmie, Umkumiut, June 2009

LIZZIE CHIMIUGAK: And these they call mermaids, they used to talk about *qukviulriit* in Yup'ik, also only shamans evidently made them appear.

Qukviulriit, those with long hair, those beings that swim in the water. Only shamans seemed to make those appear.

And when they told stories about *keggiarnat*, shamans also seemed to make them appear.

RUTH JIMMIE: What are *keggiarnat*?

LIZZIE CHIMIUGAK: They probably look like river otters. I think only shamans made them appear. I told the story earlier, Akagualriim Atii [Akagualria's father], or that person, when

Qukviulriit keggiarnat-llu, angalkut taugaam tamakut puggngatetullrulliniit

Cingyukan, Neng'uryar, Angalgaq-llu, Umkumiut, June 2009

NENG'URYAR: Makut-llu cali *mermaid*-anek pitukait Yugtun qukviulrianek qantulriit, angalkut cali tamaa-i pugtelallrulliniit taugaam.

Qukviulriit, nuyarpiit, mermi yuut imkut kuimatulit. Angalkut taugaam tamakut puggngatetullrulliniit.

Keggiarnanek-llu call' qanemciaqameng, angalkut call' pugtetungatellrulliniit.

ANGALGAQ: Keggiarnat cauluteng?

NENG'URYAR: Tua-i-w' cenkatun ayuqellilriit. Angalkut taugaam pugtetullruyugnarqait. Ak'a qanemcikellruaqa, Akagualriim Atiin, pi wani, Acaguam Atii tamakucimek tangellra Akagualria tuquqatallrani.

Acaguam Atii [Acaguaq's father] saw one of those when Akagualria was about to die.

You know how I already told the story about that one with long hair that was continually surfacing and diving in the water, heading downriver toward the ocean.

When Akagualriit Atrat [the one that the Akagualrias are named after] was about to die, when Akagualria's late grandmother was going to die, they say that small straight stretch along the river isn't long, and they say it suddenly bends down there where it exits out to the ocean.

RUTH JIMMIE: Up north?

LIZZIE CHIMIUGAK: At Qalvinraaq River. At Naruyamiut along the mouth of Qalvinraaq, at the spring camp, back when it used to be a spring camp. Acaguam Atii [Acaguaq's father] evidently saw it; that person was evidently about to die in the tent.

My, he said that one down there headed down the river, continually surfacing and diving in the water along the small straight stretch in the river, facing the ocean. A person, one of those, a *qukviiq* was surfacing and diving. They call them *qukviulriit*.

RUTH JIMMIE: Did it have a face?

LIZZIE CHIMIUGAK: He said it had long hair. He said that it continually surfaced and dived as it headed down along the small straight stretch of river.

He said as it reached the bend, it went around the bend, and [that person] died. The ones who told the story, including Noni, Noni told the story and said that [the *qukviulria*] had gone to get that person [who was dying]. She probably had one of those.

ALBERTINA DULL: She probably had [one of those] as a *napaneq* [support, foundation that keeps one alive].

LIZZIE CHIMIUGAK: She probably had one of those for a *napaneq* created by shamans. She was dying, and then died. . . .

ALBERTINA DULL: Those are probably created by shamans. But long ago, when Iquyuilnguq was about to lose her spouse, when her husband was about to get into a mishap . . . I wonder who watched him, or were they lying. . . .

Then they started telling all sorts of stories, started saying all sorts of things, and they said that that woman, they said that woman who was swimming had extremely long hair.

Who watched her? Or did that happen to him when he and the person accompanying him went their separate ways? They say the woman [who was responsible for his death] had long hair. [His

Iciw' ak'a qanemcikellrukeka nuyarpak taman' qaktaarluni anelralria kuigarkun imarpiim tungiinun.

Una tuquqatalria tauna Akagualriit Atrat, Akagualriim maurluirutii, tuquqatallrani-gguq, nakirnecuar-gguq taman' takenrituq, uani-llu-gguq qip'arrluni imarpigmun anellra.

ANGALGAQ: Qavani?

NENG'URYAR: Qalvinraami. Naruyamiuni Qalvinraam iqrani, up'nerkiviutulria up'nerkiviutullermi. Acaguam Atiin tanglliniluku; tauna tua-i tuquqatalliniluni pelatekami.

Aling, anelralria-gguq un'a qaktaarluni nakirnecuarkun kuigkun imarpik cauluku. Yuk qaktaalria tamakuciq qukviiq. Qukviulrianek pituit.

ANGALGAQ: Kegginarluni?

NENG'URYAR: Nuyarpakayallrai-gguq. Qaktaarluni-gguq qaktaarluni anelralria nakirnecuarkun.

Tua-i-llu-gguq ua-i qiptellra tekilluk' qipcimaarluku una-ll' anerneriryarturluni. Tamaa-i qanaalteng qanemcikestai Noni-q-llu, Noni-m qanemcikurallrua, taum-gguq aqvastii tua-i. Tamakucimek-wa pingqellill'.

CINGYUKAN: Napanengqellilria.

NENG'URYAR: Napanengqellill' angalkut piliallratnek. Anerneriryarturluni anernerirluni. . . .

CINGYUKAN: Tuunrangayiim-wa piliaqellikai tamakut. Taugken imumi ak'a cali iciw' Iquyuilnguq augna aipaiqatallrani uinga imna picurlaka[tallrani] . . . kia-tam tangvallruagu, wall'u-q iqluut. . . .

Tua-ll'-am qanemcinguangluteng piciatun tua-i qanengluteng, taumun-llu arnamun, arnaq-gguq tauna kuimalria nuyarpaukacagarluni.

Kia tangvagtau? Wall'u-qaa avv'arulluni, avvenrarulluni malini-llu pillermegni tuaten piuq? Taumun tua-i arnaq-gguq tauna pistii nuyarpauluni. Angullia-ll'. Angulliamiu tuaten

partner] probably happened to see it [when it happened]. Her husband got into a mishap when he climbed up, down there in the ocean during the spring. He froze to death.

LIZZIE CHIMIUGAK: My, I wonder if that one went to get him.

ALBERTINA DULL: My, that's probably so.

[Shamans] not out in the open[48]

Albertina Dull and Lizzie Chimiugak, Umkumiut, June 2009

ALBERTINA DULL: My, her husband probably cursed and caused Iquyuilnguq's death. I thought they said that Paniliaraam Atii [Paniliar's father] was a shaman.

LIZZIE CHIMIUGAK: Yes, that's what they said about him also.

ALBERTINA DULL: And his wife who he left behind, you know how they said that Paniliaraam Arnaan [Paniliar's mother] was haunted for a long time.

LIZZIE CHIMIUGAK: Yes, by that person.

ALBERTINA DULL: Up to this day, the door would even shake. My, I wonder why?

LIZZIE CHIMIUGAK: My goodness!

ALBERTINA DULL: But I think he was not out in the open. You know how they referred to those who didn't practice their shaman powers in front of people *alairumanrilnguut* [ones who haven't exposed their abilites, lit., "ones who keep themselves concealed, using their power secretively"]. That's what they say about them.

LIZZIE CHIMIUGAK: Some people who spoke of Paniliaraam Atii [Paniliaq's father] said that he exhibited some of those [shaman] qualities.

ALBERTINA DULL: They refer to those ones as *alairumanrilnguut*.

The children of shamans will have some sort of ability[49]

Albertina Dull and Lizzie Chimiugak, Umkumiut, June 2009

LIZZIE CHIMIUGAK: They say that since my mother had a father who was a shaman, she almost became a shaman. They say when Egacuayak went to her [married her], her ability went away, making it so that she wouldn't become a shaman.

ALBERTINA DULL: You know how today, the children of shamans will have some sort of ability.

---

qanell'. Tua-i tauna angutii mayucurlagluni, picurlagluni, imarpigmi iciw' unani up'nerkami. Qerruluni tua-i.

NENG'URYAR: Aling taum-kiq aqvallia.

CINGYUKAN: Ala-i, kiika-w' tua-i.

Alairumanrilnguut

Cingyukan Neng'uryar-llu, Umkumiut, June 2009

CINGYUKAN: Ala-i uingan-wa umyuarrlugcillrullikii tuquvkallrullikii Iquyuilnguq. Paniliaraam Atii-ggem im' angalkuunillruat.

NENG'URYAR: Yaa tuaten call' qanrutkellruat.

CINGYUKAN: Kia-i-w' ingna yaa-i kingunra, iciw' tua-i alangrukuyagtura'arqellra im' Paniliaraam Arnaan.

NENG'URYAR: Ala-i, taumek.

CINGYUKAN: Man'a-ll' tekilluk' tua-i waten-llu amik qiivqetaarciuraqluni. Ala-i, ciin-kiq?

NENG'URYAR: Ala-i!

CINGYUKAN: Taugaam aqpiitnek iciw' alairumanricugnarquq. Iciw' tuunriyuilnguut alairumanrilngurnek pilaqait. Tuaten-am qanrutkelaqait.

NENG'URYAR: Ak'a atam qanqalriit Paniliaraam Atiinek tamakurrluunilallruat.

CINGYUKAN: Tuaten tamakunek alairumanrilngurnek pilaqait tamakut.

Angalkut irniarit iciw' cakumyuggluaraunrilngaitellriit

Cingyukan Neng'uryar-llu, Umkumiut, June 2009

NENG'URYAR: Aanka-llu-gguq angalkumek atangqerrami angalkuuyarpiallrulliniuq. Taum-gguq tua-i Egacuayiim ulliimiu ayalliniluku, angalkuungairucelluku.

CINGYUKAN: Iciw' maa-i angalkut irniarit iciw' cakumyuggluaraunrilngaitellriit.

She would be distressed by him in her sleep[50]

Albertina Dull and Lizzie Chimiugak, Umkumiut, June 2009

LIZZIE CHIMIUGAK: And also Ungusraq, I was going to tell you a story. Evidently my *al'akegtaar* [wonderful older sister], your poor *narusvak* [*tuqluun* (kinship name) for her older sister] used to have bad dreams about him. She said that one time, when he went to get some rope . . . she would be in distress over him [in her dreams]. . . .

She said that when she asked him why he was causing her distress [in her dreams], without saying anything at all, he took the rope and quickly went out. He would cause her distress [in her dreams].

ALBERTINA DULL: My, these shamans.

Although they are shamans, they tell them not to finish their future abilities[51]

Albertina Dull and Lizzie Chimiugak, Umkumiut, June 2009

LIZZIE CHIMIUGAK: They also say that our deceased grandfather Naulalriim Atra [the one Naulalria is named after] caught an *amikuk* [legendary creature that cleans a person's body] up at Urumangnaq during the spring. He caught one in his fishnet. He, too, had some sort of [shaman] ability.

When he went reindeer hunting. He said that its antlers, this was covered with moss; it was moss.

ALBERTINA DULL: My! It had moss on it?

LIZZIE CHIMIUGAK: Yes, it had moss on it. And he said, I didn't understand what he meant, I don't know what it means. He said that although they are shamans, they are not to display their abilities so that they don't finish their future abilities. They probably tell them not to use up all their ability.

They say when he showed his ability, that's what he said. He said something, and I didn't understand him. He said they tell them not to do that. Or is it because he would shorten his life?

ALBERTINA DULL: Yes, they shorten their lives. My, I wonder why?

LIZZIE CHIMIUGAK: They also shorten their lives when they didn't kill them.

Kapiatekaqluku qavamini

Cingyukan Neng'uryar-llu, Umkumiut, June 2009

NENG'URYAR: Ungusraq-llu imna, qanemcitqatallruyaaqamken. Al'akegtaarma im' Narusvageurlurpeci qavarrluk'lallrullinikii. Caqerluni-gguq ilavkugmek aqvatellrani . . . kapiatekaqluku. . . .

Kapiatek'lallminek ciin piani-gguq qanqerpek'nani-gguq ilavkuk teguqqerluku anqerrluni tayima. Kapiatekluku.

CINGYUKAN: Aling tua-i-w' makut angalkut tua-i.

Tua-i angalkuungraata manissiigluki uknakaq nangenrilkurrluku pisqetuyaaqait

Cingyukan Neng'uryar-llu, Umkumiut, June 2009

NENG'URYAR: Cali-gguq apa'urluirutvuk Naulalriim Atra Urumangnami kiani kuvyakengyaaqellruuq up'nerkami amikumek. Kuvyakngellruuq. Ellii call' tauna caruyauluni.

Tuntussullermini. Cirunrek-gguq, una urumek qecigluni, uruuluni.

CINGYUKAN: Ala-i! Uruartarluni?

NENG'URYAR: Yaa, urutarluni. Waten-llu, taringeurlunrilkeka-ll'-am, nalluaqa, waten-llu kingunelirluku. Waten-gguq tua-i angalkuungraata manissiigluki uknakaq nangenrilkurrluku pisqetuyaaqait. Tamakut caprilutait-wa pillilriit nangenrilkurrluki pisqetuyaaqait.

Ellii-gguq tauna tua-i piyugngacini manillrani tuaten. Qaillun-am qaneryaaquq, taringellrunritaqa. Waten-gguq pisqessuicaaqait. Wall'u-qaa unguvallerkani qungakanirciqngaku?

CINGYUKAN: Ee-m, qungakanirilluki. Ala-i, ciin-kiq?

NENG'URYAR: Unguvallerkaitnek tuaten qungakanirilluki tuqutenritaqamegteki.

ALBERTINA DULL: But here, although shamans have amazing abilities, when their time comes, they die.

LIZZIE CHIMIUGAK: When the time comes for them to die, they die.

ALBERTINA DULL: Yes, they die and cannot save themselves.

CINGYUKAN: Taugken tua-i makut cang'ermeng caprilengermeng angalkut pillerkarteng tekitaqan tuquaqluteng.

NENG'URYAR: Tuqunariaqateng tuquaqluteng.

CINGYUKAN: Ii-i tuquqeraqluteng ellmeggnek-llu anirturciiganateng.

She mentioned Nayangaraqtaq when she was about to die, the shaman who had wanted to marry her[52]

Albertina Dull and Lizzie Chimiugak, Umkumiut, June 2009

LIZZIE CHIMIUGAK: They say that although men wanted to marry Paningayaq, her father never complied like in a *quli'ir* [legend]. Then they say Nayangaraqtaq, a powerful shaman, wanted to marry her.

ALBERTINA DULL: That one?

LIZZIE CHIMIUGAK: The one who would die. Her father didn't want her to marry him once again. They say when she was about to die, she mentioned Nayangaraqtaq when she was about to die, the shaman who had wanted to marry her. That one [Nayangaraqtaq] evidently killed her.

Then her poor mother said to their father, "You see, it's because you continually held her back although they've asked to marry her." Then they say when she was about to die, Nayangaraqtaq moved toward the Yukon River area, the shaman. I wonder if Qiurtaralek's wife is that [shaman's] relative.

ALBERTINA DULL: My, that's probably so.

LIZZIE CHIMIUGAK: Then, back when they didn't have telephones or VHF radios, she died. They didn't have telephones or VHF radios.

A long time after it happened, the poor people of Arayakcaaq heard about her. Jacob and his family and Pulaviilnguq and family were staying at Arayakcaaq. When they heard about [her death], her beaded jewelry . . . they used to have containers like this. They'd cut a large log and hollow it out and they probably didn't make it thick. It became a storage box. They probably made them wooden covers.

They say that wooden container was filled with beaded jewelry that belonged to Paningayaq. They say it was filled with a lot of beaded jewelry. Her things, old beaded jewelry are inside. They say

---

Tua-i-gguq tuquqataami Nayangaraqtaq tauna apeurlurluku, anerneriqataami, angalkuq tauna nuliqsuuteksaaqellni

Cingyukan Neng'uryar-llu, Umkumiut, June 2009

NENG'URYAR: Atiin-gguq nulirrniangraatgu niiyucuunaku quli'irtun Paningayaq tauna. Tua-i-llu-gguq-am Nayangaraqtam angarviim angalkum taum nuliqsugluku.

CINGYUKAN: Tauna-q' tua-i?

NENG'URYAR: Tuquarkaq. Atiin-am qessakelliniluku. Tua-i-gguq tuquqataami Nayangaraqtaq tauna apeurlurluku, anerneriqataami, angalkuq tauna nuliqsuuteksaaqellni. Taum tuqutelliniluku.

Tua-i-llu-gguq aanaurluan aatateng, "Tangrriu nulirrniangraatgu aksaupaka'arqeken." Tauna-llu-gguq Nayangaraqtaq tamaa-i tuquqataan Kuigpiim tungiinun upalliniluni, angalkuq. Augna-kiq Qiurtaralgem nulirra tungayaklia taum.

CINGYUKAN: Ala-i, ikika.

NENG'URYAR: Tua-i-llu-gguq qanercuutaitellermeggni, tuquluni. Qanercuutaunateng-gguq.

Cayaqlirluteng-am tayim' Arayakcaarmiurluut niiskiit. Jacob-iinkut tamaa-i Pulaviilngunkut Arayakcaametaurluteng. Niicamegteggu-gguq tegglii waten . . . waten aguumangqetullruut. Muragpall'er kepluku, una-llu nayugluku, qecigtuvkenak' tayim' pilallikiit. Imuurrluni tua-i qemaggvik. Patuliqerluki-ll'-am pilallrullikait muraganek.

Muragaq-gguq tauna qemaggvik tegglinek imangqertuq taum Paningayam. Ala-i tegglinek-gguq imarluni. Tayima tua-i cai uitalriit, cali akaartat tegglit. Tegglirugai-gguq taukut

when they heard of her death, [they placed them] along the point at Arayakcaaq.

niicamegteggu tuqullinian Arayakcaam cingianun.

Since Apar'aq was a shaman, he had a bowl that had been taken from a grave[53]

Lizzie Chimiugak, Umkumiut, June 2009

LIZZIE CHIMIUGAK: I recall what my father used to say, "The old village of Qanrangarmiut is over there." At that place, Tengesqauktaq, who was evidently our great-grandfather, would mention beaded jewelry that was beyond his mother's [grave]. He would mention their old house pit next to the *qasgiq*, probably thinking that someone would want to search for his mother's beaded jewelry. They evidently used to believe in taboos back in those days, and they didn't take them.

And when we'd walk among graves, when we were walking around behind Umkumiut, someone found a handmade doll that someone had made, a small doll. I think it was from along the edge of Nasgaum Atran's grave.

After taking it, she placed it down like this [and said], "There's the item that was on your grave, *pev-pev-pev* [spitting]." And after doing this, "*pev, pev, pev*." She didn't take that. I thought that they didn't take them. She mentioned that it was an item from her grave, "There's the item from your grave." And she quickly spit and wiped her hands.

It seems that they couldn't take grave goods long ago. But since Apar'aq was a shaman, he had a bowl that had been taken from a deceased person's grave. They say that he cleansed his bowl, an item taken from someone's grave.

I never forget his bowl that was this size. He had a bowl that was painted and it was square shaped, a small dish. And I would go and get it when my mother was going to give him food. His bowl was a small square-shaped bowl.

Apar'aq imna angalkuungami alailutlermek qantangqellruuq

Neng'uryar, Umkumiut, June 2009

NENG'URYAR: Aatama qanellra neq'aqalaqeka, "Qanrangarmiullret akaartat yaa-i." Tuani-ll' taum Tengesqauktaraam amauqellikemegnuk aanami yaatiini tegglirugaat-gguq aperturyaaqaqluki. Tayima-gguq qasgim elatiini, elanellerteng taun' apertulallruyaaqellinia, aanami tegglirugai kitumun cucuknayukluk' pillrullill'. Piciruitullrullilriit tamatum nalliini, pinrilkurrluki.

Waten tang elivret-llu akuliitni kanga'arqamta Umkumiut keluatni kangavsegtellemteni kina tang im' piliamek irniamek yuum piliallranek irniaruacuarmek nalkutell'. Tuartang Nasgaum Atran qunguan mengliinek.

Teguyaaqerraarluku waten tang ellikii, "Qunguutegken tamaa-i, *pev-pev-pev* [qecirturluni]." Waten-llu pirraarluni, "*pev, pev, pev*." Tegunrilkurcaaqluku taman'. Tauna call' teguyuicukluki wii umyuarteqellruunga. Qunguutiinek-gguq, "Qunguutegken tamaa-i," qecirtulaagluku-ll' unatni periqtalaagluki.

Alailutet-llu tamaa-i ilait akaar tamaani tegusciigatellrungalkait. Apar'aq taugaam imna angalkuungami alailutlermek qantangqellruuq. Tua-i-gguq cayaillrua taun' qantani, alailutleq.

Waten tang angtalriamek qantallra avauyuitaqa. Mingulegmek qantarluni yaassiigenqeggluni, miiskaarrauluni. Tua-i aqvaluku aanama-ll' tuvqakaqaku piaqluku. Qanataa-w' yaassiiguayaaq.

Back when shamans had the deceased walk around[54]

Lizzie Chimiugak, Umkumiut, June 2009

LIZZIE CHIMIUGAK: Then she said, my *al'apak* [older sister] Unangim Arnaan said to him, "He puts on old parkas and pretends to be Akista." My goodness!

Tamaa-i angalkut tuqumalriit kangarcecetullinillrata nalliini

Neng'uryar, Umkumiut, June 2009

NENG'URYAR: Tua-i-ll' qanertuq-gguq-am al'apama tang Unangiim Arnaan piluku, "Atkull'ernek all'uni Akistengungualallinill'." Ala-i!

Back when those poor people were [afraid of] *carayiit* [fearsome things]. Then she said when their mothers or older sisters died, how depressing, the poor things used to say that their mothers became *carayiit*. My, why, how depressing, they'd say that their mother had become a *carayak* [fearsome thing]. This was back when shamans had the deceased walk around. . . .

After she died, my mother told a story, since she would go to visit them during the summer in a tent. Her older daughter died just before she started doing work. She said she went inside and there was an old net hanging, and I forgot what type of fish she said was hanging right after she had died.

Poor, when my mother went inside, she said to Akugar, "Don't hang these, but if there's a picture, hang one instead."

She said the poor thing had followed an old custom. She had hung a fish and an old net, and it even had a hanging fish. When she went inside, she told her not to hang those, but to hang a picture along her doorway.

Carayagnek piurlutullratni. Tuamellu-gguq tuqukata aanait, aling alianaqvaa, wall'u-q' alqait, qaneurlulallrulriit aaniit carayaurrniluki. Aling ciin nakleng alianaqvaa, aaniit carayaurrniluku. Tamaa-i angalkut tuqumalriit kangarcecetullinillrata nalliini. . . .

Tuqullran kinguani aanaka qanemciluni ullalaamikek kiagmi pelatekami. Panigpallrii-am tuqu'urlull' castengurteqatarluni. Itertuq-gguq kuvyall'er man'a agalria ca-ll' im' neqa aganikii tuqunerrallrani.

Nakleng aanama itrami pilliniluku Akugar, "Makunek pivkenak tarenrartangqerkan tarenramek agarci taugaam."

Akaarcetuarluryaaqelliniluni-gguq. Neqa kuvyallruar-llu agarrluku neqmek-llu-gguq agautarluni. Itrami pilliniluku makunek pivkenaku tarenraq taugaam agarcesqelluku amiiganun.

They used to say that her children were too soft for her[55]

Albertina Dull and Ruth Jimmie, Nightmute, April 2013

ALBERTINA DULL: Minegtuli, the one Mancuaq married for a short while, she was the only one of Luk'aq's children who lived for a while.

RUTH JIMMIE: I thought they said Luk'aq was a shaman.

ALBERTINA DULL: She was a shaman.

RUTH JIMMIE: Her children, did she . . .

ALBERTINA DULL: They were too soft for her. They used to say that her children were too soft for her.

RUTH JIMMIE: Since she did that to them, they couldn't stay alive?

ALBERTINA DULL: Yes, they couldn't have children. They call that *qetulkelluki irniateng* [their children were too soft for them]. *?Tumkurluki*.

That's what they did.

RUTH JIMMIE: They were their shields.

ALBERTINA DULL: That's what she was like.

Qetulkenitullruit atam irniari

Cingyukan Angalgaq-llu, Negtemiut, April 2013

CINGYUKAN: Imna Minegtuli iciw' Mancuam nulirqeqallra kiimi tua-i tauna anagneruqalria Luk'am irniara.

ANGALGAQ: Luk'aq-ggem tauna angalkuuningatellruat.

CINGYUKAN: Tua-i-w' angalkuuluni.

ANGALGAQ: Tayima-qaa irniani . . .

CINGYUKAN: Qetulkai. Qetulkenitullruit atam irniari.

ANGALGAQ: Tua-i-llu-q' tuaten pilliaki unguvasciiganateng?

CINGYUKAN: Mm-m, irniangqerciiganateng. Wagg'u-q' tua-i qetulkelluki irniateng. *?Tumkurluki*.

Tuaten tua-i.

ANGALGAQ: *Shield*-aqluki.

CINGYUKAN: Tuaten ayuqellrulria.

If a shaman attacked those of us who were just normal people, we would know[56]

Albertina Dull and Ruth Jimmie, Nightmute, April 2013

ALBERTINA DULL: They used to say, and our parents would say that if a shaman attacked those of us who were just normal people, we would know. [The shaman] would go into our dream, and we would be distraught. If [a shaman] tried to harm us, we would know.

RUTH JIMMIE: Isn't that what Acac'aq experienced?

ALBERTINA DULL: Yes.

RUTH JIMMIE: You know how she said that [a shaman] was trying to catch her with a gillnet, and she said when she came upon that gillnet, it was nothing to her and she just did this to it and went to the other side of it. She told that story one time.

ALBERTINA DULL: That's what shamans do. But for some people, when their time to die comes, even if he is a wily shaman, he will die.

And Yus'uk, too, the father of Cauyaq's mother, after sleeping sometime the poor thing told a story and said that the upper part of the Kuskokwim and the Yukon Rivers were getting dark. He said many people don't come out of that dark.

What he said turned out to be true. That dark was death. And he said he himself won't come out of it. What he said turned out to be true.

My! That darkness is probably death.

And that person they called Tepsaq at Cakcaaq, they mentioned that he would ask what that dark thing was along his aura, not far away.

RUTH JIMMIE: Did he sense it?

ALBERTINA DULL: Yes, that person did. Evidently, he would die suddenly one day. Qussauyaq my dear late maternal uncle was named Tepsaq [lit., "Smelly thing"]. [chuckles]

Those people who would become shamans, they knew things, what they call *tevrunateng*[57]

Albertina Dull and Ruth Jimmie, Nightmute, April 2013

ALBERTINA DULL: Some people would see things [that others didn't] long ago. And those they called

Wangkuta-gguq yuunginani angalkum pikakut nallungaitaput

Cingyukan Angalgaq-llu, Negtemiut, April 2013

CINGYUKAN: Nauwa-m' qantulriit angayuqaput-llu wangkuta-gguq yuunginani angalkum pikakut nallungaitaput. Tua-i-w' qavamtenun ekluni, kapiatekaqluku. Pissaakakut, tua-i pissaakakut tuaten nallungaunaku tuaten.

ANGALGAQ: Acac'aq im' tuaten pilallrulria?

CINGYUKAN: Yaa.

ANGALGAQ: Kuvyakun-llu iciw' pissurninguaryaaqellrulria, elliin-llu-gguq tekicamiu kuvyaq cakevkenaku waten piluku amatairluku. Taumek qanemciqallruuq.

CINGYUKAN: Tuaten tua-i pituut angalkut. Taugken tua-i ilii man'a tuqutekaan tekiskani angalkuuqtang'ermi tua-i tuquciqluni tua-i.

Tauna-ll' tua-i Yus'uk, Cauyam Arnaan aatii tuaten-am tua-i qavarpakarluteng qanemciurlullinilria, Kusquqviinkuk-gguq Kuigpak-llu kangikek tan'geriut. Yuk-gguq, yuum-gguq amllerem anenritaa tamana tan'geq.

Cunawa-gguq ilumun. Tuquq tamana tan'geq. Ellii-llu-gguq tua-i [anngaunaku]. Cunawa-gguq ilumun.

Ala-i! Tan'gerulallilria-w' tuquq.

Cali tauna Tepsamek pilallrat tuaten Cakcaami, qantunillruat tuaten, caularta-gguq man'a anllugnerani tungulria tua-i-gguq yaaqsigpek'nani.

ANGALGAQ: Elliin-qaa elpekluku?

CINGYUKAN: Yaa, elliin taum. Cunawa-gguq tua-i erenrem iliini tua-i alqunamek tuquluni. Qussauyaq Tepsaurlullruyaaqell', Angairutka. [ngel'artuq]

Tamaa-i angalkurkat, ca nalluvkenaku apqiitnek tevrunateng

Cingyukan Angalgaq-llu, Negtemiut, April 2013

CINGYUKAN: Tua-i-w' ilait canek tangaalalriit imumi ak'a. Makut-llu apqait angalkurkat canek

angalkurkat [ones who would become *angalkut*], they would see things, and the end of firewood that they had cut would turn into faces [when they saw them]. The ones who would become shamans, they knew things, what they call *tevrunateng*. They knew things.

RUTH JIMMIE: So does *tevrunani* mean that they know things?

ALBERTINA DULL: They know things, *tevrinateng*. They call it *tevrinateng*. They know things, *tevriulluteng*.

RUTH JIMMIE: What are those faces along the end of firewood that had been cut, are they shamans, are they shamans' faces?

ALBERTINA DULL: They aren't anything, but they are just things they saw. They aren't anything, you know one who would become a shaman would see various things.

They are probably shamans who haven't exposed their abilities to people, *alairumanrilnguut* as they called them. These who don't practice their shaman powers [in public], they refer to them as *alairumanilnguut*. Although they know things, they aren't exposed, *alairumavkenateng* as they call it. They *tevrunateng*, they know things.

She constantly spoke to that dead person[58]

Albertina Dull and Ruth Jimmie, Nightmute, April 2013

ALBERTINA DULL: What do they do? Why, are they ghosts, or are ghosts shamans? Why is it that some who died became ghosts long ago? And if one of their belongings wasn't burned, that would be the cause of their seeing a ghost or being haunted. What do they do?

That's why long ago, when they died, they took off a piece of everything they were to bring with them [to the afterlife].

During that time, the first one I saw was the late Nupigaq's mother. When his/her father died at Qungurmiut, Avaq was sitting upright. And he seemed to be a very large man. His wife was next to him.

Nupigaq's mother took tallow, a small piece of tallow. She instructed [the dead], and she spoke, she spoke to that dead person. And she told him that when he arrived to his older sister and she made *akutaq*, this would be the caribou back fat that she would use.

---

tangaatulriit nauwa, eqiat-llu iquit kepellrit kegginangaqluteng. Tamaa-i angalkurkat, ca nalluvkenaku apqiitnek tevrunateng. Ca nalluvkenaku.

ANGALGAQ: Tevruitnikuni-qaa ca nalluvkenaku, tevrunaku?

CINGYUKAN: Tua-i-w' nalluvkenaku tevrinateng. Tua-i-gguq tevrinateng. Nalluvkenaku ca, tevriulluteng tua-i.

ANGALGAQ: Tamakut kegginat eqiat iquitni caugat, angalkuugut-qaa, angalkut-qaa kegginait?

CINGYUKAN: Tua-i-w' cauvkenateng ellaita tangerqengaqluki. Cauvkenateng, iciw' angalkurkaq tangaagaqluni piciatun.

Apqiitnek alairumanrilnguut pilallilriit yugnun. Tuunriyuilnguut makut alairumanritniluki pilaqait. Ca nallunrilengraatgu wagg'u-q' taugaam alairumavkenateng. Tevrunateng, tua-i ca nalluvkenaku.

Qanruqu'urluku taun' tuqumalria

Cingyukan Angalgaq-llu, Negtemiut, April 2013

CINGYUKAN: Qaill' pilartat? Ciin, alangruulartut wall'u-q' tuunrangayaulartut alangruulalriit? Ciin tuqullret ilait alangruulallruat ak'a imumi. Aklumeng-llu ilait legcimanrilkan tua-i tauna alangruutekaqluku. Qaill' pilartat?

Taumek tua-i imumi ak'a tuquaqata tua-i ca ilaiqetaarturluku tua-i ayautarkaa.

Tuani tangerqerrallrulrianga iciw' Nupigallrem aaniinek. Aatii tuqullrani tang Qungurmiuni maktaluni-am tua-i Avaq. Angulvallraungatellrulria-llu im'. Nulirra-w' tua-i caniani.

Kaugamek-am, kaugaquinermek-am aug'umek tegulluni Nupigaam arnaan. Alerqualuku qaillun tua-i qanerturluni, qanruqu'urluku taun' tuqumalria. Waniwa-llu una alqaanun tekiskan akuskan waniwa tunurkaa.

RUTH JIMMIE: My goodness!

ALBERTINA DULL: That's the only person that I heard speaking [to the deceased]. I haven't heard another. Just that one.

ANGALGAQ: Ala-i!

CINGYUKAN: Tauna tang kiingan qanerturalria niitellrukeka. Allamek niicuitua. Taun' taugaam kiingan.

One who they didn't consider to be a worthy shaman[59]

Tauna angalkukeggnerunrilkelaqengaat

Paul John, Umkumiut, June 2009

Kangrilnguq, Umkumiut, June 2009

PAUL JOHN: At this time I'm going to tell a ghost story that I've heard more than once. She was actually a person like us, but because her husband wanted to follow her and didn't want to part with her, he evidently broke the rule on purpose and caused his wife to become a ghost.

They say Qamuralriim Arnaan died, dying from complications from giving birth, *irninerrluggluni* as they say. When she gave birth to her baby, she died. That's what happened to some people in the distant past once in a while, what they call *irninerrluggluteng*.

Her baby, was it because there wasn't another woman to take care of it, they buried the baby with its mother.

Because her husband didn't want to part with her, he purposely used a tool [with a blade]. Since long ago, one of their admonishments was that when someone among them died, they wouldn't use any type of tool, they would not use a tool to carry out work.

There was evidently more than one shaman in that village, and I'm not sure how many there were, back when shamans were around.

The old village of Qissunamiut is ancient when they tell stories about it. Among the shamans there was one from Qissunamiut. And their shamans didn't consider the powers of that shaman from Qissunaq to be great, and they didn't think much of him because he had moved there from another village, not considering him to be a worthy shaman.

That one who had come from Qissunamiut, since they didn't consider him to be a competent shaman, he evidently didn't use his powers to heal people in the *qasgiq*.

They call it *tuunriluteng* when those shamans are trying to heal a person among them. That sha-

KANGRILNGUQ: Alangruq tauna qanemciq ataucirquunrilngurmek niitetulqa qanemcikqata'arqa. Yuuyaaqluni wangkucicetun taugaam uingan maligcugyaaqluku qunuksaaqetacirmini alerquun-am tua-i pitsaqutmek navegluku alangruurcetellrukii tauna nuliani.

Una-gguq Qamuralriim Arnaan tuqullinilria irninerrluggluni tua-i apqiitnek. Iciw' tua-i piipini antellermini tuqutngurrluni. Tuatnaqatuut ukanirpak pivakarluteng, wagg'u-q' irninerrluggluteng.

Tua-i-am tauna irniayagii, aulukestekailan waniw' arnamek piat, qumiliulluku qungitelliniluku tauna tua-i aanii.

Tua-i taum uingan qunuksaaqetacirmini pitsaqutmek caskuquluni. Waten-am avanirpak inerquutangqetullruameng tuqukan tua-i ilaseng ernerni tallimani caskumek caqerngaunateng, caksumek aturluteng caqerngaunateng.

Cali tamaa-i taukut nunat angalkungqelliniluteng atauciunrilngurmek, qavcinek-llu tayim' piat, angalkut imkut alaitetullratni tamaani.

Qissunamiut ukut nunallret ak'allaugut qanemciugaqameng. Qissunamiumek taumek angalkut ilangqelliniluteng. Tauna-llu-gguq Qissunamiu taukurmiut angalkuita kemyukevkenaku, tua-i tekitaukluku piaqluteng, angalkukeggnerunrillekluku.

Tauna tua-i Qissunamiunek kingunelek angalkukeggnerunrilkengatni qasgimi-llu tuunriyuitelliniluni.

Tuunrinilarait una ikayungnaqkengarteng tamakut angalkut piaqamegteggu. Elliin tua-i

man, using his ways, ways that aren't part of the ways of us [regular] Yup'ik people, when [a shaman] summons his *tuunrat* and he uses them, they used to refer to it as *tuunertaarluteng*.

Since the people of that village didn't consider that shaman to be worthy, he'd only go to a home to use his powers to heal a person when they'd ask him to use his powers. And the poor thing couldn't use his powers in the *qasgiq* since he understood that the people of that village didn't consider him worthy.

When Qamuralriim Arnaan, starting with her labor, died from complications from childbirth, her husband, before those five days were up, on purpose, taking one of those tools that you no longer see today that they call a *kepun* [adze], brought a log into the *qasgiq* and chopped it with the adze, wanting to follow his wife, wanting to die also, probably since he was so sad about losing his wife and didn't want to part with her.

After he had been chopping with an adze, that evening while the people in the *qasgiq* were relaxing, that one appeared through the underground tunnel entrance, carrying her small baby on her back.

Goodness, since they knew that she had just died, the people of the *qasgiq*, the men were all frightened, and because they were so afraid, they gathered and piled along the corner of the *qasgiq*. Qamuralriim Atii was situated behind them since she had asked where he was when she came inside.

When they suddenly gathered, when they'd push those shamans, asking him to use his powers to confront that ghost out there, out of fear they would quickly retreat, and they were even making gasping noises with their throats.

When they make this noise, making some sort of gasping noise with their throats like this, they refer to it as *nucemrrualuki*. Because [the other shamans] were so afraid, when they'd push them down, they'd quickly retreat.

They say the one from Qissunaq who they didn't consider to be a worthy shaman was the only one who didn't move from his spot, and he was the only one who was along the side wall across there. All the people of the *qasgiq* had gathered along the back wall.

When they told her that he was gone, while she was visible out along the exit, placing her hand on her forehead to shade her eyes and trying to see the area beyond them, she said, "You are lying.

taum angalkum piciryaramikun, wangkuta Yup'igni ayuquciqenrilkemteggun, wagg'u-q' tamaa-i tuunrani cayugluki aturluki piaqata tuunertaarnitullrukait-llu.

Tauna tua-i angalkuq nunalget taukut pikegtakenrilatni qasgimun taugaam, enem'un taugaam agluni tuunrisqumaaqatni tuunriaqluni. Qasgimi-llu piurlurciiganani tua-i pikegtakenrilucini taringumiimiu taukunun nunalegnun.

Tua-i-am tauna tua-i Qamuralriim Arnaan irnillni ayagneqluku apqiitnek irninerrluggluni tuquan, uinga tauna erenret talliman naavailgata pitsaqutmek, augkut tangerturanriqci maa-i keputnek pitukait, muragamek qasgimun itrulluni tua-i keputequllinilria nuliani tua-i maligcugluku umyuamikun ellii-ll' tuquyugyaaqluni qunuksaaqetacirmini tayim' nuliani pillilria.

Atam tua-i tuani keputequrraartelluk' atakuan uitainanratni qasgimiut imkut tua-ll' ugna kalvagyarakun puggliniuq imna tauna irniayaani amaqluku.

Arenqiapaa tua-i tuqunerraan nallunrilamegteggu alingelliniut imkut qasgimiut angutet tamarmeng, ugaan-llu alingem tuavet-gguq kangiramun quyurmeng tua-i qalliquurulluteng. Tauna taugaam Qamuralriim Atii iluqliqluku pugglermini yuaraku.

Tua-i quy'uqercameng imkut angalkut cingyaaqaqaceteng ugna alangruq tuunraikun piluku pisqelluku, alingluteng-gguq tagqerrnaurtut igyarateng-gguq tuaten nucemrrualuki.

Qalriuguryagluteng nucemrrualuki piniaqait igyarateng tua-i qaillun elliurqatki. Alingem ugaan tua-i cingyaaqaqaceteng tagqertaqluteng.

Tauna-wa-gguq Qissunamiu angalkukeggnerunrilkekngaat, enem'inek-gguq kiimi pektevkenani aug'um nakiqataam nunaqluku kiingan tua-i. Qasgimiut tamarmeng egkuanun qasgim quyurrluteng.

Tua-llu-gguq tua-i cataitniatgu ua-i pugumallermini unatminek elqiirluni amatiit amna alangkaussaggaarluku qanlliniuq, "Iqluuci. Keluvceni tua-i uitauq. Qamuuralriim

He is behind you. Have Qamuralriim Atii come. By using his tool, he has broken our trail and has made us distressed at this time. By breaking the rule and chopping wood with his adze, he has made us lose our trail."

Placing her hand along her forehead to shade her eyes, she said that they were lying to her that he wasn't there, and she said, "If you continue to refuse to have him come, this is what I will do to you all." While she was appearing [in the tunnel entryway], she would bend her knees going up and down, and fine soil started sprinkling down inside the *qasgiq*, its soil started to sprinkle down.

My, when she said that if they refused to let him go to her, she would do that, the one they didn't consider to be a worthy shaman, since he was the only one who hadn't retreated, stood up from where he was sitting.

When he stood, he said, "The one who really should be dealt with out there by those who are shamans, that one out there who is asking for it, you're about to leave her alone! But some of us who are considered unworthy are willing!" That's probably what he said because the people didn't consider him to be a worthy shaman.

When he stood he said, "Do any of you have dog-fur gloves? If there is someone with dog-fur gloves, they should hand them to me."

After a while, since this evidently occurred during the winter, one of the people who was in the back threw a pair of gloves at him.

All the people of the *qasgiq* were afraid of that ghost.

When he put on those gloves, he went to her and said, "Now, move toward the exit a little so that I can help you from in front of you by going down into the tunnel entryway. Let me help you in your efforts to take Qamuralriim Atii." My they were scared, they became even more afraid.

My, that ghost said, "My goodness, you shouldn't get in front of me, but go behind me, help me from behind."

That shaman said to her, "My, if I go behind you, I won't be of any use. I can help you only if I go in front of you."

My, although he thought she wouldn't comply, the ghost that was visible along the doorway moved farther toward the exit.

Atii taivkarciu. Caskuquluni tumkairtaakuk nanikuavkarlunuk waniwa. Inerquun navegluku keputequluni tumkairtaakuk."

Tua-i elqiirluni unatminek alangkarrluni iqluniluki cataitningraatgu pirraarluni waten qanlliniuq, "Taivkaryunripakaquvciu waten piciqamci." Imna-gguq uani pugumallermini uyungssualalria qasgiq-gguq man'a nevuqegtaarmek kanvallagakili, nevuminek kanvallagaluni.

Aling tua-i taivkaryunrilkatgu tuaten piciqniluk' qanrami, qanran imna tauna angalkukeggnerunrilkelaqengaat itrallrunrilami tua-i kiimi aqumgaurallerminek nangertelliniuq.

Nangercami qanlliniuq, "Nutaan-am taugken ugna picetaarutellria angalkuulriani nutaan picetaarutellria pinami uitatqataqeksi! Wangkuta taugken cakegtanrilengramta piyugluta ilaitni!" Tua-i tauna angalkukeggnerunrilkelallni pitekluku tayim' tuaten qanllilria.

Tua-i nangercami pilliniuq, "Waniwa-qaa ilasi aliumatengqerituq qimugtegnek? Aliumatellegtangqerquni atak qimugtegnek cikiqerlia."
Piqerluni tua-i uksumi pilliniami tauna qavaken quyungqalriit iliita aliumategnek milqaullukek cikilliniluku.
Tua-i qasgimiut alingluteng tamarmeng taumek alangrumek.
Taukuk tua-i aliumatek ac'amikek ullagluku pillinia, "Kitek' uaqvaqaniqaqaa, kiatevkun kalevlua ikayuqernaamken. Qamuralriim Atii tegungnaqlerpeni ukisqiqernaamken." Aling alingut, alingvallaartut taukut.

Aling, imna tauna alangruq qanlliniuq, "Arenqiapaa manumkun pinarqenritaaten tunumkun taugaam pii, tunumnun piluten ikayurnga."
Taum-am angalkum pillinia, "Arenqia, tunuvnun piyaaqekuma cassuutngungaitua. Manulirnerpeggun taugaam pikuma nutaan ikayurciqamken."
Aren, imna tauna niisngaicuksaaqengraani uaqvaqanilliniuq alangruq tauna pugumalria amigmi.

He placed his legs down [into the tunnel entry-way] in front of her, and when he was standing down there, he thanked her, "My, thank you so much for having me go in front of you."

My, after telling her that, he grasped her, "Why are you trying to cause trouble? Since you are trying to cause trouble, since you are making people afraid, I am going to bring you down underground."

My, when he placed his arms around her, they say that woman was whimpering and pleaded with him not to do that to her, pleading with him not to do that to her, that while she was in pain, she didn't want to be in great pain.

Although she was whimpering, while that shaman had his arms around her, they gradually went down. While they were gradually going down from that doorway back there, they disappeared. When they disappeared, that woman was whimpering down there, and as they went down, their sounds became quiet, her noise got quiet when she had gotten far.

When her noise was no longer audible, the one who had moved there from Qissunamiut appeared through the doorway out there.

When he appeared, when he got up, they saw that his body was covered with very fine sand, and the gloves that he had borrowed were also covered with really fine sand.

He dusted off his clothes. After dusting off his clothes, when he headed up to the place where he had been sitting, he said to the people of the *qasgiq* there, "Now, you men make your *qasgiq* here upright again!" My, after he said, "Try to make your *qasgiq* here upright," they saw that the *qasgiq* was slanted toward the doorway.

They say if that shaman hadn't dealt with her, she probably would have turned it inside out with them there; if she had caused the *qasgiq* to go downward, all the people of the *qasgiq* would probably have gone underground.

Yes, when those people finally realized it, since the *qasgiq* had slanted toward the doorway, when she was bending her knees and going up and down and soil was sprinkling down, all the shamans there helped each other to use their powers to make their *qasgiq* upright again.

That story that I used to hear about how that person who had just died turned into a ghost, I'm telling you that story as it is.

Aren tua-i kiatiinun irugni kalevvlukek aciminun, tuc'imariqercami quyaviklinia, "Aling, aren quyanarpiit-lli manulirnerpegun pivkarlua."

Aren, tuaten qanruqaarluku qet'ellinia, "Caluten uitacurlagcetaarisit? Uitacurlagcetaariavet, alingevkariavet iivkaqataramken camavet nunam acianun."

Aren, imna-gguq tua-i tegumariqercani cungiallagaqluni-gguq tuaten taun' arnaq pisqenricaaquq tua-i, pinritqaasqelluni tuaten, nangteqnginanermini nangteqvallaaryuumiitniluni.

Aren tua-i cungiallagangraan qesngallerminiu taum angalkum murungiinalliniuk. Tua-i tayima amiigmek uaken murungiinaamek nallimellinilutek. Nallimlutek-gguq pillermeggni cama-i tua-i cungiallagaqluni tauna arnaq, camatmun tayim' umingurtellinilutek, nepii niitnairulluni yaaqsigillermini.

Tua-i nepii tayima niitnairuquraqertelluku tua-ll' augna imna tauna Qissunamiunek kingunelek puggliniuq ua-i amigkun.

Maaten-gguq tang pugngan tangvagluku nugellrani piat tua-i-gguq qainga man'a qaugyaqegtaarmek nevumaluni taukuk-llu-gguq navrak aliumatek qimugtek qaugyaqegtaarmek cali tua-i nevumalutek.

Evculliniuq tua-i. Evcuggaarluni tuavet aqumgavillminun tagngami pillinii tamakut qasgimiut, "Kitag' nutaan-ata angalkuni qasgisi man'a maktanqegciu!" Aren, taum-gguq tua-i nutaan qanran, "Qasgisi man'a maktanqegciu," murilkelliniut qasgi amiigem tungiinun uvertellinilria.

Tua-i-gguq taum angalkum pinrilkani ull'ucarngatai; taukut qasgimiut tamalkuita tua-i qasgiq acitmun pivkaqaku qasgimiut tamarmeng tua-i nunam acianun iteryarngatut.

Ii-i, nutaan tua-i taukut elpeka'arcamegteggu qasgi tauna amiigem tungiinun uvertenga'artellrullinian uyungssaallrani tuani kanvallagallermini nutaan-gguq tua-i ikayuqluteng angalkut tamakut tuunriluteng maktanqeggluku tamana qasgiseng.

Tauna tua-i tuqunerraq alangruullra augna ava-i niigartelalqa, ayuquciatun tua-i elpecenun qanemcikaqa.

Now listen to me. You all go inside the church. Those of us who are disobedient, like that ghost, if we had been too disobedient while living, God will have us fall to hell although we are afraid.

Since these people here [at Umkumiut Culture Camp] have been telling you things that are beneficial, these ones here have been constantly talking to you. Like that shaman had done although she was whimpering, those of us who had been too disobedient, God will easily let us fall to hell in the last day as they call it.

I'm just briefly telling about that ghost that I used to hear of. I do know another story.

Thinking that one of you or those two up there want to talk, I'm going to say this much.

Tua-llu tua-i atam niicugniqaqercia. Tamarpeci agayuvigmun itetuuci. Niicuilngurni wangkuta tautun tua-i alangrutun Agayutem niicuipakallrukumta waten unguvallemteni kenerpagmun igceciiqekiikut nangyaryungramta.

Maa-i niicunarqelrianek qalarutengrraanermegceci ukut qalaruquralaqaiceci. Tua-i ava-i aug'utun angalkum pillratun cungiallagangraan niicuipakallerni wangkuta Agayutem kenerpagmun tuaten igcetqainauciqkiikut ernermi nangneqlirmi apqiitni.

Augna tua-i alangruq tuaten niitetulqa qanemcikqeraqa. Allamek call' nallunrilkengangqerrsaaqua.

Tua-i-w' ilasi pingkuk-llu piyugnayuklukek wii waten pitaqertua.

I saw one person who traveled to the sky using her shaman powers[60]

Elsie Tommy, Alice Rearden, and Mark John, Anchorage, January 2012

ALICE REARDEN: What about *tengautulit* [those who fly], what were they like?

ELSIE TOMMY: I used to hear about ones who flew, but only one time, the last time when we were girls, during a time when it was such that we wouldn't forget things, I saw one person who used her shaman powers who traveled to the sky, our dear little grandmother who has since passed.

ALICE REARDEN: Who was that person? Your grandmother?

ELSIE TOMMY: Little grandmother Angakaq, a female.

I saw her, when we were girls. You know how when we become girls we become such that we won't forget things; evidently she was the last person I would see, with my eyes.

She entered through the door, and she had a small wooden bucket, her small bucket had a handle. It was filled with salmonberries that had leaves on them that were very red.

ALICE REARDEN: In winter?

ELSIE TOMMY: In the winter.

I forgot to mention that she said when she entered that she picked some salmonberries from *ellam allngignaa* [the sky's open tundra]. And when she entered inside the *qasgiq*, she distributed them.

Ataucimek tuunrilriamek qilagmun ayalriamek tangellruunga

Nanugaq, Cucuaq, Miisaq-llu, Anchorage, January 2012

CUCUAQ: Tengautulit-mi tamakut qaillun ayuqellruat?

NANUGAQ: Wiinga wani tengautulit niitetullruyaaqanka, taugaam ataucirquqapiarmek nangnermi nasaurluuluta nalluyagusngairulluta, ataucimek tuunrilriamek qilagmun ayalriamek tangellruunga, maacuaraurlumtenek tayima.

CUCUAQ: Kituuluni tauna? Maacuaran?

NANUGAQ: Maacuar Angakaq, arnauluni.

Tangellruaqa, nasaurluuluta. Iciw' nasaurluurtaqamta ca nallungairulluku pitukeput; nangenruluku cunawa tangvallruaqa iigemkun.

Iterluni amigkun muragaq-wa qaltaucuarii muragaq, qaltaucuarii epuluni. Atsanek imarluni imkunek pellukutartuumalrianek kavirpak.

CUCUAQ: Uksumi-qaa?

NANUGAQ: Uksumi.

Waten imat'anem iterngami qanellrulria, ellam-gguq allngignaanek atsanek unatallruuq. Iterngami-ll' qasgimun aruquteqluki.

They smelled like salmonberries, they had turned red in their midst. That was her last time. She never went again after her father died. They say she went the last time the year after, to go pick berries from up in the sky.

ALICE REARDEN: [What is] *nunam allngignaa*?

ELSIE TOMMY: The *allngignaq* of the sky up there.

MARK JOHN: What is an *allngignaq*?

ELSIE TOMMY: A clear open area. You know how when you're traveling on land, you come upon a smooth area with nothing else on it but salmonberries or blackberries.

Atsarninaqluteng kaviriluteng imumek akunlait. Tua-i tauna tua-i nangnermilqaa. Ayanqigtellrunrituq, atami tuqullran allrakuani. Allrakuani-gguq tua-i ayallruuq nangnermek, nangniurluni pakmaken nunataryarturluni.

CUCUAQ: Nunam allngignaa?

NANUGAQ: Qiliim pakmani allngignaanek.

MIISAQ: Cauga allngignaq?

NANUGAQ: Iciw' carr'ilqaq. Nunam qaingani ayagaqavci manigcelngurmek tekitaqelriaci tua-i caunani, atsanek taugaam wall' tan'gerpagnek.

Shamans flying in the sky probably used to reach those northern lights[72]

Elsie Tommy, Alice Rearden, and Mark John, Anchorage, January 2012

MARK JOHN: What did you hear about northern lights?

ELSIE TOMMY: This is what those people used to say about them, that when the weather is going to get warm, the northern lights play. They said when they used to be low, they used to take a person up into the sky in the past, only in the past, among those people who really knew things, among those old people of long ago.

Older generations are continually replaced. They are replaced when the time comes. These older kids will replace us. These adolescents will replace us when we die. They used to say [the next generation] replaces another during a certain year. After living a long time, others replace them here on this land. Those [older] ones continually die. Yes.

I also heard about those northern lights. When we would enter and say that we have seen some northern lights making noise in the sky, going back and forth up there, they'd go back, and then go back again.

Then the people we told would tell us, "Since it's going to get warm, the northern lights are going back and forth." Indeed, when the weather was going to get warm in the past, that's what the northern lights used to do.

ALICE REARDEN: And would they make noise?

Angalkut tamakut ellam iluani qilagkun tengaurluteng tamakut tekitelallrullikait tayima qiuryat

Nanugaq, Cucuaq, Miisaq-llu, Anchorage, January 2012

MIISAQ: Qiuryanek qaill' niitelallrusit?

NANUGAQ: Tua-i-wa waten augkut qanrutek'lallrukait, nenglairteqatarqan-gguq kiuryat aquilartut. Aciqsigaqameng-gguq yugmek tengucilallruut avani, avani taugaam augkuni cam nallustepiarini yull'erni tayima ak'allarni.

Ciuliat cimirturatulriit. Piyungengaqameng cimirluteng. Maa-i cimirkaput maa-i makut ayagyuayagaat angturriaralriit. Makut wangkuta tuqukumta cimirteput, ayagyuayagaat maa-i angturrilriit. Allrakuq caurtaqan tayima yuut cimituniluki qanrutek'lallrukait. Yuulnguaqameng allanek nutaranek cimingaqluteng maani nunam qaingani. Tuquurluteng tamakut. Ii-i.

Cali qiuryat tamakut niitelallrukenka. Itraqamta ellam ilua qalrialrianek kiuryanek tangerrniluta qilagmi, utertaarluteng pagaani, utertaqluteng, allanek utertaqluteng.

Tua-llu ciunemta piciqaakut, "Tua-i-wam nenglairteqataan utertaalriit kiuryat." Ilumun nenglairteqatarqan avani kiuryat pitullruut.

CUCUAQ: Neplirluteng-llu-qaa?

ELSIE TOMMY: Yes, they used to make noise like this, "*Cugg, cugg.*" When they are low, their noise is audible, when they're close.

And I also heard the following, that they are a reflection of ice in a place where ice doesn't melt. I think the water there is murky.

Using their shaman powers, the shamans flying in the sky probably used to reach those. I heard briefly about those old shamans who used to fly through the sky. And they would also say that shamans used to travel underground when they would flee from their fellow shamans.

NANUGAQ: Ii-i, neplitullruut waten, "*Cugg, cugg.*" Aciqsigaqameng nepait alaitelartut, canimenateng.

Waten-llu niitellruluku nani tamaani cikut uruyuilngurmun tarenraq'larniluki. Tua-i-wa meq wani ecuqessiyaagngatuq.

Tuunrangayamegteggun angalkut tamakut ellam iluani qilagkun tengaurluteng tamakut tekitelallrullikait tayima. Niigarcecuaqallrenka tengautullret angalkullret qilagkun. Nunam-llu aciakun ayatullruniaqluki cal' angalkut angalkuullgutmeggnek qimagaqameng.

One who a shaman cut open using a story knife[62]

Paul John and Mark John, Bethel, February 2014

PAUL JOHN: Then those people, our late elder, as you know he died right after he turned a hundred years old. Since he watched her, the elderly lady is still alive today at Tununak, one who a shaman cut open using a story knife as a knife.

He said after cutting open her stomach, when he put a red fox snout over his nose and mouth and ate her ailment, he made a loud crunching noise as he ate it.

And he said when he was done, he put his mouth over that incision that he made along the end, there was no longer an opening, but there was just a little bit of blood along some part of it.

Since he had watched a shaman cut open and operate on his *iluraq* [cross-cousin]; that person is a real cross-cousin of our late elder. She's still alive down at Tununak, but she's an elderly woman. That elder really removed her ailment by cutting her open and eating her ailment, and his knife was a story knife. [chuckles]

MARK JOHN: Which one is she at Tununak?

PAUL JOHN: Arnangiar. Paul Albert's child.

Angalkum pilagtullra yaaruitmek uluarluni

Kangrilnguq Miisaq-llu, Mamterilleq, February 2014

KANGRILNGUQ: Tua-llu tua-i aug'um tegganriutellemta, *hundred years old*-aqerluni tuqullrulria. Tangvallrulliniamiu, cama-i arnassagaq call' unguvauq Tununermi angalkum pilagtullra yaaruitmek uluarluni.

Callarqaarlukek-gguq aqsiik, kaviarem cugg'egkenek cugg'eliuciqerluni nangtequtii tauna nerrlermini-gguq qiaryiggluni cakneq nerkii.

Tuamtellu-gguq taqngami tauna im' pilallni iqmigluku iquakun pikiini callanertairullun' tua-i, nallii-gguq taugaam auggliarluni.

Tangvallrulliniamiu taum camna ilurani pilagtuqii angalkum; ilu'urqaa taum nakmiin *elder*-airutlemta. Cama-i call' Tununermi unguvaluni, arnassagarluni taugaam. Aqpucipiarluku angalkum pilagtullinikii nerluku apqucia uluara-w' yaaruin. [ngelaq'ertuq]

MIISAQ: Naliqatgu taun' Tununermi?

KANGRILNGUQ: Arnangiar. Paul Albert-am kingunra.

This person has some abilities[63]

Mark John and Roland Phillip, Bethel, October 2006

MARK JOHN: When they mention that there are people with abilities these days, I believe it, when they mention that there are people with the ability to become shamans.

Una cakuyuulliniuq

Miisaq Anguteka'ar-llu, Mamterilleq, October 2006

MIISAQ: Maa-i piyugngalriartangqerrniaqatgu ukvelartua, iciw' angalkuuyugngalriartangqerrniaqatgu.

In the beginning of the 1980s, I went along to Anchorage when we went commercial fishing, when we flew through Anchorage [to get to our destination]. There were four of us. But I wasn't there when he did that; he did that when I was bringing some items outside.

I was carrying some items outside, but the others who were with me were in the hotel room. One person in our group accidentally slammed the fingers of someone in our group in a door, and tore this [finger]. Then after seeing it that person evidently said, "How infuriating! I needed to use this hand, too!"

Then he did that. After staying for a while, he displayed it, and there was no tear on it. It was healed. I don't usually hear stories of that person having any abilities, and I haven't heard that he has abilities these days.

ROLAND PHILLIP: He's a person with abilities.

MARK JOHN: Yes. When those people went outside, while we were loading our belongings inside the car, one of them told me, "This person has some abilities." They saw the tear, the big cut he got when he slammed his finger in the door, but he healed it by just merely doing this, saying that he needed to use it.

And again, we used to call Nuyarnerilnguq our great-grandfather, and his older brother Arnaqtaq was also a shaman. But his older brother was publicly known, we'd hear things about him. Since he was their grandfather, though my mother and others teased him about having abilities, he always denied it and said that he didn't have any abilities. But we'd hear about the things that he did here and there, how he'd use his abilities here and there.

And when his older brother would appear in people's dreams, he would stick up for those people and appear and scold his older brother about constantly meddling [with people] when he would appear in their dreams. And they would see Nuyarnerilnguq [in their dreams].

Then [Nuyarnerilnguq's] grandchild, when we went to go herring fishing over in Togiak, we were inside Metervik. They were anchored right down below Fish and Game, and they were sleeping there. And I had gone to the other side. When I woke and saw that the wind had started to blow a little, I removed my anchor and went across to the calm area thinking that it might start to get windy.

Then during the night, since there seemed to be someone near the entrance [my father] saw that that person [Nuyarnerilnguq's grandson] was sit-

1980-t ayagninratgun ilagautellruunga Anchorage-aami kuvyayarluta, Anchorage-aarkuirluta. Cetamauluta. Tuani taugaam pillrani uitallrunritua; anucillemni aklunek pillruuq.

Anucilua tua-i, ilanka taugaam tuani *room*-ami uitaluteng. Iliita ilamta pitsaqa'artevkenani ilavut patuqautelliniluku, una-ll' tua-i allegluku. Tua-i-llu tangrraarluku qanlliniuq, "Eqnarivakar! Una-ll' unateka aturyugyaaqluku!"

Tua-i-llu-gguq tuaten piqerluni. Uitaurarraarluni mania allganrunani. Tua-i mamumaluni. Tauna tua-i qaillun piuluku niicuicaaqaqa, maa-i-llu cali qaillun piuluku niicuicaaqluku.

ANGUTEKA'AR: Piyugngalriarulliniluni taugaam.

MIISAQ: Ii-i. Tua-i taukut anngameng *car*-amun caput ekurluki pillemteni iliita pianga, "Una cakuyuulliniuq." Elkenka-gguq tua-i tangerrsaaqaak, allellra, kilip'allra, patuqautellrani, tua-i mamlluku taugaam elliin waten piqerluku, aturyugniluku.

Tuamtell'-am amaumtenek augna pilallruaput Nuyarnerilnguq, anngaa-llu cali Arnaqtaq angalkuuluni tauna. Taugaam anngaa alaitelallruuq, niitnaulallruuq. Augna taugaam aanama ap'akngamegteggu ilangciarluku pilangraatni cakuyungqelallranek mecirauralallruuq, caitniluni. Taugken tua-i niitnaugaqluni caqaqulallra, tua-i-wa caaksuaralallra.

Yuuruciluni-llu, anngani qavanguitgun piaqan, ellii yuuruciluni alaitaqluni waten piqtarpakalallranek tauna anngani nunuraqluku qavanguitnun piaqan. Tangrraqluku-llu tauna Nuyarnerilnguq.

Tua-llu taum tutgarii, atama iqalluarpagcullemteni yaavet Tuyuryamun, cam, Meterviim iluani uitaluta. Ellait tua-i augkut Fish and Game-at ketiitni kicaumaluteng, qavarluteng. Wiinga-ll' akilirnermun. Anuqsaaranga'artellrani, tuani tupiima anuqengnayukluku kicairlua arvirlua uq'lirnermun.

Tua-i-llu unuumainanrani atama yulkitarngalan ugna ualirneq pilliniuq tauna tua-i aqumgaluni, uani estuulumi aqumgaluni.

ting there, seated at the table near the entrance [of the boat].

[My father said,] "Are you awake because you aren't sleepy?" Then that young person replied by saying that something is wrong with his son. And that young person is younger than me. He said something was wrong with his son.

Then we got up and listened to the radio station KDLT out of Dillingham. I heard the message, and just when we heard the message, they were looking for my father's boat from Togiak, and they said that they wanted to talk to that person. I answered the people from Togiak who were calling, and they said that there was an emergency, and they wanted that man to make a phone call.

When I notified my father, they immediately got ready, and since they wanted us to go with them, we removed our anchor and accompanied them.

He knew during the previous night that something was wrong with his son. When he phoned, his wife told him that they had medevacked him, but that his condition was improving.

I hear of other young people who have abilities these days. They could have abilities, but they don't use them.

And my *iluraq* has told me many times . . . whenever I'm walking toward him, he turns his head to look at me. He suddenly turns and looks at me and says that he senses me. He says that he doesn't usually sense the presence of all people, but that he senses my presence whenever I'm approaching him, even though he can't see me.

And recently when I saw him at Swanson's [store in Bethel], I walked toward him, and then he suddenly turned to me and faced me as he came into view in the aisle.

He suddenly turned toward me and said that he thinks that I have abilites. Then I told him, "Since you yourself probably have abilities, you can sense me." [laughs]

That person says that he can also sense other people. He said some people are easy to sense. That's why when people say that there are people who could possibly [become shamans], I believe it since I hear of people who have those types of experiences nowadays.

"Waq' qavarniilavet maktauten?" Tua-i-ll' kiullinia qaillun-gguq qetunraa piuq, taum ayagyuam. Wiinga-ll' kinguqliqaqa tauna ayagyuaq. Qaillun-gguq qetunraa piuq.

Tua-i-llu wangkuta makluta *radio*-t niicugniluki ingkut Dillingham-artat KDLT-t. *Message*-aaq niilluku, niiteqanemteggun tuamtell'-am Tuyuryamek atama angyaa yuarluku tauna tua-i qalarucugniluku. Kiuluki tua-i wii Tuyuryarmiut, piut *emergency*-rniluku tua-i *phone*-aasqelluku.

Ataka tua-i qayagaullemni, up'arrluteng maligcesqelluteng-llu piullgucirluteng-wa tua-i pisqengata, wangkuta-ll' kicairluta maliggluki.

Tua-i tuani unugmi qetunrami tua-i callra nalluvkenaku. *Phone*-allrani tua-i aipaan qanrulluku ayagarutellruniluku, taugaam assiringa'arrniluku.

Cali tua-i allanek niigartelartua ayagyuaqsing'ermeng tua-i cayugngalrianek maa-i mat'um nalliini. Tua-i-w' cangqerrsugngayaaqluteng, taugaam atuyuunaku.

Aug'um-llu cali ilu'urma pulengtaq pilaraanga tua-i . . . tungiinun ayagqama tua-i takuyalartuq. Caugarrlua tua-i piciquq elpek'laraanga-gguq. Yuut-gguq tamalkuita piyuicaaqai, elpek'laraanga-gguq taugaam taigaqama tangssunrilngermia.

Ukaqvaggun-ll'-am Swanson-aami tangerrngamku tua-i tungiinun pilrianga, caugarrlua tua-i igvarluku *isle*-ami.

Caugarrlua pianga, cangqelaryuklua qanerluni. Tua-i-ll' kiugarrluku, "Elpet-wa taugaam cangqerrngavet elpek'laqevnga." [ngel'artuq]

Tauna tua-i, tua-i-w' yuut-llu ilait elpek'larnilaqai. Tua-i elpegnaqluteng-gguq elliini pilartut. Taumek cauyugngalriartangqerrsaaqsukluku piaqata ukvelalrianga waten yuut waten maa-i niitnaqluteng pilaata.

Stories of the People from the Lower Kuskokwim Coast

I speak of things that I have heard from elders[1]

Frank Andrew, Anchorage, October 2001

FRANK ANDREW: Our ancestors did not do things in just any way. Some people have little regard for them. A person is not supposed to think little of himself, a Yup'ik person who is raised here in Alaska. They're just putting themselves down.

I cannot have little regard for [our ancestors]. And I speak of things that I heard from elders, and I explain things based on what I heard, from things that I used to hear. Since we have started meeting like this, I've said that I cannot explain things that I have not heard, because I cannot fabricate things. But I only speak of things that I have heard.

Those treated by a shaman while still in the womb and allowed to live[2]

Frank Andrew and Alice Rearden, Anchorage, October 2001

FRANK ANDREW: They especially made different kinds of *iinrut* [amulets] for their *yungcarat* [those doctored by shamans in the womb to stay alive] as they called them. A person I knew had an eagle [amulet], and he's alive today. An *angalkuk*, a *tuunrangayak* used his powers on him when he was in the womb when his parents could not have children, when he was in the womb, he used his spirit powers to work on him.

And [the shaman] told them to name him Nauyartulria [lit., "One who is growing"] when he was born. It turns out it was one of these spruce trees. [The shaman] apparently called these [spruce trees] *nauyartulriit*. They were these spruce trees, the trees out there. An eagle was perched on top of it. [The shaman] apparently had [the baby] use the perched [eagle] as a mattress; he told [the parents] to always have [the baby] use it as a mattress after he was born.

https://doi.org/10.5876/9781646427314.c014

Caninermiut Qanemciit

Niitellemnek ciulirnernek qalartelartua

Miisaq, Anchorage, October 2001

MIISAQ: Piciatun pinritut augkut ciuliaput. Yuum iliin caunrilkelarai. Ellminek
caunrilkengaicaaquq yuk, Yup'ik naumalria maani nunamteni Alaska-mi. Cavkenateng
ellmeggnek caunrilkilartut.

Wii waniw' tua-i caunrillekluki pisciigatua. Niitellemnek-llu ciulirnernek qalartelartua
waniw', nalqigciaqlua-llu tamaggun niicugnillemkun wii, niicugnilallemkun. Tua-i
niiteksailkeka waten pilangerraanerpetek aperturciigatniluku nalluniluku-ll' pila'arqa, pinilua
pisciigalama. Taugaam niicugnillemnek, niicugnillemnek qalartelartua.

Yungcarat

Miisaq Cucuaq-llu, Anchorage, October 2001

MIISAQ: Yungcarateng arcaqerluki apqait, yungcarateng tamakunek iinrulituit piciatun. *Eagle*-
aamek makunek augna nallunrilkengaqa, maa-i-ll' unguvaluni. Angalkuum, tuunrangayiim
waten qingauluku angayuqaag' irniangesciigatellragni, qingauluku tuunrangayamikun
caliaqluku.

Ankan-llu Nauyartulriamek aciisqelluku. Cunawa makucimek nekevraartumek. Makut
maa-i nauyartulrianek aterpagtelliniluki. Makuulliniluteng nekevraartut, muriit qagkut.
Misngastii-wa *eagle*-aaq. Tauna tuan' misngastii curuqevkalliniluku; ankan curuqurtelluku
pisqelluku.

https://doi.org/10.5876/9781646427314.c014

ALICE REARDEN: His nest?

FRANK ANDREW: A skin, they just dried an eagle's skin. That is what that person from Tuntutuliak who I know is like today who a shaman [doctored in the womb to live].

And then in Bethel, you know Bishop Jacob Nelson in Bethel. He was also the *yungcaraq* of a shaman. He gave him an *ikiituk* [wild celery plant] as his *napaneq* [something that keeps him alive]. He made him an *ikiituk*. And when he was born, he told them to name him Ikiituguaq [Pretend *ikiituk*]. His name is Ikiituguaq in Yup'ik. It is obvious that his medicine was *ikiituut*.

ALICE REARDEN: So he was [doctored by a shaman to live] while his mother was pregnant as well?

FRANK ANDREW: That's what they do. Shamans apparently do not [doctor] them once they are born. They do what they call *yungcariluteng* when they doctor a child to live while it's in the womb. I know of those two who were [doctored], that one from Tuntutuliak and Ikit'aq, who lives in Bethel.

This is how it works. And now, the one from Tuntutuliak did not die when he was born [because he was doctored by a shaman]. And when he got a younger sibling, he didn't die either. There came to be four of them. That couple was done when they had four children. But the others kept dying before the *tuunrangayak* doctored them. They'd die before they grew older.

And now Ikit'aq over there, the Bishop, there are three of them. Their third sibling is a female. She lives here, August's wife. You probably know her? Their older siblings did not live either at first. When the shaman used his powers to make him live, this child lived, and these two [born after him] are also alive.

ALICE REARDEN: Did they always do that?

FRANK ANDREW: When they believed in it, that's apparently what they did. On their own, they would tell the *angalkut*, the *tuunrangayiit* to do that.

ALICE REARDEN: They would name them the names of things?

FRANK ANDREW: They would name them after their *tuunrat* [spirit powers or helpers].

They called him Nauyartulria [One who is growing]. It so happens it was a spruce tree. And they called the other Ikiituguaq, the one who came from an *ikiituk*. The *tuunrangayak* out of his own choosing named them after one of his *tuunrat*. [The child's] parents did not name them.

CUCUAQ: Unglua?

MIISAQ: Amiq, *eagle*-aam amia nalliikun kinercirluku. Tua-i tuaten ayuqluni tua-i Tuntutuliarmiu maa-i tauna tuunrangayiim pillra nallunrilkengaqa.

Tuamtellu Mamterillerni ingna Jacob Nelson-aaq Bishop-aq nallunritan. Tuunrangayiim call' yungcaraqaa. Ikiitugmek napanirluku. Ikiituuvkarluku tua-i. Anngan-llu Ikiituguamek aciisqelluku. Yugtun tua-i Ikiituguaruuq. Tua-i cali taukunek ikiitugnek iinrungqellruuq tua-i nallunailngurmek.

CUCUAQ: Tua-i-qaa taun' aanii qingallrani tuaten cali?

MIISAQ: Tuaten pitulliniut. Waten anumariluki piyuitelliniit tuunrangayiit. Apqemeggnek yungcariluteng-gguq, yungcariaqameng. Taukugnek tua-i malrugnek nallunritua takumni pimallregnek, Tuntutuliarmiumek, ing'umek-llu Mamterillerni uitalriamek Ikit'amek.

Tua-i waten ayuqetulliniluni. Tua-i-llu ingna Tuntutuliarmiu yuurcami tuquvkenani. Tuamtell' kinguqlingami tuquvkenani. Cetamaurrluteng waten. Cetamanek tua-i irniangeqerlutek taqlutek taukuk. Makut taugken tuunrangayiim pivailgateng tuquurluteng. Anglivailegmeng tuquaqluteng.

Tuamtell' Ikit'aq ingna, Bishop-aq, pingayuuluteng waten. Arnamek pingayurluteng. Maantuq tayima, August-aam nulirranek. Nallunritlian? Cali tua-i ciuqlikeg' makut unguvasciiganateng pillruyaaqluteng. Tuunrangayiim tua-i yungcariluku qaillukuarani unguvaluni una, ukuk-llu cali malruk unguvalutek.

CUCUAQ: Tuaten-qaa piuratullruut?

MIISAQ: Ukveklermeggni tua-i tuaten pitullrulliniut. Ellmeggnek tua-i angalkut, tuunrangayiit qanrulluki tuatnasqelluki.

CUCUAQ: Aciraqluki-qaa cat atritnek?

MIISAQ: Tuunrameggnek aciraqluki.

Taumek Nauyartulriamek acirluk'. Nekevraartumek cunaw'. Una-ll' Ikiituguamek acirluku, ikiitugmek kangilek. Tuunrangayiim umyuani aturluku tuunrami ilaitnek acirluki. Angayuqaak acirivkenatek.

They named [the children] of the ones who aren't able to have children after their powers[3]

Frank Andrew and Marie Meade, Bethel, December 2003

That's what they're like also. They named [the children] of the ones who aren't able to have children after their powers [to allow them to live].

However, they say if a shaman creates that, if the parents or grandparents of his *yungcaraq* do not ever give him goods, for some shamans, his mind would start to *?tunirrugteng'arkauguq*. And he can cause his *yungcaraq* to become ill.

That is why they were instructed that if a shaman, one with powers [doctors someone] for the sake of the child, to always give that shaman something.

And they talk about those ones and how they *cukalluku* [?they hurry them up]. They had him use his powers on him. That was the way of those who have *yungcarat* [those they doctored to live]. They strengthen their powers and abilities like a satellite, going over to them. You know how they say they go over to satellites to strengthen the powers. They say those *yungcarat* are like that, too.

MARIE MEADE: Who would strengthen them, that shaman?

FRANK ANDREW: His *urumavik* [shaman who enables a couple to have a healthy child]. They call those shamans their *urumaviit* [ones who help in a child's conception].

ALICE REARDEN: One of the women, Theresa, the one they call Ilanaq in Toksook, said that she gains weight when the *ikiitut* grow. Then when they are going to wilt, she becomes thin. Can those who were named in that way, those who were given a *napaneq* [something that keeps one up, alive or going] do that?

FRANK ANDREW: They are all different. But I know of a person they called Unguiq [lit., "One who comes back to life"] who was also a *yungcaraq*. One with the moon up there for a *napaneq*. She is spoken of down in our village. They say that her condition was more serious when she was small.

That shaman said to her parents that if that moon happens to, you know how they say the moon dies when it goes dark [eclipses]. He said not

Kangilirluki tamakunek tuunrameggnek yung'esciigalnguut pituit-gguq

Miisaq Arnaq-llu, Mamterilleq, December 2003

MIISAQ: Tuaten ayuqluteng cali tamakut. Kangilirluki tamakunek tuunrameggnek yung'esciigalnguut pituit-gguq.

Taugaam-gguq-am angalkuq tauna tuaten pilikan, pilikuni, ilii, ukuk yungcarami taum angayuqaagken wall' apa'urluugken, camek cikiqayuilkagni ilii angalkum, umyugaa tua-i ?tunirrugteng'arkauguq. Naulluungevkarluku-ll' taun' yungcarani.

Taumek alerquuteklinikiit-am angalkum tua-i tuunralgem pikani tuaten mikelnguq pitekluku, camek cikirrarrlainarluku kesianek taun' angalkuq pisqelluku.

Tamakut-llu tamaa-i qanrutkelaqait cukalluku-gguq. Tuunritell'uku piaqluku. Piciryaraqelliniat-am tuaten yungcaralget. Pissuuceteng *satellite*-atun pinircaraqluki, ullagluki. *Satellite*-aq nauwa ullagnilaqiit pinircarluku kenrat. Tuaten-llu-gguq tamakut ayuqut yungcarat.

ARNAQ: Kia pinircaraqluki, taum-qaa angalkuum?

MIISAQ: Taum urumavian. Urumaviitnek pilarait tamakut angalkut.

CUCUAQ: Augna tang qanellrulria iliit arnaq, Theresa [Moses], augna imna Ilanamek pilaqiit Tuksugmi qanellruuq, ikiituut-gguq naugaqata uqungelartuq. Tua-llu-gguq nalayartuaqata kemgelliaqluni. Tuaten-llu-qaa tuaten aciumallret tuaten napanelget pilartut, piyugngaut?

MIISAQ: Ayuqenritut. Taugaam nallunritua Unguimek cali yungcaramek. Pik'umek iralumek, *moon*-amek pik'umek napanelek. Qanrutkumalartuq nunamteni uani. Miklermini-gguq arcaqerluni pillruuq.

Taum-gguq angalkum pia, angayuqaak piak pitsaqevkenani pikna iraluq, nalanilaqiit iciw' tan'geriaqan. Tuaten pikan, nalangraan tauna

to pay any mind to her if she dies, that if [the moon] above goes back to normal, that she would come to life following it.

They say that used to happen to her. They called that old woman Ar'aq. They say that used to happen to her. They said she'd die when the moon became dark; when it did that, she would die for a short time, and she would come to life when it got bright. Her name was Unguiq. Her namesake is down in Kipnuk, her namesake Unguiq.

ilangcivkenak' uitatesqelluku, pikna maliggluku assirikan unguirciqniluku.

Tua-i-gguq tuatnatullruuq, Ar'amek piaqluk' arnassaagaq. Tuatnatullruuq-gguq tua-i. Iraluq tan'geriaqan tuqunilaqiit; tuatnaaqan tuquaqlun' tua-i, tanqigian-llu unguirluni. Unguimek tua-i aterluni. Qipnermiuni ua-i atra uitauq, atqestii Unguiq.

They say shamans would also use their powers to doctor a child while it was inside the womb, what they called *yuungcariluteng*[4]

Frank Andrew, Alex Bird, and Marie Meade,
Bethel, December 2003

FRANK ANDREW: They say shamans would also use their powers to doctor a child while it was inside the womb, what they called *yuungcariluteng*, and they would eventually become shamans.

Before a woman gave birth, while [the baby] was inside the stomach, [the shaman] would work on [the baby] using his powers and make the child a future shaman.

And they would give [the child] a name that wasn't a namesake of a person. [The shaman] would give [the child] names of things, things that are amazing, or even great plant names. And killer whales were names too. There was someone by the name of Arrluyagaq [Little killer whale] who was doctored by a shaman.

A shaman would produce those [future shamans], those who would work to help people.

They really depended on shamans back then when these contemporary things weren't available, and before doctors came around. They couldn't be without them, they really believed in them and they tried not to break their rules either. That's how [shamans] were.

Tuunraurtarkanek-llu angalkut cal' tamakut yuungcariluteng-gguq pilitullruut

Miisaq, Apaliq, Arnaq-llu, Mamterilleq,
December 2003

MIISAQ: Tuunraurtarkanek-llu angalkut cal' tamakut yuungcariluteng-gguq pilitullruut.

Waten arnaq irnivailgan aqsiigken iluagni uitallrani tua-i caliaqluku. Tuunrangayamikun angalkuurtelluku tua-i, pikaurtelluku.

Acirluku-llu yuut atqenrilkiitnek tua-i. Cat taugaam tua atratnek, irranarqelriit atratnek acirluku, wall'u piciatun naunrakayagnek-ll' acirluku. Augkut-ll' ava-i atrulalriit arrluut. Arrluyagartangqellrulria cali yungcaramek.

Tamakunek tua-i tamaa-i pikiuraqluni tuunrangayak, caliarkanek tua-i yugnek ikayuriluteng.

Tuunraat tua tamakut cacetuqutekqapiarallrulliniit avani yaqvaarni cataitellrani makunek, yungcaristet-llu pivailgata. Nanelkauvkenaki tua, ukvekluki cakneq, inerquutait-llu navguryaaqevkenaki. Tuaten tua ayuqellrulliniut.

Shaman helping in a child's conception[5]

Frank Andrew and Marie Meade, Anchorage, September 2005

MARIE MEADE: What exactly are *urumaviit*?

FRANK ANDREW: They say if a person who could not conceive a child asked [a shaman] to intercede and help with the healthy development of their child, when [the shaman] did that [interceded] and it worked, and the child was born, the shaman would be the *urumavik* of the *yungcaraq*.

That's how it works.

MARIE MEADE: It became apparent to me some time ago that Ikit'aq was a *yungcaraq*. So, his *urumavik* was. . . .

FRANK ANDREW: Muracuar [was his *urumavik*].

MARIE MEADE: That was his *urumavik*.

My mother was also a *yuungcaraq*, but I don't know who her *urumavik* was.

Power of the *angalkut*[6]

Frank Andrew and Alice Rearden, Anchorage, October 2001

ALICE REARDEN: What are the *tuunrat* of an *angalkuk*?

FRANK ANDREW: I don't know what they are. Because I have never used [the powers] of shamans, I don't know what they are. I do not know the ways of the shamans, the way they work and use their *tuunrat*.

But they would *tuunrilluki*, what they call *tuunrilluki* [use their spirit powers to heal them]. He would let a woman sit on her bed and he would crouch at her feet. And he would wrap himself with a seal-gut rain parka and he would have her step on it. The shaman exercises his powers by going on his knees face down, with his knees flexed and legs folded toward the body when shamans work inside the home. He would constantly move those back and forth with his face covered behind the person who he was healing. . . .

But when they were [using their powers] in the *qasgiq*, when they would *nangrulluki* [stand and work to heal a person in the *qasgiq*], they would have two drummers or three.

Then down on the floor planks, they would have the person they are healing sit on a mat in the back area [of the *qasgiq*]. When they sang their *yuarulluut* [songs composed by shamans], when they were drumming, he would dance. When he would

Urumavik

Miisaq Arnaq-llu, Anchorage, September 2005

ARNAQ: Caqapiaraugat urumaviit?

MIISAQ: Waten angalkuq una yung'esciigalnguum pikani yungcarisqelluku, ikayuusqelluku, irniangesciigalnguum, tua-i tuatnakuni, piciureskan, tauna mikelnguq ankan, mikelnguum taum tauna angalkuq-gguq urumavikarkauluku yungcaram.

Tuaten ayuquq.

ARNAQ: Ikit'aq yungcaraulliniluni. Urumavingqerrluni. . . .

MIISAQ: Muracuarmek.

ARNAQ: Urumavikluku.

Aanaka-llu-wa yuungcaraullrulria, taugaam camek urumavingqellra nalluaqa.

Angalkuum tuunrai

Miisaq Cucuaq-llu, Anchorage, October 2001

CUCUAQ: Angalkuum tuunrai caulartat?

MIISAQ: Nalluanka. Angalkuum piinek piksailama nalluanka. Nalluanka angalkut cayarait, caliyarait tuunramegteggun.

Taugaam tuunrilluki, apqiitnek tuunrilluki. Arnaq ingelrini aqumevkarluk' teruanun-llu elavluni. Imarnitegnek-llu caquluni, waten tut'elluku. Ciisqumigglun' palurrluni, irugni qungcurrlukek angalkuq tuunrituuq enem'i piaqameng tamakut angalkut. Taukuk tua-i arulaqu'urlukek, caqumaluku qamiquni tuunriskengami tunuani. . . .

Qasgimi taugken piameng, nangrulluki-gguq piameng cauyarcirluteng nutaan malrugnek wall' pingayunek-llu.

Nacitni kanani nutaan, tuunriskengarteng kiavet curirluk' piluku. Yuarulluitnek aturaqameng, cauyarluteng piaqata yurarlun' tua-i. Takussagluni-gguq. Uivaaraqluni waten un'a. Pinariaqan, yag'artaqan taq'ertaqluteng.

do that, they would call it *takussagluni*. The one down there would go in circles. When it was time, when he'd suddenly extend his arms, they'd suddenly stop [drumming]. He would talk about what the person who he was healing was like.

ALICE REARDEN: He would let the people in the *qasgiq* hear what he said?

FRANK ANDREW: He would let the people in the *qasgiq* hear him. He used a seal-gut rain garment as a blanket. And they always circled in this direction [clockwise, *ella malligluku*] and not this direction. They would go around in a circle, and when they got all the way around, they would go toward the center. Then they would finally ?*angitaarluteng* facing the door of the *qasgiq*, the tunnel entryway.

They call it *takussagluteng*. I don't know how they do their work, but that is what they do. They would move toward the door, then they would back up, following their drumming. His steps would follow the drumming.

When he was ready, when he suddenly extended his arms, the drummers would suddenly stop. He would then squat and talk about what the person he was healing was like.

That's what they did in the *qasgiq*. There were sometimes two or three shamans helping one another.

It is powerful, it is apparently very powerful. But in the stories they tell, after a person was extremely ill, they would [heal him] to where he was able to walk out. And after he had been dead, they would bring him back to life and have him walk out, working on him with their shaman powers. They are actually very powerful.

Malicious shamans[7]

Frank Andrew and Alice Rearden, Anchorage, October 2001

ALICE REARDEN: Why do we sometimes hear about good and bad shamans? Did you hear that also in the past? What are those two like?

FRANK ANDREW: Shamans with malicious intent. And when they used their powers to heal a person, even though they are capable, they couldn't cure them.

And again, their fellow shaman who the people were starting to prefer because he always healed people, because he cured people, other shamans would start using their powers against him in a

Qanemciaqluni uum ayuqucianek tuunriskengami.

CUCUAQ: Niicelluni-qaa qasgim yuinun?

MIISAQ: Qasgim yuinun niitelluni. Imarnitek uliklukek. Ukatmurrlainaq-llu uivetuluteng, ukatmun piyuunateng. Uivaqluteng tua-i, kassuameng-llu tua-i qukavarluteng. Nutaan angitaarluteng qasgim amiiga caumaluku, kalvagyaraq.

Takussagluteng-gguq. Taugaam qaill' calilauciat nalluaqa, taugaam tuaten pituut. Anelraaraqluteng ataam kingupiaraqluni cauyallrat maligtaquluku. Tutmarluni tua-i cauyallrat maligtaquluku.

Tua-i-ll' pinarilliami, yag'arcan cauyalriit taq'errluteng. Uyungqerrluni-ll' tua-i nutaan qanemciluni tuunriskengami ayuqucianek.

Tuaten tua-i qasgimi pitullruut. Malruuluteng wall' pingayuuluteng ikayuqluteng caaqameng piaqluteng tuunrangayiit.

Tukniyaaquq tua-i, tukniyaaqelliniuq. Taugaam qanemcimegteggun yuk-llu naulluuqapiarraartelluku piyualuk' anevkaraqluku. Tuqumaluku-ll' piyaaqerraartelluk' unguirtelluku anevkaraqluku, tuunrangayamegteggun caliaqluku. Tukniyaaqut tua-i.

Umyuarrliqelriit angalkut

Miisaq Cucuaq-llu, Anchorage, October 2001

CUCUAQ: Ciin-gguq iliini niitelarceta assilrianek angalkunek assiilngurnek-llu angalkunek? Tuaten-qaa niicetullruuci elpeci? Qaillun taukuk ayuqak?

MIISAQ: Umyuarrliqelriit angalkut. Yuk-llu tuunritngermegteggu, piyugngangermegteggu anirturluku pisciiganaku.

Tuamtellu-gguq angalkuullgutseng yuut makut cucuksaguskiit anirtulguan, assirivkarilaan yugnek makunek, tuunrangayamegteggun assinrilngurmek pingnaquranguluku angalkut,

bad way, because he was doing good works on people. They say it was because of the goods they pay him for his service. They apparently offered them goods when they asked them [to heal]; it was like paying them.

However, they say that a shaman with good intentions would only request a certain amount of the goods they were to give them for their service. When they asked [the shaman], he would say that he asks to be given an amount by measuring the path of the person he was healing, which was [the amount of goods] that was just right for him. They say those shamans with good intent are not like their fellow shamans. They are not evil, and they do not provoke people with their powers. They do not kill others.

yugnun assilriamek calillra pitekluku. Aklut ellimerrutai-gguq pitekluki. Aklunek canek piciatun ellimetullrulliniut; tua-i akililriatun ayuqluki.

Imna-gguq taugken umyuaqellria angalkuq ellimerrutni-llu tamakut tuaten pitasqelluki taqesqelluki pituluki. Aptaqaceteng-gguq pinaurai, uum-gguq tuunritarkami tutmayararkaa cuqluku cikircet'lartuq, engelqerriinek. Tamaa-i-gguq tamakut umyuaqellriit, angalkut assilriit, angalkuullgutmegcetun ayuqevkenateng. Umyuarrlugpek'nateng, picestaariyuunateng yugnek tuunrangayamegteggun. Tuqurqivkenateng.

They called him Tairtaq[8]

Frank Andrew, Peter John, and Marie Meade, Washington, DC, February 2003

FRANK ANDREW: Out in the Yukon, about a child who had just grown.

Aqumgaciq told about that shaman who he watched.

One who raised a person from the dead. From a village of Kassurpagmiut. They called him Tairtaq. He walked in a crawling position. His legs were bent in [from being crippled].

His name was Tairtaq.

They said a *yugaq* [nonhuman being] of the wilderness made his legs shrivel. He threw a rock at him. He was sitting on a tree. It was at a time when they were fighting each other through their shaman powers.

His staff had five designs on it. That *yugaq* was young, a person of the wilderness.

Tairtaq had a regular person from his village sit back to back with him [in his kayak]. Because he could not walk, he took that person with him to help him.

The other would [attack him] with his shaman powers. That shaman would retaliate.

That *yugaq* [would retaliate against] Tairtaq. This was when he used to walk. His legs had not shriveled.

PETER JOHN: They were fighting each other.

FRANK ANDREW: They did that the whole day. I'm not

Tairtarmek aterpagtaqluku

Miisaq, Mumess'aq, Arnaq-llu, Washington, DC, February 2003

MIISAQ: Kuigpagmi qakmani mikelngurmek angliriqalriamek-wa tua-i.

Aqumgaciq-wa qanemcillrulria tangvallminek taumek angalkumek.

Unguircecilriamek. Kassurpagmiumek. Tairtamek aterpagtaqluku. Aurrurluni kangaraqluni. Qungaumalutek ukuk iruk.

Tairtamek aterluni.

Tamatum-gguq yuilqurmiurtaam yugam qungagcetellruak iruk. Teggalqumek milqerluku. Napam qaingani aqumgaluni. Tuani inglukuurutlermeggni tuunrangayamegnegun.

Ayarua-wa-gguq tallimanek qaralirluni. Ayagyuarluni tauna yugaq, yuilqurrmiutaq.

Alraparluni-llu tauna Tairtaq nunalgutminek yuunginamek. Kangarciigalami tua-i ikayuastekaminek taumek maligluni.

Tamakut-gguq, uum aipaan camek-wa tua-i, angalkuminek-wa tua-i piaqluki pitullinia. Taum angalkuum akiaqluku.

Yugam taun' Tairtaq. Piyuatullrani. Iruk qungaumavkenatek.

MUMESS'AQ: Inglukuurullutek.

MIISAQ: Ernerpak-gguq tua-i. Qaill' pitariluku taun'

sure what time of day they came upon that [*yugaq*]. Then night came, and they [fought using their powers] all night, too. They did not run out [of spirit powers].

When daylight came, his companion there, Tairtaq, started to stop for a bit, trying to recall [what he could use]. But his opponent there would counter him right away when he was done. But that Tairtaq started to hesitate and try to recall [what he could counter with].

Just when daylight came, [Tairtaq] ran out of [ways to counter him].

Tairtaq. That person [of the wilderness] told them that they both were going to die. He said he's actually not the one [who would kill them]. But the things that he had used earlier were going to [kill them].

My, because they were about to die, his companion, the regular person had him sit behind him. They were across from each other. He scattered them from his armpits saying to get out of his way. "I have warned you repeatedly knowing what will happen to you. But you go right ahead and do those things anyway!"

When he was trying to see those things, he took him along. Those [*yugat*], that kind [of being].

MARIE MEADE: A *yugaq*?

FRANK ANDREW: A *yugaq*. And *?piviirluni-am yugtarmek aturraarluni*, he threw a rock at him. The rock grazed him on this side and did not hit him directly. He immediately buckled.

Then he told him, "As long as you live, you will never stand again!" Just as he stated, he never walked again.

So his companion changed [their fate]. They kept retaliating to one another all day long. As you know, the summer day is long.

Just before sunset, that *yugaq* started to hesitate. Before too long he said that he had ran out and said that he could not recall [what to use] anymore. He got sad and said that he could not recall anything now.

That young man told him not to worry and that they would not do anything to him.

He got happy because he was not going to die.

MARIE MEADE: Yes.

FRANK ANDREW: After he was told that, he asked, "Which one of you wants to be a shaman?"

tekitellruagnegu tayim'. Unugluni-llu unugpak-llu. Nangucuunatek tua-i.

Erteqerluki tua-i tauna malia, Tairtaq tauna, uitaqalangllinilria, neq'angcarluni. Taunag-gguq taugken aipaa tua-i egmian' taq'errutaqan kiumek piaqluku. Tauna taugaam Tairtaq tua-i neq'angcalangluni.

Erteqertelluku tua-i nangutelliniluni.

Tairtaq. Taum tua-i pilliniak tua-i waniw' tuquarkaurrnilukek tamarkenka. Elliin pingaicaaqnilukek. Augkunun taugaam atullminun elliin piarkaurrnilukek.

Aren tua-i tuquqatalliniamek taum yuunginaam malian tunuminun-gguq tuavet aqumevkarluku pia. Akiqliqluteng waten. Unrek aciagnek calligtellinikai qanerluni avicesqelluni. "Inerqularyaaqekemken waten pillerkan nallunrilngurtun. Arenqialnguten ciumuarluten tua-i!"

Tamakunek-gguq tangengnaqaqami tua-i malikelaraa. Tamakunek, aug'umek.

ARNAQ: Yugamek?

MIISAQ: Yugamek. Tamaani-llu piviirluni-am yugtarmek aturraarluni taumek tua-i teggalqumek milqerluku. Maaggun-gguq ukalirnerkun agtuvlerrluku qukarturpek'naku teggalqum taum. Egmian' tua-i uyungleqertelliniluni.

Qanrutlinia, "Unguvallerpeni nangerrngairututen tua-i!" Apruciatun tua-i piyuayuirutlinilria.

Taum tua-i cimillinia malian. Ernerpag'-am tua-i kipulketaagullutek tua-i akiurtaagullutek. Kiagem erenra taktulria.

Akerta tua-i tevirarkaurrluku tauna atam yugaq uitaqalangllinilria. Tua-i ak'anun pivkenani nangniluki neq'anairutnilluni. Angnirpek'nan' tua-i qanrulluku neq'anairutnilluni tua-i waniwa.

Taum ayagyuam pillinia umyuassuugarpek'naku pisqelluku, qaill' pingaitniluku.

Angniriqertelliniluni tua-i nutaan tuquqatanritliniami.

ARNAQ: Ii-i.

MIISAQ: Qanruqaartelluni pilliniak, "Nalirteg'-mi tua-i angalkuuyugta?"

The regular person answered him that where he comes from he was not called a shaman.

But he said that person [Tairtaq] was their shaman at their village. He told him to make that one [a shaman].

He said to him, "Now you are going to become a shaman!" He said to Tairtaq, "Give him half of all material things given to you for your services without fail!"

"He has given you life!"

He told him he was finally going to become a shaman.

So they went home, they went their separate ways. After that he became a shaman.

Aqumgaciq started hearing about Tairtaq, a shaman who lived upriver from them somewhere around Urraarmiut; he was revered.

In winter, when [Aqumgaciq's] father was going to go to the Yukon, since he wanted him to take him along, they went to the Yukon.

When they arrived at Iqugmiut, when they arrived there they saw that the *curukat* [guests invited to a dance festival, lit., "attackers"] had already arrived. They were going to have Kassiyuq [Dance Festival].

So they went to the *qasgiq*. When a person who was his age made a motion to come to him, he went to him and sat down beside him. And his father there probably sat with his age group.

So that one also got him some food.

After they ate, after he ate, they took his bowl out. So he became his host.

In a little while, one of them said, "Gee, those who are getting people are taking so long to arrive!"

Because he was curious, he also asked his fellow boy, what person had they gone to fetch?

He told him that they had gone to fetch a shaman from the Kuskokwim area, and his name was Tairtaq. So he started to anticipate seeing how Tairtaq looked since he had heard so much about him.

They had installed seating in that *qasgiq*. When they were going to dance, they put in seating.

They said that there was a sick person in the village, the daughter of their elder. And she had not acquired a husband yet. She was getting critically ill.

Later on that night, when [someone] came in, he announced that the [elder] over there told them

Yuunginartaan taum kiulliniluku taum kingunermegni ellii angalkumek aprumanritniluni.

Tauna taugaam angalkuqniluku nunameggni. Pisqelluku tauna.

Pillinia-am, "Kitak' tua-i angalkuurteqatartuten elpet!" Tairtaq pillinia, "Ellimerrutevnek aklunek maliin tauna avguterrlainarluku pikiu!"

"Unguvaliraaten!"

Nutaan angalkuurteqatarniluku.

Nutaan utertelliniluteng, avvulluteng. Taum kinguani nutaan angalkuurrlun' tua-i.

Aqumgaciq-gguq niitelangelria Tairtarmek taumek qavan' kiatmeggni Urraarmiut natiitni nunaluni angalkumek; nanraumaluni tua-i.

Uksumi Kuigpagteqatallrani atani, maliksuani maliklutek Kuigpagtelliniuk.

Iqugmiunun tua-i tekillutek, tekitelliniuq, curukat tekitellrullinilriit. Kassiyuqatalliniluteng.

Qasgimun tua-i ciunillinilutek. Pitatmi aug'um, pitatekluku tua-i elliitun pitaluni nuluraqaani ullalliniluku, canianun-llu tua-i aqumluni. Atii tauna tua-i pitatminun cal' aqumellilria.

Neqkassaalliniluku tuamtell' taum.

Nererraarlutek tua-i, nerraarluni taqngami qantaa anulluku call' tua-i. Tukuqeqerluku tua-i.

Uitaqertelluki tua-i iliit pilliniuq, "Aling' yussaagegni-ll' imkugni tekicuipaa!"

Tan'gaurluullgutni call' tauna paqnayuami aptellinia cali, cameg' yussaagucianek?

Angalkussaagtut-gguq Kusquqvagmek, Kusquqvagmiumek, Tairtamek at'legmek. Neryuniungartellinilria tua-i tauna atrakun niitelaami Tairtaq qaill' ayuqucianek.

Qasgi-llu-gguq tamana aqumucillrulliniluku ak'a. Yuraqata'arqameng aqumucituit.

Naulluulriamek ilangqerrniluteng, tegganemeng taum panianek. Uingeksaunani-llu-gguq. Tua-i augtarnariniluku.

Atakurpak tua-i uitaqerluteng [kina] itrami pilliniuq ing'um-gguq qanrucesqai ilangcivkenani

to go ahead and dance because those guests had already been there a long time.

They answered him that they would not dance while he was not there.

They said that they would not dance well while he was not there and not with them. So they decided not to dance because their guest there had said the same thing.

Later on that evening before dark, one of the people who had entered said that they had just arrived outside, those people who had gone to fetch a shaman.

As they were waiting, from outside of the log frame entrance to the underground tunnel, the top of a head appeared with hands pulling back the covers. Two people quickly went out and opened it and took and pulled him up on each side of his arms, and when he came up, he looked just like a boy, he was a small man!

When they released him, he crawled to this side of the wall, and there was the door out there. He sat at the edge of the floor boards. He crawled up to it. He sat on the edge of the floor boards on the head rest and began to take his clothes off. He was a small, skinny man.

His flesh was white. His head was full of gray hair.

When he got through taking off his clothes and putting them down, the person who had gone to fetch his food came in. He placed his food in front of him. When he set them down, [Tairtaq] asked, "That person who you fetched me for, have I gotten to her in time?"

They said to him that she had ?numaaqluku earlier that day. But she hadn't done that since.

Pushing his bowl away, he said, "So now is not a time to eat!"

He told them to go and fetch her. They answered him that they could no longer walk her over.

He repeated that if he tried to cure her in the house, he would not cure her properly. But if he [doctored] her by standing up, there would be a 50-50 chance of success.

They answered him, "She is in such a state that we can't walk her over." They said it was too risky.

PETER JOHN: Yes.

FRANK ANDREW: They said that she would die [if she was moved]. He answered that even though that might happen, they should get her right away.

tua-i yuraasqelluki akaurcessiyaagniluk' allanret tamakut pillrat.

Kiugaat-gguq yurarngaitniluteng cataunaku.

Elluarrluteng yurarngaitniluteng cataunaku ilakevkenaku. Tua-i taq'iluteng, allanrita-ll' tamakut qanerniarutliniateng.

Atakuyartuqerluku tua-i tan'gerivailgan itellriit iliit qanlliniuq keggai-gguq tekitut, pissaallret angalkussaallret taukut.

Piinanratni pall'itaam uatiitnek tua-i kakangcalkitangartelliniuq ugna pakiurluku patuak. Anelraqerrlutek malruk ikirrluku inglugtun teguluku nugtelliniak tan'gaurlull'er-gguq tuar uani angucecuayaaq-gguq!

Pegcagni aurrluni mengelvalliniluni ukalirnermun, amik-wa ua-i. Nacitet ngeliitnun aqumqalliniluni. Aurrlun' tua-i tagluni. Maavet nacitet keluqliatnun aqumluni akitmun ugayallinilun' nutaan. Angucecuayaaq-gguq kemegkunani.

Qakinguarluni-gguq. Qamiqurra tua-i qiilingluni.

Qaqiarcata tua-i aturani quyurrluki elliqanrakun, payugcestii neqkainek aqvatleq itliniluni. Ketiinun tua-i ciuqerranun elliqalliniluku. Elliqaaki qanlliniuq, "Tua-i-qaa amna aqvavkaluuguci anguaqa?"

Pilliniat ernermi ava-i nuumaaqluku pillruniluku. Tuaten pinqigteksaicaaqniluku taum kinguani.

Qantani tauna kasmellinia qanerluni, "Arenqiatelliniuq nerkaunritlinilria!"

Aqvasqelluku. Kiulliniat kangaucunairutniluku.

Pulengllun' pilliuq nem'i piyaaqekuniu piluaqerngaitniluku. Nangrulluku taugaam pikuniu aipaak aturyarniluku.

Kiulliniat-am "Arneqialnguq-wa kangaucunailnguq tua-i peknertuluni pikuni." Aarnaqniluku.

MUMESS'AQ: Ii-i.

MIISAQ: Piciqniluku tua-i, piunrirciqniluku. Kiullinia tuaten pingraan, piarkaungraan kiiki aqvasqelluku. Maani tuquurangraan anguniluku,

He said that even if she dies in there, that he had gotten to her in time, and that he wanted to [doctor] her by standing up. He said that she might as well die inside the *qasgiq*.

So they finally went to fetch her. Carrying her on the sides, they brought her in.

When they brought her in, he knelt down behind her and got into a prone position, covering himself with a seal-gut parka.

After he had been down in a prone position for a long time, when he got up he told them to get a grass mat and a young bearded-seal skin for her to lie on. So they went to get those things.

He told both of her parents to come to the *qasgiq*.

So they made a mattress for her at the end of the floor boards toward the inner wall and let her parents sit by her side.

So then he let them beat the drums and started [his ceremony].

Because he could not walk, he stayed crouched down there. But he kept swaying his head to the drum beats.

After a number of *yuarulluut* had been sung, he suddenly stood up on his legs. When he stood up, he put on a seal-gut parka. His legs stretched. Then he circled the one he was healing when he stood up.

Before too long, he raised his arms and told them to stop. When they suddenly stopped, he got down by bending his legs.

As soon as he crouched, from the corner across there, from the edge of the people, a man suddenly got up. When he got up, he said that if anything happened to [the girl], he would put her in the coffin along with the person doctoring her. He was not cordial at all.

Without saying anything, [Tairtuq] told them to start again.

After he *?angitaarluni*, he circled her.

So the second time, he told them to stop. When they stopped, before he could say anything, that person retorted like before, that if anything happened to her, he would put her in the coffin along with the person who was doctoring her.

Again, without saying a word, [Tairtaq] continued a second time.

Then he told them to stop for the third time. Before he told them to stop, that same person said the same thing again.

nangrulluku piyugniluku taugaam. Maani tuquuraasqelluku qasgim iluani.

Aqvalliniluku tua-i nutaan. Akigarluku itrulluku.

Itrucatgu tua-i kiatiinun kiavet ciisquga'arrlun' palurtelliniluni imarnitegnek piluni.

Ak'anun palungqaqerluni makcami pilliniuq tupiganek-gguq amirkamek-llu cururkainek aqvallit. Aqvatliniluteng-am tua-i tamakunek.

Angayuqaak-llu taukuk tamarkegenka qasgisqellukek.

Curirluku tua-i kiavet nacitet iquatnun angayuqaak-llu avategkenun aqumevkarlukek.

Nutaan cauyartelluki ayagnilliniluni.

Piyuasciigalami-gguq tua-i kanan' lavngaurluni. Qamiquni-gguq taugaam cauyalriit maligqurluki waten elliurturluni.

Yuarulluut tua-i qavciurteqerluki nang'ertelliniluni. Nangercami-ll' imarnitek at'ellinilukek. Nenglutek iruk. Nutaan takussalliniluni nangercami.

Ak'anun-am pivkenani yag'arrluni taqesqellniluki. Taq'ercata tua-i uyungluni.

Uyungeqanrakun kangiramek agken yuut teruatnek-gguq angun ing' mak'artelliniuq. Mak'arcami pilliniuq qaillun pikan amna tuunricestiinek tapirluku qungurciqniluku. Kenkevkenani.

Tua-i camek qanerpek'nani ayagniisqelluki-am pillinikai.

Tua-i una angitaarraarluni takussarluni [uivaa].

Aipiriluni-am taqesqelluki. Taq'errutiitni-am qanerpailgan tauna-am nepelkitliniuq aug'utun, qaillun pikan tuunritestiinek tapirluku qungurciqniluku.

Ataam cameg-am tua-i qanerpek'nani aipiriluni ayagnilliniluni.

Pingayiriluni-am taqesqellniluki. Taqesqelluki-am qanerpailgan, tauna-am nepelkitliniuq aug'utun tua-i qalarrluni.

PETER JOHN: He kept saying one thing?

FRANK ANDREW: Yes. So again without saying a thing, he started again.

MARIE MEADE: He circled the one he was healing?

FRANK ANDREW: He circled the one he was healing. After the fourth time, he told them to stop.

Oh, just before he told them to stop, when he circled her, he went around in a circle and when he got to that man, he put his arms up and told them to stop. Then he went down on bended knees right away.

When he stood up, that person back there said the same thing, that if anything happened to that girl, he would put her in a coffin along with the person doctoring her.

Kneeling down he said to him up there, "You are too much! Ever since I have come down here you have been the only one making noise! This person who you plan to bury with me once she dies, there was too little compensation given to cure her! There are not enough paths for her to walk on!"

That person who had been bad-mouthing retorted, "Listen! He randomly wants more compensation! Those of you who have things to give, you must give him some!"

The people started to go out. This was at the time when they used to give material things to ask a favor [of a shaman]. They came in holding things and placed them down there in front of him. When all the things were put there, instead of having them take them away, he continued.

Before too long, when he told them to stop, he said that they had gone beyond what was necessary!

That person said to him, even though they had given too much, to go on because they would not take them back.

[Tairtaq] told him that if they did not take some away, this person would not live for long. He told them to take some away.

He started to take some of his compensation away. When they were just right, he added them on to the ones that were not enough. And since they were not going to take those back, he said along with the guests, he told them to make songs for him and that he would have gifts to give during the dance.

He finally continued. That person who kept retorting never said anything again.

PETER JOHN: Because he now understood.

MUMESS'AQ: Atauciq qaneryaraqluku?

MIISAQ: Ii-i. Tua-i-am qanerpek'nani ayagninqigtelliluni-am.

ARNAQ: Takussarluni?

MIISAQ: Takussagluni. Cetamiriluni-am taqesqelliniluki.

Aren, tuani taqesqeqatallermini takussallermini uivluni nallairamiu-ll' tua-i tauna yag'arrluni cauluku taqesqelliniluki. Uyungqerrluni-llu egmianun.

Nang'ercan-am pingna nepelkitliniur-am aug'utun, qaillun pikan tauna tuunricestii malikluku tungmagciiqniluku.

Ciisqumigarrluni qanrutlinikii piaviarluku, "Arenqiapaa-ll' elpeni! Wavet atrarraanemnek kiivet nepngulriaten! Tuquukan tang una maliklua tungmagtarkan, ellimerrutai nurutellriit! Tutmayararkai nurutellriit!"

Qanlliniur-am tauna qanlertulalleq, "Kaaka! Kilgarmun laaralria ellimerrutminek! Pikalegni piyunarqerci!"

Anuralliniluteng tua-i tayim'. Canek tua-i ellimerrluk' tamaani pitullermeggni. Tegumiarluteng iterluteng tua-i ellilerluki kanavet uatiinun. Nangeng'ata-am teguvkarpek'naki tuantelluki ayagnilliliniluni.

Ak'anun pivkenani taqesqengamiki-am pilliniuq anagarutut-gguq!

Taum-am kiullinia anagarutengraata pisqelluki tegungaitniluki.

Pillinia ilangartenrilkatki ak'anun unguvangaitniluku una wani. Ilangarcesqelluki.

Ellminek-gguq tua-i nutaan ilangarqurarai tua-i ellimerrutni. Tua-i pitacqeggiata ilaulluki tuavet nurusngalrianun. Taukut-llu tua-i tegungaitelliniitki pilliniuq allanernun ilaulluni yuarukaraasqelluni ukunun yurautengqerciqniluni.

Nutaan tua-i ayagnilliliniluni. Tauna-ll' qanleralalria pinqigtevkenani.

MUMESS'AQ: Taringarcami tua-i.

FRANK ANDREW: When he stopped, he asked those two. They answered him that she was no longer breathing.

He said to them, "It's okay, because I got here in time while she was breathing, even though she is not breathing [now], it is okay!"

Then finally after he stayed awhile, he said to them that they should separate her parents and have them settle along the lampposts behind the people and cover them with their goods. They should cover them with the goods of the people of that village who were in the *qasgiq*.

He told them not to cry sorrowfully, he told them not to be downhearted because they would ?*milqakciqniluni* [cut off his ability?]. If they were sad, they would cause him to fail, they would let him ?*milqakceciiqniluku*.

And he told those people in the *qasgiq* that if he left, they should appoint a person to check on him whenever the fifth song was sung. This was a time when the moon was full, and it was bright outside at night.

If [the one checking] saw something, he told him to quit going out. And if something should appear to them, he told them to stay quietly in the *qasgiq*. Even though they were scared, he told them to be quiet and stay still.

After he instructed them to do that, he went down into the floor door. As soon as he went down, they started singing a song. On the fifth *yuarulluk* [song of incantation], he would go outside [and check].

PETER JOHN: That checker there?

FRANK ANDREW: Yes. Just the way he was instructed, he checked for something on the moon. When the *yuarulluut* were done being sung, they would stop. He would check [the moon].

One of the times when he went out, when he came back in he said the moon, when it ?*taaluicaku* [had no shadow?], when he looked again [when it appeared], he said it looked like a dog, he said it looked like a dog. When he saw the moon as it was shining. When he came in, he told about that, and he never went back outside again.

So they waited without drumming.

After they had been like that for quite a while, vapor burped from the door! It suddenly filled the floor up to the seating section. And going up and down, [the vapor] went down. When it retreated out to the door . . .

PETER JOHN: It quickly went down.

MIISAQ: Taq'erpailuni aptelliniak taukuk. Kiulliniak anertevkanrirniluku.

Pilliniak, "Canrituq tua-i, angumariaqa anertevkarluku, angumariaqa, tua-i anerneringermi canrituq!"

Nutaan tua-i uitaqarraarluni pilliniak nanilrak nalkegnun avvlukek angayuqaak taukuk yuut pamatiitnun pamavet elkarcesqellukek, akluitnek patulukek. Akluitnek ukurmiut tamakut qasgimelnguut patulukek.

Angu iluteqesqevkenakek, umyugaak-wa tua-i angniitesqevkenaku milqakciqniluni. Angniilkagnek tua-i piciurcessngaitniluni, milqakceciiqniluku.

Nutaan alerqullinii qasgimiut waniw' ayakuni iliit paqtaartekaminek piluki, tauna tua-i yuarutet tallimaurtaqata paqtelaasqelluku. Iraluq-gguq tua-i imumek tenguqvigpaumallran nalliini ella tanqigcenani unungmi.

Camek tangerqan anenermek taqesqelluku. Cali-ll' cameg' alangrukata nepaunaki tua-i uitasqelluki qasgimi. Alingengraata tua-i uitasqelluki nepaunaki tua-i.

Tuaten tua-i alerquagurarraarluki amigkun-am kanaqalliniluni. Kanaqauciatun tua-i yuarutmek aturluteng. Tallimaurtaqata-gguq yuarulluut paqtaqluni, an'aqluni tayima.

MUMESS'AQ: Tauna pista?

MIISAQ: Ii-i. Alerquuciatun tua-i iralum tunglirnera kiartaqluku camek. Naagaqata tua-i yuarulluut-llu taukut taq'aqluteng. Paqtaqluku.

Anviirlun' tua-i, itrami pilliniuq iralum-gguq tungiinek taaluicaku iraluq piuq, pinqigtuq, tuarpiaq-gguq qimugta, qimugtengunganani-gguq piuq. Iraluq tua-i tauna ciqinqaumallra nall'arrluku pillermini. Itrami tua-i qanemcikluku anenqigtevkenani-ll' tua-i.

Uitallinilriit cauyaqsaunateng tua-i.

Ak'arrarnun tua-i uitauraqertelluki amiigat aurnermek elciallinilria! Muirrluku tua-i un'a nateq, aqumutet makut ngelkarrluki. Uyungssuarturluni-gguq tua-i acivarluni. Amigmun uavet tua-i qamqerteqertelluku . . .

MUMESS'AQ: Atraqerrluni.

FRANK ANDREW: He had told them to cover the opening with a grass mat by elevating it from the ground. He didn't cover the *pall'itaak* with the real covering.

As soon as that vapor was gone, a nose started to come out from under the grass mat out there. It was a huge nose! It started to come up. When it appeared, it was a huge dog! It was a giant dog!

When it came out, its body had no fur at all! But along its spine back there there was a small amount of fur. And the tip of its tail had a small amount of fur. And its paws had a little bit of fur. And the tip of its ears.

It kept sniffing.

It sat down out there facing the inside [of the *qasgiq*].

That dead person, this was after her parents had gone back there. I forgot to mention, he had also let them take the clothes off that [sick girl] before he went out. They put that person on top of a young bearded-seal skin and a caribou hide, too.

MARIE MEADE: They took the clothing off the dead [girl]?

FRANK ANDREW: He had them take her clothes off, yes. And he let them put her clothes just on this side of her.

It got in a prone position, *?ciuteqerluni*. Moving like this, it went around this way. It was sniffing around.

So those people in the *qasgiq* never made a sound.

When it got to the place where the mother was, I'm not sure which of the parents, when it got to his/her location, [the dog] stood taller. When it stood taller, it sniffed up toward where he/she was.

After it did that, it went around again and went past that [dead person].

When it got to the location of the [other parent] across, it stretched up once again and after it sniffed, it went toward the door, it then faced the inside [of the *qasgiq*] where that naked body was.

It approached her *?ciuterniarturluni* [twitching its ears?]. And when he reached her, sniffing her, it circled her.

When it had gone all the way around her and stopped at her legs, it began to put her lower body into its mouth up to her waist. Chewing on her, it cut her in half. Then it put its head up and began to chew on her. It was making crunching noises! And blood ran down [the sides of its mouth]. On top of those.

MIISAQ: Tupiganek-ll'-am imat'am tauna patua patusqellinikii acia qerrataurluku. Patua patupiaranek pivkenaku pall'itaak.

Aurneq taman' nangqertelluku qengag' ugkuk nuucimaarallinilutek tupigat aciatnek. Qengarpakayallraak-gguq! Tua-i nuuluki tamakut nugngiinarluni. Aliartuq-gguq qimulvall'er! Angtuaq tua-i qimugta!

Nuggliniuq melqungssagaunani qainga! Culugyumikun-gguq taugaam pavaggun melquvyagluni yaavet. Pamyuan-llu-gguq nuuga melqurrarluni. Makut-llu-gguq ipii cali melqurrarluteng. Ciutegken-llu kangkek.

Naru'urturluni-gguq.

Aqumqalliniluni uavet kiatmun cauluni.

Tauna tua-i nalamalria, angayuqaak tagumarilutek tua-i. Ugayarcetliniki-ll' imat'am anvailegmi. Tamakunek tamaa-i inguqirluki, amirkamek tuntumek-llu cali.

ARNAQ: Nalamalria-qaa ugayartelluku?

MIISAQ: Ugayartelluku, ii-i. Aturai-llu-gguq yaavet yaalirneranun ellivkarluki.

Laavellinilria-am waten ciuteqerluni. Waten elliurturluni uivellinilria ukatmun. Naru'urturluni-gguq.

Tua-i nepelkiteksaunateng qasgimiut.

Tauna-ll' tua-i aanii, naliak piagu angayuqak, nallairamiu tauna sugturtellinilria. Sugturcan tua-i pavavet naruralaryaaqellinilria nalliinun.

Pirraarlun' tua-i ataam uivelliniluni qavaggun tauna-ll' ketairluku.

Nalliaramiu-ll' tuamtell' ikna, tuaten-am call' tua-i sugturrluni cali naruraraqluni pirraarluni, anelraami, kiatmun nutaan caullinilria taum matangqalriim tungiinun.

Ciuterniarturluni-am ullagturallinikii. Tekicamiu-llu aug'utun naru'urturluku uivelliniluni.

Kassuamiu-ll' tua-i irugken nalliik, uatek iqmillinilukek qukaakun-llu, qukaa ngellekluku. Tamualuku keplinikii. Nutaan ciuggluni tamuallinikii. Qiaryiggluni-gguq tua-i! Ukugnegun tuaten augmek qurrlullagaluni. Taukut qaingat.

She was alone, her husband had died. Her husband's name was Qugyulek. He was not the real father of Aqumgaciq.

MARIE MEADE: Qucillgaq [Crane] and Qugyulek [One with a swan].

FRANK ANDREW: They both had the name of a bird. Qucillgaq [Crane] and, Qugyuk [Swan], Qugyulek [One with a Swan].

I saw her when they were at fish camp. She was their mother, Qucillgaq. She was a big old woman, she was tall.

MARIE MEADE: And there was a *yugaq*, a person of the forest?

FRANK ANDREW: That *yugaq* was a being of the wilderness. They say there were those kinds of beings in those days. They are called *yugat*.

When that person ran out of [powers], he showed his staff, saying that he was not finished [acquiring them]. But if there came to be ten designs, he would have acquired all of them. He said since the five on there were few, if there had been ten designs he would not have run out of [powers]. That's the way he explained it to him.

Those *yugat* are *ircenrraat*, they are shamans, those are evidently shamans.

They will not kill female shamans[9]

Frank Andrew and Alice Rearden, Anchorage, October 2001

FRANK ANDREW: They will not kill female shamans. They say they cannot, they are too strong for them.

ALICE REARDEN: Are female shamans too strong for male shamans?

FRANK ANDREW: They cannot [kill them], even though they are malicious. They are too strong for them. They say it is because women *qagrumaluteng* [have exploded, referring to their menstrual periods]. There used to be a shaman on this side of my village in a place they called Kangirnaarmiut named Uyangqulriim Arnaan [Uyangqulria's mother].

Uyangqulriim Arnaan. This was a long time ago. They say that woman was a good shaman. And her son Uyangqulria was also a shaman.

Although other shamans used their powers against her, they could not touch her. And she would do surgery on broken bones. While others observed her inside the *qasgiq*, she would heal those with broken bones and serious wounds.

And they say she had a knife, you know how they had wooden implements when they ?*cakel-*

Kiimellillrullinilria, uinga tayim' piunrillrullinilria. Qugyulek-gguq uinga. Aqumgacim atapiaqenritlinia.

ARNAQ: Qucillgaankuk Qugyulek-llu.

MIISAQ: Tua-i-w' yaqulegnek aterlutek tamarmek. Qucillgaq, Qugyuk-wa, Qugyulek.

Tangellruaqa taun' neqlillratni. Aanaklinikii tauna Qucillgaq Arnassagarpakayall'er, sugtuluni.

ARNAQ: Tauna-wa-gguq-qaa yugaq, napamiu?

MIISAQ: Yuilqurrmiutaq-gguq tua-i taun' yugaq. Tamakunek-gguq pitangqelallruuq avani. Yuganek aterluteng.

Tauna-ll' tua-i nangutellermini ayaruni tauna manilliniluku qaqiciiksaitniluni. Qaralii-gguq taugaam tamakut qulngureskata, qaqiciiyartuq. Carraungata-gguq augkut tua-i, talliman ukut imait, nangucanritaa-gguq qulngukata qaralii. Tuaten nalqigtelliniluku.

Ircenrraat-wa tua-i tamakut yugat, angalkuut, angalkuulliniut tamakut.

Tuqusngaitait arnat angalkut

Miisaq Cucuaq-llu, Anchorage, October 2001

MIISAQ: Tuqusngaitait arnat angalkut. Pisciigatait-gguq, arturait.

CUCUAQ: Angucet-qaa arnat angalkut arturluki?

MIISAQ: Umyuarrluungermeng-gguq pisciigatait. Caperqait-gguq. Qagrumiimeng-gguq arnat. Taumek Uyangqulriim Arnaanek angalkurtangqellrulliniuq nunama ukatiini yaani Kangirnaarmiunek aterpagingalriit.

Uyangqulriim Arnaan. Ak'a avani ciuqvaarni. Tauna-gguq tua-i angalkuq assilria arnaq. Qetunraa-w' taun' Uyangqulria angalkuuluni cali.

Angalkut-gguq tua-i piyaaqengermegteggu agturciiganaku tua-i. Navelrianek-llu-gguq pilagturituluni. Tangvagtelluni-gguq tua-i waten qasgim iluani kitugcituluni navelrianek akngirterpalrianek-llu.

Nuussingqerraqluni-gguq imumek, cakelmagluteng iciw' muragnek pilalriit.

magluteng. She had a wooden knife like that. After putting [the blade] inside her mouth and swiping it across, she would then cut open the skin of that person. That [knife] was like steel to her.

She operated on a person who had TB [tuberculosis] when she was an old woman. His parents had brought him to many different shamans and he could not be healed, and having no hope, they told [Uyangulriim Arnaan] that if she healed him, he would be her child. The [parents] gave the child to her. [They said] if he lived, they would always see him anyway because they were from the same village.

She exchanged his lungs for animal lungs; I don't know which animal's [lungs] she used. As usual, she had others watch as she cut him open, his lungs here. And she took out his lungs, and she exchanged them for one of the animal's lungs.

When she'd close it up, when she would do this, it would heal to its original form. She saved him in that way, so that he would become healthy. They say he became her little husband. That one whom she saved became her husband even though she was an old woman.

Before she died, there was a big flood in my village down on the coast. There are many hills behind our village, many hills that water does not reach.

When I began traveling, I saw that there were logs high up on top of the hills, and some of their stumps were visible and covered by land. They say that those drifted there and landed during that big flood. They were [logs] that had drifted ashore along the ocean. I'd see them, too, and those logs were visible and laying ashore on the land.

They say our home area down on the coast was covered by water. The village of Kangirnaarmiut was starting to be covered by water.

She had that boy whom she saved for a little husband, and he was probably older. When water was about to enter the houses, they went outside. She got into the kayak and was back-to-back with that one, and they were going to stay on the lee side of the house.

When the water reached a certain level, one of the people went over to that shaman Uyangqulriim Arnaan and said to her, "Goodness, can you not do something about this water?"

After a while, she said that he should get two sealskin floats, and if there were rocks, he should get two and two sealskin lines.

Tamakucimek nuussingqerraqluni muragmek. Iqmigluku-gguq waten agqaarluku tua-i, kemga-ll' tua-i pilagluku taum. Cavigtun ayuqlun' tua-i elliini tamana.

TB-lriamek-am taumek arnassagarluni pilagturillinilria. Angayuqaagken taukuk angalkunun piyaaqvigmegnek tua-i cangairucan, caperrsagulluku, anirtuqaku elliinun yuk'eciqniluku. Elliinun tua-i waniwa tunluku elkenka. Unguvakan nunalgutekniluku tangaagurciqniluku.

Lung-ai-am cimillinikai pugtautai ungungssilinramek; cam ungungssim pikaki. Tangvagtelluni-am tua-i ullirrluki, ukut wan' qat'gai. *Lung*-aak-ll' aug'arlukek, unguvalriim ungungssit iliita *lung*-agkenek cimirlukek.

Nunutaqamikek-gguq tua-i, waten piaqateng mam'aqlun' waten ayuqucimitun. Tuatnaluku tua-i anirturluku, cangairutelluku. Uiyaaqsagulluku-gguq tua-i tauna. Anirtullni tauna uiksagulluku arnassagang'ermi.

Tua-i-llu tuquvailegmi tuani ulerpiulliniluteng uani nunamni un'gaani. Kelumteni qemit amllertut, qemirugaat, mer'em tekicuunaki.

Ayagayaurtua, maani qemit qaingatni qulvaarni muriit makut nallunaunateng, qamiqunait-llu ilaita pugumaaqluteng, nunam patumaluki. Taum-gguq tua-i nallini ulerpiim tepellri tamakut. Unani cenami tepumayaaqellret. Wiinga-ll' tangaagaqluki tua-i, nallunaunateng muriit nunam akuliini tepumalriit.

Una nunavut-gguq unegna mer'em patullrua tua-i. Kangirnaarmiut tua-i ugkut nuniit atam mer'em mat'um qainginga'artellinikii.

Taumek-gguq tua-i uiyaarluni anirtullminek tan'gaurlurmek, angluni-w' tua-i pillill'. Enet tua-i makut itqatangarcaki anluteng ellamun. Qayamun ekluni alrapaqevkarlun' taumun uqrani enem uitanalutek.

Qaillun tua-i et'utariqertelluku yuut iliita ullagluku angalkuq tauna Uyangqulriim Arnaan pillinia, "Aling aren, usuuq-qaa waniw' man'a meq qaillukuaqerciigatan?"

Uitauraqerlun' pilliniuq, kitaki-gguq qerruinaagnek malrugnek pili teggalqurtangqerkan-llu malrugnek cali, taprualugnek-llu cali malrugnek.

She had them blow up the sealskin float and put a sealskin line on the end with a rock at the end. There were two of them. She told them that when they were done, they should throw the other inside the river of the village and [throw] the other one behind their village.

They complied because she was their shaman.

Those two sealskin floats were filled with air. You probably know what those sealskin floats are. They are those [inflated] seal skins. Two of those.

A person was holding them. Another person was holding the rock which was tied to a line, and they had them [swing back and forth] and throw them in the water.

When the sealskin float hit the water, it was like a rock. It sunk immediately. But that rock skidded when it hit the water. It looked like it was filled with air. The other was like that too.

After letting them do that, she said that she had made a float for the village. And when the water reached a certain level, it stopped going up. But around the village, the water rose.

And those hills back there disappeard when the water got high. The area around the village was like this [like a bowl], and the village was down below. The water level around their village stayed at that level, but the water rose around them.

When they weren't paying attention, before the water receded, while she was sitting in a kayak back-to-back with her little husband, Uyangqulriim Arnaan's face transformed into a walrus. She had become a walrus, and her big tusks were on the side of the kayak.

That's how that female shaman appeared. After a while, they saw that she turned back to her normal self. They say that woman did not let Kangirnaarmiut flood. If she had not done that, with the water being that deep, it would have covered those houses.

Also, they said that she repaired those who were hurt and bleeding. She eventually became unable to walk and stayed inside her home when she became an old woman.

When people were injured, she started to [heal people] in other homes. She'd let them take out a sealskin line and bring it to [those who were hurt], and if it was too short, they would tie another one to it. And they would stick the end onto the body of the person who was hurt and she would suck it out from her house, taking out the bleeding from her house with that sealskin line that was not hollow.

Taprualuk-gguq qerruinarmek qerrurluku iqukliliraqluku teggalqumek iqua picirluku. Malruulukek waten. Taqkata-gguq, taqkagnek unavet nunat kuigata iluanun aipaa egcesqelluku, aipaa-llu pavavet kelulirneratnun.

Angalkuqngamegteggu tua-i maliggluku.

Qertunermek tua-i imarlutek taukuk qerruinaak imkuk. Qerruinaat nallunritliaci. *Sealskin*-at imkut. Tamakucik.

Yuum tua-i tegumiaqlukek. Ingna-ll' teggalquq cali uskuriumaluni, allam call' tegumiaqluk' waten elliurtellukek mermun egtellinilukek.

Qerruinaq-llu tua-i mermun tuc'ami tuarpiaq-gguq teggalquq. Egmianun kit'elliniluni tayima. Teggalquq-gguq taugken mer'em qainganun tuc'ami kat'agluni. Qertunermek-gguq tuar' imalek. Aipaa-llu-gguq tauna.

Tuatnarraartelluki qanlliniuq tua-i-gguq nunat ukut waniw' pugtaucirai. Tuaten-llu tua-i et'utariqerluni meq cakaniirtelliniluni. Nuna taugaam avatiit mayurlun' meq.

Qemit-llu pamkut ipluteng tayim' meq quyigillrani. Nunat tua-i avatiit waten ayuqluni, nunat-wa kankut kanani. Tuaten et'utaurluni nuniit, meq taugaam mayurluni avatiitni.

Murilkevkenateng-am piinanermeggni tuani enpailgan piqalliniut tauna imna Uyangqulriim Arnaan uiyaami alrapaqurallrani, waten qayami, asvinarmek kegginangllinilria. *Walrus*-aarurtellinill', tulurpakayallraak-wa-gguq makuk qayam talirnerani.

Tua-i tanglliniluk'-am tuaten ayuqlun' taun' angalkuq arnaq. Piluteng-am tua-i piuraqerluteng pilliniat ayuqucimitun ayuqlirillinill'. Taum-gguq tua-i Kangirnaarmiut ulniurcetellrunritai arnam. Tuaten et'utaluni enet-wa taukut patuyallinikai pinrilkateng.

Cali-gguq akngirtellrianek tua-i tumarciaqellria, aunralrianek-llu. Kiituan' tua-i kangarciigalilliniuq enem'ini arnassagaurcami.

Akngirtellriartangqerraqata enem'i allami, tuatnalangellinill'. Taprualuk amimikun anutelluku agutelluku-llu, naniteqaan-llu usguluku allamek. Akngirtellriim-llu taum qainganun iqua tugrulluku enem'inek amaken pat'rarluk' aunrallra aneqluku enem'inek amaken taprualugkun tamaaggun, cupluilngurkun.

They say when she was unable to walk anymore, she started to suck out [their sickness] when she couldn't go to them in person anymore. She made a hose out of sealksin line when she became an old woman.

And then her son Uyangqulria, next to our village, not far from our river, we have hills that roll down to the ocean. Beyond them is a small river, a small stream. It has no outlet, and it is only filled by very high tide. And over at the edge of the marshland, on the tip of high ground is a small hill that is quite high. They say that is the grave of Uyangqulria. It is still over there today.

And the old village where he lived, that place is called Nukcaaq. His old village is still there today.

And his boat that he and another person went to retrieve from across the Kuskokwim River is still on top of one of the hills of Kangirnaarmiut. But its [ribs] were weathered by wind. But they are still sticking out a little from under the ground, but covered by land. It was an actual boat that an *angalkuq*, a *tuunrangayak* went to get.

They say the Kuskokwim River became wide on him [as he traveled]. His fellow shaman made that happen. He was trying to let him get into a mishap [and die].

He reached the other side of the Kuskokwim River, traveling with an old woman, with her grandchild as their third passenger.

After spending the night in the dark when they reached the other side, they woke on top of a hill, and the ocean was far down there. Not being able to bring it down [to the ocean], he left it there.

They say that malicious shaman did that to his fellow shaman Uyangqulria.

Kangarciigali'irtellermini-gguq tuaten pat'raturillruuq tungaunani pinanriamiki. Taprualugnek taugaam *hose*-aliluni arnassagaurtellermini tamaani.

Tua-llu tauna qetunraa Uyangqulria, ukaqlirrangqertukut kuimta yaakariini, qemit kanallritnek imarpigmun. Yaalirneratni-w' kuicuayaaq, kuiggayagaq. Anenrunan', ulerpiim taugaam imituluku. Ikani-w' maram engeliini, nunapiim qertulriim nuugani pengurraq waten qertuckeggluni. Taum-gguq tuani Uyangqulriim qungua. Maa-i cali piuluni ama-i.

Nunallri-w' taukut, Nukcaamek aterlun' tauna. Nunallri-gguq yaa-i cali ingkut cali uitaurluteng yaa-i.

Angyallra-w' cali tamana aqvallra Kusquqviim akianek maligluni, Kangirnaarmiut ugkut qemiita qaingatni iliita uitalun' ama-i cali. Makullri taugaam nangluki anuqem. Taugaam tua-i pugumacuarluteng nunamek caqumaluteng. Angalkum taum tuunrangayiim angyaq, yugtaq aqvayaaqellra.

Tua-i Kusquqviim-gguq nequturitellrua-gguq. Angalkuullgutiin taum pivkarluku. Picurlagcetengnaqsaaqluku.

Kusquqvak-gguq tua-i tull'uku, arnassagarmek taumek maligluni, tutgariinek pingayurluteng.

Qavartarraarluteng unugmi tuc'amegteggu, tupalliniut qemim qaingani, imarpik-wa un'a ak'aki unani yaaqvani. Atrautellerkaa tua-i capeqluku unitelliniluku tua-i tamaavet.

Taum-gguq tua-i angalkum ikiulriim piyaaqluku taun' angalkuullgutni Uyangqulria.

That *angalkuq* Uyangqulria became a walrus[10]

Frank Andrew and Alice Rearden, Anchorage, October 2001

FRANK ANDREW: That shaman named Uyangqulria, they had a Kassiyuq [dance festival during which gifts are exchanged between villages]. When the people of Qinaq requested a boat, he had them dance for his boat during the winter. Then when they distributed the gifts, one of the people of Qinarmiut, a fellow shaman took it. He caught his boat.

Asevrurrluni taun' angalkuq Uyangqulria

Miisaq Cucuaq-llu, Anchorage, October 2001

MIISAQ: Augna imna Uyangqulria angalkuq, yurallinilriit Kassiyurluteng. Qinarmiut-llu tua-i angyaryuata angyani tamana yurautekevkarluku uksumi. Tua-i-ll' aruqngameng Qinarmiut iliita taum angalkum cali angalkuullgutiin tegulliniluk'. Pitaqluku tamana angyaa.

Then during summer, across from Tuntutuliak, at the old village of Qilqanermiut, it was a village back then. That shaman who came to own the boat that Uyangqulria distributed during dancing, was living there. That person had caught [the boat].

That person from Kangirnaarmiut who gave it away during the dance festival wanted it back because he did not like being boatless. Because he was having a hard time, he left to go get it, and because he was a shaman.

He arrived at the village of Qilqaneq. The old village was located at the mouth of what they called Kuiguyuq upriver from Iinrayalleq. He was from there. They would harvest and dry salmon there and never moved to other places.

He arrived and saw that his boat was propped up next to [the new owner's] home on land. Because the one who caught it came to own it, he cherished that boat.

He went toward it and reviewed it with his shamanic powers. He saw that it could not be taken by him, that it could not be touched any longer. He would die right there if he touched it. The one who caught it had used his powers to make it untouchable. [The previous owner] could not take it, could not touch it because he would die if he touched it.

When he was thinking of returning home, a person from that village asked him what he was doing there. He told him that he had gone there to get his boat. He said to him, "There are a grandmother and grandchild who want to go to your village of Kangirnaarmiut here, and you can travel with them." He did not reply because of not being able to touch [the boat] himself.

When he showed him who the grandmother and grandchild were, he went to them. When he entered their home, he saw that it was an old woman along with her grandson.

When that old woman saw him, she recognized that Uyangqulria because she knew him, and eagerly welcomed him, asking him when he was leaving, wanting to go with him if he was going by boat. He told her that he went to get his boat, but that it was too bad that he could not take it, that he could not touch it.

After some time, that old woman said that she would have her grandson touch it. When her young grandson came inside, and I don't know how big he was, she asked him to come and dis-

Kiagan-llu tua-i ikani Tuntutuliarmiut akiatni Qilqanermiullerni, taukut nunauluteng. Taukumiungulun' taun' angalkuq piksagutestii taum Uyangqulriim yurautellranek angyamek, angyamek tamatumek. Taum pitaqellrulliniluku tua-i.

Taum yurautekestellran Kangirnaarmium umyugaan teguyunglliniluku, angyaitullni assikevkenaku angyailami. Arenqialami tua-i aqvaluk' ayalliniluni, angalkuungami-ll'.

Tekitelliniuq Qilqanermiunun tuavet. Iinrayallrem kiaqlian Kuiguyumek pitullrata paingani nunallret uitallruut. Taukumiu. Neqliaqluteng tua-i nugtaqtaayuunateng tuani.

Tekitelliniuq elatiini akivingqauralria, mayungqaluni taun' angyaa. Taum tua-i pitaqestiin angyaqsagucamiu kenekluku call' tua-i angyaqluku.

Ullagluku tua-i piyaaqellinia, tuunrangayamikun-am kiarrluku. Piyaaqellinia teguyunaitellinill' elliingulriani, agtuyunairutellrullinill'. Agtuquniu tua-i waniw' tuquciqlinill'. Taum pitaqestellran tuunrangayamikun piyailkucillrullinikii. Taum tegusciiganaku tua-i, agturciiganaku pillinill', agtuquniu tua-i tuquarkaulliniami.

Tua-i uterrnaluni umyuarteqluni pillrani iliita aptellinia cassurluku tekiararucianek. Angyani tamana aqvayaaqniluku. Taum pillinia, "Kitak' imkugnek tutgarqelriignek Kangirnaarmiunun nunavnun cakmavet ayagyulriartangqertuq man'a, maliklukek ayagniartuten." Tua-i kiunritliniluku agturciigalamiu elliin.

Tua-i apertuigakek taukuk tutgarqelriik ullallinilukek. Eniignun tua-i itrami pilliniak tua-i arnassagaurluq tauna tutgaraminek tan'gaurlurmek aiparluni.

Taum tua-i arnassagaam tangerqaamiu, Uyangqulria taun' nallunrilamiu elitaqluku, arenqiatellinikii, qaku ayagarkaucianek, maligcugluku angyakun pikan. Pilliniuq tua-i angyani augna aqvayaaqniluku, taugaam arenqiatniluku, tegusciigatniluku, agturciigatniluku.

Arnassagall'er tauna uitaqerlun' pilliniuq, tutgaraminun-gguq aug'umun agturceciiqaa. Itran tua-i tauna tutgarallerani tan'gaurlucuar', qaill' angtaria tayima, taisqelluku, unatai waten

After laughing out loud, he said to him, "Aasasilek, because he has an *?aasasik*, he will probably cure Usruar with it." Then he laughed out loud again.

He felt no compassion for him whatsoever, but he only laughed at him.

Then when he returned home, at the *qasgiq* at Kangirnaaq, when Aasasilek asked him, because Aasasilek was his grandfather, and I'm not sure who it was, he asked him about Keggsuli.

He said he saw that one who was apparently Keggsuli at Goodnews Bay.

After telling him that, because Aasasilek was his grandfather, the father-in-law of this person [pointing at Puyulkuk's picture], after saying his name, he said, "Even though the *qasgiq* of Goodnews Bay is big, it was too small for me." He asked him for what reason, "Why was it too small for you?"

"My goodness, their shaman, the great Keggsuli over there asked me, 'Is Usruar across there ill?' I told him that he was ill because I wasn't going to lie.

"After laughing, he said to me, 'Has Aasasilek tried to cure him with his powers?' I told him that you have tried to cure him with your powers because you have been. When I told him, he laughed at you, he laughed out loud at you in the *qasgiq*, and there were many people in the *qasgiq*.

"After laughing, he said to me, 'Aasasilek, since he has an *?aasasik* he will probably cure Usruar with it.' He laughed aloud again after saying this. When he said this, because you are our shaman, their *qasgiq* was too small for me to go through, even though it is large." Aasasilek did not say anything but stared at one place.

After a while, he said, "Go and get Usruar." He told them to go get his son-in-law. And he told the two drummers to get ready. He was going to use his powers, he was going to try to cure this person [in the photo, Puyulkuk] with his powers in the *qasgiq*.

Two people went to get him. They brought him inside the *qasgiq*, with his mat underneath him, with people holding him. He had them put him down below the long log support in the *qasgiq*.

When Aasasilek, this person's [Puyulkuk's] father-in-law came down, when they were going to begin, he crouched down and without letting others hear him, he said in his son-in-law's ear, "I am going to cure you because Keggsuli asked me to cure you." He had been trying to cure his son-in-law with his powers before that time.

Engel'allaggaarlun' pillinia, "Usruar-wa Aasasilgem aasasingqerrami mat'ukun anirturciqlikii." Tuamtell' ngel'allalliluni.

Takumcuksugnaunaku, temcikluku taugaam.

Tua-i-ll' utercami qasgimi Kangirnaarmi apcani taum Aasasilgem, apa'urluqliniamiu Aasasilek tauna, naliata taum pillruagu, Keggsulimek aptelliniluku.

Tangerrniluku-wa tua-i qanemcilliniluni ika-i ikna Keggsuliullilria Mamterani.

Pirraarluk' pillinia tauna apa'urluqngamiu Aasasilek, uum cakia, tuqlurraarluk' pillinia, "Mamterarmiut-llu qasgiat angengraan uumi caltuq'aqerpaa." Taum pillinia, "Camek tam picirluten, camek pilriaten caltuq'erciu?"

"Arenqiapaall' ik'umi Keggsulikayagmi angalkuatni, aptaanga waten, 'Akma-qaa tua-i Usruar naulluuguq?' Tua-i iqlungailamku nalqiguskeka naulluuniluku.

"Engel'arraarlun' waten qanrutaanga, 'Aasasilgem-qaa tuunriteksaitaa?' Nalqigulluku tua-i tuunrit'laryaaqngavgu tuunrit'laryaaqniluku. Qanrucamni tuamtell' temcikaaten, temcikluten ngel'allagtuq qasgimi, yugyagluni-ll' qasgi.

"Engel'arrarlun' pianga, 'Usruar-wa Aasasilgem aasasingqerrami mat'ukun anirturciqlikii.' Ngel'allaglun' tuamtell' tua-i waten qanrraarluni. Waten qanran, angalkuqngamteggen wangkuta qasgiat angyaaqelria, caltuq'eraqa." Qaneqsaunani tua-i taun' Aasasilek atauciq tangvallinikii.

Uitaqerluni pilliniuq, "Usruar aqvaqerciu." Nengauni piluku aqvasqelluku. Cauyararkak-llu uptesqellukek. Tuunriqatarluni, tuunritqatarluku qasgimi una.

Aqvalliniluku tua-i malruk. Itrutliniat inguqerluni curuminek, tegulaucirluku qasgimun. Kanavet-llu tua-i tugeryaramun, tugeryaram uatiinun ellivkalliniluk' qasgimun.

Atraami tua-i Aasasilek, uum cakia, waniw' piqatanga'arcata nengaumi ciutiinun pull'uni ukunun niicetevkenani pillinia, "Keggsulim anirtuusqengaten anirtuqataramken." Ciungani tuunrit'laryaaqluku nengauni.

When he used his powers on him to heal him, he used his powers on him right away. He would crouch down and blow on the base of his neck. He would blow on him here [on the base of his neck]. When he began to do that to him, he became more active, and as he sat there, he started to move his head more.

After using his powers on him for a while, he was done. And when he was done, he took off his parka. His father-in-law told him to take his parka off as well. He had him put on his parka, and his father-in-law put on his parka, too.

He finally faced the one who did this to him, Keggsuli. When [Keggsuli] would use his powers on him, he would take them and claim them. He stripped him of his powers in that way. When Keggsuli tried to use his powers on him, [Puyulkuk] would take them when they arrived and would own them.

That shaman from Goodnews Bay no longer was a shaman because his powers were all gone, because this person took them all. They became this person's [Puyulkuk's].

They tell this story. I used to see this person here all the time, my *aparuk*. This person here [Puyulkuk] used to speak to me without caution, and he didn't care whether or not I got embarrassed. [His English name was] Temple. The story is this long.

Tuunricamiu tua-i wanirpak tuunritlinikii. Tarenriryaraanun pull'un' cupurtuagaqluku. Cup'leraluku ukuakun. Cegg'angllinilria atam tuatnangani, takuskeggiluni-ll' aqumgarrarmi una.

Tuunritelnguamiu tua-i taqliniluku. Taqngami-llu atkuni yuullinikuki. Taum uum cakian atkui yuusqelluki, atkua yuusqelluku. Atkuminek acetliniluku, uum-llu atkui elliin cakian taum all'uki.

Uum nutaan tauna pisteni Keggsuli nutaan caullinia. Tuunrangayamikun piyaaqaqani, uum ciuniuraqluki piksagulluki elliin. Ugayarturallinikii tua-i tuaten. Tuunrangayamikun piyaaqaqani Keggsulim taum, uum tekitaqata teguaqluki, elliin piksagulluki.

Tauna im' tuunrangayak Mamterarmiu angalkuunrirluni tua-i, tuunrairucami tua-i, uum nangeng'aki. Uum piksagulluki.

Una watua waniwa qanemciktuat. Una tangaalguluku wii aparuka. Uum waniw' aaqevkenii qalarut'lallruanga, talluryullerkaqa-ll' pivkenaku. Temple-aaq. Waten taktauq.

They called that shaman Neq'ayaraq[12]

Frank Andrew and Marie Meade, National Museum of Natural History, February 2003

FRANK ANDREW: And sometimes the items that were bequeathed by shamans, *pinguarcuutait* [items used by shamans to request an abundance of resources], I used to see ones from Qinarmiut that were *pinguarcuutek* [two items used by shamans to request an abundance of resources], that were *aciliurcuutek* [two items used for checking what was below] that belonged to shamans, two wooden common loon models.

They would hang those two wooden common loons up there only during Kassiyuq [Dance Festival] up along the sides of the window beside each other. They would hang them when they had Kassiyuq.

When they placed them there, they'd continually go in a circle and they'd come to a stop. And

---

Neq'ayaramek pilaraat angalkuq tauna

Miisaq Arnaq-llu, National Museum of Natural History, February 2003

MIISAQ: Angalkut-ll' iliini paiciutait, pinguarcuutait, Qinarmiutaagnek tanglallruunga pinguarcuutellregnek-gguq aciliurcuutellregnek, angalkut piklukek, tuulleguagnek.

Kassiyumi taugaam yurami elliaqlukek pikavet egalrem avategkenun akiqliqlukek, muriik tua waten tuulleguak. Agarrlukek Kassiyuraqameng.

Tua-i taugken elliicetek uivvaarturlutek, arulairlutek. Piyungamek-llu uivlutek caullutek

sometimes they would go in a circle again and face each other and come to a stop. They were amazing. They didn't just randomly [move], even though there was no one controlling [their movement].

They would store the common loon models so that they would not break. They say they were bequeathed by a former shaman of Qinarmiut.

They called that shaman Neq'ayaraq. Yes, one who ran away to the Yukon. They say those common loon models were his *aciliurcuutek*.

And in the summer, when salmon were going to be abundant on the Kuskokwim, some people would see those two. They were kayakers and had wooden visors. They'd be down [on the water], especially across there when Qilqanermiut was a village. Across from Tuntutuliak on the other side of the Kuskokwim River, upriver from Kuiguyuk.

At the mouth of Kuiguyuk, where its mouth used to be, around those old villages, I used to see Qilqanermiut. That village there. It was called Qilqanermiut. They say the two of them would appear to people there. Two kayaks would be down from the bank. But then they would start sinking downward. Eventually they'd disappear into the water.

Then after disappearing for a while, a pair of common loons would appear farther away from the shore. Then they'd fly away.

They said they didn't do that all the time. They'd do that when there were going to be many salmon, they'd appear and be seen when the Kuskokwim was going to have an abundance of salmon.

They were the *aciliurcuutek* of [that shaman], the two common loon models. They'd see them as kayakers in the summer on the Kuskokwim River wearing wooden visors.

His fellow shamans lied about him, saying he had malicious intent, and made people start to torment him. Shamans were jealous of him for helping people.

When they were going to kill him, they apparently let him go to the Yukon. He left his children. And that summer, he went and got his childen from the Yukon River.

They say after a number of years, his three sons arrived at Qinaq. But Qinarmiut couldn't stop them at all even though they destroyed things.

They did that on purpose so that they would retaliate for their father if the people there should lay their hands on them. [People of Qinaq] left

arulairlutek. Irr'inaqlutek. Piciatun piyuunatek pistaileng'ermek.

Tua-i tuulleguak qemagtaqlukek tua-i pilluggngaunakek. Paiciutek-gguq taum angalkullrata Qinarmiut.

Neq'ayaramek pilaraat angalkuk tauna. Ii-i, Kuigpagmun qimaalleq. Aciliurcuutellrek-gguq tua taukuk tuulleguak.

Cali-llu kiagmi Kusquqvak-gguq neq'liqatarqan tangtulukek yuut ilaita. Qayaulutek-gguq elqiarlutek-llu muragnek. Atraumaaratuuk, ikani arcaqerlutek Qilqanermiut nunaullratni. Tuntutuliarmiut akiatni Kusquqviim akiani Kuiguyuum nuniini, kiatiini.

Kuiguyuum paingani, paillrani nunallret ilait, taukut tua Qilqanermiullret tanglallruanka. Taukuullinilriit. Qilqanermiunek aterluteng. Tuani-gguq tua-i alangruutullruuk taukuk malruulutek. Qayag' atraumaarlutek ekviarmek maaken. Kisngiinarlutek-gguq taugken acitmun. Kiituan' tua mermun pulauk.

Tua-i-llu muluqerlutek kanaggun ketvaarkun tuullgek puglutek. Tenglutek-llu-gguq tua-i nutaan.

Pirrlainayunatek-gguq. Neq'liqatarqan-gguq tua-i tuatnatullinilutek, alangruulutek Kusquqvak neq'liqatarqan.

Taum aciliurcuutellrek, taukuk tarenrak tuulleguak. Qayaulukek tangrraqlukek kiagmi tamaani Kusquqvagmi elqianek aturlutek.

Angalkuullgutain-gguq iqluqutekluku umyuarrlugniluku, nakukengevkarluku yugnun. Angalkut ciknakluku ikayurillra pitekluku yugnek.

Tuquteqataatni tua-i, tuquteqataatgu ayagcetellrulliniat Kuigpagmun. Irniari unilluki. Kiakuan-llu-gguq irniari aqvaluki qakmaken Kuigpagmek.

Allrakut-gguq qavciurteqerluki, qavciurrluki Qinarmun tekitellruut taukut qetunrai pingayun. Taugaam-gguq qaill' tua-i pisciigatellruit Qinarmiut navguingraata canek.

Pitsaqluteng ataseng tauna akinaurutnaluku yageskata, pikata tamakut. Uitatellruit-gguq

them alone when they understoond their intention. Even though they destroyed things, they didn't chastise them, since his three sons were intimidating.

They say those two common loon models were what he bequethed to Qinarmiut. He instructed them to use them when they'd have Kassiyuq until they were gone.

MARIE MEADE: When you saw those two [common loons] twice was it during Kevgiq [the Messenger Feast] or Iturka'ar [dancing with masks]?

FRANK ANDREW: I saw them when they had Kevgiq. I didn't know what they were at first. That's what they said about them. My dear grandfather, when I didn't know what they were, this person's [Peter John's] dad told me what they were when I asked him. He said their former shaman bequeathed them. They were his *aciliurcuutek*, the *aciliurcuutek* that he used.

The common loon models had just skin hangers. They were skin. He said they would store them away. They didn't mess with them and hung the two up.

When they were hung, they would remain in place syncronized. And when they wanted, they would go in a circle and face each other. And when they faced each other, they remained still. And when they didn't do that, they would be in opposite directions. They would [rotate] again when they wanted. He said they were amazing to see. Like that, they wouldn't hang still. Whenever they wanted to, they would rotate slowly, and stay in place with their backs to each other.

MARIE MEADE: Did you see them before you got married?

FRANK ANDREW: I wasn't big. But I watched them [dance] when I started to observe things closely.

When they wanted fish to be abundant, they would let shamans *aciliurluki*. And he wasn't the only one [to do that]. They were making what they would catch more available. They also wanted fish that they would obtain to be more available. They call it *aciliurluteng* [shamans checking below to make prey more available].

PETER JOHN: They wanted the entire Kuskokwim River to have an abundance of fish.

FRANK ANDREW: They wanted the fish to be available for the people who fish.

tua-i taringamegteki. Navguingraata canek qanleratevkenaki, uluryanaqngata taukut qetunrai pingayun.

Taukuk-gguq tua-i paiciutellrek tuulleguak Qinarmiunun. Tua-i alerquullukek piunrirviagnun Kassiyuraqata pilaasqellukek.

ARNAQ: Tuani-qaa taukuk tangllerpekek malrurqugnek kevgillratni wall'u-q' itrukarallratni?

MIISAQ: Kevgillratni tangellruagka. Cauciicaaqekegka-wa. Nalqigtellrukegket tuaten. Apa'urlurluma-w' imum cauciitellemkek, uum atiin nalqigtellrukek apyutkellemni cauciagnek, cauciagnek taukuk. Taumun tua-i angalkullratnun paiciuteknilukek. Aciliurcuutek-gguq, aciliurcuutellrek.

Tuulleguak waten tua-i agautarrarlutek qecignek. Qeciuluteng tua. Qemagtetulukek-gguq tua-i. Qaillukuaqevkenakek-gguq tua-i agartetulukek taukuk.

Tua-i-llu-gguq agarcacetek nutaan aug'utun tua-i maligyagullutek-llu-gguq uitaurnaurtuk. Piyungamek-llu uivlutek caullutek. Caucamek-llu uitaurlutek. Pinrilmiamek-llu-gguq kipullgullutek waten. Ataam [uivlutek] piaqlutek piyungaqamek. Irr'inaqlutek-gguq. Tuaten tua-i, uitaurlutek agayuunatek. Piyungaqamek tua uivnginaararaqlutek, tunuyullutek-llu uitauraraqlutek.

ARNAQ: Nulirturpailegpet-qaa tamaani tangellruagken?

MIISAQ: Angevkenii. Taugaam tua murilketarilua tangvallruanka.

Neqnek piaqameng paivngasqumaluki aciliurcetetullrulliniit angalkut. Kiimi-ll' taun' pivkenani. Pitarkait paivngarcarluki. Neqet-llu unakarkait paivngasqumaluki. Aciliurluteng-gguq.

MUMESS'AQ: Kusquqvak tamalkuan neqengqerresqumaluku amllernek.

MIISAQ: Paivngaliluki pisqumaluki yuut neqsutulinun.

I saw masked dancing a number of times[13]

Frank Andrew, Peter John, and Marie Meade, National Museum of Natural History, February 2003

FRANK ANDREW: They say when shamans *pinguarluteng*, they reveal those *yugat* masks. And when they were done dancing, the owner of the mask described the purpose for the mask.

I saw masked dancing a number of times. The male dancers were wearing masks.

PETER JOHN: The men who danced. A woman would dance, but a man would wear a mask.

I joined those [dancing like that], too. I wore a mask and was paired with a woman and danced. There might have been three women dancing. I sat next to them and danced. Then I stopped dancing.

FRANK ANDREW: And when they were done dancing, the shaman who owned the mask would then explain the purpose for those masks and what they do. I saw [masked dancing] in Bethel and Napaskiak.

MARIE MEADE: Those dancing with masks?

FRANK ANDREW: Yes, I also watched [masked] dancing in Qinaq. In those three places. They explained the purpose of those masks because they owned them.

MARIE MEADE: What did those masks that you saw depict?

FRANK ANDREW: They varied. Those masks didn't exactly look like something. Two of the masks had a dark line across the face [on the cheeks and nose]. It was a wide [line] underneath the eyes, this way painted with dark paint [across the cheeks].

MARIE MEADE: Did you see many masks there?

FRANK ANDREW: There were two, or there might have been three. The third one was biting onto something. I saw Qaluvialler a lot at that time. I watched that person [when he danced].

MARIE MEADE: When he was explaining [the mask]?

FRANK ANDREW: Yes, the *agayuq* [mask] that he made. He apparently saved his fellow shaman when he used his powers, the one whose name is Yugauyulria.

After asking him to look toward him, he told that person, after showing him that one that seemed to be biting on a *cupluarngalnguq*

Qavcirqunek wii tangtullrulrianga kegginaqurluteng yuralrianek

Miisaq, Mumess'aq, Arnaq-llu, National Museum of Natural History, February 2003

MIISAQ: Angalkut-gguq pinguaraqameng alaituit taugaam yugat tamakut kegginaqut. Tua-i-ll' yuraumariameng caliarit nalqiggluki taum pikestiita kegginaqut.

Qavcirqunek wii tangtullrulrianga kegginaqurluteng yuralrianek. Angutngunertat-wa augkut kegginaqurluteng pillrulriit.

MUMESS'AQ: Angutet yuralriit. Arnaq yurarluni tua-i waten, angun taugaam kegginaqurluni.

Wiinga-llu ilagautellruunga tuaten pilrianun. Kegginaqurlua arnamek aipiullua yurarlua. Arnat pingayuulliut tayim' yuralriit. Wii tua-i caniatnun tua-i aqumlua yurarlua. Tayima-ll' tua-i yurayuirullua.

MIISAQ: Yuraumariata-ll' tua-i taum angalkum pikestiita nalqiggluk' nutaan, nalqigtetulliniluki camek caliangerruciat kegginaqut tamakut. Mamterillermi tangvallruunga Napaskiarmiuni-llu.

ARNAQ: Kegginaqurluteng yuralrianek?

MIISAQ: Yaa, Qinarmiuni-llu call' tangvallrulua. Taukuni pingayuni. Nalqigtaqluki tua-i tuani tamakut kegginaqut pikngamegteki tua-i.

ARNAQ: Canguarullruat tamakut kegginaqut tangelten?

MIISAQ: Piciatun-wa. Augkut kegginaqut qaillun ayuqenricaaqellriit. Augkuk malruk maaggun tungulriamek kep'arlutek kegginaquk. Iqtuluni maani iinguag' ukuk aciagni ukatmun, tungulriamek minguumaluni.

ARNAQ: Amllerrluteng-qaa kegginaqut tuani tangller[peni]?

MIISAQ: Malruullrulriik-wa taukuk aren, pingayuullruyugnarqut. Pingayuat camek keggmiaruarluni. Qaluvialler augna tangaamallruaqa. Tauna tua-i pillrani tangvallruaqa.

ARNAQ: Nalqigcillrani?

MIISAQ: Ii-i, agayuliaminek. Angalkuullgutni augna anirtullrullinia tuunrillermini Yugauyulriamek at'lek.

Tauna tua-i qanrutellrua takuyangcarraarluku tauna manimaluku, cupluruarngalngurmek keggmialek. Yugauyulria takuyangcarraarluku

[something that looks like a pipe]. After asking Yugauyulria to look toward him, he told him that if this [mask] hadn't saved him, he would not be seen there. He said [the mask] he was holding saved him. I don't know how he [saved him]; that Yugauyulria was actually a shaman himself.

That person didn't reply to him. Qaluvialler apparently saved him when he was near death. He said that he would have died if [that mask] hadn't saved him, that he wouldn't be seen again.

MARIE MEADE: Did that mask have some [design]?

FRANK ANDREW: It was probably a *cupluyagaq* [straw, pipe] and had small line designs on it.

MARIE MEADE: At what village?

FRANK ANDREW: At the village of Qinaq.

MARIE MEADE: What about in Napaskiak, did you recognize those who were explaining [the masks]?

FRANK ANDREW: Unrapik, another shaman named Unrapik. That person also described them, that those two were his *aciliurcuutek*. Well, he said that they were for [requesting an abundance] of food.

It was a red fox mask along with a white fox mask. Two men danced wearing those masks. He said what I just said, that they were his *aciliurcuutek*. Maybe they were for requesting an abundance of fish.

Ayalpik from Bethel also explained [the purpose of a mask]. He also said that the two were for requesting the abundance of fish. I don't know what the two were, I don't know what they were made to depict. The masks looked like humans. The ones in Napaskiak, one was a white fox and the other one a red fox.

MARIE MEADE: What about in your village?

FRANK ANDREW: They never had [a masked dance] in my village, I never saw them. I didn't know what they were doing, but they told me that they would explain the purpose of their masks.

I watched them at Qinaq during the winter, and also in Napaskiak, all during winter. And in a very large *qasgiq* in Bethel before they no longer had a *qasgiq*. They never [danced] again after that.

They danced like you do today. There were many people, that very large *qasgiq* was full of people.

MARIE MEADE: They called it *agayuluteng* [masked dancing] then?

FRANK ANDREW: Yes. They probably had Itruka'ar, I don't know. When they danced with masks, it was probably when they *pinguarluteng* [shamans requested an abundance of things through masked dancing].

pillrua uum pinrilkaku tangrruuyanritniluku. Uumun taugaam anirtullruniluku. Qaill' piluku pillruagu, angalkuuyaaquq call' tauna Yugauyulria.

Kiullrunritaa tua-i taum. Qaluviallreraam taum anirtullrullinia tuquqataryaaqellrani. Taumun tua-i, taumun pinrilkaku tuquyarniluku, tangrruuyanritniluku.

ARNAQ: Tauna-qaa kegginaquq camek [qaralingqellruuq]?

MIISAQ: Cupluyagauyugnarquq kep'aruarrarluni qaralirrarluni.

ARNAQ: Camiuni tuani?

MIISAQ: Qinarmiuni.

ARNAQ: Napaskiarmiuni-mi elitaqellruaten-qaa taukut nalqigcillratni?

MIISAQ: Unrapik, Unrapik cali angalkuq. Tauna call' tua-i pillruuq, aciliurcuuteknilukek augkuk. Neqnek-wa tua-i pissuuteknilukek pillruuq.

Kaviaruar' augna kegginaquq uliiruarmek aiparluni. Kegginaquk, angutek yurarlutek taukugnek kegginaqurlutek. Aug'utun tua-i qanruteklukek aciliurcuuteknilukek. Neqnek-wa pillilriik, neq'liurcuuteklikiik.

Mamterillerni-ll' im' Ayalpik cali nalqigcillruuq. Cali taun' neq'liurcuuteknilukek tamakuk. Caugak-wa augkuk, canguaruak-wa. Yugngacaaquk tua-i kegginaquk augkuk. Taukuk tua-i Napaskiagni uliiruarulliniluni aipaa, aipaa-ll' kaviaruaruluni.

ARNAQ: Nunavceni-mi?

MIISAQ: Nunamteni piksaitut, tangvallrunritanka. Caciicaaqekenka tuatnatunillrukait taukut nalqigcilriit tamakunek kegginaqumeggnek.

Qinarmi uksumi tangvallruunga, pimi-llu Napaskiagni-llu, uksurrlainarmi. Mamterillerni-llu qasgiirupailgata qasegpall'er. Tayim' kinguani taum pinqigtevkenateng.

Yuralaucirpetun yurarluteng. Yugyapiarluteng, taun' qasegpall'er tua-i muirumaluni yugnek.

ARNAQ: Agayuluteng-gguq-qaa tuani?

MIISAQ: Ee-m. Itruka'arluteng-wa pillilriit, qaill' piat. Tuatnaaqameng-wa tua-i pitungatlinilriit kegginaqurluteng piaqameng, caaqameng, pinguaraqameng-wa pitullilriit.

MARIE MEADE: And you told us about Unrapik from Napaskiak. And you [Peter] danced there with a mask as well?

PETER JOHN: But I never heard anyone explain [the meaning of a mask] after that. . . .

MARIE MEADE: You probably danced when they danced with masks for the very last time.

PETER JOHN: Yes. They stopped [masked dancing] in our village around the 1920s. I think it was in the 1920s, in the early 20s. I think it was one of the Moravians who stopped it in Kwigillingok before 1920.

ARNAQ: Napaskiarmiunek tuaten Unrapigmek qanrutaqluta. Tua-i-llu-q' elpet tuani call' yurarluten kegginaqurluten?

MUMESS'AQ: Taugaam nalqigcilriamek niitellrunritua taum kinguani. . . .

ARNAQ: Aipaagni nangneqlikacaarmek pillratni kegginaqurluten yurallrulliniuten.

MUMESS'AQ: Ii-i. Avani arulaillrulria nunamteni. 1920-m natiini. 20-m iluani pillruyugnarquq, 20-iurrnerrarluku. Ukut wani Moravian-aat taugaam iliita arulairrngatellrua yaani Kuigilngurmi, 20-rpailgan.

Those they called *angalkut* used to explain the masks after using them[88]

Frank Andrew, Bethel, December 2003

FRANK ANDREW: Those they called *angalkut* used to explain the purpose of masks after using them. They didn't make [masks] for leisure. Ordinary people did not create masks, but only shamans revealed the masks. And after having them wear them when they danced, they'd explain their purpose. They always explained their purpose, and didn't just use them for no reason.

   That is why there is an admonishment not to use a mask to dance when one isn't a shaman. The shamans reveal them because they belong to them. And they'd let [people] wear them, and I used to watch them down the coast.

   That is why those who were composing songs for dancing would compose songs, and they would only end them with *yii-irrii* endings. They composed [songs] that were not ones of shamans. And those shamans would [compose] their own songs. And they would explain the meanings when possible and would reveal masks with them and let them wear them.

Kegginaqut-wa makut imkut angalkunek pilallrita aturraarluki nalqigcetullrukait

Miisaq, Mamterilleq, December 2003

MIISAQ: Kegginaqut-wa makut imkut angalkunek pilallrita aturraarluki nalqigcetullrukait. Ellmikun-am piyuitut. Yuunginaat kegginaqunek piyuitellruut, angalkut taugaam alairiluteng makunek kegginaqunek. Aturtelluki-ll' yurarceqaarluki nutaan kangiit nalqigtetuit, nalqigtetullruit. Nalqiga'arterrlainatullruit, ellmikun-am pivkenaki.

   Taumek inerquusngayaaquq angalkuuvkenaku kegginaqumek aturluk' yuraasqevkenaku. Angalkut pikngamegteki alailarait. Aturtelluki-llu tamaani, wiinga-ll' tangvalallruluki uani.

   Yurarcuucilriit taumek imkut piliameggnek yurarcuucirluteng, yii-irriirluki taugaam nangyararluteng. Pililuteng angalkurtaunrilngurnek. Angalkut-llu tamakut pimeggnek ellaita yuarutmeggnek. Kangiit-llu tua-i piyugngaaqamegteki waten kegginaquuluki-ll' alairaqluki, alairluk' aturcetaqluki.

Qaluvialler found and made a lot of wood available[15]

Frank Andrew, Peter John, and Marie Meade, National Museum of the American Indian, February 2003

FRANK ANDREW: That one [in the photo], this person [Qaluvialler] was a shaman. He did a rite

Qaluvialler nalkulluni tua-i muritellruuq tua-i amllernek muragnek

Miisaq, Mumess'aq, Arnaq-llu, National Museum of the American Indian, February 2003

MIISAQ: Angalkuuguq tauna, una wani. Muraguallruuq tua-i tuani Kuigilngurmi

requesting an abundance of wood [as a shaman], *muraguarluni*, while he was living in Kwigillingok, *equguarluni* [he did a rite requesting an abundance of wood]. He found and provided a lot of logs.

Yes, he constructed an *agayu* [mask]. When the wind was blowing from the south, the wind smelled of wood pitch as the logs were about to float ashore.

MARIE MEADE: Was this after he *muraguarluni* [did a rite requesting an abundance of wood]?

FRANK ANDREW: The smell of driftwood logs was wonderful.

We were told not to take wood while they were afloat before they reached their destination. We only began to take them when the wind along with the high tide floated and beached them ashore.

PETER JOHN: Only when it left them, when the water left them.

FRANK ANDREW: We were admonished about them while they were down on the ocean, not to take them as they are afloat, but they took the ones that were brought inside rivers.

MARIE MEADE: So since they don't know where they were going to drift ashore while they're afloat, where they would end up, since they're still on their journey.

FRANK ANDREW: Our area would get a supply of driftwood every spring. Sometimes there would be a lot of wood.

Qaluvialler was fun to watch when he danced, too. And while he was drumming, as he was drumming, he would groan loudly and intensely.

When he would drum alone inside the *qasgiq*. When the people of Kwigillingok would have him drum, he would groan loudly as if in pain.

Qaluvialler composed this song, honoring the spirit of the wood[16]

Frank Andrew and Marie Meade, Anchorage, September 2005

MARIE MEADE: You apparently also know the song that was composed by Qaluvialler.

FRANK ANDREW: [The song by] Qaluvialler? Which one?

MARIE MEADE: The song you sang recently [when I visited you in Kwigillingok].

FRANK ANDREW: Is it the *agayu* [request song] he composed?

MARIE MEADE: Perhaps it is. [The song composed by] Qaluvialler.

---

uitallermini, equguarluni. Nalkulluni tua-i muritellruuq amllernek tua-i muragnek.

Ii-i, agayuliluni. Ungaliarluni tua-i pillrani muragnek angerniriluni anuqii, tepsartullratni, tepqatallratni muriit.

ARNAQ: Muraguarraartelluku?

MIISAQ: Muriit tepiit narniqpiarluni tua-i.

Muriit-ll'-am pugtaluki inerquutekellruaput tegusqevkenaki ciunipailgata. Anuqem taugaam tua-i tepluki ulmek taperluni tepumariaqaki nutaan tegulangtuluki.

MUMESS'AQ: Unitaqaki taugaam, mer'em unitaqaki.

MIISAQ: Una'anlluki inerquutaqluki, pugtaluki tegusqevkenaki, taugaam kuignun itqerrutellrit teguaqluki.

ARNAQ: Natmun-qaa aterrnginanermeggni natmun teplerkaat nalluamegteggu, natmun ciunillerkaat, cali tua-i ayiita.

MIISAQ: Nunavut un' muriquratullruuq tua-i, up'nerkat tamalkuita. Iliini amllerrluteng piaqluteng muriit.

Yurarluni cali anglanarqelliniuq una wani Qaluvialler. Cauyaraqami-ll' cauyainanermini yuuniapagnaurtuq tua-i cakneq cauyainanermini.

Kiimi cauyaraqami tua-i qasgimi. Kuigilngurmiut tua-i tuaten cauyarcetaqatni akngirtellriatun tua-i yuuniapagnaurtuq qastuluni.

Mat'umek agayulillruuq muraguarluni Qaluvialler

Miisaq Arnaq-llu, Anchorage, September 2005

ARNAQ: Qaluvialleraam-ll'-am yuarutii nallunritlinian, yuaruciara.

MIISAQ: Qaluvialleraam-qaa? Cakuciq-tanem?

ARNAQ: Icivaq-wa atullren.

MIISAQ: Agayuliallra-qaa?

ARNAQ: Pilliuq. Qaluvialleraam.

FRANK ANDREW: Is it the song that goes, "It's growing *a-yii-yarraa*?"

MARIE MEADE: Yes.

FRANK ANDREW: It is growing *a-yii-yaraa*

It is growing *inga-yaraa-nga-yaa*

Ayii-ggyaa-aa-ya-ya yuraayaa

Yii-ii-rrii

My spirit,

Peer into the upper part of Kuskokwim River,

It is beginning to be covered with wood.

Ayii-ggyaa-aa-ya-ya yuraayaa

Yii-ii-rrii

Qaluvialler composed this *agayu* [request song], *muraguarluni* [honoring the spirit of the wood, to ask for an abundance of wood].

Qaluvialler [composed the song] when he lived in Kwigillingok briefly.

He composed the song right before [the driftwood was abundant in our area]. It was back in those days when a lot of driftwood used to drift ashore in our area. That one particular time [after he composed the song] lots of driftwood came to our area. The great Qaluvialler.

MARIE MEADE: What do you mean by *eqilluni*?

FRANK ANDREW: Pieces of driftwood came, a lot of driftwood was available.

MARIE MEADE: Oh, there would be a lot of driftwood around.

FRANK ANDREW: Yes.

The second [verse] talked about the Yukon River.

MARIE MEADE: Asking one to peer into the Yukon River.

FRANK ANDREW: My spirit of being,

Peer into the upper part of Kuigpak River,

The shore along the river down there,

The area up there is now covered with driftwood.

Ayii-ggyaa-aa-ya-ya yuraayaa

Yii-ii-rrii

Okay. [You] dance.

It is growing *ayii-yaraa*

It is growing

Ingaa-yaraangayaa

Ayii-ggyaa-aa-ya-ya yuraayaa

Yii-ii-rrii

You can learn to dance this very quickly because you know how to dance.

MIISAQ: Naularauq a-yii-yarraa-qaa?

ARNAQ: Yaa.

MIISAQ: Naularauq a-yii-yaraa

Nulaularauq inga-yaraa-nga-yaa

Ayii-ggyaa-aa-ya-ya yuraayaa

Yii-ii-rrii

Yugiiyamaa

Kusquqviim kangia qamna uyangesgu

Muragnek qallinguq qamna

Ayii-ggyaa-aa-ya-ya yuraayaa

Yii-ii-rrii

Mat'umek agayulillruuq muraguarluni

Qaluvialler.

Qaluvialler Kuigilngurmetqallermini.

Piqatallra tuani nall'arrluku. Eqitetullrani. Eqitellermini tua-i muriit amllepiallruut. Nall'arutellruuq-am piqatallrani. Qaluviallerakayak.

ARNAQ: Qaill' eqilluni?

MIISAQ: Muriit-wa tua-i tekilluteng, murilluki.

ARNAQ: Oh, murilluni.

MIISAQ: Ii-i.

Kuigpagmek aipirluku cali [apallillrua].

ARNAQ: Kuigpak uyangtesqelluku.

MIISAQ: Yugiiyamaa

Kuigpiim kangia qamna uyangesgu

Cenii-am un'a

Qalliinguq-am qamna

Ayii-ggyaa-aa-ya-ya yuraayaa

Yii-ii-rrii

Kitaki.

Naularauq ayii-yaraa

Nulaularauq

Ingaa yaraangayaa

Ayii-ggyaa-aa-ya-ya yuraayaa

Yii-ii-rrii

Eligarcukaaralriaten-wa yuratulriaten.

He looked and saw that it was Apaqassugaq without eyes[17]

Frank Andrew and Marie Meade, National Museum of Natural History, February 2003

FRANK ANDREW: They lied about him, they began to loathe [Apaqassugaq]. They came to the point where they killed him.

The ones who killed him returned to the *qasgiq* and went in, and that one who they killed was sitting down in his usual place in the *qasgiq*. After telling that part, the ones who tell the story say, "Being so agile, that one got into a mishap."

When they came upon him as he was traveling in the wilderness, they would kill him and butcher his body, and leave him scattered. They say they would arrive to see that he had already returned.

One day, they pried his eyes out and placed them inside a lamp and put it upside down in that old village.

They went back and arrived and saw that he was gone. They thought that he had been murdered for good.

While a person who went to fetch some food from their fish camp was in his aboveground cache, he saw a person standing up there on the back wearing snowshoes. He looked and saw that it was Apaqassugaq. He had no eyes, with hollow eye sockets. But on this part of his face, side-by-side on his temple was something sparkling. It was apparently his eyes. He thought, "So this is how this person disappeared."

MARIE MEADE: He got another set of eyes.

FRANK ANDREW: Yes. Even though that person wanted to talk to him, since he had heard that they stop speaking when they talk to the dead, while he was just thinking that to himself, that one up there said, "You will not stop speaking, even though you speak to me. There is nothing wrong with me, and I am not frightening. I can return to my home back to you all because there is nothing wrong with me. But I won't return home for the sake of children who might be terrified because of my eyes up there. There is already someone who will inherit my powers across the ocean. Do not believe [it is me] even though they name the children here in our area Apaqassugaq. He hasn't yet been born across the ocean. I am going to him now."

The village of Kangirnaarmiut used to be situated down the coast from Platinum long ago. That

Pillinia Apaqassugaullinilria iingunani-gguq

Miisaq Arnaq-llu, National Museum of Natural History, February 2003

MIISAQ: Iqluqutekluku tua-i, kenkenrirluku [Apaqassugaq]. Kiituan' tua-i pivakarluku yagtelliniat tua-i tuqulluku.

Tuqucetellri taukut uterrluteng qasgimun itliniut uitayaramini qasgimi aqumgauralria, im' tuqutellrat. Pirraarluteng-am tuaten qanemcilriit pilartut, "Piqunqessiyaagaqluni picurlalliniuq tua-i tauna."

Temii-llu navgurluku tua-i ciamlluku yuilqumi piaqan ayangssillra nall'arrluku tuqucaaqaqluku saggluku tua piciatun unitaqluku. Tekitnaurtut-gguq ak'a tekitellrullinilria.

Caqerluku tua-i, iik taukuk ikugglukek kenurramun eklukek palurutlinilukek kenurramun, nunallerni tuani.

Tua-i uterrluteng tekicaaqelliniut tayima tua-i. Tua-i nutaan tuqucukluku umyuarteqluteng.

Neqsaalriim taum neqlillermeggnun qulvarvigmi piinanermini piqalliniuq pikani iquani yuk pik' nangerngalria tanglugnek aturluni. Pillinia Apaqassugaullinilria. Iingunani-gguq, iik imaunatek. Ukugni-gguq taugaam qevlerpallaralriik akiqliqlutek ayakutaraan. Cunawa-gguq iik tua-i taukuk. Umyuarteqliniuq, "Waten cunaw' piluni pikna catairutellria."

ARNAQ: Allagnek iingluni.

MIISAQ: Ii-i, qanrucungermiu tua-i uum nalamalrianek-llu waten qalaruciaqata qanyuirutetuniluki niitelaami, umyuarteqluni piqanrakun, pikna pilliniuq, "Qanyuirusngaituten qalarutngerpenga. Qaill' pinritua, alingnarveqkenii-llu. Utercugngayaaqua nunamnun elpecenun qaill' pinrilama. Mikelngurnun taugaam tatamurratek'larnayuklua iigka pakemkuk piteklukek uterteqatanritua. Mer'umavigkangellruunga ak'a imaam akiani. Maani nunamteni Apaqassugarmek mikelnguut aterpagtaalangraitki ukveryaqunak. Imaam akiani akma piurteksaituq. Ullakataraqa taugaam waniwa."

Kangirnaarmiunek Arviirmiut uaqlingqellrulliniut tamaani avani ciuqvani.

was the place where the one who would inherit his powers lived.

Because he could not find [his eyes]. They were actually underneath that lamp turned upside down.

After telling him that, when he took a step, they said it was during the winter in cold weather. When he would step down, he would make a crackling noise. He was outside. Wearing snowshoes, he traveled toward those capes, [including Cape Newenham].

After a while, among those Kangirnaarmiut, one of them had a baby boy.

When he got a little older, at a certain age, he began drumming. When he began drumming, he would sing Apaqassugaq's *yuarulluut* [shaman songs].

That was his *mer'umavik*, the one who would inherit his powers. That is as much as I heard. Because shamans are very powerful.

I used to listen to storytellers in the *qasgiq* when I wasn't doing chores. There are many stories, but I cannot tell them when I don't know the whole story. Because I always did chores in the *qasgiq*, watching out for those who might ask for help. But when I began to work with wood, I then began listening to the complete stories in the *qasgiq*.

ANN RIORDAN: Thank you.
MARIE MEADE: Yes, thank you very much.

Tuani-gguq, taukuni-gguq cunaw' tua-i tauna mer'umavigkaa.

Nalaqesciigalamikek [iigni] tua-i. Cunawa-gguq tuani kenurrami palurusngalutek pimallinilriik.

Tuaten taugaam qanruqaarluku amllian, uksumi-gguq tua-i waten nenglem nalliini. Tut'aqan qiaryigtaqluni. Ellamenani-gguq. Tanglura'arluni tayim' ayallinilria ikegkut nuuget tungiitnun.

Taukut tua-i Kangirnaarmiut piinanratni iliit tauna irnilliniluni tan'gaurlurmek.

Angliqerluni atam angliluni tua-i qaill' pitariqerluni cauyalangellinill'. Cauyalanguq-gguq Apaqassugaam yuarulluinek atuagaqluni.

Tua-i taungullinilria mer'umavia, mer'umavigkaa. Tuaten cali taktaluku niicugnila'arqa. Tuunrangayak tukniyaaqngami caqtaallra.

Qasgimi qanengssaaralriit tua-i kevgiunritaqama niicugnilallruanka. Qanemcit amllerrsaaqut, taugaam iqupkuuluki qanemcikesciigatanka. Kevgartuagurluta pitullruamta qasgimi, ellimeqlirarkat tua-i murilkurluki. Calianek taugaam calilangama qasgimi nutaan niicugnilangluki iqukliciiluki qanemciitnek.

ELLAQ'AM ARNAAN: Quyana.
ARNAQ: Mm-m, quyanaqvaa.

He was regarded as an *alairumanrilnguq* [one who kept himself concealed][18]

Alairumanrilnguq-gguq tua-i

Frank Andrew and Marie Meade, Washington, DC, February 2003

Miisaq Arnaq-llu, Washington, DC, February 2003

FRANK ANDREW: But there was a place that was occupied during that time in a river called Iluqaaqniq. . . .

A man named Esiseq who had a wife lived there. He was a man who absolutely didn't like going after animals. He didn't like to hunt.
MARIE MEADE: What did they call the place where he lived?
FRANK ANDREW: Iluqaaqniq, Iluqaaqnirmiut. He would move to Kangirnaarmiut in the winter. He lived there during fall. It was said Esiseq was a *caangrayak* [not an ordinary person].
MARIE MEADE: Esiseq. His name sounds like a name unheard of and not an ordinary name.

MIISAQ: Augna taugaam Iluqaaqniq yungqelallruyaaqelliniuq tamaani. . . .

Esisermek, angutmek nuliarluni-ll'. Pitangyuyuitqapiarmek-gguq angutmek. Pissuneq assikevkenaku.
ARNAQ: Nunallra tauna camek piaqluku?

MIISAQ: Iluqaaqnimek, Iluqaaqnirmiunek. Kangirnaarmiunun wavet kacetetuluni. Uksuilleqluku-gguq tua-i taum. Caangrayauluni-gguq taugaam taun' Esiseq.
ARNAQ: Esiseq. Atrani-ll'tanem allayuggauvaa.

FRANK ANDREW: It was just a place where he stayed in the fall. They say he was totally unafraid of other shamans, even though they were malicious. When he got a little agitated by them, he'd cast stronger force on them, pressing them down flat. The shamans were wary of him and left him alone, even though he never used his power in public. He was regarded as an *alairumanrilnguq* [lit., "one who kept himself concealed, using his power secretively"].

MARIE MEADE: Were the shamans who used their power in public referred to as *alairumalriit* [those who were visible and did their work with people watching them]?

FRANK ANDREW: Yes. That was his fall settlement.

It was a place where he stayed in the fall harvesting blackfish. Afterward he'd move to the old village of Kangirnaarmiut. And his wife was barren and couldn't conceive.

One time when he and his wife were going home through lower Cavuneq, after picking blackberries inside that river, down below them . . . Oh, excuse me, they were going up inside [Kelliq River] just when the water was going out, to pick blackberries. And just before they reached an area where there was tundra along the upper Kelliq River, they saw a beluga whale up ahead swimming along down the river toward them.

Then his wife said, "Gosh, look at the animal coming in our direction, and it's unfortunate, you don't even have a weapon!" And just when they were about to meet it, he shoved his paddle in the mud on the riverbank and pushed, while tipping the kayak to one side allowing the beluga to swim by.

Then his wife blurted out to him, "My goodness, are you not going to go after it as always?" He was silent. As the beluga continued along, it brushed its body against [their kayak] and swam by. His wife, [wishing to get the animal], continued to complain. After it swam by, they continued on.

And another time he came upon a bearded seal perched out in the open. At that time he actually wanted to take action in pursuit of the animal, and he was about to. [Whenever he went out on the land], they say he always brought his wife along. When he saw the animal on a lump of earth along the Ilkivik River, since it wasn't too muddy, while [the seal] was on top of the lump of earth, he poked his paddle in, and just when he was about to disembark he stopped and stood still.

MIISAQ: Uksuillerraqluku taugaam. Angalkunek-llugguq alingesciiganani umyuarrliqengraata tua-i. Passiaqluki umyuani pirrlugaqan. Angalkut-llu pisciiganaku capeqluku tuunriyuilengraan. Alairumanrilnguq-gguq tua-i.

ARNAQ: Tuunritulit-qaa tangvagtelluteng alairumalrianek pilarait?

MIISAQ: Ii-i. Taum-gguq tua-i uksuillri.

Uksuarmi neqsurvikluku can'giirnek. Kacet'aqluni Kangirnaarmiunun, Kangirnaarmiullernun. Irniangyuunani-ll' nulirra.

Cavunerkun-am uaqlirkun caqerluni, kangranun unavet, nuliani-llu malikurlutek tan'gerpagqaarlutek utertellmegni, unaggun-gguq tua-i. . . . Tan'gerpagtellermegni imat'am asgurluk' imairutqatarluku tua una-i. Nunapik taman' tekiteqatarluku, Kellirmek atlek, kangra, cetuamek pairkengyartullinilriik pequarturluni cetulriamek.

Pillinia nulirran, "Aling arenqia, caskuunak tua-i arenqiateqatalria!" Pairteqatanga'arcamegnegu agaavet marayamun anguarutni kapulluku taum, akianek-am cingluku qayani uv'ayagtelluku ukatmun avitelliniluku cetuaq.

Nulirran-gguq pilraa, "Aling, tua-i-mtaq piqatanritan?" Kiuksaunaku-gguq. Keliglukek tua-i agturlukek kitullinilukek. Nulirran-wa-gguq taum arenqiacaaqekii. Kituan' nutaan ayallinilutek.

Tuamtell' maklaarmek ugtarcilliniuq. Tuani-gguq tua-i pitangyukaryaaquq, piqataryaaquq. Nuliani-gguq malikuratua.

Qarmam qaingani ugtamek Ilkivigmi, ketiinun tua wavet, pika-i tua-i qarmam qaingani uitallrani, maraskilan man'a anguarutni kapulluku, sugturrluni yuuqataqerluni-am uitanga'artelliuq una.

In a moment he said, "Nga, oh how I wish to have some young bearded seal meat!" His wife said to him, "My gosh, you aren't going to go after it like usual, are you?" He replied, "People don't catch young bearded seals in the middle of summer." He just left the young bearded seal perched there.

And again another time after they had gone deep inside Ilkivik River, up beyond Merr'aq River and above the long straight stretch along the river, and they were going back downriver toward home. At that time the water was high in the Ilkivik River. Right before they reached the mouth of Iiqaquq River they saw a herd of caribou coming down toward the long straight stretch [along the Ilkivik].

His wife said, "Move quickly and go after them while they are within reach and easy to get. They are almost down on the edge of the river!"

Then he quickly replied, "Leave them alone, they'll get to the edge when they're ready." Then as usual he just left them alone. They say that's how Esiseq was. He never got excited when he saw animals, and he didn't try to catch them. Those who knew him have said that he never pursued animals that presented themselves to him like that because he knew they were placed there by the other shamans [to try to kill him].

MARIE MEADE: He knew what was going on.

FRANK ANDREW: Yes, he knew. He knew that if he [struck the animals with a weapon], he would only hurt himself.

Uitanga'arteqerluni ngarraalliniuq, "Nga, maklaaryugpaa-ll'!" Nulirran-am pillinia, "Aling arenqia, piqatanritan-emtaq-qaa?" Kiugaagguq, "Kiapagmi maklaarcuitut." Unitelliniluku maklaar ugtalria.

Taumtell'-am pavavet Ilkiviim kiatinun, kiaqvaarnun, Merraam kiatiini, nakrem kiatiinun, ayangssilutek-am pirraarlutek utertelliniuk. Imartuluni-gguq Ilkivik. Iiqaquq taun' tekiteqatarluku tuntut atam unegkut kanaryartullinilriit nakerkun.

Nulirran pillinia, "Cukangnaqluten pikina piyunarqellratni. Tut'eqatartut!"

Kiugartaa-gguq-am, "Uitaski tuc'ungkuneng tuciiqut." Ilangcivkenaki-am tua-i. Tuaten-gguq tua-i ayuquq tauna Esiseq. Pitangyuyuunani. Pilaraat-gguq taqukiutekngamiki-gguq tamakut angalkut tamakut piyaaqengraatni piyutai.

ARNAQ: Nalluvkenaki.

MIISAQ: Ii-i, nalluvkenaki. Tamakut pikuniki ellminek akngirtarkaungami.

....

Nasgauq watched Qumaqniq of Kwigillingok who let the people burn him[19]

Frank Andrew, Peter John, and Marie Meade,
Washington DC, February 2003

FRANK ANDREW: Shamans were so fascinating to watch in those olden days. They would burn, using wood, large piled wood. They would burn outside, not in the *qasgiq*.

That woman, Nasgauq apparently watched Qumaqniq, who let the people burn him at Kwigillingok. She tells about that.

He was drumming in the *qasgiq* looking for wood. So he was looking [for wood].

When he finished drumming, when he was going to be burned, there was a lot of snow at that time. He revealed the spot where a log was. He said that he would put a marker on it, something they

Nasgaum tangvallinia Qumaqniq Kuigilngurmi yaani ekuavkalleq

Miisaq, Mumess'aq, Arnaq-llu, Washington DC,
February 2003

MIISAQ: Angalkut-am irr'inaqluteng pilallruut ak'a. Ekuagaqluteng murganek murirluteng ellilararpagnek. Ellami ekuagaqluteng, qasgimi pivkenateng.

Aug'um tangvallrem Nasgaum arnam tangvallinia Qumaqniq Kuigilngurmi yaani ekualleq, ekuavkalleq. Qanemcik'laraa.

Cauyarluni-gguq qasgimi muragkaminek yuarluni. Yualliniluni.

Taqngami-llu-gguq tua-i cauyarraarluni ekuaqatallermini tuani qanikcarpagluni-llugguq. Murak tamana nunii apertulliniluku. Nallunailkucirciqniluku camek, camek tua-i

could recognize. He pointed out its location to the two who would get it. It was under the snow. So he revealed where it was.

He said that a snowy owl would be perched where it was located, a female snowy owl, the kind [of owl] that is spotted.

When the two who went to get it left and were approaching it, as it got close, they saw a snowy owl perched on top of the snow down below where the tundra becomes marsh.

So when they were just about to get to it, because it got to the point where it couldn't look at them any longer, it flew off.

So when they got to that spot on the snow where it had been perched, they shoveled it.

They found a really nice log right under that spot, a driftwood log.

It is said that they took home a whole log and used all of it as firewood and didn't leave any part of it unused.

So he did an incantation at that time in the *qasgiq*.

So when they said that they were taking him out and because they were curious, just when the sun was setting, they went out to watch him. This was before the village moved.

They brought him up. He was wearing a seal-gut rain parka with a belt over it. And he was wearing fish-skin mittens. He was also wearing wading boots. He was using two walking sticks [one in each hand]. There were two people who were holding his arms as they went up to that place.

Just across there, just farther down from what they used to call Kuicuar, there was a high narrow piece of tundra stretching inland; so on top of that ground, just a little farther up from the village. They put down large wood piles. They used that entire log that had been chopped.

There was a breeze from the north.

They put kindling on each of its corners. And their corners were ?*cakelvagluteng*.

And they said when he got there, just before they were lit, on the north side, on the north side of the corner, he would kneel down and bow his head, and circle farther following the rotation of the universe, whenever he bowed on their corners.

When they were done, those two let him climb up on top of the wood pile.

He stood up facing the east. And he inserted his staff, striking it down on top.

So finally they lit those [piles of wood]. So the fire began to get bigger.

nallunritarkamek. Nunii apertulliniluku aqvastekagkenun. Qanikcam maa-i akuliini. Apertulliniluku tua-i.

Anipamek misngastengqerciqniluku nallii, arnacalumek, kukupcilriamek imumek.

Ayiimek tua-i taun' tekicartulliniak aqvastek taukuk, canimellilliniuq anipa im' misngauralria qanikcaam qaingani ingigutem ketiini.

Tekiteqataagni tua-i qitngayungami tengllinini.

Tekicamegnegu tua-i tauna qanikcaam qainga misngavillra, qanikciurluku.

Murakegtaarmek nalkutlinilutek caman' nalliini, tep'armek.

Cali-ggur-am ilakuiluki murak taugaam tua-i tamalkuan-gguq ut'rutetuat, tamalkuan-llu murakluku, ilakuivkenaku.

Tuunrillinilria tua-i tuani qasgimi.

Anutniatgu tua-i paqnayuami, akerta teviqatarluku, anlliniluteng tangvagyarturluteng. Nunat itraquvailgata.

Itrautellinikiit. Imarnitegnek-gguq aturluni naqungqalutek. Arilluugnek-llu aturluni. Ivrucignek-llu aturluni. Akiqliqelriignek ayarurluni. Malruulutek-gguq tass'uqu'urluku, tegumiaqluku itrarluni.

Ikegkut-wa-gguq, uani Kuicuaraam, Kuicuarmek pilallrata ualirnerani, nunapig' augna iqtuvkenani qertulun' kelutmun; tamatum-gguq tamaa-i qaingani, nunat kialirneratni. Ellilarilriit-gguq angtuanek ellilaranek. Murak taman' tua-i nangluku tua-i eqiurumalria.

Negeqvarmek-gguq anuqliarluni.

Kangiraitgun-llu-gguq tua-i ayagyaaqucirluki. Cakelvagluteng-llu kangirait.

Tekicami-llu-gguq tua-i taum qaqican kumarpailgata negeqvalirnermi, negeqvalirnermi kangiraagkenun ciisqumiggluni put'aqluni, ella maliggluku uivkaniraqluni, pusngaaqan kangiraitni.

Qaqicata tua-i taukug'-am uuggun pilukek mayurcetliniluku ellilarat qaingatnun.

Nangertelliniluni calaraq cauluku. Ayaruni-ll' kapulluku, qainganun tugqaulluku.

Nutaan tua-i kumartelliniluki tamakut. Keneq tua-i angliriyartullinilria.

MARIE MEADE: Those he had circled, they lit them?

FRANK ANDREW: Yes. When the fire grew, it engulfted those large piles of wood.

When the fire got to that person, where a wind hit that flame, it started to extend upward. So the flame completely engulfed that person. And the smoke started to go right straight upward.

When the flame engulfed him, the smoke went right straight up. The wind could not blow it away, even though it was blowing quite a bit.

When it got high, the smoke split in two. One side went south and the other one to the north against the wind. The two smoke columns were blown away.

So as they watched, that person became red hot, he became red hot like steel.

When those stacks of wood were burned thin, they crumbled and fell. When they fell, that person fell with them.

When that happened to him, they told them to go inside [the *qasgiq*]. Those who were tending to him told the people to go in.

PETER JOHN: So no one would watch him anymore?

FRANK ANDREW: Yes. They told them not to go in and out; they told them to settle inside.

PETER JOHN: They probably followed what he had told them to do.

FRANK ANDREW: So they watched him when he did that to that extent.

It was that his seal-gut parka was stuffed with wood shavings. His wading boots were also stuffed with wood shavings. Those that are highly combustible.

And he had an Arctic hare hooded garment with the fur on the outside, as a second garment outside of the seal-gut parka. That fur that is easily singed by fire.

So all night long, they drummed; they would stop and rest. And they would start again.

They say those who go through that [drum] all night. And just when the sun comes up, those who had burned arrive. When the sun came up, he arrived. They pulled him up from the door out there.

So closely examining him, they took off his clothing. They were looking for spots that a fire might have singed, spots that the fire singed.

And his seal-gut parka was not even singed or his fish-skin mittens or his wading boots. There were no spots that were singed by the fire. And his Arctic hare parka wasn't singed at all.

ARNAQ: Tamakut uivqaqullri kumarrluki?

MIISAQ: Ii-i. Amllerriami tua-i kenrem caquluki taukut ellilararpallraat.

Yuk taun' tekicamegteggu, kener' imna anuqem pillra naparrngiinalliniluni. Kenrem tua-i caqulliniluku taun' yuk. Aruvii-llu naparrngiinarluni.

Caquani tua-i aruvak qulmuraqapik tua-i waten mayullinilria. Anuqem tengtesciiganaku anuqlirrlung'ermi.

Quyigiqerluni-llu-gguq, tua-i aruvak avvluni waten. Aipaa ungalatmun ayagluni, aipaa-ll' negeqvatmun anuqa pairrluku. Tengllukek aruvak, aruviik.

Tangvainanratni tua-i yug' imna tauna kenrurtellinilria, cavigtun tua imutun kenrurrluni.

Taukut tua-i ellilarat amiliameng igtelliniluteng. Igcata tua-i yuk tauna malikluku tayim' igtelliniluteng.

Tuaten-gguq tua-i piami itresqait. Nayurtain taukut itresqelluki tangvalriit.

MUMESS'AQ: Tangvagtairutesqelluku?

MIISAQ: Ii-i. Anqetaarluki pisqevkenaki; elkarcesqelluki tua-i.

MUMESS'AQ: Picirkiutii tua-i-w' aturluku pillilriit.

MIISAQ: Tua-i-gguq tuaten pitalriamek tangvallruat.

Cunawa-gguq imarnitek taukuk ekiangqellinilriik canallernek. Ivrucik call' taukuk canallernek ekiarlutek. Imkunek ekuaqeryukaarnek.

Negilirkanek-llu-gguq melquit laqliqluki qasperluni, tunglirlutek taukuk imarnitek. Kenrem tua-i lek'aryukaarkainek melqulget imkut.

Unugpak tua-i cauyaumallinilriit; arulairluteng uitaaqluteng. Ayagniraqluteng ataam.

Tuaten-gguq tuaten pilriit unugpak pituut. Akerta-ll' tua-i pit'eqerluku tekilluteng tamakut ekuallret. Akerta tua-i pitqertelluku tekilluni. Nugtelliniluku tua-i amigmek uaken.

Yuvrirturluki tua-i aturai tamakut ugayalliniluku. Lek'allranek kiarqurluteng, kenrem lek'allranek.

Taukuk-llu-gguq imarnitek naugg'un tua-i qellugaringavkenatek, arilluuk-llu taukuk, ivrucik-llu taukuk. Tua-i kenrem piqallranek cataunatek. Taukut-llu atkuut negilirkat, naugg'un lekaumalriamek pitaunateng.

He told me that he had watched that. I wonder why they did that, let themselves be burned?

And they apparently watched him when he *egavagluni* [cooked inside a big pot]. Before they moved from Kangirnaarmiut, in a time I did not know, before I was born.

They burned five igneous rocks on the fire. And they brought a wooden *alvik* [type of bowl] where he would sit inside the *qasgiq*. They filled it with water about this deep.

When they became red hot, they pulled [the rocks] out [of the fire] and dipped them in that water. The water started to boil heavily.

Then he put his arms inside his *qaspeq* and sat on those red hot [rocks].

When he got inside, they would use holders to take the molten [rocks] over. When they'd put them under him, it would start boiling from between his fingers and toes.

He would put [the rocks] inside there through his legs. But nothing would happen to his hands. He *egavagluni* [cooked] inside there as they called it.

He also saw that person [do that], that man by the name of Qumaqniq.

MARIE: So is that the name of that person who let them burn him, Qumaqniq?

FRANK ANDREW: Qumaqniq. So with what looked like a meat roasting fork, they'd poke him a number of times here on his legs, they poked him.

When they would jab him repeatedly, from inside the bowl, there would be a striking noise.

PETER JOHN: Yes.

FRANK ANDREW: And on the other side too. They used what looked like roasting forks that were sharp. They were checking to see if he was done cooking.

PETER JOHN: They were frying him. [*chuckles*]

MARIE MEADE: And they say at Nanvarnarrlak, there was also an *egavatuli* [one who would get cooked inside a big container using his shaman ability], or one who did that.

[Ingallak] would walk on top of the water and go across using snowshoes at Nanvarnarrlak[20]

Frank Andrew, Peter John, and Marie Meade, Washington, DC, February 2003

FRANK ANDREW: I also heard about Ingallak.

Taumek tua-i tangvallruniluni qanemcitellruanga. Caaqameng tua-i tuatnatuat, legtelluteng?

Tuamtell' egavallrani tangvallrulliniluku. Kangirnaarmiunek agqurpailegmeng, nallumni tayima tua-i, yuurpailegma.

Iingarnanek-gguq tallimanek kenermun ekuavkarluki. Alvigmek-llu-gguq unglukaanek qasgilluteng cali muragmek. Mermek-gguq imirluku qaill' tua-i et'utaluni.

Kenrurcata-gguq taugaam tuani nutaan nuggluki tuavet mermun akurrluki. Qallarvangluni-gguq tua-i.

Aliirluni-llu-gguq tua-i aqumvikluki kenruringalriit taukut.

Eklermini-gguq call' tuani, tegullicirluki kenret agutaqluki. Aciirluki-gguq waten elliaqaceteng-gguq maavet qallarvanga'arrnaurtut yuarain akuliitgun.

Amlemikun-gguq uuggun ek'aqluki tuavet. Unatai-gguq taugken cakaniqsaunateng. Egavagluni-gguq tuavet.

Taumek call' tangvallrulliuq, Qumaqnimek taumek.

ARNAQ: Tauna-q' tua-i ekuavkalleq, Qumaqniq?

MIISAQ: Qumaqniq. Tua-lli-wa-gguq maniarutngalngurmek iruaken'gun uuggun kap'laqiit, kapkiit.

Tuguaraqata-gguq camaken qantam iluanek tuguaraqluni.

MUMESS'AQ: Ii-i.

MIISAQ: Akiakun-llu cali. Maniarutngalngurnek-gguq cingikegglutek. Uumatassiarluku-gguq.

MUMESS'AQ: *Fry*-arluku. [*ngel'artuq*]

ARNAQ: Nanvarnarrlagmi-llu-gguq tuaten pitulimek egavatulimek, tuaten-wa pillermek pitangqellruuq.

[Ingallak] mer'em qaingakun tanglura'arluni-gguq qerarnaurtuq tuani Nanvarnarrlagmi

Miisaq, Mumess'aq, Arnaq-llu, Washington, DC, February 2003

MIISAQ: Niitelaqeka-llu tauna Ingallak.

They say during summer when he'd use his shaman powers, when they'd ask him to use his shaman powers, [he'd go] across the river to the village, he would put on snowshoes and lace them up.
Then he would go across walking on water, *angalkilluni*. He'd put on his hood and really bundle up as
if it was winter, and this was during summer.

He would walk on top of the water using snowshoes and go across there at Nanvarnarrlak.

I used to hear about him when they told stories
about him.

And when he'd go up to the village and get on
land, after taking off [the snowshoes], he would
face the village across, and his whiskers would be
frosty. His name was Ingallak.

Even in summer, he would make it cold and
travel through the cold.

He fled upriver and became a resident of
Ayimqeryararmiut when he became an old man.
Ingallak. He was originally from the Akula area.
He was probably from that place, Nanvarnarrlak.

His namesake is at Kasigluk. Ingallak's namesakes are from Kasigluk.

MARIE MEADE: Some time ago when he was
really sick, he almost died. When he gained
awareness, he said that when he was about to gain
consciousness, [with] Nanurqalria or someone,
he said that he came up somewhere around the
former village of Nunacuarmiut. When he came
up, he regained consciousness. He is still alive
over there. After being in a coma, he regained
consciousness. When he regained consciousness,
he got well.

FRANK ANDREW: Ingallak?

MARIE MEADE: Ingallak. Someone, maybe
Nanurqalria, someone was with him when they
came up somewhere near the former village of
Nunacuarmiut. Just recently. That former village.

He said that he came up there at that time.
That's what he said when he regained consciousness. They said that he had said that.

PETER JOHN: He probably came up by his village. That
was probably his home village.

FRANK ANDREW: He was probably from that village.

PETER JOHN: They tell stories about Ingallak. He had
experienced that, too.

That person said that they made masks at his
village. That person went to get something, too. Do
you know that? The thing that Ingallak hunted, do
you know it? When he went hunting for a snowy
owl.

Kiagmi-gguq waten angalkitaqami
ikavet, kuigan tamatum akianun nunanun
angalkungcaraqatni, tanglugnek at'aqelria
cingirlukek-llu. Merem-llu tua-i qaingakun
piyualuni qerarluni, angalkilluni. Nacarluni,
umciggluni, uksutun tua-i kiagmi.

Mer'em qaingakun tanglura'arluni-gguq
qerarnaurtuq tuani Nanvarnarrlagni.
Niitelallruaqa qanemcikaqatgu.

Nunamun-llu-gguq tagluni nugngami
aug'arraarlukek kinguneni ikegkut caunaurai
ungai kanerluki, cikumaluki. Ingallak-gguq.

Kiagungraan-gguq nenglengevkarluku,
nenglekun ayatuluni.

Qimagluni-w' tauna qavavet
Ayimqeryararmiungurtellrullinilria
angukaraurrnermikun. Ingallak.
Akulmiunguyaaquq. Taukumiungullrullilria-wa
tua-i Nanvarnarrlak.

Atra Kassiglumi uitalria. Kassiglurmiut
Ingallak'laqait.

ARNAQ: Qangvar'-am naulluqapiarluni
tuquyarpiallruuq. Ellangami-ll' tua-i
qanlliniluni camani tua-i cacini nallullerminiu
ellangeqatallermini kitumun Nanurqalriamun,
kitumun-am Nunacuarmiullret natiitgun
pugellruniluni. Pugngami-ll' tua-i ellangluni.
Ama-i cal' unguvauq. Cacini nallumarraarluku
ellangluni. Ellangami-ll' tua-i assirluni.

MIISAQ: Ingallak?

ARNAQ: Ingallak. Kitumun, Nanurqalria,
kitumun malikluku pugetniluni, pugniluni
Nunacuarmiullret natiitgun. Maa-i-rpak.
Nunallret.

Pugniluni tuani. Ellangami qanerluni. Tuaten
qanerniluku.

MUMESS'AQ: Nunamikun-wa pillilria. Nunakellikii
tauna.

MIISAQ: Taukumiungullrullilria-wa.

MUMESS'AQ: Ingallak-wa tua-i tauna
qanengssakaulalria. Tuacetun-am pillrullinill' cali.

Taukut-llu-w' uitavii kegginaqillrunilaqai
taum. Tauna call' tua-i cakarculleq tua-i tauna.
Nalluan-qaa? Ingalliim call' pissullra, nalluan?
Anipasullra.

FRANK ANDREW: I don't know it. That shaman?

PETER JOHN: Yes. They also used to tell about that.

FRANK ANDREW: I haven't heard about him hunting snowy owl.

PETER JOHN: When they used to dance wearing masks.

FRANK ANDREW: I see.

PETER JOHN: They made masks. They did not have materials to make designs [attachements, decorations] on masks. You know, they didn't have anything to make designs on them.

It must have happened at Nanvarnarrlak.

FRANK ANDREW: Probably.

PETER JOHN: And somewhere near Nanvarnarrlagmiut, there was always a snowy owl on a hill. It was probably just farther up from there, somewhere there. Near there.

They did not have anything to [decorate] them with, and they did not have down feathers, since they used to make them really attractive.

So those people encouraged Ingallak to hunt that snowy owl.

I think he had two people go and check on [the hill]. In the day time. He would let them check on it.

Ingallak was using his spirit powers inside. Those two would go and check that area back there.

After a number of times, when the two went to check on that snowy owl; before [Ingallak did an incantation], before he left, he let them check on that snowy owl. There was one there as usual. So he kept letting them check on it, he was doing an incantation.

During one of the times he checked and as he was watching it, that snowy owl collapsed. It fell back, it had collapsed.

When he mentioned [that it collapsed], he told him to get it. So he went to get it and brought it down and brought it inside the *qasgiq*.

They got some wing feathers to use. So they now had material to decorate the masks. He went to get *qamurautet* [things to decorate with] at that time.

At the present time, they probably cannot do that anymore. That is what I heard about Ingallak.

FRANK ANDREW: And they said Kuicaraq somewhere near the village of Nunapitchuk, under it, he caused its mouth to get some fish, broad whitefish from the Yukon River. They said the outlet of Kuicaraq never used to have that kind of fish before that. He, Ingallak, made it come to have that kind of fish.

MIISAQ: Nalluaqa. Angalkum-qaa taum?

MUMESS'AQ: Ii-i. Cali-am qanemcik'lallruat.

MIISAQ: Niiteqaqsailkeka tang tuaten anipassullrani.

MUMESS'AQ: Tamaani-w' yuratullermeggni kegginaqurluteng.

MIISAQ: Aa-a.

MUMESS'AQ: Kegginaqiluteng. Qamurautekaunateng. Iciw' qaralircissuutekaunateng.

Nanvarnarrlagmi pilliuq.

MIISAQ: Pillilria-wa.

MUMESS'AQ: Tauna-llu Nanvarnarrlagmiut natiitni penguq tauna anipataicuunani. Kiatiitni tayim' pillilria, natiitni pia. Canirneratni.

Cakailameng tua-i qivyukaunateng-llu, imkut kenuggluki pilaameng.

Tauna-am anipa cingutelliniluku Ingallagmun taukut pisqelluku.

Paqtaarcirlun' taugaam malrugnek pilliuq. Erenrani. Paqcetaqluku.

Tauna tua-i qama-i tuunriluni Ingallak. Taukuk tua-i tangrraqluku kia-i.

Qavciliriluni tua-i paqtellragni tauna anipa tauna im' tua-i; pivailegmi taun' ciuqlirmek ayagpailegmi paqtelluku tangertelluku tauna anipa. Tua-i-am pitarluni. Paqcetaqluku tua-i piluni, tuunriluni.

Qavciliriluni tua-i anluni taum tangvakanrakun anipa taun' kitngulliniluni. Kitnguluni tua-i, kitngukunaulria atam tayima.

Qanrutekngaku pilliniuq aqvasqelluku. Aqvaluku tua-i anelraulluku qasgimun-llu itrulluku.

Niss'unga'arrluteng. Qamuranga'artut. Qamurautekassaagluni tuani.

Maa-i mat'um nalliini tuatnasciigacugnarqut. Tuaten-am cali niitela'arqa wii Ingallak.

MIISAQ: Kuicaraq-llu-gguq paugna Nunapicuarmiut natiit, aciat, igyaraa-gguq neqngevkallrua, akakiingevkarluku Kuigpagmiutarnek. Tamakungqessuitellruyaaquq-gguq Kuicaram igyaraa. Elliin-gguq Ingalliim akakiignek neqngevkallrua tamakunek.

PETER JOHN: That shaman was powerful.

So that's what is told of Ingallak at Kasigluk. And whenever he wanted to eat fresh fish, he probably went to get some. [*laughs*]

MUMESS'AQ: Angalkuq tauna tuknilliniuq.

Tuaten-am taugaam tua-i qanemciuguq Ingallak qamna tua-i qama-i Kassiglumi. Nutaranek-llu-w' neryugaqami aqvat'lallilria. [*ngel'artuq*]

While he is sleeping, through his *tarnaq*, he'll reach a different level of awareness where he can experience things[21]

Tuaggun-gguq ellangarkauluni qavamini, tarnamikun

Frank Andrew and Marie Meade, Anchorage, September 2005

Miisaq Arnaq-llu, Anchorage, September 2005

FRANK ANDREW: When [a shaman] sleeps, when he sleeps and loses conciousness, through his *tarnaq* [soul, spirit, tiny human figure resembling its owner], he'll reach a level of awareness where he can experience things in his sleep.

MARIE MEADE: What you call *alangrut* [ghosts] in Yup'ik, are they the deceased appearing to you in their physical form? Are the shamans the ones who have the power to make these apparitions appear to regular humans?

FRANK ANDREW: Shamans had apparitions [appear to people], they made them appear all the time. I, myself, personally knew that [shamans] could do that, since I caught them in my lifetime.

Those *carayiit* [extraordinary beings], our fellow people who died, when living humans see them in their physical form they call them *carayiit*. But they can't walk or run since they don't possess life. The form can't walk, since it wasn't filled with its *tarnaq*. But a shaman [with his power] helped it to move, and it could go from here to there very easily.

MIISAQ: Tua-i tauna qavaraqami, cacini nalluyagulluku qavaquni, tuaggun-gguq taugaam ellangarkauluni qavamini, tarnamikun.

ARNAQ: Alangrut-qaa tua-i tamakut tamaa-i tememegteggun pimalriit? Alangrut-qaa tuunrangayiim caliaqai?

MIISAQ: Tuunrangayiim-wa tua-i pivkalallrullinikai alangrut, paivngavkarluki. Wiinga-ll' tangvagluki nalluvkenaku tua-i, angullruamki augkut tamakut.

Carayiit tamakut, ilamta yuunrillret, carayagnek atengluteng, tangrruulria temtuumarmi. Taugaam piyualuteng aqvaqurluteng pisciiganateng, yuucimek imailameng. Tarnaan pulamanrilani piyuasciiganani. Tuunrangayiim taugaam ayagalluku, wanteqa'aqluni, wanteqa'aqluni,

---

Amulets[22]

Iinrut

Frank Andrew and Marie Meade, Anchorage, September 2005

Miisaq Arnaq-llu, Anchorage, September 2005

MARIE MEADE: The people you saw, what *iinrut* did they use?

FRANK ANDREW: They had different *iinrut*, including carvings of miniature people.

MARIE MEADE: The models of miniature people made out of ivory and driftwood.

FRANK ANDREW: They were made out of driftwood. They kept bundles of wild celery plants and some grass with the objects they used as medicine.

They also used little rocks [as amulets]. They would also tell people not to eat certain foods. Peo-

ARNAQ: Tamakut-wa takuvni tanglalten canek iinrungqelallruat?

MIISAQ: Piciatun-wa iinrungqelallrulriit yuguayaarnek tuaten.

ARNAQ: Yuguayaarnek tulunek, muraganek.

MIISAQ: Muraganek. Canek-ll' makunek ikiitugnek, caneggluyagarnek-llu nunaqlingqerrnaurtut.

Teggalqurrarnek-llu. Inerquraqluki-llu tua-i piciatun canek, neqet-llu ilait nerlaasqevkenaki inerquraqluki. Meq-llu man'a inerquutaqluku

ple were also told not to drink from water that had a current. They were told to only drink water without a current, from lakes. Those were some of the things [they did].

carvanilria. Carvanrilngurnek taugaam melaasqelluki, nanvanek. Tamaa-i tamakut.

It was hanging high up at the edge of their bed, and it was covered[23]

Frank Andrew, Alex Bird, Marie Meade, and Alice Rearden, Bethel, December 2003

FRANK ANDREW: That family that I saw down at an old fall camp, that piece was probably clay, but I didn't know what it was since it was covered with woven grass mats and I did not see it. And it had a hanging device. I didn't know what it was; it was hanging high up at the edge of their bed, and it was covered.

In December, I think it was right after Christmas, during one evening, their father took it down. And after setting it down, when he sat, his children went to him, and they placed it down in their center. He finally took the covering off of it. It was covered with what looked like the same material as a seal-gut rain parka is made from.

I was not curious about it, I didn't know what it was. It was their *iinruq* [amulet, medicine]. When he was done with them, it was like he was unclothing his children and placing them all on the floor. They did that. Both he and his wife also did that. And he didn't say a word. After covering it he closed it, and after making sure that it was completely covered, he hung it up in its place. They didn't say anything.

It seems to be one of those, I think it's an *iinruq*.

ALEX BIRD: It was probably their *iinruq*. It probably gave them strength. It was probably a way to give them strength. All shamans had little *iinrut* back then, and they even kept stones in their pockets. . . .

ALICE REARDEN: Did they have many different kinds of *iinrut*, not like the ones we saw? What kind of *iinrut* did they have, mostly what kinds? Can it be an *iinruq*, even though it doesn't resemble that, even though it isn't a pretend person like this here [at the museum]?

FRANK ANDREW: I saw many different kinds of things that were used as medicine. Some even had water. When it was time, they would sprinkle their families from [that water].

Yaani ingelrita iquatni qulvaarni agaurnaurtuq patumaluni qainga

Miisaq, Apaliq, Arnaq, Cucuaq-llu, Mamterilleq, December 2003

MIISAQ: Augkut-llu *family*-t tangvallrenka uani uksuillermi, qikuuyugnarqelria-wa augna, tupiganek caqungqerran cauciitaqa tangvanrilamku. Agautarluni-ll'. Cauciitelaqeka; yaani ingelrita iquatni qulvaarni agaurnaurtuq patumaluni qainga.

December-aaq, Alussistuam kinguani nallaiqerluku piyugnarquq, atakuyartumi caqerluni atiita atrareskii. Elliamiu-llu tua-i aqumngan, irniari imkut, irniarin ullagluku, waten qukameggnun kanavet pivkarluku. Patuirluku nutaan tauna. Imarnillugngalngugnek patuluni.

Tua-i paqnakevkenaku, cauciinaku. Iinrukekiit-wa. Qaqicamiki tua-i matarrnguarnganaki kanavet yun'i tamakut piurqiliki. Qaqillutek tua-i. Elkek-llu aipani-llu tamarmek tuatnalutek. Qaneqsaunani-ll'. Ataam cikluku caqurraarluku, umcigqaarluku tua-i pirraarluku, eniinun-am tuavet agartak. Qaillun qalartevkenateng.

Tua-i augkuciungatuq, iinrukuciungatuq.

APALIQ: Iinruklikiit-wa. Kayucauteklikiit-wa ellait. Kayucauteklikiit-wa. Iinruangqetullrulriit tamaani tamarmeng angalkut, ciimarrarnek-llu waten qemagtaarangqerrluteng. . . .

CUCUAQ: Piciatun-qaa iinrungqetullruut, aug'utun ayuqenrilengraan? Canek iinrungqetullruat carpallurnek iinrungqetullruat? Waten ayuqenrilengraan iinruuyugngauq, yuguarunrilengraan waten?

MIISAQ: Ayuqenrilngurnek tangaalartua iinrunek piyaralegnek. Ilait-llu, mernek-wa tua-i pingqelalriit. Pinariaqan *family*-teng ceqvallertarluk' waten pinaurait tuaken.

ALICE REARDEN: That was their *iinruq*?

FRANK ANDREW: I saw many different kinds, when they administered *iinrut*. They watched over them carefully and paid close attention to them. They didn't place them anywhere out in the open, but only put *iinrut* in a safe place.

But these Labrador tea plants, they are [medicine], and they are not referred to as *iinrut*. Everyone can use them since they are medicine. Their juice is good. We drink [their juice] for a hot beverage. Some people abstain from drinking tea that has *ayuq*. And my late *iluraq* [male cross-cousin] who died, Albert Beaver, would not drink tea that had *ayuq* in it, since shamans used them to exercise their powers. [*laughs*]

MARIE MEADE: He was afraid of them?

FRANK ANDREW: He was afraid of them.

CUCUAQ: Tauna-q' iinruqluku?

MIISAQ: Ayuqenrilngurnek tangaalartua, iinruaqata. Tua-i murilkelluki cakneq, cumikluki pinaurait tamakut. Cailkami uitavkaqsaunaki, nek'eggingarrlainartelluki taugaam iinrut.

Makut taugaam ayut, tua-i piugut iinrunek-llu aterpagingavkenateng. Yuum tua-i tamarmi aturyugngai iinruungameng. *Juice*-aat assirluni. Tua-i yuurqerluku piaput. Ilaita-am ayulirluki yuurqalalriit eyakelarait. Ilurairutma-ll', imna Albert Beaver-aaq ayulegmek yuurqerngaunani, angalkut-gguq picinguissuutek'laitki. [*ngel'artuq*]

ARNAQ: Alikluki?

MIISAQ: Alikluki.

Two who provoked each other through song, Murak and Pamsuq[24]

Frank Andrew and Marie Meade, Anchorage, September 2005

MARIE MEADE: Those two individuals who tried to provoke each other, *yuiratellriik*, through song, do you remember the song one of them composed?

FRANK ANDREW: Those who try to take the spirit away from each other through songs, *yuiratellriit* as they called it, composed songs to try and aggravate each other. In the lyrics of his song, the person would mention little things that the other person had done to irritate him. [They composed songs about] the things they did, the time they stole something, the things they did.

MARIE MEADE: [They'd mention in their song] little things they did.

FRANK ANDREW: Yes, the lyrics in the song would mention those things. They called it *yuiraluki* [trying to take ones spirit/life essence]. Those *yuiratellriit* apparently do that.

And when Murak [composed a song to try to provoke] Pamsuq, even though [Murak] was his cousin, [Pamsuq] at first was scared and ignored him since [Murak] was a shaman. Poor Pamsuq left [his cousin] alone at first, fearing him because he was a shaman.

I suppose that crafty Murak was presumptuous. From time to time Ikit'am Atiin would tell [Murak], "You there, leave Pamsuq alone! He's clever. When he answers you, he'll strike you with greater power."

Yuiratellriik Muriinkuk Pamsuq-llu

Miisaq Arnaq-llu, Anchorage, September 2005

ARNAQ: Yuiratellriik-llu-qaa taukuk yuarutiik nallunritan?

MIISAQ: Yuiratellriit-wa tua-i yuarutetgun. Callrit, caqallrit tua-i apalluqluki, yuiratetullinilriit yuarutetgun. Callrit tua-i teglengssakallrit waten, cat caqallrit tua-i.

ARNAQ: Qaillukuaqallrit.

MIISAQ: Ii-i, apalluqluki tamakut. Tua-i-gguq yuiraluki. Tuaten pitulliniut tamakut yuiratellriit.

Pamsuq-llu imna Muriim pillrani angalkuungan alingluni tua-i kiuksaunaku ilu'urqeng'ermiu. Uitaurluryaaqelliniuq Pamsuq, angalkuungan alikluku.

Arenqiatellilria-am Muracualler. Ikit'am Atiin pilaryaaqellinia, "Usuuq, Pamsuq pinrilgu! Puqigtuq. Kiukuniten arenqiaciiqaaten."

When he was warned, Murak would quickly respond and say, "It's okay, there is a tongue that exists [that can create words as weapons]." When [Pamsuq] finally retaliated, he did it with much determination and sting. Pamsuq was clever.

MARIE MEADE: Murak, where was he from?

FRANK ANDREW: He lived in Kipnuk. They both lived in the same village.

Yes, they were both from the same village. But Murak would stay in Urutuq sometimes, at a fall camp out there. When It'gacangaq, Ikit'am Atii stayed there, he used to stay there with him.

When he was staying there [at that fall camp], Ikit'am Atiin began warning [Murak] that Pamsuq was clever and to leave him alone.

Then when the other members of the village began urging [Pamsuq] to answer back [to Murak], one day he just came out and started to sing a song; Pamsuq apparently had already composed a song. He apparently quickly composed the song and learned to sing it.

The first ones to go. When they'd approach the village of Kipnuk they would float on by down below the village as they arrived. He began to sing a song:

He wants to come, down there
Agii-rrii-yaa
He is floating by down there
And he keeps looking back at Murak
Yii-yaraa angarragiyaraa
Yii-yaa-rraa-aa-aa
Ayayungiiyagiiyaa
Yii-rrii-nga-yaarr-ii-yaa

That one down there
He is floating by down there
Ag-iir-ii-yaa
He is floating by down there
And he keeps looking back at Murak
Iiyaraa angarragiyaraa
Yii-yaa-rraa-aa-aa
Ayayungiiyagiiyaa
Yii-rrii-nga-yaarr-i-yaa

That one down there
I've been afraid of Murak
Agii-rrii-yaa
Because he is a powerful shaman
Agii-rrii-yaa-aa
But he kept trying to provoke me
Yii-irr-iiyaa yayiirriiyaa
Agii-rrii-yaa-aa-aa
Angaarraa-aa-aa
He is floating by, down there

Kiugartelaraa-gguq, "Aren, ulutangqertuq." Kiungamiu tua-i arenqiatelliniuq. Puqigtuq im' Pamsuq.

ARNAQ: Murak tauna camiungullrua?

MIISAQ: Qipnermiunguluni. Nunalguteklutek.

Ii-i, nunalguteklutek. Taugaam Urutumi uitaaqluni caaqami Murak tauna, uksuilleruarni avani. It'gacangaq imna tuantelallrani ilalirluku uitaaqluni, Ikit'am Atii.

Tuantellermini tua-i inerqularyaaqellrullinia Ikit'am Atiin, pisqevkenaku Pamsuq puqigniluku.

Caqerluni tua-i pisquungvakaatni-am nunalgutmi, yuarutmek-am meng'elria; ak'a taqutellrullinilria yuarutmek Pamsuq. Ak'a-am taqellrullinikii tamana yuarun.

Ciuqlirmek piarkat. Unaggun ketairalarait canimarluteng Qipnermun tekicarturaqameng. Yuarutmek-am meng'elliniuq:
Taiyugtuq unani-aa
Agii-rrii-yaa
Canimartuq unani-aa
Takuyaryugluni-llu Muragmun
Yii-yaraa angarragiyaraa
Yii-yaa-rraa-aa-aa
Ayayungiiyagiiyaa
Yii-rrii-nga-yaarr-ii-yaa

Un'a agiiyaraa-aa
Canimartuq unani-aa
Ag-iir-ii-yaa
Canimartuq unani-aa
Takuyaryugluni-llu Muragmun
Iiyaraa angarragiyaraa
Yii-yaa-rraa-aa-aa
Ayayungiiyagiiyaa
Yii-rrii-nga-yaarr-i-yaa

Un'a agiiyaayaraarrai
Muragmek-qaar alingyaaqua-aa
Agii-rrii-yaa
Angarvauyaaqvakaan
Agii-rrii-yaa-aa
Taugken-qaar arenqianani picetaurluami
Yii-irr-iiyaa yayiirriiyaa
Agii-rrii-yaa-aa-aa
Angaarraa-aa-aa
Canimartuq unani-aa

Ag-iirr-ii-yaa-aa
He is floating by down there
He is floating by down there
And he keeps looking back at Murak
Yii-yar-aa-ngaa
Ag-ii-yar-aa
Yii-yaarraa-aa-aa
Ayayungiiya . . .
Yii-yagii-aa-aa

I've heard that he sulks and pouts
Ag-ii-rr-iiyaa-aa-aa
The esophagus of a *?cucuketaq*
Murak is beginning to lack things
Yii-yar-aa-ngaar agiiyaraa
Yii-yaar-aa-aa-aa
Ayayungiiyagiiyaa
Yii-rrii ngayiirriyaa
That one down there
[Pamsuq] sang this song when he answered [Murak] the first time. And even though [Murak] died [Pamsuq] continued composing songs to humiliate him. He continued to sing about him even after he died.

That was the song they sang to take their spirit away from one another. Pamsuq is my paternal uncle.

Ag-iirr-ii-yaa-aa
Canimartuq unani-aa agii-rri-ya
Canimartuq unani-aa
Takuyaryugluni-llu Muragmun
Yii-yar-aa-ngaa
Ag-ii-yar-aa
Yii-yaarraa-aa-aa
Ayayungiiya . . .
Yii-yagii-aa-aa

Qeneqtalarnilaqiit
Ag-ii-rr-iiyaa-aa-aa
Cucuketam igyamcua
Nangutmacugyaaqvaa canek Muragmi
Yii-yar-aa-ngaar agiiyaraa
Yii-yaar-aa-aa-aa
Ayayungiiyagiiyaa
Yii-rrii ngayiirriyaa
Un'a agiiyaarraa-aa-ai
Mat'umek maa-i kiullinia ciumek kiuqerraallerminiu aug'umek apallirluku. Tuqungraan-llu tua-i egmicalkivikluku. Tuqumaringraan apalluqaqluku.

Yuiratellrak elkenka. Ataatakekeka-w' Pamsuq.

The time when residents of Kuigilngurmiut ran out of food, it was Cingarturta who helped them to survive[25]

Frank Andrew and Marie Meade, Anchorage, September 2005

FRANK ANDREW: The time when residents of Kuigilngurmiut ran out of food, it was Cingarturta who helped them to survive.

That poor man, [those in Kuigilngurmiut] began thinking of ways to kill him, but they didn't touch him.

MARIE MEADE: Though he may have been able to [fight them back], he decided to just move away from them.

FRANK ANDREW: Yes.

MARIE MEADE: Back in those days, that was probably what people did [to avoid conflict].

FRANK ANDREW: Yes. More then once, there were those who left their home areas and moved over to this [coastal] area [because of fear of being killed].

MARIE MEADE: Cingarturta was a shaman.

Kuigilngurmiut neqaitullratni kanautestellrat Cingarturta

Miisaq Arnaq-llu, Anchorage, September 2005

MIISAQ: Kuigilngurmiut neqaitullratni kanautestellrat Cingarturta.

Tuquiteurlullruat tua-i tauna, taugaam agturpek'naku.

ARNAQ: Elliin-llu-wa piyugngangermiki tua-i tayima unilluki upalliniluni.

MIISAQ: Ii-i.

ARNAQ: Tuaten-w'-am tua-i pitullrullilriit tamakut.

MIISAQ: Ii-i. Qimagaullret makut tua-i qimagaulartut pulengtaq, avaken yaatemtenek ukatmun.

ARNAQ: Cingarturta tauna angalkuuluni.

FRANK ANDREW: He was a shaman.

MARIE MEADE: He was your late wife's grandfather.

FRANK ANDREW: He was her grandfather. Cingarturta.

They turned against him for some reason. Perhaps they were suspecting him of some wrong-doings.

I don't think they would have allowed them to harm him anyway. There were many who would have defended him [even if others tried to harm him]. . . .

They wouldn't have allowed them to hurt him. There were many [who would have helped him].

He apparently helped many young people, including orphans, survive during the time when there was a food shortage. Those people he helped, they were always ready to return the generosity later on when they were able to.

MARIE MEADE: Those people who were grateful.

FRANK ANDREW: Yes.

MIISAQ: Angalkuuguq.

ARNAQ: Aipairutvet apa'urlua.

MIISAQ: Apa'urluqaa. Cingarturta.

Camek-wa tua-i ayagnirluku pillikiit. Kamakluku-ll' pillikiit.

Pivkaryanricugnarqaat pingraatgu Cingarturta. Pistekai amllertut Cingarturtem. . . .

Pivkaryanritaat. Amllertut.

Tuani-ll' tua-i neqaitullratni ayagyuat elliraat-llu amlleret anagcetellrullinii Cingarturtem. Tamakut tamaa-i kellusngallruat-gguq tua-i akinauryugluku unguvallrani.

ARNAQ: Quyallret.

MIISAQ: Ii-i.

Some shamans cast spells allowing others to become intoxicated[26]

Frank Andrew and Marie Meade, Anchorage, September 2005

MARIE MEADE: [When they got intoxicated] they didn't fight and get into arguments. Did you ever hear of [alcohol-related] murders also?

FRANK ANDREW: They didn't do that. They didn't murder. They didn't partake in that.

It was the younger ones who started fighting [when they drank]. The older ones didn't do that. They didn't fight their fellow people. It was the younger ones who did that; people who were intoxicated started to change, and they'd even travel and go to other places [when intoxicated]. Some who behaved like that when intoxicated weren't good examples for their children.

And some shamans, they'd cast spells on others and allow them to get intoxicated. And that person named Qateryak, the brother of Kelissayagaq from Nightmute, they said that he filled a ladle with plain water, and after he drank a little he let an individual drink the rest. After he drank the water he got intoxicated. He'd stay drunk and not sober up. [The shaman] would be the only one who would undo the spell and finally allow him to sober up.

MARIE MEADE: A shaman did that. Did he let him drink plain water?

Angalkut-llu ilait taangiqevkarinaurtut

Miisaq Arnaq-llu, Anchorage, September 2005

ARNAQ: Picurlagalluteng piyuunateng. Tuqucilrianek-llu-qaa niicuunaci?

MIISAQ: Tuatnayuunateng. Tuquciyuunateng. Tamatumek piyuitellruut.

Makut taugaam nutaan kinguqliit callualuteng pilangellruut, ayagyuanrit tamakut. Ciulirneret tamakut tuaten pillrunritut. Ilameggnek callualuteng pillrunritut. Kinguqliit taugaam makut; tamakutgun tua-i tamaa-i taangiqellriit allaurrluteng, ayagaluteng tuaten piaqluteng ullagalluteng. Mikelngumeggnek elitnauriluaqallrunritut taangiqtullret ilait.

Angalkut-llu ilait taangiqevkarinaurtut. Augna-ll' Qateryak Kelissayagaam anngaa-gguq Negtemiu, mermek tua-i makucimek-gguq qaluqaarluku meq'erraarluku-ll' tua-i mertelluku. Taangiqluni-llu-gguq tua-i tauna. Pellugngaunaku-llu. Taum taugaam pikani taangiqenrirarkauluni.

ARNAQ: Angalkum. Mep'igmek-qaa tua-i?

FRANK ANDREW: Yes. It was Qateryak who cast a spell on Pamsuq and allowed him to get drunk [from plain water]. And he stayed drunk for a long time. He only sobered up when [Qateryak] undid the spell.

MARIE MEADE: Perhaps in the beginning people weren't happy about the introduction of alcohol. Or didn't they mind when those first ones started to drink?

FRANK ANDREW: Back in those days when elders advised them to quit, that person would immediately comply and quit. People in those days were easier to persuade. When a person was told to quit he'd immediately stop drinking without argument.

MIISAQ: Ii-i. Imna Pamsuq Qateryiim taum taangiqevkallrullinia. Tua-i pelluksaunaku tua-i. Piani taugaam nutaan assiriluni, taum pistellran.

ARNAQ: Taangaq-llu-wa tamana ciuqlirmi quyakevkenaku pillrullilriit, tamakut pingqerraallratni. Wall'u-q' canrilkelluki pillruit ciuqliit pingraata?

MIISAQ: Tua-i tamaani inerquiceteng-llu tua-i tamakut ciulirneret tamatumek taangamek taqesqelluki taqluteng. Malingngatenrullruameng tamakut ciuqliit. Inerquiceteng tua-i ciumuarpek'nateng taangayuirulluteng.

The kayaks of Asngualler and Alaqteryar, a blade couldn't cut through them[27]

Frank Andrew and Marie Meade, Anchorage, September 2005

MARIE MEADE: His kayak that he tried to chop, the story you two were telling last night. Was it the kayak owned by Alaqteryar or someone else?

FRANK ANDREW: They say the kayaks owned by the two brothers were like that. [The kayaks of] Asngualler and Alaqteryar. A blade couldn't cut through them.

MARIE MEADE: And didn't you say that they never allowed others to look inside their kayaks?

FRANK ANDREW: People were told not to look inside their kayaks before they had been smeared with blood. People were told that it would be okay and nothing would happen to them if they looked into their kayaks only after the owners had caught a bearded seal and the insides of their kayaks had been stained with the blood of their catch.

[The two men] weren't shamans, however. But it was said that their father had empowered them with something to protect them. Their father was a shaman, but I don't know who he was.

MARIE MEADE: Was the hide cover of his kayak thick?

FRANK ANDREW: I'm not sure. But no tool with a blade could cut through [the kayak skin].

MARIE MEADE: They were both safeguarded.

Asnguallrenkuk Alaqteryar-llu qayakek saskum iterngaunakek

Miisaq Arnaq-llu, Anchorage, September 2005

ARNAQ: Tauna-ima-qaa qayaa piqerturyaaqellra, akwaugaq iciw' qanemcikurallertek. Alaqteryaraam-qaa wall'u-qaa kia qayaa?

MIISAQ: Anngaqelriik-gguq taukuk qayakek tuaten ayuquk. Asnguallrenkuk Alaqteryar-llu. Saskum iterngaunakek tua-i.

ARNAQ: Qayatek-llu-qaa uyangtaarcecuunakek?

MIISAQ: Inerquusngalutek-wa qayakek augtangvailgagnek uyangtaaresqevkenakek qayakek. Taugaam tua-i maklagglutek makliim auganek uqlangareskagnek qayakek uyangtaangraata qaill' pingaitniluki.

Angalkuuvkenatek taugaam. Taugaam-gguq piyailkuciumauk atamegnek camek taumek. Camek-ll' atangqellruak angalkumek taumek.

ARNAQ: Qayaan-ima-qaa amia cakneq mamtuluni?

MIISAQ: Qaill'-wa pia. Caskum taugaam iterciiganaku.

ARNAQ: Piyailkuciumalutek.

Even though his body stayed behind he'd travel far away[28]

Frank Andrew and Marie Meade, Anchorage, September 2005

MARIE MEADE: When you speak of *cauyatulria* [one who drums], what is it that he does that he is called *cauyatulria*?

FRANK ANDREW: Because they used their drums [and sang], they called them *cauyatulit*; they used shaman drums.

MARIE MEADE: What were the drums used for?

FRANK ANDREW: *Tuunritulit* [people who conjured spirits] had drums. There's a ritual [shamans] do by standing up to conjure spirits, then there was the drum. They say the way of conjuring spirits by standing up was a way for a shaman to travel. He'd travel; that way of conjuring was a way for him to travel physically in the flesh.

MARIE MEADE: The drum?

FRANK ANDREW: He wouldn't be drumming; it was a way of conjuring spirits [and traveling].

MARIE MEADE: He would stand up and do that.

FRANK ANDREW: Yes. They say it was his way of going out and traveling. They say he ?*nenguraluni*; using his mind he would travel. Even though his body stayed behind, he'd travel far away.

But they say a shaman used the drum to look around. He would check his path ahead if he was asked to do so by the community.

And if they asked him to *pinguarluku* [request an abundance of something with his spirit powers], he'd use his drum first and check out the path he would take, and find out what he would do if he encountered something.

Long ago, in Ayikataak, that man named Aqsarpak had previously not been referred to by that name, [but his name changed and everyone started calling him that].

I'm going to tell a story.

One day his grandsons asked [Aqsarpak] to travel to the ocean, asking him to [provide] animals they would hunt.

When they told him to, that evening he took his drum and started drumming. He was going to check the trail he would be taking. This was up at Ayakataak; over at the tributary of Tagyaraq River, at Ayikatarmiut.

After he drummed for a long time, and when he was finally done he told [his grandsons] that he would like to wait and go later. He told them that

Temni uitangraan tuani yaaqvanun ayagaqluni

Miisaq Arnaq-llu, Anchorage, September 2005

ARNAQ: Cauyatulriamek-wa, qaillun pituami cauyatulriamek aprumaluni?

MIISAQ: Imumek-wa cauyameggnek cauyatuata cauyatulinek pilaqait; angalkurtarnek cauyanek.

ARNAQ: Cassuutekluki tamakut cauyat?

MIISAQ: Tuunritulit cauyangqetullruut. Tua-i nangerrluni tuunriyaraq, cauyaq-wa. Una-gguq waniwa tuunriyaraq nangerrluni angalkum ayagayaraqaa. Ayagaluni; temtuumarmi ayagayaraqluku tuunraryaraq tauna.

ARNAQ: Cauyaq?

MIISAQ: Cauyarpek'nani; tuunriryaraq taugaam.

ARNAQ: Nangerrluni.

MIISAQ: Ii-i. Ayagayaraqaa-gguq. Nenguraluni-gguq; umyuamikun tua-i ayagaqluni. Temni uitangraan tuani yaaqvanun ayagaqluni.

Una-gguq taugken cauyaq kiarcaraqluku angalkum. Ciunerkani tauna *check*-ararkauluku-llu ellimeqatni ukut nunat.

Pinguaresqelluku-ll' pikatni, cauyararkauluni tua-i ciumek yuvrirluku man'a tumkani, qaillun pikuni pillerkaa nallunrirluku.

Aqsarpak tauna Aqsarpaullrunricaaqelliniuq Ayikataagni ak'a avani.

Qanemciqatartua.

Tutgarain-am taukut ellimelliniat amci imartesqelluku, imarpigmun ayaasqelluku, pitarkameggnek piluku.

Ellimellratni-am atakuan, cauyaminek piluni cauyalliniluni. Tumkani-am *check*-aqatarluku. Kiani Ayikataagni; amani Tagyaram avayaani Ayikatarmiuni.

Cauyalnguami-llu taqngami pilliniuq, uitaqaqerli-gguq atak tang ellii. Imarpik-gguq camna pektestengqeqatalliniuq Qaluyaarmiumek.

someone was going to be traveling down on the ocean, a person from Nelson Island. He said that the person was younger than him. He told them that he would like to wait a bit and go after that person had gone.

His grandsons were adamant and quickly replied, "No, you must not wait!"

I don't know what his real Yup'ik name was before he came to be called Aqsarpak.

After not wanting to go, because his grandsons kept pleading for him to go, he reluctantly got ready.

When he was ready, they wrapped him up with a bearded-seal skin, *qilaraulluku*. They say they take off their clothes when shamans were covered and wrapped with bearded-seal skins, *qilaraulluki*. The shaman would first take off all his clothes.

After laying out a bearded seal pelt, they also brought out skin line they'd use to string through the *putut* [holes on the skin's edge made for sticks when drying it on the ground]. They also got a skin line usually attached to a spear and got it ready to use as a tether. They say [shamans] going to the ocean do that. That was how that particular [shaman] usually went.

Then after they removed their clothing, some would ask that a seal-gut parka be folded and put next to them here. [The shaman] would stretch out [on the seal pelt] with his arms down the sides of his body. Then they went around him and covered his body with the skin and tied it and bound it with the skin line. As instructed by the shaman, they stepped on him and pulled on the skin to securely wrap his whole body.

Then they tied the gangline securely to the bottom near his feet, making sure that it couldn't come off when pulled. They then picked a strong man and positioned him to hold [the line] and pull it when the time came.

When they were done [getting him ready], he laid there motionless tied up inside the bearded-seal skin.

Then in a moment, he suddenly rolled over on his belly. And as soon as he was on his belly, he darted forward hopping on four legs. Although the seal skin covering his body was dry, it suddenly got soft.

And as soon as he got to the frame entrance to the tunnel passageway he went down head first [and disappeared into the entry hole]. The skin line began unraveling and moving forward, and at times it made a hissing sound because it was moving so fast.

Ayagyuanruluni-gguq elliini. Kinguakun-gguq piniartuq uitaqaqerli ellii.

Tutgarain tamakut pilliniat, "Aren uitayunaituq!"

Kituupiarullrua-llu Yugtun tayim' Aqsarpaurpailegmi.

Qessayaaqerraarluni tua-i arenqialatni tutgarami uptelliniluni.

Pinarian tua-i qilarautelliniluku, maklagmek amilirluku. Ugayarluki-gguq qilarautaqamegteki. Aturamek tua-i cairluku tauna angalkuq ugayatuuq.

Maklak sagqaarluku waten, makucimek waten taprualugmek putuikun waten nuvuurutkainek upluteng cali. Uskurarkaanek-llu asaaqum imgutaanek waten ellegtalriamek taprualugmek, uskurarkaanek piluteng. Imartellriit-gguq tuaten pituut. Tauna tua-i tuatnatullrulliniuq.

Tua-i-gguq taugken matarcaceteng, ilaita imarnitek maavet menglemeggnun imeglukek, wavet imarnitek ellivkarlukek. Nenglluni tua-i waten piluni, talligni-ll' maavet pilukek, nenglluni tua-i makliim qainganun. Tua-i-ll' cikluku nutaan nuqilrarluku. Tull'uku-gguq tua-i cayuuraqluku kassuucetengnaqluku waten, taum angalkum alerquuciatun.

Iqua-llu yaaggun tua-i tukullgikun, it'gain tunglirneratgun taprualugmek uskuraanek qillerrluku aug'arrngairulluku. Nutaan-llu allamun angutmun pinilriamun nuqcetarkauluku.

Tua-i-gguq taugken taqngatni taklaluni tua-i uitaluni, makliim iluani nuqilrausngaluni.

Piinanratni-llu-gguq tua-i akagarrluni palu'urrluni. Palu'urcami-gguq taugken pangalegluni ayagarrluni. Imna ciilertengraan tua-i, ciilriulluku tua-i amirkaq maklak caquni.

Pall'itaak-llu-gguq tua-i nall'arcamikek kanaqerluni tayima. Nekevluni-gguq taugken, qalriayaarluni-ll' iliini nekvaqluni taprualuk cukanram ugaan.

And at the end [of the line] stood a *nukalpiaq* [accomplished hunter] at the log supporting the back end of floor planks over the firepit back there. He would hold the skin line with a piece of wood for a handle with his feet stepping on something for support, and stood ready to pull when it was time.

After [the line unraveled completely], straining, [he held on to the end and pulled], and sometimes his body would stretch forward. He'd pull again [with all his might and move back into position] when that shaman going to the ocean pulled the line.

Then one time [as he pulled], he suddenly fell backward. [The line] suddenly came toward him. The line suddenly got loose.

They say that some [shamans] travel out through holes in the ice.

They say [that shaman] from Ayikatarmiut used to travel through ice holes. He didn't travel through [entrance holes of men's houses]. They didn't bind them in seal skins [when they went]. But they would make holes on the ice [for them to go through].

And they'd plant their feet along the sides of the ice hole and stand wearing seal-gut parkas and waterproof boots; they wore garments that were usually worn for ocean hunting. They'd wear fish-skin gloves, wearing all the clothing worn by men when they hunted in the ocean. But they'd be holding walking sticks in both hands. They say that shaman from Ayikatarmiut traveled out through a hole in a lake. They'd chop the ice and make a square hole.

They say they'd have five helpers [to go with him to the hole]. They'd take him out of the *qasgiq* holding his arms when they took him to their hole in the ice. No one else would go with them.

And when he reached the hole, he'd stand right over the hole with his legs spread out [with feet planted on the sides], holding his walking sticks with the tips poked in the ice. *Qaniqluni* [He performed a shamanistic incantation invoking helping spirits]. Whenever he blew out his breath, his feet would move toward the water; his helpers would tell him to step harder into the ice.

MARIE MEADE: When he'd blow out his breath.

FRANK ANDREW: Then, though his feet fell down into the water in the hole, he'd stand on the water. His boot soles *?unevkausngalutek* on the water.

They say that after he got inside the hole, they had them put their hands right here; the five

Tauna-wa-gguq kiani tugeryarami nukalpiaq iquani. Muragmek waten teguyarirluku taprualugmek, tukerlukek irugni, tukrucirlukek waten, uqliusngakii.

Iquklican-gguq taugken tua-i cakviurluni tua-i, neng'aqluni uavet. Ataam cayugaqluku qimugaqan tauna imartellria.

Tua-i-gguq piinanermini nengugtellria taun' qetqallagluni. Alqunaq taigarrluni man'a. Qacigarrluni taprualuk.

Ilii-gguq taugken tua-i anluakun ayatuluni.

Tauna-gguq tua-i anluakun ayatullruuq Ayikatarmiutaq. Tamakutgun ayayuunani. Qilarautevkenaki pitulliniluki-gguq tuaten. Anlualirluki-gguq taugaam.

Anluam-llu avategkenun waten tull'uteng-gguq, imarnitnek taugaam aturluteng ivrucinek-llu; imarpiliurcuutnek aturluteng. Arillugluteng, qaqilluteng tua-i imarpigmi pilriacetun. Ayarurluteng taugaam inglugtun. Nanvakun-gguq pituuq tauna Ayikatarmiu. Ukilluku tua-i waten kangiriluku anluara.

Tallimanek-gguq waten kevgangqetuut yugnek. Qasgimek tua-i anulluki ayautaqluki tass'urluku tuavet anluaratnun. Yuum allam maliggngaunaki.

Tua-i-gguq taugken tekicamiu anluaq tauna avelrulluku nangerrluni, ayarugni tugrullukek waten. Qaniqluni. Cup'aqan iruk mer'em tungiinun pikanircetaqlukek; tukqanircetaqlukek.

ARNAQ: Cup'aqan.

MIISAQ: Tua-i-ll' anluamun igteng'ermi, mer'em qaingani tusngaluni. Mermi tuani tua-i ?unevkausngalutek nat'rak.

Tuaten tua-i ekumariaqan-gguq, uuggun unatait wavet ellivkatuit; qalliqurtelluki taukut

[men's] hands would be laid on top of each other. They'd place their hands on top of one another here on his crown. With the weight of their hands, he slowly went down.

Then after [his feet] got in the water they left their hands on his head and didn't remove them right away. They left them on his head for a while and finally removed them. They then returned to the *qasgiq*.

They say that was how that [shaman] traveled. They also said that my great-grandfather Pangalgalria from Qinaq traveled like that.

So that [shaman Aqsarpak] went away and traveled.

There in Ayikataak at that time there was a shaman who was visiting from another village. His name was Ungaayacungaq. He was a shaman from the edge of the northern area. He had been seated above the entrance in the *qasgiq*.

The shaman, before he traveled, had asked him to move from there and find a place elsewhere. But that shaman answered that it would be okay for him to remain there [above the entrance], to go ahead and go while he was there, that he wouldn't do anything to him.

Down on the ocean, he ran into that shaman Nagiiquyaq from Nelson Island. Nagiiquyaq was his name. He was younger than the one who would come to be named Aqsarpak.

When he ran into him, that younger [shaman] loathed him. He behaved as if he was going to attack him.

After [Aqsarpak] had acquired the "likeness" of the seal that he had come to seek, for some reason, Nagiiquyaq who he came across down in the ocean, a shaman like himself, suddenly turned against him.

So when he started to attack him, [Aqsarpak] got the *tarnaq* [soul, tiny visible likeness] of the thing he had acquired, its real soul, and he quickly pushed it behind the lace loop of his waterproof boots. But in his hand he held a mock-up piece of the real thing.

His fellow shaman Nagiiquyaq attacked and battered him.

Since he wouldn't stop attacking him, he pretended to be dead. When he left him there, [Aqsarpak] slightly opened one eye and glanced at him while he was going. When [Nagiiquyaq] looked back and saw him do that, he went to him again.

talliman. Qalliqurluki tua-i waten unateteng elliluki nangenranun wavet. Qaamait tua-i aturluki atrarturluni.

Tua-i-llu-gguq mermun tekican unateteng patgusngauraqerluki egmian' aug'arpek'naki. Akaarnun tua-i qaill' pitalriamek uitaqerceqaarluki nutaan aug'arluki. Nutaan qasgimun uterrluteng.

Tuaten-gguq tauna ayatullruuq. Tauna-ll' Pangalgalria cali amauqa cali pillrunilaraat Qinarmiu.

Tayima tua-i ayalliniluni tauna.

Allaneq-wa-gguq call' tauna angalkuq Ayikataagni tuani. Ungaayacungarmek-gguq aterluni. Qagkumiu angalkuq. Amiigem-gguq quliinlluni uani.

Tuani tua-i ayakatallermini piyaaqellinia tuaken augaasqelluku, nugtartesqelluku. Kiucullralliniuq-am ugna wanleng'ermi ayaasqelluku, qaill' pingaitniluku.

Camani tua-i imarpigmi tauna tua-i Qaluyaarmiu nall'artellinia Nagiiquyaq. Atra waniw' Nagiiquyaq. Ayagyuanruluni elliini taumi Aqsarpagkami.

Nall'artellinia tua-i taum kenkevkenaku ayagyuam. Piqatarluku tua-i waniw', piqatarnganaku.

Unangumarinrakun tua-i taumek piyukengaminek unguvalriaruamek, camek tua-i ayagniqerluni taum kenkenriqertellinikii Nagiiquyam nall'artellran tuunrangayaullgutiin, camani imarpigmi.

Tua-i yagtenga'arcani tauna, unangkengami taum tarnaa, tarnapiara, pilugumi ivrucimi putuan keluanun qerr'artelliniluku. Pinguaranek taugaam tegumiarluni.

Nangtellinikii taum tuunrangayaullgutiin Nagiiquyam.

Tua-i arenqialani tuqunguallilniluni. Unicani tua-i iimi uum ingluakun uitemssuarluni avavet tangerqalliniluku. Kingyaamiu tangqerqaamiu ataam ullalliniluku.

He then attacked him even harder this time. He'd even break his spinal cord in places. But his flesh was still in one piece. He would also take him and bring him down under, reaching the real sea salt. Nagiiquyaq [held him way down under and] let him swallow saltwater.

Then he finally pretended to be dead. And he didn't open his eyes this time. He only started going toward his home after he knew that the other shaman had left and was far enough away.

When he got near Ayikatarmiut, they had blocked his way home. That man named Ungaayacungaq who was sitting above the entrance had blocked his way home. He couldn't [pass through to reach the village]. And the person appointed to keep an eye on him couldn't do anything about it.

[When shamans went on journeys] they usually appointed a person who had the ability to see them out through the corner of the qasgiq. I think they sat on the left [corner in order to see them]. They'd sit with a cover over them and fill a bowl with water.

While the shaman was out in the ocean, they'd look [into the bowl] and watch him. Though the person wasn't a shaman, his eyes were given the power to see. When he was asked to do that, when he sat, although he wasn't a shaman, his eyes would open and could see.

He would use the [spirit guides] of that shaman, and he'd be able to see him. From inside the qasgiq, he'd be able to see [the shaman] as he did things in the ocean. Whenever he did something, he'd tell the others what he was doing.

He was the one who reported that [a shaman] had blocked his way home. He told them that he could see that he had arrived home, but was unable to reach it.

Then while he looked [into the bowl] he told the people there that he could see from the direction of the ocean a large ice floe moving. Then again he said that he could see from the direction of the upper Kuskokwim another large ice floe, too. They say ?imaqiktaaqiignek.

Then when the two [ice floes] were about to meet, he said there seemed to be a person right where they would meet. While he was reporting what he was seeing in the bowl full of water, Ungaayacungaq was sitting above the entrance, above the pall'itaak; the shaman who was visiting.

[He continued to watch the two] saying they were about to meet, and right when he told them

Nutaan nangtelliniluku. Qukaa-ll' man'a kep'aqluku, uivai kep'aqluki. Amianun taugaam uitavkarluku. Camavet-llu imarpipiamun, taryupiamun anglluutaqluku. Mer'avkarluku taryumek, taum Nagiiquyam.

Nutaan tua-i tuqungualliniluni. Uitemssuaranqigcugnaunani tua-i. Yaaqsigian taugaam tua-i nutaan uteqtarturalliniluni.

Ayikatarmiut tekicaaqellinii kinguillinikii. Imum taum Ungaayacungaam amiigem quliini uitalriim kinguillinikii, tumyaraa umegluku. Tua-i qaill' piviinani tua-i. Tangrrumastiin-llu taum tua-i qaill' pisciiganaku.

Tamakut-am tangrrumastengqetuut qasgim kangiraakun. Iqsulirnermi uitatuyugnarqut. Waten caquqerluki-am, qaltaq-llu mermek imirluku.

Tua-i angalkuq tauna imarpigmi ayaumallrani uyanglluku unavet tangvauraraqluku. Angalkuunrilngermi tua-i iik takviliumalutek tuaten. Ellimeqatni aqumekuni angalkuunrilngermi iik uitarkaulutek.

Tuunrangayiim taum caskui aturluki, alaunani-ll'. Qasgim iluanek tangvagluku tua-i imarpigmi camani callrani. Qaill' piaqan tuaten piniaqluku.

Taum qanrutekliniluku tua-i kinguillinicianek una waniwa. Tua-i qaill' piviitniluku kana-i tekicaaqniluku.

Piuraqerluni pilliniuq, tangerrluku-gguq imarpiim tungiinek angenqertangelria. Tuamtellu-gguq qamaken Kusquqviim kangian tungiinek cali angenqertangluni cali. Imaqiktaaqiignek-gguq.

Kassuucartungellragni tua-i tuani, piuraqerluni-am pilliniuq, kan'a-gguq tang kassuutellerkaagni yuuyugnarqelria. Tauna tua-i Ungaayacungaq-gguq ua-i amiigem quliinlluni pall'itaak quliigni; angalkuq allanrulria.

Kassuuteqatarnilukek tua-i tamakuk, kassuucartuarallragni kassuutniqertellukek atam

that they had met, [that shaman sitting above the entrance] suddenly fell on the floor. When he hit the floor he rolled over, and people there in the *qasgiq* quickly realized that he was already dead with blood coming out of his nose.

Then right after [he fell], they heard water splashing from the front of the tunnel entrance. And immediately after the sound of splashing water, they heard the voice of [the shaman who had traveled] telling them to help him up [through the back entrance hole].

They pulled him up through the hole and discovered that the midsection of his body was cut open. Then they dragged him into the room. Once he was inside, they took off his clothes. They took off his seal-gut parka and his waterproof boots; they took off his outer garments.

He said to his grandsons who had asked him to go [and retrieve something], "Seeing him, I had not wanted to go at first [when you asked], because I knew this was going to happen to me. You are all responsible for what happened to me. A shaman totally battered me. However, though he fought me, I got the thing you wanted. Take it from behind the loop hole of my boot sole and examine it."

They checked behind the loop hole and it was a ?*taqimlluar*. They took it and saw that it was a tiny piece of seal meat, a ?*taqemkuyagaq*. It was that.

They say that is what they do to [shamans] when they happen upon them.

After he spoke, he had them bring him back to the log headrest of the *qasgiq*, to the *tugeryaraq*, and let them pull his body belly down over the log with the part that was broken sitting right on the log.

With that tool that was like a pick-ax, that tool that was always kept in the *qasgiq* and was used for pounding, that huge hammer that was used to split wood, he let one of them take that tool and he said, "I know you chop wood. So using your wood chopping ability, using all your strength, whenever I breathe out, hit me with all your might right on the spot where I'm broken."

So that person, as instructed, did that to him. Whenever he would tell him to [hit him], his body would suddenly stretch out and saltwater would spray out of his mouth. And soon the inside of the *qasgiq* was filled with the scent of ocean salt. Then after he was hit for the fifth time, he stood up. His body recovered. They had rescued him [and brought him home].

The mighty Nagiiquyaq finally got home [to Nelson Island] after him.

ugna igtellinilria kanavet ketminun. Tuc'ami akagartelliniuq ak'a tuqullinilria, qengagmikun augmek maqluni.

Tuatnaqertelluku-llu cakmaken kalvagyaramek merpalla'artelliniluni. Merpalla'arteqerluku erinalkitliniuq tauna nugtesqelluni.

Nugtelliniat qukaa kepumaluni. Qamurluku-ll' itrautelliniluku. Nutaan tua-i kiani ugayalliniluku. Imarnitai tamakut, ivrucik-llu yuulukek; qallii yuuluki.

Tutgarani tua-i tamakut ellimerturtellni qanrutlinii, "Tangerrluku qessayaaqelrianga-am, waten picirkaqa nallunrilamku. Waniwa elpeci pivkaqevcia. Angalkum aug'um nangeskiinga. Taugaam nangtengraanga waniw' piyukengarci unakaqa. Putulrima keluani uitauq teguluku yuvrirciu."

Putulrian keluani piqalliniut taqimlluar una. Tegulliniat unkumiutaam unguvalriim kemkuinrii, taqemkuyagaq. Tua-i taunguluni.

Tuatnatuit-gguq-am tua-i nall'artaqamegteki.

Tua-i pirraarluni qavavet imumun qasgim akitiinun tugeryaramun itrautelluni, tauna kepumalria nall'arulluku tamatumun, palurtelluni waten.

Imumek ciklauraam aipaanek, kaugtuutamek imumek, muraliurcuutmek qasgimi uitatulimek, *hammer*-aarpakayagmek, muragmek qupurissuutmek, iliit tegutelluku tamatumek pillinia, "Kitak' tua-i muriutuuten. Muriulaucin aturluku, pinin ilakuivkenaku, cup'aqama tuaggun asmumallemkun piqertulaqia taumek pinirtacin ilakuivkenaku."

Tua-i-am tuatnalliniluku. Pisqaqan tua-i piqerturaqani nengqerrnaurtuq, qanmikun-gguq taugken taryumek agtaraqluni. Qasgi-llu-gguq taryurniriluni. Tallimiriani-llu tua-i tuatnarraarluni nangertelliniluni. Assiriluni temii. Tua-i unakelliniluku.

Tauna Nagiiquyakayak tekitelliniuq nutaan kinguqliuluni nunaminun.

I'm telling you this story exactly the way I used to hear it.

MARIE MEADE: Yes.

FRANK ANDREW: They say he was from Yuukiararmiut. It's an old village site that sits near the outskirts of Tununak. When I went to Tununak one time, I asked the people about that village. They told me that the old village of Yuukiararmiut was located right outside of their village.

That Nagiiquyaq lived in Yuukiararmiut.

So [Nagiiquyaq] got home. He had killed a shaman, he had taken away what that shaman had acquired. He was not disappointed, but quite boastful and blissful.

MARIE MEADE: [Bragging] that he had won.

FRANK ANDREW: Yes, [he was happy] because he won. Because he had killed [the shaman he was fighting], too.

[On his way home] just when he was about to reach Qaluyaat [Nelson Island], the point [of Qaluyaat], he saw a raven and a glaucous gull pulling and fighting over something to eat back on the beach. He watched them for a while up there and continued going home. He didn't understand the significance when he saw them doing that.

And when he went around [the point] to the "face" of Qaluyaat, he saw a red fox and a white fox play a stick game, qip'artalriik [two playing a game of jumping over a slanted pole and landing on the other side with both feet]. They were playing hard and having fun. After watching them for a while, he turned and left and didn't understand the significance of what he saw them do either.

He arrived in his village of Yuukiararmiut. When he went [into the qasgiq], and after he took off his outer garments he took out the pinguaq [imitation thing] he got from the other shaman and said, "Okay, now I'm going to inform you about this. In the days ahead, expect to hear news about what happened to a shaman from the Kuskokwim area."

They say back in those days when [a shaman] captured and killed another shaman, they always followed abstinence rules for a while. And when they went outside, they always covered their heads and always wore a belt. They'd cover their bodies very thoroughly before going outside when they'd kill a shaman. That mighty Nagiiquyaq did that [in the days following his arrival].

Then after he did that, he started to feel kind of sick. And he didn't understand why [he was feeling the way he did].

Qanemcik'lauciatun-am waniw' qanemcikaqa.

ARNAQ: Ii-i.

MIISAQ: Yuukiararmiunek-gguq nunangqertuq. Tununermiut elalirneratni nunallret. Apyutkellruanka-am Tununermiunun pillemni. Elatmeggni uitaniluki taukut Yuukiararmiullret nunallret.

Tauna tua-i tuantelliniuq Nagiiquyaq Yuukiararmiuni.

Utertelliniluni tua-i. Angalkurrluni, pitaiqengluni tuaten angalkumek. Tua-i umyugaa aciqsigpek'nani quyigluni taugaam tua-i.

ARNAQ: Win-arniluni.

MIISAQ: Ii-i, win-aami. Tuqucamiu-ll' tua-i.

Qaluyaat atam tekiteqataqerluki, nuugat, piqalliuq keluani pingkuk tulukaruunkuk narusvak-llu camek ping'umek neqairautellriik. Piavet tua-i tangvaggaarlukek, unitellinilukek. Caucingevkenaku.

Tuamtell' Qaluyaat kegginaat igvallinia, kaviarenkuk uliiq-llu qip'artalriik. Tua-i arenqianatek tua-i. Tua-i anglaniqerraarlukek taringevkenakek-am tua-i ulurlukek ayalliniluni.

Tekitelliniluni tua-i tuavet Yuukiararmiunun nunaminun. Itrami tua-i, ugayaami tauna maniluku pinguara pirraarluku pilliniuq, "Kitaki, waniw' qanrutqataramci. Niicugnikici Kusquqvagmiumek angalkumek."

Angalkurtaqameng-gguq tamaani eyakatuut. Nacaunateng-llu ellamun anyuunateng, naqugterrlainarluteng-llu. Umciggluteng an'aqluteng ellamun angalkurtaqameng. Tuatnalliniuq-am tauna Nagiiquyakayak.

Atam tua-i tuatnallmi kinguani ayuqucia assiiruterrlungllinilria. Taringeksaunaku tua-i.

Then one evening in the *qasgiq* when everyone was preparing to retire for the night, that shaman who was acting boastful and confident noticed two eyes looking in through a hole in a grass mat covering the *pall'itaak*, human eyes. Someone out there was looking in through a hole and was watching him. Then when he saw him, he smiled and disappeared from view.

[Nagiiquyaq] didn't understand the significance of what he witnessed.

When he started to wonder what was happening, after he had seen [that person], he noticed that he was feeling sicker. Then while probing further, he saw that [the shaman] who he thought he had killed, the one he fought and defeated out in the ocean, was actually just about to kill him.

He saw that the raven and gull he saw fighting over something to eat on the beach were actually fighting over his *tarnaq*.

Then he probed into the two *qip'artaalriik*, but he didn't know why they were doing that. In fact, they were the ones who would pop him. He was going to finally understand their significance when he went through the upcoming experience.

He examined [the eyes looking at him] and realized [the shaman] he thought he had killed had come to check on him.

There in Ayikataak, when his grandsons were watching [their grandfather], after that when he was asked to do a ritual, right before he was done he'd ask for a hood [for a hoodless parka] made of dog skins. And he'd ask for a pair of mittens.

Then he let them spread out a grass mat on the *aceturutet* [space between corner posts] back there, along the two *aceturutek* of the two corner posts. That area back there, the space between the two posts, they call *aceturutet*. He had them lay a grass mat there. It was placed at the part [of the *qasgiq*] that was not used to exit and enter.

Then after he put on the [hood and the gloves] and putting on a belt, he jumped down into the entrance hole in the front of the room. [And just as he did that], dried soil particles flew up from the bottom of the entrance hole. Then after he was gone for a while, their shaman appeared from what wasn't a doorway, from behind the *aceturutet* in the back corner and slowly came down to the floor. He was completely covered with soil.

Then one day one of his grandsons asked him, "Why has our grandfather begun to do this?" He answered him, "I see that the little long-tailed

Caqerluni-am qasgimi, atakumi inarteqatarluteng piinanermeggni piqalliniuq tauna angalkuq, angalkurtemiyalleq tauna, pall'itaak patuagnek, tupigaat akuliitgun iig' ugkuk, yuum iik. Qinerrluku kiavetgguq tangvaurqii. Tangerqaani-gguq quuyuaraqarraarluni tayima iptelliniluni.

Taringartenritlinia-am.

Taringcaurluku tua-i kinguani pillermini, tangellmi kinguani, ayuqucia assiitekanillinilria. Maaten-gguq tang murilkuq, imum pitaqsukellran, callullran imum imarpigmi, ellii tua-i waniw' pitaqeqatallinikii, pitaqerkaurtellinikii tua-i waniwa.
Imkuk-llu callullrek tulukaruunkuk narusvak-llu pilliniak, tarnaanek neqairautellinilriik.

Tuamtellu taukuk qip'artaalriik piyaaqelliniak ayuqucingevkenakek. Cunawa-gguq qagertestekagni waniwa. Atuqunikek-gguq cunaw' nutaan taringarkaulukek.

Pillinia imna tauna, tuqucukellran paq'ertellinikii.

Ayikataagni-am tauna tutgarain murilkellratni, taum kinguani tuunrivkaraqatni, taqeqata'arqami qimugtenek yuraryaragnek pisqelallinilria, qimugtet amiitnek yuraryaranek. Aliumategnek-llu.
Aceturutnun-gguq taugken kiavet tupigat saagartelluki, talliqiutek aceturutekegnun. Kiugna talliqiutek waten napalriik akuliik aceturutnek pituat. Tupigat tuavet saagartelluki. Amiigunrilngurkun.

Tua-i-gguq taukuk aqaarlukek naqugarrluni-llu, amigmun qeckaq'erluni uavet. Imumek-llu marayamek kinertellriamek ell'allagluni amiik kan'a. Tayima-gguq taugken tua-i muluuraqerluni, taukut aceturutet kiatiitgun amiigunrilngurkun kiaggun kangirakun, qasgim kangiraakun, atraumaarluni imna angalkuat. Qainga-gguq tua-i nevumaluk' nunarrluum kaimam.

Caqerluku-am tutgarain iliita aptellinia, "Ap'avut-tanem una qaill' pilriim waten pilanga?" Kiullinia, "Allgiayagaam nuusaartani taluutnanriryaaqellinii. Pelacaqalartua."

duck has stopped [?moving around] the three-pronged spear that he obtained. *?Pelacaqalartua.*"

It was during that time that his grandsons started calling their grandpa Aqsarpak. When he did that he apparently would go and check on the shaman [he had captured] who lived at Yuukiararmiut.

One day when the other men were having a fire bath [Nagiiquyaq] went outside. The wind was blowing from the south. Since he didn't want to partake in the fire bath and after he sat in the porch for a while, since it was warm he went out around the *qasgiq* to the back and saw his two cousins, the two who he thought nothing of, playing the game of flipping over a stick.

As soon as they saw him they got excited. They told him to hurry and flip over the stick. He told them, "Don't [ask], you two play flipping over the stick even if I don't play it." They replied, "Gosh, he is acting so high and mighty just because he's a shaman. If we were shamans like you, we'd show our ability and flip over this stick. And you, you aren't going to [flip over the stick]."

Those *qip'artaarutet* [sticks used in the competitive game of flipping over a stick] were like this. You'd poke the end [of this stick] and slant it this way, and take it like this. Then a person would throw his legs up in the air and jump over the stick to here. They call that *qip'arrluni* [he flips over the stick]. We used to play a game like that. We'd pull the stick up higher and higher [make it more vertical]. Sometimes the stick would reach this angle. That was how they used to play that game of *qip'artaaq.*

So he stood next to the stick and got ready to jump. And he jumped over it when he was ready. And as soon as he landed on the other side, the impact sounded like a bladder suddenly popping. His nose suddenly started bleeding. Then he looked at [his cousins] and saw that they were actually a red fox and a white fox; they were those two. He had popped himself and wasn't going to live too long.

And just as he looked up he saw a red fox running toward the area behind them. And he saw a white fox running toward the river. A few minutes before, he had seen them as his cousins, as humans. He realized that he had been defeated and would soon die.

They say that's what he did to him. That's why he came to be called Aqsarpak, that shaman from

Tua-i-gguq tamaani aciraat-am taum tutgarain Aqsarpagmek, ap'aseng tauna. Paq'ertelallinikii-am tua-i tuatnaaqami tauna angalkurtani Yuukiararmiu.

Caqerluni-am maqillratni anlliniuq. Ungalirluni-gguq. Maqiyuumiilami anluni elaturraani uitayaaqerraarluni, nenglailan uivluni qasgim tunua igvallinia, iluraak ukuk, imkuk tua-i canrilkenrilkengak qip'artaalriik.

Tangerqaamegen'gu nepngarutelliniak. Amci qip'artesqelluku. Piyaaqelliak-am, "Tua-i-am pivkenatek, qip'artaartek qip'artenrilngerma." Pilliniak-am, "Aling aren, cakneq-lli angalkurtemayivaa uumi. Wangkuk tua-i elpengukumegnuk angalkuulunuk, angalkuucirkaatun una qip'arcararpuk. Tua-i-am elpet piqatanrilken."

Qip'artaarutet imkut waten ayuqetuut. Kapulluku tua-i una iqua, kanarrluku-ll' ukatmun, teguluku waten. Irugni-ll' pagg'un pilukek qeckarluni wavet. Tua-i-gguq qip'arrluni. Tuaten naanguarutengqellruukut. Napaqaniraqluku una. Kiituan' tua-i waten iliini ellirtuq. Tuaten qip'artaatuut.

Urniallinilria tua-i. Piyungami-ll' qeckarluni tua-i. Tut'ellria-gguq nakacuk-gguq tuar qag'ertellria. Kakgallalliniluni-ll' augmek. Piqalliniuq imkuk nutaan taukuk kaviarenkuk uliiq-llu; uungullinilriik waniw'. Qagerrluni tua-i ellminek tua-i unguvangairulluni.

Ciugarteqanrakun-llu kaviaq kelutmun pangalegluni man' ayagartellinill'. Tauna-ll' uliiq-llu man' ketmun ayagartelliniluni tayima. Yuulukek imkuk nakmiin ilu'uqlukek tangellrek. Tua-i caviirutliniluni, tua-i yuungairulluni tua-i waniwa.

Tuaten-gguq tua-i pillrua taum. Aqsarpauruyutiin iqua, taum Ayikatarmium

Ayikatarmiut. They say Nagiiquyaq happened upon him [on the ocean] and had him go through that.

Then when winter came—spring came and it was summer. Then Nagiiquyaq died before winter.

angalkum. Taum-gguq tua-i Nagiiquyam nall'arrluku tuatnavkallrua.

Tua-i-llu uksuan—up'nerkarpak tua-i, kiagluni-ll'. Uksurpailgan-llu piunrirluni tauna Nagiiquyaq.

Aqsarpak injured and broke the hearts of Yuukiararmiut[29]

Frank Andrew and Marie Meade, Anchorage, September 2005

FRANK ANDREW: Then when winter came, people there celebrated the Messenger Feast.

Yuukiararmiut invited Ayikatarmiut [to attend the Messenger Feast challenge].

They say Aqsarpak had a best friend named Yaquq. He was a shaman, too. They were friends and could help each other out when something happened. But they say that [Yaquq] didn't hunt. And even though his wife encouraged him to hunt, he never went hunting.

And in the spring when others started obtaining seal blubber from down there, and when [his wife] said something, he'd say, "Why do you pester me? We'll eventually get enough seal oil when they *?qessanaireskata.*" [He'd say that to her] since the great Yaquq was a shaman.

When it was time, people from there went to Yuukiararmiut for the Curukaq [Dance Festival, another term for the Messenger Feast]. So, the guests danced. They let them dance.

[They sang the songs they had prepared and] finally they were ready to sing songs composed by Aqsarpak. When it was his turn, after he gave gifts to the individual who had requested something from him, *cingarturiqaarluni,* he announced that he had no more gifts to give and told the drummer to sing his song.

When they started singing, that mighty shaman let his voice out, giving his boasting cry, "Don't celebrate too early and say that he caught me. Don't celebrate too early and say that he caught me! I haven't looked back! I haven't turned my head to look back! When I turn my head and look back at you, you'd be so weak, you wouldn't be able to smash and kill a louse. When I look back at you, you'd be so weakened and find it very difficult to crush the feces of a louse. What is aggravating?" When he swung his arm up into the air he was holding an awl. After he lifted it up, he pointed his

Yuukiararmiut ircaqrui akngirtellinii Aqsarpiim

Miisaq Arnaq-llu, Anchorage, September 2005

MIISAQ: Uksuan Kevgilliniut taukut.

Yuukiararmiut Ayikatarmiunek kelegluteng.

Aqsarpak-gguq qatngutengqertuq Yaqumek. Angalkumek cali. *Friend*-aqlutek tua-i, aipartek ikayuryugngaluku qaill' pikan tua-i. Tauna-gguq taugaam tua-i [Yaquq] pissuyuunani. Watqapik nuliami-ll' pissuusqengraani pissurngaunani.

Up'nerkami-ll' waten uqunek pingaqata unaken, piyaaqaqani-gguq pinaurtuq, "Calarcia waniwa? Qessanaireskata-am uquucingciqukuk." Angalkuungami tauna Yaqukayak.

Curukarnariata curukalliniluteng tuavet Yuukiararmiunun. Yurallinilriit tua-i allanret. Yurarcetlinikait.

Aqsarpak atam tekitellinikiit. Tekicatni tua-i cingarturiqaarluni, nangutniluni yuarucetarkani atuusqelluku.

Atuusqerraarluku anerquciarallinilria tauna angalkukayak. "Pitaqaaruteksara'arpek'nii -ata-a-a. Pitaqaaruteksara'arpek'nii-at a-a-a-a. Kingyaqsaitua. Takuyaqsaitua. Takuyaqumken atam, nerestem-llu mat'um ciitellerkaa caperrsagutniaran. Kingyaqumken atam nerestem-llu mat'um anaa ciitellerkaa kalivyagutniaran. Ca nekanarqa?" Nalugarutelliniuq everquutmek. Nalugarcamiu katngitlinia, "Una-qaa waten nekanarquq?" Nutaan anlliniluni.

middle finger at it and said, "Is this aggravating?" Then [after he said that], he went out.

Aqsarpak broke the hearts of Yuukiararmiut. And there were many shamans in that village.

People summoned their shamans, since their feelings were hurt by the shaman who gave his boasting cry. Wanting to retaliate in remembrance of their former shaman Nagiiquyaq, they began looking for [a shaman] who could fight him. They finally found a shaman, a guest who had come from another village, who could fight him, but he was an elderly man. And he was older than Aqsarpak.

They decided that they would ask that [shaman to go after Aqsarpak]. So that shaman started working with his shaman powers and went after him.

Soon after he began his work, one night, all night long, the great Aqsarpak kept getting up. He couldn't stay put and kept moving, trying to find a comfortable place. He couldn't get comfortable in his own place and kept getting up.

Soon he got so desperate and asked one of his sons to go and invite his old best friend, [asking] that he should go there. "Tell him I'm in deep trouble." [He was talking about] Yaquq.

This was before the dance festivals [were held in villages], but people were starting to sing in the *qasgiq*. It was during that time that he had started to suffer.

While he waited, that great Yaquq came in looking imposing, his noble friend, his old *qatngun*.

When he came in, he quickly squatted down in front of Aqsarpak while he was lying down on his mattress. As soon as he squatted down he said, "My old best friend, what's the matter?" [Aqsarpak answered,] "I'm distressed for there are many who are against me. And I've asked my son to inform you because I'm worried, and I don't know what to do."

Then [Yaquq] stood up, laughing at the same time [and said], "My old best friend, don't be distressed!" While he said that he was turning and getting ready to go out. He took a step toward the exit and said, "Now relax and don't be distressed! I will let our ?*kitugacungall'er* flash a light at Qaluyaat [Nelson Island mountains]." [After he said that] he went out.

Not long after he left, a person ran in and said that he saw flashes of light from Qaluyaat. He said a person would move that flashing light vertically through the base of the mountains, and when it reached the other end, the light would go out.

Yuukiararmiut ircaqruit akngirtellinii Aqsarpiim. Angalkuit-llu amllerrluteng.

Angalkuarateng tua-i tamakut piluki, nekayuameng aug'umek anerquciaralriamek. Tauna angalkullerteng pitekluku, Nagiiquyaq, piyugngastiinek yuarluteng. Tua-i allanret iliitnek tamakut nalaqutliniut angukaraurrluni, angutngurrluni taugaam. Aqsarpiim-llu taum ciulirneqluku.

Taumun tua-i pivkararkaurrluku. Taum caliaqelliniluku tuunrangayamikun.

Aqsarparuk atam piuraqerluni unuumainanrani aqumnanrillinilria. Nanllikiangellinilria tua-i. Nem'ini tua-i aqumgasciigaliluni.

Arenqialiami tua-i qetunrarmi iliit pillinia qatngutlerani tauna kelgesqelluku, taiqerli-gguq maavet. "Arenqiatua-gguq." Yaquq.

Yurangvailgata tua-i, atuangluteng-gguq taugaam qasgimi. Caknengyaaqellinilria tamaani tua-i.

Piinanrani atam Yaqukayak tauna itlinilria, *friend*-akayii, qatngutlerii.

Itrami ciuqranun uyunglelliniuq acimi inangqaurlun' pillrani Aqsarpak. Uyunglerami pilliniuq, "Waqaa qatngutleraaq qaillun pisit?" [Aqsarpiim kiullinia,] "Arenqialngua-w' tua-i, amellrupakaatnga. Nasperturlua waniw' elpengcarceskemken, nanikuarrlungama."

Nangertelliniuq [Yaquq] ngel'arluni tuaten, "Qatngutleraa nanikuavkenak!" Uatmun-gguq tuaten cauluni anqatarluni. Amigmun uavet amllirlun' tuaten qanerluni, "Nanikuavkenakata! Qaluyaat kitugacungallramegnun kenurquta'arceciiqanka." Anlliniluni-ll' tayima.

Anellra umiqerluku iliit itqertelliniuq, Qaluyaat-gguq tang ikegkut kenurqutaralriit. Yuum-gguq tua-i ayautelaqai kumarutet aciitgun, iquatgun-gguq qam'aqluni.

And right after he said that, Aqsarpak began to feel better. Then, as soon as anxiety left him, he immediately got well.

Those two [shamans] behaved like that toward each other. After an encounter with that shaman, people started calling him Aqsarpak.

Aqsarpak. They say Aqsarpak was strict with following abstinence practices and followed them quite religiously. They say he had five sons. And if one [of his sons] had lost an offspring, he'd keep them back and didn't allow them to hunt all spring. Their father would watch all of his sons like that. They say he practiced and followed abstinence practices unfailingly.

When he [abstained from hunting], he would make the back area of their house become the upper end of Naryigun.

MARIE MEADE: Is [Naryigun] a river?

FRANK ANDREW: Yes. That big bay over there in our home area, the one on the outer side, where we hunt, is Naryigun. Those two that sit alongside each other; that is where there are many seals.

Naryigun. The two rivers are like this, there are two of them. The place in between the two is called Naryiga'arcaraa, the place where it goes like this. This is Ullagtaa, and here sits Naryigun.

And the island [inside] is called Aangaguk, its island. Those two islands there are *ircenrraak*. Those two [islands] out there below us are amazing. And even today they haven't changed. They are *ircenrraak*. And those who go on them shouldn't go barefoot when they are menstruating, or experiencing death or miscarriage.

Since that bay was located below their spring camp, that was where they hunted. Aqsarpak had the back area of their home become the headwaters of that channel; he made it that.

And though [his sons] began hunting after the others had started hunting, they caught more than those who went before them. They'd quickly catch animals. That was what [Aqsarpak] did after he made them abstain from hunting.

MARIE MEADE: When one of their family members died, did he let all of them abstain [from hunting]?

FRANK ANDREW: Yes. When his children lost an offspring, he'd let them follow the abstinence laws; he wouldn't let any of them hunt until [they had completed the days] it was time for them to hunt. It was when they finally went into the ocean that the shaman Aqsarpak would make the back end of their house become the headwaters of Naryigun. That [shaman] from Ayikatarmiut.

Tuaten-am piqerluku Aqsarpak tauna ayuqucia man'a assiriyartulliniluni. Aren, nanikuayugnaircami-am assiriqertelliniluni.

Taukuk tua-i tuaten ayuqellrulliniuk. Aqsarpauruyutii tua-i tauna, taum angalkum piluku.

Aqsarpak. Eyanqepiartuq-gguq tauna Aqsarpak. Qetunrangqertuq-gguq tallimanek waten. Irniarita-llu-gguq picurlallruaqan iliit, tegumiaqetui tua-i up'nerkami pissurceteksaunaki eyagtelluki. Murilkelluki atiita taum irniani tamalkuita. Eyanqepiartuq-gguq.

Tuatnaaqami-gguq tua-i neseng tauna egkua kiugna Naryigutmun kangiksagucetetullrua.

ARNAQ: Kuik-qaa?

MIISAQ: Ii-i. Man'a amani nunamteni pissuryararput keggaqliq keggna, kangirpak, Naryigun. Taukuk itukelriit; tauna tua-i unguvalriartupiartuq.

Naryigun. Waten kuig' ayuquk, waten, malruulutek. Una waniwa akuliik Naryiga'arcaraanek pituat, una waten pillra. Man'a-wa Ullagtaa, una-w' Naryigun.

Una-w' qikertaa Aangaguk, qikertartaa. Taukuk qikertak ircenrrauguk. Irranarquk kegkuk ketemteni malruk. Maa-i cali mat'um nalliini cakaniyuunatek. Ircenrrauguk. Kamilarmi-ll' itagnaqluni piyunaunani.

Kangiketuat-gguq tauna tua-i up'nerkillrata ketiini uitiin. Taum Aqsarpiim tauna kangiksagutelluku kuiguyum kangia egkumeggnun kiavet; taunguvkarluku.

Kingumek tua-i pillrung'ermeng ciuqliteng kituraqluki pitamegteggun. Patagmek unangaqluteng pitarkamek. Tuatnatui-gguq tua-i, eyagceqaarluki piaqamiki tuaten.

ARNAQ: Ilangartaqameng-qaa eyagcetaqluki tamalkuita?

MIISAQ: Yaa. Yun'i ilangartaqata, eyagceqaarluki-gguq tuaten pitui; pissurcetevkenaki tua-i tamalkuita pissurnarillerkaata ngeliinun. Ek'aqata-gguq tuaten, tauna tua-i Naryigutem kangia egkuksagucetetua enemeggnun, tuunrangayiim taum Aqsarpiim. Ayikatarmium.

I think the story I just told ends right here.

MARIE MEADE: It's a long story. Is it a story about what happened a very long time ago?

FRANK ANDREW: It's an old, old story.

MARIE MEADE: A story you heard back when you were young.

FRANK ANDREW: The back end of their river came out to Ciun River somewhere back inland. It's a small river up there surrounded by trees. They say [at the time of Aqsarpak], that was the river where the village was located. (singing)

> That up there, could it be Aqsarpak's *tuunraq*
> I'm here watching it and having fun
> *Qaa-rra*
> My spirit
> That loon up there, *?narartaalria* up there
> Up above Ayikataak
> That up there, could it be Aqsarpak's *tuunraq*
> I'm here watching and having fun
> I used to hear his *yuarulluk* [song] being sung, [a song about Aqsarpak].

A lake up inside close to Ayikataak, a small lake near where the bluff goes like this.

They say, after he traveled on it, the next morning it would be filled with frozen ice pebbles from the ocean along that river. The water in that river would be saltwater. Water there would be just like the ocean water. And after nightfall, the next day they'd see that it had already changed to normal [river water]; after it had been salt water, it wasn't saltwater anymore.

It would be like that only right after he had traveled on it.

Aqsarpak evidently let his *ircenrraat* who resided inland come and get [the body of Ungaayacungaq][30]

Frank Andrew and Marie Meade, Anchorage, September 2005

FRANK ANDREW: So, they buried Ungaayacungaq, who had fallen from above the entrance and died. Then right before it got dark Aqsarpak discovered that Ungaayacungaq, who he had killed, the one who had fallen from the *qasgiq* doorway, was just about to come after him during the night.

MARIE MEADE: Even though he had died?

Tua-i waten taktayugnarquq augna.

ARNAQ: Takluni qanemciq. Ak'allauguq-qaa tauna qanemciq?

MIISAQ: Ak'allauguq tamana.

ARNAQ: Niitelallren tamaani.

MIISAQ: Kuillrat-llu qaugna apertualallrat pamalirnerkun pamaggun Ciutem natiikun anumaluni. Napat tua-i akuliitni kuicillruar augna. Tamana-gguq tua-i kuilqaat nunaullratni taukut.

> Aqsarpiim tuunraqlia pagna
> Anglaniluanga wiinga
> Qaa-rra
> Yuugiyama
> Tuullinraq pagna narartaalria pagna
> Ayikataak quliigni
> Aqsarpiim tuunraqlia pagna
> Anglaniluanga wiinga
> Yuarullua-am tamana niitela'arqa.

Nanvaq-gguq kiugna kia-i mallegluk' waten Ayikataam taum, mat'um qemim kiugum waten pillrani, nanvaq angevkenani.

Aturraartelluku-gguq unuaquan errnaurtuq, cenii tua-i man'a akangluaryugnek imarluni, imarpiim akangluaryuinek. Mer'a taryuqapiarauluni-gguq. Imarpiim mer'atun tua-i ayuqluni mer'a. Unuggaarluni-gguq errnaurtuq waten makuurtellinilria ak'a; taryuulleq im' taryuuvkenani tayima.

Atunerraraqani-gguq taugaam tuaten ayuqetuuq.

Tua-i taukunun ircenrraminun aqvavkalliniluku nunamiuqlirnun, Aqsarpiim tauna angalkurtani

Miisaq Arnaq-llu, Anchorage, September 2005

MIISAQ: Tauna tua-i Ungaayacungaq igtelleq amiigem quliinek, tungmagtelliniluku. Unukatarluku-am tua-i tauna Aqsarapak pilliniuq, tauna-am Ungaayacungaq pitaa imna qasgim amiiganek igtelleq, unuku qaillukuaqatallinilria.

ARNAQ: Tuqullrung'ermi?

FRANK ANDREW: Yes. As soon as Aqsarpak realized that, he informed the *ircenrraat*, his helpers who reside up inland—I guess he phoned them. [*laughter*]

MARIE MEADE: So he had *ircenrraat* who were part of his life?

FRANK ANDREW: He asked them to do something to that *shaman* he had killed who was about to retaliate during the night.

The following morning, they saw that it had snowed a little during the night, and it was calm out. Then while one of the people was doing something outside and when he looked in the direction of the new burial site, he quickly noticed that it was destroyed. He went to it and looked closer and saw that it was empty. Then he noticed many, many wolf tracks in and around [the burial site].

Aqsarpak had evidently let his *ircenrraat* who resided inland come and get the body of the shaman [Ungaayacungaq] he had killed.

They say that [Aqsarpak] used to say that if people never died, all the burial sites would be burials of just shamans.

They say Aqsarpak only went after those who asked for it. He never used his power against anyone initially. He only killed those who came after him.

What was Aqsarpak's real name? I have not heard his real name.

He evidently lived before warfare times, before people started engaging in warfare.

MIISAQ: Ii-i. Elpekngamiu-am taum Aqsarpiim ircenrrani nunamiuqliit pamkut elpengcalliniluki —*phone*-arluki-wa pillikai. [*ngel'artut*]

ARNAQ: Ircenrrarluni-llu-qaa, ilakluki?

MIISAQ: Taukunun caliaqesqelluku tauna angalkurtani qaillukuaqatallinian unuku.

Ertelliniuq qaniqallrullinilria kayukita'arluni. Tupiimeng tua-i pivakarluteng iliita-am elpeka'artelliat tauna qunguq nutaraq navguumaluni. Ullagluku piyaaqelliniat imaunani. Kegluninraat-gguq taugken tumet amllepiarluteng nuniini.

Tua-i taum ircenrraminun-am aqvavkalliniluku nunamiuqlirnun, Aqsarpiim tauna angalkurtani.

Qanlallruuq-gguq yuut tuquyuilkata angalkullerrlainarnek Ayikatarmiut qungungqerrsarniluki.
Picetaarutellriit-gguq tua-i tamakut pilallrui Aqsarpiim. Ciumek-gguq piyuituq. Pingnaqesteni-gguq taugaam tua-i piunrirtaqluki.

Kituupiarua tuana Aqsarpak? Atpiara-ll' niiteksailkeka.
Anguyiim ciungani tauna pillrulliniuq, anguyangvailgata yuut.

Arnaruaq from Togiak also tried to capture his fellow shamans[105]

Tuyuryarmiu Arnaruaq angalkuullgutminek tua-i cali ingcurilleq

Frank Andrew and Marie Meade, Anchorage, September 2005

Miisaq Arnaq-llu, Anchorage, September 2005

FRANK ANDREW: There is also a story about Arnaruaq [lit., "Pretend *arnaq* (woman)"] from Togiak who tried to capture his fellow shamans. Arnaruaq who had two *nukalpiaq* husbands. But he lived in Togiak. At night he'd turn into a woman. And at daybreak, he would become a man.

Have you heard about this person? Arnaruaq lived in Togiak long ago.

The two husbands were avid whale hunters. When they hunted whales at the beach, when a whale would breach, they'd shoot their arrows toward it and yell and ask that its body be washed up at a certain spot on shore. Then they'd go home.

MIISAQ: Tuyuryarmiu Arnaruaq angalkuullgutminek tua-i cali ingcurilleq qanemciutulria. Arnaruaq nukalpiagnek malrugnek uiluni. Tuyuryarmiunguluni taugaam. Unugaqan arnaurtaqluni. Ercan-llu angutngurrluni.

Niitelaran-qaa? Arnaruaq-gguq Tuyuryarmiunguluni tua-i *long time* avani.
Uik-wa-gguq taukuk malruk arvercurtek. Imarpiim-gguq ceniinun pilutek arvercuraqamek, arveq tua-i qaktaqan, tungiinun-llu tua-i pitegcautetek pitgaulluki, qayagpagluteng tuavet tepesqelluku. Uterrlutek-llu tua-i.

Later when they were ready, they'd check the spot they mentioned and find a dead whale on the beach. The husbands of Arnaruaq. They would always hunt like that and were always provided for since Arnaruaq was a shaman.

Arnaruaq would also take drums that belonged to other shamans.

Keggutellek from Apruka'ar; he had a drum and went on journeys with his drum there in his village of Apruka'ar.

Then one day his drum disappeared. He tried to find the person responsible for the disappearance of his drum, but he couldn't figure out who it was. He lost his drum. When he wasn't going to find it, he gave up.

Then one day when he was preparing to go to Togiak, two boys wanted to go with him. So he took those two along and went to Togiak by kayak.

MARIE MEADE: They went to a place far away from Apruka'ar.

FRANK ANDREW: They arrived in Togiak. After they were guests [and ate], when they went outside, he noticed a man sitting outside a home at the end of a log nearby facing the ocean.

Keggutellek was a shaman. He thought to himself, "Perhaps the man sitting over there is Arnaruaq, the shaman who people used to talk about back home. I wish I could get closer and see what he looks like."

Then he walked toward him. As he approached, the man sitting on the log turned and looked at him with a straight face. He noticed that the one sitting was an old man. So, not coming right up to him, he sat at the opposite end [of the log].

Deciding not to stay silent, he started conversing with him. [Keggutellek] said that he had heard about a shaman named Arnaruaq there [in Togiak]. The old man responded that he was that person who he was inquiring about. He told him that he was the one, that people called him Arnaruaq.

[Arnaruaq] told him to come with him. He brought him inside his house. When he went in, he invited him in, [saying] that he was going to show him something. [Keggutellek] followed him and went into his house.

When they dropped down the *kalvagyaraq* [tunnel entryway], he noticed a huge whale vertebrae step below the entrance hole up ahead, the hole where you come up [into the main room], and there

Pinarian-gguq tauna apertullertek paqnauraak arveq tauna pitgallrak ak'a tepellrullinikii tuavet. Uik taum Arnaruam. Tuaten ayuqlutek nuqlicugnaunatek angalkuungan tauna Arnaruaq.

Cauyaiqengyugluni tauna Arnaruaq-llu angalkuullgutminek.

Apruka'armiu tauna tua-i Keggutellek; cauyarluni tua-i tauna angalkuq cauyalallinilria nunamini tuani Apruka'armi.

Pivakarluni cauyaminek paqricilliniluni. Piyaaqellinikii tua-i camun piciinaku tua-i. Tamariluku cauyani. Nataqngairucamiu tua-i taqluku.

Atam caqerluteng Tuyuryarmun ayakatallrani tan'gaurluuk malruk maligcullinikiik. Maliklukek taukuk Tuyuryartelliniluni qayatgun.

ARNAQ: Yaaqvanun amavet Apruka'armek.

MIISAQ: Tekitelliniluteng tua-i Tuyuryarmun. Allanruluteng tua-i pirraarluteng, ellamun anluteng pillermeggni piqalliniuq nem taum elatiini, muriim iquani angun ingna aqumgauralria imarpik caumaluku.

Tauna tua-i angalkuuluni Keggutellek. Umyuarteqliniuq, "Taungullilria-w' tua-i ingna niitnaulalleq, Arnaruamek aterpagtaarluku. Canianek kin' yaa-i mecikluku tangerqerliu."

Ullallinia-am. Tekicartuarallrani tangerqaamiu tangvagluku nulgaunani. Angutngurrluni-gguq tauna aqumgauralria. Mallegtevkenaku tua-i iquanun wavet aqumelliniluni.

Tua-i qanenrilkurutevkenaku qanengssaulluk' pillinikii. Pilliniuq-am niitelarniluni maani angalkumek taumek Arnaruamek. Pillinia ellii-gguq waniwauguq. Taunguuq-gguq waniwa ellii, Arnaruamek-gguq piaqaat.

Atam-gguq maligteqerliu. Nem'inun itrulluku. Itlermini maligtesqelluni maniitqatarniluku. Maligtelliniluku tua-i eniinun itellrani.

Kalvagyaraanun-gguq kalvagtuq kiugna kiaqliq tuss'ararluni arevrem uivarpallriinek, nugyaraq, uaqlia-ll' cali camek cali.

After Arnaruaq shut his eyes because of the blinding light, when he opened them he was alone. [Keggutellek] who was just there was gone. Then he realized that he had already left.

Keggutellek then went to the *qasgiq*. When he was going back to bed he told his traveling companions that they were going to go home the next day.

At daybreak, they left. Then while they were going, when the sun was straight up in the middle, he started to feel pressure in his whole body as he traveled.

Then he probed and saw Arnaruaq with his arms and hands [stretched out]. He could see that they were going down [Arnaruaq's arm], and they had reached this area [part of the way down]. He realized that [Arnaruaq had gotten hold of them and] they were on his arm going along heading toward his hand.

And since they apparently had gotten to that area, and when [Arnaruaq would bend] his arm, that was apparently when [Keggutellek] felt pressure in his body. And when [Arnaruaq] stretched out his arm, he'd feel better.

He evidently was about to kill all of them. When they got [inside the palm of his hand] he apparently was just going to pop them by clenching his fists.

[These were some of the ways] shamans used when they exercised their powers.

And as soon as Keggutellek saw what [Arnaruaq] was doing, he told his companions, "Let's stop and go to bed." And here the sun was out in the middle of the day. So they made a shelter and went to bed.

And as soon as they went to bed, [Keggutellek] got hold of the *tarnak* of his companions and kicked them toward home along with his drum. And in minutes his drum reached [home] along with the *tarnak* of the two boys.

MARIE MEADE: To their village.

FRANK ANDREW: Then he relaxed knowing that the shaman [Arnaruaq] would not be able to touch his traveling companions.

After he kicked them [to safety], Keggutellek then took off using his shaman powers. He looked back and saw [Arnaruaq] sitting down gliding and following him from behind.

Since he was worried that he might catch up with him, Keggutellek turned abruptly and decided to go to his parents' place. He headed toward the upper Yukon River to a place called Paluqtaviik, since he was getting closer. He kept fleeing trying to escape.

Arnaruaq-am tanqiullerminek uigarcaaqelliniuq kiimi tua-i. Aipaa imna tayima. Piqalliniuq ak'a anllinilria tayima.

Tua-i nutaan aggliniluni qasgimun. Inarcami ilagni taukuk pilliniak unuaqu ayagciqniluteng uterrluteng.

Ercan tua-i nutaan utertelliniut. Tua-i-ll' akerta nalleqvaqatarluku ayainanermeggni ayuqucia tenguqlinglallinilria ayainanermini.

Murilkelliniuq-am Arnaruaq waten pimaluni. Maavet-gguq tua-i ellilliniluteng ayalriit. Unatain iluita maaggun qaingatgun utertellinilriit Arnaruam talliakun.

Wavet-gguq tua-i maavet ellilliniata, ukut waten piaqaki ayuqucia tenguqlinglallinilria. Nengcaki-gguq taugken waten assiriluni ayuqucia.

Tuquciiqellinikai elliin tamalkuita. Wavet elliqata tua-i waten qes'arrluku qagertarkaulliniluki.

Tuunrangayiit pissuutait.

Keggutellgem-am imum murilkarcamiu arulairrluni ilagni pilliniak, "Tua-i arulairluta amci inarrnaurtukut." Akerta-wa-gguq pikna nalleqvalria erenret qukaatnun ellirluni. Tua-i neliurluteng inartelliniluteng.

Inarcameng tua-i taukuk maliigmi tarnakek kingunemeggnun amavet, cauyaminek taumek tapirlukek, itegmillinilukek. Cauyaa tua-i wanirpak amavet tekilluni, taukuk tan'gaurluuk tarnakegnek maligluni.

ARNAQ: Kingunratnun.

MIISAQ: Tua-i qaill' pingairullutek taukuk, pengegnairullutek, maliik taukuk, taum angalkum pingairullukek.

Tuani tua-i itegmiggaarlukek, nutaan tua-i ayakallinilria tuunraryaramikun Keggutellek. Kingyarnaurtuq-gguq Arnaruam aqumgarrarmi maligeskii.

Arenqialani tua-i uyakelliinarngarian, angayuqaagminun tua-i caqirqullinilria Keggutellek. Kuigpiim kangrani pakmani Paluqtaviigni, mallgiinaani. Qimaktarturallinilria tua-i.

MARIE MEADE: To whose parents?

FRANK ANDREW: [The parents] of Keggutellek. And when he finally arrived at their place, he dashed through the door of their house. Seconds after he went in the house, there was a violent bang, and their house shook when Arnaruaq put his hands on it.

They say in the upper Yukon River, a mountain, a rock, the white rock *uqumyak* [quartz] started to form there, with *angernagun*, cement. The house of *paluqtaviit* [lit., "big *paluqtaat* (beavers)"], cracked open when Arnaruaq slapped his hand on it.

[As soon as he entered], his father gave Keggutellek a small bow. He told him that Arnaruaq was about to look in through the smoke hole, and he told him to aim.

And just as he took that small bow and aimed, [Arnaruaq] looked in. And as soon as he looked in, he shot his arrow straight at his chest. Then they heard him roll down out there. That was when he finally killed [Arnaruaq]. They say Keggutellek killed Arnaruaq.

I think this is where the story ends.

I've just told you one of the stories [I know] for your enjoyment.

MARIE MEADE: My goodness, those mighty shamans were dangerous.

Shamans didn't get along, they were jealous of each other[32]

Frank Andrew and Marie Meade, Anchorage, September 2005

FRANK ANDREW: They say shamans would fight, they were jealous of each other. They say when a shaman used his power to do good works and helped others, and healed people from sickness, the other shamans would go against him without him knowing, trying to cause trouble for him, being jealous of him.

You see, [when people asked them for help], they'd pay shamans with things. They'd compensate them for the work, *ellimerrucirluki* as they called it. They'd give them material things.

Because of [their payments] some [shamans] would start to counter them. And they'd lie about them and try to influence others who weren't shamans to oppose them. Then those believing what they heard would begin going against them.

ARNAQ: Kia angayuqaagkenun?

MIISAQ: Taum-wa Keggutellgem. Tekiquraamikek tua-i tuani amiigagni cuukcautelliniluni. Itqertelluku tua-i eniik tauna qatngitlinilria Arnaruam patellrani unatminek.

Kuigpiim-gguq kangrani pakmani tauna ingriq, qiu, imumek uqumyagmek qaralingellruuq, angernagutmek, *cement*, taum kinguani. Ngelua tauna paluqtaviit qup'arrluku-gguq patlerminiu Arnaruam, patellrani qup'artelliniluni quligluni.

Atiin taum cikiqallinikii urluvcuarmek Keggutellek. Nuvutesqelluku Arnaruaq uyangteqatarniluku egalratgun.

Urluvcuar-llu tamana nuvluku piqanrakun uyangtelliniluni. Uyangcan qat'gaakun pitgalliniluku. Qakma-ll' akalliniluni. Tua-i nutaan piunrirrluku. Tauna tua-i Keggutellgem-gguq tuqutellrua, tauna Arnaruaq.

Waten taktayugnarquq.

Quliramek, iliitnek piamken, anglaniurcetamken.

ARNAQ: Angalkukayiit tamakut alingnaqvagtat.

Nakukutut angalkut, ciknakulluteng

Miisaq Arnaq-llu, Anchorage, September 2005

MIISAQ: Nakukutut-gguq angalkut, ciknakulluteng. Waten-gguq una angalkuq ikayurilria tuunraryaramikun assilriamek mat'umek, yuut-llu naulluulriit assirivkaraqluki, tuaten piqaquuralria angalkuullgutain makut inglukengtuat nalluani pinrillugcetaangluku, assinrilngurnek tua-i pinrillugcetaangluku, ciknakluku.

Nauwa canek akilirluki pitullrullinikait angalkut. Nunulirluki ellimerrucirluki-gguq. Aklunek tua-i cikirluki.

Tamakut tamaa-i pitekluki inglukngetullrulliniit ilaita. Iqluqutekengluki-llu pingcetaarluki tua-i, pingucetaarluki makunun angalkuunrilngurnun. Ukvertaqaceteng-gguq tua-i inglukengtuit.

Remember the story about that man named Ississaayuq who fled to the Yukon River area because they were going to murder him. Just like in that story, shamans would begin spreading gossip about other shamans, and many people would believe them and begin probing into killing that person. That was what happened to Cingarturta, too.

Those shamans didn't do good works. They lied about their fellow [shamans] who did good works [influencing others to go against them].

MARIE MEADE: They speak falsely about them.

FRANK ANDREW: Yes. They'd have others who aren't shamans despise them.

Iciw' imna qanemciq Ississaayuq tuquteqataatni qakmavet Kuigpagmun ayalleq, qanemciutulriallu. Tautun tua-i, yuut makut angalkuunrilnguut amlleret ukverrluki, angalkuullgutain piaceteng tauna tua-i tuquitungluku. Cingarturta-llu cali tuatnallrulliniluku.

Tamaa-i tamakut tamaa-i assinrilngurmek caliarluteng. Ilateng elluarrluteng calilriit tua-i iqluqutekluki.

ARNAQ: Pinguartelluki.

MIISAQ: Ii-i. Kenkenrircetaqluki makunun angalkuunrilngurnun.

Devices shamans used to put a curse on someone and make him sick[33]

Nuyarniurcuutet

Frank Andrew and Marie Meade, Anchorage, September 2005

Miisaq Arnaq-llu, Anchorage, September 2005

MARIE MEADE: The other day when you mentioned *nuyarnera*, how did you explain it?

FRANK ANDREW: The *nuyarniurcuutet* that shamans used were "devices" they used to cut up *nuyarneraralriit* [those inflicted with *nuyarnera*].

With us not knowing it, a shaman might make people sick. Their means for hunting would remain in that person they attacked while he is living. The bad thoughts that a shaman has for that person, [through their mind's eye] they see those "bad thoughts" as *nuyarneret*. People couldn't see them, but only the shamans could see that it had been planted in a person, by his *nuyarnerarallra*, the one who cursed someone.

MARIE MEADE: But a normal person can't see it.

ARNAQ: Nuyarnera imat'am uumi caunillruken?

MIISAQ: Nuyarniurcuutait-gguq tamakut imkuugut kepurissuutait nuyarneraralrianek.

Angalkut nallumteni tayima naulluuvkariluteng yugnek piciatun. Pissurcuutait, cassuutait-gguq tua-i aug'ayuunateng tuavet pikngaatnun unguvallrani. Tamaa-i umyugaa angalkum assirpek'nani taumun pimallra, tangellratni-gguq nuyarneruluni tua-i ayuquq. Yuum tangvagpek'naku tua-i, angalkum taugaam tangerrsugngaluku tuaten pimacia, nuyarnerarallrakun, alaitellrakun.

ARNAQ: Yuunginaam taugaam tangerciiganaku.

They say shamans sleep two ways[108]

Angalkuq-gguq malrugnek waten qavaryarangqetuuq

Frank Andrew and Marie Meade, Anchorage, September 2005

Miisaq Arnaq-llu, Anchorage, September 2005

FRANK ANDREW: Normal people are very perceptive and can understand when things are not normal. They say shamans sleep two ways. But normal people sleep only one way. For that reason, a normal person will know immediately if a shaman is not "thinking right" toward him, even though [the shaman] is being secretive.

He can recognize [a shaman] through his dreams.

MIISAQ: Yuunginaat-gguq nallukengengaitut. Angalkuq-gguq malrugnek waten qavaryarangqetuuq. Yuunginaq-gguq taugken ataucimek. Taumek-gguq yuunginaam angalkuq angarvaungraan tungminun qaill' umyuarteqelria nallusciigataa nallucetaangraan.

Qavangumikun tua-i elitaqsugngaluku.

MARIE MEADE: A shaman has two ways to sleep.

FRANK ANDREW: That's what they say. A shaman can sleep on two levels. He can sleep and get down very deep and stop breathing. And he can also sleep on the level that we normal people sleep. And he can also sleep a very deep sleep.

MARIE MEADE: And he can get down very deep as if he was dead.

FRANK ANDREW: [When he sleeps] he can stop breathing like a dead person. But a normal person only sleeps in one way. That's why normal people can easily understand if a shaman has ill feelings toward them, even though he doesn't want him to know. A normal person will perceive [that it is a shaman] right away in his sleep.

MARIE MEADE: And can shamans continue to use their powers [against someone], even after they had died?

FRANK ANDREW: Yes. And they say when their fellow shamans killed them, after they died, [their opponents] wouldn't be able to run anymore. If [a shaman] retaliates after he dies, he won't let [his opponent] live, even though he had been weaker [and was defeated while alive].

MARIE MEADE: [If he had been defeated by] his fellow shaman.

FRANK ANDREW: Yes. They say when shamans retaliate after they had been killed and died, they don't leave anyone alive. And it's because some of them are *yuungcarat*. They reside with the *ircenrraat*, those living beings who are not like regular human beings.

When [the shaman] died, he would be visible through that person, he would have awareness there at his *mer'umavigkaq*[35]

Frank Andrew and Marie Meade, Bethel, December 2003

FRANK ANDREW: And they say these *iinrut* have different uses. And he told me a story about how he came to be one of those [shamans]. His father was also a shaman. His father's name was Apalciq. He was also a shaman, a *tuunraq* [shaman's helping spirit, but here used as a synonym for shaman]. His son was Ayagina'ar, Akerpak. Because he was

ARNAQ: Angalkuq malrugnek qavaryararluni.

MIISAQ: Tuaten qanrutkelaraat. Malrugnek-gguq qavaryarangqertuq angalkuq. Kiveggluni tuquluni tua-i anernerunani-llu qavaryugngaluni. Qavamteggun-llu maaggun qavalaucimcetun qavaryugngaluni. Kiveggluni-ll' tuaten qavaryugngaluni.

ARNAQ: Kiveggluni tuqumalriacetun.

MIISAQ: Tuqumalriacetun anerneriulluni. Yuunginaq-gguq taugken tuaten ataucimek qavaryarangqerrluni. Taumek-gguq angalkuq nallungailkiit nallucetaangraan, tungminun qaillun iqlutun umyuarteqelria. Qavangumikun qavamikun tua-i egmian' elpekarkauluku yuunginaam.

ARNAQ: Angalkut-llu-qaa tua-i cali tuqullrung'ermeng catairutellrung'ermeng cali tuaten tamana angalkuucirteng cali aturturyugngaluku?

MIISAQ: Ii-i. Angalkuullgutmeng-gguq pitaqaqaceteng-llu, tuqumariaqameng-gguq taugaam tua-i qaillun qimagviirutetuut. Tuqumariluni tua-i akinauquni unguvavkarngaunaku nutaan, cirliqellrung'ermi.

ARNAQ: Angalkuullgutiin.

MIISAQ: Ii-i. Unguvavkariyuitut-gguq tuqumariluteng akinaulriit. Tua-i yuungcarauluteng-llu pilaameng ilait. Nunaluteng ircen'ernek, canek tua-i makunek yugtun ayuqenrilngurnek.

Tua-i tuqukuni apqiitnek tuavet, tuaggun alaitarkauluni, ellangqerrarkauluni tuani mer'umavigkamini

---

Miisaq Arnaq-llu, Mamterilleq, December 2003

MIISAQ: Makut-llu maa-i iinrut ayuqevkenateng tua-i pituluteng-gguq. Tua-i-llu tamakuurteqatallerminek qanemcitaanga. Atii cali angalkuuguq. Tauna Apalcimek atengqertuq atii. Angalkuuluni cali, tuunrauluni. Tauna-gguq qetunraa Ayagina'ar, Akerpak. Tua-i kiingan yukngamiu angalkuuvkallerkaa,

his only son, his father didn't want him to be a shaman, and he didn't teach him what he knew.

But a *tuunraq*, a shaman who had died long before that time, became captivated with him, and he began to appear to him at night outside in the wilderness, too. That one apparently captured him, even though he fled. That one turned him into a shaman.

And he said when he finally captured him, he showed him the abilities that he would acquire. He showed and explained to him what powers could be used for curing what illnesses. He explained what they were one by one.

He said that person did that to him, he turned him into a shaman. He said that he didn't know anything because he wasn't taught. But he said when he followed that person's instructions, he became a *tuunraq*, by using the instructions he was given.

MARIE MEADE: Even though that person had already died before that? He gave him instructions, even though he had died?

FRANK ANDREW: Yes. They say those *tuunrat* are different. And when they are going to die, they start looking for what they call their *mer'umavigkat* [lit., "ones who would give them a constant source of drinking water," from *meq*, "water"].

When [the shaman died], he would be visible through that person, he would have awareness there at his *mer'umavigkaq*, at his *mer'umavik*.

And he didn't know who that person was because he had not seen him before. He came to learn later on that the [shaman who passed on his powers to him] was his great-grandparent. [When] that one appeared to him inside that house in Ekvicuaq [Eek], he finally allowed him to capture him. He said he was wearing a muskrat parka without a hood. I'm starting to tell you a story. Is it okay?

MARIE MEADE: Yes, it's fine.

FRANK ANDREW: It had floor boards that were small, thin pieces of plywood like this. [The boards] *?qanermigingaluteng*, and where they connected, they would push in like this. They were those thin [pieces of wood] that were floor boards. His house in Ekvicuaq had that kind of floor boards.

He said that the door was out there, and his stove here [indicating to the right with his arm]. There were beds that were situated across from each other. He was sitting [on the bed] on this side [on the right].

While he was there, he suddenly became aware that he was sitting right in front of the door on top

angalkuusqumavkenaku taum atiin pillrullinia, elisngaaminek-llu elitnauyuunaku.

Taugaam tuunraam, angalkum taum piunrillrem ak'a agyakengluku tamaani, aliuqungluku unugmi ellami-llu yuilqumi. Taum tua-i teguurainallrullinia qimagangraan. Tua-i angalkuurtelluku taum.

Nutaan-llu-gguq tegumariamiu pissuutekainek maniilluku. Apertualluki tua-i, man'a tuavet, tuaten taumun naulluulriamek camek apqucimek pilriamun atuuyugnganiluku. Nalqigqurluki-gguq.

Taum-gguq tua-i tuaten pillrua, angalkuurtelluku. Camek-gguq ellii nalluuq tua-i elitnaurumanrilamni. Taum-gguq taugaam tua-i alerquatiikun piaqami tua-i tuunraurtelartuq, alerquatni aturturluku.

ARNAQ: Ak'a-qaa tauna tuqullrung'ermi? Tuqullrung'ermi-qaa taum alerqualuku?

MIISAQ: Yaa. Tamakut-gguq tuunraat allakaugut-am tua-i. Waten-llu tuquarkaurtaqameng yuangaqluteng mer'umavigkameggnek-gguq.

Tua-i tuqukuni apqiitnek tuavet, tuaggun alaitarkauluni, ellangqerrarkauluni tuani, mer'umavigkamini, mer'umavimini.

Tauna-llu-gguq nalluluku tangellrunrilamiu. Cunawa-gguq amauqellinikii. Taum pugvikluku tuani enem iluani Ekvicuarni teguvkallrulliniuq nutaan. Tevyulinek-gguq atkugluni negiliinani. Qanemciteng'amci. Canrituq-qaa?

ARNAQ: Yaa, assirtuq.

MIISAQ: Imkunek nacitengqelliniuq tuskacuarnek iqkilnguayaarnek waten. Qanermigingaluteng imkut, waten cingautellrit itqerrluteng pituluteng. Iqkilnguayagaat nacitngutulit. Tamakunek nacitengqelliniuq enii Ekvicuarni.

Amiik-gguq uani, kaminiara-w' tuani. Inglertarluni-gguq akiqliqelrianek. Tuani aqumgaluni ukaqliani.

Piinanermini tua-i ellangartelliniuq amiigem ciuqerrani nacitet qaingatni aqumgaluni, amiik

of the floor boards, facing the door, and the stove was here. He felt anxious like he was expecting something to happen.

After a while, he started to hear his sound, it sounded like a housefly. He said he wasn't frightened. When it became loud, the house started to shake.

While he [had his head down], the floor boards below started to come up. He was coming up. And when he was about to reach his level . . . he said those floor boards were very strong. They did not break apart, but only lifted like this.

When he was about to reach his same height, they suddenly parted and went down. He said that person's back was to him. He said he had a haircut here like this [indicating right above his ears] and his temples had a lot of white hair.

His parka made of muskrats had no hood, but it had an opening through here.

When he reached his height, he stopped moving to the height where he was sitting. When he was done, he told him to grab hold of him.

He didn't reply, but thought, "Where on his body will I hold him?" When that thought came to mind, he told him, "You can grab on here."

He pointed to these two here, these two. They were bound with what looked like spruce root. On this part of his body [his hips] was another set; on these parts of him were the bottom ones. He was thinking to take hold of the two up top [on his shoulders].

When he was just about to extend his arms [to hold him], he admonished him, "Oh no, you are about to take me on the wrong part. Take me on the bottom ones." He then grabbed hold of him there.

When he took him, he had a good grip on him. When he'd let him move, he moved easily in circles.

He started to move him around unexpectedly. He would follow his movements. When he would move him in a circle, he would go in circles easily.

After a while, he admonished him, "Stop messing with me. Listen to me now. I am going to show you something."

After doing that, the sun, you know how it becomes bright when the sun suddenly pours through the gaps in the wall when there are holes. Those kinds of [sun rays], they suddenly shone in front of him this way.

caumaluku, kaminiaq-wa-gguq una wani. Camek-gguq neryuniurluni.

Piinanrani nepii alailliniuq, ciivagtun neplirluni. Alingallanrituq-gguq. Qasturiami tua-i kakavungllinilria ena tamana.

Waten-gguq tua-i [puc'imaluni] piinanrani tamakut tuskayagaat nuulliniluki camaken. Mayulliniuq tua-i. Elliitun-llu tua-i pitariqatarluni . . . tamakut-gguq nacitet elngulliniut. Allgauteksaunateng, mayurluteng taugaam waten.

Elliitun tua-i pitariqatarluni nutaan qukviqerrluteng, atrarluteng-gguq. Tunusngaluku-gguq taum. Kepliarluni-gguq waten maaggun, qiilinglutek ayakutaraak.

Kanaqlak-wa atkua nacaunani, maaggun taugaam pugyararrarluni.

Man'a-gguq tua-i tekiteqerluku, elliitun sugtutariqerluni aqumgallrani taq'uq. Taqngami pillinia, tegusqelluni.

Kiuvkenaku umyuarteqliniuq, "Natiikun-mi waniw' teguciqsia?" Tuaten-am umyuarteqngan pillinia, "Tua-i tang teguvigkagken."

Pillinia wani ukugkenek, ukugkegnek. Nekevraarcinrarnek-gguq tuar nemrumalriik. Ukugni-wa-gguq call' aipaak; ukugkeni atliik. Taukugnegun tua-i qulliignegun umyuarteqluni tegunalukek taukuk.

Yaggnaluni tua-i piqanrakun inerqullinia, "Aullugga-i iqlukun teguqatararpenga. Atliignegun tegunga." Tegulliniluk' tua-i tuaggun.

Teguyunaqvaa-gguq tegullrani. Waten pek'arcetaqani-gguq uivqetaaqernaurtuq waten.

Qaillukuangellinia. Maligtaqulluni-gguq tua-i. Uivqetaarcetaqaku uivqetaarluni pisciigatevkenani.

Pivakartelluni-am inerqullinia, "Tua-i naanguarutekviiqnii. Niicugninga amci. Maniiteqataramken."

Tua-i tuaten piqertelluku nauw' im' akerta, pagkut-llu pagaa-i tanqiit waten ukinret, ilutmun waten akerta ukinertangqerraqan itqertaqami tanqigcenateng pitulriit akertem pillri. Tuaten tua-i ayuqellriit nengqertelliniut ciuqerranun waten, ukatmun.

FRANK ANDREW: I got up. After [drumming] for a while, he told me to sit below him and rest my legs over the pillow, and to turn my back to him.

His mother was in the back area, and her daughter was across there as well. And there was also someone at the back area of the place, her other daughter.

I sat just below in front of him on top of the head rest. He sat behind me and after that, he would blow on my back, turning off the lights.

After some time, I started to feel cold. I started to shiver and my arms [crossed on chest] started moving this way, they were lifting. It seemed that my breathing was going inward sometimes. It started to get more powerful.

Eventually, my voice started to come out unexpectedly, and I would make the sudden noise, "Ee-ee." When I got to that point, I started to hear something, and I realized that it was people laughing, those who I thought were sleeping.

When it got too much and too powerful, I twisted the bottom part of my body and fell onto the floor. When I landed, it suddenly ended. Those are apparently powerful. I told him that I was done, that I wouldn't do it again.

They are powerful. People should not think little about the abilities of shamans.

ALEX BIRD: You were fine, you went back to your normal self?

FRANK ANDREW: I was the same as before.

MARGARET ANDREWS: He was probably testing you, how you were.

FRANK ANDREW: But that person from Kipnuk, my other *iluraq*, the one named Nuqarrluk had him start drumming. He wasn't a shaman before that time and did not drum. But back when he was a reindeer herder, after encountering some kind of ghost and his disposition changed, he began to drum. The one who they called Arucuaq.

They say it's easy for a *tuunraq* [shaman] to overtake something they want. No matter what he does, even if he flees, if he wants to enter him, he can enter him, even if he doesn't want him to. That's why they say one should not disparage shamans too much. And they say even though he was killed, there is a way for him to come alive again. If he had been taken by the *ircenrraat*, he would live there.

MIISAQ: Maklua. Ak'anun tua-i piuraqerluni, pianga kitaki-gguq ketiinun wavet akitmun irugka tev'arrlukek tunulluku aqumlii.

Aanii-w' tauna kiatmi, pania-w' cali ikani. Egkuq-llu kiani cali yugluni panian aipaanek.

Aqumlua tua-i ketiinun, akitem qainganun. Qamaa-i-ll' tua-i tunumnun piluni, piluni tua-i pirraarluni, cupnauraanga tang tunumkun, kenurrat nipluki.

Atam qaillun pitariqerluku tuartang qerrutengkiinga. Qiivngelrianga talligka-ll' tang waten pinglutek ukatmun, mayuriinarlutek. Anerneqa tuartang iliini ilutmun it'ngartelalria. Tua-i tukniriinarluni.

Kiituan' tua-i tuaten elliqerluni erinaka anqertelanguq, "Ee-ee" waten-ll' pileryaglua. Atam tua-i tuaten elliqerlua cameg' imumek niitenga'artellrianga. Maaten tang pianka, engel'arturalriarullinilriit, tamakut qavaryukellrenka.

Arenqialama tua-i tukniriinaan, qipqerrluku uateka igglua natermun. Tuc'ama tua-i nutaan pellugarrlun' tamana. Tuknilliniut tamakut. Piaqa tua-i taqnilua tua-i, pinqiggngaitnilua.

Tukniut. Caunrilleksiyaagluki pissuutait piyunaitut tuunrangayiit taukut.

APALIQ: Tua-llu tua-i cangatevkanak tua-i, ayuqucirpetun ayuqluten?

MIISAQ: Ayuqlua ayuqucimtun.

QUUQAN: Yuvrillikiiten-wa, qayuwa ayuqellren.

MIISAQ: Augna taugaam Qipnermiu, cali ilu'urma allam, cauyaryaurtelluku, Nuqarrlugmek atellgem. Angalkuullrunricaaqluni cauyayuunani-ll'. Tuntulgullermini taugaam tamaani cam taum alangrum pirraanranek qaillun ellillermini tamaani cauyalangluni. Arucuarmek pilallrat.

Tuunraam-gguq piyukellni qacikaa. Cangraan-gguq qimagangraan tua-i iteryukuniu iteryugngaa, piyuumiilengraan. Taumek-gguq caunrilkessiyaayunaitaa man'a tuunrangayak. Tuqucimangermi-llu-gguq tua-i pivigkarluni tua-i. Ircen'ernek tegumallrukuni tua-i tamaantarkauluni.

If he had a *napaneq* [foundation], he would join them and stay alive[38]

Frank Andrew, Alex Bird, and Marie Meade, Bethel, December 2003

FRANK ANDREW: And if he had a *napaneq* [thing that keeps him alive given to him by a shaman], he would join those things and stay alive, the various plants that are on the land. If he has one of those for a *napaneq*, he would stay alive with them because he is one of them, be it of the water, of the air, or a land animal. They say that is how shamans are.

He would be taken from there, and even from *ircenrraat*. He would grow up with that as a foundation.

At Ingriigmiut, a shaman doctored two people from the same village to live, Cauvakayak and Angulluarluq, [who was also] Kiangqalria. Ingriik over there between Kipnuk and Chefornak, at that place.

They grew up at the same time. That one shaman [allowed them to live], in that one place; as they grew up, they weren't spoken to, and they would pick on each other as teasing cousins. And those two would speak of their village.

When they got to a certain age when they grew older, the mother of Cauvakayak . . . this is what those with powers do. [The shaman] warned his mother not to eat beluga whale, not to eat those.

Because some people break their rules, his mother broke her admonition, and she ate that to his detriment. She caused her child, the *yungcaraq* to end up a certain way, the *nukalpiaq* of the people of Ingriirmiut, their *nukalpiaq* Cauvakayak. He could not hunt, even though it was time for him to hunt.

But that Kiangqalria, when he started [to hunt] as an older man, he would go out to the ocean and would catch a lot of animals.

One day, when people spoke about him when he was an older man, when they said that Kiangqalria had caught a bearded seal, Cauvakayak put his head up after having it down smiling.

When he put his head up, he said, "We keep hearing about that *nukalpianguciq* [great *nukalpiaq*]. As if he caught more back in Ingriirmiut where we came from when we used to hunt, who was nothing but a lookout." They say those two were given abilities.

Cauluni napanerluni pillrukuni, tamakut ilagarluki unguvaarkauluni

Miisaq, Apaliq, Arnaq-llu, Mamterilleq, December 2003

MIISAQ: Cauluni-ll' napanerluni pillrukuni, tamakut ilagarluki unguvaarkauluni, caranglluut piciatun nunam qaingani uitalriit. Iliitnek napanengqerkuni tua-i unguvaarkauluni pillgutekluki ilakngamiki, mermiutauli, ellamiutauli, ungungssiuli. Angalkut-gguq tua-i tuaten ayuqut.

Tuaken tegumaaqluni, apqaitnek ircen'ernek-llu. Taun' kangikluku tua-i angliaqluni.

Ingriigmiuni angalkuq tauna nunalgutkelriignek yungcarilliniuq, Cuvakayiinkugnek Angulluarluq-llu, Kiangqalria. Ingriik ingkuk Qipnermiut akiit, Cevv'arnermiut-llu, taukumiuni.

Ataucikun anglilutek tua-i. Angalkum ataucim, nunani atauciini; angliamek tua-i qalarucimayuilnguuk-wa, nakukullutek tua-i ilu'urni[klutek] pilallinilriik. Nunamegnek-llu taukuk qanngaqlutek.

Tuaten tua-i ellirlutek angliriamek tua-i, tauna Cauvakayak aaniin tua-i . . . waten tuunralget pilalriit. Aanii-am tauna cetuanek imkunek nerlaasqevkenaku inerqullinia, tamakunek nerlaasqevkenaku.

Tua-i navtuan, navgituami yug' ilii amlleq, alerquatni-am tua-i navegluku taum aaniin, nercurlaulluku tamatumek. Qaillun ayuqlirivkarluku tauna yungcaraq waten irniani, Ingriirmiut nukalpiarat, nukalpiarat Cauvakayak. Tua-i pissurciiganani, tua-i pissurnaringraani.

Tauna taugaam Kiangqalria, angulluarluni pilangellermini, imarpigmun tua-i ayagaluni piliquulallinilria.

Caqerluni tuaten-am qanrutkellratni angulluarluk', Kiangqalria tauna maklaggniluku-am qanrutekluku pillratni, tauna Cauvakayak cikingqaumallerminek ciugcimaaralliniuq quuyurmi.

Ciugcami qanlliniuq, "Nukalpiangucimi-lli niicetaaqtanqegg'. Ima-llu-qaa kingunemegni Ingriirmiuni pingnatulallmegni pinrulallruluni, cavkenani kiarcetelleq." Pikiurumalutek-gguq tua-i taukuk pimauk.

And when they [go to] one they consider to be bright, they take that one and that one becomes his *mer'umavik*. He would become his *avneq*.

They always give them water. While they are conjuring, they ask for someone to give them water. Then he would stop conjuring, and he let them fill the dipper, and would have another person splash water on him. They say they are giving him water when he is thirsty. That is why shamans searched for what they called their *mer'umavigkat*.

Those *kit'ellriit* [shamans who went underwater] cannot be without this waterproof clothing as well[40]

Frank Andrew, Margaret Andrews, Marie Meade, and Alice Rearden, Bethel, December 2003

FRANK ANDREW: And *kit'ellriit* [shamans who went underwater using their powers] cannot be without these [seal-gut parkas], they say they never went without these, and probably those *elegtellriit* [those who burned using their powers] as well.

They say *kit'ellriit* prepared by putting on waterproof clothing, and they wore waterproof mittens, and they wore seal-gut rain parkas and waders. They got ready, they fastened and tightened the area around their face to keep out water. They say they have five helpers.

During recent times, in the old village of the people of Tuntutuliak, in Qinaq, one with the name Pangalgalria used to have five helpers when he drowned underwater, and the fifth would be his daughter.

MARIE MEADE: When they traveled to the water?

FRANK ANDREW: That place downriver from their village, Aassaqvik, one they called Aassaqvik, they say he would make a hole in the ice right where the river flows out. He would let them clear the surface of the ice. And when it was clear, they would lay down those grass kayak mats that are woven and would weigh down the corners and would leave the place.

But then [the five helpers] would take him down from the *qasgiq* holding him. And when they got to the grass kayak mats, after letting them take off the weights, they would take them off and it would not be covered, and there were no small pieces of ice on it at all.

They say they spread their legs out when they do that. They plant their feet on the edges of that

Tua-i-ll' tanqikmeggnun tuavet, teguluku tua-i taun' mer'umaviksagulluku. Taum tua-i avneqsagutarkaurrluku, piksagulluku.

Merquratuit. Tuunriinanermeggni iliiratulliniut-am mermek piqaasqelluni. Tua-i-ll' taqeqerluni tuunrillni, qaluurin imiqertelluku, waten ceqvallertarcelluni allamun yugmun. Mertelluku-gguq tua-i meqsukan. Tamana-wa tamaa-i pitekluku mer'umavigkameggnek aterpaggluki yuatuut, pitullruut angalkut.

Kit'ellriit-llu makuicuitut [meliurcuutnek]

Miisaq, Quuqan, Arnaq, Cucuaq-llu, Mamterilleq, December 2003

MIISAQ: Kit'ellriit-llu makuicuitut, makuicuitellruut-gguq, elegtellriit-llu pilliut.

Uptetuut-gguq kit'ellriit tua-i meliurcuutnek all'uteng, augkunek-llu arillugnek, imarniterluteng-llu ivrucirluteng-llu. Upluteng tua-i kegginateng-llu nungirrluki. Tallimanek-gguq waten kevgangqetuut.

Ukaqvaggun Tuntutuliarmiut nunallratni, Qinarmi tauna Pangalgalriamek at'lek kit'aqami tallimanek waten kevgangqetulliniuq, kevgangqetullrulliniuq paniminek tallimirluki.

ARNAQ: Mermun-qaa aya'agqameng?

MIISAQ: Ii-i. Ugna-am nuniita uatiini maani Aassaqvik, Aassaqvigmek acilallrat anellran-gguq ciuqerrakun anelituuq. Carrircetetua-gguq cikum qainga. Tua-i-ll' assirian imkut ikaraliitet, tupigat, sagtelluki, kangirait nanqertelluki unilluku, unitelluku.

Qasgimek-gguq taugken tua-i atraulluku taukut tegumiaqurluku. Tekicamegteggu-gguq tua-i tauna ikaraliitet taukut nanertai aug'arceqaarluk aug'arnauraat, qilaunani tua-i, cikurrluarmek-llu caunani.

Avlerrluteng-gguq pitulliniut. Anluam taum tua-i avatiinun tull'ukek waten, ayarugni-ll'

hole in the ice like this, and he'd insert his walking stick on the sides. Then using their powers, when he did something, he would plant his feet next to his [helper's] feet. They would push him farther toward the hole, and also the other person on the other side, narrowing his legs.

And after a number of times, he would suddenly get into the water. And on the water, his legs, his feet were like this. He didn't go down in the water right away.

And when he got to that point, he let them put their hands on him here, with their hands on top of each other. And he told them not to help him [put weight down on him]. But with just the weight [of their hands], just relaxed, with their [hands] on top of one another. And when they did that, they would finally start to go down. And when the bottom of his garment reached the water, it would ?nung'iqerrluni inside, the bottom of his seal-gut garment would look like this.

They would go down like that. And like he told them to, when [their hands] reached the water, they didn't remove them right away, but kept them there for a while. After he had done that, they'd return, when he had sunk.

They use these [seal-gut rain parkas] when they do that [go underwater]. These were tools for shamans; drums and seal-gut garments were their tools.

MARGARET ANDREWS: That killed him or what?

FRANK ANDREW: He didn't die.

They say they would sing all night while he was on his journey. They would rest when they'd get tired of singing, they'd rest for a short while. They'd start again. They would finally stop when he arrived.

MARGARET ANDREWS: They probably travel through song.

MARIE MEADE: When shamans do that, what do they call their songs, *yuarulluut*, or something else?

FRANK ANDREW: They call them *yuarulluut*. They say [other people] sing songs for them that they know, when they used their powers while standing. But when they used drums [to use their powers], they sang their own songs. But when they [used their powers] standing, those who weren't shamans sang for them, because they knew their songs.

ALICE REARDEN: Did they always use seal-gut garments when they were using their powers?

kapullukek. Pissuutmeggnek-gguq taugken tua-i aturluteng, qaill' piaqan, iruk it'gai kankut it'gameggnek waten ituliqerluki. Kat'um anluam tugniinun cingkaniraqluk' ik'um-llu, quukanirtellukek iruk.

Tua-i-llu-gguq qavciliriluni pian, mermun ek'arrluni. Meq-llu-gguq tua-i waten, ayuqlutek iruk, it'gai. Muruvkenani egmianun.

Tua-i-llu-gguq tuaten ellian, nutaan uuggun pategtelluni, unatait qalliqurtelluki. Tua-i ikayurluki-ll' waten pisqevkenaku. Tua-i taugaam qaamii man'a, waten elliqerluku, unaqseqerrluni, qalliqurtelluki. Tuaten-gguq pivkatuut. Nutaan-gguq tuatnaaqaceteng acitmun egilngartetuut. Man'a-llu-gguq tua-i mer'em tekicani akua, nung'iqerrluni ilutmun, waten ayuqliqerrluteng imarnitek akuak.

Tuaten-gguq tuan' piluteng atrarnaurtut. Alerquuciatun-llu taun' meq tekicamegteggu, egmian' aug'artevkenaki uitauraqertelluki. Tuaten-gguq tua-i pirraartelluku utertetuut, kit'aqan.

Tua-i atutuit makut tuaten piaqameng. Teguyaraqellrullinikait angalkut makut; imarnitet cauyat-llu tua-i teguyarallrit.

QUUQAN: Tua-i-qaa tuqulluku-qaa, wall'u-qaa?

MIISAQ: Tuquvkenani-wa.

Unugpak-gguq tua-i ayaumallrani aturpagatuut. Uitaqa'aqluteng tua-i atulngungaqameng, uitaqacuaqeraqluteng. Ataam ayanqigtaqluteng. Tekican taugaam nutaan taqluteng.

QUUQAN: Yuarutkun eglerrngaatut.

ARNAQ: Angalkut tua-i tamakut tuatnaaqameng, yuarutait-qaa canek ap'lartatki, yuarullugnek, wall'u-q'?

MIISAQ: Yuarullugnek-wa tua-i pilaqait. Nallunrilkengameggnek-gguq yuarutnek atuatetuit, nangerrluteng tuunriaqata. Taugken-gguq makutgun cauyatgun piameng nutaan ellmeggnek, ellmeggnek pimeggnek ellaita atualuteng. Nangerrluteng-gguq taugken tuaten piata, angalkuunrilngermeng tua-i atualluki elisngiimegteki yuarutait.

CUCUAQ: Imarnitegnek-qaa aturrlainarluteng tuunriaqameng?

FRANK ANDREW: They don't actually wear them, but draped them over their shoulders, then used them [to do incantations]. But they say when they are about to go on journeys, they put them on.

ALICE REARDEN: I heard they used to take their arms out of their sleeves.

FRANK ANDREW: When they didn't wear these, some *qilaraulluteng* [were wrapped in a sealskin for a spirit journey]. They folded these [seal-gut garments] and had them place them on the sides [of their bodies], on the right side. They folded them and placed them on their sides, covered with a bearded-seal skin.

And they'd thread walrus-skin line through the outer holes on the skin and tighten them very tightly. They'd take their clothes off, they were completely naked. Then they would finally put a sealskin rope on it for a harness, and appoint a person who would pull them, and get a piece of wood for a handle.

After doing that, they would [pull again]. Then after a while, he would suddenly fall back, and [the rope] would loosen.

They say when that happens, they pull them out from the entranceway. And when they pull them up and inside, they would take their [skin coverings] off and see that he was wearing the seal-gut rain garment that had been folded here. They'd be drenched.

MARGARET ANDREWS: So he had put them on, even though he was tightly bound?

FRANK ANDREW: These were some of their ways, things they did. They say when they'd do what they call *pinguarluteng* [pretending to do something], they'd sink down into the water, those [shamans] would sink in the water.

Those who fly are amazing to watch[41]

Frank Andrew, Alex Bird, and Marie Meade, Bethel, December 2003

MARIE MEADE: And did they only fly at night?

FRANK ANDREW: Those who fly are amazing to watch. They apparently fly at night seated on top of a rock. We did it at nighttime down on the coast when that shaman Ayuqsar was alive, one who is a little older than I am.

We would take his clothing off, tie him up and put a good rock underneath him. Then we'd flex

---

MIISAQ: Aturluki makut piyuicaaqait, ulikarluteng taugaam, tua-i-ll' aturluki pissuutekluki. Taugaam tuatnaaqameng, ayagluteng piqatarqameng, all'uki-gguq pituit.

CUCUAQ: Niitellruunga-llu aliteng aug'arluki.

MIISAQ: Pinrilmiameng-llu-gguq makunek ilait qilaraulluteng. Makucit imegturluki waten menglemeggnun maavet ellivkarluki, tallirpilirnermun. Imegluki menglemeggnun, maklagnek caquluki.

Putuitgun-llu qavyanek nuvluki cagniqluki cakneq tua-i. Matarrluteng, matqapiarmeng. Nutaan-llu taprualugnek uskurirluki, nuqcestekalirluki-llu, muragmek teguyararkaitnek pililuki cali.

Piyaaqerraarluku ataam piaqlutek. Tua-i-gguq taugken piinanermini, qetqallagluni kiatmun, qac'uqerrluni-llu-gguq man'a.

Tua-i-gguq tuaten piaqata, nugtetuit amiigmek waken tua-i. Nugtaqamegteki-gguq caquirnaurait, imkug' imarnitek imgumallrek maani aturlukek. Mecungqapiarlutek.

QUUQAN: At'elliak-qaa, qayuwa cagning'ermi?

MIISAQ: Makut piyarallrit maa-i, pilallrit. Pinguaraqameng-gguq kitaatuut, kit'aqluteng pituut tamakut.

Irr'inarqut atam tengautulit

Miisaq, Apaliq, Arnaq-llu, Mamterilleq, December 2003

ARNAQ: Unugmi-llu-q' kiingan tengautuluteng?

MIISAQ: Irr'inarqut atam tengautulit. Teggalqunek curirluteng tengautulliniut unugmi. Atakumi-w' pilallrulriakut uani, Ayuqsar augna unguvallrani angalkuq, ciulirnerraqa-w' ellma.

Ugayarluku tua-i qillerqelaqvut teggalqumek-llu curirluku assirturalriamek. Qunglluku-llu

---

his knees to his chest and let him sit. And they would put [his arms] down by his ankles and tie his wrists in the back. And then we'd tie these two here as well, here, having him bend his body.

And when he was done, we would sit him on top of the rock at the edge of the floor boards in the back [of the *qasgiq*]. And they would take the drum out into the entranceway of the *qasgiq*, and place it slanted [to one side] because it fit tightly. [The entranceway] was too narrow since the drum was large. They would just place the drum at a slant into the porch down below.

And they would let the drumstick fall through the cracks of the floor boards, they'd let it fall underneath the floor boards. Then they would turn the lights off.

And just as he instructed them, the ones in the back area would continually make a noise [by slapping their tongues against the front part of their lips inside their mouths]. And the ones who were below, up front would go, "Shhhh, shhhh." They'd continually make this sound, they'd continually sound out "shhh."

As they were there, they'd hear a thud entering, then something made a drumming noise. After the noise of drumming, the echoing noise started coming in. And it came up through the entryway down there. Just as it went up, there was a loud whistling noise down there. That was how fast the drumstick was beating, the one that we dropped through the gaps in the floor boards.

After a while, a large drumming noise could be heard. And the second time, when the drumming noise came from above, it suddenly went around [the *qasgiq*] in this direction. It was drumming. Then they finally sang loudly. When there was a place the song ended, it would end. And when it was over, a loud thud came from down there.

We would turn the light on and see him sitting on top of the rock biting onto the drumstick. And the drum's handle would be here, stuffed into the side of his neck with the edge of the drum leaning against the top of his knees. The drum's [handle] was here.

He would strike using his jaws, but here he was tied down. And when they were complete, when the five times [of circling the *qasgiq*] were complete, we would turn the lights on and see his bindings down there not untied, but in a pile.

MARIE MEADE: After what was complete, in what way complete?

tua-i waten aqumevkarluku. Makuk-llu pamavet waten pilukek, tayarnerikun qillerrluku waten pamavet pilukek. Ukuk-llu call' qillerrlukek maaggun, maaggun, apngevkarluku.

Tua-i-ll' qaqican teggalqum qainganun aqumlluk' nacitet iquatnun kiavet. Cauyaq-llu amiguyuanun qasgim anlluku irirrluku elliluku, caltulaan, caltuan. Iqkelkelluku, anglaan cauyaq. Irirrluku taugaam waten elliluku cakmavet elaturramun.

Kaugutii-llu nacitet aciatgun qulinerkun, nacitet aciatnun igtelluku. Tua-i-ll' nutaan kenurrat nipluki.

Alerquaciatun-am tua-i, qaugkut kiaqliit, waten elliurturluteng. Unegkut-llu uaqliit, "Shhhh, shhhh." Waten piurluteng, shhh-aaraurluteng.

Tua-i tuaten piinanratni migpalla'ar-llu itqerluni, cauyarpallarrluni ca. Cauyarpallarteqerluni-llu tua-i cauyaq, qasiarqurluni itrarluni cakma. Amigkun-llu cakma nuglun'. Nugqertelluku-ll' tua-i culuugyuugpallarrluni camna. Kaugutem cukatacia, imumun nacitet aciatnun igcetlemta.

Piuraqerluni-ll' tua-i cauyarpallarrluni. Aipiriami-ll' pakmaken cauyarpallarcami, ukatmun uivqerrluni. Cauyarluni. Nutaan aturpagluteng. Kep'arcarangqerraqan kep'artaqluni. Tua-i-ll' taq'ercan, migpalla'arrluni camna.

Kenurrarnaurtukut teggalqum qaingani aqumgaluni tua-i, kaugun-wa keggmiara. Cauyam-wa paplua maani, qerringanuni iiraani wani, ciisqugken qainganun maavet pimaluni engelii. Wanlluni tua-i cauyam pia.

Uuggun kaugtualallinii agluqugmikun, qillengqaluni taugken. Tua-i-ll' naangan, naangata, talliman ukut naangata, kenurrarnaurtukut qillrutallri kankut angicimavkenateng quyurmeng uitalriit.

ARNAQ: Cat naangata, qaillun naaluteng?

FRANK ANDREW: These five [rounds]. They apparently go around five times. When these [five rounds] were over, he'd quit. What he was doing was called *canipgurluni* [flying around using his shaman powers].

MARIE MEADE: They would turn the light off?

FRANK ANDREW: They only do it without the lights on. They'd turn them on when he was done.

MARIE MEADE: Five times? I wonder where he'd go?

FRANK ANDREW: That Milton, my little teasing cousin was always plotting things. I did not do as he wanted me to, even though Ayuqsaq was my teasing cousin. But he used to pick on him badly.

There was a long fire poker used for fire baths. I think it was inside the *qasgiq*. One day he told me when [Ayuqsaq] was going to [fly using his shaman powers], that he will swing at him with a fire poker [to try to touch him] when it's time for him to [fly].

Because they had planned to [take it] before there were people there, they pulled up the fire poker. Then he placed it on the other side of the head rest and covered it with bedding material. He would be sitting there.

They entered. When it was time and he entered, they got him ready. When he would [fly], he would apparently swing at him with that fire poker and swipe it back and forth up there. [*laughter*] He said he never touched him.

When he told him, Ayuqsaq said to him, "Even though you swipe at me, you will not touch me. Do you think that I [fly] inside this *qasgiq*? I go in circles up there *nunat anllugneratni* [along the aura/mist of the village], where you cannot reach. You won't touch me even if you try to touch me."

[Milton asked,] "How do you do that?"

He pointed at that rock, "This takes me." And he said it also takes him upside down, he would be upside down. That [rock] would take him. It was really stuck to his buttocks. That's the explanation he gave.

Ayuqsaq [said that]. Lerniq and Tengquq from Chefornak used to do that as well.

Those two actually have the same name, Tengquq and Lerniq. Those two used to do that in my presence, too, and Ayuqsaq as well.

MARIE MEADE: They would fly?

FRANK ANDREW: Yes.

MARIE MEADE: Where was Ayuqsaq from?

FRANK ANDREW: He became a resident of Kwigillingok. But he used to live around Kipnuk.

MARIE MEADE: Do those people have relatives today, do they have descendants?

MIISAQ: Talliman ukut. Tallimarqunek waten uivetulliniut. Tua-i-ll' qaqicata ukut taqluni. Canipgurluni-gguq tua-i.

ARNAQ: Kenurraq-qaa niptaqluku?

MIISAQ: Kenurraunaku taugaam pitulliniut. Taq'aqan taugaam kumartaqluki.

ARNAQ: Tallimarqunek? Natmun-kiq ayalarta?

MIISAQ: Aug'um-am Milton-aam, augna iluracungaqa picirkartuuq. Tua-i wii maligtaqullrunritaqa ilu'uqsaaqengramku Ayuqsaq. Elliin taugaam anagulluku pilaraa.

Keniurucetangqelartuq takqupagmek maqissuutmek. Iluani tua-i qasgim pingatelaryaaquq. Caqerluni-am pianga piqatallrani, keniurutmek-gguq kaalguaqerciqaa piqataqan.

Yungvailgan tua-i piciqliarutellruatgu, keniurun tauna nugtaa. Maavet-llu tua-i akitem keluanun elliluku, cururrlugnek patuluku. Wani taun' uitaarkauluni.

Iterluteng tua-i. Pinarian upluku itran. Tua-i-am tuatnaaqan tamatumek keniurutmek elliularyaaqellinia pakmavet. [*ngel'artut*] Agtuqsaitaa-gguq.

Qanrucani, Ayuqsam pia, "Kaalguangerpenga agturngaitarpenga. Mat'um-qaa qasgim iluani pilaryuklua umyuarteq'lartuten? Nunat ukut anllugneratni pakmani uivvaalartua, nuuqevni. Agturngaitarpenga agtussaangerpenga."

"Qaillun-mi piluten pilarcit?"

Teggalquq tauna niiraa, "Uum ayagat'laraanga." Kanarmi-llu-gguq uum ayagataqluk', kanarmi tua-i. Taum ayagalluku. Nepingaluni cakneq nulluugkegni. Tuaten-am nalqigtaa tamana.

Ayuqsaq. Lerniq-ll' imna pitullruuq, Tengquq-llu Cevv'arnermiu.

Taukuk atellguteksaaquk, Tengquq Lerniq-wa. Taukuk tua-i takumni pilallruuk cali, Ayuqsaq-llu.

ARNAQ: Tengaurlutek?

MIISAQ: Ii-i.

ARNAQ: Ayuqsaq camiunguluni?

MIISAQ: Kuigilngurmiungurtellruuq. Avaken Qipnermiut nuniitni uitalallruuq.

ARNAQ: Ilangqertut-qaa taukut maa-i, kinguvengqertut?

FRANK ANDREW: They have descendants. Ayuqsaq has many children. I don't know their names. They call one of them Angivran, and then there's Issurilek. I don't know some of his children.

MARIE MEADE: So in your presence, you would help one another tie him up?

FRANK ANDREW: Yes, they would tell us to tie them very tightly. He said loose [bindings] hurt a lot. But he doesn't feel anything with tight ones. They had the opposite effect. We used to tie him up really tightly.

We only did that during winter, we used to have him do that. I didn't hear that it was done for any purpose, but it was done for fun, and I didn't hear that it was done for any [shaman-related] reason.

ALEX BIRD: They did that for fun, for fun. We hear it was a good thing, it was for fun.

MIISAQ: Kinguvengqertut. Irniari amllertut Ayuqsam. Atrit-wa nallukenka. Angivramek-wa augna, Issurilek-wa. Ilait-wa nallukenka irniari.

ARNAQ: Elpeci-q' tua-i tuaten takuvni elpet ikayuqluci qillertaqluku?

MIISAQ: Ii-i. Alerqurnauraakut cagnilluki cakneq pilaasqelluni. Qacngalnguut-gguq akngirnarqut cakneq. Cagnilriit-gguq taugken uunguciinateng. Mumiggluteng. Cagniqluku qillerqelallruarput.

Uksumi taugaam pilallruukut, pivkalallruarput. Cayarauniluki-ll' niicuilkeka, naanguarutekluki tua-i pilallrulriit, cassuutnguluku-ll' niicuunaku.

APALIQ: Aquitekluku tua-i, aquitekluku. Niitellra assirluni, anglanaqluni.

And there would be a person inside the ground swimming, what they called kis'uka'arluni[42]

Frank Andrew, Bethel, December 2003

FRANK ANDREW: And when they kis'uka'arluteng, they were amazing to watch, they are apparently very amazing to watch. The wooden floor boards . . . they would hold onto the sealskin rope. And down underground would be a person. When he would swim around, the skin line would move, cutting through the floor boards, and the wooden plank [that it had gone through] would fuse together after it passed. [The sealskin line] would turn in different directions, it would go across [planks], cutting across.

We would watch it, and it was amazing to watch; on floor boards like this, the sealskin rope would cut across them, going anywhere. This was in the qasgiq.

And there would be a person inside the ground swimming, what they called kis'uka'arluni. Another person would hold onto the sealskin rope. And suddenly, it would go toward the front area [of the qasgiq]. When it got to the tunnel entrance, he would make noise and tell them to pull him out. They also tie them up when they do that.

That person used to do all sorts of things. And he would place the drum on the edge of the weight of the window and hang it there by the handle. And he would turn the lights out after tying him up.

Yuk-wam caman' nunam akuliini kuimalria kis'uka'arluni-gguq

Miisaq, Mamterilleq, December 2003

MIISAQ: Kis'ukaraaqameng tuamtell' irr'inaqpiat, irr'inaqpialliniluteng. Nacitet muriit . . . taprualuk tua-i man' tegumiaqurluku pitulliniluku. Yuk-wa im' camani nunam akuliini. Kuimarluni ayagaqan, muriit taprualuk kepluku ayagnaurtuq, kingunra tuaten mamluni muriim. Caqialuni, qer'aqtaarluni, kepelmun piluku.

Tangvagluku tua-i wangkuta, irr'inaqluni; waten muriit ayuqelriit, kepelmun taprualuk ayagaqluni piciatun. Qasgimi.

Yuk-w' im' caman' nunam akuliini kuimalria, kis'uka'arluni-gguq. Yuum allam tegumiaqluku taprualuk. Pinarian-llu tua-i uatmuqerrluni. Kalvagyaramun tekicami nepelkilluni nugcesqelluni. Cali tua-i tuaten qilleqluki pitulliniluki.

Qaillukualallruuq tauna. Cauyaq-llu pikavet qasgim egalranun nanertiin mengliikun epua piluku agarrluku pikavet. Nipluku-ll' tua-i qillerqerraarluku.

But the drumstick would whistle, and after whistling, and we couldn't sense him going up there, and immediately from the window above, there would be a loud drumming noise. And after the loud drumming noise, he would fly around and go down. When he landed on the floor boards, he would stop [making noise].

They would turn the light on, and he would be tied down, but here the drum handle would be on this side. That's what he would do, what they called *kis'uka'arluni*. He would have them feel around his body [to make sure he was secure].

Kaugutii taugken tua-i culu'ugyungluni tua-i culu'ugyuguaqerluni, mayuuciinani-ll', egmian' pakmaken egalermek cauyarpallarrluni. Cauyarpallarcami-ll' uivvaarluni atrarluni. Nacitnun tuc'ami taq'errluni.

Kumarrnaurtuq qillengqaluni, amtall' cauyaq taun' waten, ukalirnermi paplua uitaluni. Tuaten-am tua-i piaqluni, kis'uka'arluni-gguq. Cavtaartelluni.

Puyulkuk used to let us watch him[117]

Frank Andrew and Marie Meade, Bethel, December 2003

FRANK ANDREW: However, Puyulkuk used to let us watch him. He would have us watch him as he was down in the center surrounded by us.

And even though we were staring at something, as we were looking at it, it would disappear.

And we would tear up a seal-gut parka, and he would gather all the pieces together and tuck them under here, near this. Then he would cover them with his old *qaspeq*. After a while, he would open it up and take them out and they had already repaired; it would have no tears on it.

And then those pieces of twine [called] *imuat*, they used to have those long ago. He got one of those that belonged to his wife. He told us to place it in the fire, inside the stove. He had it burn, and he would let us check on it. And when the fire went out, like before, and he didn't seem to do anything. After lifting up this part, he stuck his hand in and took it out, and that twine was in its original state.

And then, that large rock that was oblong that was used for strengthening the body, he placed it in our center and told us to stare at it and not lose its whereabouts. We stared at it, not being very far from it. As we were looking at it, it felt as though we just blinked, and when we looked at it, the rock was gone.

After doing that, he did the same thing to us, and made [the rock] reappear.

After doing that, he asked what we thought about what he just did. He asked if we thought that he merely moved it somewhere else. He said that

Puyulkuk taugaam tangvagtelluni tungaunani

Miisaq Arnaq-llu, Mamterilleq, December 2003

MIISAQ: Puyulkuk taugaam tangvagtelluni tungaunani tua-i pilallruuq. Qukamteni kanani tangvagtelluni tua-i.

Murilkelluku-ll' pik'ngarput piyaaqengramta, tangvainanemteni tamarnaurtuq tayim'.

Ukuk-llu waniw' imarnitek allgurlukek piyaaqeciqerput, quyurrluki tua-i wavet-am qerrnaurai, uum nuniinun. Patuluki-ll' tua-i qaspellraminek. Uitauraqerluni taugken angparrluku anetnaurai ak'a tumallinilriit; allganrunateng.

Tuamtell' imkut pelaciniit imuat, pingqelallruut avani ciuqvani. Tamatumek-am piluni nuliami pianek. Kenermun-am ekesqelluku, kaminiamun ekluku. Elegtelluku tua-i yuvriqercetaqluku. Qamngan-llu tua-i, aug'utun-am tua-i, qaillun-llu pivkenani, pingatevkenani. Tamana-am qakgarqaarluku kauluku antaa-am ayuqucimitun tamana pelacinak.

Tuamtellam pinirtaarcuutek'lallrat teggarvall'er takaayiluni, kanavet-am qukamtenun elliluku piakut, kitaki-gguq tangvaurlarput tamariyaaqevkenaku. Tangvagluku tua-i yaaqsissaagpek'naku. Piinanemteni, cikemyaqalriakut tuar, piyaaqnaurput, piukut tayima im' teggalquq.

Tua-i-am pirraarluta, call' aug'utun piluta, alairtelluku.

Pirraarluni, nalqigtai qaillun-gguq umyuarteqceta augkunek pillrani. Natmun-gguq-qaa nugtarrluki piyukluki piukut,

they actually stay in their places, but that our eyes become blinded suddenly. That thing disappears, our eyes become unable to see it. He said that's what happens to them.

MARIE MEADE: Even though it is in its place?

FRANK ANDREW: Even though it was still sitting in its original place.

He said that's how he explains it. He said there are many shamans who are deceptive. Even if he is unable to carry out something, he just deceives.

MARIE MEADE: Puyulkuk said that? But he was not lying himself? But he had real [powers]? Did he do things for real?

FRANK ANDREW: Yes. He said that he explains things without holding secrets.

He said shamans, some of them pay others and pretend to go on journeys, and they pretend to go underwater, by paying their helpers. And they paid them with animals, that they would give them those things. They would pretend to go on journeys and not really go. He said some shamans were like that. They weren't truthful, they'd lie about going on journeys.

- -

Cupungulria, one who drums and sings to conjure her spirit powers[44]

- -

Theresa Moses, Frank Andrew, and Marie Meade, National Museum of the American Indian, February 2003

THERESA MOSES: That one [woman in Waugh photo 2738] is sewing a seal-gut garment.

FRANK ANDREW: It's Cupungulria.

Cupungulria, *igyararatuli* [one who drums and sings to conjure her spirit powers], she would drum.

The small drum, those sugar cubes that have a container about a certain width, you know what they are. Those people said her drum was about that size.

THERESA MOSES: She is sewing a young bearded-seal-gut garment. Is she left-handed?

FRANK ANDREW: She's left-handed.

MARIE MEADE: What kind of drum did you say she had?

FRANK ANDREW: Those sugar containers, the cardboard containers that weren't wide usually filled with those sugar cubes.

umyuartequkut. Nem'eggni-gguq uitalaryaaqut, taugaam-gguq iiput tangerciigalliqertellartut. Ca catairrluni nallmikun, iimta tangerciigalli'irrluku. Tuaten-gguq pilartut.

ARNAQ: Uitayaaqengraan?

MIISAQ: Uitayaaqengermi enem'ini.

Makut-gguq maa-i nalqigtelarai waten. Angalkuq-gguq amlleq iqlungartuq. Tuatnallermikun tua-i, piyugnganrilngermi tamana tua-i camek, iqluquluni taugaam.

ARNAQ: Puyulkuum? Ellii-qaa taugaam iqluvkenani? Ellii taugaam piciuluni piaqluni? Ellii-qaa piciuluni piaqluni?

MIISAQ: Ii-i. Aassaqevkenani-llu-gguq elliin nalqigtelarai.

Angalkut-gguq, ilait-llu-gguq nunulirturluki ayaguatuut mermun-llu kisnguaraqluteng, ukut kevgateng nunulirturluki. Pitarkaitnek-llu akiliraqluki, tuaten piciqniluki. Ayagpek'nateng tua-i ayaguarluteng. Ilait-gguq tua-i angalkut tuaten ayuqut. Piciuvkenateng tua-i, ayaguaraqluteng.

- -

Cupungulria, igyararatuli

- -

Ilanaq, Miisaq, Arnaq-llu, National Museum of the American Indian, February 2003

ILANAQ: Iqellria-w' taun' imarnitegnek.

MIISAQ: Cupungulria.
Cupungulria, igyararatuli, cauyatuluni.

Cauyacuar, imkut caarralat imkut tuvtat caqungqelalriit qaill' iqtutauralrianek ai, nallunrilketen. Tuaten tua-i cauyaa angtanilaqiit taukut.

ILANAQ: Maklinrarmek qilumek iqellria. Iqsungqertuq-qaa tauna?

MIISAQ: Iqsungqertuq.

ARNAQ: Camek-im' cauyangqerrniken?

MIISAQ: Saarralautellret, saarralat imkut kegglaranek imalget, caquit imkut kalikat iqtunrilnguut.

They say that her drum could fit into one of those. It was that size.

When she would *igyara'arluni* [drum and sing to conjure her powers], she would take it, and when she drummed, sometimes the drumstick would hit her face.

Paru was apparently her *uicungaq* [male teasing cousin]. Paru criticized her drum because the drumstick would hit her face. She replied that when her *tarian* [another word for *tuunraq*, helping spirit] comes near her, her drum grows into a very large drum.

MARIE MEADE: Oh. Her helping spirit?

FRANK ANDREW: Yes, she was an *igyararatuli* [one who drums and sings to conjure her powers], she would drum.

MARIE MEADE: How do they *igyara'arluteng*?

FRANK ANDREW: Her spirit powers come to her, inhabit her. They call those who do that *igyararalriit*.

Tua-llu-gguq cauyaa taukuk iluagni ekumalria. Angtacia.

Igyararaami-gguq taugken teguluku cauyaami kegginaminun kaugutii iliini tut'aqluni.

Uicungaqellinia imna Paru. Tua-i Parum-am taum cauyaa taun' uputellinikii kegginaanun-llu kaugtualallra kaugutii. Kiugaa-gguq uum, aren cuayaa-gguq una tarian mallgaqani causpakayall'ertun angtarilartuq.

ARNAQ: Oh. Tarian?

MIISAQ: Ii-i, igyararatulim, cauyatuluni.

ARNAQ: Qaillun-kiq igyararalartat?

MIISAQ: Tua-i-w' tuunraan tekilluku, kauluku. Tuatnalriit igyara'arnilaqait.

When *angalkut* became scarce, [hauntings] became rare[45]

Frank Andrew, Peter John, and Marie Meade, National Museum of the American Indian, February 2003

MARIE MEADE: Is It'gacangaq from Qipneq [Kipnuk]?

FRANK ANDREW: Yes.

MARIE MEADE: Yes. And his father is Kukukualek.

FRANK ANDREW: Their father was probably from that village. They say their father there was haunted at Kangirnaarmiut in the *qasgiq* at the end of winter.

Kukukualek. After he had gone up there, and he was coming back, using a kayak sled, at a time no one was at Kangirnaarmiut in the spring, he went there, when they had all left for spring camps. When he spent the night in their *qasgiq*. He was alone.

MARIE MEADE: How fearless he was.

FRANK ANDREW: After he ate supper, he went to bed in the *qasgiq*. He kept his light on.

While he was laying down, he heard someone walking on hard snow, talking. The voice was that of a woman. And he could tell when she entered the porch of the *qasgiq*.

She could be understood to say, "They have said a stranger has arrived! He must be very hungry!"

Angalkut-llu tua-i tayim' nurnariata, tamana nurnariluni

Miisaq, Mumess'aq, Arnaq-llu, National Museum of the American Indian, February 2003

ARNAQ: It'gacangaq-llu Qipnermiunguuq?

MIISAQ: Ii-i.

ARNAQ: Em-em. Kukukualek-wa atii.

MIISAQ: Taukumiungullrullilria-wa tua-i atii, atiit. Kangirnaarmiuni-gguq alangrullruuq taun' atiit qasgimi iqukvami.

Kukukualek. Qamavirqaarluni utertellermini qamigaukarluni, yuirutenratgun Kangirnaarmiunun up'nerkami, up'nerkillernun ayagaluteng yuirutenratgun. Qavartallermini qasgiatni. Kiimi.

ARNAQ: Alingipaa-lli.

MIISAQ: Atakutarraarluni-gguq qasgimi inarcaaqelliniluni. Kenurrani taun' kumaurtelluku.

Inangqainanrani atam qerqiugtengllinilria pamaken qalarrluni. Erinii-gguq arnauluni. Cakma-ll' tua-i itliniluni qasgim elaturraanun.

Maaten-gguq taringnariuq, "Allaneq-ggem tekitnillruat! Kaigpagtur-kiq!"

Because he couldn't do anything, he took the end of his belt, a bone, a tooth, and after wrapping [the belt] around his hand, he climbed up above the *pall'itaak* and he climbed and sat there with his legs around the rafter. Holding that, he was ready to swing at it. When she came up, he was going to whip her on her face.

He could tell that she went into the tunnel entryway. She kept saying, "They say that a stranger has arrived! He must be very hungry!"

It appeared, and there was a bowl down there, and her hand was at the end. Inside it was a baby, its belly was slit open!

MARIE MEADE: Oh, my!

FRANK ANDREW: When her head appeared, before she came up, he whipped [his belt] in her face!

The only thing he was aware of was when he whipped her. Then he lost all consciousness. When he woke up, there was daylight coming through the window. He was lying on the floor boards; he was holding on to his belt.

As soon as he woke up, he looked around, but [that woman] was not there. And that plate with a baby was not there.

He talks about that time and time again. He said that he was haunted by that at the *qasgiq* of Kangirnaarmiut.

PETER JOHN: Who was that?

FRANK ANDREW: Kukukualek. They used to get haunted.

When shamans became scarce, [hauntings] became rare. That's why I think that those apparitions were caused by shamans. When there were no longer shamans, when they became scarce, those ghosts didn't appear any more.

They say that some shamans deal with the dead. When they started to haunt people, they took them and no longer made them appear as ghosts. Some shamans [did that]. They say some of them do not deal with the dead because they do not have the expertise to deal with them.

They say shamans encourage [ghosts to appear]. When they'd ask [the ghosts who encouraged them], the shamans would try to get them to [appear to people].

It is evident that shamans make those [apparitions appear].

When there were no longer [shamans], they stopped talking about apparitions appearing to people.

Qaill' pisciigalami tua-i naqugutmi iquulqutaa eneq, keggun, tapqualuku unatminun nemruqaaluku, pall'itaak quliignun avelrulluku, wavet elliluku, agluq pagna, mayurluni. Tamatumek tua-i uqliutellinikii. Pugkan tua-i kegginaakun piqerturarkauluku.

Kalvagtelliniluni tua-i cakma. Tuaten-gguq tua-i qanerturluni, "Allaneq-ggem tekitnillruat! Kaigpagtur-kiq!"

Igvalliniuq qantaq kan'a, iquakun patgumaluku. Mikelnguq-wa-gguq imaak, aqsiik ullingqalutek!

ARNAQ: Ila-i!

MIISAQ: Qamiqurra tua-i alairan, nugvailgan, piqertulliniluku kegginarrluku!

Piqertullni-gguq taugaam tua-i elpekluku. Cacini tayim' nalluyagulluku. Ellanguq-gguq tanqigillinilun' egaleq. Nacitet qaingatni kanani taklaluni; tamana naqugutni tegumiaqluku.

Makyutmini tua-i kiarcaaqelliniluk', cataunani tayim' tauna. Tauna-llu-gguq qantarmi tamana-ll' mikelnguq tayim' cataunani.

Pulengtarmek qanemcik'laraa. Kangirnaarmiut qasgiatni taumek tua-i alangrulluniluni.

MUMESS'AQ: Kina tauna?

MIISAQ: Kukukualek. Alangruatullruut.

Angalkut-llu tua-i tayim' nurnariata, tamana nurnariluni. Taumek tua-i angalkunun pivkaumalallruyukluki umyuarteq'lalrianga alangrut tamakut. Angalkut pinanriata tua-i nurnariata nurnariluteng, tamakut pinanrirluteng alangrut.

Tamakuliutunilaqait-llu angalkut ilait nalamalrianek. Alangrukuungaqatki teguluki-gguq tua-i caliaqetuit alangruunqigcetevkenaki. Angalkut ilait. Ilait-gguq tamakuliuyuitut tua-i pisuutailnguut nalamalrianek.

Angalkut-gguq tua-i cingumalarait. Apqeraqaceteng tua-i angalkunun tua-i, angalkut picetaarluk' pillininaurait-gguq.

Tua-i angalkut pivkatullrulliniit tamakut nallunailngurmek.

Tayima tua-i pinanriata, alangrulriamek, tua-i alangrumek qanernanrirluteng.

So she was an *angalkuq*, that Arnarayar. She was not known to be one[46]

Frank Andrew, Peter John, and Marie Meade, National Museum of the American Indian, February 2003

FRANK ANDREW: And also another woman did that to their place across from Kuinerrarmiut [Quinhagak].

Even though some were well trained, they weren't known to the public in those days. And that one . . . Her name was Arnarayar. I used to see her.

She was the wife of the shaman Cingarturta, she was his second wife.

After his first wife died, he got her as a wife. They always used to stay near Ayikataag. That Caakuu used to stay with them. They also had other people who lived with them there at Paluqtat.

MARIE MEADE: Yes.

FRANK ANDREW: Her grandson, Miisaq, told an anecdote about her. Allgiar was their in-law. And also that Cingarturta.

Upriver, at its source where there were no longer trees, there were three houses. Those houses belonged to Caakuu, Alaskuk, and Cingarturta and his family, and his brother-in-law was in the same house with him. They called that place Kuiguacuarmiut.

That Allgiar got sick, his brother-in-law. So it happened that he was unable to go anywhere [to hunt].

Because he was a shaman, his father-in-law made medicine for him, but he didn't improve at all.

Then one day, they invited him, saying that they were going to drink alcohol, that they were going to get drunk.

[Those houses] are not situated close together [but spread out]. Cingarturta and his family were the farthest up. Caakuu lived up where the river bends; up farther from him was Alaskuk's house. There were three houses.

MARIE MEADE: What was the name of that river?

FRANK ANDREW: It was called Kuiguacuar. They called the place Kuiguacuarmiut. That's what he said about it.

They were getting drunk over there, across there. They were starting to get noisy across there. They were starting to ooze with songs.

Angalkuullinilria tang imna Arnarayar. Alairumanritliniuq tua-i augna

Miisaq, Mumess'aq, Arnaq-llu, National Museum of the American Indian, February 2003

MIISAQ: Cali-ll' taum allam arnam cali Kuinerrarmiut akma akiatni uitavigteng tauna call' tuatnalliniluku.

Elisngang'ermeng-gguq ilait alairumayuitut avani. Augna-ll' . . . Arnarayarmek aterluni. Tangaalguluku tua-i wii.

Angalkum aug'um Cingarturtem nuliqluku, nuliangenqiguteklukuqu.

Nakmiin [nuliami] piunrillran kinguani taumek aipangluni. Kiani Ayikataag' nuniigni uitauratullruut. Caakuumek imumek ilangqerraqluteng. Caneg' ilangqeqa'aqluteng Paluqtani kiani.

ARNAQ: Mm-em.

MIISAQ: Qanemcikaa-am tutgariin, Miisaam. Allgiarmek nengaungqertut. Cingarturta-llu tauna.

Pikani tamatum kuigem kangrani pamani napairtellran ngeliini uitaut enet pingayun. Taukut tua-i Caakuu, Alaskuk, ellait-wa taukut Cingarturtenkut nengauminek nelguterluni. Kuiguacuarmiunek piaqluki, aterpaggluki.

Naulluulliniuq tauna Allgiar nengauga. Tua-i ayagasciiganani tua-i.

Angalkuungami tua-i taum cakian tuunrit'laryaaqelliniluku, cakaniqsaunani.

Tua-i-llu-gguq-am caqerluteng kelgaat mer'aqatarniluteng, taangiqeqatarniluteng.

Tua-i mallgutenritut. Taukut kiaqliuluteng Cingarturtenkut. Kuigem-llu waten qipcartullrani wani Caakuu; keluani-w' piani Alaskuum enii. Pingyun tua-i enet.

ARNAQ: Kuik tauna cameg' aterluni?

MIISAQ: Kuiguacuarmek aterluteng. Kuiguacuarmiunek piaqluki. Taum tua-i qanemcikellrua tuaten.

Taangiqengluteng-gguq cakma, tua-i akma. Nepengluteng tua-i akma tua-i. Yuarutnek maqengluteng.

MARIE MEADE: Yeah!

FRANK ANDREW: As night fell and because they probably ran out [of booze], Cingarturta started to make noise first. He was yelling.

That Cingarturta had a bad temper. And it was because he had large eyebrows. It was so that, talking *real* loud, he approached the house!

This was right after the people of Kwigillingok had the Messenger Feast, after they had danced. They helped Caakuu take his things that he had been given; there were other sleds from Kwigillingok, and he had helpers with him.

MARIE MEADE: Yes!

FRANK ANDREW: When I got there, they were like that; [their houses] were not close together.

He came in making a lot of noise, he was yelling.

Arnarayar was sitting on the far interior of the bed, using a light, she was sewing. When he sat down just away from her, she placed her sewing on a small shelf just near her.

She faced her husband Cingarturta, the one who was yelling.

When she faced him, she said to him, "You are just too much! You are so impossible!" [chuckles]

PETER JOHN: His wife said that to him?

FRANK ANDREW: Yes, Arnarayar.

"But still this dear one who should be hunting for us . . ." (she was referring to their son-in-law) ". . . even though you use your powers to try to heal him, he remains the same! And here you should be treating him in earnest!"

They say he never answered her; he became suddenly quiet.

After she said that to him, she said to him, "Give me your *qaspeq*! Your cloth one there! Using your heat, let me [doctor him]!"

He took off his cloth *qaspeq* and gave it to her. He didn't say anything more; he stopped yelling.

Arnarayar, she just cloaked herself [with the *qaspeq*] and put its hood here, and when she went across, she went up on the bed behind him. Cingarturta was sitting on the bed with his legs stretched down to the ground.

So without talking, she was across there . . .

Since she was not near him, when Arnarayar was singing, he didn't understand what she was singing, since she wasn't loud either.

While she was doing that—Cingarturta was sitting down. And he didn't say anything. Without

ARNAQ: Ii-i!

MIISAQ: Atakuqertelluku tua-i nangutelliamenggguq nepii-am alaillinilria Cingarturtem ciumek. Qatguurluni-gguq.

Qenngartuq imna Cingarturta. Qavlurpaungami-ll'. Tua-i-ggur-am qanpagtaarluni tua-i akma tekicartulria!

Kuigilngurmiut Kevgillrata kinguani, yurallrata. Caakuu tuani aruqucetain ilaitnek itraucilluku; allamek cali ikamranek Kuigilngurmiunek allanemeng uciit ilait ikayurilrianek maligluni.

ARNAQ: Ii-i!

MIISAQ: Tekitellemni tua-i tuaten tua-i ayuqellruut taukut; mallgutevkenateng.

Itliniur-am tua-i neplirluni, qatpagaluni.

Arnarayar-gguq tuani acim iquani kiani kialirnermi, aqumluni, kenurrarluteng mingquralria. Aqumngan tua-i uatminun, mingqaani tauna ellilliniluk' qulqika'arnun wavet yaatminun.

Caullinikii atam uini tauna, qatpagalria, Cingarturta.

Caungamiu pillinia, "Arenqiapa-ll' elpekayagpeni! Cayunaitelalriaten tang tua-i!" [ngel'artuq]

MUMESS'AQ: Nulirran-qaa piluku?

MIISAQ: Ii-i, Arnarayaraam.

"Amtallu tang una anguussaagkaraurlurput . . ." (nengaugtek piluku) ". . . tuunritngerpegu cakaniryugpek'naku! Nutaan ilungluten piarkan!"

Kiuksaunaku-gguq; tua-i nepairrluni.

Qanruqaarluku pillinia, "Qasperen taiteqerru! Lumarrallraan tauna! Puqlarpenek aturlua piqernauqa!"

Matarrluni tua-i ellumarrallraminek cikilliniluku. Qanenqigtevkenani tua-i; qatguunermek taqluni.

Arnarayaraam, ulikarluni taugaam, nacaa-ll' wavet piqerluku qeraami, keluanun tagluni. Cingarturta-gguq acimi tua-i aqumgaluni irugni unavet pimalukek.

Qaneqsaunani-gguq tua-i ikani . . .

Arenqiatuq-gguq caniminun, canimetenrilan taum yuarutmek aturturallra Arnarayaraam taringenritaa, qastunrilan-llu.

Atam piinanrani—aqumgauralria taun' Cingarturta. Qaneqsaunani-ll' tua-i.

looking up, he said to her, "Easy! You are going to use the wrong thing! Do not use that on him!"

Arnarayar answered him right away, "I'm going to let him *?tuklequ'urluku!*"

I didn't know that she was a shaman when they were at Kwigillingok. I never heard that she was a shaman.

Cingarturta never said anything after that.

After a while, she stopped [doctoring him]. When she was finished with him, he got up, that one who had been lying down all that time.

She told him to rest for five days, even though he got well. After five days, she told him to go ahead and do whatever.

MARIE MEADE: Her son-in-law?

FRANK ANDREW: Her son-in-law. She healed him right away.

So she was a shaman, that Arnarayar. She was not known to be one. And I never heard that she was a shaman.

Then again one time, she told her husband Cingarturta to make a small fish trap.

Quite a ways up from where they lived, farther up from Kipnuk, there is a constant cascading stream, and up behind it is a lake. It wasn't a real creek and it was overgrown with plants. But that down there had a small slope.

PETER JOHN: There was quite a bit of water cascading down from the slope?

FRANK ANDREW: Yes. Before she used her spirit powers.

After he finished that small fish trap, taking along a cooking pot, he and Miisaq, the resident of Tuntutuliak, went together.

PETER JOHN: Yes!

FRANK ANDREW: Going together, "Let's go and set them." He wanted to take him along. So he went with him.

When they got to that little cascading creek, and after they fixed the place where they would be set, that area right downstream from the small cascading flow, they set that small fish trap. After they covered it, they went on out there and did other things.

I think they said they were getting sourdocks.

So they went back [to where they had set the fish trap]. When they got to them, he took his grass basket off before he checked the fish trap. They had just set them recently.

After he poured the sourdocks from his bucket into the grass basket, he took the covering off of that fish trap. When he raised them, he found that

Ciugtevkenani pilliniuq, "Aulluggaa-i! Iqlukun piqataran! Tamatumek piyaqunaku!"

Arnarayaraam kiugartellinia, "Tuklequ'urluku pivkaqataraqa!"

Angalkuucia-ll' wii nallullrukeka Kuigilngurmi yaani uitallratni. Angalkuuniluku-ll' niiteksaunaku.

Qanenqigtenritliniluni tua-i Cingarturta.

Pilngungamiu tua-i taqliniluku. Taqngani-ll' maktelliniluni taklauralleq im'.

Pillinia ernerni tallimani uitaqaasqelluku assiringraan. Naakata tua-i kinguani pisqelluku.

ARNAQ: Nengauni?

MIISAQ: Nengauni. Tua-i wanirpak assirivkarluku-gguq tua-i.

Angalkuullinilria tang imna Arnarayar. Alairumanritliniuq tua-i augna. Angalkuuniluku-ll' niicuicaaqellrukeka.

Tuamtellu-gguq-am taluyisqaa uini Cingarturta taluyacuarnek.

Kiatiitni-gguq qamani kiaqvaarni, Qipnermiut qavcin kiatiitni, qurrlurturalriartangqertuq, nanvaq-wa-gguq pingna. Kuiluaqauvkenani naumaluku tua-i. Kan'a-gguq taugaam igcenarrarluni.

MUMESS'AQ: Igcenamek im' qurrelvaagarluni?

MIISAQ: Ii-i. Tuunrivailegmini.

Unayaqlinia egaksuarmek-llu-gguq pilutek taqngaki taluyacuaraat tamakut, maliklutek Miisaq-ll' ingna Tuntutuliarmiu.

MUMESS'AQ: Ii-i!

MIISAQ: Maliklutek, "Civcarturnaupuk." Maliksugluku. Maligtelliniluku-am.

Tauna-ll' tua-i tekicamegnegu, qurrluciyaalria tauna, nekaat una kitugarqaarluku kan'a kanani qurrlulriim uum uakaraa, taluyacuaraat taukut civtelliniluki. Patuqerluki tua-i pirraarluk', ayallinilutek avavet canek pilutek.

Quagcinek, quagcitnilutek piyugnarquk.

Utertellinilutek tua-i. Tekicamegneki-ll' tua-i issratni yuuluku takuvailegmiki, pivailegmiki. Tua-i wanirpak, watua ava-i civtellruluki.

Qaltani tauna quagcit imai issratminun ekraarluki, tua-i patuirluki taluyat taukut. Ciugtellinii keni'irkanernek tua-i cangllinilriit

it had caught just enough to cook because they weren't big at all. They [caught those] in a very short time. They were enough to cook.

So all that fall, they would only catch that much. She was a shaman.

They kept checking it the next day. Whatever it caught didn't increase nor did it decrease.

taukut, angenrilameng-llu tua-i. Wanirpaagaq. Tua-i keni'irkanruluteng.

Cunawa-gguq tua-i uksuarpak cangtacir[kai] Angalkullinilria tua-i.
Unuaquaqan-gguq takuaqluku.
Cangtallri amllerikaniyuunateng-llu-gguq, ikeglikaniyuunateng-llu.

One with good wishes toward others[47]

Roland Phillip, George Billy, John Phillip, and Alice Rearden, Bethel, October 2006

ALICE REARDEN: What you mentioned earlier, that many of those [first Moravian helpers] were shamans. When I became aware of life, I never heard of good shamans. I used to think that they were all malicious, and since they spoke of them through the church or other places saying that they meddled with people, but I hadn't heard of good [shamans]. Did the church start talking about them in that way?

ROLAND PHILIP: People who knew what they were like talked about them. You know how this person mentioned earlier that some are malicious. I will speak of that later in what I prepared to say. I will mention something that I know. And I will touch upon the fact that they are malicious and also have good intentions. Some aren't malicious. Like this person said, some are malicious.

GEORGE BILLY: Do you understand what *umyuaqegcilria* [one with good wishes toward others, one who is thoughtful] means? *Umyuaqegcilria.*

ALICE REARDEN: Describe it.

GEORGE BILLY: He only has good wishes toward others; he only wishes them good. They have only good wishes and encouragement for young people or even others who aren't young among us. They only wish them well. They say their minds are strong.

JOHN PHILLIP: This is evidently what [Reverand Ferdinand] Drebert said about those shamans. He said these shamans shouldn't be criticized too much, that they help people. But he said the Devil is evil because he tends to meddle with people. That's what they say about it.

Now. They say the Devil, you know how they say in the Bible that the Devil fell [from Heaven].

Umyuaqegcilria

Anguteka'ar, Nacailnguq, Ayagina'ar, Cucuaq-llu, Mamterilleq, October 2006

CUCUAQ: Augna qanrutkellren, angalkuullruniluki amlleret tamakut. Wiinga tang ellangellemni tamakut angalkut, assilrianek angalkunek niicuitellruunga. Tua-i tamarmeng umyuarrliqsukluki maaggun-llu agayuvigkun naugg'un qanrutkaqluki yuliutuniluki, taugaam assilrianek niiteksaunii. Agayuviim-qaa tuaten qanruteksaurtellrui?

ANGUTEKA'AR: Yuut nallunricetaita qanrutkait. Uum-llu iciw' ava-i qanrutkellrukai watua ilait umyuarrluuluteng. Qalarutkarkamni waniku kanarciqaqa tamana. Nallunrilkengamnek qalarciiqua. Tamakut-llu kanaqerciqaqa umyuarrluuciat, umyuaqegciciat-llu. Umyuarrliqevkenateng ilait. Uum qanrutkellruciatun tua-i ilait taugken umyuarrluuluteng tua-i.

NACAILNGUQ: Umyuaqegcilria taringumaan? Umyuaqegcilria.

CUCUAQ: Kiik aperluku.

NACAILNGUQ: Assilriamun ukut ilani cingluki taugaam; assilriamun cingumaluki. Assilriamun cingluki ayagyuat wall' ayagyuanrilengraata ilaput. Cingumaluki nanramun. Tua-i-gguq umyugait tukniut.

AYAGINA'AR: Waten qanrutkelallinii Drebert-aam tamakut angalkut. Angalkut makut pissiyaayunaitniluki, ikayuqengtuniluki yugnek. Taugaam-gguq una Tuunrangayak assiituq yuliuryuami-llu. Tuaten qanrutkelaraat.

Nutaan. Tauna-gguq tua-i Tuunrangayak nutaan, iciw' maani Bible-aani qanrutkumalria

ent types of medicine, including beaver castor, menstrual blood of girls who had started menstruating, cranberries, when he finally [consumed the *kavtak*], he recovered. His dryness stopped, he was healed from then on. That's something that I witnessed. My story is over; my father went to get that person.

They probably also [healed people] in other ways.

Putting a curse on someone[49]

George Billy, Bethel, October 2006

GEORGE BILLY: A shaman who was constantly trying to heal people, one who pushed others toward good, he tried to heal people's ailments.

Since shamans weren't all alike, some had a tendency to curse people. Cursing people isn't good. They say even if someone around us snubbed us, they told us not to say anything bad about what would happen to them in their future.

[Cursing someone by saying], "Don't mind him/her. This will happen to that person." *Aniqlaayaraq* [putting a curse on someone] isn't good in that way.

It's written in the Bible that we shouldn't curse anyone. We should only have good wishes for others around us. Even if they snubbed us, or if they snub us, they tell us not to say, "You won't amount to anything when you try to accomplish something, or you won't be in a good situation." That's apparently putting a curse on someone.

These two understand what *aniqlaayaraq* means. Do you understand what *aniqlaayaraq* means? That's apparently what some shamans are like. They wish that person to come upon misfortune in their future, or they wish death upon that person. They threaten them.

That's what malicious shamans are apparently like. And even though we're just regular people, they caution us not to wish ill on the people around us, but to only have good wishes toward them. And they also tell us never to seek revenge. These two understand this.

paluqtaat, aglenraraat aglellritnek, tumaglinek, taumek tua-i piami tua-i assiriluni. Tua-i imna kineryullra kepluni tua-i, assiriluni. Tua-i tauna murilkelqa. Tua-i qanemcika nang'uq, aug'um aqvaluku tauna atama.

Call' tua-i tayima allatgun pilallilriit.

Aniqlaayaraq

Nacailnguq, Mamterilleq, October 2006

NACAILNGUQ: Augna ava-i angalkuq anirturingnaquralria, ilani assilriamun cingluk', apquciit tua-i assirivkangnaqu'urluki.

Angalkut makut ayuqenritliniameng ilait aniqlaayugluteng. Aniqlaayaraq man' assinrituq. Wagg'u-q' ilamta tangerrnakluta-llu pingraatkut agu assiitellriamek tekitarkaatnek-llu qanresqev[kenata].

"Ilangcinrilgu. Tauna tuaten piciquq." Tuaten aniqlaayaraq assiitelliniuq.

Aniqlaaqaasqevkenata igausngauq Bible-aami. Assilriamun taugaam nanramun ilavut cingluku. Tangerrnakengraatkut wall'u tangerrnakekakut waten pisqevkenata, "Qaill' pingaituten tuaten pingnaqngerpet, wall' assirngaituten." Tua-i taman' cali aniqlaayaraulliniuq.

Aniqlaayaraq taringumaak ukuk waniwa. Aniqlaayaraq-qaa taringumaan? Angalkut tuaten ilait ayuqelliniut. Tekitarkiuraqluku assiitellerkaatnun, wall' unguvanritlerkaatnun. Akeqnerrlugtaqluki.

Angalkut tuaten umyuarrliqellriit ayuqelliniut. Yuungramta-llu wangkuta aarcirturaitkut ilavut assiitellriamek cingumasqevkenaku, taugaam assilriamek. Akinauqaasqevkenata-llu cali qanrutkumauq. Taringumaag' ukuk wani.

The shaman Qamuutaq would speak in English[50]

George Billy, Bethel, October 2006

GEORGE BILLY: I used to see a shaman at Nanvarnarrlak. It so happens he was a shaman. When we'd have liesure time in the *qasgiq*, after putting on clothing, he would say things in English that we didn't understand.

One day, he put on his clothes in the morning, during a certain time of the morning, and jumped a little, "Haa, I'm hungry. I eat." [*laughter*] We didn't understand what that old man named Qamuutaq was saying.

It so happened that when white people first came around up north, he had worked on a steamboat. When white people first started to have steamboats that were able to haul supplies from the mouth of the Yukon River, Anissilleq hired that shaman as a worker, as a machinist.

I used to see that person. He lived for a long time. These two used to see that person. Then about that person, those people we caught in our early lives would say that [Qamuutaq] speaks English. It so happens that when he worked up north, he had learned how [to speak English] when he was a machinist. He was a shaman before there were many white people around.

When I was young, he would say things that we didn't understand when he was about to do things. Although we were unable to understand, he'd jump up a little and say, "I'm hungry. I eat. I eat." He was apparently hungry. He said that when he was about to go to a house and eat. [*laughter*] He spoke of the time when white people first came around and told about it.

The shaman Puyulkuk used his powers to heal me in Anuuraaq[51]

John Phillip and George Billy, Bethel, October 2006

JOHN PHILLIP: A shaman also used his powers to heal me in Anuuraaq before we moved to Kwigillingok. You've seen Puyulkuk? His name was Puyulkuk.

GEORGE BILLY: I think I have.
JOHN PHILLIP: Yes, he lived in Napakiak. Did you see him?

Angalkuq Qamuutaq Kass'acetun qanernaurtuq

Nacailnguq, Mamterilleq, October 2006

NACAILNGUQ: Angalkumek tangtullruunga Nanvarnarrlagmi. Cunaw' angalkuq. Qasgimi waten ulapeqaqamta aklurraarluni Kass'acetun tang taringelqenrilkemtenek qanernaurtuq.

Caqerluni-am aklulria unuakumi-ii erneq man' qaill' elliqerluku qecgauqertuq, "Haa, I'm hungry. I eat." [*ngel'artut*] Wangkuta taringevkenaku angukara'urluq Qamuutaq.

Cunawa qakmani kass'angqerraallratni caliqerraallrullinilria palagguutarmi. Palagguutangqerraallratni, tuaken Kuigpiim painganek agauquriyugngalriamek, taum tua-i Anissillrem calistekellrullinikii, *machine*-istekluku angalkuq tauna.
Tangtullruaqa taun'. Unguvamallruuq ak'anun. Ukuk tangtullruak. Tua-llu taumek tua-i, tua-i-ll' qanernaurtut augkut angulput, una-gguq Kass'atun qantuuq. Cunaw' calillermini qakmani elitellrullinilria *machine*-istaaruluni. Angalkuuluni tua-i, kass'at amllerivailgata.

Ayagyuarluta tua-i taringenrilkemtenek qalarrnaurtuq caqatarqami. Tua-i-am taumek taringevkarpek'nata qanlartuq, qeckaq'[erluni], "I'm hungry. I eat. I eat." Cunaw' kaigluni. Neryartuqatallermini enem'un. [*ngel'artut*] Tua-llu kass'angqerraallra taum nalluvkenaku qalamcikqallrua taum.

Angalkum Puyulkuum caliaqellruanga Anuuraami

Ayagina'ar Nacailnguq-llu, Mamterilleq, October 2006

AYAGINA'AR: Wiinga tua-i waniwa cali angalkum caliaqellruanga Anuuraami taivailemta Kuigilngurmun. Puyulkugmek tanglallruuten ai? Puyulkugmek aterluni.
NACAILNGUQ: Tuartang.
AYAGINA'AR: Ii-i, Naparyarrarni uitallruuq. Tangellruan-qaa?

GEORGE BILLY: He evidently lived there before I moved there. I used to hear of him.

JOHN PHILLIP: Puyulkuk, the one they called Puyulkuk. When we lived over there in Anuuraaq, Puyulkuk and his family lived there. I'm going to speak of what happened since it's now my turn to speak. This is how he [healed me]. I knew Puyulkuk's name at the time as thay called him Puyulkuk.

One day, my eye up there started to get bad, the right side here, the one that I shoot guns with. This was before I started shooting as a small boy, but I had become aware of my surroundings.

Now when it got worse, and it began to throb in pain, and the center [of my eye, the iris] turned white, it had formed a white spot. You see some people today who have white [on their eye]. That's how white it became. After a while, I couldn't see out of it, and it began to swell when it got that way.

I cried for two nights when my eye was throbbing in pain. I was a boy at the time before we moved to Kwigillingok, in the village of Anuuraaq right beyond the village of Kwigillingok.

Then one day, when I cried for a second night and didn't sleep from continually crying, my parents didn't sleep very well. I had one younger sister at the time, before my two siblings were born.

One morning, since they got up early long ago, when my father got up before it got bright out, he went outside. Puyulkuk and his family were living at Anuuraaq during that time. When he went outside, after being gone a while, Puyulkuk came inside. This was before I found that he was [a shaman] when I was a boy.

When he went inside—and I couldn't see out of my eye any longer. My late mother would try to remove the substance [on my eye] using a kistarkaq [strand of hair thread that was used to remove substances in the eye], since they sometimes used that to remove it, but that substance couldn't come off. It was stuck, and I couldn't see anything. My eye was throbbing and was extremely swollen.

When Puyulkuk came inside—my father was out—when he came indoors, while I was crying, he brought me in front of my mother and had me lie on my back. After laying me on my back, that person didn't seem to make any strange movements or actions, he didn't seem to do anything strange when I watched him.

NACAILNGUQ: Tamakumiungurpailegma tuantellrulliniuq. Niiteqalallruaqa.

AYAGINA'AR: Puyulkuk tua-i taun', Puyulkugmek pilallrat. Tauna tua-i Puyulkuk yaani Anuuraami uitallemteni, tamaantellruut taukut. Atam wangnun tua-i tekican qanrutkeqatarqa. Wangnun taugaam pillra waniw'. Puyulkuk tauna wani atra tua-i nalluvkenaku Puyulkugmek piaqluku.

Atam cat iliitni pivakarlua iika pakem assiirutell', una right side-aq una wani nutegcuuteka. Nut'langvailegma tan'gaurlullraulua mik'nii taugaam ellangumarilua.

Atam tua-i assiirutngellrani, imumek-llu piqerluni, engell'ugtungluni, kan'a-llu qukaa qat'riluni, white spot-aurrluni. Tanglalriaten maa-i iliini qaterluteng piit. Tuaten qat'riluni. Tangrrucesciigaliluni puvengluni-llu tuaten ellillermini.

Unugmi tua-i two nights avani qiagura'aqlua engell'ugtullrani una wani iika. Tan'gaurluulua yaani Kuigilngurmun taivailemta, Anuurami, Kuigilngurmiut yaatiitni.

Tua-i-am tuani caqerluni, unugpak tua-i aipirilua qavarpek'nii tua-i qiagura'aqlua, ukuk tang angayuqaagka qavassiyaagpek'natek. Ataucimek tamaani nayagangqellruunga nasaurlurmek, augkuk ilagka piurpailgagnek.

Atam tua-i piqerluni unuakumi tupagyaratulaameng avani ciuqvaarni, tanqigivailgan tua-i makcami, ataka tayim' anelria. Tamaantellruut Puyulkuunkut tuani Anuuraami tamatum nalliini. Anngami tua-i tayima muluuraqertelluku, Puyulkuk ug' iterluni. Tamakuurcivailemku wiinga tan'gaurlullraulua.

Atam tua-i itrami tua-i—tangrrucesciigaliluni-ll' una iika. Aug'um tua-i unistema, aanama imumek tua-i kistarkamek aug'angnaqluku pilaryaaqekiini, tamakunek aug'arituata iliini, aug'arciiganani tauna. Nepluni tua-i tangrrucesciigalilua-llu waten camek. Engell'ugturluni tang puverpagluni iika.

Atam tua-i itrami taun' Puyulkuk—tayima aataka anumaluni—itrami, qiagurallemni aanama tang ciuqerranun taillua, waten taklarceskiinga wavet neverrlua waten. Taklarcama-ll' tua-i qaill' pinrituq tauna, qaillukuanrituq tua-i, qiallukuarngatenrituq murilkellemni.

After laying me down on my back, after a while, he put his mouth over my eye. He placed his mouth here. With his head down, he seemed to briefly touch [the eye] with the tip of his tongue.

After touching it for just a second, when he removed it, the one up there started to crunch and chew just like he was crunching on candy. I listened to him as he was right above me. After a while, after making crunching noises, he swallowed it. Then after a moment, he [put his mouth over my eye] again.

After doing that again, when he got up he crunched again and this time he crunched less. He seemed [to chew] more previously. He'd get up like that, and then he went a third time, and a fourth time, and took less time [to chew] each time.

Then he went a fifth time. During the fifth time, he made a short crunching noise and was done. After doing that, when he got up, without doing anything he left.

Then after he did that, it stopped throbbing. When the throbbing stopped, since I hadn't slept, when I lay down, I fell asleep. I slept when the throbbing pain stopped.

Those boys my age, and my deceased *iluraq*, and the one who was this person's father-in-law, Egkurraq, who was my age, and my peers who were boys who lived in Anuuraaq would come and see me at that time [I was ill]. Since we'd all go sledding during the day right below my grandfather's home, those two [boys] would come and see me. After going in, they'd go out.

I slept when the throbbing pain stopped. While [I was sleeping], my mother woke me and told me to get up as the day was getting long. She woke me. When she woke me, I suddenly got up, and she told me, "You might not be able to sleep tonight. Get up now."

My eye that previously had no vision was just dazzled by the brightness. I could see above me, and everything looked bright. Immediately after, since I didn't feel any throbbing pain, immediately after I woke, I put on my skin boots and went outside.

When I went outside, I saw that my friends were at the place down the way where we used to go sledding; those boys including Luglaaq's namesake, and even my real cross-cousin, were sliding there.

Taklarcamia-ll' tua-i waten nevercama uitaqerluni iika iqmigluku. Qaneni wavet elliluku. Pusngainanermini ulumi nuuganek agtuq'erngnaku tauna, agtuq'ernganaku nuuganek.

Agtuq'erraarluku cayuamiu atam pakemna, *like candy*, qangqunga'artell', tamualuni qiaryiggluni. Niicugniluku tua-i wii pika-i qulemni uitiin. Pilngungami, qiaryigtelngungami igluku. Tuamtell' uitaqarraarluni tuamtell' piluku.

Tuaten-am pirraarluku cali makcami tuacetun tua-i qangqurluni ikeglikanirluni. Ciuqlirmi amllermek pingatellruluni. Tuaten tua-i maktaqluni, pingayiriluni-llu, cetamiriluni-llu, ikegliinarluni tuatnallra.

Tua-i-ll' waniw' tallimiriluni. Tallimiriami carrarmek qiraskarluni taqluni. Pirraarluni-ll' tua-i camek pivkenani makcami taqngami tua-i tayim' anluni.

Tua-i-ll' tauna pillran kinguani engell'ugtuirrluni. Engell'ugtuirtellrani qavaqsailama ina'artellrianga qavaqallinilua. Qavarlua tua-i caciqa engell'ugtuirtellrani tuani qavarlua.

Imkut tua-i augkut ilanka tan'gaurluut, ilurairutka-ll' augna, uum cakiqsaaqellra augna, augna Egkurraq, tauna pitateka, augkut-llu yaani Anuuraami uitalriit ilanka tan'gaurlullraat tamaantellret, paqtelallruatnga tamaani. Erenrani ilakluta ellu'urtaarturalaamta avani apa'urluma eniin ketiini, taukut tua-i paqtaqlutek. Iteryaaqerraarlutek an'aqlutek tamaani.

Atam tua-i qavarlua tua-i engell'ugtunriama. Tua-i piinanemni taum aanama tupageskiinga maktesqellua amci waten erneq takliriluku. Tupagglua. Tupagcanga tua-i uigarrlua, pianga, "Qavarkaicuartuten unuku. Amci makten."

Imna tangssuitelleq iika qitngiryugluni taugaam. Tangvagluki pagkut, tanqigtessnganani-ll' man' tangelqa. Aren egmian' tua-i, engell'ugtunrilama-ll' wanirpak tua-i tuani egmian' pilu'uglua anlua, anlua ellamun.

Anngama tua-i piunga ugkut uani ellu'urtaarvik'lallemteni ilanka; augkut-wa tua-i tan'gaurluut Luglaam-llu aug' atra ilakluku tuani, ilu'urqa-llu tauna nakmiin tuani ellu'urtaalriit.

When I went outside, they spotted me upriver. Then they ran over and came to me, watching me closely. My eye was dazzled from the brightness when I went outside. The [eye] that previously had no vision had very good sight. When they came over and arrived, they looked up at my eye from down below me and asked me, "Who healed this?" [laughter]

Since I knew his name—they usually cautioned us not to say the names of men who had become fathers—since they only called that person Puyulkuk, I said, "Puyulkuk healed it this morning."

This is [the eye] that that person healed. I know of Puyulkuk who did that. I tell about that person [who healed] in my very presence.

My eye recovered, and it's good even up to this day. But those doctors in Anchorage removed the cartaracts so that I could see better recently. They cleaned [my eye] when I started to get double vision.

Atam anngama uavet kiavet tangerqaqiitnga. Aqvaqurluteng uka-i tailuteng tangvaglua. Qitngiryugluni ellamun anllemni iika. Tua-i takvikapiarluni imna tangrrucuitelleq. Taingameng cali tekicameng wavet iika aciirlua pinauraatnga, "Kia una kitugtau?" [ngel'artut]

Atra tua-i tauna nallunrilamku- inerqutullruyaaqaitkut waten arivtaaresqevkenaki makut aataurtellriit-kiingan tauna Puyulkugmek pilaatgu, "Puyulkuum kitugtellrua unuaq."

Tua-i waniwa taum tua-i pillra. Taumek tua-i wii nallunrilkenganqertua Puyulkugmek tuatnallranek. Tauna tua-i qanemcik'laraqa takumni pilleq tauna.

Tua-i assiriluni iika waniw' tua-i man'a engelkarrluku. Taugaam amani Anchorage-aami yungcaristet takvigcavsiallruatnga cali, man'a aug'arluku misiarutellra. Iciw' malruurtellrani tangelqa clean-arluku.

When he took [his finger out] there was no cut[52]

John Phillip, Bethel, October 2006

JOHN PHILLIP: And after that, my grandfather and my father would tell me to try to place the window back onto the *qasgiq* right after a fire bath. They told me to try to place the window back onto the *qasgiq* before anyone else.

One day as usual, I was keeping watch after they had taken a fire bath in the *qasgiq*. After placing the window back on, sometimes I'd go in briefly, as they would tell us to go to the *qasgiq* as some people would ask us to carry out chores for them, so that we carry out chores for others.

Since I was watching the *qasgiq* after they had taken a fire bath, when the smoke subsided, I watched. When the smoke was all gone, I went over and saw that the fire had gone out. I placed the window back on after yelling down there [to tell them that I was about to place it on], and I placed the window back on since smoke was no longer rising. Then I immediately went inside the *qasgiq* when I was done. I saw that Puyulkuk was there.

They were naked. Then they started to put their clothes on. He put on his pants. When he put them

Aug'araa-am kilinertaunani man'a

Ayagina'ar, Mamterilleq, October 2006

AYAGINA'AR: Tua-i-ll' tua-i cali kinguani, aug'utun wani apa'urluma atama-llu pilaraanga maqinerra'ararqan qasgi tua-i cali egalingnaqesqelluku cali. Qasgi ciullegtaunii egalingnaqesqelluku.

Tua-i-am kellullua, qasgimi pillratni, maqirraartelluki. Tua-i egalirraarluku itqalartua, ilait ellimeqlituniluki iliini agesqelaasqelluta qasgimun, kevgartuasqelluta.

Tua-i-am qasgimun, maqirraartelluki tangviimki yaa-i puyuirusngiinaan kelluqurluku. Puyuirucan tua-i ullagluku piaqa qamllinilria. Egalirluku tua-i qayagauqerraarluki, puyuirutlinian egalra elliluku. Iterlua-ll' tua-i taqngama egmian' qasgimun. Piaqa-am tauna Puyulkuk tamaanlluni.

Tua-i piluteng wani, matangqaluteng piluteng. Piameng aturarluteng. Qerrulliigni all'ukek.

on, and I saw that his *iluraq* was seated across from him, the one who happened to be his *iluraq*. They were talking to one another over there.

Then a while after putting on his pants, he dug inside his pocket and took out a knife. When he took it out, Puyulkuk unfolded it.

And when he unfolded it, since he would tease his *iluraq* a lot, when he unfolded it, after telling him to look over at him, [Puyulkuk] cut off his own index finger and it became covered with blood. Just as the blood started flowing out, he placed [his finger] inside his mouth.

I was watching him since I was in awe of someone doing that. This was after the time [he healed my eye]. I watched him. When he took it out, there was no cut here. There was no cut. That's what that person did. [*laughs*]

Ac'amikek, iluraa-w' augna akiani tauna ilu'urqellinikii. Ika-i qalarullutek.

Atam piuraqerluni qerrulliigni aqaarlukek kalmiiniuqerluni nuussignek ancill', nuussignek ancill'. Ancamikek nengllukek taum Puyulkuum.

Nengcamikek-llu tua-i tauna ilurani-am ilangciaralalliniamiu pulengtaq nengcamikek takuyangcarraarluku tekni, elliin tekni, nuussimek uugun nuussimek pilakarluku augurrluni. Qurrlullautiini-ll' tua-i iqemkarluku.

Tangvagluku tua-i wii, irriama tuaten pilriamek. Taum kinguani. Tangvagluku. Aug'araa-am kilinertaunani man'a. Kilinertaunani. Tua-i tauna. [*ngel'artuq*]

Evidently, these shamans can place [cuts] inside their mouths and heal them[53]

Waten imkut iqmigluki-llu angalkut mamtetullinikiit

Roland Phillip and George Billy, Bethel, October 2006

Anguteka'ar Nacailnguq-llu, Mamterilleq, October 2006

ROLAND PHILLIP: Let me ask you a question. You are eighty-three years old. Did you [George] witness a shaman exercising his powers in your presence, did you watch him with your eyes?

GEORGE BILLY: When we were small, they called the village Paingarmiut.

ROLAND PHILLIP: Not something that you've heard.

GEORGE BILLY: I'm going to talk about something that I've witnessed.

When we were small, we were just sitting inside the *qasgiq*. There was a shaman named Qamuutaq there. He was a shaman.

You know how when a man is about to [dance during the Messenger Feast] he constructs many items that he would bring to the *qasgiq*.

Then Qamuutaq took the adze from an area beyond him, and while he was chopping wood, he made an "Eng!" noise. The [finger] that he had accidentally grazed with an adze was gone. We watched him when we were small. This person had me recall what happened with [that shaman].

Evidently, these shamans can place [cuts] inside their mouths and heal them. I happened to see that when I was small inside the *qasgiq*.

ANGUTEKA'AR: Apteqerlaken. *Eighty-three*-aartuten. Angalkumek-qaa takuq'apiarpeni camek pilriamek tangvallruuten, tangvagluku iigpegun?

NACAILNGUQ: Atam, ak'a mikluta, Paingarmiut-gguq.

ANGUTEKA'AR: Niitelqenrilkevnek.

NACAILNGUQ: Tangllemnek waniw' piqatartua.

Ak'a mikluta qasgimi uitaurtukut. Tauna-wa tua-i Qamuutaq angalkuq. Angalkuuluni.

Iciw' yug' angun piqatarqami amllernek canek taqutetuuq qasgiarkaminek.

Tua-llu tauna Qamuutaq qaill' kepun tauna yaaken yaatminek qaill' cakisnginanermini, "Eng!" Tua-i-ll' tayima tua-i maani agenkallni keputmek cataunani. Tua-i tangvagluku mikluta. Tua-i taumek neq'ercetaa uum.

Waten imkut iqmigluki-llu angalkut mamtetullinikiit. Tua-i taun' elpeka'artelqa tua-i miklua qasgimi tua-i.

They say after a while, he said, "Don't be offended." And he apparently burst out crying after saying that. [laughter] Being astonished, he apparently burst out crying when his *nuliacungaq* said to him, "Here you say you fly but aren't seen."

They say they used to travel to the moon and to the ocean down there. That's what I used to hear about those [shamans].

ALICE REARDEN: After watching it?

JOHN PHILLIP: That's all I'll say. I'm taking up your time. [laughter]

ALICE REARDEN: Did Puyulkuk not have any hair?

JOHN PHILLIP: Yes, right after he got a bald spot on his head, he left our village when he became an elderly man. He has descendants downriver. You know Eva Jenkins.

ALICE REARDEN: Yes, Eva Jenkins.

JOHN PHILLIP: My grandchild. That person. And Cauyaq, those people. Cauyaq was his son. Those are some of his children.

NOAH ANDREW: The Temples are his descendants. Alexie Temple. Those ones. They know that they're from Kwigillingok.

JOHN PHILLIP: And at Napakiak he lit a fire [using a fire-starting kit]. Those people watched him along with Willie Alexie, the lay pastor. And Mataralria watched him. I saw him in his pictures. When it lit up those two were smiling, amazed when he lit a fire.

I'm going to tell you something that I know, about the shaman Cingarturta who I witnessed[56]

Roland Phillip, John Phillip, and Alice Rearden, Bethel, October 2006

ROLAND PHILLIP: You young men here who are listening will not see [shamans] that we mentioned. There are probably some [shamans] around still, but you will not see them.

We are only talking about things that we've observed at this time, about shamans who you won't know about. I'm telling you that you will not see anyone exercising their powers. But some of you have only seen white people [performing magic], and I've seen them, too. And you've probably seen people performing magic. But you [young people] won't see [shamans] who we spoke of. We're the only ones who know about them.

Uitaqerluni-gguq qanertuq, "Tua-i cangayugyaqunaci." Qalrillalliniluni-ll' tua-i iqukluku qanrraarluni. [ngel'artut] Ucuryugluni qalrillalliniluni taum nuliacungami piani, "Elpeci tangrruuvkenaci waten tengaurnilalriaci."

Moon-artetunilarait unavet-llu cali imarpigmun. Tamakut niitelallruanka tuaten.

CUCUAQ: Tangvaurarraarluku-qaa?

AYAGINA'AR: Tuaten pitaluku. Qaritamci. [ngel'artut]

CUCUAQ: Puyulkuk-qaa tauna nuyaitellruuq?

AYAGINA'AR: Ii-i, waten tua-i patkallengqerluku ayallruuq tua-i nunamtenek angukara'urluurcami. Kinguvengqertuq uani cakma. Iciw' Eva Jenkins.

CUCUAQ: Yaa, Eva Jenkins.

AYAGINA'AR: Tutgarqa tauna. Tauna. Imkut-llu Cauyaq, tamakut. Cauyaq qetunraqaa. Tamakut tamaa-i yuin ilait.

AIGGAILNGUQ: Temple-aat taukut kinguveqekai taum. Alexie Temple. Tamakut. Nallunritaat Kuigilngurmiungucirteng.

AYAGINA'AR: Naparyarrarni-ll'-am kumarciuq. Augkut tua-i tangvagluku imum-llu Willie Alexie, tuyum, Mataralriim-llu tangvagluku, tangvalliniluku. Tarenraini-am tangellruaqa. Kumangartellrani taukuk tua-i quuyuaralriik ucuryuglutek kumarcillrani.

Nallunrilkengamnek qanemciqatartua tangvallemnek angalkugmek Cingarturtemek

Anguteka'ar, Ayagina'ar, Cucuaq-llu, Mamterilleq, October 2006

ANGUTEKA'AR: Ukuni tua-i tan'gaurlurni niicugnilriani tangerrngaituci, tangerrngaituci augkunek. Pitangqerrsaaqellilria tayima, taugaam tangerrngaituci.

Wangkuta taugaam tanglallemtenek qalartukut, nallukengarpecenek augkunek ava-i angalkunek. Qanrutamci caqtaalriamek tangerrngaituci. Taugaam kiingan imkunek kass'anek pilalrianek tangvalalriaci tayim' ilaci, wiinga-ll' tangvagaqlua. Elpet-llu tangvalallilriaten *magic*-aalrianek. Taugaam elpeci tangerrngaituci augkunek qalarutkellemtenek. Taugaam wangkuta nallunritaput.

I'm going to tell you something that I know, about a shaman who I witnessed. You know Frank Paul, Qakiur. You also saw Qakiur when he was a lay pastor downriver. His grandfather Cingarturta. They also called him Apa'urlull'er. His grandchildren called him their Apa'urlull'er, he was their grandfather, and eventually that became his name.

I watched that person [exercising his powers] downriver in Iiqaquq. That's someone who I witnessed using his powers. And he wasn't [healing] a person, he didn't seem to be. He didn't seem to be doctoring a person, but he was probably just demonstrating his ability to others.

And I also hear that these shamans who are exercising their powers cause people to see illusions. They make something visible. They cause people to see illusions. Many of us are able to see the illusion that he made appear.

When we lived in the place they called Iiqaqurmiut, people announced that Cingarturta was going to exercise his powers, Apa'urlull'er, Frank Paul's real grandfather; [Frank Paul's] mother was his daughter.

I was curious about what that person would do. Since my father participated, when the time that he had set to perform came around, when [my father] went over to the *qasgiq*, I went with him. When I went inside, I saw that Cingarturta was already there.

There were some drums there since it was during the time when they were about to have the Messenger Feast. There were drums inside the *qasgiq*. But those drums were larger, larger than these that they have nowadays—the drums that they use for entertainment dancing nowadays aren't very large. But those drums of the past used to be larger.

When people gathered inside that *qasgiq*—and there were no women, but only men, and there weren't very many people living at that place. The few people who lived there probably all gathered there.

That person [Cingarturta] went down during the evening. When I went inside the *qasgiq*, I saw that situated along the corners [of the *qasgiq*] were seal-oil lamps, lamps that weren't very bright like this.

When they filled a container with seal oil and placed a wick in it and had the end [of the wick] stick out, those [lamps] would stay lit, using seal oil for fuel. There were four lamps, one along each

Cali nallunrilkengamnek qanemciqatartua, tangvallemnek angalkumek. Frank [Paul] imna Qakiur nallunritan. Elpet-llu-q' tangellruan Qakiur tuyuullrani uani. Taum apa'urluanek Cingarturtemek. Apa'urlull'ermek-llu piaqluku. Taukut tutgarain Apa'urlullrameggnek, tua-i ap'akluku, apa'urlullrameggnek, kiituan' tua-i ateqsagutaa tauna.

Uani Iiqaqumi tangvallruaqa tauna. Tua-i tuunrilria tua-i tauna tangvalqa. Yugmek-llu pivkenani, pingatevkenani. Tuunriskengengatevkenani yugmek, taugaam tua-i ca piyugngacini tangertelluku pillilria, piyugngacini.

Makut-llu angalkut makut caqtaalriit niitelaranka tua-i-gguq tangrrualirluki pilarait. Alaicugngarivkarluku ca. Tangrrualirluki. Wangkuta amllerrluta tangerrsugngariluku tauna alaicetellra.

Taumeg-am tua-i, uani Iiqaqurmiunek pilallritni tuani uitallemteni, tuunriqatarnikiit-am tauna Cingarturta, Apa'urlull'er, Frank Paul-am apa'urlua nakmiin; panianek taum wani aanangqellria.

Tua-i paqnayuglua-am tua-i taumek. Ataka tua-i pian, pillerkiuraa tauna tekican qasgimun agellrani maliggluku tauna. Maaten itertua tua-i tamaantengllinilria tauna Cingarturta.

Cauyat-wa makut maani kevgiqatallermeng nalliini pillrulliniami. Maani qasgim iluani cauyat. Angenrulallruut taugaam tamakut cauyat makuni atuqengaitni—yuratulit maa-i anglanissaagarluteng angssaagaqsaitelalriit cauyat. Tamakut taugaam angenrulallruut tamakut cauyat.

Atam tua-i tauna tua-i yung'engan qasgi—arnartaunani-llu, anguterrlainaat taugaam tua-i, amllenrilameng-llu tuani yugyanrilameng. Yugg'ait tua-i quyurtellilriit tuavet.

Atralria tauna atakumi. Maaten-llu qasgimun itertua tuani kangiramikun imkunek uqunek kenurranek, waten tanqigpaunrilngurnek.

Ca tua-i imirluku uqumek imirluku kumarucirluku-llu iqua pugumaurtelluku piaqameng, tamakut kumauratullrulriit, uqumek piluteng. Kangiramikun cetamanek

corner of that *qasgiq*. But it was still bright inside. Everything inside the *qasgiq* was visible.

And the shaman Cingarturta went down there on the floor, and he was holding a seal-gut rain garment. Then he removed his clothing. And that place was cold since it was during the middle of winter, during the cold season. He removed his clothing and put on that seal-gut rain garment.

They mentioned that there were two types of songs that were composed in the past. They said [the songs] they called *yuarulluut*, those are the songs composed by shamans. They are called *yuarulluut*.

But the other songs were for dancing during the Messenger Feast, and they weren't shaman songs. But the other kind, the *yuarulluut*, when shamans performed and exercised their powers, their singers knew how to sing their *yuarulluut*.

Probably since they always [sang those songs] during the time when they exercised their powers, the elders there started singing those types of songs.

And that person [Cingarturta], when he put on the seal-gut rain garment, he walked back and forth down there on the floor. And it appeared as though he was continuously moving his seal-gut rain garment from the inside with his hands. He seemed to be constantly making that motion. His seal-gut rain garment appeared as though it was constantly rattling.

The entranceways of the *qasgit* up at the front down there used to be low; the [tunnel entryway] below was called the *kalvagyaraq*. When a person went outdoors, they would go down into the tunnel entryway.

And I would try to pull myself up when entering inside the *qasgiq* [as a child], too. The area underneath was covered with something when they took fire baths; you know, it was a draft hole.

That's what it was like; [the entryway] isn't the same level as the *qasgiq* [floor]. That [tunnel entryway] is called *kalvagyaraq*. It's called *kalvagyaraq*.

[Cingarturta] was down [on the floor]. After a while, he suddenly moved across the room quickly. When he got to that [tunnel entryway], it seemed that he would suddenly extend his arms from underneath the seal-gut rain garment [into the tunnel entryway], it was as though he would suddenly extend his arm out. His hands would suddenly become visible.

kenurrartarluni tamana qasgi. Amtall' tua-i ilua tanqigcenani. Cat iluanelnguut qasgim iluani tamarmeng alaunateng.

Tauna-ll' tua-i angalkuq tauna Cingarturta atrarluni kanavet, qasperek-wa tegumiak, qasperek tegumiak. Matarrluni-ll' tua-i. Nengllirluni-ll' man'a uksuungan, uksuum qukaanlami tua-i tayim' nenglem nalliini. Matarrluni qasperek taukuk all'ukek.

Makut-am yuarutet malruuluki qanrutkelallruit avani. Makut-gguq yuarullugnek pilallrit, tamakut tua-i tuunrangayiit yuarutkait. Yuarullugnek aterluteng.

Aipait taugken makut yuarutet Kevgiraqameng tua-i yurarcuutngululuteng, angalkurtauvkenateng. Taugaam tamakut aipait yuarulluut, tua-i tamakut tuunrangayiit tuunrangayagaqameng tamakunek aturtait, aturtaita nalluvkenaki tamakut yuarulluit.

Tua-i piicuitelliameng tuunriaqameng, yuut tua-i mengluteng augkut tegganret tamakunek.

Tauna-ll' tua-i, qasperek taukuk ac'amikek unani tang waten tua-i utqetaarturluni. Qasperek-llu tuartang imumek waten iluagnek qamaken unatminek-wa arulaqu'urnganakek. Tuaten piurnganani. Qasperek imkuurlutek arulaqu'urnganatek.

Ugkut amiigit qasgiit aciqsitullruuq; camna kalvagyaramek aterluni. Yuk tua-i an'aqami kalvaggluni.

Cali-ll' tua-i kiingan nuggsaakarlua nuglallrulrianga itraqama qasgimun. Camna aciat qilagluni maqiaqameng, iciw' cup'urillruluni.

Tuaten ayuquq; mat'umi qasgimi manigtatkevkenani. Kalvagyaraq taugaam tua-i taun' ateqluku. Kalvagyaramek aterluni.

Tua-i unani. Tua-ll' piinanermini cukangnaqa'arrluni anelraqerrnganani. Tuartang tuavet tekicami qasperek aciagnegun yaq'ertelalria tuavet, yaq'errnganani. Unatai alairtaqluteng.

ALICE REARDEN: Was he inside the tunnel entryway?

ROLAND PHILLIP: That person was inside the *qasgiq*. But it appeared as though he would suddenly extend his arms out toward the deep tunnel entryway. His hands would suddenly appear. He would suddenly extend his arm.

But after having them stop [singing], he would start again. After doing that for the third time, he went on his knees in the middle of the *qasgiq*, with one leg down on his knee and the other up, and he told the singers to stop singing. He had them stop [singing].

When he removed the seal-gut rain garment that he was wearing, he took it by the bottom section down there along the opening. It appeared as though his right arm was inside the seal-gut rain garment, as though he was keeping his arm extended. I watched him during that time. I watched in amazement.

After positioning himself in that way, he told people who wanted to see it to come and see it. But after saying that, he also said, "But try not to breathe inside this seal-gut rain garment." That's what he said.

And when those men across there who were closest to the exit went down, since they were wearing hooded garments, they put their heads down, [and covered their mouths with the neck area of their hooded garments].

Since I was also wearing a hooded garment, I tried [covering my mouth], too. I was curious as I was sitting next to my father. [*chuckles*]

When they'd go back up [to sit], another two would go down again. Some of them, after being down there, would say that it was apparently an adult. That's what they would say after looking inside [that seal-gut rain garment]. That's what some of them said, that it was evidently an adult. I was so very curious because of what they said.

And when the people across were done, when two people on this side went, I whispered to my father, "I'll go with you. I'll go with you." And he just nodded his head.

When it was our turn, immediately after I stood, I [covered my mouth] with my hooded garment. I thought that I might accidentally breathe inside [the shaman's seal-gut rain garment] like he had cautioned.

I went down there. When it came into view as he was holding [the seal-gut garment] open, I saw that he held his hands together [in a cup], and the area above was like this.

CUCUAQ: Kalvagyaram-qaa iluani uitaluni?

ANGUTEKA'AR: Qasgim iluani uitaluni tauna. Tauna taugaam tuavet ilutulriim tungiinun kalvagyaramun yaq'errngataqluni. Unatai-w' tua-i alairtelalriit. Yaq'errluni tua-i.

Taugken tua-i arulairceqaartelluki ataam ayanqiggluni, ayanqigtaqluni. Wani taugaam pingayiriami tuatnacimini, pingayiriami, kanavet atam qasgim qukaanun nutaan ciisqumiggluni, una irumi inglua, una-ll' napaluku, arulairesqelluki-ll' atulriit. Arulairtelluki.

Qasperek taukuk yuungamikek akuagnegun 'ggun qulirnerkun uumek teguluku. Tuartang kanani tallian una *right*-alirnera qaspereg' iluagnun pimalria, waten yagingaurnganani. Tua-i murilkelluku wii tangvallemni. Tangvagluku irriama, irr'ilua.

Tua-i tuaten pimariami waten qanertuq, paqnakestainun paqcesqelluku. Taugaam tuaten qanrraarluni cali waten qanerluni, "Ukuk taugaam qasperek iluagnun aneryaanrilkurrluci piniartuci." Tuaten qanerluni.

Tua-i-ll' ikegkuk angutek uaqlikacagaak atraamek qaspertuamek waten tang cik'arrlutek pikilik, una-w' tua-i.

Wiinga-ll' qaspellruararmek atuama tua-i naspaaqerlua. Atama caniani paqnayuglua tua-i taumek. [*ngel'artuq*]

Tag'aqagnek malruk atraraqlutek. Ilait waten qanernaurtut kanani tua-i pirraarluteng, temirtengulliniuq-gguq. Tuaten qanraqluteng tamakut tuavet iluagnun pirraarlutek. Qanraqluteng tua-i tuaten ilait, temirtengulliniuq-gguq. Tua-i paqnanaqpiarluni.

Tua-i-ll' agkut qaqicata maavet ukalirnermun, kiugkuk wani piagnek, ataka tauna agyumciaqerluku piaqa, "Maligciiqamken. Maligciiqamken." Nayangaqerluni tua-i.

Tua-i-ll' tekicatkuk, egmianun tua-i nangrutemni qaspell'erqa waten piluku iluagnun. Taum-gguq iluagnun aneryaaqernayuklua inerquutellranun.

Atrarlua tuavet. Igvaraqa tang waten pimallrani, waten unatni pimallinikai, una-ll' qulii waten pimaluni.

I saw that inside his palm was a seal. There was water inside his palm. There was water, and there was a seal down there that wasn't staying still, but it was moving around and swimming in a circle. And it would even move its hand flippers like this down there inside that person's palm. And after putting its head down in the water, when it would lift its head up, its whiskers would drip water.

ALICE REARDEN: The seal's?

ROLAND PHILLIP: The seal's whiskers. It was swimming in a circle down there. Its head was reddish in color. You've seen bearded seal heads that are reddish in color.

JOHN PHILLIP: A *tulignaq* [bearded seal with a dark belly and gray top].

ROLAND PHILLIP: They've heard of them. Apparently, since its head was reddish in color, those who saw it would say that it was an adult.

There was a seal down there. Everyone had a turn. All the people saw it. When there was no one else left to see it, that person said . . . they call the river where Iiqaquq River empties the Ilkivik River, a large river that flows all the way down to the ocean. And it was a hunting place in the spring when the men were moving; when we'd go spring camping, we'd go to the mouth of the Ilkivik River.

The one who was holding it said that he was going to place that seal at the upper part of the Ilkivik River. Here it was winter and cold outdoors at that time. In the past, some of the things they did, they allowed people to see them. They made [those things] appear.

That's what I've seen, a seal. It was moving, even its arms. Yes.

ALICE REARDEN: Was [what the shaman did] called *maklaguarluni* [performance by a shaman requesting or conjuring up bearded seals]?

ROLAND PHILLIP: He didn't say that he was going to perform a ritual to request something, but when he started, all he did was suddenly go down toward the entrance tunnel.

After saying that he was going to place it there at the upper part of the Ilkivik River, he had them sing again and he went across. After a moment of being there, like he had done before, he suddenly extended his arm. He probably placed it at the upper part of the Ilkivik River [when he did that].

ALICE REARDEN: He didn't immediately go down [into the tunnel entryway]? He didn't suddenly go down?

ROLAND PHILLIP: He didn't go outside. He didn't go outside, but stayed inside the *qasgiq*. That story is over.

Kan'a-w' tang tumiin qukaatni unguvalria. Man'a-llu tumiin avatii merluni. Merluni, kan'a-w' unguvalria tua-i uitavkenani pekluni uivvaarluni unguvalria. Unatni-llu kankut waten piluki tua-i waten elliurnaurai, patgulluki elliurnaurai kana-i tumiini. Maavet-llu mermun puqaarluni maktaqan ungai mermek kucirturnaurtut.

CUCUAQ: Taum unguvalriim?

ANGUTEKA'AR: Unguvalriim ungai imkut. Uivaarluni tua-i kanani. Qamiqurra-wa kavircenani. Kavircetellrianek tanglalriaten makliit qamiqurritnek.

AYAGINA'AR: Tulignaq.

ANGUTEKA'AR: Niitaqait. Tua-i tauna qamiqurra kavircetlinian tamakut tangtulit qanlallinilriit temirtenguniluku.

Tua-i kan'a kanan' unguvalria tua-i. Qaqilluteng-llu tua-i yuut. Tangertekai nangluteng. Nang'ata waten qanertuq tauna . . . ingna tamatum Iiqaqum un'a anellra Ilkivigmek pilaraat kuigpaller' ak'aki tua-i camavet imarpigmun ayaumatuluni. Up'nerkami-ll' pissuryaraugaqluni taukut upagaqameng angutet; up'nerkiyaraqamta yaavet painganun Ilkiviim.

Qanertuq tauna tegumiaqestii, Ilkiviim-gguq kangianun elliqataraa tauna tua-i unguvalria. Uksuq-wa man'a tua-i nengla qakemna tua-i. Ava-i tua-i waten ca pillerteng tamakut ilait yugnun tua-i tangrruurrluk' pitullinikiit. Alairtelluku.

Tua-i tauna wiinga taumek tangelqa, unguvalriamek. Pekluni tua-i, talligni. Ii-i.

CUCUAQ: Tua-i-qaa maklaguarluni?

ANGUTEKA'AR: Qanenrituq pinguaqatarniluni, camek qanellrunrituq pinguaqatarniluni, tua-i taugaam ayagniami tua-i waten atraqertaqluni pillruuq.

Tua-i qanrraarluni tuavet Ilkiviim kangianun elliqatarniluku, tua-i aturtelluki cali anelrarluni. Tuavet piqarraarluni, tua-i-ll' tuaggun cali yaq'ertelallermitun tua-i tuaten piqerluni. Tua-i Ilkiviim kangianun ellillikii.

CUCUAQ: Taugaam-qaa atraqertevkenani? Atraqertevkenani-qaa?

ANGUTEKA'AR: Aneksaunani. Aneksaunani qasgim iluani. Tua-i iquklituq augna qanemciq.

Keplialleq obtained an *avneq* and became a *shaman*[57]

Roland Phillip, Bethel, October 2006

ROLAND PHILLIP: But let me also add and end with what my father witnessed when he was young. Let me tell you about something my father witnessed and told about.

They say the first hospital was located across from Akiak, and there were medical doctors there. There was no hospital here [in Bethel] at the time, but only in Akiak. They say that doctor would travel to the villages by dogsled. That doctor would travel from place to place. Downriver, in an old village called Akulirarmiut that is no longer inhabited, and my father was from that village, from Akulirarmiut.

During winter, they announced that that white person had arrived with another person. Apparently, it was that doctor who had come from Akiak. He was probably [doctoring] people.

Then it is said that while they were sitting in the *qasgiq* in the evening, that doctor said, and my father heard him. He said that he would like to see a shaman performing using his powers. And there was a shaman at that place, and that shaman's name was Keplialleq.

My father also talked about Keplialleq. He said he was just a regular person like us, and he wasn't a shaman. But when he grew older, since he had an *urumavik* who was a shaman, they say he attempted to get an *avneq* [shaman's helping spirit, guardian or guide] and got an *avneq*. He obtained an *avneq* and became a shaman.

They mention the *avneret* [guardians] of shamans, that their *avneret* are their guardians. [The *avneq*] isn't visible, but only the shaman is visible. But that's what he mentioned, that their *avneret* are their guardians. Although other shamans were trying to attack him, his *avneq* would alert and guide the person who it resides in. And when his fellow shamans were about to attack him, [the *avneq*] would alert him. The [*avneq*] was his guardian.

That person named Keplialleq evidently became a shaman. His name was Keplialleq.

Since the doctor wanted to see a shaman exercising his powers and performing, he prepared and put on his seal-gut rain garment. Since they don't just stay down there on the floor, when he got tired, he told his singers [to start singing].

Keplialleq avnengellruuq, angalkuurrluni

Anguteka'ar, Mamterilleq, October 2006

ANGUTEKA'AR: Taugaam, taugaam cali atama tangvallminek ayagyuarluni cali iqukeqerluku cali. Qanemciknaurqa cali, atama tua-i tangvagluku qanemcikellra.

Akiarmi-gguq akiani Akiarmi ciumek *hospital*-aartangqellruuq yungcaristetarluni-llu. Wani pitaunani, Akiarmi taugaam. Tauna-gguq yungcarista nunanun waten qimugcetgun ayagatullruuq. Ayagatullruuq yungcarista tauna. Uani Akulirarmiunek pilaqait taukut yuirutellrulriit nunallret, tauna-llu ataka taukumiunguluni, Akulirarmiunguluni.

Uksuumainanrani tua-i qanllinilriit kass'aq tauna tekitniluku, maligluni. Cunawa-gguq tauna yungcarista, tuaken Akiarmek kingunerluni. Tua-i yuut piluki pillilria.

Tua-i-llu-gguq qasgimi tamaani atakumi waten uitainanratni tauna yungcarista qanertuq, atama taum tua-i niicugniluku. Angalkumek-gguq tuunrilriamek tangerrsugyaaquq, tuunrilriamek tangerrsugyaaquq. Angalkurtarluni-ll' tauna, angalkum-wa taum atra Keplialleq.

Cali tauna atama qanrutkelaraa, tauna Keplialleq. Yuunginaullruuq-gguq wangkugcetun, angalkuuvkenani. Taugaam tua-i angliriluni urumavingqelliami angalkumek avnengengnaqluni-gguq-am tua-i avnengellruuq. Avnengellruuq, angalkuurrluni.

Tamakut-wa avneret qanrutketukait angalkut avenrit, avnerit, murilkestekait-gguq avneteng. Tangrrumavkenani tua-i, augna taugaam angalkuq tua-i. Taugaam tua-i tuaten qanrutekluki, avneteng-gguq tua-i murilkestekait. Taum wani avenran angalkuq allat makut pingraatni, taum wani tauna uitavini tua-i ellalirturaqluku. Angalkuullgutain-llu piqatarqatgu elpengcaraqluku. Murilkestekluku-gguq.

Tua-i tauna angalkuurtelliniluni-am Keplialleq. Kepliallermek aterluni.

Tua-i tauna tangvagyullinian taun' yungcarista tuunrilria, tua-i upluni-am tua-i tuaten qasperegnek all'uni. Tua-i unani-am tua-i uitavkenateng pitulliniameng tamakut, pilngungami, aturteni-ll' tua-i tamakut piluki.

come true. That's how I'll answer your question, but I can also tell you a story about that.

ALICE REARDEN: Was it because they knew that person performing the ritual had the ability [to materialize what they asked for]?

JOHN PHILLIP: Since they knew that he was [a shaman], that he was capable, that he had the ability to do something like that. I will tell you a story about someone who they asked to perform a ritual to request something.

That person, at Anuuraaq where I used to live; before we moved from that village, we lived there.

People living there at the time, and even that person named Puyulkuk who I mentioned lived there. And these people, all my grandfathers lived there. And Adolf and his family lived there, and their parents lived there, all their fathers were there at the time. And that person's namesake lived there, and my aunt lived there, [Roland's] grandmother was there at the time.

There [at Anuuraaq] one day, sometimes they sent out messengers to invite another village in the fall to take part in the Messenger Feast. When they are about to have dancing, they send messengers out to invite people from a nearby village to have the Messenger Feast. They'd invite a nearby village to have the Messenger Feast. I used to see that in the past.

And then, the people who lived there, those elders there, my grandfather Ciqilaralria, and also Cegg'aq and Adolf Jimmie's father Cimigaq, and Murak, and Paruk and his family also lived there at the time, and Puyulkuk was also there. Those people were there, and Aassitugaaq and his family also lived there during that time.

During the fall, since they planned to have a Messenger Feast, they prepared. Those who decide to have a Messenger Feast evidently prepare long before the time comes to have it.

That person among them whom they called Murak lived here [in Bethel] in the past. When they moved from the coastal area, he moved here.

That person, in order to begin the process of the Messenger Feast, they sent two messengers to Kipnuk during the fall time since that was their usual custom to send the messengers during freeze-up in the fall. They sent them to Cicingmiut right above the village of Kipnuk.

And when they sent those [two messengers] to Kipnuk, they decided upon and wrote down the names of the families who would dance, and wrote

CUCUAQ: Tua-i-qaa tauna pinguarvikestii nallunrilamegteggu?

AYAGINA'AR: Nallunrilamegteggu taungucia, tamakuucia, piyugngacia, tuavet piyugngacia, tuavet. Qanemciciiqamci taumek pinguarvikellratnek.

Tauna wani, yaani Anuuraami uitavillemni; yaaken upagpailemta tuani uitaluta.

Tamatum tamaa-i nalliini augkut uitallret, augna-ll' imna qanrutkelqa Puyulkuk tamaanlluni. Ukut-llu, ukut-wa tua-i apa'urluunka tuanlluteng tamarmeng. Augkut-llu Adolf-aaq-llu tamaanlluteng, angayuqrit tamaanlluteng, atait qaqimaluteng. Augna-llu cali taum atra tamaanlluteng, acaka-llu tamaanlluni taum maurlua.

Tuani caqerluteng, waten uksuarmi avani iliini kevgituut. Waten yuraqata'arqameng kevgituut, kevgituut. Kevgirluteng taukunun yaaqlirmeggnun nunanun pitullruut. Tamakunek tanglallruunga wiinga.

Tauna tua-i, tuanelnguut taukut, tegganret taukut, apa'urluqa Ciqilaralria, Cegg'aq-llu augna cali-llu Cimigaq Adolf-aam atii, Murak-llu, cali-llu Parunkut tuanlluteng augna-llu Puyulkuk tamaanlluni. Tamakunek tamaa-i, augkut-llu Aassitugaankut call' tuanlellruut taum nalliini

Tuani tua-i uksuarmi, uksuaran yuraqatalliniameng upluteng. Uptetulliniut envaarni tamakut yuraqatalriit.

Tauna wani iliit Muragmek pilallrat maantellruuq, maantellruuq tayima. Upallermeggni un'gaken maavet pillruuq.

Tauna wani kevgillratni yaavet Qipnermun-am kevgak ayagcetagket uksuarmi waten pituameng waten qenuqami. Cicingmun pillinilukek Qipnermiut kelliitnun.

Tua-i-llu tuavet ayagcecamegteki taukut Qipnermun, taukut tua-i yurararkat atrit elliluki, piyuutait-llu elliluki tamakut.

down the gifts they requested [from people in the invited village].

And that person who they called Murak wasn't initially part of the group [that was to take part in the Messenger Feast], since the poor thing wasn't a prosperous person. And his two children were being cared for by Ikit'am Arnaan, by Jacob Nelson's mother. I am the same age as the younger sibling, Nagtaq. We were living there at Anuuraaq at that time.

After they had left, those messengers returned home. When they arrived, they had what they call *qalurraq*. Do you hear of *qalurraq*?

GEORGE BILLY: I've heard of it.

JOHN PHILLIP: What is *qalurraryaraq*?

GEORGE BILLY: I don't really understand what *qalurraryaraq* is. I only became aware once when people from Nanvarnarrlak and Paingaq had their last Messenger Feast.

JOHN PHILLIP: Since my *iluraq* asks you questions since you're eighty-three years old, and since you are older than we are, I'm only asking what that word means. That's it.

The meaning of *qalurraryaraq*, when the [messengers] arrived from the village of Kipnuk, after having brought the list of gifts they requested from their village and disclosing what they were, when they revealed the items that they had requested and would dance for, they reveal the names of their firstborn children.

They request items from all the people for the dance by naming the firstborn children of those people, requesting those items from all the people in that way.

When those two [messengers] arrived, they gave an account [of what was requested]. *Qalurraryaraq* is a way of giving an account [of what was requested].

GEORGE BILLY: Now I finally understand what it means.

JOHN PHILLIP: Yes, *qalurraryaraq* is the practice of telling a story. They gave an account of what was requested inside the *qasgiq*. The people from Kipnuk had [the messengers] return home with their own requests to that village.

Murak evidently had a real *iluraq* [teasing cousin, male cross-cousin] in Kipnuk. That person lived there.

[When they went to Kipnuk to announce the participants' names and requests] when they announced each of the names, Murak was appar-

Tua-i tauna ilakenricaaqluku Muragmek piallrat, tua-i imuurluan tua-i, waten ayuqngan, canek paivngalivkenani. Irniarak-llu augkuk Ikit'am Arnaan aug'um, Jacob Nelson-aam aaniin auluklukek taukuk. Augna uyuraa Nagtaq pitatekaqa tauna. Tuani Anuuraami uitaluta.

Atam tua-i tayima ayaggaartelluki kinguani taukuk uterrlutek kevgak. Tekicamek apqiitnek qalurrarlutek. Qalurraq-qaa niitelaran?

NACAILNGUQ: Niiteqalarqa.

AYAGINA'AR: Qalurraryaraq cauga?

NACAILNGUQ: Qalurraryaraq taringeqapiarumanritaqa. Ataucirqumek taugaam tua-i elpeka'arrluku Kevgillruut nangnermek Nanvarnarrlagmiut Paingarmiut-llu.

AYAGINA'AR: Taum aptelaaten ilu'urma *eighty-three*-arluten, wangkugni-llu ciuqliungavet tauna apyutkaqa *word*-aq kiingan. Tua-i nang'uq.

Tauna qalurraryaraq imuuguq, tekicamek tua-i tuaken Qipnermek, tamakut, ukut piyuutait agulluki, tuavet maniluki pirraartelluki, yurautekaitnek aperturluki waten irniangqerraarutait pituit.

Tamakut irniangqerraarutaitnek aprucirluteng yurautarkanek tamakunek piyugviktuit yuut tamalkuita, tua-i piyuutekluki.

Atam tua-i taukuk tekicamek qanemcilriik. Qalurraryaraq qanemciyarauguq.

NACAILNGUQ: Nutaan taringartaqa.

AYAGINA'AR: Ii-i, qanemciyarauguq qalurraryaraq. Camek qalurrarluki-am tua-i tuaten qasgimi qanemciluteng. Taukut Qipnermiut utertellukek taukuk piyuuteteng, ellait tuavet nunaun piluku.

Tauna wani Murak ilurangqelliniuq nakmiin Qipnermi. Tauna tua-i tuanlluni.

Atam tua-i wani taukut atret piuryaaqellinikait, tauna Murak ilakenritlinikiit, nalluvkenaku elliin tuanlucia. Ilakevkenaku tua-i,

ently not among them, and [his *iluraq*] knew that he lived there. He wasn't among [the people who would participate], and he wasn't set to dance. It's because the poor person had nothing and didn't have anything to give when he danced since some of us people aren't prosperous and have nothing to give. But he was a shaman. He was one of the ones who we told stories about. But he was a shaman.

When they gave the names of people who they requested gifts from, they saw that [the people of Kipnuk] had included that person [Murak]. The ones who had sent the messengers over to that village hadn't initially included [Murak].

It so happened that his *iluraq* Pamsuq had requested something from him since he knew [that he was a shaman], and he insisted that his *iluraq* be included. He insisted that he be included, even though he had nothing to give, that he would request something from him.

When they gave an account announcing who would participate, after naming others, when they got to Murak, they saw that [his *iluraq*] had requested a young bearded seal from him. When he requested something from his *iluraq*, Pamsuq had evidently said that [Murak] had no gifts to give, but that he wanted to request something that wasn't seen or visible since he had heard that he was a shaman. That's what he did.

When they finally gave the account of what the other village requested, they included that person [Murak]. When they revealed their requests, they said . . . Nagtaq's older brother is Capen'aq, and he's the older brother. His *iluraq* Pamsuq had requested a young bearded seal from his older bother [Capen'aq]. He had requested a pretend young bearded seal. He requested those which had not yet arrived, and here it was falltime and those bearded seal pups hadn't been born yet; they were far from being born at that time.

They call his older brother Capenruilnguq, Capen'aq. They said that [Pamsuq] had requested from [Capen'aq] young bearded seals that would arrive in the spring. He had requested those which weren't seen, and he ended by saying that he was a shaman. He said [Murak] had nothing to give, and that he had wanted to request those things from him as he was a shaman. I heard that since I was listening inside the *qasgiq* at the time.

They usually requested things from one person in the family when I observed them. But when his *iluraq* [Pamsuq] requested from him, he had

yurararkauvkenani. Tua-i-w' waten ayuqurluami cakaunani yurautekaunani-llu, waten ayuqngamta ilaitni yuut tua-i caitaqluta. Taugaam angalkuuluni. Augkut qanemcilput ava-i. Taugaam angalkuuluni.

Tauna atam tua-i qalurraamek piameng ilakellinikii. Maaten pilliniat ilakellinikiit tauna Murak. Ilakenricaaqluku taukut, ilakellrunricaaqluku kevgilriit ayagcecilriit yaavet.

Taum cunaw' tua-i iluriin nallunrilamiu Pamsum pillinikii tauna tuanetniluku ilakesqelluku, ilakesqelluku tauna ilurani. Cakailengraan ilakesqelluku, piyugvikciqniluku.

Maaten tua-i qanemciameng piut, makut piurarraarluki tauna tekicamegteggu Murak maklaaryugviklinikiit. Qanlliniuq tauna Pamsuq piyugvikngamiu tuavet iluraminun tauna wani cakaitniluku, tangrrumanrilngurnek, taugaam maani alaitenrilngurmek piyugvikesqelluku, niitelarniluku angalkuuniluku. Tuaten tua-i pilliniuq.

Atam tua-i tauna maaten tua-i qanemciut tauna ilakluku tuaten. Maaten qanemciameng piut . . . aug'umek Capen'amek anngangqertuq taun' Nagtaq, anngauluni. Tuavet anngaanun wani maklaaryugviklinikiit taum iluraan Pamsum. Maklaaruaryugviklinikii. Tekiteksailngurnek, tayima uksuaruluni-llu tamakut-llu maklaaraat aneksaunateng; tamatum anyugnaunateng nalliini.

Tauna wani anngaa Capenruilngurmek pilaraat, Capen'amek. Taumun-am maklaaryugvikniluku up'nerkaqu tekitarkanek taukunek. Tamakunek piyugvikliniluku tangrrumanrilngurnek, angalkuuniluku tua-i aug'utun iqulirluku. Cakaitniluku tamakunek pisqelluku angalkuuniluku. Tua-i niilluku taun' niicugniama qasgimi tamaani.

Tua-i atam ataucinek pituyaaqut murilkellemni wii, ataucirrarnek *family*-nek. ataucinek. Taugaam tauna piamiu iluraan kinguqlia-ll'

evidently included his younger sibling [Nagtaq] at that time. He had told them to request a young bearded seal pup from the older brother, from Murak. Since he didn't have anything to give, he only requested things from him that were unseen.

After requesting that from him, they added that when the young bearded seals arrived, [Pamsuq] asked that his younger sibling Nagtaq provide windless weather. Do you understand what it means when I say windless weather? He wanted it to be continuously calm when they hunted those [young bearded seals]. That's what his *iluraq* requested from Murak. When that person heard, he couldn't do anything and just listened.

One day, after [the messengers] told him [what was requested], Murak had them construct a young bearded seal out of his namesake, *murak* [wood], and he also had them make a wooden stand for it, and he placed the young bearded seal in the center.

Since I watched them make it at that time, they finished its construction. When they finished constructing that, since they asked his younger sibling to provide good weather for it, he constructed a *ellanguaq* [lit., "model world or universe"] out of split strips of straight-grained wood.

He connected all the straight-grained wood pieces inside the *qasgiq*, and he carved them extremely thin like this, and assembled them following the contour of the *qasgiq*, making them gradually smaller. I saw those, I watched them as they made them when I had started to become aware and observant.

He made a *ellanguaq* that went all the way around [the *qasgiq*], and he finished it. When they finished that *ellanguaq*, they got those—we call them *aarraangiit* [long-tailed ducks]—they [decorated it with] tail feathers and placed small feathers in between up there along that *ellanguaq*.

He had evidently asked for a young bearded seal along with good weather. That man wasn't in good health at the time, and he had lost his eyesight. He didn't have good eyesight at that time.

That person [Murak] had them make that. One day, when they finished its construction, they watched him try it. They assembled and placed that above, and when it was complete, they placed that model young bearded seal in the center.

Then after a while, they practiced by singing a song. The model young bearded seal was down

tapqulluku pilliniluku. Pillinia tauna anngaa maklaaryugvikesqelluku ellii Murak tauna. Tua-i cakailan tangrrumanrilngurmek taugaam piyugluni elliinek.

Atam tua-i pirraarluku, cali iquliraat, maklaaret tuskata, Nagtamun taumun uyuraanun ellakirtuusqelluki ellamek anuqliryunrilngurmek. Taringan-qaa, ellamek anuqliryunrilngurmek? Taukut pissuqatki quunirrlainarluku pisqelluku. Tamatumek taum wani iluraan tauna Murak piyugvikliniluku. Tua-i niicamiu taum qaillun pisciiganani niicugniluku.

Atam tua-i piinanemteni caqerluteng ukut, taum qanrucatni taum wani Murak, muragmek atellgutminek muraggarmek maklaaruivkallinikai, inguqirluku-ll' muraggarmek cali, maklaar-wa qukaanun elliluku.

Wii tua-i tangellruamku tuani piliaqellratni tua-i, taqluku. Tauna-am taqngan taumun uyuraanun ellakirtuusqengatgu unarciarrarnek tang augkunek muraganek ellangualikili.

Qasgim iluani imkut unarciat usguqu'urluki amitkacagarluki waten, qasgi maliggluku, mikliinarluku waten. Tamakut tua-i tangellruanka wii, tangvallruanka murilkessagullua pillruata.

Ellangualikili tua-i tuaten uivetmun, taqluku. Taqngamegteggu tauna ellanguaq, imkunek—wangkuta aarraanginek pituaput—teqsuqritnek, qivyurrarnek nuulirluku akulirluku pagna, tamana.

Taukunek tua-i pinguarvikliniluku maklaarmek ellakartuumaan. Tauna elluatuuvkenani angun augna tamaani-llu takviarulluni. Tangerrnanrirluni cakneq mecikenrirluni tuani.

Tua-i taum tuaten pilivkarluki. Atam tua-i caqerluni taqngamegteggu taun' tangvagceskiit naspaaluku. Elliluku tua-i tamana qaqican pikavet tauna wani maklaaruaq tauna wani maklaaruaq qukaanun elliluku.

Atam tua-i piqerluteng naspaalriit yuarutmek aturluteng piluteng. Tamana tang kanani

there in the center. That bottom wooden [ring] was there. That bottom piece was there, it would move up and down, and the young bearded seal model was in the center. [The *ellanguaq*] would move up and down. It turned out that they had attached some sort of harness to pull it. It would move up and down and was wonderful to watch.

That's what they requested from that person [Murak]. They asked him to request [something from nature] using his powers, *pinguarvikluku*. That person over there asked about *pinguaq* [something inauthentic, fake]. They requested that from him, they asked for that from him, *pinguarvikluku*.

They finished constructing that. When they finished the construction, when they were about to leave [for the Messenger Feast], they made another model. He made a miniature *ellanguaq* and placed another young bearded seal model in the center again.

When it was time, they went to Kipnuk to attend the Messenger Feast. I went along, too, since they brought me along and included me. We had an *agyuq* [gift exchange partner], and I too had an *agyuq*. Do you know what they are?

GEORGE BILLY: I know what they are. I also had an *agyuq*, I used to have an *agyuq*.

JOHN PHILLIP: This is what [it's like] to have an *agyuq*. When they had us put on clothing, when I would remove my clothing inside the *qasgiq*, I would be so shy when I accompanied them.

They would apparently request things from the firstborn child. They were referred to by their firstborn child's name. And when they sang the song, they called out that [firstborn child's] name when they requested gifts from him. And after saying that person's name, they would say, "Would Nacailnguq bring forward many young bearded seals that are unlimited down at the bay."

GEORGE BILLY: Since they would say their names.

JOHN PHILLIP: Yes, that's what they did. That's what I heard at the time. Pamsuq, his *iluraq*, composed a song for him. When they got [to Murak], since he had no gifts to give, they placed him at the front, near the people who were going [to dance] first. Then they got to Murak. When they got to him . . . at that time we went over to attend the Messenger Feast, and I went along, too.

When they got to Murak, when he was about to dance, since they brought him along, he stayed inside the porch.

maklaaruaq qukaani uitaluni. Pagna wani, man'a aciqliq uitaluni muragaq. Uitaluni tamana, uyungqetaarnaurtuq, una-ll' maklaaruaq uitaluni qukaani. Uyungqetaarnaurtuq. Cunaw' tang cayuuciluku camek pillinikiit. Uyungqetaarnaurtuq tangssunaqluni tangvallra.

Taumek tua-i piyugvikluku tauna. Pinguarvikluku. Pinguamek ingna qanellruuq. Piyugvikluk', pinguarvikluku tamatumek.

Tua-i taqluku tauna. Tua-i taqngamegteggu tauna pililuku allamek cali ayagniaraameng nutaan. Mikcuayaarmek ellanguamek pililuni qukaanun cali maklaaruaq elliluku.

Atam tua-i piyungameng curukalriit Qipnermun. Wiinga-llu maligullua tua-i ilakngatnga malikngatnga. Agyungqetullruukut, wiinga-ll' agyungqetullruunga tamakunek. Nallunritaten-qaa?

NACAILNGUQ: Nallunritanka. Agyungqellruunga-ll' wii, agyungqelallruunga.

AYAGINA'AR: Tua-i waten agyunqeneq [ayuquq]. Aturanek tang acetaqatkut, wiinga tang tua-i qasgimi matarrlua acetaqatnga talluryulallrulrianga, maligutaqama.

Waten-am makut piyugvikluki ciuqlikacagaat yukqerraarit tamakut pitulliniit. Tauna tua-i ciuqliq yuat aprutekluku. Tua-i-ll' yuarucet atuamegteggu tauna piyugvigteng tauna aperluku yuum atra, taun' piyugvikteng. Nutaan-llu apraarluku waten pilartut, "Taitnaurai-qaa Nacailnguum-qaa maklaarugarnek quk'arcunrilngurnek unani kangimi."

NACAILNGUQ: Atrit aperturluki pituameng.

AYAGINA'AR: Ii-i, tuaten tua-i. Tuaten tua-i tauna niicugnilqaqa. Taum Pamsum elliin yuarutetarkiurluki iluraan. Atam tua-i tekicatni, cakaiturluan ciuqvanun tua-i maavet, ciuqlikacagaat natiitnun maavet elliluku pilriit. Ayumian tekilluku tauna Murak. Tekicamegteggu . . . tua-i tuani curukarluta, wiinga-ll' maligullua.

Tekicatni tauna Murak, yuraqataami malikngatni elaturrami tua-i uitaluni.

When they sang, asking [Murak] to bring forward the gifts they requested, when they got to him, he had given that model bearded seal pup to someone so that he would bring it inside as a gift to present during the dance. When they got to that person, they called out the name of Murak's son, "Would Capenruilnguq bring forward the many young bearded seals that are unlimited down at the bays."

They named the bays down there, the places where they hunt. We call the places where we hunt, the bays where the channels flow out to the ocean *kangit*. We call them *kangit*. The bays are also different down there; some are good places to hunt where animals are readily available. They aren't all the same.

When they called out Capenruilnguq's name, he had someone quickly enter with the young bearded seal model. He was only holding the young bearded seal model. When he brought it inside, he danced to present it. And when the song was over, he placed it down on the floor.

And when the song was complete, they also called out and made a request to his younger brother, "Would his poor younger brother Nagtaq provide good weather." He requested windless weather when the young bearded seals arrived. These are the things that his *iluraq* requested from him.

One of them ran in with that small model *ellanguaq*, with a young bearded seal model in the center. After dancing to present it, he placed it down. They say those two were actual first cross-cousins.

And when the song was over, his first cousin *kingulluggluku* [sang a song of ridicule to him] as they call it. Do you understand what a *kingullugtaq* [ridicule song] is?

GEORGE BILLY: They talk about what he was like in his home village. That's how I understand it.

JOHN PHILLIP: He sang a ridicule song to him.

GEORGE BILLY: Yes, he talked about what he's like in his village. *Kingullugtaq* means that they mention the type of person he is in his hometown.

JOHN PHILLIP: Since that person was a shaman, because he might not produce what was requested, or that he might produce it, they sing a ridicule song for him. For that reason, they call it *kingullugtaq*.

When the song suddenly ended, Pamsuq, when it ended, included their poor father [in the song lyrics]. The song lyrics stated, "Would their poor

Tua-i-llu tauna wani taitnauraaratni tekicatni tauna Maklaaruaq piliarraq waten yugmun tunluku itrucetarkauluku yurautekluku. Tauna tua-i tekicatni, apratni Muriim taum qetunraa aperluku, "Taitnauraa-qaa Capenruilnguum-qaa maklaarugarnek quk'arcunrilngurnek unani kangini."

Kangit unkut aterpaggluki, pissuryarait. Kanginek wangkuta pissuryaraput kangiqutat tamakunek kuiguyut ciunrit, tamakut kuiguyut kanginek pilaraput. Kanginek. Tamakut tang kangit, cali tua-i unani wangkuta ayuqenritut; ilait tua-i piqayunaqluteng ilait, cat paivngalluki makut pitaqsunarqelriit. Ayuqeqapigtevkenateng.

Atam tua-i tauna apratgu kina Capenruilnguq, iliitnun taun' itqerruceskii maklaaruaq. Maklaaruaq kiingan tegumiaqluku. Itqerrucamiu tua-i yurautekluku. Taqngani-ll' yuarun kanavet elliluku.

Iquklican-llu tua-i tauna uyuraa waten piluku cali. "Ellakirturliu-qaa kinguqliurluan-qaa Nagtam-qaa ima-qaa." Anuqliryunrilngurmek ellamek piyugluni maklaaret tuskata. Taum tua-i iluraan makut elliinun pilleqluki.

Iliit-am itqerrutuq ellanguamek taumek tua-i mikcuayagauluku taugaam, qukaani-w' maklaaruaq. Yurautekraarluku elliluku. Taukuk-gguq nakmiin ilu'urqutuk.

Tua-i-llu iqukliutiini taum wani cali iluraan apqiitnek kingull`uggluku. Kingullugtaq-qaa taringumaan?

NACAILNGUQ: Kingua qaill' ayuqucillra apertualuku. Tuaten taun' taringartela'arqa.

AYAGINA'AR: Kingull`uggluku.

NACAILNGUQ: Yaa, kingua. Kingull`uggluku-w' tua-i, apaaluki kingunrin qaill' ayuqucillra tuaten.

AYAGINA'AR: Tauna wani angalkuungan pitekluku tayima aipaagni-llu pingailucia wall' piarkaucia umyuaqluku kingull`uggluku-gguq. Tauna piluku tua-i, kingull`uggluku.

Iqukliarcan-am yuarun Pamsuq iqukliutiini tapeqluku call' tauna ata'urluak. Waten yuarun-am piuq, "Kasmurra'arlikek-qaa

father push them in a sled. We don't know if he will provide many, even if he says that he does." Because he was a shaman, "We don't know if he provides many." That's the way they ridiculed him. "We don't know if he will provide many, even if he says that he does."

GEORGE BILLY: Yes.

JOHN PHILLIP: When he ridiculed that poor person in that way, Murak suddenly entered. When he came into view down there, he pretended to paddle down on the floor, facing those people, and he suddenly ran out.

That's the ritual they asked him to perform to request and conjure something, a ritual that was done in my presence. One of the times when I accompanied others to the Messenger Feast, and I don't know how many times I had gone at that time.

That passed, and his *iluraq* probably anticipated his request materializing.

They say when Murak was about to tease his cousin Pamsuq, he announced that he was going to tease his cousin Pamsuq through a song.

Then our mutual grandfather, Jacob's father, tried to warn him, "Beware, you there, Pamsuq is smart. Pamsuq is smart. Leave him alone." They say he quickly replied to their surprise, "There is a tongue." [laughs]

"There is a tongue." Apparently, that was to try to entice Pamsuq. I'm just briefly mentioning the first thing that he did.

Then they finished their dancing and ceremonies, and began to hunt. Then they hunted in the springtime out on the coast . . . The person who requested them probably anticipated the young bearded seals.

The young bearded seals arrived during the spring. They say when they arrived, the only seals that were available along the bays were young bearded seals. There were only young bearded seals. And they say the wind stopped blowing during the entire time they hunted that spring. It was never windy during the time the young bearded seals hit.

That's what they said about that. And that's what our fellow villagers also said about it. They say the person who they had asked to perform that requesting ritual delivered those all summer long, and eventually it turned into fall.

ata'urluagnek. Pilirnaucia nalluarput pilarnilangraan." Angalkuucia pitekluku. "Pilirnaucia nalluarput." Kingulluggluku-gguq tua-i. "Pilirnaucia nalluarput pilarnilangraan."

NACAILNGUQ: Ii-i.

AYAGINA'AR: Taunaurluq tua-i tuaten kingullugcani, atam itqertellria tauna Murak. Igvaarcami tua-i kanani anguaruaqili cauluki taukut, anqerrluni-llu.

Tua-i ava-i augna pinguarutiit elliinun taum takumni pinguallret. Yuralrianun maligupakarlua taukut qavcilirilua-w' tuani.

Tua-i tamana pellugluni, taugaam neryuniurutekluku tua-i pillikii taum iluraan.

Taum-gguq-am elliin Muriim tauna ilurani Pamsuq iluriuqatallrani, waten-gguq qanertuq, ilurani-gguq Pamsuq iluriuqataraa yuarutkun.

Tua-ll' aug'um apa'urlumegnuk Jacob-aam atiin piyaaqellinia, "Aulluggaa-i usuuq. Pamsuq puqigtuq. Pamsuq puqigtuq. Uitasgu." Kiugartell'ertuq-gguq-am, "Ulutangqertuq." [ngel'artuq]

"Ulutangqertuq." Cunawa-gguq tua-i waniw' Pamsumun neqciutekluku. Tua-i aug'utun tua-i augna ciuqliq elliinun pillra piaqa, qanrutkeqa'arqa.

Atam tua-i tayima taqluteng yuranrirluteng, pissungluteng tua-i tua-i tayima. Atam tua-i up'nerkami avani cenami pissurluteng tua-i tamakut . . . Taum-wa tua-i pistiita neryuniurutkellikai tamakut maklaaraat, maklaaraat.

Atam tua-i up'nerkami maklaaraat makut tut'ellinilriit, tull'uteng. Tuc'ameng-gguq tua-i, tuc'ata imna maklaarrlainarnek kangit kiingita taqukaqluki. Maklaarrlainarnek. Anuqa-llu-gguq tua-i nipluni pissullrata taktaciatun tamaani up'nerkami. Anuqliyuunani maklaaraat tut'ellratni.

Tua-i tauna tuaten qanrutkaat. Augkut-llu nunalgutemta cali tuaten. Tauna tua-i pinguarvikellrat tua-i-gguq kiagpak tamakut, uksuarluni-llu-gguq.

Then they mentioned that it was as though they were spring camping when they were hunting during the fall for young bearded seals that they had requested [they were available from spring until fall].

That's all I'll say about the time that [the young bearded seals] arrived and became available. And he provided what he had requested. They say during the time that young bearded seals were available, it was never windy. That's what those who observed that occurrence said about it. That shaman had performed that ritual in which he requested those. Since he had requested them.

GEORGE BILLY: He allowed them to materialize.

JOHN PHILLIP: Yes. Like you said earlier, since they believed in things, he gave what his cousin requested to him.

GEORGE BILLY: That's what I used to hear. They say when they request things from some shamans, they come to materialize for sure. They danced, like they were requesting things. They say that always came to materialize before there were many white people around.

Some people acquired belongings only through dance, and the orphans and the widows received a lot of food when they had the Messenger Feast. And those who didn't have materials to make skin boots were given skins first. Now? I used to hear of [shamans] performing rituals to request things.

JOHN PHILLIP: I only know of Murak who they asked to perfom a ritual to request something, and I knew about things he constructed. He made a *ellanguaq*.

That's all I'll say about how he performed the ritual to request something. Those who told the story said that they reached falltime, and that young bearded seals continued abundant up until the fall. That's what [Pamsuq] requested from [Murak].

I've also heard of those who were asking for driftwood through a ritual in the past, but they never performed the ritual in my presence, but I've heard of those occurrences.

ALICE REARDEN: So Pamsuq requested those things from Murak?

JOHN PHILLIP: Yes, he requested those things that aren't seen.

ALICE REARDEN: Where was Pamsuq from?

JOHN PHILLIP: Pamsuq, his real *iluraq* was from Kipnuk. And Murak lived in Anuuraaq.

ALICE REARDEN: When they were going to have the Messenger Feast, did the people of Kipnuk go to Anuuraaq?

Tua-ll'-am qanrutkait, tuarpiaq-gguq iliini tamakut ilait un'gani uksuarmi pilriit, up'nerkilriit-gguq tuar maani tamakut maklaarnek, piyuutaitnek.

Tua-i tauna tua-i tuaten nallunricetaqa tauna tuaten pitaluku tut'ellrat tamakut. Tauna-ll' tua-i piyullra taum elliin tuavet tunluku tamana. Anuqliyuunani-gguq maklaaraat tusngallratni tua-i. Tuaten tua-i qanrutkelaraat murilkestain. Taum tua-i angalkum tamakut pinguaqluki, kaigatekluki. Kaigatekngaki taum tua-i.

NACAILNGUQ: Piciurcelluki.

AYAGINA'AR: Ii-i. Tua-i aug'utun qanllerpetun ca ukvekluku piamegteggu, piyullra tamana tua-i elliin taum ilurami tunluku.

NACAILNGUQ: Tuaten tua-i niitetullruunga. Piyugvikaqaceteng-gguq ilait angalkut piciurtenricuitut. Tua-i camek kaigavikellriatun yurarluteng. Tua-i piciurtenricuitut-gguq tamaani kass'at amllerivailgata.

Yurakun taugaam yuk cangqetullruameng ilait elliraat aipainret tuaten neqkalingartaarluteng yura'arqata. Aminek tuaten pilugugkaitaalriit cikirtuumaaqluteng ciuqlikacaarmek. Tua-llu? Tamaa-i-gguq yurakun piyugvikaqaceteng, pinguarqata niicetullruanka.

AYAGINA'AR: Tauna tua-i Murak tuaggun yurakun tamakunek pinguarvikellratnek wiinga kiingan nallunritaqa, tamakut-llu piliallri nalluvkenaki. Ellangualiluni piluni tamakunek.

Augna tua-i aug'utun ava-i taktaluku piaqa pinguallra. Ava-i uksuarmun tekilluni tamana qanrutkaat qanemcikestain tekitellret tamaa-i uksuarmi maklaaraat. Taumek piyugvikluku.

Allanek cali tua-i muraguatullernek niitelaryaaqua, takumni taugaam piksaitut, tamakut taugaam niitaqluki.

CUCUAQ: Taum-qaa Pamsum Murak piyugvikluku tamakunek?

AYAGINA'AR: Ii-i piyugvikluku tamakunek tangrrumanrilngurnek.

CUCUAQ: Tauna-qaa Pamsuq camiungullrua?

AYAGINA'AR: Qipnermiunguluni Pamsuq iluraa taum nakmiin. Murak-llu Anuuraami tuani uitallruuq.

CUCUAQ: Tua-llu-qaa taukut tuani kevgiqatallratni Qipnermiut-qaa Anuuraamun?

JOHN PHILLIP: The people of Anuuraaq sent messengers to Kipnuk to invite them to take part in a Messenger Feast. And when they sent their messengers, they also sent their requests back to them. They would have mutual [gift exchanges and dancing] at that time. That's what dancing was like.

ROLAND PHILLIP: They called it *mumigarulluteng* [immediate reciprocation, switching roles].

AYAGINA'AR: Anuuraarmiut Qipnermun kevgirluteng. Tua-i-llu taukut Kevgiameng, utercecetuit waten piyuutait ellaitnun waten. Atunem akiqautarkauluteng waten. Tuaten yurar' ayuqellruuq.

ANGUTEKA'AR: Mumigarutniluki pitullruit.

I watched someone who tried to change the weather in the *qasgiq*[60]

John Phillip and Alice Rearden, Bethel, February 2014

JOHN PHILLIP: I also watched someone who tried to change the weather in the *qasgiq*.

He turned the wind direction like this, since that weather man evidently had the ability to change the weather using his paddle.

He would have a person go and check [the weather], he would go and check it. He would say that [the wind direction] reached this place where the paddle was pointing.

Then when it reached the west, he told him to stop when the people told him to stop. The wind started blowing from that direction. They said the weather would improve after that.

ALICE REARDEN: Who did that during that time?

JOHN PHILLIP: I don't know who the person that I watched was, but I watched him. I didn't know the name of the shaman who I watched who did that.

ALICE REARDEN: Would he let someone go and check outside?

JOHN PHILLIP: Yes, he would have another person go and check the wind. He shifted [the wind] in a circle inside the *qasgiq* using a paddle, by continually moving it. And the wind followed and shifted.

Ellaliulriamek tangvallruunga qasgimi

Ayagina'ar Cucuaq-llu, Mamterilleq, February 2014

AYAGINA'AR: Ellaliulriamek call' tangvallruunga qasgimi.

Anuqa uivvluku waten, anguarutni piluku ellaliutulliniami *weather man*-aq.

Paqcetaqluku uumun, paqtaqluk'. Tuavet ellirniaqluku anguarutem ciunranun.

Tua-i-ll' waten *west*-aq tekicaku taqesqelluku ukut taqesqengatgu. Tuaken tua-i anuqlinga'arrluni. Assiriarkaurrluni-gguq tua-i.

CUCUAQ: Kina tuani tuaten pillrua?

AYAGINA'AR: Kituuciitaqa augna tangvalqa, taugaam tangvallruaqa. Kituuciitellruaqa tauna angalkuk tangvalqa tuaten pilleq.

CUCUAQ: Ellamun-qaa paqcetaqluku kina?

AYAGINA'AR: Ii-i, allamun yugmun paqcetaqluku anuqii. Qasgim iluani uivvluku anguarutmek waten, ayagturtelluku. Anuqa-llu maligulluni ayagluni.

Their shaman evidently brought them there, and so they went by sled to survive[61]

John Phillip and Alice Rearden, Anchorage, January 2011

JOHN PHILLIP: And some fish in rivers including needlefish weren't too readily available although they were around. [Slushy snow] blocked the mouths of rivers and the current couldn't flow

---

Taum angalkuata ayautelliniluki, ikamrarluteng tua-i anangnialliniluteng

Ayagina'ar Cucuaq-llu, Anchorage, January 2011

AYAGINA'AR: Makut-llu kuiget neqait quarruuget-llu paivngassiyaagpek'nateng pilangermeng. Kuiget paingit tamakut qanisqinrem kuiget capluki, quarruuget, kuiget carvanirciigaliluteng;

anymore; [the needlefish] would only circle around when the mouths of rivers were blocked in [rivers] where there were needlefish.

Then there is another story about people who had gone to survive a famine from upriver, heading to the river of the village of Chefornak, to Urrsukvaaq, through the inland route. Their shaman evidently brought them there, he wanted to bring them there, and so they went by sled to survive.

They say their shaman was looking at a bright light that was shining down on that place. It was bright like this.

When they reached that river, that shaman told them to make an opening [along the ice]. It was pointing to where the needlefish were; perhaps it was the one who watches over us [God]. When that person saw it, that place was bright. They finally made an opening [in the ice], and using some sort of implement that fit, they dipnetted those needlefish.

But they say some people starved to death there looking at their food. Since they don't usually eat them, the people from upriver weren't used to eating them. When they'd give them some, they would say . . . the small needlefish have many eyes. It is said they would say after looking at them, "Gee, so many eyes!" [laughter]

ALICE REARDEN: Poor! They starved to death?

JOHN PHILLIP: Those who said, "So many eyes" starved to death. They didn't want to eat their food.

Although they were those [needlefish], our grandmother would bite their small heads off, and they'd have children eat them. They continually removed their small heads, their small heads, and not their bodies since they have a lot of needles on them. They'd only feed [children] their small heads. The small heads of needlefish are tasty when dipped in seal oil.

They say needlefish would help people to survive until there was an availability of food. I'm adding that to what I said.

uivvaarturluteng taugaam pilalliniluteng kuiget paingirtaqata tamaani quarruulegni.

Tua-i-ll' cali qanemcitarluni qavaken kiatiitnek anangniyalriit taukut, yaavet Cevv'arnermiut kuigatnun Urrsukvaamun, pavaggun. Taum angalkuata ayautelliniluki tamaavet ayacugluki, ikamrarluteng tua-i anangnialliniluteng.

Taum-gguq tua-i angalkuata tangvagluku waten tauna tanqik tuavet tusngalria. Waten tanqigcenani.

Kuik taun' tekicamegteggu nutaan taum angalkum callarcesqelluku. Quarruuget-gguq cunaw' tua-i waten apertuusngaluki; tua-i-wa tangvagtemta pillikai. Tanqigcenani-gguq waten taun' tangvallrani taum pillruuq tauna. Tauna callarrluku nutaan quarruugnek canek pissuucirluteng tua-i ngelqiitnek qaluluki.

Taugaam-gguq ilait tuani call' paluluteng neqkateng tamakut tangvagluki. Neryuilamegteki nalluluki makut kiaqliita. Qanernaurtut-gguq cikiraqaceteng . . . quarruuyagaat iingit, amlletuut quarruuyagaat iingit. Qanernaurtut-gguq tangvaggaarluki, "Aling iilirpaa-ll'!" [ngel'artut]

CUCUAQ: Akleng! Paluluteng?

AYAGINA'AR: Tua-i paluluteng tamakut tuaten qanellret, "Iilirpaa." Neqkateng qessakluki.

Tamakuungraata tang wangkuta aug'um maurlumta qamiquyagait kegqerluki mikelngurnun tamakut nerevkalallrukait. Qamiquyagait aug'arturluki, qamiquyagaitnek imkunek enerngalngurnek, taugaam temiit man' pivkenaku cukileliata. Qamiquyagaitnek taugken. Assiyaartut atam qamiquyagait quarruuget uqumek piluki.

Tua-i-gguq tamakut quarruuget tamaa-i kanautngutullruut avani makut quarruuget. Taukunek ava-i ilaluku piunga.

Stories of People from the Kuskokwim River

That female shaman used her small story knife to pierce the injuries of people who were hurt and she healed them[1]

John Phillip and George Billy, Bethel, October 2006

JOHN PHILLIP: When I went inside [the *qasgiq*] at Qinaq, they had two levels [of beds], and also along this area. I saw those two.

GEORGE BILLY: They called those *qulirualget* [ones with upper level beds/platforms]. They called [those types of *qasgit*] *qulirualget*. Since it had beds with two levels, they called them *qulirualget*.

Something I heard, I only heard about those in stories. An old man told a brief story in my presence, and he said that there was a *qasgiq* that collapsed with many people inside it. This was probably because [they had a dance festival] during summer. That's the story that I briefly heard.

They said many people were injured, but he said that two people, one a shaman and the other a female shaman; they said that female shaman, since they had story knives in the past, she would pierce people who were injured with her story knife on a certain place, and she healed them by allowing their wounds to bleed, removing the blood. It is said that the other shaman would also poke them with something, and he healed many people at that time.

You know how since long ago, girls used story knives to play, and they also used them beyond the capes [at Bristol Bay]. But down in the lower Kuskokwim coast, in Canineq, they had ivory [story knives], and I'd see them once in a while. But here in the tundra area or the Kuskowkim River area, they had wooden story knives.

The story knife apparently saved some people. It is said that female shaman used her small story knife to pierce the injuries of people who were hurt and she healed them.

I once saw someone pierce a person's injury [to remove the infection] in the *qasgiq*. Someone else had apparently hurt someone on his back, and his midsection here was bruised pretty badly, and it was swollen.

https://doi.org/10.5876/9781646427314.c015

Kusquqvagmiut Qanemciit

Angalkum arnam taum yaaruiksualleraminek taumek akngiringalriit kapurluk' aunraqluk' assirivkarluki

Ayagina'ar Nacailnguq-llu, Mamterilleq, October 2006

AYAGINA'AR: Qinarmiut [qasgiatnun] itlemni *two*-aagnek qulliqelriignek, maani-ll' cali. Taukuk tangellruagka.

NACAILNGUQ: Tamaa-i-gguq tamakut qulirualget. Qulirualegnek pinaurait. Aperluki tua-i, qulliqellrianek piami, qulirualget-gguq.

Niitellemnek, qalamciqauluki-am niigartellruunga augkucinek. Qalangssakalria angukara'urluq, tamaani-gguq qasgi tauna yugu'ugarnek waten amllernek imvikluku. Kiagmi-w' pilliata pillilriit. Tua-i taun' qalamci niigartelqa.

Amlleq-gguq akngirqellruuq, taugken-gguq ukuk malruk aipaa angalkuq, aipaa-w' call' angalkuq arnaq; taum-gguq arnam angalkum, yaaruitengqetullruameng imkut, yaaruitminek-gguq akngiringalriit naugg'un kapurluki, aunraraqluki assirivkallrui, tamana aug' anevkaraqluku. Angalkum-gguq taugken call' aipaan una tua-i uumek cali kapurluki amlleq-gguq ilii assirivkallrua.

Iciw' tamana avaken ayagluni man'a nasaurluut naanguaruciryaraqellruat yaaruiyaraq, nuuget-llu call' augkut yaatiitni cali atullrulliniluku. Unani-ll' Caninermi tulunek taugaam pingqetullruut, tangrraqlua-ll' iliini. Maani taugken Akulmi wall' Kusquqvagmi, muragnek tua-i pilianek yaaruitengqetullrulliniluteng.

Tua-i yaaruin anirtuqngellrulliniuq. Angalkum arnam taum yaaruiksualleraminek-gguq taumek akngiringalriit kapurluk' aunraqluk' assirivkarluki.

Ataucirqumek kap'ilriamek tangvallruunga qasgimi. Iliita-am pamaggun akngirtellinikii, qukaa man'a qiurpagluni tua-i puvluni.

https://doi.org/10.5876/9781646427314.c015

When they were about to insert a sharp object into his injury, he examined the injury briefly. Then he smeared a little bit of charcoal along the area where they were going to insert the object. Then he flattened a nail. Two people stretched the skin here, two people who were strong pulled it very tightly and held it tight.

And when they pulled the skin, as soon as he poked the object, it bled, some infected blood came out, and the person's injury was apparently infected. They let the injury bleed. And when it was good, it healed, and it no longer bled.

Tua-i-ll' kapqataamegteggu yuvriaqaqiit. Tua-i-ll' tauna tua-i kap'arkaq kangipluggarmek mingukarluku. Tua-i-ll' ussukcaq passilluku. Tauna tua-i malruk uuggun nenguggluku tua-i caknerpak tua-i qet'erpagluku pinilriik.

Tua-i-ll' nengugcan'gu, kap'leqiini augmek aunrarluni, augglugmek, assiingqaluni tauna akngirnera. Tua-i aunrarqurluku. Assirian-llu tua-i mamluni, tua-i aunranriqerrluni.

A shaman used his powers on my grandfather[2]

Elena Charles and Marie Meade, National Museum of the American Indian, April 1997

MARIE MEADE: Did shamans use these [seal-gut parkas] when they practiced their spirit powers?

ELENA CHARLES: They say long ago, in the early days shamans wore them when they did incantations. They had them make crackling noises as they sang and walked.

I saw one shaman singing when he was using his spirit powers on my grandfather. He was the only one I saw. That was the only shaman I saw when he used his spirit powers on my grandfather when he was sick.

MARIE MEADE: Was he wearing a seal-gut parka?

ELENA CHARLES: He was going in circles wearing a seal-gut parka.

MARIE MEADE: Around your grandfather?

ELENA CHARLES: My grandfather was sitting, my grandmother was sitting, and my younger sister was sitting. I think there were only three of them.

My father, I noticed that he didn't want anything to do with shamans. He didn't want anything to do with traditional abstinence practices either. They say when I was still in my mother's womb, my father had an accidental gunshot wound. Is it all right if I tell this story?

He accidentally shot himself with a bird gun when I was still inside my mother's womb. The wound was on one side of his face, and one eye was popped. They saw him approaching, and he would quickly paddle and then put his head down.

When he arrived, my dear mother and grandmother received him. And [the bleeding from his

Angalkuum tuunritellrua apa'urluqa

Nengqerralria Arnaq-llu, National Museum of the American Indian, April 1997

ARNAQ: Makut-qaa tuunriaqameng angalkut atutullruit?

NENGQERRALRIA: Ak'a-gguq avani ciuqlirmi, ciuqvaarni angalkut tuunriaqameng atutullruit. Qiaryigqurtelluki aturluteng piyualuteng.

Ataucimek angalkugmek tangellruunga atulriamek apa'urluqa tuunrilluku. Tua-i tauna kiingan tangelqaqa. Cali-llu tauna angalkuk kiingan tangelqelluku tuunrilluku tauna apa'urluqa naulluullrani.

ARNAQ: Imarniterluni-qaa pillruuq?

NENGQERRALRIA: Imarniterluni waten uivvaalria.

ARNAQ: Apa'urlurpet avatiini?

NENGQERRALRIA: Apa'urluqa aqumgallruuq, maurluqa aqumgallruuq, nayagaqa aqumgallruuq. Tua-i kiimeng pingayuunganateng.

Atam imna ataka, maaten murilkaqa angalkut tamakut piyuumiitelallrui. Eyagyarat-llu piyuumiitelallruluki. Ak'a-gguq qingaulua ataka tauna anqerrivikellruuq. Man'a qanemcikengramni canrituq?

Anqerrivikellruuq yaqulegcuutmek nutegmek wiinga qingaulua. Kegginami ingluakun, iinga-llu qagrumayaaqluni. Agiirtellria-gguq angualaakarraarluni pus'artaqluni.

Maaten-gguq tekican taum tua-i aanaurluma maurluma-llu ciuniuraak. Qayaan-llu imkut enri tekitelliniluki. Aunrallrulliniuq amllermek.

wound] reached his kayak ribs. He apparently bled a lot.

He had a very capable person taking care of him, too, my grandmother. They say my grandmother washed his open skin wound. After she washed it thoroughly, she put the skin back in place the way it was. I wonder what she put over it?

Gee, those people in the past did such a good job! My father was in great pain because they had no pain medication back in those days. He was in so much pain and would lie face down on his pillow.

When he was doing that, he said an angel came from above. Whenever he'd look down, he'd have only one eye. But when he'd put his head up, he'd have two eyes.

When [the angel] got to my father, he told him he had brought him an eye. And the angel placed the eye in his eye.

When he woke, his popped eye was a good eye. And he could see. Because of that, he didn't want anything to do with shamans.

He even cautioned me when I first started to menstruate, "Even if your mother gives you many abstinence practices to follow, don't follow them. If you want to abstain, only think about the Bible's teachings. Those abstinence practices are more important to follow."

MARIE MEADE: The one who the shaman used his powers on, was it your father or grandfather?

ELENA CHARLES: The one who the shaman used his powers on was my grandfather. He was my mother's father.

They say he was sick a year . . . those first people would go through illness for a long time before they died. Because they didn't have medication to cure them, they'd be ill for a long time. And some were ill for a number of years. They couldn't do anything.

My grandfather was apparently sick probably for two years. He couldn't swallow, he didn't eat. Because those first people were strong, even though they didn't eat for a long time, they didn't lose weight right away.

The shaman used his spirit powers on him wearing a seal-gut parka. When I was a child, or when I got a little big, I used to learn songs I heard. I didn't learn that shaman's song. I can't even remember one word from the song when I tried to remember it. I wonder what he sang?

Tua-i aulukestekegciluni-llu pillrulliniuq maurlumnek. Maurluma-gguq eruqii man'a amir' ikingqalria. Erunqegcaararraarluku-llu-gguq elliluku ayuquciatun kemganun. Camek tayima tunglilirluku piagu?

Anglilli tamakuni yugni elluarrluki pitullrulliniivaa! Ataka-gguq tauna nangteqluni cakneq iinrunek canek piitellruameng, akngirnairutsuutnek. Nangteqellria cakneq putuskami palungqaaqluni.

Tua-i tuatnallrani an'gilaq-gguq agiirtellruuq pakmaken. Waten kanatmun piaqami iinga atauciurtaqluni. Taugken ciugeskuni iik malruulutek.

Tua-i-llu tekicamiu ataka qanrutliniluku, waniwa-gguq iikaanek payugtaa. Iinganun-llu ellilliniluku taum an'gilam.

Tua-i maaten tupagtuq iinga qagrumaalleq iinguluni. Tangerrsugngaluni-llu. Tua-i taumek angalkut piyuumiitetullrui.

Wiinga-llu agleryaaqellemni inerqullruanga, "Aanavet canek eyagyaranek amllernek cikingraaten aturyaqunaki. Eyagyukuvet ingkut qaneryarat taugaam umyuaqekiki. Taukut taugaam arcaqerluteng eyagnarqut."

ARNAQ: Tua-llu-q' tauna angalkuum tuunritellra, atakellruan wall'u-q apa'urluqluku?

NENGQERRALRIA: Tauna angalkuum tuunritellra apa'urluqaqa. Aanama atakluku.

Tauna-gguq naullullruuq allrakuq . . . augkut atam ciuqliit yuut tuquqataumatullrulliniut. Iinrunek-wa anirtuastaitelaameng nangtequmaluteng ak'anun. Ilait-llu allrakuni qavcini naulluugaqluteng. Tua-i casciiganateng.

Tauna tua-i apa'urluqa naullullrulliniuq allrakurrngatuq-llu malrugnek. Igesciiganani, neryuunani. Augkut yuut ciuqliit piniameng nereksaicimangermeng-llu egmianun kemgiqercuunateng.

Tua-i taun' angalkum tuunritellrua waten imarnitegnek aturluni. Yuarutet elitetuyaaqekenka mikelnguulua niitellrenka wall'u-qaa angliyugarlua. Taum tang angalkum yuarutii elitellrunrilkeka. Camek tua-i atauciungraan-llu *word*-aq umyuaqeksaunaku neq'angcalaryaaqellrianga. Cameg'-kiq tayim' atullrua?

And down there, in the center of the people he was using his spirit powers on, they were on a woven grass mat that was made with narrow strands inside the home. And down in the center was a wooden bowl like we saw earlier, a *tumnguaq*, a man's [bowl]. In the middle [of the bowl], when I looked at it, they looked like three bearberries, those bearberries.

After he went around in circles he stopped and said, "Hurry and let him swallow the middle one of those [bearberries] down there." My grand-mother took it . . . he couldn't swallow. I wonder how he swallowed it? After that, I don't remember anything. I am done with this. This person is now going to talk. Thank you.

Kan'a-wa, qukaatni taukut wani tuunriskengain, tupiganek imkunek curunek akulkilnguarnek tupiumalrianek curungqellruut enem iluani. Kan'a-wa qukaatni imkut augkut tangllemcetun ayuqellria qantaq tumnguaq, angucetaq. Kankut-wa qukaani, wiinga tangllemni, tuartang kavliit pingayun, imkut tua-i kavliit.

Tua-i-llu tauna uivaarinanermini arulairluni qanertuq, "Kitaki, kankut qukaqliatnek igevkarru." Tua-i maurluma teguluku . . . igesciigatellruuq. Qaill' tayima tua-i igau? Tua-i tuaken ayuquciqa tayim' nalluyagutellriatun pillruaqa. Waniwa taq'uq. Una cali qalarteqatartuq. Quyana.

They say they would lean their hands down on them[3]

Alexie Nicholai, Jacob Black, and Marie Meade, Napaskiak, March 2017

MARIE MEADE: So here in Napaskiak and down [in Napakiak], when you were growing up, these ones they call *angalkut*, there used to be some. . . .

And then, probably here in this village [of Napaskiak] and for sure in villages down toward the coast also, they used to mention Qinarmiut also, they'd talk about them, that there were some good [shamans] who helped people; [there were] shamans who were like that or ones who went against people.

A good one was one who helped people. In this village or in your village downriver, do you know about the time when they were like that, or sha-mans you used to hear about, ones who helped people or those who didn't do good works?

ALEXIE NICHOLAI: I don't know about those shamans. But some people, he would cover a person's ailment with his hand and then he did something to it with his hands; some people apparently had powers to heal [ailments].

They say those who were able to heal, people would give them payment and use them. And if [that person] didn't pay him, this [ailment] would once again go bad. But when they had paid, [his ailment] would heal.

They called it *ayaperluku* [lean their hands down on something] when they treated the ailment. That's all I know about those. But some of those shamans, they apparently would heal a person.

Ayaperluki-gguq pituluteng

Apeng'aq, Nasgauq, Arnaq-llu, Napaskiaq, March 2017

ARNAQ: Tua-llu-q' maani Napaskiarni cakmani-llu tamaani angliyugallerpeceni makut angalkut apqait, pitangqetullruuq. . . .

Tua-ll', maani aipaagni nallunailngurmek avatmun-llu nunat un'gatmun, Qinarmiut-llu ukut cali apaalallruit, qalarutkaqluki assilrianek ikayurilrianek pitangqellruniluki; tuaten aprumalrianek angalkunek wall'u-qaa inglukilrianek.

Iciw' tua-i una assilria ikayurilriaruluni yugnek. Maani-qaa ukurmiuni wall'u nunavceni un'gani nallunrituci tuaten ayuqellratni wall' niitelallerpecenek angalkuullernek, nalluvkenaki ikayurilrianek wall'u assirpek'nateng pilrianek?

APENG'AQ: Wiinga-w' tamakut angalkut nallukenka. Ilait taugaam yuut, iciw' nat'liqutii yuum unatminek patuluku unatminek-llu qiallun piluku; ilait tua-i kitugcissuutengqellliniluteng.

Tamakut-gguq kitugcitulit yuut cameg' akilirluki atutuit. Akilillrunrilkuniu-llu una ataam qaillun piluni. Taugken tua-i akilillruaqata una assiriluni.

Tuaten tua-i ayaperluku-gguq qaillun aulukellni. Tuaten-am kiingan tamakut nallunritanka. Taugken tamakut angalkut ilait yuk kitugcetullrulliniluku.

They were sort of like doctors. [chuckles]

MARIE MEADE: Yes, some of them were able to do that using their powers.

ALEXIE NICHOLAI: They had powers. I only know about those two things. They say they would *ayaperluki* [lean their hands down on them]. . . .

They apparently placed their hands on their ailment and [healed it] with their hands. They leaned their hands down on it, what they call *ayaperluni* [leaning his hands down on something for support].

Then if they did well and healed their ailment, it would heal. But when people out in the public asked them to do that to them, they would pay that person with something when they did that. They say if they didn't pay, it doesn't work well.

JACOB BLACK: They mentioned what you just said, that even if they are given a small payment, they are grateful for it.

And he asked me if he gave me his ability would I accept it[4]

Alexie Nicholai and Jacob Black, Napaskiak, March 2017

JACOB BLACK: Yes, since you're talking about shamans, since you said you don't know about them too well, but I want to ask you since you're an elder, the way of becoming a shaman, how does one become one of those, become a shaman?

ALEXIE NICHOLAI: When a person was born, when they wanted him/her to be one of those, he probably would give him/her those abilities, when they wanted them to become shamans. They probably did that. That's all I know about that.

JACOB BLACK: Let me tell you a brief story. I'm asking you about those, one day these two, you've heard of Apangtak and Agagliiyaq. Especially Apangtak told me this; he was apparently my great-grandparent.

After calling me by a kinship name, he asked me if I think that he's been something [a shaman] throughout his life. I said to him, "Yes." He said he didn't know anything at all before, and he said he didn't know about the way of being a shaman. And Agagliiyaq also told me the same thing. That's what he told me.

One day, they always invited me over, and I constantly tried to help them, doing work for them. One day when I invited them to my house to eat, my grandfather Agagliiyaq said to me after call-

---

Yungcaristengullerluteng. [*ngelaq'ertuq*]

ARNAQ: Yaa, ilait tuaten piyugngaluteng pissuutmegteggun.

APENG'AQ: Pissuuterluteng. Augkuk tua-i kiigkenka nallunritagka wii. Ayaperluki-gguq pituluteng. . . .

Augna-wam tayim' unatmeggnek, nat'liqutiin nalliikun unatmeggnek piluki pitullrullinikiit. Ayaperluku tamana, ayaperluni-gguq.

Tua-i-llu tauna nat'liqun piluaqaqani assiriluni. Taugaam tamakucetaaraqameng yuut makut cailkamelnguut akiliqerluku camek atutulliniluku tauna. Akilinritaqami-gguq cali assirluni caliyuituq.

NASGAUQ: Aug'utun ava-i qanllerpetun qanqallruuk, carraquinraungraan-gguq akiliutiit quyakelarait.

Qanrullua-llu man'a-gguq-qaa pia [tunkaku] wangnun ciuniurciqaqa

Apeng'aq Nasgauq-llu, Napaskiaq, March 2017

NASGAUQ: Yaa, angalkunek qalarcavci, tua-i nallunritsiyaanritniavki, taugaam ap'arcugamken ciulirneruavet man'a-qaa angalkuurcaraq qaillun taungurcarauga, angalkuurrluni?

APENG'AQ: Una tua-i yuurtaqan taungusqumaaqamegteggu-wa pissuutekainek cikilallrullikii, angalkuurtesqumaaqamegteki. Tuaten tua-i pitullrungatellikiit. Kiingan tua-i taun' tuaten nallunritaqa.

NASGAUQ: Qanemciarteqerlamci. Tamakunek aptamken, caqerlua ukuk wani, Apangtak im' niitelaqci Agagliiyaq-llu. Taum tua-i arcaqerluni Apangtiim qanrutellruanga waten; amauqelliniluku wii.

Tuqlurraarlua tua-i, caminek pianga, ellii-gguq-qaa caugurallruyukluku umyuarteq'lartua. Piaqa, "Yaa." Nallumquuqapiarallruyaaquq-gguq man'a-llu-gguq angalkuuyaraq nalluluku. Tuamtellu cali Agagliiyaam cali tuaten qanrullua. Tuaten tua-i.

Caqerlutek, kelegturatullruagnga, ikayungnaqu'urlukek-llu tua-i cacillukek. Caqerlukek enemnun kelellemkek aug'um apa'urluma Agagliiyaam pianga tutgaraminek

ing me his grandchild that he wants to give me his ability sometime. Then when he was done saying that, [Apangtak] also told me after calling me by [a kinship] name.

And he asked me if he [gave me] his ability would I accept it. I was thinking in my mind right away since I had heard about them the way he just mentioned, I said to them that I don't know about those things at all, and I don't know what they do, and I don't know about how they become [shamans].

Then Apangtak said that he didn't have much of an ability, but they were asked by a person who wanted to pass down their ability to them. I told him that I don't know anything about that.

Then he told me, and my dear grandfather told me, no differently than this person, this is what they explained to me, that they have to teach [their ability] to someone. They also warn them about the wrong way of practicing it. And when they've learned, they give over the entire [ability] to the one who wants to accept [it]. Then they become those.

But even though those two offered [their abilities] to me, I locked out the [abilities] of both of them. [laughs] Since I didn't know about it.

ALEXIE NICHOLAI: They apparently wanted you to become one of those.

JACOB BLACK: Yes. I had heard about those two [being shamans] before that. But they apparently didn't cause anyone harm when they used their abilities by following their admonishments like he said. They apparently used it in a good way.

And they would become doctors like he just said. They had no limitations, and although one's ailment was inside the body, they would remove it. They used to be extremely capable.

He said he wasn't always a shaman. He said he was taught[5]

Jacob Black, Qemirraq, August 2017

JACOB BLACK: This is what they confessed to me. Agagliiyaq and Apangtak wanted to pass on those [shaman powers] to me, two of them did.

I told them no, that I don't know about those things. Then the father of Imuq'aq and siblings said that I should look at him. I looked at him. Then he asked me, "Now do you see me?" Then I said yes to him. Then he asked me again. He said doesn't he, to me, appear like he was always a sha-

---

tuqlurraarlua, qaku tauna elliin pini wangnun taicugyaaqluk'. Tua-ll' iquklicaku tamana, uum wani cali qanrullua tuqlurraarlua.

Qanrullua-llu man'a-gguq-qaa pia [tunkaku] wangnun ciuniurciqaqa. Tua-i tuani umyuaqa egmianun pillruuq niitelaamki aug'utun ava-i apellritun, piagka, wiinga tamakunek nalluk'acagarnilua, qaillun-llu pillrit nalluniluki, tuaten-llu piurtellrat nalluniluki.

Tua-i-ll' qanerluni una Apangtak ellii-gguq cakegtaullrunricaaquq-gguq taugaam-gguq tua-i waten apcesciullruuk yugmek naivcicuglukek. Kiuluku tua-i wiinga qaillun tamana nalluniluku.

Tua-i-ll' pilua, taum-llu call' apa'urlurluma qanrullua, uumi cangallruvkenaku, nalqiugtellruagnga elitnaurluki-gguq piyarauguq, elitnaurluku. Aarcirturluki cali atucurlallerkait. Eliskan-llu tua-i tamalkuan tunluku tuavet piyugtiinun. Tua-i tamakuurtaqluteng.

Taugaam wii taukuk *offer*-aangraagnga tamakucimek kelucausngallruagka tamarkenka. [*ngel'artuq*] Tua-i nalluamku.

APENG'AQ: Tamakuurcesqumayaaqelliniluten.

NASGAUQ: Yaa. Tua-i niitelaranka taukuk ciungani. Taugaam tua-i pinerrlugtaarlutek atullrunritliniak inerquutatek maliggluku qanellratun uum. Assillerkaakun atullrulliniak.

Aug'utun-llu ava-i *doctor*-aarurtaqlutek. Caprunatek tua-i, qamani-ll' apqucia uitangraan aug'araqluku. Tua-i caperrnaqpiatullruuk.

Tuaten angalkuugurallrunritniluni. Elitnaurumallruuq-gguq

Nasgauq, Qemirraq, August 2017

NASGAUQ: Waten apervikuallruagnga. Ukuk wani Agagliiyaankuk Apangtak-llu tamakunek tua-i naivcicugyaaqellruagnga, malruulutek.

Pillruagka, *no*, nallunilua tamakunek. Tua-i-ll' tauna Imuq'ankut aatiit tangerqerlaku-gguq atam. Tua-i-ll' tangerrluku. Tua-ll' aptaanga, "Tua-i-qaa tangrrarpenga?" Tua-i-ll' yaa-rluku. Tua-i-ll' aplua cali. Tuar-gguq-qaa wangni ellii angalkuugurallrulria? Tua-i-am wii nalluamku,

man? Since I didn't know, I said, "Yes." I said that's what I thought.

Then he said to me, "No." He said he wasn't always a shaman. He said he was taught. He apparently accepted it when that person wanted to grant him [shaman powers]. He learned how. And he became one of those.

They pretended to travel to the moon, lying[6]

Yako Andrew and Alexie Nicholai, Napaskiak, March 2017

YAKO ANDREW: Did shamans only work on a person?

ALEXIE NICHOLAI: I'm not sure how they worked. They probably even fixed the weather. [*chuckles*] They were even weather changers. And they also tried to make things more readily available, and they wanted people to obtain foods, too. . . .

YAKO ANDREW: I thought I also used to hear that those shamans used to travel to the moon. Did they indeed arrive at the moon? [*laughter*]

ALEXIE NICHOLAI: I don't think they arrived there. It's far. [*laughter*]

YAKO ANDREW: That's what I used to hear.

ALEXIE NICHOLAI: I used to hear that, too.

YAKO ANDREW: During one of the times they were telling stories, this is a story I heard. There were some shamans inside a home. Then one of them went out, saying that he was going to travel to the moon now.

Then the other also went out, he ran out saying that he was going to travel to the moon, too. Then when he got to the arctic entryway, he attempted to hide along the side and saw a person here. Then the one who had gone out second said to him, "Are you here too?" [*laughter*]

They pretended to travel to the moon, lying. That's a story I used to hear, an old [story].

They said since [the mosquitoes] were biting too much, they removed their stingers[7]

Jacob Black and Alexie Nicholai, Napaskiak, March 2017

JACOB BLACK: If that story they tell is true, they say one of the shamans, you two probably heard

"Yaa." Tuaten tua-i wii umyuarteqnilua.

Tua-i-ll' pianga, *"No."* Tuaten angalkuugurallrunritniluni. Elitnaurumallruuq-gguq. Taum *grant*-aryullraku ciuniullrullinia. Elitnaurutekluku-ll'. Tamakuurrluni-ll'.

Iralurrnguaryaaqellinilutek, tua-i iqlulutek

Qaluk'aq Apeng'aq-llu, Napaskiaq, March 2017

QALUK'AQ: Angalkut-qaa tamakut yugmek kiingan calitullruut?

APENG'AQ: Qaillun-wa calilartat. Ella-llu-w' tua-i kitugtaalleralallrullikiit. [*ngelaq'ertuq*] Ellaliurtenguluteng tuaten. Cat-llu makut paivkanircetengnaqaqluki neqet tuaten yugnun unakesqumaluki. . . .

QALUK'AQ: Niitelallruunga-llu-ggem tamakut angalkut iralurcetullruniluki. Ilumun-qaa iralumun tekitetullruut? [*ngel'artut*]

APENG'AQ: Tavaqaa tekitelartut. Yaaqsigtuq. [*ngel'artut*]

QALUK'AQ: Niitelallrulrianga-w' tua-i tuaten.

APENG'AQ: Wiinga-llu-w' tua-i tuaten niitellrulrianga.

QALUK'AQ: Caqerlua-am qalamcit iliitni, waten qalamcimek niitellruunga. Enem tua-i iluani tuani tamakut angalkut uitaluteng. Tua-llu-gguq iliit anluni enem'ek qanerluni waniwa-gguq ellii iralumun ayakatartuq.

Tua-i-llu-gguq aipaa call' tauna anluni, anqerrluni cali iralurteqatarniluni. Tua-llu-gguq elaturramun tekicami menglemun maavet iirluni piuq yug' una. Tua-i-llu-gguq taum kingumek anellrem qanrutaa, "Elpet-llu-qaa wanelmiuten?" [*ngel'artut*]

Iralurrnguaryaaqellinilutek, tua-i iqlulutek. Tuaten qalamcimek niitellruunga, ak'allamek.

Keggmassiyaangvakaata-gguq-am tua-i tamakut sugg'illruit

Nasgauq Apeng'aq-llu, Napaskiaq, March 2017

NASGAUQ: Augna cali piciullrukuni qanemciktukiit taumek, iliita-gguq-am taum

it before, about when there were too many mosquitoes, probably when they didn't have insect repellent. They said since the mosquitoes were biting too much, they removed their stingers, they made it so that they wouldn't bite anymore.

Then they said when they removed their stingers, those fish that had been around down there disappeared. After a while of having no fish, when one of the people realized what happened, he told that one to open up the stingers of mosquitoes again. When he opened them up, not long after, there were fish once again. Is that story true?

ALEXIE NICHOLAI: Yes, I heard it like that too. [chuckles]

angalkuum, niitelalliktek-wa, iciw' egturyat amllessiyaallratnek, minguitelallratni-w' pilallikait. Keggmassiyaangvakaata-gguq-am tua-i tamakut sugg'illruit, keggesciigalivkarluki.

Tua-i-llu-gguq sugg'illrateng imkut neqet piyaaqellret unani tamarluteng. Neqngengairucan-gguq iliita elpekngamegteggu tauna pillinia ataam angparcesqelluki sugg'erit egturyat. Aren angparcateng-gguq ak'anivkenani neqngartuq. Tamana-qaa piciuguq?

APENG'AQ: Yaa, wiinga-ll' tuaten niitellruaqa. [ngelaq'ertuq]

The shaman who fled from the village of Qinaq[8]

John Phillip, Bob Aloysius, and Alice Rearden, Anchorage, October 2010

BOB ALOYSIUS: That story that you told when we first arrived here before that [tape recorder] was on, about that grandmother, the grandchild, and that one who fled somewhere.

JOHN PHILLIP: Is she asking about that one who fled from the village of Qinaq?

ALICE REARDEN: She wants you to tell that story as the last story if you can.

JOHN PHILLIP: That one evidently lived there and was not originally from that village, but he moved there after marrying. He was a shaman.

[He moved to] Qinaq when Qinaq was a village.

They say the people of Qinaq had a tendency to physically abuse people. Since people had various dispositions in their stories, some also tended to be malicious.

They say when that person moved to that village after marrying and became a son-in-law, and he was a shaman there also, when one of the people there had a son, since he loved [that child], [that child] evidently became his *yungcaraq* [one doctored by a shaman]. Some [shamans] had *yungcarat*, probably wanting their *yungcarat* to live long lives. They say his *yungcaraq* in that village was a boy at the time.

And the one who was doctoring [that child] took good care of him. They evidently doctored people so that they would be in good health and live long. That's evidently what those shamans had in mind

Qinarmiunek qimalleq angalkuq

Ayagina'ar, Sliksuuyar, Cucuaq-llu, Anchorage, October 2010

SLIKSUUYAR: Imna maavet tekiteqarraallemteni, tauna ayagpailgan qanaatekellren maurluq, tutgara'urluq augna-llu natmun qimallra.

AYAGINA'AR: Qinarmiunek-qaa qimalleq augna pia?

CUCUAQ: Tauna-gguq qanemcikesqaa nangneruluku piyugngakuvgu.

AYAGINA'AR: Tauna-w' tua-i tuantellrullinilria taukumiunguvkenani taugaam nengaugilluni. Angalkuuluni.

Qinarmiunun Qinarmiut taukut nunaulallratni.

Taukut-gguq tua-i Qinarmiut tua-i-w' nangcitallruut. Ayuqenrilameng yuut augkut qanemcimeggni tua-i avani ilait, ayuqenrilameng, umyuarrliqaqluteng-llu.

Taukut-gguq tua-i tuani tauna tuavet nengaugitlermini, angalkuuluni-llu tuani, kenekngamiu taun', yung'ellrani iliit tan'gaurlurmek, kenekngamiu tauna yungcaraqellinia. Yungcaritullruut ilait, yuusqumaluki-w' tua-i ak'anun pillikait tamakut yungcarateng. Tauna-gguq tua-i tamaani tauna tan'gaurlullrauguq tua-i yungcaraa.

Tua-i-llu taum wani yungcaraqestiin tua-i qaunqelluku cakneq. Tua-i-w' canritlerkait pitekluki tamakut yungcaritullrulliniut waten akaarnun yuuqallerkait pitekluki. Tamakunek

when they did that, and so that they would live good lives also. That [shaman] evidently doctored that [child].

At some point, sickness afflicted the people of Qinaq, sickness came upon that village. Like the people of the Nushagak River area call it, it was probably *qenanaq*, an illness.

Those people evidently started to become sick and it never passed. As you know sometimes these days, sickness arrives and afflicts our village; that's what it was like.

Then when those people started to suffer from sickness, all of his fellow villagers suspected that one of having afflicted them with that sickness since he was a shaman.

The people there started to become displeased with him, they started to think he caused that sickness although he wasn't responsible, although he wasn't thinking that way.

All the people there began to suspect him. After a while, since they wouldn't stop accusing him, they took him and beat him inside the *qasgiq*, suspecting that he had given them that sickness although he hadn't given it to them. And although he explained [that he hadn't], they didn't believe him.

When they started to beat him, they brought him to the *qasgiq* and held him and tied him up so that he couldn't move and had him eat feces, and even people's feces.

They would have him eat their feces inside the *qasgiq* although he refused.

That poor thing, doing what they asked, when they'd give him [feces] he would [eat it].

One day, when they let go of him, when he felt disgust, he was thinking of leaving them and not staying there with them.

Those people there evidently took him. When they took him, they cut the skin along the soles of his feet down there so that they would flap open, cutting it and letting it flap open like this and leaving part of his skin there.

When night came, since he was in pain, after staying there, he went outside. When he went outside, that *qasgiq* . . . They had a *qasgiq*, and I saw that *qasgiq* myself. The other *qasgiq* was located downriver from that small river they used to call Avcaumcak, and the other [*qasgiq*] was located upriver from it.

He went up that river walking on foot. He left the people who tortured him.

umyuangqerrluteng tamakut angalkut pilallrulliniut, elluarrluteng-llu yuullerkait. Tua-i tauna yungcarilliniluni taumek.

Tua-i piinanratni taukut nunat Qinarmiut naulluutem tut'elliniluki, naulluun-wa tua-i tull'uni tuavet. Man'a Iilgayarmiucetun qenanaq pillill', qenanaq, naulluun.

Naulluungelliniut taukut pelluksaunateng. Tua-i iliini maa-i naulluun tekitelalria nunamtenun; tuaten ayuqluni, tuaten tua-i.

Tua-i-ll' taum, taukut tua-i naulluungellratni, taukut tamalkuita imna nunalgutain, tauna angalkuungan taumun umyuarteqluteng tauna kamakluku, taumun piyukluki.

Tauna tua-i umyugaat imkunglliniluku atawakenrilliniluku tua-i, taumun ellilartengluku taman' naulluun elliinun piyukluku, pinrilengraan tua-i tamatumek umyuarteqenrilengraan.

Atam tua-i taukut tamalkuita pingllinikiit. Tua-i piqerluteng taqngairucamegteggu teguluku tua-i nangtelliniluku qasgimi tua-i piluku, naulluutmek piluku elliinun piyukluku kamakluku pinrilengraaki. Nalqigtengraan-llu tua-i imkuvkenateng, ukvekevkenaku.

Atam-am tua-i taum wani tua-i nangtengatni, waten qasgimun agulluku tegumiaqluku qillerrluku waten pekviirluku tua-i anarturcet'lallinikiit, yuut-llu anaitnek.

Ananek tua-i anaitnek anarturcetaqluku qessangraan tuani qasgimi.

Tua-i-urluq tauna, tua-i-am pisquciat maliggluku tua-i ellaita cikiraqatni tuatnaaqluni.

Tua-i caqerluku pegcatni tua-i-w' umyugaa-w' tua-i piami, cangakuungami, unitnaluki piluki taukut ayagnaluni nayurpek'naki.

Taukut-am, pillrani tegulliniluku tua-i. Teguamegteggu alui maktelliniluki kankut it'gai, pilagluki makluki waten, amia-ll' uitavkarluku illii.

Tua-i unuan nangteqngami-ll' tamaani uitarraarluni anlliniluni. Anngami tua-i taukut qasgim, tamaaggun . . . Qasgitangqellruut tangerqallruaqa qasgi tauna wii. Avcaumciim kuiggaam aug'um Avcaumcimek pilallrata ualirnerani qasgim aipaa uitauq, aipaa-ll' kiatiini.

Tua-i tamaaggun asgurluni kuigkun ayalliniluni piyualuni. Taukut unilluki nangtesteni.

When he was about to leave, when he went out of that place, he kicked the one he loved a little and left. He put what he had experienced there not on the people of that village but to his *yungcaraq* there.

After he left, the next day, when they sensed that he was gone, they followed the tracks of that one, they followed his tracks as he was walking along that river.

They hurried since they knew that he wouldn't be walking fast since the skin along the soles of his feet had been cut open.

When he got pretty far, his tracks along the snow inside Avcaumcak River, as he was walking along, one side of his footprints became wolf tracks.

When one side started to appear like that, the people following him became reluctant to follow him.

That person continued on. Those people [following him] turned back.

The poor person continued walking along the snow and would warm up once in a while.

When he got far out there, as he was walking along, they say it was during a time when there were patches of ground where the snow had melted. They say he'd stop along the patches of ground where the snow had melted and warm up his feet, and he'd wrap them with visible grass.

While he was walking along, a home appeared ahead. He was grateful and started to walk toward it as fast as he could go.

Those two in the wilderness, they say there were two people, a grandchild along with that one's grandmother living there. But I'm not sure what gender that one's grandchild was, a girl or boy.

They say when her grandchild would go outside, one of the times when [the grandchild] went out, he/she said there was a person approaching, that a person was approaching. [The grandchild] didn't say anything else about him, but that he was slow.

[The grandchild] would go outside and see that the one who was approaching hadn't really moved any closer. Evidently it was because he would periodically stop and thaw and warm up his feet.

Eventually, it was almost night. When it was almost dark, [the grandchild] told her that the person approaching was slow.

His/her grandmother said to him/her, "Maybe it's not a person. Why is he so slow? Take my sharpening stone down there and go outside and starting from the front of our doorway out there, hold

Ayaktaami tua-i tuaken anngami umyugaa, tauna tua-i imna kenkekngani tuklerrluku ayalliniluni. Tuavet tamana elliin pillni elliluku, taukunun nunanun pivkenaku taumun taugaam yungcaraminun.

Atam tua-i ayallran kinguani unuaquan elpekngamegteggu tum'arcaaqelliniat tauna, tum'arcaaqelliniat kuigkun tamaaggun ayallrani.

Tua-i cukangnaqluteng cukangailan maa-i nallunrilamegteki makingiita ukut it'gani.

Yaaqsigiqerluni atam tumai makut qanikcarmi, kuiggaam iluani taum Avcaumcim, ayainanratni tumai makut kegluninranek inglunga'artellinilriit.

Inglunga'arcata tua-i tuaten tamakut maligcetain capeqsaguartelliniluku.

Ayalliniluni tua-i tauna. Uterrluteng tua-i taukut.

Ayagaurlulliniluni tua-i tamaani qanikcarkun urugciriqaqluni.

Avani tua-i yaaqsigiluni piinanermini, watengguq urunqingluku, urunqit alaingeqtaangluki tuaten piluki pillruuq. Urunqinun arulairluni urugciraqluk' it'gani, canegnek-llu alailngurnek nemerluki piaqluki.

Tua-i piinanrani ciunermini enet'anglliniluni tauna ciunra. Quyaluni tua-i ullagturalliniluki cukatacirramitun.

Taukuk tua-i tamaani yuilqumi, taukuk-gguq maurlurluminek aiparluni uitallruuq. Tauna taugaam caucia taum tutgariin caciitela'arqa, nasaurluuli wall' tan'gaurluuli.

Tauna-gguq an'aqami tutgara'urlua, caqerluni anngami qanertuq, man'a-gguq yug' agiirtuq, yugtangqertuq agiirtellriamek. Tua-i qaill' pivkenaku piluku, taugaam-gguq cukaituq.

Anenaurtuq-gguq cakanissiyaaksaunani tua-i taiguralria. Tua-i cunaw' tua-i arulaiqaqluni urugciriqaqluni pilliniami taukugnek it'gaminek.

Kiituan'-gguq unukatangartuq. Unukangarcan pillinia man'a tua-i cukaitniluku taiguralria yuk.

Maurluan taum pillinia, "Yuunritliuq. Ciin cukaipakarta? Kitek' arviiqa kan'a teguluku anluten keggaken enem'egnuk amiigan

it and touch the outside and go around. And when you've gone all the way around with it, place it there." She was referring to her sharpening stone, her *arviiq*.

After doing that, when he/she went outside again, he/she reported on him once again.

[The grandmother] said to him/her, after searching around digging around beyond her, she gave her grandchild beaver castor and said to him/her, "Okay, take those outside and circle our home again like you did before, and place it there once again."

Following her request once again, he/she circled the home, and then placed [the beaver castor] by the rock.

The third time, just before it was night and it was about to get dark, she said to him, "Go and get wild celery from out there." When he/she brought it inside, she said to him/her, "Now take that wild celery like I told you before, go around in a circle with it." This was her third request. "Place it on top of it."

He/she placed those there. Then her grandchild stopped going outside when it got dark.

That one slowly approached them and arrived. He arrived upon that home. He was grateful and was just resting a while before entering, watching that [home]. And he evidently used to see that [grandchild] when he/she would go outside when [the home] got close.

After the last time he/she had gone outside, he arrived outside that home.

He rested outside the home for a short while, thawing his feet before he entered.

While he was there, that home turned into a boulder, it turned into a rock. It turned into a boulder.

He was wondering what was happening to that place. As he was looking at it, it evidently turned into a beaver's home. He just stayed there although it did that. After a while, the home turned into wild celery. He had no way to [enter]. It turned into wild celery.

It would constantly transform like that, turning into a rock, turning into a beaver's home, and turning into wild celery. It would transform into those things that [the grandchild] had [put there].

That one started trying to find a path since he was a shaman. They say when it would transform into a rock like that, he had no way to enter. And he also had no way to enter when it turned into wild celery. But they say when it would transform into

ciuqerranek teguluku waten agturturluku uivusgu. Kassukuvgu-llu tuavet elliqerniaran." Ipegcautni imna arviiq teggalquq.

Tua-i pirraarluni, cali ataam anngami tangrramiu cali qanrutekluku.

Pillinia, pirraarluni tua-i yuarraarluni yaateliuqerluni tut'gara'urluni-am taun' cikillinia imkunek palqutaam aluqatkaagkegnek, cikillinia, "Kitek' taukuk anullukek aug'utun cali uivurluten enev'uk tauna, tuavet cali elliniaran."

Tua-i-am tuaten maligtaqluku uivuralliniuq enem'un tuavet, teggalqum canianun elliqerluku.

Pingayiriluni piami, pillinia tua-i unukatarluku tua-i waniwa tan'geriqatarluku, "Kitek' ikiitugmek qagaaken aqvaten." Itrucani tua-i pillinia, "Kitek' un' ikiituk teguluku aug'utun call' uivulluku." Pingayiriluni. "Qauraanun elliqerniaran."

Taukunek tua-i ellivikliniuq. Tua-i-ll' anen'ermek taqluni tauna tutgarii tan'gerian.

Tauna tua-i taiguralliniluni, tekitelliniluk'. Tekitellinia waniw' ena una. Quyaluni tua-i itqatarluni uitauraqerluni taum tangvagluku. Tauna-ll' tua-i tanglallrulliniluk' an'aqan taum, yaa-i canimellian.

Anngan tua-i anrraarcelluku una tua-i nangnermek tekitelliniluni tuavet elatiinun.

Uitaqalliniuq tua-i elatiini urugcirlukek-am it'gagni iterpailegmi.

Atam uitainanrani, tauna-am uitaqanrakun tauna imna qiururtellinilria ena tauna, teggalqurrurrluni. Qiururrluni tua-i.

Tua-i pirraarluni qaill' umyuarteqluni qaill' picianek tauna. Allamek piqerluni tangvainanrani paluqtaam neksagutelliniluku. Tua-i tuaten uitalliniluni tuaten pingraan. Piuraqerluni-am ena tauna ikiituurtelliniluni tua-i. Qaillun piviinani. Ikiituurrluni-am.

Cunawa-gguq tua-i tuaten elliurturnaluni, teggalqurrurtaqluni, paluqtaam eneksagutaqluku, ikiituurtaqluni. Taukut tua-i aturluki pillri.

Atam-am tua-i tauna tumkarcullinilria angalkuungami. Tuaten-gguq tua-i teggalquurtaqan pivigkaituq. Cali-llu ikiituurtaqan pivigkaunani. Taugaam-gguq nutaan palqutam neksagutaqaku tua-i

Stories from the Yukon River

When I was watching him, he instructed those about the masks that he would use[1]

Mary Mike and Marie Meade, St. Mary's, October 1994

MARIE MEADE: Yes. But he would instruct those who were able to carve and would have them construct masks?

MARY MIKE: When I was watching him one time there, he instructed those about the masks that he would use. I think he got someone to construct them for him.

MARIE MEADE: He described the [masks] that he would reveal?

MARY MIKE: I didn't know what some of his masks were supposed to represent.

MARIE MEADE: That one? Did that person have many masks?

MARY MIKE: He had many masks. I wonder how many there were. Two people situated across from one another would use them. They probably [danced] to the verses. He probably had someone do the dance motions.

MARIE MEADE: Those two had masks?

MARY MIKE: Yes, those ones had masks. Gee, and he would have those men who were the singers make the noises they usually make. I think he instructed them.

And those two wolves entered howling very loudly. They seemed to be [howling] first from up on top of the *qasgiq*. They would howl loudly like dogs. When it was probably time, after howling loudly, they got quiet, and eventually they reached the porch out there.

They entered making periodic noises. Gee, after entering, for some reason these two made noise down there, and then they fought. I didn't watch them, and they started to get bloody. Since I was afraid, I didn't watch.

They say some actually really do things. I think that pretend wolf does that.

And at Nunaqerraq also, or rather at Nunallerpak, when he made a mask for the last time, he evidently revealed those two. I think his masks are there at Nunallerpak up behind Qip'ngayag-miut, up behind them, that slough that has a bend.

https://doi.org/10.5876/9781646427314.c016

Kuigpagmiut Qanemciit

Tuani-wa tua-i tangvallemni, elliin taugaam alerqualuki
piminek, atu'urkaminek-wa elliin kegginaquminek

Arrsauyaq Arnaq-llu, Negeqliq, October 1994

ARNAQ: Ii-i. Taugaam cat canayugngalriit alerqualuki kegginaqulivkaraqluki?

ARRSAUYAQ: Tuani-wa tua-i ataucirqumek tangvallemni, elliin taugaam alerqualuki piminek,
atu'urkaminek-wa elliin kegginaquminek. Caliscirluni piyugnarquq.

ARNAQ: Alairarkani tamakut aperturturluki?

ARRSAUYAQ: Ilait-llu-am canguaruciilkenka kegginaqurri.

ARNAQ: Taum? Tauna-q' amllernek kegginaqungqetullruuq?

ARRSAUYAQ: Kegginaqurri tua-i amllerrluteng. Qayutuugas-kiq tayima. Akiqliqlutek taugken
aturnaugket. Tua-i-w' apallut pilaryugnarqekek. Arulastengqelaryugnarqellria waten tua-i,
arulalcirturluni.

ARNAQ: Kegginaqurlutek taukuk?

ARRSAUYAQ: Ee-m, kegginaqurluteng taukut. Aling qalriuciitnek-llu, qalriaciitnek-llu-w' tua-i
qalriavkaqlukek taukuk angutek aturtegket. Elliin alerqualukek pilaryugnarqait.

Taukuk-llu keglunraak marurpagaq'apiarlutek iteryartullrulriik. Pakmaken ciumek
qasgim qainganek pinganatek. Tua-i qimugtetun marurpagaqlutek tua-i. Pinarilliaqakek
maruarraarlutek umeqsigilutek, kiituan cakmavet pimun elaturramun ellirtuk.

Nepliqa'aqlutek iterlutek. Aling tua-llu-w' itramek qaill' pilutek ukuk kana-i neplirlutek
pilutek uirrutellriik. Wii-am tangvanritagka, augurtenglutek-llu. Wii alingama wii
tangvanritua.

Ilait-gguq atam pipiggluteng pilartut. Tauna pituyugnarquq keglunruaq.

Cali Nunaqerrami, aren Nunallerpagmi nangnermek agayulillrani taukuk cali
alairtellinikek. Tuani cali kegginaqurri tua-i uitangatut Nunallerpagmi Qip'ngayagmiut
keluatni, pia-i keluatni, aug' kuicualler qipnengqerrluni.

https://doi.org/10.5876/9781646427314.c016

MARIE MEADE: Leggleq's [masks]?

MARY MIKE: Yes. He composed a dance for the last time there. Evidently the poor thing didn't compose a dance after that. That one composed a dance when he became elderly and after he started using a cane at Nunallerpak. A small village with few residents; when those ones evidently asked him to, his family and the relatives of his family, they told him to compose a dance before he died.

MARIE MEADE: Using masks, he constructed masks?

MARY MIKE: They evidently constructed masks and danced. And my late husband and I stayed there for a while, and both of us were set to dance. Then the niece or nephew of my late husband suddenly died.

ARNAQ: Taum Legglerem [kegginaqui]?

ARRSAUYAQ: Ee-m. Nangnermek tuani arulalillruuq. Tua-i cunaw' tuakenirnek arulaliksaiteurlur'. Angutngurtengmikun tauna ayarungnermikun-llu arulalillruuq Nunallerpagmi. Yugkunateng ukut nunat, nunarraat; taukut-am pisqelliniatni ilain tungelqurmi-ll' natain tua-i tuquvailgan arulalisqelluku.

ARNAQ: Kegginaqirluki, kegginaquliluni?

ARRSAUYAQ: Kegginaquliluteng tua-i arulalliniluteng. Wangkuk-llu aipairutka-ll' tuanteqeryaaqlunuk, ?arulaarkaarcaurrlunuk-llu-am tamamnuk. Tua-llu-am uum aipairutma usrua tuquq'erluni.

Two shamans who ran into one another at the moon[2]

Mary Mike and Marie Meade, St. Mary's, October 1994

MARY MIKE: These Yup'ik people, and those shamans of the past, they'd say they knew the stars, and a powerful shaman would travel to the moon up there, the moon.

But those two shamans who ran into one another at the moon, they say they ran into each other up at the moon. That Teggalquq who had lived next to the *qasgiq* along with another from the Yukon River area who was his fellow powerful shaman.

MARIE MEADE: Did you say they ran into each other on the moon?

MARY MIKE: Yes, they say when they went to the moon, they ran into each other, was it in the winter? My late maternal uncle, that elderly man told about those two. When they lost their wives and they no longer had a female to take care of them, along with Eugene [Pete] down there, the one he raised, they used to stay with me. That one would tell stories. When we'd tell him to tell stories, since the one he raised would tell him to tell stories, the poor thing would tell stories.

He said those two shamans, one from Paimiut, this one here, Teggalquq was from Paimiut, and this one was from the Yukon River area. I forgot what he called him. I recalled [his name] earlier, but I have forgotten it already.

I think the village he mentioned was located downriver from Marshall.

This powerful shaman and this other powerful shaman, I'm not sure for what reason they went

---

Angalkuk nall'arutellrek iralumi

Arrsauyaq Arnaq-llu, Negeqliq, October 1994

ARRSAUYAQ: Yupiit makut, angalkuulriit-llu-w' tamakut cat pagkut agyat-llu natait nallunritnilaqait, angalkurpagmun iraluq-llu pakemna paqtaqluku paqtestain, iraluq.

Amtall'-am taukuk angalkuk nall'arutellrek iralumi, amtall' nall'arutellruniaqlukek pagaani iralumi. Tauna Teggalquq qasgim elatiini uitalleq allamek Kuigpagmiumek aipangqerrluni angalkurpaullgutminek.

ARNAQ: Iralumi-gguq-qaa nall'arutellruuk?

ARRSAUYAQ: Ee-m, iralurtellermeggni-gguq nall'arullutek, cami uksumi-qaa piuk? Angairutma-w' taum angukaralleraam qanemcikellrukek taukuk. Wangni aipairamek, aulukestairucamek arnamek, camna-ll' Eugene-aq-llu anglicarani-llu uitauralallrulriik. Qanemcinaurtuq tauna. Qanemcicetaarqamegni-llu-w' taum-ll'-am anglicarallran pilaani qanemcisqelluku qanemciuraurlurnaurtuq.

Taukuk-gguq-am angalkuk, Paimiu, una Paimiunguluni Teggalquq una-ll' Kuigpagmiunguluni. Camek-llu imat'am aterpagtellrukii. Ak'a-am neq'aqeryaaqellruaqa watua ak'a-am tamartuq.

Pimiut, Masercullermiut uatiitni uitalarngatuq taun' aperlaqii nuna.

Tauna angalkurpak una-ll' cali angalkurpak, cassurlutek-tam ukuk iraluq, nalluklutek tayim'

there, but the two went to the moon not knowing about one another, they evidently went to the moon. They arrived at that moon not knowing about one another. It is said those ones going to the moon fly there. They tie them inside a bearded seal skin, tying them up.

MARIE MEADE: Inside a bearded seal skin?

MARY MIKE: Yes, you know how they cut bearded seals down the belly; you know how those skins are cut down the belly. It is said they bind them up inside those and tie them up, and they place them down inside the fire pit down there, underneath the *qasgiq*.

MARIE MEADE: My!

MARY MIKE: And they put floor boards over it. They sing and they drum in that *qasgiq*, trying to get the person to go. They evidently do that to him, sing for him, probably some *yuarulluut* [shaman songs]. He leaves to a place he wants to go.

MARIE MEADE: So he and that one ran into one another?

MARY MIKE: Yes, they ran into each other at, up at the moon. When they ran into each other there, I'm not sure why, I wonder starting with what, they suddenly got mad at one another. Those two evidently got mad at one another for some reason there, Teggalquq and what was his name again.

It's because they left using their shaman powers. They weren't regular people but left having some sort of ability; they probably go in the form of their *tuunrat* also.

Since he was weaker than him, Teggalquq told him . . .

His enemy, when they fought, since he was too weak for him, he evidently told him to his face that he wouldn't have let him return home alive, but that he wanted him to tell the story about him, that he's going to have him return home near death.

MARIE MEADE: Teggalquq [told him that]?

MARY MIKE: That's what Teggalquq told him.

MARIE MEADE: Teggalquq was stronger?

MARY MIKE: Yes. He said he would have killed him then and there, but [he didn't] because he wanted him to tell about him when he returned home. He told him that he was not going to kill him, but that he was going to let him return home near death.

MARIE MEADE: Yes.

MARY MIKE: Then they left one another, they went their separate ways and retuned home. That one probably returned home, and he also returned home and arrived at his hometown.

iralurtelliuk, iraluq paqtelliak. Tua-i nalluklutek tuavet iralumun tekitellinilutek. Tengluteng-gguq pituut tamakut iralurtellriit. Maklagmun qillrulluteng, iluanun qamavet, qillerqulluteng.

ARNAQ: Maklagmun?

ARRSAUYAQ: Ee-m, iciw' makliit ullirtellaqait; amit imkut ullingqalriit. Tamakunun-gguq nemrulluki qillerqellarait, camavet-llu kenillermun kalvaggluki qasgim acianun.

ARNAQ: Ila-i!

ARRSAUYAQ: Nacicirluku-ll' qaingat. Aturluteng cauyarluteng tamaani qasgimi tamaa-i ayagcetaarluku. Tuaten-am pilalliat, atuulluku yuarullugnek-wa pillikiit. Ayagluni tua-i piyullerminun tayim'.

ARNAQ: Tua-llu-q' tauna-ll' nall'arutellinilutek?

ARRSAUYAQ: Ii-i, nall'arutellinilutek tua-i-wa pimi, pikani iralumi. Nall'arucamek tua-i tuani qaill' piak, ca-kiq tayim' ayanqelluku qenqerrutak. Tua-i camek-wa imumek tuani pilutek qenqerrutellinilriik taukuk, Teggalqunkuk, kituuyaaqell' imat'am.

Tuunraryaramegnegun-wa tua-i ayallruamek. Waten yuk'apiarauvkenatek cangqerrlutek ayallruuk; tuunrameggnek caluteng amilirluteng-llu pilallilriit.

Taum-gguq Teggalqur taun' cirlakngamiu tauna pia, qanruskii waten . . .

Tauna tua-i ingluni, tua-i yagutellermeggni cirlakngamiu qanrutliniluku wavet, anerteqluku utercecanritniluku taugaam qanemcikesqelluni ellii, waniw' anerteqevleggluku utercetqatarniluku.

ARNAQ: Teggalqum?

ARRSAUYAQ: Teggalqum qanrulluku tauna.

ARNAQ: Teggalquq pininruluni?

ARRSAUYAQ: Ee-m. Tua-i tuqucarniluku wani taugaam qanemcikesqelluni ut'reskan kingunranun. Tuqutevkenaku anerteqevleggluku utercetqatarniluku.

ARNAQ: Ee-m.

ARRSAUYAQ: Tua-i-ll' uniyullutek avvullutek uterrlutek. Tua-i-w' taun' uteqtararallrilria, ellii-ll' uterrluni, tekilluni tua-i tuavet nunaminun.

They say his body had broken bones since his enemy beat him. When he returned home he told the people that he ran into a shaman up on the moon. He said he wasn't a person but evidently a rock, that he had broken the bones on his body.

MARIE MEADE: So Teggalquq [lit., "Rock"] was like this name?

MARY MIKE: It was evidently Teggalquq. Teggalquq was his name. He was a *yungcaraq* [one doctored to live by a shaman while he was in the womb] as a rock. He crushed him repeatedly and found him weak. I forgot why they said Teggalquq went to the moon. And the other who he ran into had gone there for another reason.

> They didn't do what they had set out to do.

MARIE MEADE: They fought?

MARY MIKE: Yes, instead they fought there on that moon. And after fighting, they returned home. They evidently returned home not doing what they had gone there to do.

MARIE MEADE: Yes. I wonder what they had gone there to do?

MARY MIKE: He said Teggalquq had gone there for something and also his counterpart from the Yukon River area. He evidently had gone up there for some purpose. They both had gone on the same day, and they ran into one another.

MARIE MEADE: I wonder what they were like after they returned home?

MARY MIKE: His counterpart from the Yukon River area probably improved. But Teggalquq returned home without any injuries. But since he broke the bones of the other, he returned home in bad condition. He said to him that he was only going to send him home alive because he wanted him to tell about what he had done. But here although that one was a powerful shaman, he died when it was his time to die.

Tauna pikegtacurqevkenani-gguq tua-i qainga man'a navgumaluni aug'um inglullran nangtelliniani. Tua-i-gguq qanemciluni tekicami nall'arkengniluni angalkumek pakmani iralumi. Yuuvkenani-gguq teggalqurrullinilria, man'a-gguq qainga maa-i navgutuqluku.

ARNAQ: Atni aturluku Teggalqum?

ARRSAUYAQ: Cunawa-gguq tua-i Teggalquq. Teggalqumek wani atengqerrluni. Yungcaraullruuq teggalqurruluni. Nanqaquluku tayim' tauna cirlaklinikii. Cassurniyaaqekegket-am tuavet iralumun tauna-w' Teggalquq. Tauna call' aipaa cassuryaaqniluku nall'arkengaa.

> Tamakut piltek aturpek'naki.

ARNAQ: Callullinilutek?

ARRSAUYAQ: Ee-m, callullinilutek taugaam tua-i tuani iralumi. Calluggaarlutek-llu tua-i uterrlutek. Utertellinilutek tuani tua-i cassurlutek tuavirtellertek aturpek'naku.

ARNAQ: Ee-m. Cassuryaaqak-kiq?

ARRSAUYAQ: Cassurniyaaqluku-wam tauna Teggalquq tauna-ll' cali Kuigpagmiuqlia. Tuani camek avalissagluni mayuryaaqellinilria. Aling erneq-llu-am tauna nall'arrlukek tamarmek tuani nall'arutellinilriik.

ARNAQ: Kinguani-kiq tua-i utertellmek qaillun ayuqellruak?

ARRSAUYAQ: Tauna-w' tua-i utumariqtallilria angun Kuigpagmiuqlia. Tauna taugaam cavkenani natlugtevkenani uterrluni Teggalquq taun'. Tauna taugaam tua-i akngiqngani natii navcataqluku piani, navcacani pikegtaluaqerpek'nani uterrluni. Tua-i pilliniani, qanemcisqelluku taugaam anernemek cikirluku utercesqatarniluku. Amtall'-am tua-i nalanariani nalaurlurluni tayim' tauna angalkurpaungermi.

Our grandmother who was named Tut'angaq used to wear a *nepcetaq* [shaman mask][3]

Paul Waskey, Johnny Thompson, and Marie Meade, Toksook Bay, January 1996

PAUL WASKEY: Our grandmother who was named Tut'angaq used to wear a *nepcetaq* [shaman mask that sticks to the face]. There were four different

---

Tua-i-wa imna maurlullerput im' Tut'angaamek pilallrat nepcetatullruuq

Pugleralria Cakitelleq Arnaq-llu, Nunakauyaq, January 1996

PUGLERALRIA: Tua-i-wa imna maurlullerput im' Tut'angamek pilallrat nepcetatullruuq. Cetamanek-am atkugnek ayuqenrilngurnek

kinds of parkas over each other. Then her hands were tied behind her, she had them tied four times. After the seal-gut parka was soaked in aged urine, very aged urine. She would put them on, and they would be very dry.

It's because Tut'angaq was a shaman. Tut'angaq, no, my grandmother. She was a female. Yes, they say their women shamans were powerful.

JOHNNY THOMPSON: Men feared women shamans.

PAUL WASKEY: They were scared of women shamans.

Long ago, since I stayed with [my grandmother] over and over, she would say, and after she used her shaman powers and summoned *tukaratulit* ["those who kick," meaning *ircenrraat*, extraordinary beings], she would summon those *tukaratulit*. When they came, she would be thankful. She'd say nothing would happen out there today. [*laughs*]

MARIE MEADE: What are *tukaratulit*?

PAUL WASKEY: *Ircenrraat*, yes, from under the ground.

MARIE MEADE: She would use her shaman powers and let them come?

PAUL WASKEY: Yes, she would use her shaman powers and let them come. *Tuunrat* talk like us, but they are a little hard to understand like they are talking from inside a tank [oil barrel]. My dear grandmother would summon two [spirit helpers]. The other spoke in the Chevak dialect, and the other spoke with a northern accent. He was from up north.
Meryiggluni.

JOHNNY THOMPSON: You know, they spoke in the Chevak dialect. When they speak in their dialect, they call it *meryiggluni*. You know, the accent that Chevak people use when they speak.

PAUL WASKEY: They speak *meryiggluteng*, yes.

MARIE MEADE: And the other [spirit helper]?

PAUL WASKEY: It spoke in a northern accent.

JOHNNY THOMPSON: Speaking with a northern accent.

PAUL WASKEY: Like the people of the north.

MARIE MEADE: Stebbins? St. Michael? Elim?

PAUL WASKEY: It was like that.

JOHNNY THOMPSON: They call it *piluraluarluteng* [when they speak with the northern accent].

MARIE MEADE: From Unalakleet? The Iñupiaq people?

PAUL WASKEY: The Iñupiat. Yes, her other *tuunraq* would come to be heard speaking like the Iñupiaq people. [The spirit helper] would talk from inside the seal-gut parka. Sometimes she would tell them not to be too close and to move farther away.

MARIE MEADE: She would understand them?

qalliqluki. Tua-i talligni-ll' pamavet qillerrlukek, qillercellukek cetamarqunek. Tua-i taugken tua imarnitek teq'umun akurqaarlukek, imumun teq'ilriamun cakneq. Atnaurak ciilerpak tua-i cakneq, tua-i ciilerpak.

Angalkuullruami tauna Tut'angaq. Tut'angaq, no, maurluqa. Arnauluni. Ii-i, pinirtut-gguq tamakut arnat angalkuit.

CAKITELLEQ: Angalkut arnat angutet capirait.

PUGLERALRIA: Alikait arnat angalkut.

Tua-i akaurtellria tamaani, ellaitni-ll' uitauratullruama pulengtaq, waten qantullruuq, waten-ll' tuunrirraarluni imkunek-llu tukaratulinek, taivkatui tamakut tukaratulit. Taigaqata tua quyanaurtuq. Qakma-gguq cangaituq-gguq ernerpak. [*ngel'artuq*]

ARNAQ: Cat imkut tukaratulit?

PUGLERALRIA: Ircenrraat, ii-i, nunam akuliinek camaken.

ARNAQ: Tuunriluni taivkaraqluki?

PUGLERALRIA: Ii-i, tuunriluni taivkaqluki. Tuunraat-am wangkucicetun qanerlartuq taugaam tuarpiaq tainkam iluanek qanelria taringnaiterrlugluni. Malrugnek tauna maurlullraurluqa taivkarilartuq. Aipaa meryiggluni, aipaa-ll' qaggluni. Qagkumiunguluni.
Meryiggluni.

CAKITELLEQ: Iciw' Cev'armiut qaneryaraicetun. Qaneryarait meryiggnilarait. Cev'armiut iciw' qanraqata tua-i *accent*-ait.

PUGLERALRIA: Meryiggluteng, ii-i.

ARNAQ: Aipaa-llu-qaa?

PUGLERALRIA: Qaggluni.

CAKITELLEQ: Piluraluarluni.

PUGLERALRIA: Qagkumiucetun.

ARNAQ: Stebbins? St. Michael? Elim?

PUGLERALRIA: Tuaten-wa tua-i.

CAKITELLEQ: Piluraluarnilarait.

ARNAQ: Ungalaqlirnek? Inupiat-qaa?

PUGLERALRIA: Inupiat. Ii-i, Inupiagcetun taum tuunraan aipaa igvarlartuq. Qanerlartuq atam waken imarnitek iluagnek. Iliini-llu pilaraat ukaqsissaagpek'nakek yaaqvaqaniisqellukek.

ARNAQ: Elliin taringtulukek?

MARIE MEADE: Yes, what was the name of the place where she lived along the banks of the Qissunaq River?

PAUL WASKEY: The banks of the Qissunaq, yes, Putukulek [lit., "One that has toes"]. It's not too far from Cuqartalek.

MARIE MEADE: Where did you hear those *tukaralriit*?

PAUL WASKEY: From close by, about fifty feet from her house.

MARIE MEADE: Yes, from outside.

PAUL WASKEY: Yes, outside. They'd come to the area down below.

MARIE MEADE: Oh, below you.

PAUL WASKEY: Yes, they'd be fast underground. I wouldn't want to participate with them. [laughs]

MARIE MEADE: Yes, he and his grandmother? His grandmother beckoned them to come?

PAUL WASKEY: My dear grandmother was an old woman. She'd just discard her old woman age and always did things. [laughs]

She died as an old, old woman at Mountain Village.

JOHNNY THOMPSON: When her future *tuunraq* started to [beckon her], when she first acquired [the spirit helper], they cracked opened this part of her [top of her head], right here; she had me feel it with my hands.

MARIE MEADE: The top of her head.

JOHNNY THOMPSON: Before she got [her spirit helper], she said she used to really enjoy playing in the night in the dark in the moonlight all by herself. One day she saw a person.

PAUL WASKEY: Yes, before she went into the *qasgiq*, she said a face blocked her way.

MAN: Yes, she said she first went to the houses [to try to enter]. When she became distressed, she went up to the *qasgiq*. While she was going up, when she remembered what they used to do, she tried pressing down on it. Before it fully disappeared, when she stepped over it, as it came up, she went up with it and cracked this, but there was someone in the *qasgiq* who knew what was happening to her. She told about when she first became a shaman. When we went to Cuqartalek to spend a night, she told the story.

ARNAQ: Ii-i, tauna wani nunarrii Qissunam ceniini cauluni?

PUGLERALRIA: Qissunam ceniini, ii-i, Putukulek. Waken Cuqartalegmek yaaqsigpek'nani.

ARNAQ: Taukut tukaralriit naken niitaqluki?

PUGLERALRIA: Waken canirrarmek, *about fifty feet* eninek.

ARNAQ: Ii-i, qakma.

PUGLERALRIA: Mm-m, qakma. Tailartut camavet.

ARNAQ: Oh, acivcenun.

PUGLERALRIA: Ii-i, cama-i tua-i cukaluteng cakneq nunam akulinek. Ilaganrilliki kia. [ngel'artuq]

ARNAQ: Ii-i, elkek maurluni-llu? Maurluan taicetaarluki?

PUGLERALRIA: Arnangiarauguq atam tauna maurlullraurluqa, taugaam cegganqe[ggluni]. Arnangiaraullni eggluku cangnatutuuq. [ngel'artuq]

Tua-i arnassagaqapiaraurrluni catairutellruuq Asaacaryami.

CAKITELLEQ: Tuunrarkaan-wa taum wani pingellrani, tua-i pikliuteqarraallermini, ukucia ciilluku-llu una, 'gguun; cavcetellrua wangnun.

ARNAQ: Kakangcaa.

CAKITELLEQ: Tuani-gguq tua waten tamaa pikliupailegmiu tauna, aquiyunqegglartuq-gguq unugmi tua-i iralum nalliini, kiirrarmi-llu-gguq tua. Caqerluni-gguq tua tangerkenganguq yugmek.

PUGLERALRIA: Ii-i, tauna tuan', itqatallermini-gguq qasgimun kegginam-gguq capellrua.

ANGUN: Ii-i, tua-i ciumek-gguq maavet enenun ayagayaaquq. Arenqialingami-am qasgimun taggliniluni. Tagglermini-am tuani tua nutaan neq'aqaamiu qayuw' pilallrat naspaalliniluku tua neggluku. Tua-am pellaluaqerpailgan amllillerminiu tua tapeqluku nugulluku una tua ciilluku, taugaam alakumastengqelliniluni qasgim iluani. Tua-i tauna angalkuurteqarraallni qanemcikellrua. Tua tamaani-wa wangkuk Cuqartalegtellemegni qavartaumanginanemegni qanemcika'artellrallrua.

Because she was a shaman, she had someone make her a wolf mask by carving it[4]

Charlie Steve and Marie Meade, Toksook Bay, January 1996

MARIE MEADE: At that time of the Curukaq [Messenger Feast, from *curukaq*, "challenger, guest invited to a dance festival"] while they were there, did they use the masks, or was it at another time?

CHARLIE STEVE: That is a different one, too. On a different day, and they would do it by months, a certain month was when they held it. They would start to work on masks during a certain month when they were going to have masked dancing, and it wasn't Kassiyuq [Dance Festival].

They would display [the mask]. At the time my dear grandmother was an elderly woman. Since she was a shaman, she would have them make her a wolf mask by hollowing out a piece of wood. [The mask] would fit her.

But it was made so that the mouth here and the chin would move like this. They made it so that it would open and close. I didn't examine that [mask]. Probably from the inside, I get curious about it these days, I think it [opened and closed] when she'd squeeze it from the inside.

When she would bite herself as I watched, she used to roll this up all the way. When she pulled it out, she would drip with blood. She would stretch out her arms when she did that, even though her clothes started to get bloody.

My poor dear grandmother.

MARIE MEADE: Your poor, dear grandmother wore a mask?

CHARLIE STEVE: She was masked. I had many grandmothers there. One of them wore that kind of mask because she was a shaman, because she was one of the shamans.

MARIE MEADE: Would she also wear a mask?

CHARLIE STEVE: She wore a mask. She bit herself when she wore the mask, [bit] herself. When she was going to do it, the mouth of that wolf [mask] would open very wide. After she suddenly did it, [the mouth] would suddenly open again and [its teeth] would come off. She would bleed and get bloody. They would make sharp ivory [teeth on the mask]. They'd insert them along here [on the mask] and make them very sharp.

Angalkuungami-wa, keglunramek equgmek kegginaqulivkalallruuq ilua nayugluku

Anauterkaq Arnaq-llu, Nunakauyaq, January 1996

ARNAQ: Tuani taukut curukat-qaa tuanelnginanratni kegginaqut atulallruit wall'u-qaa allami?

ANAUTERKAQ: Allakauguq cal' tauna. Allami ernermi, iralutgun-llu piuralallruut, iraluq una pivikaqluku. Iralumi kegginaquingelallruut kegginaqurluteng piqatarqameng, Kassiyuuvkenani.

Tua maniurluki tua. Tauna maurlurluqa arnangiaraurrluni-w' tua arnaurrluni. Kegginaqumek, angalkuungami-wa, keglunramek equgmek kegginaqulivkalallruuq ilua nayugluku. Waten ngelqayagulluku.

Taugaam qanra una, tamlua cali waten elliutuliuluku. Ikirngaurcelluku-am taqluku. Yurvillrunritaqa tauna. Qamaggun tayima, watua paqnayuglartua qamaggun qetaarqani pilallrungatuq.

Keggmarqami tua ellminek, tangssugaqamni kangivarteqapiarluk' man'a keggmalallruuq. Amugartaqan augmek kucirturnaurtuq. Yagiranaurtuq tuaten pingraan, qaini tua augglainaurtengraan.

Maurlurluqa.

ARNAQ: Maurlurluun kegginaqurluni?

ANAUTERKAQ: Kegginaqurluni.
Maurlunka amllellruut tuani. Iliit tauna kegginaqungqelallruuq tamakunek, angalkuungami-wa, angalkuut ilakngatni.

ARNAQ: Ellii-llu-qaa kegginaqurluni piaqluni?

ANAUTERKAQ: Kegginaqurluni ellii. Ellminek keggmarluni kegginaqurluni, ellminek. Piqatarqami qanra taum keglunrem aitaqerrnaurtuq cakneq. Tua-i pileryaggaarluku qaill' piqaan ataam aitaqerrluni aug'arrluteng. Aunrarluni augugyirturluni. Ip'giluki pilallruit tugkarnek. Maavet kapurqelluki ipgikacagarluki.

MARIE MEADE: A female would wear a mask?

CHARLIE STEVE: She was a female. She was a female shaman.

MARIE MEADE: Then how did she do that? When she was done, did they heal?

CHARLIE STEVE: She healed them, her *tuunrat* [would heal them]. Every day, when I'd go and see her right away and I'd go in, she'd be making things, and sewing boots too. Since I wasn't shy toward her, because she was my grandmother, I would run to her and say, "My dear grandma, I want to see your arm. Yesterday I saw you, and it was bleeding when you were biting on it." She would lift it up, and there would be no wound at all. She would tell me before I made a sound that we won't get sick. And she'd say no one would die.

Then I would do something, the next year, I would go in and I would see she had made a new mask. They always burned the old masks in the fire bath. It would be a wolf mask. It was always a wolf mask. They would make one for her that looked like that.

When she would dance again, whenever she bit herself, she would suddenly bleed. I'd go over every day and when I'd enter, she would be sitting there wearing her parka with her arms out of her sleeves. I'd quickly go to her and tell her I wanted to see her [arms] again. She'd tell me that her self-inflicted bites on her arm from yesterday didn't heal. She'd say sickness would fall upon the village. She'd say some would perish. She would show [her arm] and there would be holes [bite marks]. Some didn't heal. The sickness [that would hit the village] wouldn't let them heal, wouldn't let them disappear, the sickness that would befall them.

MARIE MEADE: Did they use the masks to tell the future?

CHARLIE STEVE: Some of them. Some of them were used to tell the future.

MARIE MEADE: So that person would check what was to come in the future.

CHARLIE STEVE: Yes, using her shamanistic powers, her *tuunrat*. She would check using her [own body]. She would tear her own [skin]. Her *tuunraq* would heal her [wounds] at night. She was a very powerful shaman.

ARNAQ: Arnauluni-qaa kegginaqurluni?

ANAUTERKAQ: Arnauluni. Angalkuuluni arnauluni.

ARNAQ: Tua-ll' qaillun tauna? Taq'aqan-qaa ataam mamtullruut?

ANAUTERKAQ: Elliin mamtelallrui, elliin tuunrain. Unuaquaqan egmiinaq paqtaqamni iternaurtua calilria canek pilugunek-llu mingeqluni. Ullagarrluku tuaten, takaqenrilamku-ll' tua maurluqngamku, ullagarrluku pinaurqa, "Maurlurluu, tallin tangerrsugaqa. Akwaugaq tangellruamken aunrarcelluku keggmallerpeni." Maknauraa, waten tua-i ayuqluni, ekingssagaunani. Pianga, pinauraanga neplirpailemni, waniwa-gguq wani nangteqngaitukut-gguq. Tuqulriartangqerrngaituq-llu-gguq.

Tua-i-am calua, qakuaqan, allrakuaqan, iliini iterlua, calua, maaten pinaurtuq ataam allanek kegginaqirrlainarluni. Kegginaqut maqikelaatgu. Keglunruanek. Keglunruarrlainarnek. Tuaten ayuqluku cali pilinauraat.

Ataam cali tuani yuraraqami piluku, keggmaaqami tua aunrallagaluni. Unuaquaqan aglua iternaurtua atkullramini aliingqayagarluni uitauralria. Ullagarcamni pinauqa ataam tangerrsugluki. Pinauraanga akwaugaq-am keggmallri mamenritut-gguq. Ukut-gguq nunat nangyutem tut'eqatarai. Ilaiquciqut-gguq. Maninauraa ukinret. Ilait mamevkenateng. Tua-i-w' cangerliim tamatum mamcesciiganaku, aug'avkarciiganaku, cangerlagkaata.

ARNAQ: Maa-i-q' makut kegginaqut aprutekluki ciunerkarcuutekluki?

ANAUTERKAQ: Ilait. Ilait ciunerkarcuutekluki.

ARNAQ: Taum-wa tua-i tuaten ciunerkaq man'a yuvriraqluku.

ANAUTERKAQ: Ii-i, angalkumikun tamaaggun, tuunramikun. Ellmikun-wa yuvrirluki. Waten allgurluni pilaami ellminek. Tuunraan taum unugmi mamtaqluki. Angalkuullruuq kayuluni cakneq.

He scolded his older sister, even though she was dead[5]

Charlie Steve and Marie Meade, Toksook Bay, January 1996

MARIE MEADE: Who was your grandmother?

CHARLIE STEVE: Ungilak. She was Ungilak. Qanitaq's older sister. Qanitaq was a man. He was It'gacangaq's father. He is also my grandfather. He wasn't a shaman though.

Then when she died, their house had a window up above. They lifted her through that. They used to fold their legs in [when they prepared them for burial]. When Ungilak died. They lifted her. They say when she was about to reach the middle, it broke on one side and snapped and she fell.

Her younger sibling ran to her body. When he got to her he scolded her and said, "What did you do with your shaman powers and fall! Where are your shaman powers?" [laughs] He apparently scolded his older sister, even though she was dead. He asked what she had done with her shaman powers that she fell. He asked her where her powers are. [laughs]

MARIE MEADE: Why did she fall?

CHARLIE STEVE: The thing they were using to pull her probably broke probably because it was rotten when it got caught on something. [laughs] The poor thing that they were about to take out through the window. Her younger sibling didn't even feel pity for her and scolded her as he approached her, even though she wouldn't respond. When she landed, he quickly went to her. When he got to her he said to her, "Ungilak, where are your *tuunrat*? What did you do with your shaman power and fall?" [laughs] He called her Ungilak.

[My grandfather] used a *nepcetaq* mask[6]

Henry Teeluk and Marie Meade, Kotlik, March 2003

HENRY TEELUK: I haven't forgotten our instruction from back then. Accept what your fellow person says if you don't mind what it is. If you don't like what you heard, don't accept it. That is what the people who raised us would tell us.

I have heard many, many words of wisdom, but I have forgotten some. Then in the evenings, my grandfather would gather us young boys and talk

Nunullia taun' alqani tuqumangraan

Anauterkaq Arnaq-llu, Nunakauyaq, January 1996

ARNAQ: Maurluun kituuluni?

ANAUTERKAQ: Ungilak. Ungilauguq. Qanitam alqaa. Qanitaq, angun. It'gacangam atii. Tauna apa'urluqaqa cal' tauna. Angalkuullrunrituq taugaam.

Tua-ll'-am tuquan, pikaggun egalengqertut eniit tauna. Mayurtelliat. Imumek qungcurrluki pilallruit. Ungilak taun' tuqungan. Mayurrluku-am. Waniwa-gguq qukaqatarluku, ingluaqerluku kevkaulluni iggluni.

Taum uyuraan ullagartellia. Tekicamiu nunullia, pillia, "Angalkuten cakluki igcit! Nauwam angalkuten?" [ngel'artuq] Nunullia taun' alqani tuqumangraan. Angalkui cakluki igtellranek. Nauwa-gguq angalkui. [ngel'artuq]

ARNAQ: Ciin-kiq-tam igta?

ANAUTERKAQ: Tamana-w' arumallian natmun pillrani nuqyutni igtellinilria. [ngel'artuq] Egalerkun anteqataurluqngaat. Uyuraan-ll'-am taum tua-i kusgukevkenaku nunuqcallia-am ullagluku kiungailengraani. Piami-w' taum tuc'an ullagartelliniluku. Tekicamiu pilliniluku, "Ungilak nauwa-mi tuunraten? Cakluki tuunraten igcit?" [ngel'artuq] Ungilagmek acirluku.

Nepcetarlartuq

Teeluk Arnaq-llu, Qerrullik, March 2003

TEELUK: Alerquutvut-wa ukanirpak avaurlanrilkeka. Ilavet qanellra ciuniuqiu cangalkenrilkuvgu. Ciuniurpek'naku-llu tua assikenrilkuvgu tauna niitellren. Tavaten qanrullaraitkut imkut anglicartemta tamaani.

Ak'akika qaneryaraq niicaaqsarqa, avaurluku tuaten wii pilaama. Tua-llu wangkuta tan'gurrallerni apa'urluma tua atakumi

to us about our future and what we should do and what we are not supposed to do.

He always spoke to us. When one of our teen-aged young boy companions would go out as my grandfather was talking, he would look over at us and say, "That person [who went out] will not reach a long life. He does not listen. He doesn't want to listen to how we should live as we are living."

Whenever he said that, my body felt as though it congealed. I would suddenly feel scared to move my body when he would say that. It wouldn't be long until we heard that the person who went out died after [my grandfather] spoke like that.

My grandfather always spoke to us. I wish he could wake and come in here today, and I would let him go down there and let him use a *nepcetaq*. I would tell him, "If you don't use a *nepcetaq* mask, I won't let you eat all day." [*laughs*]

He used to use a *nepcetaq* mask. My grandfather was a powerful shaman. He didn't use his powers on people though. He would know what was going on with the people around us, though. He would tell us that he won't use his powers that he continued to use on people.

He never used [his powers] on people. I never heard that he used [his powers] on people.

Even though it was completely dark out, if he let a person walk outdoors somewhere, if he let him go he would always make a whirling sound down there. He would stop after making a whirling sound. He would tell us, "The ones I told [to go] have stopped. I think they are planning to go home. I think they are planning to come." He would go again. Here they were traveling. He would tell us that they were coming, that they have returned home. I think he had a TV.

MARIE MEADE: How did he *elevlevaarturluni* [make a whirling noise]?

HENRY TEELUK: He would make a whirling noise. What are those things? Those hooded garments, seal-gut parkas. He had those for a TV. He would watch through those and tell about it, even though they were traveling [elsewhere]. He would see them, even though they were walking. Even if he had traveled in complete darkness, he would say that he did this and that and he is doing this and that. He said that they weren't going where he told them to go, that they got scared and went home. He

katurcelluta, katurrluta qanruqu'urnauraakut ciunerkamtenek aturarkamtenek-llu, atunritarkamtenek-llu.

Qanruqu'urlallruakut. Ilavut, ilavut an'aqan, tan'gurralleraat iliit an'aqan tuani qanerturnginanermini ikavet, iivet tangekluta pinauraakut taum apa'urluma, "Tua-am augna avani yuullerkaani nurrluku anerteqciquq. Niicunriituq. Niicugnisunriituq eglertellerkamtenek anertequrallemteni."

Tua wiiurluq tua tavaten qanraqan tuarpiaq igurrlaqiinga. Qaika pektellerkaqa caperrsaguarrnaurqa tuaten qanraqan. Ak'anirpagpek'naateng-llu tua tauna tua niitnauraat tauna im' anlleq yuunrillruuniluku.

Apa'urlullrama taum qanruqu'urlallrukiikut. Waniwa-tuq tayima makluni maavet iterluni apa'urluqa tauna kanavet pivkarluuku nepcetarcetqerlaaku. Qanrulluku, "Nepcetanrilkuvet nerevkarngaitqapigtamken ernerpak." [*ngel'artuq*]

Nepcetarlartuq. Angalkurpausaaqellruuq tauna apa'urluuqa. Yugnun atusuillallrua angalkuullni. Nallusuunaki taugken avaqliput elliin. Qanrullallruakut-wa elliin, pilallruakut yugmun aturngaitniluku tamana, tamana egelrutellni elliin.

Aturlallrunritai yugnun. Niillallrunritaqa aturniluku yugnun.

Tamlek'apigtengraan-llu tua yuk-gguq pekeskuuniu esslaami, natmun ayagceskuniu, kanani tua elevlevaarturlartuq. Elevlevaarluni arulairnaurtuq. Pinauraakut, "Taukug-im' ellimellregka imkuk arulairtuk. Utertekunangatuk. Taikunangatuk." Ataam eglengaqluni. Eglercaaqlutek. Qanrutnauraakut, tamaa-gguq taiguk, utertuk-gguq. TV-ingqerrlallrungatuq tauna.

ARNAQ: Qaillun elevlevaarturluni?

TEELUK: Elevlevaa. Imkut caugat? Qasperet imkut, imarnitet. Tamakucikun TV-iingqerrlartuq. Tamaaggun tua tangkurlaraa, qanrutkurluki-llu tangek'apiggluki pektengraata. Tamlek'apik pillrungraan, qanrutkurluku waten piniluku, waten-ll' piniluku. Tavavet pisqellerminun ayanritniilukek, alingenglukek uterrnilukek tamaa. Angalkurpaullrusaaquq cakneq; yugnun atusuunaku angalkuullni man'a. Naanguaqluku taugaam.

was a really powerful shaman; he never used his powers on people. He just used it as entertainment.

I responded by thanking him, "Some day if I live and you get sick, I will help you"[7]

Martina Aparezuk and Marie Meade, Kotlik, March 2003

MARIE MEADE: Do you still dream up to this day?
MARTINA APAREZUK: Sometimes I still dream like that.

When they are going to practice those. A few times I have told them, "I may be a shaman." [*laughs*]

Back then I became really sick at the age of seven years old. There were two girls, my age. One was my husband's younger sister who died at Pastuliq at that time. I didn't eat and got very skinny.

At that time there was a shaman who came to me. I was sick at the end of November. That shaman came in and stroked me this way. I don't know what he said when he [was stroking me] here. While he was doing that, I fell asleep. I woke up, I had better awareness.

The next day he came to check on me to see how I was doing. I told him that I recovered. I never ate. After that I was hungry. He said to me, "You will be okay. You will heal now." I told him, I responded by thanking him, "Some day if I live and you get sick, I will help you."

Then he got sick. He had cancer on his tongue and it was rotting. He made me a hook. He made a hook, over there at the camp at Pastuliq. I would always spill out his urine pot and bring him food to eat. He was alone, and his son never really took care of him.

Then he made a hook for me. When he was done he said to me, "Here is a hook that I made. It will catch everything." Then it was falltime, and he died right after freeze-up. Then I went fishing with a hook. I tried it. I had so much fun at that time. There were many fishing holes around me. And even when I wanted to move [to another hole] I had so much fun. I was really catching. It was [the hook] that the shaman made.

Then soon, and no matter where I went people would ask me, "What makes you catch so much?" I would answer, "I don't know why I am catching."

Quyarraarluku, "Cam iliitni anerteqnginanemni elpet nangteqkuvet wii ikasuaciqamken"

Atangun Arnaq-llu, Qerrullik, March 2003

ARNAQ: Cali-q' maa-i qavangurtutuuten?
ATANGUN: Waten iliini-ll' tua qavangurturlartua.

Tamakunek *practice*-aaqatarqata. Iliitni pilaranka, "Wii tang angalkurungatua." [*ngel'artuq*]

Tamaani ak'a nangteqerpallruunga *seven years*-arlua. Tua-llu taukuk pitalgutegka, *same age*-agka. Aipama kinguqlia tuquluni, Pastulirmi tuquluni. Kemgiullua nersuirullua.

Tua-llu angalkurtangqerrluni tailuni. Tua November-aq nangluku nangteqlua. Tua-ll' angalkuum taum iterngami maaggun ellailuni. Camek qanellra nalluaqa maaggun pillrani. Piniinanrani-ll' tayima qavarlua. Tupagtua cellaka assiqerluuni.

Tua-ll' unuaquan paqtaanga cangatellemnek. Pikilaku assirinilua. Nersuitellruunga. Nutaan tua kaiglua taum kinguakun. Pianga, "Assiriciquten. Assiriarkaurtuten." Tua-llu teguluku wii kiukilaku, quyarraarluku, "Cam iliitni anerteqnginanemni elpet nangteqkuvet wii ikasuaciqamken."

Tua-llu tuani nangteqengluni. Ulua *cancer*-arluni aruluni. Tua-ll' manaqucikilia. Manaqucikili ikani *camp*-ami Pastuliarmi. Qurrutiinek ciqiciqu'ur[larqa] neqkainek-ll' payugtaqluuku. Kiimelami, taum qetunraan-llu nayuluaqernanrilani.

Tua-ll' manaqumcilua. Taqngami pianga, "Waniwa un' manaq un' piliaqa. Ca tamalkuan pitaqeciqaa." Tua-ll' uksuarurrluni, cikuqanrakun ellii tuquluni tayima. Tua-ll' manarlua. Uigtualuku. Ak'a tua anglanilua tuani. Avatemni-ll' ukin[ret]. Nugtarcungrema-llu tavan' anglanilua. Picuqapigglua. Angalkum piliara.

Tua-ll' piqerluni, natmun-ll' ayangrema yuut pinauraatnga, "Qayugga-wa pilriani picuvakarcit?" Piaqa, "Nalluaqa picuvakar[lalqa]."

They never caught anything. All [the fish] went to [this hook]. They never caught anything.

When they would begin to gather around me, I would move over [to another fishing hole]. Then I had fun over there, too. When I got too much, I would go home.

That hook of mine, now I don't know where it is, it was made by a shaman. I don't know where it is now. Maybe one of my brothers lost it. Whenever my brothers used my hook, they wouldn't catch. When I would use it, I would catch a lot.

MARIE MEADE: Do you not have that anymore?

MARTINA APAREZUK: Yah, it broke when they were using it. I was sad to lose it. I should have let him make lots. That shaman [made the hook].

Ellait taugken picuunateng. Pitarkat uumun tailuteng. Ellait-wa picuunateng.

Wani tau pakma quyurpaka'arqatnga avavet nugtarrlua ataam. Tava-am ataam anglanilua tavani. Arenqiarutaqama utertaqlua.

Taun' tua manaqa un', tayima natmun, angalkuum manaliaqaa. Natmun tua pillrua. Tamallrungataa iliita brother-aama. Taukut-llu brother-aama atuqatgu picuitnaurtut. Wii taugken kiima atuqumku picunaurtua.

ARNAQ: Tua-i-llu-q' tayim' avaliqenrirluku elpet?

ATANGUN: Yaa, qup'artellinian taun' atullermegteggu. Qunuksaaqaqa tauna. Umyuarteqlua ciin-tam amllernek pilivkanricia. Angalkuum taum.

He told me when he was alive, "You will live [for a long time]"[8]

Martina Aparezuk and Marie Meade, Kotlik, March 2003

MARTINA APAREZUK: I thanked him very much, and he told me when he was alive, "You will live [for a long time]. Even if animals, bears are around you, don't run away. They won't bother you."

So one day I went to pick berries down [on the coast]. Down below me not far from me were two [people] who were picking berries and they would bend down. I ignored them and continued to pick berries. Soon I lost their whereabouts.

It so happened, when my late brother saw me, he came to me. "Are you not aware?" I said to him, "I don't know anything." He said I was picking berries not too far from the bear. It didn't do anything to me, even though it was there. Since [the shaman] had said that animals wouldn't bother me, but he did say not to run away, even though I saw them. That shaman instructed me to do that.

MARIE MEADE: Who was that shaman?

MARTINA APAREZUK: He was Kiuryaq. His name was Kiuryaq. I don't know his English name. But his name was Kiuryaq. I sang his song a few weeks ago in the Potlatch, his *puallassuun* [song for a northern-style line dance]. He would dance [with his torso] undressed. I had them sing his *puallassuun*.

MARIE MEADE: Alma Keyes's dad?

MARTINA APAREZUK: Alma Keyes's dad.

MARIE MEADE: Her dad, Kiuryaq?

MARTINA APAREZUK: That is him. That song came into my mind for *puallaq* [a northern-style line

Waten anerteqlermini [pillruanga], "Qayugg', anertevkarciquten"

Atangun Arnaq-llu, Qerrullik, March 2003

ATANGUN: Tua-i-w' tuani quyaluku cakneq pillruamku, waten anerteqlermini. "Qayugg', anertevkarciquten. Cat-llu ungungssiit taqukaat pingraa[ta] qimagarca[qunak]. Pingaitaatgen."

Tua-ll' cam iliit unavet ayaglua. Piunga ketemni kanani yaaqsigpek'na[tek] cam taukuk malruulutek put'aqlutek unatalriik. Tua-ll' ilangciksaunak' tua unataarlua. Piqerluni tayim' tamarilukek.

Cunaw' anngairutma taum tangerrngamia tailliuq. "Nalluuten-qaa camek?" Piaqa, "Nalluunga camek." Carayalleq yaaqsinrirluku unatartua. Pinritlianga pekaarangerma. Tuaten qanellruami, tamakut ungungssit pingaitnilua, taugaam tangeng'erma ayakaasqevkenii. Alerqualua taum angalkum.

ARNAQ: Kituullrua tauna angalkuk?

ATANGUN: Kiuryaraullruuq. Kiuryamek atengqellruuq. Kass'atun atra nalluaqa. Kiuryaullruuq taugaam. Yuarutii-ll'-am tamaan' atuqeka icivaq Potlatch-allratni, puallassuutii. Matarrluni puallatullruuq taman'. Aturcetellruaqa puallassuutii.

ARNAQ: Alma Keyes-am-q' atii?

ATANGUN: Alma Keyes-am atii.

ARNAQ: Atii Kiuryaq?

ATANGUN: Taunguuq. Puallassuutii icivaq tayima piqerluni tua tauna-am yuarun umyuamnun

dance] a few weeks ago. I sang for them right away. I said to them, "That was a song for a shaman a long time ago." He would sing it and they'd perform a *puallaq*. It was a *puallassuun*. His namesake would remove his upper clothing and dance *puallaq*.

They did that long time ago. My husband also did that back when he used to *puallaq*. Whoever knew how to do it would undress [from the waist up] and *puallaq*. [laughs]

ek'arrluni. Egmiulluku atuuskilaki. Pianka, "Taun' tuani ak'a angalkum yuarutkaa." Aturluku puallassuutekellruat. Puallassuun. Tauna atra matarrluni puallalallruuq taman'.

Long time tavaten pit[ullruut]. Aipaqa-ll' puallatullermini. Uum nallunrilami matarrluni *shirt*-airluni puallarluni. [*ngel'artuq*].

He used to go and get [animals], and I used to see that old shaman[9]

Thomas Chikigak, Alakanuk, August 1987

THOMAS CHIKIGAK: But that one, those who were around before us are gone now, but their grandchildren are alive today. That shaman, a shaman from this village, they used to talk about him; they didn't mention exactly where he went, how he went to get [land animals] from somewhere up in the sky. He used to get [animals], and I used to watch that old shaman.

Yes, I used to watch him. During one winter like this, they let him practice his spirit powers to get one of the foods they eat, they had him go and get a land animal that they would use.

He flew away using snowshoes, those Yup'ik-style snowshoes. He evidently flew away.

That [shaman] left. Somewhere, from somewhere that he considered to be far away, he went to get that thing that people would use, and he returned.

While he was traveling home up in the sky, he saw a tundra hare here, a tundra hare that was along the edge of a hole, along the edge of a star's hole. There was a tundra hare that was crouched down and could easily fall down there, and underneath it, where people were walking, was visible.

[The shaman] was holding that thing that he went to get. As he was traveling along, he began to covet that tundra hare and thought, "The people of my village would want to have it since it's food and its fur and skin can be used."

As he approached it along his path, wearing snowshoes, since that hole wasn't far, he swept it with his snowshoes and made it fall. As he watched, when it fell, it landed on top of the land down there.

Aqvatlalria-w', wii-ll' tangvatullrukeka tauna angalkulleq

Cikigaq, Alarneq, August 1987

CIKIGAQ: Tauna taugaam, ukut, ukut nangelriit tayim' augkut ciuqlimta, maa-i-wa tutgarait taugaam anerteqellriit. Angalkulleq tauna, ukurmiut angalkullrat, tua-i qanruteklaqiit; tuani naken tayima nakqapik pillra pivkenaku, pakmaken-am naken cellamek aqvatellra tauna. Aqvatlalria-w' tua-i aqvatetulria, wii-ll' tangvatullrukeka tauna angalkulleq.

Ii-i, tangvalallrukeka. Tuani waten wani uksumi tuunrivkarluku camek, neqkat-wa iliitnek, tua-i-w' ungungssimek aqvatevkarluku nunami piarkamek, atu'urkameggnek.

Tua-i-am tengluni tanglura'arluni, imkunek *snowshoes*, Yup'igtarraagnek. Tengluni ayallinilria.

Tua-i-am ayagluni tauna. Nani tayima, naken tayima yaaqvanek ellmini tauna yuut atu'urkaat aqvallerminiu uterrluni.

Utercami pakmani cellami eglerrnginanermini piuq qayuqeggliq una, qayuqeggliq una ukinrem tuani ceniini, agyam ukinrani. Qayuqeggliq una lavngauralria igcukaarluni-ll' una-i tua-i, acia man'a yuut man'a pektellrat alaunani.

Tua-i-am tauna imna, imna tegumiaqluku aqvallni. Eglerrnginanermini ayarika'arrluku tauna qayuqeggliq umyuartequq, "Kingunrenka, tua-i-wa piqeryuumirluteng neqkaungan-llu atu'urkaungan-llu amia."

Tumekngamiu, waten tumekluku ayallermini tuaten tangluarluni, imna tauna ukineq, yaaqsinritliniaku kalegluku tangluminek igcetliniluku waten. Ama-i tangvagluku, igcami nunam qainganun tull'uni kanavet.

When he arrived, after displaying what he had gone to get inside the *qasgiq*, he evidently told them—this was before I started going to the *qasgiq*—he evidently told them that while he was traveling up in the sky, as he was returning home, when he saw a tundra hare that could easily fall that was crouched, suddenly desiring to have it, thinking to obtain it for the people in his hometown who want to catch things, who want to obtain food to eat, and also with his two sons in mind, he swept it like this with his snowshoes while it was crouched down. As he approached it, since it was along his path, using his other snowshoe, the right one, he made it fall through that hole there. He said if he wasn't mistaken, that during spring, following the lengthening of the days, that those tundra hares would increase in number.

That one had called his spirit helpers, and the moon [month]—as you know they call *iralut* [months] *unugcuutet* in the other dialect—that month ended and another came.

When the next month came, their numbers evidently started to increase. The people who were traveling, tracks were starting to be around, tracks were starting to be everywhere. In the month of March, I think just when the month of March came, many came to be seen. They were plentiful, they became plentiful, people started catching tundra hares.

And when my late older brother was a boy, the one who raised us, that one and I were adopted and raised by another family. The Stanislaus family, those who have the last name Stanislaus, these young men, they are the children of my older brother.

Four of us were adopted children. The ones who raised us, since his wife couldn't have babies, they evidently adopted four of us. I was the youngest. [My brothers and sisters and I] actually have one mother, but the Joseph's have another father, and I have another [father], and I'm the oldest in our family.

Their family has increased in number. That one, the father of the Stanislaus family, when their father-to-be was a boy, the bird gun's lever, he said that it was almost too far for him to reach during that time.

When he would travel, he would catch many tundra hares; he said there were many tundra hares. They didn't have to search for animals to hunt after that one fell.

Tua-i tekicami qasgimi tua-i imna tauna aqvakngallni pirraarluku, nasvaggaarluku, qanemcilliniluni—wii tamaa-i qasgiyaurpailegma—qanemcilliniluni pakmani cellami eglertellermini uterrnginanermini qayuqegglimek waten igcukaaralriamek, lavngauralriamek tangrrami, ayarika'arrluku, kingunermini pitqeryuumilrianun taugaam neqkangyuumilrianun tamakunun umyuaqarrluku, taukuk-llu qetunraagni neq'aklukek, tua-i tangluminek kalegluku tua-i waten lavngaurallrani. Tumekluku tumkamini maan' pian tanglumi ingluanek uumek, tallirpilirnermek, igcelluku ukinerkun tuaggun. Tua-i iqlunrilkuni waniwa up'nerkaumainanrani, erenret taklirillrat maliggluku amlleriinarciqniluki pitarkat, qayuqegglit.

Tua-i imna tua-i maani tuunriluni, iraluq—unugcuutmek avani pilaqait iraluq—tamana pillra nangluni allamek cimirluni.

Cimiqerluku amlleriinaaralliut. Ayagauralriit makut, tumliangluni man'a piciatun tumliangluni. Tua-i imna, tamaani March-am tamaan', March-aq tamaani pingatuq pit'eqerluku amlleq tangerrnariluteng. Ik'ikika tua-i nurnaunateng, nurnairulluteng, qayuqegglirqaqengluteng.

Tauna-llu anngalqa tan'gurrallerauluni tamaani, anglicartemegnuk taum, anglicaraullruukuk tauna-llu. Ingkut Stanislaus-at, taukut Stanislaus-amek *last name*-angqellriit ukut tan'gurraat, taum anngarma irniaqai.

Anglicaraullruukut *four*-auluta. Taukut anglicarteput, nulirrat-am piipingyuitelliniami wangkuta *four*-auluta teguaqellrulliniakut. Wii kinguqlikacaarqellruatnga. Ukut-am aanangqerrsaaqut ataucimek, ukut taugaam Joseph-at allamek atangqertut, wiinga-ll' allamek, ciuqlikacagaulua ilamteni tuani.

Tua-i amlleriluteng. Tauna tua-i, ukut Stanislaus-at atiit, atakaat tan'gurrallerauluni, imna tua-i tengmiarcuutem pakigyaraa, tua-i agturaa-ll' waten nuryaqiirrluarluku-gguq tua-i piaqluku tamatum nalliini.

Ayagaqami tua-i qayuqegglirqaqaqluni; ik'iki-gguq qayuqegglit. Pitarkait yuarnarqevkenateng taum igtellran kinguakun.

That old shaman was from this village. I also saw him. He's actually my grandfather, he was related to my grandfather. His children's children are living separately upstream.

My grandfather was actually a shaman, but I didn't know that he was [a shaman][10]

Fred Augustine, Edward Phillip, and Marie Meade, Alakanuk, March 2011

FRED AUGUSTINE: They say in the past, when they would make *agayut* [masks] like that, when they didn't have those [feathers to adorn their masks], their shamans would go and obtain those long-tailed duck feathers, they went and obtained some long-tailed duck feathers [for adorning their masks]. Although it was winter, they'd go and get them. I think they must have thawed the lake somehow and picked them. That's what I used to hear when they didn't have any long-tailed duck feathers [for adorning masks].

MARIE MEADE: Yes. I wonder if in your presence, I wonder if in your hometown, in your village, there were shamans.

FRED AUGUSTINE: My grandfather was actually a shaman, but I didn't know that he was [a shaman]. I only heard that he was a shaman. But we never heard that my late grandfather did anything [practiced his powers]. He was very elderly. His head [hair] was very white, and he stopped moving. He would just lie face down and not move. He stopped getting up, he stopped sitting, but he would just lie face down.

   Then one day, over at Kapuutelleq, the *curukat* [dance guests] arrived. The *curukat* left, and a number of people stayed behind. They were evidently shamans, they were evidently shamans. They were evidently going to practice their spirit powers. My grandfather there, since they were evidently going to practice their spirit powers, I was extremely curious since I hardly saw those.

   Accompanying my father, I went inside the *qasgiq*, and I sat next to him, down below him. I sat there.

   The guests there were older men; they were evidently shamans, and Angutvassuk was one of them. A person from this village, well, he had rela-

Tauna tuani ukurmiungullruuq angalkulleq tauna. Tangaallruaqa-llu wiinga tua-i. Apa'urluqsaaqluku wiinga tua-i, apa'urluma ilakluku augkut, apa'urluma ilakellruat. Irniarin waniw' irniarit kiani uitaut allakarmeng.

Apa'urluqa-ll' angalkuullruyaaquq taman' taugaam uunguciitaqa wiinga

Qapuggluk, Qavarliar, Arnaq-llu, Alarneq, March 2011

QAPUGGLUK: Tamaani-gguq tua-i-wa tuaten agayuliaqameng tamakucirkaitaqameng angalkuit allginrarcurlartut, allginrarkarcutuut. Uksuungraan aqvalluteng. Qaill' tayima urugcelluku pilarngataat nanvaq, avurlarngatut. Niitetullruunga tuaten, allginrarkaitaqameng.

ARNAQ: Ii-i. Tamaani-kiq takuvni, tamaani nauvivni, nunavni angalkurtangqetullrulria.

QAPUGGLUK: Apa'urluqa-ll' angalkuullruyaaquq taman', taugaam uunguciitaqa wiinga. Niitelarqa taugaam angalkuuniluku. Caniluni taugaam niitnaitellruuq apa'urlulqa tauna. Angulluallruuq cakneq. Nasqurra tua-i qercurpak'apik, pekcuirulluni-ll'. Tua-i waten palungqauratuluni-ll' pekcuunani. Makcuirulluni, aqumyuirulluni, palungqaurluni taugaam pituluni.

   Tua-llu caqerluteng amani Kapuutellermi curukat tekilluteng. Tua-i-am ayagluteng tayim' curukat, qayutun-llu yuut uneggluteng. Cunaw' angalkut, angalkuulliniluteng. Tuunriqatalliniluteng. Tua-i apa'urluqa tauna, tuunriqatalliniata, wiinga tua-i paqnayuglua cakneq tangerpakayuilama tamakunek.

   Qasgimun tua-i aataka maliggluku iterlua, canianun-llu aqumlua ketiinun. Aqumgaurlua.

   Ukut allanret angutngurtengluteng; cunaw' angalkuulliniluteng, Angutvassuk-llu ilakluku. Imum' makurmium, makurmiunek-wa tua-i

tives from this village, and his children live in this village today. The younger sibling or rather older brother of the father of that family. What, what did I call him. Angutvassuk, yes, Angutvassuk. He was going to practice his spirit powers. He was the only one who was a younger man, and he was going to practice his spirit powers.

Then he started. He removed his clothes, he removed his clothes, and he put on someone's *qaliruak* [ankle-high skin boots], he borrowed them.

When they drummed, he went back and forth on the floor. He was doing something, and after going back and forth, when he stopped . . . I was just a boy and wasn't big. He told me, he pointed to me and said that he had found someone to help him, referring to me. Then I quickly ran behind my father, and said I wouldn't [help him]. I stayed back there.

Then my grandfather called on me, since he used to call on me, "Cekac'-Cekac', if they want you to help them, don't be reluctant and help them. I will watch you." Since I usually listened to that one, I obeyed and finally went farther down.

He was practicing his spirit powers. After practicing his spirit powers, he called on someone else. Then there were two of us.

Then he went to us, and he instructed me to place my head here and lie face down on him, and the other person with me was situated here.

MARIE MEADE: Along his lower body?

FRED AUGUSTINE: We were side by side, we were helping one another. He said we should press down on him as hard as we could. He said after he goes . . .

MARIE MEADE: Was he lying down?

FRED AUGUSTINE: No, he was lying face down like this, he was lying face down.

He told us when he left, when he was gone, to stay. Although they took a while to arrive, he told us not to stand whatsoever.

Then he started. They were drumming. That shaman spoke. [Someone] would reply to him. It was like [someone] would reply to him from his mouth. They were talking back and forth. He was doing something, he continually made muffled noises, he made noise like a house fly, he was making loud rumbling noises.

Then after a while, from here, his mouth was next to me here. From here, those two who were continually speaking went down and got quieter. They left. And Angutvassuk's body went down. As it left, [his body] gradually went down. And even-

tungelqungqerrluni, maa-i-ll' irniari maanlluteng. Taukut wani atiita kinguqlia, anngaa. Camek, camek-ima, Angutvassuk, yaa, Angutvassuk. Tauna tuunriqatarluni. Tan'gurraqsigluni kiimi, tuunriqatarluni.

Tua-llu ayagnirluni. Matarrluni, aturani yuuluki, kia-ll' qaliruagkenek all'uni navrarluni.

Cauyaata utertaararluni natermi. Caksuggluni, utertaararraarluni arulairami . . . wiinga tayim' tan'gurralleraulua angevkenii. Pianga, niiraanga, waniwa-gguq pistekanguq uumek, wiinga pilua. Tua-llu aatama keluanun tagqerreskilii, qanerlua tuaten wiinga pingaitua. Tagumalua.

Tua-llu taum apa'urluma tuqluraanga, tuqlurlaamia, "Cekac'-Cekac', ikayuqsukatgen qessavkenak ikayuuten. Kelluciiqamken." Nutaan tua-i niitellaamku tauna, niillua tua-i atraqanirlua nutaan.

Tua-i-am tuunriluni. Tuunrirraarluni kina ataam piluku. Malruurrlunuk.

Tua-i-llu tua-i ullaglunuk, alerquagururaanga wiinga-gguq wavet, nasquqa wavet elliluku palureskilii qainganun, aipaqa-ll' maavet.

ARNAQ: Uategkenun?

QAPUGGLUK: Caniqliqlunuk, ukisqaqlunuk. Niikilauk-gguq cakneq. Ayaggaarluni-gguq . . .

ARNAQ: Inarrluni?

QAPUGGLUK: Nuu, palurrluni waten, palungqaluni.

Ayakuni waniwa, im' catailkuni tua-i uitasqellunuk tua-i. Tekitnaciangermek, anguq'apik nangercesqevkenanuk.

Tua-i-llu tua-i waniw' ayagnirluni. Cauyarluteng. Qanerturqili tauna angalkuq. Kiugaqluku. Tuarpiaq qanranek kiulaqii. Kiutaaguqu'urlutek tua-i. Caluni, em'irqurluni-w' tua-i, ciivagtun neplirluni, tua-i tem'irrluni cakneq.

Tua-llu piinanermegni, waken, wanlluni tua-i qanra canimni. Waken wani qanerturalriik taukuk atraqilik qaskelliinarlutek. Ayaglutek. Una-llu Angutvassuum kemga atrarluni. Ayallra maikluku atrariinarluni. Kiituani ukuk-llu, ukuk-

tually, and these two, these two that were like this would fall. He died. [laughter]

They were no longer there. And his body fell. But he had said when he was arriving and we could hear him, to press down on him hard, when we could hear his noise. Finally, after a long time passed, he started making noise from somewhere, from far away. When he started making noise, we did as he asked. His body was flat.

Then as he got closer, his body started to expand like this. When it was able, his arm would go into place and make a popping noise as it went into place. And his legs did that also. He was upright before his voice arrived.

And when he arrived to where he was, that person's body went back to normal. After a while, he was done.

I was wondering when he was done, "I wonder what they'll say?" They never said anything at all. Not one of them said anything at all.

That person got ready, and he put his clothes on. Not one of them said anything at all. I was extremely curious at the time. I wonder what they did. Before they said anything, and my grandfather there, two people once again carried him out using something to carry him with.

Sometimes, my grandfather there, when he'd speak for a while, his jaw would fall sometimes. But his daughter-in-law, our paternal uncle's wife who was young would quickly run to him and his jaw would make a popping noise as it went back into place [laughs] when his jaw would fall. But [his jaw] didn't always do that; it did that sometimes.

I was extremely curious about what they were doing and why when they were practicing their spirit powers. Those people, Qakurtaq, and that other person, Qakerluilaq, those who were shamans in the past were there, before they were elderly men, back when I was a boy.

MARIE MEADE: Qakurtaq?
EDWARD PHILLIP: Qakerluilaq.
FRED AUGUSTINE: Qakurtaq, Qakerluilaq; that person was from up north. Kotzebue.

He was Iñupiaq. Qakerluilaq.

He used to live in this village [Alakanuk], he became a resident of this village; he was actually from up north. They say Qakerluilaq fled from place to place and came from Kotzebue up north; Kotzebue actually has a different name, [they called them] Mali-something.

llu waten pimallrek qaillun tua-i iqunaur[tuk]. Tuquluni tua-i. [ngel'artut]

Tayima catairullutek. Tauna temii tua-i iquluni. Qanellruluni taugken agiireskuni, niitnarikuni cakneq engisqelluni, niitnarikan nepii. Tua-i cayaqliqapiggluni tua-i nepengluni naken tayima yaaqvanek. Nepngellrani tuani tua-i pisquciatun tua-i. Mamcaringaluni tua-i tauna kemga.

Tua-i-ll' ukaqsigillra maliggluku waten tua-i qerruriinaqili tauna temii. Piyunariaqami tallia nunaminun ekluni cingqullagluni ek'aqluni. Iruk-llu tuaten. Naparrluni tua-i tekipailgan tua-i erinani.

Tekilluni-llu tua-i wavet ellirluni, ayuqucimitun-llu ayuqliriluni temii taum yuum. Piuraqerluni tua-i ak'anivkenani taqluni.

Paqnayugtua taqngan, "Camek tayim' qanerniartat?" Camek qanqallrunritut caitqapik. Tua-i caiqapik iliit qanqallrunrituq caitqapik.

Tua-i upluni tauna aturarluni-ll'. Tua-i iliit camek caitqapik qanerpek'nani. Paqnayullruunga tuani cakneq. Cas'-kiq, callruas'-kiq. Tua-i camek qanqerpailegmeng, apa'urluqa-ll' tauna ataam malruulutek kevgucirluku anulluku tayim' kevegluku.

Apa'urluma taum, iliini qanertura'arqan ukuk agluquk caaqamek igtelartuk. Taum taugken ukurraan ataatamta nulirran, young-arluni, curukarnauraa tua-i agluquk-llu cingqullakarlutek eknaurtuk agluquk [ngel'artuq] igtaqamek. Kesianek taugaam piyuunatek; caaqamek piaqlutek.

Paqnayugyaaqellruunga tuani camek pillratnek tuunrillratni. Imkut Qakurtaq kina-ll' augna Qakerluilaq, angalkullret taukut tua-i tuanlluteng, angulluarpailegmeng tan'gurralleraulua wii.

ARNAQ: Qakurtaq?
QAVARLIAR: Qakerluilaq.
QAPUGGLUK: Qakurtaq, Qakerluilaq; qagkumiunguuq tauna. Kotzebue.

Iñupiaq. Qakerluilaq.

Maantetullruuq, makurmiungurtellruuq; qaugkumiunguyaaluni. Tauna-gguq tuani Qakerluilaq qimagturluni qakmaken taillruuq Kotzebue; Kotzebue allamek atengqerrsaaquq, Mali-canek.

North of [Unalakleet], Kotzebue. Kotzebue has a different name, but they call it Kotzebue today.

EDWARD PHILLIP: Do they call it Malimiut?

MARIE MEADE: Yes.

FRED AUGUSTINE: They say that shaman there, he was a shaman, they say Qakerluilaq fled from place to place. His fellow [shamans] would pursue him. But he would escape before they'd [kill him]. And he was alive for a while here. That person, Qakerluilaq died in this village some time ago. I think Qakurtaq killed him.

EDWARD PHILLIP: Qakurtaq and he were enemies, that powerful shaman. They were evidently enemies.

FRED AUGUSTINE: Then, after being at Kapuutelleq for a while, we returned home. In the evening, after eating dinner, our father would tell us various stories.

When he was doing that in the evening, he said that his father said that Qakerluilaq had arranged/ordered [the death of] Angutvassuk. That one who had practiced his spirit powers at Kapuutelleq; it so happened that Qakerluilaq arranged [his death]. They don't leave their fellow shamans alone at the opportune time; they said that's what they do. He said that his father said that [Qakerluilaq] had arranged [the death of] the one who had practiced his shaman powers.

MARIE MEADE: What exactly do you mean by *picirkirluku* [to arrange (his death)]?

FRED AUGUSTINE: They say from the start, he provided food for him to eat, he put a sheefish in his stomach.

Then in the spring, we traveled to Qip'ngayak; after a while we heard that Angutvassuk died of a stomachache. Evidently, when he arrived at Narullegarvik he fished with a fishnet along with his wife and daughter.

Then they caught a sheefish. His wife cooked that sheefish. They ate, really eager to eat, eating freshly caught fish. They say he and his daughter suddenly had a stomachache, and they died at once, but his wife didn't [die].

That's evidently what they do to them, they seem to arrange [their death] while they are doing things. They say they are malevolent. Our late grandfather used to say that shamans are malicious.

MARIE MEADE: Some of them, some of them probably are.

FRED AUGUSTINE: Yes. They say some are good, but they say there are few who are good. They say there

Negranek, Kotzebue. Kotzebue-q' allamek atengqertuq, watua taugaam Kotzebue-mek pilaraat.

QAVARLIAR: Malimiunek?

ARNAQ: Ee-m.

QAPUGGLUK: Tauna-gguq angalkuq, angalkuuluni tua-i-gguq qimagturluni eglertellruuq tauna Qakerluilaq. Ilain piyugluku. Taugaam tua-i anagaqluni pivailgatni. Maani-llu anertequmaqerluni. Maani yuunrillruuq tauna Qakerluilaq imumi. Taum-wa Qakurtam pitaqngalkii.

QAVARLIAR: Qakurtaq-llu inglukellruuk, angalkurpak tauna. Inglukellrulliniuk.

QAPUGGLUK: Tua-llu, tuantelnguamta tua-i Kapuutellermek uterrluta. Atakuararqan, atakutallemta kinguani, atamta taum qanemciurautlaraakut canek.

Tuatnallermini-am atakumi qanlliniuq, qanertuq-wa atii-gguq qanertuq Qakerluilamun Angutvassuk picirkirniluku. Tauna imna tuunrilria Kapuutellermi; cunawa tua-i picirkillrullia tuani taum Qakerluilam. Uitacuitait tamakut ilateng angalkut arenqika'arqata; pinilallruit tuaten. Atii-gguq qanertuq picirkirniluku [Qakerliulamun] tauna tuunrilleq.

ARNAQ: Qailluqapiar picirkirluku?

QAPUGGLUK: Ayagmek-gguq tuani neqkaanek pillrua, imanillrua ciirmek.

Tua-llu up'nerkami ayagluta Qip'ngayagmun piqerluta niitukut Angutvassuk-gguq tuquuq ilukaarluni. Cunawa Narullegarvigmun tekicami kuvyilliniluni nuliani-llu panini-llu.

Tua-i-llu ciirmek neqtellinilutek. Nulirran egalliniluku tauna ciiq. Nerrliut tua-i neryugluteng cakneq, nuta'arturluteng. Tua-i-gguq tuani il'uqertellruuk panini-ll', ataucikun-llu yuunrirlutek, nulirra taugken pivkenani.

Tuaten pilalliniit, tuaten cainanratni picirkitungatliniit. Assinritnilarait. Apa'urlullemta taum assiitnilarai angalkut.

ARNAQ: Ilait-wa, ilait pilalliut.

QAPUGGLUK: Yaa. Ilait-gguq assiryaaqut, taugaam-gguq ikgetut assilriit. Amllenruut-gguq ik'imek

are more who tend to be malicious. He said being a shaman isn't something to desire. He said he was a shaman, but he said he endured distress. His fellow [shamans] tended to pursue him without him knowing, they tended to [pursue him] without him knowing.

MARIE MEADE: But he would sense them?

FRED AUGUSTINE: Yes, he said when he would sense them, he wouldn't let them [kill] him.

MARIE MEADE: Using his powers? So with the help of his powers, he didn't allow them to [kill him].

umyuarteqsulriit. Cucunarqenrituq-gguq angalkuulleq. Ellii-gguq angalkuuyaaqluni, makugtuq-gguq taugaam. Ilain nalluanek pissuryugluku, nalluliluku pingnaqsugluku.

ARNAQ: Elpekaqluki taugaam?

QAPUGGLUK: Ii-i, elpekaqamiki-gguq pivkarlanrituq.

ARNAQ: Pissuutmikun? Pissuutminek ikayirluni pivkarpek'nani.

He said the following, that we may have a shaman in our family, but that he won't live[11]

Fred Augustine and Lawrence Edmund, Alakanuk, March 2011

FRED AUGUSTINE: Yes, I think so. I don't know about those shamans. He said being a shaman isn't something to desire; he said it's distressing. And he said when we were small that it's best if we don't have a shaman in our family. Then after saying that, he said the following, that we may have a shaman in our family, but that he won't live.

Then as we were living and grew older, there was someone in our family, the late younger sibling of Uuqerrulria, Ingamulria; I think you saw him, I think you saw him.

LAWRENCE EDMUND: I don't know. I don't think I saw him.

FRED AUGUSTINE: That one was a shaman. He didn't live long. Like our grandfather said, he didn't live long. Since he continually practiced his shaman powers, I think he became a shaman.

Qanellruuq waten, angalkumek-gguq ilangqerciqsaaqukut anerteqngaituq-gguq

Qapuggluk Paugnaralria-llu, Alarneq, March 2011

QAPUGGLUK: Yaa, pingatuq. Cauciitanka tamakut angalkut. Qanellruuq anglakuulleq-gguq cucunarqenrituq; makuggnarquq-gguq. Qanerluni-llu mikluta angalkumek ilangqessunaicaaqniluta wangkuta. Tua-llu qanrraarluni tuaten qanellruuq waten, angalkumek-gguq ilangqerciqsaaqukut anerteqngaituq-gguq.

Tua-llu uitaluta angliriluta-llu ilangqertukut imum' Uuqerrulriim im' kinguqliirutii im' Ingamulria; tangellrungatan, tangellrungatan.

PAUGNARALRIA: Naamiki. Tangellrunrilngataqa.

QAPUGGLUK: Tauna tuani angalkuullruuq. Ak'anivkenani tuqullruuq. Qanellracetun tua-i taum apa'urlumta ak'anun anerteqellrunrituq. Ellii-w' tuunringuaryugpakaami angalkuurtellrungatuq.

I was in awe of what I saw; someone was going to become a shaman[12]

Benedict Tucker and Marie Meade, Emmonak, March 2011

BENEDICT TUCKER: Something I saw when I suddenly became aware of life there, let me tell a brief story about what I saw here at Cevv'artelleq. I wasn't too aware, but I would do things and do chores. When I suddenly became aware there, I was in awe of what I saw; someone was going to become a shaman, Kegginacngaq's, O'Malley's younger sibling.

Waten iillayullruunga; cunaw' una angalkuurteqatalria

Cikulraaciq Arnaq-llu, Imangaq, March 2011

CIKULRAACIQ: Tuani wani cellangartelqa tua-i, waten qanemcicuaqerlii wani Cevv'artellermi. Nallumalallruaqa tua-i ayuquciqa, amtallu tua-i waten catulua tua-i castengulua. Tuani cellangartellemni waten iillayullruunga; cunaw' una angalkuurteqatalria Kegginacngaam uum wani O'Malley-m kinguqlia tauna.

Then Leggleq came inside in the early morning. When he came inside, he told me that that evening after they take a fire bath, right after the fire bath, he would check on my condition, what was causing my condition. That's what he said, that he would check on my condition that evening.

Then right after a fire bath, when he told me to go over, I went over. Leggleq placed a *qasperek* [seal-gut rain garment] here and shook it. Those drumming, including Tekcengaq, Qasqanayuk, those ones were there since they were singers.

Not long after shaking it, he stopped, he stopped. When he stopped, he said to me that my condition, that my great sorrow has caused my condition. Since I tried to hold it in and not cry, that had caused my condition.

Then he already found the cause of my condition. That Leggleq really knew things. That person would save people. I never heard that that person did anything malicious at all. He just saved people.

And Father Llorenti also spoke directly to him. He told him going in front of him that he never heard anything [bad] about him, that he had only heard that he saved people. He said that when he dies he will go up to Heaven. That's what he told him in my presence.

Tua-i-llu tauna Leggleq unuakuarmi iterluni. Itrami pikilia ataku-gguq maqirraarcelluki, maqinerrami-gguq ayuquciqa-gguq paqciiqaa, camun, camun pilqa. Tuaten qanerluni, ayuquciqa paqciiqniluku ataku.

Tua-i-ll' maqinerrami agesqenganga aglua. Leggleq imna qasperegnek waten maavet ellilukek angalalluku. Ukut cauyalriit imkut Tekcengaq, Qasqanayuk, tamakut tamaa-i aturtengulaameng tamakut.

Ak'anun tua-i angalatevkenaku arulairtuq, arulairtuq. Arulairami pianga, ayuqucima-gguq tamatum-gguq iluteqerpallma pillinianga. Qiangnaqevkenii negingalua uitiima, tamatum-gguq pianga.

Tua-i-llu ak'a alaklua. Tauna tua-i nallunritqapigtuq Leggleq imna, nallunrituq. Yuk anirtutua taum yuum. Wiinga caniluku ik'im tungiinun niicuitellruaqa tauna caitqapik. Anirtuituluni taugaam yugnek.

Imum-llu Father Llorenti-m qanaatellrua takuakun. Qanrutellrua tua-i ciuqerranun piluni, elliin camek niigarcuitellruniluku caitqapik, anirtuilarniluku taugaam niitlarniluku. Tuqukan wani Qilagmun mayurciqniluku. Tuaten qanellruuq takumni.

I sang that quliraq to you. That has evidently brought you to a good place[157]

Atuuskemken tamatumek imumek quliramek. Egelrutluaqalliniaten tamatum

Eugene Pete and Lawrence Edmund, Anchorage, December 2011

Aliuq Paugnaralria-llu, Anchorage, December 2011

EUGENE PETE: He told me, in May, in April down at Nunallerpak, he told me that the next day he would bring me across Qip'ngayagak [River] over there, and he would tell me some sort of *quliraq* [legend, tale], and I didn't know those *qulirat* [legends] myself.

Then in the early morning before the sun came up, he brought me across to the wilderness there. On top of a patch of ground from which the snow had melted, holding a small piece of cloth, he spread that out on top of a patch of ground where the snow had melted like this.

After spreading it, he said to me, "Now sit there, facing the sunrise out there." I sat there like he told me to like this, facing the dawn like this. He was behind me.

ALIUQ: Tua-i tuaten pianga, May, April-aami Nunallerpagni camani, pianga unuaqu-gguq ikavet Qip'ngayagaam akianun ayaullua quliriciiqaanga-gguq camek imumek, wiinga-ll' qulirat tamakut nallukenka.

Tua-i-ll' unuakuarmi akerta pipailgan qeraullua yuilqurrarmun tuavet. Urunqim qainganun tulvaarrakuyuarmek tegumiarluni, tauna tua-i urunqim qainganun saggluku waten.

Sagqaarluku pianga, "Kitaki tuavet aqumi, qaugkut erenret cauluki." Aqumkilii tua-i pisqutaciatun waten, qaugkut erenret cauluki waten. Ellii-w' pama-i.

Then he said to me that he was going to tell me a *quliraq* now. "Now try hard to understand it, try to learn this *quliraq* that I'm telling." I agreed with him.

Then behind me, and he didn't sing but that one back there just talked. When he had reached a certain point, he blew some air at me. I could feel the air that he was blowing back there. He said to me that he would blow air at me four times, that the fourth would be the last time.

Then when he was about to blow air at me for the last time, he said to me that he was going to blow air at me for the last time now. Then after blowing air at me for the last time, he said to me, "Did you learn that one I just sang?" I said I had. And I didn't know what he had said. And I didn't understand that one talking back there. I said I had, "Yes, I learned it." [*laughter*]

LAWRENCE EDMUND: You lied to him?

EUGENE PETE: I didn't know what it was at all.

Then he said to me, "Now, one day as you are living, when something happens to you, if something should happen to your condition, sing that. But don't forget part of it when you do." Once again, I agreed that I would [*chuckles*] but I didn't know what it was, I didn't know what it was at all.

Then after blowing air at me for the last time, he said to me, "Go ahead and stand. I'm done with you." When he told me to stand, we returned together.

In my mind, I didn't believe that anything had happened to me, I didn't believe him. "I wonder what he wants to achieve by trying to heal me?"

Then I went to bed that night. I lay down facing the exit. I had a small bed made of wood like this. When I went to bed, I finally slept.

While I was sleeping, as I became aware, I started to feel wind on my ears. I wonder what I was doing, was I sleeping or was I actually not sleeping.

When I looked at my bed, I saw that I was hovering in the air. I was moving forward along with my bed. The wind would suddenly blow at my ears. After a while, I landed, and I jolted. I was wondering, "I wonder what's happening to me?" I was very amazed.

Then the next day, when I got up, I immediately went over, I went to see him. When I went inside I told him that last night, I was moving when I gained conciousness, and that my bed was hovering in the air. Leggleq was happy, "I'm go grateful. Yesterday, over there in the wilderness, I sang that

Tua-i-ll' pianga, waniwa-gguq quliramek piqataraanga. "Kitaki tarignaurluku cakneq pikiu, elitengnaqkiu man'a quliraq antelqa." Angerluku.

Tua-i-ll' pama-i, aturpek'nani-llu qanerturluni pamna. Qaillun tayim' pitariami cupaanga. Elpegnaqluni tua-i pama-i cupellra. Pikilia cetamarqunek-gguq cupciqaanga, uumi-gguq cetamiitni nangnermek piarkaugaanga.

Tua-i-llu nangnermek cupqataamia piuq, waniwa-gguq nangnermek cupqataraanga. Tua-i-llu nangnermek cupraarlua pianga, "Augna-qaa tua-i ava-i atulqa elitan-qaa?" Angraqa. Wiinga-w' tua-i camek piciilngua. Taringevkenaku-ll' pamna qanaalria. Angqilii, "Ii-i, elitaqa." [*ngel'artut*]

PAUGNARALRIA: Iqluluku-qaa?

ALIUQ: Tua-i cauciitqapiggluku wiinga.

Tua-i-ll' pikilia, "Kitaki, cam iliini yuunginanerpeni qaillun pikuvet ayuqucin man'a qaill' pikan atuqiu tamana. Iliinek taugaam katagiluku piyaqunaku." Tua-i-am angqilaku [*ngelaq'ertuq*] cauciilkeka tua-i wiinga, cauciitqapiggluku tua-i.

Tua-i-llu cupraarlua nangnermek pianga, "Tua-i nangerten. Taq'amken." Nangerrlua pisqenganga uterrlunuk maliklunuk.

Umyuaqa tua-i wiinga qaillun, qaillun-wa pillemnek ukveqeveknii, ukveqevkenaku. "Casqellua-kiq waniw' qaillukuarutkanga?"

Tua-i-ll' inarrlua atakuan. Uatmun caulua inarrlua. Waten inglerrangqerrlua equggarmek waten. Inarcama tayim' qavalliunga nutaan.

Maaten imna qavarnginanemni, elpengyarturtua ciutegka imumek anuqliurlutek. Qaill' pillrusia, qavallilrianga-llu-w' wall'u-q' qavanricaaqua.

Maaten-am acika tangrraqa qerratallinilua. Inglertuumarma tua-i ciutmun eglerrlua. Ciutegka anuqem tekitaqlukek. Piqerluni tus'artua, qatngiarrlua-ll' wiinga. Umyuarteqkilii, "Qaillun tanem pilarcia?" Iillayuglua tua-i cakneq.

Tua-i-llu unuakuan tupiima tua-i egmiinaq aglua, ullagluku. Itrama piaqa unuk wani elpengnilua eglerrlua, acika-llu qerratallruniluku. Quyauq Leggleq. "Quyanarpiit-llu. Akwaugaq-am ikani yuilqumi atuuskemken tamatumek imumek quliramek. Egelrutluaqalliniaten tamatum."

quliraq to you. That has evidently brought you to a good place."

He wasn't lying when he told me that. Somehow, when I woke, I saw that I felt extremely good. I didn't feel heavy. I felt very good.

Iqluvkenani tua-i qanrullua tamatumek tua-i. Qaillun tua-i, maaten-am tupagtua ellaka tuaten assirpak. Imutun uqamairullua pivkenii. Assiqapiggluni tua-i cakneq ellaka.

Then Leggleq said to me, "That mink has evidently revealed what is in your future"[15]

Eugene Pete, Anchorage, December 2011

EUGENE PETE: Then when fall came, I hunted. I accompanied Lurtuli from Nunaqerraq and Itegmialria, the father of Cowboy; accommpanying those two, I left, carrying seven wooden mink traps. And that was the first time I traveled there, to the place where they normally hunted around Manumik.

Then when I set them, I set all of my *taluyaruat* [conical wooden mink traps]. When they went to check their traps, I accompanied them and left again. Then after clearing my *taluyaruat*, I would bring them up, but there would be nothing inside them. These seven caught nothing.

I was thinking, "I will take them out the next time if they don't catch." The next time, they waited for Saturday, and then I accompanied them and left. I opened them, but there was nothing inside [the traps].

I placed them in my sled and brought them home. Since I knew the sloughs around Nunaqerraq, I was thinking to set them there. I brought them there in one day.

Across from Nunaqerraq, just as I emerged, I came upon a small stream between lakes, a slough without ice. And I saw that a mink had been walking around in the area. I placed [my traps] underwater there, I set them.

Again, after a while, waiting until Saturday, I checked them. I checked those that were in the small *akuluraq* [channel connecting lakes] first. After cleaning that, I brought them up, and there was a mink. Its body [fur] was this color, it was yellow. Its small fur was about this length. And its other eye was popped, and it had no teeth at all, and its tail was cut. It was an extremely old mink. It was extremely old, and its body [fur] was yellow like this. A trading post wouldn't buy it looking like that.

Tua-i-llu Legglem pianga, "Imarmiutaam taum ciunerkan apertullinia"

Aliuq, Anchorage, December 2011

ALIUQ: Tua-i-llu uksuaran pissurlua. Imna Lurtuli maliggluku Nunaqerramek imna-llu Itegmialria Cowboy-am im' atii; maligglukek taukuk ayaglua taluyaruanek waten *seven*-aanek ucilua. Tamaavet-llu ayagpaaluglua pissurlallragnun tamaavet Manumiim avatiinun.

Tua-i-ll' civciama tamalkuita tua-i taukut civvluki wii taluyaruanka. Takuingagnek maligglukek ataam ayaglua. Tua-i-am taluyaruanka tamakut carrirraarluki mayurcaaqnaunka tayima pitaunateng. Cainarluteng ukut *seven*-at.

Umyuarteqlua, "Uumiku yuuciqanka pitenrilkata." Tua-i-am uumikuan Maqinerteqerlutek uitaqerlutek, tua-i-am maligglukek ayaglua. Tua-i-am ikircaaqanka tayima pitaunateng.

Ekluki ikamramnun ekluki ut'rulluki. Maani Nunaqerram avatiini kuicuaraat nallunrilamki tamaani tamaavet umyuartequlluki tamaavet civvnaluki. Erniqerlua ayaulluki tamaavet.

Nunaqerram akiani qakvaqerlua akulurarrarmek uumek tekitua kuicuarmek cikuunani. Man'a-wa avatiini maa-i imarmiutaq man'a pektelliniluni. Tua-i tuavet akurrluki, civvluki.

Tua-i-am caqerluku, maqinerteqerluki tua-i takuluki. Taukut ciumek akulurarrarmi uitalriit takuluki. Carrirraarluku tauna mayurtanka imarmiutar una. Waten qainga ayuqluni, *yellow*-arluni. Melqucuaraa-w' qaill' taktaurluni. Iingan-llu inglua qagrumaluni, keggutaunani-ll' caitqapik, pamyua-ll' kepumaluni. Ak'allaq'apik imarmiutaq. Ak'allaqapik tua-i cakneq, waten *yellow*-arluni qainga. Qaillun laavkaam kiputarkauvkenaku tuaten ayuqluku.

I was considering just discarding it there and leaving it, but I decided to put it in my sled. And it was the only thing I caught. The other [traps] didn't catch any at all. It was extremely old.

Then I went to Leggleq the next day. I told him that I had hunted all fall, using wooden mink traps, but that I only caught that very old one.

Gee, there were actually many wooden mink traps surrounding that place, and that one evidently didn't enter those wooden mink traps, wanting me to catch it.

I told Leggleq about that one. I told him that I caught a very old mink. Then Leggleq said to me, "That mink has evidently revealed what is in your future. You will become like it." That's what he told me.

These days, sometimes I recall it. Leggleq had truthfully spoke of my future, he knew what was in my future. Amazing! And although I wanted to believe him, I just let him be. That one really knew what a person's situation would be. And he didn't lie at all.

The next year, down at Amigtuli, along the river of Ingrill'er, I hunted. I finally was catching then. I paddled by kayak, during Christmas time, I was paddling by kayak.

Amigtuli down there never froze in the past down to its mouth. It used to have a strong current in the past. Animals would go down to it, including mink, otter, foxes, various things. The person who stayed there had a good place, he had a good hunting place.

Amazing! Sometimes I think about Leggleq. He wasn't lying at all when he told me things. That person evidently knew exactly what was in a person's future.

And a priest, Father Llorenti, spoke to that person in front of me. He said these other shamans around who were just fighting among themselves, engaging in various activities, he said those shamans were very bad people. He said they are devils.

Then I didn't just abandon that mink, but skinned it. I skinned it. And I turned it inside out [to its fur side] and hung it inside the home. And as it was hanging, it disappeared. I searched for it, I did whatever I could, but didn't find it. It was extremely old! It had become extremely weak and evidently went inside that wooden mink trap.

Nalirrugucaaqluku tauna tamaavet-llu eggluku unitnaluku, ikamramnun eketngurtaqa. Kiingan-llu tua-i pitaqluku. Taukut-am ilait pitevkenateng tayim' caitqapik. Ak'allapiaq tua-i cakneq.

Tua-i-llu tauna unuakuan Leggleq ullagluku. Piaqa wani uksuarpak pissuryaaqnilua taluyaruanek taumek taugaam ak'allapiamek pitnilua.

Aling, ik'ikika-wa taluyaruaq amllelria tamaani avatiini, taluyaruanun-llu tamakunun ekluni piqayuitelliuq tauna, wangnun cunaw' pisqelluni.

Taumek qanruskilaku Leggleq. Piaqa imarmiutarrnilua tua-i ak'allapiamek cakneq. Tua-i-llu Legellrem pianga, "Imarmiutaam taum ciunerkan apertullinia. Elliitun ellirciquten." Tuaten taum qanruskilia-am tuaten.

Maa-i caaqama neq'aklarqa. Iqluvkenani ciunerkamnek tamatumek qanerlallrulliniuq Leggleq, ciunerkaqa nalluvkenaku. Iicill'er. Ukveksungramku-llu tua-i uitaskeka. Nallunritpigtellinia yuum ayuqucirkaa taum. Iqlunritqapiggluni-llu tua-i.

Allrakuani unani Amigtulimi, Ingrillraam im' kuigani pissurlua. Nutaan tua-i pitaqlua. Anguarlua qayakun, Christmas-aam nalliini anguarlua qayakun.

Cikuyuitellrua un'a Amigtuli cakmavet paiminun. Carvanqellruuq cakneq. Pitarkat kanarvikluku, imarmiutaat, cenkaat, kaviaret, cat. Nunakegcillruuq imna nayurtii, pissurvikegcillruuq.

Iicill'er! Umyuaqellarqa caaqama Leggleq. Iqlunritqapigglua qanrutellruanga. Yuum ciunerkaa nallunritqapigtellinia taum yuum.

Agayulirtem-ll' takumni qanaatellrua tauna, Father Llorenti-m. Imkut-gguq taugken makut angalkut allat ellmeggnun caumakulluteng pilriit, qaillun piluteng piaqluteng, tamakut-gguq tamaa-i assiitqapialriit yuut angalkut tamakut. Tuunrangayaugut-gguq tamakut.

Tua-i-ll' tauna cakaarpek'naku nillarluku tauna imarmiutaq. Nillaniluku nillarluku. Ullell'uku-llu agarrluku enem iluanun. Agangqainanermini-ll' tayim' tamarluni. Tua-i yuaryaaqluku, cayaaqluku, nalaqevkenaku tayima. Ak'allapiaq tua-i cakneq! Cirlaurteqap'iggluni tua-i taluyaruanun tuavet ekliuq.

Teggalguq filled [the kayak] with ice, and he tethered them to his eyes[16]

Eugene Pete, Lawrence Edmund, and Alice Rearden, Anchorage, December 2011

EUGENE PETE: Then this person, you've heard of that shaman, the father of this family, I think Teggalquq was Qasqanayuk's father. He's well known and heard of. The children of that shaman, I'm not sure why that happens to those shamans, [his children] died.

And I don't think you saw Angussaagta's older sister when she was alive.

LAWRENCE EDMUND: I don't know her.

EUGENE PETE: Yes, you don't know that person.

Then they say Teggalquq there, when they went to attend a Messenger Feast over at Kapuutelleq, they say he filled a kayak with ice. He used two strips of hide as a harness. He inserted the two strips of hide onto his eyes, and they say he continually turned his head from side to side pulling that kayak, having someone carry him in a sled to meet the guests [attending the Messenger Feast]. Gee, that was probably very heavy. It's because nothing was impossible for Teggalquq. And he would travel to the moon.

ALICE REARDEN: What did he do to that kayak?

LAWRENCE EDMUND: He filled it with ice and he tethered [the strips of hide] to his eyes. And that kayak, he lifted it having his eyes pull the whole thing.

EUGENE PETE: After inserting the two skin strips on the kayak, then he inserted them inside his eyes.

And he inserted that strip of hide inside his eyes. He had them bring him as a passenger and moved his head from side to side as he pulled that kayak.

ALICE REARDEN: Along the water?

EUGENE PETE: Yes, although it was extremely heavy.

That great shaman evidently asked Kencialnguq to doctor his one daughter while she was in the womb so that she could live, they say, because he doesn't lie when it came to exercising shaman powers.

Yes, he said that he would. And Teggalquq evidently told that shaman that when they were done, the next year he would repay him. Teggalquq said to him that if he wanted to be good at something, if he wanted to be good at catching animals, or if he wanted to live, he would repay him with some-

Teggalqum [qayaq] cikumek imirluku, iigminun-llu petuglukek

Aliuq, Paugnaralria, Cucuaq-llu, Anchorage, December 2011

ALIUQ: Tua-llu una, angalkur' im' niitlaqen, ukut atiit, Qasqanayuum ataklarngataa tauna Teggalquq. Niiskengaulalria tauna. Taum angalkum irniari, tuatnalartat-wa tamakut angalkut caameng, tuquluteng.

Imna-ll' tua-i angunricugnarqan Angussaagtem alqaa.

PAUGNARALRIA: Nalluaqa.

ALIUQ: Ii-i, nalluan tauna.

Tua-i-ll' imna-gguq taun' Teggalquq, yaani Kapuutellermi curukallratni-gguq, qayaq-gguq imirluku cikunek. Tapengyiignek-am uskurirluku. Tapengyiik iigminun kapullukek, tamana-gguq qayaq takuyaqtaarulluku ucikevkarluni paiqaucelluni. Aling uqamaicaaquq ataki tamana. Caprilami tauna, Teggalquq tauna. Iralumun-llu ayagaqluni.

CUCUAQ: Qaillun tauna qayaq piagu?

PAUGNARALRIA: Aa, cikumek imirluku, iigminun-llu petuglukek, iigminun. Tamana-ll' qayaq kevegluku iigminun atavkarluku tamalkuan.

ALIUQ: Tapengyak qayamun kapuqaarlukek iigminun-llu kapullukek.

Iigminun-llu kapulluku tapengyak tamana. Ucikevkarluni ayaucelluni, qayaq tamana takuyartaarutaqluku.

CUCUAQ: Merkun-qaa?

ALIUQ: Ii-i, uqamaicaaqellria cakneq.

Tauna-am tuani Kencialnguq tauna angalkurpiim taum iliiravikelliniluku panini tauna atauciq yungcaqaasqelluku, iqluyuilan-gguq tuunraryaramek.

Ii-i, anglliniluni, piciqaa-gguq. Angalkuum-llu taum pilliniluku Teggalqum waniwa qaqiyuskunek allraku nunulirciqniluku. Taum Teggalqum pillia, cayukan, picuyukan qang'a-ll' anerteqsukan piyullranek nunulirciqniluku. Tuaten-gguq taum qanrulluku.

thing that he desired. They say that's what he told him.

Then from Anagciq, he accompanied others to Kapuutelleq. And when they were about to leave, when the guests going to a village to attend a Messenger Feast left, Kencialnguq stayed behind.

That [Teggalquq] evidently told him he wanted to pay him with whatever he desired. After a while, Kencialnguq told him that he desired to do that thing where he fills the kayak with ice and inserts [the harnesses] into his eyes.

They say [Teggalquq] told him that that's nothing, that it's only something that people are awed by. He told him it won't be used for a good purpose. He was so insistent [chuckles]. That's what he desired to do. [Teggalquq] thought little of it, saying that it doesn't have a good purpose.

Since he was so insistent, he taught him how to carry that out, for a story he would tell.

Then he evidently admonished him, "Okay now, when you carry it out, don't leave anything out when you carry it out. If you leave anything out, you will put yourself through hardship, you will put yourself through hardship." They say he agreed.

Then they say they went to Anagciq to attend a Messenger Feast. Just like [Teggalquq] had done, he filled that kayak with pieces of ice. And after inserting the two pieces of hide [into the kayak], he inserted them into his eyes and had them bring him to meet those attending the Messenger Feast as they approached.

They say he entered inside the *qasgiq*. [chuckles] [The other harness] couldn't come out. He suddenly cried. [laughter] They say he was sobbing and making noises, and he'd cry.

Then Teggalquq who owned that ability said to him, "My goodness, I thought I instructed you not to leave out part of it when you carry it out. You left something out when you carried it out." He'd cry out not long after. [laughter]

Since that was [Teggalquq's] ability, he removed that [harness] for him. [laughs] The person who it belonged to [Teggalquq] chided him, that he had warned him beforehand. [laughs]

Teggalquq who it belonged to removed it. Since it was his ability, he removed it. But the one using it couldn't remove it. [chuckles]

Tua-ll' Anagcimek maligutliniluni Kapuutellermun. Tua-ll' ayakataata curukat ayiita un'garrluni tauna Kencialnguq tauna.

Taum wani pillia piyullranek nunuliryugluku. Tua-i-ll' uitaqerluni taum Kencialnguum pillia taun', imna-gguq taugaam tuaten imna qayamek cikumek imirluku iigminun kapulluku tamana-gguq cucuksaaqaa.

Piyaaqaa-gguq cakaunritniluku tamana, ucurnaqnginarniluku taugaam kiingan. Camun aturngaitniluku. Arenqialaku-gguq taqiirluni [ngelaq'ertuq]. Tua-i-am piyugluku tamana, cucukluku. Cakaunrilleksaaqluku, cakaunrituq-gguq.

Arenqialan tua-i taqiiran tua-i tamatumek tua-i elicalliniluku, quli'irkaanek tamatumek.

Tua-i-ll' inerqullia, "Kitaki atuquvgu iliinek katagiluku aturyaqunaku. Katagikuvgu elpenek makugciiquten, elpenek makugtarkauguten." Angraluni-gguq tua-i.

Tua-i-llu-gguq Anagcimun curukarluteng. Tua-i elliitun tua-i qayaq tamana cikunek imirluku. Tapengyiik-llu kapuqaarlukek iigminun-llu kapullukek ayaucetliuq paiqaucelluni curukanun.

Tua-i iteryaaqluni-gguq qasgimun. [ngelaq'ertuq] Aipaa-gguq tauna pisciiganani, anesciiganani. Qalrillaga[luni]. [ngel'artut] Qalrillagaluni-gguq tuaten aarpagaluni, qiagaqluni.

Tua-i-ll' taum yullran, Teggalqum taum pillia, "Aling alerqullruamken-ggem tanem ilii katagluku pisqevkenaku. Katagiluku atullrullinian." Ak'anun-gguq tua-i pilanrituq, qalrillagnaurtuq. [ngel'artut]

Tua-i elliin pikngamiu aug'aritelliniluku tua-i taumek. [ngel'artuq] Arivellia tua-i taum yuan, inerqullruyaaqniluku. [ngel'artuq]

Elliin-wa taum Teggalqum yuan tauna aug'allrua. Elliin-wa pikngamiu tua-i aug'arrluku. Taum taugaam aturtiin aug'arciiganaku. [ngelaq'ertuq]

Requesting an abundance of wood through masked dancing[17]

Eugene Pete, Lawrence Edmund, and Alice Rearden, Anchorage, December 2011

ALICE REARDEN: What about that *quuguarluni* [act of requesting an abundance of wood through masked dancing] that you briefly mentioned? One who requested an abundance of wood through masked dancing.

EUGENE PETE: Requesting an abundance of wood through masked dancing?

ALICE REARDEN: Yes, you mentioned it earlier.

EUGENE PETE: Teggalquq, or rather Paqricilleq. You didn't see him. I saw him for three years. And he was blind. When he requested an abundance of wood through masked dancing, there was a large amount of wood. His lyrics stated that he wanted to smell the odor of spruce pitch.

Indeed those logs would smell of spruce pitch. Amazing! That one used to authentically [practice his shaman powers].

And when he would *neqnguarluni* [request an abundance of fish through masked dancing] also, he would let the Qip'ngayak River have a great abundance of fish.

LAWRENCE EDMUND: My goodness, how amazing those ones are.

EUGENE PETE: That one would do it authentically.

ALICE REARDEN: Did you watch him, did you watch him when he did that?

EUGENE PETE: I used to see him, I used to see that elderly man. And eventually, at the *qasgiq*, that elderly man used to stay inside the *qasgiq*. He had a bird-skin parka.

He had a bird parka. When they were about to take a fire bath, they would take him outside. I think you used to see Akiuk.

LAWRENCE EDMUND: I probably did, but I probably didn't know who he was.

EUGENE PETE: That Akiuk liked to talk, since he drank alcohol a lot. That person didn't lack anything when he lived. He had two inboard-engine boats.

When they went to go and attend a Messenger Feast over to Kapuutelleq, that elderly man was sitting along the corner of the *qasgiq* facing the exit wearing his parka.

Akiuk arrived intoxicated accompanying those who had gone to attend the Messenger Feast.

Quuguaq

Aliuq, Paugnaralria, Cucuaq-llu, Anchorage, December 2011

CUCUAQ: Augna-mi qanrutkeqallren quuguarluni? Quugualleq.

ALIUQ: Quuguaq?

CUCUAQ: Ii-i, watua apqallruan.

ALIUQ: Teggalquq, aren Paqricilleq. Tangellrunrilken-wa. Wiinga tangellruaqa allrakuni pingayuni tangvallruaqa. Cikmirluni-llu. Quuguallermini-am tuani palartenrilnguq qugmek. Apallungqerrluni, angeryugmek narumaayugluni.

Ilumun tua-i tamakut equut angeryugmek tuaten tepsaqnaurtut. Iicill'er! Pipigtaarlallruuq tauna.

Neqnguaraqami cali palartevkenaku Qip'ngayak neq'lircetaqluku.

PAUGNARALRIA: Ik'iki, caperrnaqlarpaa-ll' tamakuni.

ALIUQ: Pipigcaurlartuq tauna.

CUCUAQ: Tangvallruan-qaa, tangvallruan-qaa tuaten pillrani?

ALIUQ: Tangerrlallruaqa, tangerrlallruaqa angukara'urluq. Kiituani qasgimek, qasgimi uitauralartuq taun' angukaraq. Yaqulegnek atkungqerrluni.

Yaqulegnek. Maqiqata'arqata anutaqluku. Akiug' im' tangerrlallrungatan.

PAUGNARALRIA: Piyaaqellrullikeka-w', kituuciitellrullikeka tayima.

ALIUQ: Tauna tuan' Akiuk qaneryulriaruuq yuk, melguami-llu. Waten cameg' nuuqitevkenani eglertuq tauna yuk tauna. Malruk tuqtuk.

Curukallratni-ll'-am tuani amavet Kapuutellermun, tauna-am angukara'urluq qasgimi kangiraani uatmun aqumgauraurlulria taukunek atkuminek aturluni.

Tua-i-am taun' taangiqu'urluni tekilluni taun' Akiuk curukat-wa maliggluki. Inglernun-am

When he got up on top of the bed, he said to him, "*Ii-ii!* Tupaqriciller, the bad shaman, wearing a squirrel parka!" [*chuckles*] That person didn't like Akiuk because of his father, because he would bother his father.

LAWRENCE EDMUND: Those many things you said are also true, those things you saw; they are good, they are good. I didn't catch people doing those things, and I didn't see those shamans, but I'd hear about them. I didn't see them.

ugcami pia, "Ii-ii! Tupaqriciller, angalkull'er, qanganaat-wa atkui!" [*ngelaq'ertuq*] Taum imum' keneksuilkii taun' Akiuk, taumeg' ataminek, pilaaku-wa atani tauna.

PAUGNARALRIA: Ak'akika augkut qanelten augkut piciuluteng-llu, tamakut tangelten; tua-i assirtut, assirtut. Tamakunun wii angutellrunritua tuaten pilrianun, tamakut-llu angalkut tangeqsaunaki taugaam niitaqluki taugaam. Tangeqsaunaki.

They say that one that Leggleq used to start off with up there was an offering[18]

Eugene Pete, Lawrence Edmund, Denis Shelden and Alice Rearden, Anchorage, December 2011

ALICE REARDEN: I was curious about that *quugualria* [one who requested the abundance of wood through masked dancing], and how exactly they used to do that.

LAWRENCE EDMUND: When those ones would sing, they used to carry that out, *agayuliluteng* [dancing with masks] as they say, dancing with arm movements like this. When they'd do that, when they would dance with masks, they would request things.

When they'd construct *agayut* [masks to request things], and when they'd also request an abundance of wood, *quuguarluteng*, they would request them, and they'd obtain them.

EUGENE PETE: They obtained some of them.

LAWRENCE EDMUND: Yes.

EUGENE PETE: Some of them, that Leggleq, in my presence up at Amigtuli, since he constantly constructed *agayut*, he constructed an *agayuq*.

There was a ball like this up there that was about this wide. It had a twine harness that extended to the edge of the *qasgiq*, and there was someone who watched over the end of the twine.

Then there were two polar bears situated across from one another curled up. They were both polar bears sleeping.

Then as they were sleeping, that ball up there fell down. When it landed on the floor boards, it landed with a loud thud down there! Those two who were curled up suddenly got up. They circled following the universe, walking, and they were snarling. Those masks looked like real polar bears.

Mike's grandfather, Mike Andrews's grandfather, I didn't see him, but his father was around

---

Aviukarqutnguuq-gguq pikna im' ayagniuteklallra Legellrem

Aliuq, Paugnaralria, Kituralria Cucuaq-llu, Anchorage, December 2011

CUCUAQ: Taumek quugualriamek paqnayuglua qaillun piqapiarluteng pilauciitnek.

PAUGNARALRIA: Tamakut aturaqameng waten, tamana pilallruat, agayuliluteng-gguq, yagiraluteng waten. Tuatnaaqameng, agayuliaqameng-wa tuaten kaigaluteng canek pilalriit.

Agayuliaqameng-wa, canek, quuguarqameng-llu kaigaluteng, unakluki taugken.

ALIUQ: Ilait unaklaqait.

PAUGNARALRIA: Ii-i.

ALIUQ: Ilait tua-i, imna tua-i Leggleq takumni taun' Amigtulimi agayulilgulaami, agayuliluni.

Pikani angqaq waten, waten ellegtaluni. Pelacinagmek taun' uskurarluni maavet qasgim mengliinun, nayurtengqerrluni tauna pelaciniim iqua.

Ukuk-wa malruk akiqliqlutek ungelralriik nanuak. Nanuarulutek tamarmek qavarlutek.

Tua-i-ll' qavaarainanermegni, pikna imna angqaq iggluni. Nacitnun tuc'ami migpak kanavet! Taukuk mak'arrlutek imkuk ungelrallrek. Ella maliggluku uivlutek, piyualutek, uirralutek-llu. Tua-i nanuaqapiik tua-i kegginaquk.

Imna tua-i Mike-am apa'urlua, Mike Andrews-am apa'urlua, wii angunritaqa, atii

and I saw him. He would cry when he was moved by something. He evidently cried during that time, and he said, "They are going to do something great!" Then he let his voice out, and he cried without any restraint, letting out his feelings of being moved by what he saw. That's what he did.

That thing up there was evidently an offering, *aviukarqun*. The one who was taking care of it untied it and let if fall.

They say that one that Leggleq used to start off with up there was an offering.

ALICE REARDEN: What do you mean it was an *aviukarqun* [offering]?

DENIS SHELDEN: It's some kind of an offering.

ALICE REARDEN: That ball?

DENIS SHELDEN: To ask for certain things.

LAWRENCE EDMUND: Do you know what *aviukartelleq* [giving an offering] is?

ALICE REARDEN: Yes. But he said that some ball that fell was an offering.

LAWRENCE EDMUND: Yes.

EUGENE PETE: You know how when they get a small bowl, they just take a pinch and give an offering. That thing that is hanging is one of those when it lands down there. They say it is a large amount. And the small contents of this, when a person sprinkles it, they say it lands as a large amount down there.

taugaam angullruaqa. Ucuryugaqami qialartuq. Tua-i-am tuani qiallinilria, qanerluni-llu, "Pikayakatartut!" Tua-i-ll' erinani anlluku, cap'araunani tua-i qialuni, ucuryullni anqelluku. Tuaten.

Cunaw' taun' imna pikna aviukarqun. Taum aulukestiin angilluku igcelluku.

Aviukarqutnguuq-gguq pikna im' ayagniuteklallra Legellrem.

CUCUAQ: Qaillun-kiq-tanem aviukarqutnguluni?

KITURALRIA: *It's some kind of an offering.*

CUCUAQ: Tauna angqaq?

KITURALRIA: *To ask for certain things.*

PAUGNARALRIA: Aviukartelleq nallunritan?

CUCUAQ: Ii-i. Taugaam tauna ca angqaq igtelleq tauna aviukarqutnguluni-gguq.

PAUGNARALRIA: Ii-i.

ALIUQ: Iciw' waten qantarrarmek-llu piaqameng pupsugluku aviukarqellalriit. Tua-i tamakuciuguq taun' agalira tut'aqami kanavet. Amllerrluni-gguq. Uum-llu imarraa kaimaqamiu yuum amllerrluni-gguq tutlartuq camavet.

He just draped [the seal-gut parka] over himself, and just shook it[19]

Eugene Pete, Lawrence Edmund, Denis Shelden, and Alice Rearden, Anchorage, December 2011

ALICE REARDEN: When you talked about the shaman earlier, you said he did something to the seal-gut rain garment, what do they do exactly, do they put them on?

EUGENE PETE: He would shake them like this.

ALICE REARDEN: Oh, he didn't put them on?

EUGENE PETE: Yes, he didn't put them on. He just draped them over himself, and just shook them.

He just made this movement following the drumbeats.

When he would practice his shaman powers, he was amazing to see, and those floor boards would start to creak loudly, since he was heavy.

DENIS SHELDEN: Put the arms over the arms and just move it back and forth, so it's probably not really on.

Naliglukek, angalallukek taugaam

Aliuq, Paugnaralria, Kituralria, Cucuaq-llu, Anchorage, December 2011

CUCUAQ: Augna watua angalkuq qanrutkellerpegu qasperek qaillun pinilukek, qiallun piqapiaralartat, all'ukek?

ALIUQ: Angalallukek waten pilarak.

CUCUAQ: Oh, at'evkenakek-qaa?

ALIUQ: Ii-i, at'evkenakek. Naliglukek, angalallukek taugaam.

Cauyat taugaam maliggluki elliurluni.

Ucurnaqlartuq tuunriaqami, nacitet-llu tuar kekingerpak tamakut, uqamailami-w'.

KITURALRIA: *Put the arms over the arms and just move it back and forth, so it's probably not really on.*

ALICE REARDEN: Oh. Did he put on the hood of the *qaspeq*?

EUGENE PETE: He didn't put it on, but just draped it over himself.

LAWRENCE EDMUND: Eugene has many stories, since he is old.

CUCUAQ: Oh. Nacaa-qaa qasperem all'uku?

ALIUQ: At'evkenaku nalikutaqerluku taugaam.

PAUGNARALRIA: Qanemcilirtuq Eugene-aq, ak'allaurcami-w'.

I heard my father say that a shaman put a marking on it by smearing [the king salmon] with charcoal to distinguish it[20]

Lawrence Edmund, Denis Shelden, and Alice Rearden, Anchorage, December 2011

ALICE REARDEN: Are the first king salmon to arrive larger, or smaller, or what?

LAWRENCE EDMUND: Sometimes there are small ones among them. Those small ones, their roe is very small. Maybe those came from a hatchery in Canada, those that are small. But these very large ones, their roe is large. I think the ones that will eventually go to streams farther downriver, their roe is large. But those that have small [roe], I think they will eventually head far upriver.

DENIS SHELDEN: And some of those king salmon with green backs, there are many of those.

LAWRENCE EDMUND: And sometimes, long ago, there were king salmon that had a dark mark [spot] here [under their nose?]. When I went to Flat Island [at the south mouth of the Yukon River] to go fishing one time, when my father was in good health and also Joe Smith, I heard them say, I heard my father say that a shaman marked those. He said they are from the north. And [a shaman] put a marking on it by smearing it with charcoal to distinguish it; he said that's what those are. He said sometimes when those are among [the run of king salmon] there are many salmon.

ALICE REARDEN: Oh. They have a small black marking on them?

LAWRENCE EDMUND: They have a small dark marking here. He said those are the ones that a person put a marking on [to distinguish them].

Underneath, along this part of it.

ALICE REARDEN: So that's what they're like. Some people say that some of them have dark noses.

Ataka-w' qanerluni angalkum-gguq nallunailkucirluku-llu kangiplugmek mingugluku

Paugnaralria, Kituralria, Cucuaq-llu, Anchorage, December 2011

CUCUAQ: Ciuqliit-qaa taryaqviit tut'ellriit angenrulartut, wall' mikenruluteng?

PAUGNARALRIA: Iliini atam mikellrianek avungqerrlartut. Augkut mikyaalriit imlaugit mikqapiggluteng cakneq. Tamaa-i tamakut *hatchery*-mek pillilriit Canada-mek, tamakuyagaat mikluteng. Makut taugken angelriarpiit imlaugit angluteng. Tua-i carvanun tamakut uaqvanun piarkat imlaugit anglarngatut. Tamakuyagaat taugken mikellrianek pilget qavavet kiaqvanun piarkaularngatut.

KITURALRIA: Imkut-llu-wa ilait taryaqviit *with green backs*, tamakut amllerrlartut.

PAUGNARALRIA: Iliikun-llu ak'a 'gguun taryaqviit tungulriamek pingqerraqluteng. Cami-im' maani Flat Island-aami neqsuryallemni ata'urluqa cavailgan Joe Smith-aq-llu qanerlukek niitellruagka, ataka-w' qanerluni angalkum-gguq nallunailkucillrui tamakut. Negertaugut-gguq. Nallunailkucirluku-llu kangiplugmek minguguluku; tamakuugut-gguq. Caaqameng tamakut avuugaqata-gguq amllerrlartut neqet.

CUCUAQ: Oh. Tungulriarrarluteng?

PAUGNARALRIA: Tungulriarrarluteng 'gguun. Tamakut-gguq tua-i nallunailkucillri taum.

Aciakun, makucimikun.

CUCUAQ: Cunawa. Ilait-llu qanlalriit canek tungulrianek qengangqeniluki ilait.

They say one day Teggalquq flew, going to the moon[21]

Eugene Pete, Lawrence Edmund, and Alice Rearden, Anchorage, December 2011

EUGENE PETE: From somewhere around the village of Scammon Bay, he'd evidently go to St. Michael and arrive the next day.

LAWRENCE EDMUND: St. Michael is actually far away.

EUGENE PETE: They suspected that he flew.

Yes. He actually had two dogs, but he would fly with his two dogs. [*laughter*]

They say one day Teggalquq flew, going to the moon. They say he came upon a person up on the moon, a person from the north. That person evidently could fly.

They returned at night. They say his northern counterpart told him to run with him. Teggalquq was ahead. There was a full moon.

They went down. As he was going down, he looked at the person behind him, he looked at his shadow, and behind him, he was running holding up his weapon at him, his walking stick.

They say Teggalquq put on his cloak. Although he hit him, it wouldn't go inside his body.

They say he hit him twice, but that weapon didn't enter. Amazing!

They say when he reached the area out there, when he reached home, his northern counterpart told that he came upon a person, that he evidently wasn't human, that he was a rock.

And one day when he went to St. Michael, he ran into that person at St. Michael at the store. Teggalquq said to him, "You there, I think I saw you up on the moon." He said yes he had. They recognized one another.

They say when Teggalquq would fly, he would leave with a bearded-seal skin cloaking his body, having them tie him up inside a bearded-seal [skin].

It's because some of those shamans were amazing, because they did amazing things.

Caqerluni-gguq teng'uq iralurrluni taun' Teggalquq

Aliuq, Paugnaralria, Cucuaq-llu, Anchorage, December 2011

ALIUQ: Marayaarmiut natiitnek tamaaken Tacirtelalliniuq unuaquan-llu tekilluni.

PAUGNARALRIA: Yaaqsigyaaquq Taciq.

ALIUQ: Tengaurluku piyukluku pilaraat.

Ii-i. Malrugnek qimugtengqerrlaryaaquq, taugaam qimugtegni-ll' taukuk tengaurutaqlukek. [*ngel'artut*]

Caqerluni-gguq teng'uq iralurrluni taun' Teggalquq. Pakmani-gguq iralumi nall'arkengluni yugmek qagkumiumek. Tengtumilliniluni tauna, yuk tauna.

Atakumi utertelliuk. Taum-gguq tua-i negeqlian pillia aqvaquucugluku. Ellii-gguq Teggalquq taun' ciuqliuluni. Iralirluni-gguq.

Atrarlutek. Atrainanermini-gguq kinguqlini tauna tangrraa, tarenraakun tangerrluku, pamaggun caskuminek, ayaruminek uqliusngaluku, aqvaqulria.

Taum-gguq tua-i Teggalqum taum amini taman' ataa. Narulkangraani pulangaunani qainganun.

Malrurqugnek-gguq narulkaryaaqaa, it'yuunani taman' caskuq. Iicill'er!

Qakmavet-gguq tekicami kingunicami qanemciluni tauna negeqlia tauna, yugmek nall'arkengyaaqniluni, yuunritliniuq-gguq, teggalqurrulliniuq-gguq.

Tacirtellermini-ll' cam iliini nall'artelliniluku tauna Tacimi laavkaami. Pillia taum Teggalqum, "Usuuq tuarpiaq pakmani iralumi tangellrukemken." Aa-gguq. Elitaqullutek.

Teng'aqami-gguq taun' Teggalquq maklagmek amilirluni ayaglartuq, naqirqutevkarluni maklagmun.

Angalkut-wa tamakut caperrnaqngameng ilait, caperrnaungameng.

They say Qakurtaq would fly across the Alarneq River[22]

Lawrence Edmund, Anchorage, December 2011

LAWRENCE EDMUND: Qakurtaq also, Qakurtaq. Qakurtaq, they said, did amazing things.

My father said that he would help him when he would exercise his shaman powers because he would ask him to be his helper. He also used to tell stories about him.

These two, the late Suqutall'er and the father of the late husband of Panigkaq, what did they call him again? They say those two made him into a shaman, Suqutall'er and I forgot what they call the other. I used to see him.

They say when they learned [that he was a shaman], they would tie him up. Before the Alarneq River became wide, they would leave him across the Alarneq River after tying him up, bringing his drum with him. They say he would fly across the Alarneq River. They say he only got faster.

They say one day, my late grandmother, they had a tent down below the *qasgiq*, she said she would hear him up in the sky. She said there was a small tear [in the tent] in the area toward the *qasgiq*. They say one day, she looked outside it, and he was circling with his drum underneath him *cella maliggluku* [going clockwise, lit., "following the direction of the universe"] in the air.

She said after a while, back when they had sealgut windows, she said he landed on that window and went inside the *qasgiq*.

They say one day those two tied a rock onto him to drag, since he got too fast at crossing, they used an old fishnet as a towing line to drag that anchor.

They say during that time Qakurtaq was extremely desperate. But they say the very tips of his feet were sitting along the doorway, but here he was on the land. They say the poor thing was desperate, and he asked them to hurry up and take him. They say he admonished them and told them never to do that to him with a rock even though they had him do stunts, that that rock almost caused him to fall. They never did that to him again.

Qakurtaq tengnaurtuq-gguq Alarnerem akianun

Paugnaralria, Anchorage, December 2011

PAUGNARALRIA: Qakurtaq-llu-w' imna, Qakurtaq. Qakurtaq-wa caperrnarqellruniat.

Atama-gguq picecirlallrua tuunriaqan pisteksuglaani. Qanemciklallrua-llu.

Ukuk Suqutallraunrilriim imum-llu Panigkam aipairutiin atii, kitumek-im' piqerlaqiit? Taukuk-gguq angalkuurtellruak, Suqutallraam, tauna-im' aipaa kitumek piqerlaryaaqekiit. Tangerrlallruaqa.

Nallunriamegnegu-gguq qillerquurluku. Alarneq nequturivailgan, Alarnerem-gguq akianun unitaqluku qillerqerraarluku, cauyaanek, cauyaa malikluku. Tengnaurtuq-gguq Alarnerem akianun. Cukariinarluni-gguq taugaam.

Caqerluni-gguq taum maurluirutma qasgim ketiini pelatekangqerrluteng, niitnauraa-gguq tuaten pakma cellami. Allganertangqerrluni-gguq taum qasgim tunglirnera. Caqerluku-gguq uyangtaa cella maliggluku pagaaggun cauyaminek curirluni uivaalria cellami.

Piqerluni-gguq tua-i irnerrlugmek imumek egalengqetullratni, tuavet-gguq egalermun tua-i tull'uni qasgimun iterluni.

Caqerluku-gguq-am taukuk ciimagmek petugaak nangcirluku, cukariinarpakaan qerallra, kuvyallermek kicaq tauna nangciucirluku.

Kapiallruuq-gguq tuani cakneq Qakurtaq. Amtallu-gguq amigmun uavet tusngaluteng it'gai-gguq nuukackamikun, amtallu-gguq nunam qaingani uitaluni. Kapialuni patagmek teguqaurluusqelluni. Inerqurrlukek-gguq, picirkartuyarutkengraatni, tuaten pinqigcesqevkenani ciimamek, igucarpiaqapiggniluni taumun ciimamun. Tua-i pinqigtevkenaku.

And they say they would hide drums from him to no avail[23]

Eugene Pete and Lawrence Edmund, Anchorage, December 2011

LAWRENCE EDMUND: And they say they would hide drums from him to no avail. They say he would find them. One day, those two threw his drum in the water in the fall and had it float away. They say he couldn't find that drum for a while, and he continually said how unfortunate it was.

After a while, he told them to give him a strip of hide. They gave him a strip of hide, and earlier you just heard what it is. When he asked for that, they gave it to him. They say he made a snare. He lowered his snare all the way to the end through the cracks in the floor boards in the *qasgiq*.

After exercising his shaman powers, when it was at the end, he pulled that, and he evidently had snared that drum along its handle, along the very end like this. He took that one that they had thrown in the water and that had floated away.

They say there was one big drum. They'd remove its drum skin since it couldn't enter through the doorway, and they brought it in through the window by bending [the frame]. They would only use it when they'd have the Messenger Feast. They wouldn't use it during other times.

They evidently put the drum skin on that one for him. After putting the drum skin on, they placed that drum that didn't usually go inside the *qasgiq* [doorway] but only through the window inside the smokehouse. They finally told him that the drum he would use, his drum was out in the smokehouse.

Once again, they turned off the light, and that one down there started to fly. They say he quickly brought it inside the *qasgiq*, [*laughter*] that one that couldn't enter.

EUGENE PETE: Yes.

He said that any gun, although it has no bullets at all, he would shoot it[24]

Lawrence Edmund, Anchorage, December 2011

LAWRENCE EDMUND: They say one day, when they were counting people [during a census], I think

Cauyanek-llu-gguq iiriyaaqnauraat

Aliuq Paugnaralria-llu, Anchorage, December 2011

PAUGNARALRIA: Cauyanek-llu-gguq iiriyaaqnauraat. Tua-i-gguq nataqnaurai. Caqerluku-gguq-am cauyaak taukuk mermun egtaak uksuarmi, atercelluku. Tua-i-gguq nataqesciigacaaqaa tauna cauyaq, arenqiapaaraluni-gguq tuaten.

Piqerluni-gguq-am piuq tapengyagmek pisqelluni. Taum-am tapengyagmek piluku, ava-i tapengyak niitellruken. Taumek pisqengan tua-i pilliniluku. Tua-i-gguq-am negaliuq. Akulqucugkun-llu-gguq tua-i negani tamana atrarrluku qasgimi iquklilluku.

Tuunrirraarluku iquklican taun' nuqtaa cauyaq im epuakun nuukackaakun waten negallia. Atercetellrag' im teguluku.

Atauciq-gguq cauyaq ang'uq. Eciirluku-llu-gguq taugaam, amigkun iterciigatlaan egalerkun itertaqluku cuqlurrluku. Curukaraqameng taugaam atutuluku. Maani cailkami atuyuunaku.

Taumek-am tua-i eciritliak taukuk. Nutaan ecirraarluku puyurcivigmun ellilliniluku tauna cauyaq it'yuilnguq qasgikun egalerkun taugaam. Nutaan apertuutelliniluku qakma puyurcivigmi cauyarkaa uitaniluku cauyaa.

Tua-i-gguq-am kenurraq nipluku, ak'a-llu-gguq teng'anga'arrluni camna. Itqautellia-gguq-am qasgimun, [*ngelaq'ertut*] iterciigalnguq imna.

ALIUQ: Ii-i.

Tua-i-llu-gguq nutek piciatun imartaitqapigtengraan nutguciiqniluku

Paugnaralria, Anchorage, December 2011

PAUGNARALRIA: Caqerluni-llu-ggur-am yugnek naaqiluteng-wa, ca-im' tayim' Luucirpak

Luucirpak [Big Luuciq] was a translator at the time, someone named Luucirpak, probably Luucicuar's [Little Luuciq's] father.

Then those people wanted to see [Qakurtaq] doing stunts with his shaman powers. My father said that if he had known what they were going to do, he would have lit the *qasgiq* and had them take a fire bath. He said it was so cold at the time and there was frost inside the *qasgiq* since they hadn't taken a fire bath. He said it was so cold that they couldn't be without clothing.

He took his clothes off and excercised his shaman powers. He told them that he wanted to use one of their guns. Someone told him that he won't let a shaman mess with his gun. My dear father used to say, he told the story. He evidently told him that if he wants to hit an animal when he shoots it, not to refuse to give it to him to use. When he told him that, he gave it to him. He said it wasn't loaded.

He checked it and it wasn't loaded. They say after circling for a while, he shot. They say circling inside the *qasgiq*, he shot four times.

They say when they checked it the next morning, the bullets had evidently hit right into where the logs go like this up there. And the bullet casings, the bullet casings were manufactured; it had that kind of casings.

Then he said to the *kass'at* [white people] who had wanted to watch him, that any gun, down in the Lower Forty-eight states where they were from, he could shoot it even though it had no bullets at all. That one was really fit to be a soldier. [*laughter*]

And they say those people were all tangled up on top of the bed when he shot four times. Unfortunately, since it was so cold, he said he thought he would have gone on longer, but since it was so cold, he couldn't stay undressed for long.

He would kill himself, planning to go to where the deceased are[25]

Lawrence Edmund, Anchorage, December 2011

LAWRENCE EDMUND: That one gradually became more powerful. He was a shaman; they say he wasn't a very good one at first. They say those two turned him into a shaman. They say the father of the late Akagualria, his father-in-law, gave him

qanertenguluni pingatuq, Luucirpak, ca imna, Luucicuaraam-wa atii pillilria.

Tua-llu-gguq taukut tangerrsugluku picirtaarluku. Nallunritellrukuniu-gguq atama qasgiq maqivkallruyarai kumarrluku. Arenqiatuq nenglliami qasgim-llu-gguq ilua kanerluni, maqiksailata. Matangqayunaunani-gguq tua-i.

Matarrluni tua-i tuunrilliniluni-am tuaten. Pilliniluki nutgatnek taukut iliita, nutga aturyugluku. Taum tua-i piyaaqelliniluku elliin nut'ni angalkumun qaillukuarutkevkarngaitniluku. Ata'urluqa qanerlallruuq, qanemciklallrua. Pilliniluku, nutgutaqaku pitarkamun nall'arutaqluku piyukaku qunukesqevkenaku. Tuaten tua-i piani tunlliniluku. Imaunani-gguq.

Tua-i imkucirluku tua-i imaunani. Piqerluni-gguq uivaarturaqerluni, ik'iki-gguq nutegtuq. Uivaarturluni-gguq nut'gauq qasgim iluani cetamarqunek.

Pagaavet-gguq, unuaquan paqtaat imkut equut waten piatnun, tuavet-gguq qukarturrlainarluku puulit tut'elliut. Imallret-llu-gguq imkut, imallret tua-i Kass'artaat; tamakunek-gguq imallerkuiluni.

Tua-i-llu-gguq taukut kass'at pikiliki taukut tangerrsugtellni, nutek piciatun, akmani kingunratni ellaita nutgutellrukan imartaitqapigtengraan nutguciiqniluku. Nutaan taun' anguyagcuutekaq. [*ngel'artuq*]

Tamakut-llu-gguq ilarqaqluteng ingelret qaingatni nut'ganga'artellrani taun' cetamarqunek. Arenqiatuq nenglliami akaarnun piyaryuklukuarluku, arenqiatuq nenglliami matarmi uitayunailami.

Nalalluni taugaam ellminek, tuavet tuqumalriit nuniitnun ayagarkauluni

Paugnaralria, Anchorage, December 2011

PAUGNARALRIA: Kayuriinallruuq tauna. Tua-i-w' angalkuuyaaqluni; pikeggnerullrunricaaquq-gguq. Taukuk-gguq angalkuurtellruak. Taum cakian-gguq tuunraminek ingluarrvikellrua tauna Akagualrianrilriim

half his shaman powers. When he married his daughter, they say he gave him half his shaman powers. They say he wasn't a good shaman at first. Those two tied him up. And they say he would kill himself also, what they call *yugcarluni*.

They would talk about something called *qalrit* [bearded seals making their mating calls], that when they'd hear those, one of them would have a person's voice. They would call those *qalrit*.

But they say he would exercise his shaman powers, he would kill himself, planning to go to where the deceased are. They say that's what he did, choking himself with a hide strip. They say he would be extremely puffy and sick-looking and his eyes were almost coming out. But they say [the hide strip] would sever, but here he looked [dead]. But that hide strip had been extremely tight. They say he would die, he would really die and his body would get stiff.

They say they would stay like that with him in the center all night, with him dead like that. During the evening, probably in the morning, the sound of a house fly would first appear, he would start to make noise like a house fly. And they say when it reached his person, he would come alive. They say that's what he used to do.

And they say when he accidently shot himself, when he was fox hunting and he slipped . . . they say they used to admonish them not to hold the gun like this with its opening on this side. When he was doing that and fell, he accidentally shot himself on his lung.

They say he returned home. When he reached Alakanuk, the village was hovering in the air. There was no way to enter the village as it was hovering in the air. They say one of the women, when she dumped a small chamber pot and spilled it, [the village] suddenly landed on the ground, and then he finally entered.

And they say since he couldn't recover, he had them shoot him, he had Panigkaq's late husband [shoot him]. They say since that gun had no ammunition, after exercising his shaman powers like that, he put on a seal-gut rain garment, and they say they painted the place where they would shoot, and the bullet would enter with charcoal.

With that. When he opened his seal-gut rain garment, that smudge he made was a hole. They say the posts of the *qasgiq* along the corner were visible through that hole. That smudge that he made was a hole.

Atii. Taumek paniminek aipangan, tuunraminek-gguq ingluarrvikellrua. Angalkukeggnerullrunricaaqluni-gguq. Taukuk-gguq qillerquurluku. Ellminek-llu-gguq nalataqluni, yugcarluni-gguq.

Canek imkunek qalrinek qanerlalriit, tamakunek-gguq niitaqameng, iliit-gguq atam yuum waten eriniinek erinangqerrlartuq. Qalrinek piaqluki tamakut.

Taugken-gguq tua-i tuunriluni, nalalluni taugaam ellminek, tuavet tuqumalriit nuniitnun ayagarkauluni. Tuatnanaurtuq-gguq, qemilluni tapengyagkun. Tenguqlirrluni-gguq caknek iik-llu-gguq anqerteqatarlalriik. Taugken-gguq tua-i kep'arrluni, amtallu-gguq waten ayuqluni. Amtallu-gguq tauna tapengyak quumaluni tua-i cakneq. Tuquluni-gguq taugken tua-i, tuquq'apiggluni yurrluni-llu.

Qukaqmigluku-gguq taun' waten unugpak uitanaurtut-gguq tua-i, tuaten tuqumaluni. Unuumainanrani-gguq, unuakumi-w' pilallilria tayima, ciivak ciumek alairnaurtuq, nepengluni ciivagcetun. Tuavet-llu-gguq yum'inun tekicami unguirluni. Tuatnatullruuq-gguq.

Cali-gguq anqerriviklermini kaviarcurluni qurrasqiarrluni . . . inerqurrlallruit-gguq tuaten nutek-gguq waten quukataasqevkenaku cuplua ukaqliqluku. Tuatnaluni iqullermini ellminek anqerrivikluni qat'gamikun.

Uterrluni-gguq. Alarnermun-gguq tekituq nunat qerrataluteng. Qiall' it'yunaunani nunanun, aciat qerrataluni. Iliit-gguq arnat qurruksuarmek ciqiciluni kuvngaku tus'artuq waten, nutaan-llu ellii iterluni.

Assirisciigalami-llu-gguq nutegcelluni, imumek tauna Panigkam aipairutiin atiinun. Imailan-gguq tamana nutek tuaten tuunrirraarluni qasperegnek all'uni, cuputmek-gguq minugluku tauna puulim nutlerkaa.

Tamakucimek. Maaten-gguq waten ikirtaa imarnitegni ukinruluni tauna mingullra. Qava-i-gguq qasgim egkuani naparyat tangerrnaqluteng, tuaggun ukinerkun. Ukinruluni tauna mingullra.

They say since the gun wasn't loaded, the gun was facing him, since it wasn't loaded, he squeezed the trigger. They say it made a loud popping noise, and the *qasgiq* sprinkled some soil.

And they say that one back there, they probably call those things *naqugtat* [partitions of woven grass]. I forgot what else they call them. I saw those woven grass mats here. They say it fell on the other side of the woven grass mats, and they say that one across suddenly started to leak [blood]. And they say the one who shot repeatedly blurted, "oh dear" and went on his back, saying that he would be hung when the white people found out what he did.

And these two who were drumming here, their drums began to pass by each other going in opposite directions. That late father of the late Akagaralria evidently scolded those two who were drumming, bringing them to their senses. They say they [drummed] all night.

They say after a while, first as a fox, that one that sounded like a fly came up first. They say he circled the *qasgiq* as a fox first. And when he went all the way around, he became human again. And they say he never was bothered by that [gunshot wound] that he was suffering from. That Qakurtaq evidently was amazing. I used to see him, and he would call me his grandchild. And I also used to see his son there.

Imailan-gguq nutek tamana, tungiinun-gguq nutek caumaluni; imailan-gguq qet'aa. Ik'iki-gguq cingqurpak, qasgiq-llu-gguq nunamek kanevluni.

Imna-llu-gguq kiugna tayima, naqugtanek pilallikait imkut. Caneg'-im' piqerlaqait-llu. Maani tangellruunga canegnek tupiganek. Tupigat amatiitnun iggluni tayima, ak'a-llu-gguq augna qurrlullagluni. Tauna-llu-gguq nutegta arenqiapaaraluni tua-i taklartuq, waniw' agartauciqniluni kass'at nallunriqatni.

Cauyalriik-llu-gguq ukuk wani kipullgutaangarcaaqlukek cauyakek. Taum Akagaralriarunrilriim atairutiin nunurtellinilukek taukuk cauyalriik, cellangarcellukek ataam. Unugpak-gguq.

Caqerluni-gguq ciumek, kaviaruluni, tuaten tauna ciivagtun ayuqellria qaivarluni tauna. Kaviaruluni-gguq ciumek uivaa qasgiq. Kassuami-llu-gguq ataam waten yuurrluni. Tauna-llu-gguq aviraniurutkellni tayim' aviraniurutkenqigtevkenaku. Caperrnarqellrulliniuq tauna Qakurtaq. Tangtullrukek tutgara'urluminek-llu piaqlua. Qetunraa-ll' tangtullruaqa tamaani.

He told someone to try using his shaman powers to track the trail of the person who had taken the few things he was given[26]

Mike Andrews Sr. and Alice Rearden, Anchorage, December 2011

MIKE ANDREWS SR.: And then, I heard a story at Alakanuk, that long ago the people of Emmonak went to attend a dance festival and arrived. People from other places including people from Mountain Village went to watch and they arrived. They say there were many people at Alakanuk.

That one had become elderly; he evidently came from upriver, from the Yukon River up there.

They evidently included him in their distribution, and they gave him a small amount of frozen fish along with *akutat* [festive mixtures of fat, fish, and berries]. That person from upriver was grateful for the few things he was given.

Tuani kina imna tayima taukunek tuunrilluku, uigtualuku tumai taum tamakunek taum aruqukarami, aruqutmi uigtuasqelluku

Angauvik Cucuaq-llu, Anchorage, December 2011

ANGAUVIK: Tua-i-llu Alarnermi qanemcimek niitellruunga, avani ak'a ciuqvani, Imangarmiut curukarluteng tekilluteng. Naken-am camiunek qavaken-llu Asaacaryamek tuaten anglaniyalriit tekilluteng. Yugyagluni-gguq Alarneq.

Angutngurrluni-gguq tauna; qavaken-gguq kingunengqelliniluni Kuigpagmek qavaken. Aruqelliniluku tua-i ilakluku, canek kumlanrrarnek akutanek tauten. Quyatekluki taum qaugkumium aruqukarani tuakut.

Then, back when people had aboveground storage caches, as you know people in villages had aboveground caches where they stored things; back when they had those, he evidently told his hosts there at Alakanuk that since he was so grateful for the things he was given, he wanted to bring them outside to the aboveground storage cache to keep them there temporarily. And he also told them that he would cover them, and he covered them with his tarp. He evidently brought them outside. His host went with him and after clearing it, they placed them there.

They say the next day they were going to return home. They say after they ate, he went out to check on those things, since he was also thinking to return home, he went to check on the things he was given the night before. When he checked on them he saw that someone had taken them, and his tarp had been tampered with, it wasn't in its original spot. He lost those things.

They say he was very upset because he had been grateful for them. When he entered, he evidently told his host about it. And they say he had been planning to leave, to return home, but he decided not to leave.

Then in the evening, he told someone to try using his shaman powers to track the trail of the person who had taken the few things he was given, to find out which village he was from.

Then that one practicing his shaman powers told him that the one who took the things he was given, that the one who took them was evidently from upriver; that's what that shaman told him.

Then he evidently told him to try to follow that person's tracks again to see where he went to stay, to see where he arrived. Then once again after practicing his shaman powers, he told him that that one had evidently come from Mountain Village.

Then they say that one found out who that person was. Since he knew of that person who was a thief at Mountain Village, because he knew he tended to steal things, he found out who he was.

Then they say that one told him that before winter ended, the shaman evidently told the one who lost his things that [the thief] wouldn't live through the entire winter.

He told him that starting from his arms he would get an ailment, he would become unable to do things, he wouldn't be able to lift his head up

Tua-i-llu qer'angqetullrani imumi nunat qer'angqerrlalriit elliviggarnek; tamakucingqellratni, tukuni tua-i tauna Alarnermi ukut wani quyatekvakaamiki aruqutni keggavet qer'anun anucugluki, elliqeryugluki. Patuluki-llu-gguq piciqai, cingyaaminek-llu patuqerluki. Tua-i anutelliniluki. Tukuan taum maliggluku carrirraarluku tuavet elliluki.

Tua-i-gguq unuaquani uterteqatarluteng. Maaten-gguq tuaten pirraarluteng, nererraarluteng imkut paqtai anluni, ellii-ll' uterrnaluni piami, imkut unuk aruqutkellni. Maaten-gguq pii kia imum tegullrullii, cingyaara-ll' tamana pimaluni, nunamini uitavkenani. Tamariluki.

Arenqianani-gguq tua-i quyatekellruamiki. Itrami tua-i taun' tukuni qanrutliniluku. Ayagarkaullruyaaqluni-llu-gguq utertarkauyaaqluni, ayanritngurrluni.

Tua-i-llu tua-i atakumi kina imna tayima taukunek tuunrilluku, uigtualuku tumai taum tamakunek taum aruqukarami, aruqutmi uigtuasqelluku, camiungullra kangingnaurluku.

Tua-i-llu taum tua-i tuunrilriim tua-i pillia tauna-gguq tegustiit tamakut aruqutain tegustiit-gguq qaugkumiungulliniuq-gguq; qanrulluku tua-i taum angalkuum.

Tua-i-ll'-am pillia uigtualuku ataam tumai natmun tukillra, tekitellra. Tua-i-ggur-am tua-i taum tuaten tua-i tuunrirraarluni apertuutellia, Asaacaryarmek-gguq kingunengqelliniuq tauna.

Tua-i-ll' nallunrirluku-gguq tua-i taum tauna. Cunawa-gguq tauna tegucutuli tuani Asaacaryami, camek tegucugluni piyullra nallunrilamiu-gguq kangingekiliu-gguq tua-i.

Tua-llu tua-i pillia taum waniwa uksuq wani iquklipailgan, tauna uksuq iquklisngaitniluku qanrutlia angalkuum tauna imna piicilleq.

Tua-i-gguq tua-i, tua-i-gguq maaken-gguq talligminek ayagluni apqucingeciquq, qaill' pisciigaliluni, ciugtaarciigaliluni, neryuirulluni-

anymore, and he wouldn't be able to eat any longer. He told him that he would die before winter ended.

That one evidently learned what would happen to him. They say before winter ended he died. With an ailment that started in his arms, he eventually died.

It so happened that when he stole the things that were given to that person, he hurt that person's feelings by taking the things he was given, things that he had been grateful for. William Trader told me that story before he died at Emmonak when I visited William Trader in the evening. That person told me that story about how at Alakanuk, he made a person feel sad for losing things, hurting his feelings.

ALICE REARDEN: I hear that a person's mind is powerful.

MIKE ANDREWS SR.: Yes, yes, that's so, yes. When that person was sad over the loss of those things, his feelings were hurt. Nothing happened to him, but the one who stole, they say he died before winter ended.

llu. Tuaten qanrutlia taum. Uksuq iquklipailgan tuqullerkaa qanrutekluku.

Taum tua-i taringelliniluku. Tua-i-gguq uksuq iquklipailgan tuqullruuq. Maaken ayagnirluni talligminek tuquluni.

Taukunek cunawa aruqutainek taum tegutell[ermini], tauna umyugaa navgurluku aruqutainek teguiluku, quyakellrinek. Tauna tua-i imum William Trader-am Imangami tuquvailegmi qanrutellruanga taumek atakumi cenirtellemni William Trader-am. Tua-i taum qanemcitellruanga taumek Alarnermi qivruvkarluku, umyugaa navegluku.

CUCUAQ: Niitelartua yuum umyugaa tukniniluku.

ANGAUVIK: Ii-i, yaa, tua-i, ii-i. Tua-i taumun tua-i qivrullermini taukunek umyugaa navegluni. Cavkenani, tauna taugaam tegutelleq uksuq iquklipailgan-gguq tuqullruuq.

The one who raised me told me that I would know if a shaman did something to me[27]

Mike Andrews Sr., Eugene Pete, and Lawrence Edmund, Anchorage, December 2011

MIKE ANDREWS SR.: They say a person's mind, that starting with feelings of sorrow, that a regular person who isn't a shaman, one who is a regular person like this, that they can eventually kill a shaman with their mind. One's mind is powerful like that. I hear that also, that a regular person can kill a shaman. They say a person who has no shaman powers at all can kill [a shaman]. That's what I hear also. . . .

EUGENE PETE: Those regular people, as you know we are all regular people, and we have no shaman powers.

MIKE ANDREWS SR.: Yes.

EUGENE PETE: They say those [regular people] who are like that, when a shaman [confronts or attacks them in their dreams], they will know for sure [that it was a shaman]. I also knew when a shaman was doing something to me. The one who raised me used to tell me that I would know if a shaman did something to me. I knew; when [a shaman] would do something to me, I would know.

Qanrutlallruanga anglicartema taum angalkuum qaill' pikanga nallungaitniluku

Angauvik, Aliuq, Paugnaralria-llu, Anchorage, December 2011

ANGAUVIK: Umyugaa yuum-gguq piuq, iluteqellni-llu-gguq ayagneqluku cali-gguq yuunginaam angalkuunritellriim, angalkuuvkenani, waten yuunginauluni, angalkuq-gguq pitaqeciqaa umyuamikun. Tuaten tukniluni umyugaa. Tuaten-am niitlaraqa-ll' tauna, yuunginaam-gguq angalkuq pitaqeciqaa. Caitqapik cailnguum tua-i angalkum tungiinun pitaqeciqaa-gguq. Tuaten niitlaraqa-ll'-am tauna. . . .

ALIUQ: Tamakut yuunginat, wangkuta waniw' yuunginaulriakut, tua-i camek tuunram tungiinun caunata.

ANGAUVIK: Ii-i.

ALIUQ: Tuaten-gguq ayuqellriit angalkum pikani nallungaitqapigtaa-gguq. Wiinga-llu nalluyuitellruanka qaill' piaqanga angalkum. Qanrutlallruanga anglicartema taum angalkuum qaill' pikanga nallungaitniluku wangnun. Nalluyuunaki; caqa'arqanga tua-i nalluvkenaku.

And my weapon [to fight back with] would be out in the open, my club. I [fought] dogs twice; a dog attacked me. But I struck them both repeatedly.

MIKE ANDREWS SR.: Yes. [chuckles]

EUGENE PETE: I killed those two dogs. The second time, I had a dream about Thomas. A dog approached, and Thomas also walked outside. That dog approached me, snarling. The weapon I used suddenly appeared. I took it, and its weight was just right. When it arrived and I hit it, it fell face first, and that person over there [Thomas] entered. And I heard that Thomas wasn't feeling well. I think that person indeed used to meddle [with people].

LAWRENCE EDMUND: He probably did so. They used to say he did.

Although some were shamans, they didn't disclose themselves to others[28]

Eugene Pete and Marie Meade, Nunam Iqua, March 2011

EUGENE PETE: Along the shores of Qip'ngayak. That was where Qakurtaq used to live.

Taciurtalek is where Qakurtaq used to live. Some time ago, Austin went fall camping there, just after his father passed away. When he arrived, he said he didn't have a watch, and he didn't have a lantern.

He said during some time, toward evening, when it started to get dark, he said that he had no sense of time all night. He said he'd stay up. He would finally go to sleep when he felt sleepy.

He had no watch and no lantern. He had no sense of time. But he said sometimes when he felt like it, he would wake and see that it was early dawn. [chuckles]

MARIE MEADE: Who was that?

EUGENE PETE: Austin, Qakurtaq's son.

MARIE MEADE: Qakurtaq. Are *qakurtat* [northern harriers] birds?

EUGENE PETE: Yes, there is a bird that looks like an *eskaviaq* [hawk owl] that is extremely white. They call that *qakurtaq*. That is his *napan* [something that keeps one up, alive, or going].

That is Qakurtaq's *napan*.

MARIE MEADE: Was he a *yungcaraq* [one brought to life by a shaman through doctoring]? So his name was his *napan*?

EUGENE PETE: Yes.

MARIE MEADE: Was he a shaman?

Cali caskuqa paivngaaqluni, kaugtuutaqa. Malrurqugnek qimugtegnek pillruunga; caumaklua taum qimugtem. Kaugtuqtaallruagka taugaam tamarkenka.

ANGAUVIK: Ii-i. [ngelaq'ertuq]

ALIUQ: Tuqullukek taukuk qimugtek. Kinguqlirmi pillemni imumek qavangurtullruunga Thomas-aamek. Qimugta agiirtuq, cali-ll' Thomas-aaq yaa-i anluni. Taum qimugtem ullagyaaqlua uirrluni. Ak'a-am imna caskukaqa paivarrluni. Piaqa, teguqeraqa, assirpak uqamia. Tekican-llu tua-i kaugtuamni pucikarluni, ingna-ll' yaa-i iterluni. Niilluku-ll' wii tauna Thomas-aq assinritniluku ayuqucia. Qaillukuatulallrungatuq taun' ilumun.

PAUGNARALRIA: Pillilria-wa. Pinilaqiit-wa.

Ilait angalkuungermeng alaiyuitut

Aliuq Arnaq-llu, Nunam Iqua, March 2011

ALIUQ: Qip'ngayiim ceniini, ii-i. Qakurtam nunalqaa.

Qakurtam Taciurtalek. Cami-am Austin-aq uksuiyalliuq tuavet, atani-w' catairutnerakun. Tekicami cassaunani-gguq, kenurrarkaunani-llu.

Tua-i-gguq cami, atakungaqan waten, tan'geringaqan, qaill' tua-i ayuquciitnaurtuq-gguq unugpak. Pegg'arnaurtuq-gguq tua-i. Qavam-gguq taugaam piani nutaan inarrluni.

Cassaunani kenurraunani-llu. Cami tua-i pillerkaa nalluluku. Taugaam-gguq iliikun tua-i piyungami tua-i tupagnaurtuq erqaaralliniluni. [ngelaq'ertuq]

ARNAQ: Kina tauna?

ALIUQ: Austin-aq, taum Qakurtam qetunraa.

ARNAQ: Qakurtaq. Qakurtat-qaa yaqulguut?

ALIUQ: Ii-i, yaqulegmek pitangqertuq eskaviatun ayuqluni qatqapiggluni. Qakurtaq-gguq. Napatekaa tauna.

Napatekaa taum Qakurtam.

ARNAQ: Yungcaraullruuq-qaa? Napatekluku taugaam tauna atni?

ALIUQ: Ii-i.

ARNAQ: Angalkuullruuq-qaa?

EUGENE PETE: Yes, a real shaman. And after having others shoot him, he would come back to life. Anguksuar tells a story about him. I think they [shot him] in his presence. He said they shot him in the *qasgiq*. He said he collapsed. It was dark. He said after a while, he began to make noise. He evidently came back to life. [*chuckles*]

That person was a powerful shaman. But when he was about to die, they said he was extremely desperate and struggled.

MARIE MEADE: What was Qakurtaq's English name?

EUGENE PETE: John Qakurtaq.

I'm not sure about Austin either; I think he was a shaman. He was one, but he wasn't known to the public.

Yes, Austin. He died.

MARIE MEADE: Did some shamans not disclose themselves to others back then?

EUGENE PETE: Yes. Although some were shamans, they didn't disclose themselves to others. They were shamans, but they weren't disclosed.

ALIUQ: Yaa, angalkupik. Ellminek-llu nutegceqaarluni-llu unguiraqluni. Anguksuaraam-wa qanemciklaqii. Takuani pingatut. Qasgimi-gguq nutellruat. Tua-i-gguq iquluni. Tan'gercelluni. Piqerluni-gguq nepnguq. Cunaw' unguilliniluni. [*ngelaq'ertuq*]

Angalkurpak tauna. Taugaam-am tuquqatallrani nanikuanillruat cakneq.

ARNAQ: Qakurtam Kass'atun atra kituuluni?

ALIUQ: John Qakurtaq.

Austin-aaq-llu-w' imna qaill' pilarta; angalkuularyugnarquq tauna. Pilkialaryaaquq, taugaam alairumalanrituq.

Ii-i. Austin. Tuqullruuq.

ARNAQ: Ilait-qaa alairumavkenateng tamaani angalkuulallruut?

ALIUQ: Aa-a. Ilait angalkuungermeng alaiyuitut. Amtallu tua-i angalkuuyaaqluteng, taugaam alaiyuitut.

They say when shamans were nearing death, their powers started to leave them[29]

Benedict Tucker, Emmonak, March 2011

BENEDICT TUCKER: But at that time, they called that person Nutgun; because he was too overly confident, before he died, they say when shamans were nearing death, [their shaman powers] started to leave them, when they are nearing death. They couldn't help them; their shaman powers would leave them.

Nutgun requested an abundance of wood [using his shaman powers] in the past. When the *qasgiq* was back there, outside the water plant [well].

Since that [shaman] was too overly confident, before [they started], he and his younger sibling Qayaruaq there, when they were just starting, he ran out and brought the tips of willows inside and placed them here. I think it was because he was too overly confident, but he was nearing death at the time.

He evidently used to tell Cakicenaq, "Since you're constantly lacking steambath wood, this spring . . ." He said wood for taking fire baths was heading downriver.

Waten-gguq makut angalkut waten tuqullerkaat yaaqsinriraqata imkucirlarait, unitenglarait

Cikulraaciq, Imangaq, March 2011

CIKULRAACIQ: Tuani taugaam, Nutgutmek piaqluku; waten tua-i pissiyaagpakaan, tamaa-i tuquniararluku, waten-gguq makut angalkut waten tuqullerkaat yaaqsinriraqata imkucirlarait, unitenglarait, tuquniararqata. Ikayurciiganaki-am tua-i tamakut; angalkuita unitlarait.

Imumi equguallruuq Nutgun. Piani-im' qasgiq uitallrani, merviim elatiini.

Anagulluni tamana pissaagpakaami, tua-i cakneq imkut pivailgata, tauna-llu kinguqlini-im' Qayaruaq, ayagniqataarallrani waten anqerrluni ak'a uqviaret im' kangritnek itrutuq wavet-llu elliluki. Tua-i anagarulluni pivakaan pingataa, tuquniararluni taugaam.

Tua-i-llu tauna Cakicenaq pilallia, "Maqikaituravakarlalriaten, tayim' up'nerkaqu . . ." Maqikaq tayima anelrarniluku.

One shouldn't be overconfident when it comes to anything. And one shouldn't say that they are going to catch an animal or that they are going to be eating good food. That's true.

That person was overly confident saying [what he said] would come true. Then time passed. And he even told Cakicenaq that he wouldn't lack steam-bath firewood. Since Cakicenaq no longer felt inhibited toward him . . . at breakup, there was no [wood] at all, no [wood] at all.

Cakicenaq went to Nutgun and said to him, "Where are the logs for the steam bath that you promised?" [laughter]

They didn't materialize at all. One shouldn't be overly confident over anything.

Ca man' augtaqenrilnguayunaituq piciatun. Waniwa-llu pitarkaq piqatarniluku qang'a-ll' neqkegciqatarniluni qanyunaitelliniuq. Ilumuuguq.

Tauna-am tuaten anagulluni tauna tua-i piciurteqatarluni. Tayima. Tauna-ll' tua-i Cakicenaq maqikaiturangaitellerkaanek tua-i. Takaqenrilliamiu tua-i Cakicenam . . . cup'uq, caitqapik tayima, caitqapik.

Una-am tua-i Cakicenam ullagluku Nutgun pillia, "Nauwa-m' imkut akquceten maqikat?" [ngel'artut]

Caitqapik tua-i pillrunritut. Ca man'a augtaqenrilnguayunaituq.

He said this was his reply to him, "If my two pretend wolves come to materialize, although you want to have reindeer, you won't have any reindeer"[30]

Waten-gguq kiugaa, "Keglunrualleraagka-wa piciureskagnek tuntungqerrsung'erpeci tuntungqerrngailnguci"

Benedict Tucker and Marie Meade, Emmonak, March 2011

Cikulraaciq Arnaq-llu, Imangaq, March 2011

BENEDICT TUCKER: And that one, I just spoke briefly of shamans; let me talk about that one thing I know.

There were many reindeer back when we used to herd reindeer. Their numbers reached three thousand. When we would herd them, the reindeer would cover a hill.

Frances Lee and Joseph Afcan; [I'm finishing this story] since I haven't finished it. Those two believed in those things and didn't stop, and together those two would continue to practice these Yup'ik customs. Since they watched those things, they believed in the customs. And since those were their customs, since they probably didn't want to stop practicing them right away, they still continued to practice them, but they did so in secret.

Those people there, that one they called Tuucillngaq and Tutmaralria, over there, that place they call Arviqercaraq; that person who used to stay there. Dan Joe, Dan Joe married that person's daughter, Tuucillngaq's [daughter].

They used to call him Tuucillngaq and Tutmaralria.

Then those people there told him that he had caught a reindeer in secret, and they asked why he had killed that without saying anything.

CIKULRAACIQ: Augna-llu imna, angalkunek qanqalrianga; augna wani nallunritelqa qanrutkeqerlaku.

Tuntut amllellruut tuntulgullemteni tamaani. *Three thousand* tekilluku amllertarillruut. Unguaqamteki tua-i qemir' una patunauraat tuntut.

Ukuk-am Frances Lee tauna-llu Joseph Afcan-aq; iqukliteksaitelliniamku man'a. Taukuk tuani tamakut wani ukvekellruakek taukuk taqeksaunatek, aipaqu'urlutek-llu makut maani Yup'igtaat piurluki. Tangvallruamegneki tamakut, tamaani ukveq tua-i ukvekluku. Tamakut-llu piciryaraqellruamegneki, patagmek aug'aryunritliamegneki cali tuaten atu'uqluki, aassaqu'urlutek taugaam.

Tuani tua-i taukut, tauna Tuucillngarmek Tutmaralriamek-llu piaqluku, yaani, Arviqercaramek pilaqiit; tuani uitaurlallruuq. Imna Dan Joe-m, Dan Joe imna nulirtullruuq taum panianek, Tuucillngiim.

Tuucillngarmek piaqluku Tutmaralriamek-llu.

Tua-llu taukut pilliniat pitellruniluku tuntumek aassaqluku, qanerpek'naku ciin tauna tuqucillrullranek.

They used to put markings on them on their ears, putting marks on reindeer, marking them. The owner would know it belonged to him through its [marked] ear when they were about to kill them.

He told those people that he hadn't [killed a reindeer], that shaman said that he hadn't [killed one].

But Father O'Connor, the reindeer of the people at the St. Mary's mission including Joseph Afcan, they had the most reindeer. There were many of those, that Frances Lee, and all those; there were many reindeer herders.

He didn't admit it and said that he hadn't [killed one]. Although he said that, the priest, Father O'Connor said that he was lying, and that he was a shaman, that he is a liar, and he even brought up the fact that he was a shaman. He told him not to lie, [and] to leave.

Since Joseph Afcan knew what they were like, since he used to see him [practice his shaman powers] as a shaman, he followed him when he went out, when Father O'Connor told him to leave. When he reached him outside, he pleaded with him, pleaded with him, not to mind [what Father O'Connor said].

After a short silence, that shaman replied to him . . . there were no wolves around here back then. He said this was his reply to him, "If my two pretend wolves come to materialize, although you want to have reindeer, you won't have any reindeer." Since he didn't know what to do, when he went inside, he told the people there with him that he said that, that that was his reply.

We took a break [from herding]. Then that spring, in summer, the wolves arrived. They decimated [the reindeer].

Although [herders] watched over [the reindeer], [the wolves] hid somewhere, they'd hide somewhere not far from those reindeer. They say the wolves wouldn't appear when [people] were watching them. Then they'd head up to their camp, when they'd go and have coffee, those down there would suddenly make rumbling noises, when there were no longer people around. Eventually, [the reindeer] became scarce.

Since I recalled that, I'm mentioning that.

MARIE MEADE: So that priest hurt that one's feelings?

BENEDICT TUCKER: He hurt his feelings. He probably hadn't [killed a reindeer]. They used to tell us not to mistreat shamans, or they told us not to try to hurt their feelings.

Tamaani nallunailkucirlallruit ciutaitgun, alngirluki *reindeer*-aat *mark*-arluki. Tuaggun-am yuan nalluyuunaku tuquciqatarqameng ciutaitgun.

Tua-i piksaitniluni kiullinii taukut, piksaitniluni angalkum taum.

Father O'Connor-aq taugken tua-i, taukut St. Mary's-aarmiut *mission*-aarmiut *reindeer*-ait Joseph Afcan-aaq-llu taukut quyinrulluut *reindeer*-ait. Amllellruut tamakut tamaa-i, taum Frances Lee, *and all those*; amllellruut tuntulget-wa.

Assaqliniluni piksaitniluni. Pingraan taum agayulirtem Father O'Connor-aam iqluquniluku pilliniluku, angalkuuniluku-llu iqlungarniluku, angalkuullra-ll' puggluku. Pilliniluki iqluquvkenaku anesqelluku.

Taum tua-i Joseph Afcan-am nallunrilamiki, tangvalallruaku angalkuuluni, waten tangqertelluku maligtellinia kingunrakun, anellrani, anesqengaku taum Father O'Connor-am. Keggani tua-i tekicamiu qarucaaqellinia tua-i tua-i-w' qarucaaqellinia, imkucirluku tuaten cangalliuresqevkenaku.

Kiuvkenani uitauraqerluni taum angalkuum kiullinia . . . keglunertaitellruuq man' tamaani. Waten-gguq kiugaa, "Keglunrualleraagka-wa piciureskagnek tuntungqerrsung'erpeci tuntungqerrngailnguci." Arenqiatuq-gguq qaill' picirkai[lami], itrami tua-i taukut ilani qanrutlinii tuaten qanerniluku, tuaten kiuniluku.

Tua-i uitaluta. Up'nerkaan-llu kiagan, keglunret-llu tekilluteng. Nangluki.

Nayungraiceteng, waten nayuraqaitki-llu waten iirluteng natmun tuntut taukut yaaqsinrilkiitnun iirluteng. Keglunret-gguq alairngaitut kelluskateng. Tagluteng-llu waten *camp*-ameggnun kuuvviaryarturaqameng, camkut-llu-gguq tem'illagluteng yuirutaqata tua-i. Kiituani-gguq tua-i ikegliut tua-i.

Tua-i taumek neq'aqaamku qanrutkaqa tauna.

ARNAQ: Taum-emtaq agayulirtem nekayugtelluku tauna?

CIKULRAACIQ: Nekayugcelluku.
Pinricaaqellilria-llu-w' tayima. Tamakut angalkut tamaani qaill' ayuqutevkenaki

Then that elderly man said to her, "Now take it and bring it outside and throw it in the river down there." She said digging, since she knew where it was, she dug around and took it. And when she went outside and threw it in the water, after moving a while, that wooden [mask] sunk. And she said the water bubbled above where it had been.

My goodness! He did that when it was close to the time that he would die; I think he died that winter.

Tua-llu-gguq taum kiuluku anguteka'urluum, "Kitak' teguluku anulluku unavet kuigmun egesgu." Aglugluni-gguq tua-i nantellra nallunrilamiu aglugluni teguluku. Anngami-llu-gguq waten kuigmun egcani elliuqerraarluni-gguq kiskili, imna muragaq. Kingunra-llu-gguq qallarvaagarluni.

Ila-i! Tuquniarallermini; uksuan tuqullrungatuq.

Napatet and iinruq are the same[35]

Maryann Andrews, Barbara Joe, Marie Meade,
and Alice Rearden, Anchorage, April 2012

ALICE REARDEN: Just recently before we started when you were sitting over there, you had talked about, I think it was your grandmother, or your mother, you mentioned that they had a walrus as a *napateq* [thing that holds up one who was doctored by a shaman and made to live].

MARYANN ANDREWS: My mother had a walrus for a *napateq*. You know how walrus have these [tusks], those walrus; they say out of that, they used to create people [ivory figures], I used to hear that they used to create figurines.

Yes, they would make *napatet*. She said she had that kind of *napateq*. You know how I told you that I went to Alakanuk to attend a potlatch. Then the late Mary Agnes, this person here knows who she is; a great many of us were guests at her place, and Alqayagaq, Anna Pete, was also among us.

Then we went to sleep. Then my mother went to sleep. I was thinking, "She won't let the others with me sleep." Then I went to sleep, and I, being the very first one, folded up my clothing and moved to the living room. And when I finished preparing [a place to sleep], another came. [*laughter*] All night people moved, leaving my mother's room. She was snoring. She used to snore really loud. I think those walrus snore.

Then when she finally woke up, when she went down, she came to me and said, "I woke up all alone." She said she was all alone in the room. Then I said to her, "Since you wouldn't let us sleep, we moved." She chuckled.

BARBARA JOE: Poor.

ALICE REARDEN: When did she not snore again?

MARYANN ANDREWS: When she was not feeling too well, she never snored at all. And when I watched her, she looked like she wasn't breathing.

Ayuquk napatet iinruq-llu

Tauyaaq, Arnaucuaq, Arnaq, Cucuaq-llu, Anchorage,
April 2012

CUCUAQ: Uumi ayagnirpailemta ikani aqumgallerpeni qanrutkellruken tauna maurluun-wa pillill', aanan-wa pillilria asvermek napatengqellruniluku.

TAUYAAQ: Napatengqertuq aanaka asvermek. Imkut asveret waten pingqerrlalriit, kaugpiit; tamakucimek-gguq taum wani yul'ilallrulriit imkut, yul'iniluki wiinga niitelallruunga.

Ii-i, napaciriluteng. Tamakucimek-gguq napatengqellruuq. Iciwa-m qanemciskemci Alarnermun curukaliyarlua. Tua-ll' Mary Agnes-aunrilriim nallunritaa uum; eniinun tukirluta yugyakap'iggluta, Alqayagaq-llu ilakluku Anna Pete.

Tua-llu inarrluta. Tua-i-ll' aanaka inarrluni. Umyuarteqlua tua-i wiinga, "Tua-i qavarcessngaitai ukut ilanka." Tua-ll' inarcaaqellrianga tang tua-i, wiinga tua-i ciuqlikacagaulua aklunka imegluki upalrianga *living room*-amun. Taqullua-llu waniwa alla-llu tailuni. [*ngel'artuq*] Unugpak upalriit yuut, aanama *room*-aaranek anluteng. Qutugluni. Qutupiatullruuq cakneq. Qututungatut tamakut kaugpiit.

Tua-i-ll' makcaqliami, anelraami ullaglua pikilia, "Tupagtua wii kiirrarma." *Room*-ami-gguq ellii kiirrarmi. Tua-ll' wii pikilaku, "Qavarcessngailavkut upagtukut." Engelaq'aqili.

ARNAUCUAQ: Akleng.

CUCUAQ: Taugaam-ima caaqami qutuyuitellrull'?

TAUYAAQ: Nangteqerrluararqami qutuyuirtelallruuq caitqapiar. Tuarpiaq-llu imna murilkenaurturangramni-llu aneryaayuilnguq.

Then one day my late older sister and I said to her, "Why is it that when you aren't feeling well, you don't snore after usually snoring loudly?" Then she told us that the thing that keeps her alive, the walrus, seems to leave her when she's not feeling well.

You know how when we've heard about our ancestors, they would try to constantly save people from dying. I think that was what was done to my mother.

MARIE MEADE: Was your father a *yungcaraq*?

MARYANN ANDREWS: My father was a *yungcaraq* also. But I never heard the significance of his *iinruq*.

His Yup'ik name was Taqinqurraq.

And along the end of his pillow he had just a stone. I would take that pillow when I remembered that his *iinruq* was there, and it was sewn inside. I would try to look at it, I would move its stitches and try to look at it. When my mother saw what I was doing, she would take it from me.

ALICE REARDEN: Was it inside cloth?

MARYANN ANDREWS: Yes, it was sewn inside cloth. You know how we have pillows like this, and then there was another white piece of cloth that was sewn and there was a stone inside it.

It was sewn onto his pillow.

ALICE REARDEN: Are those *iinrut* and *napatet* not the same thing?

MARYANN ANDREWS: *Napatet* and *iinruq* are the same. To me they're the same.

MARIE MEADE: My mother was also a *yungcaraq*, and her name was Narullgiar [lit., "One like a weasel"]. She said that *narullgiar* was her *napateq*.

MARYANN ANDREWS: And my mother, also, this is what my mother told me, she said that walrus was her *napateq*.

MARIE MEADE: Yes. And my mother's name Narullgiar, probably because of that *narullgiq* [weasel], that the *narullgiq* was her *napateq*.

MARYANN ANDREWS: And my mother's name was Tulungulria [lit., "One who has ivory," from *tuluq*, "ivory"]. That was her Yup'ik name. And my father's name was Taqinqurraq.

ALICE REARDEN: Was [she named] Tulungulria because she had a walrus for a *napateq*?

MARYANN ANDREWS: She would snore, my mother would snore loudly, she said, since she had a walrus for a *napateq*.

Tua-llu caqerluku wiinga alqairutka-llu pillruarpuk waten, "Ciin assilinritqerqavet qutuyuirtelarcit qutup'agarraarluten?" Tua-ll' pikilikuk, tua-i-gguq-wa, yuutiin-gguq taum kaugpiim-gguq uniartelarngataa assilinriqertaqan.

Augkut wani iciw' yugnek anirtuangnaqu'urluteng-llu pilalriit niitellrit ciuliaput. Tamakuciumallrungatuq aanaka.

ARNAQ: Tauna-qaa elpet aatan yungcarauluni?

TAUYAAQ: Yungcarauluni-llu cali aataka. Taugaam taum iinruan kangianek niitellrunritua.

Yugtun atra Taqinqurraullruuq.

Tua-llu putuskami iquakun taugaam ciimarrarmek pingqerrluni. Wiinga tua-i teguluku tauna putuskaq umyuaqliutaqamku iinrua, mingqumaluni. Tua-i tang tangengnatuglaryaaqekeka, tangengnatuglaryaaqekeka kelui piluki. Aanama alakaqamia allurtaqlua.

CUCUAQ: Lumarram-qaa iluanlluni?

TAUYAAQ: Ii-i, lumarraam iluani mingquci[maluni]. Iciw' putuskangqerrlalriakut waten, tua-ll' allamek qatellriamek cali pingqerrluni mingqucimaluni ciimarmek imarluni.

Mingqucimaluni putuskaanun.

CUCUAQ: Tamakut-qaa iinrut napatet-llu allaugut, ayuqevkenateng?

TAUYAAQ: Ayuquk napatet *and* iinruq. *To me they're same.*

ARNAQ: Aanaka, aanaka-llu wiinga yungcaraullruuq, atra-wa Narullgiar. Narullgiar-gguq tauna napatekluku.

TAUYAAQ: Aanaka-ll' wani wiinga, waten pillruanga aanama, tauna-gguq kaugpak elliin napatekaa.

ARNAQ: Ii-i. Wiinga-ll' tauna cali aanama atni Narullgiar, tauna-w' tua-i narullgiq pillikii, narullgiq napatekniluku.

TAUYAAQ: Tua-llu aanama atra Tulungulriaruluni. Yugtun Atra. Atama-llu atra Taqinqurraq.

CUCUAQ: Tauna-qaa kaugpagmek napatengqellra pitekluku Tulungulriamek?

TAUYAAQ: Qututuluni wani, aanaka qututuluni cakneq kaugpagmek-gguq napatengqerrami.

They say some shamans are like doctors[36]

Barbara Joe and Alice Rearden, Anchorage, April 2012

BARBARA JOE: When I observed things, those shamans, back when they didn't have [Western] doctors, they say some shamans were like doctors. A person in pain, although he was a baby or an adult, they would use their shaman powers to doctor a person in pain. They were trying to bring them toward wellness, and they weren't doing anything malicious, they didn't push them toward malice, but they tried to heal him so that he would live, they tried to save him.

I heard one time that [Leggleq], the father of the late Tommy Moses, I used to hear that he was a shaman, but I never saw him practicing his shaman powers. We never saw those practicing their shaman powers since we used to live in the wilderness at camp back when we didn't attend school.

I heard that that person was a shaman. They said a person living in a home, although [he didn't heal] a man, but a person who was just living there . . . My mother told me a story. She was pregnant with my deceased younger sibling Joseph Gregory. Then she said Leggleq arrived at their home, and he was practicing his shaman powers to heal someone, but she never told me who he was practicing his shaman powers on. She said he was practicing his shaman powers and doctoring someone.

Then she said after practicing his shaman powers on that person, when he was done, he said there is something in the house that is worrisome. That means that there is someone in this home whose life is uncertain. Do you know the meaning of *augtarnarqellria* [something that one feels unsure of, feels hesitant about, doubtful about]?

ALICE REARDEN: Talk about it.

BARBARA JOE: Those *augtarnarqellriit* [people who one doubts will live] are like this. Although they are doctors, they may take care of a person in pain, but they find it difficult to heal them. Then if they are doubtful about them, they will say that they are doubtful that they can make them well again. They used to call that one *augtarnarqellria* [one they were doutbtful (would live)] in the past.

Then she said Leggleq said, I didn't observe this back then; she said the late Tommy Moses's father said, that he senses that inside that home, that

Ilait angalkut-gguq tua-i yungcartetun ayuqut

Arnaucuaq Cucuaq-llu, Anchorage, April 2012

ARNAUCUAQ: Murilkellemni tamakut angalkut yungcartaitellermeggni, ilait-gguq ilait angalkut-gguq tua-i yungcartetun ayuqut. Nangteqellria piipiungraan taqnerungraan nangteqellria tuunrilluku. Iciw' elluam tungiinun, ik'itmun pivkenaku, iqlutmun pivkenaku yuungnaqevkarluku taugaam, anirtungnaqluku.

Niigartellruaqa cami imna-gguq Tommy Moses-aunrilriim atii niitlallrukeka angalkuuniluku, taugaam tuunrivkarluku tangellrun[ritaqa]. Wangkuta tuunrilrianek tangssuitellruukut wangkuta yuilqurrarmi *camp*-ami uitatullruamta *school*-ayuitellemteni.

Niitelallruaqa tauna angalkuuniluku. Man'a-gguq enem iluani uitalria taum angutem ellii pinrilngermiu tauna cailkami uitalria . . . Aanairutma tuaten qanemcitellruanga. Ellii-gguq kinguqliirutemnek Joseph Gregory-mek qingarluni. Tua-llu-gguq tauna Leggleq tekilluni eniitnun tuunrilluku kina im', qanrutellrunritaanga kina imna tuunritniluku. Kina-gguq imna tuunrilluku.

Tua-i-llu-gguq tuunritraarluku taqngami qanertuq ellii-gguq man'a-gguq, elliin pivkenaku, man'a-gguq enem ilua aviranarqellriartangqertuq. *That means,* man'a-gguq enem ilua anerteqlerkaa-gguq augtarnarquq. Augtarnarqellria taringan?

CUCUAQ: Qanrutekluku.

ARNAUCUAQ: Augtnarnarqellriit tamakut waten pilartut. Una yungcartengungermeng una auluksaaqeciqaat nangteqellria, ellaita capirluku. Tua-llu capiqunegteggu qanerluteng, caperrnarquq-gguq, ellaita-gguq capiraat assirivkallerkaa. Tauna augtarnarqellriamek pituat avani.

Tua-llu tauna Leggleq-gguq qanertuq, wiinga murilkellrunritaqa tamaani; qanertuq-gguq tauna Tommy Moses-aunrilriim atii, man'a-gguq

there is something worrisome inside that house. *Aviranarqellria* [something worrisome] and *augtarnarqellria* [something one is uncertain about] are almost the same. An *augtarnarqellria*, even though they are doctors, they say they are doubtful about healing that one. They try to help that person, and when they are done trying to help that person, they say they are unable to heal that person, that he is in a state that is difficult to treat.

Leggleq evidently said that there is someone whose life is uncertain inside that home. That means that there is someone there who won't live, and he said that he sensed it.

Then Leggleq evidently told our late mother that her fetus, and here he wasn't watching it, that her fetus was something that was unlikely to live, that it was like one who won't live. They say Leggleq, the one Tommy Moses followed was like a doctor, that he was like a real doctor. That one who was like a doctor, I'm thinking that he wasn't someone who was malicious.

You know how they used to tell us when we became aware, "As you are living, don't stay with one who tends to head toward waywardness. He's a bad person." But a person who is heading toward good, one who encourages a person to live a good life with their future in mind, that person, however, is a good person.

I often think that Leggleq didn't have shaman powers that were malicious. It's because he tried to help a person whether one was a child or an adult so that one would live.

Then he evidently practiced his shaman powers on the fetus of our late mother. I didn't watch him. She was pregnant with my younger sibling.

He practiced his shaman powers [on the fetus] close to the time it would be born, and he instructed her that if anything . . . In our family that was the only person who [a shaman] practiced his shaman powers on, in our family. In our family, you know how they say they give them *napatet*; we never experienced that.

My mother used to tell us that her mother, long ago when they were small, when they were children, that her mother never followed those abstinence practices. She said her mother lived just as she observed her. But she said that the one who Piqtayumiq is named after, the late mother

enem ilua elliin alakaa, enem iluani-gguq tamaani aviranarqellriartangqertuq. Aviranarqellria augtarnaqellria-llu ayuqsarpiartuk. Una waniw' augtarnarqellria yungcartengungermeng pilaqait, capillerteng tauna capirniluku. Tua-i ikayungnaqsaaqluku, tauna ikayungnaquteteng qaqitaqan qanerlalriit una-gguq pisciigataat, caperrnarilliniuq-gguq.

Tua-i qanlliniluni tauna Leggleq una-gguq enem iluani-gguq tamaani augtarnarqellriartangqertuq. *That means*, anerteqarkaunrilngurmek-gguq yugtangqertuq tamaani, elliin-gguq alakaa.

Tua-i-llu aanairutput qanrutliniluku taum Legellrem, qumia-gguq tauna, tangvanrilmikii-wa, qumia-gguq tauna augtarnarquq, anerteqngailngurtun-gguq ayuquq. Tauna-gguq Leggleq Tommy Moses-am tua-i-wa maligcestii yuungcartetun-gguq ayuquq, tua-i yuungcarteqapigtuq-gguq. Tamana yuungcartetun ayuqellria, umyuarteqlartua assiilnguunricukluku.

Iciw' ellangellemteni pitullrukaitkut, "Man'a yuunginanerpeni iqlutmun ayagyulria aipirturyaqunaku. Assiilnguuguq." Man'a taugken elluatmun ayalria yuk ciunerkaa umyuaqluku cingumakii tamana taugken assilriaruluni.

Umyuarteqlartua tauna Leggleq assiilngurmek tamatumek tuunrangqenricukluku. Mikelnguungraan, taqnerungraan ikayungnatugturluku anerteqlerkaatun aulukellruamiu.

Tua-i-ll' tuunritliniluku tauna qumia aanairutemta. Wii murilkellrunritaqa. Kinguqlima, kinguqlimnek qumingqerrluni.

Tua-i yuurrnariani tua-i tuunrilluku alerqurrluku-llu camek piciatun . . . Tua-i *family*-mteni kiimi tauna tuunricecillruuq, wangkuta *family*-mteni. Wangkuta *family*-ni kia, imkunek-llu napacirnilaqait; tamana atullrunritarput.

Aanamta qanrutlallruakut aanii-gguq taum elliin ak'a tamaani mikellratni mikelnguullratni aanii-gguq elliin makut-gguq eyagyarat atuyuitellrui. Aanani murilkellermitun-gguq yuullruuq. Makut-gguq taugaam tua-i arcaqaq'apiaralrii atutullrui taum Piqtayumim

of my mother only practiced the most important customs. She said she instructs us following her instructions.

Then that child was evidently born. She said he was born and he seemed okay. He's still living today. But when he had a big stroke, when he was extremely ill, he had a loss of brain function, it evidently was lost.

And since he was educated in school, you know how Maryann told us yesterday that her father had just a stone for an *iinruq*. Leggleq evidently also gave him a small stone for his *iinruq*. When he married, since he probably wouldn't keep that pillow for a long time, he lost it. [*chuckles*] Poor!

atran, aanama anairutiin. Tua-i-gguq maa-i ellait alerquutai aturluki maa-i qanrutlaraitkut.

Tua-i-llu tauna mikelnguq yuurtelliniluni. Yuurtuq-gguq tua-i cangatevkenani. Maa-i cali tua-i anerteqluni. Taugaam *stroke*-arpallermini, nangteqerpallermini umyugaan ilii aug'allruuq, aug'allrulliniuq.

Ellii-llu *school*-araullruami, iciwa akwaugaq-llu Maryann-aq qanemcilria ciimarrarmek iinrungellruniluku atairutni. Tuaten-llu taum Legellrem cikiryaaqluku ciimarrarmek iinrukaanek. Nulirtuami tayima tauna ak'arpak-wa putuskaqngailamiu tayima tamallia. [*ngelaq'ertuq*] Akleng!

He takes the life that his child would have lived[37]

Barbara Joe, Maryann Andrews, and Alice Rearden, Anchorage, April 2012

BARBARA JOE: They say some shamans have shaman powers that are dangerous with an intent that is malicious. And some [shamans], wanting to live long, wanting to have a long life, and although they are his own children and relatives, being selfish, he would try to take their souls. That one who is selfish, wanting to live and not die, his children . . . This is how I heard it, that he takes the souls of his children. They say that is a malicious shaman.

MARYANN ANDREWS: So he takes the life that his child would have lived?

BARBARA JOE: Yes, he takes the life he would have lived. That is a very bad thing. When we attended school at Akulurak, when a shaman would speak, there would be many people. My, it was one who the Devil instructed. My goodness!

ALICE REARDEN: Would they recognize those people when they spoke?

BARBARA JOE: Mark spoke briefly about that and mentioned the name of that female, that her children died. He mentioned that he took the life his child would have lived, trying to stay alive himself. That is something that is very bad among us, a bad thing. Since we never became aware of life . . . Our parents and our grandmother and our

Irniami anerteqlerkaa elliin teguluku

Arnaucuaq, Tauyaaq, Cucuaq-llu, Anchorage, April 2012

ARNAUCUAQ: Tamana-gguq angalkuq ilii-gguq alingnarqellriamek ik'itmun, ik'itmun ayalriamek tuunrangqerrlartuq. Ilii cali ellminek yuumayugluni, anertequmayugluni, cali irniaqengermiki ilakengermiki-llu anernerit ellminek, ellminek arcaqakluni anernerit-gguq cali tamakut tegungnatutuluki. Ellii-am tauna ellminek arcaqakellria, ellminek taugaam arcaqakluni yuuyugluni, tuquksaunani uitayugluni, irniaminek . . . Waten niitelallruaqa irniami-gguq anerneritnek tegulluni. Tamaa-i-gguq tamana assiilnguq angalkuq.

TAUYAAQ: Irniami-qaa anerteqlerkaa elliin teguluku?

ARNAUCUAQ: Ee-m, anerteqlerkaa elliin teguluku. Tamana tamaa-i assiilnguq nutaan. Wangkuta Akulurak-ami *school*-allemteni, ilii angalkuq qanqerqan yugyagnaurtut. Ala-i tuunrangayiim-wa alerquallra. Ala-i!

CUCUAQ: Elitaqluki-q' tamakut qalartaqata?

ARNAUCUAQ: Mark-aq qanqalria tamatumek, kitumek tuani imna arnaq aperluku, irniariulluni-gguq. Qanrutkekii, irniani yuullerkaa teguluku ellii taugaam anerteqengnaqluni. Tamaa-i tamana wangkutni nutaan tamana assiilnguuguq, tua-i assiilnguq. Wangkuta ellangellrunrilamta . . . Wangkuta angayuqaagka maurlurput-

grandfather, we didn't have a person like that in our family.

They say a shaman who coaxes others [to take his powers] is dangerous[38]

Barbara Joe, Anchorage, April 2012

BARBARA JOE: They say some people, some shamans, when they are filled with gratitude when someone gives them food, too, the shaman coaxes a person [to take his powers], when he no longer feels confident that he will live.

They say the one who is coaxing someone [to take his powers] says that he doesn't have anything to pay him with. When he is grateful for something, he will want to give something in return.

He would tell the one who helped him that although he wants to give him a small payment, that he has nothing to give. They say that [shaman] is one who is coaxing someone [to take his powers]. He says he has nothing to give, but maybe he should pass down his shaman powers to that person. They say that one is one who is trying to coax someone [to take his powers]. He asks that person if it would be okay if he passes down his shaman powers to him. It is said if he gives away his shaman powers, if that person learns it, he will start to practice it.

They tell a person not to accept a shaman's offer when he coaxes him, he is told not to comply, not to accept. He is told to ignore him. They say a shaman who coaxes someone is dangerous. But they say long ago, some people asked [for his shaman powers]. When he knew a shaman [had powers] and asked for them, [the shaman] complied and gave him his shaman powers.

But they say some people didn't accept [his powers] because they were afraid of it. They tell the shaman they're fine just the way they've been living without any [powers]. And [the shaman] wouldn't get angry at him. They say one who gets angry . . . You know how you spoke of *aniqlaalria* [one who curses someone] yesterday. They say *aniqlaalria*, a person may make threats when a shaman does something to him. They will say things to offend that shaman.

Ellminek-gguq man'a angalkuq qaruyutellria alingnarquq

Arnaucuaq, Anchorage, April 2012

ARNAUCUAQ: Ilii-gguq yuum, angalkum ilii quyaqerqami-llu neqkamek payugtaqatni, quyaqerqami-llu qaruyutlartuq ellminek, anerteqlerkani capiryagutaqamiu.

Tua-i-gguq tauna qaruyutellria, qantuuq-gguq, ellii-gguq tang waniwa camek akinaurutkaminek cailnguq, piilnguq. Akinaurutkaminek-gguq ugaani quyam, camek quyaqerqami.

Ellii-gguq tang waniwa camek quyaluku nunuliqeryung'ermiu tauna ikayuasteni, ellii-gguq tang waniwa camek-gguq cakaituq. Tua-i-gguq tauna qaruyutellria. Cakaituq-gguq ellii taugaam-gguq angalkuminek, angalkuminek-gguq paiciskuniu. Tua-i-gguq qaruyutellria. Angalkuminek-gguq paiciskuniu-gguq-qaa caciqa. Tauna-gguq angalkuni cikiutekekuniu elliin, elliin-gguq eliskuniu aturyaurciiqaa.

Tamana qaruyutellria cikiqengyugluni angalkuminek angresqessuitaat, maligtaqucesqessuitaat, angresqessuunaku. Ilangcilluku. Ellminek-gguq man'a anglkuq qaruyutellria alingnarquq. Taugaam-gguq taum yuum tamaani, ak'a tamaani, yuum-gguq iliin kaigaviketua. Kaigavikaqamiu-gguq tauna angalkuq, nallunritaqamiu angalkuminek tua-i maligtaquluku cikitua.

Iliin-gguq taugken yuum iliin ciuniuyuitaa-gguq tauna alikluku. Kiutua-gguq waten tauna angalkuq, ellii tuaten ayuqenrilngermi eglerqurallra cangatenritniluni. Aam, qenqerrutevkenaku-llu. Man'a-gguq qenqerrulluni pilria . . . Iciw' akwaugaq-llu imumek aniqlaalariamek qanqalriatek. Aniqlaalria-gguq tua-i, ilii-gguq yuum aniqlaaciquq angalkum taum qaillun piqaqani, akunaluni-gguq aniqlaaluni. Iciw' qanaaluni cangayugcelluku-llu tauna angalkuq.

They say that shaman will curse a person who doesn't comply[182]

Barbara Joe, Anchorage, April 2012

BARBARA JOE: They say a shaman would try to give his powers to someone, and if they don't accept, he will threaten a person who doesn't accept by saying something, only through words. He won't do something out in the open, and he won't say, "I will do this to you." And he won't attack him directly, but will bother him in secret. They say if he bothers him in secret, he won't stop. They say he won't stop bothering that person until he gets him.

But if a person doesn't threaten him, if he doesn't curse him, he will feel compassion for him, feel pity for him. They say that is one who is feeling guilty. Although he cursed him, he is one who feels guilty. They say that one is one who is heading toward good, that he is a good person. Although he curses, following the teachings, "Although a person mistreats you, no matter what they do to you, don't ever talk back to him. Don't ever reply to that person although a person mistreats you. And although they curse you, don't ever talk back to him."

These words of wisdom that we were given in the past, they used to give us that admonishment, "Although a person does something to you, no matter what they do to you, don't ever talk back to him. Don't talk back to him as part of your body will get hurt, he won't remove any part of your body. No part of your body will be hurt, so don't talk back to him." They say not talking back is powerful, that trying not to talk back is powerful.

She learned his identity on her own in her sleep[40]

Maryann Andrews and Barbara Joe, Anchorage, April 2012

MARYANN ANDREWS: I actually became aware of life a long time ago, but one practicing his shaman powers, I actually saw one preparing to practice his shaman powers, but since I didn't watch him from beginning to end, I don't know what [shamans] are like. Because I was so afraid, I fell asleep.

Angalkuminek maligtaqutenrilnguq-gguq cali tuaten taum angalkum aniqlaaciqaa

Arnaucuaq, Anchorage, April 2012

ARNAUCUAQ: Iliin-gguq cali angalkum tuaten maligtaqutenrilnguq cikingnaqsaaqluku angalkuminek maligtaqutenrilnguq-gguq cali tuaten taum angalkum aniqlaaciqaa qanllermikun, qanllermikun taugaam. Alailqurravkenani waten-llu pivkenani, "Tuaten piciqamken." Tuaten-llu pivkenaku taugaam nalluanek, nalluanek taugaam qailliukuarulluku. Nalluanek taugaam, nalluanek-gguq *bother*-aaquniu peggngaitaa. Tua-i tauna unakumavkenaku-gguq peggngaitaa.

Iliin-gguq taugken yuum aniqlaatekenrilkani, aniqlaanrilkan naklegyagulluku, naklegyagulluk', kusguryagulluku. Tamana-gguq tamaa-i umyuarniulria. Aniqlaangraan umyuarniulria. Tamana-gguq assilriim tungiinun eglertuq, assilriaruuq. Aniqlaangraan, imkut qaneryarat aturluki, "Yuum pingraaten, cangraaten kiuqeryaqunaku. Kiuqeryaqunaku yuum pingraaten. Aniqlaatengraaten-llu kiuqeryaqunaku."

Maa-i tua-i wangkuta tamaani qanruyutvut, inerqutullruitkut tuaten, "Yuum pingraaten, cangraaten kiuqeryaqunaku. Kiuqanrilgerpegu, naten qain akngirrngaituq, naten ilangarrngaitaa. Qain-llu naten akngirrngaituq qanenrilngerpet atam kiunrilngerpegu." Kiuqanritleq-gguq una kayuuq, kayuuq-gguq kiumatenritengnaqleq.

Ellminek qavamikun alakluku

Tauyaaq Arnaucuaq-llu, Anchorage, April 2012

TAUYAAQ: Wiinga-llu ellangelqa imna akaurcaaquq, taugaam tuunrilriamek, upluni tuunriqatarluni tangellruyaaqua, taugaam taqellranun tangvallunrilamku nalluanka. Alingem tang pitaciatun wiinga qavaqerlallrulrianga.

I used to see them preparing a number of times, those who were preparing to practice their shaman powers. Out of great fear, I used to fall asleep. I cannot tell stories about the ways of shamans in any way.

And myself also, you all probably had a best friend who you played with all the time when you were small. You would play with this particular person, you really liked playing with them. That's how I was also.

But we hardly saw one another. When we'd move to Manumik in the winter, we didn't see each other all winter. But only when we moved in the spring, our parents, when our parents would move us there, we would only see one another again at Qip'ngayak. The one I used to play with is alive today.

Then one time when we were playing together, and we both had had our menstrual periods, she told me the following story. She said a shaman used to bother her in her sleep. I just listened to her. She said after he did that a number of times, after a number of times of bothering her in her sleep, she said she thought, "I wonder how I could counter him?"

Then when she had a dream about him again, when she thought of a way to counter him, she said this is how she got revenge on him, when she was desperate in her sleep, "I wonder how I should counter him?" She said the one she saw would be in the form of a dog. She would think, "I wonder how I could repay him so that my revenge would be strong?"

She said she first spread her hands like this. And after spreading them, pretending not to, she put saliva on them. And after putting saliva on them, she smeared both of these [tips of her feet] with her saliva.

Her feet. She said when she took a step, that dog started making noise right away. She said when that one started to make noise, it was Leggleq.

BARBARA JOE: My goodness!

MARYANN ANDREWS: She said he hunted her in her dream, but she said she countered him during that time. And she said when she [took a step] with the other [foot], he made noise even more.

She said when she continually approached him like that, she said she saw the fire that was burning from behind him. She said that [shaman] was extremely desperate, and she was thinking to let him fall there, but she stopped when she thought,

Qayuturqunek ava-i tangtullruyaaqua uptellrianek tuaten tuunriqatarluteng. Alingem pitaciatun wiinga qavaqatuunga. Qanemcikesciigatanka qaillun angalkut piciryarait.

Tua-llu wiinga-llu cali, elpeci-llu tayima miklerpeceni tamarpeci aiparnaarrangqerrlallruuci. Aipaqaqluku una yuk, aiparnikluku cakneq. Wiinga-llu tuaten ayuqellruunga.

Taugaam tangvaupakayuunanuk-llu. Uksumi upagaqamta Manumigmun tua-i uksurpak tangrrucuunanuk uitaaqlunuk. Upagaqamta taugaam up'nerkami angayuqaput, angayuqamta upautaqaitkut tuani Qip'ngayagmi ataam tangrrutaqlunuk. Ernerpak cali tauna anertequq aipaqlalqa.

Tua-llu ataucirqumek elliin aipaqlemegni wani aglellrurrlunuk-llu tamamegnuk elliin waten qanemcitellruanga. Ellii-gguq angalkuum qavaakun caumatullruyaaqaa. Wiinga tua-i niicugniurluku. Qayucirillrani-gguq ava-i, qayuturqunek qavaakun pillrani ellii-gguq waten umyuarteqellruuq, "Qaillun atak' piluku akiqerlaku?"

Tua-llu ataam qavanguqenqigcamiu, tua-i-w' umyuaqliucamiu tamana akiurutkani waten-gguq elliin akillrua, kapiarqellrani qavamini, "Qaillun atak' akiqerlaku?" Qimugtenguluni-gguq tauna tangerrlallra. Umyuarteqluni tuaten, "Qaillun waniw' akikumni-kiq wiinga kayuniartuq akiuteka?"

Ciumek-gguq unatni waten sagtellrui. Sagterraarluki-llu tua-i pinrilnguarluni tua-i nuaggluki. Nuagqaarluki-llu ukuk wani nuagminek tamarkenka minguglukek.

It'gagni. Tua-i-gguq amllillrani waten ak'a-ll' taun' qimugta nepengluni. Maaten-gguq imna nepnguq Leggleq.

ARNAUCUAQ: Ala-i!

TAUYAAQ: Qavaakun-gguq pissurturallruyaaqaa taugaam-gguq elliin akillrua tuani. Aipaa-llu-gguq cali piani pikanirluni.

Tuaten-gguq piurturluku ullallrani elliin-llu-gguq amna kingunra keneq ekualria tangerrluku. Arenqianani-gguq kapialuni cakneq tauna, tua-i-gguq tuavet igcetnaluku-gguq tuavet piyaaqaa, waten-gguq taugaam tua-i umyuarteqlermini

"If you bother me again, I will let you fall." The [friend] I used to play with is still alive today.

She learned his identity on her own in her sleep. She said she used to see him as a dog. She said that dog was really bothering her, was bothering her badly. She said she started to think, "I wonder what I can do to counter him?"

She said one time when she was extremely desperate, she did that, she spread out her hands and put saliva on them. And after putting saliva on them, she said she smeared it on the front of her feet. And she said when she took a step, it started making noises right away.

BARBARA JOE: My goodness!

MARYANN ANDREWS: She said when [the dog] made noise, it was Leggleq's voice.

BARBARA JOE: My goodness! I think that person was a shaman with two intentions. He tried to save people and he also bothered people. He evidently used to bother people. . . .

MARYANN ANDREWS: The way I understood it, when my best friend told me that, I was thinking, since she had nothing and since she didn't see a weapon in her sleep, after spreading out her hand and after putting saliva on it, then she wiped the front of her feet with it. Then she said when she took a step, when that one made noise in desperation, that's how I understood that, I was thinking that a person's saliva is powerful.

BARBARA JOE: It's powerful.

MARYANN ANDREWS: Since she had no weapon, since she had no knife, but she only had her saliva, that's evidently what she did.

In my understanding, since that person had no weapon, she had no knife or semilunar knife, but she only had her saliva, she evidently used that as a weapon and confronted that [shaman] with it.

They say they alert people to what is about to occur[41]

Barbara Joe, Maryann Andrews, Peter Black, Marie Meade, and Alice Rearden, Anchorage, April 2012

PETER BLACK: Since we aren't very observant, although they alert us, we don't pay attention to them. We don't [understand] the signs that they give us.

taqellrua, "Uumiku pinqigeskuvnga igcelluten piciqamken." Maa-i cali tauna aiparniarraqlalqa miklermeggni anertequq.

Ellminek qavamikun alakluku. Qimugtenguluku-gguq tangerrlallrua. Qimugtem taum tua-i caumakluku, qimugtem caumakluku cakneq. Ellii-gguq umyuarteqngellruuq, "Qaillun-kiq tayim' pikumku akiniarcia?"

Cami-gguq tua-i kapiarqellrani cakneq, tuaten pillruuq, unatni nenglluki nuaggluki-llu. Nuagterraarluki-llu-gguq wavet it'gami ciuqerranun minguulluki. Amllian-gguq tua-i ak'a-llu nepengluni.

ARNAUCUAQ: Ala-i!

TAUYAAQ: Neplirtuq-gguq Legellrem erinakluku.

ARNAUCUAQ: Ala-i! Tauna tang malruuluni angalkuullrungatuq. Yuk anirtungnaqluku cali yuliutuluni. Tua-i yuliutullrulliniuq. . . .

TAUYAAQ: Wiinga wani taringellemku, tauna wani tuaten taum aiparnaarrarma qanrutellranga waten wiinga umyuarteqellruunga, camek ellii piilami caskumek-llu qavamini tayima tangenrrilami tauna wani unatni neng'arterraarluki nuagqaarluki tua-i-ll' it'gami ciuqerranun minguulluki. Tua-i-ll' amllillrani-gguq tauna imna ak'a-ll' kapialuni neplillrani wiinga waten umyuamkun tauna taringumaaqa, una wani yuum nuaga kayulriaruyukluku.

ARNAUCUAQ: Kayulria-w'.

TAUYAAQ: Iciw' caskuilami, camek caviggarmek piilami nuaminek taugaam, pillrullinilria.

Tuar wangni taringellemni wangni wiinga iciw' caskumek piilami, caviggaunani uluarunani-llu, tua-ll' nuaminek taugaam uumek taumek caskirluni tauna pillrullinia.

Elpengcarituut-gguq

Arnaucuaq, Tauyaaq, Nanirqun, Arnaq, Cucuaq-llu, Anchorage, April 2012

NANIRQUN: Murilketailamta, waten elpengcangraitkut pamateqsuitaput. Murilkessuitaput tamana taum-llu elpengcautii.

BARBARA JOE: They also refer to dogs that cry as *elpengcarilriit* [ones that give signs that something is about to occur]. They say dogs cry when someone is going to die in their family.

ALICE REARDEN: Do they tell people to kill them?

BARBARA JOE: I never heard of anyone killing [a dog] for that reason. . . .

I never heard that they killed [the dog]. But the dog, I forgot what they experience. Since people are different, some people probably kill [the dog] out of fear. They are afraid of it since it cried.

PETER BLACK: Yes, they don't let [the owner's] sibling [kill it], but they tell someone who is not of their family [to kill it]. You don't let your close family member [kill it]. They used to have one who wasn't related to you take care of it.

ALICE REARDEN: What do you mean take care of it?

PETER BLACK: Take care of it, *aulukevkarluku*.

MARIE MEADE: They had them kill it?

PETER BLACK: I think they did. I used to hear that, too. I forgot how I heard it. That one who cried. I think they did that through shamans. [The death] affects the dog and not the person. But they only had that suffering affect the [dog] that had cried, and they had the thing that would kill the person go to the dog that had cried.

It's because people's few customs were not the same.

The shamans probably take on the forms of those. They took on the forms of those animals.

MARYANN ANDREWS: Yes.

He shortens his destination[42]

Francis Charlie, Raphael Jimmy, and Alice Rearden, Anchorage, January 2013

ALICE REARDEN: And some people say they have abilities to travel. Although a village is far away, they can arrive there right away by doing something.

FRANCIS CHARLIE: Yes, that's what some people are like. But I've never heard that there are many [with that ability]. But they say only very few are like that.

RAPHAEL JIMMY: Only very few people.

FRANCIS CHARLIE: I also know of one person, but he died.

Although a place is far . . . what they call a *piyugcetalek* [lit., "one with the ability to walk"]. He has

---

ARNAUCUAQ: Qimugtet-llu qialriit cali elpengcarilrianek pilarait. Ilangarteqatarqata-gguq qimugtet qiatuut.

CUCUAQ: Tuqutesqelarait-qaa?

ARNAUCUAQ: Tuqucilriamek tamana pitekluku niitellrunritua. . . .

Niiteksaitaqa tuqutniluku. Taugaam qimugta, qaillun im' pikata ayuqenrilameng-wa ilii yuum, iliita yuut tuqutlallikiit alikluku. Qiallruan alikluku.

NANIRQUN: Yaa, anelgutainun pivkarpeg'naku ilakenrilkiinun taugaam aulukesqelluku-llu pilarait. Elpet nakmiin ilavnun pivkarpek'naku. Ilakenrilkengavnun aulukevkalallruat.

CUCUAQ: Qaill' aulukevkarluku?

NANIRQUN: *Take care of it*, aulukevkarluku.

ARNAQ: Tuqutevkarluku?

NANIRQUN: Pilallrungatut. Wiinga-ll' taman' niigarrlallruaqa. Qaillun-llu im' niitelallruyaaqaqa. Elliinun taumun qiallermun. Angalkutgun pilallrungataat. Qimugtemun tuc'illuku yugmun pivkenaku. Taumun taugaam qiallermun tuc'illuku tauna nangyun, nalatekaa-llu tauna qimugtemun tuc'illuku taumun qiallermun.

Piciryararrait-wa ayuqlanrilameng tamakut imkut.

Amiqlallikait-wa tamakut angalkut-llu. Cat tamakut ungungssiit amiqluki.

TAUYAAQ: Ee-m.

Ciunerkani nanilicarluku

Acqaq, Angagaq, Cucuaq-llu, Anchorage, January 2013

CUCUAQ: Ilait-llu call' ayagassuutengqerrnilu[ki]. Yaaqsingraan una nuna egmian' tekicugngaluku qaill' piqerluteng.

ACQAQ: Yaa, tua-i-w' tuaten ilait. Taugaam amllermek, amllerrniluki wii niicimaksaitua. Taugaam tua-i caqapiar-gguq tuaten ayuqut.

ANGAGAQ: Caqapiaraat taugaam.

ACQAQ: Ataucimek cali nallunrilkengangqertua taugaam piunrillruluni.

Yaaqsingraan . . . piyugcetalegmek-gguq. Piyugcetangqerrluni. Tua-i amlliquni-gguq

---

a *piyugcetaq* [ability to walk]. They say if he takes a step, [the ground] folds and he is able to land far although it's close. When he takes a step, [the ground that folded] comes . . .

ALICE REARDEN: The land folds?

FRANCIS CHARLIE: Yes, his path, his path folds. He shortens his destination.

They call those *piyugcetalget*.

RAPHAEL JIMMY: They say although a place is very far, some take two steps or three and arrive. Those *piyugcetalget* are like that.

That shaman evidently put a child in her womb who wouldn't catch animals[43]

Francis Charlie, Raphael Jimmy, and
Alice Rearden, Anchorage, January 2013

RAPHAEL JIMMY: You probably didn't catch those two, who was that man who was very tall from Kuiggaq? He had a mother and father there. They used to stay at Kuiggaq. I forgot what they used to call that person.

FRANCIS CHARLIE: And did they say that he was a shaman?

RAPHAEL JIMMY: Yes. But they say although he was a shaman, it was hard to tell that he was. They say the children of that couple wouldn't live.

A shaman evidently put a baby inside that woman's womb. Then he told them not to be critical of him, that he would not catch anything at all from the wilderness, nothing at all!

Exactly as he said, they say he didn't catch anything at all from the wilderness! Be it a small mouse, or something small, he never caught anything at all. And I used to see that person, a tall man. I forgot what they called him.

ALICE REARDEN: Was he one who a shaman doctored to live while in the womb?

RAPHAEL JIMMY: Yes, the shaman gave his mother a child since she couldn't have children. They say right after they were born, her children would suddenly die; because that constantly happened [to the mother]. That shaman evidently put a child in her womb who wouldn't catch animals. That's the only way he would live. I think he would die if he caught something, probably if he hurt something.

imegluni man'a tua-i yaaqvanun canimelengraan tuc'ugngaluni. Amlliqan man'a tailuni . . .

CUCUAQ: Nunaq imegluni?

ACQAQ: Ii-i tumii, tumii imegluni. Ciunerkani nanilicarluku.

Tua-i-gguq tamaa-i piyugcetalget.

ANGAGAQ: Yaaqsikapiarangraan-gguq ilii malrugnek wall' pingayunek-llu amllirluni tekilluni-llu. Tua-i piyugcetalget tamaa-i tamakut.

Angalkum-am taum tua-i qumililliniluku taumek picuitarkamek

Acqaq, Angagaq, Cucuaq-llu, Anchorage,
January 2013

ANGAGAQ: Imkuk ukuk-wa angullrunritliktek-wa ukuk-wa pim, kituullrulria-llu ima-q' imna angulvak im' sugtuluni Kuiggarmiu? Aanangqerrluni tuani aatangqerrluni-llu. Kuiggarmi uitauratulutek. Kitumek-im' pitullrukiit tauna.

ACQAQ: Angalkuuniaqluku-llu-qaa?

ANGAGAQ: Ii-i. Taugaam angalkuungermi iciw' nallunarluni. Tauna-gguq tuani, taukuk-gguq tuani irniakek anerteqsuunatek taukuk.

Tua-llu tua-i angalkum arnaq tauna nulirra qumililliniluku. Tua-llu pilukek cangalkesqevkenaku, yuilqumek caitqapiar camek picuiciiqniluku, caitqap'ik!

Tua-i-am qanellra aturluku tauna, tua-i-gguq yuilqumek caitqap'ik! Tua-i avcelngarraungraan, carraungraan caitqap'ik picuunani. Wii-ll' tangtuluku tauna, sugtuluni angun. Kitumek-am pitullrukiit.

CUCUAQ: Angalkum-qaa yungcaraa?

ANGAGAQ: Yaa, angalkum yul'iluku taukuk tuani aanii irniangqerciigalan. Irniari-gguq tua-i an'aqameng piqerluteng tuquq'ernaurtut; tuatnauraan tua-i. Angalkum-am taum tua-i qumililliniluku taumek picuitarkamek. Tua-i-gguq kiingan anertequtekarkauluku. Piskuni camek akngirkengkuni tua-i tuquciqluni-am pingatuq, aipaagni.

FRANCIS CHARLIE: I've never heard that before. Through stories told about him, all I heard was that a shaman, because they were tired of envying those around them with children, wanting to have a child, they evidently turned to a shaman. It seems he paid [the shaman] with his kayak, they asked for a son, paying that shaman with a kayak.

ALICE REARDEN: Do they call them *yungcarat* [children doctored by shamans to live while in the womb]?

RAPHAEL JIMMY: He was a *yungcaraq*, yes. I almost recalled his name, then I forgot it. He was a tall man. He had two ears here, and another ear here that was smaller.

Tuuyak! That person I talked about, that person who was unable to catch things, Tuuyak. His name was Tuuyak.

FRANCIS CHARLIE: A giant.

RAPHAEL JIMMY: Tuuyak was a giant. Tuuyak, I just recalled it. [*chuckling*]

ACQAQ: Wiinga tuaten niiteqaqsaitua. Tua-i-wa qanemciakun, taugaam tuaten angalkum tua-i-w' cuculnguagnek makugnek ilagmegnek irnialegnek, irniangeqeryuumiryaaqlutek angalkumun tua-i caullinilutek. Tuarpiaq qayaminek nunuliucirluku, qayamek nunuliucirluku angalkuq tauna qetunrarkamegnek kaigatkellrukiik.

CUCUAQ: Yungcaranek-qaa pituit?

ANGAGAQ: Yungcarauluni, yaa. Neq'aqeryarpiarqa atra tamaq'ariluku-ll' ataam. Sugtuluni angun. Ciutengqertuq atam malrugnek, wani cali aipaa ciuksuar.

Tuuyak! Waniwa imna qanrutkelqa, picuilnguq tauna Tuuyak. Tuuyauguq.

ACQAQ: Yugpak.

ANGAGAQ: Yugpak Tuuyak tauna. Tuuyak neq'aqa'arqa. [*ngelaq'ertut*]

Even if a shaman wants to give you a *pissurcuun* [something to hunt with], don't receive it[44]

Francis Charlie, Raphael Jimmy, and Alice Rearden, Anchorage, January 2013

RAPHAEL JIMMY: In the past my mother used to thoroughly admonish us about the ways of a shaman. She told us that no matter what proposition a shaman gave us, not to accept it. And she would end by saying that what a shaman does has a bad consequence. Do you understand it?

He said that if a shaman had done something to me, that my children will die. Or I won't be able to have children. When a child is born, he dies right away. That's the consequence that is dangerous.

She would also tell us the following, "Although you don't catch things in the wilderness, even if a shaman wants to give you a *pissurcuun*, shaman's power source [lit., 'something to hunt with'], don't receive it at all. It also has a bad consequence." She said its consequence in the future is bad. I don't believe in that whatsoever today.

FRANCIS CHARLIE: And the late Kaligtuq wanted to pass down his *pissurcuun* to me.

RAPHAEL JIMMY: I see.

Yuilqumek canek watqapik pissurcuutmek angalkum pingraaten watqapiar akurturyaqunaku

Acqaq, Angagaq, Cucuaq-llu, Anchorage, January 2013

ANGAGAQ: Avani aanama inerqunqegcatullrukiikut mat'umek angalkum ayuqucianek. Angalkum cangraakut caitqapiar ciuniuresqevkenaku. Waten-llu iqulirluku angalkum-gguq una callra wani iqugglugtuq. Taringarci?

Aipaagnek-gguq angalkum pillrukanga irnianka nang'urciqut. Qang'a-llu-qaa irniangesciiganii. Irniaq yuurtaqami ak'a-ll' tuquq'erluni. Tamaa-i tamana kangia alingnarqellria.

Cali waten, waten cali pinauraakut, "Picuiqurangerpet yuilqumi, yuilqumek canek watqapik pissurcuutmek angalkum pingraaten watqapiar akurturyaqunaku. Cali iqugglugtuq." Iqua-gguq amna assiituq. Tua-i maa-i caitapik tamana ukveksuitaqa catqap'ik.

ACQAQ: Aug'um-llu wii Kaligtuunrilriim pissurcuutminek paicicuglua pillruyaaqaanga.

ANGAGAQ: Aa-a.

FRANCIS CHARLIE: I replied to him that being a careless person, although I'm pitiful, that I cannot accept it. He wasn't insistent but agreed with me.

RAPHAEL JIMMY: They say that person [has a *pissurcuun*]. They say, when he was about to die as a consequence of his *pissurcuun*, he told a story about himself, about how he got into a mishap.

He said when he saw a fox that was curled up and sleeping, he approached it by crawling toward it along its lee side here, along its lee side. He came right up to it, he came upon it. He mentioned that he circled in a particular direction, I think he said he circled it following *ella* [the world (clockwise)].

He said since he had heard of people circling things in the past, he carried that out and he circled around that fox that was curled up and sleeping by crawling, and he went all the way around it. He said the fox didn't sense him at all!

And he said when he had gone all the way around it, he suspected that it wouldn't have done anything to him if he didn't catch it. He caught that one. He said by doing that, he was responsible for causing himself pain later. They say he told that story.

ALICE REARDEN: So by doing that, he was causing himself pain later in life?

RAPHAEL JIMMY: By doing that he was causing himself pain later in life. I'm not sure what he suffered from. He became extremely weak. I wonder what kind of ailment he suffered from. He told that story himself.

ACQAQ: Wii kiullruaqa wii picuqcaunii camek naklegnarqeng'erma pisciigatnilua. Tua-i ciumuuvkenani angerlua pillruanga.

ANGAGAQ: Tauna tua-i pinggerrnilaraat. Tua-i-gguq wani, waniwa pissurcuutni tamana tua-i-w' tuqutekniaraamiu, qanemcikellruuq ellminek, picurlallni.

Kaviarmek-gguq ungelralriamek tangrrami ullagaa aurrluni 'gguun uqlirnerakun. Tua-i tekilluku waniwa tua-i waten tekilluku. Natetmun-am uivniyaaquq, tuarpiaq tella maliggluku uivnilria.

Uivelrianek-gguq-am niitellaami avani tua-i-am ellii-llu aturluku tamana kaviaq taun' ungelralria qavalria uivelliniluku waten tua-i aurrurluku tua-i kassugluku. Imum-gguq uum kaviarem caitqapik elpekeksaunaku-llu caitqap'ik!

Kassuamiu-llu nutaan aipaagnek pitaqenrilkuniu aipaagnek cayanricuklukuartuq. Tauna tua-i pitaqluku. Cunawa-gguq tua-i ellminek nangtequtekiurluni. Tuaten qanemcillrunilaraat.

CUCUAQ: Nangtequtekiurluni-q' ellminek?

ANGAGAQ: Nangtequtekiurluni ellminek. Camek tayima nangtequtengqellrua-llu. Kayuirutellruuq cakneq. Caullrua-kiq tua-i nangtequtii. Ellminek tua-i qanemcikellruuq, qanemcikellruuq-wa.

That shaman cut open her stomach with a story knife[45]

Raphael Jimmy, Anchorage, January 2013

RAPHAEL JIMMY: And for us also, in the past when I was young, I also used to hear of shamans. They mentioned how they would practice their shaman powers on one who was ill. But I never witnessed that since I never traveled to places, since I became aware of life in the wilderness. In the village, they would heal a person, or if a person's leg broke, they say that shaman would fix it right away.

We used to hear of those things. They would also tell the following stories about those shamans. Let me tell a short story, okay?

There was also a person, a long time ago, they say a woman couldn't have a child. Then that sha-

---

Angalkum taum aqsiikun pilagturluku imumek yaaruitmek

Angagaq, Anchorage, January 2013

ANGAGAQ: Cali wangkuta wani avani waten tamaani *young*-arlua, makunek-llu cali angalkunek niitaqlua. Waten una wani nangteqellria waten tuunrilluku-llu. Wii taugaam tangvallrunritua ayagayuitellruama yuilqumi tellangellruama. Nunani kitugtaqluku waten qang'a-llu-qaa irua-llu asmeskan taum-gguq tuani angalkum kituggluku wanirpaggaq.

Tamakunek tamaa-i niitaqluta pitullruukut. Waten angalkut tamakut cali qanemcikaqluki waten. Qanemcicuaqerlii-qaa?

Cali tauna, ak'a tamaani avani arnaq-gguq wani irnisciiganani. Tua-llu-gguq angalkum

man cut open her stomach with a story knife, he
cut it open with a story knife and took that child
out. And she was fine.

And that woman's stomach, after taking [the
baby] out, after cleaning inside her, he closed it
and healed it by putting it in his mouth like this,
they say he closed and healed what he had cut open
to take the child out. He healed it and closed it; and
she had no pain.

Then my wife, there was something bad inside
her stomach, about how many years now, maybe
fifteen years ago. They cut open her belly, and
the doctors took that bad thing out. Then when it
healed, I recalled that story.

They said just like the [surgery] that the doctors
had carried out, they say the shaman's [surgery]
was exactly like that. People who knew said it was
exactly like that. The [Western] doctor cut her
open with a metal knife, and that shaman cut open
her stomach with a story knife.

But they say when that shaman was about to use
that story knife on her belly, he put it in his mouth,
he put it in his mouth. They say the people who
watched said that the story knife was very sharp
like a metal knife.

That's it. Thank you.

taum aqsiikun pilagturluku imumek yaaruitmek,
yaaruitmek pilagturluku taun' mikelnguq
anevkarluku. Cangatevkenani-llu.

Tauna-llu arnaq aqsiik, anqaarluku ilua
carrirraarluku mamlluku-ll' waten iqmigluku
mamlluku-gguq tamana pilagtullni waten
mikelnguq an'arkaurrluku. Mamlluku tua-i
assiriluku; camek nangtequtmek piinani.

Tua-llu maa-i aipaqa wani iluani qamani
maani iluani ca assirpek'nani *about*, qayutuurtut
maybe fifteen years ago. Tauna maaggun
aqsiigkenkun pilagturluku tauna assiilnguq
yuungcartet aug'arluku. Tua-llu mamngan tauna
neq'akellruaqa tauna qanemciq.

Yungcarcet tua-i pillracetun-gguq imna
augna angalkum pillra-gguq tuateqapiar-gguq
ayuqellruuq. Makut nallunrilnguut tuaten-gguq
ayuqeqapiarallruuq. Yungcartem caviggakun
pilagturluku taum-llu angalkum yaaruitekun
pilagturluku.

Taugaam-gguq taum angalkum taun' yaaruin
atuqatallerminiu tuavet aqsiigkenun waten
iqmigluku pillrua, iqmigluku. Caviggartun-gguq
tua-i tangvagtain ipkapiarluni yaaruin.

Tua-i. Quyana.

These shamans who were good,
I saw a number of them[46]

Joe Phillip and Alice Rearden, Anchorage, December 2013

JOE PHILLIP: And since there were many shamans
that I caught in my life in the past, they also
mentioned those, not to say anything to them to
make them upset.

Those shamans, as you know we have doctors
today. When a certain part of our body is in pain,
we go to a doctor. Those people who I observed who
were in pain, or children also, their parents would
tell that shaman to use their spirit powers to heal
them.

They were their doctors as you know. Our doctors had no [medical instruments]. They would
heal some, but they tended to make others worse.

ALICE REARDEN: Were some shamans malicious?
JOE PHILLIP: This is what they said they were like.
Some of them, here's me, and you are a shaman.

Makut angalkut elluarrluteng pilriit,
qavcinek ukunek tangerrlallruunga

Panigkaq Cucuaq-llu, Anchorage, December 2013

PANIGKAQ: Angalkut-llu amllellruameng avani wii
angullrenka, tamakut-llu aperturluki, qaillun
nekalirluki qarucesqevkenaki-wa.

Angalkut tamakut, waten tua-i yungcartenek
maa-i pingqellriakut. Natliqaqamta
yungcartemun piaqluta. Tamakut-llu yuut
murilkellrenka nangteqellriit, mikelnguut
qang'a-llu, angayuqaarita taumun angalkumun
tuunricesqelluki.

Yungcartekellrukait-am nallunrilketen.
Yungcarteput canek piinateng. Ilait
assirninaurait, ilait taugken ilalqatmun-gguq
piyugluki.
CUCUAQ: Ilait-qaa umyuarrliqellruut angalkuut?
PANIGKAQ: Waten ayuqnilallruit. Ilait, waten-wa
wiinga, elpet-llu angalkuuluten. Wiinga

him to, that shaman would go to him and work on him with his spirit powers.

I talked about some of it just now. If he doesn't speak about it well, [the shaman would tell him], "If you don't speak of it, I cannot fix it." Then his parents would tell him, "If you have done something, don't keep it secret and tell this person about it." Then when he spoke of it, that shaman would listen to him.

When he was done, he sat down and said, "I think I will be able to fix it." He would tell his parents that. He would practice his spirit powers and work on him.

When he was done with him, he told his parents that the one who he was previously unable to fix, since he confessed, since it became easy, he had removed it. He would tell them that he won't experience that again. That's what those who I saw used to do.

Then these priests are also like that. We confess our sins and leave out things, we leave things out that we're ashamed of. They say that thing that we left out will only multiply with more bad things. It will become big again. But if we speak about all of it, it will be absolved. It's just like that [shaman] who practiced his spirit powers said.

Those people used to speak to us [about those things]. And I also learned a lot that I didn't know from priests. They used to tell us. And some of their teachings were those, they would speak of our ancestor's teachings a little, but a shorter version, the way in which I heard them in the past. They were these proscriptions that we talked about.

Tua-i ava-i qanrutkaqa ilii. Elluarrluni qanenrilkan, "Qanenrilkuvet pisciigataqa wiinga." Tua-ll' angayuqaagken piluku, "Callrukuvet kasngukevkenaku qanrutkiu uumun." Tua-llu qanrutekngamiu, angalkum taum niicugniluku.

Taqngan aqumluni piuq, "Piyuumariciqngataqa-wa." Angayuqaak imkuk qanrullukek. Tuunrilluku.

Taqngamiu angayuqaak qanrutak, imna-gguq pisciigatellni, qanruteknngaku, pisciiryariqercan-gguq aug'araa. Pinqiggngaituq-gguq tuaten. Tuaten pilallruut tamakut tangellrenka.

Tua-llu makut cali agayulirtet tuaten. Assiilnguirlalriakut tua-ll' ilakuiluta, kasnguklemtenek-llu ilakuiluta. Tauna-gguq ilakuarput assiilngurnek ilangyullra kayuciquq. Ataam angliriluni. Tamalkuan qanrutkekumteggu taugken tua-i tayim' aug'arluni. Tautun imutun tuunrilriim qanellratun.

Qanrutlallrumiitkut tamakut. Maaken cali agayulirtek wiinga, amlleq augna nallulqa nallunrillruaqa. Qanrutlallruitkut. Augkuuluteng-llu qaneryarait ilait, ciuliamta qaneryarait qanrutkecuaqernaurait taklirivkenaki ayuquciicetun niitellemtun. Tua-i makuuluteng maa-i qanaatekelput inerquutet.

He said [having the child] between them, they apparently made it die[48]

Joe Phillip and Barbara Joe, Anchorage, December 2013

JOE PHILLIP: And a person who was using his spirit powers to heal someone, it seems they said Paugnaralria [Lawrence Edmund] is here at the hospital.

BARBARA JOE: He moved to Bethel. Paugnaralria returned to Bethel to a home.

JOE PHILLIP: They call that person Lawrence Edmund. These ones, his mother and father's children tended to die back in those days and wouldn't live.

Qukaqmika'arrluku-gguq tuquvkarlalliniak

Panigkaq Arnaucuaq-llu, Anchorage, December 2013

PANIGKAQ: Cali waten tuunrilriamek, maanetnikiit tuar imna kina Paugnaralria yungcarvigmi.

ARNAUCUAQ: Pimun, Mamterillermun *move*-allruuq. Paugnaralria utertellruuq Mamterillermi *home*-amun.

PANIGKAQ: Tauna Lawrence Edmund-aamek pilaraat. Ukut wani, aanii atii-llu irniari avani tuqulallruut anerteqsugpek'nateng.

Then at Alakanuk a person they call Qakerlui-laq practiced his spirit powers and worked on them. When he practiced his spirit powers on them, he told them . . . there were the usual people at the qasgiq at the time. Their children tended to die.

Then Qakerluilaq practiced his spirit powers on them down there. After practicing his spirit powers on them, he sat down. When he sat down he told them, "This is apparently what you are like. You get angry at one another. And here your child is right there. You apparently get angry at one another. And your child is between you two [when you get angry at one another]." He said [having the child] between them, they apparently made it die.

He said if she has another child, he told his wife, "Your child will be a male." He said if he was born, they shouldn't be like that. And he told them that although they made him cry, if his fellow children made him cry, not to defend him. He told them not to be that way, and not to call one another names.

After that, Lawrence Edmund was the first [child who lived]. Then his younger siblings haven't died, but they also suffer from ailments today.

Then another person, Thomas Cikigaq [Chiki-gak]. When he used his spirit powers to heal him in the same way, that person told them that that's what they're like. He told that woman once again, "You will have a child. It will be a male." He told them not to be that way. [Their children] didn't die again. Cikigaq's chidren are alive to this day.

Tua-ll' Alarnermi tuunritak Qakerluilam-gguq uum. Tuunricamikek qanrutak . . . qasgiq yungqerrluni yum'inek. Tua-llu irniakek tamakut tuquyugluteng.

Tua-i-llu taum Qakerluilam Tuunrillukek kanani. Tuunritqerlukek aqumuq. Aqumngami qanrutak, "Waten tang ayuqellinilriatek. Qenqerraqlutek. Tauna-wa mikelnguq irniartek. Qenqerraqlutek waten uitalallinilriatek. Tauna-llu irniartek qukaqmika'arrluku." Qukaqmika'arrluku-gguq tuquvkarlalliniak.

Watua irniangkan, tauna nulirra qanrutaa, "Angutnguciquq irnian tauna." Ankan tuaten ayuqesqevkenakek. Waten-llu yuut qiarqengraatgu ilain mikelnguut qiarqengraatgu yurnakluku pisqevkenaku. Qanrutak tuaten ayuqesqevkenakek, arivutaqlutek-llu.

Taum kinguakun tauna Lawrence Edmund-aq ciuqliuguq. Ukut-llu kinguqlii tuquksaitut, taugaam maa-i nangteqluteng-llu pilartut.

Ataam cal' alla, Thomas Cikigaq. Tuaten cali tuunritlermeggniu, taum qanrutai tuaten ayuqnilukek. Tua-i-am ataam qanrutaa taun' arnaq, "Waten irniangeciquten. Angutnguciquq." Tamakucetun pisqevkenakek. Tua-i-ll' tuqunqigtevkenatek. Maa-i cali irniari anertequt Cikigaam.

Then he said that person he had gone to see was too difficult for him [to heal][49]

Tua-i-llu qanertuq capiraa-gguq ingna, tauna ullallni

Joe Phillip and Barbara Joe, Anchorage, December 2013

Panigkaq Arnaucuaq-llu, Anchorage, December 2013

JOE PHILLIP: And those shamans who heal in a good way are truthful. [The shaman] would speak of how they were.

Those people were their doctors, well, shamans were their doctors. Some people were too difficult for them [to heal]. Those ones including Qakerlu-ilaq, when they couldn't heal those who were too difficult for them, they would tell some of them that that is too difficult for him, that too much time had passed since they got the ailment. He would tell him that this was when he would die. He would tell him he couldn't do anything for him. And that person would continue to live as he said he would, and he would die when he said he would die. That [shaman] spoke to them truthfully.

PANIGKAQ: Piciuluteng-llu tamakut elluarrluteng angalkut tuunritulit. Ayuquciicetun qanrutnaurai, qanruteknaurai.

Yungcartengqellruut tamakunek augkunek, yungcartengqellruukut-wa tamakunek angalkunek. Ilaita tua-i capi'iqluki. Taukut Qakerluilaq, capilteng tamakut pisciigataqamegteki ilait waten qanrutlarait elliin-gguq capiraa tamana, akaurtellinian-gguq tuaten ellillra. Wani, wani tua-i piciqniluku, iqukliciiqniluku tamana anernera. Qaillun pisciigatniluku elliin. Imutun-llu qanellratun tauna eglerrluni, tuani-ll' piciqnillrani tua-i yuunrirluni. Tua-i elluarulluki qanrutkellrukai taum.

Then one day, they used to call the late Qemrallrunrilria's father Pissugpiar. This one, Iikilnguq was apparently the first sibling. I'm related to those ones. That person was the husband of the late older sister of my late father.

He asked for Qakerluilaq on his own. Then, at the time we were living at Kuiggaq. He told his late younger sibling, the late Qemrallrunrilria to go and get that shaman Qakerluilaq.

Then he arrived with him. When he arrived, he was our guest. Then since my dear father had some homebrew, he had that shaman drink. That person lived separately in a different home over there. When night came, he would start to make noise in desperation, yelling.

Then my father had the shaman Qakerluilaq drink some alcohol. Above the stove, he placed his legs in this position and sat. He had his head down over there, he had his head down. Then he said that person he had gone to see was too difficult for him [to heal]. He said that he cannot save him in any way. He said it had been a long time that he had been in that condition. He said that it had been a long time since he got that illness. He said he cannot save him. He said that one would die after [the river] became free of ice.

He told our father to bring some grass inside, ones used for insoles, those grasses, if we had some. Then when he brought them inside, when he took the grasses, he dispersed them in front of him and would suddenly blow on them.

Yes, the grasses. After dispersing them, that shaman [blowing] would suddenly blow air onto them.

BARBARA JOE: My goodness!

JOE PHILLIP: They said they did it four times, he said he would blow on them. After gathering them, he told them to scatter them underneath that one in pain, along his mattress. They brought them over.

And he didn't practice his spirit powers on him. When he came over, he told him that he has added this much to his life. He said right after [the river] became free of ice, that person would die. He said he couldn't go over that time [couldn't lengthen his life further].

Then we stayed there. And when it was free of ice, we headed up to Kuiguk where we used to camp in the summer. And as they were pitching their tents, they said, his wife down there said inside a boat with a cabin, at the time we had a boat with a sail. She said that he died. They headed

Tuamtell' iliini, una wani Qemrallrunrilriim atairutii Pissugpiarmek piaqluku. Uum wani, Iikilnguq ciuqliullrullinilria. Ilakanka wii taukut. Uum atairutemta alqairutiin uikluku tauna.

Tauna tua-i ellminek Qakerluilaq tauna piyugluku. Tua-i-llu, Kuiggarmi uitaluta. Taumun Qemrallrunrilriamun kinguqlirminun aqvasqelluku taun' angalkuq, Qakerluilaq taun'.

Tua-i-ll' tekiulluku. Tekicami wangkutnun tukirluni. Tua-i-ll'-am uum ata'urluma ek'angqerrami mercelluku taun' angalkuq. Tauna-wa yaa-i ama-i allakarmi uitalria. Unungaqan waten nepengnaurtuq kapialuni, aarpagaluni.

Tua-i-llu ata'urluma taum mercelluku tauna angalkuq Qakerluilaq. Tua-i pelitaam kiatiini ukatmun irugni pilukek aqumgaluni. Pusngakili waniw' ika-i, pusngaluni. Tua-i-llu qanertuq capiraa-gguq ingna, tauna ullallni. Elliin-gguq qaillun-gguq anirturciigataa. Akaurtelliniuq-gguq tuaten ellillra. Taum-gguq akaurtelliniuq-gguq apqucingellra. Elliin-gguq anirturciigataa. Waniwa-gguq cikuiqan yuunrirciquq tauna.

Tua-llu atavut taun' pia canegnek itrucesqelluku, piinerkanek, imkunek canegnek, pingqerqumta. Tua-i-llu itrucamiki teguamiki ukut can'get wavet ciuqaminun saggluki cup'lernaurai.

Ii-i can'get. Sagqaarluki angalkum taum [cupluni] cuplernaurai.

ARNAUCUAQ: Ala-i!

PANIGKAQ: Cetamarqunek piniluki, cup'lerniluki. Tua-i-ll' piluki, quyurqaarluki taum ing'um nangteqellriim acianun alliraan pianun sagcesqelluku. Tua-i tayim' agulluki.

Tuunritevkenaku-llu. Tua-i taingan qanrutaa waten-gguq taktalriamek anernera usgua. Yaani-gguq cikuiqerluku yuunrirciquq tauna. Cipcesciiganaku-llu-gguq tamana pillra.

Tua-i-ll' uitaluta. Cikuirngan-llu Kuigugmun kiavet itrarluta kiagilallemtenun. Pelatekiurinanratni-llu qanertut taun', nulirra camna qanertuq angyam iluani net'algem, tengalratulimek angyangqerrluta. Anernerirtuq-gguq una. Kuiggarmek anelrarluteng Kuigugmun, tuani-ll' tua-i yuunrirluni qanellra atuq'apiarluku.

down from Kuiggaq to Kuiguk, and he died there just like [the shaman] had said.

When some would use their spirit powers to work on someone, they spoke of exactly what a person was like. Then after speaking of him, they said to him, "Okay now, speak of what you are like. If you don't speak of it, I cannot remove it. I cannot do anything about it." [The shaman] would tell him to speak about it, even though it was shameful.

And when he spoke of it, he would sit. Then he would say that he was going to work on him now. He would practice his spirit powers, he would say, he would finish and say that he had removed something that couldn't be removed. He said that he won't go back to his previous condition, that he will recover. That's what they would tell them.

But although some were shamans, they would say that some weren't skilled and had weak powers. They say when those who don't have strong powers turn bad, their tendency to want to turn bad is strong.

And although people in the past weren't shamans, those elderly men, they knew what a person was like by looking at him. When he left, they would say, "That person is apparently like this." They spoke of what he was like, even though he hadn't spoken. They knew what he had done. That was an admonishment.

Ilait tamakut tuunriskengaqameng yuum ayuqucia qanruteklaraat ayuquciatun. Tua-i-llu nutaan qanrutkerraarluku piluku, "Kitaki man'a ayuqucin qanrutkiu. Qanrutkenrilkuvgu aug'arciigataqa wii. Qaill' pisciigataqa." Kasngunarqengraan qanrutkesqelluku.

Tua-i-ll' qanrutekngaku aqumluni. Tua-i-gguq waniwa piqataraa. Tuunriluni, qanertuq, taqluni, aug'araa-gguq una pisciigalnguq. Uterrngaituq-gguq, assiriciquq-gguq. Tuaten tua-i pilallrukait.

Ilait taugken angalkuungermeng, pikeggneruvkenateng kayuunateng-llu ayuqninaurait. Tamakut-gguq-am cali tua-i iqlucitmun piaqameng iqlucitmun-gguq pillrat kayuuq, kayuilnguut tamakut.

Tua-i augkut-llu angalkuunrilngermeng cali, angukaraat augkut ak'allaat, nalluyuitait yug' una tangerrluku. Tayima-llu ayiin qanernaurtut, "Augna tang waten ayuqelliniuq." Ayuqucia qanruteknauraat qanenrilengraan. Nalluvkenaku pillra tua-i. Tua-i inerquutnguluni.

Priests were scarce, and our ancestors weren't Christians[50]

Joe Phillip, Anchorage, December 2013

JOE PHILLIP: And our shamans, those people in the past had shamans for doctors when I became fully aware. Priests were scarce, and our ancestors weren't Christians. My grandmothers and grandfathers didn't know about God. All over the place, and even the elders of the people to the north of us [didn't know]. Some of us didn't know at all, didn't know about God. But the first priests would arrive once in a great while only in summer by boat. We would learn those things [from them]. They would give them books and tell those who could read, those who were educated in schools, to read them.

There was only a small church up at Kuiguk. They used to teach us about communion there, about prayers.

Agayulirtet nurnarluteng, agayumavkenateng-llu augkut ciuliaput

Panigkaq, Anchorage, December 2013

PANIGKAQ: Makut call' angalkuput, augkut angalkunek yungcartengqellrulriit maaten usvingua. Agayulirtet nurnarluteng, agayumavkenateng-llu augkut ciuliaput. Maurluunka apa'urluunka-ll' wii nalluluteng Agayutmek. Kegkut-llu negeqliput augkut teggnellrit [nalluluteng]. Ilaitni tua-i caitqapik nalluluta, Agayun nalluluku. Agayulirtet taugaam augkut ciuqliit caqap'igtaqameng kiagmi taugaam tekitnaurtut angyakun. Tamakut tua-i elitaqluki. Kalikanek waten cikirluki naaqitulinun elicarallernun naaqevkarlaasqelluki.

Kiani taugaam tua-i Kuigugmi agayuvicuartangqellruuq. Tuani wangkuta elicarlallruitkut kemegturyaranek, tua-i-w' agayuyaranek.

A person named Father Deschout, with a female who was educated in school at Kangilek [mission], she was our teacher. She taught us prayers and ways of communion on Saturday, at the end of the week. And there weren't many of us. There were a few of us like this. Others probably [were taught] after us. And I didn't understand them although I heard them. I didn't know what they were saying.

Those who try to live honorably at this time, live peacefully at this time.

Father Deschout-am-gguq uum, arnamek pamani elicarallermek Kangilegmek tuani, taumek elicartengqerrluta. Agayuyaranek kemegturyaranek-llu elicarluta pinauraitkut Maqinerem iquani, week-am iquani. Yugyagpek'nata-llu tua-i waten. Qavcirrauluta. Allat-llu pilallilriit kingumteggun. Wiinga-ll' taringyuunaki niitengramki. Camek qanruciitaqluki.

Tua-i elluarrluteng taugaam maa-i uitangnaquralriit nepaunateng uitalalriit watua maa-i.

They say my father's father was a very powerful shaman long ago[51]

Placid Joseph and Alice Rearden, Anchorage, December 2013

PLACID JOSEPH: They say my ancestors lived here long ago at Iqalliarvik. And I didn't know that I had family there. They say from somewhere around here, from Kuigilnguq [Kwigillingok], they left by *palkaassaq* [skin boat] in wintertime.

ALICE REARDEN: What did you say about the shaman? You know, your ancestor, how your ancestor was a shaman.

PLACID JOSEPH: They say down at Kuigilnguq, since that shaman had many children, his children, because they'd go through starvation in the spring, and since he was a shaman and knew, he traveled with his shaman power probably at night. They say he saw fish vapor here at Iqalliarvik, from Kuigilnguq which is somewhere around here. This is the mouth of the Kuskokwim. Around this area is Kuigilnguq. Some place in between, what is it called again, Scammon Bay and Nunivak. Some place around here, they call it Kuigilnguq. They say my father's ancestors left that place.

ALICE REARDEN: Your father's father?

PLACID JOSEPH: Yes, they say my father's father was a very powerful shaman long ago, back when they used to go through starvation. He apparently told them to leave and travel to the place he saw. Apparently it was to Iqalliarvik here. I keep losing its location [on the map]. [*chuckles*]

ALICE REARDEN: It's right here.

PLACID JOSEPH: It's here. Some place around here. Kusquqvak [the Kuskokwim River], around here, maybe some place around here, from the shores of the ocean.

Taum atama atii-gguq angalkuullruuq cakneq ak'a tamaani

Qavarliaq Cucuaq-llu, Anchorage, December 2013

QAVARLIAQ: Ciulianka-gguq augkut wani uitallruut ak'a tamaani Iqalliarvigmi. Nalluluku-ll' wiinga ilangqelqa-ll' tamaani. Maaken-gguq naken, Kuigilngurmek, ayallruut *by palkaassaq in wintertime.*

CUCUAQ: Qaillun-ima angalkuq qanrutkellruken? Iciw' tauna ciulian, ciuliaci tauna angalkuullrulria.

QAVARLIAQ: Unani-gguq Kuigilngurmi angalkuq tauna irnialiami, irniani, up'nerkami waten kainiqtuameng, angalkuungami-w' nalluvkenaku, tuunramikun ayagluni unugmi pillilria-wa. Neqet-gguq, neqem-gguq puyuanek tangellruuq wani maani Iqalliarvigmi naken maaken Kuigilngurmek. Una wani *mouth of Kuskokwim. Around this area* Kuigilnguq. *Some place in between,* caulria-llu, *Scammon Bay and Nunivaaq. Some place around here, they call it* Kuigilnguq. Tamaaken-gguq atama taukut ciuliari ayallruut.

CUCUAQ: Aatavet aatii?

QAVARLIAQ: Yaa, taum atama atii-gguq angalkuullruuq cakneq ak'a tamaani, kainiqtullermeggni-w' tamaani. Qanrutliniluki-am ayaasqelluki taumun tangllerminun. Cunawa-gguq wavet Iqalliarvigmun. Tamarinaurqa tayima. [*ngelaq'ertuq*]

CUCUAQ: Tang waniwa.

QAVARLIAQ: Waniwa. *Some place around here.* Kusquqvak, *around here, maybe some place around here,* imarpiim ceniinek.

ALICE REARDEN: Yes. They call the area around Kuigilnguq Canineq, they call it Canineq.

PLACID JOSEPH: They said they were from Kuigilnguq. They say that powerful shaman was from Kuigilnguq.

ALICE REARDEN: Did they mention his name?

PLACID JOSEPH: I never heard it, and they never spoke of that powerful shaman. But that one was a shaman and had a great many children.

CUCUAQ: Ii-i. Kuigilnguum avatii Caninermek pilaraat, Canineq-gguq.

QAVARLIAQ: Kuigilngurmek kingunengqerrnilalriit. Tauna-wa, angalkurpak-gguq taun' Kuigilngurmiunguuq.

CUCUAQ: Atra-qaa qanrutkeksaitaat?

QAVARLIAQ: Niitekasitaqa, qanruteksuitaat-llu angalkurpak. Taugaam tauna angalkuuluni-w' irnialirluni cakneq.

When these shamans are desperate, they aren't good leaders[52]

Joe Phillip, Barbara Joe, Placid Joseph, and Alice Rearden, Anchorage, December 2013

JOE PHILLIP: This person has probably heard about those ones long ago who were on ice that detached and drifted away.

BARBARA JOE: Ayissangaaq and others, Ayissangaaq and others from Scammon Bay.

JOE PHILLIP: Taigulria, Qakerluilaq, and Qasqanayuk.

BARBARA JOE: I see.

JOE PHILLIP: Those ones who drifted away when the ice detached. They say down in the ocean they were on ice that people had said doesn't melt. And although it was windy, they didn't break to pieces. But they say the [pieces of ice] they were on tended to fill with water from the spray. They apparently landed out there through Nome.

PLACID JOSEPH: So far away! Nome is far from the area below Qip'ngayak.

JOE PHILLIP: They say Qakerluilaq was their leader at first. That one who they used to call Qakerluilaq was a shaman.

They say he tended to travel through bad routes. Qasqanayuk apparently led his two companions. When they would move [to another piece of ice], when the [ice] they were on filled with water from the spray. They said when they got too thirsty, and when they caught ringed seals, they'd get snow from there, using some kind of container, he would fill it and place it inside [the seal] while it was warm and melt it.

From there, they apparently brought them home. All spring they apparently were down on the ocean somewhere. They apparently brought them home from Nome out there. This person [and then another person] would bring them home, and

Makut-gguq angalkut kapialuteng waten ciuqlirkaunritliniut-gguq

Panigkaq, Arnaucuaq, Qavarliaq, Cucuaq-llu, Anchorage, December 2013

PANIGKAQ: Ak'a tang imkut qecuutellri uum-llu niitellallikai.

ARNAUCUAQ: Ayissangaankut, Marayaarmiut Ayissangaankut.

PANIGKAQ: Ukut Taigulriinkut, Qakerluilaq, Qasqanayuk-llu.

ARNAUCUAQ: Aa-a.

PANIGKAQ: Ak'a taukut qecuutellri. Unani-gguq imarpigmi imkuni uitallruut uruyuitnilallritni cikuni. Anuqlingraan-llu navguyuunateng. Taugaam-gguq waten ciqrem uitaviit imangyugluteng. Keggaggun-am Nome-akun tut'elliniluteng.

QAVARLIAQ: Ak'akika! Qip'ngayiim ketiinek Nome-aq yaaqsigtuq.

PANIGKAQ: Tauna-gguq Qakerluilaq ciuqliqsaaqellruat. Qakerluilamek pilallrat angalkuuluni.

Arenqiatuq-gguq tumkaunrilngurkun eglercugtuq. Taum-am uum Qasqanayuum tua-i ilagni taukuk pillinilukek. Nugtartaqluteng tuaten piaqata uitavigteng tauna ciqrem, mermek-wa imangaqan. Meqsungvaka'arqameng-llu, waten-llu nayirnek pit'aqameng, qanikcamek tamaaken, camek-wa tua-i assigciqerluni, imirluku iluanun taum puqlanirtuumaan urugciqluku.

Tuaken-am ut'rutliniluki. Ak'aki up'nerkarpak tamaani nani imarpigmi uitalliniluteng. Keggaken nutaan Nome-amek ut'rutliniluki. Uum ut'rutaqluki kingunritnun tekiulluki. Tua-i cavkenateng. Taugaam-gguq tua-i tungurpangllinilriit.

he arrived with them at their hometown. They were okay. But they say they got extremely dark.

BARBARA JOE: Poor.

PLACID JOSEPH: From the mist of the ocean.

JOE PHILLIP: They were extremely tan.

Since there were military out there, they apparently had the military check those ones. They found out they were from here by asking them questions. Finally, they would have people heading this way take them. Eventually they reached St. Michael out there. From there, once again, others brought them here, and arrived with them at their hometowns. And I'm not sure where those people lived at the time. They arrived with them to their hometowns.

I used to hear of those who drifted away when the ice detached. And I used to see those men who drifted away to the ocean when the ice detached.

PLACID JOSEPH: Those who drifted away on the ocean when the ice detached died recently. They say when they were about to arrive at Nome, when they got onto shore ice, when the town became visible, one of them smiled and his teeth were very white.

BARBARA JOE: Poor.

PLACID JOSEPH: The entire time they were down there, they never smiled at one of their companions. But they say their youngest, their youngest among them, Tekcengaq's younger brother, when he would move them [onto another piece of ice], he would bring them through a good route down on the ocean.

When he would move them onto other large pieces of ice. They would continually go to pieces of ice, and he would move them onto pretty large ones. And they say Qakerluilaq was a shaman. They say he never recalled the possibility of using his spirit powers when he became desperate. They say that's apparently what shamans do, their spirit powers . . .

BARBARA JOE: When they suddenly panic.

PLACID JOSEPH: When they panic, they don't think about using their spirit powers. They say Qakerluilaq, I think when they started to fall asleep, they say when he went to sleep, he would place his ammunition underneath his pillow. He was thinking that if he became too desperate that he would kill his companions first and then kill himself afterward.

BARBARA JOE: Poor.

PLACID JOSEPH: Because there was no place for them to go to survive.

ARNAUCUAQ: Nakleng.

QAVARLIAQ: Imarpiim puyuan.

PANIGKAQ: Palirrluteng cakneq.

Tamakut keggani anguyagcetangqellruan tamakunun anguyagtenun yuvrircetliniluki taukut. Tua-i makurmiungullrat nallunrirluku apqaurluki. Nutaan-am ukatmurtellrianun ayaucetaqluki. Kiituan-gguq keggavet Tacimun tekitut. Taugken nutaan ataam allat nutaan tailluki, tekiulluki kingunritnun avavet. Nani-ll' uitallruat tamakut. Kingunritnun tua-i tekiulluki.

Taukunek tua-i qecuutellritnek niitellallruunga. Tangrraqluki-ll' tamakut wii qecuutellrit angutet.

QAVARLIAQ: Ukaqvaggun tamakut tuquallruut qecuutellri. Nome-amun-gguq tekitarkaurcameng tuarmun ugcameng nunat tangerrnariata iliit-gguq quuyurniuq keggutai-llu-gguq tuaten qercurpak.

ARNAUCUAQ: Nakleng.

QAVARLIAQ: Tua-i una'antellermi taktaciatun ilateng-llu quuyurnicuunaku yuuluteng. Taum-gguq taugaam young-anrata yun'erraunrata Tekcengaam kinguqlian, nuninqigutaqamiki tua-i elluatukun ayautlarai unani imarpigmi.

Nuninqigutaqamiki allanun anelrianun cikunun. Cikut tamakut ullagtaarluki ang'uralrianun nunanqigutaqluki. Qakerluilaq-llu-gguq taun' angalkuuluni. Tayima-gguq caitqapik tuunrani neq'aksuunaku nanikuallermini tua-i. Tuaten-gguq angalkut pitulliniut, tuunrateng . . .

ARNAUCUAQ: Qamqertaqameng.

QAVARLIAQ: Umqertaqameng tuunrateng neq'aksuunaki. Qakerluilaq-gguq tamaani qavarangvaka'arqameng pilarngatut, inartaqami-gguq imani akitmi acianun ellilarai. Kapiavaka'arquni ilagni taukuk tuquqaarlukek ellii-ll' tuqutnaluni kingumek.

ARNAUCUAQ: Nakleng.

QAVARLIAQ: Natmun anagvigkailameng.

ALICE REARDEN: Poor.

JOE PHILLIP: Qasqanayuk said when he told the late Billy-ll'er the story that when these shamans are desperate, they aren't good leaders. It's probably because they try to survive using their spirit powers. They say they aren't to be depended on for support when they are desperate.

PLACID JOSEPH: They say when one is desperate, shamans aren't good to have around. [laughs]

JOE PHILLIP: He said since it was like he was trying to survive alone, Qasqanayuk tried to lead them. They say those [shamans] aren't good as leaders when traveling when they are desperate. He said they want to be the only one to survive. He said since he practiced his spirit powers, they initially thought that person would help them survive, but they said he tended to travel through bad routes that weren't good to travel on.

PLACID JOSEPH: It was probably because he panicked.

ALICE REARDEN: Did they have kayaks with them?

JOE PHILLIP: Yes, they also had kayaks. They kept their kayaks since it was impossible to paddle, since it was windy. They got far down from shore. They say when the weather was calm, they would move with kayaks to another piece of ice that they saw that was stable when it was calm. They said they continually moved from one [piece of ice] to another like that.

When they would catch a ringed seal or bearded seal, they would fill their container, whatever it was with snow and place it inside [the seal] while it was warm and melt it and try to get something to drink from it.

My, the ocean isn't a place to be when one is desperate. It's overwhelming.

....

Teggalquq, that shaman who was indomitable, they say he panicked[53]

....

Eugene Pete and Lawrence Edmund, Anchorage, December 2011

EUGENE PETE: Long ago, it was a long time ago, before I was born, my father-in-law told about what happened. He said there was a large flood during Christmas. The ice was about [five feet] thick.

LAWRENCE EDMUND: It used to be thick when it used to be cold.

EUGENE PETE: The ice headed up through the marshland up there, it folded the land along the

CUCUAQ: Akleng.

PANIGKAQ: Qasqanayuk taun' qanellruuq Billy-lleraunrilria qanemcitlerminiu makut-gguq angalkut kapialuteng waten ciuqlirkaunritliniut-gguq. Tua-i-w' tuunramegteggun tayim' pilalliameng, anangnaqlalliameng. Kapialuteng-gguq cacetuqutngunritut tamakut.

QAVARLIAQ: Ilakaunritut-gguq angalkut nanikualuni. [ngelaq'ertuq]

PANIGKAQ: Kiimi-gguq anangnaqellriatun ayuqngan tua-i elliin ciuqlilirluki tua-i-w' egelrutengnaqluki Qasqanayuum taum. Egelrucetekaunritut-gguq kapialuteng tamakut. Kiimeng-gguq anangnaqellriatun pitulliniut. Tuunrituan-gguq anautnayukluteng taumun pillruyaaqut, taugaam-gguq tumkaunrilngurkun eglercugtuq.

QAVARLIAQ: Umellran-wa taun' pillikii tuani.

CUCUAQ: Qayalgirluteng?

PANIGKAQ: Ii-i, qayangqerrluteng-llu. Qayateng tua-i qelekluki anguayunaitlaan-wa, anuqlian. Kessigiluteng unani. Tua-i waten-gguq tua-i quunirqan tangvallermeggnun cikumun asvailgnurmun nugtartellartut tua-i quunirqan qayakun. Tuaten-gguq tua-i nugtartaararluteng pillruut.

Tuaten pit'aqameng nayirmek qang'a-ll' maklagmek ca una assigtarteng qanikcamek imirluku iluanun puqlanirtuumaan iluanun urugcirluku mengnaqaqluteng.

Aling, nanikuavigkaurituq una imarpik. Arenqiatuq.

....

Teggalquq angalkuq tauna caprilnguq, umluni-gguq

....

Aliuq Paugnaralria-llu, Anchorage, December 2011

ALIUQ: Ak'a imumi avani, akaurtuq, tayim' yuurpailegma-ll' wiinga, imum taum cakima qanemcikellrua. Ulerpagtuq-gguq tuani Christmas-aam nalliini. Cikuq wani qaill' tayim' can'utaluni.

PAUGNARALRIA: Can'utullruuq nengllitullrani.

ALIUQ: Pavaggun marakun tagluni cikuq kumlanrem, engeliinun nuna imegluku, tagluni.

edge of the permafroast and headed up. You've seen those [landforms] that the ice gathered at Kayangulivik. And at this time, they've grown bushes.

He said he hasn't seen a stronger wind since that time. And he said people couldn't go outside because it was hard to stand, but they'd only move by crawling. . . .

They say [the wind] was extremely strong! [It happened] long before we were born.

And the one I heard of in the past, Teggalquq, that shaman who was indomitable, they say he panicked. They say one of them brought him to his senses when he asked him why he was doing nothing. He told him to do something [with his shaman powers], not to just do nothing.

They say with a knife, he pierced the middle of his home down there, making a place for [the water] to leak out. They say the ice didn't enter it at all. They say he suddenly came to his senses; at first he panicked.

I also used to see the father of Alec-all'er's wife at Emmonak whom they called Nass'ak, Nass'ak. He got up on top of his house when the ice got closer, and they say he told a legendary tale, some sort of legendary tale, and they say he blew at it. They say when he blew at that ice, it split in two like this. They say it looked like a doorway. The ice didn't touch his home.

Qaluyartuq evidently was there when they went on top of that person's home when he was a boy. Then he said he would blow air at it like this, and he would also blow air at Qaluyartuq at the same time. [chuckles]

He said since he was blowing directly at him, he moved a little so that he could blow through here. One time he said, he told about that, and he said he shouldn't have moved out of the way of that one who was telling a quliraq. He said if he hadn't moved out of the way of that quliraq, he might have been affected somehow, and he might have been indomitable as he was living. [chuckling]

[Someone] said to him, "Why did you move out of his way?" He said that wind was extremely strong. There is no other like it. My father-in-law, although they said it was windy, he said he hasn't seen a wind comparable to that one. He said it was extremely powerful. And it brought the ice up onto land through the lowland out there although [the ice] was thick.

Ava-i augkut Kayangulivigmi tangerrlaqci tamatum cikum katurtellri. Ava-i-llu uqviangluteng cuyaqegglinek.

Anuqmek-gguq taum kinguakun tangeqsaituq. Anyunaunani-llu-gguq ellamun, nangerngayunaunani, aurrluteng taugaam pektaqluteng. . . .

Kayuqapigtuq-gguq cakneq! Ak'a nalluluta wangkuta, nallumteni tayima.

Tauna-ll' imna niiskengaqa avani Teggalquq, angalkuq tauna caprilnguq, umluni-gguq. Iliita-gguq taugaam ellangevkarluku ciin uitavakallranek. Qaillukuaqaasqelluku, ilacirluku-w' uitasqevkenaku.

Imumek-gguq caviggamek enii-gguq camavet kanaggun qukaakun-gguq kapaa, ellngarvilirluku-gguq. Watpik-llu-gguq cikum itenritaa tua-i caitqapik. Ellangarrluni-gguq; umyaaqluni.

Atauciq cali tangerrlaraqa imum' Alec-allraam Imangami nulirran atii, Nass'agmek piaqluku, Nass'ak. Enem'inun uggluni cikur yaaqsinrian quliriluni-gguq cameg' imumek quliramek, cupluku-llu-gguq. Cupngani-gguq tamana cikuq avegluni waten. Tuarpiaq-gguq amiik. Enii tauna cikum agturpek'naku.

Imna tua-i, Qaluyartuq tuantellrulliniuq taukut eniinun mayullratni tamaa-i tan'gurraurluuluni. Tua-i-llu waten-gguq cup'laraa-gguq, ellii tayim' Qaluyartuq tumekluku. [ngelaq'ertuq]

Arenqialan-gguq tumkekapigpakaani-gguq avikanirluku maaggun cupesqelluku. Qanertuq cami, taumek qanemciuq, tauna-gguq quliriliria-gguq ciin-llu-gguq tanem avitau. Avitellrunrilkuniu-gguq tauna quliraq tamana, cayarngatuq-gguq, asvailqurrauluni-llu yuuyarngatuq. [ngelaq'ertut]

[Kia] pia, "Ciin-tanem aviciu?" Kayullruuq-gguq tauna cakneq anuqa. Ayuqaituq. Ayuqiinek cakiqa imna anuqlirningraatgu taum anuqiinek tangeqsaitniuq anuqmek. Kayuqapigtuq-gguq cakneq. Cikuq-llu can'ungraan tagulluku avaggun marakun.

Akiuk was the son-in-law of [the shaman] Leggleq, that one I told you about earlier. He had his *avneq* [helping spirit] go and see how he was doing. [His helping spirit] told him that those two were fine, but that the one living on the other side of him floated away [in the flood].

Imum qanemcikellma watua Legellrem, tauna nengaukaa Akiuk. Avnerminun-am paqcelluku. Tua-i cam'um qanrulluku canritnilukek taukuk, aipaa taugaam tauna akiqlia tayim' mermun tengevkautniluku.

Old Village of Paimiut[54]

Lawrence Edmund and Mike Andrews Sr.,
Anchorage, December 2011

LAWRENCE EDMUND: They call that place Paimiullret [the historic village of Paimiut]. They say long ago when there was a great flood in the fall, that village was in the middle of ocean ice that piled up. It was the same story about the great flood that this person [Eugene] told, and he said that [Teggalquq] made a hole for the water to leak out [of the *qasgiq*]. This was during that time. They say that small village wasn't visible as it was in the middle of ocean ice that had piled. The entire area surrounding [the village] was covered by ocean ice that had piled. But the people of the small village were okay.

Paimiut is at Mernualivik [River]. . . .

They say during that time, this village couldn't be seen from ground level. They say that small village was situated in the midst of ice, in the midst of piled ice.

MIKE ANDREWS SR.: Yes. That person told a story, and I used to see her, and she told a story in my presence. She said when it flooded, it covered the entire area inland from the Bering Sea. She said at Paimiut, when the water was entering the houses, they went across to the *qasgiq*, and they carried that woman on their backs; they all gathered at the *qasgiq*.

Then she said there was a shaman among them. They say that shaman panicked, he suddenly didn't know what to do, he suddenly forgot how to save them, probably because he was afraid.

Then they say before the water entered the *qasgiq*, one of the men asked that shaman why he was not taking any action, asking why he wasn't doing anything.

He told him, along with his spirit helper, to help the people of the village there since the ice was nearly upon them.

They say all of a sudden, he came to his senses. He had panicked at first, something happened to

Paimiullret

Paugnaralria Angauvik-llu, Anchorage,
December 2011

PAUGNARALRIA: Paimiullernek tauna piaqluku. Ak'a-gguq ulerpallrani uksuarmi waten evunret qukaatni uitallruuq tauna nunaq. Imna watua qanemcikekii uum ulerpallrani, ellngarvilillruniluku. Tauna-gguq tua-i. Tangerrnaunateng-gguq taukut nunarraat taukut evunret akuliitni uitaluteng. Avatiit tamarmi-gguq tua-i evunruluni. Taukut taugaam cangatevkenateng nunarraat tuani.

Mernualivigmi Paimiut uitaut. . . .

Ukut-gguq nunat tamatum nalliini cailkamek waten tangssunaitellruut. Cikut-gguq akuliitni uitallruut taukut nunarraat evunret akuliitni.

ANGAUVIK: Yaa. Qanemcillruuq tauna tangtullruaqallu qanemciluni-ll' takumni. Tuani ulerpautiini man'a qaingirluku man'a Bering Sea-m kelua tamalkuan. Paimiuni-gguq tua-i-gguq enen'un, enen'un meq it'ngarteqataan qasgimun qerarluteng, ellii amaqluku tauna; qasgimun quyurmeng tamarmeng.

Tua-llu angalkurmek-gguq ilangqerrluteng. Tauna-gguq angalkuq qaill' piluni umluni, qaill' picirkairrluni, anirtuallerkaa qaill' nalluyaguarrluku tayima, alingami pingatuq tayima.

Tua-i-llu-gguq waniwa tua-i meq iterpailgan qasgimun, tamakut angutet iliita tauna angalkuq pillia caluku uitavakallranek qanrulluku, qaill' pian ciin uitavakallranek.

Pisqelluku tua-i tuunraa-llu ikayungnaqluki pisqelluki ukut nunat tua-i waniw' piqataaki cikum.

Nutaan-gguq tua-i ellangarrluni. Umyaaqluni, caluni, alingem pingataa. Tua-i-gguq caviggarmek

him, I think fear overcame him. They say he took a knife that he stuck in the ground down there. They say the water that went inside that *qasgiq* leaked out.

They say there was so much ice. If this here was the *qasgiq*, they say the ice parted along that *qasgiq*; far from reaching it, [the pieces of ice] wouldn't hit it. They say the pieces of ice headed inland around it, even large pieces of ice, and they didn't touch the [*qasgiq*].

Mask that sticks to one's face[55]

Lawrence Edmund and Mike Andrews Sr., Anchorage, December 2011

LAWRENCE EDMUND: Amuqan told my father [about that flood] when he went up to Cingigtuli just when winter arrived. I think [the shaman] was Amuqan's grandfather. He said [Teggalquq] blew at [the ice] coming toward them, and he said that the ice didn't touch [the village] at all. And he said that his boat had a *nepcetaq* [mask that sticks to one's face] inside it; his *nepcetaq* was in there.

MIKE ANDREWS SR.: I see.

LAWRENCE EDMUND: They say the wind was such that a boat couldn't stay put. They say [Teggalquq] went down to the river's ice, and it was such that it was impossible to stay there. They say a *nepcetaq* mask [was inside his boat]. And they say his other *nepcetaq* was inside his kayak located on top of a fish rack. They say [the ice] didn't touch that at all, but the fish rack was filled with pieces of ice.

That doorway of the *qasgiq* was about this far from the river bank, but it seems that it didn't erode. Qapuggluk [Fred Augustine] says that the land has sunk, the old village of Paimiut. They say that's the old village where Teggalquq lived, that shaman. . . .

That *nepcetaq* [mask]. They say it's a mask. They are square-shaped. It's a mask.

They say when [the shaman] Teggalquq would get stuck in shallow water also, they say those stuck to his face. They say he would put his *nepcetaq* in his boat, and wearing a *nepcetaq*, he would bring it down by carrying it.

That was Teggalquq's source of power. He would use a *nepcetaq*. He would lift things although they were heavy, having it adhere to his face. I haven't seen those, but I've heard of them.

piluni kaalguarutkaminek camavet. Tua-i ellngartuq meq tuavet qasgim iluanun.

Ik'iki-gguq cikut waten. Una waniw' qasgiukan cikut-gguq qukviutekluku una qasgiq; cayugnaitarluteng puukayuunaku. Avatiikun-gguq cikut kelutmun, cikurpiit-llu, una tayim' agtuyuunaku.

Nepcetaq

Paugnaralria Angauvik-llu, Anchorage, December 2011

PAUGNARALRIA: Imum Amuqan ataka uksuqerluku-wa Cingigtulimi, tuavet-wa tagluni qanemcitellrullinia taumek. Tauna apa'urluqngataa Amuqan. Cup'aqluku-gguq, tumekluki, cikum-llu-gguq agtuq'erpek'naki caitqapik. Cali-gguq angyaa nepcetamek imangqerrluni; tuanlluni nepcetaa.

ANGAUVIK: Aa-a.

PAUGNARALRIA: Anuqa-gguq ik'ik' qaill' angyaq tamaani uitayunaunani. Kanavet-gguq atraqili kuigem cikuanun waten, qiall' tuancunaunani. Nepcetaanek-gguq imangqerrluni. Aipaa-llu-gguq cali qayaani cali nepcetaa uitaluni, qer'ani ugingaluni. Tauna-llu-gguq agtuq'erpek'naku, amta-llu-gguq qer'at akuliit cikunek kevirluni.

Tauna watua qasgiq, amiiga waten ekvigmek yaaqsigtangatuq, amta-ll' uscuilngacaaqluni. Qapuggluum atrarnilaraa tamana nunaq, taukut Paimiullret. Taum Teggalqum nunakaa-gguq tauna, taum angalkum. . . .

Tauna nepcetaq. Kegginaquq-gguq. Waten yaassiigenqeggluteng. Kegginaqruluni.

Taum-gguq Teggalqum, en'arutaqani-llu-gguq tauna kegginaanun tamakut neptetuut-gguq. Angyaq-gguq nepcetaminek piluku nepcetarluni, atrautelallrua kevegluku.

Taum Teggalqum taman' pissuutekluku. Tuaten nepcetarluni. Uqamailengraan-llu kevtuluku nepcelluku kegginaminun. Tangeqsaitua wii tamakunek, taugaam niitellartua.

[The ice] didn't touch the two [masks], and it was as if the ice showed respect to the two. The pieces of ice didn't touch his boat, and the ice didn't touch his kayak either. They say it was actually such that they wouldn't have been able to stay in their place, but they were supposed to have blown away. They say that boat wasn't blown away, but moved down to the edge of the ice and stayed there; they say it didn't go anywhere. It was amazing. Since it's true, they told stories about that event that occurred during a flood.

I saw what might have been a *nepcetaq*, when I arrived at the old village of Kuimlill'er. I looked inside what was probably a small smokehouse that didn't have a roof and was small. There were four masks. There were masks, and one among them was a square-shaped one. It had paint on it, and it seems that its appendages were the width of toothpicks, and there were various things, animals, around it.

And I wasn't thinking. When my mother was a girl, she said she used to live there. Those were supposed to have rotted by the time I saw them. I was thinking that I would take them when I arrived again. And those wooden bowls were very clean inside.

Sometime later, I went to check on them; they were rotten. They say they put things out for people when that happens; I think they displayed those for me. I didn't take them and didn't touch them, thinking to take them when I arrived the next time. When I arrived the next time, a year later, I think it was two years later, they were completely rotten.

Pivkenakek, cikut takaqellriatun pilukek agtuq'erpek'naku-ll'. Angyaa agturpek'naku cikut qayaa-ll' cikut agturpek'naku. Qaillun uitayunaunani-gguq tengtarkauluki tamatum. Tauna-gguq tengtevkenani angyaq atrarluni kanavet cikum ceniinun tua-ll' uitaluni; natmun ayagpek'nani-gguq. Iillanaqluni. Tua-i piciungan qanemciklaqiit tamakut qanemcikestaita taum ulerpiim, ulerpallran.

Tangellruunga wiinga, nepcetaullilria-wa, Kuimlillermiullernun tekitellemni. Uyangtua puyurcivicuarallraullilria-wa qilaunani mikluni waten. Kegginaqut cetaman. Kegginaqut, tamakucimek ilangqerrluteng yaassiigenqellriamek. Mingugtuumaluni, *toothpick*-acetun ellegtangatut makut epuit, canguat, pitarkat avatiini.

Tang umyuarteqenrilngua-llu. Aanaka tamaani naskuggaurluuluni-gguq tamaantetuluni. Tamakut aruarkauyaaqluteng wii tuani tangllemki. Umyuarteqkilii uumiku tekiskuma tegunaluki. Taukut-llu qantat equut, waten tua-i carrinqegpak iluit.

Uumikuan tekicama paqcaaqanka; arumaluteng. Paivutnilaqait tuatnaaqata; paivutellruyaaqngataatnga taukut. Tegullrunritanka agturpek'naki-llu uumiku tekiskuma tegunaluki. Tekicaaqua uumikuani, allrakuani, *two years* pingatuq, arumaqap'iggluteng.

The time I gave an offering of food and water at the old village of Paimiut[56]

Lawrence Edmund, Alakanuk, March 2011

LAWRENCE EDMUND: There is an old village here, upriver from this place called Paimiut. It was an old village that existed long ago, and there is an old *qasgiq* there. And inside there are two old homes, and another *qasgiq*. They called that village Evegtulirmiut. And up above [Evegtulirmiut] up there, it's a small lake. They call that Qullicuar. Qullicuar was occupied in the past; no one lives there today.

I used to camp there in the fall. Yes, here is Qullicuar, yes.

Paimiullerni aviukarqelqa

Paugnaralria, Alarneq, March 2011

PAUGNARALRIA: Nunacillertangqertuq wani, uum wani kiatiini Paimiunek piaqluku. Ak'a nunallret, qasgillertangqerrluni-llu. Cali iluani cali nec'illrek malruk, ataam-llu qasgiq. Taukut Evegtulirmiunek piaqluki. Pakmani-ll' quliitni nanvarrauluni. Qullicuarmek tauna piaqluku. Yungqetullruyaaquq tauna Qullicuar; maa-i yuirutuq.

Tuani uksuilallruunga. Ii-i, waniw' Qullicuar, ii-i.

One time I didn't camp in the fall as I was working on the dump site here [in this village]; they had me work. When [they] traveled to the south, when they arrived from Mernualivik, they told me that there weren't any mink.

Then the next year, we went to camp in the fall. But at Bethel, I told you about the person in Bethel who told me that twice he gave an offering to the deceased, and it came to materialize; he told me that the custom of offering to the deceased is true.

Then at that place they used to call Paimiullret [the historic village of Paimiut], they say Teggalquq was a powerful shaman. He would obtain animals from the wilderness.

Then our elder told us that when the ice became thick enough so that one wouldn't fall through, we should check on the sloughs to the north of us.

When we arrived at our fall camp, we went to set a blackfish trap; since [the place where we usually set blackfish traps], the stream between two lakes was close back there, we walked to set our blackfish trap. We saw that the mink trails were unused; we saw that plants were growing on them. And we went to check those dens there, but they evidently hadn't been used; there were various plants growing on them.

And across in the slough downriver from where we were, since we usually set nets to catch tomcod at the mouth, the mink trails were also unused at that place. There were plants growing on them. We learned that there were no mink by those signs.

Then when the ice became thick, one of our companions told us that he wanted to check the sloughs to the north of us. We left. There were no mink. We only found one new [mink] track, and it was the only one when we had traveled far to the north. And when we arrived at the slough beyond the one they called Avayarraq, no tracks were there at all.

When we reached that place, I suddenly felt discouraged and thought, "I wonder how I'm going to catch mink when there are no mink?" And without saying anything I thought, "Although there aren't any, I will set my wooden mink traps. I don't want to camp here in the fall for nothing. After setting them, I will remove them." And my companions never said that there weren't any mink.

Then Halloween came. I suddenly recalled what Angaqaaq had said, that the custom of giving an offering to the deceased is true. I only had heard about the old village of Paimiut in the past and knew of them; they had said that the one who owned that *qasgiq* there was a shaman.

Caqerluta uksuiyarpek'nii maani ciqicivignek calilua; calivkarlua-wa. Ayiimeg' amavet, Mernualivigmek tekicamek piagnga imarmiutartaitniluku.

Nutaan-llu allrakuan uksuiyarluta. Taugken Mamterillermi aug'um qanrutkellruaqa augna qanemcikesteka, aviukaqluni malrurqugnek nall'arutellruniluni; pillrulua aviukarqelleq piciuniluku.

Tua-llu tauna tuani Paimiullernek pilallrat, tauna-gguq Teggalquq, ca imna angalkuullruuq cakneq. Waten yuilqumek canek pitarkanek pikarcutuluni.

Tua-llu ilamta taum, teggnemta-w' piakut ciku can'uriqercan, igutnaircan, negemteni-gguq qagaani kuiggaat paqtaaqerlaut.

Tuani uksuiyallemtenun tekicamta taluyarayarturluta; canimetlaan piani akulurami piyuagurluta taluyiryarturtukut. Imarmiutaat aprullrit atuumayuitelliniluteng; cat naunraat naumalliniluteng. Taukut-llu igtet paqcaaqluki, atuqsaitelliniluteng tua-i waniwa tua-i; cat naunraat naumaluteng.

Ikani-llu uatemteni kuicuarmi iqalluarcuucirlaamta-ll' taum painganun, tamaani cali aprulluut imarmiutaat atuumavkenateng. Cat naunraat naumaluk'. Tamaaggun taugken nallunrirluku imarmiutaitellra.

Tua-llu can'uriqercan ilamta taum piakut paqtaaryugluki kuiggaat negemteni. Ayagluta. Imarmiutaunani. Atauciqap'igmek nutaramek tumciluta tua-i kiingan ak'aki negeqvanun ayagyaaqluta. Tamana-llu Avayarrarmek pilallrata yaaqlirraa kuicuar tekitarput, caitqaq'apiar tumtaunani tua-i caitqapik.

Tuavet tua-i tekicamta umyuaqa cap'illagtuq, "Qaill'-kiq pilua imarmiutarcarcia waten imarmiutaunani?" Qanerpek'nii-ll' umyuartequa, "Tua-i piilengraan taluyaruanka civerqeciqanka. Elliinginaq maavet uksuiyaryunritua. Tua-i civerqerraarluki yuuniaranka ataam." Ilanka-ll' taukut qanyuunateng imarmiutaitniluku.

Tua-i-llu Halloween-arluni. Neq'aqa'arqa-am imum Angaqaam qanrutkellra, aviukarqelleq piciuniluku. Tauna taugaam niitaqluku Paimiullret taukut wii nalluvkenaki; tuani yuat, taum qasgim pikestii angalkuullruniluku.

I told my companions that I wanted to go down to the old village of Paimiut and give an offering of water, food, the few things that we had to Teggalquq, asking him to provide us mink that we were to hunt. My companions urged me to do so.

I got ready, and Ay'arruq gave me snuff to bring, and since he evidently had candy, he gave me one. Then when I arrived there, I didn't see a mink track.

After facing my snowmobile toward the area I came from, I dug into the ground after thoroughly clearing [the snow off]. After filling the cup half full, I headed up and entered that old *qasgiq*. Since the fire pit was visible, I was thinking, "Teggalquq probably used to call on his spirit helpers here."

This is what I told him first, that we are his descendants, that he was our great-grandfather through our distant ancestors, that we want him to provide us with mink that we will hunt all fall, that we are not capable of [making mink available], that we cannot do anything about them. I was speaking by myself there.

And I told him that I had heard that when he was alive he used to obtain things, that I was going to give him some water and food that he lacked. I gave an offering of those few things that I had brought with me. And when I was going to give an offering of that snuff, I told him that this is tobacco, that they call it snuff in English, that if they chew tobacco, to divide it among them.

And when I was going to offer that candy, I said to him that this is something tasty, that we eat these things they call candy in English, that if they have children, to divide it among their children.

After giving him the offerings, when I was going to return home, I told him again, "Okay, be grateful because a person won't come to you from afar and give you water and food that you lack. Provide us the mink that we are going to hunt this fall." Then I returned home without seeing any tracks.

When I arrived, our elder told me, "Gee, you didn't take long." I told him that since I was in a hurry, I didn't take long. And we didn't leave again. Then the next day, when I was going to set [mink traps], I told my companions, "We should check in the back area [inland] first." I wanted to check that place.

We left. We didn't see mink tracks. When we reached the upper narrow part of Mernualivik,

Pianka ilanka wii cakmavet Paimiullernun anelrarlua ca im' Teggalquq aviukarcarturyugluku mermek, neqmek, carramtenek-wa, paivutqaasqumaluta makunek imarmiutarnek pissurarkamtenek. Ak'akik' ilama tua-i pisqellua tua-i.

Uplua tua-i, taum-llu Ay'arrum *snuff*-amek taquillua, *candy*-ngqelliniami-llu ataucimek. Tuavet tua-i tekicama imarmiutarmek-llu tumcivkenii.

Kingutmun cauqaarluku massiinaqa, elakilii carrinqegcaararraarluku. Caaskaq qukarluku tagngama tuavet qasgillermun itrama, tangerrnaqngan kenillra, umyuartequa, "Wani tayim' tuunrilallrulria tauna Teggalquq."

Ciumek qanrutaqa, waten tua-i qanrutaqa, wangkuta elliinun kinguliaraqniluta, wangkuta avaggun ciuqvaggun amauqniluku, uksuarpak makunek pissurarkamtenek imarmiutarnek paivutqaasqumayaaqniluta, taugaam wangkuta capirniluku, qaill' pisciigatniluki. Waten tua-i qanaalua kiima.

Piluku-ll' niitelarniluku canritellrani pikarcutullruniluku, nuuqellranek mermek pilarniluku neqmek-llu. Taukut tua-i aviukaqluki carraat ayautellrenka. Tauna-ll' *snuff*-aq piqataamku piaqa, una cuyauniluku, *snuff*-anek pilarniluki Kass'atun atritnek, iqmitukata avqiuresqelluki.

Tauna-llu *candy*-q piqataamku piaqa, una neqnirqellriaruniluku nertuniluki *candy*-nek Kass'atun atellget wangktua pilarniluki, mikelnguarangqerqata mikelnguaraitnun avqiuresqelluki.

Taukut tua-i, pirraarluku, uterteqataama ataam piaqa, "Kitek lingrayugluten, yuum-llu waten kia yaaqvanek ayagluten nuuqellerpenek mermek pingaitaaten neqmek-llu. Paivutqerniarpekut makunek uksuaq pissurarkamtenek imarmiutarnek." Uterrlua-ll' tayim' tumcivkenii.

Tekicama tua-i taum teggnemta pianga, "Aling, ak'aninrituten." Piaqa, cukangnaqu'urlua piama ak'aninritnilua. Ayanqigtevkenata-ll' tua-i. Tua-i-ll' waniw' unuaqu civciarkaungama ilanka pianka, "Pavavet tang wangkuta ciumek paqteqaalta." Paqcugluku.

Ayagluta. Imarmiutarmek tumciksaunata. Pakmavet Mernualiviim quurneranun tekitukut,

EUGENE PETE: Yes, I think he was. Probably [he did that] because he was.

MIKE ANDREWS SR.: Yes, he used to practice *qelayaraq* [a shamanistic ritual in which a patient's ailment is determined by tying a string around another person's head or foot and testing it by pulling on it to see if it could lift easily or couldn't be lifted, which determined the extent of the illness].

EUGENE PETE: He used to carry out the practice of *qelayaraq*.

MIKE ANDREWS SR.: Yes.

LAWRENCE EDMUND: *Qelatulit* [those who practiced divination], they tied something around a person's head and continually pulled up on it.

　　They say that's what they did, and they say some people did that to their feet.

MIKE ANDREWS SR.: They used to do that to their legs also, or to a person's head.

EUGENE PETE: One time that Terussaq, he tied his foot, and Aluuyaq evidently entered drunk while he was performing *qelayaraq*. [*chuckles*]

　　When Aluuyaq entered, he took away his *qela* [instrument with which he carried out *qelayaraq*], and Aluuyaq asked him why he was doing that. [*laughs*] And he opened the stove and placed the object with which he was carrying out *qelayaraq* inside the stove and burned it. [*laughs*]

　　When drinking he was sort of a mean person. He didn't care whether or not a person would be offended, and he wasn't afraid of shamans at all! [*chuckles*]

ALICE REARDEN: For what reason did they *qelayaraq*?

LAWRENCE EDMUND: Perhaps they were trying to save people.

EUGENE PETE: I'm not sure why that [person] down there [couldn't be lifted]. Although he tried [to pull it up], this bent also; he couldn't lift it.

　　But sometimes he could pull it up, and sometimes he couldn't.

LAWRENCE EDMUND: They say it's easy to [lift] when it agrees.

MIKE ANDREWS SR.: They say if you lift it, even a person's head, if you lift it, it will mean yes if you lift it. But they say if you can't lift it, [it means no].

EUGENE PETE: I tried it when I was curious about that. [*chuckling*] I did it just to try it. When it wasn't going to work, I was thinking that maybe they lied when they did that, that that person pretended he couldn't [lift] that one. It isn't impossible [to lift]. It's like this.

ALICE REARDEN: What do they use, a tether?

LAWRENCE EDMUND: They tie it with something, they tie it with something.

ALIUQ: Yaa, pilaryugnarquq. Pilliami-wa'.

ANGAUVIK: Ii-i, qelatullruuq.

ALIUQ: Qelalalria.

ANGAUVIK: Ii-i.

PAUGNARALRIA: Qelatulit tamakut yugmek, nasqurrakun qillerrluku ipuurluku pilartut.

　　Tuaten-gguq, ilait-llu-gguq it'gameggnek pilartut cali.

ANGAUVIK: Irumegteggun-llu piluteng pilallruut, qang'a-ll' nasqurranek yuum.

ALIUQ: Caqerluni-ggem tauna Terussaq-gguq waten it'gaminek qillrulluku tauna, taangiqluni-am Aluuyaq itliniluni qelainanarani. [*ngelaq'ertuq*]

　　Taum tua-i Aluuyam itrami qeliinek allurrluku pillia Aluuyam cakiurluku tuaten pillranek. [*ngel'artuq*] Pelitaaq-llu ikirrluku qelatii taun' pelitaamun eqiulluku. [*ngel'artuq*]

　　Taangiqaqami taangiqerrluglallruami tauna. Yuk cangayullerkaanek pilanritaa, angalkut-llu alikenritqapigtai! [*ngelaq'ertuq*]

CUCUAQ: Canaluteng-gguq qelatullruat?

PAUGNARALRIA: Anirtuangnaqluteng yugnek pilarngatut.

ALIUQ: Qaillun-wa piaqameng pisciigatlarta kan'a. Tua-i cangraani man'a-llu perluni; nalugciiganaku.

　　Caami taugaam tua-i nalugluku, caami-ll' tua-i pisciiganani.

PAUGNARALRIA: Pisciryarlartuq-gguq angraqami.

ANGAUVIK: Kevkuvgu-gguq yuum-llu nasqurra, tuaten kevkuvgu tua-i waten pimaciquq, *it means yes* kevkuvgu. Taugken kevegciigalkuvgu.

ALIUQ: Wii uigtuallruyaaqua paqnayuglua-am tamatumek. [*ngelaq'ertut*] Tua-i ellmikun tua-i. Pingairucan tua-i piaqa, umyuartequa, iqluquluki pilaryukluki, pisciigalngualaryukluku tauna. Pisciigatenrituq. Tua-i waten ayuquq.

CUCUAQ: Camek aturluteng, uskuramek?

PAUGNARALRIA: Camek qillerrluku, qillerrluku camek pilartut.

They probably used skin rope long ago when they didn't have store-bought things. They would tie their heads with something.

MIKE ANDREWS SR.: Yes, my wife was one of those. I went camping in the fall once at Taciurtalek.

EUGENE PETE: I see.

MIKE ANDREWS SR.: At that place, the wife of Qakurtaq, his second wife from up north, that person carried out the practice of *qelayaraq* and my wife's was the head [she tried to lift]. My wife was the head for one who was practicing *qelayaraq*.

Using something, she just tied it here, and placed a small pillow down. They tied this, and the piece of wood was attached to that. Nothing was wrong with my wife, and she wasn't feeling differently, and nothing was wrong with her after that. My wife was the head for one who was carrying out the practice of *qelayaraq*.

EUGENE PETE: One of those didn't affect me. I tried many times, but it didn't have any effect.

MIKE ANDREWS SR.: I see.

LAWRENCE EDMUND: And we also, back when we used to sleep at the *qasgiq*, we tried it, and I didn't obtain anything. But Fred Rock actually obtained [a divination].

MIKE ANDREWS SR. AND EUGENE PETE: I see.

LAWRENCE EDMUND: There were many of us who tried it. [*laughs*] Fred Rock was the only one who obtained a *qela*.

MIKE ANDREWS SR.: Then that person, Aqevtan, Aqevtan and I, is he Kaligtuq's grandchild?

EUGENE PETE: I see.

MIKE ANDREWS SR.: It was spring and the days were longer. We went down to the *qasgiq*, Aqevtan and I, since that person and I were close friends.

When we entered [we said], "Let's you and me try *qelayaraq* just to try." We said that, just the two of us.

We were across from one another, down on the floor on top of the floor boards, and I carried out the practice of *qelayaraq*, I carried out *qelayaraq* on my leg. While I was [pulling], I [pulled this] and it couldn't [be lifted]. [*laughs*] I found out that the lace of my boot had gotten caught on something, and couldn't [pull up].

We suddenly stood up and we quickly ran outside making loud clanking noises! [*laughs*] Those [ties] there, and the piece of wood that was tied here, it was clanking loudly as we ran outside! And when we got outdoors, I took that and he took his and threw it! [*laughs*] We didn't go inside again.

When we just tried out *qelayaraq*.

Tamaani-w' tapengyagnek pilallrullilriit ak'a avani waten makunek piitellermeggni. Makucinek qillerrluki canek nasqurrit pilarait.

ANGAUVIK: Yaa, aipaqa-llu tamakuciullruuq. Uksuillruunga tuani atauucirqumek Taciurtalegmi.

ALIUQ: Aa-a.

ANGAUVIK: Tuani, imna Qakurtam nulirra, kinguqliq imna qaugkumiu tauna qelaluni, aipaqa nasquqluku. Aipaqa-llu qelalriim pikellrua nasquqluku aipaqa.

Camek tayim', maaggun taugaam qillerrluku, akiciqerluku. Una-am qillerrluku, tua-i-ll' equg' man'a tuavet pimaluni. Cavkenani aipaqa, qaillun-llu ayuqevkenani, qaillun-llu ayuqevkenani taum kinguakun. Tua-i aipaqa nasqurrullruuq taumun qelalriamun.

ALIUQ: Agtullrunritaanga wii tamakucim. Tua-i piyaaqaqa tua-i pulengtaq tua-i tayima piituq.

ANGAUVIK: Aa-a.

PAUGNARALRIA: Wangkuta-llu-wam qasgimi qavatuluni-w' tamaani, uigtuaquyaaqukut, wiinga-ll' cangellrunritua. Imna taugaam Fred Rock-aq unangyaaqellruuq.

ANGAUVIK ALIUQ-LLU: Aa-a.

PAUGNARALRIA: Yugyagluta-w' tua-i uigtuallruyaaqukut-am. [*ngel'artuq*] Fred Rock-aq taugaam tauna qelangyaaqluni.

ANGAUVIK: Tua-llu wangkuk imna-llu Aqevtan, Aqevtan imum Kaligtum tutgara'urluqlaraa-qaa?

ALIUQ: Aa-a.

ANGAUVIK: Up'nerkangluni-wa erenret takliriluteng. Qasgimun atrartukuk, ellii Aqevtan-llu wangkuk aiparnaarraqlaamegnuk tauna-llu.

Itramegnuk tua-i, "Uigtualunuk kitek qelanguaqerluk wangkuk." Qanerlunuk kiirramegnuk.

Akiqliqlunuk tua-i natermi kanani imkut nacitet qaingatni, wiinga-ll' qelalua, irumkun qelalua. Piinanemni tua-i una piaqa pisciiganani. [*ngel'artuq*] Cunaw' tayima camun tayima piluguugma nagtelliniluni cingia, maavet pisciiganani tua-i.

Nang'errlunuk tua-i kallagpak ellamun anqerrlunuk! [*ngel'artuq*] Tamakut, imna-ll' wani equk-llu qillerngaluni, kallagpak ellamun anqerrlunuk! Keggavet-llu tekicamnuk tamana teguluku elliin-llu eggluku! [*ngel'artuq*] Itenqigtevkenanuk.

Qelanguarlunuk-wa pillmegni.

LAWRENCE EDMUND: Those carrying out *qelayaraq*, I think they tried to heal people, I think they also try to heal people, trying to heal those with some sort of ailment.

MIKE ANDREWS SR.: Yes, they used to try to heal a sick person.

LAWRENCE EDMUND: They tried to heal a person. They say that person who carried out *qelayaraq* would try to heal that person. If that person had some sort of ailment or something, they'd do that to that person, trying to heal him. I think that one who carries out *qelayaraq* heals that person if needed.

MIKE ANDREWS SR.: If this one cannot [lift up], if you can't lift it, this is what I heard, that it means no [and is a bad sign]. They would know through their leg. But if you lift it like this, it means yes [and is a good sign], and if it can't [be lifted], it means no. They knew through that.

LAWRENCE EDMUND: They call its name, their *qela* [spirit], talking to it, trying to heal a person with an ailment. I think that's what they do.

MIKE ANDREWS SR.: Yes. Yes and no. If it cannot [be lifted], if it cannot [be lifted], they cannot heal the person. But if you [lift it] it means that that person can easily be healed. Yes and no, although it didn't say anything.

ALICE REARDEN: [Lifting] the leg of that one who is in pain or his head?

MIKE ANDREWS SR.: No, not the one in pain, but they only try to heal that person [in pain].

My wife was one of those because she let them use her head [as a *qela*]. Nothing was wrong with her though.

But my buddy and I ran outside during that time, we ran out making loud clanking noises. [*laughs*]

PAUGNARALRIA: Tamakut qelalriit yugnek anirtuavikengnaqluteng-llu pilarngatut, yuut-llu anirtuangnaqluki-ll' pilarngatut, anirtungnaqluki camek nangtequtelget-llu.

ANGAUVIK: Ii-i, anirtuangnaqluku yuk pitullruut.

PAUGNARALRIA: Anirtungnaqluku yuk. Tauna qelatulim taun' yuk anirtungnaqluku tuatnalartut-gguq. Camek nangteqkan qang'a-ll' cakan tuatnaluku anirtungnatugluku-ll'. Tauna anirtularngataa qelalriim pinarqekan.

ANGAUVIK: Una tua-i pisciigalkan, kevegciigalkuvgu, waten-am niitellruaqa, *it means no*. Tuaggun irumikun nalluvkenaku. Taugken kevkuvgu waten *it means yes*, pisciigalkan-llu *no*. Tuaggun nalluvkenaku.

PAUGNARALRIA: Apqerluku tauna pilaraa ca im' qelaseng qanaalluku, camek yuk nangtequtelek anirtungnaqluku. Tuaten pilarngatut.

ANGAUVIK: Ii-i. *Yes and no*. Pisciigalkan tua-i, pisciigalkan anirturciiganaku. Taugken tua-i pikuvgu anirtuqainaulliniluku. *Yes and no*, qanenrilngermi.

CUCUAQ: Taum-qaa nangteqellriim irua wall' qamiqurra?

ANGAUVIK: Qang'a nangteqellria pivkenaku, anirtungnaqluku taugaam.

Tuaten tua-i aipaqa tamakuciullruuq nasqumikun. Cavkenani taugaam.

Tuani taugaam anqertellruukuk tauna-llu *buddy*-qa-llu, kallagpak tua-i anqerreskiluk, aqvaqurlunuk. [*ngel'artuq*]

I used to hear about those who used divination on a person who had an illness[58]

Margaret Andrews and Frank Andrew, Bethel, December 2003

MARGARET ANDREWS: When they carried out *qelayaraq* [divination through lifting one's body parts], I used to hear about *qelatulit* [ones who use divination to determine a patient's ailment] back then, a person who had an illness, I think women also did shamanistic incantations.

Qelaluteng-wa qelatulit tamaani niillaqenka yug' una nangyutlek [qelaluku]

Quuqan Miisaq-llu, Mamterilleq, December 2003

QUUQAN: Qelaluteng-wa, qelatulit tamaani niillaqenka, yug' una nangyutlek, arnaungermeng-llu qelatullruungatut.

They let one who had an illness come, let him lie down on a pillow, and tied him here around the head. They put a tether on that and put a piece of wood where it is tied. [The one performing the divination] then sits on the floor and begins to pull on it.

They say they would pull it toward him. They say when his sickness is not quite right, his head would be heavy. When that happens he stops and instructs him not to eat certain foods. That is what I used to hear. That is probably what [others] do too. Do you know about *qela* [divination]?

FRANK ANDREW: Are you asking about *qelat* [divinations]?

MARGARET ANDREWS: Yes. They tie a piece of wood to their heads and continuously pull on it. I call them "junior *tuunraq*."

I don't think other customs were associated with that when they told about it. But they were instructed to abstain from eating certain foods or not to do certain activities.

They also told them not to get close to young girls who just started their first menstruation. I think they were admonished against those also. I never heard too many other things about *qelasaraq* [divination].

Nangyutlek taivkarluuku, inarcelluku akicirluuku, nasqurrakun maaggun qillerrluku. Tauna uskuralirluuku equgmek qillrutaa tuavet imkucirluni. Aqumluni natermun nuqiaararlun'.

Taigartaraluni-gguq. Tua-gguq nangyutii tauna qayuwetaqan uqamaitlartuq-gguq nasqurra, qamiqurra. Tauaten-gguq piaqan pitaarsaaqluku taqluku inerqualaraat cat ilaitnek neqkat. Tuaten-am niillarqa. Tuaten-wa pilallilriit-llu. Qelamek-qaa nalluuten?

MIISAQ: Qelanek-qaa?

QUUQAN: Ii-i. Nasqurritgun imumek imkucirluki equgmek muragmek qillerrluku nuqit'arluuki. Wii aug' acirlaranka *junior* tuunraq.

Cameg' allamek cacirsaitellruungatuq qanrutkaqamegteggu. Taugaam inerqurilarngaatut cat ilaitnek neqkat, qanga-llu calrianun pisqevken'aku.

Makunun-llu aunrarpailulrianun-llu pisqevken'aku yuunerrarnun, mallguuresqevkenaki tamakut. Inerqurilarngatut tamakunek-llu. Allamek amllermek niillanriitaqa tuaten qelasaraq tauna.

One who had the ability to come back to life[59]

Nick Andrew, Bethel, January 2006

NICK ANDREW: Since he has given it over to me, I'm going to speak briefly of *ircenrraat* [other-than-human persons], but it's not a long story.

Up between Kuicaraq [Johnson River] and Akuliqutaq is a small river. That is a long [river], and the place where the river ends flows out to Kuicaraq, quite a ways up the river. But the place where it heads downriver, it flows out down below the place they used to call Kuvuartelleq. The place where it's about to exit is a very large open marshy area where a lake has dried up. And there are many grassy knolls that sink. There is a very large grassy knoll. The one who told me stories is an *angalkuq*; he's actually from Nanvarnarrlak. He apparently resided there all the time when he was able to.

And he also has an older brother there, at Nanvarnarrlak. They say his name is Qamuutaq, a powerful *angalkuq*.

Unguiryugnganilleq

Apirtaq, Mamterilleq, January 2006

APIRTAQ: Aren-wa augkunek cali taicagu wangnun ircenrrarnek qanemciqaqatartua, takenrituq taugaam.

Piani atam Kuicaram Akuliqutaam-llu akuliigni kuicuartangqertuq. Tak'uq tamana, egmiumallra-ll' cali qamavet Kuicaramun anumaluni kiaqvani. Una taugaam uatmurtellra Kuvuartellermek pilallrata kiatiikun anumaluni. Anqatallrani tuani qass'uqitvagtangqertuq. Ikiki-ll' evinret imkut, kit'etulit. Evinerpaller'. Augna imna qanemciceteklalqa angalkuuguq; aug'um-wa pingkumiunguyaaquq Nanvarnarrlagmiunguuq. Tuani tua-i uitauratullruulliniuq tamaani piyunarqellermini.

Cali-llu amaqlingqerrluni tuani, Nanvarnarrlagmi. Atengqerrnilaraat taun' Qamuutarmek, angalkurpagmek.

He said that he slept overnight there when he arrived, since he was sleepy. When he woke in the morning, there was a very heavy fog, and there was no visibility. There were many people chasing an animal down there, making loud noises. They were apparently *ircenrraat* who were chasing sea mammals. They were very loud.

He said that it got bright and the fog lifted. He said that [the *ircenrraat*] got quiet when the fog lifted, and there was nothing there. It so happens that he would die that fall.

When my wife and I went to summer fish camp, we went up to bring him and his wife some fish and some fish to cook as well; we stayed in the same place as them. In the evening, I would go to them since he would tell various stories.

He told a story and said that an *angalkuq* who was keeping watch over him had killed him. But he said that in the spring when he paddled and spent a night out, he said that when he gained awareness at that time, a small person was setting a deadfall trap. (I don't know how their deadfall traps look.)

That one tried [to kill him] with that, but because he knew what he was doing, he didn't allow him to [kill him]. Then suddenly from up [in the air] he saw a spear coming toward him through the air. Although he tried to move, he couldn't move. Since he couldn't move, he ducked to dodge it. They say that one died for I think he said what was one week. His wife said that he didn't arrive for one week.

When he became aware of his surroundings down there, he searched for a way to return. He said while he was there, when he came upon a wild celery plant, he appeared through there. Then he told me that if he happened to die in my presence, that I should bind his body and place him where no one would see, placing him in a good place on the land.

I told him, since I always teased him, I said to him, "How will I do it? You will rot." He said no, that he would return, that he would come back to life. He said that he had come back to life before that time. He said that it wasn't difficult for him to return.

We spent the summer there. And when it was time for us, we brought him over. During the fall, not long after we moved, the poor thing died. When he died . . . Or no, he had started to become ill at that time.

Our priest whose name is Wassilie was alive at the time. When he arrived, when he went to let him

Qavartartuq-gguq-am tuani tuavet tekicami, qavarniami tua-i. Maaten-gguq unuakumi tupagtuq tairvagluni tua-i kiarrnaunani. Ikiki-gguq-wa camkut malirqellriit, nepsarpak. Cuna-gguq ircenrraat malirqellriit imarpigmiutarnek. Nepsarpak-gguq tua-i.

Tua-i-gguq tanqigiyaaquq, taituirulluni. Nepairtut-gguq imkut taituirucan, cataunani. Uksuaqu cunaw' tuquciqluni, catairuciiqelliniluni.

Kiagillmeggni-am aipaqa-llu, itraullukek nulirra-llu, cikiqaquurnalukek egaarkakegnek tuaten; nunalgutekluki. Tua-i atakuaqan wii ullaglarqa qanengssaaralaan waten canek tua-i.

Qanengssaarluni, aug'umun angalkumun tarikesteminun tuqucaaqellruniluni. Taugaam ellii up'nerkami anguarluni pillermini, qavartallermini, aa, maaten-gguq tuani cellanguq, yucuar una naneryamek civcilria. (Qaillun-llu tamakut tayim' ayuqelartat naneryait.)

Tua-i-gguq taugg'un pingnaqsaaqluku taum nallunrilamiu-w' pivkarpek'nani. Tua-llu-gguq atam piqerluni maaten piuq pagken man', imkut-wa caulartat kapsuutet, agiirtellria, pagken tua-i cellarrlainarkun. Arenqiatuq-gguq pekcaaqengraan pisciiganani. Pektesciigalami acitmun avilluku. Tua-i-gguq tuan' tuqumallruuq *one week* piniyugnarquq. Taum-wa nulirran pillrukii *one week* tekicuitellruniluku.

Camani tua-i cellangami kiarrluni ataam uterrvigkaminek. Tamaani-gguq tua-i piinanermini ikiitugmek tekicami, taugg'un pugellruuq. Tua-llu pilaraanga waten, pitsaqa'artevkenani takumni catairuskuni kemni nemrulluku yuum tangvanrilkiinun ellisqelluku nunakegcarluku nunam qainganun.

Piaqa, piurlaamku-llu, piaqa, "Qaill-mi piciqsia? Aruciquten." Qang'a-gguq uterciiquq-gguq, unguirciquq-gguq. Ak'a-gguq ciungani unguillruuq. Capinritaa-gguq utertellerkani.

Tua-i kiagiluta. Upagnariamta-ll' anelraulluku. Uksuarngan, anelrallerput ak'anivkenaku tua-i catairuteurlurluni. Catairutellrani . . . Aren tuani imat'anem naulluungluni.

Imna agayulirtevut Wassilie-mek atlek anerteqluni. Tekican, agturcecartullrani, pia,

take communion, he said to him, he used to call him his *iluraq*, "Iluq, if I die, and although you are up [in your village], you will know [that I've died]."

At that time, at night, during the early morning, past five o'clock sometime, the poor thing died. I wasn't thinking anything, and I didn't think of hiding his body.

I went outside right away and went down to my boat after having a small meal, and I went to go get that priest with my boat. And I never thought anything.

It so happened, when I arrived, he immediately got ready. I didn't really talk to that person either. I went inside and found that he had prepared to leave. It so happened that when he died, the bell rang at five o'clock in the morning. I told him, "You are already prepared; I've come to get you." Then we went down and left, and we returned home.

Only after a year had passed, that came into my mind. "Our grandfather probably came back to life underground." They say he was a shaman. Well, those two, they say that his elder brother was a powerful shaman.

Someone from our village also, up in Kuicaraq, not far from the place that I just told the story about, the weather suddenly became stormy as he was traveling by dogsled.

Since he was overwhelmed [by the weather], he went underneath a large hill along Kuicaraq River. There are many hills there, and there are trees.

He said that when he got to a place that was good to stop, since he wouldn't return home, and he wouldn't get there if he tried, he stopped. He said that as he was sitting there, during the evening, someone started talking up there.

He said that the one who I told the story about, the one who was supposed to come back to life, would refer to him as his grandchild. But he had never seen that person up at Nanvarnarrlak. He heard someone say, "Grandchild, don't feel desperate. Nothing will happen to you. I'm watching over you." He would look around, but there was no one there.

Then he told him, "I'm going to give you some directions on how to get to my fall camp. In my fall camp, there are many frozen blackfish for you to feed your dogs. When the sun comes up and you leave . . ." Then he showed him a trail that he could take through the trees. He gave him recognizable markers to follow.

iluraminek pilaraa tauna, "Iluq, catairuskuma qamaanlengerpet nallungaitarpenga."

Tua-i tuani tua-i unugmi, unuakuurtengluku, tallimanek kaullran amatιιni tua-i anerneriurlurluni. Cameg' umyuarteqenritua, iillerkaa-ll' im' kemgan umyuaqenritaqa.

Egmian' anlua atrarlua angyakun, nerqerraarlua, angyamkun aqvaaqa tauna agayulirta. Camek-llu umyuarteqsuunii.

Cunawa tang tuani tekicama egmian' uptuq. Qanrutsiyaayuilamku-ll' tauna. Maaten itertua upingaluni. Cunawa tang tuani anernerillrani kulukuunaq, agayuviim kulukuunaa qayiartellinilria *five* 'klaak unuakumi. Aren imna, tua-i piaqa, "Upingalliniuten; tua-i waniw' aqvaamken." Atrarlunuk-llu tua-i ayaglunuk, uterrlunuk.

Allrakuq kassugngan taugaam nutaan umyuamnun ekluni. "Atag' imna apa'urlurput unguillruyaaqngatuq tayim' caman' nunam iluani." Angalkuullruuq-gguq. Taukuk-wa, una-llu-gguq amaqlia angalkurpauguq.

Augna-am cali nunalgutka qavani Kuicarami, tamatum qanemcikellma yaaqsinrilkiini cellaqerrutelliniluku tua-i, qimugcirluni pillrani.

Tua-i-llu-gguq arenqialami pengurpallraam acianun piluni, Kuicaram ceniini. Pengut tamaan' amllelartut, napangqerraqluni-w' pilall'.

Utumalriamun-gguq tekicami kingunisngailami elluaciqngailami-llu pingnaqkuni, arulairluni. Uitaurainanrani-gguq unuumainanrani pakmaken qanelriartanguq.

Taum-gguq tua-i qanemcikellma aug'um, unguirarkauyaaqellrem, tutgarminek-gguq taun' pilaraa. Tauna-gguq taugken ellii piani Nanvarnarrlagmi tangssuunaku. Qanelriartanglliniuq, "Tutgar' nanikuanrilu. Arenqialluggngaituten. Nayuramken." Kiarcaaqnaurtuq-gguq yugtaunani.

Tua-llu-gguq pia, "Alerquaqataramken uksuillemnun ayallerkarpenek. Uksuillemni tuani kuv'at amllertut can'giiret qimugcitkaten. Waniw' ereskan ayakuvet . . ." Apertuaquralliniluku-ll' tua-i napani tumkaanek. Elitaqnarqellrianek-gguq tua-i apertuulluku.

When the sun came up, he left. He said he would recognize those places that [the dead shaman] had told him about, those markers, and even trees. He arrived at a fall camp, and the blackfish that he had told him about were there. They stayed there. When the weather improved, he returned home.

During the spring, when summer came, my grandfather, the one who had taken my mother from the village of Nunacuaq and brought up there, he had a trading post up along Kuicaraq River, and he raised foxes there. He also had reindeer.

When summer came, he also had a boat, a very large boat, with a four-horse Johnson motor. They would go to that place through Kuicaraq to meet the barge to get his supply of food. When he was about to do that, he wanted to bring that person along. He agreed, and they left.

He said they arrived at Nanvarnarrlak, they docked, and there was a man who was sitting outside of a home. He faced him. He went up since he was visible up there. When he was about to reach him, he said to him, "Hello grandchild. Have you forgotten my voice? When you were in a desperate situation during the winter, I helped you." He then recognized his voice.

That's how long it is.

Ercan tua-i ayalliniluni. Tua-i tamakut-gguq elitaqaqluki apertullri, nallunailkutat, cat, napat-llu taukut. Tekitelliniuq uksuillermun, tua-i apertullri-ll' taukut can'giiret tamaanlluteng. Tamaani tua-i uitaluteng. Ella assirian utertelliniluni.

Up'nerkaan, kiagngan, apa'urluqa tauna, aanama itraucetkellra, piaken Nunacuarmek tegustekellra, kiani Kuicaram ketiini kipusvingqelartuq, kaviarnek-llu qunguturarluni. Tuntui-wa cali.

Kiagaqan-am, angyangqerrluni cali angyarpall'ermek, massiinaa-wa imna *four horse*-aq Johnson-aaq. Taukunun tailartuk Kuicarakun sun'aq piarrsaagluku neqkautni aqvayarturluki. Tuaten-am piqatallermini tauna imna maliksullinia. Anglliniluku tua-i, ayallinilutek.

Nanvarnarrlagmun-gguq tekituk, culurtuk-gguq, angun pingna aqumgauralria enem elatiini. Caugartaa. Tag'uq-gguq tangerrnaqngan pia-i. Tekitniaraan-gguq pia, "Waqaa tutgar'. Tua-i-qaa erinaka nalluyagutan? Uksuq imumi nanikuallerpeni wii ikayuallruamken." Nutaan elitaqluku erinii.

Tua-i-w' tuaten taktalria.

Lawrence Edmund of Alakanak, Eugene Pete of Nunam Iqua, and Mike Andrews
Sr. of Emmonak sharing stories during a Lower Yukon elders gathering, December
2011. All three elders have since passed away. Ann Fienup-Riordan.

Stories from Qissunaq

They say when they catch up to that [shaman],
they will strip away [his powers]

Joe Ayagarak and David Chanar, Chevak, December 1987[1]

JOE AYAGARAK: But those who I used to see at Qissunaq, after going our own ways and gathered together [in one place], around forty years, in 1940, around there, the men who I had seen who were no longer active, there were three of them who were the same age in the *qaygiq*. When they'd tell stories, they'd help one another. And with their eyes closed, they'd fix the story they told. What they shared was something that would have been good to put in books and to be recorded on tape. I really regret what might have been.

DAVID CHANAR: Gee, I came a little too late.

JOE AYAGARAK: Yes. [*laughs*] When they'd speak, the three of them would face each other. When this one would make a mistake, one of them would take over [the story] and speak about what happened for a while. They would burst out laughing from time to time. [*chuckles*] It's because they were really imagining what they were talking about.

And these shamans, after practicing their spirit powers, when they spoke of them, they also spoke of those. When they imagined them in their minds [as they spoke]. They especially imagined the people of long ago, our ancestors.

These ones pursuing their fellow shamans, when they chased them, when they caught up with the ones who they were pursuing somewhere, then they captured them, they flattened their ways of practicing their spirit powers. They finished them.

And when there was no way for him to escape, they didn't let [that shaman] know, they didn't allow his body to be aware [that they had flattened his spirit helpers].

But when he noticed his body, that shamans [had gotten his spirit powers], when he suddenly became aware of it, he would inflate his spirit helpers that could be inflated since they belonged to him. Starting with that, he would attack the one who [tried to flatten his spirit helpers].

https://doi.org/10.5876/9781646427314.c017

Qissunamiut Qanemciit

· ·

Tava-i-gguq tau angukunegteggu ugayaqerluku

Ayagarak Cingurruk-llu, Cevv'armiut, December 1987

AYAGARAK: Taugaam imkut tangtullrenka Qissunami waten tamarqerraaluta piamta quyurcaaqellemteni, *forty*-m taugaam, *forty years* tamaani avatiini, 1940, tamaani, angutnaaneng imkuneng cananrilrianeng tangtullemneng, waten pingayuugut taukut egelrallgutkelriit qaygimi. Qanengssaagaraqameng waten ikayuququrluteng. Waten-ll' uisngavkenateng tau, tamana taugaam qanemciyeng kituggluku. Nutaan tau kalikamun elliyunaqsaaqluni waten *tape*-anun-llu elliyunarqellruyaaqelliniluteng maaten. Uurcaralrianga tua-i cakneq.

CINGURRUK: Aren, tainaciaqallrulliniunga.

AYAGARAK: Ii-i. [*ngel'artuq*] Waten qanerturaraqameng caulluteng pingayuuluteng. Uum, una alartaqan uum iliita teguqerluku waten pillra qanrutkuraqaqluku. Nenglallakaqluteng. [*ngelaq'ertuq*] Tangrruam ugaani tamatumeng qanrutkengameggneng.

    Makut-llu angalkut, waten tuunrirraarluteng, qanrutkellrit, cali tamakuneng piluteng. Waten tangrruareluki cat piaqamegteki. Makut maan' arcaqerluki tangrruatuit tamakut cuut ak'a, wangkuta augkut civuliamteneng.

    Malirqaralriit makut angalkuullgutmeggneng, waten-am malirqaraaqamegteki, nani angukunegteki malirqarakengateng tamakut, tava-i-ll' teguluki, makut tuuneryarait mamcarqelluki. Tau nangluki ellmeggni.

    Tua-i-ll' anagviiruskan, taugken elliinun nalluvkarluku, uumun kemganun nalluvkarluku tamana.

    Taugken-am waten alakarareskatgu man' temni, pillrullra angalkugnun, elpengarareskuni, qerruryugngalriit elliin tuunrani qerruqtarluki pikngamiki. Tamaaggun ayagluni tauna pisteni curugciqaa.

https://doi.org/10.5876/9781646427314.c017

But if the one he was attacking was paying attention to the possibility that he might become aware [that he was being attacked], he would sense it and they would suddenly fight. Then he would finally attempt to pursue him.

They say when they do that, all those who are able to see using spirit helpers move toward the edge. They want to watch those two who are going to challenge one another.

They say those are just like movies, like watching TV. They say when they get going, those who lack [power] lose, and they head up. They say only powerful shamans do that, their powerful ones among them.

Then they say when they catch up to that one, they will strip away [his powers] and let him go. They will finally take away his spirit helpers and claim them, or they will discard the ones that aren't good to keep. [chuckles]

DAVID CHANAR: So that's what they would do?

JOE AYAGARAK: Yes.

DAVID CHANAR: Then when they did that to them, that one they [pursued] lost, as they say?

JOE AYAGARAK: Then that one they stripped [of powers], that one would make it so that he would die [eventually].

DAVID CHANAR: He would die?

JOE AYAGARAK: Yes. Even though he is to die, he makes it so that he will die before him. They will let him go with a time [to die].

DAVID CHANAR: Yes.

Taugken-am taum civunran murilkengamiu elpenga'artellerkaa, cali elpeka'arrluku caugaruciiqut. Nutaan tau malirqaraqatarluku.

Tavaten-gguq tavatnaaqata, imkut kiyartetuaralriit tuunratgun maaggun ketvatuut tamalkurmeng. Tangerrsugluni taumeng ingluqrutellriigneng.

Tangercitaatun-gguq tua ayuqeqapigtut taukut, TV-t taukut. Makut-gguq tavaten eglengaqameng waten nuryagutellriit katagluteng, tagluteng tavaten. Taugaam-gguq tau angarvauguralriit tavaten pituut, makut kayulriarit.

Tava-i-llu-gguq tau angukunegteggu ugayaqerluku tua pegteciqaat. Makuneng tuunraineng nutaan tegulerluk' pikurluki, qang'a-ll' makut piknailnguut egqaqluki. [ngelaq'ertuq]

CINGURRUK: Tuaten-emtaq tua-i piaqluteng tua-i?

AYAGARAK: Ii-i.

CINGURRUK: Tua-llu-q' tuaten pikateng, tauna ciunrat apqiitnek lose-alleq?

AYAGARAK: Tauna-ll' ugayaqengaat tau tuquarkauluku taum im' piluku.

CINGURRUK: Tuquarkauluni-qaa?

AYAGARAK: Ii-i. Tuquarkaungermi-w' elliin civumini tuquarkauvkarluku. Wagg'u-q' tau tekiterkirluku tua peggluku.

CINGURRUK: Mm-m.

The people of Qip'ngayagmiut were looking inside, [looking at] the one they were trying to pursue and catch, Kenirmigpak[2]

Joe Ayagarak and David Chanar, Chevak, December 1987

JOE AYAGARAK: The following is something that I imagine in my mind, even though I hear of shamans doing that. I imagine that person who they call Kenirmigpak, [the one named] Ciutairutleq. He is our ancestor. He was from Qissunamiut.

And he wasn't a distantly related relative. He was somehow related to my father's father.

DAVID CHANAR: Yes.

JOE AYAGARAK: When he was an old man, he lived in the *qaygiq*, although that poor thing had a

Uyangteqtaalliut Qip'ngayagmiut, kat'umeng pitarkameggneng Kenirmigpagmeng

Ayagarak Cingurruk-llu, Cevv'armiut, December 1987

AYAGARAK: Uumeng taugaam wii tangrruatuunga tavaten angalkuneng niitetungerma pilrianeng. Una taugaam tangrruatuaqa Kenirmigpagmeng pitukiit Ciutairutleq. Wangkuta civuliaqerput. Qissunamiunguluni.

Cali-ll' yaaqsissiyaagpegnani. Aatama atiin cakluku tauna.

CINGURRUK: Mm-m.

AYAGARAK: Waten-am angutnaaraami, qaygimiuvatuami, taugaam

partner named Atsaruaq before. They were allies, they were partners. When they'd attack them, *?qivirqaqacetek*-ll' [and they would ?_?] they would turn to that [shaman] and *?tekiterkiqa'aqluku* [give him something to come upon in the future]. They were allies, they were partners.

One day, since there was a village up north called Qip'ngayagmiut or Amigtulirmiut to the north of Scammon Bay, around there, in the evening when the people of the *qaygiq* were about to go to sleep, he put on his little mittens and went down, since they always had inside entrance holes.

When he went down, when he fell down [the entrance hole], he headed down, he was wondering why there were people singing from up ahead of him. He was offended by those singing in the area up ahead since he was going out, since he was going outdoors. He stopped for a second and listened, and they were singing down there.

Then the people inside were speaking for a while, and the lamp cast a shadow on the entrance opening downward. After singing, they finished and started speaking. They were about to start another [song]; when they struck the drum again, he headed out toward the exit and there were people out there who were practicing their shaman powers up ahead of him outdoors.

And he looked back, but he didn't know what to do and stayed there.

When he closed his eyes and tried to think of what to do, he saw that they had already flattened his spirit helpers. He didn't know what to do.

He said when the woman back there struck the drum, her two lengths of hair started to stretch out following the beating of the drum, going out. They were coming his way. And when it reached him, when they reached him, they went behind him, following the beating of the drum.

And when the [two lengths of hair] encircled him, once again following the beating of the drum, they pulled him. He *?_teqeryaaquq* with as much strength as he had, but he slipped and headed slowly inside.

Then when he reached the entrance hole, those shrunk.

But they say he had an *iluraq* [male cross-cousin] there, a real cross-cousin who had married someone there and who was living there as a son-in-law. The people up there, the people of Qip'ngayagmiut kept looking inside. [They were looking at] the one who they were trying to pursue and catch, Kenir-

aipaurlungqellruyaaqluni waten wagg'u-q' uumeng Atsaruarmeng. Waten iliklutek, paatnaqlutek. Piaqacitek, ?qivirqaqacetek-ll' caugarrluku tau ?tekiterkiqa'aqluku. Iliklutek tau, tau paatnarraqlutek.

Piuraqerluni-am tau, qagaani nunatangqerrami Qip'ngayagmiuneng qang'a-ll' Amigtulirmiuneng qagaan' Scammon Bay-rmiut negratni tamaani, atakumi inarteqataata ukut qaygimiut aritvacualleragni ay'arrlutek atralliniluni, pugyarangqetuameng kesianeng.

Atraami-am ig'arcami anelraryaaquq, ciinggguq man' civunraneng cat qamkut aturciqat. Atulrianeng tau cangayukarluni civunemineng anngami, cillamun anngami. Arulaiqerluni piuq tau cakmaa-i atulriit.

Tava-i-llu-gguq tau qamkut qanerturaqerluteng, kenurram-llu una pugyaraq acitmun akiqerrluku. Aturturaqerluteng tau taqluteng qanengluteng. Ayagniqatartut allameng; cauyaq kaugngatgu uavet piqertuq tuunrilriit qaugkut civunraneng cillami.

Kingyaryaaquq-llu tau, qaill' picirkaunani uitaluni tavani.

Maaten-gguq tang qelemqerluni cillangcaqertuq tuunrayarai-llu makut mamcarqelliit ak'a. Qaill' picirkaiteqerluni.

Cauyaq-gguq kaugluku kiugum arnam, waken nuyak neng'uk cauyaq kaugturallra maliggluku anlutek. Uka-i. Tekicamiu-llu-gguq, tekicamegnegu amatairluku, tuamtell' cauyaq kaugturallrak maliggluku.

Kassuamegnegu tuamtell' cauyaq maliggluku cayugturluku. Tau ?_teqeryaaquq-gguq kayungtacimitun qurrasqilluni itraarluni.

Tava-i-ll' pugyaramun nallairucamiu qungagluteg' imkuk tayim'.

Taugaam-gguq ilurangqertuq tamaani, nakmiin iluremineng nengaugitauluni tamaani. Pikegkut uyangteqtaalliut Qip'ngayagmiut. Kat'umeng pitarkameggneng Kenirmigpagmeng; Kenirmigpauluni tau tamaani.

migpak down there; his name was Kenirmigpak back then.

His *iluraq* was thinking at the time, "Those ones over there, I hope that they catch a powerful shaman, the most difficult to catch." That's what he thought. After a while, the people there started to turn to him. The two who were drumming were without clothes since it's hot when they practice their shaman powers. I know that since I also used to be in the *qaygiq* around those practicing their shaman powers.

The people there started to tell him to hurry, "Hurry and go see that one down there, he's from your village, you will know him. Is that one down there indeed Kenirmigpak?" And this one went down smiling, "These ones should hurry and kill him."

He looked in on him, and when he tilted his head up, my, it was his dear *iluraq* down there. My, when he suddenly felt guilty, even though he smiled up at him, he didn't reciprocate and headed up and tucked himself underneath the bench and lay down on his back.

The people around were demanding, "Is that one down there indeed Kenirmigpak?" He didn't want to reply when he felt guilty. He was upset over him since he was his real *iluraq*.

The other of the two drummers asked him. There was a full urine container near him.

They say when he tilted his head up, he was looking around for a way to escape underneath the floor boards. And they say the window above, the *?kapellri* all had someone manning them. They were guarded by the spirit helpers of those who were practicing their shaman powers.

But they say that one up there who had pierced a hole and moved . . . we call those *?kapsuiltelleruat*. That was the only spot up there that wasn't manned [by a spirit helper].

Since they were all different back then, and people are all different today too, that one who was drumming suddenly got angry and took the urine container and threw it on the floor. When the urine container landed, it splashed all over. And those practicing their spirit powers all lost awareness, they forgot what they were doing.

But they say Kenirmigpak, even though aged urine landed on him, on that . . . you know how in the past along watery paths, we used to see those small things that spring up, those water beetles; he transformed into one of those and shot himself through that [hole] up there.

Taun' ilurii waten umyugarturtuq tavani, "Amkut angarvallermeng piskilit, angalkut caperqataatneng." Umyugarturlun'. Piqerluku tau pinga'artelliat ukut. Ukuk-wa cauyalriik mata'arqaupiarmek kiircitetuami tamana tuunriaqata. Wii-ll' tuunrilriani taugaam qaygitullruama.

Ampiarangaartaat ukut, "Am' kan' tangerrsartuqarru, nunalgutkan, nallungaitan. Ilumun-qaa tua-i kan'a Kenirmigpauguq?" Quuyurmi-ll' una atralliniluni, "Am-gguq ukut pitaqekilitgu."

Uyanglluku-gguq tauna, civuvartuq-gguq, aren, iluraurlua kan'a. Aren, qessanayullallermini-gguq tau quuyuarniartengraani-ll' pikavet, akiqerpeg'nak' tagluni ingleret aciatnun qerrluni avavet iggagtelliniluni.

Ukut-gguq nepngutqeryaaqaat, "Ilumun-qaa tau kana-i Kenirmigpauguq?" Kiuyugpeg'nak qessanayullermini. Ilutequtekluku-wa tua iluraqngamiu nakmiin.

Apqaqeryaaqluku taum cauyalriim aipaan. Qurrun-wa nuniini-w' muiqaaralria.

Tavani-gguq tau civuvartellermini anvigkaminek kiyarteqeryaaquq mat'um nacitet aciatni. Pikna-llu-gguq tang egaleq, kapellri pagkut tamalkurmeng cungqellrulriit. Taukut tuunrilriit tuunraitneng nayurkarluteng.

Pikna-gguq taugaam kapsaaqerraarluni im' nugtara'artelleq . . . tamakut ?kapsuiltelleruanek wangkuta pituaput. Kiimi taugaam pika-i cuunani.

Ayuqsuilameng tamaani cali-ll' maa-i ayuqsuilnguut cuut, qenqerrluni tauna cauyalria qurrun teguqerluku natermun egtellia. Qurrun-gguq-am tuc'ami picimitun ciqruq. Imkut-llu-gguq taukut tuunrilriit ciilaseng nalluyaguarrluku, qaill' piciiteqerluteng.

Tauna-gguq tang tau Kenirmigpak, teq'um tut'engraani, imukun . . . nau ak'a tumlleruarni mermi petgayagalriit imkut cungavyeruaraat tangtukput; tamakucimeng amiliqerluni pik'ukun tau nutgutliuq.

He landed outside, he got out through ?*Qiurng-*
aliaq. And when he landed outside, he took off
?*piyugcitarluni*.

They say when they ?*piyugcitallrat*, there are no
tracks, when they fly.

They lost him from there.

When he arrived at Qissunaq in the flesh, when
he entered, he scolded them. He had left in the evening the day before. They had pulled him. He practiced his shaman powers.

Back in those days they really valued their shamans. And when they'd practice their shaman
powers, they wouldn't go against them or tell them
not to. They would just immediately agree with
them [when they wanted to practice their shaman
powers].

And they say when he was done practicing his
shaman powers, one of them asked him what he
was doing, "So are they not going to do anything
to you now?" He said it's okay. He said they could
have lived long if they hadn't fooled around. He
?*tekiterkirturluki* [made a future for] all of them, he
lined them up and put them in their places.

I just finished that [story].

Cillamun tull'uni, anluni Qiurngaliarkun.
Cillamun-ll' tuy'utmini piyugcitarluni
ayakalliniluni.

Piyugcetallrat man' tumailngaraqluku pituniit,
teng'aqata.

Tayima tau tamariluku tavaken.

Tekicami-am Qissunamun kemegtuumarmi,
iterngami nunurluki. Waniw' atakumi akwaugaq
ayallruyaaquq. Taumun cayugyaaqellrulliniluku.
Tuunrililuni.

Tamaani pirpakqapiareluki pitulqait
makut angalkuteng. Tuunriksuraqata-llu tau
naiggngaunaki pisqevkenaki-ll' inerqurngaunaki.
Angerluk' taugaam egmian'.

Tuunrinermeng-llu-gguq tua-i taqngami,
naliata tayim' aptellinia qaill' picianeng,
"Tava-llu-qaa tua caarkaunrirluten?" Canrituq-
gguq. Picingssanrilkuneng-llu-gguq-am
anerteqnertuuranruyarluteng. Tamalkuita tau
tekiterkirturluki, *line up*-arluki ellilallii.

Augna ava-i iquklitaqa.

Aperyarat

Glossary[1]

· ·

Note: In the Yup'ik language, nouns ending in "q" are singular, nouns ending in "t" are plural, and dual nouns end in "k."

aciirulluni. One going underground, to the place below (from *aci-*, "below").

aciliurcuutek. Two items used by a shaman to check below (from *aci-*, "below").

aciliurluteng. Shamans checking below to make prey more available (from *aci-*, "below").

agayu/agayuq/agayut. Mask(s) to request things, song(s) requesting things.

Agayun. Christian God.

Agayuyaraq. Masked dancing requesting future abundance; also Itruka'ar.

akigarluku. Carrying something evenly between several people, as when a person is carried on a grass mat into the *qasgiq* to be healed.

akutaq/akutat. Mixture(s) of fat, fish, and berries.

alairumalriit. Shamans who were visible and did their work with people watching them (from *alair-*, "to appear, to come into view").

alairumanrilnguq/alairumanrilnguut. Shaman(s) who were not visible, one(s) who kept themselves concealed, using their power secretively (from *alair-*, "to appear, to come into view").

alairyuaralria. Novice shaman (lit., "one who is just appearing").

alangruq/alangrut. Ghost(s), apparition(s), thing(s) that appear unexpectedly.

alerquun/alerquutet. Admonition(s), proscription(s), instruction(s) (from *alerqur-*, "to instruct, advise, offer guidance").

aliurtuq/aliurtut. Ghost(s), apparition(s), supernatural presence(s).

amiingirluku. A ghost blocking a person between the entryway and exitway of the tunnel leading into a *qasgiq* or home (from *amiik*, "door, entranceway").

anerneq. Spirit, soul, breath.

Anerneq Tanqilria. The Holy Spirit.

angalki-. To perform shamanic acts; also *angalkumirte-*.

angalkuq/angalkuk/angalkut. Shaman(s); also *kallalek, tuunralek* (lit., "person with a *tuunraq* [spirit helper]"), *tuunrangayak.*

angalkurkat. Ones who would become *angalkut* (shamans).

angarvak. Powerful shaman.

aniqlaayaraq. Putting a curse on someone.

https://doi.org/10.5876/9781646427314.c018

anllugneq. Aura emanating from a person or place.

apqara'arcuun/apqara'arcuutet. Shaman's drum(s) (lit., "device[s] for asking," from *apqara-*, "to ask about something").

apqara'arluteng. When shamans communicate with their *avneret*, asking about something (from *apqara-*, "to ask about something").

apqaraun/apqarait. One(s) that serve shamans; means by which shamans do their work; their shaman power(s) (from *apqara-*, "to ask about something").

arula/arulaq. Dance (from *arula-*, "to be in motion, to move back and forth, to dance").

atellgun. One having the same name as another, usually those named after the same deceased person (from *ateq*, "name," plus *-llgute-* "fellow").

ateq. Name.

atlirneq. Thing placed underneath a person by a shaman (lit., "something underneath").

atlirnirluki. A shaman placing a requested object, but one not received, under someone to make the person sick (lit., "placing something underneath them").

augtarnarqellria/augtarnarqellriit. Person/people who one doubts (will live); something one feels unsure of or hesitant about.

aurneq. Mist or vapor, especially vapor rising from a warm object in the cold or coming with the presence of a ghost or apparition.

aviukarqun. An offering to request things in the future.

aviukaryaraq. Process of giving an offering of food and water to the dead, to animals, or to the land.

avneq/avneret. Shaman's "other half" (from *avek*, "half"); shaman's helping spirit(s) (identified with the voice of the dead shaman who gave him his power); felt presence of something immaterial; ghostly humming noise coming from a corner of the house; shaman's guardian(s) or guide(s).

avnir-. To perform shamanic practices (?using the spirit of the dead).

avulluksagute-. To become aware of a shaman intending to kill people.

ayapercuutet. Hands to lean down on for support (from *ayaper-*, "to lean on one's hands, to support oneself with one's hands").

ayaperluni. Healing with one's hands (lit., "resting one's hands down on something for support," from *ayaper-*, "to lean on one's hands, to support oneself with one's hands").

ayapetulit. Healers, those with healing hands (lit., "ones who lean down on their hands for support," from *ayaper-*, "to lean on one's hands, to support oneself with one's hands"); also *unatellget*.

caangrayuk. Not an ordinary person.

caarrluk. That which one is going to have as an illness (lit., "dirt, debris, transgressions, evil spirit, sin").

caavtaaryaraq. The way of feeling with one's hands and finding wounds (from *caavtaar-*, "to feel around, to grope, to play a game of blindman's buff").

caavtaatulit. Those who feel around with their hands and find wounds (from *caavtaar-*, "to feel around, to grope, to play a game of blindman's buff"); also *cavcitulit*.

canipqurluni. One flying around using his shaman powers.

capkuciryaraq. The process of covering one who was dying with the life of another person, who would die instead; using another person's life to cloak oneself.

carayak/carayiit. Extraordinary being(s) (lit., "terrible fearsome thing"), ghost(s), monster(s), bear(s).

carayar-. Attempt to murder (of a shaman).

cauyatuli/cauyatulit. One(s) who drum; shaman(s) who drum to go on journeys (from *cauyaq*, "drum").

cavcitulit. Those who feel with their hands and find wounds (from *cavte-*, "to feel or touch intentionally with one's hand").

Curukaq. Dance Festival (from *curukar-*, "to attack"); also Kevgiq.

curukat. Guests invited to a dance festival (lit., "attackers," from *curukar-*, "to attack").

egavatuli. One who would get cooked inside a big container using his shaman ability.

elegtellriit. Shamans who burned using their powers.

ella maliggluku. Going clockwise (lit., "following the direction of *ella* [world, universe]"); also *cella maliggluku*.

Ellam Yua. Person of Ella (the Universe).

ellangqurrulluni. Going into the sky world (from *ella*, "world, universe").

ellanguaq. Model *ella* (universe), round hanging device hung in the *qasgiq* and moved up and down during a performance.

ellimerrucirluki. Paying shamans for their work, according to what they request (from *ellimer-*, "to request to perform a task, to order").

elpengcarilriit. Ones that give signs that something is about to occur (from *elpengcar-*, "to notify, to make aware").

elucira'arluki. Making known what something is like, such as what is making them sick (from *eluciq*, "shape, form, condition, what something is like").

elumar-/elumaar-. To fly with the aid of shaman power; also *luumar-, luumaar-.*

eyagyaraq/eyagyarat. Abstinence practice(s) following birth, death, illness, and first menstruation.

igyararatuli/igyararalriit. One(s) who drum and sing to conjure their powers (from *igyaraq*, "throat").

iinruq/iinrut. Amulet(s), charm(s), medicine(s).

iivkarluki. Lowering ghosts by putting one's hands on them to make them disappear (from *iivkar-*, "to fall or lower from a height").

iluq. Vocative form of *iluraq* (cross-cousin).

iluraq/ilurat. Male cross-cousin(s) of a male, cousin(s).

imarnin/imarnitek/imarnitet. Seal-gut rain parka(s).

imartelleq. One who journeyed into the ocean (from *imarpik*, "ocean").

inerquun/inerquutet. Prohibition(s), proscription(s).

iqlungalria/iqlungalriit. False shaman(s), liar(s) (lit., "one who lies").

ircenrraq/ircenrraat. Other-than-human person(s), said to live underground in hilly areas; place(s) where extraordinary things occur; also *tukaratulit.*

Itruka'ar. Masked festival; also Agayuyaraq.

kacell'uteng. People gathering at their winter settlement.

kalvagyaraq. Tunnel entryway to the *qasgiq* (from *kalvag-*, "to go down, usually into the ground").

kap'iluni. One poking or making an incision to heal an ailment.

kap'issuun. Implement for piercing patients during traditional medical treatment.

kapun/kaputet. Poking instrument(s) with wood handle and thin metal tip, needle(s); also *kap'issuun.*

kass'at. Non-Natives, white people.

Kassiyuq. Dance festival during which gifts are exchanged between villages.

keggiarnat. Huge otter-like creatures that shamans cause to appear.

kegginaquq/kegginaqut. Dance mask(s) (from *kegginaq*, "face").

Kevgiq. Dance Festival; Messenger Feast; also Curukaq.

kingullugte-. To berate with a ridicule song recounting a person's misdeeds.

kis'uka'arluni. One swimming through the ground.

kit'ellriit. Shamans who travel underwater, wearing seal-gut garments and using their powers (from *kit'e-*, "to fall into water, to sink, to drown").

kitengkayuli/kitengkayulit. One(s) who kick (from *kitengkar-*, "to kick").

mer'umavigkaq/mer'umavigkat. One(s) to whom a shaman gives his powers after he dies, becoming the *avneq* of his *mer'umavigkaq* (lit., "one who would give him a constant source of drinking water," from *meq*, "water"); also *mer'umavik.*

nangrulluki. Shamans standing and working to heal a person in the *qasgiq* (from *nangerte-*, "to stand up").

napan/napaneq/napanret/napateq/napatet. Amulet(s) or name(s) given to a person by a shaman (lit., "support[s] or foundation[s] that keep one up or alive," from *napa-*, "to stand upright").

naparta/napartet. Thing(s) that hold up one who was doctored by a shaman and made to live (from *naparte-*, "to set upright"); thing(s) that keep them alive.

nemertayagaat. Children who died (lit., "small ones who are bound"); also *qillerqayagaat.*

nepcetaq/nepcetat. Shaman's mask(s), said to stick to the face without any visible support (from *nepte-*, "to stick or adhere"); also *tukaraun, yug'aq.*

nukalpiaq/nukalpiat. Great hunter(s) and provider(s).

nuyarneq/nuyarneret. Bad thought(s) shamans use to make people sick (from *nuyarnir-*, "to feel the body warmth of an unseen person").

nuyarneraralria/nuyarneraralriit. One(s) who curse someone (from *nuyarnir-*, "to feel the body warmth of an unseen person").

nuyarniurcuutet. Devices shamans used to put a curse on someone and make him sick (from *nuyarnir-*, "to feel the body warmth of an unseen person").

pall'itaak. Removable log frame entrance to the underground tunnel passageway into the *qasgiq.*

pamyulget. Insects resembling worms found in vole caches that give one who finds them healing hands (lit., "ones with a *pamyuq* [tail]").

paterturyaraq. Way of or ability to suck out illness (from *pater-*, "to suck or soak up").

pinguarcuutet. Items shamans used to request an abundance of resources.

pinguarluteng. Shamans revealing meanings of masks used to request abundance; shamans requesting an abundance of things using their spirit powers (lit., "pretending to do something," from *pinguar-*, "imitation, inauthentic thing").

pissuun/pissurcuun/pissuutet. Power source(s) or helper(s) of a shaman (lit., "something to hunt with").

piyugcetalek/piyugcetalget. One(s) who take a step and their path folds, shortening the distance to their destination (from *piyua-*, "to walk," lit., "ones with the ability to walk").

piyunarqucilget. One(s) with abilities and authority, from *piyunarquciq*, "authorization."

puqlii. Its warmth, its heat (from *puqla*, "heat, warmth").

qanemciq/qanemcit. Story(s), historical tale(s).

qaniqelria/qaniqelriit. One(s) performing shamanic incantations (from *qaniqe-*, "to perform a shamanic incantation invoking spirit helpers").

qaniqun/qaniqutet. Shaman's incantation(s) invoking helping spirits and protecting one from illness (from *qaniqe-*, "to perform a shamanic incantation invoking spirit helpers").

qanruyun/qanruyutet. Oral instruction(s).

qasgiq/qasgit. Communal men's house(s); also *qaygiq* (Cup'ik).

qelatuli/qelatulit. One(s) who use divination to determine a patient's ailment (from *qela*, "spirit"; *qela-*, "to practice divination").

qelayaraq/qelayarat. Divination(s); shamanistic ritual(s) in which a patient's ailment is determined by tying a string around another person's head or foot and testing it by pulling on it to see if it could or couldn't be lifted easily (from *qela*, "spirit"; *qela-*, "to practice divination"); also *qelasaraq*.

qelqun. Shaman's paraphernalia.

qilaraulluku. Wrapping a shaman in a bearded-seal skin for a spirit journey.

qillerqat. Those who are tied (from *qillerqe-*, "to tie repeatedly and securely").

qillerqayagaat. Small ones who are tied or bound, meaning children who have died (from *qillerqe-*, "to tie repeatedly and securely"); also *nemertayagaat*.

qukviiq/qukviulria/qukviulriit. Being(s) with long hair that swim in the water and that shamans cause to appear.

quliraq/quli'ir/qulirat. Legend(s), tale(s), sometimes used by a shaman to request things from spirits.

qupurruyuli. Being belonging to a shaman that helps people in distress at sea (from *qupe-*, "to split, to crack").

quuguarluni. Act of requesting an abundance of wood through masked dancing (lit., "pretend *quuk* [firewood]"); also *eguguarluni*.

takullugluni. One displaying unusual behavior portending someone's death.

takussagluni. Shaman circling the person he is healing, following the direction of the universe *ella maliggluku*, clockwise.

tangrruarluni. Seeing the future in a vision (lit., "something like seeing," from *tangrruar-*, "to hallucinate, to have visions").

tari/tarian/tariit. Spirit(s); also *tuunraq*.

tarnaq/tarneq/tarnat. Soul(s) of person(s), spirit(s), tiny human figure(s) resembling its owner, tiny visible likeness(es).

taru/taruq. Person, human being (used instead of *yuk* in some areas, and may have been a shaman's word elsewhere).

tengautulit. Those (shamans) who fly (from *tenge-*, "to fly").

tevrunateng/?tevrinateng. They knew things (referring to shamans).

tukar(ar)-. To explain the mask during a dance, said of shamans.

tukaratulit. Little people (from *tukara-*, "to make rumbling noises welcoming shamans," lit., "those who kick with both feet, from a lying position [from underground]"); also *ircenrraat, tukaralriit*.

tukaraun. Shaman's mask, song, or figurine.

tukni-. To be strong, potent or powerful in any sense, including the use of shamanic powers.

tuunriyaraq/tuunriyarat. Way(s) of practicing their spirit powers; spirit helpers.

tuunralek/tuunralget. Shaman(s) (lit., "person[s] with a *tuunraq* [spirit helper]"); also *angalkuq*.

tuunrangayak/tuunrangayiit. A term sometimes used for shaman(s); also evil spirit(s), the Devil/devils, Satan.

tuunrangcarrluni. Shaman waiting for his *tuunrat* (shaman powers or spirit helpers) to come.

tuunraq/tuunrat. Shaman's spirit helper(s) or guide(s), familiar spirit(s), spirit power(s); also *tari*.

tuunritulit. Ones who use spirit power, ones who conjure spirits (from *tuunri-.* "to use spirit power, to traffic with familiar spirits").

umyuaq. Mind, mental activity.

umyuaqegcilria. One with good wishes toward others, one who is thoughtful (from *umyuaqeci-*, "to have good thoughts").

umyuarrluut. Those [shamans] who were malicious, the Devil's helpers (from *umyuarrliqe-*, "to have malicious thoughts or evil intentions").

unatekat. Things found in vole caches that give one healing hands (from *unan*, "hand").

unatellek/unatellget. One(s) with healing hands (lit., "those with *unatet* [hands]"); also *ayapetulit.*

unguva. Life, life spirit.

urumavik/urumaviit. Shaman(s) who help in a child's conception; shaman(s) who enable a couple to have a healthy child, known as a *yuungcaraq* (from *uruma-*, "to be warm [of a person]").

yua. Life essence, its person (from *yuk*, "person, human being").

yuarulluk/yuarulluut. Song(s) composed by shamans and performed by others in the *qasgiq* during the time a shaman is taking a journey or using his power; song(s) used to obtain what is desired.

yugaq/yugat. Nonhuman being(s) of the wilderness (lit., "doll[s], human figurine[s]").

yug'aq. Shaman's mask or representation of his familiar spirit.

yugcarluni. Shaman killing himself, then coming back to life.

yugtaarluteng. Shaman healing a sick person by crouching down beside him/her, draped in a seal-gut parka.

yuiraluki. Trying to take someone's spirit or life essence (from *yuk*, "person, human being").

yuiratellriik/yuiratellriit. two/those who provoke each other and try to take the spirit away from one another through song.

yuliur-. To deal with or bother people through shamanic power.

yuuciq. Life, lifeline, immortal soul.

yuun. A voice that identified a dead person and could be summoned by a shaman.

yuungcaraq/yuungcarat. One(s) doctored by a shaman while still in the womb and allowed to live; one(s) medically treated by a doctor (lit., "one doctored to become a person"); also *yungcaraq.*

yuungcariluteng. Shamans using their powers to doctor a child while still in the womb.

Notes

··

Chapter 1: *Kalikam Ayagnera* / Introduction

1. For discussions of shamanism in Alaska see Burch 1971; Fienup-Riordan 1994, 1996, 1997; Fienup-Riordan, Rearden, and Meade 2009; Fortuine 1986; Hawkes 1913; Himmelheber 1993; Lantis 1946, 1966, 1990; Mather 1985; Morrow 1984; Mousalimas 1995; Nelson 1899; Oswalt 1963; and Spencer 1959. For shamanism in other parts of the Arctic see Balikci 1963; Blodgett 1979; Bogoras 1904; Borre 1994; Hughes 1958; Merkur 1985, 1991; Oosten 1976, 1981, 1989, 1997; Rasmussen 1930, 1931, 1932; Saladin d'Anglure 2001; Saladin d'Anglure and Morin 1997; and Sonne 2017. Work in the early 2000s with elders at Nunavut Arctic College in Iqaluit is especially relevant (Laugrand and Oosten 2006, 2010, 2012; Oosten and Laugrand 2002; Oosten, Laugrand, and Remie 2006; Saladan d'Anglure 2001). During these meetings information was shared in group settings similar to CEC topic-specific gatherings and during the same time period that some of our most valuable documentation work with Yup'ik elders took place.

2. My discussion of topic-specific gatherings draws from our book, *Ellavut / Our Yup'ik World and Weather* (Fienup-Riordan and Rearden 2012). I have also drawn from the introduction I wrote for *Words of the Real People: Alaska Native Literature in Translation* (Fienup-Riordan 2007b) as well as an essay I published in Roger Sanjek's 2015 edited volume, *Mutuality: Anthropology's Changing Terms of Engagement*.

3. For detailed accounts of specific gatherings and what they taught about salmon, birds, sea mammals, and land animals respectively, see Fienup-Riordan et al. 2020.

4. Fienup-Riordan 2005a and Rearden, Meade, and Fienup-Riordan 2005; Fienup-Riordan 2005b and Meade and Fienup-Riordan 2005; Andrew 2008 and Fienup-Riordan 2007a; and Fienup-Riordan and Rearden 2012 and Rearden and Fienup-Riordan 2011.

Chapter 3: *Angalkut Yuungcaristengulallrat* / Shamans as Healers

1. Inuit elders also indicated that healing had been the major task of shamans. According to Boas (1964[1888]:592–3): "The principal office of *angakut* is to find out the reason of sickness and death or of any other misfortune visiting the natives. The Eskimo believes that he is obliged to answer the *angakoq*'s questions truthfully" (Laugrand and Oosten 2012:242).

2. Compare Hughes (1958:80) for the Siberian Yup'ik people.

3. This distinction is made differently in the Canadian Arctic, where animals as well as humans are said to have *tarnat* (Laugrand and Oosten 2012:103, 112).

4. In the Canadian Arctic, one initiation technique for a shaman was to put moss containing living things such as insects and caterpillars from underground on the skin of one's arm and stay still while they sucked on it (Laugrand and Oosten 2012:214).

5. Anthropologist Robert Spencer (1959:309–10) also noted the importance of confession in healing among the Iñupiat, and Frédéric Laugrand and Jarich Oosten (2012:242–44) found the same thing to be true among Canadian Inuit: "A patient could only be healed if he confessed his transgressions in public, so that other people as well as non-human agencies would hear. . . . The body and mind were connected . . . In many cases illness was caused by transgression that hadn't been acknowledged."

6. Descriptions of Inuit head-lifting go back to the sixteenth century, and it was practiced in a great variety of ways (Laugrand and Oosten 2012:309). Boas (1901:135) described how a thong was put around the head of a person lying down next to the patient. The thong attached to the end of a stick was held by a shaman, who summoned the soul of a dead person and then asked questions as to the outcome of the disease, which the dead responded to by making it impossible to lift the head if the answer was affirmative. Laugrand and Oosten (2012:310) noted that head-lifting was described as both divination and as a healing technique. If it worked it was like medicine, and it could be played around with and tested. It was generally considered a weak technique that could be used by anyone, and young people were allowed to practice using it (Laugrand and Oosten 2012:319, 322).

Chapter 5: *Cauyatuli* / One Who Drums

1. Others tell this story, including Michael John (June 2008:240–43) and Elsie Tommy (February 2010:69–71, in Rearden et al. 2021:124–29).

Chapter 10: *Iqua* / Conclusion

1. Frank Andrew tells another version of the Ississaayuq story in his book *Paitarkiutenka / My Legacy to You* (2008:321–33).

Angalkut Agayumaciq-llu / Shamanism and Christianity

1. CEC tape collection. Yupiit Piciryarait Museum Gathering, with Frank Andrew, Margaret Andrews, Alex Bird, Joan Hamilton, Noah Andrew, Mark John, Marie Meade, Alice Rearden, Freda Jimmie, and Ann Fienup-Riordan. Bethel. December 16, 2003. Tape 4, pages 118–25.

2. CEC tape collection. Bethel Workshop with David Martin, Paul John, Theresa Moses, Elsie Mather, Walter Therchik, Marie Meade, Alice Rearden, and Ann Fienup-Riordan. Bethel. April 2, 2001. Tape 1, pages 5–13.

3. CEC tape collection. Bethel Workshop with David Martin, Paul John, Theresa Moses, Elsie Mather, Walter Therchik, Marie Meade, Alice Rearden, and Ann Fienup-Riordan. Bethel. April 2, 2001. Tape 1, pages 5–13.

4. CEC tape collection. Nunaput Gathering with Paul John, John Phillip, Nick Andrew, Peter Jacobs, Golga Effemka, Joe Asuluk, Anthony Oney, Glenn Azean, Magdalene John, Alice Rearden and Ann Fienup-Riordan. USFWS Refuge, Bethel. January 20, 2006. Tape 7, pages 426–45.

5. CEC tape collection. Nunaput Gathering with Paul John, John Phillip, Nick Andrew, Peter Jacobs, Golga Effemka, Joe Asuluk, Anthony Oney, Glenn Azean, Magdalene John, Alice Rearden, and Ann Fienup-Riordan. USFWS Refuge, Bethel. January 20, 2006. Tape 7, pages 446–62.

6. CEC tape collection. Nunaput Gathering with Paul John, John Phillip, Nick Andrew, Peter Jacobs, Golga Effemka, Joe Asuluk, Anthony Oney, Glenn Azean, Magdalene John, Alice Rearden, and Ann Fienup-Riordan. USFWS, Bethel. January 20, 2006. Tape 7, pages 446–62.

7. CEC tape collection. Lower Yukon Men's Gathering, Anchorage, with Raphael Jimmy, Denis Shelden, Francis Charlie, Mark John, Alice Rearden, and Ann Fienup-Riordan. Anchorage. January 16–17, 2013. Tape 8, pages 358–61.

8. CEC tape collection. Interview with Frank Andrew and Noah Andrew with Marie Meade, Alice Rearden, and Ann Fienup-Riordan. Anchorage. September 27, 2005. Tape 4, pages 178–79.

9. CEC tape collection. Interview with Frank Andrew and Noah Andrew with Marie Meade, Alice Rearden, and Ann Fienup-Riordan. Anchorage. September 28, 2005. Tape 7, page 281.

10. CEC tape collection. Yupiit Piciryarait Museum Gathering with Frank Andrew, Margaret Andrews, Alex Bird, Joan Hamilton, Noah Andrew, and CEC staff Mark John, Marie Meade, Alice Rearden, Freda Jimmie, and Ann Fienup-Riordan. Bethel. December 18, 2003. Tape 8, pages 302–303.

11. CEC tape collection. Yupiit Piciryarait Museum Gathering with Frank Andrew, Margaret Andrews, Alex Bird, Joan Hamilton, Noah Andrew, and CEC staff Mark John, Marie Meade, Alice Rearden, Freda Jimmie, and Ann Fienup Riordan. Bethel. December 18, 2003. Tape 8, pages 303–307.

Qaluyaarmiut Qanemciit / Stories from Nelson Island

1. Ann Fienup-Riordan tape collection. Interview with Tim Agagtak and Magdaline Sunny with Ruth Jimmie and Ann Fienup-Riordan. Nightmute. July 17, 1985. Tape 2, pages 20–27.

2. Ann Fienup-Riordan tape collection. Interview with Tim Agagtak and Magdaline Sunny with Ruth Jimmie and Ann Fienup-Riordan. Nightmute. July 17, 1985. Tape 2, pages 28–34.

3. Ann Fienup-Riordan tape collection. Interview with Tim Agagtak and Magdaline Sunny with Ruth Jimmie and Ann Fienup-Riordan. Nightmute. July 17, 1985. Tape 2, pages 35–36.

4. Ann Fienup-Riordan tape collection. Interview with Tim Agagtak and Magdaline Sunny with Ruth Jimmie and

Ann Fienup-Riordan. Nightmute. July 17, 1985. Tape 2, pages 36–38.

5. Ann Fienup-Riordan tape collection. Interview with Tim Agagtak and Magdaline Sunny with Ruth Jimmie and Ann Fienup-Riordan. Nightmute. July 17, 1985. Tape 2, page 39.

6. Ann Fienup-Riordan tape collection. Toksook Bay Mask Exhibit. Interview with Dick Anthony of Nightmute by Marie Meade. Toksook Bay. January 1996. Tape 8, pages 36–48.

7. Ann Fienup-Riordan tape collection. Toksook Bay Mask Exhibit. Interview with Dick Anthony of Nightmute by Marie Meade. Toksook Bay. January 1996. Tape 8, pages 49–51.

8. Ann Fienup-Riordan tape collection. Toksook Bay Mask Exhibit. Interview with Dick Anthony of Nightmute by Marie Meade. Toksook Bay. January 1996. Tape 10, page 153.

9. Ann Fienup-Riordan tape collection. Interview with Dick Andrew by Marie Meade and Ann Fienup-Riordan. Bethel. August 16, 1992. Tape 1, pages 6–7.

10. Ann Fienup-Riordan tape collection. Interview with Dick Andrew by Marie Meade and Ann Fienup-Riordan. .... August 16, 1992. Tape 1, pages 8–9.

11. CEC tape collection. Yup'ik Science Steering Committee meeting with Paul John, Frank Andrew, Noah Andrew, Andy Paukan, Elsie Mather, Joan Hamilton, Marie Meade, Theresa John, Mark John, Alice Rearden, and Ann Fienup-Riordan. Yupiit Piciryarait Museum and Cultural Center, Bethel. August 27, 2003. Tape 3A, pages 27–28.

12. CEC tape collection. Kevgiq Gathering with Frank and Noah Andrew, Paul and Martina John, Benedict Tucker, Simeon and Anna Agnus, Marie Meade, Denis Shelden, Freda Jimmie, and Ann Fienup-Riordan. CEC office, Bethel. May 9, 2003. Tape 1B, pages 39–40.

13. CEC tape collection. Kevgiq Gathering with Frank and Noah Andrew, Paul and Martina John, Benedict Tucker, Simeon and Anna Agnus, Marie Meade, Denis Shelden, Freda Jimmie, and Ann Fienup-Riordan. CEC office, Bethel. May 9, 2003. Tape 1B, pages 42–51.

14. CEC tape collection. Kevgiq Gathering with Frank and Noah Andrew, Paul and Martina John, Benedict Tucker, Simeon and Anna Agnus, Marie Meade, Denis Shelden, Freda Jimmie, and Ann Fienup-Riordan. CEC office, Bethel. May 9, 2003. Tape 1B, pages 52–58.

15. CEC tape collection. Nelson Island Women's Gathering, Whitehouse B&B, Bethel. Albertina Dull, Martina John, Helen Walter, and Theresa Abraham, with Alice Rearden and Ann Fienup-Riordan. Whitehouse B&B, Bethel. November 5, 2007. Tape 3, page 164.

16. CEC tape collection. Nelson Island Project Newtok Elders' Gathering, #2. Michael John and Joseph John with Alice Rearden and Ann Fienup-Riordan. Newtok School, Newtok. June 4, 2008. Tape 7, pages 35–36.

17. CEC tape collection. Nelson Island Project Newtok Elders' Gathering, #2. Michael John and Joseph John with Alice Rearden and Ann Fienup-Riordan. Newtok School, Newtok. June 4, 2008. Tape 7, page 37.

18. CEC tape collection. Nelson Island Project Newtok Elders' Gathering, #2. Michael John and Joseph John with Alice Rearden and Ann Fienup-Riordan. Newtok School, Newtok. June 4, 2008. Tape 7, pages 40–41.

19. CEC tape collection. Nelson Island Project Newtok Elders' Gathering, #2. Michael John and Joseph John with Alice Rearden and Ann Fienup-Riordan. Newtok School, Newtok. June 4, 2008. Tape 8, pages 54–63.

20. CEC tape collection. Nelson Island Project Newtok Elders' Gathering, #2. Michael John and Joseph Patrick with Alice Rearden and Ann Fienup-Riordan. Newtok School, Newtok. June 4, 2008. Tape 9, page 127.

21. CEC tape collection. Nelson Island Project Newtok Elders' Gathering, #2. Michael John and Joseph Patrick with Alice Rearden and Ann Fienup-Riordan. Newtok School, Newtok. June 5, 2008. Tape 12B, pages 255–60.

22. CEC tape collection. Nelson Island Project Newtok Elders' Gathering, #2. Michael John and Joseph Patrick with Alice Rearden and Ann Fienup-Riordan. Newtok School, Newtok. June 5, 2008. Tape 14, pages 260–67.

23. CEC tape collection. Nelson Island Women's Gathering, #2. Elsie Tommy, Martina John, Mary George, and Ruth Jimmie with Alice Rearden and Ann Fienup-Riordan. Vicky Malone's House, Bethel. March 30, 2009. Tape 3, pages 122–24.

24. CEC tape collection. Nelson Island Women's Gathering, #2. Elsie Tommy, Martina John, Mary George, and Ruth Jimmie with Alice Rearden and Ann Fienup-Riordan. Vicky Malone's House, Bethel. March 31, 2009. Tape 7, pages 303–304.

25. CEC tape collection. Nelson Island Women's Gathering, #2. Elsie Tommy, Martina John, Mary George, and Ruth Jimmie with Alice Rearden and Ann Fienup-Riordan. Vicky Malone's House, Bethel. March 30, 2009. Tape 5, pages 191–96.

26. CEC tape collection. Nelson Island Women's Gathering, #2. Elsie Tommy, Martina John, Mary George, and Ruth Jimmie with Alice Rearden and Ann Fienup-Riordan. Vicky Malone's House, Bethel. March 30, 2009. Tape 5, pages 197–204.

27. CEC tape collection. Nelson Island Women's Gathering, #2. Elsie Tommy, Martina John, Mary George, and Ruth Jimmie with Alice Rearden and Ann Fienup-Riordan. Vicky Malone's House, Bethel. April 1, 2009. Tape 8, page 373.

28 CEC tape collection. Nelson Island Women's Gathering, #2. Elsie Tommy, Martina John, Mary George, and Ruth Jimmie with Alice Rearden and Ann Fienup-Riordan. Vicky Malone's House, Bethel. April 1, 2009. Tape 8, page 378.

29. CEC tape collection. Nelson Island Women's Gathering, #2. Elsie Tommy, Martina John, Mary George, and Ruth Jimmie with Alice Rearden and Ann Fienup-Riordan. Vicky Malone's House, Bethel. April 1, 2009. Tape 8, page 380–82.

30. CEC tape collection. Nelson Island Women's Gathering, #2. Elsie Tommy, Martina John, Mary George, and Ruth Jimmie with Alice Rearden and Ann Fienup-Riordan.

Vicky Malone's House, Bethel. April 1, 2009. Tape 8, page 384.

31. CEC tape collection. Nelson Island Project. Interview with Albertina Dull and Lizzie Chimiugak by Ruth Jimmie and Ann Fienup-Riordan. Umkumiut. June 24, 2009. Tape 2, page 73.

32. CEC tape collection. Nelson Island Project. Interview with Albertina Dull and Lizzie Chimiugak by Ruth Jimmie and Ann Fienup-Riordan. Umkumiut. June 24, 2009. Tape 3, pages 113–20.

33. CEC tape collection. Nelson Island Project. Interview with Albertina Dull and Lizzie Chimiugak by Ruth Jimmie and Ann Fienup-Riordan. Umkumiut. June 24, 2009. Tape 3, page 123.

34. CEC tape collection. Nelson Island Project. Interview with Albertina Dull and Lizzie Chimiugak by Ruth Jimmie and Ann Fienup-Riordan. Umkumiut. June 24, 2009. Tape 3, pages 124–26.

35. CEC tape collection. Nelson Island Project. Interview with Albertina Dull and Lizzie Chimiugak by Ruth Jimmie and Ann Fienup-Riordan. Umkumiut. June 24, 2009. Tape 4, pages 132–36.

36. CEC tape collection. Nelson Island Project. Interview with Albertina Dull and Lizzie Chimiugak by Ruth Jimmie and Ann Fienup-Riordan. Umkumiut. June 24, 2009. Tape 4, pages 136–37.

37. CEC tape collection. Nelson Island Project. Interview with Albertina Dull and Lizzie Chimiugak by Ruth Jimmie and Ann Fienup-Riordan. Umkumiut. June 24, 2009. Tape 4, page 146.

38. CEC tape collection. Nelson Island Project. Interview with Albertina Dull and Lizzie Chimiugak by Ruth Jimmie and Ann Fienup-Riordan. Umkumiut. June 24, 2009. Tape 4, pages 147–48.

39. CEC tape collection. Nelson Island Project. Interview with Albertina Dull and Lizzie Chimiugak by Ruth Jimmie and Ann Fienup-Riordan. Umkumiut. June 24, 2009. Tape 4, pages 148–49.

40. CEC tape collection. Nelson Island Project. Interview with Albertina Dull and Lizzie Chimiugak by Ruth Jimmie and Ann Fienup-Riordan. Umkumiut. June 24, 2009. Tape 4, page 172.

41. CEC tape collection. Nelson Island Project. Interview with Albertina Dull and Lizzie Chimiugak by Ruth Jimmie and Ann Fienup-Riordan. Umkumiut. June 24, 2009. Tape 4, pages 174–75.

42. CEC tape collection. Nelson Island Project. Interview with Albertina Dull and Lizzie Chimiugak by Ruth Jimmie and Ann Fienup-Riordan. Umkumiut. June 24, 2009. Tape 5, pages 193–98.

43. CEC tape collection. Nelson Island Project. Interview with Albertina Dull and Lizzie Chimiugak by Ruth Jimmie and Ann Fienup-Riordan. Umkumiut. June 24, 2009. Tape 5, pages 208–16.

44. CEC tape collection. Nelson Island Project. Interview with Albertina Dull and Lizzie Chimiugak by Ruth Jimmie and Ann Fienup-Riordan. Umkumiut. June 24, 2009. Tapes 5 and 6, pages 225–27, 233.

45. CEC tape collection. Nelson Island Project. Interview with Albertina Dull and Lizzie Chimiugak by Ruth Jimmie and Ann Fienup-Riordan. Umkumiut. June 24, 2009. Tape 6, page 234.

46. CEC tape collection. Nelson Island Project. Interview with Albertina Dull and Lizzie Chimiugak by Ruth Jimmie and Ann Fienup-Riordan. Umkumiut. June 24, 2009. Tape 6, pages 241–45.

47. CEC tape collection. Nelson Island Project. Interview with Albertina Dull and Lizzie Chimiugak by Ruth Jimmie and Ann Fienup-Riordan. Umkumiut. June 24, 2009. Tape 6, pages 246–47.

48. CEC tape collection. Nelson Island Project. Interview with Albertina Dull and Lizzie Chimiugak by Ruth Jimmie and Ann Fienup-Riordan. Umkumiut. June 24, 2009. Tape 6, pages 251–52.

49. CEC tape collection. Nelson Island Project. Interview with Albertina Dull and Lizzie Chimiugak by Ruth Jimmie and Ann Fienup-Riordan. Umkumiut. June 24, 2009. Tape 6, page 252.

50. CEC tape collection. Nelson Island Project. Interview with Albertina Dull and Lizzie Chimiugak by Ruth Jimmie and Ann Fienup-Riordan. Umkumiut. June 24, 2009. Tape 6, page 252.

51. CEC tape collection. Nelson Island Project. Interview with Albertina Dull and Lizzie Chimiugak by Ruth Jimmie and Ann Fienup-Riordan. Umkumiut. June 24, 2009. Tape 6, pages 253–54.

52. CEC tape collection. Nelson Island Project. Interview with Albertina Dull and Lizzie Chimiugak by Ruth Jimmie and Ann Fienup-Riordan. Umkumiut. June 24, 2009. Tape 6, pages 255–56.

53. CEC tape collection. Nelson Island Project. Interview with Albertina Dull and Lizzie Chimiugak by Ruth Jimmie and Ann Fienup-Riordan. Umkumiut. June 24, 2009. Tape 6, pages 256–57.

54. CEC tape collection. Nelson Island Project. Interview with Albertina Dull and Lizzie Chimiugak by Ruth Jimmie and Ann Fienup-Riordan. Umkumiut. June 24, 2009. Tape 6, pages 259, 261.

55. CEC tape collection. Nelson Island Project. Interview with Albertina and Katie Dull by Ruth Jimmie and Ann Fienup-Riordan. Nightmute. April 22, 2013. Tape 1, page 40.

56. CEC tape collection. Nelson Island Project. Interview with Albertina and Katie Dull by Ruth Jimmie and Ann Fienup-Riordan. Nightmute. April 22, 2013. Tape 1, pages 40–41.

57. CEC tape collection. Nelson Island Project. Interview with Albertina and Katie Dull by Ruth Jimmie and Ann Fienup-Riordan. Nightmute. April 22, 2013. Tape 2, pages 65–66.

58. CEC tape collection. Nelson Island Project. Interview with Albertina and Katie Dull by Ruth Jimmie and Ann Fienup-Riordan. Nightmute. April 22, 2013. Tape 2, pages 66–67.

59. CEC tape collection. Umkumiut Culture Camp with Paul John, Simeon and Anna Agnus, Sophie Agimuk, and Moses Tulim. Umkumiut. June 2009. Tape 1, pages 13–19.

60. CEC tape collection. Alaska Marine Science Symposium presentation with Elsie Tommy, Mark John, Alice

Rearden, and Ann Fienup-Riordan. Anchorage. January 20, 2012. Tape 1, pages 13–14.

61. CEC tape collection. Alaska Marine Science Symposium presentation with Elsie Tommy, Mark John, Alice Rearden, and Ann Fienup-Riordan. Anchorage. January 20, 2012. Tape 1, pages 27–29.

62. CEC tape collection. Yukon Project Steering Committee Meeting with Paul John, John Phillip, Noah Andrew, Simeon John, Andrew Boyscout, Francis Charlie, Denis Shelden, Ray Waska, Eva Malovich, Steve Street, Vivian Korthius, Uma Bhatt, Peter Beniki, Hajo Eicken, Peter Pulsifer, Mark John, Alice Rearden, and Ann Fienup-Riordan. USFWS Refuge, Bethel. February 4, 2014. Tape 2, page 70.

63. CEC tape collection. Atertayagaq Gathering. George Billy, John Phillip, Roland Phillip, Frank Billy, Aron Lake, with Mark John, Alice Rearden, Freda Jimmie, and Ann Fienup-Riordan. USFWS Refuge, Bethel. October 13, 2006. Tape 6, pages 192–94.

Caninermiut Qanemciit / Stories of People from the Lower Kuskokwim Coast

1. CEC tape collection. Interview with Frank Andrew and Noah Andrew by Alice Rearden, Veronica Kaganak, and Ann Fienup-Riordan. Anchorage. October 16, 2001. Tape 7, page 181.

2. CEC tape collection. Interview with Frank Andrew and Noah Andrew by Alice Rearden, Veronica Kaganak, and Ann Fienup-Riordan. Anchorage. October 16, 2001. Tape 7, pages 182–83.

3. CEC tape collection. Yupiit Piciryarait Museum Gathering with Frank Andrew, Margaret Andrews, Alex Bird, Joan Hamilton, Noah Andrew, and CEC staff Mark John, Marie Meade, Alice Rearden, Freda Jimmie, and Ann Fienup-Riordan. Bethel. December 16, 2003. Tape 4, pages 129, 130.

4. CEC tape collection. Yupiit Piciryarait Museum Gathering with Frank Andrew, Margaret Andrews, Alex Bird, Joan Hamilton, Noah Andrew, and CEC staff Mark John, Marie Meade, Alice Rearden, Freda Jimmie, and Ann Fienup-Riordan. Bethel. December 18, 2003. Tape 8, page 303.

5. CEC tape collection. Interview with Frank Andrew and Noah Andrew with Marie Meade, Alice Rearden, and Ann Fienup-Riordan. Anchorage. September 27, 2005. Tape 6, page 247.

6. CEC tape collection. Interview with Frank Andrew and Noah Andrew by Alice Rearden, Veronica Kaganak, and Ann Fienup-Riordan. Anchorage. October 16, 2001. Tape 7, pages 184, 185

7. CEC tape collection. Interview with Frank Andrew and Noah Andrew by Alice Rearden, Veronica Kaganak, and Ann Fienup-Riordan. Anchorage. October 16, 2001. Tape 7, page 196

8. CEC tape collection. Storytelling during winter blizzard with Frank Andrew, Theresa Moses, Peter John, Noah Andrew, Marie Meade, and Ann Fienup-Riordan. Capital Hill Suites, Washington, DC. February 18, 2003. Tapes 30B and 31A, pages 178–201.

9. CEC tape collection. Interview with Frank Andrew and Noah Andrew by Alice Rearden, Veronica Kaganak, and Ann Fienup-Riordan. Anchorage. October 16, 2001. Tape 7, page 199.

10. CEC tape collection. Interview with Frank Andrew and Noah Andrew by Alice Rearden, Veronica Kaganak, and Ann Fienup-Riordan. Anchorage. October 16, 2001. Tape 9, page 245.

11. CEC tape collection. Interview with Frank Andrew and Noah Andrew by Alice Rearden, Veronica Kaganak, and Ann Fienup-Riordan. Anchorage. October 22, 2001. Tape 13, pages 350–55.

12. CEC tape collection. Work in Collections with Frank Andrew, Theresa Moses, Peter John, Noah Andrew, Marie Meade, and Ann Fienup-Riordan. Museum Support Center, National Museum of Natural History in Suitland, Maryland. February 13, 2003. Tape 11, pages 518, 527.

13. CEC tape collection. Work in Collections with Frank Andrew, Theresa Moses, Peter John, Noah Andrew, Marie Meade, and Ann Fienup-Riordan. Museum Support Center, National Museum of Natural History in Suitland, Maryland. February 11, 2003. Tape 6, pages 272–75.

14. CEC tape collection. Yupiit Piciryarait Museum Gathering with Frank Andrew, Margaret Andrews, Alex Bird, Joan Hamilton, Noah Andrew, and CEC staff Mark John, Marie Meade, Alice Rearden, Freda Jimmie, and Ann Fienup-Riordan. Bethel. December 16, 2003. Tape 4, page 141.

15. CEC tape collection. Examining Leman Waugh photographs with Frank Andrew, Theresa Moses, Peter John, Noah Andrew, Marie Meade, and Ann Fienup-Riordan. National Museum of the American Indian, Washington, DC. February 13, 2003. Tape 22, pages 24–27.

16. CEC tape collection. Interview with Frank Andrew and Noah Andrew with Marie Meade, Alice Rearden, and Ann Fienup-Riordan. Anchorage. September 27, 2005. Tape 5, pages 195–97.

17. CEC tape collection. Work in Collections with Frank Andrew, Theresa Moses, Peter John, Noah Andrew, Marie Meade, and Ann Fienup-Riordan. Museum Support Center, National Museum of Natural History in Suitland, Maryland. February 13, 2003. Tapes 12 and 13, pages 591–93.

18. CEC tape collection. Storytelling during winter blizzard with Frank Andrew, Theresa Moses, Peter John, Noah Andrew, Marie Meade, and Ann Fienup-Riordan. Capital Hill Suites, Washington, DC. February 16, 2003. Tape 25, pages 34–37.

19. CEC tape collection. Storytelling during winter blizzard with Frank Andrew, Theresa Moses, Peter John, Noah Andrew, Marie Meade, and Ann Fienup-Riordan. Capital Hill Suites, Washington, DC. February 16, 2003. Tape 30A, pages 166–71.

20. CEC tape collection. Storytelling during winter blizzard with Frank Andrew, Theresa Moses, Peter John, Noah Andrew, Marie Meade, and Ann Fienup-Riordan. Capital Hill Suites, Washington, DC. February 16, 2003. Tape 30A, pages 173–76.

21. CEC tape collection. Interview with Frank Andrew and Noah Andrew with Marie Meade, Alice Rearden, and Ann Fienup-Riordan. Anchorage. September 25, 2005. Tape 2, page 46.

22. CEC tape collection. Interview with Frank Andrew and Noah Andrew with Marie Meade, Alice Rearden, and Ann Fienup-Riordan. Anchorage. September 27, 2005. Tape 5A, page 179.

23. CEC tape collection. Yupiit Piciryarait Museum Gathering with Frank Andrew, Margaret Andrews, Alex Bird, Joan Hamilton, Noah Andrew, and CEC staff Mark John, Marie Meade, Alice Rearden, Freda Jimmie, and Ann Fienup-Riordan. Bethel. December 16, 2003. Tape 4, pages 137–38.

24. CEC tape collection. Interview with Frank Andrew and Noah Andrew with Marie Meade, Alice Rearden, and Ann Fienup-Riordan. Anchorage. September 27, 2005. Tape 5, pages 200–205.

25. CEC tape collection. Interview with Frank Andrew and Noah Andrew with Marie Meade, Alice Rearden, and Ann Fienup-Riordan. Anchorage. September 27, 2005. Tape 6, pages 226–27.

26. CEC tape collection. Interview with Frank Andrew and Noah Andrew with Marie Meade, Alice Rearden, and Ann Fienup-Riordan. Anchorage. September 27, 2005. Tape 6, pages 243–44.

27. CEC tape collection. Interview with Frank Andrew and Noah Andrew with Marie Meade, Alice Rearden, and Ann Fienup-Riordan. Anchorage. September 27, 2005. Tape 6, pages 244–45.

28. CEC tape collection. Interview with Frank Andrew and Noah Andrew with Marie Meade, Alice Rearden, and Ann Fienup-Riordan. Anchorage. September 28, 2005. Tape 6, pages 248–61.

29. CEC tape collection. Interview with Frank Andrew and Noah Andrew with Marie Meade, Alice Rearden, and Ann Fienup-Riordan. Anchorage. September 28, 2005. Tapes 6 and 7, pages 261–69.

30. CEC tape collection. Interview with Frank Andrew and Noah Andrew with Marie Meade, Alice Rearden, and Ann Fienup-Riordan. Anchorage. September 28, 2005. Tape 7, pages 260–70.

31. CEC tape collection. Interview with Frank Andrew and Noah Andrew with Marie Meade, Alice Rearden, and Ann Fienup-Riordan. Anchorage. September 28, 2005. Tape 7, pages 271–79.

32. CEC tape collection. Interview with Frank Andrew and Noah Andrew with Marie Meade, Alice Rearden, and Ann Fienup-Riordan. Anchorage. September 28, 2005. Tape 7, pages 280–81.

33. CEC tape collection. Interview with Frank Andrew and Noah Andrew with Marie Meade, Alice Rearden, and Ann Fienup-Riordan. Anchorage. September 28, 2005. Tape 7, page 281.

34. CEC tape collection. Interview with Frank Andrew and Noah Andrew with Marie Meade, Alice Rearden, and Ann Fienup-Riordan. Anchorage. September 28, 2005. Tape 7, page 282.

35. CEC tape collection. Yupiit Piciryarait Museum Gathering with Frank Andrew, Margaret Andrews, Alex Bird, Joan Hamilton, Noah Andrew, and CEC staff Mark John, Marie Meade, Alice Rearden, Freda Jimmie, and Ann Fienup-Riordan. Bethel. December 16, 2003. Tape 4, pages 125–29.

36. CEC tape collection. Yupiit Piciryarait Museum Gathering with Frank Andrew, Margaret Andrews, Alex Bird, Joan Hamilton, Noah Andrew, and CEC staff Mark John, Marie Meade, Alice Rearden, Freda Jimmie, and Ann Fienup-Riordan. Bethel. December 16, 2003. Tape 4, page 131.

37. CEC tape collection. Yupiit Piciryarait Museum Gathering with Frank Andrew, Margaret Andrews, Alex Bird, Joan Hamilton, Noah Andrew, and CEC staff Mark John, Marie Meade, Alice Rearden, Freda Jimmie, and Ann Fienup-Riordan. Bethel. December 16, 2003. Tape 4, pages 132–34.

38. CEC tape collection. Yupiit Piciryarait Museum Gathering with Frank Andrew, Margaret Andrews, Alex Bird, Joan Hamilton, Noah Andrew, and CEC staff Mark John, Marie Meade, Alice Rearden, Freda Jimmie, and Ann Fienup-Riordan. Bethel. December 16, 2003. Tape 4, pages 135–37.

39. CEC tape collection. Yupiit Piciryarait Museum Gathering with Frank Andrew, Margaret Andrews, Alex Bird, Joan Hamilton, Noah Andrew, and CEC staff Mark John, Marie Meade, Alice Rearden, Freda Jimmie, and Ann Fienup-Riordan. Bethel. December 18, 2003. Tape 9, page 338–39.

40. CEC tape collection. Yupiit Piciryarait Museum Gathering with Frank Andrew, Margaret Andrews, Alex Bird, Joan Hamilton, Noah Andrew, and CEC staff Mark John, Marie Meade, Alice Rearden, Freda Jimmie, and Ann Fienup-Riordan. Bethel. December 18, 2003. Tape 9, pages 340–43.

41. CEC tape collection. Yupiit Piciryarait Museum Gathering with Frank Andrew, Margaret Andrews, Alex Bird, Joan Hamilton, Noah Andrew, and CEC staff Mark John, Marie Meade, Alice Rearden, Freda Jimmie, and Ann Fienup-Riordan. Bethel. December 18, 2003. Tape 9, pages 344–48.

42. CEC tape collection. Yupiit Piciryarait Museum Gathering with Frank Andrew, Margaret Andrews, Alex Bird, Joan Hamilton, Noah Andrew, and CEC staff Mark John, Marie Meade, Alice Rearden, Freda Jimmie, and Ann Fienup-Riordan. Bethel. December 18, 2003. Tape 9, page 348.

43. CEC tape collection. Yupiit Piciryarait Museum Gathering with Frank Andrew, Margaret Andrews, Alex Bird, Joan Hamilton, Noah Andrew, and CEC staff Mark John, Marie Meade, Alice Rearden, Freda Jimmie, and Ann Fienup-Riordan. Bethel. December 18, 2003. Tape 9, pages 348–50.

44. CEC tape collection. Examining Leuman Waugh photographs with Frank Andrew, Theresa Moses, Peter John, Noah Andrew, Marie Meade, and Ann Fienup-Riordan. National Museum of the American Indian. February 13, 2003. Tape 23, page 39.

45. CEC tape collection. Examining Leuman Waugh photographs with Frank Andrew, Theresa Moses, Peter John, Noah Andrew, Marie Meade, and Ann Fienup-Riordan. National Museum of the American Indian. February 17, 2003. Tape 29A, pages 105–109.

46. CEC tape collection. Examining Leuman Waugh photographs with Frank Andrew, Theresa Moses, Peter John, Noah Andrew, Marie Meade, and Ann Fienup-Riordan. National Museum of the American Indian. February 17, 2003. Tape 29A, pages 119–25.

47. CEC tape collection. Atertayagaq Gathering, with George Billy, John Phillip, Roland Phillip, Frank Billy, Aron Lake, with Mark John, Alice Rearden, Freda Jimmie, and Ann Fienup-Riordan. USFWS Refuge, Bethel. October 13, 2006. Tape 5, pages 166–67.

48. CEC tape collection. Atertayagaq Gathering, with George Billy, John Phillip, Roland Phillip, Frank Billy, Aron Lake, Mark John, Alice Rearden, Freda Jimmie, and Ann Fienup-Riordan. USFWS Refuge, Bethel. October 13, 2006. Tape 5, pages 168–71.

49. CEC tape collection. Atertayagaq Gathering, with George Billy, John Phillip, Roland Phillip, Frank Billy, Aron Lake, Mark John, Alice Rearden, Freda Jimmie, and Ann Fienup-Riordan. USFWS Refuge, Bethel. October 13, 2006. Tape 5, page 171.

50. CEC tape collection. Atertayagaq Gathering, with George Billy, John Phillip, Roland Phillip, Frank Billy, Aron Lake, Mark John, Alice Rearden, Freda Jimmie, and Ann Fienup-Riordan. USFWS Refuge, Bethel. October 13, 2006. Tape 5, page 172.

51. CEC tape collection. Atertayagaq Gathering, with George Billy, John Phillip, Roland Phillip, Frank Billy, Aron Lake, Mark John, Alice Rearden, Freda Jimmie, and Ann Fienup-Riordan. USFWS Refuge, Bethel. October 13, 2006. Tapes 5 and 6, pages 173–76.

52. CEC tape collection. Atertayagaq Gathering, with George Billy, John Phillip, Roland Phillip, Frank Billy, Aron Lake, Mark John, Alice Rearden, Freda Jimmie, and Ann Fienup-Riordan. USFWS Refuge, Bethel. October 13, 2006. Tape 6, page 177.

53. CEC tape collection. Atertayagaq Gathering, with George Billy, John Phillip, Roland Phillip, Frank Billy, Aron Lake, Mark John, Alice Rearden, Freda Jimmie, and Ann Fienup-Riordan. USFWS Refuge, Bethel. October 13, 2006. Tape 6, page 178.

54. CEC tape collection. Atertayagaq Gathering, with George Billy, John Phillip, Roland Phillip, Frank Billy, Aron Lake, Mark John, Alice Rearden, Freda Jimmie, and Ann Fienup-Riordan. USFWS Refuge, Bethel. October 13, 2006. Tape 6, pages 179–80.

55. CEC tape collection. Bethel Steering Committee Meeting with Paul John, John Phillip, Noah Andrew, Simeon John, Andrew Boyscout, Francis Charlie, Denis Shelden, Ray Waska, Eva Malovich, Steve Street, Vivian Korthius, Uma Bhatt, Peter Beniki, Hajo Eicken, Peter Pulsifer, Mark John, Alice Rearden, and Ann Fienup-Riordan. Bethel. February 5, 2014. Tape 6, pages 188–89.

56. CEC tape collection. Atertayagaq Gathering, with George Billy, John Phillip, Roland Phillip, Frank Billy, Aron Lake, Mark John, Alice Rearden, Freda Jimmie, and Ann Fienup-Riordan. USFWS Refuge, Bethel. October 13, 2006. Tape 6, pages 183–89.

57. CEC tape collection. Atertayagaq Gathering, with George Billy, John Phillip, Roland Phillip, Frank Billy, Aron Lake, Mark John, Alice Rearden, Freda Jimmie, and Ann Fienup-Riordan. USFWS Refuge, Bethel. October 13, 2006. Tape 6, pages 189–92.

58. CEC tape collection. Atertayagaq Gathering, with George Billy, John Phillip, Roland Phillip, Frank Billy, Aron Lake, Mark John, Alice Rearden, Freda Jimmie, and Ann Fienup-Riordan. USFWS Refuge, Bethel. October 13, 2006. Tape 6, page 195.

59. CEC tape collection. Atertayagaq Gathering, with George Billy, John Phillip, Roland Phillip, Frank Billy, Aron Lake, Mark John, Alice Rearden, Freda Jimmie, and Ann Fienup-Riordan. USFWS Refuge, Bethel. October 13, 2006. Tape 6, pages 197–211.

60. CEC tape collection. Bethel Steering Committee Meeting with Paul John, John Phillip, Noah Andrew, Simeon John, Andrew Boyscout, Francis Charlie, Denis Shelden, Ray Waska, Eva Malovich, Steve Street, Vivian Korthius, Uma Bhatt, Peter Beniki, Hajo Eicken, Peter Pulsifer, Mark John, Alice Rearden, and Ann Fienup-Riordan. Bethel. February 5, 2014. Tape 6, page 187.

61. CEC tape collection. Interview with John Phillip by Alice Rearden, Mark John, and Ann Fienup-Riordan. Anchorage. January 19, 2011. Tape 5, pages 128–29.

Kusquqvagmiut Qanemciit / Stories of People from the Kuskokwim River

1. CEC tape collection. Atertayagaq Gathering, with George Billy, John Phillip, Roland Phillip, Frank Billy, Aron Lake, Mark John, Alice Rearden, Freda Jimmie, and Ann Fienup-Riordan. USFWS Refuge, Bethel. October 13, 2006. Tape 10, pages 351–52.

2. Ann Fienup-Riordan tape collection. Work at the National Museum of the American Indian with Elena Charles, Annie Blue, Henry Alikayak, Andy Paukan, Marie Meade, and Ann Fienup-Riordan. New York City. April 17, 1997. Tape 14 (Day 9), pages 433–35.

3. CEC tape collection. Napaskiak Whitefish Gathering #3 with Alexie Nicholai, Yako Andrew, Jacob Black, Ralph Nelson, Marie Meade, and Ann Fienup-Riordan. Napaskiak. March 15, 2017. Tape 7, pages 284–85, 288.

4. CEC tape collection. Napaskiak Whitefish Gathering #3 with Alexie Nicholai, Yako Andrew, Jacob Black, Ralph Nelson, Marie Meade, and Ann Fienup-Riordan. Napaskiak. March 15, 2017. Tape 7, pages 286–87.

5. CEC tape collection. Qemirraq field trip with James Nicholai, Jacob Black, Ralph Nelson, Marie Meade, and Ann Fienup-Riordan. Qemirraq. August 16, 2017. Tape 1, page 15.

6. CEC tape collection. Napaskiak Whitefish Gathering #3 with Alexie Nicholai, Yako Andrew, Jacob Black, Ralph Nelson, Marie Meade, and Ann Fienup-Riordan. Napaskiak. March 15, 2017. Tape 7, page 289.

7. CEC tape collection. Napaskiak Whitefish Gathering #3 with Alexie Nicholai, Yako Andrew, Jacob Black, Ralph

Nelson, Marie Meade, and Ann Fienup-Riordan. Napaskiak. March 15, 2017. Tape 7, page 289.

8. CEC tape collection. National Park Service Regional Gathering, Anchorage, with Paul John, John Phillip, Nick Andrew, Martin Moore, Bob Aloysius, Moses Paukan, Mark John, Alice Rearden, and Ann Fienup-Riordan. Anchorage. October 17, 2010. Tape 9, pages 400–413.

Kuigpagmiut Qanemciit / Stories from the Yukon River

1. CEC tape collection. Interview with Mary Mike by Marie Meade. St. Mary's. October 19, 1994. Tape 3, pages 12–14.

2. CEC tape collection. Interview with Mary Mike by Marie Meade. St. Mary's. October 19, 1994. Tape 4, pages 21–25.

3. Ann Fienup-Riordan tape collection. Interview during Yup'ik mask exhibit opening with Charlie Steve and Paul Waskey by Marie Meade and Ann Fienup-Riordan. Toksook Bay. January 21, 1996. Tape 1, pages 1–11.

4. Ann Fienup-Riordan tape collection. Interview during Yup'ik mask exhibit opening with Charlie Steve and Paul Waskey by Marie Meade and Ann Fienup-Riordan. Toksook Bay. January 21, 1996. Tape 1, pages 46–49.

5. Ann Fienup-Riordan tape collection. Interview during Yup'ik mask exhibit opening with Charlie Steve and Paul Waskey by Marie Meade and Ann Fienup-Riordan. Toksook Bay. January 21, 1996. Tape 1, pages 49–50.

6. CEC tape collection. Interview with Henry Teeluk by Marie Meade and Alice Rearden during Kotlik Messenger Feast. Teeluk home in Kotlik. March 28, 2003. Tape 4, pages 101–102.

7. CEC tape collection. Interview with Martina Aparezuk by Marie Meade and Alice Rearden during Kotlik Messenger Feast. Aparezuk home, Kotlik. March 28, 2003. Tape 5, pages 119–22.

8. CEC tape collection. Interview with Martina Aparezuk by Marie Meade and Alice Rearden during Kotlik Messenger Feast. Aparezuk home, Kotlik. March 28, 2003. Tape 5, page 122–23.

9. Ann Fienup-Riordan tape collection. Interview with Thomas and Cecelia Chikigak by David Chanar and Ann Fienup-Riordan. Alakanak. August 11, 1987. Tape 91, pages 76–79.

10. CEC tape collection, Yukon Project village planning meetings, Alakanuk meeting with Denis Shelden, Lawrence Edmund, John and Paula Ayunerak, Fred Agustine, Edward Phillip, Marie Meade, and Ann Fienup-Riordan. Alakanuk community hall. March 10, 2011. Tapes 21 and 22, pages 1077–84.

11. CEC tape collection, Yukon Project village planning meetings, Alakanuk meeting with Denis Shelden, Lawrence Edmund, John and Paula Ayunerak, Fred Agustine, Edward Phillip, Marie Meade, and Ann Fienup-Riordan. Alakanuk community hall. March 10, 2011. Tape 22, page 1085.

12. CEC tape collection. Yukon Project village planning meetings. Emmonak meeting with Ray Waska, Benedict

Tucker, Mike Andrews Sr., Marie Meade, Mark John, and Ann Fienup-Riordan. Emmonak tribal office. March 9, 2011. Tape 16, pages 778–82.

13. CEC tape collection. Yukon Men's Gathering with Eugene Pete, Mike Andrews Sr., Lawrence Edmund, Denis Shelden, Mark John, Alice Rearden, and Ann Fienup-Riordan. Anchorage. December 6, 2011. Tape 1, pages 35–37.

14. CEC tape collection. Yukon Men's Gathering with Eugene Pete, Mike Andrews Sr., Lawrence Edmund, Denis Shelden, Mark John, Alice Rearden, and Ann Fienup-Riordan. Anchorage. December 6, 2011. Tape 1, pages 37–39.

15. CEC tape collection. Yukon Men's Gathering with Eugene Pete, Mike Andrews Sr., Lawrence Edmund, Denis Shelden, Mark John, Alice Rearden, and Ann Fienup-Riordan. Anchorage. December 6, 2011. Tapes 1B and 2A, pages 39–42.

16. CEC tape collection. Yukon Men's Gathering with Eugene Pete, Mike Andrews Sr., Lawrence Edmund, Denis Shelden, Mark John, Alice Rearden, and Ann Fienup-Riordan. Anchorage. December 6, 2011. Tape 2, pages 49–51.

17. CEC tape collection. Yukon Men's Gathering with Eugene Pete, Mike Andrews Sr., Lawrence Edmund, Denis Shelden, Mark John, Alice Rearden, and Ann Fienup-Riordan. Anchorage. December 6, 2011. Tape 2, pages 52–53.

18. CEC tape collection. Yukon Men's Gathering with Eugene Pete, Mike Andrews Sr., Lawrence Edmund, Denis Shelden, Mark John, Alice Rearden, and Ann Fienup-Riordan. Anchorage. December 6, 2011. Tape 2, pages 54–55.

19. CEC tape collection. Yukon Men's Gathering with Eugene Pete, Mike Andrews Sr., Lawrence Edmund, Denis Shelden, Mark John, Alice Rearden, and Ann Fienup-Riordan. Anchorage. December 6, 2011. Tape 2, page 58.

20. CEC tape collection. Yukon Men's Gathering with Eugene Pete, Mike Andrews Sr., Lawrence Edmund, Denis Shelden, Mark John, Alice Rearden, and Ann Fienup-Riordan. Anchorage. December 6, 2011. Tape 2, pages 75–76.

21. CEC tape collection. Yukon Men's Gathering with Eugene Pete, Mike Andrews Sr., Lawrence Edmund, Denis Shelden, Mark John, Alice Rearden, and Ann Fienup-Riordan. Anchorage. December 6, 2011. Tape 3, pages 98–99.

22. CEC tape collection. Yukon Men's Gathering with Eugene Pete, Mike Andrews Sr., Lawrence Edmund, Denis Shelden, Mark John, Alice Rearden, and Ann Fienup-Riordan. Anchorage. December 6, 2011. Tape 3, pages 99–100.

23. CEC tape collection. Yukon Men's Gathering with Eugene Pete, Mike Andrews Sr., Lawrence Edmund, Denis Shelden, Mark John, Alice Rearden, and Ann Fienup-Riordan. Anchorage. December 6, 2011. Tape 3, page 101.

24. CEC tape collection. Yukon Men's Gathering with Eugene Pete, Mike Andrews Sr., Lawrence Edmund, Denis Shelden, Mark John, Alice Rearden, and Ann Fienup-Riordan. Anchorage. December 6, 2011. Tape 3, pages 101–103.

25. CEC tape collection. Yukon Men's Gathering with Eugene Pete, Mike Andrews Sr., Lawrence Edmund, Denis Shelden, Mark John, Alice Rearden, and Ann Fienup-Riordan. Anchorage. December 6, 2011. Tape 3, pages 103–104.

26. CEC tape collection. Yukon Men's Gathering with Eugene Pete, Mike Andrews Sr., Lawrence Edmund, Denis Shel-

den, Mark John, Alice Rearden, and Ann Fienup-Riordan. Anchorage. December 8, 2011. Tape 11, pages 438–40.

27. CEC tape collection. Yukon Men's Gathering with Eugene Pete, Mike Andrews Sr., Lawrence Edmund, Denis Shelden, Mark John, Alice Rearden, and Ann Fienup-Riordan. Anchorage. December 8, 2011. Tape 11, pages 440–41.

28. CEC tape collection. Yukon Project village planning meetings. Nunam Iqua meeting with Eugene and Anna Pete, Peter Strongheart, Denis Shelden, Marie Meade, and Ann Fienup-Riordan. Nunam Iqua. March 11, 2011. Tape 23, pages 1200–1205.

29. CEC tape collection. Yukon Project village planning meetings. Emmonak meeting with Ray Waska, Benedict Tucker, Mike Andrews Sr., Marie Meade, Mark John, and Ann Fienup-Riordan. Emmonak tribal office. March 9, 2011. Tape 18, pages 907–908.

30. CEC tape collection. Yukon Project village planning meetings. Emmonak meeting with Ray Waska, Benedict Tucker, Mike Andrews Sr., Marie Meade, Mark John, and Ann Fienup-Riordan. Emmonak tribal office. March 9, 2011. Tape 18, pages 911–13.

31. CEC tape collection, Yukon Project village planning meetings, Alakanuk meeting with Denis Shelden, Lawrence Edmund, John and Paula Ayunerak, Fred Agustine, Edward Phillip, Marie Meade, and Ann Fienup-Riordan. Alakanuk community hall. March 10, 2011. Tape 20, pages 1032–33.

32. CEC tape collection. Lower Yukon Women's Gathering with Barbara Joe, Maryann Andrews, Mary and Peter Black, Mark John, Marie Meade, Alice Rearden, and Ann Fienup-Riordan. Anchorage. April 11, 2012. Tape 6, page 239.

33. CEC tape collection. Lower Yukon Women's Gathering with Barbara Joe, Maryann Andrews, Mary and Peter Black, Mark John, Marie Meade, Alice Rearden, and Ann Fienup-Riordan. Anchorage. April 11, 2012. Tape 7, pages 275–76.

34. CEC tape collection. Lower Yukon Women's Gathering with Barbara Joe, Maryann Andrews, Mary and Peter Black, Mark John, Marie Meade, Alice Rearden, and Ann Fienup-Riordan. Anchorage. April 11, 2012. Tape 7, page 278.

35. CEC tape collection. Lower Yukon Women's Gathering with Barbara Joe, Maryann Andrews, Mary and Peter Black, Mark John, Marie Meade, Alice Rearden, and Ann Fienup-Riordan. Anchorage. April 11, 2012. Tape 8, page 279–82.

36. CEC tape collection. Lower Yukon Women's Gathering with Barbara Joe, Maryann Andrews, Mary and Peter Black, Mark John, Marie Meade, Alice Rearden, and Ann Fienup-Riordan. Anchorage. April 11, 2012. Tape 8, pages 297–300.

37. CEC tape collection. Lower Yukon Women's Gathering with Barbara Joe, Maryann Andrews, Mary and Peter Black, Mark John, Marie Meade, Alice Rearden, and Ann Fienup-Riordan. Anchorage. April 11, 2012. Tape 8, page 301.

38. CEC tape collection. Lower Yukon Women's Gathering with Barbara Joe, Maryann Andrews, Mary and Peter

Black, Mark John, Marie Meade, Alice Rearden, and Ann Fienup-Riordan. Anchorage. April 11, 2012. Tape 8, pages 302–303.

39. CEC tape collection. Lower Yukon Women's Gathering with Barbara Joe, Maryann Andrews, Mary and Peter Black, Mark John, Marie Meade, Alice Rearden, and Ann Fienup-Riordan. Anchorage. April 11, 2012. Tape 8, pages 303–304.

40. CEC tape collection. Lower Yukon Women's Gathering with Barbara Joe, Maryann Andrews, Mary and Peter Black, Mark John, Marie Meade, Alice Rearden, and Ann Fienup-Riordan. Anchorage. April 12, 2012. Tape 9, pages 336–38, 347.

41. CEC tape collection. Lower Yukon Women's Gathering with Barbara Joe, Maryann Andrews, Mary and Peter Black, Mark John, Marie Meade, Alice Rearden, and Ann Fienup-Riordan. Anchorage. April 12, 2012. Tape 10, pages 373–74.

42. CEC tape collection. Lower Yukon Men's Gathering with Raphael Jimmy, Francis Charlie, Denis Shelden, Mark John, Alice Rearden, and Ann Fienup-Riordan. Anchorage. January 16, 2013. Tape 6, pages 240–41.

43. CEC tape collection. Lower Yukon Men's Gathering with Raphael Jimmy, Francis Charlie, Denis Shelden, Mark John, Alice Rearden, and Ann Fienup-Riordan. Anchorage. January 16, 2013. Tape 6, pages 275–77.

44. CEC tape collection. Lower Yukon Men's Gathering with Raphael Jimmy, Francis Charlie, Denis Shelden, Mark John, Alice Rearden, and Ann Fienup-Riordan. Anchorage. January 16, 2013. Tape 6, pages 294–96.

45. CEC tape collection. Alaska Marine Science Symposium presentation with Raphael Jimmy, Mark John, and Ann Fienup-Riordan. Anchorage. January 25, 2013. Tape 1, pages 18–19.

46. CEC tape collection. Alakanuk Elders Gathering with Barbara Joe, Joe Phillip, Placid Joseph, Alice Rearden, Mark John, and Ann Fienup-Riordan. Anchorage. December 3, 2013. Tape 1, pages 30–31.

47. CEC tape collection. Alakanuk Elders Gathering with Barbara Joe, Joe Phillip, Placid Joseph, Alice Rearden, Mark John, and Ann Fienup-Riordan. Anchorage. December 3, 2013. Tape 3, pages 71–73.

48. CEC tape collection. Alakanuk Elders Gathering with Barbara Joe, Joe Phillip, Placid Joseph, Alice Rearden, Mark John, and Ann Fienup-Riordan. Anchorage. December 3, 2013. Tape 3, pages 74–75.

49. CEC tape collection. Alakanuk Elders Gathering with Barbara Joe, Joe Phillip, Placid Joseph, Alice Rearden, Mark John, and Ann Fienup-Riordan. Anchorage. December 3, 2013. Tape 3, pages 75–78.

50. CEC tape collection. Alakanuk Elders Gathering with Barbara Joe, Joe Phillip, Placid Joseph, Alice Rearden, Mark John, and Ann Fienup-Riordan. Anchorage. December 4, 2013. Tape 5, page 159.

51. CEC tape collection. Alakanuk Elders Gathering with Barbara Joe, Joe Phillip, Placid Joseph, Alice Rearden, Mark John, and Ann Fienup-Riordan. Anchorage. December 5, 2013. Tape 8, pages 248–50.

52. CEC tape collection. Alakanuk Elders Gathering with Barbara Joe, Joe Phillip, Placid Joseph, Alice Rearden, Mark John, and Ann Fienup-Riordan. Anchorage. December 5, 2013. Tape 10, pages 338–42.

53. CEC tape collection. Yukon Men's Gathering with Eugene Pete, Mike Andrews Sr., Lawrence Edmund, Denis Shelden, Mark John, Alice Rearden, and Ann Fienup-Riordan. Anchorage. December 6, 2011. Tape 3, pages 89–92.

54. CEC tape collection. Yukon Men's Gathering with Eugene Pete, Mike Andrews Sr., Lawrence Edmund, Denis Shelden, Mark John, Alice Rearden, and Ann Fienup-Riordan. Anchorage. December 6 and 7, 2011. Tapes 4 and 7, pages 186, 284–85.

55. CEC tape collection. Yukon Men's Gathering with Eugene Pete, Mike Andrews Sr., Lawrence Edmund, Denis Shelden, Mark John, Alice Rearden, and Ann Fienup-Riordan. Anchorage. December 7, 2011. Tape 7, pages 285, 288–89.

56. CEC tape collection, Yukon Project village planning meetings, Alakanuk meeting with Denis Shelden, Lawrence Edmund, John and Paula Ayunerak, Fred Agustine, Edward Phillip, Marie Meade, and Ann Fienup-Riordan. Alakanuk community hall. March 10, 2011. Tape 19, pages 978–83.

57. CEC tape collection. Yukon Men's Gathering with Eugene Pete, Mike Andrews Sr., Lawrence Edmund, Denis Shelden, Mark John, Alice Rearden, and Ann Fienup-Riordan. Anchorage. December 7, 2011. Tape 6, pages 245–51.

58. CEC tape collection. Yupiit Piciryarait Museum Gathering with Frank Andrew, Margaret Andrews, Alex Bird, Joan Hamilton, Noah Andrew, and CEC staff Mark John, Marie Meade, Alice Rearden, Freda Jimmie, and Ann Fienup-Riordan. Bethel. December 16, 2003. Tape 8, page 308.

59. CEC tape collection. Nunaput Gathering with John Phillip, Nick Andrew, Paul John, Peter Jacobs, Golga Effemka, Joe Asuluk, students Anthony Oney, Glenn Azean, Magdalene John, and CEC staff Alice Rearden and Ann Fienup-Riordan. USFWS Conference Room, Bethel. January 20, 2006. Tapes 6B and 7A, pages 239–44.

Qissunamiut Qanemciit / Stories from Qissunaq

1. Ann Fienup-Riordan tape collection. Interview with Joe Ayagarak by David Chanar. Chevak. December 16, 1987. Tape 103, pages 35–36.

2. Ann Fienup-Riordan tape collection. Interview with Joe Ayagarak by David Chanar. Chevak. December 16, 1987. Tape 103, pages 36–41.

Aperyarat / Glossary

1. The primary source for this word list is Steven Jacobson's *Yup'ik Eskimo Dictionary* (2012), providing etymologies generally as well as specific shamanic vocabulary (Jacobson 2012:1190), with additions provided from elder interviews.

References

....

Alaska Department of Labor. 2010. American Community Survey Site. http://live.laborstats.alaska.gov/cen/acsarea.cfm.

Anchorage Daily News staff. 1986. "People in Peril." *Anchorage Daily News.* Anchorage, AK.

Andrew, Frank. 2008. *Paitarkiutenka / My Legacy to You.* Alice Rearden and Marie Meade, transcriptions and translations. Ann Fienup-Riordan, ed. Seattle: University of Washington Press.

Andrew, Frank, and Alice Rearden. 2007. "Aanakallii Ner'aqallii / I Have Eaten My Mother." In *Words of the Real People: Alaska Native Literature in Translation,* ed. Ann Fienup-Riordan and Lawrence Kaplan, 68–83. Fairbanks: University of Alaska Press.

Angaiak, Susie. 1991. "Letter to the Editor." *Tundra Drums* (Bethel, AK). p. 3.

Balikci, Asen. 1963. "Shamanistic Behavior among the Netsilik Eskimos." *Southwestern Journal of Anthropology* 19:380–96.

Becker, A. L. 2000. *Beyond Translation: Essays toward a Modern Philology.* Ann Arbor: University of Michigan Press.

Berman, Matthew. 2014. "Suicide Among Young Alaska Native Men: Community Risk Factors and Alcohol Control." *American Journal of Public Health.* Published online April 2014 at www.iser.uaa.alaska.edu.

Blodgett, Jean. 1979. *The Coming and the Going of the Shaman: Eskimo Shamanism and Art.* Winnipeg Art Gallery.

Boas, Franz. 1901. "The Eskimo of Baffin Land and Hudson Bay. From Notes Collected by Capt. George Comer, Capt. James S. Mutch, and Rev. E. J. Peck." *Bulletin of the American Museum of Natural History* 15(1):1–370.

Boas, Franz. 1964 [1888]. *The Central Eskimo.* Lincoln: University of Nebraska Press.

Bogoras, William. 1904. *The Chukchee.* Leiden: E. J. Brill.

Borre, Kristen. 1994. "The Healing Power of the Seal: The Meaning of Inuit Health Practice and Belief." *Arctic Anthropology* 31(1):1–15.

Burch, Ernest, Jr. 1971. "The Nonempirical Environment of the Arctic Alaskan Eskimo." *Southwestern Journal of Anthropology* 27(2):148–65. (Reprinted in *Iñupiaq Ethnohistory: Selected Essays,* ed. Erica Hill, University of Alaska Press.)

Dauenhauer, Nora Marks, and Richard Dauenhauer. 1999. "The Paradox of Talking on the Page: Some Aspects of the Tlingit and Haida Experience." In *Talking on the Page: Editing Aboriginal Oral Texts,* ed. Laura Murray and Keren Rice, 3–42. Toronto: University of Toronto Press.

Eliade, M. 1970. *Shamanism: Archaic Techniques of Ecstasy.* London: Routledge and Kegan Paul. (*Le shamanisme et les techniques archaiques de l'extase.* Paris: Payot, 1951.)

Fienup-Riordan, Ann. 1986. *When Our Bad Season Comes: A Cultural Account of Subsistence Harvesting and Harvest Disruption on the Yukon Delta.* Monograph Series 1. Aurora: Alaska Anthropological Association.

Fienup-Riordan, Ann. 1988. *The Yup'ik Eskimos as Described in the Travel Journals and Ethnographic Accounts of John and Edith Kilbuck, 1885–1900.* Kingston, ON: Limestone Press.

https://doi.org/10.5876/9781646427314.c019

Fienup-Riordan, Ann. 1990a. *Eskimo Essays: Yup'ik Lives and How We See Them.* New Brunswick, NJ: Rutgers University Press.

Fienup-Riordan, Ann. 1990b. "*Selaviq*: A Yup'ik Transformation of a Russian Orthodox Tradition." In *Eskimo Essays: Yup'ik Lives and How We See Them.* New Brunswick, NJ: Rutgers University Press.

Fienup-Riordan, Ann. 1991. *The Real People and the Children of Thunder: The Yup'ik Eskimo Encounter with Moravian Missionaries John and Edith Kilbuck.* Norman: University of Oklahoma Press.

Fienup-Riordan, Ann. 1994. *Boundaries and Passages: Rule and Ritual in Yup'ik Eskimo Oral Tradition.* Norman: University of Oklahoma Press.

Fienup-Riordan, Ann. 1996. *The Living Tradition of Yup'ik Masks: Agayuliyararput / Our Way of Making Prayer.* Seattle: University of Washington Press.

Fienup-Riordan, Ann. 1997. "Present Yup'ik Recollections of Past Shamans." In *Shamanism/Christianization/Possession*, ed. Bernard Saladin d'Anglure and Francoise Morie. *Études/Inuit/Studies* 21(1–2):229–44.

Fienup-Riordan, Ann. 2000. *Hunting Tradition in a Changing World: Yup'ik Lives in Alaska Today.* New Brunswick: Rutgers University Press.

Fienup-Riordan, Ann. 2005a. *Wise Words of the Yup'ik People: We Talk to You because We Love You.* Lincoln: University of Nebraska Press.

Fienup-Riordan, Ann. 2005b. *Yup'ik Elders at the Ethnologisches Museum Berlin: Fieldwork Turned on Its Head.* Seattle: University of Washington Press.

Fienup-Riordan, Ann. 2007a. *Yuungnaqpiallerput / The Way We Genuinely Live: Masterworks of Yup'ik Science and Survival* Seattle: University of Washington Press.

Fienup-Riordan, Ann. 2007b. "Introduction: Yupik and Iñupiaq Literature in Translation." In *Words of the Real People: Alaska Native Literature in Translation*, ed. Ann Fienup-Riordan and Lawrence D. Kaplan. Fairbanks: University of Alaska Press.

Fienup-Riordan, Ann. 2010. "Yup'ik Perspectives on Climate Change: 'The World Is Following Its People.'" *Études/Inuit/Studies* 34(1).

Fienup-Riordan, Ann. 2015. "If You Want to Go Fast, Go Alone, If You Want to Go Far, Go Together." In *Mutuality: Anthropology's Changing Terms of Engagement*, ed. Roger Sanjek, 61–78. Philadelphia: University of Pennsylvania Press.

Fienup-Riordan, Ann, ed. 2018. *Yuuyaraq / The Yup'ik Way of Being.* Fairbanks: Alaska Native Language Center.

Fienup-Riordan, Ann, and Alice Rearden. 2012. *Ellavut / Our Yup'ik World and Weather: Continuity and Change on the Bering Sea Coast.* Seattle: University of Washington Press.

Fienup-Riordan, Ann, and Alice Rearden. 2016. *Anguyiim Nalliini / Time of Warring: The History of Bow-and-Arrow Warfare in Southwest Alaska.* Fairbanks: University of Alaska Press and Alaska Native Language Center.

Fienup-Riordan, Ann, Alice Rearden, and Marie Meade. 2009. "Tumaralria's Drum." *Shaman* 17(1/2):5–27.

Fienup-Riordan, Ann, Alice Rearden, and Marie Meade. 2017. *Qanemcit Amllertut / Many Stories to Tell: Tales of Humans and Animals from Southwest Alaska.* Fairbanks: University of Alaska Press.

Fienup-Riordan, Ann, with Alice Rearden, Marie Meade, David Chanar, Rebecca Nayamin, and Corey Joseph. 2020. *Nunakun-gguq Ciutengqertut / They Say They Have Ears Through the Ground: Animal Essays from Southwest Alaska.* Fairbanks: University of Alaska Press.

Fortuine, Robert. 1986. "Shamans and Seal Oil: Health and Healing in Traditional Alaska Native Societies." Anchorage: Alaska Native Medical Center, Indian Health Service.

Gapp, S. H. 1928. *Where Polar Ice Begins: The Moravian Mission in Alaska.* Bethlehem, PA: Comenius Press.

George, Otto. 1979. *Eskimo Medicine Man.* Portland: Oregon Historical Society.

Goforth, J. Pennelope. 2003. *Sailing the Mail in Alaska: The Maritime Years of Alaska Photographer John E. Thwaites, 1905–1912.* Anchorage: Cybrrcat Productions.

Hawkes, Ernest W. 1913. "The Inviting-In Feast of the Alaskan Eskimo." *Canada Department of Mines, Geological Survey Memoir 45, Anthropological Series 3.* Ottawa.

Himmelheber, Hans. 1993. *Eskimo Artists.* Fairbanks: University of Alaska Press.

Hughes, Charles. 1958. "Translation of I. K. Voblov's 'Eskimo Ceremonies.'" *Anthropological Papers of the University of Alaska* 7(2):71–90.

Hymes, Dell. 1981. "*In Vain I Tried to Tell You*": Essays in Native American Ethnopoetics. Studies in Native American Literature 1. Philadelphia: University of Pennsylvania Press.

Jacobson, Steven A. 1984. *Yup'ik Eskimo Dictionary.* Fairbanks: Alaska Native Language Center, University of Alaska.

Jacobson, Steven A. 1995. *A Practical Grammar of the Central Alaskan Yup'ik Eskimo Language.* Fairbanks: Alaska Native Language Center, University of Alaska.

Jacobson, Steven A. 2012. *Yup'ik Eskimo Dictionary*, Second Edition. Fairbanks: Alaska Native Language Center.

Kawagley, Oscar Angayuqaq. 1989. Yup'ik Ways of Knowing. manuscript. University of British Columbia, Vancouver.

Kilbuck, Edith. 1888. Letter to Papa, February 21. Box 9:1A. Kilbuck Collection, Moravian Archives, Bethlehem, PA.

Kilbuck, Edith. 1894. "Journal. Extracts. Bethel, Alaska. January 8, 1894." *The Proceedings for the Society for Propagating the Gospel Among the Heathen* 1894:60.

Kilbuck, Edith. 1895. Unpublished Journal, February 28, 1895. Kilbuck Collection, Moravian Archives, Bethlehem, PA.

Kilbuck, John Henry. 1889. "Report to the PEC. May 30, 1889." *The Moravian* 34(33):519–21.

Kilbuck, John Henry. 1892. Journal to Edith Kilbuck, January 26, 1892. Unpublished manuscript. Kilbuck Collection, Moravian Archives, Bethlehem, PA.

Krauss, Michael. 1980. *Alaska Native Languages: Past, Present, and Future.* Fairbanks: Alaska Native Language Center Research Paper No. 4. 110 pages.

Lantis, Margaret. 1946. "The Social Culture of the Nunivak Eskimo." *Transactions of the American Philosophical Society* (Philadelphia) 35:153–323.

Lantis, Margaret. 1959. "Folk Medicine and Hygiene, Lower Kuskokwim and Nunivak-Nelson Island Area." *Anthropological Papers of the University of Alaska* 8(1):1–75.

Lantis, Margaret. 1966. *Alaskan Eskimo Ceremonialism.* Seattle: University of Washington Press.

Lantis, Margaret. 1990. "The Selection of Symbolic Meaning." In *Hunting, Sexes, and Symbolism*, ed. Ann Fienup-Riordan. *Études/Inuit/Studies* 14(1–2):169–89.

Laugrand, Frédéric B., and Jarich Oosten. 2006. "Connecting and Protecting: Lines and Belts in the Canadian Arctic." *Anthropological Papers of the University of Alaska* 4(1):133–47.

Laugrand, Frédéric B., and Jarich Oosten. 2010. "Qupirruit, Insects and Worms in Inuit Shamanic Traditions." *Arctic Anthropology* 47(1):1–21.

Laugrand, Frédéric B., and Jarich Oosten. 2012. *Inuit Shamanism and Christianity: Transitions and Transformations in the Twentieth Century.* Montreal and Kingston: McGill-Queen's University Press.

Litecky, Ahnie Marie Al'aq David. 2011. "The Dwellers Between: Yup'ik Shamans and Cultural Change in Western Alaska." Master's thesis, University of Montana, Missoula.

Mather, Elsie P. 1985. *Cauyarnariuq [A Time for Drumming].* Alaska Historical Commission Studies in History No. 184. Bethel, AK: Lower Kuskokwim School District Bilingual/Bicultural Department.

Mather, Elsie P. 1995. "With a Vision Beyond Our Immediate Needs: Oral Traditions in an Age of Literacy." In *When Our Words Return: Writing, Hearing, and Remembering Oral Traditions of Alaska and the Yukon*, ed. Phyllis Morrow and William Schneider, 13–26. Logan: Utah State University Press.

Meade, Marie, and Ann Fienup-Riordan. 1996. *Agayuliyararput, Kegginaqut, Kangiit-llu / Our Way of Making Prayer, Yup'ik Masks and the Stories They Tell.* Seattle: University of Washington Press.

Meade, Marie, and Ann Fienup-Riordan. 2005. *Ciuliamta Akluit: Things of Our Ancestors.* Seattle: University of Washington Press.

Merkur, Daniel. 1985. *Becoming Half Hidden: Shamanism and Initiation among the Inuit.* Stockholm: Almquist and Wiksell International.

Merkur, Daniel. 1991. *Powers Which We Do Not Know: The Gods and Spirits of the Inuit.* Moscow, ID: University of Idaho Press.

Miyaoka, Osahito, and Elsie Mather. 1979. *Yup'ik Eskimo Orthography.* Bethel, AK: Kuskokwim Community College.

Mooney, Sean, and Chuna McIntyre. 2019. *Yua: Henri Matisse and the Inner Arctic Spirit.* Phoenix, AZ: Heard Museum.

Morrow, Phyllis. 1984. "It Is Time for Drumming: A Summary of Recent Research on Yup'ik Ceremonialism." In *The Central Yupik Eskimos*, ed. Ernest Burch Jr. *Études/Inuit/Studies* Supplementary Issue 8:63–93.

Morrow, Phyllis. 1990. "Symbolic Actions, Indirect Expressions: Limits to Interpretations of Yupik Society." *Hunting, Sexes and Symbolism*, ed. Ann Fienup-Riordan. *Études/Inuit/Studies* 14:141–58.

Mousalimas, Soterio A. 1995. *The Transition from Shamanism to Russian Orthodoxy in Alaska.* Oxford: Berghahn Books.

Nelson, Edward William. 1899. *The Eskimo about Bering Strait.* Bureau of American Ethnology Annual Report for 1896–1897, Vol. 18, Pt. 1. Washington, DC: Smithsonian Institution Press. Reprinted 1983.

Oosten, Jarich G. 1976. *The Theoretical Structure of the Religion of the Netsilik and Iglulik.* Meppel: Krips Repro.

Oosten, Jarich G. 1981. "The Structure of the Shamanistic Complex among the Netsilik and Iglulik." *Études/Inuit/Studies* 5(1):83–98.

Oosten, Jarich G. 1989. "Theoretical Problems in the Study of Inuit Shamanism." In *Shamanism Past and Present*, ed. Hihaly Hoppal and Otto von Sadovsky, 2:331–42. Budapest: International Society for Trans-Oceanic Research Books.

Oosten, Jarich G. 1997. "Amulets, Shamanic Clothes and Paraphernalia in Inuit Culture." In *Braving the Cold: Continuity and Change in Arctic Clothing*, ed. C. Buijs and J. Oosten, 105–30. Leiden: Center of Non-Western Studies.

Oosten, Jarich, and Frédéric Laugrand, eds. 2002. *Inuit Qaujimajatuqangit: Shamanism and Reintegrating Wrongdoers.* Inuit Perspectives on the Twentieth Century 2. Iqaluit: Nunavut Arctic College.

Oosten, Jarich, Frédéric Laugrand, and Cor Remie, eds. 2006. "Perception of Decline: Inuit Shamanism in the Canadian Arctic." *Ethnohistory* 53(3):455–77.

Oswalt, Wendell. 1963. *Mission of Change in Alaska: Eskimos and Moravians on the Kuskokwim.* San Marino, CA: The Huntington Library.

Oswalt, Wendell. 1973. "The Kuskowagamiut." In *This Land Was Theirs.* New York: John Wiley and Sons.

Oswalt, Wendell. 1990. *Bashful No Longer: An Alaskan Eskimo Ethnohistory, 1778–1988.* Norman: University of Oklahoma Press.

Phillip, Joshua. 1988. Tape recorded interview and transcript. 88CAL049. BIA ANCSA 14(h)(1) Historical Places and Cemetery Sites Collection, Alaska and Polar Regions Collections, Rasmuson Library, University of Alaska Fairbanks.

Rasmussen, Knud. 1930. *Observations on the Intellectual Culture of the Caribou Eskimos: Iglulik and Caribou Eskimo Texts.* Vol. 12(2–3) of *Report of the Fifth Thule Expedition 1921–24.* Copenhagen: Gyldendalske Boghandel.

Rasmussen, Knud. 1931. *The Netsilik Eskimos: Social Life and Spiritual Culture.* Vol. 8(1–2) of *Report of the Fifth Thule Expedition 1921–24.* Copenhagen: Gyldendalske Boghandel.

Rasmussen, Knud. 1932. *Intellectual Culture of the Copper Eskimos.* Vol. 9 of *Report of the Fifth Thule Expedition 1921–24.* Copenhagen: Gyldendalske Boghandel.

Rearden, Alice, and Ann Fienup-Riordan. 2011. *Qaluyaarmi-uni Nunamtenek Qanemciput / Our Nelson Island Stories: Meanings of Place on the Bering Sea Coast.* Seattle: University of Washington Press.

Rearden, Alice, Marie Meade, and Ann Fienup-Riordan. 2005. *Yupiit Qanruyutait / Yup'ik Words of Wisdom.* Lincoln: University of Nebraska Press.

Rearden, Alice, Marie Meade, Mark John, and Ann Fienup-Riordan. 2021. *Ircenrraat / Other-than-human Persons in Southwest Alaska.* Fairbanks: Alaska Native Language Center.

Reed, Irene, Osahito Miyaoka, Steven Jacobson, Pascal Afcan, and Michael Krauss. 1977. *Yup'ik Eskimo Grammar.* Fairbanks: Alaska Native Language Center, University of Alaska.

Sahlins, Marshall. 1999. "Two or Three Things That I Know about Culture." *The Journal of the Royal Anthropological Institute* 5(3):399–421.

Saladin d'Anglure, Bernard. 2001. "La construction de l'identite chamanique chez les Inuit du Nunavut et du Nunavik." *Études/Inuit/Studies* 25(1–2):191–215.

Saladin d'Anglure, Bernard, ed. 2001. *Cosmology and Shamanism.* Interviewing Inuit Elders 4. Iqaluit: Nunavut Arctic College.

Saladin d'Anglure, Bernard, and Francoise Morin. 1997. *Shamanism/Christianization/Possession. Études/Inuit/Studies* 21(1–2):229–44.

Samuel Fox Museum. 2021. Exhibit label. Dillingham, Alaska.

Shield, Sophie, and Ann Fienup-Riordan. 2003. *Qulirat Qanemcit-llu Kinguvarcimalriit / Stories for Future Generations: The Oratory of Yup'ik Eskimo Elder Paul John.* Seattle: University of Washington Press.

Sonne, Birgitte. 2017. *Worldview of the Greenlanders: An Inuit Arctic Perspective.* Fairbanks: University of Alaska Press.

Spencer, Robert. 1959. *The North Alaskan Eskimo: A Study in Ecology and Society.* Bureau of American Ethnology Bulletin 171. Washington, DC (Reprinted in 1969).

Swann, Brian. 1994. *Coming to Light: Contemporary Translations of the Native Literatures of North America.* New York: Random House.

Tedlock, Dennis. 1983. *The Spoken Word and the Work of Interpretation.* Philadelphia: University of Pennsylvania Press.

Tennant, Edward A., and Joseph N. Bitar, eds. 1981. *Yupik Lore / Yuut Qanemciit: Oral Traditions of an Eskimo People.* Bethel, AK: Lower Kuskokwim School District Bilingual/Bicultural Department.

Thalbitzer, William. 1930. "Les magiciens esquimaux, leurs conceptions du monde, de l'ame et de la vie." *Journal de la Societe des Americanistes* (Paris), n.s., 22:71–106.

Woodbury, Anthony C. 1984. "Eskimo and Aleut Languages." In *Arctic*, Vol. 5, *Handbook of North American Indians*, ed. David Damas, 49–63. Washington, DC: Smithsonian Institution Press.

Index

....

Page numbers followed by f indicate illustrations; page numbers followed by n indicate notes.

About the Authors

··

Ann Fienup-Riordan has lived and worked in Alaska since 1973. She has written and edited more than twenty books on Yup'ik history and oral traditions. Her most recent book with the University of Alaska Press is *Yungcautnguuq Nunam Qainga Tamarmi / All the Land's Surface Is Medicine: Edible and Medicinal Plants of Southwest Alaska.*

Alice Rearden is a fluent Yup'ik speaker and teaches Yup'ik at Bethel Regional High School. She was primary translator and oral historian at the Calista Elders Council and has coedited and translated for numerous books on Yup'ik history and oral traditions, including *Yungcautnguuq Nunam Qainga Tamarmi / All the Land's Surface Is Medicine: Edible and Medicinal Plants of Southwest Alaska.*

Marie Meade is a fluent Yup'ik speaker and an expert translator. She teaches Yup'ik at the University of Alaska Anchorage. She has coedited and translated for numerous books on Yup'ik history and oral tradition, including *Yungcautnguuq Nunam Qainga Tamarmi / All the Land's Surface Is Medicine: Edible and Medicinal Plants of Southwest Alaska.*